Kai Bird

SIMON & SCHUSTER

NEW YORK LONDON
TORONTO SYDNEY
TOKYO SINGAPORE

John J. McCloy

The Making of the American Establishment

THE CHAIRMAN

SIMON & SCHUSTER
Simon & Schuster Building
Rockefeller Center
1230 Avenue of the Americas
New York, New York 10020

Designed by Levavi & Levavi
Manufactured in the United States of America

1 2 3 4 5 6 7 8 9 10

Picture research by Natalie Goldstein

Library of Congress Cataloging-in-Publication Data
Bird, Kai.
The chairman : John J. McCloy, the making of the American establishment / Kai Bird.
p. cm.
Includes bibliographical references and index.
1. McCloy, John Jay, 1895–1989. 2. Statesmen—United States—Biography. I. Title.
E748.M1457B57 1992
973.9'092—dc20
[B] 91-44255
CIP

ISBN: 0-671-45415-3

For Susan

CONTENTS

Preface 13

Introduction · A Memorial 15

Book I: The Making of a Wall Street Lawyer **21**

Chapter 1 · A Philadelphia Youth: 1895–1912 23

Chapter 2 · Amherst Years: 1912–16 37

Chapter 3 · Harvard Law School and the War Years: 1916–21 47

Chapter 4 · Wall Street: 1921–30 57

Chapter 5 · Black Tom: McCloy's Wilderness of Mirrors 78

Chapter 6 · Cravath, the New Deal, and the Approach of War 96

Book II: World War II **115**

Chapter 7 · Imps of Satan 117

Chapter 8 · Internment of the Japanese Americans 147

Chapter 9 · Political Commissar 175

Chapter 10 · McCloy and the Holocaust 201

Chapter 11 · Victory in Europe 228

Chapter 12 · Hiroshima 240

Book III: Wall Street, the World Bank, and Germany **269**

Chapter 13 · A Brief Return to Wall Street 271

Chapter 14 · The World Bank: "McCloy über Alles" 284

Chapter 15 · German Proconsul: 1949 308

Chapter 16 · The Dilemma of German Rearmament 332

Chapter 17 · McCloy and U.S. Intelligence Operations in Germany 345
Chapter 18 · The Clemency Decisions 359
Chapter 19 · Negotiating an End to Occupation 376

Book IV: The Eisenhower Years 389
Chapter 20 · Chairman of the Chase Manhattan Bank: 1953–60 391
Chapter 21 · McCloy, McCarthyism, and the Early Eisenhower Presidency 403
Chapter 22 · Ike's Wise Man 441

Book V: The Kennedy Administration 493
Chapter 23 · Arms Control Czar 495
Chapter 24 · The Cuban Missile Crisis 522

Book VI: LBJ's Wise Man 545
Chapter 25 · The Warren Commission, a Brazil Coup, Egypt Again, and the 1964 Election 547
Chapter 26 · McCloy and Vietnam: 1965–68, NATO Crisis, Secret Middle East Negotiations 569

Book VII: Elder Statesman 1969–89 611
Chapter 27 · The Establishment at Bay: The Nixon–Kissinger Administration 613
Chapter 28 · McCloy and the Iran-Hostage Crisis 641

Twilight Years 655
Notes 665
Archival Sources 756
Interviews 757
Bibliography 759
Acknowledgments 774
Index 777

"I am not sure who the chairman of the Establishment is today. . . . By a thrust of sheer intuition, though, I did get the name of the 1958 chairman and was rather proud of myself for doing so. In that year, I discovered that J. K. Galbraith had for some time been surreptitiously at work in Establishment studies, and he told me that he had found out who was running the thing. He tested me by challenging me to guess the man's name. I thought hard for a while and was on the point of naming Arthur Hays Sulzberger, of The New York Times, *when suddenly the right name sprang to my lips.* 'John J. McCloy,' *I exclaimed. 'Chairman of the Board of the Chase Manhattan Bank; once a partner at Cadwalader, Wickersham & Taft, and also in Cravath, de Gersdorff, Swaine & Wood, as well as, of course, Milbank, Tweed, Hope, Hadley and McCloy; former United States High Commissioner in Germany; former President of the World Bank; liberal Republican; chairman of the Ford Foundation and chairman—my God, how could I have hesitated—of the Council on Foreign Relations; Episcopalian.'* " 'That's the one,' *Galbraith said."*

RICHARD H. ROVERE, 1961
The American Scholar

PREFACE

This is the first full-scale biography of John J. McCloy. Hundreds of books published in the last thirty years mention McCloy in a paragraph or a footnote. Most books dealing with World War II, postwar Germany, the Kennedy assassination, the Vietnam War, the Cold War, the CIA, or the atomic bomb also mention something of McCloy's role. Thomas Schwartz's *America's Germany* provides a study of McCloy's tenure as high commissioner in occupied Germany. And one book, *The Wise Men,* by Walter Isaacson and Evan Thomas, summarizes his career together with that of five other members of the Establishment. But it is astonishing how little has been published altogether, and how few Americans are familiar with an individual who had so much to do with running the postwar world.

McCloy himself was reluctant to see a biography written, and when I began this project ten years ago, he took the unusual step of sending a letter to the editor of *The New York Times Book Review,* disavowing the work. He tried to persuade both me and my publisher to abandon the book. Two years later, however, he agreed to a series of meetings, and then interviews. For a brief time, he attempted to write a short memoir of his own, but that project never came to fruition. After nine long interviews during the years 1983–86, he and his family once again made known their desire that no biography be written of him. Because of increasing press criticism for his role in the Japanese American internment and the decision not to bomb Auschwitz, McCloy feared any biography would treat him in a hostile fashion. But his reluctance also came from his deep-seated aversion to seeing himself singled out. Lawyers of his generation and background did not like to see their names in print.

In addition to interviews with McCloy, this book is based on interviews with more than a hundred of his friends and associates. (Some of these interviews were conducted by a former colleague.) Several hundred Freedom of Information Act requests resulted in the release of thousands of pages of formerly classified documents from the State Department, the CIA, the FBI, and many other government agencies. Finally, I gathered more than eighty thousand pages of archival material from the National Archives, the German and British official archives, all eight presidential libraries, and numerous private archives, including McCloy's own private papers housed at Amherst College.

I hope this book will be read as something more than a conventional biography. McCloy's life story is also a story of the American Establishment, that elusively defined elite which in many respects still exerts its influence over the democratic polity. McCloy spent his life serving this Establishment, and in most instances he was truly the best representative of this elite club. At the same time, on issues in which the Establishment left a questionable legacy, it can best be examined through the life of one of its more admirable members.

INTRODUCTION: A MEMORIAL

They came quietly, dressed in dark winter overcoats and furs, and crowded into the Brick Presbyterian Church on the fashionable Upper East Side of Manhattan. By 3:00 P.M., there was standing room only inside the church, and some two hundred people, including a throng of reporters, gathered in front of television monitors set up in the basement. Outside, black limousines lined the streets for a block in each direction, and a few policemen stood guard at the doors of the church.

This was an intimate gathering of a self-selected aristocracy of lawyers, bankers, corporate chiefs, and government officials. They were representatives of the old American Establishment, come to pay their respects to the man known as their chairman, John J. McCloy.

They were from institutions he had served for nearly seven decades: lawyers from the Wall Street firms of Milbank, Tweed, Hadley & McCloy, Cravath, Swaine & Moore, and Cadwalader, Wickersham & Taft; investment bankers from Kuhn, Loeb and commercial bankers from Chase Manhattan Bank; and corporate officers from AT&T, Westinghouse, Dreyfus, Squibb, Allied Chemical Co., Metropolitan Life Insurance Co., the Mercedes Benz Corporation, and all the major American oil companies.

Many were members of the Council on Foreign Relations, and most belonged to the same clubs he had joined long ago: the New York City Bar Association, the Century Club, the Bond Club, the Links, the Anglers' Club, and such elusive associations as the discreet Nisi Prius luncheon club, where two members from each of the city's leading law firms met each month to discuss politics, the law, and business affairs. Former colleagues from the Ford Foundation, the Rockefeller Foundation, the American Council on Germany, the Atlantic Institute, and the Aspen Institute had come. Filling the pews were also men from the World Bank, honoring the man who, forty years ago, had served as midwife to that pillar of the postwar international financial system.

In this crowd, the few politicians and foreign dignitaries seemed almost inconsequential. McCloy would have been amused by the presence of Richard M. Nixon, a man whose bitterness at being shunned for so long by the Establishment had done much to destroy his presidency. But there he was, sitting in the front pew, flanked by the former chancellor of Germany, Helmut Schmidt, and James A. Baker III, the newly sworn-in secretary of state, who would read a letter of homage from President George Herbert Walker Bush.

Despite the resemblance to a state funeral, this was an intimate affair of the Establishment, organized by McCloy's colleagues from Milbank, Tweed. The ushers were men who, though not always known to the public, ran the country's leading institutions. There was the former chairman of the Federal Reserve Board, Paul A. Volcker. McGeorge Bundy, the national-security adviser in the Kennedy and Johnson administrations—whom McCloy had selected as president of the Ford Foundation—served as an usher. So too did Perry Richardson Bass, the Texas oil billionaire; Richard M. Furland, the chairman of Squibb Corporation; Peter G. Peterson, once chairman of Lehman Brothers; Shepard Stone, a Ford Foundation and Aspen Institute officer; and Cyrus R. Vance, another corporate lawyer who served as secretary of state in the Carter administration.

When the last available seat had been taken, organ music filled the chamber and the congregation rose to sing the hymn "A Mighty Fortress Is Our God." Following the reading of McCloy's favorite Psalm 121, handsome, silver-haired Alexander Forger, the lead partner from Milbank, Tweed, walked briskly to the pulpit and gave the first of nine eulogies. He was followed by former West German President Karl Carstens, former Chancellor Helmut Schmidt, Secretary of State Baker, former Secretary of State Henry Kissinger, David Rockefeller, McCloy's two young grandsons, and, finally, his only son, John J. McCloy II. They praised a man who, in Forger's words, "was never impressed with his own self-importance."

Though he died virtually unknown to most of his countrymen, to these men he was the embodiment of all that was worthy and sound about America. President Bush's letter, read by James Baker, called him "one of the giants and true heroes in the history of this country. He was a trusted advisor of American Presidents from Franklin Roosevelt to Ronald Reagan." He never "flagged in pursuing the private and public good. . . . He was a regular presence, always reliable . . . a pioneer in arms control." The president noted that perhaps his "greatest success" took place in early postwar Germany, where McCloy for three years wielded virtually dictatorial powers over the lives of millions of Germans.

Helmut Schmidt labeled McCloy the "architect of Germany's rehabilitation from an occupied country to an independent state." Karl Carstens said he had been "a wise man who had sound judgments about events and men." David Rockefeller suggested McCloy had been unafraid to take politically unpopular stands, and cited his opposition to the atomic bombing of Hiroshima and his insistence on providing asylum in America for the shah of Iran in 1979.

Kissinger, whose own career owed much to the late "chairman," compared him to the godfather of a United Europe, Jean Monnet, and observed that McCloy asked of his associates not cleverness, but simple common sense. "John McCloy never served in the Cabinet of any president," Kissinger said, "and after 1952, never occupied a full-time position in government. Yet few Americans have had a greater impact on their time."

When the politicians and statesmen had finished speaking, the youngest grandson, Rush Middleton McCloy, a neat, handsome boy who bore a striking resemblance to his grandfather at that age, approached the podium. He remembered how his "Big Papa" had taught him to hunt and fish, and always, always to "run with the swift." He was, said the boy, "a loving, caring man who always had a lap to crawl into." And "if Dad and Mom said, 'No,' I only had to ask Big Papa."

McCloy's son, John J. McCloy II, an investment banker, reminded his audience that "Father never liked having attention drawn to himself." And it was true, the chairman had shunned the limelight. McCloy preferred the shadows of power, the inner recesses of the decision-making process, where men of similar background, usually lawyers like himself, sat in a room together and rationally took the measure of a problem. Rarely in his long career did he attract controversy. Always congenial, he invariably left the impression with his bureaucratic opponents that he was actually sympathetic to their concerns. He could fire a man, and there would be no hard feelings later. As his son now recalled, "Eric Sevareid said Dad had no enemies. . . . He never wanted to take advantage of anything or anyone."

McCloy had been a lively, athletic man with the chunky body of a wrestler and a bald head. He smiled easily, and with a mischievous gleam in his brown eyes told the kind of stories that made him a popular dinner companion. For almost all of his nearly ninety-four years, he had an abundance of physical energy; on the tennis court he always charged the net. Married to the same woman for fifty-six years, he had been, as David Rockefeller now reminded his audience, "a devoted husband and father." Kissinger thought him "more like a jovial gnome than a preeminent New York lawyer. . . ." To friends and critics, he was an immensely likable man.

No one, however, including McCloy, ever claimed that he was a brilliant jurist or an intellectual. Though he read widely and could "yellow-pad" his legal memorandums in half the time it took most lawyers, he was not a man given to introspection. His intelligence was that of a working lawyer, trained in the tradition of Paul Cravath, the creator of the great New York law factories at the turn of the century, to break any problem down into all its pieces and then laboriously put it together again. "Brilliant intellectual powers are not essential," Cravath once explained to an audience at Harvard Law School. "Too much imagination, too much wit, too great cleverness, too facile fluency, if not leavened by a sound sense of proportion are quite as likely to impede success as to promote it." McCloy fit the Cravath mold perfectly.

John J. McCloy's life mirrored the rise of the American empire. Through his life story as an influential corporate lawyer and presidential adviser, one can understand how power works in the wealthiest and most powerful nation-state created in human history. At one time or another, he was an assistant secretary of war, president of the World Bank, high commissioner to occupied Germany, chairman of Chase Manhattan Bank, chairman of the Ford Foundation, chairman of the Council on Foreign Relations, and chairman of the President's Advisory Committee on Arms Control and Disarmament. He was legal counsel to all "Seven Sister" oil companies, a board director for a dozen of America's top corporations, and a private, unofficial adviser to most of the presidents in the twentieth century. He was the ultimate power-broker, a man who was virtually chief counsel to the American century. As John F. Kennedy once described him, he was a "diplomat and public servant, banker to the world, and Godfather to German freedom. . . . He has brought cheerful wisdom and steady effectiveness to the tasks of war and peace."

His story also encompasses the rise of a new national elite, composed largely of corporate lawyers and investment bankers, who became stewards of the American national-security state. Beginning in the 1920s, these men formed an identifiable Establishment, a class of individuals who shared the same social and political values and thought of themselves as keepers of the public trust. Unlike the British Establishment, from which the term is borrowed, the American Establishment was dedicated not to preserving the *status quo,* but to persuading America to shoulder its imperial responsibilities. Most of these men modeled themselves after Henry Lewis Stimson, that paragon of an American lawyer, gentleman, and statesman. One of the country's earliest corporate lawyers, Stimson served as either war secretary or secretary of state to Presidents William Taft, Herbert Hoover, Franklin Roosevelt, and Harry Truman. His politics became the yardstick by which other members of America's twentieth-century Establishment judged themselves and the world. A Theodore Roosevelt Republican, Stimson acted out his mentor's motto to "speak softly and carry a big stick." A fervent internationalist, Stimson believed America should engage itself with the rest of the world and always be willing to negotiate with its adversaries within forums like the World Court, the League of Nations, and, later, the United Nations. But he also was a founding member, together with another liberal Republican lawyer, Grenville Clark, of the pre–World War I "military-preparedness movement," which ingrained in a generation of young Americans, including McCloy, the notion that the peace could only be assured by thoroughly preparing for war. Stimson bequeathed a complicated blend of toughness, idealism, and rationality to the men who considered him their mentor. Like him, they became part American puritan and part imperial warrior, dedicated to building a Pax Americana.

Later in life, McCloy used the Latin word *gravitas* to describe the few men of sound judgment, men in whom the republic placed its trust, not because of their status or rank, but because they possessed a balanced, centered understanding of the complexities of life. " 'Gravitas' did not imply age or brilliance, and, least of all," McCloy said, "a style or school of thought. It means a core, a weight of judgment and honest appraisal." These few men of *gravitas* were entitled to the public's trust, for only they were capable of dealing with what McCloy frequently called the "imponderables" of public policy.

McCloy was only one of the most influential members of an elite group, but, partly due to the breadth and longevity of his career, he was without doubt the most important member of this Establishment. Alone among his peers, he managed to straddle for nearly five decades the interlocking directorships of corporate America, the federal government, and the country's leading public-policy and philanthropic foundations. For much of his career, he was in a position to grease the machinery that powered postwar American society. When something went wrong, when a crisis occurred, he was invariably a man whom presidents called to their side, whether it was in World War II, postwar Germany, the Cuban missile crisis, or the aftermath of a presidential assassination.

He was a modest, almost unpretentious man. John Kenneth Galbraith had dubbed him the "Chairman of the Establishment," but that was a description McCloy abhorred. He preferred to call himself a mere "legman," and liked to point out that his origins were humble. He was, in fact, the son of a woman who made her living working as a hairdresser in the homes of well-to-do Philadelphia families. A strong-willed woman, Anna McCloy molded her son to become a different kind of servant to America's ruling elite.

Well into his eighties, McCloy could still be called, by *Harper's* magazine, "the most influential private citizen in America." But simple longevity does not explain how one man could wield such influence. Character had something to do with it. His congeniality, personal modesty, and commonsensical demeanor evoked trust. Unlike some of his peers—such as Averell Harriman or Lewis Douglas—McCloy had no political ambitions. His politics were less a matter of ideology than simple pragmatism. He had no constituency—except for his ties to Rockefeller family interests on Wall Street—and even in this case, for most of his career, he managed to make it seem that he was always able to rise above these private interests in order to discern the public interest. He was the quintessential chairman of the American Century.

BOOK I

The Making of a Wall Street Lawyer

CHAPTER 1

A Philadelphia Youth: 1895–1912

"John, always run with the swift. You might someday come in second."

COACH JOHN PLANT
THE PEDDIE SCHOOL

All his life, John Jay McCloy knew he had been born on the wrong side of Philadelphia's "Chinese Wall," a massive, blockwide stone viaduct which once physically and symbolically segregated the upper classes in the city center from the poor of North Philadelphia. Built by the countr largest corporation at the time, the Pennsylvania Railroad, the W provided westward-bound trains an elevated route out of the city, tow the new "Main Line" suburbs. McCloy always remembered it as a so divide, a barrier his mother was determined he would cross.

At the turn of the century, Philadelphia maintained a strong ser class. "Proper Philadelphia gentlemen" were rapidly setting the sta for a national aristocracy of talent and wealth based largely on th Coast. The common interests of these merchants, investment b and corporation lawyers lay in free trade, internationalism, and th sion of American power abroad. Culturally, "Philadelphia gen were generally groomed in a few select New England boarding and then attended Harvard, Yale, the University of Pennsy Princeton. They socialized at exclusive men's clubs, vacationed resorts in Maine, Cape Cod, or the Adirondacks, and had ped could usually be inspected in the *Social Register.* All the attrib

establishment—the private-school education, the men's clubs, even the *Social Register*—were Philadelphia inventions.

The country's oldest private club, the Fish House, was founded in 1736, a few years before the earliest of London's famous clubs. The Philadelphia Club followed in 1834, and the Old Philadelphia Rabbit Club started up in 1861. The Union League and the Rittenhouse Club soon followed. These exclusive clubs—the Fish House limited its membership to thirty men—imposed aristocratic and courtly standards on the city's social life. Every day the city's leading bankers, brokers, doctors, businessmen, and lawyers—men with names like Biddle, Cadwalader, and Bingham—came to the Philadelphia Club's stately brick home at 13th and Walnut to eat, drink, and discuss the city's affairs. It was, in the words of one social historian, "probably the most compact and inviolable little group of aristocrats in America."[1]

Everyone knew everyone else. These men had usually grown up together, gone to the same prep school together, and married into families known to one another. Many of them were of Quaker merchant ancestry, though most now attended "high" Episcopalian church services. Such names as Wharton, Wister, Morris, Rush, and Ingersoll had played prominent roles during the American Revolution. A hundred years later, these families still constituted the inner circle of what it meant to be a "Proper Philadelphian." Their personal code of conduct was derived from Quaker middle-class money values, a blend of virtuous materialism and aristocratic aloofness. The Protestant work ethic ordained that piety, frugality, and hard work would be rewarded by material success. At the same time, it was considered unseemly to make a public spectacle of one's wealth or power.

For this reason, few "Philadelphia gentlemen" sought political office.
highly educated and righteous men possessed a sense of public
but they preferred to fulfill their civic and charitable obligations
he public limelight, within discreet voluntary associations. Simi-
hose to exercise their power indirectly, from behind the scenes
their contacts with other men of means. More than in any
merica, Philadelphia's club men represented a cohesive and
nent. It was an establishment to which the McCloys had

o Philadelphia as poor Scotch-Irish immigrants
oos. As devout Presbyterians, they stood outside
hment, but they were a rung above the Irish
an immigrants of the mid-nineteenth century.
r, McCloy's grandfather William McCloy
62, Amelia, twenty-seven, gave birth to a

son, whom they named John Jay McCloy. This was McCloy's father, a quiet, handsome young man who dropped out of high school to earn his livelihood.

When he was barely twenty years old, in December 1882, John Jay McCloy landed a job as a clerk with the prestigious Penn Mutual Life Insurance Company. This was an achievement for a youth with little education and no experience. Established in 1847, Penn Mutual in the 1880s was a highly respectable institution in Philadelphia society. Its officers were members of all the right clubs and listed in the *Social Register.* McCloy started as an actuarial clerk earning $600 a year. It was tedious, meticulous work, but it suited him. "Persistency," said a Penn Mutual officer, "may be set down as one of the qualities of a life insurance agent."[2]

McCloy fit the mold, and his steadiness did not go unrewarded. Each year his salary rose about $100, until by the early 1890s he was paid $1,400 *per annum*—a more than handsome wage. In 1891, he married Anna Snader, twenty-seven, a pretty, independent-minded woman of poor Pennsylvania Dutch stock. In the summer of 1892, she gave birth to William Snader McCloy.

Earlier that year, McCloy's status at Penn Mutual had dramatically improved. In February, the supervisor of applications, policies, and death claims died, and McCloy, who had risen to chief clerk, was selected to take his position. This placed him among the top fifteen employees in the company's Philadelphia headquarters. His salary rose from $1,550 in 1891 to $2,000 in 1892. That year they made a 50-percent down payment on a $7,600, plain two-story row house at 2136 North 19th Street, a mile north of the Chinese Wall. It was a two-mile walk to Penn Mutual's new offices on Chestnut Street, or John McCloy could take the trolley that ran past his front door.

In this solid middle-class house on Sunday, March 31, 1895, Anna McCloy gave birth to a second son. She had wanted to name him John Jay, after his father. But at the christening, Anna's father insisted that the boy carry his mother's maiden name. Because neither Anna nor her self-effacing husband was willing to argue the point, the child was baptized John Snader McCloy. But in just a few years, young "Jack" would suddenly announce that he had changed his middle name, dropping the "Snader" for "Jay."

The high-school dropout had done well by his family. By the time his second son was born, the supervisor of applications and death claims was earning more than $3,000 a year. He was not part of good Philadelphia society, but he had a window onto it. One of his best friends at Penn Mutual was the company's medical doctor, J. Allison Scott. "He was from the Philadelphia elite," young Jack McCloy would remember, "from the right part of town, across the Chinese Wall."[3]

With Dr. "Al" Scott's encouragement, McCloy, Sr., began to study Latin. He took to carrying Latin exercise books on the trolley to work and, with Scott's encouragement, began to write little pieces of Latin verse in spidery green ink. When another Penn Mutual colleague commented that "one had to know Greek to be an educated person," he told Anna that he only wished he had time to study Greek as well, and wanted to be sure that his sons learned both classical languages.[4]

Despite his friendship with Dr. Scott, John McCloy hoped his two sons would study the law. The lawyers at Penn Mutual possessed a certain status and prestige independent of their rank in the corporation. One of the lawyers representing the company at this time was a thirty-three-year-old attorney named George Wharton Pepper. McCloy was introduced to Pepper by Dr. Scott, who had married Pepper's younger sister, Frances. Through their friendship with the Scotts, the McCloys became known to the Peppers as decent, hardworking people. Because they lived north of the Chinese Wall, John and Anna McCloy never became a regular part of the Peppers' social calendar. But Anna would always regard George Pepper as someone whom she could approach for advice. Over the years, the lawyer was to become young Jack's first mentor and role model.

The aristocratic cadence of the Pepper name was matched by the man's debonair good looks, his "Old Philadelphia" breeding, and his University of Pennsylvania education. He played the British sport cricket, not American baseball. He was president of the elite Rittenhouse Club, a major fund-raiser for the Episcopalian Church, and a partner in the prestigious law firm of Biddle & Ward. He was a paragon of the "Philadelphia lawyer," a term dating back to Andrew Hamilton's defense of John Peter Zenger in Colonial America's earliest case involving the freedom of the press. Such lawyers were known for their advocacy of private interests; few Philadelphia lawyers ever made a reputation for their careers on the bench. They were advocates, not judges.

George Pepper's paying clients were usually corporations, such as the Union Traction Company, a monopoly that controlled Philadelphia's trolley system. As a young attorney, he frequently defended the company against damage suits arising from accidents suffered by passengers. As with Penn Mutual and other corporate clients, his job was to keep the company out of court. "Lawyers," Pepper wrote in his memoirs, "as a class have always been unpopular."[5] Sensitive to the fact that this was particularly true of corporate lawyers, Pepper early in his career cultivated a patrician sense of "trusteeship" in questions involving the public interest.

"The so-called 'corporation lawyer,' " he wrote, "when he deserves to be scolded, is one whose offense does not consist in representing a corporation or in being disloyal to his client but in allowing fidelity to that client to dim or black out entirely his sense of public duty."[6] Only lawyers, he believed, possessed the disinterestedness necessary to discern the greater public good. Such attitudes were typical of paternalistic Philadelphian society.

Pepper's sense of civic duty did not include running for elective office. Gentlemen lawyers did not, he believed, "itch for public office"; his attitude mellowed somewhat in later years, when he reluctantly accepted an appointment to a U.S. Senate seat. (He proved to be a poor politician and was quickly defeated at the polls.) He believed that lawyers like himself and Elihu Root, New York's foremost corporate lawyer, best exercised their influence on the commonwealth from afar. Such lawyers were a class apart, and John McCloy, Sr., the self-conscious high-school dropout, dreamed of nothing better for his two young sons than that they should enter the ranks of such men.

Young Jack McCloy was four and half years old in December 1899, when epidemics of diphtheria, typhoid, and cholera swept through Philadelphia. The young were especially vulnerable. Two-year-old Edward T. McCloy, a cousin, died first, and then his brother, William, age seven, came down with diphtheria: a fever and a severe sore throat gradually swelled until the boy could hardly breathe. He died in December 1899. Jack always remembered William as a bright, athletic boy whom he had been told to emulate.

Only thirteen months later, John McCloy, Sr., had a heart attack. Lying on his deathbed, he said to Anna, "Make sure John learns Greek."[7] McCloy left a widow and son with no income. Penn Mutual had refused to insure his life because their doctors had detected a heart murmur, stemming from a mild heart attack he had suffered during the Great Blizzard of 1888.

Three weeks after his death, at the end of a board meeting at Penn Mutual, trustee Noah Plympton eulogized McCloy. No one mentioned that the company had refused life insurance to their own supervisor of applications and death claims. But the trustees did vote to pay his widow the balance of his salary for the year 1901.[8] McCloy had worked eighteen years at Penn Mutual; he was a top officer in the company when he died, and his widow had little more than $3,000 to make her own way in life and support her six-year-old son.

Anna McCloy's immediate concern was Jack's education. For a brief time, she enrolled him as a day student at a cheap orphanage school in the city. But the boy didn't like it, so she had him transferred to Thaddeus Stevens School, a neighborhood public school. Like most middle-class Philadelphians, she had a low regard for the free public-school system, and assumed she would someday send her son to a private school.[9]

Earmarking the $3,000 payment from Penn Mutual for Jack's education, Anna set about earning money. She hired herself out as a home nurse, but this didn't bring in enough money, so she taught herself hairdressing. Starting out with her contacts at Penn Mutual, Anna gradually established a reputation as a fine hairdresser. Among her customers were some of Philadelphia's best-known society ladies, including George Pepper's wife, Charlotte, the daughter of a distinguished Yale professor. "She had a rich clientele," McCloy remembered. Anna rose each morning by six and carried her large sack of materials to "do heads" across the Chinese Wall, where her customers lived. "She never made more than 50 cents an hour," recalled McCloy. Other customers included Agnes Repplier, a nationally known essayist, and the families of H. H. Furness, a philanthropist and famous Shakespearean scholar; John Wannamaker, the department-store magnate, who was then known as the "Prince of Merchants"; and Samuel Disston, the manufacturer of the world-famous "Disston saw" and one of Philadelphia's leading businessmen.[10]

Anna's pleasing personality made of these men and women of Philadelphia society not only clients, but friends of a sort. Furness gave her a set of Shakespeare for her young son. Others, like the Disston family, gave her secondhand toys from their own children's castoffs. A pretty, vigorous, and intelligent young widow, she managed to make a small but decent family income. In the eyes of men like Pepper, Wanamaker, or Disston, Anna's social standing was higher than that of a mere domestic servant. As a contemporary author described these "working" society women, "Some act as secretaries to wealthy women; others are house decorators; another does dressmaking; still another provides 'afternoon tea.' This makes no difference in their social standing. In Philadelphia a gentlewoman raises the dignity of her work to her own level: she herself never sinks."[11] And Anna was the kind of woman who coveted respectability more than money.

Three years after her husband's death, Anna sold their row house on North 19th Street to a speculator. She made enough money to buy another house, not far away, at 874 North 20th Street. In this small, two-story row house, Anna and Jack were joined by Anna's two spinster sisters, Sarah "Sadie" M. Snader, forty-two, and Lena M. Snader, thirty-two.

This is the family McCloy remembers. "Sadie did hats and my mother did heads," he quipped. "She worked for a milliner whose brother worked at Penn Mutual. Lena, the younger one, was the cook and housekeeper. She provided me with all the fun. . . . She took me to Fairmount Park and Willow Grove where Sousa's band played and the roller coasters were. She saved her nickels and dimes and paid our entrance fees to the zoo and the circus."[12]

Young McCloy was taught that appearances were important. Every

Saturday morning, he watched Aunt Lena scrub their front stoop. "Lena used to polish those front marble stoops until you could see your face in them," he recalled. "Doing the front," as the washing of the stoops was called, was very much a Philadelphia ritual. The standards were set, of course, by the servants of those living on Walnut Street, across the Chinese Wall. A magazine article of the period observed, "It is a point of honour to have the five or six white marble steps immaculately clean, and the swish of the water and the knocking of the scrubbing brush are dear to the ears of every true Philadelphian."[13] Aunt Lena upheld the McCloys' honor on this score.

Anna was the major breadwinner in the household, and Aunt Lena spent the most time raising Jack. There was little if any male presence. Anna tried to be a disciplinarian, invoking the name of her dead husband. She would point to the picture of him kneeling in the grass with a handkerchief carefully placed beneath his knee, and tell Jack, "There, see how neat your father was?"[14]

But as he grew older, Jack became an athletically active, rowdy youngster. He and his friends played around the railroad yards, where McCloy recalled being "chased from time to time by what we called railroad dicks, always more exciting to run from than mere cops."[15] He also took to visiting the Philadelphia Baseball Park at North Broad and Huntington, about a mile down the road, or the Baker Bowl at Broad Street and Lehigh Avenue, where he watched professional baseball players like the great Napoleon Lajoie play America's national pastime.

Philadelphia had two major-league teams, the Phillies and the Athletics. The latter were managed by Cornelius McGillicuddy, known as "Connie Mack," who in the five-year stretch from 1910 to 1914 led the Athletics to four American League pennants.[16] McCloy was thrilled when one day the groundskeeper let him on the field while the "A's" were practicing. "They were the best, why, I guess they were the best team ever," recalled McCloy. "I was on speaking terms with 'Home Run' Baker, Eddie Collins, and Connie Mack. I used to shag flies for them." For a while, he became a regular, spending all his after-school hours hanging about the field.[17]

During the summers, Anna followed her hairdressing clientele to one of the fashionable summer camps in the Adirondack Mountains. One summer, they went to the Ausable Club, a beautiful lakeside resort frequented by Wall Street lawyers and businessmen and their families. Anna would "do heads" and arrange for Jack to work as a chore-boy, delivering wood, milk, and ice to the campsites with a shoulder yoke. When he was a little older, he had jobs maintaining tennis courts or acting as a guide for mountain climbers. On free afternoons, McCloy would go trout-fishing in the Bouquet River or hunt squirrel with a single-shot .22-caliber rifle.

Later, the summer exodus took them to the more exclusive Maine retreats on Mount Desert Island. Roughly fifty miles in circumference and cut halfway through by an arm of the ocean, the island was notched by picture-postcard harbors and crisscrossed by deep freshwater lakes and nine mountain ridges rising to fifteen hundred feet.[18] Anna's best client, Mrs. George Pepper, had gone to Mount Desert every summer since her marriage. Her husband described the island as "an ideal vacation-ground for anybody who loved mountains and sea and enjoyed the companionship of people of culture." By people of culture, Pepper meant men like Jacob Schiff, founder of the investment banking firm of Kuhn, Loeb & Co., and Charles W. Eliot, president of Harvard University.[19]

As one of the island's few hairdressers, Anna made her rounds on foot or bicycle, and when Jack was finished with his chores (often chopping wood for the Peppers), he sometimes accompanied her. He felt at ease around the vacationers. The outdoors was an equalizer, and any condescension was reserved for the island's taciturn natives, who had to make a year's living from the visitors during a short summer season. McCloy was part of the summer crowd.

But back at school, Jack did not excel, and soon Anna decided to send him away to a boarding school. "She wanted to get me away from the petticoat government there on 20th Street," explained McCloy. "[With] all those women in that house, she thought I needed some male influence." Anna consulted George Pepper, who discouraged her from sending Jack away to school, arguing that she could hardly afford the expense.[20] Refusing to be dissuaded, Anna turned for further advice to George Johnson, one of her late husband's friends from Penn Mutual. Johnson, a Quaker, recommended a Friends school in Concordville, Pennsylvania. The Maplewood Institute, founded in 1862, had a sound reputation as a preparatory school for young men bound for college or careers in business. The headmaster, who had been educated at both Swarthmore and Harvard, taught not only Latin but Greek as well; remembering her husband's injunction that Jack must learn Greek, Anna made her decision. "She was a very literal-minded person," explained McCloy. After all, Maplewood didn't work out.

"I can remember," said McCloy years later, "my mother sitting me down and telling me, 'Now, John, this is going to be tough. You will be very homesick and will want to quit. You will just have to be tough and remember your father.' Well, I knew it was going to be rough, but when I arrived, they stuck me in a bare room all by myself. There was no bed or anything. And then they completely forgot about me. I was supposed to be registered, but they just forgot all about me. It got dark, hours went by, and I ended up spending the whole night alone in that empty room. . . . I remember that night as if it happened yesterday."[21]

Perhaps it was this inauspicious arrival or the school's Quaker austerity but McCloy disliked Maplewood. Despite its idyllic rural location on a lovely tract of wooded land, Maplewood did not emphasize athletics. This was an obvious drawback for a boy who loved the sports field. Nor did he make any progress on the academic front. After a short time, Anna took him out of the school; in 1907, she decided to try another boarding institution, The Peddie Institute.[22] Anna's only reservation about Peddie was that the school was by background Baptist. She told Jack to "be a Presbyterian and don't let those Baptists convert you."

After the boy's traumatic registration experience at the Maplewood Institute, Anna made sure Jack was properly settled into The Peddie Institute. One morning in mid-September 1907, she and Jack took the train to Hightstown, New Jersey, a ride of an hour and a half from Broad Street Station. Hightstown was a village of some two thousand inhabitants, located about halfway between Philadelphia and New York. They walked to Wilson Hall, a four-story brick Victorian structure, the largest of the half-dozen buildings on the tree-lined campus. There they met Roger W. Swetland, Peddie's principal since 1898. A tall, balding man, Swetland consciously imitated the dean of New England headmasters, Dr. Endicott Peabody of Groton School. A Peddie education, Swetland advertised, would cultivate "those habits of self-reliance and self-control which are essential to a well-rounded manhood." Behind his back, Peddie boys irreverently called him "Old Baldy," or, more fearfully, "The Eagle."[23]

Swetland had large ambitions for what he called his "Greater Peddie." He hoped the school could "fill the gap between the modern high-priced boarding school for boys and the old-time cheap academy."[24] By shunning either extreme of "extravagance" or "impecuniosity," Swetland had created in Peddie an educational "middle ground" for the sons of "those who occupy the middle ground financially in the industrial and economic world."[25] Swetland's approach must have appealed to Anna McCloy's middle-class sensibilities. Here was a man who aspired to give her boy an education equal to that at Exeter or Andover, but at middle-class rates.

After Anna paid the school bursar $200, half the yearly rate for tuition, room, and board, Jack was escorted upstairs and unpacked his trunk. He shared a sparsely furnished room with one other boy. This was to be his home, with the exception of summers in Philadelphia and Bar Harbor, for the next five years. In 1907, there were fewer than eighty other boys at Peddie. Attendance at Bible study and the church of your choice in Hightstown every Sunday was mandatory. But religion was only a backdrop to the boys' regular curriculum. There was a science laboratory, which boasted a domed observatory with a four-inch telescope, and a library with ten thousand books.

Swetland emphasized a vigorous athletic program, and in 1904 had spent the phenomenal sum of $25,000 to build a modern gymnasium, complete with an indoor running track, a swimming pool, an exercise room, showers, and needle baths. There was a large athletics field with space for football and baseball, a pond for boating and skating, gun traps, and seven tennis courts.

Behind Wilson Hall, near the lake, was the dreaded "guard path," where any infraction of Peddie rules was paid for by walking fifty, seventy-five, or even a hundred rounds of the worn circular dirt path. A physical chore, certainly, but its real purpose was to make a public spectacle of the offender's humiliation. Those who walked the guard path were satirized as "pilgrims" of "extreme devotion."[26] It was punishment by ridicule, and Swetland found it highly effective. McCloy later remembered Swetland as a "wise, vigorous, deeply religious man." But he also feared him: ". . . I have a hard time thinking of him as ever having feared anybody, human or divine. The muses sing of the terrible wrath of the godlike Achilles, but to me Achilles' wrath was mere petulance compared to the really noble outbursts of which 'The Eagle' was sometimes capable."[27]

The most frequent cause of "guard" duty was infraction of Swetland's regulation forbidding the boys to leave their rooms after certain hours. Inevitably, many boys considered it a contest to see how often they could sneak out of the Wilson Hall dormitory by sliding down a rain pipe. Many "walked guard" for smoking cigarettes. Young Jack McCloy was, from all accounts, a frequent traveler on the guard path, at least in the first few years of his Peddie tenure.

"Oh, was he mischievous," recalled a classmate, Amzi Hoffman. "He was capable of all kinds of tricks . . . being out after hours, getting caught going up the rain pipe . . . or [he] might have gotten a guard penalty for not having good marks."[28]

McCloy was still not the best of students. His friend Amzi, who had started school late, was five years older. McCloy nicknamed him "Amazia." Amzi took a fair amount of ribbing for being an exemplary student, but McCloy nevertheless began to take his cues from the older boy. Hoffman recalls McCloy as someone who knew how to "take advantage of the opportunities. Lots of times I would know the answer to a question in class and sort of half give the answer under my breath, only half-audible, and he'd stick his hand up and give the same answer and get credit for it."[29]

It took McCloy more than a year to realize "what I could achieve."[30] Even after that, his grades were usually only a bit above average. The turning point was a Greek-language class, which he began to take in his second year, fifty minutes a session, five days a week. For some reason, perhaps because his mother had drummed into him his father's injunction that "John must learn Greek," he excelled. The Greek instructor, Herbert Winters, whom the boys nicknamed "Wintees," made him memorize hundreds of lines from Homer's *Illiad* and Xenophon's *Cyropaedia;* for the rest of his life, he could and often did recite these lines. In his eighties, he recalled fondly how "Wintees" had made him pound out the rhythm of the Greek verse with his feet, until he could "smell the dust, sweat and blood of the Scamander Plain."[31]

McCloy was one of the youngest members of his class. Shorter than most of his classmates, he had grown into a handsome, baby-faced young teenager with a shock of neatly parted brown hair. He had a well-scrubbed, all-American look about him; only his eyes betrayed a certain playful intelligence. His friends would always remember the roguish gleam in his eyes. He would never lose that brazen, mischievous expression. Even when he was a grown man, an old friend, an army general, would write him, "You always were impish with Generals. Like a girl, you do it with your eyes."[32]

He still loved sports, but his light, short frame made it difficult for him to get on any of the varsity teams in baseball or football. John D. Plant was the school's "physical director," and without question the most popular member of the faculty. "The 'Old Roman,' as we called him," remembered McCloy. "Tireless, cheerful, patient . . . he inspired us to play, or play at, all sports."[33] He was a strong, short, barrel-chested man with a mane of blondish hair swept straight back over his forehead. His round, flushed red face always had a friendly smile for his boys.[34] He was the only man on campus in whom every boy could confide his problems. For McCloy, the coach quickly became somewhat of a father figure. Plant exhorted his boys to play hard; those who hesitated received a kick in the rear. McCloy remembered, "If you flinched a tackle in football, the next day you were apt to find a jersey in your locker with a yellow streak down its back. It was pretty brutal."

Plant told McCloy, "John, always run with the swift. You might someday come in second." "It was good advice," he later recalled. "I took it to heart in all things. I always tried to play tennis with superior players. It's axiomatic. If you are always challenged by a superior player, sooner or later, if you are sound in body, you must someday beat the other fellow."[35]

With Plant's coaching, McCloy soon learned to play an aggressive game of tennis, a skill that served him well the rest of his life, opening doors that might otherwise have remained closed to someone of his social background. In 1911, when a tennis team was formed for the first time since 1907, eighteen boys tried out. Only five were chosen, and McCloy was ranked second. They had matches with teams from Princeton Preparatory School, ten miles down the road, the Drexel Institute, and Lawrenceville Prep, a preparatory school that catered to boys of wealth.

During his junior year, McCloy began to shine. That year he won the Hiram E. Deats, '91, Greek Prize, given to those who show the best scholarship in Greek during their junior and senior years. The prize brought an award of $10.[36] He was becoming more confident of himself and socially more gregarious: "I found you could raise your voice and talk out loud in the world."[37] Invited to join practically every one of the fraternities on campus, McCloy chose the oldest and most prestigious club, Alpha Phi. Founded in 1872, it had chapters at twelve other preparatory schools on the East Coast. Members got together for elaborate meals paid for by dues McCloy had to ask his mother to forward. Peddie had become a surrogate family. As with boys from similar elite prep schools, the camaraderie he enjoyed from his fraternity also served to inculcate in him a self-conscious sense of exclusivity. His Peddie class yearbook pictured a dapper McCloy, hair neatly slicked down, wearing a tweed vest and jacket, with a tie and large shiny pearl tie-pin. The photo was captioned, "So young but oh so wise." He had become a proper young gentleman, acculturated to the upper-class values common to a private-boarding-school life style.

In his last year at Peddie, McCloy, who had registered four years earlier as John Snader McCloy and had always signed his name "John S. McCloy," began to call himself John Jay McCloy. He told his friends that he had decided to name himself after John Jay, the nation's first Supreme Court chief justice. "That just tickled him," recalled Amzi Hoffman. It made a good story, and he told it with a characteristic twinkle in his eye, as if to say that he knew it for the joke that it was. He really did aspire to be a lawyer, because that was what his father had wanted. But it was his mother's wish as well. Widowed now for eleven years, Anna Snader McCloy had refused to remarry, and now that her only son was about to go off to college, she was determined that he use his late father's middle name.[38]

His grades had improved enough by his senior year so that he could begin to think about going to a good university. To pass a subject at Peddie, one had to score at least 75 percent. But Swetland refused to "certify" any student in a subject for university unless he had a score of 85 percent. In his last year, McCloy mustered this grade in most of his subjects, and higher in Greek. (He was also captain of the tennis team.) He assumed that he would enter the University of Pennsylvania, which would mean he could live at home.

Swetland had other ideas. He thought the boy, once so nonchalantly oblivious to discipline, had developed some of what he liked to call "Peddie character." He wanted such students to aspire to something better than even the University of Pennsylvania. It was part of Swetland's "Greater Peddie" strategy to have as many of his students as possible break into one of the elite Ivy League universities. Some of his "boys" were now in Princeton, Yale, Brown, and Amherst.[39] At the last, Swet-

land had placed two Peddie boys from the class of 1907.[40] Now Amzi Hoffman, the school's valedictorian in 1912, had been accepted at Amherst, as well as another McCloy classmate, Theodore "Gus" Edwards.

When the possibility of Amherst was broached with Anna McCloy, she resisted the idea; she had always thought the University of Pennsylvania was the best place for her son. Many "Proper Philadelphians," such as George Wharton Pepper, were alumni of Penn. And, of course, Jack could live at home. But at Swetland's urging, she began to reconsider. "I told her," Swetland wrote to Hoffman on July 19, 1912, "that if we could arrange for Jack to room with you, I thought it would be a splendid arrangement for the boy. You know Jack needs someone to act as ballast for him in order to get the best results out of his work. That I should expect you to do. Jack has the making of a splendid man in him, but he needs some one to steady him and hold him down to serious work during his college life." Swetland set the plot further in motion by closing his letter with the firm instruction that Amzi immediately write McCloy, "telling him of your own plans, and urging him to go with you."[41] In short order, McCloy consented.

He left Peddie a self-assured young man. He now had the simplicity of manners and easy dignity that mark many adolescents groomed in a prep-school cocoon. The private-boarding-school experience had taught him, in the words of his coach, to "run with the swift." He had learned that a little perseverance would allow him to compete with the best. The Spartan quarters and close comradeship of boarding school had also taught him to get along with his peers. As he later described the life of a boarding-school student: "He lives, eats, plays and studies with his fellow students and, of necessity, adjusts himself to their characteristics and attitudes." He even thought the experience was more democratic than a public-school education: ". . . true democratic forces can operate more effectively in the private school. . . . The student becomes freed from the local family and community prejudices and attitudes to a much greater degree than is the case of the public school student. . . . The outward symbols of class or other distinctions are lost more rapidly and more completely in the whole-absorbing community of the school than they are apt to be in the public school."[42] He had experienced a kind of class acculturation. As the sociologist C. Wright Mills wrote, America's elite private prep schools "perform the task of selecting and training newer members of a national upper stratum. . . ." Like Groton, Andover, or Saint Mark's, Peddie served to transmit upper-class values, and as such it was a "force for the nationalization of the upper classes."[43]

McCloy believed Peddie had given him a superior education. Private-school graduates, he said, "had the poise, the balance, the instincts, the training out of which leaders came in the largest proportions." As evidence, he cited a statistic that 65 percent of those listed in *Who's Who* were educated in private schools.[44] The son of a hairdresser, McCloy was grateful that Peddie had given him opportunities beyond his origins, beyond Philadelphia's Chinese Wall. He now had one of the requisites for membership in the Eastern Establishment: a prep-school credential.

CHAPTER 2

Amherst Years: 1912–16

"I firmly believe that there are times when a man must *fight, I believe it as firmly as I believe in loving my mother."*

JOHN J. MCCLOY, 1915

Soon after arriving at Amherst, McCloy and his classmates clambered up to the balcony of College Hall to witness the inauguration of the college's new president, Alexander Meiklejohn. It was October 16, 1912, a brisk and bright autumn day; the trees blanketing the campus were awash with orange, red, and yellow foliage. Scores of students were kept standing outside, waiting to squeeze into the packed hall. Inside, everyone sat impatiently in anticipation of seeing a new era begin. The last such inaugural had been seventeen years before, and the relatively young man about to speak to them represented a break with the past. Meiklejohn, forty, had a certain flair for the dramatic, a talent that did not fail him on this occasion.

From his perch in the balcony, McCloy looked down on the new college president, a short, gaunt man with a dimple on his chin and wire-rim spectacles balanced atop a long, thin Roman nose. Physically, he was not an impressive-looking figure; only his blue-gray eyes betrayed the man's forceful personality. As he began to speak, the audience realized this was not to be just another college sermon. Meiklejohn intended to criticize the college and its faculty. They had just heard their retiring president, George Harris, tell them, "The aim of a college is not to make scholars. The aim is to make broad, cultivated men . . . socially refined, and gentlemanly . . . with sane, simple religion, all in proportion. . . ."[1] Meiklejohn, in contrast, declared, "The college is primarily not a place of the body, nor of the feelings, nor even of the will; it is, first of all, a place of the mind. . . . To be liberal a college must be essentially intellectual." Ideas and a freewheeling questioning of everything, even religion, were to take precedence over the athletics department, or fine arts, or Bible study. Meiklejohn announced that his function, like that of other faculty members, was to "stand before his pupils and before the community at large as the intellectual leader of his time. If he is not able to take this leadership, he is not worthy of his calling."[2]

One of McCloy's classmates, Scott Buchanan, who later became a noted philosopher and the principal architect of the "Great Books" curriculum of Saint John's College, remembered the scene vividly: "At the end of the address I didn't know exactly what had happened nor exactly what had been said. The air had been tense, many people were puzzled, and some people were ready to be angry."

In that first year, the "Prexy," as Meiklejohn was nicknamed by the students, disrupted a number of Amherst traditions. At compulsory daily chapel, he replaced the regular Bible readings with quotations from his favorite philosophers, such as Epictetus, or poets, such as Robert Burns. Several old professors were forcibly retired, and young men filled with brash talk of socialism and agnosticism took their place. Meiklejohn's tenure at Amherst was stormy; he was fired by the trustees in 1923. But it turned him into a seminal figure in the history of liberal-arts colleges in America. And his essential liberalism—a blend of idealism and cold, analytical thought—influenced McCloy all his life.

McCloy took Meiklejohn's course in logic, which met in a dingy chemistry-lecture hall adorned with periodic-table charts. One hundred students sat on wooden benches while "Prexy" held forth. "He would begin," recalled Julius Seelye Bixler, a McCloy classmate, "with a selection from the *Euthypro* or perhaps the *Phaedrus*. Then, eyes flashing, and voice trembling with excitement, he would carry the battle to us, testing our comprehension of what had been said, summoning us to debate, challenging us to criticize his thought and our own. There was nothing namby-pamby about his use of the discussion method. . . . On occasions, before the closing bell, a kind of incandescence would descend on us, and the embers of the argument would burst into blazing flame. Afterward we realized that the experience had touched us where we lived."[3]

Bixler, Buchanan, Lewis W. Douglas—later McCloy's brother-in-law—became lifelong "Meiklejohn men." Not everyone, however, was so moved by the president's magnetism. Intellectually and temperamentally, Meiklejohn had the same moral certitude as another college president, Woodrow Wilson, who that November had just been elected president of the United States. He could be tactless with his critics.

McCloy's attitude toward the man was one of qualified respect.[4] He was entertained by Meiklejohn's unorthodox ideas and respected the president's willingness to debate vigorously both sides of any question: ". . . one came prepared for some new thought or some new personality every morning we climbed up the hill. I do not suggest that the entire student body was stirred every bleak week-day morning to a high level of intellectual speculation by the manner in which Meiklejohn conducted the Chapel services, but most of the students were intrigued and for a few minutes, at least, they had a new thought or an unusual point of view on which to ponder as they went off to their first classes. [He] had a way of stirring your thoughts on every contact you had with him."[5]

But the constant intellectual banter made McCloy uncomfortable. "To me, he never seemed relaxed and you found it difficult to relax in his presence simply because he made you keep on your toes when you talked to him."[6] Despite his nonathletic appearance, Meiklejohn played cricket, soccer, and an excellent game of tennis. McCloy, who had joined the tennis team soon after arriving on campus, became a regular on the court with Meiklejohn. The college president played to win. "To my great chagrin," McCloy recalled, "he once licked me, and he never let me forget it."[7] Intellectually, Meiklejohn never let up; even on the tennis court he was always turning the conversation to such weighty subjects as "What is justice? What is friendship? What is truth?"[8]

Such unrelenting intellectual stimulation had its effect; McCloy got into the habit of staging "reading debates" for himself, whereby he read books on similar topics with widely divergent points of view.[9] Never brilliant, he worked hard to earn his usual B's and occasional A. His favorite courses were in philosophy, Greek, and the American Civil War. His classmates remember him as a "competent . . . but not conspicuous" student.[10]

Some of the young professors Meiklejohn hired were left-wing in their politics. Walton Hamilton and Walter Stewart in the economics department, and Raymond Gettel in political science advocated greater government intervention in the nation's economy.[11] Some of the faculty were openly socialist and in their spare time taught workers in neighboring towns how to read. Meiklejohn himself encouraged students to donate their time to "classes for workers" in nearby Springfield and Holyoke.

McCloy, however, did not have a yen for teaching the working class how to read. He was still the hairdresser's son, struggling to better his own status in life. While the college gave him a small scholarship to meet the $140 annual tuition, he waited on tables to help pay for his room and board. Altogether, it cost about $750 annually for an Amherst education, and Anna's hairdressing money covered the bulk of this. During his freshman year, while rooming with Amzi Hoffman and Gus Edwards in a dormitory, he joined Beta Theta Pi, one of the cheaper fraternities.

Though a scholarship student and relatively poor, McCloy chose friends that were more often than not of a different class. His future brother-in-law was a case in point. Lewis W. Douglas was one of the richest men in McCloy's class. The son of an Arizona copper-mining magnate, Douglas had the easygoing self-assurance of a young man born to wealth, and soon established himself as a "big man on campus." He joined the most expensive and fancy of fraternities, Alpha Delta Phi, and, unlike McCloy, quickly assumed positions of leadership among his peers. He became class treasurer, and led a revolt that first year against the excessive "hazing" of freshmen by older fraternity boys. "Lew" Douglas had strong views about everything and didn't hesitate to voice them. Indeed, McCloy thought him a bit sanctimonious.[12] Gradually, however, the two men established a friendly rivalry, competing for grades and arguing over politics. This rivalry set a pattern, not only at Amherst, but later, in their careers on Wall Street and in government. Although they often disagreed, each judged himself partly by his measure of the other's career.

In the evenings, McCloy, Douglas, and other Amherst friends occasionally took a trolley ride toward South Deerfield, or joined other students at Dick Rahar's beer garden. On weekends, they often took long hikes across the Holyoke mountain ridges; afterward, they'd spend 50 cents to eat creamed spinach and chicken at one of the local restaurants.[13] Saturday nights, the frat houses hosted dances attended by women from nearby Smith and Mount Holyoke colleges. McCloy, however, was not known for "fussing" or "twosing," as dating was called. On this score, Lew Douglas clearly outshone him. Douglas spent a lot of his free time chasing women at Smith College; the Class of 1916 yearbook noted: "Jack McCloy and Lew Douglas hold the two ends of the fussing record."[14]

When McCloy returned to Amherst for his junior year in the autumn of 1914, the campus was consumed by talk of the European war that had just broken out. Articles advocating first the German and then the Allied cause were published in the *Amherst Monthly.* Most students were inclined to favor the Allies, and some thought America might someday be dragged into the fight. But early in the debate, President Meiklejohn strongly aligned himself with President Wilson's policy of neutralism and nonintervention. He discouraged what became known on the campus as the "preparedness movement," and refused to introduce military training into the curriculum, as suggested by many alumni and students. He was accused of pacifism.

On this issue, McCloy opposed his "Prexy." Everything he read about the war, particularly the accounts of alleged German atrocities committed in Belgium, struck an emotional chord; he was repelled by "things German." In the face of Prussian militarism, a policy of military preparedness seemed only good sense. He felt so strongly about the issue that, in the spring of 1915, he and three other students announced that they were going to attend a military training camp in the summer.[15] At Plattsburg, he had the formative political experience of his life.

Most Americans were unconcerned about the war in Europe until the afternoon of May 7, 1915. On that day, a German submarine fired a torpedo into a Cunard passenger liner off the coast of Ireland. The *Lusitania* sank within eighteen minutes, and 1,195 of her 1,959 passengers and crew members drowned. One hundred and twenty-four Americans died, bringing the European war home to America. *The New York Times* called upon the Wilson administration to demand that "the Germans shall no longer make war like savages drunk with blood."[16]

Grenville Clark, thirty-two, heir to a banking and railroad fortune and a senior partner in the firm of Root, Clark, Buckner & Howland, was so upset at the news that he couldn't work that day. He told his law partner, Elihu Root, Jr., that inaction was intolerable. Two days later, Clark called together some of his friends to discuss what they could do. Clark had noticed an article in the newspaper about an upcoming military training camp for students at Plattsburg, New York. Picking up on the idea, he suggested to his friends that they form a "businessmen's camp." The idea met with approval, and by June 14, 1915, Clark had arranged for General Leonard Wood to speak to a packed audience on the subject at the Harvard Club. A veteran of Theodore Roosevelt's "Rough Riders," General Wood was an ardent interventionist. Over a thousand lawyers and other professional young men listened as he praised the sacrifices being made in the European trenches and warned that the United States had to prepare itself to join the struggle. Afterward, Bernard Baruch, the Wall Street financier, donated an initial $3,000 to prepare the camp at Plattsburg.

Thousands of circulars and application blanks were soon mailed out to colleges and various alumni lists on the Eastern Seaboard. McCloy may have heard of Plattsburg through one of these fliers, but it is more likely that George Wharton Pepper provoked him into joining the camp. Pepper signed up for the first businessmen's camp, scheduled for August, and McCloy joined a training session for students beginning on July 6, 1915. "It seemed to me that all the right people went," McCloy recalled many years later.[17] They were certainly an elite group of students: Out of a total of 613 trainees, Harvard boasted the largest contribution with 76, followed by Yale with 62, and Princeton with 48. The rest came from similar colleges, such as Dartmouth and Bowdoin, and a few prep schools, such as Andover.[18]

Plattsburg was a small town of ten thousand residents. The army camp was located outside the town, on the shore of Lake Champlain and had a breathtaking view of both the Green Mountains and the Adirondacks.[19] McCloy arrived on the afternoon of July 5, to be greeted at the depot by a group of army officers and escorted to the camp, where he paid $27.50 for the privilege of four weeks' training ($17.50 for food and $10 for a uniform).[20] After a medical examination, he was taken to a stretch of ground sloping toward the lake where sixteen rows of conical tents had been pitched.

The next morning, he rose at 5:15 A.M. to begin the day with a cold shower, followed by group calisthenics and a quick breakfast. He and his squad, members of Company A, were issued rifles and taught how to care for them. The rest of the morning was devoted to marching drill. Noon mess was wolfed down by the hungry trainees, and then the students were allowed a choice of "voluntary work" in the afternoons. McCloy concentrated on rifle practice and learning to play soldier on horseback. He was good on the rifle range, and terrible on horseback. Some recruits were thrown from their horses so often that they joked it was "aviation" they were learning, not "equitation."[21]

At the end of each day, with his buttocks often blistered from the afternoon scrimmage with the saddle, McCloy was moved by a spine-tingling exercise in ceremonial patriotism. As the "colors" were lowered, and after the "retreat" was sounded by bugle, the entire camp came to attention as "The Star-Spangled Banner" was played. "I do not believe anyone in the camp," McCloy wrote a few weeks later, "no matter how tired or how blue he felt, ever 'stood retreat' without having a tiny thrill run up his spine."[22]

When the four-week session was over, he requested permission to remain for the businessmen's camp session, beginning on August 8. He and a few other enthusiastic students, including Archie Roosevelt, one of Theodore Roosevelt's sons, settled in for another four weeks. He was now in very special company. One major organizer of the businessmen's camp, DeLancey K. Jay, was a descendant of both John Jay and John Jacob Astor. Jay had recruited "the best & most desirable men" from as far away as Buffalo, Chicago, and Cleveland.[23] Standards were extremely high. Of the twelve hundred men who attended the camp that summer, more than 90 percent were college graduates.[24] Included were New York Police Commissioner Arthur Woods; Ralph W. Page, son of the U.S. ambassador to London; and Willard Straight, a millionaire then working for J. P. Morgan & Co. The previous year, Straight had founded *The New Republic,* which, of course, was running articles in support of preparedness.[25]

There were, indeed, so many men of substantial wealth that the press quickly dubbed Plattsburg the "millionaires' camp." It was reported that "the butterflies of Newport and Bar Harbor complained that life was desolate, since the best of their young men were at Plattsburg."[26]

McCloy used his month-long "veteran" status to make himself known to a few of these men, and his relationship with George Pepper helped smooth the way. He became friends with Jay J. Scandrett, twenty, a nephew of J. P. Morgan partner Dwight Morrow. He so impressed Morgan partner Willard Straight that he was offered a job in the Philippines with a Morgan-affiliated company. He turned the proposition down.[27]

The businessmen's camp routine was similar to what McCloy had just gone through in the previous month—except for the level of propaganda. As one historian later put it, "Plattsburg was not just a military training camp, it was, in a way, a secular retreat for a whole generation. There, amid simple, material surroundings, the upper-class elite underwent a conversion experience of patriotism. . . ."

In the evening, the men sat around fires, listening to army officers talk about the inadequate state of the nation's defenses. Grenville Clark often spoke, and McCloy was fascinated by the charismatic lawyer's words. General Wood, who had come to supervise the camp, believed such sessions were as important as the daily rifle drills. The first week, Wood told the men that William Jennings Bryan's recent assertion that the country could easily be defended by a million citizens springing to arms between sunrise and sunset was "a perfectly asinine statement."[28] America, he warned, could easily be invaded by a relatively small army, only three hundred thousand men.[29] Wood was a jingoist and an alarmist, and although he was under orders not to say anything that would undermine the Wilson administration's official stance of neutrality between the Allies and the Germans, the Plattsburg trainees came to recognize their potential enemy. Reporters heard the men singing this ditty while on the march:

We're Captain Kelly's company
We're neutral to a man
But if we have to lick the Dutch
You bet your life we can. [30]

These and other remarks were reported in the daily papers around the country, causing jitters in Washington, and increasing tension between Wilson and Wood. The Plattsburg general then invited Theodore Roosevelt to address the trainees. Roosevelt showed up early on the morning of August 25, wearing his familiar Rough Rider outfit. He spent the day watching McCloy, his son Archie, and twelve hundred other men in the camp perform maneuvers against regular U.S. Army units.

That evening, after supper, McCloy sat on the grass as Roosevelt stood by a campfire and delivered one of his more saber-rattling speeches.[31] As the sun set against the Green Mountains, Roosevelt started out by congratulating the men for "fulfilling the prime duty of free men." He then condemned all "professional pacifists, poltroons, and college sissies who organize peace-at-any-price societies." The crowd applauded, and when Roosevelt paused and said he would not accept applause from any who didn't feel a "burning sense of shame" for what had been done to Belgium, the men cheered even more wildly than before."[32] The next morning, the former president's remarks were front-page news across the country. Public opinion was polarized. Editors like Oswald Garrison Villard of *The Nation* inveighed against Roosevelt and the entire "war-mongering" preparedness movement.

But the youthful McCloy was greatly taken by both Roosevelt and his stirring appeal to the idea of military service. Congress held hearings in which some disgruntled Plattsburg students charged that "rookie" trainees were being turned into hardened militarists. McCloy's attitude was reflected in an unsigned editorial in the *New Republic,* probably written by his friend Willard Straight, on "The Plattsburg Idea" of national service: "The associates of this camp do not propose to militarize the American nation. They seek rather to civilize the American military system. . . ."[33]

Certainly, Plattsburg was a peculiarly privileged form of public service, performed in the company of the nation's brightest and wealthiest individuals. But that was precisely its appeal: here were privileged men who voluntarily gave themselves over for the national good. This experience gave McCloy a new set of role models, younger versions of his mentor George W. Pepper.

When the camp was over on September 6, McCloy accompanied Pepper up to Bar Harbor, where his mother had gone on her annual pilgrimage.[34] After a few weeks' vacation, he returned to Amherst for his senior year. Once back on campus, McCloy plunged into the "preparedness" debate with a two-thousand-word article in the *Amherst Monthly* entitled "Why Not the Camp?" Unaware of his painful encounters on horseback, the editors identified McCloy as "connected with the cavalry at Plattsburg."[35]

The article demonstrated that he had fully digested Greenville Clark's campfire sermons. With boyish earnestness, McCloy publicly swore allegiance to the kind of political affiliations to which he would remain constant for the rest of his life. He declared himself a heartfelt patriot, an internationalist, a pragmatist devoted to "collective action," and a critic of appeasers and pacifists. Echoing both Clark and Roosevelt, he wrote, "I firmly believe that there are times when a man *must* fight, I believe it as firmly as I believe in loving my mother." He argued that the violation of Belgium's neutrality by Germany was one such instance; it was a great crime that had to be punished. Whereas critics of the war inveighed against the senseless slaughter of millions in brutal trench warfare, McCloy made a highly romantic appeal to his fellow students' sense of self-sacrificing idealism: "Instead of continually referring to the crime of Europe, it should rather be considered a blessing that men should die for the righting of such a crime."

He fervently defended TR's militancy: "Theodore Roosevelt said there were some things worse than war. Because Roosevelt said it, strange as it may seem, the statement ipso facto is not wild militarism. Incidentally, if some people wasted less breath calling Roosevelt names and considered more carefully some things that he says, they might accomplish more."

He attacked pacifists by quoting Christ: "I bring not peace but the sword." Of passive resistance he wrote, "They say it hasn't been tried but it would work. They have great faith in it. I have just as great faith that it won't work, and anything that I can do to hinder that experiment being tried, I'll do."

He reasoned with his Amherst peers that "war is an ever-present possibility. This summer war talk was rife. It would have taken but little to plunge the country into war. People would no more have hesitated because of the size of the army than they ever did." He dismissed the popular idea that either the army officers or Wall Street was pushing the country into war. "The notion," he wrote, "that it is the military men who make wars is wholly false. They do not vote, they do not urge their views, they simply do what they are ordered to do. The ones that order them are not the group of financiers in a corner in Wall Street either, it is not the President. It is the people in the last analysis. The man in the street in nine cases out of ten would have the country go to war before the officer would.

"Justice never was and never will be provided by the weak," McCloy concluded. ". . . Crime and intrigue among nations will stop only when nations take a stand against them, and a very decided stand."[36]

The article established his reputation in his senior year at Amherst as a leader of the "preparedness" camp, and it expresses a political philosophy that he subscribed to for the rest of his life. Military preparedness in itself was a simple idea, but for men like Teddy Roosevelt, Grenville Clark, and Henry Stimson, it formed the basis for a world-view eventually shared by a whole generation of "Stimsonians." McCloy bought into this philosophy at an early stage.

In their last year at Amherst, McCloy and Douglas had both inched their averages to above 90, making them eligible to graduate *cum laude.* Douglas had no clear idea of what he wanted to do next, but McCloy had set his heart on Harvard Law School. He didn't even bother to apply to any other law school, and was ecstatic when Harvard accepted his application.[37]

His class yearbook named him a "stellar performer," but Douglas won the familiar accolade "most likely to succeed."[38] Their collegiate rivalry did not end with graduation. Douglas announced that he would join McCloy for the August session at Plattsburg. There the two friends competed on the rifle range. Douglas, who had grown up in the West handling guns, was an excellent marksman, but McCloy, who had already gone through two Plattsburg sessions, managed to equal his high score of 448 out of a possible 450.[39]

McCloy was not the only veteran to return to Plattsburg in 1916; 85

percent of the men trained in 1915 came back, including George Pepper, Mayor Mitchel, Willard Straight, the Roosevelt sons, Hamilton Fish, Jr., and Elihu Root, Jr. One notable newcomer was former Secretary of War Henry Stimson, forty-nine, who was given the temporary rank of acting lieutenant and allowed to command some cavalry troops. (Though Stimson was practically blind in one eye, he shot well, and the doctors obligingly pronounced him fit for active service.) It is quite possible that Pepper introduced "Lieutenant" Stimson to "Lieutenant" McCloy sometime during their cavalry exercises, but there's no evidence that they established any memorable relationship.[40]

It was a much larger camp than in 1915; more than seven thousand trainees went through the program that summer. President Wilson had come around to endorsing the "Plattsburg Idea" the previous November, saying, "We have it in mind to be prepared, not for war, but only for defense. . . ."[41] General Wood, however, had in mind something more when he wrote a friend about the August camp: "We are putting over the sentiment for universal training and perhaps that is the most important thing we can do."[42] Wood believed war was a certainty. And from the perspective of many of the men stomping through the mud of Plattsburg, there was already evidence that it had arrived on American shores. On the night of July 29, 1916, a week before Wood wrote his friend about the need for a draft, a terrific explosion tore apart Black Tom Island in New York. Millions of rounds of ammunition and other explosives bound for the Russian front were destroyed, and the newspapers reported that the police suspected sabotage. As he left Plattsburg on September 6, 1916, for Harvard, McCloy could not help wondering how long he would be left alone to study the law.

CHAPTER 3

Harvard Law School and the War Years: 1916–21

"In the synthesis of thinking that must shape the Great State, the lawyer is in many ways the coordinator, the mediator. . . ."

FELIX FRANKFURTER

Harvard Law School has been called a republic within the republic, a high citadel and a clearing house for the Establishment. To study law at Harvard qualifies one to become part of the governing mechanisms of the American state, and the friendships students form open doors for the rest of their careers. For McCloy, Harvard was the final stepping-stone into the Establishment. It made him part of a tradition that included men like Henry Stimson, Elihu Root, and Oliver Wendell Holmes, Jr.

"I have a quasi-religious feeling about Harvard Law School," Felix Frankfurter once said. "I regard it as the most democratic institution I know anything about. By 'democratic,' I mean regard for the intrinsic and nothing else."[1] Frankfurter was only thirty-three in 1916, when McCloy arrived on campus. A Jewish immigrant, the son of a cloth peddler in Manhattan, Frankfurter was awarded a professorship in 1914, a move embodying Harvard's commitment to pure meritocracy. But the flip side to this egalitarianism was a seductive elitism.[2]

The rules of the game were simple: "What mattered was excellence in your profession," recalled Frankfurter, "to which your father or your face was equally irrelevant. And so, rich man, poor man were just irrelevant titles to the equation of human relations."[3] What mattered to a first-year student was making the *Harvard Law Review,* an honor determined strictly by the year-end examinations. The competitive pressure on McCloy was intense. He was both awed and intimidated by Harvard, and compared his move from Amherst to Cambridge to traveling from the Greek provinces to the sophisticated atmosphere of ancient Athens. "I had to work harder than everyone else there," McCloy recalled. "I wasn't as smart. . . . All those boys from Groton and Exeter had a better education than I did at Peddie."[4]

One of his Amherst classmates, Homans Robinson, the son of a Springfield, Illinois, lawyer, also entered Harvard Law that year, and McCloy decided to share a room with him. They paid $50 per month for a room in a private home off campus.[5] Charles A. Wolfe, another first-year student, took the only other room in the house, and the three of them worked hard that year to keep up with their studies. "The first year there's a preoccupation with survival," Frankfurter recalled of his own Harvard christening, "and you don't know, nobody knows how good he's going to be at anything in a contest in which he hasn't been tested."[6]

McCloy earned a little extra cash and the occasional steak dinner by washing dishes at a steak-and-seafood house in Boston called Durgin Park.[7] He, Robinson, and Wolfe socialized very little. Whereas many men joined one of the traditional "law clubs," where one could have a substantial dinner, they took most of their meals at Memorial Hall, the cheapest eating place on campus. McCloy played a little tennis with a few of his fellow students, including Wallace C. Chandler, another first-year man, whom he regularly beat.[8] But for most of that year, he was hard-pressed to keep up with his studies.

Harvard had been the country's foremost law school for nearly two generations when McCloy arrived in 1916. Founded in 1817, the school came into its own in 1870, when a young lawyer named Christopher Columbus Langdell was appointed dean. Langdell conceived the "casebook method" of teaching law. Until then, students had listened to abstract lectures on the principles of law, and after a year or two were graduated. Langdell's Socratic approach required a student to read up on a particular case and be prepared to dissect it under close questioning from his professor.

By 1916, the school's staff included such noted legal scholars as Joseph H. Beale, Samuel Williston, Eugene Wambaugh, Edward H. Warren, Austin Scott, Frankfurter, and Roscoe Pound. The last had been appointed dean in March 1916. McCloy studied with all of these men. Pound, who wore a green eyeshade, taught torts and equity. Williston handled commercial contract law, Scott did trusts, Beale lectured on taxation and "conflict of laws," and Frankfurter covered criminal law, jurisdiction and procedure of federal courts, and municipal corporations.[9]

Williston wrote what is still considered the bible on contracts; McCloy later said he was "the best contracts man ever."[10]

They were all towering figures in the legal community, but McCloy's favorite professor was Beale.[11] Beale and Williston, both of whom had been on the faculty since 1890, represented the "entrenched common-law tradition."[12] This conservative school of legal thought was under severe attack at the time from such "radicals" on the faculty as Frankfurter and Pound, the nation's leading proponent of the "sociological-jurisprudence" movement. Frankfurter thought of himself and Pound at the time as infiltrating Harvard with a "Trojan horse of what [Learned] Hand calls our 'heretical thinking.' "[13] McCloy gravitated toward the traditional camp. Perhaps Beale's orderly, logical approach to the law appealed to his mind. Frankfurter thought Beale "dogmatic" and complained, "He could straighten out the greatest confusion. Everything had to fall in its place. He didn't allow for any untidiness, and of course the law is as untidy as life with which it deals. . . ."[14]

Frankfurter was not a favorite of McCloy's. "He only paid attention to the bright students," McCloy recalled, "the ones sitting in the front row. . . . Frankfurter never paid attention to those in the back. I later used to chide him about how he ignored us."[15] Frankfurter's favorites were those like Dean Acheson (a year ahead of McCloy), Leo Gottlieb, and Archibald MacLeish, who were quick-witted, articulate and self-confident. They sat in the front row, willingly taking the brunt of Frankfurter's hard-edged banter. They were also invited back to the professor's home for afternoon tea sessions where the conversation often turned to politics. But this was not McCloy's experience; sitting in the back rows, he was one of those who, even if he did get called upon by Frankfurter and gave a partially correct answer, would promptly be upstaged by someone from the favored front row.[16]

McCloy's other classes were led by equally demanding personalities. Professor Edward H. "Bull" Warren, who taught property law, demanded that students reply to his queries with accurate, tersely stated summaries of all the facts in a case. He once called upon an unprepared student who replied incoherently at great length. Warren let him finish and then said, "Sir, that was a splendid example of a diarrhea of facts and constipation of ideas. I hope you haven't ordered your shingle, for you won't need it."[17]

If the regimen was brutal, it was also seductive. After a few months, McCloy found himself, in Frankfurter's words, being "sucked into the law by the very atmosphere of the place." He patiently read the casebooks and suffered through the Socratic classroom confrontations. "I had to run as fast as I could to keep up," McCloy recalled.[18] His long first year was neither distinguished nor dishonorable; it was, in fact, a familiar Harvard story. The precocious Frankfurter himself had spent the first few months of his own Harvard Law student experience muttering, "This is too fast a crowd for me."[19] Initially intimidated by both the faculty and his fellow students, McCloy just missed making the *Harvard Law Review* by the end of the year. He was disappointed, but the competition had been fierce. Dean Acheson and Archibald MacLeish made the *Review,* and so too did Donald Swatland, a brilliant classmate with whom McCloy was on friendly terms.

There had also been distractions to take his mind away from the law books. The war news from Europe in 1917 was increasingly ominous, and McCloy felt sure that he would soon be in uniform again. Although the *Harvard Crimson* and other student publications in 1915 had criticized the preparedness movement, the university's president, A. Lawrence Lowell, was an early convert. Feelings ran high on the campus between the pacifist and preparedness camps. One law student remembered with some bitterness, "If you were pro-war, you were a hero. If you were a pacifist, which indeed I was, you were just a no-goodnick."[20]

Frankfurter was no pacifist, but he thought the preparedness movement was financed by big business and influenced by "sinister, ignorant forces." He thought the worst of McCloy's commanding general at Plattsburg: "The preparedness views of Leonard Wood make me wholly impatient—he has no vision about this country that goes beyond a German General's."[21]

On this as on many other issues at Harvard, Frankfurter was in the minority. By the summer of 1916, the university had established a Reserve Officers' Training Corps (ROTC) undergraduate course for the next academic year.[22] When President Wilson finally asked Congress for a declaration of war in early April 1917, the campus quickly began to look like a military garrison. Hundreds of ROTC students were immediately sent off to Plattsburg. McCloy was ordered to return to Plattsburg by the afternoon of May 14, 1917.[23]

As a three-time veteran of the camp, McCloy thought himself professionally superior to most of his peers, who were in the greatly expanded camp for the first time. Hoping to win a commission in the regular army by the end of the summer, he decided to specialize in field artillery. "The work is getting more and more complicated," he wrote his mother in June. "We have exams each day on the stuff and I am not getting along any too well on them. My chances are pretty slim in this game for a commission at the end of the camp. . . . So I guess my chances of getting to France with the 1st shift are thin."[24]

He may always have felt he had to work harder than most, but he invariably succeeded. On August 15, he won a provisional commission as a second lieutenant in field artillery, and by the end of the month was temporarily assigned to the 19th Cavalry. Anna must have been relieved when, instead of being shipped off to the front on the "1st shift," her son was assigned to Fort Ethan Allen in Vermont.

For the next nine months, McCloy was shuttled between various army camps and kept busy on training exercises. He wrote his mother frequently, thanking her for the little parcels she mailed containing chocolate, apples, and various other foods. Once she sent him a warm quilt and told him to sew the sides together to make a sleeping bag. McCloy demurred, writing, "Sleeping bags are usually a nuisance. They get so sweaty. . . ." He worried about his mother as much as she did about him. When Anna was looking for a new place to live in Philadelphia, he wrote her, "Do promise me that you will get a good place. I'll give you something out of each month's check that will help out. . . . If you only knew how much better I'd feel if you were well fixed."[25]

More than anything else, he was impatient to get across the Atlantic Ocean, and gave much thought to acquiring the right equipment for every contingency. In March 1918, he wrote Anna from Charlotte, North Carolina, and instructed her to pay $125 for his own private riding saddle. "When I leave for France," he explained, "I want to feel fully equipped for anything that may happen. . . ."[26] This was a considerable expense for Anna, but she promptly sent him the saddle.

His saddle worries were quite genuine. Though he still lacked grace atop a horse, his usual persistence again caught the eye of one of his superiors. His commanding officer, Brigadier General Guy H. Preston, ran into him just after a long ride. "One day at Fort Ethan Allen," Preston wrote McCloy years later, "I walked behind you after you had been riding and I could see blood all over your pants. I said to myself that any son of a bitch who could keep riding with that much pain must be a damn good officer." Preston asked McCloy to serve as his aide-de-camp, a coveted position in any army. When he pointed out to the general that the army hadn't issued him orders for the job, Preston snapped back, "Pay no attention; I'm certified to have an aide." Such informality resulted in McCloy's being carried for some months on the official army lists as AWOL.[27]

General Preston, fifty-three, was a gruff career cavalry officer with an earthy sense of humor. When McCloy met him, he was organizing a field-artillery brigade, explaining, "I learned what a trajectory was while pissing against the schoolhouse wall."[28] He regaled his aide with stories of his battles in the Dakotas with the Sioux Indians. (In December 1890, Second Lieutenant Preston was "commended" for his "courage and endurance" at Wounded Knee, where at least 153 Sioux men, women, and children were massacred.) McCloy always remembered him as the general who "fought the Indians on the Plains," and years later would underline this aspect of his CO's career to emphasize how few years separated America, the global power, from America the conqueror of Indians. As a nineteenth-century cavalry officer, Preston believed in America's manifest destiny. With the Indians pacified, he had remained in the cavalry and later served in the Spanish-American War. McCloy grew very fond of Preston; over the years, the general became a father figure—to the point where Preston began signing his letters to him, "Love, Dad."[29]

Preston and McCloy shipped out for France with the 160th Field Artillery Brigade in late July 1918. Stationed in the Toul sector with the Second Army, McCloy didn't see action until October and November. Even then, he recalled, his "combat service was rather drab."[30] His unit lobbed artillery shells against Germans positioned across the Moselle River for several weeks. The Armistice was signed just before he and his men were to assault the city of Metz.

On Armistice Day, November 11, 1918, McCloy was sitting with Preston on the parapet of a trench outside Metz, watching French prisoners being released by the defeated Germans. During the next few months, he served in the army of occupation, and saw a good bit of Germany. On March 1, 1919, he was transferred to General John J. "Black Jack" Pershing's headquarters at Chaumont. By this time, Preston had introduced him to all the leading figures of the American Expeditionary Force, including General Pershing, Colonel George C. Marshall, and Colonel Douglas MacArthur. He also introduced him to the best-known hero of the war, Colonel William J. Donovan. The winner of a half-dozen medals, including the Congressional Medal of Honor, Donovan had already been named by the newspapers back home as "Wild Bill." "He had the mark of bravery and leadership written all over him," McCloy later recalled. "I remember how much I then envied him, his elan, his spark, and his record."[31]

Occupation duty at Chaumont left some time for recreational activities, and, characteristically, McCloy was still trying to "run with the swift." On the tennis court, he frequently played with some of France's most celebrated pros. One day he had a chance to play with a rising young French champion, Suzanne Lenglen. Later that year, Lenglen became a Wimbledon champion. Known as "The Goddess," she was rather short-tempered, and on those rare occasions when she felt herself about to be beaten, she might sometimes abruptly walk off the court. This time, McCloy was down four games to love when General Pershing himself walked into the bleachers to watch the play. "Why, he was my commanding general," remembered McCloy. "I just set to work, serving very hard, running to the net, calling the ball very close, doing whatever I could to win. When I pulled even with her four games to four, she just turned and walked off the court."[32]

At the end of June 1919, McCloy was promoted to the temporary rank of captain, and then shipped home with Preston. His mentor tried to persuade him to make a career of the army. McCloy stood in awe of professional military men like Marshall, Donovan, and MacArthur. But his two years away from Harvard had not shaken his ambition for a legal career. Sitting in Camp Lee, Virginia, waiting to be discharged, he opened a few of his old law books. "One evening McCloy came to eat with me at my camp table in the mess hall," Preston wrote later. "I saw he was preoccupied. Finally he exclaimed, 'General, that abstract law is beautiful stuff!' I glanced at him and saw his face was radiant as an angel's. I said at once, 'Mac, I'll never again ask you to stay in this man's army. Your destiny is too manifest.' "[33]

Harvard had changed. Enrollment had dropped from a high of 857 when McCloy left in 1917 to a low of 68 just before the Armistice.[34] The elitist luncheon clubs had so shrunk that most were completely disbanded. Ten thousand Harvard men had served in the war, half as officers.[35] The students who returned were older and impatient to get on with their careers. McCloy rented an apartment in Cambridge, and his mother decided to move from Philadelphia to take care of him. Anna was now fifty-five, and for the rest of her long life she frequently lived with her son. Finances were tight as usual, so he made a little extra money teaching squash and handball as he resumed his studies. "At first it was not easy," McCloy recalled. "In fact, it seemed dull, terrible to be sitting in a classroom, reading and rereading cases after having commanded a field artillery battery in the greatest war in history. The studies didn't seem to bear much relationship to the war. Gradually, however, I caught on."

Politically, the postwar mood turned nativist and reactionary, and the country was becoming polarized by a growing and militant trade-union movement. Attorney General A. Mitchell Palmer warned that a "blaze of revolution" threatened to destroy American life, "licking the altars of churches, leaping into the belfry of the school bell, crawling into the sacred corners of American homes, seeking to replace marriage vows with libertine laws, burning up the foundations of society."[36] In January 1920, when Palmer arrested more than five thousand suspected "radicals" in over thirty cities around the country, Frankfurter and a group of his colleagues in the law school condemned the warrantless arrests. Frankfurter and Zachariah Chafee, Jr. an assistant professor since 1916, wrote a brief that was instrumental in obtaining the release of some of those arrested. Chafee wrote a *Harvard Law Review* article in April 1920 that vigorously criticized the government's prosecutions under the Espionage Act. And when the Supreme Court upheld the convictions anyway, Frankfurter, Chafee, Pound, and a number of other Harvard Law School personalities signed a petition for clemency addressed to President Wilson.

Such controversies spilled over into the student body, where opinion became just as polarized. The *Harvard Advocate* was filled with articles reflecting the views of the two camps, described as "those who would like to see all the Reds and near-Reds dangling from lamp posts, and those who believe that free speech is an absolute right. . . ."[37] But McCloy was only a witness, never a participant in these political arguments. Not part of Frankfurter's favored inner circle, he had no personal involvement in the professor's political battles. Unlike Dean Acheson, who under Frankfurter's influence emerged from Harvard Law School a Democrat, McCloy distrusted the trade-union movement and counted himself a Roosevelt Republican. He no doubt agreed with an April 1920 editorial Archie MacLeish wrote on "The Liberalism of Herbert Hoover." Hoover's brand of liberalism had no "old World" roots, papered over "class lines," and was thoroughly American in its emphasis on individual "opportunity and flexibility." Hoover was a liberal, wrote MacLeish, "who has not forgotten that liberalism signifies *progressive* reform, and that in progression there is present the idea of development out of things that have been."[38]

College men in general greatly admired Hoover's career, and this was particularly true of war veterans who were hearing of his efficient war relief operations in postwar Europe. Hoover's reputation for an "open-minded ability to find constructive remedies for grievous situations" had caused his name to be bandied about as a possible presidential candidate by the spring of 1920. But no one seemed to know whether the great engineer was a Republican or a Democrat. In the event, Warren Harding was nominated by the Republicans, with Calvin Coolidge, an Amherst man, as his vice-president. McCloy voted Republican.

Politics did not absorb much of his attention at Harvard. McCloy was, as usual, spending more time than most of his classmates poring over the case histories. Outside the classroom, he began to take tutoring jobs to earn a little more money for tuition. During the summer of 1920, he took his mother up to Mount Desert Island and, instead of chopping wood for George Wharton Pepper, hired himself out as a tutor of history and law. One day Anna urged him to approach the Rockefellers for a job. In 1910, John D. Rockefeller, Jr., had bought a majestic mansion of solid Maine granite perched atop a cove at Seal Harbor. The estate, called the Eyrie, had 104 rooms and a manicured Oriental garden surrounded by a fence adorned with tiles shipped from the Great Wall of China.[39]

Such a formidable setting would have led any young man of McCloy's background to hesitate. But Anna insisted that there was no harm in presenting oneself at the front door and asking for employment. She had knocked on many such doors in the course of soliciting clients. McCloy climbed the hill to the Eyrie three times before he "had the nerve to ring the doorbell."[40] When he told the butler his business, he was curtly informed that the Rockefeller sons already had tutors, and the door was slammed in his face.

This humiliation was only momentary. By the end of that summer, he was teaching the young Rockefellers sailing in the little harbor below the Eyrie. Rockefeller, Jr., was forty-six years old and had five sons and one daughter, Abby, who was seventeen at the time. John D. 3rd, Nelson, Laurance, Winthrop, and young David ranged in ages from fourteen to five. It was a fleeting relationship, but it set the terms for what turned out to be a lifelong association with the Rockefellers. David was so young at the time that he would scarcely remember the episode. But in the eyes of the other boys, McCloy would always seem a teacher, a mature figure, closer in authority to their father's generation than to their own. In later years, McCloy always referred to Junior as an elder due the greatest respect, whereas the sons were etched in his mind as those youngsters he had taught sailing so many years ago.

Back at Harvard for his last year, McCloy concentrated on corporate or commercial law, and relished courses with Austin Scott, a vivacious, intense young professor who paced neatly back and forth in front of his class as he lectured. At the age of thirty-seven, Scott was already probably the country's foremost legal scholar on trust law, a relatively new and exciting field. The Standard Oil trust controlled by John D. Rockefeller, Sr., had been broken up only a decade earlier. Since then, corporate executives had been paying their lawyers to ensure that they did not become the targets of antitrust legislation. McCloy enjoyed the problem-solving aspects of the trust cases he studied; corporate law seemed more concrete than the subjective and highly political legislative and constitutional law taught by professors like Frankfurter and Chafee.

His ambition was to seek a job with a large Philadelphia firm specializing in corporate work, an intention that Frankfurter would have scorned. Private practice, Frankfurter wrote in 1913, "means putting one's time in to put money in other people's pockets."[41] Frankfurter's prejudice was in part affected by his own early experiences with anti-Semitism on Wall Street. But he had also hated the work and had jumped at the opportunity to work for Henry Stimson as an assistant attorney general. He encouraged his brightest students to do the same, arguing that no corporate lawyer could affect the public interest.

Frankfurter's mentor, Justice Louis D. Brandeis, took another view. Brandeis had made himself a millionaire working for some of the country's major corporations. He strongly believed that in a democratic society lawyers in particular were trained to distinguish the public interest from the narrow private interests of the moment, and that knowledge of the law made it possible for them to rise above petty, material interests. Far from saying, as Frankfurter did, that a lawyer could not serve the public interest while working for a corporation, Brandeis merely complained that too many lawyers in modern society were suspending their judicial good judgment and independence of mind.

In the spring of 1905, Brandeis chastised an audience of Harvard Law students, including Frankfurter: "Instead of holding a position of independence, between the wealthy and the people, prepared to curb the excesses of either, able lawyers have to a large extent, allowed themselves to become adjuncts of great corporations and neglected the obligation to use their powers for the protection of the people."[42]

The difference between Brandeis and Frankfurter was ultimately one of temperament. Before joining Harvard's faculty, Frankfurter had written himself a memo justifying the move. Among other things, he suggested, "In the synthesis of thinking that must shape the Great State, the lawyer is in many ways the coordinator, the mediator, between the various social sciences." Citing the "easily accountable dominance of the lawyer in our public affairs," he speculated that only to lawyers would fall the task of mediating between the powerful private and public interests characteristic of any modern industrial society. The battles ahead would center on the "shaping of a jurisprudence to meet the social and industrial needs of the time. . . ."[43]

McCloy left Harvard with ideas about his new profession not so dissimilar. Like Frankfurter, he saw his role as an impartial mediator, objective, rational, and capable of discerning the greater public interest. Unlike Frankfurter, he saw no conflict between this and working for large corporate interests. In the spring of 1921, he graduated with more than respectable marks and left to seek work in Philadelphia.

CHAPTER 4

Wall Street: 1921–30

"Brilliant intellectual powers are not essential. Too much imagination, too much wit, too great cleverness, too facile fluency, if not leavened by a sound sense of proportion are quite as likely to impede success as to promote it."

PAUL CRAVATH

McCloy's role model was still George Wharton Pepper, and upon returning to Philadelphia he went straight to the distinguished lawyer and asked for a job. Pepper's firm, Pepper, Bodine, Stokes & Schoch, was the leading firm in the city. Pepper's senior partner, Bayard Henry, had founded the prestigious Lawyers' Luncheon Club, and the firm represented some of Philadelphia's leading corporations. In a few months, Pepper, fifty-four, would be appointed to the U.S. Senate seat then occupied by a dying Boies Penrose, boss of the Republican machine in Pennsylvania for the last twenty years. To Anna it only seemed natural and right that her son should go to work for her late husband's colleague. Pepper had already taken into the firm Ernest Scott, the son of the late Dr. Al Scott, her husband's close friend.

Pepper was friendly and polite as ever, but he bluntly told McCloy, "Now, listen John, I know your family well. When your mother wanted to send you away to school, I was against it. I didn't think she could afford it. I was wrong about that, but I am not wrong about this. I know Philadelphians. It is a city of blood ties. You have good grades, but they don't mean anything here. Family ties do. Even when I started out here it was difficult and slow. It would be impossible for you. You were born north of the Chinese Wall, and they'll never take you seriously in this town. In New York, however, your grades will count for something."[1]

Years later, McCloy would remember this little sermon from his Philadelphia patron word for word and smile. He knew right away that

Pepper was not snubbing him; it was the city. There was no point wasting the formative years of his legal career in a city that would never really accept him. McCloy didn't brood about it for a minute, but the same day, after informing Anna of the discouraging interview, he took the train to Manhattan—and left behind the Chinese Wall forever.

It might not have seemed the best of times to look for a job. The years 1920–21 were years of serious recession. Unemployment throughout the 1920s never fell below 5 percent, and during the '21 recession it was much higher.[2] When the Republicans elected Warren Harding to the White House, the Federal Reserve clamped down on post-Armistice inflation. Government food-relief operations in Europe were halted, and the price of U.S. wheat plummeted. Whole sectors of the economy were in trouble, including such blue-chip industries as railroads and steel.

But when businesses falter, America's lawyers find their offices overflowing with clients in need of sound legal advice. McCloy made the rounds of all the major New York firms and received seven or eight offers. He accepted a position as an associate with Cadwalader, Wickersham & Taft, because "it was a very prestigious firm. There was George Wickersham, the former attorney general, and Henry W. Taft, the brother of the president."[3] The business community regarded the firm as particularly well qualified to defend corporations from antitrust suits; Wickersham, who as attorney general for four years under President Taft had vigorously prosecuted monopolistic behavior, now used his talents on behalf of the defendants.

There were more than a dozen associates and thirty-four nonlegal staff, making the company one of Manhattan's earliest law factories. In 1921, the firm collected $734,278 worth of fees, 31 percent of which was used to cover expenses. That left a hefty pretax profit of $506,652 to be divided among the eight partners.[4] Cadwalader was doing well, and the potential rewards if McCloy made partnership were considerable.

But from the beginning he found the pace at Cadwalader "slow" and the firm's atmosphere "very traditional."[5] McCloy gravitated toward the corporate and securities work supervised by William Lloyd Kitchel. Because many of Kitchel's clients were troubled railroads, McCloy found himself specializing in this field.

His annual salary of $1,000—plus bonus—was good money in 1921. Real income in 1920 had risen less than 5 percent above the rates for 1899. The subway fare was a nickel, first-class postage was 2 cents, and a seven-course meal could be had at a number of Italian restaurants in Greenwich Village for $1.10.[6]

Because he wanted to be as close as possible to the West Side Tennis Club, McCloy rented a bachelor's room from a family in Forest Hills. Next door lived a professional tennis coach who befriended McCloy and used him to warm up the women pros.[7] He once won a set in an informal match from another native Philadelphian, William Tilden, Jr., the reigning Wimbledon champion, who was turning tennis into a big-money spectator sport. McCloy talked up his little victory and won the reputation on Wall Street as the lawyer who had beaten "Big Bill" Tilden.

On some evenings, McCloy visited Manhattan's flourishing speakeasies in the company of a pint-sized, somewhat impish little man named Benjamin Buttenwieser. "Benny" was five years younger, born, in his own words, "Not with a silver spoon in my mouth, but platinum."[8] He had graduated from Columbia University in 1917, at the age of seventeen, and though he had wanted to become a poetry professor, his family persuaded him to work as a clerk-runner for Kuhn, Loeb & Co., the investment-banking house that rivaled the House of Morgan. McCloy met Buttenwieser in the course of working for Cadwalader on a Kuhn, Loeb railroad receivership.

With his dark, bushy eyebrows and wide, easy grin, Buttenwieser made up in zest and energy what he lacked in physical stature. His bristling self-assurance and easy nonchalance charmed McCloy. They began to double-date around town, taking their women to the theater and then to a nightclub for some dancing. By his late twenties, McCloy had lost almost all the hair from the top of his head. He had a stocky frame, but his weight was all muscle and he was quick on his feet. He did not exactly cut a debonair figure, though he was nevertheless handsome in a pleasant sort of way. His self-assurance, his easy smile, and the brightness in his eyes suggested to women that this was a man who knew his way about town.

The early twenties were exciting years to be a young lawyer in New York. Beginning in 1919 with the formation of the General Motors Acceptance Corporation, Americans were learning how to buy on credit everything from cars to furniture. After the 1920–21 recession, the economy boomed, and lawyers could not help benefiting. The Cadwalader firm's revenues jumped more than $200,000 in 1922, to $942,879.[9]

McCloy was also witnessing an intellectual renaissance in the city. A half-dozen new book-publishing firms were established, *The New Yorker* was founded, and in 1921 the Council on Foreign Relations was created by a group of New York lawyers and investment bankers. The Council eventually became a second home to McCloy, but at the time he was still too young to join its ranks. He was, however, well aware of its activities; his boss, George W. Wickersham, was chairman of the board. Other, more senior Cadwalader men were active members of the Council and such private clubs as the Metropolitan. For the moment, McCloy confined himself to a membership in the New York City Bar Association, which maintained a plush parlor and library in midtown.

Much of McCloy's work at Cadwalader involved railroad receiverships or working to protect Cadwalader's corporate clients from antitrust or regulatory actions by the federal government. Typically, this meant burying the government lawyers in mountains of paper. In one case, involving Bethlehem Steel's acquisition of a rival steel company, McCloy inundated the Federal Trade Commission with fourteen thousand pages of testimony. The Supreme Court eventually upheld the merger, which helped accelerate a trend toward large corporate mergers. The Bethlehem Steel case also gave McCloy the opportunity to work with several senior lawyers from Cravath, Henderson & de Gersdorff. He liked what he saw of the Cravath men: Carl de Gersdorff and Hoyt Moore were extremely hard-working and demanded as much from their associates. McCloy's Harvard Law classmate Donald Swatland, a Cravath man who had assisted him on the reorganization of the bankrupt Denver & Rio Grande Railroad, began to encourage McCloy to switch firms.

McCloy was tempted, in part because his speakeasy companion Benny Buttenwieser had been introducing him to the select world of Kuhn, Loeb, which was invariably represented by Cravath and had its offices in the same building.

By 1920, when the patriarch of the firm, Jacob Schiff, died, Kuhn, Loeb was second only to the House of Morgan; over the years, it had syndicated some $10 billion worth of loans for various corporations and governments all over the world. When Buttenwieser showed McCloy around the office in the early 1920s, there were only five resident partners: Otto H. Kahn; Mortimer L. Schiff, Jacob's son; Jerome J. Hanauer; Paul M. Warburg, who had married a Loeb daughter; and Felix M. Warburg, who had married Jacob Schiff's only daughter, Frieda. None of these names were unknown to McCloy; indeed, he had met Felix and Frieda Warburg and their four sons and one daughter during a summer at Bar Harbor. His mother had occasionally done Frieda's hair those summers.

Buttenwieser and his peers at Kuhn, Loeb referred to themselves as part of "Our Crowd," or the "One Hundred," to differentiate themselves from the "Four Hundred" families of New York's gentile social elite. The Loebs, Kuhns, Warburgs, Buttenwiesers, Altschuls, Lewisohns, Lehmans, and other "Our Crowd" families traced their origins to Germany and were in one way or another part of New York's clannish Jewish banking community.

Though not members of "Our Crowd," two younger Kuhn, Loeb men that McCloy met were remarkable personalities in their own right. Both Lewis L. Strauss and Sir William Wiseman were to become lifelong friends. Strauss had served as Herbert Hoover's secretary during the war and came to Kuhn, Loeb in 1919. As for Wiseman, McCloy was intrigued to learn that this British gentleman had been the head of London's intelligence operations in North America during the war. Wiseman had set up an elaborate network of British agents, largely to counter the effort of German saboteurs to slow the shipment of war supplies to Britain. After the war, he decided to remain in New York, and in 1921 joined Kuhn, Loeb.

Young men like Wiseman and Strauss had lunch with people like Robert Cecil, the English lord and Tory politician, and William Randolph Hearst, and made deals every day worth hundreds of thousands of dollars.[10] McCloy was strongly attracted by the idea of working with such wealthy and influential Cravath clients. He also wanted work that involved traveling abroad. Much of Kuhn, Loeb's business was syndicating war reconstruction loans for Europe, and Cravath handled all these transactions. So, after three years with Cadwalader, on December 1, 1924, McCloy moved just around the corner into Cravath's offices at 52 William Street. He was now part of the exacting "Cravath system."

Temperamentally, McCloy already fit the Cravath mold. Neither brilliant nor easily distracted by his imagination, he instinctively exercised the qualities that Paul Cravath had spent a lifetime inculcating into a generation of young lawyers: a relaxed common sense and an intuitive grasp of the proportion of any problem thrown his way.

Until Cravath came along, law partnerships had been an informal, fluid collection of lawyers who came and left on whim. Instead of seeking new partners by enticing lawyers with established reputations, Cravath intended to create an institution capable of perpetuating itself by training its future partners from within its own ranks. He planned to hire each year a few of the best law-school graduates from Harvard, Yale, and Columbia. To qualify, these men usually had to be Phi Beta Kappa and law-review editors.

Cravath abolished the practice, still common at the time, of having unpaid clerks in the office study the law in preparation for passing the bar. Cravath actually paid his law clerks a regular salary, starting at $50 a month in 1908.

These clerks were molded and trained under the close supervision of a Cravath partner. Robert Swaine, a partner since 1917, described the discipline in the firm's privately printed history: "Under the 'Cravath system' a young man watches his senior break a large problem down into its component parts, is given one of the small parts and does thoroughly and exhaustively the part assigned to him. . . ."[11]

After a few years, it was either up or out. If an associate failed to make partnership after a period of five or six years, he was let go to make room for others. Unlike Cadwalader, Cravath hired no associates, let alone partners, because of their familial connection to members of the firm. No Cravath men were to have any financial connection to the firm's clients, since that might impede their objectivity. The firm was not to traffic in anything so petty as "political influence."

All of this appealed to McCloy, who had found quite different assumptions about the law prevailing at Cadwalader. He liked the idea of practicing "pure law" inside Cravath's meritocracy. Even so, it was unusual for Cravath to recruit a lawyer from a rival firm. Perhaps Cravath decided to make one of his exceptions to the "system" because McCloy had been sponsored by Don Swatland, who was just a year away from becoming a partner himself. Another factor was that Cravath's partners were swamped with work generated by the economic boom of the 1920s; they desperately needed some experienced men. As at Cadwalader, McCloy's clients were investment bankers, corporations such as Westinghouse, the Radio Corporation of America, Bethlehem Steel Co., and a variety of railroads. In his first year with Cravath, McCloy earned about $3,500, surpassing what his father had been making at his death in 1901.

A year before McCloy joined in 1924, the firm had only five experienced partners: Paul Cravath, Carl de Gersdorff, Hoyt Moore, Robert Swaine, and Douglas M. Moffat. In the following year, three more partners were named, and in the next five years, the firm expanded from thirty-three associates serving eight partners to forty-six associates serving thirteen partners. The nonlegal staff grew from seventy to 104. An office manager was appointed, and the antiquated practice of copying all outgoing letters into letterpress books was abandoned. In 1927, a Paris office was opened to handle the firm's increasing business in foreign securities. Cravath was clearly not a stagnant place for an ambitious young lawyer.

Paul Cravath, sixty-four in 1925, ruled the firm much as he had since 1906, as, in the words of Francis T. Plimpton, an "absolute Czar."[12] Six feet four inches tall, and weighing 240 pounds, Cravath intimidated anyone who came within his view. His piercing eyes were set behind a pair of gold-rimmed pince-nez, and his massive head was topped by a shock of iron-gray hair. He made no pretense of simplicity, but dressed expensively, almost like a dandy. His temper was fearsome, and he never hesitated to display contempt for his inferiors. J. D. Robb, a young associate at the time, recalled, "There were two very formidable figures who used to be seen on Wall Street: J. P. Morgan and Paul D. Cravath, and their derby hats, unlike ours which were nicely rounded, were flat-topped. Their very presence emanated power and instilled awe."[13]

Early in his career, Cravath had established a reputation as a lawyer with the mind of a businessman. He cultivated business leaders like George Westinghouse and Jacob Schiff, and soon both Westinghouse Electric and Kuhn, Loeb were his clients. In the years of Teddy Roosevelt's "trust-busters," Cravath became nationally known as a defender of the robber barons. The Hearst newspapers called him a public malefactor. *The New Yorker* wrote, in mock sympathy, "Those were bitter days for

Cravath. . . . He became, for the public, a symbol of rapacious Capital."[14] John W. Davis, later a Democratic presidential candidate, decided in 1917 against becoming a Cravath partner in part because he thought the firm "distinctly the counsel for the predatory rich."[15]

By the time McCloy arrived at the firm, Cravath had somewhat mellowed in both temperament and reputation. Swaine wrote, "The Cravath who returned from World War I was a much more human person than the prewar Cravath. His role during the war was that of an advisor, constantly seeking to reconcile the differing points of view of strong men of vigorous personalities. He acquired tolerance. He learned that few men are unfailing in their judgements and he became less sure of his own and less insistent that everything be done his way."[16]

He also began to develop some interests outside the law, interests becoming a man who was now taking statesmanlike positions in the public debate over the League of Nations, the World Court, and the settlement of European war debts. Like Henry Stimson, Cravath thought "men of wealth and power had special obligations to the community. . . ." In Cravath's case, he began to think of himself as a steward of the country's foreign policy. When the Council on Foreign Relations was organized in 1921, Cravath became a director and vice-president. He contributed funds to the Council's new publication, *Foreign Affairs,* edited by Hamilton Fish Armstrong. Cravath argued in the pages of *Foreign Affairs* that the United States should recognize the communist regime in the Soviet Union and encourage East-West trade. He thought the Treaty of Versailles was a "millstone around the neck of economic Europe," and that Germany would never be able to pay "anything approaching the indemnity imposed on her. . . ."[17]—views that McCloy would soon begin to echo.

Cravath was not the only strong personality in the firm. Hoyt Moore was notorious for wearing out the young associates with his marathon binges of work late into the night, night after night. Moore, Harvard Law '04, was known as a "slavedriver."[18] Moore, recalled McCloy, "wasn't happy unless he was working. . . . If he didn't have something to do, he'd go around and ask to work on a brief."[19] Moore's obsession with petty detail suited Paul Cravath's purposes; he wanted men with patience to break a problem down into all its possible legal components and laboriously solve it.

McCloy worked long hours, but he also managed to bring himself into the social circles of Cravath's most valued clients. With the death of Paul Cravath's friend Jacob Schiff in 1920, a younger generation had begun taking control of Kuhn, Loeb. Sometime in 1925–26, McCloy became good friends with Frederick Warburg, twenty-eight, the eldest grandson of Schiff. "Freddie," as he was known to everyone, had just joined Kuhn, Loeb after serving a stint with his uncle Max's merchant banking firm,

M. M. Warburg, in Hamburg, Germany. Because Freddie was Felix Warburg's son, it was ordained that he join the family firm, and he proved to be a competent, if overly conservative, banker. But his heart was not in it.

He was an easygoing and lighthearted young man, whose only real passion in life was sports. At the time McCloy met him, Freddie was an avid lawn-tennis player and routinely enticed the tennis pros from Forest Hills to play with him at the family's estate in White Plains. When Freddie learned of McCloy's tennis prowess, he too became a frequent visitor to White Plains.[20]

It did not escape Paul Cravath's notice that McCloy regularly socialized with such Kuhn, Loeb personalities as Freddie Warburg and Benny Buttenwieser.

In the summer of 1925, McCloy hired William O. Douglas as a Cravath associate. Though he would someday, as a Supreme Court justice, be known as a populist and a critic of corporate America, Douglas, upon graduating from Columbia Law School, decided to try out Wall Street before returning to his native Washington. He chose Cravath because "everyone there seemed earnest and frank, and not at all pretentious." McCloy recalled that Douglas "was not on our list" of those the firm was hoping to recruit from that year's batch of law-school graduates. "He was a little off the beaten track. . . . In fact, he looked like a singed cat. But then he told me what he had done to get a legal education and I was interested because I had worked my way through law school, too. He talked about his background and how hard life had been. I told Bob Swaine, 'I think this fellow's got something.' "[21]

Swaine told McCloy he could have Douglas but the young lawyer would have to share McCloy's office. Douglas was hired at an annual salary of $1,800 and moved into McCloy's tiny office. There was barely room enough for two desks; McCloy took the one next to the only window. "In those days," McCloy explained, "you may not have been a partner, but if you had a desk by a window it counted for something."[22]

Both men worked closely with Don Swatland, whose fits of temper could rival Swaine's. They sometimes stayed up all night preparing papers that had to be filed in court sharp at nine o'clock the next morning. The two men would order out for steak dinners and then puff away all night on stogies to keep themselves awake.[23]

About the same time, McCloy received his first mention in a daily newspaper. The case involved yet another railroad reorganization, this time the nation's largest railroad bankruptcy. By 1925, the Chicago, Milwaukee & St. Paul Railroad (known as the St. Paul) was running a $2-million annual deficit, and $50 million worth of refunding bonds were to mature that year. St. Paul's management turned to Cravath to prepare the inevitable receivership. What Cravath did was not illegal, but in a few years the case became the subject of contentious congressional investigations.

"Bill Douglas and I worked on the details of the St. Paul reorganization under Swatland's supervision," McCloy recalled. "Supervising the logistics of the massive reorganization was late night drudgery. There was some looking up of the law, but not too much, because there was not too much law on the books. It was mostly organizing a very big job. We prepared titles and deeds of transfer. There were trips to Chicago and leg work for the investment banks. It didn't require legal genius to do it; it did require a lot of hard work."[24]

With assets of more than $700 million, the St. Paul reorganization was a major case for the firm. Paul Cravath himself and Swaine took the lead on making all the major decisions. Cravath's strategy in such reorganizations was promptness: everything depended on getting first in line for the receivership. So, when St. Paul's management quietly approached Kuhn, Loeb (their bankers) about the need for a receivership, Cravath lawyers immediately began drawing up the papers. Under Swaine's supervision, McCloy started work on the drafts a full two months before there was any public hint that the St. Paul was going under.[25]

While McCloy was diligently drawing up the receivership papers and taking various affidavits, the major holders of St. Paul stock and the men who had appointed the company's board of directors, William and Percy Rockefeller and Ogden Armour, were quietly selling out. In a short time, few of the railroad's directors had any stock at all in their own company. Theoretically, the numerous small shareholders, owning more than $400 million worth of stock, had a voice in running the company. In practice, however, the board had been self-perpetuating since 1913. The directors' only allegiance seemed to be to the troubled railroad's bankers, Kuhn, Loeb and the National City Bank.[26]

In anticipation of the receivership, Kuhn, Loeb needed a legal device whereby none of the some forty thousand individual investors, scattered all over the country, could attempt to exercise collective control over the reorganized railroad. To this end, McCloy, Swatland, and Douglas drafted an enormously complicated and wordy document. Max Lowenthal, a Senate investigator who later wrote a small book about the case called *The Investor Pays,* observed that, if an ordinary investor "had attempted to explore the documents, he would have perished in the jungle of impassable words."[27]

The document had no table of contents and no index. The language was all but impenetrable; one sentence ran to 2,250 words. Buried throughout the proposed receivership document was this essential fact: in order for any shareholder to participate in the receivership, he must give an unqualified proxy to the bankers. The document also gave the lawyers the right to set a deadline for shareholders to submit their shares in return for certificates in a new company. This put pressure on any shareholders who might wish to challenge the receivership in court. If they lost, and the deadline for agreeing to the Cravath receivership had passed, then they would be ineligible for any compensation at all. In these circumstances, it was not long before the Cravath receivership committee controlled an absolute majority of all shares.

The lawyers made sure that a friendly judge would acquiesce in a Cravath receivership, and a new company was quickly incorporated in Delaware; the newspapers reported the appointment of McCloy as the youngest-ever president of a railroad company, and a photo of him looking very youthful in his army captain's uniform was published alongside the story.[28] Over at Kuhn, Loeb, Buttenwieser referred to the new company as a "dummy corporation."[29]

All that remained was for McCloy and Douglas, appointed vice-president of the new entity, to attend the auction of the bankrupt St. Paul. Because the defunct railroad had been incorporated in Butte, Montana, the Cravath lawyers and Kuhn, Loeb bankers had to take the train out west in mid-November 1926.

The *New York Times* correspondent reported from Chicago, "When the Olympian of the Chicago, Milwaukee & St. Paul Railroad leaves this city at 11 o'clock tomorrow night it will bear a group of bankers, railroad officials and lawyers representing probably a quarter billion dollars in purchasing power. . . . It seems practically certain that the Reorganization Committee backed by Kuhn, Loeb & Co. and the National City Bank will buy in the property."[30]

An independent bidder for the property was hardly likely. The only other investment bank capable of handling such large refinancing bonds was the House of Morgan. But in those days the two rivals rarely, if ever, engaged in bidding wars against each other. When rumors were floated in Wall Street that the House of Morgan might back a minority faction of stockholders against the Kuhn, Loeb reorganization, a Morgan official took the trouble to deny the report firmly, explaining that "it would not be fair to Kuhn, Loeb & Co."[31]

When McCloy and his party arrived in Butte, there were no other bids at the auction. It was a cold, snowy day when the train pulled into the station. A crowd of Butte citizens were there to greet the luminaries, who included Pierpont V. Davis, vice-president of National City Bank; Jerome J. Hanauer, operating head of Kuhn, Loeb; and Frederick H. Ecker, chairman of the bondholders' committee formed by the Cravath lawyers. The auction was scheduled to be held on the steps of the station, but the steps were so icy that at the last moment a table was set up just inside. The auction master took twenty-two minutes to read the legal notice of sale, and then he announced that there were no bids other than Kuhn, Loeb's. A *Chicago Daily News* reporter wrote, "A festive air pervaded the hearing. The reorganization group were in high spirits and they bubbled over with good feeling as the proceeding continued and no semblance of opposition manifested itself."[32]

The trip was a significant financial success for the lawyers and bankers. Kuhn, Loeb and National City Bank billed the reorganized St. Paul railroad $1,044,000 for their banking services. Cravath submitted bills for more than $450,000. Neither McCloy nor Douglas seemed troubled by the roughshod treatment they had accorded the independent stockholders. A few years later, Douglas would write articles attacking the selfishness of Wall Street. But his colleagues, McCloy included, can recall no such qualms on his part at the time. "I don't remember any ideological interchange between Douglas and me at Cravath," said McCloy. "We just talked about how to get the day's business done. How do we get our ducks in a row? What consents do we have to get? Who on the bondholders' committee is important? Who should we talk to at the banks? Bill Douglas wasn't the passionate crusader then."[33]

Almost immediately the St. Paul reorganization became a popular symbol of Wall Street greed. Complaints were filed with the Interstate Commerce Commission (ICC), and a group of disgruntled stockholders went to court to challenge the high fees paid the bankers and lawyers. For the next five years, Cravath lawyers found themselves hauled before ICC investigators or federal judges to explain their conduct. Swaine defended the high fees he charged St. Paul as an "ordinary business arrangement." Angry St. Paul stockholders fought the Cravath fees to the Supreme Court. It was not until 1931 that the court, in a five-to-three decision, upheld Cravath's fees. Justices Stone, Holmes, and Brandeis dissented, charging Cravath with "failure to conform to those elementary standards of fairness and good conscience. . . ." Justice Stone called the fees "wasteful and extravagant" and argued that Cravath's conduct would serve to undermine the public's confidence in the railroads.[34]

His prediction proved correct, for though the ICC ultimately approved Cravath's reorganization plan as a "lesser evil," the railroad was back in receivership within a few short years. Even Swaine had to acknowledge that the legal system had failed: "The discussion brought to public attention the artificiality of the consent receivership, the fictitious nature of the railroad foreclosure sale and defects in the conventional procedure which had earlier been pointed out even by counsel criticized in the St. Paul reorganization."[35]

Off and on throughout 1926–27, McCloy worked with Swatland, Douglas, Swaine, and others on similar corporate reorganizations. He thrived on the sixteen-hour workdays, and enjoyed "getting our ducks in a row." His only ambition was to be named a Cravath partner. Not everyone had the physical stamina or patience to endure both the long hours and the often tedious nature of the work. Bill Douglas pined for his beloved Northwest and the outdoors. "I don't think he ever had his heart wholly in his work," McCloy remembered. "The work at Cravath was pretty much of a grind."[36] Douglas, in fact, had seen enough of both New York City and corporate law, and had concluded that "the practice of law required predatory qualities."

When Douglas left the firm in January 1926 for eight months in the West, McCloy remained, content to clock the long hours needed to win a partnership. Despite his long hours, he was not asocial. Quite the contrary, he was one of the most popular associates in the firm.

His circle of acquaintances now included a group of rising young bankers and businessmen who became lifelong friends. In 1925, Cravath managed an offering of $30 million in bonds placed by Brown Brothers in Norway.[37] As a consequence of this and other bond business with Brown Brothers, McCloy met Robert Abercrombie Lovett, a Yale graduate of the same age. Lovett's father, chairman of Union Pacific, was a neighbor of Paul Cravath's on Long Island. The younger Lovett had spent one year at Harvard Law and then, in the autumn of 1921, decided a legal career was not to his taste; he joined Brown Brothers, a major investment-banking firm, working initially as a "runner." A tall, handsome young man with a wry sense of humor, Lovett had been born into the kind of privileged class McCloy so respected. At Yale, one of his best friends was F. Trubee Davison, the son of Henry Davison, the J. P. Morgan & Co. partner. While McCloy was learning to ride horses at Plattsburg, Lovett and Davison put together the "Aerial Coast Patrol No. 1," more popularly known as the "First Yale Unit." Davison's father financed the entire operation, and the boys trained in their seaplanes headquartered on the Davison estate at Peacock Point on Long Island.[38]

They were scoffed at in the newspapers at the time as the "millionaires' unit." When Lovett's and Davison's seaplane had to make an emergency landing one day in the East River, the two young men calmly went off to have lunch on Davison's yacht, moored nearby.[39]

They were not quite the dilettantes they made themselves out to be; when America finally entered the war, Lovett distinguished himself as an expert dive-bomber and came home from Europe with a Navy Cross. By the time McCloy met him in the mid-1920s, Trubee Davison was an assistant secretary of war, supervising the air force in the Coolidge administration. Davison had married Dorothy "Dot" Peabody, daughter of the famous headmaster of Groton. The Davisons were also good friends of Lew and Peggy Douglas in Washington, where Douglas was serving his first term as Arizona's sole congressman.

Davison took to inviting McCloy out to play tennis on the grass courts at his Peacock Point mansion. McCloy found another tennis partner at Brown Brothers: Henry "Harry" Brunie, an amiable but quiet young investment banker. Brunie was good enough to have played at Wimbledon, and could more often than not beat McCloy. "I was just as good as he was," claimed McCloy, "but kept my nose to the grindstone [at Cravath] a bit more."[40]

Another rich young man in this charmed circle was W. Averell Harriman. A few years earlier, Harriman had inherited Union Pacific from his father, the legendary robber baron Edward H. Harriman. About this time, Cravath handled a $13.5-million securities issue for W. A. Harriman & Co., a small investment bank set up by Harriman after his father's death. McCloy and Harriman may have met in conjunction with this work, but more likely they were introduced at one of many weekend parties hosted by Lovett or Davison on their Long Island estates. Compared with Lovett, McCloy thought Harriman a lightweight. "Most of the people who worked with Averell on Wall Street," McCloy recalled years later, "felt he did not pull his weight, and that he was not too bright. . . . He was good-looking, affluent, and very aloof back then, which made him quite a lady's man. I once attended one of those lavish polo parties and felt out of my milieu. He had an air about him, one that Lovett never sought to affect."[41]

McCloy was thrown in with this crowd of young investment bankers because their banking firms needed Cravath's legal expertise in handling a rising volume of business in European securities. Prior to World War I, most of Cravath's international work involved representation of European institutional investment in American securities. By 1919, the flow of capital from Europe to America was almost completely reversed. Now American investors were looking for opportunities in European markets, and they turned to Cravath for legal advice. This new business more than replaced that lost from Cravath's European clients. In 1927, the firm found it profitable to send Chester McClain, a partner in the firm and a good friend of McCloy's, to open a Paris office.[42]

McClain was swamped with work, much of which required him to travel throughout the continent. In response to his request for assistance, the firm sent McCloy, who based himself in Milan, where a large number of Italian investment-banking houses were headquartered. Working out of rented living quarters, McCloy was more or less his own boss.

His securities work kept him on the road many months out of the year, traveling throughout Italy, Greece, France, and Germany. On one occasion in late 1928, he was sent to Athens in connection with a $54-million bond issue to finance reclamation work in Struma, Philippi, and Thessaly. Before McCloy had hardly begun to negotiate the legal guarantees attached to the bond, he was stricken with a case of dengue fever that required hospitalization for several weeks; in his eagerness to return to work, McCloy checked out of the hospital long before he had fully recovered. Walking down the cobblestone road leading from the hospital, he encountered a herd of goats entirely blocking the road. He stepped to the side, was pushed up against a wall, stumbled, and fell. "It seemed as if the whole herd of goats passed over me," he recalled years later. Still delirious, he made his way back to the hospital in a fog.[43]

A large number of the European bonds McCloy negotiated defaulted within a very few years. In retrospect, Swaine explained, "If, in the light of hindsight, it seems that many such issues were put on the American market without adequate economic justification, it should be remembered that American bankers and investors were being encouraged by the national Administration to invest in the rehabilitation of Europe and the development of Latin America with faith in the future rather than regard for the past."[44]

Swaine's recollection, however, was a little too self-serving. The investment-banking community in New York, led by the House of Morgan and by Kuhn, Loeb, took the lead on these loans, because there was a great deal of money to be made in floating new securities.[45] German bonds, for instance, in these years earned a very respectable 7 or 8 percent. The investment bankers who managed such bonds took their fees off the top: thus, of the $1.2 billion in loans to Germany from 1924 to 1930, the bankers earned $50 million in fees alone.[46]

Many of the securities were risky from the beginning. To be sure, the loans were necessary to rebuild the war-torn European economies. But most of these countries also had large war-loans to pay off, or, in the case of Germany, hefty reparation payments due the Allied governments. Not surprisingly, in order to make their private reconstruction loans more marketable, New York's investment bankers encouraged leniency on the repayment of this government-to-government debt. Financiers like Otto Kahn, Thomas Lamont, Benjamin Strong, and Paul Warburg urged the U.S. government to forgive the interest for three to five years on the approximately $10 billion the European Allies owed Washington.[47]

McCloy and a whole generation of New York's "bankers' lawyers" came to believe strongly that the war debts and German reparations were both unwise and unfair. He regarded his work on European securities in the 1920s as an almost altruistic private program of war reconstruction. "What took place after World War I was the forerunner of the Marshall Plan," McCloy remembered. "But back then the rehabilitation of Europe was done in a private capacity. Practically every merchant bank and Wall Street firm, from J. P. Morgan and Brown Brothers on down, was over there picking up loans. We were all very European in our outlook, and our goal was to see it rebuilt."[48]

He made a number of trips into Germany in 1927–28 and witnessed the debilitating effects of spiraling inflation and speculation on the economy. His Warburg clients at Kuhn, Loeb still had relatives, not to speak of large financial interests, in Germany. During these years, McCloy assisted in some of the transactions of the Warburg family's International Acceptance Bank, set up to finance German industries. Paul Warburg himself was continually lobbying U.S. officials to make large-scale loans to Europe.

Anticipating the arguments made two decades later in behalf of the Marshall Plan, Warburg and Kahn raised the specter of the Bolshevist threat to Germany.[49] But for the most part they argued that European loans were needed in order to expand free trade. Warburg went so far as to suggest that the United States should throw open its doors to European imports and pay for them with the gold the Allies had used to pay for U.S. war materiel. By assuming the role of "the world's banker," he argued, New York would in fact become the world's financial and commercial center.[50]

Financial power was indeed shifting in these years from London to New York. A headlong rush for high profits made American bankers extend large loans to shaky European clients. Otto Kahn spoke of the fierce "competition by American bankers for European and foreign issues in general through the two mad years of 1926 and 1928, when, just as in 1929, nothing counted but pieces of paper. . . ."[51] Kahn described to Senate investigators in 1933 how dozens of "American bankers sat in half a dozen South and Central American states, or in Balkan states," engaging in "cutthroat competition, one outbidding the other foolishly, recklessly, to the detriment of the public, compelling him to force bonds on the public at a price which is not determined by the value of that security so much as by his eagerness to get it. . . ."[52] Some of Cravath's clients were more speculative than others. Throughout the 1920s, National City Bank of New York, for instance, was run by the flamboyant and aggressive Charles E. Mitchell. He made a large number of loans to German municipalities and industrial ventures, many of which later defaulted. Arrested in 1933 for tax evasion, Mitchell was represented by Cravath lawyers, who managed to have him acquitted.[53]

On returning to New York in late 1928, McCloy found himself in the midst of a stock-market frenzy. The country was reveling in what seemed to be unending prosperity. Herbert Hoover had been nominated by the Republicans for the presidency and was running against the Democrats' Alfred E. Smith, the first Roman Catholic to run for president. A poll showed Hoover the overwhelming choice of Wall Street lawyers. Paul Cravath raised money for the Hoover campaign, as did Robert Swaine, George Wickersham, William Lloyd Kitchel, Trubee Davison, and many other of McCloy's colleagues.[54] There was little doubt of the outcome; the Republican-managed economy seemed to be booming, and Hoover easily outspent his opponent. The "Chief," as he was affectionately known from his years as a mining engineer, won in a landslide.

Hoover's popularity on Wall Street did not necessarily translate into universal optimism about the direction of the economy. Paul M. Warburg was one of the few pessimists. Throughout the 1920s, he had been a Cassandra; he was known on the "Street" as "the sad Mr. Warburg," to distinguish him from his brother Felix, "the happy Mr. Warburg."[55] In March 1929, he urged the Federal Reserve to intervene, arguing that if "unrestrained speculation" was not halted it was sure to "bring about a general depression involving the entire country." One businessman retorted that Warburg was "sandbagging American prosperity."[56]

To some extent, the notion of a "New Era" of American prosperity was just a myth. Prosperity was skin-deep in many parts of the country; throughout the decade, 30 percent of the nation's coal miners were unemployed. Wages in general remained low, and in 1928 workers in many industries took wage cuts. That year, in Baltimore, a survey conducted by city policemen found the real unemployment rate to be 42.5 percent. And there was no social-welfare net to speak of.[57]

Wall Street, however, was blind to these disparities. "Leaders among America's bankers and industrialists," Swaine observed, "thought they had found the secret of perpetual prosperity."[58]

For not a few, the secret lay in insider trading. "We conducted business very differently prior to the establishment of the SEC," recalled Benny Buttenwieser.[59] In 1928, he quietly used his inside knowledge of an impending sale of railroad stock to make a quick $5,042.21 personal profit.[60] Blair & Co., a Cravath client managed by Jean Monnet, maintained a preferred list of fifty-eight prominent individuals who were cut in on favorable stock offerings. So too did Goldman, Sachs, another investment-banking house, on whose board sat John Foster Dulles. Such practices were common, even among the best of Cravath's clients.

By 1929, after four and a half years at Cravath, McCloy had labored conscientiously for the firm's most important clients: Kuhn, Loeb & Co., E. R. Squibb & Sons, Shell Union, Blair & Co., and a host of railroads and banks. He was regarded by even the difficult Swaine as someone the partners could rely on to perform meticulous work. Socially speaking, he traveled the same circuit of parties and cultural events as did the most senior Cravath partners and clients. Like Otto Kahn and Paul Cravath, who succeeded each other as chairmen of the Metropolitan Opera, he was frequently seen at the opera, dressed in full white tie and tails.[61]

As a noticeably eligible bachelor, McCloy was a constant dinner guest at the homes of Chester McClain, Don Swatland, and Maurice "Tex" Moore, where after a formal sit-down dinner the usual dozen guests would adjourn for cigars and a couple of rounds of bridge.[62] Everyone regarded him as a member of the Cravath family.

So it was hardly a surprise that on July 1, 1929, McCloy was offered a Cravath partnership. Years later, when many Cravath associates waited at least ten years for the partnership plum, Wall Street lawyers often remarked that for McCloy to have won a Cravath partnership after less than five years was an extraordinary feat. But for a brief time in the 1920s, things were different. This generation of lawyers, like McCloy, were often veterans, whose careers or legal education had been interrupted. McCloy had also had nearly four years with another firm before coming to Cravath. By 1929, he was already thirty-four years old.

A Cravath partnership was a singular achievement and carried with it considerable financial rewards. McCloy's partnership earned him at least $15,000 his first year, at a time when fewer than 6 percent of Americans earned more than $3,000 a year.[63] With the promotion came his own private room in the firm's new offices on the twenty-seventh and twenty-eighth floors of a thirty-seven-story building at 15 Broad Street, just south of the Morgan building. Paul Cravath personally supervised the decor. Each partner's room was outfitted exactly alike: simple mahogany desks, brown leather chairs, a matching divan, cream-colored walls, and a plain beige carpet. The only exception to this comfortable but blandly uniform setting was Cravath's own office: he had dark-green leather chairs and oyster-white walls. McCloy could have earned more money working for one of his investment-banking clients, or in his own private practice,[64] and it may have been rather dreary and dull, but this was where he wanted to be.

There was something magnetic about being part of the Cravath team. "Tex" Moore's wife, Elizabeth Luce Moore (Henry Luce's sister), attributed this "great attraction" to the variety of the work. "It is never boring. There's always a new challenge. . . . Each company has its own problems, and got into them in different ways. So to extract them, and put them together again, is just very interesting, [and] always different."[65] Another part of it was the simple prestige, and the security of being associated with a firm that, in good times or bad, would always have a host of wealthy clients.

Within four months of McCloy's partnership, the fever of intoxicating speculation finally broke and the market crashed on Tuesday, October 29, 1929. A week later, Cravath wrote his English friend Lord Beaverbrook, the British Canadian newspaper magnate, "We are having a shake-up in the stock market unequaled in the memory of living man. . . . Many fortunes have been lost and many very rich men are now only moderately rich."[66]

McCloy's personal finances were untouched by the October crash. All of his Cravath earnings had gone to supporting himself, his mother, and his two spinster aunts, Lena and Sadie, who still lived in Philadelphia. He had no stocks to lose in the market. And by autumn he had less wordly concerns on his mind. At the age of thirty-four, he was finally in love. In August 1929, just after winning his Cravath partnership, he had taken his vacation in Arizona, where he wanted to see the Grand Canyon. On the train back to New York, he entered a carriage and caught a glimpse of the back of Congressman Lewis Douglas's head. "I didn't know if I wanted to sit with him: he could be quite a bore. Then I saw an attractive woman sitting next to him, and I thought I would go up to talk with him."[67]

The "attractive woman" was Peggy Zinsser Douglas, Lew's wife. Peggy enjoyed McCloy's company on the train and made a point of telling him about her unmarried older sister, Ellen Zinsser. When they arrived in New York, Ellen was standing on the platform to greet them. McCloy took an instant liking to this tall, elegant brunette. She had a high forehead, long, dark eyebrows, high cheekbones, an almost classic Roman nose, and a full, engaging smile. She was the kind of woman who put people at ease upon their first meeting. Her family used a German word—*Fingerspitzengefühl*—to describe her talent in dealing with awkward social situations. Outgoing and uncomplicated, she possessed not only grace and charm, but considerable wit and intelligence.

Her family background and upbringing were quite different from McCloy's. Her father, Frederick G. Zinsser, owned a chemical company founded by her great-grandfather, who had come to New York from Germany in 1848. He had been mayor of Hastings, and his brother August, a banker and real-estate executive, was listed in the New York *Social Register.* His other brother, Hans Zinsser, a noted Harvard biologist, later wrote the bestseller *Rats, Lice and History.*

Ellen, her sister, Peggy, and her brother, John, grew up in a spacious Victorian manor, called Locust Wood, overlooking the Hudson River at Hastings-on-Hudson. Ellen's German nanny had taught her German, and as a child she had traveled in Europe and lived for several months in Paris. At Smith College, she majored in French.[68]

In the 1920s, Ellen and Peggy Zinsser were well known and popular in the New York social scene. "Everyone knew the Zinsser sisters," said Benjamin Buttenwieser.[69] Their friends noticed more than the usual bit of sibling rivalry. Freddie Warburg, one of McCloy's closest friends, nicknamed Ellen and Peggy the "Sun sisters," a reference to the scheming and intrigue that went on among the sisters of that famous Chinese nationalist family.[70]

Peggy had clearly made an exceptional match in 1921 by marrying the sole heir of the Phelps-Dodge copper fortune, Lew Douglas, who by 1926 was Arizona's congressman. Douglas had actually first dated Ellen, but the elder Zinsser sister evidently enjoyed her independence. She was working part-time at Lord & Taylor, a fancy, upscale clothing store in Manhattan, when she first met McCloy. By that time, she was already thirty-one years old, unusual for an unmarried society woman in those years. Balding, stocky, and not much of a dresser, McCloy was not the man most people thought Ellen Zinsser would end up marrying. His prospects as a Cravath partner were promising, but he had no property, and he certainly did not move in Ellen's café-society circles. And, as Ellen was to learn later, he had a possessive mother who still from time to time camped out in his apartment. Archibald MacLeish, who liked McCloy, nevertheless thought he "was not much of a catch for Ellen Zinsser compared with Lew Douglas."[71]

Ellen was dating a number of other men, but McCloy had been smitten and set about in his determined fashion to court her. He soon learned that she "was hell-bent on doctors. . . . I had a rival. He was a successful doctor named Davison who had recently bought a rather spectacular black and white wire-wheeled Cadillac roadster. It was quite impressive. . . . Ellen was enamored of that damn roadster. I was competing with Davison, and this doctor could buy and sell me. . . . I bought, out of some very spare funds, a secondhand Cadillac of the same model, only it was red and had bright wire-wheels. I drove it up to Hastings . . . and parked it along side the doctor's, who was calling on [Ellen]. I was quite broke, but I remained in the competition."[72]

McCloy's courtship campaign was waged in the midst of Zinsser family outings, picnics, and softball games. Luckily, the Zinssers had a tennis court, which allowed him to display his prowess in games with Ellen. "Things followed nature's course," remembered McCloy.[73] They were married on April 25, 1930, a day of record freezing temperatures and snow squalls, in a small Episcopal ceremony held at 8:00 P.M. in the Zinsser home at Hastings-on-Hudson. The room was lit by candlelight. Ellen wore a gown of white lace and held a bouquet of white orchids. Harry Brunie was best man, while Peggy Douglas and Ellen's sister-in-law, Mrs. John S. Zinsser, were bridesmaids. Among the guests were Lew Douglas, of course, and F. Trubee Davison, who had become an assistant secretary of war in the Hoover administration.[74]

The honeymoon had been dictated by Cravath, since McCloy had been assigned to replace Tex Moore in the firm's small Paris office. So, five days after their marriage, the couple boarded a ship for France, taking with them the red "courtship roadster" that Ellen so liked. In Paris, they had some difficulty finding an apartment within their means. Someone eventually referred them to a member of the Tiffany family who had a luxuriously decorated and fully furnished apartment for rent at 175 Rue de L'Université, near Les Invalides, on the Left Bank. McCloy was sure the almost palatial apartment would be too expensive, but Ellen charmed the owner. "Someone spilled something," McCloy recalled, "and Ellen took such good care of it that Madame Tiffany said, 'You can rent it for whatever you want to pay.' "[75]

She enjoyed driving about Paris in the splashy red Cadillac roadster. In an attempt to give McCloy a smattering of French, she hired a tutor who turned out to be a former mistress of Toulouse-Lautrec, the hunchbacked painter notorious for his liaisons.[76] From her frequent letters home that spring, her brother concluded, "She certainly seems contented and happy."[77] McCloy was now considered to be very much part of the Zinsser household. Ellen's brother reported to Douglas in May, "I got a letter this morning from our crazy brother-in-law in Paris. He greatly resents the appellation of 'baldy,' which fits him so well, and threatens in typical legal fashion to use dire financial reprisals with his New York connections, if I do not desist. Otherwise, he seems to be quite well, and tells me confidentially that his wife is not half bad."[78]

McCloy had his office at 3 Rue Taitbout, not far from their apartment. By that time, a number of major Wall Street firms had established themselves in Paris: White & Case, Root, Clark, Howland & Ballantine, Cadwalader, Wickersham & Taft, and Sullivan & Cromwell. Unlike these firms, the Cravath office did not solicit much business from the local American business community and instead worked almost exclusively on bond and security matters initiated at the New York office. Much of this meant simply a continuation of McCloy's work on the sale of European bonds in the American security markets. The clients were the usual crowd of investment bankers, including J. P. Morgan & Co., Kuhn, Loeb & Co., and Seligman, Blair, and Hallgarten.

The bond work required McCloy to travel frequently to Germany, Holland, and his old haunts in Italy, particularly Milan. But he and Ellen spent most of their time in Paris, and he managed, as usual, to find time to play hard as well as work hard. They had a tennis game nearly every week with Francis Plimpton and his wife, Pauline. Plimpton also played touch football with McCloy on the Bois du Boulogne. "It attracted a great deal of attention from the French," Plimpton said, "who never could figure what the hell was going on. McCloy was a very vigorous touch football player."[79]

The acquaintanceship with the Plimptons turned into a lifelong friendship. Plimpton was five years younger than McCloy, but they had much in common. He too had graduated from Amherst and gone on to Harvard Law School, where he was a protégé of Frankfurter's.[80] McCloy also socialized with Allen W. Dulles, thirty-seven, who was then serving as Sullivan & Cromwell's representative in Paris. Like McCloy, the future director of the Central Intelligence Agency traveled frequently to Germany on business. McCloy also saw a great deal of Lowell Weicker, the son of the owner of Squibb & Sons. Weicker and his wife, Mary, had been in Paris since 1927, when he bought a failing perfume company. By 1933, when they returned to New York, the company was well in the black. Mary Weicker grew to be close to Ellen in Paris. "She always knew what was going on [in society]," Weicker recalled of those times.[81]

In the autumn of 1930, Peggy Zinsser paid an extended visit. She found Ellen "very much in love with her husband."[82] Ellen was unhappy about only one thing in Paris. She wanted children, and she was not getting pregnant. She told several friends, including both Pauline Plimpton and Mary Weicker, that she had consulted a number of doctors in Paris in an attempt to find out what was wrong. The doctors could not help the couple.

For McCloy there were other distractions. In early September 1930, he received a cable from Cravath instructing him to attend a case scheduled for argument at The Hague. Cravath's client, Bethlehem Steel, claimed that it had been German secret agents who had triggered a massive explosion in New York harbor in 1916, destroying millions of dollars' worth of Bethlehem munitions. Like many Americans, McCloy had read the sensationalized newspaper accounts of espionage and sabotage associated with the "Black Tom" suit. That summer, the case had been reported in front-page headlines blaring "U.S. Suit Bares 'Atrocities' of German Spies" and "Mites of Evidence Linked Patiently as U.S. Drafts Black Tom Claim on Reich." Earlier that year, *The New Yorker* had published a cartoon of a man on bended knee, telling his young lady friend, "Diane, darling, you're the first real experience in my life since the Black Tom disaster."[83] As McCloy hastily reviewed the facts of the case in preparation for the arguments at The Hague, he realized how different this case was going to be from his usual corporate work. He thought the briefs read like scenarios from one of E. Phillips Oppenheim's popular spy and detective thrillers.[84]

CHAPTER 5

Black Tom: McCloy's Wilderness of Mirrors

"The whole sordid Black Tom–Kingsland episode has served one good purpose, however. It has shown the need in this country of an efficient counter-espionage system in time of peace as well as war."

WASHINGTON EVENING STAR EDITORIAL, 1939

In the summer of 1916, three-quarters of all the American ammunition shipped to the European war was loaded from New York harbor, and much of it passed through the Black Tom terminus, a maze of railroad tracks and warehouses that sat upon a spit of land, an island really, hard by the Statue of Liberty. At 2:08 A.M. on July 30, 1916, a thousand tons of dynamite, nitrocellulose, gasoline, and shrapnel shells caught fire and exploded, tearing the island apart. A million dollars' worth of window glass alone was shattered in downtown Manhattan. The blast was felt across Long Island and northern New Jersey, and as far away as McCloy's native Philadelphia. Exploding artillery shells inflicted $100,000 damage on the Statue of Liberty. Five hundred frightened immigrants on neighboring Ellis Island had to be evacuated. Fire alarms were set off all over New York, and panic-stricken crowds roamed the streets, some people thinking this was the beginning of a foreign invasion—or Armageddon. Surprisingly, only four people died.

That summer, McCloy was in Plattsburg, New York, training to become a soldier, but most Americans were still opposed to foreign entanglements. America's role as an arsenal for the British, French, and Russian Allies was not popular, particularly among recent immigrants from Ireland, the Austro-Hungarian Empire and the czar's Russia. Also, many of the country's intellectuals opposed the arms shipments. Two days after the Black Tom disaster, Lincoln Steffens, the dean of muckraking journalism, wrote his sister, "Wasn't that a bully blow-up of ammunition in New York? Think of the lives it saves—in Europe."[1]

The morning after the explosion, *The New York Times* reported that ninety-nine chemical and ammunition plants had been damaged or destroyed since the outbreak of the European war. And six months later, on January 11, 1917, a munitions factory in Kingsland, New Jersey, caught fire; within four hours, eight carloads of dynamite and some five hundred thousand artillery shells exploded. The next day, two hundred tons of gunpowder exploded at a Du Pont factory in Haskell, New Jersey. Such a string of accidents, all destroying ammunition bound for the European Allies fighting Germany, caused investigators to suspect sabotage.

After Germany surrendered in 1918, an international arbitration body, the German-American Mixed Claims Commission, was established to settle the war-damage claims of both German and American companies. A panel of two commissioners, one each from Germany and the United States, plus an "umpire," proceeded to compensate hundreds of companies. For years, however, the Commission left unresolved the sabotage claims arising from the Black Tom and Kingsland explosions. These were difficult to prove and politically controversial.

By the time McCloy was brought into the case in 1930, any leads had long gone cold. To make matters worse, the lawyer initially hired to represent the sabotage claims, Amos Peaslee, was unorganized and, as the date for the Hague hearing approached, he found himself overwhelmed. Barely six weeks before the scheduled arguments, the Germans had filed 966 pages of fresh exhibits, leaving him no time to research credible rebuttals.[2] In panic, he requested assistance from Cravath, which represented one of the sabotage claimants, Bethlehem Steel Company. As one Cravath lawyer later explained, rather uncharitably, "He was getting kind of desperate, and Peaslee, when he was losing, always wanted to get someone else to help." So McCloy found himself taking a train from Paris to The Hague. He was told that all he had to do was show up and "wave the flag."[3]

The hearings took place in the chambers of The Hague's gloriously ornate Peace Palace, built by Andrew Carnegie. By 1930, the Peace Palace had hosted dozens of such tribunals. With its delicate spirals and elaborately carved arches, it seemed as fragile as the whole idea of an international court of justice. As he entered the Palace and heard the sharp echo of his heels clicking on the gaudy marble floor, McCloy was intrigued by the atmosphere of the place. At thirty-five, he considered himself to be a hardheaded man, and certainly not naïve about nation-state conflicts. He believed in military preparedness in the tradition of Grenville Clark and Teddy Roosevelt, but he was also a lawyer's lawyer, and, like Clark, he harbored hopes that someday international law would adjudicate more sovereign disputes than force of arms. Influenced by Clark, he believed the only thing wrong with the League of Nations was that it did not have stronger judicial powers. For the moment, however, The Hague was the closest the world had to an international court. Taking his seat in the Peace Palace's great hall, he felt a little as if he had been invited to argue a case before an international version of the Supreme Court.

After only a few days of listening to the commissioners question Peaslee's evidence, McCloy cabled Cravath in New York and predicted that the suit would be defeated.[4] Peaslee, he thought, was a pleasant enough fellow, but rather incompetent. He didn't have the Cravath discipline, and in this case he simply hadn't gotten his "ducks all lined up in a row." This was all the more unfortunate since Peaslee had been handed some rather startling evidence by the chief of British naval intelligence during World War I, Admiral W. Reginald Hall.

Affectionately known as "Blinker" Hall because of his habit of rapidly blinking his eyelids when addressing his men, the admiral was a living legend in the intelligence profession. Hall had created "Room 40" in London's Old Admiralty Building, where throughout the war German wireless cables were intercepted and painstakingly decoded.

Peaslee had charmed the admiral in their first meeting in London, and subsequently persuaded him to hand over a treasure trove of 264 decoded German intelligence intercepts which described German sabotage activities in the United States during the period of American neutrality, 1914–17. The most incriminating document came in the form of a cable from German Foreign Undersecretary Arthur Zimmermann to the German Embassy in Washington, D.C. Dated January 26, 1915, the cable informed the German military attaché in Washington, Captain Franz Joseph von Papen, "In the U.S. sabotage can be carried out in every kind of factory for supplying munitions of war."

The son of an old Catholic noble family, von Papen had been posted to America in 1914 as military attaché. With an extraordinary budget of several million dollars, he directed an extensive network of sabotage agents operating in Canada, where a number of munitions factories and railroad bridges were blown up. Von Papen's brazen activities eventually came to the attention of U.S. authorities, and in December 1915 he was expelled. All of this was part of the public record when Peaslee took on the sabotage cases at The Hague. Von Papen himself did not deny the sabotage operations in Canada, but he insisted that he had never engaged in such activities on U.S. soil.

McCloy could see that the Zimmermann cable alone was not sufficient to prove the case. But as Peaslee explained to him at The Hague, the intelligence intercepts obtained from Admiral Hall had provided him with another lead. Although none of the intercepted cables specifically mentioned Black Tom, they did name a number of von Papen's agents, including Friedrich Hinsch, Fred Herrmann, and Paul Hilken. After considerable detective work, Peaslee had tracked the last of these agents, Hilken, to his home in Baltimore.

Hilken had been born into a wealthy German American family; his father was the honorary German consul in Baltimore. The family had for years been the shipping agent for the large German shipping company North German Lloyd, and now Paul Hilken was a cultivated gentleman of leisure.[5] When initially confronted by Peaslee, he was evasive, changing his story several times. Not until May 16, 1930, did Hilken finally agree to bare his soul; on that date, he formally refuted his previous sworn statements and related a most remarkable story.[6]

Hilken claimed that, at the outbreak of the war, von Papen had taken over a network of German American security guards employed by Paul Koenig, chief of security for the Hamburg-Amerika passenger-ship line. Hilken said he was recruited into the von Papen network, and early in 1916 spent two months visiting Germany. Sometime in February 1916, he had a meeting with the German General Staff in Berlin. There he met Frederick Laurent Herrmann, a Brooklyn-born German American who had been recruited in 1914 into the German Admiralty Secret Service at the age of nineteen.[7]

For the next two years, Herrmann, a tall, blond-haired youth, lived in England, ostensibly studying forestry but actually spying on the British fleet. In February 1916, he was expelled by the British, who had suspicions, but no proof, of espionage. Herrmann was then recalled to Berlin, transferred to the German Army's Secret Service, and, along with Hilken, given instructions to organize the destruction of munitions plants in the United States and the distribution of anthrax germs among cavalry horses and cattle bound for Europe.

To accomplish this task, he was given several hundred newly designed "incendiary pencils." Though one could actually write with them, these lead pencils contained a glass tube of sulfuric acid, chlorate of potash, and sugar. When the tip of the pencil was cut with a penknife, the sulfuric acid would slowly seep into the mixture of sugar and chlorate of potash, eventually producing combustion.[8] Simple in design, these "pencils" were perfect instruments for the surreptitious setting of fires in munitions plants.

In addition, Hilken told Peaslee that he was willing to testify about the activities of Friedrich Hinsch, the captain of a German ship that docked in Baltimore in September 1914. Hinsch had contacted Hilken, who gave him cash, a supply of incendiary pencils, and some deadly anthrax serum. Hilken claimed that Captain Hinsch quickly organized a team of Negro dockworkers and day laborers to inject thousands of mules, cattle, and horses with the anthrax serum as they were boarded on ships bound for the European battlefields. Sometimes as many as half the animals would die crossing the Atlantic. Shortly after the Black Tom explosion, Hilken said he had paid Hinsch $2,000 for pulling off the job.

While Hilken's new affidavit had the German High Command linked to the alleged sabotage at Black Tom, Hilken was unable, at least in 1930, to produce any supporting documentary evidence. In order to corroborate his testimony, Peaslee tracked Fred Herrmann down in Santiago, Chile, where he had found a job after the war with the National City Bank of New York. Herrmann's subsequent testimony substantiated Hilken's story, but, unfortunately for the American claimants, before leaving Chile, Herrmann, in need of money, had gone to the German Embassy and signed a statement denying the sabotage charges. Obviously, this fact would be used by the Germans to discredit Herrmann's testimony before the Commission.

Peaslee had other pieces of evidence to present at The Hague, but these too were either denied outright or discredited by the German lawyers. By this time, von Papen was a prominent member of the Prussian legislature and a leader of the monarchist Catholic Center Party. He had married the daughter of a wealthy Saar industrialist, and in just two years he would become the chancellor of Germany. He denied ever having heard of the Black Tom explosion. And he ridiculed the charges against him by arguing that the Zimmermann telegram was at most "only an authorization, and not an order" to engage in sabotage.

McCloy saw that these categorical denials from high-ranking German officials had greatly weakened the American case. He watched helplessly as Peaslee introduced one affidavit after another, only to have the German lawyers cast doubt on their reliability. As fantastic as their tale of spying seemed, McCloy wanted to believe in the Hilken-Herrmann story. It was a pity, he thought, that Peaslee had not come prepared with sufficient documentary evidence to support the affidavits of witnesses who were, after all, fairly disreputable characters, self-confessed secret agents, murderers, and men who had proved themselves willing to lie under oath.

The commissioners evidently came to the same conclusion about Peaslee's case, for on November 15, 1930, they announced their unanimous decision in favor of Germany. They did not doubt that Hilken and Herrmann were in fact German agents operating under the orders of the German General Staff. But because they had changed their stories so often, both the German and the American commissioners discounted their claims to have been responsible for Black Tom. Herrmann and Hilken were "liars, not presumptive, but proven."[9]

The American claimants nevertheless decided to file an appeal. For the next four months, McCloy devoted all his time to Black Tom, reviewing the old evidence and seeking new evidence throughout Europe.[10] Carrying pictures of Hinsch, Herrmann, and Hilken, he spent much of his time in Germany, trying to track down possible witnesses.[11]

"Every sort of thing was involved," he later recalled. "I was having to meet shady kinds of characters in dives, the worst kinds of bars, even houses of ill-repute."[12] He often took Ellen with him on these detective missions, and on one occasion had her tail a suspect.[13]

Some of the leads proved illusory. In January 1931, he was given the name of a Russian count living in Berlin who might be helpful. Count Alexander Nelidoff was rumored to have in his possession documents that could prove Germany's guilt in the sabotage cases. It took him weeks to locate the count in Berlin; even then, McCloy was worried that Nelidoff could not explain how he had acquired the documents. But from his description of them, McCloy thought they might easily be worth the asking price of a couple of thousand dollars. One day, as they sat negotiating in his hotel room, the telephone rang. It was a call from the Cravath office in Paris. While talking on the phone, McCloy decided he needed to take some notes and, not having a pencil handy, looked about the room. Seeing two mechanical clip pencils in Nelidoff's vest pocket, he gingerly leaned across the table and plucked one.

With a look of sudden panic crossing his face, Nelidoff jumped up, pulled a handkerchief to his face, and fled from the room. Startled by this strange behavior, Ellen, who as usual had accompanied McCloy to Berlin, went to the door and looked out. Nelidoff was standing in the corridor, shaken, and now embarrassed. He went back inside with Ellen and, when McCloy got off the phone, explained that the other mechanical clip pencil was actually a tear-gas pistol. He reached for the other pencil from his vest pocket, slowly took off its cap, and showed the McCloys four small pellets.

"If you had snatched this from my vest," Nelidoff said, "instead of the pencil, a poisonous gas would have been released, and we should have been unconscious in a few seconds."

His suspicions aroused by this odd little melodrama, McCloy told the count he would pay him his price but only after the documents had been authenticated by an expert. On April 18, 1931, Nelidoff turned over a batch of papers, any number of which could have led the Mixed Claims Commission to reverse its decision. After a cursory examination of the documents by a handwriting expert, McCloy paid Nelidoff several thousand dollars and then cabled news of his discoveries to his clients in New York.

Only then did McCloy call Admiral Hall and inquire as to Count Nelidoff's background. Was he known to British intelligence? The obliging Hall contacted his colleagues at the British Secret Intelligence Service, and one of their number gave McCloy a full briefing on Nelidoff. To his consternation, he was told that Nelidoff was the chief of a network of private forgery experts based in Berlin. A free-lancer in the intelligence business, he was known to have been used by the German Secret Service to plant forgeries with foreign governments. McCloy had become the victim of a double agent, an experience that underscored for him the value of the kind of intelligence bureaucracy run by the British.

It was a shock for McCloy to learn that the case "was riddled with forged documents."[14] It was one thing for the Germans to withhold evidence or even offer testimony that told less than the full truth. Such aggressive tactics were to be expected. But to hire an agent to plant forged evidence before the Commission was beyond the pale.

At just about the time McCloy was entangled with Nelidoff, new, ostensibly genuine evidence was found across the Atlantic. Hilken and Herrmann, angered by the Commission's harsh pronouncement that they were "liars, not presumptive, but proven," renewed their search for documentary evidence to support their stories. Hilken claimed to have found in his attic a bizarre secret message written in lemon juice on an old pulp magazine called *Blue Book.* The secret writing was legible only after the page had been warmed with a hot iron. The message was partly written in numbered code, the numbers referring to pages in the magazine where pinpricks had been made in certain letters. After substituting the pinpricked letters for the numbers from the page with lemon-juice writing, anyone could read the message. It had been sent in April 1917 by Herrmann in Mexico to Hilken in Baltimore, and was so indiscreet as to mention the names of the individual saboteurs responsible for the explosions at Black Tom and Kingsland: two Austrian anarchists, Michael Kristoff and Theodore Wozniak. (Kristoff was presumed dead, and Wozniak was a paid witness for the German case.) The secret message also named the saboteurs' superiors, Hinsch, Frederick Maguerre, Rudolf Nadolny, Herrmann, and Hilken. The message even referred to the Black Tom explosion. If it could be accepted by the Commission as genuine, the "Herrmann Message" alone proved the American case. Peaslee was elated, thinking the secret message was all the documentation the Commission needed to reverse the Hague decision. But McCloy thought his colleague was once again underestimating their German adversaries.

After nearly fourteen months in Cravath's Paris office, McCloy boarded a French passenger liner in Le Havre. Six days later, on June 29, 1931, the ship docked in New York harbor. He had returned just in time to help file before the Commission the final petition to reopen the Black Tom case based on the "Herrmann Message." And as he had feared, the Germans had come up with a means to question the authenticity of this curious new evidence. They now argued that Herrmann had indeed written the message with invisible ink onto a 1917 *Blue Book* magazine—but that he did this in 1931, not 1917. Consequently, for a time the case became a battle between the two sides' handwriting experts. Unless McCloy could somehow prove that the Germans had tampered with the evidence, it was beginning to look as though he would fail as Peaslee had failed.

McCloy was beginning to acquire a philosophy about the intelligence business. Early in 1932, he eagerly read a best-selling book on intercept intelligence by Major Herbert Yardley, who, until he was dismissed by Secretary of State Stimson in 1929, had been in charge of the State Department's secret "Black Chamber," where transatlantic cables were intercepted and decoded throughout World War I and afterward.

Henry Stimson thought Yardley's *American Black Chamber* was a "very disturbing book," and he had tried to prevent its publication. Historians have since argued whether Stimson actually ever made the famous comment "Gentlemen do not read each other's mail," but there can be no doubt of his disapproval of cable and wireless intercepts. "It disturbed me a great deal," Stimson wrote in his diary on February 20, 1933, "but made me very thankful that I had stopped the whole nefarious practice in the beginning of my term. . . ." McCloy disagreed; his dealings with the British and German secret services convinced him that intercept intelligence was an integral part of any modern intelligence bureau. He was also delighted to see that Yardley's book contained intercept material substantiating McCloy's claim that German intelligence had been blowing up munition dumps in 1916. Some of the deciphered messages even mentioned the use of "lead pencil sticks" to cause explosions.

The professional judgment of veterans of the intelligence game such as Admiral Hall and Sir William Wiseman gave him the confidence to persevere. Their belief that anything was possible in this wilderness of mirrors allowed him to hope that new facts could turn the case around. Still, he was disappointed when, on December 3, 1932, the Commission once again ruled in Germany's favor. His only consolation was that this time the Commission's vote had not been unanimous: the American commissioner dissented. McCloy took this as an indication that he should not give up.

For those not initiated into the double-sided logic of the intelligence business, his faith in the case now seemed a matter of sheer stubbornness.

The situation looked hopelessly muddled. "It was hard to keep all the crisscrosses of the case in mind," McCloy later admitted. "You met yourself coming back; it was a maze." He now understood that, if the Germans were responsible for Black Tom, it was only to be expected that they would protect their subterfuge with another layer of subterfuge. Covert operations launched by a nation in the midst of war had nothing to do with the law; they were a matter of national security. It was possible that otherwise honorable men might now use dishonorable methods to cover up for their country's misdeeds.

His law partners had good reason to be skeptical. For one thing, Adolf Hitler's rise to power in Germany in early 1933 made it seem unlikely that the Germans would ever honor a successful award to the American claimants. Franz von Papen, the man who McCloy believed had organized Germany's initial sabotage operations, was now Hitler's vice-chancellor. Ben Shute, a young summer intern in the Cravath office that year, recalls, "Jack suffered from only one thing in the office, and that was that he had the Black Tom thing for so long that it just looked hopeless to so many. Swaine was getting discouraged. . . . I suspect that Ellen was the only one who believed in him at one point. . . . If Jack had wanted to drop it, I think they [the senior partners] would have agreed in a minute."[15]

But by now, Black Tom had become his personal hobby, a welcome respite from the usual run of corporate law. Early in 1933, he went to Washington to plead his case before Stimson. It was a cold January morning when he walked into Stimson's office, next door to the White House. The acerbic sixty-five-year-old secretary of state gave him a half-hour just before lunch to make his argument. He failed. Stimson flatly refused even to review the sabotage claims again, let alone to urge the Mixed Claims Commission to reopen the case. In his first documented encounter with the crusty old man who would later have so much to do with his career, McCloy seemed to make no impression; Stimson even misspelled McCloy's name in his diary for the day.[16]

Not even this rebuff dampened McCloy's determination to reopen the case. Gradually, his persistence began to pay off. After Roosevelt's inauguration in the spring of 1933, McCloy discovered "evidence of collusion of a most extraordinary nature." The Germans had bribed one of McCloy's own handwriting experts to discredit his own expert testimony. In addition, he learned that some of Germany's witnesses had been paid large sums to testify to falsehoods.

On the basis of this evidence of German fraud, the Commission umpire, Justice Owen Roberts, decided on December 15, 1933, almost exactly a year after his first decision, to reopen the sabotage cases. It was the first real victory achieved by the American claimants.

The day the decision was announced, McCloy boarded a ship bound for Ireland, where he hoped to track down yet another long-lost witness to the German sabotage rings. From British intelligence files, McCloy had learned that James Larkin, an Irish nationalist and labor-union organizer, might know a great deal about German sabotage operations. British intelligence agents had kept Larkin under surveillance when the Irish radical fled to the United States in 1914. Moreover, Larkin freely admitted that during the war he had had personal knowledge of von Papen's sabotage operations in New York. This had been enough to send McCloy on his way to Dublin, where Larkin, the general secretary of the Workers' Union of Ireland, now lived.

For shipboard reading, he took a batch of documents on Larkin dug out from the War Department's archives. Born in 1875, Larkin came to New York in November 1914, and did not return to Ireland until early 1923. In the interlude, he became a good friend of Bill Haywood, the colorful chief of Industrial Workers of the World, and an active IWW organizer himself. In November 1919, he was indicted for "preaching anarchy," and the New York courts sentenced him to five years in prison. His cause was taken up by Roger Baldwin, founder of the American Civil Liberties Union, and in January 1923 he was pardoned by Governor Alfred Smith.[17] In short, the man McCloy was about to interview was a legendary radical on both sides of the Atlantic Ocean.

Not until shortly after Christmas was McCloy able to arrange an interview with Larkin in the presence of the Irishman's solicitor. This first meeting between the Wall Street lawyer and the union leader got off to a cool start. Larkin said he was sorry that McCloy seemed to have gone to so much trouble to see him, but he was not interested in helping any "monied interests." McCloy did not allow this refusal to end the matter; over the next few days, he patiently cultivated the charismatic Irishman, pointing out that, if his clients lost the case, other "monied interests," such as the North German Lloyd Steamship Company, would benefit. Larkin agreed that this "would be most unjust," since those German steamship interests "through their officers and employees were important instruments of sabotage utilized by the German government in America."

"Then purely in the interests of justice," McCloy said, "you should furnish me with whatever information you have."

Larkin hesitated for a moment and then said he might be prepared to give him a "brief statement." Several conversations and three days later, McCloy finally persuaded him to tell his whole story. The union leader began dictating from memory shortly before lunchtime and was not finished until 12:15 A.M. That same night, McCloy took him to the U.S. Consulate, where he had a sleepy consular officer notarize the document. After driving Larkin to his home on Wellington Road and saying goodbye, McCloy didn't get to bed until 2:00 A.M. He rose early that morning and caught the 8:00 A.M. boat for London.[18]

Larkin's affidavit was better than McCloy could have hoped. The Germans had been strongly attracted to Larkin's forceful personality, recognized him as a leader of stature among Irish Americans, and accepted him informally into their innermost councils. He had been courted by German officials, including Captain Franz von Papen. Larkin said a Captain Karl Boy-Ed, a German naval officer who helped von Papen to direct the sabotage campaign, offered him $200 a week "to organize a group of men, non-Germans, to work along the waterfront, as the Germans were under too strict a surveillance." He was even taken to a demonstration of an incendiary device made of white phosphorus. On one occasion, they discussed a plan to destroy the "Jersey City terminus," otherwise known as Black Tom. His affidavit was filled with remarkable detail, including names, dates, and places of meetings. The only disappointment was that Larkin could give no firsthand corroboration of what actually happened at Black Tom or Kingsland. But his statement went very far to establish that von Papen and other high-ranking German officials had been involved in sabotage.

Back in New York, McCloy spent weeks verifying the facts contained in the Larkin affidavit. There was only one incident related in the affidavit that puzzled McCloy. Larkin said that the German saboteurs often used to meet in a New York art gallery on Fifth Avenue owned by someone named Unstengel. He had hesitated over pronunciation of the name, but he was quite certain about the location of the art store and described in detail the upstairs room in which the conspirators met.[19]

Through an anonymous tip, McCloy soon learned that the mysterious "Unstengel" was none other than Dr. Ernst Franz Hanfstaengl, then employed as Adolf Hitler's foreign-press spokesman. Hanfstaengl—or "Putzi" as he had been known at Harvard—was a towering six-foot-four-inch German with an American mother. His family owned a publishing business in Munich and a high-class art store on Fifth Avenue in New York City. Educated in the United States, Putzi had society connections that allowed him to meet men like Pierpont Morgan and Henry Ford. At Harvard he had known Walter Lippmann, T. S. Eliot, and John Reed. While running the family art store in New York, Putzi took most of his meals at the Harvard Club, and there he formed a passing friendship with a rising young state senator, Franklin Roosevelt.

For all these connections, Putzi remained a staunch German nationalist, and during the war he had only avoided internment by hiring as his attorney former Secretary of State Elihu Root. After the war, he went back to Munich, where he was introduced to Adolf Hitler and participated in the 1923 Munich Beer Hall Putsch. Thereafter, his wit and love of practical jokes made him a bit of the court jester in Hitler's inner circle. His vigorous piano playing, particularly of Hitler's favorite Wagnerian themes, seemed to soothe the Nazi leader's nerves.

President Roosevelt had not forgotten his German friend, and soon after his assumption of the presidency, he sent a private emissary to Hanfstaengl. Roosevelt hoped that, in view of their long acquaintance, Putzi would do his best with Hitler to prevent any "rashness and hotheadedness." The president was quoted as saying, "Think of your piano playing and try and use the soft pedal if things get too loud."[20]

McCloy was unaware at this time of Hanfstaengl's back channel to the president. All he knew was that now both Hitler's vice-chancellor, von Papen, and his foreign-press chief, "Putzi" Hanfstaengl, were implicated in the Black Tom conspiracy. When Hanfstaengl visited America briefly in 1934, McCloy tried to obtain an affidavit from him on Black Tom. Hanfstaengl brushed him off. At this stage in his career, the Nazi official had every reason to keep his silence about those mysterious meetings in his art shop on Fifth Avenue.

By 1936, McCloy was beginning to feel that he finally had his "ducks all lined up." New facts had begun to turn the case around. He had learned that, if he was to defeat the Germans at this game of intrigue, he had to be willing to use a bit of guile and deception. Among other things, he helped smuggle a historian into an Austrian archive where a batch of military documents were found reporting on sabotage operations in America. He also hired detectives to shadow German officials affiliated with the case, and once he asked the phone company to trace their telephone calls.

The Germans could not help suspecting that in the next hearing before the Mixed Claims Commission their case might not prevail. That summer, Hermann Goering, *Ministerpräsident* of the Third Reich, indicated that Germany was now amenable to an out-of-court settlement. Hitler delegated a top aide to Minister Without Portfolio Rudolf Hess, Hauptmann von Pfeffer, to be his personal representative in the negotiations.

Soon afterward, the American claimants sent a delegation to Munich to begin the discussions. McCloy, accompanied by Ellen, arrived late on the evening of June 28, 1936, and checked into the luxurious Regina-palast Hotel. The next day, Monday, June 29, the lawyers were told that Hitler's representative, von Pfeffer, was in town and meeting with the Führer to discuss the sabotage cases. For the period of the negotiations, July 1–10, von Pfeffer was the Americans' primary contact with the Nazi government. Only once during their stay in Munich did McCloy meet with a high-ranking Nazi official, and even then his appointment with Rudolf Hess was brief and perfunctory.

In retrospect, McCloy would always say that from this experience in dealing with Nazi officialdom he had come to expect the future conflagration. "It was terrifying. All those goose-stepping soldiers. I could feel war in the air. . . . I knew then that they were a bunch of thugs." While they were in Munich, the Nazis celebrated the tenth anniversary of their first party congress, and Hitler proclaimed Nazi rule eternal.[21] The decidedly martial atmosphere made such an impression on Ellen that years later her dreams were sometimes haunted by images of Nazi Germany.

Despite the oppressive atmosphere, McCloy's negotiations with the Germans went surprisingly well. Von Pfeffer made an offer which the claimants found to be more or less satisfactory. Over the next few days, McCloy was frequently on the phone to New York, consulting with his clients and other lawyers about the German conditions.

When a settlement had been reached, the Germans hosted a celebratory dinner in a Munich restaurant. At the end of the meal, McCloy's host suddenly stood up and requested that a phonograph be placed on the table. A record was placed on the turntable, and McCloy, expecting music, was suddenly dumbfounded to hear his own voice talking by phone to his Cravath colleagues in New York. All his transatlantic phone calls had been recorded. The Germans, not a bit embarrassed to demonstrate that they had tapped his phone, roared with laughter at his obvious discomfort.[22]

While waiting for the Germans to ratify the final agreement, the McCloys and the other lawyers went to Berlin to attend what the Nazis were advertising as the "biggest show on the earth," the 1936 Summer Olympics. As a courtesy, the German Foreign Office arranged for the McCloys to sit next to Goering in Hitler's private box at the new Olympics stadium. He felt as if he had been given a "window on the center of the Nazi regime."[23] Amid the sporting events, the Nazis put on a dazzling military spectacle with thousands of goose-stepping soldiers and a band blaring the overture of Wagner's opera *Rienzi.*[24]

Upon his return to Munich, McCloy discovered that the agreement he had negotiated with von Pfeffer seemed to be coming unstuck. The German authorities still had not ratified the settlement. McCloy waited in Munich, hoping that the Nazis would sign the accords and end the case. Finally, after two weeks, his patience gave out and he left Germany empty-handed.

Only in New York did he learn what had happened. A few American attorneys whose corporate clients had something to lose by a settlement of the sabotage claims had undermined the Munich agreement. Prior to 1930, a number of U.S. banks and corporations had received compensation for war losses not contested by Germany from the Mixed Claims Commission. Actual payment was from a limited Special Deposit Fund of monies contributed by both Germany and the United States. These funds could not be fully distributed to the "award-holders" until all outstanding claims before the Commission were settled. Since there was a limited pot of money, the award-holders stood to gain a higher percentage of their awards if the sabotage cases were dismissed.

Award-holders included Chase National Bank (controlled by Rockefeller interests), Standard Oil, Guaranty Trust, Western Electric, Singer Manufacturing Co., and various insurance firms. Most of these companies had actually received 100 percent of their initial losses, or more. But they also insisted on receiving the full value of the interest payments due on their awards.[25]

McCloy was aware of the opposition by Chase Bank and other award-holders, but he was startled to learn that Chase had sent a lawyer to Germany to lobby against the agreement. Then, in the autumn of 1936, he heard of an incriminating letter addressed to Hitler's treasurer, Reichsbank President Hjalmar Schacht. McCloy quickly managed to obtain a copy of the letter, signed by Joseph C. Rovensky, a vice-president of Chase National Bank.[26]

The letter urged Schacht to scuttle the negotiated agreement, and warned the German banker that "numerous institutions in America" were determined to "use every means at their command" to void the agreement. McCloy thought this language could make Rovensky or Chase Bank itself liable for prosecution under the Logan Act, which prohibits private citizens from interfering in the conduct of U.S. foreign policy.[27] He contacted the FBI, but after a year and a half, Justice Department officials concluded they would have to get Schacht, von Pfeffer, and other high-ranking German Foreign Office officials to testify in American courts. That seemed out of the question, so the assistant attorney general recommended the case be dropped.

By the end of the 1930s, McCloy's legal career was indelibly linked to one case. Friends on Wall Street inevitably described him to strangers as the Black Tom man, and they would tell the stories McCloy himself so frequently told, of spies, messages written with invisible ink, and intercepted radio ciphers. These were entertaining stories, but McCloy's friends sometimes wondered if the case would ever amount to anything. With the collapse of the Munich accords in 1936, the Mixed Claims Commission resumed its deliberations, acting as if the near settlement at Munich had never happened. The Commission's 1936 decision to reinstate the sabotage claims to where they stood prior to the 1930 Hague decision required a whole new set of briefs, reply briefs, and oral arguments. The Germans dragged their feet, and thus succeeded in stretching out the process for almost two years.

The delays gave the American claimants time to dig up further evidence in the files of the Eastern Forwarding Co., the firm owned by the

Hilken family in Baltimore. "The Ahrendt postscript," McCloy recalled, "was the clincher."[28]

Carl Ahrendt, a German American employee of the Eastern Forwarding Co., had testified that he had no knowledge of Hilken's or Herrmann's sabotage activities. But in a letter dated January 19, 1917, eight days after the Kingsland fire, Ahrendt had written a damning postscript in an otherwise innocuous business letter to Hilken. As an afterthought, he congratulated Hilken:

> Yours of the 18th just received and am delighted to learn that the von Hindenburg of Roland Park won another victory.
>
> Had a note from March who is still at the McAlpin. Asks me to advise his brother that he is in urgent need of another set of *glasses.* He would like to see his brother as soon as possible on this account.[29]

It had already been established that Herrmann frequently used the alias March, that he was staying at the McAlpin Hotel in January 1917, and that the "glasses" he needed were the same glass incendiary tubes disguised as pencils that were used at Black Tom and Kingsland. Ironically, this sensational piece of evidence had always been within their grasp, and it was mere bad luck that it had not been discovered in 1933, when the Hilken papers were first subpoenaed. Had this occurred, the case might have been settled that year. But now there could no longer be any doubt as to the outcome. The Ahrendt postscript had been discovered just in time to be filed before the Commission's final oral arguments, scheduled for the autumn of 1938.

About the same time, Ellen, at the age of thirty-nine, finally found a doctor who was able to perform a "miracle," as one friend put it. "They had just about given up hope," says one friend, "when Johnny was born." Ellen had the baby at Lennox Hospital, where McCloy was on the board of directors. "He phoned," says Mrs. Mary Weicker, "and said, 'We have a son. It is Johnny. Come and meet me for a glass of champagne at the Carlyle.' Well, I went to the Carlyle and had that glass of champagne. He was so excited. And then I looked across the room and there was sitting Mrs. Adams, the headmistress of Buckley School. I told Jack my children would probably be expelled because their mother had been seen drinking champagne at noon. Jack just laughed."[30] After Ellen came home from the hospital, the McCloys celebrated Johnny's birth with a large party to which they invited practically everyone they knew in New York.[31]

That August, McCloy, Ellen, and their new son vacationed at the Ausable Club in Keene Valley, New York.[32] And though he caught plenty of salmon, his month in the countryside turned into a working vacation: he had once again been assigned the "laboring oar" to produce the first draft of the final Black Tom brief.

Filling reams of yellow legal pads with his practically indecipherable handwriting, he laid out the major evidence: the Zimmermann telegram, the Herrmann message, the Ahrendt postscript, the Larkin affidavit, the British Secret Service intercepts, and the incriminating cables obtained from the Austrian archives. He also placed special emphasis on the duplicitous and fraudulent character of the German evidence.[33]

When done, McCloy had an impressive document. In November 1938, he came down to Washington to prepare for the oral arguments before the Mixed Claims Commission. He knew his strong point was not oral presentation, so he had former U.S. Attorney General William Mitchell present the case. Using McCloy's notes, Mitchell argued that "there were high German officials . . . who were quite willing to testify falsely. They may have been men who in private life would not be guilty of misstatement, but they seem to have had a point of view about their country which made them justify in their own mind anything which would defend the Fatherland from embarrassing charges."[34]

The commissioners adjourned on January 26, 1939, and McCloy was confident of a favorable decision. On March 1, the two commissioners conferred with Umpire Justice Roberts, and when it became clear that Roberts was now ready to rule in favor of the sabotage claimants, the German commissioner announced his immediate "retirement." Justice Roberts requested the German government to appoint a replacement, but in the meantime ruled that the sabotage claimants had proved their case.

Awards of nearly $50 million were entered on behalf of the sabotage claimants. These were immediately contested in federal district court by the American award-holders, led by Chase Bank, who claimed that, since the German commissioner had retired, the Commission could not make a ruling. The case was eventually brought to the Supreme Court; McCloy worked on the brief, which was submitted to the full Court on November 29, 1940, and on January 6, 1941, the court upheld Justice Roberts's decision.

The Supreme Court's action became a landmark decision in the field of international law. Since the Germans had withdrawn their commissioner, the Court could have ruled that the arbitration board technically had not made a decision. By refusing to accept such an argument, the Court struck a blow for the concept of international arbitration. As McCloy argued, "It would make a farce of the proceedings and a travesty of international arbitration, were it possible for one Commissioner, by withdrawing at the last moment, to frustrate or impede a final decision."[35] Forever afterward, McCloy would cite his Black Tom experience as evidence that international arbitration was an imperfect but viable tool. Over the years, this conviction fueled his support for internationalist institutions.

On a less lofty plane, Black Tom finally paid some dividends. "Amos [Peaslee] was determined above all else," said Ben Shute, "to become a rich man, and he succeeded pretty well."[36] Peaslee's special arrangement with his clients made him a millionaire four times over; he personally received $4.4 million in attorney's fees.[37]

McCloy did not do nearly as well, but he was not hurting. Cravath paid him $94,105 in 1941, more than double his partnership share of 1940. "I was just getting into the so-called big money," he said. "I thought I was being richly paid."[38] In addition, Peaslee, evidently realizing that McCloy had unduly contributed to his sudden wealth, gave him a small portion of his contingency fee. McCloy's recollection was that this amounted to between $10,000 and $25,000.

Black Tom made a number of people a great deal of money, but McCloy was also rewarded in another currency. He had acquired a reputation as one of the country's foremost experts on German spies at a time when the United States had no central intelligence service, and only a tiny and neglected military intelligence. He had firsthand knowledge of the structure and capabilities of the British and German intelligence bureaucracies, and had dealt personally with numerous German agents and double agents. He was friends with such veterans of British intelligence as Admiral Reginald Hall and Sir William Wiseman.

McCloy thought these experiences had taught him some broad lessons about the craft of intelligence. In the coming years, these "lessons" became to him matters of absolute conviction. Spying in the twentieth century, he believed, was a sophisticated business carried out by well-financed institutions. It was no longer an isolated occurrence or something confined to wartime. Having proved the existence of the German spy ring responsible for Black Tom, McCloy was now psychologically prepared to be a ready believer in all spy rings.

Black Tom was by no means the only spy case widely publicized in the years immediately after World War I. Thousands of "suspicious-looking" foreigners, communists, union organizers, and immigrants of any kind were placed under surveillance by private vigilante groups such as the American Protective League. Together with a surge of nativist prejudice against postwar immigrants, the spy scares contributed to the "Palmer Raids" of 1919–20, when hundreds of individuals were arbitrarily arrested for subversive activities. Gradually, after the hysteria died down, many Americans recognized that it had all been much ado about nothing. Of the thousands arrested under the U.S. Espionage and Sedition Act, only a handful were convicted, including one German officer, Captain Franz von Rintelen. And even Rintelen hadn't accomplished anything with his spying. It is easy, then, to see why so many of McCloy's colleagues had been skeptical of the claims he made for Black Tom. The cast of characters—Fred Herrmann, Paul Hilken, Count Nelidoff, James Larkin, "Putzi" Hanfstaengl, Franz von Papen, and all his agents—seemed to be taken out of a pulp spy novel, but McCloy had proved it to be nonfiction. The Black Tom conspiracy always had its skeptics, and now McCloy would always be skeptical of the skeptics. Not surprisingly, in 1940, he had few doubts that German intelligence had once again targeted neutral America for infiltration and sabotage.

Others in Washington came to similar conclusions. The *Washington Evening Star* editorialized that the Court's decision "climaxes, but does not end, a true story international intrigue as weird as any tale ever conceived by writers of popular fiction. . . . The whole sordid Black Tom–Kingsland episode has served one good purpose, however. It has shown the need in this country of an efficient counter-espionage system in time of peace as well as war."[39]

Because America had been unprepared for the German intelligence offensive in 1915–16, McCloy believed the United States should create its own intelligence capabilities before it had to do so in the midst of war. He was also prepared to have the government do things in the name of national security that might offend certain "constitutional" sensibilities. Wiretaps, mail intercepts, and the decryption of foreign radio messages were essential techniques for any intelligence organization. Henry Stimson, he believed, was wrong to have thought that "gentlemen do not read each other's mail," and wrong to have closed down the Black Chamber. Black Tom had taught him that such scruples were naïve.

CHAPTER 6

Cravath, the New Deal, and the Approach of War

"In America there are neither nobles nor men of letters, and the people distrust the wealthy. Therefore the lawyers form the political upper class and the most intellectual section of society."

ALEXIS DE TOCQUEVILLE

McCloy's relentless pursuit of German saboteurs for nine years had often seemed a bit quixotic, particularly in the context of the Great Depression. As the seams of American society ripped apart, the great Wall Street law factories became more important than ever before in adjudicating the country's political and economic disputes. Cravath was no exception. With the lucrative market for handling securities drying up, Cravath once again began handling a great number of receiverships.

When McCloy returned from Paris in 1931, the firm appointed him managing partner. Black Tom consumed more of his time than any other case, but as managing partner he had to spend nearly half his time assigning cases, interviewing new associates, supervising the production of briefs, and attending endless meetings. If there was a problem between partners, McCloy's task was to solve it during their regular Monday luncheons. Not surprisingly, being managing partner was considered a headache, because it took one away from the law. But McCloy was good at it; he was personally popular, and he smoothed the abrasive edges of Robert Swaine, who as the most active senior partner, was the ultimate boss. "He [Swaine] was a very able guy," recalled one young associate, "but a little rough; in fact, he made more enemies than he should have because he was so rough. . . ."[1] Young associates like Howard Petersen and Ben Shute, who were both hired by McCloy in 1933, recall working seventy hours a week. "I worked Saturdays and Sundays for years," says Petersen.[2] The firm churned out an endless stream of legal documents, as systematically as Ford Motor Company turned out automobiles. And McCloy was the factory's foreman, the man who ensured that the papers were written, the affidavits collected, and the briefs filed on time.

It was not always the most stimulating work, and Cravath was not always on the winning side. As managing partner, McCloy became involved in many bitter corporate battles. But some tasks were less onerous, such as the one McCloy and Swatland performed for Jean Monnet, who became one of McCloy's closest friends and collaborators. Part philosopher and part international financier, Monnet devoted much of his political life to burying age-old animosities between the French and the Germans. Some would later call him the "godfather" of a united Europe; in the 1920s and '30s, however, Monnet was a low-profile but powerful Wall Street operator.

Back in 1929, Monnet had been invited to a party in Paris, and among the dinner guests were an Italian businessman and his twenty-year-old wife, Sylvia. Monnet, forty, instantly fell in love with Sylvia: "She was very beautiful. We forgot the other guests. . . . We soon decided that we must be together for life."[3] Unfortunately, Sylvia had married under Italian law, which did not allow for divorce. Five years later, when Monnet and Sylvia decided to formalize their liaison, they sought the European equivalent of a Mexican divorce: meeting in Moscow on November 13, 1934, Soviet civil authorities granted Sylvia a divorce from her Italian husband and a marriage to Monnet. Bound for New York from Moscow, Monnet was worried that U.S. authorities might not recognize Sylvia's standing as his wife. So he wired Cravath, and both Swatland and McCloy were there at dockside to see that Monnet and Sylvia made it ashore.[4] Sylvia charmed everyone in New York, and in particular Ellen McCloy. The two women soon became close friends.[5]

By 1932, the once-favorable consensus on Wall Street concerning the merits of the great engineer in the White House had broken down. Many of McCloy's friends believed Herbert Hoover was incapable of restoring confidence in the economy. McCloy's brother-in-law, Lew Douglas, hoped the Democrats would elect a "real leader in 1932."[6]

Hoover had been elected with the strong backing of Kuhn, Loeb partners and other investment houses that represented clients with large investments abroad. In 1928 he had had the support of the internationalist business community, but by 1932 only protectionist interests, led by the Du Ponts, still supported the president. Other than the House of Morgan, aligned with Du Pont and other domestic-based industries, most investment bankers had switched to the Democratic Party. Winthrop Aldrich of Chase National Bank, James A. Moffett of the Standard Oil Company of New Jersey, banker James Warburg, and the Rockefellers all supported Roosevelt. They did so not only because they had given up on Hoover's inactivity in the face of the financial crisis, but also because Roosevelt had assured them of his commitment to a balanced budget.[7]

McCloy was not impressed by Roosevelt; he thought his appeals to the masses with rhetoric about the "forgotten men" and promises of a "new deal"[8] unnecessarily flamboyant and decided to cast his vote again for Hoover. In November 1932, Roosevelt won by nearly seven million votes, but McCloy was pleased that the president-elect soon nominated Lew Douglas as his budget chief.[9] From his Wall Street offices, McCloy wrote to his brother-in-law, "The feeling here is that it is the best appointment Roosevelt has made yet."[10] Douglas was a conservative Democrat, a firm believer in a balanced budget and lower federal spending. He thought the country could dig its way out of the depression only by a negotiated reduction or even cancellation of intergovernmental debts. In November 1932, he wrote the columnist Walter Lippmann that a revival of world trade was essential: "If the debt question can be readjusted currencies will automatically become stabilized. When currencies are stabilized, tariffs . . . can then be lowered."[11]

These were views endorsed by McCloy and many of his investment-banking friends. On March 7, 1933, he wrote Douglas, "The crisis that we are going through at the present time will require all the courage that the President indicated he had in his inaugural address. All of you must be thinking and working hard and if Roosevelt can formulate and have enacted a program which will avoid the stagnation of business I will be willing to concede that he is a great and courageous man. . . . To my mind the only one clear beneficial remedy that will certainly do good, irrespective of what other remedies may be applied, is to balance the budget."[12]

Douglas heeded this advice and soon drafted an austerity budget which called for reducing the salaries of federal employees by $100 million and cutting military spending from $752 million to $531 million by 1934. Even veterans' benefits were to be cut by $400 million. But at the same time, Roosevelt was creating new programs, such as the billion-dollar-a-year Agricultural Adjustment Act, which paid farmers not to plant their fields. These expenditures caused Douglas and other fiscal conservatives to wonder where the president was leading them. "I never know when some new and foolish idea is going to be sprung," he wrote his father.[13] He was particularly incensed when, in the spring of 1933, he walked into the Red Room of the White House and a grinning FDR said, "Congratulate me. We are off the gold standard." Douglas wanted to resign. This time FDR persuaded him to remain.[14]

These were the worst years of the depression, but Cravath lawyers and many others from the professional classes were doing well. The McCloys lived in Beekman Place, a fashionable high-rise complex on the Upper East Side of Manhattan. They were not unaware of their good fortune; McCloy later recalled long bread lines and men in worn pinstripes, standing on street corners, selling apples. But he and Ellen were now people of considerable social standing. They were listed in the *Social Register*, and Ellen was known around Manhattan for her volunteer work in behalf of various charities. In the evenings, they hosted small dinner parties for their friends and frequently attended the Metropolitan Opera. McCloy was a member of the usual clubs associated with the Wall Street scene: the New York Bar Association, the University Club, Grolier, and Broad Street.[15]

But closest to his heart was the Anglers' Club, located in two rooms above the Fraunces Tavern on Broad Street, where General George Washington had been given a farewell banquet by his fellow officers. Founded in 1906, the Anglers' was one of New York's most exclusive all-male clubs; membership was limited to 265 men devoted to fly-fishing salmon and trout. The club went to great lengths to preserve its anonymity; it neither advertised its existence nor encouraged growth. With membership came a reciprocal membership in the exclusive Flyfishers Club of London.[16] President Calvin Coolidge was a member until his death, and so was Herbert Hoover. McCloy became a member in 1933, and over the years helped to raise money for its operations.[17] He frequently took his lunches there on weekdays.

Lew Douglas had first introduced McCloy to fly-fishing, and he had taken it up with a passion. Every summer, he cast his lines into the west branch of the Neversink River or the Ausable River, both in the Catskills. McCloy considered the latter one of the best trout streams in the Eastern United States.[18] Douglas was a frequent companion on these expeditions, as were Dean Acheson, Chester McClain, Chauncey Parker, and Harry Brunie, all of them bankers and lawyers.[19]

In the summer of 1933, McCloy took two weeks away from the office to join Lew Douglas on a fishing expedition to the Jupiter River, on Anticosti Island in Canada. The brothers-in-law never enjoyed each other's company so much as when they were fishing salmon. But they were always rivals. Together with some friends and a couple of guides, they made their way up the Jupiter by horse-drawn boats. Arriving at the Jupiter's traditional campsite, the guides commented that few sportsmen had explored much of the wilderness farther upriver. "The River went straight up 12 miles, and then went perpendicular," recalled McCloy. "I said to Lew, 'For God's sake, if I were a salmon I wouldn't stop at that corner of the Jupiter.' " He challenged Douglas to accompany him the next day up the river. "Early the next morning I tried to wake Lew and he just told me to go off by myself, he wanted to sleep."

The story he told upon his return was, according to Douglas, an example of "Jack McCloy's amazing imagination." Claiming that he alone now "knew the secrets of the Upper Jupiter," McCloy said he had discovered a bend in the river where he had caught thirty-four salmon, one right after another. Unfortunately, he couldn't back up this fish story, since there had been no room in his saddle bags to bring all those fish home. His campmates were skeptical. For years afterward, Douglas loved to tell the story—at his brother-in-law's expense—of how Jack McCloy claimed to have ridden horseback seventeen miles up the river and back, and then "raised, hooked, played and beached (he had no net) thirty-four salmon and had hooked a beaver which, fortunately, had disengaged itself from Jack's fly. All of this within the short span of nine hours . . . I do not question Jack's veracity, but I admire his bountiful imagination. It is this which makes him what he is, including a skillful fisherman."[20]

On these fishing expeditions, both Douglas and Dean Acheson, who had become undersecretary of the Treasury in 1933, complained bitterly to McCloy about their boss in the White House. In October 1933, Acheson was finally fired by Roosevelt, and everyone thought Douglas would be next. He had, after all, been far more outspoken in his criticisms than Acheson. Douglas and McCloy were incensed by Acheson's firing. Douglas wrote his father, "The Administration has lost real ability in Acheson . . . and has acquired stupidity and Hebraic arrogance and conceit in [Henry] Morgenthau." In December, he wrote a friend that he was "heartbroken" over the drift in the administration. He knew he was being used for political purposes: "The high command is using me now for only two purposes: first to complete the 1935 budget, and secondly, as a decoy to . . . conservative elements."[21]

At Cravath, McCloy was surrounded by men who thought Douglas should have resigned with Acheson. The ambivalence the senior Cravath partners felt toward FDR during the first one hundred days had turned to bewilderment by the end of the year, and then outright hostility. By January 1934, Paul Cravath was writing a friend, "Roosevelt is adopting very radical measures under the influence of his Brain Trust advisors and is causing great alarm among the New York standpatters with whom I associate." Swaine complained bitterly that the administration's financial policy had become "Tax and tax, spend and spend, elect and elect."[22]

Swaine was now encouraging the firm to participate in a number of the legal challenges mounted by the business community against the New Deal. One such instance was the "Chicken Case." In the first hundred days of the Roosevelt administration, Congress had passed the National Industrial Recovery Act (NIRA). Under the act, "codes of fair competition" were issued, designed to prevent the growth of monopolies. Swaine believed that, with the act, "America adopted the planned economy of authoritarian government." So, when the Supreme Court agreed to review the constitutionality of the NIRA in *U.S.* v. *Schechter Poultry Corporation,* Cravath eagerly agreed to assist Schechter's counsel. It did so, said Swaine, in the interest of its major steel client, Bethlehem Steel, which had a large stake in seeing NIRA overturned.[23]

Cravath entered the Chicken Case only two weeks before it was argued in the Supreme Court. As managing partner, McCloy had to marshal the firm's resources in a rushed attempt to meet the court's deadline. The brief they produced argued that Congress lacked the power to regulate intrastate businesses, even though the eventual product might be sold across state lines. The court agreed, and in a unanimous decision it declared the NIRA unconstitutional. McCloy and his Cravath colleagues had dealt Franklin Roosevelt his first decisive defeat.

Meanwhile, Lew Douglas was increasingly disaffected and shocked by the unprecedented measures taken by the White House to deal with the depression. Speaking of the New Dealers, he told one friend, "They want to destroy every ideal we have. . . ." He singled out brain trusters Louis Howe, Rex Tugwell, and Attorney General Homer Cummings as "three really bad men among the crowd, because they were sly and always dangerous." Despite such strong language, Douglas said in March 1934 that he wouldn't leave until he was fired, because in the meantime he could at least save the country a little money.

But later that year, it became too much for him. While visiting his in-laws at the Zinssers' Locust Wood estate, Douglas suddenly asked McCloy whether he should resign. His old friend encouraged him to make the break. "He was making up his mind," says McCloy, "and talked to me a great deal. I was sympathetic to his problem. Lew was a budget balancer and FDR pretended he was, but had another account going at the same time. Lew thought this fraudulent. . . . He thought he had been betrayed."[24] Douglas also now thought Roosevelt's "brain trust" had been infiltrated by communists. Tugwell, he said, was "a Communist at heart. . . . He is surrounded with the young Harvard Law School group, all of whom are Communists." Jews too were part of the conspiracy to destroy the capitalist system. More than once, Douglas spoke to his friends about "Hebraic influence" and blamed the New Deal's faults on the Jewish race: "Most of the bad things which it [the administration] has done can be traced to it. As a race they seem to lack the quality of facing an issue squarely."[25]

McCloy never put such anti-Semitic thoughts to paper. His opinions were never so extreme nor so forcefully articulated as his voluble brother-in-law's. He was a more tolerant and liberal man than Douglas, but he was also a man of his times and class. And in Wall Street during the 1930s, few men challenged the notion that, as a rule, Jews were socially pushy and arrogant, particularly when placed in positions of power and influence. The "best" Jews, of course, behaved differently. The Warburgs, the Buttenwiesers, the Strausses—the kind of assimilated "Our Crowd" German Jews whom McCloy counted as his friends—did not ask to be seated in public positions of power. Nor did they expect to make careers for themselves in places like Cravath or to be admitted to the elite private clubs that were a daily part of McCloy's life. McCloy did not question such social segregation, nor did he seem to insist on it. Such as they were, his prejudices regarding Jews were passive.

Douglas's visceral anti-Semitism, however, was provoked by Morgenthau. A few days after his chat with McCloy, he flew into a rage while listening to a speech by the Treasury secretary on the radio. He angrily called it the "most dishonest utterance coming from a Secretary of the Treasury I ever heard."[26] By the time he handed in his resignation a few days later, the federal deficit was running at more than $6 billion.[27] Given his obsession with balancing the budget, it was surprising he had remained even eighteen months in the New Deal. After spending a few weeks in retreat at the Zinsser home with his in-laws and the McCloys, Douglas went abroad for a while and then decided to take a job with the American Cyanamid & Chemical Corporation in New York.[28]

Douglas's departure from the administration was a turning point in Wall Street's relations with Roosevelt. Thereafter, the tenor of the country's political discourse became increasingly bitter and partisan. At a Harvard annual *Crimson* dinner in 1935 where Lew Douglas gave a speech blasting the New Deal, Felix Frankfurter responded by reading a fictitious telegram addressed to the *Crimson* editors from the president, himself a former *Crimson* editor: "I once heard Uncle Theodore say, 'I love Harvard men as individuals, but I always feel more comfortable when most of them are against me, because then I am quite sure that most of the country is for me.' "[29]

Many of those Harvard friends of McCloy's who had voted for Roosevelt in 1932, like James Warburg, had come around 180 degrees. Warburg wrote a best-selling book in 1935 in which he suggested that the 1936 election would come down to a choice between dictatorship or democracy. Though conservative Democrats like Dean Acheson and Lew Douglas were publicly committed to Roosevelt's defeat in 1936, the Republicans were not offering much by way of an alternative. As Paul Cravath wrote a friend, "The party lacks intelligent and liberal leadership, and no strong Presidential candidate seems to be in sight."[30]

The Republicans nominated Kansas Governor Alfred Landon. Landon's first choice as a running mate, Lew Douglas, was vetoed by party

leaders who wanted a Republican.[31] Douglas instead became an informal adviser to Landon, frequently commenting on the candidate's speeches. James Warburg advised Landon on foreign policy, and other disaffected Democrats lent their support. A weak candidate to begin with, Landon managed to alienate even the anti–New Deal business community in September 1936 when he attacked the reciprocal tariff treaties negotiated by Secretary of State Cordell Hull. The internationalist, corporate wing of the business community feared another wave of protectionism more than they did Roosevelt. On October 18, Warburg, who could always be relied on for drama, suddenly announced his switch back to Roosevelt. A few days later, Dean Acheson followed suit. Douglas issued a statement saying he would vote for Landon as a protest vote against Roosevelt.

Like his good friend Jeremiah Milbank, the treasurer of the Republican Party, McCloy had preferred Hoover over Landon for the Republican nomination.[32] Like Acheson and Douglas, he was distressed by Landon's protectionist leanings. So was that grand old Republican Henry Stimson, who decided to back out of the Landon campaign. But McCloy, who valued consistency in everything, including his politics, remained a loyal party man and reluctantly voted for Landon. Others in the Wall Street community swallowed their pride and turned back to Roosevelt. Sidney Weinberg, of Goldman, Sachs, returned to the Roosevelt campaign and raised more money for it than any other individual. James Forrestal of Dillon Reed, Averell Harriman of Brown Brothers, and even such conservative Texas oil men as Sid Richardson, Clint Murchison, and W. Alton Jones came aboard. Chase National Bank lent the Democratic Party $100,000.[33] Roosevelt won in an even bigger landslide, with Landon carrying only Maine and Vermont. The debacle represented a watershed for the Republican Party. The nationalist, high-tariff wing of the party had been soundly trounced, in part because McCloy and other like-minded internationalists had basically sat out the campaign. The party had learned a lesson it would apply four years later.

Before and after the election, it sometimes seemed as if Roosevelt's New Dealers viewed the New York bar as members of a criminal class. The depression had not abated, and in the minds of many Americans, Wall Street lawyers were to blame. Cravath lawyers in particular became a symbol of Wall Street's exploitation of the workingman. Hardly a year went by in the 1930s when some Cravath partner was not hauled before a congressional committee and asked to defend the firm's clients and practices. Armed with subpoena powers, these investigations gave the American public an unprecedented view of the internal workings of New York's financial and legal community. Swaine later grudgingly admitted that such investigations were probably "a necessary prophylactic in a democratic system of private enterprise. . . ." But he complained that some were conducted with "brawling that would shame a police court. During the New Deal years they implemented the President's determination to drive the 'money changers' from the 'temple' and often were reckless in unjustifiable innuendo against responsible heads of life insurance, banking, and industrial corporations."[34] Swaine wrote from personal experience.

In the autumn of 1937, a number of McCloy's colleagues, including Benny Buttenwieser and Bob Swaine, spent weeks testifying before the Senate Committee on Interstate Commerce. McCloy himself escaped questioning, but his name repeatedly cropped up in the testimony. The Committee was chaired by the populist senator from Montana, Burton K. Wheeler, but Senator Harry Truman of Missouri presided over most of the hearings. Armed with a congressional subpoena, the Committee counsel, Max Lowenthal, rummaged through the files of both Kuhn, Loeb and Cravath, and discovered not a few documents embarrassing to both firms.

Lowenthal, who had been one of Frankfurter's "front-row" protégés at Harvard Law School, concentrated his investigations on Kuhn, Loeb's near monopoly of the business of railroad reorganization. From 1924 to 1937, Kuhn, Loeb had made profits of more than $11 million on railroad bankruptcies. And yet many of these "reorganized" railroads floundered after only a few years and had to go through yet another reorganization. Questioning Buttenwieser, Truman caustically observed that some of these reorganizations "did not last much longer than a baby carriage."[35]

Inevitably, the investigation focused on the 1925–28 reorganization of the Chicago, Milwaukee & St. Paul Railroad, one of the first cases McCloy had worked on when he arrived at Cravath. The Committee had obtained Cravath's log sheets, which showed that McCloy had begun preparing the receivership papers for the St. Paul a full two months before there was any public hint of default. Swaine was grilled repeatedly as to why McCloy was assigned such work without any client. He lamely explained that he had ordered McCloy to do the work "on my own. . . . I was trying to keep myself informed, and to be prepared with [receivership] papers that I thought might be needed on any turn in the situation."[36]

Truman was unconvinced. It seemed to him that Kuhn, Loeb had decided from the beginning that a receivership was inevitable. Cravath lawyers had consequently conspired with the St. Paul directors to preserve the assets of the troubled railroad for the exclusive benefit of the bankers.

If Cravath's reputation was muddied in the hearings, Kuhn, Loeb's was blackened. One of its partners, George W. Bovenizer, described how the firm had set up a scheme to provide some of its most valued clients with a virtually riskless investment. Ten presidents of major railroads and banking clients, including two of McCloy's best friends, Robert Lovett and Jean Monnet, had been invited to participate in a Kuhn, Loeb syndicate of securities without having to make any personal investment. Furthermore, they were guaranteed that, if the syndicate sustained any losses, these would be covered by Kuhn, Loeb. As Senator Wheeler observed, "It appears that the 'participation' was really a free ride with no risk of loss to these gentlemen, does it not?"[37]

There was worse to come. McCloy's oldest friend at Kuhn, Loeb, Benjamin Buttenwieser, was forced to confess to insider trading. Internal Kuhn, Loeb documents obtained by Senator Wheeler revealed that in 1927–28 Buttenwieser had bought and sold some $125,000 worth of Wabash Railroad stock, transactions based on inside knowledge of an impending sale of a large block of Wabash stock. Senator Wheeler asked Buttenwieser if it were true that he had made a profit of $5,042.21 on the transaction. Buttenwieser replied, "That is correct, sir. At the time, I was a clerk at Kuhn, Loeb & Co. It was not done through Kuhn, Loeb & Co.'s office. They would certainly not have permitted it. I was a 26-year-old clerk at the time, and I have since learned better habits. . . . I think I have learned my lesson, and I never did it again."[38] What Buttenwieser did was not against the law in 1928. But it was when he testified in 1937.

The Wheeler-Truman hearings reinforced the image of Wall Street investment bankers and their counsel as men whose shrewdness warranted the public's distrust. The bankers had labored to present themselves, in the words of Otto Kahn, as men who "could afford to be disinterested." Kahn had likened the relationship between investment bankers and their clients to that of a doctor with his patient. During the 1933 Senate investigations into the causes of the crash, conducted by Frederick Pecora, he had argued that, if only a few of these men, like himself, had been accorded the "moral influence" possessed by the governor of the Bank of England, the Crash of 1929 might have been prevented.[39]

Four years later, Senator Wheeler sarcastically asked Buttenwieser, "How many of these patients of yours are sick at the present time?" And Wheeler concluded: "This notion that investment banking is a profession is continually used to protect the monopoly which these bankers have built up. . . . On the most charitable basis, they failed to live up to the ordinary standards of prudence and care, to say nothing of the high degree of skill they always claim."[40]

This indictment of investment banking, a profession that McCloy had spent the better part of his legal career serving, was given wide currency. In the atmosphere of the New Deal in 1937, when millions of American workers were still standing on bread lines, Lowenthal's Senate investigation made many of McCloy's friends and closest colleagues public targets of class hatred. These were bitter, partisan times, and men like

McCloy, Lew Douglas, Robert Lovett, and Robert Swaine believed themselves to be unjustly and irresponsibly libeled by Roosevelt and his ideologically motivated minions.

McCloy resented being pilloried for conduct that he believed to be sound legal practice, carried out in the best interests of his private clients. If he and his colleagues at Cravath had not acted in the way they did, he felt, many more large corporations would have been completely destroyed by small creditors. What he had done was not only good for the investment bankers who controlled the largest blocs of assets in these corporations, but it was also good for the country as a whole. Lawyers, he believed, could discern this larger public interest precisely because only men imbued with the law truly had the capacity for objectivity and disinterestedness. To McCloy's mind, the general public interest was defined as a collection of competing private interests. Only lawyers learned to discern the public interest, because only lawyers went through the daily process of representing the interests of private clients. This attitude colored McCloy's view of politicians, particularly politicians such as Franklin Roosevelt or Harry Truman, who seemed all too willing to fan the fires of class resentment. The New Deal investigations of Wall Street reminded him how easily the politicians capitulated to what Alexis de Tocqueville had called the "ill-considered passions of democracy."

By the late 1930s, McCloy was a prominent member of the New York bar, a scene far removed from the political controversies of Washington. In those years, Wall Street was still a fairly small and self-contained society. That autumn, Felix Warburg, whom McCloy had known since his summers in Maine, died. The funeral would become the occasion for a major gathering of New York's legal and financial establishment. Lewis Strauss sent out a cable the day after Warburg's death to McCloy and three dozen other old friends, requesting their presence as ushers. McCloy accepted, as did Sidney Weinberg (Goldman, Sachs & Co.), Julius Adler *(New York Times)*, Pierpont Davis (Brown Brothers Harriman & Co.), Morris Waldman (American Jewish Committee), George Brownell (Davis Polk), and other New York lawyers and financial leaders.[41]

Warburg's funeral in a sense marked McCloy's own coming of age in Wall Street society. He was not himself a financier, nor would he ever have the riches of a Felix Warburg or an Averell Harriman. But men like John D. Rockefeller, Jr., were known to consult him on matters of business and philanthropy. And because Rockefeller sought his advice, so too did the rest of Wall Street. His status in the company of such men of wealth was not that of an equal, but these uncrowned members of the American aristocracy depended upon his legal talents to insulate their wealth and social status from the uncertainties of a democratic republic.

If Washington passed legislation regulating their businesses, it was his job, and the job of other Wall Street lawyers like him, to find a way to make that law work in their interest. His was a role that had been aptly described by Tocqueville a hundred years earlier. Lawyers in America, wrote the Frenchman, are "arbiters between the citizens," and perform a function essential to any democratic society. But because their legal training imbues them with an aristocrat's "instinctive preference for order," Tocqueville had concluded that in America "lawyers provide the only aristocratic element naturally able to combine with elements natural to democracy." By the 1930s, the American legal profession, concentrated in the Wall Street law factories, had become a class apart. McCloy was now a bona-fide member of the Establishment.

Another sign of his enhanced status in society was the summons he received in the late 1930s to join the most exclusive of Wall Street luncheon clubs, Nisi Prius. Literally Latin for "unless, before," *nisi prius* is the legal term for a law that takes effect at a specified time unless cause is subsequently demonstrated why it should not. Nisi Prius was organized in 1925 by Arthur Ballantine, who had been a member of a club by the same name in Boston before moving down to New York. The Boston club gatherings were somewhat rowdy affairs, where the members put on satirical skits featuring prominent lawyers about town. They had even published a small tabloid newspaper which printed outlandish reports on the activities of thinly disguised members.

Transplanted to Manhattan, Nisi Prius became a staid version of its Boston predecessor. "It was the elite of the bar then," McCloy said. "I remember thinking that it meant I was coming along. . . . It was quite an honor in those days."[42] With the exception of Harrison Tweed, a Democrat and a man of unorthodox wit, the original members were a decidedly conservative lot. Winthrop Aldrich, a name partner at Murray, Prentice & Aldrich, and Rockefeller, Jr.'s brother-in-law, was a founding member. Ballantine was quick to recruit John Foster Dulles of Sullivan & Cromwell. Robert Swaine, representing Cravath; George Roberts of Winthrop, Stimson, Putnam & Roberts; and George S. Franklin, of Cotton & Franklin, were founding members. So too were Lansing P. Reed, Walter Hope, Francis McAdoo, Frank L. Polk, Elihu Root, Jr., Harold Otis, Joseph Cotton, and Grenville Clark, all from prestigious Wall Street firms. "These were fellows I looked up to," McCloy recalled.

George Roberts seems to have been responsible for McCloy's invitation to join the club. They had met on the tennis court and become good friends. "He was a passable tennis player," McCloy said. "He called them close." There were twenty-eight members, who met for weekly Monday luncheons in a room reserved at the Broad Street club. As a rule, each of the major Wall Street law firms was represented by one or at most two of its senior partners. New members were accepted with the unanimous approval of the club. Anywhere from six to ten club members would show up at the Monday luncheon, and as time went by the practice became to have someone at the table volunteer to introduce a topic for conversation. The discussions ranged from national and international politics to the law. "We'd talk about anything," says McCloy. "Sometimes people brought legal problems and asked for help. At other times, we'd talk about the city or politics."[43]

Gradually, the club became a venue where the leading lawyers of the country could informally keep in touch with one another and air their political views in the company of men they considered "sound." Confidentiality was the rule. To this day, members are reluctant to talk about the group. McCloy was a natural candidate, both as a senior partner from the number-one firm in the city and as a congenial raconteur who often regaled the older men with stories about the Black Tom case or his dealings with the growing federal bureaucracy in Washington. With Nisi Prius, McCloy was now part of the innermost circle of the country's legal aristocracy.

Shortly after winning the Black Tom case in 1939, McCloy received an invitation to join yet another club. Since its founding in 1921, the Council on Foreign Relations had gradually become a regular meeting ground of the Establishment's inner circle. The reason for this was quite clear. As American financial interests expanded abroad, men of influence in the private sector found it necessary to become conversant in matters of foreign policy. The Council sought to fill this need in the elite atmosphere of a New York society club.

McCloy was delighted to join the Council's ranks, and soon was regularly attending the Council's dinner seminars in the company of such pillars of the Wall Street community as Paul Cravath, Frank Altschul, Frank L. Polk, Allen Dulles, and Russell C. Leffingwell. (Lew Douglas became a Council director in 1940.) By the end of Roosevelt's second term, in 1940, the kind of men who gravitated toward the Council's internationalist world-view were of two minds about the administration. Counting themselves as fiscal conservatives and Republicans, they still disapproved of the New Deal. But they were also increasingly alarmed by events in Europe, and if war were to break out, they knew Franklin Roosevelt was no isolationist.

The Council was not particularly interested in propaganda, or publicity campaigns to counter widespread isolationist sentiment. That was a function for less elite organizations, some of which Council members would soon help to fund. The Council wanted to influence the War Department, not the American people. They wanted to engage in war-planning, and planning for a postwar Pax Americana. Soon after Hitler invaded Poland in September 1939, Hamilton Fish Armstrong and Walter H. Mallory of the Council went to Washington to propose a joint "War and Peace Project" with the State Department. Their idea was to provide the State Department with outside expert advice on global strategic issues. In December 1939, the Rockefeller Foundation gave the Council an initial $44,500 to begin the project. Allen Dulles, Norman H. Davis, Jacob Viner, Whitney H. Shepardson, and other Council members began to draft policy papers. Soon they were exerting direct influence on the White House; even before Germany overran Denmark in April 1940, Roosevelt had on his desk a memo from the group proposing that he announce that the United States considered Danish-owned Greenland part of the Western Hemisphere and therefore covered by the Monroe Doctrine. That autumn, the War and Peace Project produced a memo outlining the measures needed "to achieve military and economic supremacy for the United States within the non-German world."[44]

Such interventionist views were far outside the mainstream of American opinion. Most Americans would have been aghast to learn of the Council's sweeping war plans. Even on Wall Street there was no consensus on the Nazi threat. Many of McCloy's peers outside the Council on Foreign Relations were not convinced that European fascism threatened U.S. interests. Leading Republicans such as Herbert Hoover and Foster Dulles had made it clear that they thought some of the German demands were reasonable. Several years earlier, Dulles had given a speech at Princeton University in which he suggested that Europe was now divided between "dynamic" nations, such as Germany and Italy, and "statis" nations, like England and France. Though the Nazis might be temporarily "distasteful," it was not worth a war to stop them.[45] Even after the British abandoned the Czechs at Munich in 1938, Dulles had not changed his mind about Germany. McCloy thought such attitudes naïve and shortsighted. He was shocked by the Munich capitulation, and when war came in Europe, both he and Lew Douglas joined an avowedly prowar propaganda group, the Committee to Defend America by Aiding the Allies, organized by the prominent journalist William Allen White.[46]

Douglas also joined the Council for Democracy, a lobbying-and-public-relations outfit organized by C. D. Jackson, Henry Luce's right-hand man at *Time* magazine. Under Jackson's direction, the Council became an effective and highly visible counterweight to the isolationist rhetoric of the America First organization, led by Charles Lindbergh and Robert Wood of Sears & Roebuck. With financial support from Douglas and Luce, Jackson, a consummate propagandist, soon had a media operation going which was placing anti-Hitler editorials and articles in eleven hundred newspapers a week around the country.

As these organizations tried to proselytize the country for a coming war, a migration of lawyers from Wall Street to Washington commenced.

The first Cravath man to leave the firm was Howard C. Petersen, a young associate whom McCloy had hired in 1933. Petersen took a job in the War Department, working with Grenville Clark, the same lawyer who in 1915 had inspired the Plattsburg military training camps. Fervent internationalists, Petersen and Clark served under an equally fervent Kansas isolationist, War Secretary Harry H. Woodring. It was Woodring who in 1938 took credit for the decision not to put the B-17 bomber into production. By 1940, many in the Roosevelt administration wanted him out. Frank Altschul, a partner with the investment-banking firm of Lazard Freres and a director of the Council on Foreign Relations, and Thomas Lamont, the J. P. Morgan partner, began a campaign in the spring of 1940 to have Woodring replaced by Henry Stimson, the Wall Street establishment's consensus candidate for any position of power in Washington.[47] He had already been secretary of war and of state. A lawyer who personified "soundness," Stimson could certainly run the War Department the way the men associated with the Council on Foreign Relations wanted it run—if only Franklin Roosevelt could be persuaded to get rid of Woodring.

"Roosevelt was not one to fire anyone," Petersen recalled. "He was terrible—he would procrastinate forever. Finally, Clark contacted Julius Ochs Adler, vice-president of the New York Times Company, and they printed a fictitious leak that Woodring was about to go."[48] That precipitated Woodring's resignation. And then, on the afternoon of June 19, 1940, as the Republicans gathered to nominate their candidate for president, Roosevelt offered the post to Stimson. In accepting, Stimson told Roosevelt that, while he would be loyal to him as commander-in-chief, he owed him no political loyalty, he was still a Republican. And he warned that he would brook no political interference in running the War Department. Stimson liked FDR personally, but strongly disapproved of the New Deal. He abhorred Roosevelt's budget deficits and his "appeals to class feeling."[49]

Roosevelt, of course, was reaching out to liberal, internationalist Republicans in order to build a coalition government for the coming war. Simultaneously, he was keeping the country in suspense as to whether he would run for an unprecedented third term. That same week, the Republican Party nominated Wendell Willkie as their dark-horse candidate for president. Willkie had come to national prominence for leading the fight against the Tennessee Valley Authority (TVA), the New Deal's showcase public utility, as president of the Commonwealth & Southern, a private utility holding company.[50] He had made a fortune on Wall Street, sitting on the board of the Morgan-dominated First National Bank of New York.[51] But he now cast himself as a "good ol' boy" from Indiana, an image Interior Secretary Harold L. Ickes sarcastically caricatured as "just a simple barefoot boy from Wall Street."[52] Unlike Senator Robert Taft

(Republican from Ohio), the Republican front-runner for the nomination, Willkie was also an internationalist and a free-trader. These qualities endeared him to Wall Street and the Eastern wing of the Republican Party.

The McCloys were enthusiastic Willkie supporters. On the last day of the convention, Ellen went to Philadelphia with a group of fellow supporters and was in the galleries, chanting, "We want Willkie," as he was nominated. McCloy himself did not attend the convention, but he was very quickly brought into the campaign by his friend Jeremiah Milbank, a major Willkie fund-raiser. He and Milbank worked closely together during the campaign, largely writing fund-raising letters to their contacts in the New York financial community. McCloy in turn recruited Ben Shute to handle the correspondence, turning the Cravath offices into an unofficial finance committee for the Willkie campaign.[53]

Nearly all of McCloy's friends were on the Willkie bandwagon, including such financiers as Sidney Weinberg, Frank Altschul, and Lew Douglas, who lent his name to "Democrats-for-Willkie," a committee that independently raised nearly $400,000 for the campaign.[54] Meanwhile, Roosevelt won renomination without ever announcing that he would seek another four years in the White House. Willkie ran a vigorous campaign, particularly on domestic issues, but the race was overshadowed by the European war, where the Battle of Britain was raging. Roosevelt used both his incumbency and the European war to his political advantage. During one of his few campaign tours, the president said, "You can't say that everyone who is opposed to Roosevelt is pro-Nazi, but you can say with truth that everyone who is pro-Hitler in this country is also pro-Willkie."[55]

McCloy was offended by such rhetoric. On September 13, 1940, he wrote Acheson, "It is amazing to me what contrasts this man Roosevelt can present. The destroyer deal [wherein Britain received fifty U.S. destroyers in return for long-term leases on British bases in the Western Hemisphere] was a stroke of real statesmanship but his speech to the Teamsters Union might just as well have been written by [French Socialist Prime Minister Léon] Blum."[56] He told Acheson he thought it "ridiculous" that Roosevelt could suggest "that every element in the country, except labor, must make sacrifices in order to defend the country."

Lew Douglas had been intimately involved in putting together the destroyer deal. On July 11, 1940, he gave a dinner for eleven friends, all of whom felt America had to do something more concrete to aid Britain. Many of these men simply felt that it was time the United States declare war on Germany. Douglas expanded the group in succeeding weekly meetings, which became known as the Century Group because their gatherings were frequently held in the Century Association club. McCloy was not a formal member of the Century Group, but many of his friends were. The Group's membership overlapped heavily with the Council on Foreign Relations and the Committee to Defend America by Aiding the Allies. Francis P. Miller, organizational director of the Council on Foreign Relations; Whitney H. Shepardson, a Council director; and Stacy May, another Council regular, were members. So too were James Warburg, Joseph Alsop, Will Clayton, Dean Acheson, Frank Polk, and Allen Dulles. On July 25, 1940, the group met and drafted a legal memo instructing Roosevelt how he could circumvent the Neutrality Act's prohibition. The memo suggested that Roosevelt simply describe the destroyer deal as a defense measure. On August 1, Miller and four others went to Washington and pitched their ideas to the president and several Cabinet members. The next day, their proposal was approved by the full Cabinet, and by September Britain had signed the agreement.[57]

That Douglas and other staunch Willkie supporters could in the midst of the campaign work so closely with the Roosevelt administration is an indication of their true priorities. However much the Wall Street community felt repulsed by Roosevelt's political demeanor and domestic agenda in 1940, on matters of war and peace there was a growing affinity. As the situation in Europe disintegrated, opinion among American investment bankers and businessmen with interests abroad rapidly began to coalesce behind those who believed it was time for America to assume world leadership. The Century Group literally wanted America to become "top dog," in the words of James Conant, president of Harvard University, who began to attend the irregular meetings that autumn. Douglas wrote Conant in October 1940, "Our endeavor and England's endeavor, it seems to me, should be aimed at the reconstruction of a world order in which . . . the United States must become the dominant power. . . . I see little hope in my lifetime if this remains undone."[58]

Conant agreed: "I believe the only satisfactory solution for this country is for a majority of the thinking people to become convinced that we must be a world power, and the price of being a world power is willingness and capacity to fight when necessary. . . ."[59]

By 1940, a clear consensus had thus developed in such elite and overlapping organizations as the Century Group, the Council on Foreign Relations, and the Council for Democracy: the United States must soon replace the British Empire as the world's dominant economic and military power. McCloy, closely associated with many of the men active in these groups, couldn't have agreed more. As a matter of politics, he and his friends regarded Willkie as the preferable candidate to carry out this broad agenda. But toward the end of the campaign, Willkie came under strong pressure from the Taft wing of the Republican Party to differentiate himself from Roosevelt's foreign policies. Two weeks before election day, Willkie began emphasizing, "A vote for Roosevelt is a vote for war." Willkie, who had previously supported the destroyer deal for Britain, now called it "the most dictatorial act ever taken by an American President."[60]

McCloy, of course, disagreed; from his point of view, there was nothing wrong with stretching the chief executive's powers a bit in order to achieve the larger goal of saving the European democracies. He soon became intimately involved with that effort when, in mid-September 1940, he got a call from Stimson asking him to come down to the War Department for a few days. Stimson said he needed him to work as a temporary consultant on how to defend the country against German sabotage. Stimson's law partner, George Roberts, had recently introduced the McCloys into Stimson's small social circle at the Ausable Club, where both families had cottages. Stimson now knew of McCloy as a "top-notch" tennis player and an expert on German intelligence matters.[61]

On September 16, 1940, Stimson told General Sherman Miles, chief of Army G-2 intelligence, to hire McCloy as a part-time consultant. That night, the war secretary wrote in his diary, "I have been trying to get the State Department and the Department of Justice to connect with McCloy ever since I have been here but they have made no progress on it, so I finally decided to take him on in the War Department until they begin to realize how much he knows. He is the man who handled the Black Tom case. . . . McCloy knows more about subversive German agents in this country I believe than any other man."[62]

Stimson's call could not have come as a complete surprise to McCloy. That autumn, Black Tom seemed to be happening all over again. The newspapers were filled with stories of mysterious munition explosions in New Jersey factories, the sinking of ships in New York harbor, and congressional investigations of Nazi and communist spy rings. On September 12, 1940, a terrific explosion at a powder plant in Kenvil, New Jersey, destroyed ammunition bound for England and killed dozens of employees. The headlines throughout late September and October announced, "Hitler's Plot for War on U.S. Includes Bombings" and "FBI on Scent of Plot to Wreck U.S. Arsenals."[63] The left-wing New York daily, *PM,* reported in September that "U.S. naval intelligence agents intercepted incendiary bombs disguised as lead pencils, made in Germany. . . . A saboteur has only to split one of these harmless looking pencils and leave it in a plant. Hours later it will spread a fire almost impossible to extinguish."[64] Stimson had reason to call on the lawyer who had broken open the Black Tom case.

So it was that, even before the election, McCloy found himself in Washington, working for the Roosevelt administration. He still would not vote for the man, even if the rapid pace of events seemed to leave FDR the only politician capable of leading the American public into a new "world order." In any case, on November 5, 1940, in the largest turnout ever, forty-nine million, twenty-seven million voted to give the president his third term.[65] Roosevelt had his mandate—and little more than a year left to put together a war council.

BOOK II

World War II

CHAPTER 7

Imps of Satan

"We have as much chance of ignoring this war as a man has of ignoring an elephant in his parlor. . . ."

JOHN J. MCCLOY
SEPTEMBER 19, 1941

In the beginning, McCloy's arrangement with the seventy-two-year-old Stimson was very informal. The two men simply agreed that the younger lawyer would work "on and off" as a consultant to Army Intelligence a couple of days each week.[1] At forty-five years of age, McCloy exuded the athletic energy of a man ten years younger. His habitual double-breasted, baggy gray suits, topped off with a Stetson felt hat, made him appear shorter than his five-foot-ten-inch frame. He walked with a long, quick stride, the gait of a man who still played an aggressive set of tennis at least once a week. His closely shaven, unblemished face showed little sign of wear; only a few crow's-feet wrinkles around his eyes betrayed his early middle age. He smiled easily, and his brown eyes brightened as he engaged in conversation. He had a weakness for good cigars, but as a substitute, visitors to his office frequently saw him popping chocolate drops into his mouth from a bowl on his desk. He enjoyed telling stories, often at too great length. But he also had the patience of a listener.

The army officers who encountered him in these first few weeks on the job found that, unlike many such civilian appointees, McCloy was not full of himself. He wore the easy self-assurance of someone who felt no need to intimidate underlings. In meetings, his demeanor was informal and deferential. He often sat in silence, leaning back in his chair, his eyes closed, while lightly running his right hand back and forth across the hairless dome of his head. One might have thought he was not listening until the end of the meeting, when he would open his eyes and, in the most concise and agreeable language, summarize the salient points made by everyone in the room.

Initially, McCloy concentrated on sabotage investigations, poring over FBI reports on the security of plants manufacturing defense items.

Almost immediately, he saw that any effective antisabotage effort would require a centralized intelligence organization. But there was little coordination between the FBI and the intelligence branches of the army and the navy. Army G-2 had a staff of only eighty and a budget to match it. The Office of Naval Intelligence (ONI) had fewer than twenty attachés to cover the entire globe.[2] Only the previous summer had the FBI begun to set up an organization, the Special Intelligence Section, to cover Latin America.[3]

Yet these three organizations all claimed that, if war came, they were prepared to execute their intelligence tasks, and to do so without sharing their assets. McCloy thought this unrealistic and complained about "how small a concept of the picture we now have."[4] Exercising all his charm, he tried to persuade the rival intelligence chiefs to coordinate their work.

Part of the problem stemmed from personality clashes; General Sherman Miles of Army G-2 complained of J. Edgar Hoover's "dictatorial attitude."[5] Army and naval intelligence were reluctant to share their material, particularly when it came to sensitive coded communications intercepts. In September 1940, the Army's Signal Intelligence Service (SIS) successfully built a duplicate of the PURPLE machine used by the Japanese to encode their cables. McCloy was briefed on this breakthrough, and later that autumn he persuaded the reluctant military brass that this special intelligence should be shared with the British.

In his unobtrusive manner, he was quietly becoming an unofficial coordinator of intelligence matters. In early November, he submitted a draft of a report on counterpropaganda to Interior Secretary Harold Ickes, General Miles, and Stimson. Among other things, he charged that Hitler had prepared "a barrage of ideas to precede his mass attacks," and that the twelve million German Americans had not been insulated from this "virus." He concluded, "Only a well-organized and well-financed bureau or department could counter-act this new weapon of war." Attached was an organizational chart of "Department X," which looked suspiciously like a highly centralized intelligence organization. A "Director and his Staff" reported directly to the secretaries of war and state and the attorney general. Below the "Director" were dotted lines of "liaison" to G-2, ONI, the FBI, and "Treasury Sources." And below them were ten counterintelligence units, each assigned to a separate target group. One unit was assigned to "Counter-work in U.S. among Germans." Another unit was to conduct counterpropaganda in Germany. There were similar units for Italians, French, Czechs, Poles, and "all other races" in the United States.[6]

Miles and Ickes thought McCloy's proposed "Department X" was exactly what was needed. Taking his cue from Ickes, Stimson too thought McCloy's estimation of the danger of German propaganda was sobering.

None of these men questioned the propriety of having a government agency secretly plant propaganda in newspapers read by American citizens. McCloy was not insensible to such civil-liberty concerns, he just discounted them in the present emergency. He acknowledged to General George C. Marshall, the army's chief of staff, "It is a distasteful job to organize a propaganda weapon but in these days the Army cannot ignore the necessity for it any more than the Army can ignore the necessity for artillery or an air force. . . ."[7]

Over the next few months, Ickes doggedly pushed the idea of a centralized propaganda agency. But Roosevelt, while never saying no, refused to submit any concrete legislation to Congress. If McCloy's specific proposal died, some of his ideas nevertheless resurfaced in a few short months. In the meantime, his name became closely associated with the growing debate inside the administration over the country's intelligence needs.

Black Tom continued to grip him. When the FBI passed him a report in mid-November concluding that there was no evidence of sabotage in the recent spate of factory explosions, he told J. Edgar Hoover, "The fact of the matter is that if there is any German sabotage, it is probably being done with the use of devices which destroy themselves and leave no trace. . . ."[8]

To be sure, McCloy was not alone in giving credence to the dangers of sabotage. That summer, a book entitled *The Fifth Column Is Here* was a best-seller.[9] Newspapers all over the country, regardless of their political orientation, were running stories claiming that sabotage and fifth-columnist conspiracies were rampant. The left-wing New York daily, *PM,* observed that settlements of Japanese American truck farmers had "a consistent habit of springing up around places like the Bremerton Navy Yard on Puget Sound" and other military installations.[10] When Hoover complained that such sensationalized reporting fostered public hysteria, McCloy responded, "Some of the widespread publicity and near-hysteria may have a salutary effect. . . . Guards are being strengthened all round, and precautions are increasing not only against sabotage but against accidents."[11]

By November 1940, Stimson was using McCloy as his favorite troubleshooter, someone who could monitor "everything that no one else happened to be handling."[12] Some officers in the War Department began to resent his far-flung activities. General Marshall's assistant, General Thomas T. Handy, warned a colleague, "He's peppery. He's got his nose into everything."

What worried Stimson in the autumn of 1940 was lagging war production. How could one orchestrate an increase in military goods when the nation was still officially at peace? The army's own expanding needs were not being met, let alone the requirements of the British.

British armament needs were a particular problem, because Congress had not yet authorized the transfer of certain categories of weapons. Consequently, McCloy soon found himself trying to construct a legal rationalization for what the administration wanted to do without congressional approval. Roosevelt wanted to sell the British twenty B-17 heavy bombers and munitions. The law, however, specified that nothing could be sold to the British that was needed for the United States' own security. Congress had also barred the sale of certain munitions and aircraft unless the army certified them obsolete. McCloy's solution was ingeniously simple. In return for our selling the British the twenty B-17 bombers, London agreed to place a production order for at least twelve hundred bombers prior to March 1, 1940. This allowed the War Department to certify that the sale would benefit U.S. security by dramatically increasing aircraft production capacity. Regarding the munitions, the department merely stated that the bombs sent with the B-17s were obsolete. A willing Congress accepted these "certifications," though a minority angrily denounced the whole thing as a charade.[13]

Everyone was aware that such rationalizations might not withstand close congressional scrutiny, and McCloy constantly had to reassure Stimson that he could handle the legal proprieties. It was widely assumed among Washington insiders that McCloy was pushing the war secretary to the edge of illegalities. One day, at a Cabinet meeting, the president asked Stimson for his opinion on whether certain supplies could be sent to the British. In response, Stimson began reading from a memo on the subject prepared by McCloy. As he came to the conclusion of McCloy's arguments for why the supplies could be sent, Stimson suddenly found himself reading aloud, "Of course, this is illegal as hell, but—" and stopped short. Roosevelt laughed and, leaning back in his chair, teasingly said, "Why, Henry, you old Republican lawyer." The story was repeated all over town, and among young New Dealers like Joseph L. Rauh, who had just finished clerking for Justice Frankfurter and was then working in the president's Office of Emergency Management, it was told to McCloy's great credit.

It soon became apparent that such legal artifices were temporary measures. The magnitude of British requirements—estimated at $5 billion—would force the president to seek a congressional mandate. Something more had to be done than merely hornswoggling accounts in the War Department. On December 16, Roosevelt returned from a short sailing vacation down the Eastern Seaboard and suggested to Morgenthau that he now had in mind legislation that would allow Washington to "lend" the British guns and ships which they could return in kind at the end of the war. He said, ". . . it seems to me that the thing to do is to get away from the dollar sign. . . ."[14]

One evening, as the president's idea was percolating through Washington, McCloy was at dinner with his old law professor Felix Frankfurter, who had been nominated to the Supreme Court in January 1939. When the topic of British armament needs came up, McCloy mentioned that he thought America's role in this war was to be an "arsenal of democracy." Hearing the phrase from McCloy's lips, Frankfurter's eyes lit up; he told his friend never to use it again.[15] On Christmas Day, the justice wrote Roosevelt a short letter in which he urged him to use the phrase in his next speech. The president said he "loved" the metaphor.[16]

By this time, McCloy was not the only "young man" assisting Stimson. The war secretary had recently brought Robert Lovett, one of McCloy's investment-banking acquaintances, down from New York to work exclusively on air power. Lovett told a reporter, "My business was banking, now it's airplanes." McCloy admired Lovett's command of statistics, and his mildly profane humor. Behind his quiet owlish exterior, Lovett possessed a sharp wit; he could quote Dorothy Parker and George Santayana in the same breath.[17]

In addition to McCloy and Lovett, Stimson had also hired Harvey H. Bundy, who had served him as assistant secretary of state during the Hoover administration. These men formed an unusually close working relationship. All three occupied adjoining offices just down the hall from the secretary, who was forever shouting unintelligible orders to them over an interoffice "squawk box." Occasionally Stimson's temper got the better of him. McCloy and Lovett used humor to deflect such angry outbursts, telling his wife, Mabel, that he was a bad-tempered tyrant who "roared like a lion." Out of his presence, Lovett and McCloy began to refer to their boss as "Stimmie." For his part, the secretary called McCloy and Lovett the "Imps of Satan."[18]

Of the three aides, McCloy was the closest to the Stimsons. Both in the office and at Stimson's Woodley estate in Northwest Washington, D.C., he spent more time with "the Colonel," as he called him to his face, than did any of the other aides. Bundy's demeanor was rather straitlaced. Lovett could be cold and aloof, and even his humor was of the dry, cutting kind. He had little of McCloy's energy or patience in dealing with the bureaucracy, and when confronted by disagreements was apt to mutter, "To hell with the cheese. Let's just get out of this trap." McCloy was the consensus builder, the kind of man who could chair a meeting of people holding violently opposing views and emerge with a concrete list—scrawled on his ever-present yellow legal pad—of "what everyone seems to be saying." He called it "yellow-padding."[19]

On December 18, Stimson went to see FDR and got the president's approval to appoint both McCloy and Lovett as "Special Assistants to the

Secretary of War" at a salary of $8,000 each.[20] McCloy had formally terminated his Cravath partnership on December 7, 1940, though he viewed this break as a temporary separation, not a divorce. In fact, his career as a corporate lawyer would never be the same. After New Year's, Ellen and Johnny, now two years old, moved with him into a small house in Georgetown he rented from an old army friend for $75 a month.[21] Their new home, at 3303 Volta Place, had all of Georgetown's antique charms. It was a low-slung, two-story brick house with a tiny garden in the back. Adjacent to the house was a park where Johnny could play.

All this represented a major break with the past. In his new circumstances as a public servant, McCloy was paid less than 20 percent of his previous annual earnings on Wall Street. His household expenses alone in Washington averaged $10,000 a year. On top of this, he was still supporting his two aunts and his mother as well. Even so, he could afford to take the large salary cut. After twenty years in a Wall Street law practice, he had cash savings and securities worth $106,246, a sizable sum in 1941.[22]

Over Christmas week, which he spent in New York and Hastings-on-Hudson, McCloy had turned his mind to preparing a memo for Stimson on the war economy. "The warfare of today," he wrote, "is increasingly a question of industrial capacity to produce the ability to make, day after day, year after year, planes, ships, arms, and equipment. We must overtake and surpass in this connection an efficient, well-organized nation which is and has been devoting for a number of years the major part of its efforts to the job of preparing and fighting a war." Citing figures that showed that Germany was spending some $60 billion a year on war production, versus America's 1940 budget of about $10 billion, McCloy complained, "Business is going on in the country as usual, and it cannot go on as usual if we are to build up our capacity to anything like German dimensions. . . . To triple or quadruple our present effort requires that radical things be done to our existing economy. Obviously the job demands industrial planning of a high order on the part of the Production Boss."[23]

The problem, of course, was that there was no "Production Boss" with the power to dictate production schedules to private industry. Roosevelt, at least for the moment, was disinclined to take this step, fearful of criticism that by doing so he would be creating a "super-Government."[24] But Stimson was "startled" enough by McCloy's memo that he called the president in the afternoon and conveyed the gist of the critique. There is no record of FDR's response, but the very next day the president gave his famous "Arsenal of Democracy" fireside chat. Both McCloy and Stimson were delighted with it; their only complaint was that the president could not now cross the line into overt war. Stimson predicted,

". . . we cannot permanently be in a position of toolmakers for other nations which fight. . . ."[25]

As 1940 came to a close, the secretary and his newly appointed special assistant already felt at war. Lying ahead was the first major battle: Lend-Lease.

The day after his fireside chat, the president asked Henry Morgenthau to draft a Lend-Lease bill. Roosevelt sensed that the moment had arrived to obtain blanket authority from Congress to produce weapons necessary for the defense of America, Britain, and any of her allies. He wanted the authority up front, and told Morgenthau, ". . . no R.F.C. [Reconstruction Finance Corporation], no monkey business . . . no corporations . . . We don't want to fool the public, we want to do this thing right out and out."[26]

Over the next few weeks, McCloy made himself invaluable to both Morgenthau and Stimson in the Lend-Lease fight, rewriting testimony, lobbying, and keeping them informed of who was saying what on Capitol Hill. Everyone realized that there would be strong opposition. Senator Robert Taft was ridiculing the idea that one could "lend" military hardware; he said it was like chewing gum: "Once it had been used, you didn't want it back."[27] McCloy wrote Stimson's testimony for his appearance before the House Foreign Relations Committee, and sat next to him at the witness table during the four-hour ordeal.

When the Senate threatened to water down the president's basic control over Lend-Lease, McCloy used his "yellow-padding" skills to rewrite the measure. The new language turned the amendment on its head: instead of Congress's having to approve the disposal of each batch of defense supplies overseas, the president could make those decisions on his own—unless Congress imposed a specific restriction. The key figure in the Senate on this issue, Senator James F. Byrnes of South Carolina, accepted this language grudgingly, and agreed that McCloy should spend the rest of the week on the Hill answering "any questions of a technical character."[28]

McCloy set up a cot in the offices of the Senate Foreign Relations Committee so he could be on hand at any hour. Over the next couple of days, he worked with Byrnes to fend off any other amendments to the bill. At one point in the debate, as Byrnes stood in the Senate chamber, he signaled to McCloy to join him. Only senators are allowed a seat in the Senate chamber, so McCloy had stationed himself nearby, in a section reserved for the page boys. For the remainder of the debate, reporters in the press gallery were amused at the spectacle of the balding lawyer popping up from his page-boy pew to whisper suggestions into the ear of the distinguished senator from South Carolina.

All but one amendment was voted down by 10:00 P.M. on Friday, March 7, and on that one McCloy quickly drafted alternative language so diluting the amendment that Stimson called it harmless. The next morning, Washington woke up to the heaviest snowfall in years. The Senate nevertheless met and finally passed Lend-Lease by a margin of sixty to thirty-one. The same day, Senator Pat Harrison of Mississippi called on Stimson, who recounted in his diary, "He wanted to know who the very useful and energetic man was that I had sent up to the Senate to help them on the Lease and Lend Bill and then I told him the history of John McCloy. I found thus that he [McCloy] had made his usual impression on his new job in the Senate."[29]

Both Stimson and McCloy considered Lend-Lease an important precedent, a victory for everyone who believed the modern presidency should possess powers commensurate with America's new role as a global power. Influenced by his peers in the Century Group and the Council on Foreign Relations, McCloy felt the time had come for the United States to replace Great Britain as the world's foremost power. Through Lend-Lease, the White House acquired the kind of broad executive powers normally exercised only during war. McCloy and others in the Roosevelt administration justified such sweeping powers on grounds of national security. Congress, they argued, could not quickly carry out the day-to-day decisions necessary to defend the country's security. The president could always report to Congress on what had been done, but, in order to achieve the objectives of Lend-Lease, the chief executive had to be able to plan and redirect large resources within the domestic economy. All this constituted an extraordinary grant of power to the Executive.[30] Lend-Lease was only the beginning. Soon the umbrella of national security would justify the construction of a powerful national-security bureaucracy.

On a personal level, the Lend-Lease battle won McCloy important contacts on Capitol Hill; he was now a familiar figure to dozens of congressmen and senators. Stimson began to use him to explain War Department actions to the key congressional leaders, and before long the Washington press corps recognized him as an authoritative source of news out of the War Department. Eugene Meyer, the publisher of the *Washington Post,* made it a habit to drop by McCloy's office as often as twice a month for an off-the-record chat on the war. With a man like Meyer, McCloy could be blunt about stories he would rather not see in print. In return, what the *Post* publisher learned from McCloy "was enormously helpful in guiding the *Post*'s general policies," according to Meyer's biographer.[31]

As a rule, McCloy didn't like dealing with the press, and he wasn't so expert at using them as men like Harold Ickes, Henry Morgenthau, or Tommy "The Cork" Corcoran, the consummate New Dealer and influential Washington lawyer. But on a one-on-one basis he established a rapport with a few reporters working for the best papers. In 1941, James Reston returned from *The New York Times'* London bureau and moved into a Georgetown house across the street from McCloy. Soon it became clear that McCloy was a frequent, though unnamed, source in Reston's stories. Joe Alsop was another reporter McCloy counted as a friend. "If you lived in Washington," McCloy recalled, "he tried to pump you all the time by inviting you to dinner. Anyone who was doing any [war] planning had someone on a newspaper as an ally, to leak."[32]

Drew Pearson was one columnist McCloy came to avoid. He thought Pearson a "blackmailer" who would routinely "call you up and threaten to publish a document unless you talked to him."[33] Walter Lippmann was a different matter. McCloy did not always agree with the senior columnist's views, but he trusted him enough to pass him Army G-2 intelligence reports.[34] They corresponded frequently, and Lippmann was careful to respect McCloy's wish not to be cited as a source in his columns. Arthur Krock was another reporter who cultivated McCloy, though their relationship cooled in early 1941, when Justice Frankfurter warned McCloy that the acerbic *New York Times* bureau chief was hostile to the administration.

Frankfurter was a constant and powerful influence on McCloy and, for that matter, Ellen. The justice always made a point of cultivating the wives of his numerous contacts. One evening in 1941, when Joe Rauh's wife observed that she hadn't heard from Frankfurter for some time, Ben Cohen, one of FDR's braintrusters, remarked, "Well, I guess it's Mrs. McCloy now."[35]

Since the Frankfurters lived around the corner from the McCloys' Georgetown home, the two couples frequently invited each other over for dinner. Their wives were shopping companions about town; in the evenings, the two men regularly took walks together around Georgetown, discussing the day's events. Frankfurter wrote McCloy brief notes and on occasion lengthy memos on everything from administration appointments to comments on the European war. Stimson encouraged these visits with the justice, visits he labeled to the "caves of Abullum," as a means of keeping himself abreast of thinking among inner-circle New Dealers.[36] As a result, McCloy became Frankfurter's eyes and ears within the War Department.

Throughout the first half of 1941, McCloy used his influence to put the country on a war footing. He became a fervent advocate of air power, and tried to convince Chief of Staff General Marshall that the air weapon had been misused during the last war. He and Lovett fought to win the Army Air Corps a good measure of autonomy, if not actual independence. For the moment, Marshall blocked this move. But they did persuade the president to expand production of heavy bombers—only nine were scheduled for delivery in June 1941—to some five hundred a month.[37]

McCloy and Lovett worked well together, though they constantly teased each other and openly competed for Stimson's affections. One day Lovett walked into Stimson's office and interrupted "the Colonel," who promptly roared at him to get back to his own work. Out in the hallway, he bumped into McCloy and mischievously told him, "Stimson wants to see you right away."[38] But McCloy was now close enough to "Stimmie" to be able to respond in kind to the elder man's fits of temper. Once, when Stimson called from the White House and shouted over the phone, "Where are my goddam papers?," McCloy coolly replied, "I haven't got your goddam papers," and hung up.[39]

Stimson's style was to find reliable men to whom he could delegate enormous authority, men whose "zealous omniscience" for detail would allow him the time to concentrate on larger policy issues. In McCloy and Lovett, his "heavenly twain," Stimson had found the men he needed.[40] He decided to promote both to positions as assistant secretaries. On April 22, 1941, they were sworn into office. The next day, in the *Washington Post,* Leon Pearson, the columnist Drew Pearson's brother, noted that McCloy had initially been hired to investigate German sabotage, and reported, "He believes present-day German sabotage has much more finesse than the sabotage of World War I. Instead of blowing up munitions arsenals . . . the Germans are using 'more ingenious devices of destruction.' McCloy declines to be very specific about this, but he intimates that the corruption of labor leaders and the strengthening of the Communist hand are part of the new pattern."[41]

McCloy was still obsessed with the sabotage issue. Throughout early 1941, he was forever passing on to army intelligence rumors about various suspected saboteurs and their possible connection to a rash of strikes in American defense factories. One Saturday at the end of April, he visited J. Edgar Hoover and told the FBI director there might be "foreign money, either Nazi or Communist," behind the strikes. Hoover agreed, but said it was impossible to obtain evidence of this without employing extraordinary investigative methods, which were prohibited by the attorney general. Bringing up the Black Tom case, McCloy suggested that the only evidence of any use in the old sabotage cases came from either confessions or what he termed "second-story methods." Hoover agreed "emphatically" and said that, if he could obtain the "authority to organize what he termed a 'suicide squad,' created exclusively for the purpose of seeking evidence of foreign stimulation of sabotage of any form, whether direct or indirect, he knew he could accomplish results." McCloy endorsed the idea and said Stimson had already "gotten clearance" from both the president and Attorney General Robert Jackson that morning to see that the FBI was released from "certain restrictions." McCloy said he was to meet with the attorney general on Monday to "get his confirmation" of this fact.[42]

What they wanted from the attorney general was authorization for wiretapping. The law on this investigative practice had recently changed. Supreme Court decisions in 1937 and 1939 had led Attorney General Jackson to issue an order on March 15, 1940, prohibiting all FBI wiretapping. But two months later, the president told Jackson he thought the court "never intended" to prohibit wiretapping in "grave matters involving the defense of the nation." Citing the danger of sabotage and fifth-column activities, he authorized Jackson "to secure information by listening devices" in cases involving "persons suspected of subversive activities . . . including spies." Roosevelt emphasized, however, that wiretapping should be kept to "a minimum" and limited "insofar as possible to aliens."[43]

When McCloy and Undersecretary of War Robert P. Patterson saw Jackson late on Monday afternoon, they urged the formation of a special FBI unit to use wiretapping and other "second-story" tactics against strike leaders in munitions plants. McCloy used Hoover's term "suicide squad" to describe the unit to Jackson. He argued that, to obtain results, agents "must be given the authority to use any methods, except personal violence. . . ."[44] Jackson was not persuaded. And after the two men left, the more he thought about it, the angrier he got. The next day, he wrote a tough memorandum to the president, objecting in the most strenuous terms to the entire project. He reported that McCloy and Patterson "stated you had given a 'green light' to a proposition which seems to me extremely dangerous." He argued that such "lawless methods" as McCloy was requesting, which he described as wiretapping, "stealing of evidence," "breaking in to obtain evidence," and "unlimited search and seizures," would quickly become known, causing "bitter controversy" and "permanent" damage to the FBI.[45]

Despite this broadside, McCloy did not change his mind. In a memo to Stimson, he defended his position and even went on the offensive against the attorney general. With Stimson's approval, he sent Jackson a sharp letter asserting that it was "fanciful" to suppose that foreign agents were not behind the recent strikes. Not backing down an inch, he reiterated the necessity for such measures as the "interception of messages by mail, wire, etc.—methods, in short, without which both Mr. Hoover and Mr. Tamm [Assistant Director Edward Tamm] stated most explicitly to me before our talk, that the F.B.I. cannot obtain proof of foreign activity."[46]

Ten days later, Jackson replied in a letter that indicated that McCloy's tough-minded pragmatism was beginning to wear the attorney general down. He defended himself by observing that he was trying to persuade congressional committees to legalize such investigatory practices. Regarding interception of the mails, Jackson said he had modified postal regulations so that suspected letters could be held "long enough to obtain a search warrant. . . ." He suggested that to resort now to means outside the law "would certainly prejudice our chance to get the many improvements in the law which I am seeking." Still, having conceded this much to McCloy, Jackson ended with this warning: ". . . the unrestricted investigation methods you advocated could not be used with the type of young college men, mostly lawyers, who now compose the F.B.I. . . . Frankly, I would be afraid of any other kind of men. The man who today will rifle your desk for me, tomorrow will rifle mine for someone else."[47]

McCloy was stymied for the moment. But in the early summer of 1941, a wiretap bill came before Congress that would authorize most of what he wanted. Roosevelt, who had let his subordinates argue among themselves in the spring, now tacitly gave the bill his support. So did Jackson and Hoover, who on the evening before the congressional vote chose to announce the arrest of thirty-three German spies in New York.[48]

The timing of Hoover's spy roundup was intended to sway votes on Capitol Hill. For McCloy, the arrests were proof that he was not mistaken that there were espionage rings operating in America similar to those funded by the Germans in 1915–16. At least one member of the ring had been involved in sabotage operations during World War I.[49]

It would become clear in the trial that the FBI was capable of catching foreign agents without wiretapping. One of the group's early recruits, William G. Sebold, was an FBI double agent. As the radio operator for the ring, Sebold had been able to give the FBI a chance to screen every bit of intelligence sent back to Hamburg. There had been no need, therefore, to break this particular spy ring. In short, Hoover had been running a classic counterintelligence operation which he decided to compromise for the twin political objectives of demonstrating the Bureau's prowess and trying to persuade Congress to add wiretapping to his investigative arsenal.[50]

He lost his gamble. On June 29, despite the torrent of publicity given the arrests in New York, the House turned the measure back by a vote of 154 to 146. This did not stop the FBI from wiretapping suspected alien spies and some individual labor leaders such as Harry Bridges. Jackson and his successor, Francis Biddle, both maintained they had the right to authorize wiretaps in specified sabotage and espionage cases. Although the wholesale use of wiretapping by the kind of "suicide squad" proposed by McCloy and Hoover was blocked, the seed had been planted. In the years to come, the arguments McCloy had advanced in behalf of such extraconstitutional tactics would be resurrected repeatedly to justify a broad range of covert activities carried out in the name of the national-security state.

If the FBI was to be forbidden certain activities, McCloy determined that the creation of a centralized intelligence agency—an idea he had been working on since the previous autumn—was a top priority. In the summer of 1941, he wrote Mayor Fiorello H. La Guardia of New York, "I am somewhat obsessed with the necessity of establishing a propaganda or information bureau for our defense. . . . It is more essential than artillery. . . ."[51]

He was not the only one obsessed with such things. Partly at the instigation of William Stephenson, a millionaire Canadian businessman who was sent to New York in 1940 by Churchill as chief of British Security Coordination, Bill Donovan was now pressing the administration to set up a central intelligence organization. At one point, a British intelligence officer, Commander Ian Fleming—who later wrote the James Bond spy thrillers—sent Donovan a memo urging him to obtain the services of McCloy as his "chief of staff." Donovan knew Stimson was unlikely to release his trusted aide, but he was already using McCloy to advance his plans. Sometime in the spring of 1941, the two men met and discussed how best to "sell" the proposed intelligence agency. No record of this meeting has been found, but it is known that McCloy made "certain suggestions" to Donovan, possibly including the idea that the head of such an agency should be given the seemingly harmless title of "coordinator of information." Donovan's proposal received formal presidential backing on April 4, 1941.[52]

McCloy had proposed just such a "coordinator" of intelligence the previous autumn. Since then, there had been more reasons than ever before to appoint a "referee" between the three intelligence groups. In February 1941, J. Edgar Hoover and General Sherman Miles had such a violent falling out that for a time the two men weren't on speaking terms. Hoover accused Miles of extending his G-2 surveillance of subversives into civilian defense plants, a territory Hoover considered his own.[53]

Things got so bad that Stimson for a time considered firing Miles and finding a replacement who could work with Hoover. For McCloy, the dispute underscored the need for a system of centralized intelligence headed by one coordinator. His problem, however, was to find a way to persuade his own people in army intelligence—and, most notably, General Marshall—that such a coordinator would not interfere with the army's access to raw military intelligence. Miles warned Marshall that Donovan was attempting "to establish a super agency controlling all intelligence." Such a move, he said, "would appear to be very disadvantageous, if not calamitous."[54]

Donovan brought matters to a head on May 31, 1941, when he drafted a memo outlining the establishment of a "Service of Strategic Information." He first showed the memo to Navy Secretary Frank Knox, and then to McCloy, both of whom were sympathetic. On June 3,

McCloy passed the document to Stimson with a note saying he wanted to talk with him about it.[55] Later in July, he met with Stimson and Donovan to hammer out an agreement. Donovan helped to diffuse some of Marshall's opposition by agreeing not to take military rank. At this point, McCloy pulled out a diagram Marshall had drawn up that delineated the "routine channels" for the dissemination of intelligence reports. Marshall's diagram had all of Donovan's reports passing through G-2 and naval intelligence before reaching the president's desk. Donovan objected, pointing out that the president had assured him direct access. Indeed, he had told Roosevelt he wouldn't accept the job without certain guarantees: he wanted to report only to the president, he wanted access to the president's secret funds, and he wished to be assured that all government departments would be instructed to provide him with information upon demand. Roosevelt had agreed, though the two men also agreed that nothing should be put in writing.

With Stimson's concurrence, McCloy now drafted a compromise based on artful language. On paper, Donovan's routine intelligence reports would pass through War Department channels. But Donovan was assured that "he should have access to the President whenever he desired—that that was necessary to his position and it would be anyhow inevitable with the President's temperament and characteristics."[56] McCloy specified that Donovan would report through the War Department's Joint Planning Division, though he was authorized to carry out "supplementary activities" when requested by the president.[57] The latter, of course, was a reference to whatever "second-story" operations Donovan might carry out under presidential orders. His other alterations were wholly designed to emphasize the "civilian" character of the new organization. These changes in language made it possible for McCloy and Donovan to win the military's consent to the creation of something unprecedented in the history of the American republic, a civilian intelligence agency. That summer, Donovan set up a shop that in one form or another has never closed its doors.

He used his position as coordinator of information to build the framework of what would soon become the Office of Strategic Services (OSS). In the years ahead, McCloy could always be counted on to defend the spymaster against his opponents in the bureaucracy. The OSS thrived, and McCloy eventually saw the infant spy agency he had helped create become a major pillar of the national-security state: the Central Intelligence Agency.

By the spring of 1941, McCloy had a hand in so many different issues that others in the bureaucracy started to come to him for news about their own departments. Undersecretary of the Navy James Forrestal, who had known McCloy on Wall Street, took to coming by the McCloys' Georgetown home in the evenings to catch up on the day's war news. So too did Frankfurter and Dean Acheson. On the rare occasions when McCloy was not the first to learn an important piece of news, Stimson would wryly suggest that his assistant "must be weakening."[58]

War production was still a major worry. McCloy and others in the War Department struggled with what amounted to a contradiction between their commitment to the principles of private enterprise and the absolute necessity of increasing war production. Because industry was not cutting back on the production of consumer items, war-production quotas were not being met. That spring, McCloy realized that the gap would have to be filled by massive government intervention in the economy. He began having discussions with Lew Douglas and others in the business community, who conveyed their worries about what such a move might mean for the country's postwar economy. They feared that the cycle of boom, inflation, and sudden depression experienced in the aftermath of the previous war would occur all over again. Stimson encouraged him to think about the issue, and on April 23 he sat down and wrote out a memo entitled "The Problem of War Organization, Post-War Readjustment."

He began by observing that, "Large as the war effort appears in comparison with recent years, it is inadequate in view of the needs. . . . The proportion of our national income devoted to armament is minute compared with that of the totalitarian powers. Business as usual, 'guns and butter' concepts should be discarded. . . ." He bluntly stated, "The war effort will necessarily entail extensive centralization of power. . . ." The government would have to force industry to restrict consumer production and allocate raw materials for war production. New "governmental emergency organizations" were needed to administer what economists came to call a "command economy." All this was a given. But what concerned McCloy was how centralization could be effected without making it a permanent feature of the economy. He warned that "the political or governmental emergency organizations should provide their own termination, but unless economics 'permits' such termination, it may not be realized." Though centralization was necessary to win the war, it could also permanently alter the "American way of life." If it was not managed properly, the country risked a postwar depression "so severe that dissatisfaction from unemployment, deflation, etc. may sweep over all political organization, all principles, all legal guarantees."[59] The war effort, in other words, might build a permanent socialist economy.

His answer was a set of policies designed to ensure that Roosevelt's emerging "command economy" would be entirely transitory. First, instead of creating new industrial capacity, the government should whenever possible restrict consumer production. This would help restrict inflation and the dangers of any postwar collapse in demand. Second, "Where war expansion is unavoidable, it should be made, so far as possible, temporary in nature." Stringent excess-profit taxes should be levied. Wage rates, he said, should not be allowed to increase, and the work week should be increased from forty to forty-eight hours. Rationing and price controls would have to be used, but "as little as possible."[60]

The policies McCloy advocated in April 1941 were those that generally governed the administration of the entire war-economy for the next four years. The Office of Production Management, the Supply, Priorities and Allocation Board, and the War Production Board—uniformly staffed by Republican business executives—operated much as the "emergency organizations" McCloy described in his memo. Whenever possible, pickle plants were temporarily transformed into pontoon plants, and General Motors turned out tanks instead of private automobiles.[61]

Americans still did not think of themselves as a nation at war, but McCloy and his friends—men like Lew Douglas, Frankfurter, Acheson, Lovett, and Bundy—talked among themselves as if Congress had already declared war. Douglas, for instance, wrote Frankfurter early that summer, "Time is slipping away from us and with it, I fear, victory."[62] Worse, they feared that the American people were not behind them. Even at Harvard that June, the orator of the Class of '41 concluded his speech by saying, "Fellow classmates—let us avoid being sent overseas."[63]

McCloy was appalled by such isolationist sentiments, and did everything he could to prepare the country to intervene in a war that was not going very well. Hitler seemed prepared to invade Britain at any moment. In the Far East, the Japanese armies continued to advance inside China. On April 13, 1941, Tokyo surprised everyone by signing a neutrality pact with the Soviets. This seemed to confirm Britain's isolation in Europe and utter dependency on America. On June 22, however, the strategic situation dramatically changed. Hitler abruptly invaded the Soviet Union. Like Churchill, who quickly embraced his new ally, both McCloy and Stimson felt only relief that Hitler's armies would at least for a time be occupied elsewhere. But they estimated that Hitler's diversion to the East postponed an invasion of Britain by only a few months. On July 2, as the Germans rapidly advanced all along the Russian front, McCloy hit bottom: "The news from the war in Russia is getting worse and worse. . . . Altogether, tonight I feel more up against it than ever before."[64]

As Washington's humid summer season unfolded, McCloy spent a little more time outside the city. The war news was universally dismal, but he had the personal satisfaction of anticipating the birth of a second child. At the age of forty-two, Ellen was once again pregnant. She spent much of the summer out of Washington's heat, with her family in Hastings-on-Hudson. In July, she gave birth to a daughter, whom they named Ellen.

McCloy managed to couple his frequent visits to see his wife and new daughter with several fishing expeditions. That summer, Lew Douglas introduced him to another avid fly-fisherman, Representative Willis Robertson of Virginia. It was the beginning of a lifelong friendship. In August, he and Robertson flew up together for a long weekend of fishing on the Little Moose River in the Adirondacks. Lew Douglas joined them and later wrote another occasional fishing partner, Senator Tom Connally of Texas, about the trip: "You may have seen McCloy when he was in earnest about this fishing business, but if you haven't, I can assure you that all he needs to completely disguise himself is an egg beater. He has practically everything else hanging around his neck except the gadget that breaks eggs and a mill stone—and I suppose his brother-in-law serves as that."[65]

McCloy had met Senator Connally, the chairman of the Senate Foreign Relations Committee, during the Lend-Lease debate. In August, during the emotional debate surrounding the vote on extending the draft for another year, he got to know such leaders in the House as John McCormack and Sam Rayburn. He was shocked when the House decided by only one vote—203 to 202—to extend the draft for another year, and complained to Grenville Clark, "The vote constituted about as good news as Hitler has had for a good many months. In my judgement something should be done about the Republican Party. There seems to be a group now in control who are determined to ride the issue of isolationism as the best means of getting home to office and be damned about the country."[66]

McCloy and many other interventionists, however, were greatly exaggerating the influence of the isolationist camp. After more than a year of unofficial war, opinion polls showed that a majority of the American people favored intervention. Whatever their frustrations, the fact was that interventionists like Stimson, Clark, and McCloy had won every major battle in the last year: the destroyer-for-bases deal, Selective Service, Lend-Lease, convoying, and now the extension of the draft.

But these political victories were not enough for those who believed America was already part of a global war. On September 19, 1941, McCloy flew out to Jackson, Michigan, to address the Michigan Bar Association. His language was blunt and alarmist: "We have as much chance of ignoring this war as a man has of ignoring an elephant in his parlor. . . ."[67] He estimated the Germans had three hundred divisions, totaling some nine to ten million men. By comparison, he warned, the United States had only thirty-three divisions, and the German air force "is as large as our entire army." Not meaning to sound defeatist, he ended by asserting that America had the resources, or would soon have them, to respond to "any task."[68]

He was quite right. Despite the isolationists, a reluctant Congress, and the inefficiencies of private industry, the country's minuscule army of 1940 had grown into an enormous military establishment by the autumn of 1941. There were now six times as many combat divisions ready for action as in 1940. The army had grown from 260,000 men in May 1940 to an anticipated 1.5 million by the end of 1941. The air corps had grown from 6,000 pilots to 22,000 pilots in the same period. Whereas only 2,500 aircraft had been manufactured in all of 1939, almost that many were being produced each month by the end of 1941. Some estimates later concluded that U.S. armament production was already greater than the combined production of Germany, Italy, and Japan.[69]

These facts were not generally known at the time. The perception was often just the reverse; newspapers focused on the German Army's technical prowess and string of victories. If any attention was paid to American war production, reporters were apt to chase stories on waste and labor agitation. When Walter Lippmann read McCloy's speech, he asked for an appointment to discuss the defense buildup. The columnist worried that America could not sustain its own large military capacity and simultaneously supply Britain and the Soviet Union with the supplies they so desperately needed to hold off the Nazi onslaught. America, he thought, should cut its own military forces and serve only as the arsenal for the war efforts of others.[70]

Their meeting in late September did not go well. McCloy was constantly interrupted by phone calls. Initially, Lippmann seemed impressed by his factual description of the country's war production capacity, but afterwards he wrote a column proposing a reduction in the size of the U.S. Army. In response, McCloy circulated a long memo blasting his position: "The underlying fallacy in the Lippmann theory lies in the belief that the greatest industrial nation in the world when joined with the British Empire cannot supply enough for itself and those now in the shooting stage of war. True, we cannot supply all the needs at once but the Lippmann point of view is merely opportunism today at the expense of the insurance of ultimate victory."[71]

His dispute with the famous columnist served to confirm his suspicions of intellectuals like Lippmann. Such pundits, he thought, were too easily swayed by fancy ideas and their own introspective opinions. They lacked, McCloy felt, the lawyer's training to look for the "cold figures." But he was also convinced that the American people would not make the sacrifices necessary for a "maximum production effort" unless they were producing in large measure for their own troops. He therefore equated Lippmann's call for a reduction in U.S. troop strength as nothing less than a step toward appeasement: ". . . a negotiated peace is at the root of the Lippmann article—not a complete victory." Talk of an eventual negotiated peace between Britain and Germany, leaving the Nazis in control of continental Europe, was not uncommon. But for McCloy America was already at war, and he would settle for nothing short of a German surrender.[72]

Unknown to Lippmann, throughout that summer McCloy had been working on a set of highly secret war plans to guide the president in the event America entered the war. "Victory Parade" stipulated the creation of a ten-million-man army, half of which would be used in an invasion of Nazi Europe by July 1943. The plan postulated that, in the event of a two-ocean war, the United States would concentrate first on defeating Germany. News of such grandiose contingency plans might have been deadly political ammunition in the hands of America Firsters. But McCloy and others working on "Victory Parade" had so far been successful in keeping it a secret.

Roosevelt had requested such an overall strategic road map the previous July, and ever since McCloy had been meeting regularly with General Leonard T. Gerow, chief of the War Plans Division, to discuss the plan. Late in July, he sent Gerow "his shot" at a reply to the president's request. He and Gerow had a basic dispute over how one could properly estimate what it would take to defeat the Germans. Gerow's initial war plan started with the number of troops the Germans had at present equipped—estimated then at forty to fifty armored divisions—and then calculated how many American troops would be needed to defeat them. McCloy thought it was all wrong to "use manpower as the sole base." Shouldn't, he asked Gerow, war-production capacity, not troop levels, be the key variable?[73]

Gerow assigned the task of drafting a response to his aide, Major Albert C. Wedemeyer, a bright young officer who had spent several years studying the German military machine.[74] McCloy was told, "It would be unwise to assume that we can defeat Germany by simply outproducing her. . . . Wars are won on sound strategy implemented by well-trained forces which are adequately and effectively equipped."[75] Gerow's textbook approach to the problem prevailed for the moment.[76]

McCloy didn't give up. There was nothing clever or strategically brilliant about his approach to the problem. He simply began with the fairly unorthodox assumption that modern warfare was foremost a matter of economics, not manpower or troop deployment. Such views naturally irked some of the professional military officers around him. Gerow, Wedemeyer, and others sometimes thought McCloy was entirely too sure of himself, and found his intrusions into their discussions irritating.[77] In this instance, McCloy's figures were regarded by Gerow and others in the War Planning Division as verging on the fantastic. In an undated memo prepared around September 1941, McCloy argued that the anti-Axis powers would need a minimum preponderance of three to one in equipment over the enemy in order to prevail. He called for tripling present production of all armaments, particularly tanks, citing the heavy loss of tanks by the Soviets over the summer as an example of the kind of losses that should be expected in an offensive against the Nazis.[78] "Victory Parade" was a constantly evolving document, but at every meeting of the War Plans Division to discuss the plans, McCloy could always be counted on to argue the case for larger war-production estimates and a larger army.

Throughout the autumn of 1941, he worked at a feverish rate. War production, Lend-Lease operations, and intelligence issues were all a routine part of his daily agenda. He was also troubleshooting problems with the press and irate members of the public. His public-relations style was blunt, even heavy-handed. When *Time* magazine ran a critical story on army morale, he simply called up Henry Luce and lodged a vigorous complaint.[79] And when a prominent Ithaca, New York, clergyman wrote to criticize an army officer in Colorado who had barred his men from attending a church hosting America First meetings, McCloy wrote a long letter back in which he argued, "We have to restrain our liberties to preserve them, and in my judgement, we should be prepared to restrain them far more than the country now gives indication of being willing" to accept.[80]

This was particularly true, he believed, for Americans of Japanese and German ancestry. In mid-September, he spent a week touring military installations throughout the West. Since July, when Roosevelt had placed an embargo on oil shipments to Japan, tensions on the West Coast had risen dramatically. Newspapers reported the presence of Japanese "agents in every mountain pass, working in every railroad division, in almost every harbor and ship company, gathering detailed information."[81] Americans of Japanese ancestry were widely suspected to be involved in such subversive activities.

McCloy was well aware of the source of these reports. While in San Francisco he was told of the exploits of Lieutenant Commander Kenneth D. Ringle, a naval-intelligence officer who had investigated Japanese intelligence capabilities on the West Coast. Employing "second-story" methods with the assistance of the FBI, Ringle had burglarized the Japanese Consulate in Los Angeles and analyzed a "truckload of documents." The material contained the names of agents and some Japanese sympathizers on the West Coast. Ringle's investigation led to the arrest in June 1941 of Itaru Tachibana, a Japanese naval officer posing as an English-language student. Ringle believed that Tachibana's eventual deportation effectively destroyed Tokyo's espionage capabilities on the West Coast.

But for McCloy, the success of the Ringle-FBI burglary operation only confirmed his belief that sabotage was a real danger. There were, after all, more than one million aliens in the country of German, Italian, or Japanese origin.[82] The numbers in Hawaii were particularly disturbing to any army officer contemplating fifth-column risks; the islands contained 160,000 individuals of Japanese descent, of whom 37,500 were foreign born.[83]

The threat of sabotage still made headlines: in September 1941, Congressman Martin Dies told newspapermen that "the potential Japanese spy system in this country is greater than the Germans ever dreamed of having in the Low Countries."[84] But it was McCloy who was regarded as the objective outside expert on sabotage, and the confidence placed in him by Stimson, Ickes, and many others gave his opinions added weight, both within the administration and among the reporters he briefed in off-the-record sessions. For more than a year now, he had stressed the subject in conversations with Marshall, Miles, Stimson, Hoover, Ickes, and anyone else who would listen. And yet, for all the talk of sabotage, very little evidence had been unearthed by any of the intelligence organizations that the Germans or the Japanese had the kind of covert capabilities that would justify McCloy's worst fears. Hoover, for one, was pretty much convinced that the arrests of Tachibana in California and the thirty-three Nazi spies in New York over the summer had effectively crippled Axis sabotage capability.[85]

McCloy nevertheless remained less than sanguine about the country's counterintelligence successes, and one reason may well have been his access to a unique source denied Hoover. Earlier in the year, General Marshall had drawn up what he called a "Top List" of individuals allowed to inspect the "Purple" or "Magic" intercepts of decoded Japanese diplomatic cable traffic. The list was formally confined to the president, the secretaries of state, war, and navy, and the directors of army and naval intelligence.[86] But in practice, as many as a dozen lower-ranking aides, including McCloy, were also seeing Magic intercepts. "It crossed my desk every morning," he recalled.[87]

Magic allowed him to believe that he could know with near certainty what the Japanese were capable of and what their intentions were in the Far East. Ultimately, however, even Magic had to be interpreted, and for most of those reading the material, including McCloy, the intercepts tended merely to confirm what they wanted to believe about Japanese intentions. In the months prior to Pearl Harbor, anyone reading Magic might reasonably conclude that a war in the Far East was imminent. But McCloy, Marshall, and others always thought the first attack on American installations would come in the form of sabotage. There was little evidence in Magic to confirm this, and the telltale clues that Tokyo was planning an air attack were either ignored or analyzed and then dismissed.[88]

There were four Purple decrypting machines in Washington in 1941, and by November they were decoding an average of twenty-six daily messages between Tokyo and her most important embassies and consulates abroad.[89] On September 24, 1941, Tokyo's Foreign Ministry sent a cable to its Honolulu consulate requesting elaborate reporting on the exact positions of every U.S. naval vessel anchored in Pearl Harbor. This cable, which later became known as the "bomb-plot" message, wasn't translated until October 9, 1941, when an alert G-2 officer, Colonel Rufus C. Bratton, brought it to the attention of Stimson and Marshall. Magic cables routed to Stimson often passed through McCloy's hands first. Both men presumably saw the unusual message, but its significance did not register on either of them.[90]

In late November 1941, Marshall issued any number of warnings to his commanders in Hawaii, and though he also ordered them to initiate air reconnaissance, most of his messages emphasized that "subversive activities may be expected." Not surprisingly, the army commander in Pearl Harbor, General Walter C. Short, acknowledged these warnings by moving his forces in Hawaii to Alert No. 1, which called for "a defense against sabotage, espionage and subversive activities without any threat from the outside."[91]

Though it is more than likely that McCloy saw General Short's message before it landed on Stimson's desk, his entire orientation during the previous fifteen months made him the last man in the War Department to question whether the general might be placing an unjustified priority on the sabotage threat. Lying on his desk that day was General Miles's latest intelligence estimate concerning the "subversive situation" on the West Coast. The report, dated November 25, claimed the Japanese had a "well-developed espionage network along the Pacific Coast."[92] McCloy did not doubt it.

As tensions mounted, he came into his office on the morning of December 4, 1941, to discover that disaster had struck. Someone had leaked the War Department's highly classified "Victory Parade," the detailed set of war plans on which he and very few others had been working since the previous July. The isolationist *Chicago Tribune* and other McCormick papers around the country published portions of the plan, word for word. The *Tribune* called it "a blueprint for total war," which it was.[93]

Stimson came back that evening from a trip to New York to find McCloy and a couple of other aides gathered at his home and wearing "very long faces." The secretary was unhappy with the leak; all the same, he couldn't help being amused at the uncharacteristic glumness he saw in McCloy: ". . . for the first time in my observation of him McCloy was sunk. But the picture of this occurrence during my one day of absence rather tickled my funnybone and I cheered them up. The thing to do is to meet the matter head on and use this occurrence if possible to shake our American people out of their infernal apathy and ignorance of what this war means."[94]

McCloy thought he knew who had leaked the memo. Only five individuals had copies of the plan: Stimson, Marshall, McCloy, Gerow, and Major Albert Wedemeyer, General Gerow's aide in the War Plans Division. Wedemeyer had studied at the German War College in Berlin from 1936 to 1938, and had returned from Berlin with a profound admiration for the equipment and capabilities of the German Army. A number of U.S. officers had similar experiences in the 1930s and were known at the time as members of the "Potsdam Club," so named after the Berlin suburb where the War College was located. Dean Rusk, working in G-2 at the time, recalled they "were so pessimistic as to be almost pro-German."[95]

McCloy also believed Wedemeyer's work on "Victory Parade" reflected a "defeatist attitude." For his part, Wedemeyer had a low opinion of McCloy. He thought the assistant secretary was the kind of man who "would invariably agree with higher authorities, but would assert himself and swing his weight around in contacts with subordinates." So there was already ill-will between the two men when McCloy called Wedemeyer into his office. The army major saluted the assistant secretary and, in the absence of any invitation to sit down, remained standing at attention. On those rare occasions when he showed his anger, McCloy's eyes, usually the most disarming thing about him, became cold and hard. He would tilt his large, balding head down and look at you from beneath a darkened, furrowed brow. Now he rose from behind his oversized mahogany desk, framed on either side by the American flag and the flag of the assistant secretary of war, and said with a hard edge to his voice, "Wedemeyer, there's blood on the fingers of the man who leaked the information about our war plans."[96]

Wedemeyer was shocked, and challenged him to repeat the accusation in his presence before Stimson. McCloy looked at him in silence for a long moment and then dismissed him.[97] McCloy nevertheless had already conveyed his suspicions to the FBI, and he wanted the perpetrator court-martialed.[98] So, when Wedemeyer returned to his office, he found two FBI agents waiting for him. Under questioning, he admitted that he felt the United States should not be involved in this war—or at least in a war against Germany. Like ex-President Herbert Hoover (in the aftermath of the Nazi invasion of the Soviet Union that summer), he favored letting the two totalitarian powers wear each other down.[99] As such, Wedemeyer's political and strategic views seemed to provide motivation for the leak. The FBI investigation was inconclusive, however, and no one was ever indicted.[100]

Stimson held a press conference on Friday, December 5, and tried to dismiss the importance of the plans by saying, "They have never constituted an authorized program of the government."[101] But he was being disingenuous. The problem was that many Americans, Wedemeyer included, believed the president was duplicitous. The Victory plans were not, as Stimson stated, merely contingency plans. They were plans for a war which—as the secretary would admit to his diary but not in public—the administration was already waging. What angered the isolationists most by the end of 1941 was their conviction that the president was skirting very close to the law. Few were in a better position to know this than Stimson and McCloy. Whether it was the allocation of transition funding for British arms in the months prior to passage of Lend-Lease, the dodging of the neutrality laws, or the investigation of labor union activists for sabotage, McCloy had always urged unrestricted action. It was this combination of unfettered activism and infectious optimism that had made him so useful to the administration throughout 1941.

By December 5, 1941, many Americans both in and out of government felt that a shooting war was very near. Those with access to Magic did not need to speculate; they knew war was only a matter of days away, and now the intercepts were about to hint at the exact hour it would begin. Because he felt "something was going to happen that weekend," McCloy canceled an out-of-town appointment so he could be in his office both days.[102] He arrived at 10:05 A.M. on Sunday morning, December 7, 1941, and went directly to the secretary's office, where he and Stimson talked briefly about the apparent impasse in the Japanese negotiations. Shortly afterward, Stimson left for a meeting with Hull and Knox at the White House.[103] Marshall was out horseback-riding. Earlier that morning, the last paragraph of a long transmission from Tokyo to the Japanese Embassy in Washington had been deciphered. Translated, the cable made it clear that Tokyo expected something of great moment to happen by 1:00 P.M. Washington time. The intelligence officer monitoring Magic that morning, Colonel Bratton, quickly decided he had to find someone in the military chain of command who could issue a warning.[104]

He did not think to inform McCloy, the highest-ranking civilian in the War Department that morning, who was sitting in his office just down the hall. Instead, Bratton tried reaching General Marshall at his home, but the general had just left for his horseback ride. Marshall did not return the call until 10:30, and it took another hour and half after that to issue a warning to Hawaii. This last warning was sent via Western Union teletype, and did not arrive until hours after the 1:00 deadline.[105]

By then, two waves of 360 Japanese aircraft had in the course of one hour sunk three battleships and damaged three more so badly they had to be put out of action. The surprise attack killed 2,335 military personnel and another 68 civilians. For the foreseeable future, the Japanese Imperial Navy now seemed capable of dominating much, if not all, of the Pacific Ocean.

McCloy was one of the first civilians in the War Department to hear the news. Even then, his instincts turned to the threat of sabotage. "My first thought was to protect the president," he later recalled. "What came to mind was to send a detachment of Marines to the White House. . . . I immediately began doing what I could to implement plans for the security of the nation's capital."[106] On his orders, armed guards were stationed around the White House, the Capitol, and other major buildings in the city. In the company of Sherman Miles and an army officer named Ulysses S. Grant (grandson of the president), he marched two blocks down to the Navy Department. "When we walked into Knox's office," McCloy recalled, "his aide, who happened to be a Southerner, said, 'Here comes the entire Union Army.' "[107]

While Stimson spent a large part of the afternoon at the White House with the president, McCloy received "urgent" requests from military officials on the West Coast for instructions on how to prepare for a possible follow-up attack on the mainland. In response, he ordered into effect civil-defense plans that provided for blackouts and traffic restrictions.[108] Stimson too was worried about sabotage. One of his first impulses was to start "matters going in all directions to warn against sabotage. . . ."[109]

At 4:00 P.M., McCloy convened in his office a meeting of the chiefs of the various armed services. Stimson then came in and gave them all a "little pep-talk." Afterward, he sat around with McCloy, Marshall, Grenville Clark, Lovett, Miles, and Patterson, discussing what form the declaration of war should take. Only by the end of the day did the full dimensions of the disaster become clear. Even so, Stimson felt somehow relieved: "When the news first came that Japan had attacked us, my first feeling was of relief that the indecision was over and that a crisis had come in a way which would unite all our people."[110]

McCloy agreed. The country may have been psychologically unprepared to take the final plunge into formal war, but now there was an indisputable consensus. There would be no consensus, however, on how the surprise attack could have happened.

If the public greeted the attack with simple incredulity, those reading Magic felt quite different emotions. McCloy saw right away that Pearl Harbor was first and foremost a failure of intelligence. The extraordinary secret weapon had been misused. The ability to read the enemy's diplomatic traffic had lulled those on the Magic distribution list into an unwarranted confidence. General Douglas MacArthur's chief of intelligence,

General Charles A. Willoughby, later observed, "The sequence of [Magic] messages referred to, had they been known to a competent intelligence officer . . . would have led instantly to the inescapable conclusion that Pearl Harbor naval installations were a target for attack. . . ."[111]

The failure in the system was plain to see; no one person on the Magic distribution list was in charge of cataloguing and cross-indexing the intercepts. Years later, William Friedman, the man who had originally broken the Japanese code, remarked that those on the Magic distribution list had "had the messages only for so short a time that each message represented only a single frame" in a "long motion picture."[112] No one was allowed to hold on to the intercepts long enough to distinguish a pattern.

Hired more than a year ago for his expertise on intelligence matters, McCloy, one might have thought, would now be forced to share some of the blame for this intelligence failure. But, perhaps because he wasn't in any obvious line of command, no one questioned his role. To his credit, he had argued for a more centralized control over intelligence matters than existed in G-2. However, the one step taken in this direction, the appointment of Bill Donovan as coordinator of information, precipitated no review of G-2's handling of Magic. Donovan wasn't even on the list to receive the intercept material.

Only in the aftermath of Pearl Harbor did McCloy hire someone whose exclusive job it would be to provide long-term, in-depth analysis of Magic traffic. Sometime in December, he began having discussions on the problem with Alfred McCormack, one of his old Cravath partners. Within a few weeks, he had persuaded Stimson to hire McCormack "to brief the magic papers and cross index them so that they will form a really useful basis for inferring what the enemy are going to do."[113]

The days and weeks immediately following the surprise attack were a period of frenzied activity, and McCloy was not immune from an atmosphere that at times approached hysteria. For the first couple of nights, he rarely left the department. Late Monday evening, he called Stimson at Woodley to report that "an enemy fleet was thought to be approaching San Francisco." A few minutes later, he had to call back with the news that it had been a false alarm.[114]

Sabotage was still foremost in the thoughts of most War Department officials. Within twenty-four hours of the attack, the FBI and local police had detained 736 Japanese aliens on the West Coast in what the Los Angeles *Times* called a "great man hunt." Four days later, the number of Japanese aliens in detention had risen to 1,370.[115] All those detained could be found on a Justice Department master list of "subversive and "dangerous" aliens, prepared months in advance of Pearl Harbor. The FBI believed the detention of those on the list would effectively end any serious possibility of widespread sabotage. A few days after Pearl Harbor, the *Los Angeles Times* advised its readers, "Let's not get rattled."[116]

But such appeals for calm on the editorial page were contradicted by the tenor of the newspaper's reporting, which focused on the possibility of imminent Japanese raids up and down the West Coast. Such reports merely underscored the general public's instinctive explanation for the astonishing Japanese successes; few could believe that the enemy was not operating without the assistance of an elaborate network of spies. Even the most skeptical military minds believed for a time that a Japanese invasion of the West Coast was possible, if unlikely.[117]

With Germany's formal declaration of war on the United States, McCloy and other officials debated whether the country's resources should be concentrated against Japan or Germany. Public opinion was certainly inclined toward defeating the Japanese first and then turning on Germany. Winston Churchill naturally opposed this course, and in order to thwart an "Asia-first" strategy, he wired Roosevelt immediately after Pearl Harbor to say that he intended to visit Washington to review "the whole war plan."[118]

During the next few days, McCloy met frequently with Stimson, Lovett, and Harvey Bundy to discuss preparations for the president's conference with Churchill. McCloy opened their deliberations by handing Stimson a draft of the overall "strategic situation."[119] This was basically a revised version of the "Victory Plan" McCloy, Wedemeyer, and others had written in the months prior to Pearl Harbor. McCloy's latest draft accepted what he called the "grand strategy of the war—the defeat of Germany first." But he startled Stimson by arguing that German forces should first be engaged in North Africa and the Middle East. Both Stimson and Marshall disagreed vehemently, believing it essential that a "second front" be opened in Europe as soon as possible by means of a cross-Channel invasion of northern France.

McCloy argued that North Africa—and, indeed, the entire Middle East—constituted a "gravity center" from which Russia could be supplied. "Above all," he wrote, "the loss of this area would give Hitler oil—the thing he needs most and must have in order to prevail. It must constantly be borne in mind that the greatest oil deposits of the world are in this area." Denying Hitler access to Middle Eastern oil was the key to Germany's defeat. "The line North Africa–Iraq–Iran must be held. . . . With it held firmly in Allied hands, Hitler is confined to his European conquests, which from the point of view of the real fruits of victory are very slight." He correctly pointed out that up to this point the Soviet Army had successfully denied Hitler access to the oil fields of the Caucasus. As a result, he warned, Hitler would "seek it [oil] a different way soon."

He explicitly warned against "over-defending" other war sectors, including the North Atlantic "life line to Britain," and even the U.S. military installations along the West Coast and in Hawaii, which he estimated "in all probability" were "only subject to raiding attacks." Other than in North Africa, he believed that only in Australia should U.S. forces be built up heavily in order to check the Japanese advances.[120] Stimson rejected McCloy's arguments and, in preparation for Churchill's visit, wrote his own memo that day, giving Roosevelt all the reasons why an American expeditionary force should be built up in Britain. Though Marshall and most other military men supported this view, the matter was far from settled.

Churchill arrived in Washington on December 22 and moved into the White House, where he slept in a large bedroom across the hallway from Harry Hopkins, the president's closest confidant. The next day, the first of many meetings—known as the Arcadia Conference—took place between Roosevelt, Churchill, and their respective advisers. Everyone agreed on the broad principle of defeating Germany first. But there was sharp disagreement on how this should be done. As McCloy listened to Churchill, whom he had just met for the first time, he realized that the British prime minister was thinking very much along the lines of his December 20 memo, rejected by Stimson only three days earlier.

Churchill argued that Allied forces in 1942 should concentrate on the occupation and control of the whole of French West Africa and the entire North African shoreline from Casablanca to Cairo. On the Pacific front, a holding action should be attempted which would not "absorb an unduly large proportion of United States forces." Looking ahead to 1943, he posited not a single massive invasion of the European continent, but a series of smaller invasion forces landing in such widespread points as Norway, Denmark, Holland, Belgium, France, Italy, and "possibly the Balkans." In this scenario, the ultimate defeat of Germany would occur when "internal convulsions in Germany"—sparked by "economic privations" and an Allied bombing offensive—toppled Hitler from within. He hoped that such a strategy would avoid the inevitably high casualties associated with a frontal invasion of the continent and a ground invasion of the German homeland.[121]

Underlying Churchill's cautious approach was the assumption that the Soviets would by themselves continue to hold off the great bulk of German ground divisions on the Eastern front. As McCloy's December 20 memo had put it, ". . . the manpower problem seems to be solved there." Almost as an afterthought, he concluded that the "Russians should have, and richly deserve," all the supplies that "limited means of access" permits. But a second front on the European continent was not necessary, not in 1942, and maybe not even in 1943. Instead, Hitler could be "confined" to Europe and eventually driven to surrender or, in Churchill's scenario, toppled by his own people in revolt.[122]

Roosevelt was surprisingly receptive to Churchill's proposed "Operation Super-Gymnast," telling him "it was vital to forestall the Germans in Northwest Africa. . . ."[123] Accordingly, early on in the three-week series of meetings, the president gave his qualified approval to "Gymnast" even though Stimson and Marshall were firmly opposed to sending American troops to theaters they considered "peripheral" to an invasion of Western Europe. Marshall went so far as to tell Roosevelt that Gymnast was "a very dangerous operation."[124] Germany's defeat, he believed, would ultimately require a single major invasion across the English Channel.

Marshall favored a European strategy with three distinct components. First, he argued, a large joint British-American expeditionary force should be built up in Britain and trained for an eventual cross-Channel invasion of the continent. He later code-named this buildup in Britain Operation Bolero. Second, this force had to be prepared, in the event the Soviet front seemed about to collapse, to mount an emergency invasion of Europe as early as the autumn of 1942. Third, if this emergency invasion, later code-named Sledgehammer, was unnecessary in 1942, Marshall planned a decisive cross-Channel invasion, code-named Roundup, for the spring of 1943.[125]

No clear-cut resolution between these two radically different strategies was achieved during the Arcadia discussions. But it is clear that the postponement of this decision ultimately opened the road to implementing much of what McCloy had outlined in his December 20 memo. There were compelling domestic political reasons for the North African invasion. As Marshall explained it, "The President considered it very important to morale, to give the country a feeling that they are in the war . . . to have American troops somewhere in active fighting across the Atlantic."[126] If a major invasion of Europe could not be launched in 1942, a smaller invasion by American troops of North Africa might be a politically suitable substitute. So, despite Marshall's conviction that Super-Gymnast would delay a cross-Channel invasion, the seeds had been planted for a joint Anglo-American invasion of North Africa. This was the most fateful "nondecision" to emerge from the Arcadia Conference as it eventually led to a year-long delay in the opening of a second front.

Some concrete decisions were made during Churchill's three-week visit. On December 28, Stimson took McCloy along "as a recorder and helper of my memory" to a meeting in Roosevelt's White House study. Once inside, Stimson handed Roosevelt another McCloy memo, this one a revised estimate of war production projecting that $27 billion worth of production capacity for various munitions had not yet been contracted.[127] As a result, in discussions later with Lord Beaverbrook, a member of Churchill's entourage in charge of British war production, 1942 production targets rose 70 percent over what they had been only three weeks earlier, before the United States entered the war. The number of aircraft scheduled for production rose from 12,750 to 45,000, and the previous 1942 goal of producing 262,000 machine guns was nearly doubled.[128] America's tremendous industrial capacity, underused for more than a decade, was now about to supply all the weaponry necessary for a two-ocean global war.

One day early in 1942, Marshall called McCloy into his office and asked him to "check out" a new officer working in the War Plans Division. "His name was Eisenhower," recalled McCloy. "So I went down to meet this man; I don't think I ever told him that I had been sent to spy on him."[129] Brigadier General Dwight D. Eisenhower had been called to Washington one week after Pearl Harbor and assigned by Marshall as Gerow's deputy. Marshall was already impressed by the affable, hardworking career officer. In the weeks since the attack, Eisenhower had been working furiously on finding means of supplying reinforcements to his old boss in the Philippines, General Douglas MacArthur. His common sense and lack of pretense elicited trust even from men inclined to oppose him. Unlike McCloy, he sometimes displayed a red-hot temper, but even such outbursts were quickly followed by self-deprecating humor and the appearance of his characteristically lopsided grin. He had initiative and, unlike Gerow, he was willing to make decisions without bothering Marshall with every detail. In short, "Ike," as he was known throughout the army's officer corps, was very much a man in McCloy's mold. The two established an immediate rapport. McCloy gave Marshall a glowing endorsement of Eisenhower, who shortly thereafter was appointed to take General Gerow's place as chief of the War Plans Division.

On January 6, 1942, Stimson escorted his wife and Ellen McCloy up to Capitol Hill once again, this time to hear Roosevelt's State of the Union speech. The president pledged in soaring rhetoric to fight the enemy until German and Japanese militarism were eliminated: "We will hit him, and hit him again, wherever and whenever we can reach him." Stimson expressed satisfaction that the speech had finally knocked "the last bottom out of the old isolationist ideas. . . ." Two days later, McCloy held a press conference to praise the American public's response to the war, citing the nearly sixty thousand young men who had volunteered for military service in the month of December as "overwhelming proof of great eagerness to serve." He told reporters that it was the American habit "to reach for a gun and not a bottle of soothing syrup" when attacked.[130]

CHAPTER 8

Internment of the Japanese Americans

"You are putting a Wall Street lawyer in a helluva box, but if it is a question of safety of the country, [or] the Constitution of the United States, why the Constitution is just a scrap of paper to me."

JOHN J. MCCLOY, 1942

A week after the U.S. war began, Secretary of the Navy Frank Knox returned from a whirlwind inspection of Pearl Harbor and announced, "I think the most effective 'fifth column' work of the entire war was done in Hawaii, with the possible exception of Norway."[1] The statement did much to encourage the press to focus on the alleged fifth-column network of Japanese spies on the West Coast. Even though J. Edgar Hoover told the Justice Department that "practically all" of those Japanese aliens he thought to be a security risk were now in custody, on the West Coast the highly publicized arrests only seemed to legitimize the idea that all Japanese were suspect.[2]

Then, on January 4, 1942, Damon Runyon, a syndicated Hearst columnist, reported that a radio transmitter had been discovered in a Japanese boarding house. The report had no basis in fact, but Runyon nevertheless concluded, "It would be extremely foolish to doubt the continued existence of enemy agents among the large alien Japanese population."[3] Soon West Coast politicians began issuing similar warnings. On January 16, 1942, Congressman Leland M. Ford of Los Angeles wrote Stimson demanding that "all Japanese, whether citizens or not, be placed in inland concentration camps."[4]

The 120,000 Japanese and American citizens of Japanese ancestry who lived in California, Oregon, and Washington actually constituted a small minority. But they were far more visible than many other, larger ethnic communities. More than two-thirds of these people had been born in the United States and thus were American citizens, known as Nisei. Their parents were called Issei, and under U.S. immigration laws they were prohibited from acquiring citizenship however long they may have lived in America.

When Stimson had delegated the West Coast security problem to him in late December, McCloy was not entirely ill-disposed toward the "enemy aliens." He thought, for instance, that those who volunteered for military service should be given U.S. citizenship. Upon learning of this, Justice Frankfurter jocularly wrote him, "For a Tory—I am told you are a Tory, aren't you?—you seem to be awfully tender even about 'enemy aliens' who are able to fight for Uncle Sam."[5]

Initially, there was no consensus within the War Department on how to control enemy aliens, let alone citizens of Japanese ancestry. The army's chief law-enforcement officer, Provost Marshal General Allen W. Gullion, argued in the earliest of these meetings for a mass evacuation. Gullion's position, however, was not supported by General John DeWitt, the officer in charge of the Western Defense Command area. An evacuation was also firmly opposed by the Justice Department's representative, the young New Dealer James H. Rowe, Jr., who had recently been appointed by Roosevelt as a deputy to the attorney general.

McCloy had not been called upon to take a position on the issue until late January 1942. Strictly speaking, the Justice Department, not the War Department, was responsible for enemy aliens. But as the weeks went by in January, the pressure grew on McCloy to intervene and mediate what was becoming a jurisdictional dispute between the two departments. General DeWitt, who in late December had thought a mass evacuation impracticable, was beginning to be persuaded otherwise. He was not a man possessed of strong political principles; according to Biddle, he had a "tendency to reflect the views of the last man to whom he talked."[6] Soon he was referring to the Japanese Americans as an "enemy race."[7]

General Gullion, who had continued to press for a major evacuation, now ordered a young lawyer with the rank of an army captain to serve as his personal liaison to DeWitt in San Francisco. Captain Karl Bendetsen was no stranger either to the issue of enemy aliens or to McCloy himself. Earlier in 1941, Bendetsen had seen McCloy as often as once a week to report to him on odd assignments within the War Department. Among other things, McCloy had asked him to study various contingency plans for the internment of enemy aliens in the event of a war with Germany.[8]

During the last three weeks of January, Bendetsen practically commuted between Washington and San Francisco; he was the one man within the War Department who had studied the enemy-alien problem, and was in constant contact with DeWitt, various California politicians, and the West Coast congressional delegation on Capitol Hill. He had a "can-do" attitude about everything in his job, and by the end of January, he had convinced himself and DeWitt that the evacuation of over a hundred thousand Japanese would not be such a difficult task. McCloy, however, was still uncommitted.

Meanwhile, political pressure to do something dramatic about the West Coast security situation continued to rise. On January 30, a West Coast congressional delegation meeting informally in Washington formulated a detailed evacuation plan that provided for the forcible internment of those Japanese, "whether aliens or not," who failed to submit to "voluntary resettlement and evacuation as a patriotic contribution."[9] At this meeting, Bendetsen violently disagreed with Rowe and another Justice Department official, Edward J. Ennis, director of the Justice Department's Alien Enemy Control Unit. Rowe and Ennis saw plenty of legal problems and no military justification for the evacuation of American citizens of Japanese ancestry. Bendetsen disagreed, however, and promptly took the initiative to phone DeWitt with news of the proposal. He urged DeWitt to prepare a report that could be used to convince Stimson and McCloy that such an evacuation was a clear military necessity.

In the meantime, Rowe and Ennis persuaded Attorney General Biddle to obtain Stimson's consent to schedule a meeting on Sunday, February 1, 1942, to resolve the issue. Stimson delegated McCloy to represent the War Department. McCloy showed up at the meeting with both General Gullion and Bendetsen. Also in attendance, and clearly in the opposite camp, were Biddle, Rowe, Ennis, and J. Edgar Hoover. The same day, the FBI chief wrote a memo for Biddle in which he attacked the army's intelligence capability on the West Coast for exhibiting signs of "[h]ysteria and lack of judgement."[10]

Seizing the initiative, Rowe began with a personal attack on Bendetsen, suggesting that he and the Western congressmen were encouraging people to get "hysterical." When Rowe flatly stated there "was no evidence whatsoever of any reason for disturbing citizens," Biddle chimed in and confirmed that the Justice Department would have nothing to do with any interference with citizens, "whether they are Japanese or not."

"They made me a little sore," Gullion commented later. In fact, he was so offended by this criticism of the military that a heated argument ensued. Gullion insisted that the military situation out on the West Coast was so precarious that General DeWitt might indeed have to "get all the Japs out. . . ." McCloy had kept his own counsel throughout this exchange. But now, with his own War Department officers under attack, he interrupted to tell Biddle, "You are putting a Wall Street lawyer in a helluva box, but if it is a question of safety of the country, [or] the

Constitution of the United States, why the Constitution is just a scrap of paper to me."[11] For McCloy, it was simply a question of whether the removal of the Japanese Americans was a military necessity. He was fully prepared to allow the military authorities to make this judgment. Now, as tempers flared, he suggested to Biddle that the commander of the "men on the ground," General DeWitt, should be given a chance to assess the situation. He indicated that if DeWitt favored an evacuation on grounds of military necessity then the War Department would probably concur. After some discussion, Biddle agreed to postpone a decision until DeWitt's position could be clarified, and on this note the meeting was adjourned.[12]

McCloy's indecision up to this point in the debate is critical to understanding the events that were to follow. After the meeting, Gullion, the prime backer of a mass evacuation, knew that McCloy was "pretty much against interfering with citizens unless it can be done legally." But he had also heard the assistant secretary refer to the Constitution as "just a scrap of paper." He was convinced McCloy could find a legal way around the Constitution; the problem, as he told Clark, was that "they [Stimson and McCloy] are just a little afraid DeWitt hasn't enough grounds to justify any movements of that kind."[13]

Two days later, on February 3, McCloy met with Stimson, Gullion, and Bendetsen in an effort to resolve the War Department's position. Gullion began by reporting that DeWitt "thinks he has evidence that regular communications are going out from Japanese spies . . . to submarines off the coast." McCloy and Stimson accepted these assertions without requesting any hard evidence.[14]

Later that afternoon, McCloy got on the phone with DeWitt. The general promptly tried to win his consent for organizing a "voluntary" evacuation of both citizens and aliens of Japanese ancestry. He explained that only "all male adult Japanese" over the age of eighteen, whether "native or American born," would voluntarily be evacuated from an area of California defined as a combat zone. He assured McCloy that this meant they had only to contemplate the removal of some twenty thousand individuals.

McCloy asked a few obvious questions, such as, "The bad ones, the ones that are foreign agents, that are sympathetic to Japan, will not volunteer, will they?" When DeWitt had no answer to this point, McCloy gently dismissed the idea that a voluntary evacuation could solve the problem. He told DeWitt there were "bound to be cases, I should think, where some of them would not move, and in that case we would be up against the question as to whether we could move against the American citizen of Japanese race." After referring to the "many complications involved in a compulsory movement of any great size," McCloy proposed his own solution. The "best way to solve it," he said, was to establish limited military reservations around airplane plants, forts, and other military installations and "exclude everyone—whites, yellows, blacks, greens—from that area and then license back into the area those whom we felt there was no danger to be expected from."

DeWitt at first didn't understand the point, and McCloy had to go through it again patiently and explain that this way "we cover ourselves . . . in spite of the constitution."

The general objected that licensing all those civilians to allow them to remain in the restricted zones would be "quite a job." McCloy responded, "I think you might cut corners" and announce that all those in certain categories could take their time to come in and obtain a permit. "In the meantime," he said, "the Japs would have to be out of there. . . ." DeWitt agreed to think about McCloy's idea, but warned him, "Out here, Mr. Secretary, a Jap is a Jap to these people now. . . ."

"I can understand," McCloy replied. He then assured DeWitt that there were legal complications, but that ultimately the War Department favored some kind of evacuation to solve the security problem on the West Coast.[15]

So, by February 3, 1942, McCloy had more or less reconciled himself to taking some kind of action against the Japanese Americans on the West Coast. He was still one step removed from endorsing a full-fledged compulsory internment program. But his consideration of even quasi-legal means to exclude one group of citizens from the West Coast on the basis of race opened the door. Convinced that McCloy's position would be the War Department's position, General Gullion wrote an ominous memo on February 6 warning the assistant secretary, "If our production for war is seriously delayed by sabotage in the West Coastal states, we very possibly shall lose the war. . . . From reliable reports from military and other sources, the danger of Japanese inspired sabotage is great. . . . No half-way measures based upon considerations of economic disturbance, humanitarianism, or fear of retaliation will suffice." This toughly worded memo seems to have finally swept aside any lingering misgivings McCloy felt about a mass evacuation.[16] Half-measures would not do.

His concerns now shifted from whether such measures were necessary to how they should be implemented and under whose authority. On February 10, he went over the maps of the West Coast with Stimson, surveying the large areas from which DeWitt proposed to evacuate all Japanese Americans. Like Biddle, Stimson still had some constitutional doubts. "The second generation Japanese can only be evacuated," he wrote in his diary, "either as part of a total evacuation, giving access to the areas only by permits, or by frankly trying to put them out on the ground that their racial characteristics are such that we cannot understand or trust even the citizen Japanese. This latter is the fact but I am afraid it will make a tremendous hole in our constitutional system to apply it."[17]

Still, such sensibilities were beginning to seem almost frivolous, given the worsening military situation in the Pacific. Singapore was on the point of falling to Japanese forces, who seemed invincible as they hopped from one island to another in the South Pacific. Stimson thought it quite possible that, should the Japanese achieve naval dominance in the Pacific, they might then "try an invasion of this country."[18] Given this drastic estimate of the military imponderables, his constitutional scruples weakened rapidly. By way of an analogy, he reminded McCloy of the fire chief's right to "raze a building in order to shut off the course of a fire through a city block."[19] The logic of military necessity now made almost anything possible.

On February 11, McCloy urged Stimson to find out whether the president was "willing to authorize us to move Japanese citizens as well as aliens from restricted areas."[20] The secretary tried to arrange an appointment with Roosevelt but was told he was too busy. Instead, a phone call was scheduled, which finally came through about 1:30 P.M. "I took up with him the West Coast matter first," Stimson noted in his diary, "and told him the situation and fortunately found that he was very vigorous about it and told me to go ahead on the line that I had myself thought the best."[21]

So informed by Stimson, McCloy immediately called Bendetsen out at the Presidium military headquarters in San Francisco and told him "we have carte blanche to do what we want to as far as the President is concerned. . . . He states there will probably be some repercussions, but it has got to be dictated by military necessity, but as he puts it, 'Be as reasonable as you can.' "[22]

Roosevelt had never been a strong civil libertarian.[23] As far back as 1936, he had speculated that "every Japanese[-American] citizen or noncitizen" seen to be meeting Japanese ships calling at Pearl Harbor should be put on "a list of those who would be the first to be placed in a concentration camp in the event of trouble."[24] Like other presidents before him, Roosevelt simply assumed extraconstitutional powers during wartime. In his brief conversations with Biddle on the subject, the president had repeatedly emphasized that this must be a military decision. "Nor do I think," recalled Biddle, "that the constitutional difficulty plagued him."[25]

The morning after Roosevelt gave his carte blanche to Stimson and McCloy, the most influential syndicated columnist in the country, Walter Lippmann, published a column with the inflammatory title "The Fifth Column on the Coast." Without citing any source, he claimed, "It is a fact that communication takes place between the enemy at sea and enemy agents on land." That there had not yet been any "important sabotage on the Pacific Coast" might only indicate that the Japanese were holding back "until it can be struck with maximum effect." He concluded that "nobody's constitutional rights include the right to do business on a battlefield."[26]

In McCloy's mind, Lippmann's views only confirmed the wisdom and political inevitability of a mass evacuation. Over at the Justice Department, Biddle may have given up, but his two aides, Rowe and Ennis, were still battling against any mass evacuation. On February 17, Rowe drafted a letter to Roosevelt to go out under Biddle's signature which again pointed out that "the military authorities and the F.B.I." had yet to produce evidence of any concrete military necessity.[27] As Rowe sat writing his letter, General Mark Clark was telling Stimson and McCloy that the army's General Headquarters was opposed to a mass evacuation and was unwilling to allot DeWitt any additional troops for evacuation purposes.[28] So McCloy was well aware that the momentous decisions being made were based on contrary evidence. That morning, he jotted in his diary a brief note reflecting his mood: "Dangers too for the reason of yielding to local pressures which demand intelligent action, it is a problem but I'm afraid no easy solution or one which will not be criticized whatever way we move. It is clear, however, we must act with full responsibility and dispatch."[29]

That evening, he attended a meeting in Biddle's living room with Rowe, Ennis, Gullion, Bendetsen, and one other Justice Department official, Tom Clark.[30] The meeting quickly turned confrontational when Rowe and Ennis launched into an exposition of why a mass evacuation of citizens would be unconstitutional. "The argument waxed hot," recalled Rowe, who was unaware that a draft evacuation order ready for the president's signature was in Gullion's pocket. When Gullion abruptly pulled it out and read it aloud, Rowe couldn't believe it. "I laughed at him," Rowe recalled later that year. "The old buzzard got mad. I told him he was crazy." But Biddle made it clear that he had agreed to support an evacuation order on the grounds that the president had decided that it was a matter of military judgment. Ennis was so upset he almost cried. "I was so mad," Rowe said, "that I could not speak at all myself and the meeting soon broke up." On their way back to the Justice Department, Rowe had to convince Ennis not to resign his position in protest.[31]

Over the next two days, McCloy, Biddle, and Gullion polished the draft of Executive Order 9066, which was then signed by the president on February 19. It authorized Stimson to "prescribe military areas . . . from which any and all persons may be excluded" and gave the War Department the right to license the "right of any person to enter, remain in, or leave" these prescribed areas.[32] In short, it gave DeWitt sweeping legal powers to regulate exactly the kind of restricted military zones originally proposed by McCloy in his phone conversation with the general on February 1. No direct mention was made of Japanese Americans, but none was necessary.

The signing of Executive Order 9066 later came to be regarded as one of the most controversial decisions associated with McCloy's career. In 1981, the American Civil Liberties Union belatedly called it "the greatest deprivation of civil liberties by government in this country since slavery."[33] More than any other individual, McCloy was responsible for the decision, since the president had delegated the matter to him through Stimson. This does not exonerate Roosevelt, but at the very least it was McCloy's job to determine if military necessity justified such draconian measures. Neither during the war nor since has it been shown that any Japanese Americans engaged in sabotage.[34] Why, then, did McCloy become an advocate of mass evacuation? One answer is simple racism, particularly evident in Stimson's attitudes. Another is that McCloy and Stimson were "led by the nose by second-rate people like Colonel Bendetsen."[35] And it was true, as James Rowe recalled, that at the time McCloy was "distracted and distraught with a large number of problems." But he also possessed a unique combination of predilections that made him particularly vulnerable to Bendetsen's and Gullion's arguments. Black Tom had convinced him that the enemy would inevitably engage in sabotage.[36] Ever since Amherst and his enthrallment with the military-preparedness movement, he had been instinctively swayed by national-security arguments. Theoretical objections to strong action on civil-libertarian grounds were indications of soft thinking.

This attitude was reinforced by men McCloy respected. Soon after the evacuation decision, Justice Frankfurter, for instance, told him, ". . . you are dealing with important imponderables, and let me remind you that the fellow who put the term 'imponderables' into the vocabulary of affairs was 'blood and iron' Bismarck."[37] A month later, he told McCloy that he was handling the Japanese American problem with both wisdom and appropriate hardheadedness.[38] Coming from a Supreme Court justice who might well have to rule on the constitutionality of the evacuation, this was greatly reassuring to McCloy.

Another major factor was McCloy's exposure to intelligence sources. Some observers in recent years have cited evidence of Japanese American disloyalty in such special intelligence sources as the Magic intercepts.[39] There is no doubt that McCloy was reading Magic intercepts of Japanese diplomatic traffic at the time of the evacuation decision. But, as in the question of how much warning the Magic cables should have given him regarding the attack on Pearl Harbor, it is difficult to determine whether this intelligence information was a factor in his thinking. McCloy himself, in testimony before a congressional commission forty years later, did not mention the intercepts.[40]

Only a handful of Magic cables, out of thousands intercepted, might have conveyed the impression that Tokyo had recruited both alien Japanese and Japanese American citizens for espionage work. For instance, a Magic intercept dated May 9, 1941, contained a message from the Japanese Consulate in Los Angeles: "We also have connections with our second generations working in airplane plants for intelligence purposes."[41] This is a significant claim, but later, in the autumn of 1941, when a Magic cable does provide Tokyo with information on airplane production from specific plants, the same information can be found in published newspaper reports.[42]

Prior to Pearl Harbor, there had been no systematic analysis of Magic intercepts. So any references McCloy saw in the Magic intercepts to Japanese American espionage were fleeting and impressionistic. A meticulous analysis of the intercepts, in fact, would have shown that the intelligence information cabled back to Tokyo came almost exclusively from "legal" espionage conducted by Japanese diplomats out of their embassy and consulates.[43] Even the covert, "illegal" espionage coordinated out of these Japanese consulates was not very sophisticated or extensive. One Magic intercept, for instance, reveals that, as late as May 1941, the Japanese Embassy was reporting that "only about $3,900 a year is available for actual development of intelligence. . . ."[44] The few agents hired were invariably Caucasian Americans or German nationals.

Whereas such Magic evidence was highly ambiguous, McCloy also had access to intelligence that firmly dismissed the potential for sabotage. The president's own private intelligence system, run by Jay Franklin Carter, a journalist and personal friend, provided him with additional information. Using White House funds, Carter frequently undertook confidential investigations of various matters for Roosevelt. When Roosevelt requested an assessment of the West Coast situation in the autumn of 1941, Carter assigned the task to a wealthy Chicago businessman named Curtis B. Munson. The resulting report concluded that the American-born Nisei were 90 to 98 percent loyal and "are pathetically eager to show this loyalty. . . . They are not oriental or mysterious, they are very American. . . ."[45]

McCloy read the Munson report, and had what he called an "unsatisfactory" briefing from both Munson and Carter just one week before Pearl Harbor.[46] He thought of Munson as an amateur, and in his discussions with Biddle, Rowe, and other Justice Department officials, he never even mentioned the report.

He must have found it harder to dismiss the expertise of the Office of Naval Intelligence's foremost Japanese specialist, Lieutenant Commander Kenneth D. Ringle, the man who had broken the Tachibana spy ring. After Pearl Harbor, Ringle wrote a ten-page report on the "Japanese Question," in which he estimated that fewer than 3 percent, or about thirty-five hundred individuals, might pose a security risk.[47] Most of these were already detained, and he urged the "custodial detention" of the remainder, even if they were citizens. He attacked any mass evacuation plan as "very unwise, since it would undoubtedly alienate the loyalty of many thousands of persons who would otherwise be entirely loyal to the United States. . . ." In short, he advised that "the entire 'Japanese Problem' has been magnified out of its true proportion. . . ."[48]

McCloy nevertheless relied on a three-page Army G-2 assessment that, without reference to Ringle's report, came to an opposite conclusion. Submitted in early February, the G-2 report suggested that Tokyo's "espionage net containing Japanese aliens, first and second generation Japanese and other nationals is now thoroughly organized and working underground."[49] But it contained no specific charges of espionage or any evidence to support these conclusions.

Insofar as McCloy based his decision regarding the evacuation on any intelligence sources, they were meager and incomplete. An advocate of centralized, objective intelligence, he nevertheless in this instance gave credence only to that information developed by his own department. Nor did he tell any of his adversaries in the Justice Department that the intelligence assessments concerning the "military necessity" for a mass evacuation were ambiguous, to say the least.

It is hard not to conclude that McCloy allowed his fears of sabotage and his penchant for decisive action to sweep aside any other considerations. In the aftermath of Pearl Harbor, he was willing to take the kind of harsh steps from which other civilians shrank. And as a lawyer he believed he had found a way around the Constitution in the interest of taking whatever action was necessary to defend the country. Among those of his contemporaries who disagreed with the evacuation, many would blame McCloy for the decision. Biddle, for one, never forgave him, and in his memoirs reflected that, "If Stimson had stood firm, had insisted, as apparently he suspected, that this wholesale evacuation was needless, the President would have followed his advice. And if, instead of dealing almost exclusively with McCloy and Bendetsen, I had urged the Secretary to resist the pressure of his subordinates, the result might have been different."[50]

When Executive Order 9066 was signed, McCloy hoped that a well-organized evacuation could be accomplished slowly, quietly, and without noticeable hardship. On February 20, he sent DeWitt a detailed list of instructions: the elderly should not be disturbed, the evacuation should be accomplished in gradual stages, and all private property had to be protected.[51] He made it clear that he expected DeWitt to report by phone and in writing to him on an almost daily basis.

Several thousand Japanese—Nisei and Issei—had already voluntarily removed themselves from the immediate coastline, and it was still McCloy's intention that the great bulk of these people gradually and voluntarily resettle outside the military zones designated along the coast. Soon, however, it would become clear that voluntary exclusion would not work, for the simple reason that Americans in areas to the east were unwilling to receive the Japanese into their communities.[52]

By the first week of March, McCloy decided the situation required a personal visit to the West Coast. Before leaving on March 7, he gave Stimson a memo outlining the War Department's plans. He informed him that a number of temporary relocation camps had been selected where the evacuees would initially be housed in tents. And, on the recommendation of General Eisenhower, he had selected Milton Eisenhower, the general's younger brother, to serve as the head of a War Relocation Authority. Milton, he said, had made a "most favorable impression," and he intended to take him along on an inspection tour of the West Coast and Hawaii.[53]

The next day, at 6:00 A.M., McCloy flew to San Francisco, where he and Eisenhower met with DeWitt, Bendetsen, and other military officers involved in the evacuation. He also talked at length with Lieutenant Commander Ringle, who "greatly impressed" him with his "knowledge of the Japanese problem along the Coast."[54] Ringle still believed that a mass evacuation was unnecessary. Though this assessment must have given McCloy pause for thought, he never seriously considered trying to undo what had already been decided. But in the weeks ahead, he sometimes seemed to act as if Ringle's views had registered.

His trip to the West Coast was educational in other ways. The morning after he arrived in San Francisco, some two hundred members of the Japanese American Citizens League convened a three-day emergency conference to discuss the impending evacuation. McCloy was introduced to its leaders and heard that the organization had already voted to assist the authorities in whatever evacuation plan was effected. A JACL official, Saburo Kido, declared, "We are gladly cooperating because this is one way of showing that our protestations of loyalty are sincere."[55]

On the final day of the conference, McCloy demonstrated that he had not failed to listen. As the featured speaker that day, he said, "We know that the great majority of citizens and aliens are loyal," he said, "and being appreciative of that, we are most anxious to see that you don't suffer any more than necessary the loss of property values. . . . We want to have conditions [in the camps] just as humane and comfortable as is possible to have them. Above all, we want to give you protection."[56]

At a time when most government officials were demanding an evacuation on grounds of "military necessity" or outright racism, this speech presaged many of the themes used during the war, and later, to justify what was generally seen as a regrettable but necessary policy. Already, in McCloy's mind, the evacuation decision had become somewhat benign. Collectively, Japanese Americans were a potential security threat, but as individuals they were victims of war's circumstances. Implied was the idea that, if racism was involved, it was not the government's racism, but the government's desire to protect the Japanese Americans from the racism of other citizens, that required an evacuation. In return, these Oriental citizens had to understand that their war duty was to cooperate.

This was a message that this particular group of Japanese Americans was prepared to accept in a mood of subdued resignation. After the speech, one of the JACL's leaders, Masao Satow, walked up to McCloy and invited him to join a group of delegates who intended to have dinner in Chinatown.

A surprised McCloy said, "Did you say Chinatown? Aren't the Chinese hostile toward you fellows? Aren't you afraid to go down there?"

"No, sir," replied Satow. "They're Chinese and we're Japanese, but we're all Americans. Come on, join us."[57]

McCloy accepted the invitation and joined Satow and his friends in what became for the JACL officials a memorable dinner with the assistant secretary of war, a man whom many of them now began to regard as a friend of sorts. Among others, McCloy got to know for the first time JACL's Washington representative, Mike Masaoka. He took an instant liking to this bright, gregarious, and articulate twenty-six-year-old; it was the beginning of a lifelong friendship. Masaoka impressed upon McCloy the idea that he and other Americans of Japanese ancestry were as loyal as any other citizens. "We think, feel, act like Americans," Masaoka had said to a congressional committee in San Francisco only a few days before meeting McCloy. "We, too, remember Pearl Harbor. . . ."[58] Though Masaoka endorsed an orderly but compulsory evacuation plan, he clearly did not envisage that his people would be interned behind barbed wire.[59] Nevertheless, his compliant attitude made it that much easier for a resettlement program to evolve into a policy of indefinite internment.

Two days after his dinner in Chinatown, McCloy and DeWitt agreed to put Colonel Bendetsen in charge of the evacuation program. Though the army was still ostensibly talking of a "voluntary migration," Bendetsen quickly began building two large "reception centers" to "provide temporary housing for those who were unable to undertake their own evacuation, or who declined to leave until forced to." By March 20, he had selected the sites for fifteen "assembly centers" and given the Army Corps of Engineers until April 21 to complete construction of the camps. A week later, DeWitt issued an order prohibiting any further "voluntary" evacuation of Japanese Americans inland. Henceforth, both Nisei and Issei were in effect prisoners of the army. Only about nine thousand Japanese Americans had taken the opportunity to migrate inland before the freeze order. (Japanese Americans already living in the East, well out of the exclusion areas, were never interned.) That left more than a hundred thousand for Bendetsen's assembly camps.[60]

McCloy, meanwhile, had left San Francisco on a plane bound for Hawaii. The trip gave him something of the sensation of being on the front line: "It was a grim place. At night there was a blackout so deep and so complete that it was eerie."[61] Upon his return, he told a packed news conference that a mass evacuation of the Japanese Americans from Hawaii was "impossible." Too many of them, he explained, were providing essential labor for "defense projects" such as fortifications and new roads. He even attested to the loyalty of these Japanese workers by describing some of them as "keen and enthusiastic."[62] None of the reporters present questioned why an evacuation on the West Coast was deemed a military necessity when a much larger and more concentrated population of Japanese Americans, living in the midst of the Pacific battlefield, was thought essential to the national defense.

The first phase of the mandatory evacuation did not begin until a few days later, on March 31. There were inevitable logistical problems, delays, and reports of inadequate facilities. The less attention accorded the whole affair, McCloy thought, the better. He went so far as to issue instructions throughout the government that every effort should be made to limit any publicity surrounding the evacuations. Even so, complications arose that constantly threatened to bring unwanted publicity.

For one thing, the army had to define who was of Japanese ancestry. In the first week, dozens of Nisei married to Caucasian Americans requested individual exemptions from the evacuation orders. So as not to tear families apart, McCloy encouraged his army colleagues to issue a few such individual exemptions, but DeWitt and Bendetsen had simply denied all such requests. Although initially McCloy had instructed that persons over the age of seventy should not be disturbed, in practice everyone was evacuated. Soldiers even went into at least one orphanage run by Caucasian priests and took into custody infants of partial Japanese extraction.[63]

On April 6, 1942, McCloy tried to bend this policy by writing Bendetsen a note about the case of one Keizo Tsuji, an associate pastor in a "100 percent white U.S. citizen" Phoenix, Arizona, church. The pastor of the church was protesting Tsuji's forced evacuation on the grounds that it "violates the rights guaranteed us in the Constitution . . . since it restricts persons of one extraction while it permits persons of another extraction to be exempted." McCloy recognized that this was undeniable and told

Bendetsen, "I wonder whether as a matter of law and as a matter of policy it might not be well to include some exemptions of Japanese as well as Germans and Italians."[64]

He reasoned that a few such exemptions could well give the government the evidence it might later need in the courts to prove that the evacuation was not administered strictly on the basis of race. In response to McCloy's suggestion, the army's Office of the Judge Advocate General drew up a number of exemptions, all of which dealt with mixed-blood and mixed-marriage cases. Initially, anyone with as little as one-sixteenth Japanese blood was considered subject to the evacuation orders. Under the new rules, those with less than one-half Japanese blood and "whose backgrounds have been Caucasian" were to be exempt. Families consisting of a Japanese wife, a non-Japanese husband, and their mixed-blood children were exempt. But a Caucasian woman married to a Japanese American citizen, if she wished to live with her husband, had to follow him into the camps.[65]

None of these categories fit the case McCloy had initially raised, that of a Japanese male in whose behalf the Phoenix pastor had petitioned. The Office of the Judge Advocate General told DeWitt that in their opinion there were no grounds on which to free the individual mentioned by McCloy other than the "*apparent* harmlessness of the individual. It goes without saying that there may be many such individuals among the Japanese." The army's lawyers concluded that to make an exception in one case would open the floodgates to thousands of appeals.[66]

McCloy made no effort to press the issue. In the meantime, Milton Eisenhower, confirmed in his job as head of the newly created War Relocation Authority, was having his own problems. On April 7, at a Salt Lake City meeting of Western governors, he presented a plan for the rapid resettlement of the evacuees from the "assembly centers" into rural communities across the West. His idea was to house the evacuees in fifty to seventy-five camps modeled after the Civilian Conservation Corps. The residents would be allowed to come and go as they pleased and, if they could, obtain jobs at prevailing market rates in the surrounding agricultural communities.

To Eisenhower's surprise, his plan was met with nearly universal denunciations. Except for the governor of Colorado, all the governors said they would have no evacuees in their states unless they were kept under constant guard. The attorney general of Idaho, Bert Miller, voiced the most extreme opinion when he urged that "all Japanese be put in concentration camps, for the remainder of the war. . . . We want to keep this a white man's country." Such statements shocked and profoundly depressed Eisenhower. "That meeting," he recalled later, "was probably the most frustrating experience I ever had."[67]

Eisenhower nevertheless caved in to the governors and agreed that the evacuees would remain under armed guard within what he was now calling the "reception centers." On returning to Washington, he met with McCloy, who promised his assistance in finding suitable sites for the camps on isolated stretches of federally owned land.[68] By this time, more than four months after Pearl Harbor, the first actual evacuations had begun from Japanese American communities up and down the West Coast into the "assembly centers" devised by Bendetsen. Most of these assembly centers were hastily converted racetracks, fairgrounds, and parking lots.

The assembly centers were a far cry from what McCloy had promised would be "comfortable" camps, or what another official had described as "normal communities." Years later, an evacuee described the conditions at one assembly center, the Santa Anita racetrack, in this fashion: "We were confined to horse stables. The horse stables were whitewashed. In the hot summers, the legs of the cots were sinking through the asphalt. We were given mattress covers and told to stuff straw in them. The toilet facilities were terrible. They were communal. There were no partitions. . . . It had extra guard towers with a searchlight panoraming the camp, and it was very difficult to sleep because the light kept coming into our window. . . ."[69]

McCloy had left the West Coast before the mass evacuations began in the first week of April, so he had no firsthand exposure to the conditions inside the assembly centers. He was, however, aware that people were being put up in makeshift shelters on racetracks and fairgrounds. This was to be regretted, but it was also, in his view, a temporary inconvenience mandated by the circumstances of war.

Some of his friends in the administration were shocked by what McCloy was willing to do in the name of national security. That summer, he got into an argument with Harold Ickes over the exercise of martial-law powers in Hawaii. The interior secretary blamed a "weak governor" for having surrendered virtually all civilian authority to the War Department. McCloy stubbornly refused to allow his generals to relinquish any of their powers despite Ickes's appeals. After one angry confrontation over the issue, Ickes's assistant secretary told him that McCloy had said "he did not care whether it was constitutional or not, that there were times when even the constitution could justifiably be disregarded." Ickes commented in his diary, "This may be true, but whether or not it should be disregarded on the say of the Army alone is doubtful. . . . I like McCloy a lot and I have seen him more than any of the other men in the Army but I have been told that he is more or less inclined to be a Fascist and this would not surprise me. I know of my own knowledge that he is strong and able."[70]

This, of course, was not the first occasion on which McCloy's seeming disregard for the Constitution had been so cavalierly expressed. He had privately conveyed similar sentiments to both Biddle and J. Edgar Hoover when it came to discussing the evacuation order or, in the case of Hoover, whether it was permissible to wiretap union leaders suspected of sabotage. In his view, military necessity justified any measure.

Few individuals outside the War Department were in a position to dispute exactly what conditions constituted grounds for "military necessity." Initially, no one denied the possibility of military raids on the West Coast. But then, in the first week of June 1942, the U.S. Navy achieved a decisive victory at the Battle of Midway, sinking four Japanese aircraft carriers and numerous other ships. The Pacific was no longer a Japanese lake. A few days later, McCloy boasted to Ickes over lunch, "We caught them before they were ready to be caught. . . ."[71]

After Midway, McCloy knew that the threat of air raids, let alone a full-scale invasion of the West Coast, had practically vanished. But by that time, the evacuation of Japanese Americans into assembly camps was nearly complete. More than ninety thousand Nisei and Issei were now living in sixteen different assembly centers, and, despite the decisive naval victory at Midway, no one in the War Department considered rescinding the evacuation order. To the contrary, McCloy was disturbed that by the end of the month only three of the more permanent "relocation centers" would be open.

A week later, *The New Republic* added to his worries by publishing a devastating critique of conditions inside the camps. In a story entitled "Concentration Camp: U.S. Style," a Japanese American internee described in graphic detail the soldiers armed with machine guns in guard towers, the barbed wire surrounding the camps, the filthy condition of the converted horse stables, and the "stinking mud and slop everywhere."

Such public controversy only quickened McCloy's desire to transfer responsibility for the internees from the army to the civilian War Relocation Authority. But after only two months on the job, the WRA's Milton Eisenhower was severely depressed by what he had come to regard as an unconscionable task, a veritable "nightmare."[72] The only Japanese Americans he had been able to "relocate" outside the camps were a small percentage of college-age Nisei. These had been reluctantly accepted as students by a few Eastern universities after intense lobbying by the American Friends Service Committee.[73]

Eisenhower's unhappiness was matched by McCloy's dissatisfaction with his management of the problem, and by mid-June both men agreed that a new WRA director should be found. One evening soon afterward, Eisenhower attended a party at the home of one of his former Department of Agriculture colleagues, Dillon S. Myer. After playing Myer's piano for a while, Eisenhower took his friend aside and urged him to accept the job. When Myer asked if Eisenhower really thought he should do it, Eisenhower said, "Yes, if you can do the job and sleep at night." He confessed he hadn't been able to do so himself.[74]

Myer took the job anyway, and brought to it the zeal and efficiency that his predecessor had lacked; in the months ahead, he rapidly finished fifteen permanent "relocation centers" spread throughout California, Utah, Idaho, Arizona, Wyoming, Colorado, and Arkansas. By the end of the year, the camps housed 106,770 internees.[75] Each camp was about one square mile and contained tar-papered barracks, schools, communal kitchens, churches, and recreation centers. Though they were not exactly normal communities, under Myer's administration the camps gradually became more livable.

For all the problems attending to the evacuation, McCloy nevertheless believed that things had been managed surprisingly well and humanely. That summer, he dictated a memo for his files praising the army's conduct: "I wonder if anyone realizes the skill, speed and humanity with which the evacuation of the Japanese has been handled by the Army on the West Coast? I am struck with the extreme care that has been taken to protect the persons and goods and even the comforts of each individual. Certainly an organization that can do a humane job like this and still be a fine fighting organization is unique—and American."[76]

The arrest on June 13, 1942, of four German saboteurs spotted by a Coast Guardsman burying their uniforms and explosives in the sands of a Long Island beach confirmed all of McCloy's assumptions that the enemy would engage in sabotage. He was not surprised that two of the saboteurs were German Americans; this only confirmed everything he had learned from his Black Tom experience. But it did not mean that he felt compelled to urge the relocation or internment of German Americans. He recognized that this was impractical, given the large numbers and the widespread integration of the German ethnic minority in American society. That German Americans had committed sabotage nevertheless provided justification for interning the Japanese Americans.

Taken into custody by the FBI, the four German agents were found to have a large supply of explosives, detonators, maps of key bridges, railroads and locks on the Ohio River, plans of various industrial plants, and more than $82,000 in American dollars. There was no question of their intent to commit sabotage. Under interrogation, the two German American agents turned state's evidence and admitted that they had been brought to Long Island by a German submarine, U-boat No. 202. They also volunteered the information that another team of saboteurs was scheduled to land elsewhere on the East Coast. J. Edgar Hoover's men scoured the Eastern shoreline, and though they missed the second team's landing, by June 27 the FBI had arrested four more agents, who had landed by submarine in Florida.[77]

McCloy believed the saboteurs should be tried *in camera* and executed within days.[78] The Justice Department objected, and after considerable argument, a compromise was reached whereby the attorney general was allowed to prosecute the case but in a special martial-law court. McCloy was infuriated, however, when the trial opened on July 8, accompanied by one of J. Edgar Hoover's orchestrated press extravaganzas. The names of the saboteurs were published, and the FBI naturally was given all the credit for their apprehension. When it was over, six of the eight saboteurs were electrocuted on August 8, a month after their trial had begun and only six weeks after the first of them had been caught. But none of this mollified McCloy. He believed an elementary principle of counterintelligence had been violated by even announcing the names of the saboteurs and revealing to the Germans how many of their agents had been caught. In a memorandum to Stimson, he observed, "The FBI has now had its bath of publicity. . . . It [the trial] violated every principle of counterespionage and sabotage. The Germans know now who was apprehended, and . . . how they were apprehended."[79]

He thought, "Even a democracy can afford to execute a spy a few days after he is caught red-handed."[80] A war was going on, and he believed any overly fastidious observance of such constitutional rights as due process could risk the outcome of the battle. His attitude went far beyond the merely instinctive reactions of a wartime citizenry. He possessed a fully developed national-security philosophy, assigning to the executive arm of government sweeping powers.

Others in the Roosevelt administration were alarmed by the spread of such views and the growing power of the War Department. McCloy was perceived by many of his colleagues as a symbol of this trend toward a military mind-set. Attorney General Biddle complained that the army was "taking over the control of internal security in this country." Angered by McCloy's interference in the sabotage cases, Assistant Attorney General James Rowe wrote a memo in October warning Biddle that the Justice Department had to resist the War Department's encroaching powers. "These isolated instances, and there are many more," wrote Rowe, "indicate a disregard of the military mind for intellectual protest. I am perfectly well aware that Jack McCloy is an intelligent, reasonable human being. I am even more aware of the terrific pressures exerted against him by the brass hats . . . but I do believe in adapting our techniques to defend ourselves. The Department of Justice is relying upon Maginot Line thinking and the Army Panzers already hold both of our coasts and soon will hold most of the control of internal security in the United States."[81] Rowe urged Biddle to fight back like J. Edgar Hoover, who "keeps the Army on the run, and they respect him for it." But Biddle was not the bureaucratic player that Hoover was, and Rowe had very few allies. In this war, even the civil-libertarian community was becoming infected with the national-security mind-set.

Late in the summer of 1942, McCloy had a chance to renew his friendship with Alexander Meiklejohn, when the former Amherst president came to Washington on behalf of the American Civil Liberties Union to monitor the government's policies regarding Japanese Americans. A noted civil libertarian, Meiklejohn had nevertheless written Roger Baldwin the previous spring in defense of the evacuation. "The Japanese citizens, as a group, are dangerous both to themselves and to their fellow-citizens," wrote Meiklejohn. "And, that being true, discriminatory action is justified."[82] But with the evacuation completed, Baldwin now wanted Meiklejohn to persuade the authorities to allow the internees to leave the relocation centers for jobs away from the West Coast.[83]

When Meiklejohn arrived in Washington, he quickly learned that McCloy seemed to be "near the bottom of things" concerning any questions on the relocation camps. He informed an ACLU official that McCloy was "one of my favorite Amherst boys [*cum laude,* 1916] whom I used to lick at tennis . . . and so I'm likely to get the low-down. . . ."[84] On August 5, the two old friends got together for dinner to reminisce about Amherst and discuss the relocation camps. Using an argument suggested by Baldwin, Meiklejohn said that a liberal furlough policy would result in the absorption of the Japanese Americans into the mainstream of American community life.[85] McCloy indicated he had an open mind about the issue and said that something would be decided after he came back from an inspection of the West Coast in September.

Accompanied by Bill Donovan and Al McCormack, McCloy spent the third week of September on the West Coast.[86] But after numerous meetings with DeWitt and Bendetsen, he came back to Washington with more doubts about the Japanese Americans than ever before. Upon his return, he wrote Meiklejohn a letter that reveals the extent to which the policy of temporary, protective evacuation had now become a policy of long-term internment:

> We would be missing a very big opportunity if we failed to study the Japanese in these Camps at some length before they are dispersed. We have not done a very good job thus far in solving the Japanese problem in this country. . . . These people, gathered as they now are in these communities, afford a means of sampling opinion and studying their customs and habits in a way we have never before had possible. We could find out what they are thinking about and we might very well influence their thinking in the right direction before they are again distributed into communities.

> I am aware that such a suggestion may provoke a charge that we have no right to treat these people as "guinea pigs", but I would rather treat them as guinea pigs and learn something useful than merely to treat them, or have them treated, as they have been in the past with such unsuccessful results.[87]

Only a few weeks later, McCloy warned Myer against subjecting "the Nisei to further Issei contamination" and suggested that native-born Americans should be segregated insofar as possible from exposure to Issei culture.[88]

After consulting at length with McCloy, Myer eventually issued a set of regulations governing the release of internees from the camps. Three kinds of passes were allowed: short-term emergency passes; restricted passes for work gangs employed off camp, invariably as crop-pickers; and indefinite furloughs. In order to qualify for an indefinite furlough, an internee had to undergo an extensive investigation. References were required from "preferably Caucasian persons," and each internee was asked to sign a pledge of allegiance to the United States and agree to serve as an informant "regarding any subversive activity . . . both in the relocation centers and in the communities in which you are resettling." They were instructed to stay away from large groups of Japanese and asked to "try to develop such American habits which will cause you to be accepted readily into American social groups." Finally, those wanting out of the camps were asked, "Can you furnish any proof that you have always been loyal to the United States?"[89]

Very few internees, particularly in the beginning, were willing to subject themselves to these humiliating conditions. And yet Meiklejohn did not object to the regulations: he reported back to the ACLU that, although there were extensive "conditions" attached to any leaves, "they are, I think, essentially reasonable limits arising out of the Evacuation situation."[90] The ACLU board and national committee had by now already voted by a margin of two to one not to mount a direct constitutional challenge to the evacuation order.[91]

This did not mean that the War Department did not have to worry about legal challenges to the internment. Four cases were now before the courts, involving four different challenges to the evacuation orders. Gordon K. Hirabayashi, Mitsuye Endo, Minoru Yasui, and Fred T. Korematsu had each decided independently to defy the evacuation orders or, in Endo's case, apply for a writ of *habeas corpus*. Endo's *habeas corpus* petition was first reviewed in July 1942, but the federal district judge on the case let months pass before making a ruling. Korematsu, however, was convicted of violating the curfew and evacuation orders on September 8. Yasui was tried in June, but here too the judge let months go by before making a ruling. Hirabayashi's trial was not scheduled until October. In all these cases, McCloy was aware that there was a good chance the judges might rule against the government. By mid-September, he was so worried that some federal judge might grant a writ of *habeas corpus*—or, worse, issue an opinion vacating the evacuation order—that he took the precaution of drafting a piece of legislation that would suspend the writ of *habeas corpus* for all citizens, including those of Japanese ancestry.[92]

His fears were nearly realized when, on November 16, 1942, the judge in the Yasui case finally issued his opinion. Judge James A. Fee pointed out that Congress had not declared martial law or suspended *habeas corpus.* So long as civil courts were functioning on the West Coast, Fee wrote, "military necessity cannot be so imperative that the fundamental safeguards" of the Constitution "must be abandoned."[93] But this blow was mitigated by Fee's curious finding, against all the documentary evidence, that Yasui was not a U.S. citizen, and that therefore, as an alien, he could be convicted of having violated the curfew.

McCloy called Judge Fee's decision an "indiscretion," and again made preparations to have Congress suspend *habeas corpus* rights for all citizens.[94] As it happened, the resolution of the other cases was less than expeditious: Gordon Hirabayashi was convicted in October, but his appeal and those of Korematsu and Endo would not reach the Supreme Court for many more months. For the time being, the internment program had survived its first legal challenge.

A few weeks after Judge Fee's decision, conditions inside one of the largest internment camps, Manzanar, resulted in an explosion. A crowd of internees, angered by the authorities' use of JACL *inu* ("stool pigeons" or informers), marched on the camp jail. There they ran into a wall of armed troops hastily brought to the scene. When the crowd refused to disperse, tear-gas grenades were thrown, and then, in the confusion, a number of shots were fired. Two internees were killed and eight seriously wounded.[95] In the aftermath of this and other, less serious disturbances in the camps, Dillon Myer proceeded, with McCloy's approval, to build a special maximum-security camp at Tule Lake, California, where troublemakers and any vocally resentful internees could be isolated. By the end of 1942, a program of temporary evacuation and relocation had become a bureaucracy dedicated to the indefinite incarceration of tens of thousands of citizens in concentration camps.

For the remainder of the war, no issue absorbed more of McCloy's time than the internment. He certainly did not consider it the most important of the dozens of matters that crossed his desk each month. But it was the most persistent. Over time, as it became clear that whatever security justification might have existed for the internment was no longer remotely credible, he fought a rearguard battle to justify the original decision. For him, it was a matter of defending the War Department's reputation. He was particularly anxious that the Supreme Court not declare the internment unconstitutional.

In this context, in mid-January 1943, McCloy called Mike Masaoka, the JACL's Washington representative, into his office. The War Department, McCloy said, would soon announce the formation of an all-Nisei volunteer combat regiment. Masaoka had been lobbying McCloy for months to subject his people to the draft, or at least allow them to volunteer for military service. At first he was disquieted by McCloy's proposal for a segregated, all-Nisei combat team; he would have preferred a simple application of the Selective Service laws. But McCloy soon persuaded him that an all-Nisei combat regiment would receive greater recognition than if a few thousand Nisei volunteers were scattered throughout the army.[96] A few days later, the War Department announced that it hoped to recruit up to three thousand volunteers from the internment camps. Masaoka was the first to volunteer.

The idea that Japanese Americans interned for possible disloyalty should now be allowed to put on a uniform sharply divided the War Department. General DeWitt opposed the proposal, saying, "There isn't such a thing as a loyal Japanese."[97] But in Washington that spring, the Supreme Court was scheduled to hear arguments on the various internment cases, and McCloy was convinced that an all-Nisei combat team could provide proof of the government's good-faith efforts to determine the loyalty of those interned. It was evidence, he argued, that the internment was not governed by mere racial prejudice.

For the same reason, he argued, the War Department should authorize the WRA to determine the loyalty or disloyalty of individual internees and release in large numbers those thought to be loyal.[98] Unfortunately, a political mistake was now made that complicated the prospects for any early mass release. As a prelude to accepting volunteers for the all-Nisei combat unit, McCloy had one of his aides compose a questionnaire designed to determine the loyalty of potential recruits. Among other questions, the internees were asked whether they were willing "to serve in the armed forces of the United States on combat duty" and "forswear any form of allegiance or obedience to the Japanese emperor." Instead of being given only to potential volunteers, the questionnaire was circulated to all internees. This led to widespread doubts in the camps, where parents of draft-age sons feared the proposed segregated Nisei combat team was designed for suicide missions. Many others were offended by the questionnaire, since it implied they had an allegiance to the Japanese emperor. In the event, 86 percent of the internees answered affirmatively to both questions; but this left 10 percent, who now were labeled the "No-No" group. Such evidence of militancy by a sizable minority convinced Stimson and McCloy to defer any mass release until after the Supreme Court heard oral arguments on the internment cases.[99]

The faulty questionnaire also resulted in far fewer than the three thousand volunteers McCloy had expected for his 442nd Regiment. Because of the anger and resentment accompanying the bitter debate inside the camps over the offending loyalty questions, only 1,181 Nisei initially stepped forward. To compensate for the shortfall, twenty-six hundred Nisei were recruited from Hawaii, where, of course, there had been no internment and no smoldering resentments. After training at Fort Shelby in Mississippi, the special combat team was shipped overseas that summer and quickly became distinguished for its exploits in the Italian theater. The 442nd eventually sustained the most battle casualties—and decorations—of any comparable unit in the army.[100]

In the meantime, McCloy did everything he could to ensure that the Supreme Court did not suddenly declare the internment unconstitutional. One day in the spring of 1943, he found on his desk two printed copies of a long document entitled *Final Report, Japanese Evacuation from the West Coast.* General DeWitt proposed to release this report, written largely by Colonel Bendetsen, to the Justice Department for use in the oral arguments before the Supreme Court. Reading it over later that evening, McCloy became so alarmed that at 11:15 P.M. he placed a call to Bendetsen in San Francisco. First he rebuked Bendetsen: "I thought it was arranged that we were to get a galley of it before you printed it up." Then he told the colonel, "I'm distressed about it. . . . There are a number of things in it now which I feel should not be made public."[101]

What disturbed McCloy most was DeWitt's preface. If, as DeWitt claimed, it was "impossible" under any conditions to determine the loyalty of this "tightly-knit racial group," then the War Department would seem to be taking the position before the court that the Japanese as a race were disloyal.[102] McCloy knew the court would not accept this foolhardy assertion, and so he quickly had Bendetsen rewrite the report. The final version simply stated that "no ready means existed for determining the loyal and the disloyal with any degree of safety."[103] This language neatly sidestepped any racial implications. Even so, McCloy was worried enough by the report that he decided for the moment to withhold its release.

Oral arguments before the Supreme Court on the three cases challenging the constitutionality of the internment began on May 10, 1943. At least five of the justices had some reservations about the exclusion orders. But in the context of war, each justice wished to avoid having to question the right of the commander-in-chief and his officers to make military judgments. In short, every effort was made to decide each of the three cases on the narrowest, most technical grounds possible. Fred Korematsu's case was sent back to a lower court for a ruling on the legality of the exclusion order. Three weeks later, Minoru Yasui was convicted on the narrow ground of violating a curfew order. Similarly, the court upheld Gordon Hirabayashi's conviction for violating the curfew order, but evaded any decision on the constitutionality of the evacuation order itself. A ruling on the critical constitutional issues was in effect postponed until the Korematsu case was once more brought before the court, the following year.

As the legal historian Peter Irons has shown, all these decisions were greatly influenced by Justice Frankfurter. Irons quotes Philip Elman, Frankfurter's law clerk in 1943, explaining the justice's strong defense of the War Department in this fashion: "Frankfurter was not only very close and devoted to Roosevelt, but he was even more devoted to Henry Stimson. There was also Jack McCloy, a close friend who owed his job to Frankfurter. I don't think he regarded McCloy as a litigant. . . ."[104] McCloy had met with Frankfurter the week the justices were deciding these cases; admittedly, he saw Frankfurter as a neighbor or talked to him on the phone practically every week of the year. At the very least, Frankfurter's friendships with McCloy, Stimson, and the president ensured something less than judicious objectivity.

In the meantime, the court's delay gave McCloy the opportunity to set up a Japanese American Joint Board empowered to review the loyalty of individual internees. By then, nearly ten thousand internees had been released on furlough and allowed to relocate themselves to jobs or universities in the East. But that still left not quite a hundred thousand living in the camps. Using the ill-fated questionnaires circulated among all internees earlier in the year, McCloy's loyalty board now proceeded to classify each Japanese American in three categories: white, brown, and black. An individual classified as "white" would be cleared for employment in vital war plants; "brown" signified that the individual could be released though there were some doubtful bits of information in his file; and "black" meant the internee should be segregated from the rest of the internees. All of those in the "No-No" group were thus categorized. Almost all of the internees labeled "black" were gradually segregated and incarcerated in the special high-security camp at Tule Lake, California. Over the next year, the Joint Board investigated nearly thirty-nine thousand individual cases and recommended the furlough of more than twenty-five thousand internees. Half of the approximately 12,600 recommended for continued incarceration were released anyway by the War Relocation Authority.[105]

McCloy had started this process precisely in order to demonstrate to the Supreme Court that the government was making a good-faith effort to determine the loyalty of citizen internees. But the court did not schedule final oral arguments on the remaining internment cases until October

1944. By that time, pressure had been building for a complete end to the internment. At the end of 1943, Attorney General Biddle had written Roosevelt that the "concentration camps" were repugnant to the principles of democratic government.[106] Shortly afterward, supervision of the War Relocation Authority was transferred from McCloy's control into the hands of Harold Ickes. The secretary of the interior lobbied throughout the spring of 1944 to release all loyal Japanese Americans.

In early June, Ickes bluntly warned Roosevelt that the exclusion was "clearly unconstitutional in the present circumstances" and predicted that "the continued retention of these innocent people in the relocation centers would be a blot upon the history of this country." Roosevelt was unmoved, and replied that it would be a mistake to do anything "drastic or sudden." Ten days later, McCloy went to the White House to discuss a proposal to allow a "substantial number" of Japanese Americans to return to California. Afterward, he called the West Coast commander to say, "I just came from the President a little while ago. He put thumbs down on this scheme. He was surrounded at the moment by his political advisors and they were harping hard that this would stir up the boys in California and California, I guess, is an important state."[107]

With the 1944 presidential election on the horizon, McCloy was telling his closest friends that he was going to vote Democratic for the first time in his life. Like many Americans, he found it hard to imagine ending the war without Roosevelt at the helm. He told Ickes that, though he instinctively opposed a fourth term, the "effect on morale would be terrific" if Roosevelt were not re-elected. Stalin, he said, "would be justified in seeking a separate peace," and Hitler could assure the German people that all they had to do was to hold their belts tight for a few months more, when the coalition against them would be broken up."[108]

Politics now dictated the president's, and consequently McCloy's, attitude toward the question of an end to the internment. Whereas, earlier in the year, he had been somewhat inclined to find an unobtrusive way to release the internees, McCloy now almost single-handedly blocked every step toward an early release. Later that summer, General Charles S. Bonesteel, the newly appointed West Coast commander, repeatedly tried to persuade McCloy to suspend the exclusion orders. When pressed, McCloy finally made it clear to Bonesteel that "we shall have greater opportunity for constructive plans at a date somewhat later than November 6th."[109] An end to the internment would have to await the election.

To prolong the internment, McCloy now also had to ensure that the War Department's cases before the Supreme Court were not undermined. An unfavorable ruling would precipitate an immediate and probably chaotic release of the internees. In addition, McCloy's own reputation was at stake, since he was so closely associated with both the decision to authorize mass internment and its implementation.

One Saturday morning at the end of September 1944, he discovered a major problem while reviewing the Justice Department's brief to the court on the Korematsu case. Early in 1944, he had quietly released General DeWitt's *Final Report* on the evacuation. He did so believing that the evidence it cited of nefarious Japanese American activities would persuade the court to uphold the evacuation. But he had not counted on the stubborn doubts of one Justice Department official, Edward Ennis, the same man with whom he had clashed over the evacuation order in February 1942.

Ennis and his assistant, John Burling, decided to alert the court to the fact that DeWitt's *Final Report* contained false information. They inserted a footnote in the Korematsu brief that flatly stated that the Justice Department had information disputing the evidence contained in the DeWitt report. The footnote specifically asked the court to disregard the report,[110] and without the DeWitt report the justices would have no direct evidence before them of any Japanese American collusion with the enemy. Inclusion of the footnote severely damaged the War Department's case that military necessity required the mass detention of thousands of American citizens.

When McCloy stumbled across the footnote in the page proofs of the Korematsu brief, he immediately called in Adrian Fisher, a bright young army lawyer who had joined his office the previous December, and asked him to have the footnote removed. Fisher called Ennis, who informed him that he could do nothing: the brief was already at the printer's. When McCloy learned of this, he quickly phoned Solicitor General Charles Fahy; in response to his pleas, Fahy had the printing presses stopped at noon on September 30. Over the next few days, heated negotiations took place between McCloy and Fisher in the War Department and Ennis, Burling, Fahy, and other Justice Department officials.

Ennis and Burling refused to budge, and wrote a memo to their superiors strongly arguing that the Justice Department had an ethical obligation to repudiate the DeWitt report. They pointed out that DeWitt had asserted that Japanese Americans had engaged in "overt acts of treason." They concluded, "Since this is not so, it is highly unfair to this racial minority that these lies, put out in an official publication, go uncorrected."[111]

At one point, Ennis and Burling threatened to refuse to sign the briefs if the footnote was pulled. The presses had to be stopped a second time. But if the two Justice officials were adamant, so too was McCloy. Finally, in an effort to achieve a compromise, one of Ennis's superiors, Herbert Wechsler, hastily drafted a vaguely worded alternative footnote, which read: "We have specifically recited in this brief the facts relating to the justification for the evacuation, of which we ask the Court to take judicial notice; and we rely upon the Final Report only to the extent that it relates to such facts." Though Fisher and McCloy would have preferred no footnote at all, this almost nonsensical language was vastly superior in their eyes to any clearly worded refutation of the DeWitt report. After five days of digging in his heels, McCloy had won his point. In retrospect, he had probably also saved the government's case, for if such liberal justices as William O. Douglas had been made aware that the Justice Department considered the army's evidence to be "intentional falsehoods," the court might easily have reached a different decision.[112] As it was, in October 1944 the court decided by a six-to-three margin to uphold Korematsu's conviction for disobeying the exclusion orders.

Virtually at the same time, Justice Douglas wrote the court's unanimous decision to free Mitsuye Endo. Evading the central constitutional issue of whether the War Relocation Authority had the right to detain disloyal citizens, the court decided to free Endo on the narrow grounds that the WRA "has no authority to subject citizens who are concededly loyal to its leave procedures." This meant, of course, that the WRA would have to release all but those Japanese Americans who had been determined disloyal.

The court's decisions were made, but they would not be published until December 18, 1944. One day earlier, the army announced that Japanese Americans regarded as loyal would be released after January 2, 1945, and permitted to travel anywhere in the United States. This resulted in the release of some fifty thousand internees; but twenty thousand Japanese Americans, labeled as "troublemakers" and segregated at the Tule Lake facility, remained incarcerated. It would be many months before these embittered resisters of the internment were released.

Altogether, the outcome could not have made McCloy unhappy. The court had avoided censuring the army, and on narrow grounds it had upheld the constitutionality of the original exclusion order. True, the Endo decision made any prolonged internment impracticable. But the internment was no longer necessary anyway, and now that the elections were over, it had become politically possible to end the always troublesome administration of the camps.

More than any other official, McCloy was responsible for the internment of the entire Japanese American community inside barbed-wire camps for three years. His arguments had carried the day against the Justice Department's constitutional concerns when the original decision was made in February 1942. He had allowed the early "relocation" program to evolve into a policy of forcible internment. And he had repeatedly made it possible to prolong the internment for political reasons long after any military justifications for the action existed. Had it not been for his careful legal defense of the War Department's policies, the Supreme Court might well have declared the entire enterprise unconstitutional.

McCloy always regarded what happened to these people as a natural consequence of the war. More important, he never doubted that for reasons of national security the president of the United States could do whatever he thought necessary to defend the country, including placing thousands of citizens behind barbed wire. A constitutional travesty, the internment was a political success, and an indication that McCloy's national-security philosophy was becoming part of the national consensus.

CHAPTER 9

Political Commissar

"[McCloy was] very intelligent and interesting. . . . He seemed much more like a fellow member of the House of Commons or a minister in a British Cabinet than the ordinary American politician. I was able to say some things to him about the situation here which I cannot get [Robert] Murphy to understand."

HAROLD MACMILLAN
ALGIERS, FEBRUARY 1943

The world war transformed America, bringing it out of ten long years of depression and stagnation. A centralized, government-directed war economy did for the country what the New Deal had failed to do. Throughout these years, the War Department became an unprecedented power center in Washington's gallery of bureaucracies. Its influence on foreign policy soon surpassed that of the State Department's, and its interests intruded on issues normally handled by the departments of Treasury, Justice, Interior, and Commerce. In the world's first "total war," the American military's priorities had become the country's priorities. And within this most powerful of federal departments, it was McCloy's job to see to it that the military's interests prevailed over any "civilian" priorities. The constitutional rights of Japanese Americans had wound up on the wrong side of this equation, and so too did antitrust laws, labor rights, and the Jewish American community's desire to rescue European Jewry from the Holocaust. African Americans, on the other hand, found McCloy a cautious ally in their efforts to persuade the government to take the first steps toward desegregation of the army. In these and many other "civilian" issues, McCloy represented the military. He became the country's first national-security manager, a sort of "political commissar" who quietly brokered any issue where civilian political interests threatened to interfere with the military's effort to win the war.[1]

One evening late in July 1942, *The New York Times'* Arthur Krock happened to drive by McCloy's Georgetown home just as McCloy was leaving for dinner. Krock later sent him a joshing note describing what he had seen: "There you were, dressed in spotless white linen and what (at a distance) seemed to be gleaming pumps and a Sulka evening bow-tie—with a skimmer covering the only part of you where nature has not showered every gift—there you were being handed out of your door by a government blackamoor. . . . There you were, on your way to who knows what stimulating mental and social encounters. . . . How I envied you. . . ."[2]

At forty-seven, McCloy was still a relatively young man in a city dominated by men of Stimson's generation. He relished the quiet power he wielded in the nation's capital, a city that still preserved the intimate atmosphere of a small Southern town. His was not a household name outside of Washington, but on Capitol Hill or in the salons of Georgetown, he was a familiar fixture. His easy informality also made him an accessible source of information to the press. That August, *Time* magazine ran a short, friendly profile of him which mentioned only in passing his role in the Japanese American internment. "Affable and efficient," wrote *Time*'s writers, "he hurries conversation along with a pleasant 'yep, yep,' puffs away at thick cigars, flicks the ashes deftly into a wastebasket four feet away, occasionally extracts a bell-shaped chocolate drop from a pile on his desk. His duties have included everything from handling administrative details of the Army training program to moving Japanese off the West Coast. Everyone who knows him gives him top marks."[3]

Among other administrative tasks, McCloy supervised the construction of new office quarters for the War Department. The army wanted to build a five-sided, four-million-square-foot building, the largest office-complex in the world.[4] But long after construction had commenced, Roosevelt continued to tinker with the architectural plans, making small changes that delayed the project. On several occasions, McCloy tried to intercede through FDR's personal aide, "Pa" Watson, but each time he had been put off with the message that the president thought he could improve the plans.

Finally, a Secret Service official visited McCloy's office one day and reported that the president needed a personal favor from the War Department. Could McCloy find suitable accommodations for an enemy alien, an old Harvard friend of Roosevelt's, named Ernst "Putzi" Hanfstaengl? McCloy recognized the name from his Black Tom investigations. Hanfstaengl had fled his job as Nazi Germany's foreign-press spokesman in 1937, after a falling out with Hitler, and had ended up in a Canadian internment camp when the war broke out. He had appealed to Roosevelt, who now wanted his old friend brought to Washington in the care of the U.S. Army. McCloy saw at once the political delicacy involved in such a request; the president wished to help his old friend but also to insulate himself from certain embarrassment if it became known that he had somehow extended favors to Hitler's former "court jester."

The "somewhat ungracious idea" occurred to McCloy to exchange Hanfstaengl for Roosevelt's final approval of the Pentagon construction plans. McCloy told the Secret Service officer he could probably take care of Hanfstaengl but that he would need a particular favor from the president. A short time later, the Pentagon plans came back signed, "OK, FDR." Soon afterward, McCloy was in a White House meeting when the president was wheeled in. Upon seeing the assistant secretary of war, Roosevelt said, "Hello, McCloy, you blackmailer." When the others in the meeting asked what he meant, the president laughed and said, "Never mind, he understands."[5]

After the Pentagon was completed in 1942, many people gave it poor reviews. When Harold Ickes had a chance to see it, he declared the number of offices without windows "unpardonable." The interior secretary noted for his diary, "I would even have preferred a sky-scraper rather than subject employees to such working conditions." Because McCloy had supervised the project in its final stages, the press took to calling it "McCloy's Folly."[6] This did not stop Drew Pearson from reporting in his "Washington Merry-Go-Round" column, "Newsmen who know Assistant Secretary of War John McCloy agree with the sergeant in his office who says, 'He's really rated as the most cleverest man in this building.' "[7]

Off and on during the early part of the war, McCloy participated in the debate over where and when to open a second front against Nazi-occupied Europe. Immediately after the Midway victory in June 1942, Churchill visited Washington again, since he feared Roosevelt might be "getting a little off the rails. . . ."[8] Specifically, the prime minister was worried about a comment Roosevelt made to Lord Louis Mountbatten, then serving as chief of combined operations, that the Allies might still have to make a "sacrifice" cross-Channel invasion of France in 1942 in order to keep the Soviet Union in the war.[9] He had also heard that both Stimson and Marshall were stubbornly pushing ahead with preparations for a full-fledged invasion in 1943, code-named Operation Bolero. Churchill was determined to sidetrack any such early cross-Channel attack. Shocked by the recent loss of Tobruk to Field Marshal Rommel's forces in the Libyan desert, he once again urged Roosevelt to commit American troops to North Africa. FDR was inclined to do what Churchill asked, but he had to contend with the opposition of his war secretary. Stimson bluntly warned the two heads of state that "if we were delayed by diversions I foresaw that Bolero would not be made in '43 and that the whole war effort might be endangered. . . ."[10] In the end, Roosevelt characteristically tried to give both Stimson and Churchill what they wanted. On paper, Churchill agreed that a cross-Channel invasion in 1943 would be pursued with "all speed and energy."[11] Depending on Russian need, an emergency cross-Channel invasion, code-named Operation Sledgehammer, would be considered for the autumn of 1942. But the British prime minister insisted that if Sledgehammer was found to be improbable, the Allies "must be ready with an alternative."[12] Furthermore, they agreed that the alternative of a landing in North Africa—Operation Gymnast—would be explored in all its details, though a decision could be postponed until September.[13]

McCloy thought the president should leave strategic planning to such military professionals as Marshall. He believed it "took a hard-driving, ruthless man to win a war and that the President was not of this type."[14] Nevertheless, he disagreed with Marshall's estimation that only a cross-Channel attack into the heart of Nazi Europe would win the war. He shared the same reservations Churchill had about Operation Sledgehammer, feeling that, ". . . even after a most terrific assault from the air and water, there would be German fortifications and German troops ready to resist our advance." If the Allied assault troops were thrown back, a very good possibility, the "whole free world will feel discouraged."[15] Throughout the summer, he tried to impress upon Stimson the importance of Middle Eastern oil and the strategic viability of a North African operation. Stimson would have none of it; he began to call McCloy his "Middle Easterner," and regularly threw him out of his office whenever he started to argue the point.[16]

The issue came to a head on July 8, when Churchill cabled Roosevelt that under no circumstances would Britain participate in a cross-Channel invasion in 1942. Instead, he said, Operation Gymnast, a landing in French West Africa, posed "by far the best chance for effecting relief to the Russian front in 1942." Gymnast "is the Second Front of 1942."[17]

Stimson, Marshall, General Thomas T. Handy, Admiral Ernest J. King, and the rest of the American High Command were outraged by Churchill's unilateral decision. Stimson raged that "if they [the British] persist in their fatuous defeatist position . . ." he would recommend that an ultimatum be issued. On July 12, he accepted a memorandum for Roosevelt drafted by Marshall and Handy which warned that, if "the British won't go through with what they agreed to, we will turn our backs on them and take up the war with Japan."[18] After having a "vigorous discussion" with McCloy over the issue, Stimson thought his arguments "had pretty well knocked that [McCloy's Middle Eastern views] out of him."[19] McCloy, in his amiable fashion, may have left that impression with his boss, but he was not in fact convinced. Nor was Roosevelt, who quickly vetoed the ultimatum.[20]

Instead, the president ordered Marshall, Harry Hopkins, and Admiral King to join General Eisenhower in London in order to reach immediate agreement with the British on strategic plans for the remainder of 1942. In London on July 22, Marshall did his best to convince the British Cabinet that "without Sledgehammer we were faced with a defensive attitude in the European theatre."[21] The British, however, were steadfast in their opposition. Two days later, Marshall told his British counterparts that Roosevelt had agreed to scrap Sledgehammer in favor of an expanded North African invasion, now to be called Operation Torch. This news greatly angered Joseph Stalin, who had been promised that the British and Americans would open a second front in Europe sometime in 1942. He protested the decision in most emphatic terms, telling Churchill in a cable on July 23 that "the Soviet government cannot acquiesce in the postponement of a second front in Europe until 1943."[22] There was, however, nothing Stalin could do except to hope that his troops could hold the Eastern front. Many British and American lives were no doubt saved by the decision to delay a cross-Channel attack. But these lives were paid for at the cost of many more Soviet lives. This fact cast a pall of bitterness and distrust among the Allies for the duration of the war—and long afterward.

In retrospect, it is easy to see that the decision to invade North Africa delayed the decisive cross-Channel invasion of Europe until 1944. Churchill, McCloy, and other critics of Sledgehammer may have been right that a premature cross-Channel invasion in 1942 could have been very costly. And there is no reason to question their judgment regarding the importance of the Middle Eastern theaters, both for their oil resources and as a supply route to the Soviet Union. Hitler himself had focused much of German strategy on seizing the Caucasus oil fields from the Soviet Union and pushing the British out of Egypt. But by the time the decision was made to divert resources from a cross-Channel invasion of Europe to an invasion of North Africa, the British had finally halted the advance of Rommel's armies at the first Battle of El Alamein, on July 1–3, 1942. Egypt and the Middle Eastern oil fields to the east were secure, and therefore the justifications McCloy had given Stimson for a North African invasion ever since December 1941 were no longer so compelling. Stimson and Marshall were never impressed by these arguments to begin with, and now had only acquiesced to Torch in the face of Churchill's intransigence. They were convinced that a strategic mistake had been made which would prolong the war.

The invasion of North Africa began at midnight on November 8, 1942, and it immediately precipitated a political crisis within Allied ranks. Eisenhower had been assured by his own intelligence people that the Vichy French troops would lay down their arms without a fight. The president's emissary to the Vichy government, Robert Murphy, was sure that the Vichy would respond to an appeal for cooperation broadcast by General Henri Giraud, a French general of some stature who had recently escaped from a Nazi prison in France. But Murphy had greatly miscalculated Giraud's stature, and the Allied troops encountered fierce resistance at several points. Within three days, Eisenhower's troops were in control of Casablanca, Oran, and Algiers; but they had suffered eighteen hundred casualties, and continued resistance by Vichy troops now jeopardized Eisenhower's major objective, Tunis. When Ike discovered that Admiral Jean Darlan, the commander-in-chief of all Vichy forces in France, happened to be in Algiers on the night of the invasion, he quickly authorized a deal: in return for his cooperation, Darlan would be made high commissioner of Allied-occupied North Africa. On November 13, Darlan met Eisenhower in Algiers and accepted these terms.

As soon as the Darlan deal became public knowledge, there was an outcry in the American press, which depicted Darlan quite accurately as a Nazi collaborator and an anti-Semite. McCloy, however, had no doubts about the Darlan agreement.[23] If Eisenhower thought it had saved lives, then Washington had to support him. In any case, since the collapse of France in June 1940, Roosevelt had continued diplomatic relations with Marshal Henri Pétain's government and denied recognition of General Charles de Gaulle's Free French Committee. Both Stimson and McCloy had supported Roosevelt's Vichy policy. McCloy's early attitude toward de Gaulle had been influenced by his good friend Jean Monnet, who thought the general sounded like a dictator.[24] Over the next few months, however, both Monnet and McCloy began to alter their views.

In this, McCloy was influenced by Walter Lippmann, who had met de Gaulle in August 1942. Treated to an hour-long monologue of the general's opinions, Lippmann had returned to give a speech in which he proclaimed de Gaulle and his French National Committee the "true leaders of the French nation."[25] Lippmann was decidedly critical of the Darlan affair. After being read a cable from Eisenhower justifying the deal, he sent McCloy a long memorandum on "Our Relations with Darlan." Lippmann acknowledged the military necessity of using Darlan, but he skewered the War Department for a failure of political intelligence: "On the critical points of resistance and collaboration in North Africa, General de Gaulle's intelligence service was more accurate than our own, and it will be a grievous error to continue to ignore it." He told McCloy that Washington's attitude should be that Darlan "is being spared from the consequences of his treachery to France and to the Allies by making partial restitution for his crimes." The admiral should be compelled to "annul step by step the Vichy decrees" that discriminated against Jews.[26] Lippmann's arguments impressed McCloy, and his pragmatic instincts led him to conclude that, if de Gaulle and his "Fighting French" could do more for the war effort, then Washington should deal with the imperious general.

Viewed from Washington, the situation in North Africa had now become a major political embarrassment. The president issued a statement backing Eisenhower, but emphasized the "temporary" nature of the arrangement. By the end of November, it was clear that Eisenhower had paid a high political price for marginal military gains. Churchill, who had pushed so ardently for the North African campaign, now complained, "I never meant the Anglo-American Army to be stuck in North Africa. It is a spring-board and not a sofa."[27] With twenty-five thousand new German troops landed in Tunis, and Eisenhower spending a good deal of his time on political matters in Algiers, the North African front was indeed beginning to look like a sofa.

Then, on Christmas Eve, a French royalist named Bonnier de la Chapelle disposed of the Allies' most embarrassing irritant by assassinating Admiral Darlan. Motivated by his royalist political beliefs, the assassin nevertheless had been supplied with a weapon and encouraged by the British Secret Operations Executive.[28] McCloy was not aware of the plot, but he certainly welcomed its outcome. Several days later, he wrote Walter Lippmann a short note saying, "I hope the de Gaulle people can work out a policy which will permit them quickly to fight with Giraud."[29] These sentiments marked McCloy as a Gaullist, particularly in an administration that was still vigorously promoting de Gaulle's remaining rival, General Giraud.[30]

Though it eliminated a political embarrassment, Darlan's assassination did not lay to rest the animosities between de Gaulle's Free French organization and the Giraudists. Eisenhower did not have the patience to deal with such political annoyances; he was tired of all these "Frogs," these "little, selfish, conceited worms that call themselves men."[31] In early January 1943, he begged that McCloy be sent to handle political affairs in occupied North Africa. Marshall liked the idea, if only because he thought it would allow Eisenhower to concentrate on capturing Tunis. But when he approached Stimson and explained that Eisenhower needed McCloy as a "loan" for a "month or two," Stimson balked. Informed of Marshall's request while on vacation in North Carolina, Stimson immediately phoned McCloy and had him fly down to discuss the proposed "loan" in person. Over dinner, Stimson told McCloy that, though it was important not to disappoint Eisenhower, he had decided that, if his most valuable aide was to be loaned, he was going to write the terms of the contract. When McCloy returned to Washington the next day, he had in his pocket strict instructions to spend no longer than a month in North Africa.[32]

McCloy was ecstatic. At last he would get a tour of the front lines. The trip was set, though his departure date was postponed until after the president returned from his meeting with Churchill in Casablanca. A few days later, he had a private session with the president, who typically spent the entire meeting telling stories about his recent trip. Later that afternoon, McCloy and Ellen came by Stimson's for tea, and everyone was amused at his description of his first private meeting with FDR.[33]

Before leaving for North Africa, McCloy hosted a party for Harvey Bundy's son William, who was marrying Dean Acheson's daughter, Mary. The marriage and McCloy's party were major events on Washington's social calendar that month, bringing together dozens of Washington's wartime elite. McCloy enjoyed these social events, but on occasion he found some Washington affairs far too lavish. Earlier in January 1943, he had told Ickes about a recent dinner hosted by Bernard Baruch. Food of all sorts was extravagantly stacked across buffet tables, and half the guests, said McCloy, seemed to be high-ranking army and navy officers, while the other half "consisted of very rich people from Long Island." Ellen had cast her eye over the affair and called it all very "vulgar."[34]

On February 10, 1943, McCloy boarded a plane for North Africa. Five days later, having flown by way of Brazil, Gambia, and Senegal, his party of eight arrived in Casablanca. On the plane, McCloy devoured a number of reports about the political mess in North Africa. One of these focused on the fact that Vichy restrictions against Jews were still actively enforced in Giraud's North Africa. The Gaullists—and the American press—were having a field day excoriating this blatant marriage of Eisenhower's North African occupation with French fascism. McCloy realized his first task would be to convince Giraud to abrogate any of the Vichy laws discriminating against Jews. In this, he had the good fortune to be assisted by Jean Monnet, who arrived in North Africa the same month to become Giraud's political adviser.

The two men spent much of the next few weeks trying to educate Giraud—and Eisenhower—on the political and public-relations realities of the Jewish question. On March 1, just before leaving for an inspection of the front lines, McCloy admonished Eisenhower, "Things are moving too slowly toward the liberalization of restrictions on personal freedom. I can find no good reason why the Nazi laws still obtain here."[35] A few days later, Eisenhower and Giraud began dismantling the Vichy Nuremberg laws, specifically the quotas placed on the number of Jews allowed to engage in various professions and businesses.

McCloy's political savvy in such matters was warmly welcomed by the newly appointed British resident minister for North Africa, Harold Macmillan, whom he met on February 26. Only four days earlier, Macmillan had survived a plane crash and had suffered severe burns across much of his face. But he made a point of briefing McCloy and greeting him at a formal welcoming dinner. He noted in his diary that McCloy was "very intelligent and interesting. . . . He seemed much more like a fellow member of the House of Commons or a minister in a British Cabinet than the ordinary American politician. I was able to say some things to him about the situation here which I cannot get Murphy to understand."[36]

Through Macmillan and Monnet, McCloy's previous impression of de Gaulle's Free French was reinforced. All three men that spring could see that the politically adroit and ambitious general was rapidly undermining Giraud's authority as high commissioner. Regular French soldiers and French merchantmen were defecting to join the "Fighting French" forces. In popular demonstrations in the streets of Algiers, the crowds changed de Gaulle's name. The reality, as Monnet and others told McCloy, was that de Gaulle was no longer a mere symbol of French resistance. Even within occupied France itself, the organized resistance publicly swore allegiance to Charles de Gaulle. Built up and financed by the British since 1940, de Gaulle could now be discarded only at the risk of serious political and even military setbacks. American policy, in this instance guided by Roosevelt's personal dislike of the Frenchman, was simply unrealistic. So, throughout the spring of 1943, while ostensibly serving as a political adviser to Giraud, Monnet quietly worked to achieve a peaceful transition of political power into the hands of de Gaulle's French Committee of National Liberation. As Ambassador Murphy complained later in a memo to Roosevelt, "Jean Monnet arrived with a definite objective—to sell French unity. . . . He counts greatly on the support of Jack McCloy and Felix Frankfurter."[37]

Eisenhower had little time to absorb such political dynamics. McCloy had arrived in Algiers in the midst of Ike's first direct command of a set-piece military engagement, the Battle of the Kasserine Pass in Tunisia. Nothing had gone right. Rommel won a clear tactical victory, destroying hundreds of tanks and half-tracks, and inflicting more than five thousand American casualties at little loss to his own forces. Despite this humiliating defeat, McCloy still felt that Eisenhower was the right general in the right place. In an effort to shore up Ike's confidence, he wrote him, "I have opposed the Germans in many ways during my adult life. They have a way of testing your complete strength and they are most apt to bring you to the point of exhaustion before you prevail. I have no doubt . . . that your strength will withstand any test they can apply."[38]

McCloy spent a brief time at the battlefront during this period and grilled dozens of officers and enlisted men on everything from battle tactics to supplies. One day, during a tour of the front lines, he observed a soldier having difficulty firing a bazooka. He promptly got out of his jeep and showed the soldier how to assemble and fire the gun.

After three weeks in North Africa, Stimson impatiently began cabling his assistant to return home immediately. So, on March 9, 1943, McCloy and his party finally boarded a C-54 aircraft bound for America. A full week later, the plane landed safely in Charleston, South Carolina, where Stimson had been vacationing. The war secretary immediately took his favorite aide to the local clubhouse and spent the rest of the afternoon and evening listening to his "adventures which were very thrilling and interesting."[39]

McCloy had returned convinced more than ever of the inevitability of de Gaulle's political ascendancy. For the next few months, he quietly tried to educate Stimson and the president on the realities of the political situation in North Africa. Taken by Stimson one day to a Cabinet meeting, he put in a pitch for recognition of de Gaulle's status. Roosevelt brushed aside these arguments; seeing how annoyed the president was, Harry Hopkins noted on a piece of White House stationery, "One more crack from McCloy to the Boss about de Gaulle and McCloy is out of here."[40]

Throughout the war, McCloy was privy to the highest-level decisions on how to manage it. At the Trident Conference, held in Washington in May 1943, he was constantly by Stimson's side, taking notes and whispering into the secretary's ear. Through two solid weeks of negotiations, he watched as the Allied leaders renewed the debate on when to open a second front in Europe. Stimson was thoroughly annoyed with Churchill for "trying to divert us off into some more Mediterranean adventures."[41] He was greatly relieved when Roosevelt finally insisted upon and received British agreement to a date for a cross-Channel invasion of France. Operation Bolero—the buildup of an invasion force in Britain—would now result in a cross-Channel attack (Operation Roundup) by May 1944. As Stimson and Marshall had feared, the opening of a second front had been postponed by the invasion of North Africa. Roosevelt and Churchill were well aware that Stalin had never considered the occupation of North Africa a substitute for a second front. Now they agonized over how to tell him that a second front would not take place in 1943. As a substitute, they decided to promise Stalin that an invasion of Italy from North Africa—Operation Husky—would take Hitler's major ally out of the war. Informed of these decisions, Stalin complained in an angry cable that this left "the Soviet Army, which is fighting not only for its country, but also for its Allies, to do the job alone, almost single-handed, against an enemy that is still very strong and formidable."[42]

McCloy was aware of one other closely guarded decision reached at Trident. Churchill and Roosevelt formally agreed that their two countries would pool their scientific expertise in the production of "Tube Alloys," the code name for the project to develop an atomic bomb. McCloy was one of a handful of War Department officials aware of the Manhattan Project. He, Harvey Bundy, Robert Lovett, and George L. Harrison (a president of New York Life Insurance Co. who moonlighted for Stimson as a special civilian consultant) were cautious about what they said to one another about the project. It was rarely mentioned in the office; instead, Stimson would sometimes lead a discussion on it in the privacy of his Woodley estate. None of Stimson's aides were really competent to discuss the mechanics of the experimental weapon, but they were quite aware of its unique potential. The bomb was always in the back of McCloy's mind. Sometime late in 1942 or in 1943, he had visited the closely guarded facility at Oak Ridge, Tennessee, where an entirely new town was being built to accommodate some thirteen thousand workers.[43] A great deal of money was obviously being spent by the Manhattan Engineering District; after being shown around the construction site, he thought it was all just too complex for him to grasp. Indeed, the project was so expensive and so secret that Stimson sometimes worried that Congress might censure him for spending so much money on such a speculative venture.[44]

Another problem thrown on McCloy's desk in the spring of 1943 concerned the War Department's treatment of veterans of the Abraham Lincoln Brigade, who had fought with the Loyalists against Franco in the late 1930s. Some five hundred veterans of the antifascist fight in Spain were serving in the U.S. Army. Many of them were educated, officer-candidate material, but most were politically leftist or had once been members of the Communist Party. Consequently, as Brigade veterans were about to complete their officer training, an army security check frequently resulted in a recommendation for their dismissal from officer training school. Denied a commission, these "premature" antifascists were often still eager to volunteer for combat duty. But the army refused them even this opportunity, and instead placed them in labor battalions or low-security logistics units.

In April 1943, Harold Ickes wrote a stiff letter to Stimson, complaining that such discrimination was "shocking."[45] When similar complaints began to appear in press reports, McCloy requested an internal investigation. He quickly learned that two months earlier the War Department's security board had issued a new policy "to remove the discrimination between Communists and others in the Army which prevented known Communists from having combat duty." Henceforth, party members would be allowed to qualify for combat units; communists would be treated "just as any other soldier. . . ." There was, however, a catch: those individuals with current "communistic tendencies" could remain with their regular units "unless the circumstances of the case are unusually aggravated and the individual is in a sensitive organization."[46]

McCloy was told that in practice this meant that many Brigade veterans were disqualified: ". . . if a soldier was formerly a Communist that fact will, of course, be considered in determining whether or not he should be commissioned. . . ." The individual might still receive a commission if he was no longer a party member, had never been an active party leader, and had a record indicating "complete freedom from Communist influence."[47] McCloy considered this a pretty fair compromise.

Throughout the remainder of the war, his office served as an informal court of appeals for many leftists and Lincoln Brigade veterans. Over lunch one day late that summer, he acknowledged to Ickes that Americans who had fought for Loyalist Spain were still being discriminated against in the army. But he said he was trying to do all he could to allow all those Brigade veterans who "are not Communists and who have not been too radical" to have their officer commissions. As Ickes wrote in his diary, "McCloy thinks that it is perfectly foolish to penalize a man simply on the ground that he is a radical. . . . McCloy says that they [Lincoln Brigade veterans] are not only good soldiers but much smarter than the average."[48]

On the other hand, McCloy sanctioned punitive measures against individuals who openly advertised their Communist Party affiliations. If an officer candidate had once expressed radical opinions or had fought Franco in Spain, these facts alone would not be held against him. But evidence of current communist beliefs—such as attending Young Communist League dances or having current subscriptions to Communist Party publications—was another matter. During the rest of the war, dozens of officer candidates with such black marks on their security files were dismissed from officer training school and immediately sent overseas to a combat unit.[49] A reform that had begun by allowing Lincoln Brigade veterans to volunteer for combat duty had now become part of a systematic policy: alleged communists were automatically ordered into the front lines of combat.

That summer, McCloy focused on another issue of discrimination, that against Negro soldiers. Before the war was over, some eight hundred thousand blacks would serve in the U.S. Armed Services. The army's racial policies had remained unchanged since World War I; blacks served in segregated units and were not allowed the use of recreational facilities frequented by white soldiers. None of these segregated units could expect to see combat. Black morale was so low that by the summer of 1943 the army was, in the words of one army historian, reaping a "harvest of disorders."[50] Race riots broke out at army installations in California, Mississippi, Kentucky, Texas, and Georgia. The judge advocate general labeled these racial disorders acts of "mutiny."[51]

Stimson and Marshall turned to McCloy to handle the crisis. When similar riots had occurred the previous summer, Stimson had appointed McCloy chairman of something called the Advisory Committee on Negro Troop Policy. Created in August 1942, the McCloy Committee, as it was known, had been dormant for most of the year.[52] McCloy had been content to study the problem of Negro morale, evaluate specific racial incidents, and receive recommendations on the training and assignment of black soldiers. He was aware of Stimson's racial attitudes and recognized that the War Department was not prepared to launch any radical experiments in racial integration.

Stimson simply believed that Negroes were too backward to be relied upon to fight in a modern army. He scorned Eleanor Roosevelt and the "foolish leaders of the colored race" for seeking full "social equality." This, Stimson believed, could never happen "because of the impossibility of race mixture by marriage."[53]

One of these "foolish leaders" was Judge William H. Hastie, dean of Howard University's law school, who in 1940 had been selected by Roosevelt to serve as Stimson's civilian aide on Negro affairs. To Stimson's annoyance, Hastie had assumed an activist stance within the department, urging the department to experiment with some kind of plan that would lead to the progressive integration of the armed services. By late 1941, his proposals were still not particularly radical: he advocated only the assignment of a few qualified Negroes into regular army units. But even such a gradualist approach was rejected by Stimson and Marshall.[54]

Judge Hastie, however, repeatedly argued that segregation was "the most dramatic evidence of hypocrisy" in a war America was supposedly fighting in defense of democratic values. Didn't such racial segregation give the lie to America's ringing denunciations of Nazi Germany's racial theories? After one such lecture from Hastie, McCloy told the judge, "Frankly, I do not think that the basic issues of this war are involved in the question of whether colored troops serve in segregated units or in mixed units and I doubt whether you can convince people of the United States that the basic issues of freedom are involved in such a question." Moreover, McCloy observed, some Negroes "do not seem to be vitally concerned about winning the war." If the war was lost, he said, the black community would suffer disproportionately. They ought to demonstrate their unswerving cooperation in the war effort now, in the hope that racial relations would improve after the war.[55]

Despite this reprimand, Judge Hastie made some progress against the army's policies, and most of the time he found in McCloy an ally. In late 1942, he had brought to McCloy's attention the fact that the Women's Army Auxillary Corps was still segregating Negro candidates in officer training school. This was at a time when most other such schools had been quietly and informally integrated, at least in the classroom. McCloy took measures to integrate the school.[56] There were other such victories, most notably the establishment of an aviation unit at Tuskegee where qualified Negroes were trained to fly combat aircraft.

By January 1943, however, Judge Hastie was tired of such marginal progress and decided to submit his resignation. Segregation was still practiced in military-post theaters, blood-plasma banks, mess halls, and recreational facilities throughout the armed services. He complained that even those Negroes who were receiving combat training, such as the 99th Fighter Squadron, were not being used in combat. Such continued injustices, he said, brought into question "the sincerity and depth of our devotion to basic issues of the war." Hastie concluded that he could best accelerate reforms as a "private citizen who can express himself freely and publicly."[57]

The judge's decision to go public had an almost immediate effect: stung by Hastie's criticisms, the chief of the air staff wrote McCloy a week later promising that the all Negro 99th Fighter Squadron would see combat. For the next six months, Hastie and other Negro civilian leaders kept up the pressure on the War Department to change its policies. But not until the summer of 1943, when racial disorders erupted on many army facilities, did the McCloy Committee ask the army to take some concrete steps toward racial integration. Citing "riots of a racial character" at six army bases around the country, McCloy wrote Marshall that he thought it was time the army changed its policies. All these incidents, he said, had been incited by some specific allegation of discrimination. He urged that the army now adopt a policy of nondiscrimination regarding any base privileges, housing, or recreational facilities. Negro soldiers should be subjected to the same disciplinary standards as whites. "Discipline," he told Marshall, "is not a matter of intelligence."[58]

Marshall responded to McCloy's July memo by urging base commanders to prevent individual acts of discrimination. Racial incidents could be avoided if base commanders censured "improper conduct of either white or negro soldiers, among themselves or toward each other." Regarding base facilities, Marshall fell back on an assertion of equal treatment, and ordered that "adequate facilities and accommodations will be provided negro troops." This could have amounted to empty words, but later that month, McCloy persuaded the adjutant general to issue orders that henceforth all base recreational facilities would be open to any soldier, irrespective of race.[59] As official policy, its effect took some time to permeate day-to-day army practice, and for the remainder of the war McCloy was occasionally forced to rebuke individual commanders for not integrating their officers' clubs. But there was no doubt that black leaders felt a measure of vindication in focusing their campaign for integration on the army.

The integration of army recreational facilities was a significant and highly visible step toward racial integration, not only within the military, but in American society at large. It was, however, a far cry from integrated combat units. And, with the exception of the 99th Fighter Squadron, McCloy did not persuade Marshall and Stimson of the wisdom of allowing black soldiers combat experience until the summer of 1944, when manpower shortages became acute. He then argued, "With so large a portion of our population colored, with the example of the effective use of colored troops (of a much lower order of intelligence) by other nations, and with the many imponderables that are connected with the situation, we must, I think, be more affirmative about the use of our Negro troops."[60]

This time, General Marshall agreed to the experimental transfer of regimental combat teams from the 92nd and 93rd divisions to the Italian front. Advance elements of the 92nd Division arrived in Italy in July and performed well in combat. Their performance paved the way for further small shipments of black troops overseas. These troops quickly became a source of pride to the black community, and McCloy made sure their experiences were widely publicized in black newspapers at home.[61]

Late in the war, he could even sound a little boastful, arguing in a letter to the editor of the *Washington Post* that the army had "largely eliminated discrimination against the Negroes within its ranks, going further in this direction than the country itself."[62] Discrimination had certainly not been eliminated, but he could truthfully say he had done more to break down the barriers of segregation within the army than any other white government official.

By the summer of 1943, the war on all fronts was going well for the Allies. North Africa had been conquered, MacArthur's forces were steadily clearing the Japanese from the South Pacific, the air war was taking a severe toll on Germany's civilian population, and, most important, the third Nazi summer offensive in as many years against the Soviets had again been stymied. Soon Stalin's forces took the offensive, pushing the Germans back at Orel. Simultaneously, a British-American invasion force landed in Sicily and encountered less resistance than had been expected.

McCloy was optimistic enough about the impending campaign in

Italy that in mid-June he came into Stimson's office and speculated that Italy might soon sue for peace.[63] Stimson was not nearly so optimistic. In London that July, he distressed the British by once again "passionately advocating an early shock offensive across the Channel."[64] McCloy still disagreed. Over lunch one day not long afterward, he told Harold Ickes that ". . . Stimson had not changed his mind. He still thought that we should have landed somewhere on the coast of France [instead of North Africa in 1942]. McCloy said that if we had done this our casualties would have been terrific and perhaps when we had struck North Africa it would have been too late."[65]

McCloy and Ickes now made a habit of lunching together as often as once a month. The iconoclastic New Dealer invariably found McCloy full of gossip and well informed about events. On one occasion, they discussed the air war against Germany. That summer, Allied Bomber Command had moved from precision bombing of specific war-production factories and military installations to experimenting with fire-bombing. The most successful of these attacks occurred over Hamburg on the evening of July 27, 1943. In one night, Allied bombers dropped enough bombs to engulf the entire city in flames; at least forty-five thousand Germans were killed, most of them women, children, and the elderly.[66] If McCloy had any doubts about such fire-bombing, he did not express them to Ickes. On the contrary, he hoped that "once we get over the hump" the bombing raids would be able to inflict terrible damage with fewer crew losses.[67] Ickes did not disagree.

In mid-November 1943, Stimson decided to send McCloy as his representative to the Allied conference in Cairo. Fearful that Churchill would once again try to delay the invasion of France (the prime minister was at the moment asking Eisenhower to divert landing craft for an invasion of Rhodes), Stimson gave McCloy a "pep talk" on Overlord, as the cross-Channel invasion plan was now code-named. He told his aide that he was entrusting to him a task of immense responsibility, and he emphasized the "importance of giving a lead and courage to a lot of doubtful men."[68] His sermon ended, Stimson boarded a plane bound for his Highhold estate in New York, where he planned a few days' rest.

A couple of days later, McCloy was in the air himself, traveling with Lew Douglas, Sir John Dill, and several staff officers. He wrote in his trip diary, "There is something of a very concrete nature to accomplish and it will mean taking part in an historical incident. How far away from 874 North 20th Street [his childhood home in Philadelphia] it all is; yet it all ties back to there. . . ."[69]

The plane took the tedious wartime route, through Brazil to West Africa. Flying across the Atlantic, he had a long talk with Dill, chief of the British Joint Staff Mission in Washington. Like most British officials, Dill disparaged the need for a cross-Channel attack, telling McCloy, "By all standards Germany should give in by January. . . ." McCloy thought otherwise and diplomatically cautioned his friend, "We have to expect another tough blow from them before we win."[70]

Upon landing in Cairo on the afternoon of November 20, 1943, McCloy was driven to the Giza district, on the outskirts of the city. Quarters were reserved for him and Douglas in Villa 22 on the famous Mena House estate, where the conference would take place.[71] The site overlooked the three Great Pyramids. In a short note back to Stimson, McCloy observed, "We rest on the site of the Battle of the Pyramids and at least forty centuries look down upon us. I trust that our efforts will prove more lasting than were Napoleon's in this area."[72]

Because the president was not scheduled to arrive for two days, McCloy, Douglas, and twenty-one other passengers took off in a four-engine C-54 plane for a day-long excursion to Jerusalem. They almost didn't make it. Fifteen minutes after takeoff, the plane's number-two engine sputtered and died. As they were approaching Lydda Airport in Palestine, their number-three engine sputtered as well, but the plane landed safely on three engines. McCloy immediately reported the incident and told military intelligence that he suspected sabotage; the subsequent investigation, however, revealed nothing.[73]

This one-day visit to Palestine gave McCloy his first direct exposure to the political problems surrounding Zionism. An American Franciscan priest named Father Pascal took his party around Jerusalem on a guided tour. They visited all the usual holy places, including the Holy Sepulcher, which McCloy thought "tawdry." Soon their conversation turned to the "Palestine question" and specifically the "Jews' disregard of the Arab," concerning which McCloy concluded, "I gather there was a good bit of bitterness. . . ."[74]

Back in Cairo that Sunday evening, he had dinner at the home of the U.S. minister to Egypt, Alexander C. Kirk. Also invited were Lew Douglas and Averell Harriman. McCloy had not seen Harriman for many months. Only the previous October, Harriman had been shifted from London to become Roosevelt's ambassador in Moscow. At one point in the evening, Harriman took McCloy aside and emphasized that the Russians firmly believed that it was well within the powers of America and Britain to "take more [Nazi] divisions off their front than we had thus far accomplished." And though they now took for granted that Overlord would be launched the following spring, they also wanted the Allies to do something, somewhere, during the current winter season.

Over the next few days, McCloy had several long luncheons with General Marshall, Bill Donovan, and his British counterparts. In between these meetings, he found some army officers who could play a decent game of tennis and even took some time out with Marshall for a tour of the Great Pyramids. At noon on Thanksgiving Day, he was summoned to the Kirk villa for a photo session. The president, Churchill, Chiang Kai-shek, and all their top aides gathered in the garden to pose for the photographers. It was a dry, warm, and thoroughly pleasant day. McCloy stood next to Harry Hopkins on the fringe of the group. Harold Macmillan described the scene for his diary: ". . . it was really like a sort of mad garden party in a newsreel produced of *Alice in Wonderland.*"[75] Afterward, McCloy had lunch with Roosevelt, Hopkins, and Lord Leathers, the British minister for war transport. On the agenda was a discussion about civil-affairs matters, specifically Allied policy for occupying Germany.

The British had already passed to the president a copy of Operation Rankin, a contingency plan for the occupation of Germany if there were a sudden collapse of Nazi authority in Berlin. Rankin envisioned dividing Germany up into a number of occupation zones. When McCloy cabled Washington for instructions as to whether the United States preferred to be allocated a northern or a southern occupation zone, he received back an "eyes-only" cable saying that the State Department had no view. Moreover, he was told that Secretary of State Hull only wished that it be emphasized in any negotiations over Rankin that "no advantage shall accrue to the U.S. or to any of our allies" from any such occupation zones.[76] This struck McCloy as evading the realities. The United States was going to have to make some political choices before the war ended, and McCloy believed they should be made in Washington, not London.

He warned Hopkins, "On every cracker barrel in every country store in the U.S. there is someone sitting who is convinced that we get hornswoggled every time we attend a European conference." As the war progressed toward a favorable conclusion, he argued, the GIs would want to return home and the American people would wish "to liquidate the European involvement." These tendencies, McCloy told Hopkins, would ultimately be "fatal to both British and American interests." The British had to recognize, he thought, that it was in their interest to have the postwar future of Europe determined in Washington, not London.[77]

This was not a simple jurisdictional dispute. McCloy could see that the British were prepared to strike deals with the Soviets that the Americans were not yet ready to contemplate, and he felt frustrated that Washington hadn't given more thought to these political issues. "I get the impression," he wrote Stimson, "from my observations of how this conference operates that British military strategy is greatly influenced by British political strategy. . . . They act as if they believe thoroughly Clausewitz's doctrine that military and state policy are interwoven and that one is merely the other in a different form." He then went on to complain that, whereas the British political strategy was pronounced, the "*lack* of one on our side has been just as pronounced."

He asked Stimson if the United States intended, in the aftermath of the war, to assert any economic or political interests outside its own borders. If so, such interests should be carefully defined, "so that our military people can act on it." He suggested the United States ought to know now what "economic or other concessions we seek in Europe or the Pacific. . . . Our concept of what [is] the best re-arrangement of boundaries in Europe from an economic, military and political point of view should be known." He suggested the formation of a special committee with representation from the State Department, the army, and the navy to "define our post-war policy. . . ." Such an interdepartmental committee, he said, would communicate directly with the Joint Chiefs of Staff, "so that it can guide their military policy both during the war and after."[78] (Stimson eventually acted on McCloy's suggestion by appointing him chairman of a newly formulated State-War-Navy Coordinating Committee in 1944.)

McCloy's brief at Cairo was civil affairs and occupation policy. But Stimson had asked him to keep him informed on the crucial decisions relating to Overlord. On this matter, he witnessed considerable rancor between the British and the Americans. Stimson had pleaded with Roosevelt to seize the initiative from the British, and this is exactly what the president did upon his arrival in Cairo. Roosevelt and Hopkins made it clear from the beginning that they were absolutely committed to a cross-Channel attack within six months. Churchill said he was "a hundred percent for OVERLORD," but then proceeded to talk about how important it was to capture Rome. Afterward, Harry Hopkins snidely told the prime minister's personal doctor, Lord Moran (Sir Charles Wilson), "Some of us are beginning to wonder whether the invasion will ever come off." Stalin had agreed to meet Roosevelt and Churchill at Teheran on November 28, and Hopkins warned that, if Churchill continued to promote diversions from Overlord, "You will find us lining up with the Russians."[79]

The presidential party and Churchill left for Teheran on November 27, leaving behind McCloy, Douglas, and many others to await the results of the first face-to-face meeting with "Uncle Joe" Stalin. While they were gone, McCloy had little to do. He played some tennis and went sightseeing around Cairo. One day he saw Eisenhower and briefly discussed with him the furor set off a few days earlier by a Drew Pearson column that had reported that General George S. Patton had slapped two enlisted men in a Sicilian military hospital. McCloy decided to pay Patton a visit after the conclusion of the Cairo conference.

Roosevelt and his entourage were due back from the Teheran negotiations on December 2. But McCloy had been reading minutes of some of the Teheran meetings, and that morning he air-messaged a brief letter to Stimson on what had been decided. The substance of the negotiations had focused on Overlord. Churchill had indeed once again tried to push his allies into some Balkans operations. But Stalin had forcefully rejected any campaign that would result in a delay in Overlord. In a pointed reference to Churchill's schemes, he stated that the Soviets considered all efforts in the Eastern Mediterranean "diversionary." Throughout this meeting, McCloy reported, Stalin was very direct and emphatic: "In fact, in many cases I got the impression that Marshal Stimson was talking and not Marshal Stalin."[80]

In Washington three days later, Stimson read McCloy's summary of Teheran and exclaimed, "I thank the Lord that Stalin was there. In my opinion, he saved the day. He was direct and strong and he brushed away the diversionary attempts of the Prime Minister with a vigor which rejoiced my soul."[81] Stimson had finally seen his views triumph at Teheran. A firm date was set for Overlord; the cross-Channel attack would take place in May 1944. Both the Balkans operation and a proposed amphibious landing in Burma were abandoned, since either would result in the diversion of scarce landing craft from Overlord.

Churchill, however, viewed Roosevelt's conduct at Teheran as something of a betrayal.[82] The prime minister had put off Stimson, Marshall, and other cross-Channel advocates as long as he could. And now the distrust the Americans felt toward Churchill, a distrust engendered by his evasive conduct over the last two years, had cemented their resolve to brook no further delays. Cairo and Teheran were thus turning points in both the war and the Anglo-American relationship. In the future, the Americans would dictate the course of the war, a role commensurate with their overwhelmingly superior contribution to the war effort. American and British troops, commanded by an American general, would finally be committed to an invasion of France and an advance upon Berlin from the west, while Soviet troops moved in from the east.

Marshall and Stimson had been arguing for two years that the closest path for an attack on Berlin lay across the English Channel. Now there were indications from the Soviets that, the longer the Americans waited, the less concerned the Soviets were about opening a second front. The Soviet offensive on the Eastern front was meeting with such success that winter that a sudden collapse of Germany could not be ruled out. In that event, Stalin's troops would occupy all of Germany. If American forces were to play any decisive role in the outcome of the war, they had to be committed against the German heartland as soon as possible. Besides, Roosevelt and Hopkins believed that they could work well with Stalin. In the midst of the Teheran conference, Hopkins told Lord Moran, who was Churchill's confidant as well as his personal physician, "The President knows now that Stalin is 'get-atable' and that we are going to get along fine in the future."[83] McCloy understood and even concurred in the Overlord decision, but he still had worries about the military risks associated with the operation.

With the Cairo conference winding down, McCloy boarded a plane bound for the Italian front, where he intended to survey civilian-control problems. Upon landing in a rainstorm in Palermo, Sicily, he met with General George S. Patton. He had a soft spot for this troublesome general; he was quite simply awed by the man's bravado. In this meeting and in another session on his way back through Palermo, Patton quickly won his sympathy. After hearing the general's explanation of the slapping incident, McCloy wrote in his diary, "Patton felt himself beached, was contrite but still in a fettle. He told me of the incident and described the emotions he felt when he moved from the man with his arm shot off to the whimperer whom he slapped and shook. Patton has the chemicals that make him a leader in battle. The Sicily campaign he ran was magnificent and the soldiers like him and feel proud of having been in his army."[84]

Subsequently, McCloy sent Eisenhower a memo reporting that "Patton was a bit downcast but soldierly. He was not very intelligent the way he handled himself, but [Abraham] Lincoln's remark when they got after Grant comes to mind when I think of Patton—'I can't spare this man—he fights.' I hear that the hubbub is dying down in the States."[85] Instead of reprimanding Patton, McCloy told him he was an "inspiring leader," and promised him an army to command in Europe. Afterward, Patton confided to his diary, "I think my luck is in again."[86]

After Palermo, McCloy headed for Naples, where he visited General Mark Clark, who took him on a tour of the front lines near Caserta. "We got in jeeps and buzzed up the line to the front," McCloy wrote in his diary. "It was more like the last war than anything I had seen thus far, a muddy bruised road with trucks and vehicles of all sorts pounding along. Guns, trucks, and storage all along the route, and cannonading ahead . . . There was heavy artillery fire from our side and I saw a number of air missions. The mountain side was full of bursts and every now and then you could hear small arms fire. It was rough terrain. Supplies had to be man-handled up the approaches. . . ."[87]

Soon afterward, tired and now anxious to return to Washington, McCloy left Italy on a flight for Algiers. There he once again saw Eisenhower, who was busy trying to organize his departure for London to take command of Overlord. Ike still felt beleaguered by his difficult relations with General de Gaulle, who by now had assumed sole command of four hundred thousand Free French troops. After evaluating the situation, McCloy concluded that these French forces would never be properly utilized unless de Gaulle was accorded the political recognition he demanded. Eisenhower agreed, and begged McCloy to change Washington's policy.[88]

McCloy knew just how hard this would be. At Teheran, the president had agreed with Stalin when the Soviet dictator observed that, though de Gaulle might represent the "soul of sympathetic France," the "real physical France engaged under Pétain is helping our common enemy Germany. . . ." Stalin concluded that this "real physical France" should be punished for its collaboration.[89] Roosevelt agreed and thought the French nation should be treated as an occupied country, not an ally, as de Gaulle would have it.

McCloy was not unaware of these political factors, but they weighed little in comparison with the simple military advantages to be gained by giving de Gaulle what he wanted. Besides, from his close dealings with the Gaullists, and particularly from the assessments of Jean Monnet, he felt the difficult general's ultimate political ascendancy was inevitable. With the D-Day landings scheduled to occur in less than five months, he knew he had little time in which to change Roosevelt's mind. He began his campaign by writing a memo to Stimson urging a rapprochement with de Gaulle. Given that the French general had recently won the allegiance of all the resistance groups operating inside France, the success of Overlord, he argued, might well be substantially improved if Eisenhower could coordinate his cross-Channel attack with well-timed sabotage and guerrilla actions. Even after a successful landing, the resistance groups and the French Committee's cooperation might be essential in order to preserve Eisenhower's lines of communications. Failure to recognize the Committee's authority, he warned, might lead the resistance groups to conclude that "we intend to adopt a pro-Vichy policy."[90]

Stimson was only partially persuaded by these arguments. He shared the conviction with Roosevelt that France was headed for civil war and that Washington should do nothing to identify itself with one faction over the other.[91] McCloy's military-necessity argument convinced Stimson that the French Committee's political authority should be recognized—but only in those coastal portions of France designated by the Allies as combat zones during the invasion. McCloy thought that impractical, and proceeded to bombard his boss with memos. At one point, an annoyed Stimson suggested that McCloy had been seduced by the "blandishments" of Jean Monnet, a charge McCloy hotly denied: "I seek one thing only—military advantage and help to Overlord."[92] Eventually, Stimson relented and agreed to "make an assault on the President who has been pretty stubborn with his distrust of de Gaulle."[93]

On the day they were scheduled to see the president, Stimson received word that his sister had suffered a stroke in New York, so he sent McCloy to the Cabinet meeting alone. McCloy got to make his pitch at the White House, and came away thinking that he had won Roosevelt's approval for a limited recognition of de Gaulle's Committee.[94] He now sat down to write a specific set of instructions for Eisenhower on how to deal with the French resistance. When these were forwarded to Roosevelt for his signature, they were returned substantially altered. The president's changes would make it very difficult for Eisenhower to conclude any formal arrangement with the Committee. Refusing to give up, Stimson and McCloy rewrote the instructions once again, and finally, nearly two months after he and Eisenhower had agreed that U.S. policy toward de Gaulle would have to change, Roosevelt finally signed the new directive. Less than three months before D-Day, Eisenhower was now authorized to communicate with French resistance groups through the French Committee and recognize certain immediate postliberation responsibilities in local administration by the Gaullists. McCloy felt his perseverance in presenting sheer realities had finally altered official Washington's policies toward de Gaulle.[95]

In the coming months, however, the general's imperiousness and Roosevelt's distrust conspired to undo these practical arrangements. The matter eventually came to a head over the highly symbolic issue of whether de Gaulle would recognize the newly designed French currency to be used by Allied troops. Earlier in the year, McCloy had accompanied Henry Morgenthau to the White House, where they discussed the issue with Roosevelt. The president was sick in his bed when they entered his room. McCloy had been told by Monnet that de Gaulle would not recognize the currency unless it had the words "République Française" printed across the paper to distinguish it from the Vichy regime. De Gaulle, of course, always referred to the "République," not merely "France." Roosevelt picked up on this immediately, and objected, "How do you know what kind of government you will have when the war is over. . . . Maybe we'll have an emperor again."

McCloy tried to deflect this by suggesting, "If you fix it 'République Française,' then there is one less worry that de Gaulle is going to be a dictator."

"I have heard all these arguments," replied Roosevelt. "De Gaulle is on the wane."

Overruled once again, Morgenthau and McCloy left the White House incredulous that Roosevelt could not see past his prejudices. McCloy told Morgenthau, "I am going to prophesy that in the not too distant future Churchill will make up with DeGaulle . . . and it is going to leave the President high and dry all by himself."

Later that spring, Churchill did mend his relations with the stubborn French general. But Roosevelt still refused to extend full recognition. So, as D-Day approached, de Gaulle acted as if he had no need of Eisenhower. Invited to London just a few days before the landings, and informed of the invasion plans, de Gaulle was less than supportive. He called the French occupation currency printed in Washington and awaiting distribution by the invading troops *"faux billets"*—"counterfeit currency." Once the landings were under way and Eisenhower read a proclamation over the radio calling upon the French people to obey his orders, de Gaulle refused to endorse Eisenhower's statement. McCloy was shocked, and told Morgenthau that de Gaulle's behavior was "just outrageous."[96]

The strength of the French resistance inside France, however, quickly made de Gaulle's stature irreversible. Large portions of the countryside were in open revolt. Concentrating on the railways that could have transported German reinforcements to Normandy, the resistance cut 314 rail lines and attacked an additional 211 lines. Donovan's OSS had supplied the partisans with over a thousand bazookas and other armaments. The French resistance could easily claim credit for delaying the advance of German reinforcements by several days, a critical difference for the landings, which might easily have been repulsed had there been one more armored German division in the vicinity of the beaches.[97]

In the midst of directing the massive invasion, Eisenhower had conflicting instructions from London and Washington regarding relations with the French Committee.[98] One of his aides told McCloy on June 13, over a secure phone, that Ike didn't care one way or another, as long as there was some kind of agreement worked out between the British and the Americans on one side and the French Committee on the other. McCloy assured Eisenhower's aide, "The President has got it all right, I pounded it into him and what we can do about it. . . . I will convey this to the President and we will keep constantly after it in order to do all we can to help Eisenhower out."[99]

McCloy's memos to the president made it clear that, in the view of U.S. military observers in Normandy, "de Gaulle seems to be generally accepted as the coming leader."[100] By D-Day plus eight, even Stimson was beginning to come around. On June 14, he admitted to McCloy, "I think the President's position is theoretically and logically correct, but . . . it is not realistic."[101] At McCloy's urging, that evening Stimson met with Roosevelt and urged him to extend provisional recognition to de Gaulle while simultaneously extracting pledges that he would not interfere in the free election of a postwar government. Roosevelt refused once again, saying it was a "moral issue" he could not ignore.[102] The president assured Stimson that de Gaulle would fade away as non-Gaullist resistance groups were uncovered by the advancing Allied troops.

In the end, Roosevelt's suspicions of de Gaulle had to give way to military realities. As McCloy had foreseen, within weeks of the Normandy invasion large chunks of liberated French territory had to be governed. De Gaulle's French Committee was the only obvious government. So, in early July, McCloy scripted the negotiations for a visit by de Gaulle to

Washington. By the time the French general left a few days later, Roosevelt had reluctantly issued a statement recognizing his government.

The usually astute president had misjudged the situation. He had wanted to impose a hard peace on France, specifically stripping her of her Indochina colonies and perhaps even the French possessions in West Africa. By waiting to deal with de Gaulle until after D-Day, he had allowed the Frenchman to capitalize on the popularity that was already his as the symbol of French resistance. Now the French would demand their share of the victor's spoils, instead of being punished as collaborationists. McCloy was not unaware of these political consequences. But in his view, military necessity dictated dealing with de Gaulle in the summer of 1944, just as military necessity had required dealing with Admiral Darlan in the autumn of 1942. As the War Department's man, McCloy was always the pragmatist.

De Gaulle was only one of many problems associated with D-Day that required McCloy's attention in the spring of 1944. Just two months prior to D-Day, Stimson and Marshall sent him to London, where he was instructed to cable them a general assessment of Eisenhower's plans for the cross-Channel attack. Upon his arrival, McCloy was given the secret code name of "Junior," and Eisenhower arranged for his inspection of "all principal headquarters" throughout England.[103] At SHAEF headquarters outside of London, he discussed with Ike every possible contingency related to the invasion. These were tense and weighty times for Ike, who was glad to have McCloy around to help deal with the ever-troublesome French and to reassure Winston Churchill regarding Overlord.

With the invasion that he had put off for so long about to happen, the British prime minister was in a morose, even fatalistic mood. He told Eisenhower during this period, "I am in this with you to the end. If it fails, we go down together."[104] One afternoon, just as McCloy stepped out to keep an appointment with his British counterpart at the War Office, word came that the prime minister wanted to see him. Upon his arrival at 10 Downing Street, he was taken by Churchill to the Cabinet Room. This was the place, Churchill joked, "where all the mistakes are made." The prime minister always thought of McCloy in relation to Stimson, that uncompromising advocate of a cross-Channel attack. When Stimson's name came up in conversation, the prime minister humorously referred to him as that "thruster." Though Churchill knew McCloy was late for his meeting at the War Department, he insisted that he join him in the dining room for a "delicious meal," washed down with generous portions of white wine, port, and brandy.[105] Finally, McCloy excused himself, and the prime minister volunteered to drive him to his appointment. Along the way, he said, he would give him a tour of London's war scars. The two men walked out through the rear garden, past a bomb crater that had only recently narrowly missed the prime minister's residence, and then climbed into a chauffeured car.

McCloy was sure the driver had "carrot eyes" as he sped them through the blacked-out London streets. First they visited a park where Churchill's daughter Mary served with an anti-aircraft battery. She was clearly annoyed when her father remarked loudly that her unit had yet to shoot down anything.

Next stop was the bombed-out ruins of the House of Commons. Puffing on cigars, the two men walked amid the ruins. Churchill spoke about the building's architecture and his desire to rebuild it after the war. They then went to the nearby House of Lords, where Churchill took a seat and reminisced: "When I look across the well of this house, I see the faces that should be here. . . . Sixteen thousand killed at Somme in one morning . . . It was a hecatomb. . . . I cannot afford to preside again over the loss of a British generation."[106]

By this time, it was almost midnight. As Churchill went on in this vein, McCloy understood finally that the prime minister's meandering, nocturnal tour of blacked-out London had a purpose: to impress on Stimson's favorite troubleshooter why he had so long opposed the great venture that was about to be launched across the English Channel.

A few days later, McCloy flew into Washington, where he told Stimson in a thirty-minute briefing that "everything is going very well for the invasion plans."[107] The next evening, Stimson had the McCloys over for dinner, over which they discussed the trip at length. Despite Churchill's midnight expressions of doubt, McCloy reported "a feeling that there is no disposition on the part of the British to hold back . . . Montgomery is confident and the P.M. is secure." He recommended that more landing craft be sent to the theater, in addition to another two naval cruisers and their attendant destroyers. Regarding Operation Overlord itself, he thought the only "uncertain factors" were weather and security. "If the weather guess is wrong, many complications can ensue. If the time and place are tipped, it will be precarious." But, to offset these uncertainties, McCloy reported there was little that Eisenhower's "talent for coordination and straightening out could not deal with."[108]

CHAPTER 10

McCloy and the Holocaust

"We are alone. Tell me the truth. Do you really believe that all those horrible things happened?"

JOHN J. MCCLOY TO WORLD JEWISH CONGRESS OFFICIAL
DECEMBER 1944

On the eve of D-Day, and in the midst of McCloy's campaign to reorient the administration's policy toward de Gaulle, a new and terrible problem was brought to his desk. Under pressure from Morgenthau, the president had finally, on January 22, 1944, agreed to establish a unique agency, the War Refugee Board (WRB), "to take all measures within its power to rescue the victims of enemy oppression who are in imminent danger of death. . . ."[1] Roosevelt had specified that he wanted Stimson, Hull, and Morgenthau to supervise the WRB's activities, and, inevitably, Stimson delegated this matter to his assistant secretary.

McCloy was not unaware of the reports concerning Hitler's war against the Jews and other minorities in Nazi-occupied Europe. No one reading the newspapers in the last two years could have been ignorant of the news filtering out of Europe. As early as December 1941, the *New York Herald Tribune,* a paper noted for its skeptical treatment of Nazi atrocity stories, had concluded that what was happening in Europe was nothing short of "systematic extermination."[2] Only a month later, Reinhard Heydrich, chief of the Reich's Main Security Office, communicated Hitler's "Final Solution of the European Jewish Question" to an assembly of Nazi officials at Wannsee on January 20, 1942.[3] During the two years prior to the creation of the War Refugee Board, some three million Jews were systematically shot, gassed, or worked and starved to death. British and American newspapers during these years published numerous stories conveying the genocidal character of these mass killings. In June 1942, for instance, Polish authorities in exile in London released a report by the

Warsaw Jewish socialist organization, the Bund, which calculated that seven hundred thousand Jews had been killed in Poland alone. The substance of this report was broadcast by the BBC in London and carried by *The New York Times* and other American newspapers. Citing firsthand accounts, the report revealed for the first time that as many as a thousand Jews per day were being killed in mobile gassing trucks.[4]

In response to these reports, "Stop Hitler" rallies were held in a number of American cities to protest the "extermination of Jews . . . [by] forced labor, in concentration camps or as victims of experiment in poison gas factories."[5] Some commentators suggested that such incredible atrocity stories were reminiscent of the false reports of German baby-killings manufactured by British propaganda during World War I. But by the end of 1942, some of the country's most prominent journalists were leaving no doubt as to the credibility of such reports. On December 13, 1942, Edward R. Murrow told his listeners on a CBS broadcast, "What is happening is this: millions of human beings, most of them Jews, are being gathered up with ruthless efficiency and murdered. . . . The phrase 'concentration camp' is obsolete, as out of date as 'economic sanctions' or 'nonrecognition.' It is now possible to speak only of extermination camps."[6]

By this time, the Roosevelt administration had received confirmation of the press accounts from its own official sources. Only a few days before Murrow's broadcast, Roosevelt told a delegation of visiting Jewish leaders, "Representatives of the United States government in Switzerland and other neutral countries have given us proof that confirms the horrors discussed by you."[7] There was confirmation, and yet there was disbelief. The State Department's specialist on Jewish affairs, R. Borden Reams, in December 1942 was still telling people that reports of mass murders were "to the best of my knowledge . . . as yet unconfirmed."[8] There was still no fundamental comprehension of either the enormity of the evil or the possibility that something could be done to slow the killing. Such paralysis extended even into the Jewish American community. *The New York Times* editorialized about the "world's helplessness to stop the horror while the war is going on. . . ."[9] The consensus among the leadership of the established Jewish organizations was that the best way to aid European Jewry was to bring about an early defeat of Hitler.

Hillel Kook, a former associate of Menachem Begin's in the "revisionist" Zionist organization, Irgun, was one Jewish leader who believed otherwise. Kook, who went by the name of Peter Bergson outside of his native Palestine, had originally been sent to New York to serve as Irgun's liaison in America. When early reports of the Holocaust surfaced in the American press, Bergson abandoned his Irgun activities and turned his energies toward various rescue schemes. In July 1943, he formed the Emergency Committee to Save the Jewish People of Europe, which financed an advertising campaign demanding that the administration establish a special government rescue agency.

Despite this publicity, Roosevelt probably would not have agreed to the formation of the War Refugee Board had it not been for Henry Morgenthau. Until December 1943, the Treasury secretary had been content to let the State Department handle the question of Jewish-refugee rescue. Morgenthau then learned that the State Department had blocked for more than six months a scheme to rescue seventy thousand Rumanian Jews in exchange for $170,000 in Rumanian currency. Worse, Morgenthau learned that the State Department had also hidden from him a cable from the U.S. Legation in Switzerland that confirmed the existence of Hitler's plan to exterminate the Jewish people.[10] In a meeting in late December, he confronted the official in charge of European affairs, Assistant Secretary Breckinridge Long, and bluntly asked him if he was an anti-Semite. Long denied it. Then, in early January 1944, Morgenthau's staff wrote a devastating critique of the State Department entitled "Report to the Secretary on the Acquiescence of This Government in the Murder of the Jews." The report charged that the State Department was "guilty not only of gross procrastination and willful failure to act, but even of willful attempts to prevent action from being taken to rescue Jews from Hitler."[11]

Within days of receiving this report, Roosevelt agreed to establish the WRB. On February 1, 1944, Stimson took McCloy with him to the Board's second session. Presiding over the meeting was John Pehle, the Board's acting executive director. McCloy knew and liked Pehle, who had been a high-ranking lawyer on Morgenthau's staff.[12] Stimson dreaded the prospect of even attending the meeting, since he believed nothing of substance could be done to help the Jews short of winning the war. But Pehle was able to report that the WRB was accomplishing quite a bit. Licenses had been issued to the World Jewish Congress to allow that organization to transfer funds abroad in order to finance the evacuation of refugees from France and Rumania into Spain, Switzerland, and North Africa. Another operation might facilitate the evacuation of more than five thousand abandoned children from France at a cost of $600,000. Yet another program had been arranged with the Union of Orthodox Rabbis of the United States and Canada to finance an underground operation whereby Jewish refugees in Poland could be encouraged to seek refuge in Hungary. In order to do this, Pehle had persuaded the State Department to approve the direct transfer of hard currency into enemy-occupied territory. Finally, Pehle reported that, in cooperation with the Rumanian government, some sixty-four hundred Jewish internees had been transferred from concentration camps to Bucharest.[13] Stimson came away from the meeting quite pleased. It appeared that, contrary to his expectations, the new Board would be able to accomplish something concrete.[14]

In fact, by this time it was very late, almost too late, to do anything to save what remained of European Jewry. Since the existence of Hitler's plan for a Final Solution had been confirmed in late 1942, millions had died while the State Department blocked all efforts to ransom Jews or otherwise encourage them to seek refuge in the United States, Turkey, Switzerland, Palestine, or other possible havens. With the exception of Hungary, where a Jewish community of nearly one million remained intact, most other Jews still alive in Europe were now in Polish and German concentration camps. To rescue them would require military action.

But as McCloy learned soon after his first meeting with the WRB, military action had already been ruled out. Upon being apprised of the creation of the new agency, the British government inquired whether the presence of the secretary of war on the Board indicated that Washington intended to use parachute troops to free the Jews from any of the various concentration camps. In response, Pehle cleared a cable with the State and War departments informing the British that "it is not contemplated that combat units will be employed in rescue operations unless the rescues are the direct result of military operations."[15]

The Joint Chiefs of Staff already had a policy on rescue operations, which was to reject them out of hand. This stance had been established in November 1943, when the World Jewish Congress appealed to the War Department to ship some four thousand refugees stranded on the Adriatic island of Rab. These refugees had only recently been freed by Yugoslav partisans from Nazi concentration camps in Yugoslavia and transported to Rab. The island seemed about to be captured by the Nazis, so the Yugoslav Embassy in Washington appealed for military transport to shuttle the refugees to Allied-occupied Italy. A week before McCloy attended his first meeting of the War Refugee Board, he was informed that the theater commander in the area had investigated the matter and "determined that the military situation did not permit the rendition of direct assistance to these refugees, the majority of whom were Jews." The commander assured Washington, however, that as in the past he would care for any refugees who managed to reach the safety of Italy "as a result of their own efforts."[16] McCloy did nothing to reverse this decision.

Lack of shipping was not the reason these concentration-camp survivors could not be rescued. At that very moment, the army was transporting thousands of non-Jewish refugees from Italy to Egypt. McCloy himself reported that plenty of shipping was available in the Mediterranean to transport these refugees.[17] The real motive for refusing to rescue the Rab Jews in November 1943 was the fear among the Joint Chiefs of Staff that the rescue of the Rab refugees "might create a precedent which would lead to other demands and an influx of additional refugees."[18]

From the beginning, McCloy was personally skeptical of using combat troops to rescue concentration-camp internees. In late January 1944, Pehle had suggested to him that a message should be cabled to all theater commanders ordering them to undertake whatever refugee rescue operations they thought consistent with the war effort. Before passing on Pehle's proposal to Marshall's office, McCloy scribbled on it, "I am very chary of getting the Army involved in this while the war is on."[19] Marshall and his people were disinclined to divert combat troops from conventional military targets; higher civilian authorities would have to persuade them that extraordinary political and humanitarian factors existed to justify such a diversion of military resources. As Stimson's liaison to the War Refugee Board, McCloy was in a unique position to initiate any serious consideration of military operations designed to rescue Jews. He and perhaps Harvey Bundy were the only civilians in the War Department who had both the sufficient authority and knowledge to set such a policy in motion. But War Department records make it clear that, from the very beginning, neither McCloy nor any other official believed there was cause to challenge the military's initial rejection of the idea.

Like many other people both in and out of government, McCloy had read the published accounts of Hitler's extermination policies with some skepticism. He regarded the Germans as a particularly cruel enemy; even as a young man, he had felt a near-visceral hatred of Prussian militarism. But as a veteran of World War I, he also distrusted atrocity stories. On top of this, the reports coming out of Europe were just too horrible to be entirely credible. Not only were the sources of these reports largely Jewish, and thus perhaps self-serving, but the American Jewish community itself appeared divided over just how serious was the catastrophe that had befallen European Jewry.

One of those who doubted the horrific reports was McCloy's Georgetown neighbor Justice Felix Frankfurter. In the summer of 1943, Frankfurter had listened to a detailed briefing by a Polish-underground courier named Jan Karski on what was happening inside the Polish extermination camps. Disguised as an Estonian prison-guard, Karski had been smuggled into the death camp at Belzec. In the autumn of 1942, he had made his way to London and Washington, carrying with him a report of what he had seen in Belzec. Karski's written report had the full endorsement of the Polish government-in-exile; he was specifically ordered to request Allied intervention to stop the killing machine. His report described the entire process, from the roundups in the ghettos to the "mass exterminations" conducted in gas chambers. "Wherever the trains arrive," Karski wrote, "half the people arrive dead. Those surviving are sent to special camps at Treblinka, Belzec and Sobibor. Once there, the so-called 'settlers' are mass murdered."[20]

By the time Karski, a Polish Catholic, was ushered in to see Justice Frankfurter in the late summer of 1943, he had already personally briefed

President Roosevelt, Secretary Stimson, and OSS Chief William Donovan.[21] None of these men seemed shaken by what he said, and their questions all focused on the military capabilities of the Polish underground or, in the case of the president, on political matters affecting postwar Poland.

Karski hoped to elicit a more profound reaction from Frankfurter, who after all was a prominent Jewish figure and an active Zionist. When the justice arrived at the Polish Embassy in Washington and was introduced to Karski, he immediately came to the point. "What is happening," he asked, "to the Jews in your country? There are many conflicting reports."

For the next twenty-five minutes or more, he listened in silence as Karski graphically described what he had seen inside Belzec. At the end of the lecture, the justice paced back and forth in silence for another ten minutes and finally said, "A man like me talking to a man like you must be totally frank. So, I say that I am unable to believe you."

Startled, the Polish ambassador, a personal friend, exclaimed, "Felix, you cannot tell this man to his face that he is lying. The authority of my government is behind him."

"Mr. Ambassador, I did not say that this young man is lying. I said that I am unable to believe him. There is a difference." At that, Frankfurter extended both his arms and waving his hands, murmured, "No, no." He then turned around and walked out.[22]

Frankfurter was not the only Jewish friend of McCloy's who could not bring himself to believe the news. Karski also briefed Walter Lippmann, but, unlike other columnists who heard Karski's story, he—the only Jew among them—decided not to write about it. Such disbelief on the part of two men whom McCloy respected and trusted certainly influenced his own opinion. As late as December 1944, long after there could be no doubt whatsoever about what had happened in the Polish death camps, McCloy still could not shake his disbelief. That month he told A. Leon Kubowitzki of the World Jewish Congress, "We are alone. Tell me the truth. Do you really believe that all those horrible things happened?" Years later, Kubowitzki commented, "His sources of information, needless to say, were better than mine. But he could not grasp the terrible destruction."[23]

Such disbelief explains McCloy's inaction in dealing with this issue over the next several months. But at least one source of his disbelief came from within, specifically from his own attitude toward Jews. He was not an anti-Semite, nor did he harbor the nativist sentiments of a Breckinridge Long. But he shared some of the same prejudices as were held by many men of his generation and social standing. Until 1933, social discrimination against Jews—the exclusion of Jews from clubs, hotels, and summer resorts—was much more in evidence in the United States than in Germany.[24] Nearly all the Ivy League schools observed quotas limiting the number of Jewish students. The Wall Street legal profession was itself highly segregated; if you were a Jew, even a Harvard-educated Jew, you would not find yourself offered a partnership at Cravath or most of the other "downtown" firms.

A genteel, upper-class anti-Semitism pervaded much of the social scene to which the McCloys belonged in the prewar years. Most, if not all, of his clubs barred Jews. His own father-in-law refused to do business with Jews as a matter of principle.[25] By all accounts, McCloy generally took people as they were and paid far less attention to such strictures than most men in the Wall Street crowd. He had long-standing friendships with men like Benny Buttenwieser, Frederick Warburg, Eric Warburg, and other Jews. But these were invariably highly assimilated Jews, or Jews who, like Lippmann, made a point of distancing themselves from their heritage. And despite such friendships, McCloy sometimes went out of his way to observe the social proprieties concerning Jews. Once, during the war years, a young Jewish lawyer working on Wall Street was told by a friend that McCloy had asked him to invite a few eligible bachelors to a coming-out party for a Washington debutante but had specified that no Jews should be brought along.[26]

It is unclear how much, if at all, such petty social discrimination helps to explain McCloy's initial chariness to use combat troops for rescue operations. Stimson, for one, tended to consider any publicity about Jewish affairs or Zionism an unfortunate breach of etiquette.[27] Such personal instincts were only reinforced by the confusion and disarray displayed by American Jewish leaders. If Rabbi Stephen Wise, Peter Bergson, and other Jewish leaders had presented a common front, if the leading newspapers in the country had given the Holocaust reports the coverage they deserved, if such political factors had so coalesced as to make rescue operations a political priority, McCloy might easily have played a positive role. If Frankfurter had been moved to action by Karski's eyewitness testimony, McCloy might well have become an advocate of aggressive rescue operations. In the scheme of things, he was not wedded to his position. In his view, the matter was simply not important compared with such problems as helping Eisenhower establish contact with the French resistance.

Indeed, almost from the very beginning of his involvement with the War Refugee Board, it quickly became apparent that his position would be one of benign obstruction. The rescue of European Jewry could not be allowed to interfere with winning the war; there were any number of war-winning measures that had to take priority over the plight of the Jews. One such issue was whether the British should be pressured to open their immigration doors into Palestine.

In January 1944, the mainstream American Zionist organizations persuaded a number of legislators to introduce a sense-of-Congress resolution urging the United States to ensure "that the doors of Palestine shall be opened for free entry of Jews into the country . . . so that the Jewish people may ultimately reconstitute Palestine as a free and democratic Jewish commonwealth."[28] The resolution quickly garnered wide support, and observers thought its passage was assured. Though purely advisory, such a resolution might have saved some lives. Thousands of Jews in Bulgaria, Rumania, and Hungary possessed exit visas issued by their respective Nazi puppet governments. But these could be used only by those who were guaranteed a port of disembarkation. Too often no such guarantee had been made. Nevertheless, the British, the State Department, and the War Department all had serious reservations.

After seeing a copy of the measure, McCloy undertook a quick study of the issue. He read the language of a similar resolution introduced in 1922, talked with Middle East experts in army intelligence, and read over a number of reports on the Palestine problem. This exercise only confirmed the impressions he had picked up during his short visit to Jerusalem three months earlier: unrestricted Jewish immigration into Palestine was sure to exacerbate tensions in the region. In addition, he had since become aware of negotiations pending with Saudi Arabia to lay a new oil pipeline from the Persian Gulf to the Mediterranean. He felt certain that passage of the Zionist resolution would cause the Saudis to reject the pipeline project, and thereby deny U.S. Armed Forces a ready reserve of one billion gallons of oil. With Stimson's concurrence, McCloy therefore decided to testify against the resolution in executive session before the House Foreign Relations Committee. Stimson thought the whole idea had been planted by Drew Pearson, "who has as usual inferred a huge conspiracy against the Jews. . . ."[29]

After clearing his draft testimony with Marshall and others in the War Department, McCloy went up to Capitol Hill in mid-March and forcefully explained why the resolution would endanger the war effort. He reminded the congressmen that "there is a high degree of tension in Palestine between the Arabs and the Jews and that each side have substantial quantities of arms." After referring to the numerous attacks by Arabs on Jewish settlements, aimed at discouraging Jewish emigration, he warned, "We are dependent not only upon peace in the area but our lines of communication throughout Africa are to an important degree dependent upon the cooperation and goodwill of the Arab." He stated that one of the critical Persian Gulf supply routes to the Soviet Union ran through territory inhabited by Muslims. Even more important, he told the congressmen, was the threat of losing Middle Eastern oil: "The Abadan refinery at the head of the Gulf is the only Allied source of aviation

gasoline outside the Western Hemisphere. . . . It would require a substantial number of troops to protect them in the event of disorders."[30]

McCloy was not opposed to the establishment of a Jewish state at some time in the future. But as he told Marshall, he believed it best to "postpone without prejudice to either side [Arab or Jewish] this issue for determination after the war when military considerations will be less acute."[31] He and other War Department officials might well have tolerated a resolution that simply urged the British to open up temporary emergency camps in Palestine from which Jewish refugees could be repatriated elsewhere after the war. Peter Bergson's Emergency Committee to Save the Jewish People of Europe urged Congress that spring to adopt just such a resolution. But such a compromise measure was harshly attacked by Rabbi Stephen Wise and other members of the American Jewish establishment since it might set a precedent for the expulsion of Jewish immigrants in Palestine after the war. When it became clear that McCloy's testimony made passage of the Palestine resolution unlikely, a number of congressmen suggested to the American Zionists that the language endorsing a Jewish commonwealth should be cut, leaving only the appeal for open immigration into Palestine. Tragically, even this compromise was rejected by Rabbi Wise. As the historian David S. Wyman later wrote, "The unavoidable conclusion is that during the Holocaust the leadership of American Zionism concentrated its major force on the drive for a future Jewish state in Palestine. It consigned rescue to a distinctly secondary position."[32]

We know today that Hitler had made the complete extermination of European Jewry a major war-aim; even while on the defensive in 1944, the Nazis diverted substantial troops, supplies, and vital railroad facilities to carry out the Final Solution. Not comprehending this fact, McCloy and others in the War Department failed to take any extraordinary measures to thwart this Nazi war-aim.

As long as the War Refugee Board's activities did not interfere with military priorities, McCloy supported Pehle. He backed the WRB chief when Pehle proposed that the Spanish government be officially asked to open its borders to refugees fleeing Nazi-occupied France.

McCloy also supported Pehle's efforts to have the president issue to the Nazis another set of warnings that their crimes against the Jews and other civilians would be punished. Throughout the spring of 1944, he received weekly summaries of the WRB's activities, and he must have felt that whatever could be done for the Jews was being done. In Turkey, the WRB representative persuaded the government to permit two hundred Jews every ten days to transit Istanbul on their way to Palestine. That spring, the Rumanian government agreed to evacuate forty-eight thousand Jews from Transnistria to the Rumanian interior, where they would not be in the path of retreating German troops. But for this intervention, these Jews would not have survived the war.[33] The Irish government was persuaded to take in five hundred Jewish refugee children, and Pehle reported similar small steps toward aiding refugees in Portugal, Switzerland, and Sweden.[34]

In late March, Pehle proposed that the president announce that the United States would temporarily accept "all oppressed peoples escaping from Hitler." In a memo prepared for Roosevelt, he argued that no rescue program could be effective unless escaping refugees could be assured a haven, at least until the end of the war. He hastened to add that, though few Jews would actually have to come to the United States, Washington had to set an example before other countries would open their borders. All the president had to do, suggested Pehle, was to issue an executive order allowing refugees to enter the United States on a temporary basis, without going through immigration procedures. This proposal had the strong support of Morgenthau. But Stimson believed that Roosevelt ought not throw open America's borders without first consulting Congress: "I fear that Congress will feel that it is the opening wedge to a violation of our immigration laws."[35]

On the morning of March 31, 1944, Stimson called McCloy into his office to debate the issue. Since Congress was very unlikely to approve any formal loosening of U.S. immigration restrictions, was the situation urgent enough to justify unilateral presidential action? According to Stimson's diary, McCloy urged caution, even though on other occasions, when it involved national-security matters, he had advised the president to circumvent Congress. The Jewish-refugee problem, however, was not a matter of national security. As a result, later in the day Stimson called in Pehle and rejected his draft; eventually, Roosevelt accepted a compromise whereby temporary haven was offered to one thousand refugees, largely Jews from southern Italy.

This was a pittance, and McCloy knew it. He was not completely callous toward the suffering of these refugees, but, like many of his peers, he had worried throughout the war about army morale and feared doing anything that might awaken nativist, isolationist sentiments. He felt that buried in the back of the minds of a good majority of American soldiers was the "unbelievable" thought that this war might have been started by "Jewish capitalists." Anti-Semitism and racial prejudice were so deep-rooted that, if "the men come into the Army with these prejudices, it is going to be hard to eradicate them."[36] It was prudent, therefore, to do nothing that could suggest to the troops or the American public that the war was being fought in behalf of the Jews.

This attitude paralyzed McCloy when it came to dealing with any issue associated with Jewish interests. The initiative and courage he routinely displayed when dealing with equally controversial issues—such as the matter of racial discrimination in the army, or whether to offer army commissions to veterans of the Lincoln Brigade—was missing when it came to dealing with the War Refugee Board. In the summer of 1944, his lack of interest became a critical, even decisive factor in the fate of some four hundred thousand Hungarian Jews. In mid-June, an official of the Agudath Israel World Organization, a group representing ultra-orthodox American Jews, wrote a series of letters to various high-ranking officials in Washington, pleading with them to do something to impede the deportation of Hungary's Jews. The letters, written by Jacob Rosenheim, were forwarded to John Pehle at the War Refugee Board. Rosenheim asserted that hundreds of thousands of Hungary's Jews were being transported by rail to Polish death camps. Unlike previous vague appeals to rescue such victims or find a safe haven for them, this time Rosenheim requested that the Allies bomb the rail junctions of Košice and Prešov. This action, he argued, would at least slow the extermination process. But he warned that "the bombing has to be made at once, because day after day less people [sic] could be saved and it would be very soon too late for the rescue."[37]

Information on the Hungarian deportations had been available for some weeks. As early as April, even before the deportations actually began, Gerhardt Riegner of the World Jewish Congress in Geneva informed Rabbi Stephen Wise that the Germans were now planning to exterminate the last large Jewish community still intact on the European continent. A few weeks later, United Press reported that three hundred thousand Hungarian Jews had been forced into assembly camps. On May 10, *The New York Times* reported that the Budapest government "is now preparing for the annihilation of Hungarian Jews." A week later, the *Times* published a report that the first batch of Jews had left the Hungarian countryside for "murder camps in Poland." This was, in fact, remarkably accurate reporting: the first trains bound for Auschwitz had left only three days previously.[38]

Some of the information that persuaded Rosenheim to request the bombardment of the rail lines out of Hungary was based on the testimony of two Jews who had escaped from Auschwitz on April 10. Making their way by foot at night, and sleeping by day, they crossed into Slovakia on April 21. There the two escapees, Rudolf Vrba and Alfred Wetzler, made contact with the Jewish underground and wrote a thirty-page report detailing what they had seen at Auschwitz. Both men had survived more than two years in the death camp, largely working as registrars. In this capacity, they had plenty of opportunity to observe the millions of Jews processed through the camp. Vrba and Wetzler were determined to escape, to bear witness and warn the Hungarian Jews of what awaited them upon deportation. The previous January, Vrba had seen the Nazis construct a new railroad ramp leading right up to one of the gas chambers in the Birkenau section of Auschwitz. "The purpose of this ramp," Vrba wrote years later, "was no secret in Birkenau, the SS were talking about 'Hungarian Salami' and a 'million units'. . . ."[39]

The Vrba-Wetzler report for the first time placed a name on the main extermination camp, Auschwitz, and described in incredible detail its operations, and specifically the gas chambers:

> It holds 2,000 people. . . . When everybody is inside, the heavy doors are closed. Then there is a short pause, presumably to allow the room temperature to rise to a certain level, after which SS men with gas masks climb on the roof, open the traps, and shake down . . . a "cyanide" mixture of some sort which turns into gas at a certain temperature. After three minutes everyone in the chamber is dead. . . . The chamber is then opened, aired, and the "special squad" [of slave laborers] carts the bodies on flat trucks to the furnace rooms where the burning takes place.[40]

This report reached Budapest and the leadership of Hungarian Jews by early May, and by mid-June it was passed by Allen Dulles in Switzerland to Roswell McClelland, the War Refugee Board's representative in Geneva. McClelland did not doubt the veracity of the Vrba-Wetzler testimony; it merely confirmed everything else he had heard about the Polish death camps, and was corroborated by the testimony of a non-Jewish Polish military officer who had also escaped from Auschwitz. On June 24, he sent a three-page cable to Pehle in Washington reporting, "There is little doubt that many of these Hungarian Jews are being sent to the extermination camps of Ausehitz (Oswiecim) and Birke Nau (Rajska) in western upper Silesia where according to recent reports, since early summer 1942 at least 1,500,000 Jews have been killed. There is evidence that already in January 1944 preparations were being made to receive and exterminate Hungarian Jews in these camps. Soon a detailed report on these camps will be cabled."[41]

This was the only reference to the Vrba-Wetzler report in McClelland's cable. He had, not unreasonably, decided to devote a separate, longer cable to summarizing their gruesome testimony. But even this shorter cable of June 24 described in considerable detail, citing numerous sources, the horrific circumstances of the Hungarian deportations, and how hundreds must have died for lack of air and food during the three-day train journey to Poland. He also conveyed the request of "all sources of this information in Slovakia and Hungary that vital sections of these [railway] lines, especially bridges . . . be bombed as the only possible means of slowing down or stopping future deportations." However, he then added a disclaimer: "This [request] is submitted by me as a proposal of these agencies and I can venture no opinion on its utility."[42]

On the very day McClelland sent his cable, Pehle saw McCloy in his office and discussed Rosenheim's bombing proposal. Pehle made it clear that he "had several doubts about the matter"— specifically, whether it would be appropriate to use military personnel for such a purpose, and whether the rail lines could be put out of action long enough to make any difference to the Hungarian Jews. In a memo afterward, Pehle recorded that he had made it "very clear to Mr. McCloy" that he was not, "at this point at least, requesting the War Department to take any action on this proposal, other than to appropriately explore it." McCloy assured him that he would "check into the matter."[43]

A day or two later, Pehle told McCloy about his receipt of the McClelland cable and promised to send him a copy. On June 29, it reached McCloy's desk with a cover note directing his attention to the request to bomb the "vital sections" of the rail lines.[44] By this time, the Operations and Planning Division (OPD) in the War Department had generated a response to Jacob Rosenheim's June 18 request that the Hungarian rail lines be bombed.

OPD had received a query on the bombing proposal on June 23. Three days later, Lieutenant General John E. Hull, an assistant chief of staff and the immediate deputy to Lieutenant General Thomas T. Handy, approved a reply. (Lieutenant General Handy was at the time visiting England and the Normandy invasion beaches.)[45] General Hull, or whichever of his aides drafted the reply, conducted no study of the military viability of bombing the rail lines. Instead, Hull merely relied on the War Department's February 1944 internal memorandum stating as a matter of policy that "the most effective relief which can be given victims of enemy persecution is to insure the speedy defeat of the Axis."[46]

McCloy discussed this recommendation with his personal aide, Colonel Al Gerhardt, and concluded there was no reason to overrule General Hull's estimation. McCloy instructed Gerhardt to "kill" the matter. But then, on July 3, 1944, Gerhardt finally passed him the June 29 note from Pehle with the attached cable from McClelland. Gerhardt wrote, "I know you told me to 'kill' this but since those instructions, we have received the attached letter from Pehle. I suggest that the attached reply be sent."[47] McCloy inquired no further about the issue and merely signed Gerhardt's suggested response. It was to be the first of many letters he would sign refusing to take military action against the death camps: "The War Department is of the opinion that the suggested air operation is impracticable. It could be executed only by the diversion of considerable air support essential to the success of our forces now engaged in decisive operations and would in any case be of such very doubtful efficacy that it would not amount to a practical project."[48]

The single assertion of fact in this letter, that the Auschwitz rail lines could be bombed only by "the diversion of considerable air support," was not true. Long-range American bombers stationed in Italy had been flying over the camp since that spring. Aerial-reconnaissance photos had been taken of the Auschwitz camp and a neighboring I. G. Farben petrochemical plant on April 4 and June 26, 1944, the latter date just one week before McCloy wrote Pehle that such an air operation was impracticable.[49] Indeed, a few weeks later, U.S. bombers extended the air war against Germany's synthetic-fuels plants to regions very close to the death camps. And late in the summer, a few bombs actually fell on the Monowitz camp, a part of the Auschwitz complex, and injured some three hundred slave laborers.[50]

There is no question that the tens of thousands of inmates in the death camps themselves wished and prayed for Allied bombing raids, even at the risk of their own death. Primo Levi, an Italian partisan captured and imprisoned in Auschwitz in 1944, later wrote, "As for us, we were too destroyed to be really afraid. The few who could still judge and feel rightly, drew strength and hope from the bombardments. . . . But the greater number bore the new danger and the new discomforts with unchanged indifference: it was not a conscious resignation, but the opaque torpor of beasts broken in by blows, whom the blows no longer hurt."[51]

Nevertheless, in a letter to the War Refugee Board on July 1, Leon Kubowitzki, head of the Congress's Rescue Department, warned that the gas chambers could not be destroyed by aerial bombardment, for "the first victims would be the Jews who are gathered in these camps." Instead, Kubowitzki proposed that the Soviets be asked to send in paratroopers "to seize the buildings, to annihilate the squads of murderers, and to free the unfortunate inmates." Since it was highly unlikely that the Soviets would act on such a request, Pehle viewed it as a prelude to a request for the use of American troops. He didn't even bother to pass this proposal on to McCloy, because, as he told Morgenthau two months later, "we did not feel justified in asking the War Department to undertake a measure which involved the sacrifice of American troops."[52]

Members of Pehle's own staff disagreed with him; one of his staff aides, Benjamin Akzin, was so shaken by McClelland's June 24 cable that five days later he wrote a memo making a strong argument for bombing not the rail lines but the gas chambers themselves. To do so, he argued, would force the Germans to spend considerable time and resources to reconstruct the gas chambers "or to evolve elsewhere equally efficient procedures of mass slaughter and of disposing of the bodies." In the meantime, many lives would be saved. Akzin told Pehle it was a "matter of principle" and that in any case the Auschwitz complex itself was an important military target, containing "mining and manufacturing centres." Finally, he said, the Allies should not be deterred by the fact that a large number of Jews would probably be killed in any such military operations: ". . . refraining from bombing the extermination centres would be sheer misplaced sentimentality, far more cruel a decision than to destroy these centres."[53]

Here, at last, was a cogent and compelling argument for the use of military force. Akzin clearly accepted the basic fact, that fifteen thousand Hungarian Jews were being deported each day to Auschwitz, where one had to assume that most were executed. At that very moment, twelve thousand Jews were being gassed each day in the Auschwitz camps, and by August as many as twenty-four thousand were killed in a single day—a record throughout the Final Solution.[54] McCloy, however, was never shown Akzin's memo, and Pehle's own doubts and the halfhearted manner in which he conveyed the bombing proposal reinforced McCloy's judgment that this was something the War Department should stay away from.

Still, as the evidence accumulated in the latter half of June and the first week of July, Pehle began to have second thoughts. On July 8, McClelland, in Switzerland, cabled him an eight-page summary of the Vrba-Wetzler report. Although Pehle would not see the complete text of this graphic description of the mass killings until the autumn of that year, McClelland's summary persuaded him to raise the issue of military action once again. But he did so in a fashion clearly designed to protect the War Refugee Board's record and lay the onus for a refusal to use military force against the death camps on others in the War Department. In a July 15 memorandum for the members of the War Refugee Board, copies of which were sent to Stimson and McCloy, Pehle first summarized the Board's general response to the Hungarian crisis. He cited the Board's efforts to get Hungarian refugees out of the country or protect them with Swedish passports. The latter scheme had been instituted in cooperation with the government of Sweden, which at the WRB's request had accredited a young and prominent businessman named Raoul Wallenberg as their attaché in Budapest. About to leave on his rescue mission, Wallenberg, thirty-one, was promised whatever assistance the WRB could extend. After outlining these and various other schemes to rescue Hungarian Jews, Pehle tried to set the record straight on the question of military operations:

> As the situation in Hungary has become increasingly desperate, the Board has received several proposals that certain military operations might take place with the possible purpose of forestalling or hindering German extermination operations. One of these was a suggestion that the railways leading from the points of deportation to the camps be bombed. This particular suggestion was discussed with Assistant Secretary of War McCloy. After careful consideration of the matter, the War Department ruled that the suggested air operation was impracticable. . . .

> It has been suggested that the concentration and extermination centers be bombed in order that in the resultant confusion some of the unfortunate people might be able to escape and hide. It has also been suggested that weapons be dropped by parachute simultaneously with such bombings. Finally, it has been proposed that some parachute troops be dropped to bring about disorganization and escape of the unfortunate people. Arrangements are under way for the examination of these proposals by the competent military authorities.[55]

Attached to this memo were copies of the cables Pehle had received from McClelland in Switzerland and the Board's representative in Sweden, Iver C. Olsen. These cables were so definitive and detailed in their description of the plight of Hungary's Jews that there could be little doubt of the consequences of inaction.

Olsen's July 1 cable from Stockholm described in sickening detail the industrial character of the killing factories. He said the latest news from Budapest concerning the treatment of Jews "is so terrible that it is hard to believe and that there are no words to qualify its description." He reported that, in a conservative estimate, over six hundred thousand Jews had been either killed or deported:

> According to the evidence, these people are now being taken to a place across the Hungarian frontier in Poland where there is an establishment at which gas is used for killing people. It is said by Boheman [a Swedish Foreign Ministry official] that these people of all ages, children, women and men are transported to this isolated spot in box cars packed in like sardines and that upon arrival many are already dead. Those who have survived the trip are stripped naked, given a small square object which resembles a piece of soap and told that at the bath house they must bathe themselves. The "bath house" does in fact look like a big bathing establishment. . . . Into a large room with a total capacity of two thousand packed together closely the victims are pushed. No regard is given to sex or age and all are completely naked. When the atmosphere of the hall has been heated by this mass of bodies a fine powder is let down over the whole area by opening a contraption in the ceiling. When the heated atmosphere comes in contact with this powder a poisonous gas is formed which kills all occupants of the room. Trucks then take out the bodies, and burning follows.[56]

McCloy received a copy of this cable, but there is no record of his reaction to it. And though he and Pehle again discussed the military option, there is no formal record that Pehle followed up on his July 15 assertion that "competent military authorities" would examine the proposals to bomb the gas chambers or effect some kind of rescue operation with paratroopers. A genuine determination of the viability of any such operations would have to have been made in the office of General Henry H. "Hap" Arnold, the man in charge of the U.S. air arm. But there is no record in Arnold's papers that the issue was ever brought to his desk.[57] Evidently, McCloy still did not really comprehend or believe that mass extermination was being carried out on an industrial basis, for, after his talk with the assistant secretary, Pehle dropped the issue.[58]

Meanwhile, in London, a summary of the Vrba-Wetzler report had reached the Foreign Office on July 4, and the next day, in Parliament, Anthony Eden acknowledged that "many persons have been killed" in the course of these "barbarous deportations."[59] On the following day, Eden raised with Churchill the matter of bombing the death camps. He told the prime minister that the idea had "already been considered" but said that he was now in favor of it. On July 7, Churchill wrote Eden, "You and I are in entire agreement. Get anything out of the Air Force you can, and invoke me if necessary."[60]

Unlike McCloy, Pehle, and others in Washington, not only did Churchill instantly believe the Auschwitz reports, but he was willing to authorize military operations against the death camps.[61] A few days later, he told his foreign secretary, Anthony Eden, "There is no doubt that this is probably the greatest and most horrible crime ever committed in the whole history of the world, and it has been done by scientific machinery by nominally civilized men in the name of a great State and one of the leading races in Europe."[62]

Eden immediately acted upon Churchill's authorization and wrote a letter to British Secretary of State for Air Sir Archibald Sinclair. Referring to the "appalling persecution" of Hungary's Jews, Eden then asked for the Air Ministry's opinion as to the "feasibility" of bombing either the rail lines or the camps themselves. He told Sinclair, "I very much hope that it will be possible to do something. I have the authority of the Prime Minister to say that he agrees."

Sinclair's reply a week later echoed McCloy's own negative assessment. He told Eden that interrupting the railways to the death camps "is out of our power." Sinclair pleaded that "the distance of Silesia [in the region of Auschwitz] from our bases entirely rules out our doing anything of the kind." He explained that, whereas the distances were too great for British night bombers, "It might be carried out by the Americans by daylight but it would be a costly and hazardous operation. It might be ineffective, and even if the plant was destroyed, I am not clear that it would really help the victims." Nevertheless, Sinclair said he would try to present all the facts of the situation to the Americans, not knowing that McCloy had already rejected the idea. In the event, no formal British request was made on the subject, partly because over the next month the Air Ministry failed to obtain copies of the layout and exact location of Auschwitz, information that rested in the files of the Foreign Ministry.

In short, Churchill's request that Eden "get anything out of the Air Force you can" on bombing the death camps floundered in the face of the same military mind-set prevalent in the War Department. Scarce British pilots could not be risked for a nonmilitary target.[63]

While Churchill was an advocate of bombing Auschwitz, there is no evidence that Roosevelt was ever approached about the matter.[64] Both the president and McCloy, however, took a strong interest in another scheme to rescue the Hungarian Jews. This scheme—known as the "Brand affair"—may well have influenced McCloy's attitude toward the bombing question. On May 19, 1944, two Hungarian Jews arrived by small plane in Istanbul. One of the passengers, Joel Brand, a member of a Hungarian Zionist organization called the Relief and Rescue Committee, brought word of a startling offer. The man Hitler had placed in charge of the Final Solution, Adolf Eichmann, was prepared to exchange one million Jews in return for ten thousand trucks and various other supplies such as coffee, soap, and tea. Eichmann assured Brand that he would demonstrate his good faith by releasing several thousand Jews just as soon as Brand could return with word that the Allies could in principle agree to send the trucks.

Brand was quickly picked up and detained by the British in Cairo for interrogation. McCloy was informed of this development almost immediately, as was Roosevelt. The president wrote Ira Hirschmann, the War Refugee Board representative in Turkey, to determine the authenticity of the offer. He told Hirschmann to try to keep the door open in indirect negotiations as long as there was even a "remote possibility of saving lives."[65]

Not surprisingly, most military officers in the War Department reacted with skepticism to the idea of trading trucks for Jews. McCloy thought the proposal "bizarre," and he decided to follow the matter closely; verbatim transcripts of Brand's interrogation in Cairo were on his desk by late July 1944.[66] But he and other War Department officials were more interested in what Brand's interrogation told them about Nazi morale. In the end, the Soviets demanded that the whole idea be abandoned on the grounds that it probably represented an attempt by the Germans to explore the possibility of a separate peace on the Western front. Brand's mission thus ended in failure.

In the meantime, Jewish groups in New York had not given up on the military option. In early August, McCloy received another appeal for bombing the death camps, this time from Leon Kubowitzki, the same World Jewish Congress official in New York who had previously warned against bombing. Kubowitzki's message was actually passing on an appeal from Ernest Frischer, a member of the Czech government-in-exile. As before, McCloy allowed Gerhardt to draft the reply, which used much the same language as before to reject the request. Without investigating the matter or contacting air commanders in the European theater, McCloy again asserted that such bombings would require the "diversion of considerable air support. . . ." The only new element in this letter was the rather curious statement that "there has been considerable opinion to the effect that such an effort, even if practicable, might provoke even more vindictive action by the Germans."[67]

Nahum Goldmann, president of the World Jewish Congress, learned that the Allies were running bombing missions near Auschwitz by reading *The New York Times,* which briefly reported on the Silesia raids in August and September. Between July 7 and November 20, 1944, at least ten fleets, numbering up to 357 heavy bombers, dropped their loads within thirty-five miles of Auschwitz. Sometime that autumn, Goldmann went to see McCloy in his Pentagon office and personally raised the bombing issue with him. Goldmann maintained an apartment in Washington during the war years and knew McCloy as a friend of both Felix Frankfurter and Henry Morgenthau, Jr.

Years later, Goldmann, who always admired McCloy, wrote of this meeting: "McCloy indicated to me that, although the Americans were reluctant about my proposal, they might agree to it, though any decision as to the targets of bombardments in Europe was in the hands of the British." (This was not the case.) McCloy told Goldmann to see his good friend Sir John Dill, head of the British Joint Staff Mission in Washington. Goldmann recalled his hour-long confrontation with Dill as "one of the most unforgettable and depressing of my long career." Dill immediately rejected the idea, first on the grounds that such bombings would kill thousands of prisoners. When Goldmann argued that these prisoners were doomed anyway, Dill declared that British bombs had to be saved for military targets. Goldmann then pointed out that the Royal Air Force was already bombing the I. G. Farben factory only a few miles from Auschwitz and that "the few dozen bombs needed to strike the death camps would not influence the outcome of the war. . . ." Dill was unmoved by these arguments, and by the end of the meeting Goldmann bitterly accused the British field marshal of a "lack of human understanding for the terrible tragedy of the extermination camps." Dill responded that he thought Goldmann "discourteous," and on that note the two men parted company.[68]

If in this instance McCloy succeeded in assigning responsibility to the British, on other occasions the War Department rationalized that it was a matter for Soviet consideration. At the end of September, the Polish government-in-exile once again made a request through the War Refugee Board to have the death camps bombed. The Poles said they had received evidence from their sources in Warsaw that the pace of the exterminations had increased. Pehle decided in early October to transmit this new request to McCloy, but he did so with a note merely advising him to look it over "for such consideration as it may be worth." McCloy's assistant, Colonel Gerhardt, passed Pehle's note to McCloy and recommended that "no action be taken on this, since the matter has been fully presented several times previously." He reminded McCloy that "it has been our position, which we have expressed to WRB, that bombing the Polish extermination centers should be within the operational responsibility of the Russian forces."[69]

That the bombing should be a responsibility of the Russians represented a new rationale. In fact, there is no evidence that the issue was raised with the Soviets, even though there was an easily available excuse to do so. Only a month before, a group of American correspondents toured the Majdanek death camp, near Lublin, which had recently been overrun by Soviet troops. The reporters wired home detailed descriptions of the gas chambers, the crematoria, and the mounds of human ashes.[70] If the War Department had really intended to raise the issue of bombing the death camps with the Soviets, no one would have had to spend any time convincing the Russians of the facts.

Finally, in early November, Pehle made one last request for a bombing mission against the Auschwitz and Birkenau death camps. He had at last received the full thirty-page text of the Vrba-Wetzler report, and its contents shocked him into action. He wrote McCloy another letter, this time pulling no punches. Enclosing copies of the two escapees' reports, Pehle told McCloy, "No report of Nazi atrocities received by the Board has quite caught the gruesome brutality of what is taking place in these camps as have these sober, factual accounts of conditions in Auschwitz and Birkenau. I earnestly hope that you will read these reports." In his cover note, Pehle emphasized that the destruction of large numbers of people "apparently is not a simple process." The eyewitness reports, Pehle said, show that the Germans were devoting "considerable technological ingenuity and administrative know-how in order to carry out murder on a mass production basis. . . ."

Pehle then "strongly" recommended "destroying the execution chambers and crematories in Birkenau through direct bombing action." He acknowledged that, "Until now, despite pressures from many sources, I have been hesitant to urge the destruction of these camps by direct, military action. But I am convinced that the point has now been reached where such action is justifiable if it is deemed feasible by competent military authorities." As if he knew that these military authorities would be reluctant to bomb a nonmilitary target, Pehle then tried to make the military case for bombing the death camps. Krupp, Siemens, and Buna factories—manufacturing hand-grenade casings—could be destroyed in the vicinity of the camps. Many German soldiers guarding the camp would be killed, and the morale of the Polish underground would be "considerably strengthened." Finally, a number of prisoners might escape in the confusion resulting from the bombings. As evidence of this, Pehle enclosed a recent *New York Times* article on the British bombing of a German prison camp in France where a hundred French resistance fighters condemned to death had escaped in the aftermath of the bombing.[71]

McCloy or Colonel Gerhardt routinely passed Pehle's letter over to OPD. Six days later, Lieutenant General John Hull, recently promoted to chief of OPD, wrote McCloy a military evaluation of Pehle's latest proposal. Hull was the general who had given McCloy a quick negative evaluation of a similar proposal the previous June. This time he flatly stated, "The target is beyond the maximum range of medium bombardment, dive bombers [needed for precision bombing] and fighter bombers located in the United Kingdom, France or Italy." Hull asserted that the use of heavy bombers based in Britain would require a round-trip flight "unescorted of approximately 2000 miles over enemy territory." He then went on to tell McCloy that U.S. strategic air forces could not at this "critical stage of the war" be diverted from "the destruction of industrial target systems so vital to our effort. . . ." Hull concluded that the proposed bombing was "unacceptable from a military standpoint . . . and the results obtained would not justify the high losses likely to result from such a mission."[72]

Again, Hull had not consulted any of his commanders in the European theater, and no systematic study of the proposed mission was conducted. Contrary to what he told McCloy, bomber missions were flying over Silesia, targeting synthetic-oil plants adjacent to Auschwitz. Nor were these missions sustaining high losses. Even if it was determined that only dive-bombers could do the job, Hull was wrong to say that such bombers could not have traveled the necessary distance. P-38 dive-bombers had made a longer run from their bases in Italy to destroy oil refineries at Ploieşti the previous June. If Hull had taken the time to make a few inquiries, he quickly would have learned these facts. If McCloy had expressed any strong personal interest in a positive reply, Hull's response might easily have been different. As it was, Colonel Gerhardt received Hull's evaluation and once again merely incorporated Hull's language into a draft reply to Pehle for McCloy's signature. The letter concluded on a personal note: "I know you have been reluctant to press this activity on the War Department. We have been pressed strongly from other quarters, however, and have taken the best military opinion on its feasibility, and we believe the above conclusion is a sound one." Without commenting on whether he had even read it, McCloy then enclosed the Vrba-Wetzler report for return to Pehle's files.[73]

This ended Pehle's efforts to persuade McCloy to have the death camps bombed. Ironically, the only attempt to destroy one of the death camps was made by the tortured inmates themselves. One month earlier, on October 7, a band of courageous inmates in Birkenau had organized a suicidal uprising and managed to destroy by fire one of the camp's crematoria.[74] The ultimate tragedy lay in the number of lives that could have been saved if the Allies had bombed the gas chambers of Auschwitz and Birkenau at any time during the summer of 1944. If McCloy had pushed through a bombing order in mid-August, some hundred thousand Hungarian Jews in Auschwitz would have been spared death by gassing.[75] With the gas chambers destroyed, the Nazis would have been forced to suspend the industrial scale of their murders.

McCloy bears substantial responsibility for this misjudgment. It was his job to handle such civilian political matters brought to the attention of the War Department. Repeated requests of various Jewish leaders and organizations to bomb the death camps were not lost in a bureaucratic maze; the requests, together with the terrifying evidence, found their way to the right man, probably the only official in the War Department who possessed sufficient power and personal competency to persuade the government to make the rescue of European Jewry a military priority.

If John Pehle, Nahum Goldmann, and others had persuaded him of the merits of such an operation, there is little doubt that McCloy's characteristic diligence would have quickly resulted in a bombing attack on the Polish death camps. McCloy's mistake was one of omission. He allowed his instinctive chariness of "getting the Army involved" to govern his responses.[76] Though given more information than any other high-ranking official in Washington, he chose not to study the issue. When confronted with eyewitness reports, he chose not to believe. Like many others grappling with these unimaginable events, he lived in what the Protestant theologian W. A. Visser't Hooft called "a twilight between knowing and not knowing."[77]

He was not consumed with prejudice, as were many others in the government, such as Breckinridge Long. But he shared with Stimson and many of his peers some of the unconscious petty stereotypes of Jews common to the period. One of these was that Jews could be their own worst advocates, that any aggressive advocacy on their part was somehow grating and impolite. This view, while wholly unexceptional in McCloy's social milieu, reinforced the skepticism McCloy and others felt about the reports of a Jewish Holocaust, particularly when the sources of the reports were Jewish. Finally, it is important to record that at least one of the Jewish Americans with whom he worked could tag him with anti-Semitism. Henry Morgenthau, Jr., genuinely liked McCloy, but early in the summer of 1944 the Treasury secretary lost his temper at a Cabinet meeting when informed that McCloy was complaining about the army's having to take care of Jewish refugees. Though McCloy wasn't in attendance, Stimson was there, and returned that day to dictate a memo asserting that someone in the Cabinet had labeled McCloy an "oppressor of the Jews."

Morgenthau quickly heard that McCloy was deeply offended, so, early the next morning, he invited him over to his home in order to clear up the matter. McCloy came right to the point by saying, "I understand that I was criticized at Cabinet. . . . Somebody in Cabinet said that I was the oppressor of the Jews. That is a terrible thing." Without specifically denying that he had called McCloy an "oppressor of the Jews," Morgenthau reassured him that "there was no criticism of you. . . ." The two men then proceeded to have an amicable conversation about refugee policy. McCloy volunteered that he had found a camp to house eighteen hundred Jewish refugees and asked, "How many people are they really proposing to bring over?" Morgenthau assured him that only a "token" number would be brought into the United States. McCloy then made it clear to Morgenthau that the army was always willing "to be the over-ground railway to bring these people out." He explained that the army in Italy would feed and care for such refugees only during transit: "We have twenty thousand Italians a night coming through the line in Southern Italy. It is a very difficult military question. We have got our hands full." Morgenthau said he understood, and both men agreed that ultimately the United Nations Refugee and Relief Agency (UNRRA) would have to take care of refugees once they had made their way south of the army's front lines. With the issue settled, they parted as friends.

But, clearly, McCloy had been shaken by Morgenthau's accusation. Immediately after this meeting, Morgenthau told Pehle, "Frankly, the fellow was bothered." He told Pehle he was glad he had acted promptly to diffuse the issue, and confessed of McCloy, ". . . the fellow is a human fellow."[78]

Henry Morgenthau was not wholly immune to McCloy's persuasive charms, which may explain why he was now about to be outmaneuvered on the critical issue of Germany's future. For many months, McCloy had been crafting a set of policy directives to guide the U.S. Army as it began to occupy German territory. By August 5, 1944, the progress of Allied troops in France was such that McCloy could tell Harold Ickes over lunch that he "would not be surprised if we would be through with the war in Europe in about a month."[79] If Germany should now suddenly collapse, two policy directives drafted by McCloy on policy for occupying Germany, together with an army handbook spelling out the directives in detail, would immediately become effective. McCloy's directives reflected the army's policy of restoring law and order to a war-devastated Germany as rapidly as possible. But the directives and the handbook could easily be characterized as a blueprint for a soft peace. The army handbook instructed occupation authorities to "subsidize essential economic activities where necessary" and "reconstruct German foreign trade. . . ." The army was supposed to be prepared to ensure a food supply averaging two thousand calories a day for each German. "International boundaries will be deemed to be as they were on 31 December 1937."[80]

In early August, Morgenthau and his aide, Harry Dexter White, met with Eisenhower in France. The supreme commander indicated in strong terms that he favored letting "Germany stew in its own juice," at least for the first several months of Allied occupation. He gave Morgenthau a copy of the draft army handbook on occupation policy and, according to Morgenthau, indicated his disapproval of it. Eisenhower's major concern at the time seemed to be that any talk of a soft peace might disrupt relations with the Soviets; he was anxious to see them resume their offensive on the Eastern front.[81]

As a result, Morgenthau came back to Washington determined to change the McCloy directives. On August 25, he called up the assistant secretary and said, "Now, look, I just feel somebody's got to take the lead about let's be tough to the Germans, see?" Morgenthau said he was going to show the president a synopsis of the army handbook on occupation policy.[82] McCloy must have been surprised by what happened next. The very next morning, Roosevelt sent Stimson a stinging memo which began, "This so-called 'Handbook' is pretty bad." The president said he saw no reason to have the U.S. Army of Occupation build a "WPA, PWA, or a CCC for Germany." He asked Stimson to revise the handbook and warned him, "The German people as a whole must have driven home to them that the whole nation has been engaged in a lawless conspiracy against the decencies of modern civilization."[83]

With this, Stimson and McCloy knew they would have to toughen the initial draft of what now became known as JCS 1067. Simultaneously, Morgenthau and his people, including John Pehle, went to work on their own draft of a plan for Germany's occupation. On September 4, 1944, Morgenthau had McCloy, Stimson, Harry White, and Harry Hopkins over for an informal dinner. It was a "pleasant dinner," according to Stimson, "but we were all aware of the feeling that a sharp issue is sure to arise over the question of the treatment of Germany. Morgenthau is, not unnaturally, very bitter. . . ."[84]

Morgenthau had quite a different assessment of the dinner. In a phone conversation the next morning with Hopkins, he sarcastically mimicked Stimson's views: "All you've got to do is let kindness and Christianity work on the Germans."

Hopkins replied, "Oh, boy . . . But fundamentally, I think it hurts him so to think of the non-use of property [referring to Morgenthau's desire to shut down the Ruhr Valley industries]. . . . He's grown up in that school so long that property, God, becomes so sacred."

At the end of this conversation, Morgenthau proposed that Stimson had another motive: "Of course, what he wants—he didn't come quite clean—what he wants is a strong Germany as a buffer state [to the U.S.S.R.] and he didn't have the guts to say that."[85]

Morgenthau didn't think McCloy was much better. About the same time, he weighed in against a suggestion from Eisenhower that McCloy be named high commissioner of an occupied Germany. He told Hopkins on another occasion, "McCloy isn't the man to go. . . . After all, his clients are people like General Electric, Westinghouse, General Motors, and Stimson's are too."[86]

By this time, Roosevelt had appointed Hopkins, Stimson, Morgenthau, and Cordell Hull to a committee to decide the issue of policy toward Germany. By early September, Morgenthau had a draft of his own plan, which envisioned the total destruction of all German heavy industry, specifically any industry related to arms manufacture. It called for the pastoralization of Germany, though light industry would be allowed to produce basic consumer items. The country would be broken into two independent states, and the highly industrialized Ruhr Valley would become an international zone forbidden to trade with the rest of Germany.

Stimson thought the proposal most unwise, and over the next few weeks he, McCloy, and Morgenthau jockeyed to influence Roosevelt on the issue. Stimson was willing to incorporate some aspects of Morgenthau's plan—specifically, the idea of internationalizing the Ruhr Valley. On September 7, he had lunch with McCloy and Jean Monnet to talk over that scheme. Unlike Morgenthau, Monnet had no intention of stripping the Ruhr of its steel industries or flooding its coal mines. Rather, Monnet hoped to have the Ruhr produce for the benefit of all Europe. He was even willing to see the Soviets serve as one of the "trustees" to manage the Ruhr's factories. On this point Stimson agreed, but, to his surprise, McCloy expressed considerable alarm at "giving this addition to Russia's power."[87]

By September 9, it was beginning to become clear that Stimson and McCloy would lose the battle. They met that day with Roosevelt, and the president abruptly said he was inclined to let the Germans eat from "soup kitchens."[88] Shortly afterward, Roosevelt left for a conference with Churchill in Quebec. Unknown to either Stimson or McCloy, he allowed Morgenthau to attend the conference. A few days later, when they learned of Morgenthau's presence in Quebec from the newspapers, McCloy became despondent. "I have never seen him so depressed as this made him," Stimson recorded for his diary. "It is an outrageous thing. Here the President appoints a committee . . . and, when he goes off to Quebec, he takes the man who really represents the minority and is so biased by his Semitic grievances that he is really a very dangerous advisor to the President at this time."[89]

Two days later, Stimson learned from McCloy that Roosevelt had indeed accepted Morgenthau's counsel and rejected the War Department's occupation plans. The decision seemed firm, since not only Roosevelt but also Churchill had endorsed the Morgenthau Plan. Stimson angrily dictated for his diary, "I have yet to meet a man who is not horrified with the 'Carthaginian' attitude of the Treasury. It is semitism gone wild for vengeance and, if it is ultimately carried out (I cannot believe that it will be), it as sure as fate will lay the seeds for another war in the next generation."[90] McCloy agreed. Both as a veteran and as a lawyer in Europe during the 1920s, he had long ago concluded that the "tough peace" imposed on Germany at Versailles was a major cause of the next war.

As was his habit when upset by a turn of events, McCloy had lunch with Harold Ickes the next day. After complaining about Morgenthau's "back door" tactics, he asked Ickes what he thought should be done with the Germans. Ickes at first jocularly suggested that they "all ought to be sterilized," but after discussing the matter agreed that, "much as I hate the Germans and mistrust them, I do not believe that a vindictive peace would mean anything but another war. . . ." Both men agreed that "Morgenthau ought not to have anything to do with this matter for the simple reason that he is a Jew and the charge will be made that through him the Jews are dictating peace terms that no one in the end will be willing to accept."[91]

McCloy felt very strongly about this issue. But whether he had anything to do with leaking the terms of the Morgenthau Plan to the press two weeks later is a matter for conjecture. Someone gave *The New York Times'* Arthur Krock specific details of both the plan itself and how Morgenthau had pushed it through over the opposition of the president's other advisers. Morgenthau was furious, and though McCloy was the obvious suspect, he could not bring himself to believe that the assistant secretary was responsible: "I don't think McCloy would go out and deliberately cut my throat . . . [or] stab me in the back."[92] Krock was one reporter whom McCloy liked and felt willing to talk with during this period of the war. In any event, Krock's articles, and subsequent revelations by Drew Pearson, created a furor. Most editorialists came out against the president, partly on the argument that a hard peace would encourage Germany to fight to the bitter end. By the end of the month, Roosevelt was wondering whether he had misjudged the political pulse of a hard peace for Germany. He called up Stimson and intimated that he had almost decided that he had made a "false step."[93] He said he really didn't intend to make Germany a purely agricultural country. Later, over lunch, he grinned broadly at Stimson and confessed, "Henry Morgenthau pulled a boner."[94]

By the end of October, McCloy and Stimson were clearly winning the public-relations battle against Morgenthau's "Carthaginian" peace. But by then it was also clear that the optimistic talk in August of an early collapse of Germany was misplaced. The Germans had finally dug in on their borders and created a stable front. Eisenhower and Marshall now knew the war would not end in 1944.

CHAPTER 11

Victory in Europe

"There is complete economic, social and political collapse going on in Central Europe. . . . We are going to have to work out a practical relationship with the Russians."

JOHN J. MCCLOY TO PRESIDENT HARRY S. TRUMAN
APRIL 1945

The struggles surrounding the Morgenthau Plan, the end of the Japanese American internment, and the question of whether to bomb the Polish death camps were only three of many weighty issues crossing McCloy's desk in the autumn of 1944. He was also working on proposals for a war-crimes tribunal, and following up on some of the financial initiatives agreed upon at the Dumbarton Oaks conference in August, which created two pillars of the postwar system, the World Bank and the International Monetary Fund. Simultaneously, he was involved in negotiations with the Saudis for use of airfields in the Arabian Peninsula. And he was beginning to turn his attention to Soviet-American relations. One evening in October, over dinner, he and Ellen received a particularly pessimistic briefing from Averell Harriman on secret-police methods in the Soviet Union. In contrast to Marshall, Roosevelt, and many others in the administration, McCloy had always been skeptical of the prospects for maintaining the "Grand Alliance" in the postwar period. What Harriman had to tell him about Soviet power and intentions greatly worried him.

On the other hand, these worries did not alter his views on the politically sensitive question of whether members of the Communist Party should be allowed to receive officer commissions. This issue, raised and settled by McCloy earlier in the war, was repeatedly resurrected by Army G-2 types in the summer and autumn of 1944. Exasperated by this pattern of overzealous security investigations, he wrote Marshall in June to complain that G-2's actions could "result in a War Department 'red scare' which would penalize perfectly loyal Americans for honestly held opinions on controversial topics."[1] When Major General Clayton Bissell, G-2's assistant chief of staff, raised the issue once again late in 1944, McCloy firmly instructed him that past membership in the Communist Party was not evidence of disloyalty.[2] A few months later, in February 1945, McCloy was required to testify before a special congressional subcommittee appointed to investigate the appointment of army officers with alleged communist sympathies. Under harsh questioning from congressional conservatives, McCloy refused to change his position. The army, he said, would investigate and dismiss officers found to be disloyal; but left-wing sympathies, or even proof of lapsed membership in the Communist Party, would not constitute grounds for dismissal.[3]

All of these issues, of course, were important and politically sensitive, and therefore justified the personal attention McCloy gave to them. But it was also obvious that he was spread too thin. "He has taken over so much that he can't do it all," Stimson recorded in his diary that autumn. By now, Washington society assumed McCloy was running the War Department. One morning he was embarrassed to read a rare front-page editorial in the *Washington Post* suggesting that he should shove his "Colonel" aside and become secretary of war. He knew that Stimson at the age of seventy-eight was slowing down, and had confided to Ickes that he sometimes had to struggle to keep the secretary awake in late-afternoon meetings. But he still respected the "Colonel's" judgment, and his loyalty to the man left no room even to consider the idea of replacing him. When the publisher of the *Washington Post*, Eugene Meyer, wanted to follow up his editorial with an in-depth profile, McCloy refused to see the reporter assigned to the story.[4]

Less than three weeks later, Stimson shouldered McCloy with an additional burden by designating him the "recorder" for a revived "Committee of Three," consisting of Stimson, the newly appointed Secretary of State Edward R. Stettinius, and Secretary of the Navy James V. Forrestal. Both Stettinius, a former General Motors executive, and Forrestal, a Dillon, Read & Co. investment banker, perhaps because they assumed the aging Stimson would not appear at many of its meetings, urged that McCloy attend in order to "formulate" the Committee's agenda.[5] Stimson quickly concurred.

The Committee of Three rapidly became the venue for the most important decisions in the remainder of the war. Decisions made there were carried out on an administrative level by McCloy, in his capacity as chairman of yet another organization, the State-War-Navy Coordinating Committee. SWNCC, as it was known, was a direct precursor of what later became the National Security Council. Its creation, and the appointment of Stimson's powerful aide as its chairman, were essentially a ratification of the War Department's *de facto* supremacy in foreign affairs. As chairman of SWNCC, McCloy would now devote the remainder of the war to the larger issues of a postwar peace. Much remained to be decided. Would the United States join a postwar United Nations? Would the Manhattan Project produce an atomic weapon and, if so, should it be used to end the war and keep the postwar peace? On what basis would the Allies occupy and govern Germany and Japan? And could the Soviet-American alliance survive the defeat of fascism?

McCloy's added responsibilities did not please everyone in Washington. Henry Morgenthau felt Stimson's aide was monopolizing far too much information, particularly on the sensitive issue of occupation policy for Germany. In early January 1945, he learned from a State Department official that McCloy was excluding Treasury officials from all meetings on the controversial policy directive for Germany—JCS 1067. Not one to be bypassed, the crusty Treasury secretary drafted a tough memo warning the president that it would be very difficult to stamp out German militarism:

> The more I think of this problem and the more I hear and read discussion of it, the clearer it seems to me that the real motive of most of those who oppose a weak Germany . . . is simply an expression of fear of Russia and communism. It is the 20-year-old idea of a "bulwark against Bolshevism"—which was one of the factors that brought this present war down on us. . . . There is nothing that I can think of that can do more at this moment to engender trust or distrust between the United States and Russia than the position this Government takes on the German problem.[6]

McCloy disagreed with these sentiments, but recognized Morgenthau's influence with the president: over the next few months he made an effort to work with the Treasury secretary. The two men agreed that Germany should be politically decentralized, and perhaps even dismembered, and that her heavy industry should be restricted enough to destroy her capacity to make war. McCloy opposed the kind of blanket "pastoralization" favored by Morgenthau, but he did not envision a soft peace. When the State Department, behind McCloy's back, got Roosevelt to sign off on a "Draft Directive for the Treatment of Germany" that failed even to mention dismemberment, McCloy, in "great excitement," immediately called up Morgenthau.

"This business is all pretty delicate," he told the secretary, "because of the relations with the State Department, but I think that now, in the light of the fact that they went off on a frolic of their own . . . that . . . we've got a right to sulk on it."

Morgenthau quickly agreed, saying of the State Department plan, "It's damnable, an outrage."[7]

While Stimson took a vacation in Miami for ten days, McCloy worked with Morgenthau and his aide, Harry Dexter White, on a rebuttal of the State Department's March 10 memo. The document asserted that the State Department's position contradicted decisions reached at both the Quebec and Yalta conferences.

At Yalta in February 1945, Roosevelt had made any number of concessions to the Soviets in recognition of the obvious preponderance of power they possessed in Eastern Europe. Some of these were hedged in vague language that later became the source of much Soviet-American wrangling. But the agreements on Germany were far less ambiguous. Divided into four zones, occupied Germany was to pay reparations on the order of $20 billion, half of which would go to the Soviets. Moreover, it was understood by the Americans that four-power control over the industrial Ruhr valley would be necessary to ensure that these reparations were paid. The $10 billion in reparations that Stalin expected could not all come from the Eastern, less industrialized zone of occupied Germany. This essentially meant a hard peace, in which Germany's industrial production would be taxed heavily and closely administered by the four occupying powers. As McCloy and White now reminded Roosevelt, at Yalta the Allies had agreed that "we should aim at the greatest possible contraction of German heavy industry as well as the elimination of her war potential. . . . The occupying forces should accept no responsibility for providing the German people with food and supplies beyond preventing starvation, disease, and such unrest as might interfere with the purposes of the occupation."[8] McCloy went along with this language, while reminding Morgenthau that Stimson opposed the stronger language embodied in the Quebec Agreement. He argued that no final decision on German policy should be reached until both State and the War Department had had a chance to discuss the matter. When Morgenthau saw Roosevelt later that afternoon, the president consented to a procedure whereby McCloy, Harry White, Assistant Secretary of State William L. Clayton, and several other officials would jointly work out a new draft directive for Germany.

Over the next few days, McCloy mediated between the State and Treasury factions in a fashion that led all, including Morgenthau, to believe that deep down he agreed with their position. Despite their disagreements, Morgenthau was not immune to McCloy's sometimes playful charm. One day, as he was about to leave his office for a particularly difficult meeting with Morgenthau, McCloy was inspired to borrow a miniature spy-camera developed by Donovan's technicians in the OSS. Morgenthau, he remembered, had placed a hidden microphone in his desk, which many of his visitors knew he used to tape-record their conversations. That day, as the meeting began, McCloy pulled the camera from his pocket and ostentatiously began snapping pictures of everyone in the room. When a startled Morgenthau demanded to know if he was taking photographs without his permission, McCloy grinned and replied, "Well, since you've been recording everything without our permission, I thought you wouldn't mind if I did too."[9] After a moment of embarrassed silence, everyone in the room laughed.

McCloy gradually persuaded Morgenthau that their positions on postwar Germany were not so far apart. He got the Treasury secretary to admit that "it is one thing to have communications and a railroad, and it is something else to have an OPA [public-works program]." After a crucial March 22 meeting with the president, McCloy made a point of briefing the prickly Treasury secretary: Roosevelt had told him, "I don't want you to eliminate German industry—not at all. . . . I want you to change the character of it. . . . I'm not for throwing salt into the mines." Morgenthau took this news with surprising equanimity and told McCloy he actually appreciated his frankness. "It may sound silly," he said, "to say thank you because when I'm treated squarely it is so unusual that I have to say thank you. . . . It has happened so rarely in Washington. . . . It's a pleasant surprise."[10]

The next day, McCloy, Morgenthau, and Will Clayton ironed out a final version of a paper entitled "Summary of U.S. Initial Post-Defeat Policy Relating to Germany." The document had a little bit for everyone concerned. Morgenthau was pleased that it incorporated some strong language from his original plan, providing "programs of industrial disarmament and demilitarization." The Germans would have to pay reparations, but they would not be allowed to rebuild their heavy industry in order to pay for those reparations. All members of the Nazi Party would be removed from public office or positions of responsibility in private companies. Nazi leaders would be tried, and the army demobilized. These tough peace terms were offset, however, by language that permitted the occupation authorities in each zone to re-establish centralized organs to control such "essential national public services as railroads, communications and power . . . finance and foreign affairs, and . . . production and distribution of essential commodities." Germany would not be allowed to starve. Morgenthau, McCloy, and Clayton signed the document, and later that afternoon the president himself initialed it.

Stimson thought it a "fairly good paper," while Morgenthau told members of his staff that the March 23 document represented "the first step toward a kind of peace which I think will last. . . ." He was actually ecstatic at his victory over the State Department crowd, whom he called "Fascists at heart."[11]

He considered McCloy a loyal ally in this bureaucratic warfare, but McCloy's efforts had produced a document so flexible that it could sanction almost any kind of policy. In fact, a few weeks later, McCloy came back from an inspection trip of Allied-occupied Europe convinced that key elements of the German economy had to be rebuilt just to maintain law and order.

Before leaving for Europe, he was called to the White House for an unscheduled meeting with the president. When he entered the Oval Office, Roosevelt greeted him with a raised, straight-arm Hitler salute: "Heil McCloy—Hochkommissar für Deutschland." He explained to a startled McCloy that he was offering him the job of high commissioner of occupied Germany. McCloy responded that placing a civilian in such a job immediately after the conclusion of hostilities might be a serious mistake. He said the problems facing a war-ruined Germany could only properly be dealt with by a military general, preferably one with logistical training. When he suggested General Lucius Clay, who had won widespread admiration for his handling of the Pentagon's logistical problems, a suddenly weary Roosevelt replied, "Oh, McCloy, I'm too tired to argue with you."[12]

On his fiftieth birthday, March 31, 1945, McCloy boarded a C-47 military-transport plane bound for Paris. Eisenhower's armies were rapidly closing in on the heartland of the German state, and the civilian leadership in the War Department felt they needed some firsthand reporting on conditions inside occupied Germany. Over the next few weeks, he visited Rheims, Luxembourg, Brunen, Cologne, Frankfurt, and eventually London before leaving for Washington on April 18. He managed to see Generals Eisenhower, Omar N. Bradley, Leonard T. Gerow, George S. Patton, and dozens of other commanders on the rapidly advancing front lines.

McCloy felt overwhelmed by the devastation he saw; entire German towns were being systematically obliterated as the Allied armies advanced into Germany. When he saw the supreme commander on April 5 in Rheims, he warned Eisenhower against any unnecessary destruction of German infrastructure. Eisenhower's troops were then wrapping up a battle against 150,000 German troops trapped in the Ruhr Valley, and, from McCloy's perspective, the war was won. He was already worried about occupying and governing a defeated enemy.

Soon afterward, he caught up to the Sixth Army on the Southern front just as its commander, General Jacob Devers, readied an artillery bombardment of Rothenburg, one of Germany's most beautiful medieval walled towns. McCloy had visited Rothenburg in the 1920s, and he remembered that when he was a child his mother, Anna, had shown him etchings of the town's spired skyline. In addition, his own children's nursemaid originally came from Rothenburg.[13] When Devers happened to show McCloy the bombardment targets for the following morning, McCloy said, "Jakie, the war is so far along, do you have to bomb this town?" Devers agreed not to, and soon thereafter he managed to persuade the German commander to surrender the city.[14]

Between April 6 and 9, three American armies, including Patton's Third Army, advanced fifty miles a day. McCloy had to move quickly to catch up with Patton's army on April 7. When Patton expressed the hope that as soon as the war in Europe was over he would be transferred to the Pacific front, McCloy confided in him that the United States was developing an atomic bomb, which, he said, might make an invasion of the Japanese home islands unnecessary.[15] Patton was disappointed, since he did not look forward to playing the politically delicate role of an American proconsul in occupied Germany. A few days after McCloy moved on, Patton wrote him, "Yesterday I saw the most horrible sight I have ever seen. It was a German slave camp. . . . We took all the soldiers we could to see it, as I believe it is one of the best arguments against fraternization that I know."[16]

McCloy returned to Paris on April 12, 1945, and late that evening he was roused from his bed in a VIP house at Versailles and told that Franklin Roosevelt had died. He scribbled in his diary, "It is absolutely impossible to think of its implications. . . . The press of current and impending events leaves no time to speculate on his position in history."[17]

The evening before his death, Roosevelt had been talking of McCloy with Henry Morgenthau. The Treasury secretary had reminded Roosevelt, "McCloy is away you know."

"McCloy is all right now," replied Roosevelt, "but he was all wrong about de Gaulle, but I explained things to him and now he has been loyal to me."

"I am glad you feel that way," Morgenthau said. He noted in his diary that evening, "I was glad to hear the President say that because I think some people around town have been trying to poison him against McCloy. . . ."

Before Morgenthau left his old friend for the last time, he gave him another lecture about the importance of ensuring a weak Germany in the postwar period. "A weak economy for Germany means that she will be weak politically, and she won't be able to make another war. . . . I have been strong for winning the war, and I want to help win the peace."

"Henry," said the president, "I am with you 100 percent."[18]

About the same time, in Paris, McCloy had a long talk with General de Gaulle at a small dinner party hosted by the French general and his wife. They too discussed the fate of Germany, but came to rather different conclusions. Far from destroying German industry, de Gaulle agreed with Monnet. He said he wished to see the Ruhr Valley under international control so that its industries could produce "for the benefit of all Western European countries." He also indicated that France would need the entire production output from the Saar coal mines, and some coal from the Ruhr as well. Germany, they agreed, should be dismembered, but its economy would have to be rebuilt, if only to aid in the reconstruction of war-torn Europe.[19]

Moving on to London, McCloy attended a memorial service for Roosevelt in Saint Paul's Cathedral, where he stood near Churchill and King George VI. The boys' choir sang the "Battle Hymn of the Republic"—too slowly, McCloy thought. He was amused to see Churchill do a little jig with his feet upon hearing the words "Oh be swift, my soul, to answer Him, be jubilant, my feet." As McCloy was leaving the church, he looked back and saw the prime minister standing bare-headed, his figure framed between two columns. A shaft of sunlight fell on his face, and McCloy could see that he was sobbing.[20]

Ellen greeted McCloy at the airport upon his arrival back in Washington on the afternoon of April 19, 1945. Despite the long air journey, he drove straight to the Pentagon. There Stimson took him aside in his private study and listened to his firsthand observations of the situation in Germany. He spoke of "near anarchy" and said it was "something that is worse than anything probably that ever happened in the world." He painted a "picture of a country that has been filled up with slaves drawn from the surrounding nations, over whom the Germans have sat on as slave-drivers and have been working to death . . . and the slaves in turn are running riot through the country."[21]

Soon afterward, he held a press conference in which he stated that "one cannot exaggerate" the complete destruction of the entire European industrial base. Local food supplies would run out completely within a month or two. Referring to German war atrocities, he said that the machinery for punishing the "lower elements" of German war criminals was already being set in motion, while the Allies were still debating how to punish the top-ranking hierarchy of the Nazi regime.[22]

One subject he did not discuss at his press conference was his growing doubts about the future of U.S. relations with the Soviet Union. With Europe in such disarray, he privately wondered how the United States would deal with the reality of Soviet military might. On the Monday following his return to Washington, he and Stimson were rehearsing McCloy's briefing of the new president, Harry S. Truman, when Stimson was suddenly called to an emergency meeting at the White House. Truman wanted to know how to deal with V. M. Molotov, the Soviet foreign minister, who had just arrived in Washington. In an initial encounter with the new president, Molotov had tried to convey the absolute strategic importance to the Soviet Union of a friendly regime in Poland.

Molotov thought he was on firm ground, since at Yalta Roosevelt had agreed that no anti-Soviet government would be allowed to take power in states bordering on the Soviet Union. In return, the Soviets had agreed that "the Provisional Government which is now functioning in Poland [i.e., the Lublin government, dominated by the communists] should therefore be reorganized on a broader democratic basis with the inclusion of democratic leaders from Poland itself and from Poles abroad." Though there was a vague reference to free elections, Roosevelt had specifically dropped any language calling for supervised elections. Roosevelt himself, in a subsequent letter to Churchill, called the agreement on Poland a "compromise" in which it was understood that the Lublin government would form the basis for a broadened coalition government.[23] (This did occur in June 1945, when the Lublin Poles brought into their Cabinet five prominent noncommunist Poles.) Molotov thought his government had every right to expect the Lublin Poles to be seated at the upcoming San Francisco conference on the United Nations. Truman, however, had not been briefed on the subtleties of what had been agreed to at Yalta, and it was now his instinct to stand up to the Russians. He suggested to his assembled advisers that perhaps Molotov should be told with brutal frankness that they had to abide by their agreements, that Yalta was a two-way street.

Stimson, however, urged caution. He told Truman that "the Russians perhaps were being more realistic than we were in regard to their own security." He reminded the new president that the Soviet Union had always "kept its word" on "big military matters," and, indeed, "had often done better than they had promised."[24] Stimson was leery of coming to an impasse with Russia "on an issue which in my opinion is very dangerous and one which she is not likely to yield on in substance."[25]

Stimson was disturbed by the tone of the meeting, but he returned from it to tell McCloy that he thought his words of caution had persuaded Truman to deal with Molotov's demands in a realistic vein. Later that evening, however, Truman did just the opposite, telling Molotov in the bluntest language possible that he expected the Soviet Union to carry out its agreements regarding free elections in Poland. Molotov protested, "I have never been talked to like that in my life." Truman snapped back, "Carry out your agreements and you won't get talked to like that."[26] With this undiplomatic exchange, the meeting was over.

The following evening, Truman received a cable from Stalin himself. The Soviet dictator made it clear that he felt that Yalta had recognized his right to establish in Poland a government friendly toward the Soviet Union. "Besides everything else," warned Stalin, "this is demanded by the blood of the Soviet people abundantly shed on the fields of Poland in the name of the liberation of Poland." Neither Britain nor the United States, he pointed out, bordered on Poland. He then reminded Truman that the Soviets had not been consulted in the formation of governments for

Belgium or Greece, precisely because the Kremlin recognized the "importance of Belgium and Greece for the security of Great Britain."[27] Clearly, if Soviet interests in Poland were to be challenged, then the West could expect the same in countries they considered within their sphere of influence.

On the same day he read Stalin's angry note, Truman received an oral briefing from McCloy, who emphasized that the United States had to find a way to work with the Russians. Truman was impressed enough to ask McCloy for a quick written report. This McCloy had on Truman's desk by the evening of April 26, and its message was sobering. McCloy told the president, "There is complete economic, social and political collapse going on in Central Europe, the extent of which is unparalleled in history unless one goes back to the collapse of the Roman Empire, and even that may not have been as great an economic upheaval. . . . In this atmosphere of disturbance and collapse, atrocities and disarrangement, we are going to have to work out a practical relationship with the Russians. It will require the highest talents, tolerance and wisdom in order to accomplish our aims."[28]

Though tensions were rising between the United States and the Soviet Union, McCloy, Stimson, and many others still believed that, with a lot of hard work, a "practical relationship" with the Russians was both possible and desirable. Truman, however, was not a man to see these things in any but black-and-white terms. From the very first days of his presidency, he had decided that in dealing with the Russians he would have to "lay it on the line."[29]

And now there was the factor of the bomb. The day before McCloy delivered his report to Truman, Stimson gave the president a forty-five-minute briefing on the political ramifications of the atomic bomb. "Within four months," Stimson wrote, "we shall in all probability have completed the most terrible weapon ever known in human history, one bomb which could destroy a whole city." Moreover, he warned, the United States could not expect to maintain a monopoly over this awesome power. The Soviet Union would inevitably develop the same technology "within a few years." Stimson suggested that international control of the weapon would be difficult; nevertheless, "the question of sharing it with other nations, and if shared, upon what terms, becomes a primary question of our foreign relations."[30] Truman stoically read through Stimson's entire memo in his presence, asked no questions, and agreed to Stimson's request that an *ad hoc* Interim Committee be established to advise him on the use of the bomb. Stimson came away from the meeting pleased. His carefully prepared memo had made the point: this was a weapon the Russians could someday acquire on their own, and its destructive power was such that the two powers would someday have to cooperate with each other in regulating its use. But for Truman, fresh from his confrontation with Molotov, the real news was the simple fact that the United States was about to acquire a revolutionary weapon the Soviets did not have.

None of these men, including McCloy, had a fully developed view of how to deal with the Soviet Union. Of them all, Truman was the most insecure. He easily took personal offense at Stalin's or Molotov's language, and responded impetuously. Stimson, characteristically, could see many sides to the same argument, and over the next few months he agonized over his doubts; he ended up voicing, at one time or another, every nuance of the issue. McCloy's views, by contrast, were neither extreme nor erratic. At the end of April, as he headed for the San Francisco meetings on the United Nations Charter, where many in the administration feared a complete breakdown in U.S.-Soviet relations would take place, he summed up his own mood in a diary entry: "It is little wonder that as they [the U.S. and the U.S.S.R.] emerge in their own and the eyes of everyone else as the two greatest powers that they should walk stiff-legged around the ring a bit."

Clearly, he felt much more sanguine than Truman. Things might naturally get a little rough, but with time and hard work a "sound working base" could be established with the Russians.[31] This was his instinctive judgment, and he would return to it again and again in the years to come.

By the time McCloy arrived in San Francisco, the delegates had already spent a full week debating the ground rules for the United Nations, a new international organization designed to keep the peace in the postwar period. A number of petty issues had been resolved, though with considerable rancor. Now the delegates faced a central question: would the United Nations tolerate the formation of regional security blocs, and, specifically, would the new international organization recognize the legitimacy of unilateral intervention by the great powers within their respective security blocs? On this point, McCloy had quite definite views: nothing in the U.N. Charter should invalidate the Monroe Doctrine, which for more than a hundred years had sanctioned U.S. intervention against European or other outside influences in the Western Hemisphere. The logic of this position, of course, would sanction similar unilateral interventions by the Soviets in their sphere of influence. While McCloy was willing to go quite far toward recognizing the reality of the Soviet military presence in Eastern Europe, he wished also to retain some kind of limited, but defined, American access to countries like Poland, Rumania, and Czechoslovakia. Even more important, America's right to intervene promptly in Western Europe could not be delegated to an international body. A telephone conversation he had with Stimson on May 8, 1945, underscores the dilemma:

MCCLOY: I've been taking the position that we ought to have our cake and eat it too; that we ought to be free to operate under this regional arrangement in South America, at the same time intervene promptly in Europe; that we oughtn't to give away either asset. . . .

STIMSON: I think so, decidedly, because in the Monroe Doctrine . . . we've gotten something that we've developed over the decades. . . .

MCCLOY: Now, she [Russia] will say, "All right, we'll give you that, but give us that same thing in Europe and Asia." If we do that I do think there's an argument that we cut the heart out of the whole world organization—is it worth doing that? . . .

STIMSON: Well, you don't think that Russia is going to give up her right to act unilaterally in those nations around her which she thinks so darned—are useful, like Romania and Poland. . . .

MCCLOY: Uh, no . . .

Recognizing the inevitable, McCloy still could not help feeling uneasy about sanctioning the formation of such regional security blocs. He warned Stimson that this might mean "we finally have a good big regional war one of these days."[32]

Within a week, McCloy had supervised the drafting of an article of the U.N. Charter recognizing the right of "collective self-defense" regardless of whether or not the Security Council acted in any particular conflict. Accepted by the Soviets, Article 51 later became the basis for the two powers' string of regional security pacts around the world.

By May 10, 1945, McCloy was back in Washington, where he briefed Stimson, Marshall, Undersecretary of State Joseph Grew, Navy Secretary Forrestal, Averell Harriman, and other officials. Everyone in the room seemed to agree that McCloy had done the right thing by standing firm on the regional question.[33] Afterward, Stimson invited McCloy, Harriman, and Harvey Bundy to stay for lunch. Harriman gave them all a "gloomy report" on the prospects of working with the Soviets. "He didn't think," Stimson recorded for his diary, "there was any chance of getting the seeds of liberalism into Russia. . . ." Harriman bluntly warned that though "Russia is really afraid of our power or at least respects it . . . she is going to try to ride roughshod over her neighbors in Europe. . . ." Stimson "very confidentially" raised "our problem connected with S-1 [atomic bomb] in this matter."[34] Indeed, ever since Roosevelt's death, Stimson had begun to spend more and more of his time weighing the matter of the bomb and its possible effects on U.S. relations with the Soviets.

CHAPTER 12

Hiroshima

". . . really, we ought to have our heads examined if we don't explore some other method by which we can terminate this war. . . ."

JOHN J. MCCLOY TO PRESIDENT TRUMAN
JUNE 18, 1945

On May 14, Stimson had a long conversation with British Foreign Secretary Anthony Eden that focused almost entirely on the progress of the Manhattan Project. McCloy and Marshall joined them for lunch, and afterward Stimson summed up his views on the bomb for McCloy:

> I told him this was a place where we really held all the cards. I called it a royal straight flush and we mustn't be a fool about the way we play it. They can't get along without our help and industries and we have coming into action a weapon which will be unique. Now the thing is not to get into unnecessary quarrels by talking too much and not to indicate any weakness by talking too much; let our actions speak for themselves.[1]

Stimson's attitude at this point conformed with McCloy's conviction that though the Russians could be difficult, a "practical relationship" with them was in America's interest. The atomic bomb, which both men fully expected to be a technical success within a month, was merely one more reason why the Russians would have to become less recalcitrant in their dealings with the West.

The next morning, McCloy served as "recorder" for a meeting of the Committee of Three in which Stimson, Forrestal, and Undersecretary of State Joseph Grew discussed various problems with the Soviets arising from the Yalta accords. A few days earlier, Grew had handed McCloy a memo that posed a series of tough questions regarding the Soviets: what kind of pressure was the United States willing to exert to ensure that the Soviets kept their half of the agreement? How important was it to Washington now to obtain Soviet entry in the war against Japan? Should the United States agree to a joint U.S.-Soviet occupation of Japan or insist on a purely American occupation? These questions, Stimson thought, "cut very deep and in my opinion are powerfully connected with our success with S-1" (the atomic bomb).[2]

In what Stimson described as a "pretty red hot session," the men proceeded to discuss the points Grew had raised. They worried that, once they entered the war in the Far East, the Soviets would begin to backtrack on their Yalta promises to recognize the Chiang Kai-shek regime and stay out of China. Stimson felt it might be "necessary to have it out with Russia" on these matters. But he forcefully argued that such questions were for the moment "premature." The United States needed to postpone talking about these questions until after the atomic bomb had been tested. He was worried that Truman had agreed to meet Stalin and Churchill on July 1, which was at least two weeks before the first possible atomic test: ". . . it seems a terrible thing to gamble with such big stakes in diplomacy without having your master card in your hand."[3]

Six days later, after mulling the whole matter over with McCloy, Marshall, and his other advisers, Stimson sent the State Department a formal reply to Grew's May 12 list of questions. Regarding the question of Russian intentions, he reported that "it appears we can bring little, if any, military leverage to bear on the Russians in so far as the Far East is concerned, unless we choose to use force."[4] Nor did he think that Washington could influence whether the Soviets would enter the war against the Japanese. Their decision to do so or not would be based strictly on their own national interest. And from his perspective, it really didn't matter, since the war against Japan was almost won.

Although a conventional invasion of the Japanese home islands had to be prepared, both Stimson and Marshall recognized it might not be necessary. As Stimson phrased it in a reference to the atomic-bomb project, "Fortunately, the actual invasion will not take place until after my secret is out."[5]

On May 16, 1945, McCloy helped Stimson prepare a memo for Truman on the situation in both the Far East and Europe. Once again, he urged restraint and advised the new president to deal realistically with the Russians. Truman was told that, because it would take many months to redeploy U.S. forces to the Far East, he had more time for "diplomacy" vis-à-vis the Soviet Union than "some of our hasty friends realize." The real problems in dealing with the Soviets lay in Europe, not the Pacific. "Pestilence and famine" would likely sweep Central Europe the following winter, leading to "political revolution and Communistic infiltration." Stimson and McCloy took for granted that the Soviets would control much of Central Europe. "Our defenses against this situation," they argued, "are the western governments of France, Luxembourg, Belgium, Holland, Denmark, Norway, and Italy. It is vital to keep these countries from being driven to revolution or Communism by famine." Consequently, U.S. and Canadian wheat surpluses would have to be shipped to Western Europe that summer. But in the long term, they advised the president, "We must find some way of persuading Russia to play ball."[6]

Stimson and McCloy were greatly relieved when Truman accepted their advice to reschedule the meeting in Potsdam with Stalin after the first atomic test: "We shall probably hold more cards in our hands later than now." Like Stimson and McCloy, Truman assumed the Soviets would become more forthcoming on Poland and other issues when informed of a successful test of the new weapon.[7]

He was not the only official in Washington who hoped the atomic bomb would persuade the Russians to "play ball." James F. Byrnes, the man whom Truman had designated as his representative on the Interim Committee, was certain the bomb would make the Soviets more manageable in Europe. A conservative South Carolina politician, Byrnes hoped to persuade the Soviets to withdraw their troops from Hungary, Rumania, and other parts of Eastern Europe. Russia, he said, "might be more manageable if impressed by America's military might."[8]

Unlike Byrnes, Stimson and McCloy had no real expectations that the Soviets would withdraw from their defensive sphere of influence in Eastern Europe. But they nevertheless hoped that the expected American monopoly over the atomic weapon would dampen Russian ambitions and persuade them that their sphere of influence should be porous enough to tolerate some Western trade.[9] Whether the bomb would actually have to be used in combat in order to demonstrate its power was a different question. By the end of May, McCloy began to differ with his "Colonel" on the question of whether the bomb would be necessary to end the war in the Far East. The latest intelligence estimates suggested the Japanese were in fact very close to a surrender. As early as mid-April, the Joint Intelligence Committee had concluded that the Japanese were hoping only to modify the surrender terms so as to preserve the institution of the emperor.[10] Then, in mid-May, Allen Dulles reported from Switzerland that the resident Japanese minister, Shunichi Kase, had expressed interest in mediating a cessation of hostilities. This caused OSS chief Bill Donovan to write the president, "Kase believes that one of the few provisions the Japanese would insist upon would be the retention of the Emperor as the only safeguard against Japan's conversion to Communism. Kase feels that Under Secretary of State Grew, whom he considers the best US authority on Japan, shares this opinion."[11] Grew, in fact, did share this assessment and believed the war would end quickly if Washington issued a statement explaining that unconditional surrender did not carry with it the dethroning of the emperor.

Soon McCloy was arguing with Stimson that there was every reason to believe the new Japanese Cabinet headed by Prime Minister Kantaro Suzuki, a recognized moderate, was looking for a face-saving way out of the war.[12] On May 28, he went so far as to recommend that the phrase "unconditional surrender" be dropped altogether: "Unconditional surrender is a phrase which means loss of face and I wonder whether we cannot accomplish everything we want to accomplish in regard to Japan without the use of that term."[13] Even if in the end the bomb had to be used, McCloy was now persuaded of the importance of giving the Japanese both a fair warning and some kind of assurance that the institution of the emperorship would not be destroyed. The next day, he drafted a memo with Marshall's approval that reflected the chief of staff's views on the use of the bomb. Marshall suggested that the first target of the bomb should be "straight military objectives such as a large naval installation. . . ." If the Japanese still did not capitulate, Marshall said, then "we ought to designate a number of large manufacturing areas from which people would be warned to leave—telling the Japanese that we intended to destroy such centers." He emphasized that "every effort should be made to keep our record of warning clear. . . . We must offset by such warning methods the opprobrium which might follow from an ill-considered employment of such force."[14]

But two days later, on May 31, 1945, Marshall failed to press these views in a meeting of the Interim Committee.* It was at this all-day meeting that the initial decision was made to drop the bomb on Japan without warning. (Because he was not a member of the Interim Committee, McCloy was not present.) The transcript shows no real debate took place about whether to use the bomb. During their lunch break, Stimson and some of the scientists discussed whether a demonstration of the bomb somewhere could serve as a substitute for a surprise atomic attack. But Robert Oppenheimer dismissed the idea, saying he could think of no practical demonstration of the weapon. The other scientists present did not dispute this judgment.[15]

After lunch, Stimson "expressed the conclusion, on which there was general agreement, that we could not give the Japanese any warning; that we could not concentrate on a civilian area; but that we should seek to make a profound psychological impression on as many of the inhabitants as possible." Stimson agreed with James Conant's suggestion "that the most desirable target would be a vital war plant employing a large number

*The Interim Committee consisted of Henry Stimson, George L. Harrison, James F. Byrnes, Undersecretary of the Navy Ralph A. Bard, Assistant Secretary of State William L. Clayton, Dr. Vannevar Bush (director of the Office of Scientific Research and Development), Dr. Karl T. Compton (president of M.I.T.), and Dr. James B. Conant (chairman of the National Defense Research Committee and president of Harvard University). Also attending the May 31, 1945, meeting were Generals Leslie R. Groves and George C. Marshall, Harvey Bundy, Arthur W. Page (an assistant to Stimson), and the four members of the Scientific Advisory Panel: Ernest O. Lawrence, Enrico Fermi, Arthur Compton, and Robert Oppenheimer.

of workers and closely surrounded by workers' houses."[16] Stimson, before and after this meeting, repeatedly voiced his objections to saturation bombings of civilian targets, but in this instance concurred in the atomic targeting of civilian workers' homes.

The prevailing assumption, that the bomb should be used against the Japanese in order to shorten the war, was not challenged. (As early as April 23, 1945, General Groves had told Stimson, ". . . the target [for the atomic bomb] is and was always expected to be Japan."[17]) Stimson assured the assembled scientists that he did not regard the bomb "as a new weapon merely, but as a revolutionary change in the relations of man to the universe." And yet, even though everyone acknowledged that this was a unique device—or, in Stimson's words, a potential "Frankenstein which would eat us up"—it would nevertheless be used like any other weapon in the U.S. arsenal.[18] There was also general acknowledgment that "fundamental knowledge of this subject was so widespread" that the secret of the bomb could not long be maintained as an American monopoly. But when Marshall suggested inviting two prominent Russian scientists to witness the first test, he was firmly rebuked by Byrnes. The minutes of the meeting record Byrnes as expressing the general consensus that the United States should "push ahead as fast as possible . . . to make certain that we stay ahead and at the same time make every effort to better our political relations with Russia."[19] No one suggested that the two activities might be contradictory.

On June 6, Stimson conveyed the Committee's recommendations to Truman. But the decision was still not set, if only because many officials could see that the war might now end much sooner than any had thought. Along with other top-ranking War Department officials, McCloy was aware that on the last day of May the OSS had reported on another Japanese peace feeler, this time by the counselor of the Japanese Legation in neutral Portugal. The OSS source reported that the Japanese diplomat had declared that the "actual peace terms were unimportant so long as the term 'unconditional surrender' was not employed." The Japanese, the OSS reported, "are convinced that within a few weeks all of their wood and paper houses will be destroyed."[20]

By mid-June, McCloy felt nearly certain that any U.S. invasion of the Japanese home islands was unnecessary. By contrast, Stimson was confused and appeared overwhelmed by conflicting emotions. On the evening of June 17, he was also suffering from one of his migraine headaches when McCloy stopped by Woodley to talk about the whole question of a Japanese surrender. Stimson was scheduled to attend an important meeting the next afternoon, at which the president would be asked to approve the initial land-invasion plans. The Joint Chiefs had proposed that the first attack take place on November 1 against the southern Japanese home island of Kyushu; Marshall estimated U.S. casualties in this initial operation would run on the order of thirty-one thousand. That night, McCloy argued with Stimson that the entire operation was unnecessary. "We should have our heads examined if we don't consider a political solution," he bluntly told Stimson.[21]

Truman, he said, ought to be told to make a personal appeal to the Japanese emperor. An unconditional surrender of Japanese military forces could be effected, he argued, if the Japanese were assured that the emperor's position could be preserved in a constitutional monarchy. McCloy then suggested that Truman's message to the emperor could end with an ultimatum, threatening use of a terrible new weapon that could destroy whole cities with one blow. He was certain that such a political overture, combined with the ultimatum, would almost surely bring about an immediate surrender. Appealing to Stimson's sense of moral statesmanship, he suggested that, if such an overture did not bring about a capitulation, America would find itself on firmer moral ground if the bomb was used.[22]

Stimson seemed to agree. He told McCloy he would make the case for such an appeal at the meeting the next afternoon. But later that evening, feeling very worn out, he called McCloy and said, "Jack, I'm not up to going to that meeting tomorrow. I'll arrange with the White House to have you take my place."[23] The next afternoon, however, soon after McCloy walked into the 3:30 P.M. meeting in the White House, Stimson showed up, having dragged himself out of bed.

The meeting began with Truman's asking the assembled generals for their military recommendations. In retrospect, McCloy considered this meeting an unfortunate example "of confining large questions on the conduct of the war to purely military considerations. . . ."[24] Too often, he felt, the civilian leadership, out of deference to military judgment, ended up ignoring important political considerations. Roosevelt had encouraged this practice, and his inexperienced successor would conduct such meetings in the same fashion. General Marshall spoke first, and by the time he had outlined the contingency plans for a full-scale invasion of the Japanese home islands, there seemed nothing more to be said.

Even Stimson seemed resigned now to the invasion plans, despite the concessions he had made the previous evening to McCloy's views. The most he could muster was a vague comment on the possible existence of a peace faction among the Japanese populace: "I do think," he told Truman, "that there is a large submerged class in Japan who do not favor the present war and whose full opinion and influence have not yet been felt. . . . I feel something should be done to arouse them and to develop any possible influence they might have before it becomes necessary to come to grips with them."[25]

It was left to a military man, Admiral William D. Leahy, the president's acerbic military aide, to point out an obvious political fact: an insistence on absolute, unconditional surrender would surely stiffen Japanese resistance. Leahy voiced his skepticism on the need for any invasion.[26] Truman commented that he didn't believe the American public was willing to end the war on any other terms, but he admitted that, when he had last talked to congressional leaders, he had left the door open to modifying the terms. Preparations for an initial invasion that autumn, he said, should proceed. But then, according to McCloy's recollections, Truman made it clear that he wanted the Joint Chiefs to "return for further instructions before the preparations arrived at a point beyond which there would not be further opportunity for a free choice on the part of the President." (In his memoirs, Admiral Leahy put it more bluntly: "The invasion itself was never authorized."[27])

Since the president had given his approval to the contingency plans, the Joint Chiefs now began to rise to their feet, thinking that the meeting was over. But Truman suddenly said, "No one is leaving this meeting without committing himself. McCloy, you haven't said anything. What is your view?" The assistant secretary of war turned to look at Stimson, who quickly said, "Say what you feel about it."

McCloy began: "Well, I do think you've got an alternative and I think it is an alternative that ought to be explored and that, really, we ought to have our heads examined if we don't explore some other method by which we can terminate this war than just by another conventional attack and landing."[28] He repeated to Truman the proposal for a political overture to the emperor that he had outlined to Stimson the evening before. As he described it, McCloy made it clear that he thought the war had progressed to such a state that there was now a "question of whether we needed to get Russia in to help us defeat Japan."[29] This argument carried significant weight, since many of those in the room, like McCloy himself, were beginning to worry about the prospect of having Soviet troops occupy Manchuria or portions of Japan itself in the postwar era. If the war with Japan could be ended without Soviet assistance, why give them the chance to establish a foothold in this region? Truman responded warmly to this argument, telling McCloy, "That's exactly what I've been wanting to explore. . . . You go down to Jimmy Byrnes and talk to him about it."[30]

McCloy then suggested that perhaps the Japanese ought to be told "that we had the bomb and that we would drop the bomb" on them if such surrender terms were not promptly accepted.[31] Though everyone in the room was cleared for knowledge of the Manhattan Project, no one had felt it appropriate to mention the subject. There was a feeling that somehow McCloy had broken a taboo. He recalled later that he sensed the "chills that ran up and down the spines" of his colleagues.[32] He ventured, "I think that our moral position would be better if we gave them specific warning of the bomb." At this, a number of the assembled military officers protested that the bomb had yet to be tested and might not even explode when dropped from an airplane. In response, McCloy backed down a bit from his suggestion of a warning: "If you don't mention the bomb, at least mention in general terms what its capacity is, something in the nature that with one blow we would wipe out a city. They'll know what we're talking about."[33]

After more discussion, Truman instructed McCloy to "give further thought to this message but don't mention the bomb at this stage."[34] Truman was indicating that, while he thought some kind of political overture might be warranted, he was still inclined to keep the bomb a secret until it could be dropped.[35] McCloy's dialogue with the president influenced Stimson, who in the weeks afterward began to focus heavily on the need to change the terms of surrender. Stimson could see from the tone of the discussion that, barring a sudden surrender by Tokyo, the bomb would be used. This was an assumption that no one in the meeting seriously questioned, though it was not directly discussed. But McCloy had altered the agenda by pointing out that the war, one way or another, would certainly be long over before November 1, the earliest scheduled invasion of Japan.

By speaking the unspoken, McCloy had dramatically shifted the terms of the debate. Now it was no longer a question of invasion. What had been a dormant but implicit option now became explicit. The soon-to-be-tested bomb would end the war, with or without a warning. And the war might even end before the bomb was ready.

The following morning, on June 19, the Committee of Three met, with McCloy acting as a recorder. The acting secretary of state, Joseph Grew, argued that it really wasn't even necessary to backtrack from a demand for unconditional surrender. "We must occupy Tokyo," Grew said; no compromise peace could be tolerated. All that needed to be done was to explain "what we meant by unconditional surrender in such a way which might induce them to desist from further hostilities." He suggested that Washington notify the Japanese that eventually "they could determine for themselves the nature of the particular political structure they wanted for the future so long as it did not incorporate any of the militaristic elements."[36]

Both Stimson and McCloy agreed with these sentiments, and during the next week they drafted a memo for the president outlining the arguments for giving the Japanese such assurances. By this time, most of the president's advisers—including McCloy, Stimson, Forrestal, Leahy, and the Joint Chiefs—more or less accepted the proposition that a modest change in the surrender terms might soon end the war. On June 26, at another meeting of the Committee of Three, Stimson, Forrestal, and Grew, with McCloy present, also agreed that any such clarification of the surrender terms should be issued well before an invasion and with "ample time to permit a national reaction to set in." They agreed that "Japan is susceptible to reason" and that there was every reason to avoid an outright invasion. A "carefully timed warning" should include the following elements: a characterization of the "varied and overwhelming force" the United States was about to bring to bear on Japan; the "completeness of the destruction" this force would entail; an assurance that the Allies did not intend to "extirpate the Japanese as a race or to destroy them as a nation"; and a statement that occupation troops would withdraw from Japan as soon as there was established "a peacefully inclined government, of a character representative of the masses of the Japanese people." Stimson and McCloy suggested that, if they were to add a statement to the effect that the Allies would not "exclude a constitutional monarchy under her present dynasty, it would substantially add to the chances of acceptance." There was general agreement even on this controversial last point, and before the meeting broke up the secretaries asked McCloy, two State Department officers, and a representative of the Navy Department to draft the actual language for such a statement.[37]

As usual, McCloy became the leading "oarsman" in drafting this critical language. As instructed by Truman, he did not mention the atomic bomb; instead, a vague threat was made to inflict "utter devastation of the Japanese homeland." But in a separate note to Stimson he was careful to say that he thought a reference to the atomic bomb could be "readily introduced."[38] As he drafted it, Paragraph 12 of the surrender terms specified that the occupying forces of the Allies would withdraw after the establishment of a peacefully inclined government. And, most important, it specified that this government "may include a constitutional monarchy under the present dynasty. . . ."[39] McCloy acknowledged to Stimson that this was the "most controversial" point and might "cause repercussions at home. . . ." But without it, he said, "those who seem to know most about Japan feel there would be very little likelihood of acceptance."[40]

Over the weekend, McCloy flew up to Hastings-on-Hudson to visit Ellen and the children. He had taken copies of the draft proclamation and phoned Washington to dictate some minor changes in the wording. Back in Washington on July 2, he went over the final draft, and then Stimson personally handed it to the president later that day. Truman brusquely gave it his tentative approval. McCloy thought it fair, clear, and firm; without really compromising on the principle of unconditional surrender, the language in Paragraph 12 gave the Japanese just enough assurances to persuade them to end the war.[41] Though the proclamation did not yet include a direct warning on the atomic bomb, McCloy hoped Truman might be persuaded to insert this once the scientists successfully demonstrated they actually had a weapon ready for delivery.

In the meantime, Navy Undersecretary Ralph A. Bard, who had been sitting in on the deliberations of the Interim Committee, had made his own appeal for a bomb warning, directly to the president. The Chicago financier had become convinced, like McCloy, that the "Japanese war was really won." On June 27, he had written a formal dissent from the Interim Committee's recommendation not to issue a warning. His top-secret memo argued the merits of giving Japan a "preliminary warning" two or three days prior to dropping the bomb. Four days later, Bard took his case to the White House in person. "For God's sake," he told the president, "don't organize an army to go into Japan. Kill a million people? It's ridiculous."[42] Truman dismissed these arguments with the comment that the idea of a bomb warning had already been considered.

Under the influence of Jimmy Byrnes, the president was now moving in quite the opposite direction. Early in his presidency, there was no man on whom Truman relied more than the former South Carolina senator and Supreme Court justice. Truman sometimes felt this "politician's politician" should have occupied the Oval Office in his place. In 1944, before he had been tapped by the Democratic Party bosses to replace Henry Wallace as Roosevelt's running mate, Truman had agreed to nominate Byrnes for the job. When Roosevelt died, one of Truman's first acts was to call Byrnes to his side and promise to make him secretary of state, a move not received very graciously by Washington's foreign-policy community. Though he knew nothing of foreign affairs, Byrnes always had a strong opinion. "Mr. Byrnes," said Dean Acheson, "is not sensitive or lacking in confidence."[43] Within weeks of Roosevelt's death, the smooth South Carolinian was quietly known about Washington as the "assistant president." All the evidence suggests that, during the spring and early summer of 1945, Byrnes had influenced Truman to think of the atomic bomb as a diplomatic weapon, something that "might well put us in a position to dictate our own terms at the end of the war."[44] As the president's personal representative on the Interim Committee, he had taken every opportunity to shoot down suggestions of demonstrating the terrible force of the bomb, or sharing the "secret" of its existence with the Soviets.[45] And now Byrnes was about to take steps to ensure that McCloy's political overture to the Japanese, embodied in Paragraph 12 of the surrender proclamation, was eliminated.

On July 3, 1945, Stimson and McCloy went over to the White House to see Byrnes sworn in as secretary of state. Later that afternoon, in a private meeting with Truman, Stimson solicited a reluctant invitation from the president to "be somewhere near" him at the upcoming Potsdam conference. He pointed out that this would mean he would have to go to Berlin and asked if he could take McCloy along. Truman said, "All right," and a relieved Stimson rushed back to the Pentagon to prepare for the trip. When Truman did not invite Stimson and McCloy to accompany him on the cruiser USS *Augusta,* they made their own travel plans. Stimson decided to take another ship, while McCloy took a plane to Europe on July 8.[46]

Truman left Washington on July 7. Sailing with him aboard the *Augusta* were a number of his Missouri poker-playing companions and Jimmy Byrnes. In between poker games, Byrnes persuaded Truman to review his decision to accept McCloy's draft of the surrender proclamation. Byrnes had been impressed by former Secretary of State Cordell Hull's view that Paragraph 12—regarding the permissibility of a constitutional monarchy—sounded "too much like appeasement."[47] With no one on board to argue otherwise, Truman cut the last sentence of Paragraph 12 by the time they arrived in Antwerp on July 15, eliminating any assurance to the peace factions in Tokyo that the emperor might be allowed to retain his throne.

This decision was never altered, even when new evidence of the emperor's intentions became available that week from intelligence intercepts. Before Stimson, McCloy, and other officials left for Potsdam, they had been shown an intercept strongly indicating that the emperor himself had requested his war Cabinet to seek a peace settlement. It seemed Hirohito wished to dispatch a special Japanese ambassador to Moscow under orders to request the Soviets, then still neutral, to act as intermediaries with the Americans and British. As Truman, Stimson, and McCloy were traveling toward Potsdam, Washington intercepted a July 13 cable from Japanese Foreign Minister Shigenori Togo to his ambassador in Moscow that made Tokyo's intentions clear: "Unconditional surrender is the only obstacle to peace. . . ." In another cable, Togo instructed his ambassador in Moscow to obtain an interview with Molotov before the Soviet foreign minister left for the Big Three conference at Potsdam. Molotov should be told, said Togo, that "it is His Majesty's heart's desire to see the swift termination of the war. . . ."[48]

McCloy's plane arrived in Berlin shortly before Truman's. Greeting him on the tarmac was Averell Harriman, who had also managed to get himself invited to the conference. Andrei Gromyko, the Soviet ambassador to Washington, was there as well, and all three waited for Truman's plane to land before driving into Potsdam. After settling in at one of the large lakefront villas formerly occupied by a colony of German filmmakers, McCloy had lunch with Harriman and, later in the afternoon, discussed the Japanese war with Stimson.[49]

Unaware that Byrnes had persuaded Truman to cut out the language concerning the emperor in Paragraph 12, McCloy still considered the draft surrender proclamation incomplete. Just before leaving for the Big Three summit, he told Grew, "There are impending two matters of great significance: one, the possibility of Russian entry into the Pacific War and, two, the event with which Secretary Byrnes is fully familiar." By this veiled reference to the atomic bomb, McCloy indicated to Grew that he assumed that, if the bomb was to be used against Japan, "the warning paper, of course, will have to be rewritten to take this into account."[50]

On their first full day in Potsdam, McCloy, Harvey Bundy (Stimson's personal assistant), and the war secretary sat in the garden outside their villa and set to work drafting yet another memo to the president. Delivered to Byrnes on the evening of July 16, the memo stated that the right "psychological moment to commence our warnings to Japan" had arrived. Referring to the intelligence intercepts of Japanese diplomatic-cable traffic, they argued, ". . . the recent news of attempted approaches on the part of Japan to Russia, impels me to urge prompt delivery of our warning." If this warning did not bring about a surrender, then "the full force of our newer weapons" should be marshaled against the Japanese.[51]

That same afternoon, Stimson received an "eyes-only" cable from George Harrison, the War Department's watchdog for the Manhattan Project, in Washington, who reported on the test of the first atomic bomb carried out that morning at Alamogordo, New Mexico. Harrison said the "results seem satisfactory and already exceed expectations."[52] Stimson was visibly jubilant. "The Secretary cut a gay caper," McCloy wrote in his diary, "and rushed off to tell the President and Jimmy Byrnes about it." He caught the president coming back from a tour of the ruins of Berlin that evening and showed him the cable. The news, however cursory, immediately buoyed the president, who was scheduled to meet Marshal Stalin for the first time the next day. Later, when more detailed reports came in on the success of the Trinity test, McCloy observed that Truman and Churchill went off to their next round of negotiations with Stalin "like little boys with a big red apple secreted on their person." McCloy himself was sobered by the news. He wrote in his diary that night, "I hope it does not augur the commencement of the destruction of modern civilization. In this atmosphere of destruction and the callousness of men and their leaders, the whole thing seems ominous."[53]

For the remainder of the conference, the fact that the atomic bomb was at last an operational weapon was always uppermost in the minds of American officials. Early the next morning, Stimson made a point of showing the cable to Byrnes and made yet another plea for both an explicit warning on the bomb and an assurance to the Japanese that unconditional surrender did not mean an end to the emperorship. This time Byrnes unequivocally rejected both ideas, saying he spoke for the president.[54] Byrnes and Truman were isolated in their position; they were rejecting a plan to end the war that had been endorsed by virtually all their advisers. Just hours before the news from Alamogordo arrived, the U.S. Joint Chiefs of Staff meeting in Potsdam with their British counterparts had agreed that the "unconditional-surrender" formula should be changed or reinterpreted so as to assure the Japanese that the emperorship would be preserved. Perhaps because they were well aware of Byrnes's opposition, the Combined Chiefs of Staff then formally recommended that Churchill personally raise the matter with Truman.[55]

But it was evidently too late to change the president's mind. Truman himself was now counting on the bomb, perhaps to end the Pacific war and certainly to ameliorate some of his diplomatic problems with the Soviets. Shortly after meeting Stalin for lunch that day, the president noted in his private diary, "Believe Japs will fold up before Russia comes in. I am sure they will when Manhattan appears over their mainland."[56] He could feel so certain of this because on July 16, the same day he learned about the successful test of the bomb, he was informed of the Japanese emperor's effort to have the Russians negotiate a surrender. He characterized the deciphered message as the "cable from [sic] Jap Emperor asking for peace." McCloy said much the same thing in his own diary that day: "Hirohito himself was called upon to send a message to Kalinin and Stalin. Things are moving—what a long way we have come since that Sunday morning we heard the news of Pearl Harbor." Clearly, both men suspected the war could end in a matter of days.[57]

By the opening of the Potsdam conference, Truman had concluded that Soviet entry into the war was probably unnecessary.[58] McCloy had always been rather indifferent to whether the Soviets entered the Pacific war or not. He never thought it was "much of a trading point. . . ." And now, if it could be argued that it was quite unnecessary—given "the nearness of Japanese collapse,"—it might even be undesirable, because the Soviets could then have a claim in administering an occupied Japan.[59] If at one time the Americans had thought a mere Soviet declaration of war would have enough "shock value" to push the Japanese out of the war, they now felt the bomb could do the same thing. Moreover, according to Edwin Pauley, delegated by the president to handle the negotiations with the Russians on reparation issues, Truman also said he felt the bomb "would keep the Russians straight."[60] Later in the conference, when Stalin seemed particularly intransigent, Truman assured Stimson that he would not back down before the Soviet ruler. He could do so, the president inferred, by "relying greatly upon the information as to S-1 [atomic bomb]."[61]

In the midst of these deliberations, McCloy heard from Allen Dulles in Switzerland of another Japanese peace feeler. According to the OSS representative, Japanese individuals connected to the Bank for International Settlements had approached Per Jacobsson, a bank official, and informed him that their government wanted to surrender. As Dulles reported it, Tokyo was hesitating only over the term "unconditional surrender": "They wanted to keep their emperor and the constitution, fearing that otherwise a military surrender would only mean the collapse of all order and of all discipline. . . ." McCloy thought this so significant that he arranged to have Dulles flown to Potsdam immediately to report in person to Stimson. When Dulles arrived, on July 20, he received an "attentive hearing" from the secretary of war.[62] McCloy thought there was "something behind it, but just how substantial I do not know."[63] Taken together with the Magic intercepts, Dulles's information was one more indication that the Japanese were close to collapse. Now it was only a question of whether they would surrender soon enough to avoid an atomic bombing. As McCloy confided to his diary, "Maybe the Secretary's big bomb may not be dropped—the Japs had better hurry if they are to avoid it."[64]

On the morning of July 24, Stimson told Truman that an atomic bomb would be available to drop on a Japanese city soon after August 1. A second bomb would be ready by August 6. This meant that both bombs would hit Japan before the Soviets were scheduled to enter the war in mid-August. The war might well be over before Russian troops could invade Manchuria. This suited Truman. When Stimson then tried once again to raise the issue of clarifying the surrender terms regarding status of the emperor, the president again demurred. The most he would say was that perhaps some kind of verbal assurance could be transmitted to the Japanese if "they were hanging fire on that one point. . . ."[65] Two days later, the Potsdam Proclamation was issued without either an atomic warning or any assurance concerning the future of the Japanese royal dynasty.

Stimson was frustrated, worn out, increasingly depressed by the distrust he saw all around him. Byrnes had made a point of excluding him from all the critical roundtable meetings between Truman, Churchill, and Stalin. Almost from the beginning of the conference, Stimson complained in his diary that Byrnes was "hugging matters in this Conference pretty close to his bosom." Byrnes turned him down even when Stimson asked if McCloy could be squeezed into the main deliberations in his place. McCloy himself confided in a letter to Ellen that "we have not been in the middle of the ring."[66] Averell Harriman too was excluded, much to his annoyance. As Harriman recalled later, "Stimson also had plenty of free time. So we sat in the sun together outside his villa talking about when and how the Japanese might be brought to surrender, and how to deal with the Russians after the war."[67]

Stimson may have wished to issue the Japanese a warning, but he never voiced any doubts about whether the bomb should actually be used against the Japanese. General Eisenhower happened to be dining with Stimson when a long cable arrived conveying the details of the Trinity test. The secretary of war said they were going to drop this stupendous weapon on the Japanese. Eisenhower sat in silence, thinking it wasn't his place to disagree. But as he listened to Stimson talk of the destructive power of this new weapon, he became more and more depressed. So, when Stimson suddenly asked for his opinion of the bomb, Eisenhower said he was against its use. As Ike recalled the conversation, he argued, "First, the Japanese were ready to surrender and it wasn't necessary to hit them with that awful thing. Second, I hated to see our country be the first to use such a weapon. Well . . . the old gentleman got furious."[68]

McCloy agreed with Eisenhower, but with his boss more or less excluded from the higher councils of the conference, he found little opportunity to exert any influence in these matters. One evening, he was among the guests invited to dine with Truman, but this was largely a social affair, where everyone was entertained by the piano playing of a sergeant from Philadelphia named Eugene List.[69] In the one brief conversation he had with the president, McCloy spoke of Germany rather than the bomb and Japan. He told Truman that he felt the Soviets' intention to strip her occupation zone of all industry might well lead to a permanent division of Germany into East and West zones.[70]

With time on his hands, McCloy made several tours of Berlin's ruins. He wrote Ellen, "You would be appalled by it and you would think you were dreaming." A few days later, he wrote, "Berlin is a depressing place, a most depressing place. I saw a group of people . . . and children tearing up a carcass of a horse that had fallen dead in the streets from God knows what disease—it was horrible. The people look pale and dead looking, tho they say a night club is running in the city. There are Russian soldiers everywhere."[71] One day, he and an American general drove into Berlin and found their way to Hitler's bombed-out bunker in the middle of the city. They argued their way past a Russian sentry and, armed with flashlights, walked through the Führer's study and living quarters. McCloy's companion retrieved several chairs from the wreckage of Eva Braun's ornate bedroom and presented one of them to the assistant secretary of war. That night, he confessed to his diary, "I feel as if I were very much of a looter."[72]

While Stimson tried unsuccessfully to persuade Truman and Byrnes to issue the Japanese a warning on the bomb, McCloy spent most of his working hours at Potsdam in meetings with the Russians on the question of reparation payments. Given the Russian negotiating style, these were grueling affairs. Some sessions lasted until two in the morning. Bored by the endless haggling, McCloy in one such meeting got out his pen and began a letter to Ellen: "The Russians say Italy, to whom we are now paying over $50 million for relief purposes, should pay $6.5 million as reparations which only means that we pay for Russian reparations. The

Russians say . . . if the U.S. saw fit to promise them relief that is our affair. They did not ask us to do it."[73]

Despite such problems, McCloy felt the Soviets were "difficult and stubborn, but not impossible." The Americans on his delegations, he thought, might even be missing "a good chance at an agreement by fencing too much."[74] The central problem lay in the fate of Germany. Six months earlier, at Yalta, Roosevelt had agreed to use the general figure of $20 billion as a rough estimate of what the Germans should pay in reparations, half of which was reserved for the Soviets. Now Byrnes declared this figure "impractical" and refused to discuss any specific amount at all. Because McCloy was skeptical that Germany would be capable of paying any reparations, he concurred with Byrnes's position, saying that it would be a "great mistake . . . if the amount of reparations . . . [were] absolutely fixed now."[75] In a paper on the subject, McCloy and Stimson advised Truman, "The Russian policy on booty in eastern Germany is rather Oriental. It is bound to force us to preserve the economy in western Germany in close cooperation with the British."[76] In the end, Molotov agreed to an American proposal that each power satisfy its reparation claims from its occupation zone. This solution, of course, indirectly encouraged the Soviets to solidify their hold over East Germany. The Soviets might have been persuaded to demand less in reparations from Germany, Austria, and Italy if they had been assured of extensive lend-lease credits from the United States. But in May they had been abruptly told these loans would cease. This gave the Soviets all the more reason to take an uncompromising stand on control of Eastern Europe. Now, particularly in the wake of the successful Trinity test, Byrnes and Truman were trying to roll back some of the very specific understandings reached at Yalta concerning Eastern Europe. This was bad enough from the Soviet perspective. But worse in their eyes was the fact that they were being asked to loosen their grip on such border states prior to any U.S.-Soviet agreement on the fate of Germany. With sole possession of the atomic bomb, the Americans may no longer have feared Germany, but for the Soviets it was a different matter.[77]

McCloy had no illusions about the nature of Soviet rule. "The Russians," he wrote in his diary, "are actually posing as 'democrats' in spite of practicing totalitarianism in its most complete form (and getting away with it even in our own press)."[78] But as he demonstrated during the negotiations at San Francisco, he was willing to deal with them realistically and, unlike Byrnes, acknowledged their *de facto* sphere of influence in Eastern Europe. It was unfortunate that the Russians had "moved in like locusts on the Germans," and stripped whole factories of their equipment. "Yet in many respects," he wrote Ellen, "they cooperate fully with us in working out problems."[79] He thought Byrnes's negotiating style only made a difficult situation worse. "When there was controversy," Harriman recalled, "he [Byrnes] would pour oil on the waters."[80] McCloy was disturbed by the "atmosphere of rather deep suspicion" that pervaded the Potsdam conference: he acknowledged Byrnes to be "astute and experienced," but on the whole he thought the president's closest advisers were neither "particularly intellectually-minded" nor "enlightened."[81] In all the discussions he had heard at Potsdam, McCloy confided to his diary, "there was no clear evidence of an outstanding mind." This judgment stood for the president as well. He thought Truman was "less composed" and spoke with "less of an air of thought and experience about him" than either Stalin or the new British prime minister, Clement Attlee. "He always gives me the impression of too quick judgment."[82]

By July 24, Stimson was completely exasperated with Byrnes and Truman. He bluntly complained to the president that he had been excluded from too many of the Potsdam deliberations, to which Truman brusquely replied that he could leave at any time. Stung, Stimson finally decided to return to Washington. He left McCloy behind to find out what he could on the remainder of the Big Three deliberations.[83]

That same afternoon, McCloy learned from Marshall that after the end of the plenary session Truman had walked over to Stalin and "casually mentioned . . . that we had a new weapon of unusually destructive force." "Uncle Joe," as McCloy called him, expressed no surprise or particular interest, and remarked only that he hoped the United States would make "good use of it against the Japanese." But the Soviet ruler had not failed to catch the implied threat. That evening, he told Marshal Georgi K. Zhukov, the Soviet Army commander, "They simply want to raise the price. We've got to work on Kurchatov [the Soviets' chief of atomic research] and hurry things up."[84]

McCloy and Stimson had repeatedly emphasized the importance of apprising Stalin about the existence of the bomb, if only as a first step toward placing atomic technology under international control. Stimson, however, still thought the bomb might, if only in the short term, give the United States some diplomatic leverage over the Soviets. The more the secretary listened to Harriman's descriptions of Stalin's secret police, the more he became inclined to demand of the Soviets some degree of internal liberalization in return for a share in the control of atomic technology. Only a month earlier, he had speculated in his diary on the "quid pro quos" that might be expected for sharing nuclear secrets.[85] McCloy, however, thought it highly unlikely that any atomic horse-trading could impose Western-style democracy on the Soviet Union. "Personally," he wrote in his diary, "I think they have their political religion and we have ours." This same pragmatic instinct led him to conclude that, as difficult as the Soviets might be, some kind of *modus vivendi* would eventually have to be reached with them in order to control this "revolutionary" source of destructive power.[86] So McCloy was pleased that Truman had informed Stalin, however vaguely, of the new weapon.

The very next day, on July 25, Truman used a *National Geographic* map of Japan to pinpoint the four potential targets on which the first bomb would be dropped: the industrial cities of Hiroshima, Nagasaki, Kokura, and Niigata. He then gave his approval for the bombing; henceforward, unless the president countermanded this order, the bomb would be dropped as soon as it was ready. Twenty-four hours later, the watered-down version of McCloy's surrender proclamation was issued to the press and broadcast over the radio. Simultaneously, U.S. signal intelligence intercepted another message from the Japanese foreign minister to his ambassador in Moscow. Tokyo still would not accept unconditional surrender, but Togo wished his ambassador to "communicate to the other party [the U.S.] through appropriate channels that we have no objection to a peace based on the Atlantic Charter." This amounted to a significant signal, since the Charter constituted a liberal statement of British and American war aims. Togo pleaded that it was "necessary to have them understand that we are trying to end hostilities by asking for very reasonable terms in order to secure and maintain our nation's existence and honor." By this Togo unmistakably meant the preservation of the emperorship. "Should United States and Great Britain remain insistent on formality," Togo concluded, "there is no solution to this situation other than for us to hold out until complete collapse because of this point alone." This intercept was quickly deciphered and passed along to Truman, Byrnes, and no doubt McCloy, at Potsdam.[87]

A few days later, McCloy received another military-intelligence report, which concluded that the enemy "would be receptive to a peace that would allow Japan to continue its 'self-existence.' " From his intelligence briefings, McCloy was well aware that by the spring of 1945 most Army G-2 specialists believed the Pacific war would soon be over. Few of these intelligence specialists thought Soviet entry into the war would be necessary.[88]

Forrestal too was convinced that the Japanese were ready to surrender, and on July 28 he arrived in Potsdam with more copies of Japanese cable intercepts which he hoped would demonstrate this fact.[89] Like McCloy, he too felt that "we may need the Emperor to stabilize things in Japan" and effect a quick surrender of Japanese troops in Manchuria.[90] Nevertheless, Truman and Byrnes let the clock run on the atomic bomb.

On the same day as Forrestal arrived in Potsdam with his intercepts, Japan's prime minister gave his country's answer to the Allies' demand for unconditional surrender: "The Potsdam Proclamation, in my opinion, is just a rehash of the Cairo Declaration, and the government therefore does not consider it of great importance. We must 'mokusatsu' it."[91] The Japanese decision to "ignore" the Proclamation was no surprise to any of the American officials involved in developing the surrender policy. They had been repeatedly told that the Japanese would not accept unconditional surrender without an assurance regarding the emperor. Truman and Byrnes did not expect Tokyo to accept the Potsdam Proclamation before the bomb could be dropped. A few days later, when Stalin formally communicated the Japanese peace overture to Truman, the president quickly agreed with Stalin's observation that it represented nothing new.

McCloy hung around until the conference finally broke up on August 1. By that time, the Big Three had come to agreement on a *de facto* division of Germany. Stalin had told Truman, ". . . the Soviet delegation . . . will regard the whole of Western Germany as falling within your sphere, and Eastern Germany, within ours." Truman agreed but asked whether Stalin intended to have this division of Germany reflected in Europe as a whole. Did the Soviet ruler envision "a line running from the Baltic to the Adriatic"? Stalin did.[92]

McCloy had no basic disagreement with the accords reached at Potsdam. He favored a division of Germany and the destruction of her war-making capabilities. "This situation," he wrote in his diary, "is better than the constant distrust and difficulty we would have with the Russians over their being in our zones."[93] He was also pleased that the Allies had affirmed their intention to conduct a trial of Nazi war criminals. At the Quebec conference in September 1944, Roosevelt had casually agreed with Churchill that the top Nazis should be summarily executed. When McCloy had reported this to Stimson, the secretary immediately set him to work on an alternative. McCloy gathered a group of War Department lawyers, headed by Lieutenant Colonel Murray C. Bernays, to iron out a proposal for an international war-crimes tribunal. Bernays, a Lithuanian Jew who had immigrated to America at the age of six, eventually proposed that the Nazis should be tried not only for their individual crimes but for participating in a criminal conspiracy as well. McCloy liked the idea, and convinced Stimson that the concept of a criminal conspiracy was a valid contribution to international law. At Potsdam, the Allies agreed to negotiate the details of a war-crimes tribunal in a series of meetings in London.

On the critical issue of Poland, the Western Allies agreed to recognize a provisional government of national unity based on the Soviet-backed Polish communists. New boundaries gave Poland a large slice of formally German territory. Everyone recognized that Poland would fall within a Soviet sphere of influence.

The Potsdam Declaration would haunt the American political landscape for years to come. Conservatives would argue that the agreements amounted to a giveaway. But this argument assumes that the West had anything to "give away." Read carefully, the Declaration merely reflected the military positions of the respective powers on the ground, and postponed a reckoning of otherwise difficult political imponderables. A Council of Foreign Ministers was established, scheduled to meet in London in September. Regarding Germany, each of the four occupying powers was granted authority in its respective zone, but a four-power Control Council was headquartered in Berlin and empowered to coordinate the Allied occupation. On paper, occupied Germany was to "be treated as a single economic unit." In principle, the Americans had given away nothing that they controlled on the ground, and they had left open the opportunity for joint American-Soviet accommodation on the future of Germany.

McCloy had predicted when the conference opened that, despite the "exasperations and frustrations of dealing with the Russians," an agreement would be reached.[94] On the whole, he believed the Potsdam Declaration of August 2, 1945, was the best one could expect.

Now he packed up and, before returning to Washington, flew off on a quick inspection tour of Germany, Austria, and Italy. The State Department had concluded that Italy was in serious danger of being lost to "subversive elements," and that more food aid and other emergency relief would be needed to stem the growing popularity of the Italian left. McCloy reported that U.S. Army officers in the field found civilian conditions in such disarray that they felt "that to remove all American troops from Italy would encourage violent outbreaks."[95]

He was in Rome on the morning of August 6 when he was awakened with the news that Hiroshima had been hit with an atomic bomb. An American general asked him, "Is this all it's cracked up to be?" McCloy replied, "Yes. It's bigger than anything you've ever thought about." Truman, aboard the USS *Augusta,* exclaimed, "This is the greatest day in history."[96]

In Tokyo, the Japanese Cabinet, not certain what had happened in Hiroshima, dispatched a physicist to the city with instructions to determine if the bomb was indeed an atomic weapon. Hiroshima had been devastated; at least a hundred thousand people were killed almost instantly.* Two days later, when Truman had not countermanded his original attack order, a second bomb was dropped on Nagasaki, killing another seventy thousand people.[97] The Japanese Cabinet was still paralyzed, but the emperor intervened on August 10 and sued for peace. With the Swiss acting as intermediaries, Washington was informed that Hirohito himself had commanded his government to accept the Potsdam surrender terms "with the understanding that the said declaration does not comprise any demand which prejudices the prerogatives of His Majesty as a Sovereign Ruler."[98]

*By the end of 1945, the death toll in Hiroshima from injuries and lethal radiation would run to more than 140,000.

Hirohito's message pointedly reminded Washington that several weeks earlier Tokyo had asked the then neutral Soviets to render their "good offices in restoring peace vis a vis the enemy powers." The only barrier to a surrender at that time had been an assurance that the institution of the monarchy would not be abolished. Now, even after two atomic bombs, the same assurance was being demanded. Upon receiving the Japanese message, Truman met with Stimson, Byrnes, Forrestal, and several other of his closest advisers. On August 8, 1945, the Soviet Union had entered the war against Japan, and Byrnes saw no reason to compromise. "I cannot understand," he said, "why we should go further than we were willing to go at Potsdam when we had no atomic bomb, and Russia was not in the war." He warned Truman that accepting anything less than unconditional surrender might precipitate a "crucifixion of the President." This time Stimson did not defer to the secretary of state. He made a forceful argument that the "question of the Emperor was a minor matter compared with delaying a victory in the war which was now in our hands."[99] Delaying the inevitable victory would give the Soviets time to advance their forces into Manchuria, a factor that carried great weight with Truman.[100] Forrestal then proposed a compromise, which Truman sanctioned: they would accept the offer to surrender with language that referred both to the emperor's authority and the terms of the Potsdam Proclamation. Byrnes wrote the message and released it for broadcast the following morning.

Throughout the next twenty-four hours, McCloy worked with Byrnes and Stimson in drafting details of how the surrender would be formally effected. He was constantly on the phone to Byrnes and in meetings with Stimson.[101] At the end of the day, a message was sent to the Japanese informing them that, unless General MacArthur was notified of a cessation of hostilities, the Allied forces would continue full-scale military operations. Stimson had wished to suspend all strategic bombing, but in a Cabinet meeting it was decided only to halt any further atomic bombing. (Another bomb would have been ready by August 17 or 18.[102]) Giving evidence that only then was he beginning to realize the enormity of the event, Truman confessed that the thought of "wiping out another 100,000 people was too horrible." As Henry Wallace recorded in his diary, the president "didn't like the idea of killing, as he said, 'all those kids.' "[103]

In Moscow on August 8, Ambassador Harriman and his top aide, Minister-Counselor George Kennan, went to see Stalin in his Kremlin office. Ostensibly, their mission was to talk about Soviet progress against Japanese forces in the Far East. But the real agenda was to gauge how the Soviet ruler was reacting to news of the American atomic attack. After discussing briefly how far Soviet forces had advanced into Manchuria, Harriman pointedly raised the issue of the atomic bomb and asked what effect Stalin thought it would have on the Japanese. The Soviet ruler said he thought the bomb might give the Japanese a "pretext" to surrender. Harriman then observed that "it was a good thing we had invented this and not the Germans." Stalin volunteered that he had been told by his own scientists that it was indeed a "very difficult problem to work out." Soviet scientists, he said, had tried but failed to produce such a weapon. Harriman said that "if the Allies could keep it and apply it for peaceful purposes it would be a great thing." To this vague hint of some kind of atomic cooperation in the future, Stalin agreed, and observed that this would mean the end of war and aggressors. "But," he warned, "the secret would have to be well kept."[104]

Any chance, however, that the United States might invite the Soviet Union to share in the control of the atomic bomb was rapidly fading. On this issue Stimson again had further thoughts. Returning from Potsdam, where he had opposed any sharing of nuclear secrets, he began to torment himself with doubts. Utterly exhausted, he left on August 12 for the Adirondacks, for what he hoped would be several weeks of rest. McCloy called him there on the afternoon of August 14 to tell him that the Japanese had finally accepted the terms drafted four days earlier. The war was at an end. The next day, McCloy flew up to join him at his Saint Hubert's mountain retreat. There the two men had time to reflect on what had happened. They had "long and painful thoughts about the atomic triumph." McCloy was now routinely referring to it as the "primordial weapon." As Stimson recalled later, they asked themselves, "Granting all that could be said about the wickedness of Russia, was it not perhaps true that the atom itself, not the Russians, was the central problem? . . . And was it practical to hope that the atomic 'secret'—so fragile and short-lived—could be used to win concessions from the Russian leaders as to their cherished, if frightful, police state?"[105]

After a few days of such talk, McCloy flew back down to the Pentagon to work on a memo designed to encourage the president to share control over the atom with the Soviet Union and Great Britain. But Jimmy Byrnes remained, according to Stimson, "radically opposed to any approach to Stalin whatever." The secretary of state was looking ahead to the London foreign ministers' meeting scheduled for early September; he told McCloy, "The Russians were only sensitive to power and all the world, including the Russians, were cognizant of the power of this bomb, and with it in his hip pocket he felt he was in a far better position to come back with tangible accomplishments even if he did not threaten anyone expressly with it."[106]

McCloy tried to suggest that an American monopoly over atomic technology could not exist for long—there were no real atomic secrets. But Byrnes insisted that it was a matter of production capabilities and that it would be a "long time before they [the Soviets] were at the stage where we were now." Seeing that Byrnes's mind was pretty much made up, McCloy "did not feel it wise to argue the point further. . . ."[107] Though not encouraged, he returned to the Adirondacks and spent the last week of the summer finishing his memo on atomic policy. Ellen had taken the kids to Saint Hubert's earlier in the month, so the family was able to share at least part of their vacation together. McCloy was eager to teach his young son a little fishing. Unfortunately, one day, when the family was fishing from the banks of a nearby stream, Ellen slipped and badly bruised her thigh on the sharp rocks, forcing her to remain in bed for the rest of the vacation. Still, it was a peaceful interlude. Ellen, according to Stimson, was a "great joy" to Mabel Stimson, and the "Colonel" himself always felt invigorated by the presence of the McCloy children. This would be, however, the last such gathering of Stimson's adopted family. The secretary had decided to tender his resignation soon, and McCloy himself began to ponder what he should do now that the war was over.[108]

On September 11, 1945, Stimson sent the memo drafted by McCloy on the bomb over to the White House. In a cover note, he explained that, although he was still convinced of the ultimate importance of changing the Russian attitude on individual liberties, "I have come to the conclusion that it would not be possible to use our possession of the atomic bomb as a direct lever to produce the change." Such internal democratic reforms would come only "slowly and gradually"; in the meantime, "we should not delay our approach to Russia in the matter of the atomic bomb. . . ."[109] The memo itself was even more blunt: "To put the matter concisely, I consider the problem of our satisfactory relations with Russia as not merely connected with but as virtually dominated by the problem of the atomic bomb. . . . For if we fail to approach them now and merely continue to negotiate with them, having this weapon rather ostentatiously on our hip, their suspicions and their distrust of our purposes and motives will increase." It was a matter of "saving civilization not for five years or for twenty years, but forever."[110]

Neither Stimson nor McCloy would ever really back away from this position during the rest of their public careers. But their September 11 memo was much too late. By that time, Byrnes had gone to London for the foreign ministers' conference, and he would come away from those meetings complaining that the Soviets didn't "scare."[111] The Cold War had already begun, and over the next few months the inevitable frustrations that arose in working with the Soviets would convince many American policy-makers that any degree of cooperation was not worth the trouble. McCloy too felt these frustrations, but there was a profound difference between his view and the attitude of Byrnes and other hard-liners. The difference lay in the bomb. For McCloy—and Stimson—the existence of the bomb made all the difference. With the bomb, there could never be another war unless those waging it were prepared to destroy civilization. Atomic warfare was unthinkable. This view, however, was not universal. Less than two years later, Byrnes wrote a book in which he argued that, if the Soviets refused ultimately to withdraw their troops from East Germany, the United States should be prepared to adopt "measures of last resort" to force them to comply. "We should not start something," he warned, "we are not prepared to finish."[112] McCloy and Stimson thought talk of pre-emptive atomic warfare both immoral and, pragmatically speaking, unnecessary. There would, in fact, never be a time in the tension-filled years of the early Cold War when McCloy believed the Soviets intended to wage a war of aggression in Western Europe.

In retrospect, McCloy would always believe the decision to drop the bomb had been mishandled. He told this to his closest friends at the time, men such as Forrestal, and he maintained the position over the years.[113] He was more than a little bit skeptical over an article Stimson published in February 1947 defending the decision. "I knew Stimson as well as any man alive," he recalled years later, "and while after the war he wrote an article for *Harper's* defending his decision, I know in his soul there were doubts. He lay awake at night before the decision thinking about the consequences of dropping it on a civilian target, a city of that size."[114]

McCloy saw Byrnes as the primary advocate of using the bomb; Byrnes had repeatedly rejected McCloy's suggestions to give the Japanese an explicit warning, and Byrnes had deleted McCloy's assurance to the emperor in the first draft of the Potsdam Proclamation. He also felt that Byrnes could only have had such influence because of the character of the man who now occupied the White House. Truman, he thought, was "a simple man, prone to make up his mind quickly and decisively, perhaps too quickly—a thorough American." This was not a great president, "not distinguished at all . . . not Lincolnesque, but an instinctive, common, hearty-natured man."[115] And in the matter of atomic diplomacy, Truman's instincts led to decisions that were, in McCloy's view, neither measured nor sound.

McCloy's access to intelligence intercepts had convinced him that the atomic bombing of two Japanese cities had been unnecessary. He had been aware that the emperor had thrown his weight against the militarists, and for a surrender that was all but unconditional. Though some have argued in retrospect that Truman and Byrnes could not be certain the militarists would obey their emperor's wishes to surrender, virtually all the president's advisers except Byrnes felt otherwise.

McCloy also believed the atomic bombing had crucial moral consequences. He and other officials had been well aware, particularly after the Trinity test, that the atomic bomb was not just another weapon. "We knew it was an incredible thing," he recalled.[116] "God give us the intelligence and character," he wrote in his diary, "to use it for good purpose."[117] When it was used to end a war that was already over, he could not help fearing the moral consequences for his country. He was not alone: Admiral Leahy, General Eisenhower, and many others associated with the Manhattan Project repeatedly expressed doubts about the morality of atomic bombing.* As the years passed, McCloy came to emphasize the immorality of the Hiroshima decision: "I feel very strongly that if we had found a way to have a politically negotiated surrender, and had not dropped the bomb, we would today be in a stronger position morally. . . . We should have given the Japanese a warning at least of what we had. In the postwar world, it would have made an enormous difference."[118]

In the end, however, McCloy had to resign himself to the fact that on one of the most critical issues of the war—how it was to end—his advice was ignored. So it was with some irony then that on September 7, 1945, he received a phone call from the White House. Truman was holding up a ceremony in which he was to be presented with the formal surrender documents, recently signed by MacArthur and Japanese representatives aboard the USS *Missouri.* At the last minute, the president remembered that McCloy was the man who had chiefly drafted the documents, and he wanted him to be part of the ceremonies. So McCloy rushed over to the White House, where Marshall, the Joint Chiefs, Stimson, Forrestal, Acheson, and several other officials were impatiently waiting. After the usual press photos were taken, McCloy and Stimson returned to the Pentagon, where they talked about the atomic bomb. Before leaving the War Department, both men wished to see a change of direction in the administration's atomic policies. But the time left to either of them in government service was now very short.

A few days later, just before Secretary of War Stimson left for his Highhold retreat for the last time, he presented McCloy and Lovett with Distinguished Service Medals, one of the country's highest-ranking civilian awards. (Lovett too had decided to resign, after five years of supervising America's air war.) As McCloy stood to receive the medal, his eye was drawn to the portrait of Elihu Root, Teddy Roosevelt's secretary of war, hanging behind Stimson's desk. Root had been one of Stimson's mentors, and now McCloy could not help thinking that Stimson was passing on to him a tradition. Later that night, he wrote in his diary, "I felt a direct

*In just a few weeks, McCloy would have the opportunity to see from an airplane the devastation wrought by the Hiroshima bomb. One of his colleagues traveling with him described the scene: "We looked out and then gasped. . . . [Hiroshima was] so flattened that nothing was left except red dust which lay feet deep. The color recalled Pompeii; the completeness of the ruin brought to mind the ancient prophecy that not one stone should be left standing on another. We were appalled and physically were sickened. . . ." A few days later, McCloy declined an invitation for an on-the-ground inspection of the city, saying, "We have seen enough bombed cities."

current running from Root through Stimson to me. They were the giants."[119]

With Stimson gone, McCloy was eager to leave as well, if only because he felt it was time to get back to Wall Street and earn some decent money. But before doing so, he had agreed to take a five-week trip around the world, with an eye to giving the department an overview of America's new responsibilities. In Europe, he traveled with Averell Harriman, who was in a most pessimistic mood about the prospects for Soviet-American collaboration in the postwar world. In London, he told McCloy that he thought the "Russians are truly troubled" by the way in which the "people on the border states are reacting to them and the way the other powers are lining up against them."[120] He feared the situation would feed their natural paranoia and lead to a blowup. McCloy's instincts were always more optimistic than Harriman's. In his view, the Soviet Union was an economically backward state, exhausted by its herculean war effort. The Soviets could be difficult and troublesome, but the American military officers dealing with them in occupied Europe assured McCloy that cooperation was still possible. He agreed—assuming that the United States continued its military presence in Europe and resisted the temptation to fall back into its prewar isolationist ways.

The pressures to demobilize, however, were enormous. At one point in his European tour, he encountered a crowd of raucous GIs who shouted at him, demanding to know when they could return home. He handled the situation with humor, jocularly feigning deafness. But demobilization was not an issue that could be put off very long. And in the meantime, coming to some kind of working agreement with the Soviets was of "prime importance."[121] In large part, that meant establishing a practical relationship with the Soviets in Germany and Eastern Europe, based on the Yalta accords. To McCloy, the problem was to find a way to recognize the Soviet sphere of influence in Eastern Europe, particularly on security issues, without shutting the door to democratic freedoms and American business and media interests.

This point was brought home to him in a dramatic fashion when he and Harriman arrived in Soviet-occupied Budapest. The Hungarian Smallholders Party, a noncommunist party, had just won a majority in free elections supervised by the Soviets, and throngs of jubilant Hungarians were celebrating in the streets. As McCloy and Harriman made their way to the U.S. Embassy, they found the road blocked by a crowd of Hungarians waving the American flag. "Here was the hope of the world," McCloy later recalled, "the American flag." The incident reminded him how necessary it was to maintain an American presence in Europe. "We give the population hope against the Russian fear," he cabled back to Washington. "Opposition to Russian pressures gains encouragement by our mere presence."[122] For the same reason, he recommended that the

United States keep its troops in Austria, where Soviet troops also resided, and put any loans to Eastern Europe on hold until the Soviets demonstrated that their security presence would not block the introduction of democratic governments.

His position, therefore, was a complicated one, a blend of realism and idealism. He did not envision war with the Russians. But he believed that, by forcefully exercising American power, by imposing a "Pax Americana," Washington would help the postwar world become more receptive to American values of democracy and free-market economic principles.[123] At the same time, he was willing to accept the geomilitary consequences of the war and of Yalta. The Soviets had, after all, sustained the major burdens of winning the war against German fascism, and were entitled to the fruits of victory. This specifically included the right to secure borders and the influence of a major power over its immediate neighbors. Unlike Harriman or others who approached the Soviet problem as a matter of ideology or grand strategy, McCloy thought of it as a legal task, a matter of negotiating concrete arrangements with the Soviets.

His legalistic approach to these matters was illustrated at the end of his journey, when he flew into Tokyo with instructions from Truman and Marshall to confront General Douglas MacArthur on occupation policy. The Japanese capital, he wrote in his diary, was a "fantastic place. . . . The town is burnt out—miles and miles of it with nothing but rusty and burnt tin carpeting the area. . . . You have to convince yourself that there was recently a city here." But even Tokyo's devastation was thrown in the background by the "spectacle of MacArthur."

MacArthur was not used to hearing himself disputed, and was astonished that McCloy was talking back to him. The assistant secretary, in fact, had been sent to Tokyo with instructions to force MacArthur to comply with Washington's policies. Specifically, McCloy told MacArthur that at the very least he must make a show of consulting with the Soviets over occupation policy, as specified at Yalta. Accordingly, Washington wanted MacArthur's consent to the establishment of an Allied Advisory Council—with token Russian membership—which would advise him on occupation policy. Washington was at that very moment trying to win Soviet acceptance of a similar Allied Council to supervise the occupation in Eastern Europe. Obviously, if MacArthur refused to accept such a Council in Allied-occupied Japan, the Soviets would have an excuse to refuse to admit a Council in Eastern Europe.

McCloy and the strong-willed MacArthur spent hours over the next few days arguing over whether American interests lay predominantly in Europe or, as MacArthur insisted, in the Pacific. The argument, according to McCloy, turned to a shouting match. "I fought to get my words in," he wrote in his diary, "and by sheer might and main succeeded."

Angrily pacing the floor, MacArthur protested that he wanted nothing to do with the Russian "Bear" and would not sit with any occupation council. He talked of the "God-given authority we now had here," and accused McCloy of "sacrificing our tremendous interests in the Pacific" in order to obtain "inconsequential advantage" in Eastern Europe.

McCloy disagreed, saying that the "Atlantic was not to be written off just yet," that America had "great interests in middle Europe," where two world wars had begun. He pointed out that we were now "face to face with the Russians right in Germany," and it would be a mistake "if we did not solve all our problems on a world wide basis from here on, rather than on a 19th century localized approach." Echoing what he had told Stimson the previous spring at the founding of the United Nations, he explained that the United States could not "take a unilateral position in the Pacific," ignoring the doctrine of Allied consultation on all occupation questions, without allowing the Russians to do the same in Eastern Europe.

MacArthur was threatening to resign until McCloy calmly reminded him that he was a soldier who had been given high responsibilities and could not "indulge" himself in the luxury of quitting. "He quickly sobered up," McCloy wrote in his diary, "and said no more along that line." The two men then got down to the business of working out a practical arrangement that would allow MacArthur to exercise supreme power while satisfying Washington's diplomatic needs with the Soviets. As McCloy put it, "We harangued and argued, finally getting the real points of issue determined, and I finally got him to state what he would do and what he did not want to do."[124] McCloy quickly "yellow-padded" out language establishing an Allied Council, but one that had only "advisory" powers. All in all, it was a most remarkable performance, one that MacArthur would never forget. No one else throughout the long war had stood up to MacArthur and walked out of the confrontation with the general's good will in hand. In good Cravath tradition, McCloy had broken the problem down into all its pieces and put it back together in a fashion that satisfied everyone.

Just before leaving Tokyo, he cabled Washington his overview of the situation in occupied Japan. Basically, he had no disagreement with MacArthur's intentions, which were to use his absolute powers to remake Japanese society. "We have now in our hands an extraordinary opportunity to make steady progress in the Far East. . . . From my observation of other theatres of occupation throughout the world, our objectives are hampered in some cases by quadripartite rule and the sharp conflict of ideologies. . . . Here, by reason of the almost exclusively American character of the victory in the Pacific, we have been able to achieve the supreme command."[125]

MacArthur continued to rule Japan and the Philippines with absolute powers. An Allied Council was formed with Soviet representation, but, true to McCloy's assurances, it exercised virtually no power over the American shogun, who proceeded to impose democratic institutions on the Japanese from the top down. The experiment in tyranny succeeded in producing a functioning democracy. Not only had McCloy helped MacArthur preserve his supreme authority, but in a few years he would attempt to do in Germany what the general was doing in Japan.

McCloy recognized that America had emerged from the war with global economic and military powers unmatched by any ancient or modern empire, and where those powers were "supreme," McCloy was unwilling to bargain them away. Upon his return to Washington, after flying twenty-seven thousand miles in thirty-six days, he stayed up late one night collecting his thoughts for the last speech of his term in the War Department. NBC Radio broadcast it nationwide. He pounded away on two themes. First, only strong American leadership could "bring this world into some semblance of balance again," and therefore U.S. troops had to remain abroad in order to convince the rest of the world that "we have what it takes to carry through in peace." Second, finding a way to deal with the Soviet Union was "the A-1 priority job. . . ."[126]

Afterward, on November 24, 1945, he spent his last day in office as assistant secretary of war. "What a tangle of emotions and thoughts it all produces," he wrote in his diary. "I go at the close of a great adventure, but there is so much work ahead that you cannot fail to have misgivings at leaving."

BOOK III

Wall Street, the World Bank, and Germany

CHAPTER 13

A Brief Return to Wall Street

". . . it can readily be demonstrated that Mr. McCloy and his partners have been, to say the least, unusually friendly to the Soviet Union and sympathetic to the Communist cause."

ANTHONY PANUCH
DEPUTY ASSISTANT SECRETARY OF STATE

Five years had passed since McCloy had left Wall Street, and though he had always assumed that when the war was over he would return to Cravath, now that it was about to happen he felt a little bit ambivalent. He feared having to "get back to humdrum things," and was still tempted by government service. "We are at a windy corner of history," he wrote in his diary. But, "As interesting as it is, I must make my living again."[1] He still considered himself a lawyer, and Cravath was his home. His friends at Cravath, men like Don Swatland and "Tex" Moore, naturally assumed he would be returning to the firm. A partner might leave temporarily for government service, but once he returned to the law, it was unheard of for a senior partner to join any but his original law firm. So, one morning in November 1945, McCloy walked into the Cravath offices at 15 Broad Street and greeted his old friends. Always a popular presence in the firm, McCloy was expected to bring back a wealth of expertise and contacts after five years at an elevated level in Washington. And he certainly expected to be given all the prerogatives and financial rewards of a senior partner.

One man did not see it that way. As the negotiations commenced on the partnership share he would receive, McCloy could see that Robert Swaine was less than enthusiastic. "They were telling me," he recalled, "not that I shouldn't come back, but that I shouldn't have any grand ideas." Swaine had never gotten along with McCloy, but he also sincerely believed that those who had left the firm in World War I had never amounted to much when they returned. To Swaine's mind, leaving the firm, even for a temporary stint of public service, was a sacrilege, an abandonment of the cloth.[2]

Swatland and Moore tried to intervene and persuade Swaine that McCloy's wartime experience would be an enormous asset to the firm. "We couldn't budge Swaine," recalled Moore. Nor would McCloy accept less. It was partly a matter of money: tens of thousands of dollars separated the partnership cut of a name member of the firm like Swaine from McCloy's partnership ranking when he had left the firm in 1940. But to McCloy, it was also a matter of prestige and power. He wanted to have a hand in directing the firm. Ellen was telling him that, after all that he had done in running the War Department for five years, he deserved a lot more than Swaine was offering.

By the time negotiations came to a head, Swaine was not even talking to McCloy. When he decided to reject McCloy's final offer, he told Swatland to convey the news. But Swatland went to Moore and said, "Oh God, he's a great friend of mine; it's really not for me to do." So Moore made a date to meet McCloy at the Racquet Club: "I told him," he recalled, "that I was terribly, terribly sorry, that I was grieved, that Swaine was adamant on this particular thing, and he was managing partner."[3]

By then, McCloy had several other offers. Despite their disagreement over atomic policy, Secretary of State Jimmy Byrnes offered him the ambassadorship to Moscow. "It was most flattering and disturbing," McCloy confided in his journal, "for no one can deny the challenge that lies ahead." He was also approached about taking on the presidency of his alma mater, Amherst College. A particularly stunning offer came from the Rockefellers, who offered him the lucrative presidency of Standard Oil of California. In his fashion, he pondered at great length the merits of all these jobs, and consulted with a wide range of friends. Harold Ickes discouraged him from taking the ambassadorship. As for Amherst, he thought McCloy lacked the intellectual temperament for a college president. And if he was going to go into the oil business, Ickes wanted McCloy to join him in a small consulting partnership. But McCloy did not think of himself as a businessman, least of all an oil-company executive. And yet he felt the need to make some money, so in the end he turned down both the college presidency and the Moscow job. He couldn't imagine dragging his family off to the spartan existence of the U.S. Embassy in Moscow. He also wanted to spend more time with his family. "Now that the war is over," seven-year-old Johnny had asked one night at dinner, "can I have my daddy back too?"[4]

The more McCloy thought about it, the more he figured it was time to return to the law. If Cravath wouldn't have him back on his terms, he would go to another firm. Sometime that autumn, after rumors began circulating on Wall Street of his falling out with Swaine, Nelson Rockefeller approached him with an attractive idea. Why not, he said, join the Rockefeller family's law firm, Milbank, Tweed, Hope & Hadley?[5] A mid-sized firm, specializing in estate and corporate law, Milbank, Tweed was not top-heavy with senior partners at the moment, and would welcome the fifty-year-old McCloy into its fold. The firm was even willing to make him a name partner.

Ever since that day long ago when he had knocked on the door of the Rockefeller summer home in Bar Harbor, McCloy had been attracted by the aura of the Rockefellers. As a senior partner with Milbank, Tweed, he'd have the status he had sought at Cravath. He wanted a base from which he could, like Stimson, engage in disinterested public service while ensconced within the protective womb of an elite private law practice.

Don Swatland negotiated the deal for him. The firm's partners had no problem with his financial demands, and in order to make room for him on their already crowded shingle, the deceased "Hope" was dropped to make way for "McCloy." One partner joked that they had "given up Hope to rely on McCloy."[6] On January 1, 1946, the partners mailed out formal, embossed cards announcing the new name of the firm: Milbank, Tweed, Hadley & McCloy.

Milbank, Tweed—or Milkweed, as it was irreverently known among its employees—tolerated quite a different class of lawyers from the meritocracy of the Cravath factory. There were the usual number of hardworking, conservative lawyers like the seventy-three-year-old Albert G. Milbank. But the dominant personality in the firm was the sixty-one-year-old Harrison Tweed. And Tweed was an eccentric, free-spirited man who flouted many Wall Street conventions. For him, the practice of law had to be "fun."[7] He favored rumpled tweeds and polka-dot bow ties over the profession's pinstripe uniform. He worked standing, at a large desk in the center of the room, built high enough so that he could write without taking a seat. Instead of the usual English office decor, he had his own oil paintings, mostly landscapes, hung on walls painted dark blue.[8] He was an earthy sort of man, who didn't hesitate to drive off the public from his private stretch of beach on Long Island by parading naked up and down the shoreline.

Unlike Cravath's austere managing partner, Tweed had an irreverent attitude toward the legal profession. He once wrote, "I have a high opinion of lawyers. . . . They are better to work with or play with or drink with than most other varieties of mankind." He had served the Rockefeller-family interests for most of his professional career, but he had also spent ten years as president of the Legal Aid Society, a charitable organization devoted to providing free legal services to the indigent. In short, he would not object, like Swaine, to any of McCloy's extracurricular activities.[9]

Milbank, Tweed's most important client was always the Rockefeller family's bank, Chase National. The bank and the law firm were all part of the family. As Tweed himself put it, the law firm operated under "the Rockefeller surveillance."[10] The president of Chase in 1946 was Winthrop Aldrich, the younger brother of John D. Rockefeller, Jr.'s wife, Abby. Aldrich had started out in the family law firm, later became president of the family bank, Equitable Trust Company, which in turn merged with Chase National Bank. Out of this banking merger was created Milbank, Tweed in 1931. Ever since, the firm had not only provided legal counsel to Chase and other family corporate investments, but also handled all of the large Rockefeller family's highly centralized personal finances. As a result, Milbank, Tweed maintained one of the largest trust-and-estate departments of any major law firm in the country.

McCloy quickly felt at home. He was his own man in a firm where his partners allowed him the discretion to choose his own clients and cases. There was, however, one unspoken reason why he had been recruited into Milbank, Tweed, and this became evident later that spring, when he became embroiled in a delicate case that threatened the very basis of the Rockefeller estate. As Rockefeller, Jr., explained it to his personal lawyer, Thomas M. Debevoise, "McCloy knows so many people in government circles . . . [that] he might be in the way to get information in various quarters about the matter without seeking it, or revealing his hand."[11]

At the time, Rockefeller, Jr., was worried that the government might reopen its 1911 antitrust decree against Rockefeller oil interests. The original Standard Oil trust had been broken up under antitrust laws in 1911, and Rockefeller-family interests were prohibited from using their influence over the oil companies in a manner that would resurrect the old monopoly. Suddenly, in the spring of 1946, McCloy's wartime luncheon companion, former Secretary of the Interior Harold Ickes, who had gone into the oil-consulting business, publicly charged that John D. Rockefeller, Jr., was violating the terms of the 1911 dissolution decree. Together with two other high-powered antitrust lawyers, Thurman Arnold and Abe Fortas, Ickes petitioned the Justice Department to investigate the matter. Part of Ickes's motivation was a personal vendetta: he was angered that one of his assistants during the war, Ralph K. Davies, a deputy petroleum administrator, had not been given the presidency of Standard Oil of California. (Once an executive vice-president of Standard, Davies supported government controls during the war, earning him the distrust of his former colleagues in the business. They now called him "socialist-minded."[12]) Ickes's charges were nevertheless serious enough so that the SEC agreed to investigate.

In fact, John D. Rockefeller, Jr., owned almost 6 percent of Standard Oil of California stock, making him the single largest shareholder. In private, his own lawyers acknowledged that these shares were "enough to make his voice have some influence." Worse, Rockefeller had intervened with the board of directors to block the selection of Davies as president of the company.[13] Ickes charged that Rockefeller had regularly intervened to select the executive heads of other oil companies operating under the 1911 antitrust injunction. If it could be proved that this had resulted in a restraint of commerce, the terms of the 1911 decree could be reopened. If that happened, the Rockefellers might be forced to divest themselves of any interest in the oil companies.

McCloy was the perfect Rockefeller representative, because he was known to the other antagonists in the case as an objective intermediary. He had the basic trust of all the prickly personalities involved, including Ickes, Ralph Davies, and Abe Fortas, and the job they were fighting over was one McCloy had turned down. He could, and did, call up all of these men, and was perfectly frank with them. The SEC investigation dragged out into the autumn of 1946, but after numerous depositions the case was dropped. By then, it had generated some unfavorable publicity, but, partly because of McCloy's handling of the matter, the SEC's investigators were deflected.

Within a week of settling into his new offices at 15 Broad Street, McCloy assumed a variety of extracurricular responsibilities. Frankfurter wrote from Washington to warn him of the "difficulties you will encounter in playing your part as a citizen—that is in deciding what good causes to take on and what are beyond your hours and energy."[14] McCloy was well aware that too many outside interests might interfere with his "effort to again get the feel of the law."[15] But he could not resist.

One commitment he made was to become an active member of the Council on Foreign Relations. He was particularly interested in a major study the Council was conducting of Soviet-U.S. relations. So too was the thirty-one-year-old David Rockefeller, who had recently begun to take an active interest in Council affairs. Rockefeller had his college roommate, George S. Franklin, a lawyer bored with his law practice, write up the Council's conclusions in a report intended for publication. It quickly became apparent, however, that no consensus existed on how Washington should treat Moscow. Franklin's draft report tried to make the case for a policy combining a measure of firmness with a historical understanding of legitimate Soviet fears. He suggested that Washington had to recognize Moscow's "vital interests in having governments not unfriendly to her along her western frontier." Whenever possible, the Soviets should be treated as equals, Franklin wrote, and this might include a sharing of nuclear secrets.[16]

McCloy more or less shared these views. Early in December 1945, the Council hosted a black-tie dinner in his honor at their new and elegant quarters in the Harold Pratt House on East 68th Street in Manhattan. He told his dinner companions, "Thus far we have gotten along with Russia fairly well." There would be difficulties, but "Russia's concepts and example will wilt before ours if we have the vigor and farsightedness to see our place in the world."[17] To him, dealing with the Soviets was a simple matter of firm diplomacy and vigorous economic competition.

The Council study group, however, was split down the middle, and in the end such influential Council members as Frank Altschul and Isaiah Bowman killed the Franklin report as too mild an assessment of Soviet intentions. Altschul went so far as to say, "The problem that we face with Russia today is essentially the same one faced by Hitler."[18]

Such divisions within the Council reflected a growing polarization in America. Early in 1946, the well-known publicist Herbert Bayard Swope coined the term "Cold War" to describe the contentious nature of Soviet-U.S. relations.[19] Curiously enough, those, like McCloy, who had personally dealt with the Soviets were not immediately swept up by such early Cold War sentiments. And because McCloy really didn't fear the Soviets, J. Edgar Hoover would soon accuse him of "pro-Soviet leanings," particularly for his views on the issue of sharing the secrets of the atomic bomb.[20] Atomic policy was now on the front burner of the Truman administration's agenda. Though the Soviet press was complaining that the United States and Britain were engaging in "atomic diplomacy," the Kremlin nevertheless surprised Washington in January 1946 by supporting the formation of a U.N. Atomic Energy Commission.[21] As a result, the United States had to come up with a plan for dealing with the issue. So, barely a week after arriving at Milbank, Tweed, McCloy got a call from Secretary of State Byrnes. If he would not go to Moscow as ambassador, Byrnes asked, would he at least agree to serve on a State Department committee, chaired by Undersecretary Dean Acheson, to study atomic-energy policy? Still fascinated by the atomic bomb, McCloy couldn't resist accepting.

Joining him on the Acheson Committee were James Conant, the president of Harvard and a former member of the Interim Committee, Major General Leslie R. Groves, former head of the Manhattan Project, and Dr. Vannevar Bush, director of the president's Office of Scientific Research and Development. Acheson knew these men well, but he felt sure that all these "big shots," with the exception of Bush, lacked any technical knowledge of nuclear physics. How could they advise the president—who Acheson thought had no understanding himself about atomic matters—how to control this exotic technology if they hadn't "the faintest idea what it was"?[22] So he very quickly appointed a panel of scientific consultants, led by David Lilienthal, the head of the Tennessee Valley Authority, to advise his committee. Over the next ten weeks, the Acheson

Committee met on weekends to work out a detailed proposal for the international control of atomic energy and the bomb.

McCloy tried to acquire an elementary knowledge of nuclear physics. It was rough going. First he turned to J. Robert Oppenheimer, a member of the Lilienthal panel of consultants. Of all the scientists McCloy had met during the war, no one had made a deeper impression on him than "Oppie." Niels Bohr, the Danish Nobel Prize physicist, had introduced them early in the war years, when Oppenheimer was a candidate to head the Manhattan Project. McCloy thought of him as a man of wide culture, possessed of an "almost musically delicate mind," an intellectual who was simultaneously a man of "great charm." Oppenheimer agreed to try to explain nuclear physics to McCloy one night after dinner at Acheson's home in Georgetown. Pulling out a blackboard, he began drawing little stick figures representing electrons, neutrons, and protons chasing one another about in unpredictable ways. After McCloy and Acheson asked one bewildered question after another, "Oppie" finally walked away from the blackboard, saying, "It's hopeless. I really think you two believe neutrons and electrons *are* little men."[23]

McCloy nevertheless felt he could easily spend all his time for two months studying "the atomic bomb business" and still be "fascinated."[24] Gradually, he picked up a little understanding of atomic physics from one of Oppenheimer's colleagues, Professor Isidor I. Rabi. The political implications of what he was learning tended to confirm his own predilection toward comprehensive, international control over atomic energy.

Oppenheimer's views quickly began to dominate the Acheson-Lilienthal Committee deliberations. The physicist started with the proposition that the peaceful exploitation of atomic energy was inextricably linked to the technical capability of producing a bomb. One could not do the first without acquiring the capability to produce an atomic weapon. He concluded that, given this reality, an international agency should monopolize atomic energy, and apportion its benefits as an incentive to individual countries not to build atomic weapons. He argued that "without world government there could be no permanent peace, that without peace there would be atomic warfare." In the absence of a world government, Oppenheimer suggested that any answer to controlling this weapon of total war must include the creation of an international Atomic Development Authority. In short, in the field of atomic energy there must be a "partial renunciation of sovereignty" by all countries.[25]

McCloy, Acheson, and most everyone else on the State Department committee accepted Oppenheimer's views, and the physicist became the primary author of the report they turned over to the president in mid-March. But there were some disagreements. McCloy, for instance, accepted Oppenheimer's assertion that the bomb itself had revealed the "secret" of atomic physics, and that, short of international controls, one could expect the Soviets to develop their own bomb within a very few years. General Groves disagreed, arguing, among other things, that there was no uranium in the Soviet Union. (This proved to be false.) Groves sought to prolong the U.S. atomic monopoly by achieving global control over all uranium supplies. He did not really believe the Soviets would agree to surrender any sovereignty over atomic matters, but he knew some kind of offer had to be made, and this one was as good as any. In his mind, Oppenheimer's proposed Atomic Development Authority would serve as an atomic league empowered to punish any country attempting to build a bomb. Acheson, McCloy, Bush, and Conant did not sign on to this view. They were genuinely alarmed by the long-term dangers of another total war, this time waged with nuclear weapons, and endorsed Oppenheimer's plan in a sincere effort to abolish such weapons altogether.[26]

McCloy approached this whole problem as a lawyer. Given the right kind of international institutions, nations, he thought, could be required, like individual citizens, to act within the framework of the law. His own experience during the Black Tom case had vindicated for him the principle of international arbitration. There was no better time than now, at the dawn of the nuclear age, to take a major step toward the formation of a world government. He and the others on the Acheson Committee were well aware how controversial their proposals would seem to the American public. And so there were some second thoughts when they met for four days with the Lilienthal panel at the beautiful Dumbarton Oaks mansion in Georgetown. There they sat in the mansion's great conference hall, a room of somber elegance, discussing how to avoid an apocalypse. From the walls, which towered nearly three stories high, hung magnificent tapestries; a shaft of sunlight bathed El Greco's painting *The Visitation* in one corner; a Byzantine cat sculpted in ebony sat encased in glass.

When they had finished reading Lilienthal's draft aloud, Acheson looked up, removed his reading glasses, and said, "This is a brilliant and profound document." In succeeding days, however, some significant changes were made. Dr. Bush suggested that the final report should make it clear to the American people that the proposed Atomic Development Authority would assume control over nuclear facilities only in "stages." The theoretical secrets of the bomb, for instance, might be turned over to the Russians immediately. But control over uranium mines and other facilities would only gradually be relinguished, perhaps in return for some kind of *quid pro quo* from Stalin. Bush suggested, for instance, that Stalin might be persuaded to "open up" Soviet society to Western journalists and academics as a sign of good faith. McCloy, Groves, and Conant were, to different degrees, persuaded by Bush's arguments. Lilienthal and Acheson, however, thought it simplistic to think that the U.S. atomic monopoly could be traded for internal Soviet reforms. As a compromise, Lilienthal agreed to insert some language about a "staged" implementation of the plan, but refused to specify any timetables. McCloy and all four other members of the Acheson Committee then signed on to the final report.[27]

Truman and Byrnes officially accepted the Acheson-Lilienthal Report, and Byrnes made a pretense of saying that he was "favorably impressed."[28] He was, in fact, shocked by the sweeping scope of its recommendations, and attempted to limit the report's influence by having the president appoint a conservative to negotiate atomic matters at the United Nations. There was considerable sentiment within the Acheson-Lilienthal group to have McCloy selected for this job. But within a day of the submission of their report, the president selected, at Byrnes's suggestion, Bernard Baruch, the financier and dabbler in public affairs. Acheson was appalled, and so too was McCloy. Lilienthal wrote in his diary, "When I read the news last night, I was quite sick. . . . We need a man who is young, vigorous, not vain, and who the Russians would feel isn't out simply to put them in a hole, not really caring about international cooperation. Baruch has none of these qualities."[29]

For his part, Baruch made it clear that he did not consider the Acheson-Lilienthal Report official policy. Nor did he need any advice from the scientists: "I knew all I wanted to know," he told Bush. "It [the bomb] went boom and it killed millions of people. . . ."[30] He would rely on his own advisers—two conservative bankers, Ferdinand Eberstadt and John Hancock, and Fred Searls, Jr., a mining engineer and close personal friend. All three men happened to be investors in the same uranium mining corporation, and were alarmed by the very idea that such privately owned mines might be turned over to an international Atomic Development Authority.[31] This smacked of socialism. None of these men seriously contemplated turning over control of U.S. nuclear weaponry to an international body. Baruch thought of the American bomb as the "winning weapon," and was soon telling Oppenheimer that he saw his job as a matter of "preparing the American people for a refusal by Russia."[32]

Soon after his appointment, Baruch met with Searls and Eberstadt in his limousine while waiting to catch a train at Penn Station in Manhattan. When the elderly financier expressed "great reservations" about the Acheson-Lilienthal Report's recommendations, Searls said that he had heard that the report was the "result of a concerted effort by a wide group who would like to have had McCloy appointed to the United Nations Atomic Energy Commission."[33]

Searls's source for this information was undoubtedly Donald Russell, who shared his distrust of internationalists like McCloy and Acheson. Russell, a South Carolinian who had been Byrnes's law partner, had been struggling for several months with McCloy over the organization of postwar intelligence. At the end of the war, McCloy had supported a plan by his former Cravath partner Al McCormack to merge remnants of Bill

Donovan's OSS apparatus into a centralized intelligence group within the State Department. They had the support of Acheson, and initially, Byrnes. But then Don Russell, from his position as assistant secretary of state for administration, proposed an alternative plan whereby each geographic bureau within the department would conduct its own intelligence collection. Byrnes was trying to decide between the "Russell Plan" and the "McCormack Plan" at the very moment when the controversy over the Acheson-Lilienthal Report broke.

Russell thought the report's recommendations lent credence to an astonishing set of charges against McCloy that had been circulating in Washington ever since the previous autumn. Russell's assistant, Deputy Assistant Secretary Joseph Anthony Panuch, was convinced that McCloy was a subversive. In mid-November 1945, just as their struggle over intelligence organization was heating up, Panuch had written his boss a detailed, five-page memo of charges against McCloy: "I could see that you found it hard to believe that Mr. McCloy could possibly have any connection with Communism . . . [but] it can readily be demonstrated that Mr. McCloy and his partners have been, to say the least, unusually friendly to the Soviet Union and sympathetic to the Communist cause."[34]

Specifically, Panuch charged that McCloy and McCormack had "permitted officers with known Communist leanings (as reported by the F.B.I.) to sit in positions where they could influence the trend of intelligence."[35] Soon such charges were appearing in Congress, where on March 14, 1946, one congressman suggested that individuals with "strong Soviet leanings" who had once worked in the War Department could now be found working in the State Department. McCormack angrily denied the charge in a public letter, but Panuch was not about to give up the offensive. He now wrote a memo arguing that the integration of these left-wing OSS officers into the State Department, as envisioned by the McCormack Plan, was part of an attempt to shift the center of gravity in foreign policy-making "from a national to an international orientation via the supranational United Nations Organization." The result, he warned, would be "a socialized America in a world commonwealth of Communist and Socialist states. . . ."[36]

Shortly afterward, Secretary Byrnes accepted the Russell Plan for a decentralized intelligence apparatus, and McCormack submitted his resignation in late April 1946. McCloy was disgusted with the whole affair, but his belief in the need for a centralized intelligence bureaucracy remained unshaken. If it could not be built within the State Department, he thought, perhaps it could find a home elsewhere. Such a possibility, of course, was something J. Edgar Hoover naturally regarded with apprehension. He had, in fact, circulated derogatory information about McCormack just before Congress voted not to fund the new intelligence office.[37]

In this context, Hoover now questioned the loyalty of McCloy, Acheson, and a half-dozen other government officials associated with atomic-energy policy. The charges were contained in a long letter he sent on May 29, 1946, to one of Truman's closest aides, George E. Allen. Saying that he thought Allen and the president would be interested in information furnished by a "source believed to be reliable," Hoover reported "there is an enormous Soviet espionage ring in Washington operating with the view of obtaining all information possible with reference to atomic energy. . . ." He then listed McCloy, Acheson, Herbert S. Marks (a young lawyer and Acheson assistant who had served on the Lilienthal board), Howard C. Petersen (the new assistant secretary of war), Henry Wallace, Alger Hiss (who was then still working in the State Department under Acheson), and a number of others. All these individuals, he said, "are noted for their pro-Soviet leanings," mentioning in particular Hiss and McCloy. Hoover linked some of these individuals to Nathan G. Silvermaster, an alleged Soviet agent.[38]

Truman may never have seen this particular letter, and if he did, one can assume he gave it no credibility. Hoover himself must have known that such charges were ridiculous and that his "reliable informant," probably J. Anthony Panuch or Donald Russell, was politically motivated. The FBI chief passed on such allegations to the White House only because it suited his own agenda, which was to prevent the creation of a rival central intelligence agency. He also just happened to be wiretapping Oppenheimer's phone that spring, and so was privy to the scientist's attempts to lobby various government officials against what Baruch was now doing to water down the Acheson-Lilienthal proposals.[39]

Hoover forwarded this information to Baruch, which naturally made the prickly financier even more determined to go his own way. He chose to disregard the opinion of most scientists and decided that the Soviets would not be able to build their own atomic bomb for twenty years. If so, he believed there was no reason to relinguish the American monopoly anytime soon, and he now began to toughen the Acheson-Lilienthal Plan by adding a number of conditions: the Soviets would have to give up their veto right over any action by the new atomic authority; any nation violating the agreement would immediately be punished by atomic attack; and, before being given access to any nuclear secrets, the Soviets would have to submit to a survey of their uranium resources and an inspection of their nuclear-research facilities.[40]

McCloy and the other members of the Acheson-Lilienthal committees only learned the full import of these amendments to their plan in mid-May, at a meeting hosted by Baruch and Eberstadt. It did not go well. McCloy and Acheson vigorously objected that such an early emphasis on punitive provisions would doom the plan. There was no such thing as complete security, McCloy angrily told Baruch, and it would be "presumptuous" to suggest such harsh and automatic penalty provisions. The

Soviets would never agree to these conditions, particularly at a time when the United States was continuing to build and test atomic weapons. What Baruch was proposing was not cooperative control over the bomb, but an atomic league designed to prolong the U.S. monopoly. Everyone present was taken aback that McCloy had so uncharacteristically vented his anger. The next day, Justice Frankfurter wrote his former student, "I am told that it was a real bull fight—and that you were so disgusted with the gentleman on the other side that you just sputtered 'dust in the air.' "[41]

Baruch and Eberstadt remained unshaken in their views, and the following month presented to the United Nations what became known as the "Baruch Plan." McCloy was not surprised when it was promptly rejected by the Soviets. Later, Dean Acheson concluded, "It was his [Baruch's] ball and he balled it up. . . . He pretty well ruined the thing."[42] An early opportunity had been lost to prevent a nuclear-arms race between the two major powers, and McCloy always felt that Baruch was to blame.[43]

At the end of June 1946, Ellen and the children moved to the family retreat in the Adirondacks for the summer. McCloy visited them on weekends, and took some time off to go fishing. His six-month law practice at Milbank, Tweed was beginning to pick up, when he suddenly received an intriguing offer. A month earlier, Eugene Meyer, the publisher of the *Washington Post,* had taken on the presidency of the International Bank for Reconstruction and Development. The "World Bank"—and its sister institution, the International Monetary Fund—had been created at the Bretton Woods conference and were supposed to finance the postwar economic recovery. Ostensibly part of the United Nations system, the Bank and the IMF were finally incorporated at a meeting in Savannah, Georgia, in March 1946. McCloy had observed the Bretton Woods deliberations with great interest, and so was more than a little bit tempted when Meyer called him one day and offered him the position of general counsel to the Bank.

He thought the idea "flattering." He was still finding it difficult to get back to the law. His corporate cases just couldn't compare to the excitement of public policy-making. But after thinking about it for a week, he wrote Meyer, "Though I would probably have a more interesting time dealing with the extremely important problems of organization and policy . . . I cannot help but feel the timing is wrong." It would not be "appropriate or sound for me to leave my new firm and the connections I have just made so shortly after my return from Washington."[44] Still, he was interested enough in the World Bank to take the trouble to recommend someone as a substitute—his old Cravath partner Chester McClain. A frequent fishing companion, McClain had spent the entire war years at

Cravath, and McCloy thought he might welcome a stint in Washington. Meyer jumped at the suggestion and used McCloy to recruit McClain in July.

Barely five months later, Meyer stunned the financial community when he suddenly announced his resignation. He had found the whole business an enormous headache. Partly because of disputes between member nations, most particularly the United States and Britain, and partly because of distrust on Wall Street, he had not been able to sell a single bond or issue any development loans. He had also found himself embroiled in a debilitating conflict with his own board of executive directors, in particular the U.S. executive director, Emilio G. Collado. A brilliant thirty-six-year-old, Harvard-trained economist, "Pete" Collado had spent his entire professional life in the Roosevelt administration, working with such liberal personalities as Harry Dexter White at the Treasury Department and Alger Hiss in the State Department. Meyer consequently considered him a brash young New Dealer, and they didn't get along. Collado and the executive directors from other nations believed Meyer should run the Bank according to policy voted upon by the board. They were eager to issue as many loans as possible, and quickly. When Meyer refused one day to approve an early loan to Chile, Collado pounded the table, demanding that the loan be approved. Meyer calmly refused, saying the Bank was not a relief agency. But such constant disputes with Collado took their toll on the seventy-one-year-old Meyer, and in December 1946 he resigned. He told his secretary, "I could stay and fight these bastards, and probably win in the end, but I'm too old for that."[45]

His departure sparked speculation in Wall Street that the nascent institution would never recover. Russell Leffingwell, a J. P. Morgan & Co. partner, wrote Meyer that it would be a "bad setback for the bank."[46] In London, the *Financial Times* voiced fears that the World Bank might now become a "universal soup kitchen" and its monies "used for financing vote-catching reconstruction schemes propounded by the starry-eyed politicians of many nations."[47]

CHAPTER 14

The World Bank: "McCloy über Alles"

"Jack, you'll never have to worry about what to do after the World Bank. There will always be a place for you and people who will want you."

FREDDIE WARBURG, 1947

"Pete" Collado had a feeling he had overplayed his hand. As U.S. executive director, he still possessed a virtual veto over the Bank's activities. But without a president, the Bank was rudderless and in danger of running aground. Collado knew that he was too young to aspire to the presidency himself. So now, in consultation with his fellow board members, he began casting about for Meyer's replacement. Several prominent bankers were approached, including Graham F. Towers, governor of the Bank of Canada. But he declined, saying that a U.S. citizen had to lead the Bank if its credibility on Wall Street was to be restored. Collado then remembered that Meyer had tried to persuade McCloy to become the Bank's general counsel. During the war, working at the Treasury Department, he had occasionally run into Stimson's aide, and they had worked together briefly at Potsdam.[1] With the backing of Treasury Secretary John W. Snyder, Collado flew up to New York two days before Christmas 1946.

Though it was a wet, snowy day, Collado failed to wear galoshes or a proper overcoat, and by the time he arrived at the Waldorf Astoria for his appointment, he was shivering and had a cold. Worse, McCloy quickly made it clear that he was not inclined to take on the job. "Pete," he said, "you've made such a hell of a mess of it, you don't think I'm going to move into that damn thing?" Collado returned to Washington that day with only McCloy's halfhearted promise to think about it, and spent the next two weeks in bed with the flu.[2]

In his methodical manner, McCloy now sought the counsel of his friends. He was aware that Lew Douglas himself had turned down the job when it had been offered to him the previous spring. Not surprisingly, Douglas discouraged him, but others urged him to take the job. One day, he went out to visit Freddie Warburg at his Middleburg, Virginia, horse farm. Sitting out on the veranda, smoking a cigar, and looking across the expanse of his wealthy friend's beautiful estate, McCloy told Warburg, "I think it's time to earn some money for my family." But Freddie could tell that McCloy was actually quite inclined to take the job: "Jack," he said, "you'll never have to worry about what to do after the World Bank. There will always be a place for you and people who will want you."[3]

Some of McCloy's Wall Street colleagues saw in his possible appointment an opportunity to take control of the World Bank away from the New Deal crowd represented by "Morgenthau and those clucks."[4] Harold Stanley, president of Morgan Stanley & Co.; Baxter Jackson, president of Chemical Bank; Randolph Burgess, vice-chairman of National City Bank; and George Whitney, president of J. P. Morgan & Co. all encouraged McCloy. Whitney thought that, if its operations could be run on a "sensible and restrained basis," then McCloy "was the ideal man to head the Bank."[5]

But after a fortnight of consideration, McCloy formally turned the job down. It seemed to him that the Bank's bylaws were such that the presidency had all the responsibility and the executive-board members, in particular the U.S. director, had all the power. When informed of his reasons, Snyder and Collado went separately to New York to make their personal appeals. Soon the fact that McCloy was being courted for the job was reported in the press. *Time* said he was on the point of saying "I do," but then "saw the bride's family," meaning Collado and the other executive directors. Among "knowing Washingtonians," reported the magazine, Collado had an "increasing fondness for having his own way. . . ."[6] McCloy actually had no personal animosity for Collado; he thought of him as a bit "liberal," but there was nothing personally objectionable in that.[7]

The problem was the structure of the World Bank itself, the fact that the Articles of Agreement adopted at Bretton Woods placed a preponderance of power in the hands of the directors. As the Bank's first annual report made clear, "matters of policy determination" were the responsibility of the twelve executive directors. The president confined himself to "administrative" questions, "subject to the general direction and control of the Executive Directors."[8] McCloy had sought the advice of Eugene Black, vice-president of Chase National Bank and one of Wall Street's best-known bonds salesmen. Black had just returned from an inspection of war-torn Europe, and he was impressed with the potential importance of the World Bank. But he confirmed that the real power rested with the U.S. executive director, who controlled 37 percent of the Bank's shares. Black advised that he not accept the presidency unless he got the right to select the U.S. director.[9]

So, on February 17, 1947, McCloy went down to Washington for a meeting with the non-American board directors. He presented what the British bluntly called an "ultimatum." Eugene Black would replace Collado as U.S. executive director, and simultaneously Black would take charge of the Bank's bond operations. Robert L. Garner, a gruff, no-nonsense banker and businessman, would become the Bank's vice-president. Moreover, McCloy announced he would not take the post unless he was given a free hand in all of the Bank's loan decisions. He, as president, would decide whether to present a loan package for approval to the board, not the other way around. If these terms were not acceptable, he and his team were ready to return to New York that afternoon. There was some grumbling that his conditions violated the spirit of the Articles of Agreement. But, given the current impasse and the Bank's "diminishing" capacity to function, the non-American directors reluctantly agreed. Even then, McCloy said he would not finally accept the job until he was satisfied that the only potential buyers of the Bank's bonds, the New York commercial banks and insurance companies, were likely to cooperate. At the conclusion of the meeting, the British director reported back to London that McCloy "was at times unnecessarily truculent. . . . What happens now I don't know but I must say that dirt is a disagreeable diet."[10]

The British at that moment faced dire economic conditions brought on by a growing balance-of-payments deficit and exacerbated by one of the most severe winters in a century. The Labour government in London was desperate for dollar loans to finance necessary food and fuel imports. They had been led to believe at Bretton Woods in 1944 that the World Bank had been established precisely in order to prevent the kind of postwar fiscal crisis they now faced. The Bank's inactivity was "imperilling" a general European recovery. London interpreted McCloy's ultimatum as further evidence that Washington intended to renege on its Bretton Woods commitments. One British official bitterly complained, "It [the World Bank] was not set up to finance ordinary commercial schemes which are 100 percent financially sound. . . . It was set up to promote the schemes of reconstruction which were socially desirable, but which were so uncertain financially that the risk was to be shared among the governments of the world. . . . It is waiting for 'projects' of the 'gilt-edged' variety, instead of getting on with the reconstruction of the world."[11]

Such criticisms quickly made their way into the British press. While

McCloy went back to New York to consult with a variety of bankers and insurance-company executives, the *Financial Times* reported, ". . . on Mr. McCloy's insistence, the U.S. Government is accepting a greatly restricted concept of the Bank's role, thus foreshadowing much smaller World Bank lending in the next two years than was previously anticipated."[12]

This was not, indeed, the kind of Bank that Harry Dexter White had first envisioned in 1942. White had been to Treasury Secretary Henry Morgenthau what McCloy had been to Stimson. A hard-driving and imaginative man, he was one of the New Deal's most powerful bureaucrats. At the end of the war, he became U.S. executive director of the Bank's twin, the International Monetary Fund. Though Lord John Maynard Keynes and others contributed to the early discussion among the Allies, it was essentially White's 1942 draft proposal that was adopted at Bretton Woods. He was adamant that the Bank not become merely a rich man's club; it should be truly international and function as a global central bank for development and war reconstruction. In principle, enlightened opinion in New York's financial circles—as evidenced by some of the Council on Foreign Relations' study reports—conceded that some kind of "international agency" should stimulate foreign investment after the war, so as to prevent a repeat performance of the post–World War I disruptions in world trade. But Wall Street was disinclined to turn such a task over to such an ideologically committed New Dealer as White.[13]

By early 1947, White could see that the political tides were running against him; he announced his resignation, effective the end of March. Still, he was hopeful that in the next two years America would lend on the order of $10 billion around the globe, and as to his own plans, he was determined to attempt to "recreate the New Deal" by promoting the political fortunes of Henry Wallace.*[14]

McCloy had had his own conflicts with White during the 1944 debate over the Morgenthau Plan to create a pastoral Germany, and though their relations had been amiable on the surface, he was not sorry to see White leave Washington. From his point of view, any association between the Bank-Fund group and prominent New Dealers like Harry White would only make it more difficult to sell the Bank's bonds on Wall

*Within the year, White was named at a congressional hearing by Elizabeth Bentley, a former Communist Party member, as having spied for the Soviet Union. White vigorously denied the accusation before a congressional committee, and then a few days later died of a heart attack. His supporters over the years have demonstrated that the evidence against him was unreliable, but neither has White been fully vindicated. Some historians suggest that recently declassified intercept intelligence indicates that White had indeed been in communication with Soviet diplomats stationed in Washington. But the circumstances of these contacts leave open the question of whether he was operating as a Soviet asset.

Street. As he now moved in the direction of accepting the post, McCloy began assembling his own team of men to take with him into the Bank. Finally, on the last day of February 1947, newspaper headlines proclaimed, "McCloy to Head World Bank on His Own Terms."[15] In London, a witty British Foreign Office official sarcastically wrote his own headline for the day's news: "McCloy über Alles," a play on the German slogan "Deutschland über Alles" ("Germany over the World").

The next day, at a press conference, McCloy insisted that personality conflicts had not led to the two-month delay in his appointment. There was a role, he said, for the Bank in war reconstruction; the world could not remain "half rubble and half well-built." But he had to be sure that the Bank could become "a going concern rather than a mere distributor of its own capital." That meant it had to be able to sell its own securities on Wall Street. In practice, if the Bank was to rely for most of its capital on the sale of securities, then it could expect to issue very few loans over the next few years. On paper, the Bank had pledged assets of nearly $8 billion, but only 20 percent of this sum would be in hand by early summer, virtually all of it from the United States and Canada. Obviously, unless McCloy intended to ask the United States to increase its capital pledges by an enormous magnitude, war-torn Europe could expect to receive very little assistance from the World Bank.

That was exactly the message McCloy intended to convey to Wall Street. For the next two years, he planned to run the Bank as if its clients were private Wall Street investors and not the forty countries that had joined in the hope of receiving development aid. Some observers were slow to see what was happening. Soon after McCloy's selection, Hugh Dalton, an influential British MP, wrote U.S. Treasury Secretary John Snyder that he hoped the "way is now clear for the Bank to go full steam ahead. . . . It is essential that it should now act quickly and positively, and give concrete proof of its powers by beginning operations at once. I have said as much to McCloy."[16]

McCloy, however, cringed whenever he saw references in the press to the "$8 billion bank," and did everything he could to lower the public's expectations regarding future loans. At the end of March, he had Black propose to the executive directors a firm rule that the Bank not loan more than the sum of the U.S. and Canadian subscriptions to the Bank. The British director reported back to London that such a regulation "fairly obviously represents at least part of the price which the New York market insists on having as the condition of its support of the Bank issues. . . ."[17] A week later, the British learned from McCloy that in all probability the Bank would lend nothing like as much as $1 billion a year: if so, "it will be utterly ineffective as a substantial contributor towards world recovery. This whole story seems to point to the conclusion that the Bank and the Fund can now probably be written off as agencies for good and can merely be reckoned as instruments for the enforcement of dollar diplomacy."[18] Not surprisingly, tensions between the executive board and McCloy were high. At one early meeting, as McCloy opened the proceedings by introducing Black and Garner to the board, Sir James Grigg, the British director, muttered, "Here goes a meeting of the Chase Bank."[19]

While the British and other non-Americans groused about how they were being ignored or worse, McCloy, Black, and Garner set about organizing the Bank along commercial lines. As a token of his good wishes, Nelson Rockefeller had loaned them his house, a handsome structure on Georgetown's Foxhall Road, together with its well-stocked larder and bevy of servants. For three months, the men shared the mansion while their wives remained in New York. This arrangement allowed them the privacy they needed to concentrate on the work at hand. "We were often up until one or two in the morning," recalled Black. "My job was to create a market for securities; Garner's job was to set up a loan apparatus. McCloy was quite insistent that things be run on a conservative basis, with the proper loan conditions."[20]

Wall Street greeted McCloy's coup d'état at the Bank with mixed emotions. *American Banker,* a mouthpiece of the investment-banking community, applauded Collado's removal as a sign that the Bank would now be "guided by the philosophy that it must minimize political consideration and maximize economic factors in making its loans. . . ."[21] *The New York Times* editorialized that McCloy's ascension was "a symbol of new hope."[22] But there was still talk around Wall Street that perhaps the Bank's as yet unissued securities should be taken off New York State's "legal list" of bonds eligible for purchase by the savings-and-loan industry. And a number of other state legislatures were still refusing to allow pension funds and insurance companies to invest their monies in World Bank bonds.[23] Memories were long on Wall Street, and many brokers could still remember the 1930s, when 34 percent of all loans to foreign governments were in default. Only the Finns had repaid their World War I debts in full.[24] So the idea of further lending to foreign governments was not very attractive to most private investors.

In an effort to turn the situation around, McCloy, Black, and Garner spent much of April on the road, giving speeches at bankers' conventions and lobbying various state legislatures. McCloy told an audience of the Chartered Life Underwriters at New York City's Town Hall that the Bank "would operate in a goldfish bowl," that its securities would be listed on the New York Stock Exchange and comply with all the SEC's reporting regulations. Political loans of any kind, he told these potential investors, were "definitely excluded." Despite these assurances, many were still skeptical. After listening to one such presentation by McCloy, Gene Black overheard a member of the audience mutter, "I wouldn't touch those bonds with a ten-foot pole."[25]

In May 1947, McCloy told 350 members of the elite Bond Club in Manhattan that the mere fact that the World Bank intended to sell its bonds on the open market would help to ensure that it remained free of political pressures. If investors learned otherwise, he said, "The word would spread. It would be killing the goose that lays the golden egg."[26] In one way or another, of course, politics permeated the Bank's activities. McCloy had joined the Bank the same month that the British withdrew their troops from the civil war raging in Greece, an action that had precipitated the Truman Doctrine. The world faced a stark choice, Harry Truman said, between two ways of life, communist and democratic. As Truman himself summarized it in his memoirs, this was a "turning point" in U.S. foreign policy. From now on, "whenever aggression, direct or indirect, threatened the peace, the security of the United States was involved."[27]

Not everyone in the foreign-policy establishment was comfortable with such an open-ended commitment to intervene against the spread of communist governments anywhere. After seeing an early draft of the speech, George Kennan, then director of policy planning at the State Department, voiced his strong objections to Dean Acheson and others in the State Department.[28] Like McCloy, Kennan believed that Russia's resources were already so severely taxed that the Soviets had no intention of expanding outside the sphere of influence Yalta and Potsdam had accorded them in Eastern Europe. "I personally," he wrote in the autumn of 1946, "have no fear about our being able to contain the Russians for the foreseeable future, if we handle ourselves reasonably well."[29] Kennan's influence, however, was already beginning to wane, even as he stood at the apex of his foreign-service career.

In this context, the World Bank's lending policies could not help having great political ramifications. By April 1947, Chile, Poland, France, and several other nations had already submitted loan applications. Early that month, McCloy decided that the first loan would go to the French. At a moment when the Cold War was beginning to move into high gear, there were compelling political reasons to shore up the French government. The Communist Party of France had won for itself a minor position in the coalition government, and Washington feared that it might increase its mandate in the next elections. "The Communists were at the throat of the French," Kennan recalled a year later. "A pall of fear, of bewilderment, of discouragement, hung over the continent and paralyzed all constructive activity."[30] The French wanted $500 million, not for specific projects—a road, a power plant, or an irrigation system—but in "general-purpose" funds to finance imports of food, fuel, and industrial machinery. This was exactly the kind of loan that ordinary commercial bankers would avoid, the kind of loan that had gone into default in the 1930s. But it was what the French needed to revive their economy. And so, though he had not initially been prepared to endorse such lending, McCloy was quickly convinced by the Bank's senior economists that Europe's war-torn economies needed such balance-of-payments assistance.[31]

The terms would be tough: The Bank would lend only half of the requested $500 million, Bank officers would monitor end use of the funds, and the French government would have to pledge that the repayment of the Bank's loans would have absolute priority over any other foreign debt. Furthermore, the Bank would closely supervise the French economy to ensure that the government took steps to balance its budget, increase taxes, and cut consumption of certain luxury imports.[32] The French protested that such conditions infringed on their sovereignty.[33] But when McCloy refused to budge, they reluctantly agreed to his terms. Simultaneously, the State Department bluntly informed the French that they would have to "correct the present situation" by removing any communist representatives in the Cabinet. The Communist Party was pushed out of the coalition government in early May 1947, and within hours, as if to underscore the linkage, McCloy announced that the loan would go through.[34] Even then, he warned that the French would not receive the loan until the Bank successfully floated $250 million worth of bonds on the New York market.

For the next several months, McCloy and Black worked on little else but the first bond offering, now scheduled for July 15, 1947. They decided to offer two bonds, one issue of $100 million, ten-year bonds paying 2.25 percent, and a second issue of $150 million, twenty-five-year bonds paying 3 percent. Normally, such a bond offering would be marketed by one or two of the major investment houses on Wall Street. But because the Bank's securities were still an unknown commodity, these firms would have charged a hefty fee for underwriting the sale. So, instead, McCloy and Black decided to market the securities through hundreds of independent brokers across the country. Letters were sent out to 2,650 dealers, promising them a guaranteed commission twice the rate paid for the sale of similar corporate bonds. Over seventeen hundred dealers agreed to participate in the sale, and on the appointed day McCloy, Black, and Garner stationed themselves on the floor of the New York Stock Exchange and waited anxiously for the first bids. At 10:02 A.M., two minutes after the opening of the market, McCloy formally accepted the first bid for $100,000 worth of the twenty-five-year bonds at three points above the offering price. After two hours of spirited bidding, it was announced that both bonds had been heavily oversubscribed. At a luncheon for McCloy immediately afterward, the president of the New York Stock Exchange, Emil Schram, called it a "historic moment."[35] *Newsweek* printed a photo of a beaming McCloy, clearly relieved that his gamble had paid off.[36]

Of course, the investors, largely banks and insurance companies, were assuming very little risk on bonds that paid a higher-than-average interest.[37] As Sylvia Porter, financial editor of the *New York Post*, observed, it had been "the sort of bond sale investment men must dream of as they ride the Banker's Special and think their thoughts of heaven."[38] But because the market fears the unknown, McCloy felt he had to make the Bank's first offering particularly attractive. Even so, Standard & Poor's, the market's best-known rating service, gave the Bank's securities a rating of A, the minimum grade necessary for a bond to be eligible for purchase by an institutional investor.[39]

McCloy felt that his conservative strategy of slowly building confidence in the Bank had been vindicated. But there were many who believed such a course was undermining the fundamental purpose of the Bank. The executive directors, and many of the Bank's staff economists, believed these first two issues were far too small for the task at hand. Even assuming scaled-back lending levels, the British Labour government still hoped that the Bank might quickly begin lending on the order of $1 billion annually. In fact, under McCloy's tenure the Bank would never loan even half that amount.[40] That summer, the British were particularly resentful. "It seems to me extraordinary," wrote one British official, "that these bodies [the IMF and the Bank] should be doing so miserably little. . . . After all, great hopes were raised by Bretton Woods and we ourselves have made big international concessions as a contribution to enable the Bank and the Fund to get a good start. How can we accept all these burdensome obligations and see nothing done in return?"[41]

Not only the British, but the French too were unhappy with the Bank's unambitious stance on war reconstruction. That spring, French Foreign Minister Georges Bidault had bitterly complained to Secretary of State George C. Marshall that the Bank had cut their request in half. France was pressed to the wall, he said, and needed substantial economic assistance in order to "avoid a civil war" with the communists. Bidault was well aware that an appeal on such political grounds might evoke a response from Washington. Only the previous year, Marshall's predecessor, Jimmy Byrnes, had justified a $650-million bilateral credit to the French by arguing that it would help to "combat this Russian influence." Marshall told Bidault that he was aware of the "delicate political situation in France" and would have a personal chat with McCloy to see what could be done.[42]

McCloy, of course, explained how the Bank's lending operations were constrained by its ability to sell its securities on the New York and Canadian financial markets. When he talked to Marshall that spring, the Bank had not even sold its first bond. He said that it would be a long time, perhaps years, before the Bank would be in a position to lend billions of dollars. If European recovery required massive new loans, then the American taxpayer would have to finance a bilateral program. Will Clayton,

George Kennan, Dean Acheson, and many others influenced Marshall's attitude on this question, but since he was president of the institution specifically created to deal with war reconstruction, McCloy's views weighed heavily. Over the next few weeks, a consensus emerged within the Truman administration that some kind of bilateral European Recovery Program (ERP) should be proposed to Congress. Marshall unveiled the new idea at a Harvard commencement address on June 5, 1947.

This idea—the Marshall Plan—was the something more that was needed to get Europe's basic economy moving. Acknowledging that the world's needs surpassed the Bank's capabilities,[43] McCloy lobbied vigorously for the congressional appropriations that would make the Marshall Plan a reality. He warned it would be a waste of taxpayers' money if too little aid was given; anything less than the $6.8 billion the Truman administration was requesting would amount to a relief program, not a program aimed at full economic recovery.[44] But Congress would not act quickly on the controversial measure, to the consternation of Undersecretary of State Robert Lovett, who felt the world was edging toward war. "At no time in my recollection," Lovett wrote that summer, "have I ever seen a world situation which was moving so rapidly toward real trouble." McCloy was not nearly so pessimistic as Lovett. He thought that the British pound crisis was exaggerated, and that Europe in the long run had all the resources and manpower to become once again a major economic power.[45] He even refused to have the Bank fund food aid as a temporary measure until Marshall Plan aid arrived. "Europe itself must make the major contribution to the solution of all these problems. . . . Outside assistance is vital, but it represents a small percentage of the total effort." The Bank, he flatly stated, was "not in the stop-gap business."[46]

And, despite the political confrontation with the communists in France, or perhaps even because of it, he was unwilling to approve that country's request for the additional $250 million. Such a loan, he thought, could not be justified to the Bank's Wall Street investors. Truman and Lovett bowed to the logic of this argument, and reconciled themselves to the fact that the World Bank was no substitute, even in the interim, for massive bilateral aid. At the end of September 1947, Truman told a group of congressmen in the Cabinet Room, "We'll either have to provide a program of interim aid relief until the Marshall program gets going, or the governments of France and Italy will fall, Austria too, and for all practical purposes Europe will be Communist." Such presidential rhetoric persuaded a special session of Congress to appropriate almost $600 million in interim aid for France, Italy, and Austria.[47] By this time, the World Bank had issued three more loans: $195 million to the Netherlands, $40 million for Denmark, and a small $12-million loan for Luxembourg. Together with the $250-million French loan, these four loans were the first and the last of the loans McCloy would make to Europe. In the years to come, the Marshall Plan would make the Bank's operations in Europe redundant.[48]

Later, when it became apparent that the administration would successfully fight back efforts by Senator Robert Taft and other conservative Republicans to cut Marshall Plan aid by one-third, some newspaper columnists speculated that McCloy would soon leave the Bank to head the European Recovery Program.[49] McCloy himself was tempted, if only because he knew that, in comparison with the Marshall Plan, the Bank "was a row boat next to the Queen Elizabeth."[50] But, having spent less than a year with the Bank, he could not easily be considered a candidate; Paul Hoffman, president of the Studebaker Corporation, got the job instead.

By restricting the Bank's involvement in European reconstruction, McCloy could claim that, insofar as the Marshall Plan was motivated by political considerations, he was keeping the Bank's lending operations free of politics. And as Hoffman's boys over at the ERP began pumping $13 billion worth of American goods and services into Western Europe, he took every opportunity to distinguish their activities from his own, even to the point of criticizing the liberal terms of Marshall Plan aid. "If the [Marshall] Plan merely turns into another grant of dollars . . .," he wrote John Foster Dulles at his Sullivan & Cromwell law office in November 1947, "it will have done more harm than good."[51]

Notwithstanding such disclaimers, politics repeatedly intervened to influence Bank policy. By the end of 1947, it seemed to the British and most of the other executive directors that the Bank under McCloy had become a U.S. "monopoly."[52] This was demonstrated most graphically by McCloy's handling of a loan application from the communist-dominated coalition government of Poland. In one of the first loan applications to the Bank, in 1946, the Poles had requested $600 million to buy coal-mining equipment from the West. In the spring of 1947, the Poles had renewed their request, scaling it down to a more reasonable $128.5-million loan. But McCloy had decided to give priority to the French loan, and that spring *The New York Times* reported that, though the Polish loan was considered "a sound investment," it had so far been blocked by the U.S. government, "which fears the political effect of such a credit to Poland's Communist-led government."[53]

In June 1947, McCloy sent a Bank team to Poland to evaluate the coal project. The resulting staff report was favorable, and that autumn McCloy visited Poland. He came away strongly impressed with the potential the Polish coal industry had for supplying Western Europe with a much-needed energy source. But on his way back, he stopped off in London and saw Churchill, who said he was opposed to the whole notion of lending Western capital to Eastern Europe. A revived Germany, he said, not Poland, was the key to European stability. McCloy responded that many Europeans, particularly in the East, found the prospect of a revived Germany profoundly unsettling. Besides, a loan to Poland might save the country "from complete subjugation" by the Soviets. So, when he got back to Washington, he formally opened negotiations for a loan of some $50 million. At the same time, he realized that the Bank could not make the loan without the support of the Truman administration.[54]

Within a couple of weeks, it became clear that Truman's State Department would oppose the loan.[55] McCloy did not announce a negative decision, but he began to back off from the proposal. Because it would be awkward to admit that the loan had been rejected on political grounds, he privately made it known to the British and other interested parties that he now thought his Wall Street investors would not approve. This annoyed the British, who favored the loan, arguing that it would "help to prevent increased dependence on the part of Poland on the USSR. . . ." One British diplomat, after talking to McCloy, commented, "For what it is worth, my impression of McCloy's remarks . . . is that he tends to use the New York market as a convenient scapegoat for avoiding difficult decisions. I should have thought that if he really wanted to, he could make a small loan to Poland out of the $250,000,000 which he raised recently in New York."[56]

Instead, in their negotiations with the Poles, McCloy and Garner now began to raise conditions that they knew to be unacceptable. They demanded that Poland first stabilize its currency according to guidelines issued by the International Monetary Fund.[57] Instead of $45 million, the Bank's loan committee suggested $25 million, and even that was to be contingent on the Poles' agreeing to sell their coal to Western Europe and use the hard-currency proceeds to make payments on the Bank's loan. Poland's executive director at the Bank and its ambassador in Washington—both anticommunists—tried to persuade their government to accept these unusually tough terms. But, since they had originally sought $600 million, the $25 million the Bank offered now was hardly incentive enough for the Polish communists to agree to such concessions.[58]

Simultaneously, a firm consensus developed within the Truman administration rejecting the notion that Western aid might help preserve the coalition government in Warsaw. As an intelligence report from the newly created CIA evaluated the situation a year later, ". . . any assistance from the West to Poland would only contribute to the ultimate enhancement of the Soviet Union's war potential . . . [and] would have a demoralizing effect on anti-communist segments of the Polish population. . . ."[59] So, finally, in mid-1948, Eugene Black told McCloy that he had been formally instructed by the Truman administration to vote against any loan for Poland. McCloy then suspended all further negotiations with the

Poles, who protested in the United Nations that for some "sinister reason" the World Bank had killed the loan. Citing the rejection of a similar proposed loan to Czechoslovakia, the Poles charged that the United States was using the Bank to wage economic warfare against Eastern Europe. Moreover, they angrily pointed out that the Bank's two major loans, to France and the Netherlands, were in amounts that in effect compensated these two colonial powers for their respective military expenditures in Vietnam and Indonesia.[60]

McCloy retorted that he did not regard communist countries as *prima facie* bad risks for Bank loans. The Bank, he said, was seriously considering loans to Yugoslavia and Finland, both of which were then thought to be part of the Soviet bloc. But Averell Harriman had independently come to the same conclusion as the Poles. While visiting Paris in 1948, Harriman, who by then was the Marshall Plan's special representative in Europe, cabled Acheson "pointing out that French spending in Vietnam was about as much as we were giving them in Paris." Acheson sharply rebuked Harriman, telling him that Europe and not the Far East was his responsibility.[61]

If the Bank under McCloy was showing signs of emerging as a viable financial institution, its loyalties were obviously to the Western world, and, more specifically, to the United States. This was not the intent of its Bretton Woods creators, who had assumed that the Soviet Union would play a major part in the Bank's activities. At Bretton Woods, the Soviets themselves had demonstrated that they were willing to participate in the Bank as a full member. One indication of this had come just before the conference adjourned, when they agreed to raise their subscription to the Bank from $900 million to $1.2 billion. By the time the Bank opened its doors in 1946, however, Soviet-American relations had sharply deteriorated. Stalin had been angered by Truman's abrupt cancellation of Lend-Lease, and dismayed that his repeated requests for $6 billion in postwar credits were ignored for months.[62]

Still, some American officials had been perplexed when Stalin refused to join the World Bank and IMF. In February 1946, officials at the U.S. Treasury Department cabled the U.S. Embassy in Moscow and asked for an explanation of Stalin's behavior. They got Kennan's famous eight-thousand-word "Long Telegram," probably the most debated piece of foreign-policy analysis ever written by a U.S. diplomat. Kennan argued that Soviet behavior could only be explained by the traditional Russian sense of paranoia and inferiority toward the West. The refusal to take their place in the Bretton Woods institutions, and their increasing hostility on other issues, was motivated by deeply rooted historical insecurities, not by their worn-out ideology.[63] Stalin had simply decided to do what czars in the past had done when confronted by a rich and powerful neighbor in the West—withdraw into the isolation and self-sufficiency of the great Russian land mass.

Kennan claims in retrospect that his policy prescription—containment—was misunderstood, that he believed the Soviet challenge was political in character, and that the Soviets did not intend to risk war with the West. But there is no disputing that Kennan's analysis did contain the rationale for a host of U.S. economic and political initiatives which the Soviets quickly perceived as a policy of aggressive encirclement.

Arguably, Soviet-American relations might have been very different if war reconstruction aid had been forthcoming in 1946–47. The economic motivations for the Soviets to tighten their control over Eastern Europe in order to extract reparations from East Germany, Poland, and Hungary would have been less compelling. Of course, all of Europe was in need of such war reconstruction aid, and if it had been funneled through the World Bank, as was originally intended at Bretton Woods, the course of the Cold War *might* have been different. But America did not decide to allocate the necessary funds until late in 1947, and then it was done within the political context of the Marshall Plan, a vehicle the Soviets perceived as inimical to their sphere of influence in Eastern Europe. During the ensuing Cold War, McCloy's World Bank became neither a truly internationalist institution nor the crucial one in the scheme of European war reconstruction. That was left to the Marshall Plan, which succeeded brilliantly in its aim of integrating Western Europe into the West.

By early 1948, McCloy could see that, if the Bank was to have any impact, it would have to be among underdeveloped countries in Asia, Latin America, and Africa. That year, he made two month-long trips to Latin America, and in a speech in Bogotá, Colombia, he declared that the "American republics constitute an area of special interest for the Bank at this time." To the distress of many Latins, however, he then emphasized that the Bank's lending in Latin America was intended to "blaze the trail for private international investments." This was not what his audience wanted to hear. He refused to budge when challenged by a Mexican economist who rose from the floor and, to great applause, suggested such investments should be made by governments, not private investors.[64] The billions in Marshall Plan aid then being appropriated by the U.S. Congress might look like substantial sums. But, McCloy argued, in the long run the World Bank might be able to stimulate a much larger flow of private capital for development purposes. Such aid, he said, would be much more effective than "any program which is dependent upon political appropriations and the legislative conditions of the moment."[65] It was the same argument, turned around, that he had used to persuade private investors back on Wall Street to buy Bank bonds. But it sounded less than convincing to a Latin audience in Colombia. In fact, McCloy was dead wrong. It would be two decades before private commercial bankers began lending substantial amounts to the developing world, and many of those loans were to default over time. Direct foreign investments are still inconsequential compared with official bilateral and international aid flows. Loans and grants made by the World Bank itself greatly surpass private foreign investment in most of the poorest developing countries.[66] Such low levels of both official and private capital flows did little to contain the turbulent political forces sweeping the developing world.

Despite the bleak economic conditions McCloy saw all over the continent, only Chile received two World Bank loans, totaling $16 million, that spring, and even this small amount was lent only after he forced the Chileans to reach a settlement with their foreign bondholders on some $170 million worth of defaulted debt. McCloy thought it essential to set a precedent that the Bank would not loan to any country unless all previous defaulted debts had been rescheduled or paid up. This infuriated many Latins, who grumbled that the Bank had become a mere bill-collector for Wall Street. But McCloy had his way, and the principle has been applied to all subsequent lenders.

Over the next year, McCloy approved loans for several other Latin countries. He made another trip south that autumn, and then, in early 1949, toured Central America. In Nicaragua, the country's dictator, Anastasio Somoza, took him to a baseball game where the third baseman made numerous errors. Afterward, McCloy was entertained at a dinner during which several Nicaraguan officials made windy speeches pleading for Bank lending. When it was finally his turn to speak, McCloy broke the icy atmosphere by turning to Somoza and saying, "What Nicaragua needs most is a good third baseman." Still, upon his return, he told Bob Garner that he had observed that those countries ruled by dictators were in "better condition."[67]

By this time, the Bank was considering loans in twenty countries throughout the world. But total Bank lending since McCloy had taken charge was still less than $500 million. Though the Bank's reputation on Wall Street had never been more sound, it was still not doing the job of a development bank. In the wake of violent riots that broke out in Colombia in 1948, the Truman administration began to feel pressured to mount some kind of "Marshall Plan" for Latin America. Critics in the press and Congress suggested that the World Bank was incapable of providing large new levels of development aid. Congress debated whether or not to expand the government-funded Export-Import Bank, an institution established to stimulate U.S. exports. McCloy now regarded the "Eximbank" as a rival. By the end of 1947, it had extended some $1.1

billion in credit to Latin America alone, and in 1948 Congress appropriated the Eximbank another $500 million for such lending. Moreover, the Eximbank could make these loans at 3.5 percent, and Marshall Plan loans carried an even lower rate, 2.5 percent. McCloy knew of some countries that had abruptly suspended loan negotiations with the World Bank when they thought it possible to obtain the same funding at lower interest rates. If this continued, he warned, the Bank would have to "curtail, or perhaps even to suspend, its operations."[68]

Early in 1949, McCloy decided to take his worries to the president. He wrote Truman an eighteen-page memorandum defending the Bank and sharply criticizing both the Marshall Plan and the Eximbank. Any further U.S. war reconstruction or development loans, he argued, should be made through the World Bank, and not on a bilateral basis. He stressed that he was not opposed to further U.S. aid flows: "I urge only that such additional assistance be in the form of grants rather than in the form of illusory loans. . . ." Because the World Bank was an international institution, he argued, it was in a better position to "resist political pressures and to allocate its resources on a sound economic basis." To the extent that loans were made by the Bank, the United States would be "relieved of both the burden and the odium of being creditor to the world. . . . The pressures now being exerted for 'Marshall Plans' for Latin America and for the Far East bear witness to this." He recognized that the United States had "important political objectives" in Latin America, but he did not believe that throwing more money at Latin America could advance these objectives, and it might "only serve to stir animosities."

If necessary, he argued, the Bank could easily handle a lending program of $500 million annually, and even more if the U.S. government decided to enlarge its capital contributions: "Accordingly, it is difficult to see any economic justification for the United States now engaging in a new and enlarged program of international development financing."[69]

Much of this was sound advice. His perception of how much the developing world could absorb in foreign aid may have been overly pessimistic. But he was certainly right to argue that if the United States—for humanitarian or even outright political reasons—wished to increase its capital flows to the developing world, then it made good sense to do so through an international institution like the World Bank. But in 1949 such arguments carried little political weight. Truman didn't even bother to respond in writing to McCloy's memo, and instead, just passed it on to Dean Acheson in the State Department.

Two weeks later, at his inaugural in January, the president unveiled a massive new lending program that came to be known as "Point Four." Designed to provide bilateral loans and grants to developing nations in Asia, Africa, the Middle East, and Latin America, Point Four was everything McCloy had just recommended against. Ironically, for a few days, authorship of the president's proposals was attributed to McCloy. In fact, McCloy and the Bank's vice-president, Bob Garner, were aghast. Garner wrote in his private diary that Truman's speech was "another indication of impulsive bungling." McCloy's misgivings soon made their way into press. Four days after Truman's speech, the *New York Post*'s columnist Marquis Childs reported, "McCloy has made no secret of his concern for the status of the World Bank."[70] With Marshall Plan aid for Europe and Point Four aid for the developing world, what was the Bank's role to be?

The problem, of course, was that the U.S. Congress, impressed by Truman's Cold War admonishments, was willing to fund bilateral aid programs, but unwilling to appropriate the same funds to be administered through an international bank. McCloy resigned himself to this reality, telling *The New York Times* that the Bank would simply have to take a back seat to Point Four aid in the developing world.[71] Privately, he complained to Bernard Baruch, "I must say I think the fear of Communism and its encroachments does have such a deep-seated base that Congress and the people are going to respond for some time to the thought that dollars can help destroy the menace. What rather appalls me is the number of people today in the Government who are disposed to rationalize every foreign problem in terms of further United States aid. . . ."[72] It seemed to Baruch, Harriman, and his other friends in Washington that McCloy was showing signs of frustration with his position at the Bank. Rumors that spring began to circulate that he might tender his resignation, even though he had served only two years of a five-year term.

McCloy had a number of reasons to leave the Bank. For one thing, relations with his executive directors were worsening. More than once he expressed the opinion that men of greater stature could be recruited to the board if it met once every three months instead of each week. Many of these directors found themselves subjected to considerable criticism from their domestic constituencies. Why had Bank lending been so frugal? They in turn began to vent their frustration with McCloy, who rarely consulted with them. He admitted, "I'd go to a meeting and tell them that the Bank's mission had departed for Guatemala. Then I'd go to the next meeting and tell them the mission had arrived in Guatemala." As the Bank's secretary put it, in understated form, ". . . he might have been guilty of letting the board go by default once or twice." Once, when the directors lined up for a group photo with McCloy, one official joked, "Why don't the members pose with their rubber stamps in their hands?"[73]

McCloy frequently ruffled feathers by cutting across formal lines of responsibility. He enjoyed showing up unannounced at a program officers' meeting and questioning all the people attending about their work. But the information he gathered in this manner was often anecdotal. As the

Bank staff grew to several hundred professionals, he left the day-to-day management of the building to Bob Garner, even though the two men did not get along. Garner was a difficult personality, temperamental and extremely protective of his own authority. "It was obvious to me," Garner wrote in his memoirs, "that McCloy and I were not on the same wave length. . . ."[74] Garner was a stickler for details and orderly procedures, administrative qualities that McCloy simply did not care to develop. Gradually, McCloy began to spend more and more of his time on non-Bank activities.

Shortly after returning from his first tour of Latin America in the spring of 1948, McCloy was recruited by a government task force to study the growing intelligence bureaucracy. J. Edgar Hoover had lost his crusade to prevent the creation of a civilian Central Intelligence Agency when President Truman signed the National Security Act of 1947. Soon the CIA became the most rapidly expanding agency in the government. Insiders boasted to one another that it would be "bigger than State by '48."[75] And, indeed, by the summer of 1948 it had a larger presence in Washington than the State Department, while the reports of its agents stationed overseas already carried greater cachet with the White House than did analysis written by foreign-service officers. Increasingly, the Agency operated on its own, as a virtually autonomous arm of the foreign-policy bureaucracy, almost a government within a government. All this happened pretty much out of the limelight of public attention. In 1948, however, McCloy participated in a classified study of the CIA, which gave him the opportunity to become intimately knowledgeable about the broad reach of U.S. intelligence activities around the globe.

Worried by a burgeoning postwar federal bureaucracy, President Truman appointed ex-President Herbert Hoover in the spring of 1948 to chair a commission to study means of streamlining the government. The Commission on Organization of the Executive Branch of the Government set up shop on K Street in downtown Washington. On defense and intelligence matters, Hoover decided to appoint his old friend Ferdinand Eberstadt as chairman of a task force to study the national-security establishment. It was a logical choice for Hoover, since he trusted the judgment of this hard-boiled, conservative investment banker. But the selection rankled James Rowe, Jr., one of the few liberal Democrats appointed to the Commission.

Rowe personally disliked Eberstadt, telling Dean Acheson he was a "stinker."[76] He believed Eberstadt and James Forrestal, who was now secretary of defense and also a member of the task force, would bring a right-wing attitude toward any review of the growing intelligence establishment. Rowe would have preferred the selection of McCloy as chairman of the task force, even though he and McCloy had clashed so violently over the internment of the Japanese Americans during the war. As Rowe explained his feelings about McCloy in a letter to Acheson that spring: "I don't like him [McCloy] much either . . . but I think the Elihu Root–Henry Stimson tradition of civilian control over the military (while not all that it should be) is a hell of a lot better than the Eberstadt-Baruch-Forrestal mumbo jumbo. I am a man who knows a lesser evil when I see one and therefore I plump for McCloy."[77] As it happened, McCloy was selected by Hoover to be a member of the task force, chaired by Eberstadt. As usual, he was one of the few men acceptable to both a James Rowe and a James Forrestal.

McCloy welcomed the diversion. Throughout the spring and summer of 1948, he sat in on weekly meetings of the Eberstadt Task Force, where he was allowed the opportunity to question CIA Director Rear Admiral Roscoe H. Hillenkoetter, George Kennan, Bill Donovan, Frank Wisner, Lyman Kirkpatrick, and dozens of other officials in the State Department, the CIA, and the National Security Council.[78] These encounters constituted a virtual refresher course in the status of intelligence matters at a critical moment in the Cold War.

McCloy had no qualms about the Agency's growing number of covert operations. Since his Black Tom days, he had been enamored of "black-bag jobs," paid informants and intercept intelligence. In 1947, Truman had specifically assigned the CIA responsibility for covert psychological operations. These covert duties were expanded in June 1948, when the president approved NSC directive 10/2, a document drafted by George Kennan. NSC directive 10/2 gave the CIA responsibility for "propaganda, economic warfare; preventive direct action, including sabotage, anti-sabotage . . . subversion against hostile states, including assistance to underground resistance movements, guerrillas and refugee liberation groups, and support of indigenous anti-communist elements."[79] This rather sweeping language suggested that the Agency was authorized to engage in everything short of outright warfare on the communist world. Years later, Kennan denied that this had been his intention. "It did not work out at all the way I had conceived it. . . . We had thought that this would be a facility which could be used when and if an occasion arose when it might be needed. There might be years when we wouldn't have to do anything like this." As things turned out, once begun, covert operations quickly seemed to provide an answer to every crisis.

Early in 1948, prodded by Forrestal, the CIA had secretly begun subsidizing the election campaigns of anticommunist politicians in France and Italy. Similar payments were made to anticommunist newspapers and labor unions in both countries. In Italy, the Agency spent $10 million, and Forrestal was elated when the communists suffered a decisive electoral defeat that spring.[80] Forrestal became a fervent advocate of covert action.

McCloy regularly played tennis with the hard-driving defense secretary, and afterward, over dinner or drinks, Forrestal frequently regaled him with stories about the Agency's wide-ranging covert operations in Europe. McCloy fully approved of these operations, but he could also see that his friend had become obsessed with the Soviet threat. Forrestal was the kind of high-strung, passionate individual who tended to see the world in extremes anyway. Within a year, his obsessions would turn to outright paranoia and lead to a complete mental collapse, and then suicide.

Cold War tensions heightened dramatically in June 1948, when the Soviets—in response to the American decision to introduce a new currency in West Germany—imposed a land blockade of West Berlin. McCloy was playing tennis with Forrestal one day that summer when the defense secretary confided to him that the military governor in Germany, General Lucius Clay, wanted to dispatch a column of tanks to break the blockade. Forrestal said he feared this would provoke a full-scale Soviet invasion of Western Europe, an event for which the United States was militarily unprepared. McCloy was alarmed by this news; sending tanks down the *Autobahn* might needlessly provoke a war that he believed the Soviets had no desire to fight. And yet he agreed that Washington had to do something. So, when Lovett called him a few days later and asked what he thought of the notion of airlifting supplies into Berlin, McCloy endorsed the idea. It was, he thought, just the right measure of resolution. After Lovett got off the line, McCloy called General Henry "Hap" Arnold, who had directed the army's air arm during the war, and asked him whether it was feasible to supply a city the size of West Berlin by air. Arnold thought it possible, and shortly thereafter Lovett persuaded Truman to support an airlift. When Clay continued to insist that an armored column was the right approach, Lovett had McCloy call his old friend in Frankfurt and explain that it just was not going to happen.[81]

The Berlin crisis underscored for McCloy that Washington needed to be able to respond to Soviet challenges in Europe with something other than mere military hardware. The atomic monopoly was not enough, and the United States could never hope to match the Soviets in terms of combat-ready divisions stationed on the ground in Western Europe. He discounted the possibility that the Soviets intended to invade Western Europe, but this did not mean there wasn't a threat. A larger, better-financed intelligence apparatus, he believed, would afford Washington another offensive weapon in the political struggle with the Soviets, and a measure of defense against the possibility of another Pearl Harbor. America, with its new global responsibilities, had to have the knowledge and capability to intervene anywhere. As he questioned CIA officials brought before the Eberstadt Task Force, McCloy demonstrated his desire to see the Agency expand both its capabilities. The Agency's deputy director, Brigadier General Edwin Wright, told him that his chief limitation was time, not money. With a budget that year of some $70 million, the Agency had all the money it needed; in fact, that year the CIA returned to the Treasury millions of dollars it had found impossible to spend.[82]

By the end of 1948, the Eberstadt Task Force was ready with its recommendations. On the critical issue of covert operations, McCloy and the other members of the task force concluded that "those responsible for operations in CIA should be given considerable autonomy."[83] The Agency, they believed, should be doing more, particularly in the field of covert propaganda: "The battle for the minds of men may decide the struggle for the world. The Committee found present facilities and mechanisms for the waging of psychological warfare inadequate."[84]

Such advice opened the floodgates to a massive new program of covert activities. That autumn, a special unit, the Office of Policy Coordination, was organized within the CIA to run covert political-action operations. A former OSS officer and wealthy lawyer, Frank Wisner, was brought in to run the unit. Under Wisner's vigorous direction, OPC rapidly mounted large-scale, ongoing covert operations around the globe. He operated with the most liberal administrative autonomy, reporting only sporadically to the heads of the State Department, Defense, and the CIA. As a measure of its activities, from 1949 to 1952 Wisner's unit grew from 302 personnel to 2,812, plus 3,142 contract agents overseas. Wisner was soon tapping into local currency counterpart funds generated by the Marshall Plan to fund his operations in Europe. In 1949, his budget was $4.7 million; three years later, it had risen to $82 million. By their recommendations, McCloy and his colleagues on the Eberstadt Task Force bore a heavy responsibility for what Wisner was now calling his "mighty Wurlitzer."[85]

On a personal level, McCloy's experience with the Eberstadt Task Force increased his itch to leave the Bank. Dramatic events were happening all over the world. In February 1948, a communist-dominated government seized power in Czechoslovakia. From his seat at the World Bank, McCloy felt left out. But with the upset re-election of Harry Truman in November 1948, there seemed little possibility that the one job he really wanted—secretary of state—would become vacant. Nor could he easily imagine going back to the law. Early in 1949, he complained to Bernard Baruch of the New York law firms: "They are busier, if anything, than they ever were, and they make just as much money, but instead of their work being as it was when I first came down to practice law in terms of productive projects such as putting together groups to build or expand railroads, public utilities, industries, etc., today their work is almost all defensive. They deal with taxes, anti-trust suits, litigations, Government administrative work almost exclusively."[86] That was not for him.

Early in April 1949, McCloy learned that his brother-in-law had suffered an appalling injury to his eye while fly-fishing on the river Test in England. While he was casting a heavy wet salmon fly, a sudden gust blew Douglas's line back, snaring his left eye with the hook. In agony, he had to be carried three-quarters of a mile across muddy ground and then driven fifteen miles to the nearest hospital, in Southampton. The hook was removed, but the damage to the eye was such that doctors were uncertain whether it would require an operation. McCloy had Bank business in London anyway, but when he learned these details of the accident, he boarded an early plane for London and spent the next few weeks trying to comfort his old friend. In the event, the doctors decided not to operate, but Douglas's vision was so poor that for the rest of his life he wore a distinctive black eye-patch.[87]

McCloy also had something of importance to discuss with Lew Douglas. President Truman had called him into the White House and offered him the job of high commissioner for occupied Germany: "the toughest job in the Foreign Service." Startled, McCloy had remarked to the president that this was not the first time he had been offered the post; he described to Truman how Roosevelt had greeted him with a Nazi salute and the words "Heil McCloy—Hochkommissar für Deutschland."[88] McCloy now told Douglas that he was considering the job, but that he did not want the Bank's vice-president, Robert Garner, to succeed him.[89]

While McCloy was in London, the American papers were publishing reports that he was Truman's first choice for the high-commissioner position. When he returned to Washington on April 28, he told reporters that his mind was not made up. After discussing the matter with Dean Acheson for two hours, he still hesitated. He had learned from Douglas that Clay had clashed frequently with both Acheson and Averell Harriman over various political issues. Harriman felt Clay was demanding an inordinate share of the Marshall Plan's Economic Cooperation Administration (ECA) revenues for Germany's exclusive benefit. Clay also found it difficult to accept Washington's orders to remain neutral over internal German politics, since he could not abide the abrasive leader of the Social Democratic Party (SPD), Kurt Schumacher. The more McCloy learned about the job, the more he had to admit that he was "somewhat appalled by the difficulties. . . ." When Truman urged him publicly to take the job, in early May, McCloy made it clear he would do so only if certain conditions were met. He wanted a "free hand in picking people" to assist him, and an assurance that "no substantial decisions on Germany" would be made "without consultation with me." In addition, he would not take the job unless he had full authority over ECA monies dispensed in Germany.[90] This was not all. He also wanted Truman to name Eugene Black as his successor at the World Bank. The president agreed to this deal; Black was nominated for the Bank presidency, and a presidential executive order was signed giving McCloy full control over ECA monies in Germany. Only then did McCloy send Truman a brief note accepting the job of high commissioner.[91]

McCloy left the World Bank with ambivalent emotions. Under his two-year administration, the Bank had made loans totaling some $650 million; forty-eight countries were now members of the Bank; its bonds on Wall Street were regarded as good risks; and the projects he had chosen to fund in both Europe and the developing world were all considered sound economic investments. In an article for *Foreign Affairs* entitled "The Lesson of the World Bank," McCloy wrote that all these things were "satisfying" accomplishments. "They are not spectacular in any sense," he observed, "but they represent the fruit of much intensive work."

It was clear, however, that he was well aware of the Bank's shortcomings. Many people had harbored ambitious expectations for the Bank, and now he acknowledged the "consequent disillusionment when the spectacular failed to materialize." His critics, he admitted, believed that the Marshall Plan and other bilateral U.S. aid had relegated the Bank to "a role of secondary and minor importance. . . ." In his defense, McCloy argued that such a view was shortsighted. Marshall Plan aid was scheduled to end in 1952, and the World Bank, he predicted, would soon begin to finance a "considerable expansion of productive facilities within Europe itself." This was never to happen. By 1952, Western Europe was poised for a major economic boom, and had no need for the Bank's relatively high-interest loans. As for Eastern Europe, McCloy had been forced by the Truman administration to back out of negotiations for loans to communist-dominated Poland and Czechoslovakia. Both countries eventually pulled out of the Bank. Poland, Hungary, and Rumania would not become Bank members until the Cold War began winding down in the 1980s.

Turning to the less developed world, McCloy tried to explain why the Bank had not been able to do more. "Development," he wrote, "is not something which can be sketched on a drawing-board and then be brought to life through the magic wand of dollar aid." The Bank had learned that there were severe limits on the ability of these poor nations to absorb foreign capital. The rate of development could be accelerated by well-planned, economically viable projects. "But it must never be forgotten that low productivity and living standards are as much the product of poor government, unsound finance, bad health and lack of education as of inadequate resources or the absence of productive facilities."

Forty years later, development economists would have no dispute with these observations. It is still difficult to design projects in the poorest countries of Africa, the Indian subcontinent, and Latin America that directly improve the lives of the poorest of the poor. But today the World Bank is not in any sense a "secondary" institution. It has become a financial colossus, pumping out nearly $20 billion in loans annually, dwarfing investments made by private commercial bankers.[92]

McCloy had thought that in the long run only the free flow of private capital could ever make "a significant inroad on the world's development needs." This too proved to be wrong. The private bankers today take their lead from the World Bank, and in the countries with the greatest need for investment, private capital flows are negligible. The World Bank of the 1970s, '80s, and '90s more closely resembles Harry Dexter White's vision of a global New Deal agency than the conservative institution McCloy administered.

McCloy acknowledged that there might come a day when it would be politically possible to increase dramatically economic assistance to the developing world. If so, he strongly felt that any such expanded program of development assistance should be administered "under international rather than national auspices." Washington no doubt would have liked to maintain control over its foreign aid in order "to secure immediate bargaining advantages." But nothing would create more ill-will toward America, he argued, "than to have other nations of the world over a long period of time regard the United States Government as their principal source of capital." Moreover, his experience at the Bank had reinforced his faith in the utility of international agencies. He told readers of *Foreign Affairs* that, unlike the United Nations, which had become a group of national, highly partisan representatives expressing the views of their respective governments, the World Bank was developing a truly international civil service, "whose loyalty is only to the Bank itself. . . ." In these times of "knife-edged political tension," he argued, one needed men and institutions capable of "objective nonpolitical analysis of the issues."[93] At the height of the Cold War, such internationalism might sound a bit rarefied, an odd article of faith for a man in McCloy's position. But McCloy's actual practice was more pragmatic. When Cold War politics had interfered with Bank business, he had not objected. And now he was going to Germany, the cockpit of the Cold War.

CHAPTER 15

German Proconsul: 1949

"I had once a chief, a very great chief [Henry Stimson] during the war who kept telling me all the time the way to trust a man is to trust him, and when you don't trust him, hit him."

JOHN J. MCCLOY, 1949, FRANKFURT

News of McCloy's long-awaited acceptance was greeted with near-universal acclaim. *The New York Times* editorialized, "Here is a job to fit the man, and a man to fit the job."[1] James Reston said his old friend and neighbor was a "man who can cuss out a general or win over a Senator, or out talk a diplomat or knock the chip off a reporter's shoulder. . . ."[2] McCloy would need all these abilities to carry out Washington's agenda in Germany. Americans had come a long way from the anti-German sentiments of only three years earlier. Occupied Germany—divided sharply between East and West—was now seen by many Americans as a new battleground.

The Truman administration had been inching toward the consolidation of a West German state for at least two years, although knowledgeable men inside the administration were well aware that such a move would provoke the Soviets to consolidate their hold on East Germany, a much smaller and less industrialized zone. In November 1947, Marshall had privately warned his colleagues that the Soviets would probably respond by asserting their control over Czechoslovakia as a "purely defensive move."[3] Neither Marshall nor Kennan believed the subsequent Czech communist putsch of February 1948 presaged a hot war. A few officials had felt otherwise—in particular, James Forrestal.[4] But his had been a minority view. McCloy's attitude was more representative; he had always favored military preparedness, and so supported the Truman administration's defense buildup. But, like Kennan, he discounted any intent on the part of the Soviets to wage an aggressive war in Europe so soon after they had sustained such horrific losses in the war against fascism. To his mind, the pressing issue of the moment was not the Kremlin's intentions in Europe, but Washington's. What did the West intend to do with Germany? A stable Germany would do much to contain the growing frictions between Washington and Moscow.

Four years after the end of the war, the Western Allies were ambivalent about the Germans. McCloy shared that ambivalence. Revelations of the Holocaust had marked the Germans indelibly as a people responsible for singular crimes against humanity. These memories would not fade. The slightest evidence of German nationalism was dissected in the Western press for evidence of neo-Nazi resurgence. At least on paper, de-Nazification regulations still barred hundreds of thousands of former Nazi Party members from positions in the government or from leading any large industrial concerns. In the American zone, German businesses were subject to decartelization policies; such great industrial and chemical combines as the I. G. Farben empire were slowly being carved up into smaller companies. In varying degrees in the American, French, and British sectors, the occupation authorities in 1949 were still carrying out a program of dismantling major German industries. German machine tools, steel plants, synthetic-oil plants, and a wide variety of other factories were being shipped back to England and France or simply destroyed.

But pressures were rising to end all but the most cosmetic of these occupation policies. For one thing, the occupation was costly. West Germany, cut off from its grain-producing provinces to the east, could not feed itself. The British had to impose bread rationing on their own people, something unnecessary throughout the war, in order to feed Germans in the British sector. The British and Americans together were spending some $700 million a year to support their troops in Germany and administer the country.[5] The Americans were pouring millions of dollars of Marshall Plan aid into Germany to get the economy functioning at a basic level. By 1949, some officials in the Truman administration believed that many of the occupation's more stringent features—such as the dismantling of German plants—had become counterproductive. One could not simultaneously punish Germany and rebuild her economy.

Each step that General Clay had taken toward restoring the German economy in the period 1947–49 had inevitably stimulated an impassioned debate back in America on the political future of Germany. From Moscow's perspective, any revival of Germany under the umbrella of the Western occupation forces warranted immediate defensive measures. Not only might a West German state pose a potential military threat, but it would end forever Soviet hopes of obtaining any substantial reparations from the Ruhr industrial basin. In June 1948, General Clay had decreed a currency reform in the Western sectors of Germany designed to bring the economy off the debilitating and costly black market that had developed in the postwar years. The Soviets saw the currency reform as a major step toward creating a separate economic and political unit out of the Western sector. Within days, the Soviets had imposed a land blockade on the Allied sectors in West Berlin. If the West had decided to create a West German state, the Soviets felt compelled to take similar steps in the East. Berlin would naturally become the capital of any such East German state, and therefore the Allies would have to withdraw from their enclaves in the city. This, at least, was the message the Soviets intended to convey with the blockade.[6]

In Washington, the message was read as a brazen violation of Allied agreements reached at Potsdam. Truman would not negotiate under such circumstances, and the subsequent airlift into Berlin clearly demonstrated Washington's determination to hold on to Berlin. To underscore the point, Truman sent a squadron of B-29 bombers reconfigured for atomic weapons to air bases in Britain.[7] (Atomic bombs themselves were not sent.) Confronted with such resolve, the Soviets backed down, and on May 12, 1949, just a week before McCloy's appointment as high commissioner was announced, they ended the blockade. By that time, the political blocs dividing Europe had hardened. The North Atlantic Treaty Organization (NATO) had been founded in April, and a consultative body of West German politicians authorized by Clay had drawn up a constitution of "Basic Laws" to govern a future West German parliamentary state.

It was clear that a turning point in the Cold War had been reached. The "German problem" was about to be decided. Not everyone in the Truman administration was strongly disposed toward creating a West German state. George Kennan believed such a state would inevitably become the focus for nationalist and irredentist forces and would "be neither friendly nor frank nor trustworthy from the standpoint of the Western occupiers."[8] He advocated a unified, demilitarized, and neutral Germany, and he thought this was something the Soviets would be willing to negotiate. Walter Lippmann was taking the same line in his influential column, arguing that the partition of Germany, and therefore Europe, was "transitory."[9] But this view was in the minority; the Truman administration, McCloy included, was too suspicious of Soviet intentions and unwilling to relinquish West Germany to an uncertain neutral status. Moreover, many Americans, not to speak of most French citizens, questioned whether Germany should ever again be united, under any circumstances. McCloy, who as a child had been exposed to a popular turn-of-the-century loathing of Prussian militarism, and who had seen his country dragged into world war twice by the Germans, held similar reservations. Though he was persuaded that a rational U.S. policy required that the West Germans now be built up, he nevertheless had to "fight back his revulsions."[10]

In May 1949, desperate to maintain some semblance of four-power

Allied control over Germany, the Soviets requested another meeting of the Allied foreign ministers. Dean Acheson called in a select group of State Department reporters for an off-the-record briefing. He felt he could be absolutely frank with these men, all veterans of the diplomatic beat, and he told them essentially what he told McCloy: "Our fundamental attitude is to go ahead with the establishment of a Western government [in Germany] come hell or high water." If the Soviets proposed unification of East and West Germany, unification would have to take place under the just-promulgated Bonn Constitution. The United States would reject any proposal for all-German elections. If the Russians wanted unification, they would first have to have elections in East Germany supervised by all four powers. Only then would the Allies allow the West Germans to enter into negotiations with the East on unification. Acheson knew that such conditions, which would lead to the creation of a unified Germany firmly in the Western bloc, would not find acceptance in the Kremlin.

More than any other event, this fundamental decision—that it was better to live with the risks of a Cold War with the Soviets than to unify Germany under Soviet terms—set the Cold War in concrete: as long as the Soviets felt compelled to respond to the creation of a West German state with one of their own in the East, a prolonged period of East-West animosities and suspicion was guaranteed. Both Washington and Moscow were willing to pay this price rather than risk the creation of a unified Germany aligned with either bloc.[11] Kennan's alternative for a neutral, permanently demilitarized Germany makes clear that there were choices. And those who disagreed with Kennan, including Acheson and McCloy, realized that the course they had embarked upon with Germany was problematic. There was always the danger that, after the West Germans had been restored to economic health and full sovereignty, the bonds of culture, language, and economics would create unrestrainable nationalist forces dedicated to unification. Over the next four decades, McCloy would occasionally express doubts over the two-Germany policy and marvel that it had lasted. In 1949, his assignment was the creation of a modern parliamentary state with a free-market economy. It was not an easy task. As he and Ellen began packing up their belongings for the trip to Germany, he grinned at a reporter interviewing him for a cover-story profile in *Time* and quipped, "No doubt about it, it's going to be a windy corner."[12]

The job as America's "proconsul" in Germany was the most prominent position McCloy had yet occupied. For the first time, his name was to become familiar to an audience beyond the East Coast Establishment of New York bankers and lawyers and foreign-policy makers in Washington.

The portrait drawn of him in *Time* was of a self-assured, energetic man whose reasonableness in all things made him adept at dispelling tensions in human conflict. "McCloy has learned to gauge how far people can be pushed, to hold out in good humor but dogged firmness through protracted debate." That he was a Republican who had worked in Democratic administrations was another sign of his reasonableness. He believed in the free market, but that did not mean, he explained to *Time,* that the "government should not operate in certain important social fields." It was just "important to keep a force opposed to the monolithic state. If you destroy the incentive and initiative of free enterprise, you bring everything down to a low, undistinguished level of life." Some New Deal liberals were "totalitarians" when it came to placing controls on the economy, but on foreign-policy issues he thought some old-guard Republicans were less "enlightened" than many Democrats. A more succinct summary of the Establishment's political outlook in 1949 could not be made.

Time introduced its readers to a fifty-four-year-old man it described as "indefatigable." On family vacations in the Adirondacks, *Time* said, McCloy would be up to go fishing at 4:00 A.M., and later in the day would drag his family up Iron Mountain for a long, invigorating climb. "After a hike with him," Ellen McCloy joked to the *Time* reporter, "we all come home on our hands and knees." He was a man who abstained from both coffee and tea, but had an occasional Scotch and soda. He still smoked cigars, but never at home, where Ellen had forbidden him. When he traveled, he took along a copy of the *Oxford Book of Verse.* He was a voracious reader, starting early in the morning, when he made a habit of propping a book up by the bathroom mirror so he could read while shaving. He regularly staged "reading debates" for himself, whereby he read four or five books simultaneously, all on the same subject but from different points of view. Now, he was reading up on Germany. Ellen told a *Time* reporter visiting their yellow brick Georgetown home, "He always worries over a new job."[13]

The U.S. Senate unanimously confirmed McCloy's nomination in mid-June, and afterward he told reporters that he hoped the Germans were not "following false gods again."[14] He went to the White House, where Truman gave him characteristically simple marching orders: "Mr. McCloy, call them as you see them and we will support you."[15] A week before leaving for Europe, he checked in with his colleagues at the Council on Foreign Relations, who honored him with a dinner at Pratt House.[16] In New York, he made arrangements for his mother, Anna, and his aunts to be taken care of in his absence. Among other things, Acheson promised to have a young naval officer from a nearby base look in on Anna, who was a healthy eighty-five-years of age. Ellen and the children would travel to Germany by ship in July. On June 30, Ellen, the kids, and Anna saw him off at the airport, where he boarded a U.S. Air Force plane bound for Paris and Frankfurt. As he got on the plane, he told *The New York Times* that his goal was the establishment of a democratic Germany. "The American people should understand there can be no solution in Germany in three months, six months or a year. These are long range problems and they are building a new economic and a new social life. It is my opinion that things are never as bad as they seem, nor as good as they seem. . . . Even if progress is made in ten years, it is good."[17]

On stepping off the plane in Frankfurt, he was asked by reporters when he planned to assume his duties; he replied lightheartedly, "I guess right now. I'm here."[18] The very next day, he took off for West Berlin, as if to underscore the U.S. commitment to the city. Though the blockade had been lifted more than a month earlier, the United States was continuing to operate its airlift, which had now flown in some two million tons of supplies. As military governor, he was greeted on the tarmac by two military bands, one white, one black. After the ceremonies, he held his first formal press conference and told reporters that he hadn't decided where to place his headquarters, but that he imagined he would have a "spot in Bonn, certainly a base in Frankfurt," and would routinely visit Berlin.[19]

Reporters were struck by his easy informality, which contrasted sharply with the military decorum and precise answers they had received from General Clay. *Newsweek* described him as "short and plump, wearing a dark-brown suit, white shirt, and striped tie, his balding dome gleaming under the klieg lights, McCloy made a striking contrast with the memory of the trim, slight soldierly Clay." He fingered heavy tortoiseshell reading glasses as he stood talking to reporters. Whereas Clay always had crisp, concrete answers, McCloy spoke slowly and often hesitated, before confessing that he was not familiar with a particular matter. When asked whether he had any hopes for the unification of Berlin, he paused, grinned, and said simply, "I have hopes."[20]

From Berlin, he took off on a hectic, ten-day swing through West Germany, meeting dozens of German and American occupation officials. But as far as the reporters could tell, aside from this display of whirlwind activity, McCloy was making no newsworthy decisions. While he made himself accessible to the press, it quickly became evident that either he really had nothing to say or he was playing things close to his chest. By the end of the month, the new high commissioner was beginning to get a bad press. The tone of reporters' questions became "markedly unfriendly," and the *Washington Star* suggested that his relations with the press had "deteriorated alarmingly to the point of open resentment."[21]

In the War Department or at the World Bank, he had always dealt one-on-one with a few select opinion-makers—a Walter Lippmann, a James Reston, or a Joe Alsop. But in those elite relationships the rules were different, and McCloy now found that dealing with a pack of the working press in large press conferences was a different matter. He needed help. His rapport with the press did not improve until later that autumn, when Arthur Sulzberger lent him the services of a *New York Times* reporter named Shepard Stone. The smooth-talking Stone spoke fluent German, knew a wide range of German personalities, and was adept at handling his former colleagues.

Stone began to turn things around the first day he arrived in Frankfurt. He walked into the Allied High Commission for Occupied Germany (HICOG) headquarters just as McCloy was beginning a press conference. Standing at the back of the room, he listened as a reporter asked the high commissioner if he had received a letter from Adenauer. McCloy had indeed just received such a letter, on a matter of some passing controversy. But because Adenauer had phoned him that morning to say he was withdrawing the letter, McCloy had promised the chancellor not to speak of it to the press. When questioned by a reporter who obviously knew that such a letter had been sent, McCloy stuck by his promise. The press conference ended with many reporters grumbling that McCloy had been less than truthful. Afterward, he asked his aides, "Did I do the right thing?" They assured him that he couldn't have handled it in any other fashion. He then turned and asked his new press adviser if he agreed. Stone replied, "Well, Mr. McCloy, I think you made a mistake. You never tell an untruth to a newspaperman." If you had just said 'No comment,' everyone would have understood." McCloy replied, "I think you're right," and immediately called in the reporter and offered an apology. From that day on, things improved.[22]

Actually, in the first month of McCloy's tenure, the press had missed a major story. Prior to McCloy's arrival, the U.S. military government had deferred a decision on whether to promulgate a "General Claims Law" providing some 850 million deutsche marks in compensation to victims of Nazi repression. Clay had favored the law, but his deputy, Major General George P. Hays, had decided the proposed law should be held up until the new German parliament (Bundestag) could be elected in August. Harry Greenstein, Clay's and now McCloy's adviser on Jewish affairs, took the matter to the new high commissioner. He protested that the German Bundestag would never pass such a controversial bill so early in its existence. All McCloy's other advisers and the British military governor, General Brian Robertson, were opposed, but McCloy found Greenstein's arguments persuasive. He also had on his desk a "Dear Jack" letter from a member of the Warburg clan, Edward M. M. Warburg, chairman of the American Jewish Joint Distribution Committee, based in New York. McCloy had known Eddie as the younger brother of his old friend and frequent tennis partner Freddie Warburg. Instead of entering the family banking profession, Eddie had taken over many of his late father's positions in various Jewish philanthropic institutions. Warburg now wrote McCloy that it had come as a "real shock" to learn that the bill had been deferred to the Bundestag.[23] McCloy did not want to ignore a plea from a Warburg; on July 18, less than three weeks after arriving in Germany, he decided to promulgate the law under his powers as military governor.

Greenstein was pleased that McCloy had seen fit to overrule General Hays and all his other advisers. He wrote him, "While the embarrassment to you in reversing a decision may be temporary, the injustice to the victims of Nazism will be permanent if the present decision is permitted to stand. Fundamentally, as you so very well put it, the issue is a moral one."[24] That's how McCloy saw it, as a moral and political issue, not a military matter. He told Greenstein that, during his recent ten-day inspection of the U.S. sector, a leading German figure had shocked him by saying, "I hope, Mr. McCloy, you will forget the Auschwitzes and the Dachaus and other concentration camps, and think in terms of the new Germany we are trying to rebuild." McCloy had replied, "So far as I am concerned, I cannot forget the Auschwitzes and the Dachaus and I do not want the German people to forget them either. If they do, they will start their new German state in an atmosphere of moral degeneration and degradation."[25]

At the end of the month, McCloy visited Heidelberg, where Greenstein had arranged for him to speak to a small gathering of German Jewish leaders. Barely sixty thousand Jews were still living in Germany at this time, and many of those were planning to emigrate to America or Israel. He told them that the well-being of the German Jewish community would be "one of the real touchstones and the test of Germany's progress. . . ."[26] Early in August, on the eve of elections to form the first democratic government in Germany since the Weimar Republic, McCloy made his reparations decision public. *The New York Times* hailed the reparations law and reported that it was the result of an "extraordinary and virtually one-man battle on behalf of the measure by John J. McCloy. . . ."

In late July, Ellen arrived in England with Johnny and young Ellen. While she waited for McCloy to ferry them by plane into Germany, she took the children to see the ruins of Coventry. She knew they would soon be living among the destruction inflicted by Allied bombing in Germany, and she wanted to be sure they had an indelible impression of the destruction wrought by the Germans.[27] For the first time in their nearly twenty years of marriage, Ellen was about to become a visible partner in McCloy's career. Her good taste had always been an asset to him in their circle of friends in Washington and New York. But now, by virtue of her fluent command of the German language, she could become a spokeswoman for her husband. Ellen had strong feelings about what had happened under the Third Reich. She shuddered to remember the regimented nation she had seen during their 1936 visit to the Munich Olympics. And in her public role as the high commissioner's wife, she did not hesitate to speak her mind. Once, while talking before a German women's group, she asked them to look around the hall: wasn't it true that most of them had been limp washrags *(Waschlappen)* during the Hitler years?

To the West German public, the McCloys quickly became a household name, the "first family" of occupied Germany. Ellen had three official residences to run, in Frankfurt, Bonn, and Berlin. McCloy's main office was established in the old I. G. Farben building, one of the few large buildings in downtown Frankfurt that had escaped Allied bombardment. On his desk he had a direct "Red Line" phone to the Department of State, and a similar phone by his bed at home. German newspapers reported on their comings and goings, and much attention was given to the fact that Johnny, eleven, and Ellen, eight, were being tutored in German and had German playmates. Their mother, in fact, made a practice of speaking only German to them, and it wasn't long before their English began to suffer.[28] The children and their pets—a canary named Hansel, Judy the boxer, and a little beagle named Punchy—initially spent most of their time in the household set up in Bad Homburg, a pleasant spa twenty kilometers outside Frankfurt. The requisitioned mansion was surrounded by several acres of woods, enclosed by a tall wire fence.[29]

They had an equally spacious home sitting on a bluff above the Rhine outside of Bonn, and yet another set of living quarters in West Berlin. McCloy favored the home outside Bonn: it had a tennis court. The family had two diesel trains available for their use, the larger of which had belonged to Hitler. Dean Acheson remembered this train as "very fast and very smooth."[30] One carriage became McCloy's "office on wheels," while he also had the use of a sleeping car and dining car. He and Ellen practically lived on those trains as they commuted between Berlin, Frankfurt, and Bonn. A frequent topic at the breakfast table each morning was "who was going to take the big train and who would use the little one."[31] Their travels were such that the passage of regularly scheduled commuter trains were often delayed to make way for the high commissioner's train. McCloy would think nothing of abruptly ordering his train halted so he could step down and play a little tennis.[32]

As military governor, he was assigned a number of enlisted men for use as household servants. One such servant was Corporal Gates Davison, the son of McCloy's old friend Trubee, who had attended the McCloys' wedding in 1930. Davison had been shipped to Germany with a psych-warfare unit, but when the army brass learned he was a "McCloy cousin," he ended up working in the McCloy household, largely for Ellen. As soon as his ship arrived in Hamburg, Ellen phoned to ask if he was off duty that night. When he said yes, Ellen replied, "Good, I'll send the train to pick you up." Ellen was protective of her servants and took full advantage of her prerogatives. When Davison was thrown in the brig one night for playing tennis during reveille, she called the army officer in charge and said, "This is Madame High Commissioner, and I want you to release Corporal Davison this very minute." She had a dinner planned that evening for a group of Hollywood movie stars, and needed all the help she could get. The officer told her he couldn't release Davison without freeing all the men detained with him. Ellen said, "Fine, release them all and send them right over."[33]

McCloy relished the powers of his new job, and the life that went with it. He had taken a substantial pay cut to come to Germany—from a tax-free $30,000 to a taxable $25,000. But the houses, the trains, the chauffeured limousines, the bevy of servants, and all the other perquisites of the job were more than enough compensation. To his friends, he seemed able to enjoy the privileges of office without losing what Acheson called his "judgment and good nature—an expansive, happy nature with no littleness, suspicion or jealousy about it."[34] People were charmed to see that in him power had not turned to conceit. When Freddie Warburg and his wife visited the McCloys, they remembered one day when they were out for a drive in the countryside and encountered a carload of Germans struggling to change a flat tire. McCloy stopped the car and he and Freddie got out and helped them jack up their car. When the job was done, one of the Germans turned to Freddie and said, pointing to McCloy, "But that looks like Herr McCloy." Freddie grinned and said, "It is."[35]

After barely a month in Germany, McCloy flew back to Washington to recruit additional personnel and consult with Truman and Acheson on the imminent end of military law. With elections scheduled for August 14, the Allies planned to transfer most of their governing powers to the new, civilian German government. McCloy would relinquish his title as military governor, but as a member of the Allied High Commission for Occupied Germany (HICOG), he and the two other commissioners planned to retain broad authority over certain well-defined areas such as security, de-Nazification, decartelization, reparations, and foreign affairs. In addition, the high commissioners could decide at any moment to resume complete authority should the new German government develop renewed fascist tendencies.[36]

In Washington, McCloy agreed that these developments would allow him to cut American HICOG personnel from twenty-two hundred to no more than fourteen hundred. He had already hired Chester McClain as his general counsel, and he decided to retain the services of a career foreign-service officer, James Riddleberger, as his political-affairs officer.

He had wanted to make his old Kuhn, Loeb friend Benjamin Buttenwieser deputy high commissioner. But questions had been raised in Washington, both about Buttenwieser's qualities as a diplomat and about the appropriateness of placing an American of German Jewish ancestry in the number-two slot. So McCloy agreed to give General Hays the title of "deputy," and made Buttenwieser his "assistant commissioner." He assured Acheson in an "eyes-only" telegram that this would leave his friend in a "less exposed position." Buttenwieser was "most keen and energetic. Believe we can handle his rough edges and my personal relations with him such that I feel can always terminate without embarrassment."[37]

When he went to see Truman to report on all these developments, he found the president a bit bored. After McCloy briefed him for nearly a half-hour, Truman interrupted and said, "OK, McCloy, I sent you over there to run that country. . . . If I think you're doing wrong, you'll hear from me. Now let's talk about the Civil War."[38] McCloy rather welcomed the president's hands-off attitude, and certainly preferred it to Roosevelt's backdoor meddling. But it also worried him that Truman seemed to have no strong views on how Washington should handle the German problem. With the election of a German government, McCloy realized momentous decisions would have to be made on the future of Europe. Privately, he was telling his own staff that the American occupation in Germany might end in as little as eighteen months.[39] Much remained to be done, and in the meantime, as James Reston pointed out in the *Times,* the election was about to change McCloy's role from one of "supreme boss" to that of "supervisor—a much more subtle and difficult relationship."[40]

He arrived back in Germany in time to witness the elections. To his relief, and the surprise of most observers, the conservative Christian Democratic Union (CDU), led by the seventy-three-year-old Konrad Adenauer, won a slim plurality of the popular vote. The left-of-center Social Democratic Party (SPD), which had been expected to win, was a narrow second. It seemed more than likely that, with the support of the centrist Free Democrats and some fringe right-wing parties, an essentially "bourgeois bloc" in the new Bundestag would elect Adenauer chancellor.[41] *The New York Times* reported that McCloy and other U.S. officials made "no secret of their satisfaction over the victory of the conservative parties. . . ."[42]

Given McCloy's larger agenda—the creation of a stable parliamentary democracy in the Western sectors of occupied Germany—he could have found no better collaborator than Konrad Adenauer. Despite his age, and though he was virtually unknown to most Germans, Adenauer had a fortunate mix of credentials. As mayor of Cologne during the 1920s, he had maintained intimate personal friendships with the Ruhr Valley's leading industrialists and their bankers.[43] Because he opposed the "socialism" in the National Socialist Party's policies, and because he was repelled by the Nazis' lawlessness, Hitler dismissed him from office in 1933. Allowed to retire at age fifty-seven, he spent all the years of the Third Reich secluded in a Catholic monastery on the Rhine or at home, tending his private garden. In 1944, Hitler imprisoned him and his wife, Gussi Zinsser, whose hatred of the regime was even greater than his own.[44] Politically, he was fiercely anticommunist and firmly wedded to free-market economics.

More important for the task McCloy had in mind, Adenauer was a peculiar sort of German nationalist. He was a Catholic Rhinelander, and every cultural and religious fiber in his body was repelled by anything Prussian. He disdained the Prussian military tradition and regarded the largely Protestant East Germans as almost another nationality. He thought it a historical tragedy that Bismarck had been able to link the Rhineland's fate to that of Prussia and its godless capital, Berlin.[45] The Prussians, he thought, were inevitably drawn by the facts of geography to deal with the great Russian power to the east, whereas the interests of his own Rhinelanders lay to the West. In 1920, he had even toyed with separatist politics, though in the end he had felt compelled to oppose a group of radical separatists who attempted, with French support, to declare an independent republic in the Rhineland. He favored a federalist system for Germany in which a strong, autonomous Rhinish state could counterbalance the power of Prussia.[46] If the Allies wanted to keep greater Germany divided, Adenauer was well suited as the future chancellor of a separate West German state.

Little of this was generally recognized at the time of his election. But a month later, in mid-September 1949, when the Bundestag elected him chancellor by one vote, the *London Times* observed, "According to his lights, he is a good European—but it is a Europe which ends at the borders of the Old Roman Empire and excludes a great part of his own country. He will be satisfied to pay lip service to the ideal of German unity without pressing for it too strongly."[47]

McCloy was generally aware of Adenauer's views, and from their earliest conversations he had been struck by how often the chancellor referred to the Holy Roman Empire, as if it were a recent chapter in German history. They had met formally in mid-July at a meeting of the Consultative Council. But after the election, McCloy took Buttenwieser along with him one evening to pay a private visit. Buttenwieser remembered that it was "darker than Erebus and we only had a vague idea of the exact location of Adenauer's home." When they found it, perched atop a steep hill, Buttenwieser climbed a concrete staircase with fifty-three steps while McCloy, who had sprained his ankle playing tennis that morning, waited below. The door was opened by Adenauer's son, Paul, a Catholic priest, who confirmed that, indeed, they had found the right house. At this point, McCloy limped up and introduced himself. The chancellor shook hands and said in German, *"Ich glaube wir sind verwandt."* Not comprehending, McCloy turned to Benny and asked, "What did he say?" Buttenwieser replied, "He said, 'I believe we are related.' "[48]

McCloy was unaware that Adenauer's second wife, Gussi, was a Zinsser, distantly related to Ellen McCloy's grandfather. Gussi Zinsser had died in 1948, probably from leukemia, though her health had deteriorated greatly during her imprisonment in the last year of the war. Even this personal connection did little to break the ice. "Der Alte"—"the Old One"—as Adenauer was known, relied on his natural reserve and formality to keep other men at a distance. Theodore White, who was then a foreign correspondent in Europe for the left-wing American Overseas News Agency, once described him as a "stiff old man, who walked as if his legs were hinged by rusting joints." His aloof demeanor was accentuated by the haunting, almost forbidding appearance of his face. Tight, pale skin pulled across prominent cheekbones and a flat nose-bridge made him look slightly like an elderly Oriental gentleman. His eyes were cold and unsmiling.[49] Acheson once remarked that Adenauer seemed determined to waste no energy on unnecessary "movement, gesture, voice or facial expression. He moves slowly, gestures sparingly, speaks quietly, smiles briefly. . . ."[50] Wilhelm Grewe, a young German lawyer who later became ambassador to Washington, observed that Adenauer "was a man full of distrust."[51] He was everything, in fact, that McCloy was not: tightly controlled, austere, authoritarian, a man seemingly embittered by two widowhoods and an as yet unhappy political career. It would take all of McCloy's natural geniality and high-spirited prodding to draw this man out.

Initially, McCloy was not particularly impressed by Adenauer. His age alone suggested he was probably going to be simply a transition leader. McCloy also thought Adenauer was "not above striking a pose for political effect."[52] His prickly personality, his pride, and his extreme formality only made McCloy's task more difficult. Admittedly, his mission was to turn over sovereignty to a West German parliamentary government. But this was to be done gradually, and each step was to be accompanied by demonstrations on the part of the Germans that they had mended their ways. Adenauer's avowed intention was to accelerate this process as much as possible. His attitude had shocked the world earlier that spring, when he asserted that the German military leaders who had surrendered to the Allies in 1945 had "no mandate from the German people to submit to the terms of unconditional surrender."[53] And during the recent political campaign, he had bluntly warned, "The foreigners must understand that the period of collapse and unrestricted domination by the Allies is finished."[54] Such unilateral pronouncements suggested the new high commissioner and the new chancellor could be on a collision course.

McCloy did what he could to allay the German's suspicions. In their private conversations, he made it clear that he looked with sympathy on German desires to exercise greater sovereignty. Nor was it any secret within the HICOG bureaucracy that McCloy had brought a new perspective with him on dealing with the Germans. He told a meeting of the military governors in early September, "I had once a chief, a very great chief [Stimson] during the war who kept telling me all the time the way to trust a man is to trust him, and when you don't trust him, hit him. If we take too nervous a position at this stage, in the week before the Bonn Government is set up . . . we may be defeating our own purpose."[55] In fact, McCloy's willingness to deal civilly with the Germans was making some veteran HICOG staffers unhappy. In another meeting, later that month, McCloy nodded his head in agreement when an aide told him, "There are some people that still think that the way to treat a German is to kick him in the pants every ten days . . . and they are dismayed by the friendly approach."[56]

McCloy agreed that Adenauer was "naturally inclined to be somewhat authoritarian," particularly in his dealings with the press. But he did not think the chancellor had a "dictator complex." One day he told his staff, "You know, you see businessmen that have a way of delegating work. . . . Well, he is not such a great delegator."[57]

Attending to Adenauer's prickly expectations in matters of protocol was not easy. Under the terms of the new "Occupation Statute," McCloy and the British and French high commissioners had chosen as their official headquarters the shiny, snow-white Petersberg Hotel, a palace of a luxury hotel built before World War I in the Siebengebirge mountains just south of Bonn. McCloy was enamored by the Old World charm of the hotel, with its scenic view of Bonn and the Rhine River far below. But Adenauer suspected the high commissioners had meant to convey some symbolic message by their choice of the Petersberg, and he disliked traveling up the mountain's steep and winding road. A few days after his election in the Bundestag as chancellor—by a margin of one vote, and that cast by a former Nazi—McCloy arranged for a ceremony in which the high commissioners would formally greet the new chancellor and hand him a copy of the Occupation Statute.

When "Der Alte" arrived at the front door of the Petersberg on the rainy afternoon of September 21, 1949, the commissioners were not there to greet him. Their meeting was running late, so McCloy just sent word that Adenauer should make himself comfortable in the hotel's lobby. The old man took this as an insult and refused to come in out of the rain. McCloy was quickly apprised of the situation and went out to make amends. After walking up to the stiff figure standing outside, he whispered, "I can well imagine what you're thinking. Surely you're thinking of Canossa." Adenauer looked at him for a moment, and then cracked a thin smile. He was astonished that any American could recall how in the eleventh century Pope Gregory VII had similarly humiliated the German King Henry IV by keeping him waiting outside the Italian castle of Canossa for three days.[58]

Once inside, the three commissioners lined up on a carpet placed in the middle of a large drawing room. Adenauer immediately read some symbolic significance into the carpet, if only because he and his delegation of five Cabinet members had been asked to stop short of it while the speeches were made. So, when the French high commissioner, François Poncet, stepped forward to greet him, Adenauer seized the moment and advanced onto the carpet himself. Having claimed for himself what he took to be equal ground, he then went on the offensive with a well-prepared speech urging the high commissioners to revise the brand-new Occupation Statute in a "liberal and generous manner," transfer greater authority to his government, and thereby "hasten the further political development of our country."[59]

Once he had thus served notice that he intended to negotiate long and hard for greater sovereign powers, Adenauer handed the commissioners a copy of the Basic Law of the Federal Republic of Germany. Champagne was served, and it was only forty-five minutes later, as the German delegation was leaving, that the commissioners remembered that they had forgotten to hand Adenauer his copy of the Occupation Statute. A French diplomat rushed up to Adenauer's personal assistant, Dr. Herbert Blankenhorn, and pushed the offensive document into his hands, saying, "N'en parlons plus—Let's not talk about it any more."[60]

Adenauer could be petty and difficult, but over the next two months McCloy began to acquire a genuine respect for this hard man's patience, physical stamina, shrewdness, and biting wit. The chancellor still disliked coming to the Petersberg Hotel. On one occasion when they were about to enter its foyer, McCloy rather disarmingly explained that he "felt at home" in the mountain retreat. Adenauer stopped in his tracks and quipped, "In that case, Mr. McCloy, after you."[61]

McCloy found it more difficult, if not impossible, to establish a cordial relationship with Adenauer's chief political rival, Kurt Schumacher. The SPD chief had all of Adenauer's faults and few of his graces. A Prussian Protestant and lifelong bachelor, Schumacher was a dedicated socialist and fierce anticommunist. During World War I, he had lost an arm, and as the result of twelve years in a Nazi concentration camp, which he survived with considerable courage, he had to have a gangrenous leg amputated. He moved about physically supported by a strikingly statuesque blonde woman named Annemarie Renger. Much later, she became a president of the Bundestag, but at the time her constant presence accentuated the already bizarre appearance of this one-armed, one-legged man. He was a proud, stubborn individual, an impassioned and gifted orator, and a politician impatient to inaugurate Germany's inevitable "socialist reformation."[62] Unlike Adenauer, whose obeisance to the goal of reunification was perfunctory, the socialist leader considered the re-establishment of the Germany pulled together by Bismarck a major priority. This goal set him at cross-purposes with McCloy's agenda.

The two men got off to a bad start soon after McCloy's arrival. Hearing that Schumacher was scheduled to speak at Roemer, outside of Frankfurt, McCloy drove over and stood at the back of the crowd. Later, when Schumacher learned of McCloy's presence in the crowd, he accused the high commissioner of spying on him. McCloy soon determined that Schumacher was a "powerful hater and rabid nationalist," and even a "dictator" when it came to ruling over his party.[63]

By comparison with Schumacher, McCloy soon realized that Adenauer was a compatible partner. They had terrible disagreements over narrow policy questions, such as when the high commissioners ordered a 20-percent devaluation of the German mark. And yet, as Adenauer tried to accelerate McCloy's timetable, they shared the larger goal of creating a strong West German state wedded to parliamentary democracy and free-market economics. For this purpose they were knowing coconspirators; Adenauer deftly used Schumacher's pan-German nationalism to portray himself as the "reasonable" German, while McCloy used Adenauer's intransigence to persuade his fellow commissioners to make the next concession toward greater German sovereignty. This was to be a pattern for the next three years. The press, the German people, and indeed sometimes even Washington did not always understand the nature of their collaboration. *The New York Time*'s C. L. Sulzberger later concluded that Adenauer "pulled plenty of wool over McCloy's eyes. . . ."[64] Some wags were soon calling the chancellor the "Real McCloy," so often did it seem that the chancellor was manipulating the high commissioner.[65] At the same time, Adenauer's political opponents at home and his critics abroad portrayed him as an American marionette.

On October 1, 1949, the Soviets officially protested the formation of Adenauer's government as a violation of the Potsdam agreement. One week later, an "All-German Government" was formed in Berlin; it was dominated by members of the Communist Party, but the Foreign Ministry and several other Cabinet posts were given to members of the Christian Democratic Union of East Germany. A manifesto was issued demanding the abolition of the Occupation Statute in West Germany, an end to the dismantling of German industry, the withdrawal of all foreign troops, the restoration of German sovereignty, and the unification of East and West Germany. An SPD collaborator of the East German communists, Otto Grotewohl, was named chancellor of the German Democratic Republic.

These events underscored for McCloy and Adenauer the difficulty of keeping Germany divided. The East German manifesto spoke to all the resentments West Germans felt over the continuing occupation, and particularly toward the dismantling of German factories. In the wake of the challenge posed by the formation of an East German government, Adenauer escalated his demands for greater sovereignty by calling for an end to all dismantling. He knew that McCloy was already receptive to a change in policy.[66]

Eric Warburg had returned to Germany to reclaim the family banking business in Hamburg. Immediately after the war, Warburg had been part of the U.S. Army team that had interrogated Hermann Goering. His family had tried to dissuade him from returning, but Eric, despite his American ways, was still very much a German. He and McCloy frequently talked that autumn of 1949, and Eric was shocked to learn that his old friend believed the Allies should complete their dismantling program. The Germans, said McCloy, should be treated as "the Romans did the conquered Germanic tribes, by breaking their swords over your knee in front of them." This comment sparked a violent argument between the two men, with McCloy insisting that "something has to be done after all that has happened." After a heated discussion, they parted company. Warburg thought that he had been unable to budge McCloy from his position. But the next morning, McCloy called and asked Warburg to consult his friends in the German business community and draw up a list of those factories that he thought should be spared.[67]

Over the next few weeks, McCloy orchestrated a campaign to persuade Washington and his fellow commissioners to change the policy. Early in October, he told a German reporter that the dismantling program was a "lost cause," and when that created a storm of protest, he suggested that he had been speaking off the record. But soon afterward, the *London Times* quoted him as criticizing what he called "aimless dismantling."[68] Acheson jocularly complained that "McCloy just can't keep his mouth shut." McCloy, in the meantime, was telling Acheson that German opposition to dismantling was "not inspired by Nazi influence." On the contrary, he said, its harshest critics came from the left and center of the political spectrum. "We [should] avoid the mistakes that we made after Weimar," he warned, "where we were rather hasty to give up to the wrong government things we had long begrudged to a better one."[69]

The growing public debate was uncapping strong emotions inside Germany. In some instances, British troops had to protect German workers hired to dismantle some factories. British Foreign Secretary Ernest Bevin accused McCloy of using "pressure tactics."[70] But McCloy and Adenauer kept the pressure up. At a meeting of U.S. ambassadors in

Paris—attended by Lew Douglas and David Bruce, the U.S. ambassador to France—McCloy got to the heart of the matter by raising the question of "a united Germany versus a truncated Germany." The French, he pointed out, were firmly opposed to the reunification of Germany. But if Germany was to remain divided, and the Western portion of it brought into a federation with Western Europe, certain concessions had to be made. The French must learn that a truncated Germany "could hardly be considered" a menace. Adenauer would cooperate, he reported, because he was "strongly and favorably disposed for the federation of Germany into Western Europe." But he would insist on an "equal partnership in the economic field. . . ." This meant, of course, that what McCloy called the "horrible problem of dismantling" had to be resolved.[71]

Back in Germany, Adenauer requested a meeting with the high commissioners at Petersberg to discuss the issue again. When François Poncet suggested that the Germans were still not politically enlightened enough to be trusted with heavy industry, Adenauer caustically observed that he did not wish to acquire the reputation of "blackmailing the Council or trying to squeeze concessions from it on the basis of Soviet moves, but that if action were not taken along the lines he suggested, all of Western Europe would fall in the Soviet orbit."[72]

In another encounter, Poncet suggested that the chancellor would only be satisfied when the high commissioners were gone altogether. "That's putting it too strongly," Adenauer replied. "But I wouldn't mind if they turned into gay butterflies, or something of the kind." The Frenchman retorted, "That wouldn't do; you'd catch us in a butterfly-net." "In that case," snapped Adenauer, "you'd declare butterfly-nets to be banned weapons."[73]

The situation came to a head when Secretary of State Dean Acheson visited Germany in mid-November. This gave Adenauer the opportunity to sue for Acheson's confidence and force a new round of Allied concessions. Acheson was charmed by the chancellor. And he was equally struck by the frankness with which Adenauer explained his private support for the continued division of Germany. "Eastern Germany has always looked towards Russia," he told Acheson and McCloy. He desired wholehearted cooperation with the French and believed the German people would back him on this and reject the nationalist policies of the SPD. In Dr. Schumacher, he told Acheson, one would find a "typical East German." At one point in their conversation, he turned to McCloy and told him to cover his ears. Then he turned back to Acheson and said that McCloy "had a real warm-hearted understanding of the German problems. . . ."[74]

Afterward, an incident occurred that became a milestone in Adenauer's political career. The chancellor escorted Acheson and McCloy to the train station, where a large crowd had gathered in the hopes of catching a glimpse of the secretary of state. When their darkened limousines had sped past the crowd and into the station, Acheson turned to Adenauer and suggested that they really ought to walk back out into the square and greet the people. Adenauer agreed; as the crowd realized what was happening, cheering broke out and then, as Acheson recalled, "everything exploded." The people surged past the police lines and picked up Adenauer, Acheson, and McCloy and carried them to the high commissioner's train. After a half-hour of bedlam, the train finally got under way. Acheson and McCloy agreed that, "while we had fouled up the protocol of the departure, we had introduced a desirable element of democratic disorder into the political life of the Federal Republic. And Adenauer had had a popular triumph."[75]

With Acheson's backing, McCloy now forced his fellow commissioners to enter into serious negotiations with Adenauer. Over a period of ten days and long nights, the commissioners hammered out what became known as the Petersberg Agreement. McCloy insisted on the night sessions, hoping to wear down the opposition to any further concessions. The seventy-three-year-old Adenauer kept to the pace, but the French and British officials tired. "Reason would take command and speech falter," wrote Acheson, "as dawn began to break, and with it, the horror of resumption at ten o'clock the same morning."[76]

In the end, the commissioners agreed to the substance of Adenauer's demands: Seventeen major plants were struck from the dismantling list, and all dismantling was ended in West Berlin. Germany would be allowed for the first time since the war to build oceangoing vessels, and she would be permitted to produce up to eleven million tons of steel annually. In addition, Germany would be allowed to set up consulates abroad and join such international institutions as the World Bank and the Council of Europe. In return, Adenauer made a number of concessions: he pledged to keep Germany disarmed and to cooperate with the Allied Military Security Board; he also agreed to recognize the Ruhr Authority, which had been set up by the Allies to manage this industrial region. Adenauer really had no choice but to accept both of these points. Demilitarization was a given, and as for the Ruhr Authority, it was already an established fact, and German recognition at least gave him representation on the Authority's board.[77]

These concessions nevertheless led to a great outcry in the Bundestag. One SPD leader charged that it would lead to a "nationalism of a dog on a chain." Schumacher called Adenauer a "Chancellor of the Allies"—a charge for which he was suspended from the parliament for a period of six months.[78] McCloy was appalled by this vitriolic exchange, and yet felt unable to intervene directly. Instead, he quietly called in several high-ranking CDU leaders and suggested that the entire incident had contributed to a "lack of confidence" generated throughout the world in "the ability of the Germans even to conduct serious parliamentary debate. . . ." As a result, the CDU leaders approached Schumacher, who willingly extended an apology, and within twenty days he was reinstated in the Bundestag. McCloy knew it was only a "minor truce," but it would at least relieve some of the tensions for a time.[79]

The Petersberg Agreement greatly added to Adenauer's stature; if there had been any doubt before, Adenauer now acted as if he was indeed the head of a sovereign state. Within days of the Agreement, he spoke out on an issue of extreme sensitivity to the Allies. He did it in his own typical manner, by granting an exclusive interview to an obscure reporter, on this occasion from the Cleveland *Plain Dealer.* Such trial balloons could more easily be denied, if need be, than if he spoke with a resident correspondent. Germany, he said, would never rebuild its own army, but if the Allies wished, Germany might be willing to contribute military units to an integrated European army. There was an immediate outcry, both in America and throughout Europe, against this merest hint of a rearmed Germany.

McCloy was aware that Adenauer was not the first to venture into these controversial waters. The idea of a West German contribution to the defense of Europe had recently been broached by a number of Western military experts. General Clay himself had suggested just such a German contingent in a speech in Boston on November 20. The chairman of the Joint Chiefs of Staff, General Omar Bradley, had made a similar suggestion, as had Field Marshal Montgomery in a recent talk at the Council on Foreign Relations. Although McCloy was familiar and even sympathetic with the arguments advanced by these men, he still felt that the timing was wrong. He told Adenauer that he felt he would be better off not talking about it at all, that whatever he said would be bound to be misunderstood as simple agitation for a German army. Confidentially, he told an old Wall Street friend in mid-December, "It is a problem that one day we shall have to face. . . . We can't leave Germany with a Soviet trained East German army to take over the whole country. I frankly do not know what the solution is as yet, but I am quite clear that now is not the time to react to the East German developments on the military side."[80]

It was true that the East Germans had been allowed by the Soviets to build up their internal police force into what was beginning to appear to be a small army, even equipped with a few tanks. But the military threat came from the presence of Russian troops in East Germany. Though publicly the Truman administration made much of this potential threat, its intelligence assessments of Soviet intentions dismissed the possibility of a Soviet invasion of Western Europe. In fact, the CIA feared the opposite, that the Soviets might in 1949 choose to withdraw their troops from East Germany, and thus accelerate the political pressures on Western Europe to disengage from NATO's military buildup.[81]

The real threat was political. Early in November 1949, the Soviets had made their policy explicit when Politburo member Georgi M. Malenkov announced that the Kremlin would endorse free elections in a unified Germany if the new state would agree to be neutral and demilitarized.[82] If the Soviets made their proposals attractive and credible, the West Germans might find them irresistible. Adenauer said as much to Acheson in November, when he expressed the fear that the Soviets might soon withdraw their troops from East Germany.[83]

In this context, the issue of whether West Germany was to rearm was not a military question, but one of whether Germany was to remain divided. Schumacher and the SPD were outraged by Adenauer's suggestion of a German contingent in a European army precisely because they viewed such a step as closing off the possibility of reunification. Adenauer viewed the issue in political terms: "Rearmament might be the way to gaining full sovereignty for the Federal Republic. This made it the essential question of our political future."[84] Content for the moment with having raised the issue, Adenauer now decided, at McCloy's urging, to let it simmer for a while.[85]

Less than six months after arriving in Germany, McCloy felt rather pleased about his tenure. At an end-of-the-year press conference, he hailed the election of a West German government and the signing of the Petersberg Agreement as two major achievements. The future, he said, now rested not so much with the high commissioners as with the Germans themselves. He then made a point of saying that the touchstone of whether they would be able to develop a liberal state remained their attitude toward Jews. There had been a number of "debasing" incidents of anti-Semitism, but he said such things had been strongly criticized in the German press.[86]

At the time, McCloy's hopes for German democracy seemed overly optimistic. The next day, *The New York Times* published a poll showing that 60 percent of all West Germans could not name their own elected chancellor.[87] Nor had German attitudes toward Jews changed. It was common knowledge among HICOG employees that even Jewish Americans like Buttenwieser still encountered quite a bit of anti-Semitism.[88] And many Germans were openly clamoring for the end of the de-Nazification program and the release of imprisoned Nazi war criminals.[89] Even with Adenauer, McCloy found it difficult to discuss de-Nazification. The chancellor steadfastly ignored his arguments that more attention should be paid to cleansing the German civil service of its "authoritarian, Bismarckian" influences. He told Adenauer that it was one thing for "little Nazis" to take their place in the community, but many Americans were worried by the prospect that prominent Nazis might regain their influence.[90] Two former Nazis were in Adenauer's first Cabinet: Dr. Hans Christoph Seebohm, minister of transportation, and Dr. Thomas Dehler, minister of justice. Seebohm was an ultranationalist who in 1951 publicly denounced the "monstrous crime the victors had committed against Germany, Europe and the whole world." *Der Spiegel* later described him as a "prototype of the eternal Nazi."[91] That both men had faithfully served the Third Reich and now had seats in Adenauer's Cabinet disturbed McCloy. In addition, one of Adenauer's closest advisers, Dr. Hans Globke, had been an influential civil servant in the Nazi Interior Ministry. Globke was one of the co-authors of the notorious Nuremberg racial-purity laws of 1935, and had helped to write the 1933 emergency legislation that gave Hitler dictatorial powers. Yet Adenauer, who chose to believe Globke's claim that he had attempted to mitigate legal measures already demanded by Hitler, was now relying on him as a private, unofficial adviser.[92] When questioned about his controversial aide, Adenauer told McCloy, "I can't run the country without him."[93]

Other prominent men with unsavory backgrounds gradually became part of Adenauer's "kitchen Cabinet," including such wealthy and powerful financiers as Hermann Abs and Robert Pferdmenges. Both men had collaborated with the Nazis, and though they were not prosecuted at Nuremberg, they were placed on the Allied war-criminal list. Abs knew Adenauer from the 1920s, when they served as fellow directors of the Deutsche Bank, one of the "big three" German banks. Pferdmenges controlled the Oppenheim banking house in Adenauer's hometown of Cologne, and the chancellor had long counted him as his most intimate friend. They were kindred spirits, men of culture and conservative judgment, and Adenauer came to rely on their advice regarding a wide range of issues.[94] (In later years, McCloy himself would count both bankers as personal friends.)

That the chancellor required the services of such men made it difficult to persuade the German public that lower-level Nazis should be purged from the civil service. By 1949, the policy of de-Nazification had run its course. Immediately after the war, U.S. occupation authorities had identified 3.6 million indictable individuals for political or war crimes—or 20 percent of the population in the U.S. sector. This unmanageable number was eventually cut down to about 930,000 individuals, who were processed through a total of 169,282 trials. Over 50,000 were convicted, and 806 death sentences were handed down, of which 486 were carried out. Hundreds of thousands of these individuals were fined, imprisoned, or forced out of civil-service or other white-collar jobs. Inevitably, justice was administered unevenly: thousands of schoolteachers and low-ranking civil servants who had been pressured to join the Nazi Party were penalized by the de-Nazification courts, while prominent industrialists who had given millions to the party—but never joined it—went untouched.[95] Such inequities discredited the process to the point where many genuinely anti-Nazi Germans hesitated to testify against their countrymen. When pressed, some Germans began to argue that the Führer had lost his mind only in the last several years of the war, that the crimes against humanity were his crimes, and those who carried them out were unavoidably following orders. Moreover, as the West German state came to be perceived as a bulwark against the communist East, a small but newly vocal right wing suggested that Hitler's mistake had been to fight the West instead of turning the full force of Germany's armor against the Kremlin. Even Germans in the political center now found it easy to argue that those condemned to death for their services to the Third Reich—known as the "red-shirts" for the prison garb they wore that signified their capital offenses—should be shown some mercy.

It was in this atmosphere that a delegation of distinguished German lawyers came to see McCloy in November 1949 about the convicted Nazi war criminals still in prison. The lawyers spoke of a "miscarriage of justice" and urged McCloy to consider a general amnesty, or at least to establish some kind of parole board to review the sentences. They particularly wanted him to reprieve those war criminals facing the death sentence. McCloy's response to this initial appeal was to tell the lawyers that he didn't know whether a review of the sort they were talking about was appropriate, but that certainly anybody could bring to his attention evidence of a miscarriage of justice. As to the death sentences, he pointed out that they had been stayed, pending court appeals. That did not mean, he warned, that "some or all of those sentences would not be carried out." He then asked the head of the delegation whether he had read the record in any of these cases. As McCloy recounted to his staff, the man "hesitated just long enough to say 'yes' to convince me that he hadn't." It was a shame, McCloy said, that the Nuremberg war-crimes proceedings on these cases had not been published in German.[96]

If McCloy was thus initially disposed to take a hard line on the war-crimes cases, the machinery within the HICOG bureaucracy was beginning to move in the opposite direction. In part, this was McCloy's own responsibility. General Clay had told McCloy he regretted that he had been unable to leave a clean slate regarding the pending death sentences. McCloy mistakenly interpreted this to mean that the sentences had not been reviewed; in fact, Clay had already reviewed the cases and confirmed the sentences. Only the Supreme Court appeals prevented him from carrying out the sentences prior to McCloy's arrival. Nevertheless, in October, McCloy requested a memo from the Justice Division of HICOG on whether he had the power to "alter, after confirmation, the sentences imposed by the military tribunals at Nuremberg." He was promptly told that, indeed, he had the power to do just about anything he wished.[97]

And now the Germany that McCloy was attempting to rehabilitate began to pressure him into exercising that power. In November 1949, the archbishop of Cologne wrote the high commissioner a plea for clemency in behalf of the war criminals awaiting execution. The archbishop argued that these men had already suffered the anguish of awaiting execution for two years, and that, "thereby, they have already repented." He pleaded with McCloy to take into account that these men had "acted by orders of higher headquarters. . . ." McCloy was initially inclined to tell the archbishop that it was his "impression" that "there are some offenses so shocking and so criminal in their aspect that it would be most difficult to find any possible basis for clemency." He wanted, in fact, to tell Washington that he was prepared to carry out the executions as soon as the final appeals before the Supreme Court were rejected. But these impulses were set aside when his old friend and general counsel, Chester McClain, informed him that HICOG was "working on a plan for a parole board for the war crimes cases. . . ." McCloy was always willing to reconsider his initial judgments, and if McClain had set in motion the bureaucracy to do this, he would not stand in his way.[98] It was a decision filled with momentous consequences.

Telford Taylor, one of the American prosecutors at Nuremberg, provided McCloy with a hint of the controversy he would soon face if he took the road to clemency. Those condemned to death, Taylor wrote to McCloy at the end of the year, included the administrative head of the entire concentration-camp system, Oswald Pohl, and the leaders of the special SS killing squads who carried out the slaughter of some one million Jews and others during the invasion of the Soviet Union. "They are, without any question, among the most deliberate and shameless murderers of the entire Nuremberg list, and any idea of further clemency in their case seems to me out of the question."[99] There is no record of McCloy's reply.

CHAPTER 16

The Dilemma of German Rearmament

"Germany always had two bosses: one, the General Staff, and the other the Rhine industrialists. We still have the latter only a little chastened. Let us not take on the other for a while."

MCCLOY TO HENRY STIMSON
JUNE 28, 1950

McCloy was genuinely appalled by the tendency of the German public to turn "squalid butchers into patriots and martyrs."[1] He was annoyed by appeals in behalf of proven war criminals, particularly when unaccompanied by any recognition of the crimes these men had committed. Always an avid reader of history, he was now developing a strong interest in what little was known of the German resistance to the Third Reich. He had met and became good friends with such resistance figures as Elizabeth Struenck, Inge Scholl, and Fabian von Schelabrendorff.[2] The courage displayed by the handful of German students who paid with their lives for publicly opposing Hitler deeply impressed him, and led him in later years to assist his son in researching a Princeton undergraduate thesis on the topic. The resistance, in fact, was never more than a handful of individuals, some of whom were motivated by less-than-democratic ideals. Some were monarchists, and some had willingly participated in the regime's Judeocide. The Nuremberg prosecutors were shocked to learn that one of the army officers involved in the July 20 plot to assassinate Hitler had served as the commander of an Einsatzgruppen mobile killing squad used to carry out the first large-scale murders of Jews on the Eastern front. If McCloy gradually came to exaggerate the strength and importance of the noncommunist resistance, it was nevertheless astute of him to emphasize its symbolic value in building a new, democratic Germany.[3]

In this frame of mind, McCloy answered an appeal by the pope's personal representative in Bonn for a blanket amnesty of all war criminals. Writing early in 1950, he told Bishop A. J. Muench, "I do not believe that world opinion generally is prepared to accept the proposition that those crimes have yet been sufficiently atoned for or that the German people should now be allowed to forget them." But he also informed the church leader that as a matter of law he was interested in establishing a parole board where "reasonable and proven grounds" for individual clemency might be considered.[4]

By mid-January, his staff had already drafted the charter for just such a clemency board; the guidelines specified that the board would not review the decisions of the Nuremberg or other war-crimes trials on any "questions of law or fact."[5] In other words, the proposed parole board was not to undermine the legitimacy of the Nuremberg decisions by questioning either the unique legal grounds on which the Germans were tried, or the facts introduced as evidence in each case. McCloy was not one of those in the New York legal community who had scoffed at the war-crimes trials, and he had no intention now of overturning those decisions. Back in 1946, when the Nuremberg trials were in progress, he had bitterly complained to Acheson about the "ignorance" displayed by most of his colleagues in their attitude toward the proceedings.[6] Now, as high commissioner, he proposed that his parole board should recommend clemency only in those few cases where some individuals' sentences were deemed excessive when compared with similar cases.

There was one aspect of the whole business that made him uneasy. Clay had left him the unsavory task of carrying out the executions of sixteen war criminals sentenced to death. Publicly, he displayed a businesslike attitude toward the task, telling the press that it was his desire "to dispose of these [death sentences] as promptly as possible but in a dignified and just way."[7] But privately, when making the argument to Acheson for establishing a clemency board to review the death cases, he wrote, ". . . my own conscience is involved and though I am quite prepared to make the ultimate decision and accept ultimate responsibility, I require the help of such a group." Acheson quickly gave his assent, "inasmuch as you feel so strongly. . . ."[8]

As McCloy cast about for possible candidates to sit on his clemency board, reports began to surface that the high commissioner intended to review the war-crimes cases. The mere hint that the death sentences might not be carried out led a convention of the Jewish War Veterans of America to vote a resolution calling on McCloy to reject all pleas for clemency. *The New York Times* suggested that he had once again postponed the death sentences out of consideration for German public opinion. Simultaneously, the *Times* and other papers were running a series of stories early that year suggesting that Nazism and ultranationalists were again on the rise in Germany. During a brief trip back to the United States, McCloy told a Boston audience that, though "some evil embers are lying about," the Neo-Nazi threat was greatly overrated.[9]

He returned to Frankfurt in early February 1950, determined to correct the public's perception of his handling of the Germans. A few days later, in Stuttgart, he spoke to an audience of fifteen hundred Germans who sat in shocked silence as he bluntly told them that it was still far too early to contemplate any changes in the Allied occupation powers. The German people were still far too "apathetic or negative" in their political attitudes. In his judgment, there was still "too much traditionalism and authoritarianism in German life; . . . many undesirable former Nazis and nationalists were finding their way back into important places. . . ." He was determined, he said, to use all his powers to prevent Germany from ever again endangering the peace in Europe, and that meant, among other things, that "there will be no German army or air force." He then rebuked Adenauer's minister of justice, ex-Nazi Dr. Thomas Dehler, for suggesting that Germany's postwar difficulties were the fault of the Allies.

The New York Times hailed this new tough line and observed, ". . . no United States official in the last eighteen months has talked to the Germans about Germany as Mr. McCloy did today."[10] The next day, he had a three-hour meeting with Adenauer, who, when asked whether the meeting had been friendly, snapped, "You saw how he [McCloy] walked to the door with me and how we shook hands." Afterward, McCloy admitted the chancellor was reluctant to talk about his Stuttgart speech: "He was very disturbed about it, very upset."[11]

Not everyone, however, was convinced by this choreographed display of "getting tough with the Germans." The liberal *New York Post* suggested that one firm speech wasn't enough, that the Germans wouldn't get the message until the last of the Nuremberg death sentences were finally carried out. The New York *Compass,* a left-liberal paper, observed, "McCloy has talked back at the Nazis before this. And he has then gone right ahead building his so-called free democratic German puppet state on a broad base of Hitler sympathizers and anti-Semites."[12] The truth was that he just did not believe the Nazis were a threat any longer. No doubt there would be incidents, such as when a right-wing member of Adenauer's governing coalition in the Bundestag publicly questioned the authenticity of the Holocaust, inciting a fistfight outside the parliament.[13] And later that spring, he would be forced to condemn as a "disgrace" a rash of desecrations of Jewish cemeteries and synagogues.[14] But McCloy placed enough confidence in his executive powers—which included extensive intelligence surveillance and wiretapping of neo-Nazis—to conclude that such incidents were of little political significance. Even though many

Germans might still harbor anti-Semitic prejudices, the experience of total war and unconditional surrender had sapped them of any desire to participate in another totalitarian movement. Quite the contrary: polls commissioned by McCloy's public-affairs man, Shep Stone, revealed that most Germans were politically apathetic and decidedly antimilitarist.

The real challenge, McCloy believed, was still the difficult problem of how to create a democratic, pro-American state out of the Western half of a divided Germany. The threat to this U.S. foreign-policy priority came from the left, not the right, and in the months ahead he would have to find ways of broadening Adenauer's political base while stalemating the left-wing forces of the SPD. It was Schumacher's attractive vision of a unified Germany, achieved at the cost of neutralization and permanent demilitarization, that threatened McCloy's agenda in 1950. He realized that broadening Adenauer's base necessarily meant making the right kind of symbolic concessions on matters of national pride. A discreet end to the unpopular de-Nazification proceedings would measurably improve the standing of Adenauer's coalition government, allowing the chancellor to portray himself as the one politician who could win back German sovereignty. Still, it was a thin line McCloy had to walk.

When Adenauer appealed to him in April 1950 to commute the remaining sixteen death sentences on the grounds that the German Basic Law prohibited capital punishment, McCloy replied, "The enormity of the crimes for which these defendants were convicted exceeds the bounds of normal imagination." But then, while strongly defending the legitimacy of the Nuremberg proceedings, he told Adenauer that he had now established a procedure for reviewing each case to determine whether there were any "circumstances justifying clemency in individual cases."[15] A month earlier, he had finally selected three men to serve on a clemency board: David W. Peck, a New York State Supreme Court justice; Frederick A. Moran, chairman of the New York Board of Parole; and Brigadier General Conrad E. Snow, assistant legal adviser to the State Department. Peck had many years' experience as an appeals judge, Moran was familiar with American parole practices, and Snow could provide expertise on issues of international law.

There was just one shortcoming: time. Peck could not begin work until July 10 and had to return to the bench by September. Moran was willing to make a preliminary visit to Germany that spring for several weeks to begin work, but essentially the three men would have only forty days to review the judgments in twelve cases involving 104 defendants. Even McCloy had originally thought the review would take sixty days.[16] By contrast, Clay's lawyers had taken seven months to review just one of these cases. Given the time allotted, it just wasn't physically possible for the review panel to read through the hundreds of thousands of pages of briefs and transcripts. So they didn't. The transcripts relating to the trial of Alfried Krupp—contained in several large coffinlike packing cases—were hauled into HICOG headquarters but sat unopened all summer. Instead, the Peck Panel, as it became known, simply read the three thousand pages of verdicts and then opened hearings on each of the cases. Moran interviewed each of the convicted war criminals, and the panel as a whole heard appeals from some fifty lawyers representing the defendants. But, in a most unusual procedure, no opportunity was given to the prosecutors, like the chief of counsel to the war crimes tribunal, Brigadier General Telford Taylor, to rebut any of this testimony. One of Taylor's assistant prosecutors, Benjamin B. Ferencz, was still in Germany, but his offer to consult with the panel went unanswered.[17]

McCloy was not involved in any of these details; having selected his clemency board and agreed to the forty-day timetable, he now left them to conduct the review as they saw fit.

In the spring of 1950, McCloy was far more worried about the course of the Cold War than he was about the fate of a few convicted Nazi war criminals. In testimony before Congress, he warned that the Russians were exerting enormous political pressure on America's position in Germany: "The struggle is immediate and intensive. We in Germany feel that we are facing a critical point in history. . . ."[18] The Nazis were a residual issue, left over from the war; a resolution of their cases, one way or another, would evoke a certain political symbolism. But to McCloy's mind, this was nothing compared with the urgent task at hand. Early that year, the Soviets again made an effort to head off the creation of a West German state by offering to hold a plebiscite on German reunification. The prospect of a unified, demilitarized, and neutral Germany still had enormous appeal, both inside West Germany and among some Frenchmen. McCloy was disturbed to see the centrist French paper *Le Monde* editorialize that spring that all of Europe should become a "neutral third force" between East and West. He hated to see the Soviets seize the initiative on the evocative issue of German unity. It was essential, he said, to convince the West Germans that "integration with Western Europe does not, therefore, connote a writing off of the East."[19] This was to be a hard task, since it seemed clear to all observers that every step West Germany took toward integration with the Western alliance was a step away from unification.

Men like Schumacher and the popular Protestant-church leader Pastor Martin Neimoller were winning substantial support by criticizing Adenauer and the Allies for their lack of progress on unification. In response, McCloy took to publicizing Jean Monnet's dream of a united federation of Europe. In London that April, he gave a widely quoted speech in which he stated that "no permanent solution of the German problem seems possible without an effective European union."[20] A few days later, he tried to dampen German expectations for unification by bluntly warning that the Western powers might not end their occupation of Germany for another five years. The Allies would not leave until they felt satisfied that they had nurtured a mature liberal-democratic state. The longer the barrel of the gun, he explained to one reporter, "the more accurate the shot." Many Germans, he said, did not understand that "other countries still distrust them, and at times feel towards them a resistance not far short of revulsion."[21] The Allied occupation, in other words, would not end until the West Germans clearly aligned themselves with the West. Reunification, if it were ever to occur, would have to happen on Western terms, and the resulting German state could in no sense become a neutral, third force between East and West.

In other comments that spring, he stated that the West might soon be prepared to end the enemy status of West Germany, but only if the Germans "behave themselves." He told Adenauer that a revision of the Occupation Statute would depend on the "progress Germany makes toward democracy." As part of his carrot-and-stick strategy, he made it clear that Germany could regain control over its Ruhr Valley heavy industry only if it agreed to the French "Schuman Plan" to share steel and coal production with its West European neighbors. Crafted by Jean Monnet, the Schuman Plan was specifically designed as the first step toward the creation of a single, unified West European market. Adenauer had no problem with the idea, realizing that its economic benefits would do much to help him persuade his constituents to bury century-old antagonisms against the French and to cast their lot with the West. At a time when West German unemployment had hit a high point of 13.3 percent, any plan that would allow the Germans to increase steel and coal production was a Godsend.[22]

In myriad other ways, McCloy constantly used his sweeping powers to intervene in German affairs, prodding Bonn to institute the most elementary reforms in democratic government. When he was told by his staff that Germans who had served on the de-Nazification boards were now being blackballed by their countrymen as "traitors," he ordered the state governments to guarantee these individuals jobs in the civil service.[23] In April, he forced Adenauer to adopt a "co-determination" law, requiring large employers to give their workers some participation in corporate decision-making. He also angered the prickly chancellor by vetoing a tax bill that gave high-income taxpayers an enormous break. He initially vetoed a bill on civil-service reform that he thought not sufficiently democratic, and only relented when Adenauer promised that the law would be liberally applied. In a speech in late May 1950, he again lectured the German people on their "moral obligation" to restore to Jews that property "which is justly theirs."[24]

At times he encountered such astonishing displays of German arrogance that he lost his temper. In mid-June, he addressed an elite group of fifty industrialists in Düsseldorf and afterward was incensed when the president of the Essen Chamber of Commerce stood up and publicly complained about high occupation costs, excessive taxes, and the failure of the Allies to solve the economically costly problem of absorbing the tens of thousands of refugees pouring in from East Germany: "If Churchill and Roosevelt," said the German business leader, "felt like giving Stalin presents at the expense of Germany, then the Americans and British should foot the bill." McCloy, his voice shaking with anger, interrupted, "Don't forget that America's high taxes are the result of German aggression. Don't forget who started this war. Whether or not you gentlemen here are responsible personally for it, remember the war and all the misery that followed it—including your own—was born and bred in German soil and you must accept the responsibility. . . . Don't weep in your beer." The stunned industrialists sat in silence and then applauded him loudly. He went on to predict that someday the Ruhr would again be "big and strong," but in the meantime the world would be watching to see whether German industrialists would use their power to support or to stifle the country's fragile democracy.[25]

Afterward, Shep Stone, a witness to the scene, wrote in his diary, "Boss gets mad and hits him so hard all Ruhr is groggy. . . . Some of them [German industrialists] aren't such poisonous eggs. Some even understand that democracy might mean good business, even if they don't get the idea that it is a wonderful thing in itself."[26]

Nine days later, on June 25, 1950, hundreds of thousands of North Korean troops poured across the armistice line McCloy and Dean Rusk had once drawn across the 38th parallel to divide the communist-occupied North from the American-occupied South Korea. McCloy was as shocked by the attack as anyone, and immediately realized that the war in the Far East made a military buildup in Western Europe an urgent necessity. But three days after the attack, he could not get out of his mind the image of the Düsseldorf industrialists whining to him about their problems. In what was to be his last letter to Henry Stimson before his beloved "Colonel" died, McCloy vented his worst feelings about the Germans, telling Stimson that "the arrogance of their thinking was the greatest crime of all because they had the capacity to know." And though he acknowledged that there were "strong liberal elements in modern Germany," he could not bring himself to support the creation of a German army. To do so, he feared, "would mean the abandonment of all serious efforts to nurture the German state into a liberal constructive element in Europe." In the past, he wryly observed, "Germany always had two bosses: one, the General Staff, and the other the Rhine industrialists." Referring to his recent encounter in Düsseldorf, he told Stimson, "We still have the latter [the industrialists] only a little chastened. Let us not take on the other for a while."[27]

The remarkable thing about these candid and highly confidential sentiments is that they did not last. Within two weeks of having written these words to his mentor, McCloy was already beginning to shift his position. Given the aura of crisis and uncertainty generated by the events in Korea, perhaps this shouldn't be too surprising. He had told Stimson that the events in Korea were "too fresh for me to form any conclusions." But it did not take long before many West Germans and Americans speculated that Korea might just be a rehearsal for a full-fledged invasion of a much more valuable prize—the German industrial heartland of Europe. On July 3, 1950, just a week after the attack, McCloy told reporters, "It has become increasingly self-evident in the last year that the East zone government is nothing more than a puppet of the Soviet regime. Since the attack on South Korea it has become clear to all the world what dangers are inherent in these puppet governments." He then announced that he was ready to reconsider his rejection only twelve days earlier of Adenauer's request for a central West German police force of twenty-five thousand men.[28]

He could not help being affected by the atmosphere of near hysteria all around him. Adenauer's personal assistant urgently requested two hundred automatic pistols to defend the Chancellory from any possible communist-inspired uprising. A dozen members of the Bundestag visited McCloy's political officer in Bonn, Charles W. Thayer, and requested permission to carry firearms. "There's not a gram of cyanide to be bought," explained one Bundestag member to Thayer. "My colleagues have cleaned out the market to be prepared to take their lives when the Communists come." McCloy recognized these symptoms of hysteria, and when Thayer cabled Washington an account of the panic sweeping Bonn, he called up his young aide and angrily told him, "Washington is having enough trouble without your worrying it with reports of German panic."[29]

He tried to reassure the Germans by announcing that in principle the security of West Germany was synonymous with the security of the Western powers themselves. Twice in the next couple of weeks, he said, "I do not believe there is going to be any attack," and underscored his conviction by saying that he had invited his eighty-six-year-old mother to visit him in Frankfurt.[30] That is what he was saying in public. In private, he had his doubts. On July 12, 1950, he met with Adenauer just before the chancellor left for a much-needed month-long holiday in Switzerland. Since early May, Adenauer had been recovering from a bout of pneumonia. For a while, McCloy had thought he was going to have to find a successor for the elderly German.[31] Even now he found him "still a little weak—mentally, morally and physically." The chancellor had a bleak outlook on the world that summer, and complained of the "real vacumn in all Western preparations. . . ." In the event of a Russian attack, he pleaded with McCloy to allow his people to take up arms. Military preparedness was an argument McCloy never found easy to dismiss, and he was rather taken aback by Adenauer's deeply pessimistic attitude. If the Soviets intended to duplicate their aggression in Korea, the military equation in Germany was pretty stark: some 110,000 U.S. troops were stationed in Germany that summer, facing a Soviet force which some officials claimed was ten times as large.[32] McCloy was not convinced that the Soviets had any such intentions, but he did come away from his talk with Adenauer profoundly impressed by a simple political argument for some form of rearmament, even if it was only a symbolic token force. As he cabled Acheson a few days later, "If no means are held out for Germans to fight in an emergency my view is that we should probably lose Germany politically as well as militarily without hope of regain. We should also lose, incidentally, a reserve of manpower which may become of great value in event of a real war."[33]

This July 18 cable quickly caused a small furor inside the State Department. The sudden shift in his thinking gave considerable ammunition to those, like Paul Nitze, Averell Harriman, and George Kennan, who were trying to persuade Acheson to change U.S. policy on the question of German rearmament. In this inner circle of policy-makers only Henry Byroade, head of the German desk within the department, hesitated. The nation's youngest army general to come out of the war, and now a rising star in the State Department, Byroade disliked the idea of German rearmament. He was particularly uncomfortable with McCloy's initial idea to allow individual Germans to join U.S. combat regiments. But by the end of July, McCloy and his staff had come up with a more sophisticated plan. Instead of creating German mercenaries or even establishing a national German army, they proposed that German units be mustered as part of a European Defense Force. McCloy thought a "genuine European army" would prove to be far less provocative to the Soviets and, indeed, less worrisome to many Europeans, than a purely German army. He warned, however, that Germany would have to participate in any such scheme as a "substantial equal" with French, British, and other units.[34]

He realized that any such scheme, however gingerly presented, was bound to invite considerable controversy. To prepare the public for a change in policy, McCloy now began speaking to the press, at first vaguely, about German security needs. In late July, he told one radio audience that U.S. troops could defend Germany without any German assistance. But, he added, "I suppose there would be very many Germans who would be prepared and anxious to defend Germany in the event of an attack. . . ." Adenauer thought McCloy was moving too slowly, and upon his return from Switzerland he told the high commissioners that he was "incensed and angry" about their attitude. McCloy tried to assure him that the Soviets would not attack until that long-distant day when they felt they had achieved nuclear parity with America. In reply, Adenauer voiced his doubts about whether Washington would ever use nuclear weapons in the event of a Korea-type attack in Germany.[35]

These West German doubts about the credibility of U.S. nuclear deterrence were to become a recurring theme in German-American relations over the next four decades. McCloy realized the only policy that could assuage German fears was an increased American commitment of ground troops, a costly alternative. Even Schumacher, who by mid-August had come out for German participation in a European Defense Force, tied that participation to a "powerful increase in the U.S. military establishment in Germany."[36] That would happen in time, but in August 1950 the Truman administration was absorbed by the war effort in Korea, where American troops were taking a beating.

In the meantime, McCloy gave Adenauer his approval in late August for the creation of a ten-thousand-man federal police force. He then called in a group of reporters to his hideaway quarters in Koenigstein, outside of Frankfurt, and held an informal, off-the-record discussion on the rearmament question. After serving some fine German pilsner beer, he outlined his views. When one reporter pointed out that many Germans since the war seemed to be less than enamored with the idea of rearmament, McCloy answered, tongue in cheek, "Why, just give me a brass band and a loudspeaker truck. Then let me march from Lake Constance in the south to the Kiel Canal up north, and I will have a German army of a million men behind me—all eager-eyed."[37] In fact, he was well aware that neutralist and antimilitarist sentiment was on the upswing.[38]

This did not stop him from taking Adenauer's case for rearmament to the Truman administration and orchestrating a policy change. Just before he boarded a plane to attend a foreign ministers' conference in New York in early September, he was handed a long memo from Adenauer proposing that Germany be allowed to establish a quasi-military "protective police force" of some 150,000 men. The document had actually been drafted the previous evening, with the close assistance of Charlie Thayer.[39] McCloy was not taken aback by the proposed numbers, but he still favored the political advantages of a European Defense Force over anything that could remotely look like a resurrected Wehrmacht. In Washington, he met with Truman and pushed the EDF concept, and afterward told reporters that the West Germans should be allowed to arm themselves against a possible attack.[40] At this point, he was still out in front of the administration, which had not yet decided which way to go. But he couldn't keep himself from telling reporters what he thought: "It seems so difficult to say to these people [the Germans] that you can't share in the defense of your country if you're attacked. If that sounds like rearmament, then it's rearmament."[41]

McCloy and Adenauer collaborated so closely together on rearmament partly, of course, because they recognized that Western Europe could not appear to have a credible military deterrence in the long run without German participation. But both men had political considerations as well. Adenauer saw rearmament as the shortest path to sovereignty. McCloy thought it was necessary in order to stem neutralist sentiments, and—no less important—keep Germany divided. As he had written Truman on September 10, 1950, the occupation could not as a practical matter continue much longer after Germany contributed forces to a European army. Negotiations would have to begin to put the American occupation forces on a new footing. And though he had wished to achieve further "democratization" within the fabric of German society, "certain of the things we would like to see done in Germany will not be completed." Nevertheless, he argued, "we are forced to accept this as unavoidable in order to attain the larger objective of binding Germany to the West."[42]

Truman was convinced by these arguments and the day after receiving McCloy's memo, approved the concept of a European Defense Force. The EDF would have one supreme commander, and the chain of command at the top would be integrated, but the actual troops would function in national contingents. Germany was to contribute ten to twelve divisions. A few days later, Acheson and McCloy brought the package proposal to the ministers' meeting in New York, where a storm of criticism greeted them. The French called it the "bomb at the Waldorf." The worst feature of the plan, argued its critics, was that the Americans proposed to let the Germans begin assembling their ten divisions immediately, even before the European army had been established. The British were as opposed as the French. After a week of often bitter arguments, the foreign ministers adjourned and McCloy expressed his deep frustration to Acheson: the military threat was urgent, he thought, and time was of the essence. But uppermost in his mind was the "fear that Germany would drift away from the real desire of most people in West Germany to become incorporated into a Western community." The French attitude in the talks was forcing a "neutrality complex" on the Germans. If the Germans didn't get their army now, in the context of a European army, it would happen someday outside the context of NATO or an integrated European army. The French, of course, would strenuously oppose such an event, and traditional Franco-German animosities might easily lead to "the old dance of death."[43]

Arguments over McCloy's EDF dragged on throughout that autumn, and the issue threatened to tear apart Adenauer's own government. The popular and widely respected minister of the interior, Gustav Heinemann, resigned in protest, telling Adenauer, "God has twice dashed the weapons from our hands. We must not take them up for a third time." McCloy did not underestimate the strength of antiarmament sentiment; in November he worried about those "in Germany who are striving to avoid any definite action aligning Germany with the West. . . . This group is very large—Heinemann, Noack [a pacifist and university professor], Niemoller—are not isolated figures by any means." He felt the political balance was delicate enough so that he could no longer lightly issue any more public "diktats"—such as vetoing the chancellor's tax bill—without severely undermining Adenauer's position.[44]

Though on occasion McCloy found Adenauer "querulous and uninspiring" as a leader, Adenauer was nevertheless a "thorough Westerner."[45] This could not be said for his equally irascible SPD rival. To McCloy's distress, Schumacher—while supporting in principle the idea of an EDF—was still doing everything he could to keep the door open to reunification. In what was widely seen as an attempt to head off the rearmament of Germany, the Soviets that October once again proposed a four-power agreement on Germany, providing for both reunification and a formal peace treaty which would restore to Germany full sovereignty. The Soviets seemed to have only one condition: the fulfillment of the Potsdam agreement regarding the demilitarization of Germany.[46]

Late that autumn, in one of their rare lunches, Schumacher told McCloy that he "was prepared to buy unification of Germany possibly at the cost of temporary neutralization, his argument being that once Germany was reunited, it would be strong enough to resist all Communist pressure."[47] Schumacher's attitude was anathema to McCloy, not only because he had visceral doubts about the whole idea of a reunited Germany, but because even a "temporary neutralization" would spell the end of NATO.

In public, Adenauer too fully supported unification, but in private he was telling McCloy that he "felt it much wiser and better from all points of view to renounce for a time the thought of a reunited Germany rather than provide for a united Germany under Soviet influence. . . ." A neutral, unarmed Germany would, he said, be attracted to the East just as "a giant magnet [would] draw a filing to it."[48]

The rearmament of Western Europe became an even more urgent priority after November 24, 1950, when thousands of Chinese troops crossed the Yalu River and pushed General MacArthur's forces deep into South Korea. McCloy was now willing to concede a great deal of his powers as high commissioner in order to win agreement on a European defense. Late in November, he wrote Acheson that rearmament had to be accompanied by a renegotiation of the Occupation Statute. What he had in mind was to put Allied relations with the Germans on a "contractual" relationship, whereby the Germans would undertake certain obligations while Adenauer's government in Bonn, for all practical purposes, would be treated as a sovereign power. As long as rearmament was carried out "within the framework of a European defense structure," French fears of the Germans could be assuaged. And because German contingents would be accorded the same status as French units, such an approach might generate "a popular appeal to the German spirit of self-defense and loyalty to West European unity powerful enough to drown out Schumacher's drum-beating. . . ."[49]

By this time, Jean Monnet, again working behind the scenes, broke the deadlock with an alternative program for European defense. Eventually unveiled as the "Pleven Plan"—named after the French prime minister—this program proposed a thoroughly integrated European army of one hundred thousand men; the German and other national contributions would come in the smallest possible contingents. McCloy initially worried that the national units would be so small—as low as thousand-man battalions—that the military effectiveness of the army would be seriously compromised. But he nevertheless thought it was a step in the right direction and persuaded Adenauer to sign on to the plan. Negotiations stretched out many months, but in the meantime Washington agreed to increase its troop strength in Europe, and late in 1950 Dwight Eisenhower left the presidency of Columbia University to become supreme commander of NATO forces in Western Europe.

Eisenhower was initially rather critical of the proposal for a European army, complaining that it included "every kind of obstacle, difficulty and fantastic notion that misguided humans could put together in one package."[50] But under McCloy's gentle prodding, he changed his mind after six months in Europe. McCloy also realized that Ike's presence in Europe could help sell the whole concept to the Germans. So, during a visit by Eisenhower to Bad Homburg, McCloy arranged for several German generals to attend a cocktail party in honor of the NATO supreme commander. Ike had once publicly vowed never to shake the hand of a German officer, but on this occasion he knew what was called for and strode up to a former German general and stuck out his hand. The gesture deeply impressed Adenauer and the other Germans in the room. Afterward, when the guests had departed, Ike turned to Mrs. McCloy and said rather sheepishly, "Ellen, I hope I did well."

CHAPTER 17

McCloy and U.S. Intelligence Operations in Germany

"Mr. McCloy directed that we smoke out EUCOM [European Command, U.S. Army] on the matter to see how far they would go in helping to find this character [Klaus Barbie], and to get more details as to just how embarrassing it would be to them (CIC) if he were turned over to the French."

HICOG LETTER TO U.S. EMBASSY IN PARIS
JUNE 20, 1950

In the autumn of 1950, occupied Germany was the primary domicile for a host of covert intelligence operations aimed at containing, if not rolling back, the Soviet empire in Eastern Europe. McCloy was a man ideally suited to oversee these operations: both his work on Black Tom and his supervision of U.S. intelligence activities during the war inclined him to approve a broad range of intelligence activities. As high commissioner, he authorized extensive intelligence collection from a network of agents in both West and East Germany, a variety of paramilitary operations behind the Iron Curtain, and a sophisticated and expensive propaganda campaign designed to persuade left-of-center European intellectuals to oppose communist political influence. Thousands of Germans from all walks of life—including numerous politicians, labor-union officials, schoolteachers, and journalists—were drawn into this intelligence network as informants, agents of influence, and propagandists. And as was the case with the

Soviets—who were building a similar intelligence network—some of these agents had extremely unsavory backgrounds.

A case in point is the controversial matter of one Klaus Barbie. That autumn, while McCloy was trying to find an acceptable means of rearming the West Germans, the U.S. Army's Counter-Intelligence Corps (CIC) was preparing the escape from Europe of former Gestapo officer and convicted war criminal Klaus Barbie. In the years since, the Barbie affair has become a potent symbol of U.S. postwar collaboration with ex-Nazis for purposes of intelligence gathering. Barbie was a Nazi thug, who enjoyed whipping his victims, kicking them in the head, or stringing them upside down from hooks. As the Gestapo chief in Lyon, he had two tasks: break the resistance, and accelerate the deportation of French Jews to the death camps in the East. He had executed both tasks with cold efficiency. With the assistance of an informer, in 1943 he captured Jean Moulin, the most prominent French resistance leader. Soon afterwards, he tortured Moulin to death. In 1943–44, Barbie facilitated the deportation of some seventy-six thousand French Jews, including the infamous case of forty-one Jewish children, aged three to thirteen, from an orphanage in Izieu.

After the war, Barbie eluded arrest, though he was listed as early as 1945 in the Allies' CROWCASS directory of suspected war criminals. In February 1947, he climbed out a bathroom window as U.S. Army intelligence agents kicked down his front door. But later that same year, a former Abwehr officer, Kurt Merk, persuaded a regional branch of the army's CIC that Barbie could be of use in running a string of agents in occupied Germany. In short order, he was supervising CIC's most productive network of agents, the "Petersen Bureau." He impressed his American handlers by infiltrating the Bavarian branch of the Communist Party with an agent recruited by an SS friend who had served as a concentration-camp guard. If his CIC recruiters were initially ignorant of his background, it was not long before they were told of Barbie's reputation in Lyon. Nevertheless, his CIC superiors decided that his "value as an informant infinitely outweighs any use he may have in prison."[1] By 1949, he had become so knowledgeable about CIC operations, including some operations he was running to infiltrate French intelligence, that his CIC handlers could not risk having him extradited to France. His background as a war criminal became a public embarrassment in 1949–50, so the CIC allowed Barbie to escape from Europe through a "rat-line" organized by a Croatian priest and former Nazi collaborator operating out of the Vatican. Barbie and his family quietly made their way to Bolivia, where he established himself as "Klaus Altmann," a well-to-do businessman with close connections to the intelligence services of both countries. Only in the 1970s was his true identity revealed by the Nazi-hunter Beate Klarsfeld, and finally, in 1983, he was extradited from Bolivia and returned to France, where he eventually stood trial for crimes against humanity.

Only then were hard questions asked about how McCloy as high commissioner could have allowed his intelligence apparatus to harbor such a man. A U.S. Justice Department investigation exonerated McCloy of any direct responsibility for Barbie's escape to Latin America. The Justice Department probe, however, led to a formal U.S. apology to the French government. Washington admitted that Barbie had worked for U.S. intelligence, that he was a known war criminal, and that he had nevertheless been allowed to escape French justice. The Justice Department's chief investigator, Allan A. Ryan, Jr., concluded that Barbie was an isolated case, that he had been employed by U.S. Army counterintelligence without the knowledge of McCloy, and that his escape was the result of a cover-up by a few intelligence officers.

However, that a man like Barbie could be used and protected by U.S. intelligence in occupied Germany was a matter of policy, not accident. Nor was he an isolated case. In the context of the Cold War, at a time when McCloy and his colleagues felt themselves to be field commanders on the front line of the ideological battle to contain the communist political challenge, the disagreeable character of agents like Barbie was usually of small consequence. Indeed, that some of these men had once worked for the German enemy and had specialized in anti-Soviet work on the Eastern front was precisely why they were assets to U.S. intelligence. What mattered in the intelligence game, as McCloy knew all too well from his Black Tom work, was whether these agents were producing hard intelligence.

In the spring and summer of 1950, just as the Barbie case was becoming a sensation in the French press, McCloy had become concerned about communist infiltration of the Bavarian police force and various other West German governmental institutions. In a number of his weekly staff meetings that summer, he emphasized the importance of monitoring communist subversion and cited in one instance how HICOG intelligence had "intercepted a Communist communication running from KPD [the German Communist Party] headquarters to a local unit. . . ."[2] This was precisely the type of intelligence on KPD subversion of the Bavarian police force that Barbie was then providing his CIC handlers. Though he had no idea who the agent was who had provided this material, McCloy was ill-disposed to allow anything to jeopardize the collection of such intelligence. He regarded clandestine information of this sort as the first line of defense against the very real threat of Soviet political subversion and psychological warfare.

Initially, McCloy did not take much personal interest in the Barbie case; in the spring of 1950, the problems of de-Nazification had taken a back seat to the priority of establishing a viable West German state aligned with the West. The French allegations against Barbie were just one more irritant in Franco-German relations. But as the year progressed, McCloy was to become more aware of the special kind of controversy the Barbie case was generating in France. There Barbie was known as the "Butcher of Lyon."

HICOG officials began to realize the gravity of the matter in March 1950, when the French high commissioner wrote that Franco-American relations would be severely damaged if Barbie was not handed over. Then, in April, a French court put on trial René Hardy, the man most Frenchmen suspected of having betrayed Jean Moulin to Barbie. In the course of the trial, Hardy's defense lawyer let loose a bombshell: it was "scandalous," he said, but nevertheless a fact, that U.S. military authorities in Germany were protecting Barbie from extradition for "security reasons."[3] French newspapermen now rushed to the Americans for comment. Was it true that Barbie was under the protection of HICOG? A U.S. Army press spokesman tried to fend off the reporters with a terse "no comment," but this naturally made the allegation seem all the more plausible.

With the French repeatedly demanding his extradition, Barbie had become a minor but annoying matter of intelligence administration. Both Washington and the U.S. Embassy in Paris cabled McCloy for guidance on what the French should be told. HICOG had to come up with some answers. McCloy met repeatedly in late April and early May with the men in his office handling the Barbie cable traffic: Benjamin Shute, his old Cravath colleague who was then serving him as director of HICOG intelligence; James D. Riddleberger, his chief political-affairs officer; General Counsel Robert R. Bowie; and Assistant General Counsel John A. Bross. These men were his closest advisers, particularly on intelligence matters.

HICOG's standard line up to this point was that Barbie's whereabouts were unknown. The French knew otherwise, since French police officials had interviewed Barbie in the presence of CIC officials on several occasions. In the midst of the Hardy trial, it was now a common assumption among the French public that U.S. authorities in Germany were protecting Barbie. The U.S. Embassy in Paris was almost frantic for any information to counter what they knew was rapidly becoming an anti-American propaganda bonanza for the French left. In response, HICOG's legal office prepared a warrant for Barbie's arrest; this document was ready for Bowie's signature on May 1, 1950, but he never signed it. On May 2, 1950, HICOG's Public Safety Branch cabled the U.S. Embassy in Paris to say that the allegations that Barbie was being protected were "unjustified and unwarranted."[4] The next day, however, HICOG cabled that this information "may possibly be inaccurate or incomplete." New, unofficial information had been passed through the

U.S. Army chain of command that CIC had known where Barbie was as recently as April 28. HICOG accordingly advised the Paris embassy to say nothing more about the case "until we communicate with you further."[5] HICOG was in considerable disarray, and at least one official refused to believe that CIC had been in contact with Barbie for almost three years and had just now conveniently lost track of him. James McGraw, HICOG's chief public-safety officer, was so incredulous that he told his superiors on May 5, 1950, that he wouldn't have anything more to do with the case.[6]

Over the next several weeks, McCloy's close advisers tried to figure out how to respond to the French extradition request. On May 5, John Bross was informed of "rumors that Barbie has been seen in Munich."[7] A day or two later, Bross's boss, Robert Bowie, drafted a letter to the French in which he reported that HICOG had "recently received clues which may enable us to find him [Barbie]."[8] This letter was never sent to the French, because Bowie and Bross had second thoughts about whether they wanted to encourage the French government. Instead, it was decided that Riddleberger would verbally brief the U.S. embassy in Paris over the weekend. Riddleberger evidently had learned a great deal more about CIC's employment of Barbie, for that Monday, May 8, 1950, the Paris embassy cabled Washington, "Secret information brought by Riddleberger indicates Barbier [sic] case has highly embarrassing possibilities to put it mildly."[9] But the official records do not make it clear just how much Riddleberger knew. Had he learned that Barbie was still in a CIC safe house, or had he merely conveyed the almost equally embarrassing news that CIC had known of his whereabouts as recently as April 28?

In either case, Riddleberger now knew that he was dealing with a delicate intelligence matter. Obviously, up until a week earlier, CIC agents had still had access to Barbie. HICOG had therefore already been put in the position of lying to the French, who had been told repeatedly since 1949 that Barbie could not be located in the American zone. There must have been a good reason why CIC had worked with Barbie and evidently had continued to work with him until very recently. In any case, for the rest of May, McCloy allowed the issue to drift, letting his HICOG public-affairs spokesman state merely that the Barbie case was under investigation. In fact, he had apparently been given intelligence information that led him to hope that the whole controversy would die down. From Paris, he and Riddleberger went to London for an Allied meeting with Acheson and other State Department officials. There he and Riddleberger took Henry Byroade aside and told him that the French government "no longer desire Barbier's [sic] presence in France."[10] Exactly how McCloy acquired this impression is not clear, but the most likely source was CIC itself. That same week, the commander of the counterintelligence unit in Region XII, where Barbie was working, reported, ". . . this entire Hardy-Barbie affair is being pushed as a political issue by left-wing elements in France. No strong effort has been made by the French to obtain Barbie because of the political embarrassment his testimony might cause certain high French officials."[11] In other words, Barbie could finger any number of prominent French politicians who during the war had collaborated with the Gestapo. CIC also believed that the French resistance groups pressing for Barbie's extradition were all left-wing organizations dominated by the Communist Party.[12] If the whole controversy was just a political gambit on the part of the French left to attack their opponents, as McCloy indicated to Byroade in London in mid-May, perhaps it would blow over.

He was wrong. On May 8, René Hardy was acquitted for the second time, and an enraged French public blamed the Americans for not allowing Barbie, the star witness against Hardy, to be extradited from Germany. By the end of May, under pressure from French resistance veterans, the French government had once again requested Barbie's apprehension. They also sent another stiff note to the State Department, summarizing their "unsuccessful attempts [to] obtain Barbier's [sic] extradition through HICOG." Byroade promptly cabled McCloy, requesting guidance and pointing out the obvious, that the French were not going to give up.[13]

McCloy now turned back to his political-affairs division and asked them to begin pressing the military chain of command for an explanation. As one of Riddleberger's deputies explained to his counterpart in the Paris embassy, "Mr. McCloy directed that we smoke out EUCOM [European Command, U.S. military authority in occupied Germany] on the matter to see how far they would go in helping to find this character, and to get more details as to just how embarrassing it would be to them (CIC) if he were turned over to the French."[14] McCloy fully understood the problem. CIC had employed an accused war criminal, and now several tough questions had to be answered. Was HICOG willing to risk the damage to Franco-American relations if Barbie was not turned over to the French? Or was Barbie's value as an agent, or his knowledge about CIC operations, such that he should be turned over to the French only as a last resort? McCloy knew enough about the intelligence business to realize that the bureaucracy now had to make a judgment on whether Barbie, if found, should be handed over to the French. By the end of May 1950, he had already accepted the possibility that there might be circumstances under which Barbie could never be transferred to the French, whatever his crimes. This set the stage for an internal cover-up of the whole affair by his own intelligence people.

Actually, CIC had already made that judgment in a meeting on May 4, 1950, at CIC headquarters, where it was decided "that Barbie should not be placed in [the] hands of [the] French. . . ."[15] As one CIC officer put it, ". . . due to his [Barbie's] position as key agent in nets formerly employed, and due to his long association with C.I.C., SUBJECT [Barbie] knows more about C.I.C. targets, modus operandi, EEI's, etc., than most C.I.C. agents."[16] Most embarrassing, he had personally directed CIC's counterintelligence operations aimed at infiltrating French intelligence. This fact alone made it imperative for the CIC to keep Barbie out of French hands. Barbie knew, for instance, the names of dozens of CIC informants whom he had helped to infiltrate the communist parties in both Germany and France. CIC was convinced, based on information developed by Barbie from these agents, that the French police and intelligence bureaus had been thoroughly infiltrated by the French Communist Party.[17] Under these circumstances, the highest-ranking CIC officers were easily persuaded that Barbie should never be turned over to French interrogators.

Having made the decision, CIC now had to decide what to tell McCloy. Since the high commissioner had already been told that Barbie no longer worked for CIC, the easiest thing to do was to tell a second lie. So, on June 16, 1950, General Robert Taylor, the chief of army intelligence in Germany, sat down with several of his men and told McCloy's personal representative, Ben Shute, that CIC had not used Barbie since May 1949. According to Shute's notes of the meeting, Taylor also added that CIC had "not been in touch with him [Barbie] since late April 1950 and does not know his present whereabouts."[18]

Shute took CIC's assurances back to McCloy and his new political-affairs officer, Sam Reber. On the critical question of whether Barbie's extradition would prove to be a costly embarrassment, Shute concluded, "A complete disclosure by Barbie to the French of his activities on behalf of CIC would not endanger any present intelligence operations, but would furnish the French with evidence that we had been directing intelligence operations against them." It is always awkward to be caught spying on one's ally. Shute's recommendation was nothing if not pragmatic: ". . . the policy question presented is of whether U.S.-French relations would be more damaged by delivery of Barbie, assuming we could find him, than by non-delivery. We are in a position to make a statement to the French about our termination of his employment and about our loss of contact with him and take a chance that the German police will not pick him up even though we make a formal attempt to have that done." After consulting with Shute about all this, Reber and his deputy, E. Allan Lightner, Jr., suggested that HICOG should request the U.S. military to join in the search for Barbie "only as a last resort," and then only if the French continued to press the issue.[19]

Throughout the summer and autumn of 1950, HICOG routinely told the French that "continuous efforts to locate Barbie are being made."[20] But no search of any kind was conducted.[21] German police and HICOG public-safety officers had long ago checked the obvious leads, and they were given no authority to search CIC installations or safe houses. All the while, Barbie continued to work for CIC, culling informants' reports, largely on the activities of the German Communist Party, and for these services he continued to draw a salary.[22]

For the moment, Barbie was safe, and with him CIC's cover-up. But as long as extradition remained a possibility, Barbie's handlers remained uneasy. Finally, in December 1950, CIC stumbled upon the existence of a "rat-line" occasionally used by its CIC counterpart in Austria to extricate informers and spent agents from Europe to Latin America. For a relatively small sum, Barbie was smuggled out of Europe in March 1951, and given a new life in Bolivia.[25]*

When the Barbie affair became a scandal in the early 1980s, McCloy was interviewed about the case, both by the Justice Department's Allan Ryan and by numerous journalists. He told everyone he had no recollection of Barbie or the French struggle to have him extradited. His closest aides, old friends like Robert Bowie, John Bross, and Ben Shute—whose names appear on many of the cables and reports associated with HICOG actions in the case—had a similar response. In their minds, the Barbie matter had been a truly minor piece of business, something that at the time was never resolved and had no consequences. Over the years, it simply faded from memory.

The records they left behind, however, show that they were aware of the dilemma Barbie posed for army intelligence. McCloy did order his people to "smoke out" from the army just how embarrassing it would be to hand Barbie over to the French. But in the end, his closest advisers concluded that a thorough search for Barbie should be conducted only "as a last resort," if the French demands became too onerous. Naturally protective of army intelligence, HICOG, under McCloy, made it easy for the CIC's cover-up of Barbie to survive any scrutiny.[26]

*During this same period some ten thousand Nazi war criminals of one stripe or another gradually made their way out of Europe and into the United States.[23] Many of them used the same "rat-line" operated out of the Vatican that rescued Barbie. Most managed to emigrate to America illegally, by lying about their backgrounds. But hundreds were brought into the United States by the CIA on grounds of national security, or for reasons similar to the ones given by Barbie's CIC handlers. Dozens of Nazi rocket scientists who had committed war crimes in the course of their service to the Third Reich were also brought to America during the early postwar years in a program code-named "Operation Paperclip." McCloy was well aware of this operation and others that served to enlist the services of war criminals. Operation Paperclip, in fact, was suddenly reactivated right after the start of the Korean War, when the Pentagon approved "Project 63," a million-dollar program to evacuate up to 150 German scientists in the event of a Russian invasion of Western Europe. The purpose of Project 63 was to deny the Soviets access to this scientific talent, and even the most ardent Nazis were recruited.[24]

In retrospect, the Barbie case is a classic example of how policy-makers in the early postwar years overrated covert intelligence, something McCloy in particular had been prone to do ever since the Black Tom case. Most of Barbie's intelligence consisted of secondhand gossip or gleanings from local newspapers. Some of it was certainly tainted information, fed to him by Germans with Nazi records who had been "turned" by the Soviets. Barbie wasn't worth protecting. He was a war criminal who should have been brought to justice in 1950. McCloy must share some responsibility for the postponement of justice for more than thirty-three years.

Nor was Barbie an isolated case; he was merely a notorious one. Barbie may have been a captain in the SS, and a Gestapo chief in occupied France, but in the spring of 1950, HICOG was using men with far worse credentials. At the end of March 1950, McCloy was deciding whom he should appoint as head of the West German Secret Service. Benjamin Shute, as director of HICOG intelligence, recommended General Reinhard Gehlen, a man who had personally served Hitler as head of military intelligence for the Eastern front.[27] During the war, Gehlen had conceived the idea of organizing right-wing, anti-Soviet Ukrainians and other Slavic nationalists into small armies and guerrilla units to fight the Soviets. Many of these partisans, including those who joined the notorious Belarus SS Brigade operating in Nazi-occupied Byelorussia, were involved in the grisliest of the mass killings on the Eastern front.[28] He was also responsible for a brutal interrogation program of Soviet prisoners of war.[29] In short, Gehlen was as guilty a war criminal as many of the men tried at Nuremberg. But as the war came to an end, he had the foresight to photograph the most important of his intelligence files and bury them in the Bavarian Alps. Upon his capture by U.S. Army CIC personnel, he convinced his interrogators that his files and the knowledge he possessed about anti-Soviet networks operating in the East could be invaluable. By August 1945, he was being interrogated in Washington, D.C., by a team of OSS officers headed by Frank Wisner. Eleven months later, he was back in West Germany, operating for Army G-2 intelligence what became known as the "Gehlen Organization," collecting intelligence on the Soviets from networks of anticommunist informants in East Germany, the Ukraine, and elsewhere in Eastern Europe. In 1949, Gehlen signed a contract with the CIA—reportedly for a sum of $5 million a year—which allowed him to expand his activities into political, economic, and technological espionage.[30] Gehlen's "Org"—the "firm"—was now safely ensconced in a walled-off little community in the small town of Pullach, just south of Munich. Here Gehlen built a self-contained intelligence community, with its own homes, stores, and schools for the children of his analysts.

The "Org" was riddled with former SS, SA, and Gestapo men. Some of these men, like the notorious Dr. Franz Six, were veterans of the SS's Amt VI (Department 6), a section of Nazi Germany's main security headquarters. Dr. Six and other officers recruited by Gehlen in 1946 had led Einsatzgruppen mobile killing squads on the Eastern front.[31] Some of them, like Dr. Six, were almost by chance traced down as war criminals and tried by U.S. military tribunals. Dr. Six was convicted in 1948 and sentenced to twenty years' imprisonment.[32] Such were the "experts" Gehlen recruited for his intelligence net immediately after the war.

In 1950, when McCloy accepted Shute's recommendation and appointed Gehlen as an adviser to Adenauer on external intelligence, the Soviet Union was the number-one target of U.S. intelligence. Though McCloy never put much credence in the threat of a Soviet invasion of Western Europe, he did fear communist subversion of West German society. It seemed only logical to tap the knowledge of Germany's top expert on the Russians.

Ironically, years later, West Germany would be racked by more than one spy scandal when it turned out that some of Gehlen's top intelligence officers, men with Nazi records, had all along been working for the Soviets.[33] Still, in the spring of 1950, McCloy had heard only good things about General Gehlen, whom he thought of as a valuable CIA asset.[34]

Intelligence collection was a booming business in Germany during the summer of 1950. Frank Wisner's "mighty Wurlitzer," which McCloy had helped to set in motion while serving on the Eberstadt Task Force on intelligence in 1948, was running at high speed, and nowhere was it more active than in Western Germany. Wisner had already absorbed the Gehlen Organization in 1949, but he also employed hundreds of his own German and exiled Slavic contract agents, whose mission was to provide human intelligence on the Soviet bloc. Many of these agents had Nazi backgrounds. In addition, the CIA was financing paramilitary units composed of anticommunist refugees from Latvia, Lithuania, the Ukraine, and other portions of Eastern Europe. These émigré guerrilla units—ready to be used in the event of a full-scale war—were disguised inside "Labor Service" units initially established after the war to assist the U.S. Army of Occupation.[35]

Beginning in 1949–50, Wisner and Gehlen used one of these Labor Service units to train some 250 Albanian guerrillas for a series of mini-invasions of communist Albania, one of the more unfortunate covert operations carried out during McCloy's tenure as high commissioner. His own CIA liaison officer, Lawrence de Neufville, came up with the idea of using a Labor Service unit as a cover. Gehlen selected the Albanians for the operation; not surprisingly, most of them were veterans of the Albanian fascist collaborationist organization, Balli Kombetar. These were men who had deported Albanian Jews to Auschwitz and served in the Nazi-sponsored Albanian SS Skanderberg Division. Their leaders—Midhat Frasheri, Xhafer Deva, Hasan Dosti, and others—had emigrated to the United States under CIA sponsorship in 1949, to use CIA money to organize the National Committee for a Free Albania.[36]

Since the entire operation was being warehoused out of a Labor Service unit stationed outside of Heidelberg, McCloy's authorization was required before any of the guerrillas could be parachuted into Albania. The CIA's Lawrence de Neufville and then a CIA contract officer named Michael Burke cleared the operation with McCloy. The high commissioner was well aware of the sensitivity of running such a program from German soil, so he instructed his close aide and friend Colonel Al Gerhardt to stipulate that, once the Albanian commandos arrived on German soil, they were to be kept in complete isolation. If ever caught, they had to be unable to tell their interrogators where they had been trained. Burke found a large, walled villa outside Heidelberg where the Albanians could prepare for their mission in complete seclusion. A veteran OSS officer, Burke had been recruited by one of McCloy's Wall Street colleagues, Franklin Lindsay, who in 1950 was the European director for the CIA's covert-action arm, the Office for Policy Coordination. Burke was a colorful individual who later ran the New York Yankees baseball club when they were owned by CBS, and later still became head of Ringling Brothers Barnum & Bailey Circus. He had excellent rapport with McCloy, played softball with him, and socialized frequently in the high commissioner's rarefied circle. Once a month, he briefed McCloy and Ben Shute on active intelligence operations. "McCloy was cued into the intelligence world," Burke recalled later. "You could talk to him in shorthand about operations. . . . He always had questions, but they tended to be about policy things, rather than operational details." The high commissioner "didn't want to know when you were dropping an agent," but he was always familiar with the broad outlines of an operation.[37]

Burke vividly recalled discussing the Albanian operation with McCloy, who easily gave his authorization for both the paratroop drops and similar, even more dangerous, overflights of the Soviet Ukraine.[38] These latter overflights were used to test Soviet radar defenses and to parachute agents into the Ukraine with the intention of stimulating an eventual uprising. As with the Albanian agents, many of the Ukrainian agents were former Nazi collaborators. All of these paramilitary operations were ill-fated. If the missions were not compromised by the Soviet double agent Kim Philby, the Soviets were tipped off by one of the many men they had infiltrated into the Gehlen Organization. Dozens of the guerrillas were picked up by the Albanian police, almost as soon as they landed. In 1954, the Albanian communists tried and executed over four hundred agents and individuals who had come into contact with the operation. The Ukrainian operation ended in the same fashion, and many agents lost their lives before the CIA finally concluded that penetration of the Soviet bloc in this manner was not, as Gehlen had estimated, a feasible venture. McCloy learned the lesson too. "We didn't know how tough the Soviets were," Burke said. "McCloy came back [from Germany] as a sensible advocate of secret intelligence activity, but not whole networks of resistance." It was obvious the Soviets could easily penetrate such large networks and roll them up anytime they wished.

There were other intelligence fiascos. Burke had been brought in to replace de Neufville because there were too many covert operations without any oversight. "It was a hell of a mess," Burke claimed. "They had a lot of relatively inexperienced people running a lot of lousy operations."[39] For instance, in 1950 the CIC began training a hundred members of a neofascist group called the League of Young Germans. Led by a former Luftwaffe officer named Gerhard Peters, these Young Germans were mostly Waffen-SS and Wehrmacht veterans. These men were provided with machine guns, grenades, and other light arms and schooled in guerrilla techniques that would enable them to stay behind Soviet lines in the event of a full-scale invasion. Then, in 1952, German police by happenstance arrested one of Peters's men and discovered a hit list of two hundred Social Democratic Party politicians, all targeted for assassination in the event of a Soviet invasion. Embarrassed U.S. officials had to admit to *The New York Times* that they had been funding the paramilitary training of these "young Germans, many of them former soldiers. . . ." A German Bundestag investigation later revealed that the CIC had actually paid the Peters group an extra 12,000 deutsche marks per month for political activities such as the infiltration of SDP conventions.[40]

There is no indication that McCloy was aware of such rogue operations, but, given his tacit approval of the growing intelligence establishment, one had to expect such things to happen, particularly when the CIC and the CIA began sponsoring paramilitary activities. Though McCloy himself was not enamored of the rollback strategy, and did not think the Soviet Union was vulnerable to such attacks, as high commissioner he signed off on these ventures. They were sold to him as "pinprick" activities: the overflights of the Soviet Union gleaned valuable information on Soviet air defenses, and even if the Ukrainian agents might not be able to spark a mass uprising, they could send back economic and political intelligence. Given the Cold War atmosphere of the times, it would have required a major critique for McCloy to have overruled Washington's authorization of such activities, and he was not inclined to run against this tide.

On the contrary, there were many things about the burgeoning intelligence establishment that he fully endorsed. Throughout his tenure, he repeatedly defended surveillance operations using mail interception and wiretapping of a wide variety of individual German citizens, including some SPD Bundestag members. Such practices, he told Washington, were necessary in order to monitor "communist activities." The largest chunk of the CIA's budget in Germany during these years went to financing Radio Free Europe and Radio Liberty, whose propaganda activities McCloy strongly supported. Even in the summer and fall of 1950, when many officials feared the Korean War was a test run for an invasion of Europe, McCloy still believed the Cold War would be won mainly with ideas, not arms. First Radio Free Europe, and a year later, in 1951, Radio Liberty, began beaming a blend of objective news and propaganda into Eastern Europe and the Soviet Union. Though the cover story for both was that they were privately funded, the CIA in fact provided the bulk of their $30–35-million budget.[41]

McCloy also promoted other covertly funded informational activities, including subsidies for the publication of various books—both German and American books in translation—that might stimulate "good and positive thoughts in Germany."[42] In February 1951, he proposed an elaborate psychological-warfare offensive to fund "specific newspapers, magazines, film producers, labor organization, churches, farm organizations and refugee groups on a selected and confidential basis." Such funds, McCloy told a meeting of U.S. ambassadors in Frankfurt, "would make it possible for these groups to undertake projects considered desirable and necessary in an all-out psychological offensive but which might not be financially remunerative." The "closest coordination" between public affairs and intelligence officers "would be required to organize such activities."[43] About this time, the CIA began to buy newsprint for Axel Springer's publishing firm, and similar subsidies were given to Melvin Lasky's Berlin magazine, *Der Monat.*[44] McCloy took a personal interest in Lasky's publication precisely because he could see that its anticommunist but left-of-center intellectual stance was making inroads with German Social Democrats and the intellectual community in Berlin. Lasky was able to publish such well-known authors as Arthur Koestler, Bertrand Russell, George Orwell, and even Jean-Paul Sartre. The magazine dealt with a broad range of cultural affairs, but every issue contained articles criticizing the totalitarian nature of the Soviet system. McCloy recognized that *Der Monat*'s editorial formula gave it a credibility that other American propaganda outlets did not have with the typical European intellectual. Nothing was more important, he thought, than to discredit neutralist sentiments in the SPD, and there was no better way to do this than to win the battle for Germany's intellectuals.

To this end, in June 1950, the CIA funded the inaugural convention in Berlin of the Congress for Cultural Freedom. Lasky's *Der Monat* helped promote the event, which was organized by a salaried CIA officer, Michael Josselson. The two men managed to gather more than a hundred European and American intellectual celebrities—including Sidney Hook, Arthur Koestler, and Hugh Trevor-Roper—for four days of oratory celebrating the noncommunist left. The SPD mayor of West Berlin, Ernst Reuter, McCloy's favorite politician in Germany, gave the opening speech.[45] One writer denounced the "clever imbeciles" on the left, who preached neutrality in the face of the bubonic plague. The largely German audience applauded wildly when it was announced that President Truman had ordered American troops into Korea. At the open-air closing ceremonies, attended by some fifteen thousand West Berliners, Koestler, the forty-five-year-old author of the anticommunist novel *Darkness at Noon*, read aloud a "Freedom Manifesto" which rejected neutralism and called for a peace based on democratic institutions. He concluded by shouting, "Friends, Freedom has seized the offensive."[46]

A permanent organization was established out of this first Berlin meeting, and over the next seventeen years it would build offices in thirty-five countries, employing a staff of 280.[47] In the early years, it sponsored any number of arts and writers' "festivals" as part of a sophisticated campaign of psychological warfare against communists and fellow-travelers. A half-dozen magazines were sponsored to spread the message, the most prominent and long-lasting of them being *Encounter*, in London, of which Melvin Lasky became editor. All of these activities were funded by the CIA, and in some years the cost was as high as $900,000. McCloy thought this money well spent. Later, when he was about to leave Germany, he took the trouble to write the Ford Foundation and, referring to *Der Monat*, encouraged the Foundation to "help to carry on certain operations which the future [U.S.] Embassy may find it difficult to continue, but which are of great significance to United States objectives in Germany."[48] The Ford Foundation obliged.

He was also aware that the CIA in these years was funding dozens of individual German politicians, labor leaders, and journalists. These payments were made out of "unvouchered funds" available to the director of central intelligence. Tom Braden, who was a senior Agency officer in the early 1950s before turning to journalism, recalled that in some instances these payments could be as high as $50,000: "Politicians in Europe, particularly right after the war, got a lot of money from the CIA. . . . There was simply no limit to the money it could spend and no limit to the people it could hire and no limit to the activities it could decide were necessary to conduct the war—the secret war."[49] Such payments became common in West Germany during McCloy's tenure, and led in later years to the funding of such anticommunist men of the left as Willy Brandt.[50] Though McCloy was not necessarily apprised of each and every payment, he certainly condoned the policy. In his mind, such intelligence activities were a necessary tool to be used in creating a democratic West German state.[51]

CHAPTER 18

The Clemency Decisions

"Why are we freeing so many Nazis?"

ELEANOR ROOSEVELT TO MCCLOY, 1951

At dawn each morning, Alfried Krupp, once the sole proprietor of a half-billion-dollar industrial realm, rose from his cot in Landsberg Prison and donned the red-striped denim uniform of a convicted war criminal. In 1950, the eldest son of Gustav Krupp seemed to have lost everything the family dynasty had acquired in over three hundred years of empire-building. At Nuremberg, the Allies had wanted to put Gustav in the docket, but the old man had no longer been of sound mind. Since the prosecutors had intended to try the son as well, they made him the centerpiece of their case against the Nazi industrialists. In the course of the trial, it became clear that he was not merely a stand-in for his father. The trial took nine months and generated over four million words of transcript. Alfried had been a particularly enthusiastic young Nazi. At the age of twenty-four, in the summer of 1931, he had joined the SS Fördernde Mitgliedschaft as a sponsoring member and began contributing money to the Nazi Party.[1] Throughout the 1930s, when Germany was engaged in its massive and illegal rearmament program, Alfried supervised the Krupp firm's production of artillery, submarines, and other war materials. From 1937 on, Alfried and his father regularly had access to state secrets and traded intelligence information with Hitler's Abwehr. In those years, he was an even more devoted admirer of the Führer than his elderly father. In 1943, soon after Gustav suffered a crippling stroke, Alfried was elevated to the position of chairman of the board and sole owner of all Krupp properties. At this time, he issued a directive assuming "full responsibility" for the family enterprise.[2]

That same year, he actively pushed the firm into producing fuses at a plant in Auschwitz, where concentration camp inmates were used as slave laborers. It was not a matter of accepting slave workers thrust upon the firm by the SS; in many instances, Krupp initiated the request for such labor, and he signed detailed contracts with the SS, giving them responsibility for inflicting punishment on the workers. Thousands of such slave workers died of malnutrition, beatings, and disease.[3] The Nuremberg tribunal was given overwhelming evidence, in the form of Krupp internal memorandums, placing direct responsibility for such practices on the sole owner of the firm. In 1948, Alfried was sentenced to twelve years' imprisonment and stripped of all his property. Convicted and imprisoned with him were nine members of his board of directors.

After more than two years in prison, however, Krupp's prospects began to improve. On paper, the Americans had confiscated all his property, but veteran Krupp managers loyal to the family still ran the firm, ostensibly awaiting decartelization and the distribution of Krupp assets to new owners. Then, in June 1950, North Korean troops stormed across the 38th parallel; on the Korean peninsula, at least, the Cold War had suddenly turned hot, and many in the West feared Korea was only a prelude to a Soviet invasion of Western Europe. At a minimum, the war in the Far East gave added urgency to rebuilding West Germany's economy, which in turn would enhance the military strength of Western Europe. And because German steel was needed for armaments bound for Korea, late in October McCloy lifted the eleven-million-ton limitation on German steel production.

Ten days later, Alfried Krupp met with his board of directors for the first time since his arrest. McCloy allowed the Landsberg Prison warden to reserve a conference room on the prison grounds where the Krupp *Direktorium* could gather. Alfried entered the room in his red-striped prison denims and took a seat at the head of the table. In this surreal atmosphere, smoking American cigars and eating fruit brought in from the outside, Krupp discussed the finances of increasing the Ruhr's production. By this time, he and his lawyers had been quietly told that his release from Landsberg was "only a question of a short time." His family was hoping that he might be home by Christmas.[4]

The rumors were true. McCloy's clemency-review panel, led by Justice Peck, had submitted their report on August 25, 1950. They had worked long hours each day for six weeks, including Saturdays and Sundays, to read all the judgments. And despite the complicated nature of the evidence, the three members of the clemency panel quickly decided that their task was not so difficult as they had anticipated.[5] A consensus had developed whereby they found it easy to recommend substantial reductions of sentences in most of the cases. To do so, they disregarded many of the Nuremberg judges' conclusions. After reading through their report, John M. Raymond, one of the lawyers who had conducted General Clay's review of the sentences, wrote McCloy's chief legal counsel, Robert

Bowie, and warned him, "The basic difference in the approach adopted by the [Peck] Board from the one that we took in reviewing the cases is that the Board, while accepting specific findings of fact, did not feel bound by the findings drawn as conclusions from the facts. . . . We felt that where the Court had seen the sentences and heard all the evidence, the bulk of which necessarily was not referred to in the judgment, it was in a better position to draw conclusions than we were."[6] In other words, the Peck Panel second-guessed the conclusions of the Nuremberg judges without having heard all the evidence. This should have set off alarm bells for Bowie, but it did not, perhaps because Raymond himself concluded that he basically had no quarrel with the Peck Panel's approach.

So Bowie and his deputy, John Bross, passed on the panel's recommendations to McCloy. They also told the high commissioner that Judge Peck wanted a chance to present his conclusions in person, and pointed out that, though it would be impossible to explore the details of each of the ninety cases, they thought McCloy could "cross examine Judge Peck on a number of individual cases selected at random. The purpose would be to attempt a spot check of the validity of their recommendations." Bowie suggested that McCloy should set aside a half-day to review the matter.[7]

In the end, McCloy met with the Peck Panel for a couple of hours on the afternoon of August 28 to discuss their report, which recommended the reduction of sentences or immediate clemency in seventy-seven of the ninety cases, including commutation of seven of the fifteen death sentences. Judge Peck acknowledged: ". . . if we have erred we have erred on the side of leniency."[8]

Regarding Krupp, the Peck Panel suggested that his twelve-year sentence be reduced to seven years and that the order confiscating his property be rescinded. Peck argued that the Krupp sentence was disproportionate and unfair when compared with similar sentences given other German industrialists. Friedrich Flick, who had been convicted of similar crimes, had been sentenced to only seven years, and none of his property had been confiscated. (The Flick case must have been on McCloy's mind that week, since he had released the former steel baron just three days earlier for good behavior, after Flick served only five years.[9]) More important, the Peck Panel directly challenged the Nuremberg judgment case by arguing that the Krupp firm was not directly responsible for the use of slave labor. Because the Peck Panel had not discussed the evidence with Telford Taylor or other prosecutors of the original case, they found it easy to accept the representations of Krupp's defense counsel, and concluded that "Hitler ordered concentration camp inmates assigned to the [Krupp] concern . . . and that concentration camp inmates allocated to the concern were under the strict control of the Gestapo, and their food, billets and discipline beyond the jurisdiction of the firm."[10]

McCloy decided to reserve final judgment until he could consider the matter at greater length, but he left the meeting impressed by the arguments made in behalf of Krupp. He was more concerned about the Peck Panel's other recommendations, regarding the commutation of death sentences and the reduction of so many sentences involving men who had been concentration-camp guards or had otherwise participated in the Nazi killing machine. Over the next two and a half months, he meditated on various cases. Inevitably, word leaked that the high commissioner was weighing the merits of a general or partial clemency. When a German newspaper editor wrote him protesting the possibility, McCloy quickly responded, "Any clemency action I take will not come as the result of pressure from any organized campaign, Nazi or otherwise."[11]

But there was a campaign, and the political pressure brought to bear on McCloy was enormous. In mid-November, Adenauer wrote him asking for a "commutation of all death sentences" and the "widest possible clemency for persons sentenced to confinement."[12] Early in January 1951, a Munich organization calling itself the Christian Aid Committee inundated McCloy with letters and cables pleading for the commutation of all the Landsberg inmates. He received personal pleas from former German resistance figures such as Inge Scholl, whose own sister and brother were executed by the Nazis. Many of these pleas, like that of Kurt Schumacher, were based on a principled opposition to capital punishment, which had been outlawed under the German Constitution. A Bundestag delegation visited McCloy's office and bluntly told him that he should modify the death sentences, given the "political and psychological factors at a time when Western Germany was being called upon to make a military contribution to Western defense." McCloy bristled at this argument and told the German parliamentarians that, though he would make every effort to temper justice with mercy, "If our relations depend on these individual cases, then our friendship hangs on a thin thread indeed."[13] He said that the many petitions he had received had only "convinced him that the German people did not understand what the trials were about or what the defendants had done."[14] At one point that autumn, his mail began to contain occasional death threats against him and his family. He had to acknowledge that he faced "a well organized conspiracy to intimidate me."[15]

However much McCloy denied it, the campaign did influence him. Benjamin Ferencz, the only one of the Nuremberg prosecutors still working in Germany at the time, recalled that McCloy was in a "generous and kindly" frame of mind, and "anxious to make a gesture toward the Germans."[16] In mid-October, he commuted the five-year sentence of Baron Ernst von Weizsäcker, who as a Nazi Foreign Office official had been convicted of complicity in the deportation of some six thousand Jews from France to Poland in March 1942. Von Weizsäcker's aristocratic lineage and his résumé as a respected member of the old-guard German diplomatic establishment made him a popular candidate for clemency.[17] That there was no outcry against this individual act of clemency may explain why McCloy was so unprepared for the storm of controversy that would soon envelop him.[18]

Early in November 1950, he sent John Bross back to Washington to convey his tentative decision to carry out nine of the fifteen German death sentences. Acheson sat down with Truman on November 16 and explained McCloy's intentions. The president concurred that day, and Acheson quickly cabled McCloy that he had White House backing for whatever he did.[19] Ten weeks later, when McCloy made his decision public, he confirmed the death sentences of only five of those condemned.

Why had he changed his mind on four of the death sentences? German public opinion was an obvious answer. Politics was another. Adenauer's popularity in the opinion polls had fallen to 24 percent in late 1950, while support for the antirearmament SPD had risen to 40 percent. The SPD won local elections that November campaigning as the party of peace. McCloy cabled Washington that the situation "is not good and may be serious. . . . Adenauer's outright championship of the West has to be supported. We can see no one else who has taken a similar stand."[20] Rearmament of Germany was HICOG's number-one priority in that bleakest of Decembers, when it seemed for a moment that General MacArthur's forces might be pushed completely off the Korean peninsula. Adenauer was the only German leader willing to support German rearmament on American terms, and there was no better way to assist him politically than to do what was most popular on the clemency issue. On December 5, when Adenauer wrote McCloy a letter specifically urging clemency for Krupp,[21] the high commissioner replied, ". . . of the Krupp case I will give, I assure you, proper weight and attention to the comments and recommendations you make in your letter."[22]

For all these reasons, McCloy was inclined to accept the Peck Panel's recommendations on the Krupp case without delving too deeply into the Nuremberg record. Understandably, he was far more concerned with the death cases, and even went to Landsberg to talk personally with some of the inmates. "Some, particularly the generals, were arrogant; they deliberately turned their backs," he later told the historian William Manchester. "But others were quite decent. They walked right up and shook hands with me." He didn't ask to see the prison's most famous inmate, Alfried Krupp.[23]

After putting off Adenauer repeatedly, McCloy promised that he would announce his final clemency decisions shortly after the first of the year. Toward the end of January 1951, he closeted himself in his home for days, reading and rereading the Peck Report and the original Nuremberg judgments. Charlie Thayer, his political liaison in Bonn, later recalled, "His nerves got tauter and tauter, his temper shorter and shorter." Finally, he set himself a deadline, January 31, to announce his decisions. On the evening of January 30, a German Defense Office official showed up at Thayer's residence and pleaded that someone should make one last appeal to McCloy. If the death sentences were sustained, he said, the European Defense Community would never happen. Thayer called in Sam Reber, McCloy's political counselor, and the three men argued the issue for another hour. Twenty yards away, Thayer knew that McCloy was locked in his study, trying to come to a firm decision. The evening was growing late when two more Germans drove up; as they got out of their limousine, Thayer recognized Adenauer's advisers on defense matters, Generals Adolf Heusinger and Hans Speidel. They warned that, if the Landsberg prisoners were hanged, the prospect of "Germany as an armed ally against the East was an illusion." Speidel had a personal interest in the matter, since his brother General Wilhelm Speidel was one of the "red-striped" Landsberg convicts. Thayer and Reber argued with the Germans well past midnight, and finally, when Thayer's living room was strewn with copies of the Bible, Shakespeare, Milton, and other books the Germans were using to bolster their pleas for mercy, Reber agreed to go in and see McCloy. By this time, according to Reber, the high commissioner had already made his decision.

The next day, it was announced that five of the fifteen death sentences would be carried out, and that the sentences of sixty-four out of the remaining seventy-four war criminals had been reduced. Fully one-third of the Landsberg inmates would be released immediately, including Alfried Krupp and eight members of his board of directors who had been convicted with him. Thayer's friend from the German Defense Office called to say, "Your visitors of last night asked me to tell you that they think it's the best solution we could have hoped for under the circumstances."[24]

No other decision McCloy made in his years in Germany aroused greater furor than this mass clemency. Most Germans strongly approved the commutation of sentences and criticized the decision to hang five of the prisoners, all of whom had directly participated in mass murders. Adenauer himself called upon McCloy to reconsider the executions. But outside of Germany, the decisions were greeted with a mix of outrage and incredulity that only five years after the war such men could be freed. British and French newspapers harshly criticized McCloy, as did such old friends as Winston Churchill. The *Washington Post* published a Herblock cartoon depicting a smiling McCloy opening Krupp's cell door, while in the background Stalin snapped a propaganda photo. Telford Taylor was furious, and wrote a piece in *The Nation* calling the decision an act of "political expediency." Taylor argued that, "Wittingly or not, Mr. McCloy has dealt a blow to the principles of international law and concepts of humanity for which we fought the war." Taylor was incensed that he and the other Nuremberg prosecutors had not been consulted.[25]

Eleanor Roosevelt wrote McCloy to ask, "Why are we freeing so many Nazis?" Congressman Jacob Javits protested that the Krupp family's entire fortune should be forfeited for "misdeeds against humanity."[26]

McCloy's critics were right to characterize his decisions as a mass clemency. That's what it was, if only judged by the sheer numbers of war criminals released. But they overlooked the fact that it might have been worse. McCloy had actually been rather more severe in his sentencing than the Peck Panel. He accepted the panel's recommendations in fifty out of the ninety cases; but in twenty-four cases—most of them involving Einsatzgruppen veterans, SS concentration-camp guards, and doctors who had experimented on concentration-camp inmates—he imposed stiffer sentences than recommended by the Peck Panel. In another sixteen cases, he imposed less severe sentences than the clemency board proposed. Remarkably, he had rejected nearly half of the Peck Panel's recommendations. Such a dramatic discrepancy underscores the personal responsibility he assumed for the clemency decisions. Once he had appointed the Peck Panel, the easy thing to do would have been to leave the matter entirely in its hands. Instead, he had looked at each of the cases and made his own decisions. Now he would have to defend them.

He told Eleanor Roosevelt that the defendants hadn't had the opportunity for an appellate review of their cases, as would be normal in the American and British judicial systems. In fact, as McCloy well knew, General Clay's legal staff had conducted such a review and confirmed all but a handful of the sentences. Regarding Krupp, he had stated in his clemency announcement, "I can find no personal guilt in defendant Krupp, based upon the charges in the case, sufficient to distinguish him above all others sentenced in the Nuremberg Courts." Specifically, the confiscation of personal property was "repugnant to American concepts of justice."[27]

The Nuremberg judgments, of course, were reached not under precepts of American law, but under an amalgamation of international law, and expropriation was provided for in the proceedings. Other war criminals besides Krupp had their property confiscated.[28] Flick was not subjected to confiscation only because his holdings were in corporations traded on the public stock exchange. Confiscation in his case would have been a complicated affair, and injured the assets of other shareholders in his companies. This was not the case with Krupp, who was the sole proprietor of all Krupp enterprises.

McCloy told Javits, "I am inclined to think that the son [Alfried] took his [Gustav's] place in the dock largely because his father was on his death bed at the time."[29] For years afterward, McCloy advanced this explanation, telling interviewers, "We tried him reluctantly and the confiscation troubled me. I consulted my French and British colleagues, and they agreed with me. My feeling—it was a feeling—was that Alfried was a playboy, that he hadn't had much responsibility. I felt that he had expiated whatever he'd done by the time he'd already spent in jail. Oh, I don't doubt that he'd supported the Nazis early; he was a weakling."[30] In a private letter to a friend, he explained, "This man, you know, was not the real Krupp . . . but was a son who came into the board late in the war and exerted very little if any influence in the management of the company." He was also "doubtful" that Krupp was really guilty of the slave-labor charge.[31] But, then, he had not read the Nuremberg evidence against Krupp. Nor was it clear that Alfried had been tried for the crimes of his father. The Nuremberg prosecutors had intended to try both the father and the son from the very beginning.

McCloy's strongest justification for clemency in the Krupp case was that the industrialist's twelve-year sentence was "out of line with sentences for crimes of similar gravity" in other cases.[32] "When considered according to a standard of fairness," writes the Harvard-trained historian Thomas Schwartz, "McCloy's actions emerge as a reasonable attempt to temper justice with mercy in a series of difficult and complex cases."[33] McCloy used this argument in answering Eleanor Roosevelt: "After detailed study of this case, I could not convince myself that Alfred [sic] Krupp deserved the sentence imposed upon him."[34]

It was true, of course, that the Nuremberg trials issued a wide variety of sentences, even in roughly comparable cases. McCloy thought it only reasonable to revise these sentences according to some standard-of-fairness criteria. But this approach revealed a misunderstanding about what had happened at Nuremberg, where prosecutors like Telford Taylor were forced by constraints of time and practicality to make an example of only a small fraction of the Germans who could be tried for major war crimes. A relatively small group of men from certain categories—Nazi Party leaders, diplomats, the police and army, the party organizations, and big business—were carefully chosen as a representative indictment of the German state that had initiated war. Many more industrialists and business leaders, such as one of Hitler's personal bankers, Hermann Abs, could have been chosen for prosecution. Abs escaped the docket, according to some of the Nuremberg prosecutors, only for lack of time. As such, these were political trials, and there was nothing particularly fair in a judicious sense about who was chosen for prosecution. All these men were indictable, and many more could have been tried and convicted. Short of keeping the Nuremberg tribunals active for years on end, the interests of justice required judgment against a select few whose position and crimes were politically symbolic of the Nazi era. Krupp stood trial not only because he had approved the use and gross mistreatment of slave workers, but precisely because his name was Krupp. McCloy never accepted this salient fact, explaining to a friend, "I could see no reason to keep this man in jail merely because his name was Krupp."[35] Actually, not to have convicted a Krupp would have been an appalling omission, for one could not make a convincing example of the Nazi who ran death camps like Auschwitz without prosecuting at least several of the men of wealth, position, and influence in German society who directly profited from concentration-camp slave labor. Krupp bore a special responsibility, not only because he was guilty of using slave labor and plundering, but also because as a Krupp he was the most recognized symbol of all those German industrialists who aided Hitler. McCloy was correct to observe that Krupp had been singled out but, in many people's judgment, incorrect not to see the political justice of that act.

The Nuremberg proceedings were remarkably judicious, and, considering the crimes committed, many of those convicted got off with relatively lenient sentences. Krupp's could have been far more severe than twelve years in prison and forfeiture of all his property. His sentence was more severe than Friedrich Flick's seven-year term because at Nuremberg it was demonstrated that Krupp's use of slave labor was far more extensive than Flick's. But it was nevertheless true that some of those convicted of being accessories to mass murder received lighter sentences than Krupp. McCloy's well-intentioned attempt to second-guess the Nuremberg judges and somehow make the various sentences internally consistent inevitably led to a reduction of many sentences to some common denominator. This was particularly true of the cases involving industrialists.

He had a hard time equating the crimes of an Einsatzgruppen commander like Otto Ohlendorf, a man who admitted his personal responsibility for the death of upward of ninety thousand people, with the war profiteering of German businessmen.[36] Late in 1950, he observed that too often many of the "big Nazis" were receiving lighter fines and sentences from the German de-Nazification tribunals than "little Nazis." He explained this phenomenon to Washington by saying, "The 'big Nazi' referred to was sometimes a man of influence, possibly a devoted Nazi, who made large contributions to the party and urged his employees to join. But he may have been a benevolent employer, and one who never persecuted anyone. So when he came before his peers and neighbors who sat on the courts, these people had no grievance against him. . . . On the other hand, the 'little Nazi' . . . was assessed a heavier penalty. It was too much to expect these farmers, artisans and work-a-day people to reason that had it not been for the benevolent 'big Nazi' with his big contributions to the party, hoodlums and Gestapo could not have prospered."[37] Though he could understand the special culpability of the "big Nazis," when it came to a wealthy and politically well-connected man like Krupp, he suspended his good judgment.

It was bitterly cold at 9:00 A.M. on February 3, 1951, when the Landsberg Prison doors swung open and Alfried Krupp walked out. Behind him were twenty-eight other freed prisoners, including eight of his fellow Krupp directors.[38] The men were greeted by a bevy of foreign correspondents, German reporters, and cameramen ready to record the event. Now that he was once again the "sole proprietor," Krupp was a national celebrity. Jack Raymond of *The New York Times* cabled his editors that Alfried was "greeted like a returning hero. . . ." Later that morning, at Landsberg's finest hotel, while the press corps was kept at bay, Krupp hosted a breakfast for his fellow directors and friends. As a gesture of welcome, the hotel's owner uncorked two bottles of champagne, which naturally led the press to report that Krupp had had a "champagne breakfast." Alfried later recalled, "Two bottles for forty people—it didn't seem like too much. But Mr. McCloy was very annoyed." The subsequent press conference only made things worse. Alfried came across as cool, imperious, and unrepentant. "My life," he told reporters diffidently, "has always been determined by the course of history, not by me."[39]

Many Germans assumed the timing of McCloy's clemency decision was directly related to the Korean War. Fritz Ter Meer, the convicted I. G. Farben executive who was freed by McCloy in August 1950, drolly observed, "Now that they have Korea on their hands, the Americans are a lot more friendly."[40] McCloy sharply resented any such implications, telling William Manchester, "There's not a goddamn word of truth in the charge that Krupp's release was inspired by the outbreak of the Korean war. No lawyer told me what to do, and it wasn't political. It was a matter of my conscience." He could rightly point out that he had appointed the Peck Panel prior to the outbreak of the war. But people like Benjamin Ferencz, who admired McCloy and talked to him frankly, recall, "At the time there was a sense of panic about the Russians, a feeling that there was an urgent need for an understanding with the Germans. McCloy couldn't detach himself from that atmosphere."[41]

Domestic German political considerations certainly weighed heavily on McCloy's mind. By 1951, McCloy's priorities were the restoration of West German sovereignty, the building of a European Defense Force with German assistance, and the creation of a West European economic community centered on the sharing of the Ruhr's coal and steel industrial production. To these ends, he needed the cooperation of West Germany's business community. The Ruhr industrial heartland had to be revived, and quickly. McCloy himself acknowledged that he feared "a hell of a howl if I let the confiscation [of Krupp's property] go through."[42] By this time in his tenure as high commissioner, he was beginning to come under the influence of such prominent business leaders as Hermann Abs, the astute and powerful chairman of the Deutsche Bank, and one of the Krupp family's bankers.[43] Abs, Hans-Gunther Sohl, Kurt Birrenbach, and even his old friend Eric Warburg probably encouraged the high commissioner to release Krupp. When it happened, the restoration was greeted with universal acclaim among the Ruhr's business leaders. Baron von Lersner, of the Vereinigte Stahlwerke, wrote McCloy, "The liberation of Alfried Krupp has rejoiced our economic leaders."[44]

Krupp may have had his freedom, but the disposition of his property was still an open question. McCloy insisted that the Krupp industrial empire was still subject to HICOG's decartelization laws, and this meant the industrialist might be forced to sell off much of his steel and coal interests. Negotiations began in September 1951 and continued for a grueling eighteen months. Krupp just stalled for time, knowing that German sovereignty was soon to be restored. Meanwhile, no buyers stepped forward to make any offers on his Ruhr properties. The Ruhr barons and most of the German people regarded the Krupp concerns as something of a national trust and resented McCloy's efforts to see it dismantled. In the end, long after McCloy left Germany, Alfried signed a document pledging to segregate his heavy industry from his other holdings and to keep out of the armaments business. He had no intention of carrying out this pledge, and by 1953 a Krupp plant was actually assembling jet fighters in collaboration with an American firm. Krupp was back in business.

Krupp was only the most sensational of McCloy's clemency decisions in 1951. He also dramatically reduced the sentences of all the remaining convicted doctors who had experimented on concentration-camp inmates. One doctor was paroled immediately for time served, and the life sentences of five others were reduced to fifteen or twenty years. Freed also were four of the seven high-ranking Nazi judges who had administered Gestapo justice. Nearly half of those convicted in the concentration-camp case were paroled.

The most troubling clemency decisions, however, occurred in the Einsatzgruppen case. McCloy told his staff in early January 1951 that some of these men "have committed crimes that are historic in their magnitude and horror." He did not reveal that the Peck Panel had already recommended clemency in a large number of the cases, but the transcript of this meeting depicts a man struggling to reconcile himself with the unpleasant task at hand. "There are some, I am convinced," he said, "who, if they are not innocent—I wouldn't apply 'innocent' to these people—are not deserving of the death penalty, but there are some who, by reason of remoteness or protest, are, in my judgment, entitled to clemency. . . ."[45] He said he hadn't yet made his final decisions, but as he later explained to Judge Peck, he had discovered some "little new evidence that tended to indicate some clemency" in the case of one condemned man. "Having some doubt in my mind about him, there were three others that I felt uneasy about if I let him off."[46] What he meant was that evidence had been submitted by defense counsel claiming that some of these individuals had at some point attempted to evade orders to round up and kill Jews. This seems to have been an important factor in a few of his clemency decisions.[47] But it still does not explain why he found cause to reduce the sentences of most of those convicted in the Einsatzgruppen case. Two prisoners out of the twenty convicted were freed immediately; thirteen others had their sentences reduced.[48]

True, he confirmed the death sentences of five men who directly participated in mass killings. These included Einsatzgruppen leaders like Otto Ohlendorf and Paul Blobel, who was responsible for the Babi Yar massacre of thirty-three thousand Jews. Also slated for execution was Oswald Pohl, the chief administrator of the concentration camps, whom McCloy called a "slave driver on a scale probably never before equalled in history."[49] But it is still difficult to fathom how McCloy could make a distinction between someone like Pohl and any number of the Einsatzgruppen officers whom he decided to parole. Why execute Einsatzgruppen leaders like Blobel, and reprieve other members of the extermination squads? When the documentary record is explicit on this point, the distinctions he made were rather curious. For instance, in the case of an SS officer who confessed to having personally executed fifteen hundred Jews, McCloy reprieved the man because he had later refused to carry out any further murders.[50]

At Nuremberg and afterward, the Americans had always stressed the idea that individual German officers could and should have refused certain orders. In 1951, McCloy and other HICOG officials were still trying to convince the German public that "superior orders" was not a defense. The Peck Panel itself had been astonished and disappointed to learn "that the majority of the defendants still seem to feel that what they did was right, in that they were doing it under orders. This exaltation of orders is even more disturbing as an attitude than as a defense."[51] So, in a perverse sense, politics required the singling out for clemency of an SS officer who had, belatedly, resisted an "illegal" order. Forgotten, for the moment, was the enormity of the crime to which this individual had confessed. The Nuremberg judges used the fact that some officers had successfully refused "illegal" orders as evidence that all the defendants could have resisted such orders from the very beginning.[52] Evidence of resistance after the fact was no defense at Nuremberg. But now, in the wake of the clemency decisions, it seemed that any war criminal who gave evidence of having resisted such orders at any time could be rewarded with a reduction in his sentence.[53]

All of these clemency decisions are difficult to explain. For example, in the case of SS Lieutenant Heinz Hermann Schubert, the Peck Panel recommended that Schubert's death sentence be reduced to eight years. McCloy's legal aides suggested that this was "perhaps going too far," so he commuted the sentence to a full decade.[54] The only reason either McCloy or his clemency panel stated for such a sharp reduction was that Schubert was "a relative subordinate" and that "he did not know why the individuals were being executed."[55] Schubert, however, was one of only three officers to whom SS General Ohlendorf said he routinely assigned the task of supervising mass executions. Schubert's own signed confession and testimony at Nuremberg stated that he had personally supervised a "special action" at Simferopol in which seven or eight hundred people were machine-gunned to death. From October 1941 to June 1942, he served as Ohlendorf's adjutant, in which capacity he had full access to all the Einsatzgruppen chief's correspondence and other files. He freely admitted that he had carried out inspections of these "special actions" so as to ensure that they were carried out according to Ohlendorf's strict orders: "For a short time, when the people who were to be shot were already standing in their positions in the tank ditch, I supervised the actual shooting. . . . I know that it was of the greatest importance to Ohlendorf to have the persons who were to be shot killed in the most humane and military manner as possible because otherwise—in other methods of killing—the moral strain [*seelische Belastung*] would have been too great for the execution squad." No wonder many Americans found it difficult to fathom how the Peck Panel could have read of these things and then recommended clemency for such a man.

McCloy's clemency decisions contain little internal logic as to why one mass murderer was condemned to death and another given a commutation. It is clear, however, that the high commissioner was under intense political pressure from a broad spectrum of German society to commute as many sentences as possible. McCloy also found the prospect of placing his signature on a death warrant extremely distasteful. On the other hand, he was well aware that these men had committed unspeakable crimes and the judgments at Nuremberg should not be discredited by too sweeping a reduction of sentences. He attempted to construct a balanced clemency package, one that could be seen as a reasonable compromise by most Germans and the makers of public opinion in the West. In this he failed, for the Germans generally thought he had not been lenient enough, and the rest of the world saw his action as one of mass clemency dictated by simple political expediency.

McCloy believed otherwise, telling his critics that he had acted strictly on the basis of his own conscience. His liaison in the State Department, Henry Byroade, acknowledged on Capitol Hill that "it appeared that we were trying to buy the Germans. I must tell you that I have never seen anything hurt anybody so much, because this was a question of McCloy before God."[56] McCloy would always remember how he had agonized over individual cases; he told his staff that he was "becoming an expert on the Landsberg cases."[57] But he actually had neither the facts nor the time to review the evidence accumulated at Nuremberg over a period of many months. Compared with the reviews conducted by Clay's lawyers—who typically wrote fifty pages on each individual case—McCloy's clemency-panel reviews were skimpy and incomplete, amounting to a few paragraphs each.[58]

He failed to understand—or had forgotten—that one of the fundamental purposes at Nuremberg had been to make an example of only a few of the thousands of war criminals who could have been convicted. By freeing Alfried Krupp and his fellow directors, he discredited the whole notion that German industrialists shared in the responsibility for what had happened during the Holocaust. Tampering with the individual sentences handed out to Einsatzgruppen killers allowed many Germans to harbor doubts about the truth of all the Nuremberg judgments.

HICOG's public-opinion surveys demonstrated that for most Germans the clemency confirmed their suspicion that the Nuremberg judgments had been "victor's justice."[59] McCloy had not meant to do it, but the Landsberg clemency decision discredited the unique international judicial process that he himself had helped to create back in 1945.

Throughout the spring of 1951, McCloy became increasingly disturbed by the tenor of the German reaction to his clemency package. While, outside Germany, McCloy was attacked for being too soft, inside Germany he was deluged with appeals to commute the remaining death sentences. More than a thousand letters arrived at HICOG headquarters complaining that he had not been lenient enough; McCloy was shocked at the fanatical nationalist tenor of many of these letters. He was also disturbed that, for a solid month after the clemency decisions were announced, neither Adenauer nor any other major German politician came to his defense.[60]

The nature of the appeals, even when they came from prominent German church and civic leaders, demonstrated that the German people still had no understanding of the crimes committed by the Third Reich. McCloy wrote the archbishop of Cologne, who had made an appeal for Oswald Pohl's life, "It has been a source of great concern to me that many of the leaders of German thought . . . instead of recognizing the enormity of the conduct of the condemned war criminals and the justice of their punishment, rather manifested a tendency to put my words and those of my officials under a microscope for the purpose of detecting flaws which, whether they be genuine or unsubstantial, have nothing to do with the main issues involved in these cases." He protested that, if anything, he had erred on the side of "leniency, and not of severity."[61]

And yet, repeatedly that spring, he was forced to reconsider his decisions. Once he stayed up until 2:00 A.M. studying yet another appeal from a German law student in behalf of SS Brigadier Erich Naumann, who had been condemned to death for commanding an extermination squad on the Russian front. But his mind was made up, and the more he studied the documents, the more certain he was that the five men he had condemned to death should hang. He told Naumann's benefactor, "I hope you will one day take the time to read the records in these cases so that you can judge for yourself the extent of the murders which these 'Einsatzgruppen' committed. Conservatively estimated they were engaged in the business of slaughtering seven to ten thousand people a day and Naumann was the head of one of the big four organizations which did this horrible work. It is hard for the imagination to grasp it but it actually took place and every objective German should one day realize this and convince himself of it. I say this not for the purpose of fixing guilt, but in the hope that the average German may see it as a phenomenon which did, at one time, afflict his country and which must in the future be recognized and avoided."[62]

Such appeals to good sense fell on deaf ears, for it was apparent that Germans across the political spectrum were opposed to having the death sentences carried out. The hangings had been postponed several times that spring, because of last-minute appeals to the U.S. Supreme Court, and members of the local contingent of foreign correspondents could see that McCloy was anxious to put the whole business behind him. Drew Middleton of *The New York Times* pointed out to his readers that no American official had come to Germany with a "more sincere desire to help the Germans gain a position of trust and responsibility in Europe than did Mr. McCloy. . . ." And yet, Middleton reported, "Now he is the target for such vilification and abuse as no other American official in Germany has received during the occupation. He has striven not to become embittered and it will be interesting to see how long he can maintain his calm under abuse. . . . If this is the way the Germans treat their friends, it is not surprising they have so many enemies."[63]

Felix Frankfurter no doubt read Middleton's dispatch, and even though his court was then considering some of the appeals from the death sentences, the justice wrote his old friend a note of reassurance: "I am sure that the decisions you reached you reached on the basis of those relevant considerations of conscience. . . . Happily you have not only the wisdom to understand that one must find serenity in the consciousness of one's own duty done, but also the self-discipline to wrest that serenity from deflecting influences no matter how irritating or distorting."[64] Finally, on

June 6, 1951, after all the appeals had been rejected, the five men sentenced to death—in addition to two others, condemned in a separate review by General Handy—were hanged. After it was all over, McCloy wrote Frankfurter, thanking him for the court's expeditious dismissal of the final appeals: "It might have become almost farcical if action had not been taken when it was. It was a most unpleasant ordeal, but in connection with it I think I experienced some human reactions that had never come my way before."[65]

The whole business had been a distasteful experience which taxed his conscience and characteristic equanimity. But afterward, he never expressed any regrets. When William Manchester confronted him with a set of excerpts from the Nuremberg transcripts that tended to contradict everything he had said about the Krupp case, he looked at the material and commented, "That's ancient history."[66] For him, what was important was the task at hand, the creation of a democratic West German state aligned with the West. The Nazis belonged to history. Nuremberg was necessary to establish a modicum of symbolic justice, but he lacked any feelings of vengeance for those who had perpetrated the crimes. This attitude extended even to the highest-ranking Nazis still imprisoned in the four-power prison in Spandau. After visiting Spandau in January 1951, he told the British and French high commissioners that he thought a review of those cases was warranted. This did not happen only because the Soviets refused to consider any clemency for men like Rudolf Hess and Albert Speer.

As McCloy was leaving Germany, an incident occurred that in retrospect illustrates both his basic good intentions and his naïveté. He had established a program whereby German adolescents were given the opportunity to spend a year living in the United States. In the summer of 1952, he heard that Albert Speer's sixteen-year-old daughter, Hilde, had been barred from enrolling in the program because of her father's conviction as a war criminal. McCloy thought this visitation of the father's sins upon the daughter misplaced, so he raised the matter with Dean Acheson, who quickly overruled U.S. immigration authorities. In the meantime, McCloy arranged for young Hilde to spend her year in Hastings-on-Hudson, where she stayed with a neighbor of his in-laws. One day that year, McCloy invited Hilde Speer for tea at the Zinsser household and had a frank but easygoing discussion with the teenager about her father. The conversation left a strong impression on the child; shortly afterward, she wrote a letter to her father in which she referred to her visit with the former high commissioner and asked some heartfelt questions: "What I cannot understand is how these educated people did not turn against him [Hitler] when he began persecuting the Jews. . . . I know that at the end you were no longer in agreement with him. But what I do not understand is why you did not break with him in 1940."

Albert Speer wrote back to his daughter an equally frank letter, explaining, "The fault is mine and expiation there must be. . . . I am one of the few taking the view today that the Nuremberg trial, despite its defects, was necessary." But, oddly enough, McCloy as early as 1951 thought Speer, comparatively speaking, as much entitled to clemency as any of the other men he had freed. Later in the 1950s, he wrote Speer's wife, "I have a very strong conviction that your husband should be released and would be very happy if I could do anything to expedite such release."[67]

Speer served out his sentence, as he rightly should have, for of all the high-ranking Nazi leaders convicted at Nuremberg none had more responsibility and effective power than the minister of armaments. Like many people, McCloy had been impressed by Speer's contrition at Nuremberg. Alone among all those indicted, Speer had openly acknowledged his ultimate responsibility for everything that had happened under the Third Reich, though in the same breath he had carefully made it clear that he had never had specific knowledge of the systematic killings in the concentration camps. He was a murderer, he said, but one who had known nothing about the deaths of his victims. Speer preserved this stance through several best-selling books after his release from Spandau, but historians who have plumbed the Third Reich's archives know that this was a myth.[68] As armaments minister, Speer was as knowledgeable about the concentration camps as some of the men whom McCloy executed. McCloy's "strong conviction" that Speer deserved clemency can be explained only by his ignorance of the record and his characteristic sympathy with a man who otherwise seemed to be well bred, highly educated, and sensible. After he had spent less than two years as high commissioner, his hard-nosed attitude toward the Nazis had mellowed. Only six years after the war, these men and their singular crimes were truly ancient history.

CHAPTER 19

Negotiating an End to Occupation

"Our [decision-makers] . . . were unwilling to contemplate at any time within the foreseeable future, under any conceivable agreement with the Russians, the withdrawal of United States forces from Germany. . . . Our stand meant in effect no agreement with Russia at all and the indefinite continuance of the split of Germany and Europe."

GEORGE KENNAN, 1952

The clemency decisions left McCloy tired and emotionally drained. After two years as Germany's "proconsul," he was hoping that he could soon return to private life. But it was Dean Acheson's intention to "hang onto McCloy's coattails in Bonn" until the occupation could be formally liquidated.[1] This would be complicated, because one couldn't negotiate a formal peace treaty: that would require Soviet compliance, and presumably the unification of Germany. So, instead, Washington decided to enter into a "contractual agreement" with Adenauer's government that would restore German sovereignty in the three Western Allied occupation zones in all but four issues: the protection of Allied troops stationed in West Germany, Berlin, the question of unification, and any future overall peace settlement. Talks commenced in May 1951, and by September the broad outlines of such a contract had been agreed upon.

The negotiations then hit a snag on several delicate matters involving German rearmament and the future rights of the Allies to intervene in the event that West Germany became a totalitarian state. The French were most reluctant to see Germany rearmed and worried about relinquishing too many Allied prerogatives too early. And though it was

McCloy's job to hammer out a compromise that might assuage French fears without offending German pride, personally he found it difficult to shed his own deep-seated prejudices regarding the threat of German nationalism. The talks were often filled with acrimony. On one occasion, François Poncet flatly announced that the "essential principle" governing the relationship between the Allies and Germany—the fact of the 1945 unconditional surrender—could not be changed. Incensed, Adenauer retorted that this did not give the Allies "the right to keep such a country occupied for an indefinite period." To Adenauer's surprise, McCloy took the side of the Frenchman in this argument and reminded him that the Germans had repudiated treaties in the past and that the American stake in the "middle of Europe is an extremely important one. We're not going to play around with that until we're sure where we stand."[2] He assured the angered chancellor that the Allies intended to end the occupation someday, but it would not happen without mutual trust and long-term guarantees. Never again, he argued, could the Germans wage war against France, and that meant that, before full sovereignty could be restored to the Bonn government, the Allies had to be sure that West Germany was firmly wedded to the Western alliance.

He turned the same argument against the French position, and tried to persuade the French that concessions had to be made in order to nudge the Germans into a permanent West European union. In Paris that September, he told Monnet and a roomful of French officials that "Germany would in all probability be armed in some form in the near future in any event, but whether armed or not she would constitute a real danger if she did not wholeheartedly align herself with the West. . . ." In almost apocalyptic terms, he warned, "There were those among the Germans who felt that Germany might have one more bid for power left in her. Many of these took now the feeling that Germany's role should be one of balance between the forces of the East and the West. Joined with the East or with the threat of going to the East, she could exhibit tremendous pressures on France." He concluded that "this was a very solemn moment and no time for France to equivocate or draw back in respect to Germany. If constructive steps were not taken immediately, I could foresee the loss of our whole position in Western Europe, the re-creation of a really dangerous Germany, and the fundamental success of Soviet policy and influence in Western Europe."[3]

This line of reasoning rather unsettled the French. They were being asked to believe that, in order to keep Germany divided, with its Western portion firmly aligned to the Atlantic alliance, Adenauer should be allowed to rearm. But the French were far more skeptical than McCloy that Germany could be kept divided in the long run. The division was unnatural, and might only become a source of tension in the future. Far better, thought the French government, would be a resumption of serious four-power talks to settle once and for all the fate of Germany. And if the Soviets would not negotiate a permanent solution of the German problem, the last thing the French wanted to see was a rearmed West Germany. The Pleven Plan for a European Defense Force was still on the table, but the French refused to consider the possibility that German contingents for such a force might be mustered before the European army was firmly established. Adenauer's position, of course, was that Germany would not participate in a European army other than on an equal basis with the French. On this contentious point, the contractual talks floundered throughout the autumn of 1951.

McCloy became increasingly impatient, and began stepping up the pressure on both parties. Acheson bluntly told French Foreign Minister Robert Schuman that, without a German army, Washington's aid to France would dry up.[4] In November, McCloy publicly announced that the time had come to allow the Germans to become equal armed partners in a united Europe. He called upon Europeans to abandon what he called their "nationalism and cynicism."[5] In December, he told a gathering of German politicians that West Europeans must unite or perish.[6]

West European unity in this context was actually a metaphor for the more or less permanent division of Germany. McCloy and Adenauer might on occasion pay lip service to the idea of reunification, but both men felt that it should only happen if East Germany were someday integrated into the Western alliance. Adenauer's political opponents in Germany recognized this all too well. As the contractual negotiations proceeded, Schumacher denounced in ever more bitter terms what he regarded as the betrayal of German interests in the East. In his view, the rearming of West Germany—and the contractual agreements—were "merely a cover for the perpetuation" of Germany's occupied status.[7] Schumacher's attitude infuriated McCloy, who had given up any hope of influencing the iconoclastic SPD leader. Adenauer told him, "Schumacher [is] crazy; you either get married or you don't."[8]

One did not have to be a military expert to conclude that the purpose of rearming West Germany was to keep the country divided. A rearmed West Germany certainly offered no credible defense against the Soviet Union's now vastly superior conventional forces. Adenauer's military advisers knew the Soviets were stronger in 1952 than during the war, when two hundred German divisions had failed to stem the Soviet assaults.[9] The proposed creation of ten German divisions as the heart of a European army could at most pose a symbolic deterrence to a Soviet invasion. In reality, as McCloy and most U.S. intelligence estimates concluded, the Soviets had no intention of starting a land war, and if they did, the only real deterrent was the American nuclear arsenal. Rearmament for Adenauer was the path to West German sovereignty, just as for McCloy it was a means of keeping Germany divided and well outside the dangerous shoals of neutralism. So

Schumacher was not far wrong to suggest that rearmament would merely mean a continued occupation—or, in Adenauer's terms, a "marriage" of American and West German interests. Repeatedly during the contractual negotiations, McCloy made it clear that he was willing to make all sorts of concessions as long as Washington retained iron-clad guarantees that Allied troops would remain in West Germany and that the country would commit itself to the Western alliance. If this amounted to a permanent occupation, so be it. What was important, McCloy believed, was that it be done with the enthusiastic support of most West Germans.

This could be made palatable to both the Germans and the French only if rearmament occurred within the context of a Western Europe moving in the direction of federation. So it was that McCloy, Acheson, and other American spokesmen in these years repeatedly emphasized European unity. McCloy was greatly heartened when, in early 1952, the Bundestag voted overwhelmingly to approve the Schuman Plan. He called it "an important date in the history of the new Europe."[10] The Schuman Plan's provisions for sharing various coal and steel resources laid the foundation for what later became the Common Market and the European Economic Community. But these institutions were a long time coming, and in the near term, McCloy was soon disappointed that the Schuman Plan did not lead to more immediate steps toward a United States of Europe. Nor did it accelerate French acceptance of a European Defense Force.

German rearmament was certainly the most contentious issue under negotiation. But emotions flared as well on the delicate matter of whether the Allies would retain any rights to intervene in West Germany's internal affairs in the "case of a dangerous threat to German democracy."[11] On this issue, just as he had on the question of rearmament, McCloy took a rather hard-line anti-German view. Just as Germany could not be allowed to rearm except within the context of a European Defense Force, neither could it be trusted to guarantee its own democratic form of government. Whereas Henry Byroade and the State Department favored a more or less unqualified restoration of German sovereignty, McCloy insisted that the contractual agreements contain some kind of "Monroe doctrine for democracy" that would allow the Allies to intervene against any totalitarian trends in German society. Publicly he might be willing to defend the Germans and praise their growing democratic instincts. But privately he still had serious doubts. Speaking with all the moral force at his command, he expressed to a gathering of the high commissioners his "deep anxiety lest the tender plant of German democracy, whose roots were not yet deeply set, might wither and die if Allied support, present since 1945, were now withdrawn."[12]

In September, he and Byroade separately wrote Acheson letters laying out their arguments. McCloy warned that Germany could still take a totalitarian path if Adenauer were to leave the scene or the economy took a turn for the worse. He begged Acheson to consider an Allied guarantee of German democracy. It was "supremely important." Byroade in turn argued that such a provision constituted such a "serious infringement of Germany sovereignty" that it might actually stimulate nationalist forces.[13] In the end, McCloy won this argument, partly thanks to the support of the British and French. Article five of the final contractual agreement restoring German sovereignty reserved for the Allies the right to proclaim a state of emergency if confronted with a "subversion of the liberal democratic order."[14]

By early 1952, McCloy could point to agreement on a broad range of issues. But the negotiations seemed to drag on interminably, with disputes cropping up over such issues as how to share the cost of Allied troops stationed in Germany, and whether the French should continue trying various German war criminals. In January, McCloy went on a skiing vacation and came back with a broken ankle; while convalescing, he wrote Frankfurter to complain that "things are at sixes and sevens again and I am almost depressed."[15] He began to think seriously once again of leaving Germany and returning to private life.

Then, in March 1952, the Soviets launched a "peace offensive" that threatened to derail all of McCloy's efforts. Stalin called for the resumption of four-power talks to negotiate a final peace treaty for Germany. The Soviet leader endorsed the reunification of Germany based on free elections and the withdrawal of all foreign troops no later than one year after the signing of a peace treaty. Moreover, to the surprise of many in Washington, he said Germany should be allowed to establish its own army, as long as the country did not enter into a military pact with any of its former enemies. Democratic rights would be guaranteed for all Germans, including all former German soldiers and Nazis. Stalin obviously had calculated that such a package might so regalvanize neutralist sentiments within Germany that the United States would be forced to postpone the integration of West Germany into the American military alliance.

The Soviet proposal immediately won widespread support among many Germans, particularly among SPD voters. Polls indicated that a majority of all Germans favored at least a postponement of the contractual negotiations in order to explore the Soviet offer. Even Adenauer's own minister for all-German affairs, Jakob Kaiser, urged a favorable response, particularly after the East German regime announced its acceptance of Bonn's proposal for an all-German electoral law as a basis for discussions.[16] McCloy was so dismayed by these developments that he wrote Acheson, volunteering this time to stay on in his post a while longer: ". . . since there is so much need for keeping the pressure on the contractuals and the financial arrangements, I feel I should not come home. . . . The Soviets are playing their heaviest cards as one expected they would do to deflect our policy of European integration. . . ."[17]

A neutral, reunified, and rearmed Germany was "unthinkable" for McCloy. But even he recognized that to reject Stalin's offer out of hand would be a diplomatic and public-relations disaster. So, in what later became known as the "battle of the notes," the Allies desperately tried to make the Soviet initiative appear to be less than reasonable. They suggested that before any all-German elections could be held, the United Nations should be allowed to inspect the conditions for free elections inside East Germany. They also demanded that the reunified German state should be freely allowed to join any political or military alliance. To no one's surprise, both points were brusquely rejected by the Soviets, and over the next few months the peace initiative died.[18]

Historians have since learned that the Allied assessment of Soviet intentions was anything but uniform. Some British and French officials believed Stalin's proposal was more than a propaganda stunt. Many Germans still believe a unique opportunity to achieve unification was lost in 1952. A unified, neutral Germany would have left NATO stillborn, an empty shell of a military alliance. Likewise, without East Germany, the Warsaw Pact would not have been the same. Unless one believed the Soviets were prepared to risk nuclear war by invading Western Europe, the European continent would have evolved alternative security arrangements, less dependent on the two nuclear superpowers. The Cold War might have taken quite a different trajectory.

But at the time, McCloy and his peers were unwilling to gamble on the uncertainties of a neutral Europe. Certainly, they feared such a Europe might drift toward communism. But an even greater fear was the prospect of a unified Germany, unfettered by any outside constraints, once again dominating Europe. Better to keep Europe divided into separate military pacts, and shoulder the risks of a Cold War with the Soviets, than to live with a unified Germany. George Kennan noted in his diary that autumn, "Our [decision-makers] were basing their entire hopes on the ratification of the German contractuals and the European Defense Community, and they were unwilling to contemplate at any time within the foreseeable future, under any conceivable agreement with the Russians, the withdrawal of United States forces from Germany. . . . Our stand meant in effect no agreement with Russia at all and the indefinite continuance of the split of Germany and Europe."[19] McCloy, Acheson, and most other American policy-makers disagreed with Kennan, who had left the State Department in 1949 precisely because his views on the German question were being ignored. In retrospect, McCloy remained certain he had done the right thing: "We made unthinkable another

European civil war. We ended one of history's longest threats to peace."[20] If the Germany that had waged two world wars was ever again to be unified, it should not happen for many, many years. And in the meantime, he believed, nothing should stand in the way of integrating the Western portion of Germany into the American-financed Atlantic alliance.

Working in close collaboration with Adenauer, McCloy now stepped up the pace of the contractual negotiations, promising Washington that the treaties could be signed in late May. In order to meet this deadline, he forced the negotiators to keep a grueling schedule. He and the elderly chancellor wore down their argumentative British and French colleagues by sheer physical stamina.[21] Some all-day sessions stretched on until five-thirty in the morning, and then resumed again at ten o'clock. The British high commissioner claimed he had never suffered so "punishing an ordeal."[22]

With the full knowledge that Washington was insistent on concluding the treaties as quickly as possible, Adenauer skillfully took advantage of the situation to extract further concessions from the high commissioners. At one point, when the chancellor raised yet another minor objection, McCloy looked up from reading the draft treaty and muttered, "Oh, all right, that's concession Number 122 so far."[23] Most of the time, Adenauer found the American high commissioner to be a sympathetic partner.[24]

When Adenauer tried, however, to use the contractual negotiations to get a better deal in his bargaining with representatives of world Jewry over reparations, McCloy balked. Earlier, Adenauer had appointed two German intellectuals with impeccable anti-Nazi credentials as his negotiators with the Jews. In preliminary talks, these men had agreed in principle to start negotiations on the basis of Israel's claim of 3 billion German marks. Adenauer had told them and the World Jewish Congress's Nahum Goldmann that German reparations to world Jewry were a matter of morality. But then, in mid-May, he began to modify the money issue, apparently on the advice of his financial adviser, Hermann Abs, the financier who had narrowly escaped prosecution at Nuremberg for war crimes. On May 19, 1952—only days before the scheduled signing of the contractual agreement—Abs informed the Israelis that Germany could now only afford to ship 100 million marks' worth of goods in the following year. Nor could he commit Germany to a total amount in coming years; this, Abs said, would depend the level of American aid to Germany. The Israelis declared this offer to be "entirely inadequate" and broke off negotiations. At this point, Adenauer's own negotiators denounced Abs and handed in their resignations, telling the press, "The issue here . . . is our debt of honour to the Jews." Simultaneously, Goldmann wrote a letter to Adenauer protesting the German position, and forwarded a copy to McCloy.

The high commissioner stepped in behind the scenes and made it clear that Abs's position was unacceptable. Within forty-eight hours, McCloy was on the phone to Goldmann in Paris with the news that he could expect to hear "some important news within the next few hours." True to his word, in several hours a German Foreign Ministry official called Goldmann to say that an emissary was on his way to Paris. On the following day, the Germans agreed to the 3-billion-mark figure. Goldmann forever felt indebted to McCloy.[25]

On that same day in Bonn—May 23, 1952—Acheson arrived for the signing of the contractual treaties and was immediately briefed at McCloy's office in Bad Godesberg. Even at this late date, the French were dragging their feet, demanding additional guarantees against the possibility that Germany might again one day pose a threat to European peace. In addition, they wished to tone down some language in the treaties that might preclude negotiating a deal with the Soviets for a comprehensive German peace treaty at a later date. Acheson, McCloy, and Adenauer once again adopted the tactic of all-night negotiating sessions, so tiring French Foreign Minister Robert Schuman that he kept dozing off. More concessions were made, including a pledge that the United States would help France finance her military operations in Indochina.[26] Finally, on Monday morning, May 26, 1952, a signing ceremony was held in the German senate chamber. Afterward, Acheson announced, "On behalf of the President of the United States and the American people, I welcome the Federal Republic on its return to the community of nations."[27]

This was an exaggeration, for Germany was not quite a sovereign nation again. The Allies still reserved the right to intervene in German internal political affairs in the event of an emergency. And they retained their powers in Berlin and certain contractual rights to deal with the issue of reunification and the security of their troops in Germany. There was also a clause on the deconcentration of German industry and banking which was distinctly unpopular. Most Germans, in fact, thought the contractual treaty was nothing to celebrate, and many took to the streets to demonstrate against the whole event. Schumacher, whose health had so deteriorated that he was confined to his bed, issued a public statement condemning the "McCloy-Adenauer coalition" and suggested that "whoever approves the General Treaty ceases to be a German."[28] A member of Adenauer's own coalition government privately told McCloy that he would "rather see Russians march in than assist voluntarily in reducing [the] Federal Republic to [the] status of [a] puppet."[29]

McCloy discounted such criticism and regarded the treaties as a fitting cap to his tenure as high commissioner. A twenty-nine-year-old Harvard scholar named Henry Kissinger disagreed. Building on his experience in occupied Germany with U.S. Army counterintelligence, Kissinger in 1952 had gotten himself hired as a consultant to the president's Psychological Strategy Board, a new, rather shadowy executive agency that was supposed to help coordinate covert intelligence with sophisticated propaganda programs. He happened to be visiting Germany the week the contractual treaty was signed, and wrote a report highly critical of the treaties and McCloy's administration. He believed McCloy had concentrated on the "framework of legal relationships and neglected the psychological climate which would make these relationships effective." He observed that German reaction to the contractual treaty could best be summed up as "hysterical." The signing ceremony itself, he reported, had led to an "outburst of anti-American feeling. . . ." The high commissioner's timing had been all wrong; the United States should not have rejected the Soviet offer to have a four-power conference on Germany, and the treaty should have been "advertised as a last resort, not as the beginning of a new era in European policies." Instead, the way it was done allowed the Soviets to shift "the onus for the division of Germany on the U.S." Neutralist sentiment was spreading so rapidly that a "reverse Titoism is by no means impossible. . . ." A new approach was needed, Kissinger warned, "lest Germany be swallowed up by the Soviet orbit." The United States should appear as the "advocate" of, not the barrier to, German unification.[30]

Kissinger's report was a pretty fair reflection of the opinions he had heard from a broad range of German academics, newspaper editors, and other intellectuals. What he was saying—that the contractual treaty was likely to perpetuate the division of Germany—was apparent to everyone. Many Germans did not believe that Washington could keep Germany divided for long without precipitating a war. The division was too artificial to last. McCloy's critics, however, failed to understand that he was well aware of the historical forces behind German unification. He sought quite consciously what one diplomatic historian, Wolfram F. Hanrieder, has called a "reversal of truly historic proportions."[31] It was his and Adenauer's gamble that they could—with a combination of economic incentives and a strong American military presence—force the postponement of any reunification for a generation or two, time enough perhaps to win the "struggle for the soul of Faust" and create a new Germany.[32] They could not, of course, reveal their intentions in this matter; on the contrary, both McCloy and Adenauer so often felt compelled to proclaim their support for unification that the public rationale for the foreign policy they actually pursued seemed transparently contradictory. This at various times gave rise to a credibility gap with the German public.

Early in June, McCloy made a short visit to the United States to promote the German treaties. In his only public appearance, he spoke before a Philadelphia audience gathered in a meeting hall named after one of his mother's old hairdressing clients, John Wanamaker. "A democratic system of government," he proclaimed, "is now thoroughly developing in Germany and the people of Europe are coming together in building a new order in their own defense." In Washington he successfully lobbied the Senate for early ratification of the contractual treaty, saying there was one threat to the emergence of a peaceful and progressive Germany, and that it came from the Kremlin. "The Communists," he warned, "are now engaged in a mighty campaign to prevent German ratification of the agreements. . . ."[33] He called the treaty "solid proof of our desire for a peaceful alliance" with the new West German state.[34] It was precisely this kind of talk that worried the French, who now began to feel that they had been bludgeoned into accepting both the contractual agreements and the treaty for a European Defense Community (EDC), which had been signed the following day in Paris. From the perspective of most Frenchmen, all the Americans seemed to care about was the rearmament of Germany, and it worried them that the Germans were already predicting that they would have five hundred thousand men under arms by 1954.[35] General Charles de Gaulle bluntly told *The New York Times'* correspondent C. L. Sulzberger that the EDC was just plain "idiocy." He predicted it would never pass muster in the French Parliament: "I will do everything against it. I will work with the Communists to block it. I will make a revolution against it. I would rather go with the Russians to stop it."[36]

For two years, the French sulked, and then, in May 1954, they fulfilled de Gaulle's prediction and refused to ratify the EDC. The idea of an integrated European army was a dead letter, and with it any prospect for an early political union of Western Europe rapidly faded. Instead, in 1955 Washington negotiated West Germany's admittance to NATO, at which time the Bonn government became unconditionally sovereign in its internal affairs. To the unease of many Europeans, Germany began to muster its own national army. In his haste to negotiate the contractual agreements, McCloy had settled for a cosmetic arrangement that quickly fell apart. He had failed. But by the time this failure had become apparent, it really didn't matter. The Cold War had resumed its trajectory, and the possibility of a four-power negotiation of the "German problem" had once again receded. Instead, an increasingly vibrant and economically strong West German state was taking its place in the Atlantic alliance. This had been his major goal all along.

After three years in Germany, the high-commission era ended. "We are closing out this great adventure," McCloy told a gathering of his senior officers, "which has involved so much American wealth and so much American energy."[37] Shortly afterward, on a warm day in July 1952, he, Ellen, and their two children—who now both spoke fluent German—

boarded the passenger ship *America* and sailed out of Bremerhaven harbor into the North Sea. Upon their arrival in New York eight days later, reporters asked him his views on the 1952 presidential campaign. He replied simply that he was a registered Republican and "well-disposed" to the candidacy of Dwight D. Eisenhower. This was an understatement: he had been encouraging Ike to run for office for some time. They had resumed their friendship while Eisenhower was stationed in Europe as supreme commander of NATO, and McCloy was well aware that some of Ike's closest New York friends, such as Lucius Clay, Maurice "Tex" Moore, and George Whitney, had begun to lay the groundwork for a presidential campaign as early as the summer of 1951. And though he did not now take any public position in the Eisenhower campaign, privately he continued to advise the Republican nominee on foreign-policy issues and helped draft at least one major speech for the candidate.[38]

He had left Germany with the intention of returning either to the law or to some position in private industry. With the brief exception of his year at Milbank, Tweed in 1946, he had been supporting his family—which still included his mother and two aunts—on a government salary since 1940. At the age of fifty-seven, he now felt a pressing need to make some money once again. He just wasn't sure how he wanted to do it, and whether he could find something that would still allow him to sustain his interest in foreign affairs. After a month-long vacation with Ellen and the children, he took on a short-term consulting project with the Ford Foundation. They wanted him to chair a task-force study on the problems of world peace. This suitably lofty subject would allow him to take stock of his opportunities for a few months. At the back of his mind, however, lay one immodest thought. He knew Ike respected and felt comfortable with him, and if his old friend won the election in November, it was possible that he might be nominated for the one job in government he still coveted, secretary of state.

When Eisenhower won the election by a large margin, there was speculation in the press almost immediately that McCloy would become Acheson's replacement. But there was another candidate for the job to whom the Republican Party felt obligated, John Foster Dulles. And though Ike did not know him well, it was assumed by many in the campaign that Dulles was the top candidate. When Eisenhower reportedly said he preferred McCloy as his secretary of state, he was given all sorts of reasons why McCloy was politically unsuitable. His aides explained that the Taft wing of the party thought McCloy too closely identified with "international bankers" and "Roosevelt New Dealers." He was, after all, a good friend of "red" Dean Acheson and had worked at the highest levels for both the Truman and Roosevelt administrations. And though a Republican, they argued, McCloy was too well connected to the liberal East Coast Establishment. Finally, it was whispered, Republican business interests out west regarded McCloy as a Rockefeller man. Hadn't he worked as a director of the Rockefeller Foundation, and wasn't he associated with the Rockefeller law firm? "Every Republican candidate for President since 1936," Taft had complained when he lost the nomination to Eisenhower, "has been nominated by the Chase Bank."[39] One could not reach out to Taft Republicans and simultaneously appoint to high office a staunch internationalist like McCloy. If Dulles had much the same background, at least he was a conservative Republican who hadn't associated himself with the New Deal.

Despite these arguments, Eisenhower waited three weeks before making a decision. And then, according to one account, he reluctantly agreed to anoint Dulles, but suggested that McCloy should become undersecretary of state with the understanding that Dulles would become a White House adviser after a year, paving the way for McCloy to take charge of the State Department. According to C. D. Jackson, who was about to become Ike's "special assistant for psychological warfare" in the White House, Dulles accepted the proposal and then asked the president-elect if McCloy had been approached. Eisenhower said no, and suggested that Dulles put the proposition to him. Accordingly, Dulles phoned him for an appointment. McCloy later recalled the curious circumstances of the meeting.

Instead of explaining Ike's proposal, Dulles asked him what he thought of certain men as candidates for the job of undersecretary of state. At the top of the list was Lew Douglas, and naturally McCloy enthusiastically endorsed his brother-in-law. Finally, after talking about the merits of several other candidates, Dulles asked McCloy if he would take the job for a short time, later to be promoted into the slot of secretary of state. McCloy asked where Dulles would go in that event, and the Sullivan & Cromwell lawyer replied he would move over to the White House, where he expected to advise the president on all major foreign-policy matters. Upon further queries, McCloy learned that Dulles expected him to manage the State Department strictly "from the administrative point of view." Since this did not sound as if he would have the full powers of a secretary of state, McCloy politely declined the offer. "That wasn't for me," he later recalled. "I wasn't just going to 'mind the store' while Dulles was running foreign policy." Eisenhower was so informed, and only much later did McCloy learn from Walter Bedell Smith, who had become undersecretary of state, that Dulles had misrepresented the president's proposal.[40]

McCloy had never much liked Foster Dulles, and this incident certainly did nothing to warm relations between the two lawyers. But in any case, by the time Dulles came to see him he was already seriously considering a lucrative prospect in the private sector. Robert Taft was soon to learn how right he was to think that the Rockefellers regarded McCloy as one of their own. When the chairman of Chase National Bank, Winthrop Aldrich—a Rockefeller in-law—was nominated by Eisenhower as ambassador to London, the bank's directors immediately thought of McCloy as his possible successor. John D. Rockefeller, Jr., had already resumed his friendship with McCloy, and invited him to return to the Rockefeller Foundation as a director. Clearly, the Rockefellers would welcome him as chairman of the family bank. So, one day in late November, Aldrich went to see McCloy and explained the duties of a Chase banker. McCloy was intrigued by what he heard, and they agreed to talk at greater length.

BOOK IV

The Eisenhower Years

CHAPTER 20

Chairman of the Chase Manhattan Bank: 1953–60

"New Chairman McCloy is a man adept at talk that is affable, wide-ranging, informative, discreet and effective."

FORTUNE MAGAZINE, 1953

By the first week of December 1952, McCloy had struck a deal with Aldrich. He would be paid $150,000 a year plus benefits—the same as Aldrich—with a promise that, if he stayed with the bank until the age of sixty-five, he would receive an annual pension of $75,000.[1] In addition, stock options and profit sharing would put his annual earnings well into six figures. McCloy saw in the chairmanship of Chase a position from which he could both earn a sizable amount of money and still influence the direction of U.S. foreign policy. The bank job not only permitted him such extracurricular activities, but actually demanded it. As he recalled later, ". . . the bank appealed to me, as it was both a national and international institution, with broad connections in industry and banking here and abroad."[2]

Soon after he and Aldrich concluded their negotiations, the press announced the name of the new Chase chairman and made a point of mentioning that McCloy would continue his work with the Ford Foundation on international matters.[3] At the same time, he was consulted by both the president and the president-elect. Eisenhower talked with him about German matters. McCloy encouraged Ike to select Harvard President James B. Conant as the new high commissioner to Germany.[4] Simultaneously, President Truman, Felix Frankfurter, and Dean Acheson persuaded him to serve on an *ad hoc* committee headed by Justice Learned Hand to review the loyalty of John Carter Vincent, a Foreign Service officer accused by Senator Joseph McCarthy of being a communist. McCloy was reluctant to take the job and told Frankfurter that he really didn't know how "all this fits with just starting work as Chairman of the Board of Chase National Bank. . . ." Believing it was a matter of "real principle," Frankfurter chided him, "If the Chairman of the Chase prevents you from doing jobs like that, you better call in Barton or Bernays or some other great advisors on business efficiency and public relations for the reorganization of your shop." Both Frankfurter and Acheson were certain of Vincent's loyalty and equally certain that Justice Hand, McCloy, and others on the committee would exonerate the diplomat. McCloy, "for the sake of principle," began reading through the Vincent case records. But before he could reach any conclusions, the new secretary of state, John Foster Dulles, wrote Justice Hand, requesting him to drop the matter. Dulles had decided to review the case himself and very shortly afterward announced that Vincent was neither a security risk nor disloyal. He concluded, however, that Vincent should be dismissed, because his reporting from China had failed "to meet the standard which is demanded of a Foreign Service officer. . . ." This abject display of political cowardice disgusted Acheson, and also annoyed McCloy, who was already highly critical of the political attacks being made on the foreign-policy bureaucracy.[5] Indeed, by the time Dulles announced his decision in the Vincent case, McCloy had already publicly criticized McCarthyite attacks on the State Department.

Starting on January 10, 1953, he gave the first of three speeches as an invitee of Harvard's prestigious Godkin lecture series, named after Edwin L. Godkin, the late publisher of *The Nation.* Ellen accompanied him up to Cambridge, where they stayed in the Harvard president's home. James Conant had agreed to take the high commissioner's job in Germany, and so the McCloys, together with Shep Stone, who dropped by in the evenings, briefed the Conants on what they should expect in Germany. On the evening of the first Godkin lecture, the former and future high commissioners were given a standing ovation by an audience of four hundred students and faculty. McCloy chose as the title of his addresses "The Challenge to American Foreign Policy." That summer, they were compiled into a slim volume and published by Harvard University Press. Given a forum in which most speakers usually wax philosophical about grandiose principles, McCloy's message characteristically contained a set of fairly prosaic prescriptions for the ills of American foreign policy. The challenge, he said, was not primarily military but political, ideological, and economic. The rise of anti-Americanism in Western Europe had to be dealt with by U.S. diplomats possessing "the vision of the statesman, the insight of the philosopher and the healing powers of the doctor."[6] West Europeans, he explained, feared America's rashness might expose them to the full horrors of atomic warfare. Our representatives had to demonstrate an ability to strike just the right balance between boldness and caution in dealing with the Soviets. The danger to the West, he argued, came from the threat of disunity among our West European allies. The French had to be reassured that we would never allow the Germans to dominate France again. The Germans had to be persuaded that their future lay in West European unity. And the British had to be encouraged to support European economic integration. These complicated diplomatic tasks could not, McCloy said, be achieved by a State Department whose loss of prestige in recent years had seriously impaired its morale and effectiveness abroad.[7]

Empowering the "striped-pants" set at the State Department with greater authority and responsibility to conduct U.S. foreign policy rubbed directly against the grain of conventional wisdom. McCloy even made a point of praising one of Senator Joseph McCarthy's chief targets, Secretary of State Dean Acheson. He launched a thinly veiled attack upon McCarthy's simplistic view of communism. America, he argued, was antagonizing some of the very people in Europe who ought to be Washington's natural allies, particularly European socialists, who he said were generally "liberal-minded individuals" and "almost uniformly bitterly opposed to Soviet Communism." But he also lamented that "our intellectuals have not exerted the influence that they might have on the thinking abroad. . . ." For McCloy, the Cold War had become a war of ideas with the Soviets, and he was alarmed that America's shock troops, the country's intellectuals, were refusing to join the battle. In a veiled reference to McCarthy, he criticized "the many dangers of irresponsible and one-sided investigative procedures. . . ."[8]

Perhaps because he failed to attack McCarthy by name, the cursory press stories carried by *The New York Times* and other papers on the speech failed to dramatize his message. Nor did McCarthy—for the moment—respond to the attack. That would come later. But McCloy left Harvard feeling he had spoken his mind.

Back in New York on January 19, 1953, McCloy formally took charge of Chase Bank. Almost immediately, he was faced with a personal challenge. The bank's annual shareholders' meeting was scheduled to take place that week. Aldrich was already in Washington, preparing for his ambassadorship in London, and the bank's veteran president, Percy J. Ebbott, was in bed with a bad case of the flu. McCloy, on the job only a few days, had to preside over what in the past had often proved a fairly raucous affair. He had read accounts of disturbances at previous meetings, where disgruntled shareholders had disrupted the proceedings with sharp questions aimed at the chairman. He also knew he would be seen by some shareholders as a novice to the world of commercial banking. So, as he walked into the room, he decided on the spot to try to defuse the atmosphere with a little self-deprecating humor.

As he sat down to chair the meeting, McCloy acknowledged that he was very much a "new boy" on the block. He wryly confessed that the last job he had held in a commercial bank was as a schoolboy in Philadelphia, when he worked briefly as a runner for Drexel & Co. He then told a story about a condemned horse thief standing on the gallows who turns to the sheriff and says, "This is the first time I've ever done this, Sheriff. Would you go a bit easy until I sort of get the hang of the thing?" At this, his audience burst into sustained applause and laughter.[9]

Actually, in financial terms, Chase's shareholders didn't have much to complain about. Earnings per share over the previous year had jumped nearly 20 percent.[10] The one unhappy event in the previous year that shareholders were anxious to have explained was the collapse of negotiations conducted by Aldrich to merge with the Bank of Manhattan. Everyone recognized that, if Chase Bank was to keep pace with its rivals, it would have to expand its retail banking facilities. The Bank of Manhattan had what Chase did not—a large number of retail branches throughout the city. By contrast, Chase had what the much smaller Bank of Manhattan did not—a large portfolio of loans to major American corporations. In 1951, Aldrich had begun negotiations with the head of the Bank of Manhattan, J. Stewart Baker. Aldrich actually persuaded Baker to sign a merger agreement on August 17, 1951, which would have given Chase deposits of $5.9 billion and eighty-three branch offices, making it the largest bank in the city, and the second largest in the country. To his surprise, a few days later, Aldrich opened his morning newspaper to read a page-one headline announcing that the merger deal was off. Baker had unilaterally issued a press statement explaining that "legal obstacles" required an end to the negotiations. Aldrich was later told that the Bank of Manhattan's lawyers had discovered that the bank's charter, issued by the State of New York in 1799, required unanimous consent from all of its shareholders in order to sell its assets to Chase. Aldrich was sure this was merely an excuse to cover Baker's last-minute doubts. Though he was deeply offended by Baker's behavior, Aldrich still thought the merger attractive enough that in November 1952 he tried once more to reopen negotiations. But personal relations between the two men were so strained that the discussions went nowhere.[11]

News of the renewed negotiations had nevertheless leaked, and when McCloy walked into his first annual shareholders' meeting in January, he was asked whether the deal was still a possibility. In response, he said with quiet authority that the merger proposal was "quite dead" and that any detailed discussion of the incident would be "quite out of place here." The shareholders seemed satisfied with this and other answers he gave to their questions. He also orchestrated the defeat of a resolution hostile to the bank's management which would have limited any bank officer's profit-sharing compensation to $200,000 annually and placed a cap of $25,000 on pensions. There must have been some raised eyebrows when stockholders were told that McCloy would be earning the same salary as Aldrich, who, after all, had been with the bank for eighteen years. But the man's affable demeanor made it hard for anyone in the room to object. One stockholder known for his troublesome questions even stood up and complimented McCloy's handling of the meeting. "I can see," he told him, "from the way you are presiding that you are the right man in the right place." The next day's *New York Times* reported, "The Chase meeting yesterday was one of the most peaceful in the history of the bank."[12]

McCloy's job was one of lofty supervision, not intimate direction, of Chase's day-to-day operations. He was taking charge of an institution that processed $165 billion in checks every year and carried $2.6 billion in loans and mortgages. But the clearing of all these checks and the extension of loans was far removed from McCloy's desk. The bank's president, Percy Ebbott, who had been with Chase since 1929, ran the mundane aspects of the operation with a bevy of senior vice-presidents. "He held my hand," McCloy recalled later.[13]

"The chairman's first duty might be described as talk," reported *Fortune* in a profile of McCloy later that year. Certainly, part of the chairman's job was ambassadorial. He was the public symbol of a financial institution intimately associated with the Rockefeller dynasty. All together the Rockefellers owned about 5 percent of Chase's stock, which in practice represented a controlling interest. The entire history of the bank was intertwined with the Rockefeller fortune. It had been created by the family and had always been managed by a board trained to keep one eye on the family's interests and desires. John D. Rockefeller, Jr.'s son David was a thirty-eight-year-old vice-president, and clearly an unspoken part of McCloy's job was to groom the youngest Rockefeller son to take charge of the family bank. *Fortune*'s editors casually commented that part of his new job was to preserve "the dignity of its [Chase's] own name and that of its Rockefeller stockholders. . . ." A natural Rockefeller envoy, McCloy had known David and his father since teaching some of the boys sailing thirty-odd years earlier at Bar Harbor. He had provided legal counsel to the family and had lent his name and reputation to the family's law firm, which itself had been created by the family to represent both its personal interests and those of Chase. The family trusted his common sense and discretion. In an era when the Rockefeller name still evoked popular resentment and opprobrium, McCloy's disarming personality could be counted on to diffuse criticism. "New Chairman McCloy," observed *Fortune*'s editors, "is a man adept at talk that is affable, wide-ranging, informative, discreet and effective."[14]

Soon after his first stockholders' meeting, McCloy decided that, in an effort to get to know his employees and how the bank functioned, he would go around the building and introduce himself. So, one morning at nine o'clock, he started on the ground floor and greeted everyone he met with the words "Hi, I'm Jack McCloy." He told his colleagues, "I'm finding out what the bank is about." For some weeks, he began his day in this manner, trying to work his way up the building, floor by floor. He did not, of course, succeed in meeting all nine thousand of Chase's employees, but he quickly won a reputation for his easygoing familiarity.[15]

Symbolism aside, it was primarily McCloy's job at Chase to keep himself in a state of perpetual conversation with the bank's major clients. He called the whole process "working the economy, keeping it moving." From the beginning, the chief executive officers of America's largest corporations came to him, and often offered him a seat on their boards of directors. Within months, he became a director of AT&T, Metropolitan Life Insurance Co., and Westinghouse Electric Co.[16] (Typically, such directors were paid $5,000–20,000 a year for attending board meetings.) On these interlocking corporate boards sat dozens of officers from other banks and corporations, and during the conversations he had with these and other businessmen about town, often over the phone but frequently at one of Wall Street's luncheon clubs, McCloy would solicit new corporate depositors and opportunities to lend Chase money.

When McCloy joined Chase, 75 percent of its outstanding loans were to large corporations. This made the bank particularly vulnerable to the vagaries of a recessionary cycle. With the incoming Eisenhower administration promising to end the Korean War, it was apparent that 1953–54 was going to be a period of recession. Chase loans fell nearly 9 percent over the next two years, while the nation's GNP declined 1.4 percent in 1954. Despite these trends, McCloy adopted an aggressive banking strategy. Reserves held against demand deposits were lowered, and he approved a dramatic increase in the bank's foreign-exchange transactions. To compensate for the decline in demand for loans to corporate clients, he approved a huge increase in the bank's portfolio of government securities.[17]

A few of McCloy's colleagues thought that for a "new boy on the block" some of these policies were brashly taken and not a little risky. One such critic was George Champion, a senior vice-president in the bank who was known as a "bankers' banker." With Chase since 1930, he had been assigned during the depression to a troubled New Orleans bank indebted to Chase. For two years, he had grappled with depression conditions and the constant interference of politicians like Senator Huey Long. The experience confirmed his rockbed conservatism and left him with an indelible distrust of government. He disliked any hint of self-promotion and was once overheard telling a security analyst, "We're not going to be pressured into showing profits." In 1952, he had been promoted to direct Chase's domestic department, making him a candidate for the chairmanship. He was clearly disappointed when Aldrich passed over him to choose McCloy.[18]

Champion had always believed the bank's ratio of reserves to loans was too low, and so of course disapproved when McCloy lowered reserves even further. McCloy's international ventures also made him uneasy. When Chase was considering a loan to a copper mine in Mexico, Champion automatically opposed it upon learning that the mine was owned by the Mexican government. "We are not here," he complained, "to socialize the world."[19]

Champion was equally unhappy when, in 1954, McCloy approved an unprecedented international credit transaction whereby Chase joined the International Monetary Fund and the U.S. Treasury in a $30-million loan to the Peruvian government for currency stabilization. To Champion's horror, the loan was approved without the Peruvian government's having to offer any collateral. Instead, the government in Lima agreed to an IMF-supervised program of fiscal reform. Such IMF economic-stabilization agreements were later to become common, but Chase's participation in this loan was the first occasion on which a private bank entered into such an arrangement.[20]

Balancing Champion's conservatism on such matters was young David Rockefeller. Before McCloy came aboard, Rockefeller had served an apprenticeship in the international department of the bank. He was younger and less experienced than Champion, but his name and future in the bank assured him a powerful voice in its affairs. Rockefeller was not one to worry about such mundane aspects of the business as deposit-to-loan ratios. Brimming with self-confidence that he could fulfill the role destined for a Rockefeller, he had a natural reserve and a serious demeanor that suited the profession he had chosen within the family business. He had strong opinions about how he wished to see Chase operated, but he needed someone like McCloy to glide him past his own occasional awkwardness.

McCloy found in Rockefeller an ally for his plans to push the bank into aggressively expanding its international activities. Unlike Champion, who hadn't traveled much in Europe, let alone the developing world, Rockefeller had traveled abroad much of his life. After coming back from a couple of scouting trips to Brazil sometime in the early 1950s, he became completely sold on the idea of international expansion.[21] Ever since the depression, the normal practice at Chase's international department was to conduct its foreign business through a correspondent bank abroad.

Loans were never given directly to a foreign corporation, most transactions were very short-term, and an emphasis was placed on financing trade or commodities. In short, Chase and virtually all other major U.S. banks took few risks when it came to doing business abroad. Champion wanted to keep it that way, and even in the international department there was a great deal of resistance to any rapid expansion of loans.

But McCloy's World Bank experience had convinced him that there were plenty of banking opportunities abroad that could both earn a profit and contribute to development in places like Nicaragua, Brazil, and Egypt. Finding such profitable ventures in the developing world was quite a difficult task. Champion made it more difficult by demanding that these projects have the "right people with adequate skills."[22]

International lending grew slowly. By the end of 1954, Chase was the third-largest bank in America. But it still only had foreign branches in eight countries, and these branches held modest deposits of $445 million and loans of only $120 million. Though Chase held the record for deposits by foreign-correspondent banks, roughly $650 million, most of this money was placed in New York merely to handle trading transactions.[23] Thus, neither foreign nor U.S. bankers were making many long-term investments in one another's economies, a fact McCloy deplored. But he realized that, if the bank was going to move abroad in a major way, it would take time to change attitudes.

In the meantime, he had been pondering Aldrich's failure to negotiate a merger with the Bank of Manhattan. After only a few months on the job, he persuaded himself that there were good reasons to pursue the deal. To compete on its home turf, Chase absolutely needed to expand the number of its retail banking branches throughout the city. If it did not, National City could well overwhelm Chase before McCloy even had a chance to position the bank for an expansion abroad. To build these branches up from scratch would take time; the easiest route to domestic expansion lay in merger. Convinced that the Bank of Manhattan's Stewart Baker had firmly shut the door to further negotiations, McCloy turned his eyes to the House of Morgan. J. P. Morgan & Co. was then a relatively small but highly prestigious "silk-stocking" bank. It did not possess the retail banking branches McCloy sought, but the idea of taking over what remained of the Morgan financial empire appealed to him. One day, he grabbed his hat and walked over to see George Whitney.[24]

Whitney had been a J. P. Morgan partner since 1920, and McCloy had known him since at least the 1930s, when both men were members of the Piping Rock country club. McCloy feared his suggestion of a merger might seem presumptuous to the patrician Morgan partner. So, in pitching the idea to him, he made a point of saying that he was prepared to step aside as chairman if Chase and Morgan could be joined. To his surprise, when McCloy asked, "Are you interested or is there no sense in my talking further about this?," Whitney replied, "Keep talking. Keep talking." However, two other Morgan partners, Harry Davison and the younger Tommy Lamont, got wind of the negotiations and put a stop to them. "With all their Morgan traditions," recalled McCloy, "they put their foot down and said they would 'never, never, never' merge with anybody else, least of all Chase."[25]

McCloy then decided to take a second look at the Bank of Manhattan. He soon came across the brief prepared by the law firm of Dewey, Ballantine, which was used by Stewart Baker to justify his decision to back out of the merger. New York State banking laws did provide for the disposition of any bank's assets by a simple majority vote of shares, but the Bank of Manhattan's 1797 charter did not contain any provision for merger or consolidation of its assets in the face of minority shareholder opposition. Dewey, Ballantine argued on the basis of an old legal precedent (the well-known Dartmouth College case) that Bank of Manhattan shareholders could only approve a merger into Chase by a unanimous vote.

McCloy didn't think much of the Dewey, Ballantine brief, and believed the lawyers had inappropriately applied the Dartmouth-case analogy merely to provide Baker with an excuse to stop the merger.[26] Yet, now that the charter problem had been raised, some Bank of Manhattan shareholder was bound to tie up any renewed merger attempt in lengthy litigation. In pondering the problem, McCloy suddenly saw a simple solution: "I made up my mind that if the merger was worth doing, it was worth putting it around the other way. Instead of having the Bank of Manhattan merge into Chase, have Chase merge into the smaller Manhattan."[27] As one magazine later described the transaction, "Jonah swallowed the whale."[28] Such a maneuver precluded any question of having to obtain unanimous consent from Bank of Manhattan's shareholders, since they would only be voting to acquire Chase's assets, not dispose of their own. The maneuver would, however, require Chase to abandon its own charter, which meant the bank would leave the National Banking System and operate under the Bank of Manhattan's New York State charter. The national comptroller of the currency, among others, was horrified when he learned of McCloy's intention, but to McCloy it mattered little whether Chase operated technically under state or national regulations. In fact, though there was some prestige attached to having a national charter, New York State banking regulations were more lax than national regulations. Thus, under a state charter, Chase could make larger loans than the Bank of America could operating under a national charter.[29]

To keep the negotiations secret as long as possible, McCloy broached the idea to Stewart Baker in the banker's Park Avenue apartment. Two years older than McCloy, Baker looked and played the part of a patrician New York banker. His family had been involved with the Bank of Manhattan since 1799, and his father had headed the bank before he became chairman in 1932. Baker and McCloy ran in slightly different circles; Baker was a Princeton man and a golfer, and belonged to a different set of clubs from those McCloy frequented. Still, the two men had a passing acquaintance, and much of Baker's reticence melted away when McCloy suggested that a merger could be achieved by retaining Manhattan's old charter. Baker had realized all along that the two banks complimented each other. But, as with the Morgan partners, family history and sentiment had made him reluctant to preside over his bank's disappearance. McCloy promised that if the merger went through the new bank would be called the Chase Manhattan Bank, thus assuring the survival of the older bank's name. In addition, while McCloy would become chairman of the new bank, Baker would be named president and chairman of an executive committee of the board.

All that remained was for McCloy to convince his own shareholders—and the government—that the merger would benefit both the bank and the larger public interest. Critics pointed out that the record-breaking merger would make Chase Manhattan the second-largest bank in the country, with total resources of $7.6 billion. Only the San Francisco–based Bank of America, with resources of $8.3 billion, would be larger. Congressman Emmanuel Celler, a Brooklyn Democrat and chairman of the House Judiciary Committee, told the press, "This is too big a merger. . . . It would give an all powerful oligarchy a stranglehold on New York banking."[30]

McCloy denied that the merger would produce "anything resembling a banking monopoly," and pointed out, "There are some 14,000 commercial banks in the nation and it is really hard to conceive of any industry in the country where competition is keener." Chase's major competition in terms of retail banking, he argued, already had comparable numbers of local branch offices. National City Bank had seventy-four offices, Manufacturer's Trust had 112, and the Chemical Corn Exchange Bank had ninety-eight branch offices. The merged Chase Manhattan Bank would only have eighty-seven offices out of a total of some 560 banking offices operated by fifty-seven different banks throughout the metropolitan area. "It should be apparent at a glance," McCloy said, "that this merger would result in an intensification of competition in the city rather than a lessening of competition."[31]

He was right on one level to suggest that the merger would allow Chase to compete more effectively than before in the same retail banking services provided by such competitors as National City Bank. But Justice Department studies at the time demonstrated that bank deposits in New York City were increasingly concentrated in a few institutions, a trend being duplicated throughout the country. In each of sixteen major financial centers across the nation, two leading banks invariably owned more than 40 percent of all commercial banking assets, and in nine of these sixteen cities, the two leading banks owned more than 60 percent of all bank assets.[32] Small banks were being pushed out of business.

Critics were also unhappy about the appearance of further encroachments by Rockefeller interests upon the city's banking system. The New York State superintendent of banking wrote McCloy to question whether the merger would raise a conflict-of-interest problem. He pointed out that the Bank of Manhattan owned a minority share in the largest bank in Westchester, New York, the County Trust Co. Since the Rockefeller brothers held a substantial interest in both a competing bank, the National Bank of Westchester, and Chase Bank, the superintendent questioned whether such interlocking ownership by "Rockefeller interests" created a potential conflict of interest.

McCloy hotly denied the obvious, that the Rockefeller family together did indeed have a controlling interest in Chase. This denial mirrored the family's long-standing policy of keeping as much public distance as possible between itself and its large stock holdings. As John D. Rockefeller, Jr., explained in a letter to his sons, "This policy protects us both from the embarrassment of investigating personal grievances, answering personal requests, and from the danger of taking any position which suggested control in the slightest degree of the activities in which a large stock interest might imply a more direct connection. It has proven such a wise policy that I urge all you boys to adopt it for the protection of the family."[33] In fact, the family's stock in Chase during this period and for several decades afterward always represented more than 5 or 6 percent of all voting stock. Such percentages are commonly regarded as signifying *de facto* control. In the case of the National Bank of Westchester, the Rockefeller brothers together owned 19 percent of that bank's shares, while the Bank of Manhattan owned 6.6 percent of its competitor, the County Trust Co. The conflict of interest was clear, and in recognition of this fact, McCloy, while continuing to deny Rockefeller control of Chase, nevertheless promised the banking superintendent that, if the merger was allowed to go through, Chase Manhattan would not vote its County Trust stock without the approval of the superintendent.[34] Based on this pledge, the superintendent withdrew his objections.

One more hurdle remained: approval from Chase's own constituents at a special shareholders' meeting. This turned into what McCloy called "a regular Donnybrook Fair." In describing the scene for Justice Frankfurter later that day, he wrote, "A man named Gilbert really tried to tear things apart. He made such a to-do that at one time I did not know whether we would get through the meeting or not. . . . It was one of the most remarkable exhibitions of hysteria I have ever seen." In the end, the troublemaker wore out everyone's patience, and 86 percent of the bank's shares were voted in favor of the merger.[35]

McCloy's victory touched off a virtual explosion in bank mergers around the country. Chase's own major competitor, the National City Bank, quickly engineered a similar merger with the much smaller First National Bank, giving the renamed First National City Bank assets of $7.2 billion.[36] The trend toward larger banks eventually precipitated two pieces of banking legislation unfavorable to Chase interests. Three months after the Chase merger, Congressman Celler introduced a bill that would specifically subject banks to the Clayton Antitrust Act. McCloy came down to Washington to testify against Celler's bill on numerous occasions until finally, in 1960, Congress passed the Bank Merger Act. This bill subjected mergers of all federally insured banks to government approval. Critics of the merger also managed to have Congress pass the Bank Holding Company Act of 1956, which for the first time brought bank holding companies under the direct regulation of the Federal Reserve. The government would now have the right to decide, on the basis of size alone, whether particular bank mergers or acquisitions were not in the public interest. A senior vice-president of Chase later concluded that both measures proved to be a "severe handicap to the bank's strategy for expansion."[37]

There were other unforeseen dividends. Though McCloy promised Baker that he had no intention of ever abandoning the old Manhattan charter, certain of its provisions proved to be so antiquated that in 1965 McCloy's successors brought Chase back into the national banking system. In addition, according to the author of a history of the bank, the merger "fueled a contest between the banks in which size became an end in itself. Eventually this contributed to actions by Chase that produced heavy losses. . . ."[38] Still, for the remainder of McCloy's tenure, Chase reaped many concrete benefits from the merger. The retail banking side of the business grew from Manhattan's solid base. Profits and dividends paid out throughout the rest of the 1950s were more than respectable. Many years later, McCloy's associates would look back on his tenure as chairman and realize that under his stewardship the bank had reached its zenith.

CHAPTER 21

McCloy, McCarthyism, and the Early Eisenhower Presidency

"Oh, they're not burning books," said Eisenhower.
"I'm afraid they are, Mr. President," McCloy replied. "I have the evidence."

DARTMOUTH, 1953

Throughout his first few years at Chase, McCloy was never exclusively a banker. He regularly attended meetings of the Council on Foreign Relations and continued to serve as a special adviser on international projects to the Ford Foundation. Germany was an obsession, and he kept in touch with developments there by talking on the phone—often on a weekly basis—with his old friend Eric Warburg and Hermann Abs, the Deutsche Bank chairman who was one of Adenauer's closest financial advisers. Just before leaving for his new job as high commissioner, James Conant dropped in at 18 Pine Street to lunch with McCloy and Shep Stone. Conant's Senate confirmation had been far from certain. There had even been talk of Eisenhower's withdrawing the nomination in the face of opposition to the Harvard president from the right wing of the Republican Party, including Senator Joe McCarthy. Fortunately for Conant, McCloy had sent an early private message to Adenauer requesting that

Bonn cable its approval of the nomination. Adenauer had quickly complied, so for the White House now to withdraw the nomination would cause the chancellor embarrassment. McCloy and Adenauer both felt that any further delay in Conant's confirmation would adversely affect the Bundestag's ratification of the Allied-German peace treaties. The German chancellor bluntly told the press that in the period since McCloy's departure from Germany seven months earlier, the United States had been "disastrously unhelpful." Such comments from across the Atlantic helped to keep the pressure on the Eisenhower administration to stand fast on Conant's confirmation, and McCloy's personal lobbying of the chairman of the Senate Foreign Relations Committee, Senator Alexander Wiley of Wisconsin, proved decisive. Yet McCloy was troubled that the confirmation of a man of Conant's stature had aroused such partisan fireworks.[1]

Conant's confirmation battle underscored for him how far the country had slipped away from the ideal of a bipartisan foreign policy. Senator McCarthy was apparently going to make life as difficult for the new Republican administration as he had for the Democrats. His investigations of the State Department and the Voice of America were unrelenting. He was now focusing on the State Department's overseas libraries, which he claimed carried books with "tainted ideas" on their shelves. Included in McCarthy's list were books by Dashiell Hammett, former Communist Party leader Earl Browder, and Sol Auerbach. The State Department under Foster Dulles had quickly announced that its book policy had changed: henceforth such authors would no longer be carried in its libraries.

McCloy was unhappy with this intimidation of State Department officials. On the other hand, in his opinion liberals too had abused the power of congressional investigation. So, on April 2, 1953, he gave a speech to the New York State Chamber of Commerce in which he reiterated some of the criticisms of congressional investigations he had made three months earlier at Harvard. He complained that too many civil servants were being "knocked about" these days. "We are beginning to suspect too many of our Government servants—too many of our neighbors—and we are inclined to follow some of the methods of the totalitarians in doing so." Again without mentioning McCarthy by name, he complained about the use of innuendo and one-sided presentation of facts. But in an effort to place himself in the political center, he then suggested that such tactics had been pioneered by early New Deal investigations. "If the liberals had been more expressive when the so-called Congressional investigations of the 1930s were studiously violating personal rights and when business was the target there would have been less likelihood of excesses in this day and age." He noted with irony that Alger Hiss, who served as a counsel to one such 1930s congressional investigation of the munitions industry, had recently been sent to prison for perjury.[2]

McCloy had personal reasons to resent the 1930s congressional investigations, which had sullied the names of not a few of his friends, including Paul Cravath, Jean Monnet, Benjamin Buttenwieser, and Hoyt A. Moore. But the comparison was unjust. In the New Deal's investigations of big business, individuals were singled out for business practices—such as insider trading—that even the business community acknowledged to be wrong by any ethical standard. In contrast, the McCarthy investigations engendered an atmosphere of pervasive fear, whereby government officials and private citizens who had nothing at all to hide nevertheless felt intimidated. Many of McCarthy's victims, once subpoenaed to appear before his committee, found it impossible to obtain legal counsel. This certainly was not the case during the New Deal, when the targets of congressional investigations were vigorously defended by batteries of lawyers from the most prestigious Wall Street firms. Back in the 1930s, McCloy's colleagues felt outrage, not fear, at Congress's prying into their business practices. But if, as Telford Taylor complained at the time, the analogy wasn't apt, McCloy and many of his peers found it a useful stance from which to criticize McCarthy's charges.[3] *The New York Times* applauded his speech in an editorial condemning the current abuses of Congress's investigatory powers but also suggested that this "arrogance of committees did not originate yesterday." The *Times* too chose not to name McCarthy as the chief culprit.[4]

McCloy and *The New York Times* were not the only ones reluctant to condemn McCarthy by name. Walter Lippmann, still an occasional tennis partner of McCloy's during the 1950s, personally sympathized with McCarthy's victims, but rarely ventured to write about the issue.[5] Few, if any, nationally recognized Republicans had spoken out against McCarthy up to this time. The president himself, to the frustration of certain of his aides, was unwilling to speak out. "I really believe," Ike wrote in his diary that April, "that nothing will be so effective in combating this particular kind of trouble-making as to ignore him. This he cannot stand."[6]

But by the spring of 1953, Eisenhower and McCloy were about to learn that if they waited for McCarthy to overreach himself many of their policies could be destroyed in the meantime. Only a few days after McCloy's Chamber of Commerce speech, McCarthy dispatched two of his investigators on a fact-finding mission to Europe. Roy Cohn and G. David Schine spent two weeks looking for politically suspect books lying on the shelves of U.S. Embassy libraries, and for the suspect officials who tolerated such books.

Almost as soon as they had arrived in Bonn, Cohn announced that

McCarthy's Committee on Government Operations wanted Theodore Kaghan, the deputy chief of public relations for HICOG, to return to Washington for questioning about his political activities in the 1930s. Kaghan had met with Cohn and Schine in High Commissioner Conant's office (Conant was back in the United States) and had initially refused to answer their questions. But then Cohn revealed that Kaghan had written a play in 1939 defending the right of the workingman to go on strike and that he may have sympathized with the left-wing Republican government during the Spanish Civil War. Kaghan defiantly called Cohn and Schine "junketeering gumshoes" and said he was perfectly willing to testify under oath as to his anticommunist credentials. "I have spent more time superintending anti-Soviet broadcasts, pamphlets, newspapers and news agencies than Senator McCarthy's two travelling spies have spent in school."[7] For such boldness, Kaghan received no support from the State Department, and was brought back to Washington for questioning by McCarthy.

With Kaghan's fate in doubt, HICOG announced only two days later that 137 Americans and more than seven hundred Germans were being stricken from the U.S. government's payroll as of July 1. This force reduction had already been in the cards, but in a seeming effort to placate McCarthy's investigators, HICOG had taken the opportunity to fire two high-ranking officials known to be on McCarthy's list of suspects. From McCloy's perspective, the most distressing of these two cases involved the firing of Joseph M. Frankenstein, editor of "America Dienst," a German-language news service sponsored with HICOG funds. Frankenstein's job was to place news features with American themes in German newspapers. He ran a sophisticated operation; his features were not mere propagandistic tracts, and most Amerika Dienst stories were picked up almost exclusively by the opposition Social Democratic newspapers. McCloy had sanctioned the operation as high commissioner and believed it to be one of the most successful means of exposing left-of-center Germans to American views. He was therefore understandably distressed to hear in early April that Frankenstein had been fired. Cohn evidently precipitated the firing after learning that Frankenstein was married to Kay Boyle, a short-story writer and liberal-magazine contributor, who in years past had made small donations to various groups that now appeared on the attorney general's list of subversive organizations.[8]

Kaghan and Frankenstein were not the only ones among McCloy's former HICOG officials to be targeted by McCarthy. Newspaper reports in April speculated that McCarthy was also taking "special interest" in Sam Reber, now serving Conant as deputy high commissioner.[9] That trusted members of McCloy's intimate circle were being slandered was bad enough, but it was somehow worse that such careers were being destroyed in a circus atmosphere in which the brash young Roy Cohn had assumed the role of prosecutorial ringmaster and court jester.[10]

McCloy did not publicly come to the defense of any of the HICOG officials forced out of office. But in mid-May, he decided to take his complaints to Eisenhower. When he called the White House and said he needed to see the president, he was quickly given a half-hour appointment for May 26, 1953. He had not seen Eisenhower since the inauguration festivities, and as was his practice, he prepared for the meeting by writing out on a yellow legal pad his "talking points." In general, he wished to impress upon Eisenhower the damage McCarthy was inflicting on America's reputation in Europe. But he also wanted to prod the president into making a press-conference statement defending those HICOG propaganda programs under attack from McCarthy. He handed Ike a detailed memo describing the influence of HICOG's chain of "Amerika Haus" libraries, explaining that these libraries contained some books critical of the United States, critical of the Eisenhower administration, and even critical of McCloy's tenure as high commissioner. The Germans, he said, who used these libraries came away impressed that these information centers were "really centers of democratic thought, of freedom." It was "sheer poppycock" to say that such a program had been "communist inspired."

Regarding the Kaghan case, he defended the propaganda chief's loyalty and, in a direct slap at Foster Dulles, complained that the "higher levels of the State Department did not help this man defend himself before the committee in spite of his long and effective service." (By this time, Kaghan had already resigned, saying, "When you cross swords with Senator McCarthy you cannot expect to remain in the State Department. . . ."[11]) Citing the words of a leading German radio commentator, he warned the president that "McCarthy makes it so easy for the world to become anti-American. . . ."[12] In short, McCloy argued that the White House had to do something to stop the senator from Wisconsin.

Eisenhower didn't dispute McCloy's facts, but he still felt that a direct presidential response would only dignify McCarthy's charges. So, once again, he decided to keep his silence. As it happened, on the following morning *The New York Times* announced that HICOG was eliminating Frankenstein's controversial Amerika Dienst press service and closing down one-quarter of all the American libraries in West Germany.[13] McCarthy had won this round. Earlier in the year, he had forced the resignation of McCloy's popular consul general in Munich, Charles Thayer, and before the summer was out, he would also force the resignation or transfer of two other former McCloy aides in HICOG, Sam Reber and John Paton Davies. In the meantime, frightened HICOG officials began to purge Amerika Haus libraries of any books appearing on the State Department's list of proscribed books. These included books written by Theodore White, Edgar Snow, Owen Lattimore, Howard Fast, Langston Hughes, and Jean-Paul Sartre.[14]

A few days after seeing the president, McCloy was incredulous to learn from his own sources in Germany that HICOG officials had actually burned some of these books. Such a thing deeply offended his reverence for the printed word. He may have thought Jean-Paul Sartre's writings "poppycock," but burning the French philosopher's books seemed an act of barbarism. Over the next few weeks, McCloy couldn't stop talking about it. Then, on June 14, 1953, he found himself at Dartmouth College, where he, his old friend Grenville Clark, Sherman Adams, the president's chief of staff, and Joseph Proskauer, the chairman of the New York State Crime Commission, were to be awarded honorary law degrees. Eisenhower was scheduled to give a short address. Standing around with the president, waiting for the commencement ceremonies to begin, McCloy turned to Proskauer and started to tell him about how books were being burned in American libraries abroad at the instigation of Senator McCarthy. Overhearing only part of the conversation, Eisenhower moved closer to McCloy and asked, "What's this, what's this?"

"I was telling about the burning of State Department books abroad," replied McCloy.

"Oh, they're not burning books," said the president.

"I'm afraid they are, Mr. President," McCloy replied. "I have the evidence."

Eisenhower fell silent as McCloy launched into a speech about the virtues of the American libraries: "And the value of those books," he said, "was that they were uncensored. They criticized you and me, and Dean Acheson and anyone else in Government. The Germans knew they were uncensored and that was why they streamed into our libraries. . . ."[15]

At that moment, Eisenhower was called to the podium, where he gave one of the very few speeches of his presidency in which he directly attacked McCarthyism. Speaking without notes, he specifically denounced "book burners" and told his audience of Dartmouth students, "Don't join the book burners. . . . Don't be afraid to go in your library and read every book as long as any document does not offend your own ideas of decency. That should be the only censorship. How will we defeat communism unless we know what it is?"[16]

Even this roundabout criticism of McCarthy created a political storm. Though the president had again refrained from naming McCarthy, most newspapers reported the speech with banner headlines and left no doubt of Eisenhower's target. McCarthy himself was furious and, according to Drew Pearson, assigned one of his staff to find out who had prompted the president to make such an attack. The information was not hard to ferret out, since McCloy himself talked widely to his friends of his own role in the speech. As a result, McCarthy's staff quietly began an investigation of McCloy's career, which in turn later led them to focus their attention on the issue of communist subversion in the U.S. Army.

In the meantime, to the disappointment of McCloy and many other liberal Republicans, Eisenhower began to backtrack. McCarthy's private protests to the White House successfully prevented the broadcast of Eisenhower's speech by the Voice of America. Worse, only five days after his Dartmouth speech, Eisenhower told a press conference that he had not meant to urge the reading of books by communists or books that advocated revolution, nor would he tolerate "any document or any other kind of thing that attempts to persuade or propagandize America into communism." McCarthy quickly applauded the president for this "commendable clarification."[17]

In retrospect, historians came to regard the Dartmouth speech as a precarious beginning to the end of McCarthy's powers of political intimidation, and McCloy would always take some satisfaction in having instigated the affair. But at the time, the episode seemed merely to underscore the senator's powers.

Only three days after Eisenhower issued his "clarification," McCloy came to the White House for one of the president's intimate stag dinners. He was one of fourteen tuxedoed guests that evening. Others included such old friends as Bernard Baruch, Milton Eisenhower, Arthur Hays Sulzberger, and Dr. Henry M. Wriston, the president of Brown University. Seated across from him at dinner was Sid Richardson, a Texas oil man who was then one of America's wealthiest individuals. Richardson had met Ike aboard a train traveling from Texas to Washington, D.C., in December 1941.[18] The two men had kept in close touch since the end of the war, and Ike now counted the oil magnate as one of his closest friends. For years, Richardson had kept the Eisenhowers' freezer stocked with hundreds of pounds of Texas beef, sausage, and hams.[19] As president, Eisenhower consulted Richardson on oil and economic matters and used the Texan to influence the newly elected Senate minority leader, Senator Lyndon B. Johnson.[20]

That evening, Richardson took an instant liking to McCloy and invited him to visit his farm in Texas. In a very short time, their friendship would also include some business dealings. But on this occasion, the dinner talk was all politics. McCloy was seated between Milton Eisenhower and Attorney General Herbert Brownell, Jr. The president began by asking his pastor to say grace. And then, over vichyssoise, the men discussed the Korean War and the Rosenberg spy case. The Rosenbergs had been executed two days earlier, after the president had refused to intervene, and he confessed that he had felt under great strain. Only toward the end of the evening, when the men had adjourned to Eisenhower's study, did they discuss McCarthy. As he had before, McCloy tried to impress upon Eisenhower the necessity for defending his civil servants from scurrilous attacks. But Eisenhower once again recited the reasons why he felt it would be unwise for him to condemn McCarthy by name or get into the business of answering specific charges.[21]

McCloy was not convinced, but the president sounded persuasive to Sid Richardson, who wrote him shortly afterward, "Your not having the jitters nor being scared gives me a lot of confidence. . . ." Eisenhower emphasized his determination to keep above the fray by replying, "I am going to declare my independence of partisan quarrel and let others fight such things out to the bitter death."[22]

The practical effect of this, from McCloy's point of view, was a great loss of face abroad. German visitors to America were returning home saying that it was no longer possible to have a frank discussion, that American officials were constantly looking over their shoulders to see if anyone else was listening. *The New York Times* suggested that Gestapo tactics were being used to root out HICOG officials suspected of subversion.[23] Such reports disturbed McCloy, and in private conversations with friends in Washington and New York he blamed the secretary of state for not defending his employees. Indeed, shortly after Eisenhower's "book-burning" speech, when he learned from High Commissioner James Conant that McCarthy intended to subpoena Glen Wolfe and other HICOG officials, McCloy went to see Foster Dulles and told him in no uncertain terms that the State Department could not allow it to happen. As a result of this meeting, the State Department informed McCarthy that it was unwilling to spend the money to have such HICOG witnesses flown back from Germany. McCloy was relieved, but thought Foster Dulles could have been much more forthright in defending his employees. Drew Pearson, not one of McCloy's favorite reporters, got wind of these complaints and in late June published a one-sentence item in his column reporting that what McCloy had to say about Foster Dulles would "sizzle newsprint."[24]

It was true. But McCloy didn't like to see his views appear in print, and certainly not in Pearson's column. He promptly sat down and wrote Dulles a note that called Pearson's report "nonsense" but also reminded the secretary, "I have said what I have told both you and the President that I think you must defend your own Department people where they have done a good job for you and I have been irritated that no one in Congress or the Government has challenged McCarthy. . . ." Dulles replied briefly a week later, only to say that he had to concentrate on larger foreign-policy problems.[25] McCloy thought this quite lame.

Shortly afterward, an incident occurred that brought home to McCloy in a personal fashion just how pervasive McCarthyism had become. In July, he learned from Bethuel M. Webster, an old friend and president of the New York Bar Association, that FBI agents were running around town asking questions about McCloy's loyalty. Webster said agents had asked him if McCloy could be trusted with classified documents. Similar questions were being asked about former OSS chief Bill Donovan. Webster thought the FBI's questions so absurd that he wrote Eisenhower, "I wonder if the security clearance business is not going too far." Though Ike promised to investigate the matter, J. Edgar Hoover was commended later that same year by Deputy Attorney General William P. Rogers for having blocked thirty-three presidential appointments solely on the basis of "character investigations."[26]

In McCloy's case, there are several possible reasons for the FBI's investigation of him in 1953. The first and simplest explanation was that he was being considered for a presidential appointment. He had, in fact, already accepted an appointment in June, to the president's Commission on Foreign and Economic Policy. As a director of Westinghouse Corporation, he had applied for a routine clearance in order to be able to have access to classified information on the corporation's nuclear-energy contracts. But this hardly warranted the kind of FBI scrutiny McCloy was subjected to that summer. Certainly of more interest to Hoover was that by the summer of 1953 McCloy was informally associated with the handful of men in the Eisenhower administration who were advising the president on a variety of foreign-policy and intelligence matters. Within days of the 1952 election, Hoover had approved a suggestion from one of his top aides to write up summary reports on everything the Bureau knew about "the small group of people he felt were very close to President-designate Eisenhower."[27] McCloy was on the list, and the nineteen-page report subsequently compiled on him contained a laundry list of gossip, innuendo, and unsubstantiated allegations of communist sympathies. It pulled together such highlights from his FBI file as the 1945 anonymous letter to President Truman charging McCloy with being the "vigorous leader of a pro-Communist group within G-2 [army intelligence]. . . ."[28] Even worse, however, from the Bureau's point of view, were reports that McCloy had "no love for the FBI." Hoover himself scrawled on one memo, ". . . our relations with McCloy were never encouraging."[29]

Hoover was also aware that McCloy was frequently consulted by C. D. Jackson, the newly appointed chief of the Psychological Strategy Board, a White House agency that Hoover regarded as a rival intelligence group. As such, McCloy was privy to some of the nation's best-kept secrets. Jackson had worked under McCloy on psychological-warfare operations in North Africa during the war; subsequently, he had returned to his job in the Time-Life conglomerate as Henry Luce's right-hand man. From his present job in the White House, he was dedicated to rousing the intelligence community to action-oriented covert operations. In addition to Jackson, Hoover was well aware that McCloy was closely associated with Allen Dulles, John Bross, William Bundy, and other CIA officials.[30] Hoover instinctively tried to keep tabs on any rival intelligence organizations. And since Joe McCarthy in the summer of 1953 was also investigating the CIA, Hoover had one more reason to scrutinize McCloy's file.

The best explanation for Hoover's interest in McCloy lies in the politics of McCarthyism. The FBI chief and McCarthy were by now good friends. They regularly lunched together at Harvey's Restaurant in Washington. Two of McCarthy's top investigators were former FBI agents. Roy Cohn himself first met J. Edgar Hoover during the Rosenberg trial, and later remarked in his memoirs that he had always been able to work "well and closely with older, powerful men" like the FBI director.[31] Furthermore, McCarthy's own staff members have since said that the FBI regularly gave Roy Cohn access to confidential Bureau reports on various individuals.[32] Hoover's security file on McCloy, as mentioned earlier, also contained a copy of his 1946 memo to Truman advising the president that McCloy was alleged by FBI sources to be a member of a communist spy ring in Washington. It is not known whether Hoover leaked this particular memo to McCarthy; some of the relevant FBI papers are still classified. But, gauging by the senator's subsequent attacks on McCloy later that year, it is entirely likely that Hoover gave McCarthy portions of McCloy's file and confirmed leads developed by Cohn.

In any case, by the summer of 1953, Hoover certainly was aware that McCarthy had begun digging into McCloy's background. (Drew Pearson later reported that McCarthy's boys were even looking into such mundane things as whether Ellen McCloy had used her HICOG chauffeur for personal business.) There were plenty of men in Washington and New York who were willing to feed McCarthy's suspicions about McCloy. Westbrook Pegler, the conservative columnist, didn't hesitate to voice his suspicions about McCloy to Lew Douglas himself. Pegler couldn't understand how McCloy could have retained Benjamin Buttenwieser in his job as deputy high commissioner in Germany "after B and his wife, both, had shown sympathy almost to point of affection for Alger Hiss."[33]

While these right-wing Republicans were trying to tag McCloy—at the very least—as insufficiently anticommunist, the Chase National chairman was doing his best to find private funding for various covert operations then funded by the CIA. In his opinion, one of the worst features of McCarthy's investigations was the harm they could inflict by exposing or terminating some of Washington's most promising covert operations. He had always encouraged the propaganda activities of the CIA's International Organizations Division, the branch of the Agency that was then funding the Congress on Cultural Freedom (CCF). As high commissioner, he had sanctioned the founding of this organization in West

Berlin's Titiana Palace Theater in June 1950. Since then, the CCF had sponsored dozens of successful anticommunist cultural events across Europe and was now publishing some twenty generally highbrow periodicals designed to influence European intellectuals. These included such magazines as *Encounter* in London, *Socialist Commentary* and *Der Monat* in Germany, *Forum* in Vienna, *Tempo Presente* in Rome, and numerous others. None of these publications could survive without Agency funding. Because these periodicals attempted to appeal to the non-Marxist left, they published material written by socialists and did not automatically support every aspect of U.S. policy. It was easy to see that McCarthy would have a heyday if he was allowed to investigate any of these CIA operations. McCloy feared that the senator's attacks on the U.S. propaganda apparatus in West Germany threatened to disrupt the subsidies given numerous West European publications and such CIA entities as Radio Liberation and Radio Free Europe.[34]

McCarthy's attack on the CIA came to a head on July 9, 1953, when Roy Cohn called the Agency to demand that William Bundy testify on why he had contributed $400 to Alger Hiss's defense fund. Bundy was then a special assistant to the deputy director of intelligence. To McCarthy's surprise, Allen Dulles refused to allow Bundy to testify and rejected a subpoena demanding the testimony of the Agency's legislative counsel. For the moment, McCarthy backed off, largely because Vice-President Richard Nixon advised him that he didn't have the support in his own Senate committee, the Permanent Subcommittee on Investigations, for a confrontation with the CIA. McCloy was greatly relieved.

By the late summer of 1953, the Eisenhower administration had made covert action a major pillar of its foreign policy. Eisenhower himself felt that covert operations were "just about the only way to win World War III without having to fight it." He rejected the notion endorsed by the 1952 Republican convention of "rolling back" Soviet control of Eastern Europe. This was impractical and might lead to general warfare. But he, like McCloy, believed that there were many things that could be done on a covert level that might greatly diminish Soviet influence over the period of a decade or more. So, in the spring of 1953, he authorized a major review of the country's Cold War strategy in a series of seminars code-named Project Solarium. The resulting study urged the president to prosecute an "intensified cold war covertly using a national program of deception and concealment from public disclosure and Soviet discernment."[35]

Project Solarium set the tone for much of the Eisenhower administration's foreign policy over the next eight years. C. D. Jackson, forever an energetic proselytizer of covert action, wrote in his diary that year, "He [Eisenhower] is convinced that psychological warfare should not be the pet mystery of one or more Departments of the Government, but should be the entire posture of the entire Government to the entire world."[36]

That August, the president approved a joint CIA-British operation in Iran to restore the shah to his throne. The coup succeeded on August 22, 1953, supervised in Teheran by the Agency's Kermit Roosevelt. The same week, Eisenhower wrote McCloy, inviting him to attend a special stag dinner to raise private funds for the CIA-sponsored National Committee for a Free Europe. "Quite frankly," wrote Ike, "I believe you will be asked to take the leadership, within your industry, in support of their campaign."[37]

McCloy was fishing in Arizona with Lew Douglas that month, but came back to the East Coast in plenty of time to attend the dinner on September 23. Henry Ford II, Bedell Smith, and the corporate executive officers of Standard Oil, Paramount Pictures, AT&T, General Motors, the U.S. Steel Corp., and other companies attended. McCloy sat across the table from Allen Dulles. (The press was not allowed to know the subject of the dinner or the fact that Dulles was attending on an off-the-record basis.) C. D. Jackson was there to give the pitch soliciting corporate contributions for the National Committee for a Free Europe. A representative of the Heritage Foundation agreed to coordinate a private fund-raising campaign. Some money was no doubt raised in this fashion, but over the years the Committee continued to draw the vast bulk of its budget from the CIA.[38]

While the Eisenhower administration continued to draw upon McCloy's intelligence expertise, Germany remained his highest priority. More than a year after he resigned as high commissioner, it was clear to everyone in the State Department that, when it came to German policy, private citizen McCloy was still a major player. In part this was simply because Adenauer and other German officials chose to use McCloy as a back channel to Eisenhower.[39] Throughout the Eisenhower presidency, Adenauer knew he could count on McCloy to make the German case in Washington. Indeed, it seemed sometimes as if the former high commissioner served as the chancellor's own private envoy to Washington.

For some time, he had delayed a long-planned visit back to Germany, and finally, on October 17, 1953, he set sail aboard the *Queen Elizabeth*. Accompanying him was Shep Stone, now an official of the Ford Foundation. Five days later, he was having lunch in Bonn with Adenauer and the entire German Cabinet.[40] He tried to reassure Adenauer on the one issue that troubled all Europeans about the Eisenhower administration: McCarthyism. As the widely read Hamburg newspaper, *Die Welt*, suggested, many Europeans worried that, in dealing with McCarthy, Eisenhower would ultimately bow to the views of the "conservative majority of Republican Congressmen who look to East Asia" rather than Europe as the focal point of U.S. strategic interests. The revival of America's latent isolationism—directed at Europe, but not Asia—was a scenario that gave Adenauer's conservative constituency nightmares. This was particularly true at a time when the Soviets had launched another "peace offensive" calling for a neutral, unified, but demilitarized Germany. *Die Welt* went so far as to question whether Foster Dulles or Joseph McCarthy was running American foreign policy.[41] Though McCloy, of course, had his doubts about Dulles, he tried to persuade Adenauer that Eisenhower himself was ultimately in charge and would not turn his back on the West Germans.

Adenauer must have wondered, however, how much stock to place in such assurances when the very next week McCloy himself was personally assaulted by McCarthy. In a Chicago speech attacking the "bleeding hearts" who opposed his investigative methods, McCarthy singled out McCloy for criticism. He said the former high commissioner "had been considered for Secretary of State, but fortunately President Eisenhower was too smart." Linking McCloy with those opposed to his investigations, McCarthy told his audience, "We can't treat these people with a lace handkerchief. You can't go on a skunk hunting expedition with a top hat and silk handkerchief. . . . The closer we get to the nerve center, the louder and louder will be the screams."[42]

McCarthy's attacks were now escalating. While McCloy was in Germany, the senator was holding a series of hearings to investigate new charges developed by Roy Cohn that the U.S. Army had been infiltrated by communists. By this time, Cohn had no doubt become aware of the controversy surrounding McCloy's 1945 testimony to Congress on the army's policy toward leftists. McCarthy chose not to use this information just yet, and instead had Cohn elicit testimony in closed-door hearings on charges that a communist spy ring had established itself inside the army's Signal Corps Center at Fort Monmouth, New Jersey.

Far from standing up to McCarthy, as McCloy had suggested to Adenauer it would, the Eisenhower administration now attempted to appease the senator. In late October, the administration announced that 1,456 federal employees had been fired. And on November 6, Attorney General Herbert Brownell gave a speech charging that President Truman had nominated Harry Dexter White to be director of the International Monetary Fund in 1946 despite his knowledge of FBI reports that McCarthy said proved him to be a Soviet agent. On national television Truman angrily denied this and charged that the Eisenhower administration "has fully embraced, for political advantage, McCarthyism." To this, the Wisconsin senator demanded equal time, and in a network speech on November 24 he shocked the administration by characterizing Eisenhower's foreign policy as the same kind of "whining, whimpering appeasement" displayed by Truman. He specifically criticized the administration for not having fired John Paton Davies, McCloy's former political counselor.[43] (Davies was then serving at the U.S. Embassy in Peru.)

McCarthy's attack precipitated a sharp debate within the White House on how to respond. C. D. Jackson told *The New York Times'* James Reston that he thought the senator had "declared war on Eisenhower." Privately, Jackson thought McCarthy was attempting "to establish McCarthyism as Republicanism." He wrote in his diary, "Wonderful syllogism—I [McCarthy] am the only effective rooter-outer of Communists; there are still Communists in Government (Davies). . . . Therefore unless Eisenhower roots them out my way, he is a harborer of Communists." But other White House aides disagreed, and feared the president would lose votes on the Hill for his domestic program if he were to condemn McCarthy. Eisenhower, in the meantime, told Foster Dulles that he hadn't even bothered to read McCarthy's speech. A shocked Jackson complained, "This place is really falling apart." But Jackson didn't give up, and bluntly argued in a White House staff meeting, ". . . this Three Little Monkeys act was not working and would not work, and that appeasing McCarthy" was poor tactics. A few days later, however, the president was still adamant and blustered, "I will not get in the gutter with that guy." Even after a great deal of Jackson's "needling," the most Ike would do was to tell a press conference on December 2 that he would "protect the rights of loyal Americans."[44]

By this time, McCloy was back in America, and, like Eisenhower, he chose not to respond to McCarthy's attack upon him. Instead, he decided it would be prudent to distance himself from McCarthy's critics. In a speech at the Waldorf-Astoria calling for acceptance of West Germany by the European economic community, he took the trouble to reiterate his own anticommunist credentials. He acknowledged that there had been an "astounding" number of dupes and traitors in the United States. He even criticized the "casualness" with which previous administrations had treated the problem of communist infiltration of government agencies.[45]

But even such accommodating words did not keep McCarthy from launching another personal attack. Two weeks later, the senator claimed that Telford Taylor and McCloy had plotted to protect 125 German communists allegedly employed in the offices of HICOG.[46] McCloy was unbelieving. He couldn't countenance that he, of all people, was becoming one of McCarthy's most prominent targets. That November, he had been elected chairman of the Council on Foreign Relations. He was a trustee of the Ford Foundation, a director of the Rockefeller Foundation, and one of the president's most valued private advisers. And yet none of these prestigious positions counted for much in the mind of Joe McCarthy. On the contrary, given the isolationist context of McCarthy's charges, McCloy's internationalist résumé made him a natural target of the senator's loyalty investigations. Worse, the White House was still trying to placate McCarthy. Only a week after his most recent attack on McCloy, the senator was invited to have lunch with the president. There

Attorney General Brownell graciously outlined for the senator a "new offensive" against subversion. The administration, he said, would consider introducing legislation barring the Communist Party and legalizing wire-tap evidence in spy cases. McCarthy walked out of the luncheon and told his friends, "Ike's really learning. Now he's asking my advice."[47] It was true.

By the end of 1953, caution and appeasement characterized Eisenhower's strategy in handling the volatile senator. Above all, individual victims of the witch-hunt could expect to receive no support from the White House. Early in December, the FBI had received an allegation that J. Robert Oppenheimer was a communist spy; Eisenhower immediately ordered Lewis Strauss, chairman of the Atomic Energy Commission, to place a "blank wall" between Oppenheimer and any classified information.[48] A full-scale investigation was launched against the physicist, whom McCloy regarded as a trusted colleague. In a few short months, McCloy would be called upon to testify in his behalf. But before that happened, he would first have to defend himself.

On February 7, 1954, in a speech before a dinner crowd of a thousand at an Eagles' Club in Madison, Wisconsin, McCarthy associated the Democratic administrations of the past twenty years with an "unbelievable, inconceivable unexplainable record of the deliberate, secret betrayal of a nation to its mortal enemy, the Communist conspiracy." He then singled McCloy out by name, charging that the former assistant secretary of war had issued an order for the destruction of all U.S. Army intelligence files on communists. "Clearly, thus the record shows," McCarthy said, "that not only were Communists assigned to key jobs but an attempt also was made to keep any succeeding Administrations from knowing where and who the traitors were." Reached at his home in Manhattan that evening by wire-service reporters, McCloy branded the charges as "absolutely, utterly and completely untrue." He said he had never had any records destroyed at any time, adding, in a jab at McCarthy, "I've been a Republican longer than he has."[49]

Three days later, in Los Angeles, McCarthy told reporters, "I was in error on that." It was one of the rare occasions during his Senate career when McCarthy actually retracted an allegation.[50] Evidently, he had not carefully read the information dug up by Roy Cohn on McCloy, and had gotten the story wrong. McCloy, he conceded, had not ordered the destruction of any files on communists; but, he announced, McCloy had signed orders, when he was assistant secretary of war, to commission known communists as army officers. This allegation, of course, was quite true; McCloy had signed numerous memos during the war, largely at the urging of his friend Harold Ickes, ordering the army not to discriminate against leftists, veterans of the Lincoln Brigade and even admitted former communists who claimed their party membership had lapsed.

Placed in the uncomfortable position of having to defend himself politically against facts he knew to be more or less correct, McCloy subjected himself to a rare interview with Drew Pearson. The widely read liberal columnist was startled by McCloy's vehemence. "He is always eloquent, but not usually impassioned," wrote Pearson that night in his diary. "This time he was passionate on the question of McCarthy." McCloy told him, "McCarthy talks about twenty years of treason. I was part of that administration and I served with Republicans and Democrats, men like Henry Stimson, Bob Patterson, Bob Lovett. . . . We won a war that extended all over the world and touched every shore and after the war we managed to keep the economy of the world prosperous. That was a great achievement and I'm proud of it. And it was not accomplished by traitors."[51] McCloy then gave Pearson all the details behind Eisenhower's well-known "book-burning" speech, including his own role in encouraging the president to condemn McCarthy. This was a good news story, and Pearson was delighted to have it.

Two days after seeing Pearson, and less than a week after McCarthy's latest broadside, McCloy gave a speech in Philadelphia before an audience of a thousand business and civic leaders. Once again without mentioning McCarthy by name, he tried to place the issue of subversion in some kind of reasonable perspective. "We will make a great and fatal mistake," he said, "if we believe that the main issue lies in determining how many Communists there were or now are in our Government. When the smoke clears away it will be found that, serious as the infiltration may have been, our own fundamental strength has not been impaired. And if there were 10 times as many as we thought, it would still be a problem which we can deal with. It is simple compared to the main issue." He then tried to convince his audience that the battlefield lay not at home but abroad, "along the streets of Berlin, in the villages of India and Burma," and the success or failure of this war against international communism depended on the "character of the political leadership we give to the world."[52] This was a psychological brand of warfare, and though McCloy did not speak of McCarthy, he did not have to; clearly, the senator from Wisconsin was not the kind of man to win the hearts and minds of German Social Democrats, not to mention the neutralist-minded Nehrus of the developing world.

McCloy also reiterated the argument he had made a year ago, that the excesses of McCarthyism had been induced by the New Deal's investigations of Wall Street. This was a line of argument that Felix Frankfurter found bothersome. The justice gently admonished McCloy that he rather wished he "would risk plainer talk even to the gentry whom you addressed." He then made an analogy between present-day conservatives who rather relished the spectacle of McCarthy's attacks on liberals, and those German conservative leaders who believed Hitler could be controlled. McCloy quickly wrote back, saying he understood "the implied rebuke." In his defense, he wrote, "The best way that I have found to get a response to the excesses of the present situation from conservative groups is to point to their own interests. They can recall how they were harassed and their motives maligned by a lot of zealots in the Roosevelt days. . . . So when McCarthy's bully boys go to work, these people sit back with a certain sense of satisfaction. The minute, however, that they see their position is related, they come to their senses."[53]

Frankfurter did not let the argument rest there. A week later, he protested, "But surely you are not equating [previous liberal congressional abuses] with the pervasive evil and the deep gashes cut into our national life by the McCarthy performances and the tolerance of them. Nobody knows better than you the differences of degree are so enormous as to be almost differences in kind. . . . Really Jack, do not equate things that are of very different orders."[54] To this firm rebuke, McCloy had no reply.

While Frankfurter thought his former law student's public stance against McCarthyism was not aggressive enough, McCloy and many other like-minded Republicans thought much the same of Eisenhower's handling of the senator. That spring, McCarthy repeatedly humiliated the president, making it clear that his next target of investigation was the U.S. Army.

Finally, one day Lucius Clay told Ike over the phone, "This fellow got too powerful—people [are] scared to do anything about him. I'm willing to bet he has information on honorable discharges [of communists] while you were Chief of Staff."[55] Eisenhower vigorously protested that McCarthy could never prove such a thing, but he had good reason to fear otherwise. After all, if McCloy could be implicated, why not Eisenhower himself? It was in such an atmosphere that administration officials like C. D. Jackson and Henry Cabot Lodge now pleaded with the president to step in behind the scenes and undercut McCarthy's Senate Subcommittee's powers of investigation. Tactically, they thought the first step was to get rid of Roy Cohn. From his post in New York as United Nations ambassador, Lodge wrote to advise that this was the time to use "the documentation on Private S. [David Schine]."

For some months—and with Eisenhower's knowledge—Army Counsel John Adams had carefully compiled a thirty-four-page chronology describing the number of occasions when McCarthy and Roy Cohn had exerted pressure on the army to give preferential treatment to David Schine, who had been drafted into the army the previous autumn as a private. Cohn had first tried to get his friend Schine an officer's commission and, when that failed, had arranged for Schine to receive so many overnight passes that Private Schine was hardly ever on base. Lodge told

Eisenhower that the Adams chronology, "if published, would have an utterly devastating effect."[56]

On March 9, 1954, the Eisenhower administration finally made its move against McCarthy. The senator was invited to lunch with Defense Secretary Charles Wilson, who described the army report and then warned the senator that the chronology would be given to the press if Roy Cohn wasn't dismissed immediately. McCarthy told Wilson that the army could go to hell. After two hours, with a pack of reporters waiting outside, Wilson emerged from the luncheon to say only that he had "no arguments" with the senator about the issue of communists in the army. To the public, of course, this looked like another surrender, since only a few days earlier McCarthy had accused the army of "coddling" communists—a charge which Wilson had then said was "just plain tommyrot." Now McCarthy told reporters that he was only trying to help the army clean out "the few rotten apples." He then explained that these few "undesirables" had gotten into the army in the first place as a result of a 1944 "McCloy order." The next day the *Washington Post* reported that the order McCarthy referred to was a "secret order" issued on December 30, 1944, under which communists and their sympathizers were not to be discriminated against by the army unless a "specific finding" of disloyalty to the United States could be made. This time, McCarthy had his facts right, and, given the current political climate, McCloy was well aware that he was vulnerable.[57]

McCarthy was obviously not going to drop his charges against him, and if the senator were not diverted, the chairman of Chase National Bank might find himself being interrogated by McCarthy's committee. Public opinion, however, was beginning to swing against the senator. The evening before McCarthy's latest attack on McCloy, millions of television viewers had tuned into CBS's Edward R. Murrow's "See It Now" program and listened to a "report on Senator Joseph R. McCarthy told mainly in his own words and pictures." The film clips showed the senator at his worst, picking his nose, sneering at witnesses, and making crude jokes about nationally respected figures. The results were devastating: in the weeks ahead, Murrow's CBS office received mail that ran fifteen to one against McCarthy.[58]

At this point, three days after McCarthy's latest charge against McCloy, Pearson devoted a lengthy column to explaining why "revenge" had motivated McCarthy to attack McCloy. The senator, he reported, had learned that Eisenhower's Dartmouth book-burning speech had been inspired by McCloy. Thereafter, McCarthy had sent his investigators to dig into McCloy's career. This was how McCarthy had discovered McCloy's association with the army order barring discrimination against communists. Pearson reported that McCloy's decision, moreover, had been shared by Stimson, Marshall, and the entire General Staff of the army.[59] These were, indeed, more or less the facts.

By now, Eisenhower must have realized that, if McCarthy was given the opportunity, he would go after the records of McCloy, Stimson, Marshall, and other prominent friends of the president. He would want to know why citizens with security files that indicated they were members of the Communist Party were allowed to fight in World War II, let alone receive officers' commissions; and in the hysteria of 1954, safeguarding common civil liberties was not a politically acceptable reason. McCloy's particular vulnerability was not the sole, or even the major, motivation for the president's decision to go on the offensive, but his predicament helped precipitate the timing of Eisenhower's decision.

So, two days after Wilson warned McCarthy about the existence of the "Adams Chronology"—the senator called it "blackmail"—the White House ordered its release to the press.[60] The result was a political bombshell. Within days, the Senate agreed to hold hearings and investigate the charges against Roy Cohn. The army-McCarthy hearings began a month later.

But in the meantime, just a week after the release of the Adams Chronology, an unsubdued McCarthy told a wildly cheering crowd of South Chicago automobile dealers that he would never be a "rubber stamp" for Eisenhower. And once again he took the trouble to name McCloy as the individual responsible for allowing communists to infiltrate the army.[61] The next day, on March 19, McCloy went to see Eisenhower. There is no record of what these two old friends said to each other in this moment of personal crisis, but McCloy was not one to request a meeting without having something quite clear to tell the president. The press reported that he had requested the appointment, and the White House released no details on the meeting's agenda. The *Washington Star* pointedly identified McCloy as "one of Senator McCarthy's targets in the Senator's running battle with the Army. . . ."[62]

Soon, however, the Wisconsin senator's political career would be in ruins. During the course of the seventy-two televised sessions of the army-McCarthy hearings, millions of Americans saw McCarthy up close for the first time. The climax of this piece of political theater occurred when the army's chief counsel for the hearings, Joseph Nye Welch, interrupted one of the senator's more slanderous tirades and asked, "Have you no sense of decency, sir, at long last? Have you left no sense of decency?" When it was over, a resolution was introduced in the Senate condemning the "unbecoming" behavior of the junior senator from Wisconsin. Finally, on December 2, 1954, after three days of angry debate, the Senate voted sixty-seven to twenty-two to censure McCarthy. The senator's political career was dead, though "McCarthyism" would continue to poison the American political landscape for years to come.

While Congress prepared to hold televised hearings on the Cohn-Schine matter, a related drama was unfolding offstage. Back in December 1953, the FBI had forwarded to the White House the latest accusations against J. Robert Oppenheimer. With the exception of one item, all the charges had already been thoroughly investigated, most recently in 1948, when the Atomic Energy Commission had reviewed Oppenheimer's record and cleared him for classified work. The only new item related solely to the physicist's opposition on moral and policy grounds to the development of the hydrogen bomb. But his critics, including Lewis Strauss, the strong-minded chairman of the AEC, considered this an indication that Oppenheimer might have been, through all these years, a Soviet agent, and so formal charges were filed against the physicist.

On the morning of Monday, April 12, 1954, Oppenheimer appeared before a specially appointed loyalty-review board in Washington. For legal counsel he brought with him Lloyd K. Garrison, a soft-spoken New York lawyer whom Oppenheimer knew as a trustee of the Institute for Advanced Studies. Sitting in judgment were Gordon Gray, a forty-five-year-old former secretary of the army under Truman; Thomas Alfred Morgan, a retired chairman of the Sperry Corporation; and Ward V. Evans, a chemistry professor. Gray headed the board of inquiry. McCloy thought highly of both Gray and Morgan; he had worked with Morgan during the previous year as a trustee of the United Negro College Fund in New York.

As the "Gray Board" sat down to begin hearing testimony in the case, the public at large was completely unaware that charges of disloyalty had been brought against America's most famous nuclear scientist. The veil of secrecy over the case, however, lasted hardly a day. Fearing a leak, Garrison had taken the precaution of providing James Reston with copies of both the AEC charges and Oppenheimer's reply. Reston had promised to hold the story as long as possible, but that first afternoon Garrison received a call saying that news of the Gray Board's existence had leaked out. The *Times,* Reston determined, would have to run the story.

The next morning, McCloy opened his paper to see the scandal spread across much of the front page. Though he found the news profoundly "disturbing," he was nevertheless glad that Scotty Reston had brought out the story "before McCarthy tries to claim credit for it." McCloy rejected out of hand the very idea that Oppenheimer might have been a Soviet agent. During the war, he had seen enough of the physicist to feel the man's personal magnetism. "I was intrigued by Oppie," recalled McCloy later, "and didn't give a damn if he was sleeping with a mistress who was a communist."[63] He had seen Oppenheimer as recently as January 23, 1954, at a meeting of the Council on Foreign Relations' Study Group on Soviet-U.S. Relations.[64] The Study Group—which included Averell Harriman, Dean Rusk, Robert Bowie, McGeorge Bundy, and Arthur Dean—had been meeting regularly at the Princeton Inn for almost a year. McCloy would always remember the physicist talking of the two nuclear powers trapped "like two scorpions in a bottle," and he shared Oppie's concern that "this awful force that we had released . . . did not become a destroyer of civilization."[65] But he was also sometimes baffled by Oppenheimer, and that morning he sat down and wrote Frankfurter a note conveying his mixed emotions about the case:

> Knowing firsthand the tremendous contributions that this man made to the development of our position in atomic weapons, I can't conceive of any real disloyalty on his part no matter what his early associations were. What always puzzles me about these scientists and intellectual cases is their disposition to play with Communist theories at the same time that they must be aware of the doctrines of controlled thought which the Communist philosophy involves.[66]

Still, he had no doubt that the whole affair was ridiculous. Three days later, he wrote Eisenhower, bluntly telling the president that a security investigation of a man like Oppenheimer "is somewhat like inquiring into the security risk of a Newton or a Galileo. Such people are themselves always 'top secret.' " Ike lamely replied that he hoped the "distinguished" Gray Board would exonerate the scientist.[67]

McCloy's attitude was not shared by many men, and fewer still were willing to defend the physicist publicly. After reading Oppenheimer's security file in the autumn of 1952, Robert Lovett called it a "nightmare."[68] But Lloyd Garrison was able to assemble an impressive list of well-known figures to testify in behalf of his client. The list included Nobel laureates Enrico Fermi, Isidor I. Rabi, and Hans Bethe, and such policy-makers as George Kennan, Vannevar Bush, and Karl T. Compton. Toward the end of the hearings, and after all these men had testified, Garrison persuaded Gray to allow him to interrupt the presentation of the government's case with a last-minute defense witness—John J. McCloy. (Garrison had known McCloy since Harvard Law School, and the two men now saw each other occasionally at luncheons sponsored by the exclusive "Nisi Prius" club.) This last-minute testimony produced some of the most memorable exchanges of the trial. The entire five-hundred-thousand-word transcript of the hearing was soon leaked; excerpts of McCloy's statements were highlighted in *The New York Times,* and radio commentator Fulton Lewis, Jr., read large portions of the transcript over the air. To the delight of liberals and Oppenheimer's defenders, McCloy raised issues that went to the heart of such security trials.[69]

He asserted there was nothing that gave him any reason to suspect Oppenheimer of disloyalty. If anything, he said, it had been his impression during meetings of the CFR's Soviet Study Group that the physicist was more "militant" than others in the Study Group on the question of dealing with the Soviet Union. But then McCloy went on to question a basic assumption of the entire proceedings by challenging the Gray Board's definition of security:

> I don't know just exactly what you mean by a security risk. I know that I am a security risk and I think every individual is a security risk. . . . I think there is a security risk in reverse. . . . We are only secure if we have the best brains and the best reach of mind. If the impression is prevalent that scientists as a whole have to work under such great restrictions and perhaps great suspicion in the United States, we may lose the next step in this [nuclear] field, which I think would be very dangerous for us.[70]

Members of the Gray Board and their counsel, Roger Robb, were greatly troubled by this argument, for it suggested that there were no absolutes in matters of security, that a value judgment had to be made on the merits of each individual. This would be a particularly difficult exercise in the case of Oppenheimer, whose personality was as complicated as the mass of contrary information contained in his thick security file. How, for instance, could one weigh the single most damaging piece of evidence against Oppenheimer, the so-called Chevalier incident? Early in 1943, one of Oppenheimer's closest friends, the novelist Haakon Chevalier, had informed him in a casual conversation held in the physicist's kitchen that a British chemical engineer known to both men had recently volunteered that he had a channel by which to convey scientific information to the Soviets. Oppenheimer immediately said he would have nothing to do with any such effort. Oppenheimer's security problem arose subsequently, when it became clear that he had delayed reporting the incident. Worse, in an effort to protect Chevalier's identity, he had lied to security officers about the details of the conversation.[71]

In evaluating the security risks stemming from this incident, McCloy would require the Gray Board to weigh Oppenheimer's willingness to lie in order to protect a friend against his value to the country as a theoretical physicist. Under cross-examination, Robb countered with an analogy: did the chairman of Chase National Bank employ anyone who for some time had associated with bank robbers? "No," said McCloy, "I don't know of anyone." And if a Chase branch manager had a friend who volunteered that he knew some people who planned to rob the bank, wouldn't McCloy expect his branch manager to report the conversation? McCloy, of course, had to answer, "Yes."

This was damaging to Oppenheimer's case, and more so when Gordon Gray returned to the analogy a short time later in his cross-examination: "Would you leave someone in charge of the vaults about whom you have any doubt in your mind?"

McCloy was forced to say no, but then quickly interjected that, if an employee of doubtful background nevertheless "knew more about . . . the intricacies of time locks than anybody else in the world, I might think twice before I let him go, because I would balance the risks in this connection." He then illustrated the point by revealing that as high commissioner in Germany he had given his approval to a program (later identified as Operation Paperclip) that recruited Nazi scientists for well-paid, classified work in the United States. When it came to the mind of Dr. Oppenheimer, he said, "I would accept a considerable amount of political immaturity in return for this rather esoteric, this rather indefinite, theoretical thinking that I believe we are going to be dependent on for the next generation."[72]

In his summation speech, Garrison echoed this argument—indeed, made it central to his case—by pleading that "we must not devour the best and most gifted of our citizens in some mechanical application of security procedures and mechanisms." But in the end, this reasoning convinced only one of the three members of the Gray Board. Gordon Gray and Tom Morgan concluded that Oppenheimer was a security risk. Though the physicist was a "loyal citizen" who had "an unusual ability to keep to himself vital secrets," Gray and Morgan concluded that his security clearance should not be restored, on the grounds that "any person whose absolute loyalty to the United States is in question . . . should be rejected for government service."[73]

McCloy wrote Frankfurter, "What a tragedy that one who contributed so much—more than half the bemedaled generals I know—to the security of the country should now after all these years be designated a security risk. I understand the Admiral [Lewis Strauss] is annoyed at my testimony but great God what does he expect? I was there when Oppie's massive contribution was rendered and know there is so much more to say but what's the use?"[74]

Frankfurter tried to reassure him, writing, ". . . you opened a good many minds to a realization of the profound importance of your 'concept of an affirmative security.' " Both Frankfurter and McCloy agreed between themselves that AEC Chairman Strauss was the chief culprit in the case. Several years earlier, Oppenheimer had publicly ridiculed Strauss's knowledge of physics before a congressional committee. The opinionated admiral had been stung by this public humiliation. In addition, McCloy and Frankfurter felt certain that the admiral's policy dispute with Oppenheimer over the H-bomb program had colored his judgment. In their eyes, the result had been a personal tragedy for Oppenheimer, and a blot on the record of the Eisenhower administration.[75]

The Oppenheimer affair occurred at the beginning of the end of McCarthyism. While the Gray Board was deciding to take no notice of the "imponderables" in determining the scientist's loyalty (Isidor Rabi called the exercise "writing a man's life"), the army-McCarthy televised hearings were teaching America something about the ugliness associated with political witch-hunts.

McCloy fared better in the eyes of history for his role in this ugly chapter of American history than did most of his peers. Few of his colleagues in Establishment circles—Democrat or Republican—ever spoke out publicly against McCarthy. The self-defined stewards of the public interest stood by passively through most of this national trauma. Privately, they were disgusted by the methods and antics of the Wisconsin senator, and, significantly, they never took seriously the threat of subversion. But they nevertheless kept their silence, doing nothing when the targets of McCarthyism were just a few left-wing New Dealers and "popular front" intellectuals. Only very late in the game did a few of them—and, most particularly, McCloy—intervene. He gave his president blunt and forceful advice, and this made a difference. On the other hand, even McCloy hesitated too long, and sometimes coupled his criticism with ill-considered comparisons to the New Deal investigations of Wall Street. He did not publicly defend the careers or reputations of his own HICOG officers. And when he finally did go public with his views, it was in his own self-defense. For the times, however, even this limited response displayed a remarkable degree of political courage.

Ironically, during that same spring of 1954, when he was having to defend himself against McCarthy, McCloy was busy brokering a clandestine relationship between the CIA and the country's wealthiest philanthropical institution, the Ford Foundation. Henry Ford II had personally recruited him onto the Foundation's board in early 1953, and by the spring of 1954, McCloy was dropping in two or three times a month to talk with Shep Stone or Don Price, a vice-president of the Foundation's International Areas division. A year earlier, he had arranged for the Foundation to give the Council on Foreign Relations $100,000 to fund its Soviet Study Group, a project undertaken in consultation with the State Department. By now, the Foundation's funding of projects in the international field was expanding quite rapidly. Soon it became clear that the U.S. government had an obvious interest in some of these overseas projects. Throughout these years, Allen Dulles, Frank G. Wisner, Bedell Smith, and other CIA officials repeatedly approached the Foundation to fund Agency projects and provide access to Foundation officials or fellows abroad for use in intelligence-gathering.[76] "I can remember the unease we had over that," McCloy recalled years later. "I was skeptical about it because it had some risks to the reputation of the foundation. These people were too intelligence-minded. . . . [They] consistently thought of the Ford Foundation as an institution of intelligence-gathering. I was a little nervous about that."[77]

Frank Wisner, the mercurial chief of the Agency's Office of Policy Coordination (OPC), was particularly zealous. By 1953, OPC had a budget of more than $200 million annually, and Wisner was running clandestine operations all over the world. "Wisner was a great talker," McCloy recalled, "and he had great ideas about what the Ford Foundation ought to be doing."[78]

The pressure from the Agency was considerable. In one meeting sometime in early 1954, Dulles and Wisner told McCloy and Price that they "hoped the Foundation would take a steady and long-term view." According to Price's notes of the meeting, "There were some risks involved, and . . . the obvious limit would be when the government of the host country was really playing the communist game . . . but there were going to be a lot of in-between situations in which you could do business with a neutralist country. It would be great, they thought, if the Foundation were in the Middle East which was a wide open and flexible situation. . . ."[79]

Soon afterward, with McCloy's concurrence, Don Price made the rounds in Washington, seeing Allen Dulles, Wisner, various State Department officials, and Kermit Roosevelt, the Agency man credited with engineering the collapse of Prime Minister Mohammed Mossadegh's government in Iran the previous summer. Price came away from these meetings believing that, "in general, our [Foundation] objectives and the U.S. national objectives ought to be in harmony although we would not take the word of government officials as to what that harmony ought to consist of [and] we ought not ever to be engaged in joint operations with any U.S. government agency."[80]

McCloy agreed with these general sentiments; he valued the Foundation's independence and did not wish to see it taken over by the intelligence bureaucracy. "I was conscious of keeping the Ford Foundation's shirts just as clean as I could," he recalled. But ever since the Black Tom case, he had always been intrigued with things clandestine, and Allen Dulles's stories could be quite seductive. Describing Dulles as being buried in the "cloak-and-dagger business," McCloy recalled how he was "always coming to me to ask me to get the Ford Foundation to help behind the Iron Curtain. . . . He would give me a tale of what was going on, and if it didn't give me the shivers, it should have."[81]

These discussions with various CIA officers caused considerable debate among Foundation officers and trustees during the first six months of 1954. Finally, on May 21, 1954, in an effort to formulate a standard policy within the Foundation on how to handle such government-sponsored projects,

Don Price wrote a memo on the whole problem. He set four ground rules. First, such projects would be recommended only when they were already the kind of projects the Foundation "normally supports." Second, such projects would be "infrequently recommended. . . ." Third, "In all such cases, three members of the Board of Trustees—the Chairman, Mr. McCloy, and the President—will be in possession of all the facts regarding the interest of the government and the action recommended will have their previous approval." And fourth, "Such projects may then be put before the Board without identifying the government's interest in them. . . ."[82]

Years later, when asked about this unusual arrangement, McCloy defended it as a means of limiting the CIA's involvement with the Foundation. "We set up this group so that no one else in the Foundation would be approached. I recall the element of concern that we had—you could hardly get your mind addressed to one thing before another came up, with its ball of fur."[83] Price and McCloy feared that, if there was a blanket prohibition on dealing with the CIA, the Agency would simply recruit individual Foundation officers. Price's ground rules required the CIA to go through McCloy, and it was made clear to Allen Dulles that any other contacts would jeopardize the Foundation's willingness to cooperate. Price bluntly told Dulles, "Look, the first time you meddle with our boys, we'll quit this whole program."[84]

This understanding may have restricted the CIA's approaches to individuals within the Foundation, but over the next few years McCloy's three-man committee approved a number of CIA-initiated projects. When the Agency again requested funding for the Congress on Cultural Freedom, McCloy sent Price to talk with Dean Rusk, then president of the Rockefeller Foundation, which McCloy had rejoined the previous year as a member of the board of trustees. Though Rusk was unwilling to have the Rockefeller Foundation get involved, Price came away from the meeting ready to recommend the funding to McCloy. In short order, the Foundation approved a three-year grant of $500,000 to subsidize various magazines published in French, English, and Spanish. Price and other Ford Foundation officers were well aware of the political nature of such activities: the purpose was to make European "intellectual leaders more militant in protecting freedom and combatting Communist effort[s]. . . ."[85]

As the years passed, McCloy set some limits to the CIA's inroads into the Foundation. At one point in the 1950s, the Agency asked for a list of Foundation officers and recipients of Ford Foundation fellowships working abroad. When the CIA indicated that these individuals might be asked to engage in a little free-lance intelligence-gathering, the Foundation again debated whether it should cooperate. Don Price had several long talks with Allen Dulles and his aide Richard Bissell, who himself had worked for a short time at the Ford Foundation. According to Price, he eventually reached an understanding with the Agency: "I had solemn promises from Dulles and from Bissell that they would not meddle with fellows while they were in that status, but they would be free to recruit them later on." Henceforth, only the names of Foundation fellows whose grants had already expired were regularly forwarded to the CIA.[86] Similar arrangements between the CIA and dozens of other foundations quickly became quite commonplace.[87]

Throughout the Eisenhower presidency, as he had during the war, McCloy served as Ike's private political counselor. Unsure of his own political instincts, Eisenhower deferred to the lawyer who had so often extracted him from delicate political problems during the war. Whether the issue of was McCarthyism, Germany, intelligence operations in Europe, or how to handle the controversial Bricker Amendment, Ike listened to McCloy.[88]

He was Ike's hidden vizier, but he was also a simple friend. The two men enjoyed each other's company, and they often tried not to talk politics. Looking ahead to a meeting in a few weeks' time, McCloy could write, "I hope we don't have to talk 'business' all the time."[89] Alone, they often shared their mutual passion for Civil War history. That spring, McCloy sent Eisenhower a rare copy of the *Freemantle Diary*, an eyewitness account of the Battle of Gettysburg. He suggested that the tree from which the author had observed the battle might be found on Eisenhower's own 246-acre Gettysburg farm. The president said he would certainly "investigate the matter of the tree."[90] For his part, Eisenhower admired McCloy, just as he admired all such pillars of the business community, for the practical power he exercised. He felt comfortable around businessmen like Pete Jones, Bill Robinson, Bob Jones, Sid Richardson, Bob Woodruff, and Dillon Anderson precisely because these were men of means, and therefore, thought Eisenhower, they could afford to be disinterested about public affairs.* "These were men of discretion," Eisenhower later wrote in his memoirs, "men, who, already successful, made no attempt to profit by our association."[91] (Eisenhower himself, however, profited enormously from these friendships; some of the same businessmen gave him all his suits, stocked his freezer with food, and built him a summer cabin at Augusta, Georgia.[92]) Though busy men themselves, they could always find the time to entertain the president. McCloy was not a golfer, and was thus not so visible a member of the president's

*W. Alton "Pete" Jones was president of Cities Services Co., a Texas oil company; William Robinson was an advertising-and-sales executive of the *New York Herald Tribune;* Robert Tyre Jones was president of the Joroberts Corporation, which marketed Coca-Cola abroad; Bob Woodruff was another Coca-Cola executive; Sid Richardson was an independent and wealthy Texas oil man; and Dillon Anderson was a Houston lawyer.

"gang" as men like Ellis Slater and Bill Robinson. But he was nevertheless sometimes there, in the background, watching the president play his favorite sport. On at least one occasion, in February 1954, he used a Chase National Bank plane to ferry himself and the rest of Ike's "gang" down from New York in order to keep a golf date with the president at the Augusta National range.[93]

Naturally, McCloy and other businessmen who shared Eisenhower's friendship in these years also shared the president's political philosophy. No one considered Ike a profound political thinker, but he possessed a coherent and distinctive political philosophy. Like McCloy, he had been a lifelong Republican, and if his professional military ethics had not prevented him from voting, he would have voted Republican in every presidential race with the exception of 1944, when he thought the war effort dictated the re-election of Roosevelt. Drawing on much of Herbert Hoover's managerial approach to politics, Eisenhower's political creed in retrospect has been described by one historian as a commitment to a "corporate commonwealth." Like McCloy, he abhorred any visible signs of class conflict and regretted the "drift toward statism" initiated by the New Deal. Instead, he hoped to see business, labor, and the government work together harmoniously for the greater public good. By and large, of course, only men of means from the corporate world could occasionally afford to appear disinterested, and this may help to explain Ike's instinctive admiration for the kind of men who stood at the top of corporate empires. Politicians, by contrast, were to be distrusted precisely because they catered to an alleged popular will, which in the view of Eisenhower was no more than the pleading of selfish "pressure groups." The businessmen to whom he gravitated were invariably the kind of internationalist "corporate liberals" who identified themselves as liberal Republicans. These men were not rock-ribbed conservatives; they did not intend to roll back Social Security, and they believed the federal government had a role to play in the "maintenance of prosperity." Politically speaking, there could not have been a better match between Eisenhower and McCloy.[94]

Eisenhower also felt a certain personal empathy for McCloy. Both men had spent long years in public service, during and after the war, and the president felt almost protective of McCloy's opportunity now to recoup some financial gain from his position at Chase National. Early in 1954, when Eisenhower learned from a mutual friend that McCloy was being pressured to head yet another government study group, he promptly wrote Foster Dulles a short note saying, ". . . Jack McCloy has made more than his full share of sacrifice through his long period of government service and . . . we should not 'pressure' him if anyone else can possibly do the job."[95]

McCloy was indeed busy with Chase business. One day, while he was poring over the bank's loan portfolio, he noticed that a number of very sizable loans had been made at an unusually low interest rate to two Texas oil men, Sid Richardson and Clint Murchison. He had met Richardson at Eisenhower's stag dinner the previous year. Feeling a little nervous about the size of such a low-interest loan, McCloy picked up the phone and called Richardson. The expansive Texan had heard that McCloy enjoyed hunting quail, and so he insisted that before they talked business the banker should come down to Texas for a little hunting on his ranch. McCloy accepted the invitation, and took with him to Texas a fine English "Boss" hunting gun he had just purchased from a retiring member of the Chase board. Richardson explained that they would be hunting the quail from a Landrover. McCloy said he'd prefer to walk, but his host insisted that he ride on the front extension of the Landrover—at least in the beginning. Grinning broadly, the Texas oil man said he could "walk" his quail later, if he still wished. They had not gone far when the largest rattlesnake McCloy had ever seen came close enough to attack him. He blasted the snake with his shotgun more than once before killing it. But this was only the beginning. As they bounced across Richardson's ranch that day, he ended up shooting far more rattlers than quail. After McCloy killed yet another snake, Richardson grinned and asked if he still wanted to "walk" the quail. When a chagrined McCloy quickly declined, Richardson suggested it was time to talk about those loans. He asked if he should shift the loans to one of Chase's competitors, and when McCloy said no, the Texan told McCloy not to worry, that the loans were secure.

Early in 1954, Richardson and his partner, Clint Murchison, were enticed by Robert R. Young, the "Populist of Wall Street," into a deal that promised quick profits. For several years, Young had been trying to take control of the New York Central Railroad Company, worth in the neighborhood of $2.6 billion. Chase National Bank had some time earlier been appointed trustee of eight hundred thousand shares of Central stock, representing one-eighth of all outstanding shares, a trusteeship that came about primarily because Percy J. Ebbott, who served under McCloy as president of Chase National, also happened to be a director of New York Central Railroad Company. In that capacity, Ebbott had voted along with the rest of Central's board against one of Young's earlier takeover bids. By early 1954, Young had readied yet another assault on Central; but he feared that Ebbott would once again vote the eight hundred thousand shares held in escrow by Chase Bank against him. At this point, Young decided to bring in Richardson and Murchison. He arranged for the two Texans to buy Chase's eight hundred thousand shares without putting up any of their own money. They merely had to vote these shares for Young's slate on Central's board, and he would arrange for a temporary loan to buy the shares. The two Texans were also given an option to sell their shares back to Young's syndicate with a guaranteed profit of some $10 million; Richardson and Murchison had nothing to lose. In an episode that must have reminded him of his railroad-takeover work as a young lawyer with Cravath in the 1920s, McCloy facilitated the sale to Richardson and Murchison of the eight hundred thousand Central shares held in trust by Chase. New York Central's management considered the unusual arrangement highly improper and lodged a protest with the Interstate Commerce Commission. The ICC held hearings but did nothing to stop the sale. In the meantime, Central's management fought what they considered to be a hostile takeover and refused to give the two Texans seats on the board of directors.

When the two oil men arrived in New York for negotiations with Central's management, they drove straight from the airport to McCloy's East Side apartment in Manhattan. McCloy served in his usual role as intermediary, and arranged meetings between the Texans and Central's management. A bitter proxy fight, however, could not be avoided, and eventually Young won control of New York Central. Young's victory proved to be fatal both for him and the railroad; after sustaining serious losses in early 1958, he committed suicide. New York Central never recovered financially; it eventually merged with the Pennsylvania Railroad, and this amalgamated railroad went bankrupt in 1970. Rarely did such tales of corporate conflict find their way into the pages of *The New York Times,* but this one did, giving a public hint of how important the Chase chairman was to men of business like Sid Richardson.[96] Clearly, what McCloy had done did not serve the public interest, but by the time Penn Central went bankrupt, no one would remember his role in the corporation's downfall.

Early in 1954, *The New York Times* published a photograph of McCloy and Averell Harriman talking to Secretary of State John Foster Dulles. The occasion at New York's posh Hotel Pierre was as much in honor of McCloy's becoming the new chairman of the Council on Foreign Relations as it was for the dour Dulles. McCloy presided over the Council dinner and introduced Foster Dulles as the evening's guest of honor and main speaker. More than three hundred of the Council's members attended this major event on the city's social calendar. Dozens of McCloy's oldest friends showed up, including Averell Harriman, Allen Dulles, Ben Buttenwieser, Eric Warburg, Francis Plimpton, George Roberts, David E. Lilienthal, and Cass Canfield, a book publisher and now one of McCloy's frequent tennis partners. There were also many former colleagues from HICOG days, such as Shep Stone, Robert Bowie, Ben Shute, and Eli W. Debevoise, the last two of whom had returned to their respective law firms. In addition, such old New York acquaintances as Henry Luce, Paul Nitze, Arthur Dean, Roswell L. Gilpatric, Emilio G. Collado, Clarence Dillon, Lloyd K. Garrison, Herbert Bayard Swope,

George Ball, Samuel K. C. Kopper, Juan T. Trippe, Thomas J. Watson, Walter J. Levy, Howard C. Petersen, Thomas S. Lamont, and John W. Davis came to celebrate McCloy's ascendancy to the chairmanship.[97] Such a turnout from among the leaders of the New York business and legal communities suggested that under McCloy's chairmanship the CFR would be stepping outside its clubbish private quarters at Pratt House and assuming a higher profile than ever before.

Early in Eisenhower's first term, many Council members had regarded Foster Dulles with skepticism. In Council seminars he was thought to be rigid in his thinking and not a little sanctimonious. McCloy and many other Council members thought his policies simplistic, partly because he was tying U.S. prestige to a string of artificial regional-security pacts stretching around the globe, and partly because he had endorsed a defense strategy based on massive nuclear retaliation for any Soviet act of aggression. Both propositions seemed inflexible and dangerous. Worse, McCloy thought Dulles's stance actually put the United States on the defensive in the propaganda war with the Soviets. He felt the administration was losing its bearings.

During the summer of 1954, McCloy and C. D. Jackson had several long talks in New York over what they agreed was a chaotic state of affairs. Jackson had promised to assist Ike for only one year in the White House, and by April 1954 he was back in New York. Almost immediately, Eisenhower became "acutely conscious of the gap" left by Jackson's departure.[98] Given Eisenhower's hands-off managing style, he had depended on Jackson to stimulate debate, churn ideas around, and "bat things up to him. . . ."[99]

White House morale was low, and Jackson's was not the only departure that year. Before the end of the summer, the president's special assistant for national security affairs, Robert Cutler, would also submit his resignation, citing, among other factors, "the conduct of certain Republican Senators. . . . A 'Party' which relies upon these untrustworthy men makes me sick at heart."[100] Though the senator from Wisconsin no longer seemed invincible, McCarthyism had taken its toll. Even Foster Dulles, who usually exuded an air of unquestioning devotion to Eisenhower, now agreed with Jackson that Ike's "exaggerated desire to have everybody happy, everybody like him, prevents him from making clean cut decisions and forces him to play ball with the last person he has listened to." Jackson concluded in his diary that Ike might be a "wonderful man, every right instinct, the man to fulfill Arthur Vandenberg's 'bipartisan leadership America-out-of-crisis' dream. [But] May well go down to ignominy and defeat."[101] Jackson was always sounding the alarm bell, but in the summer of 1954 there could be no mistaking the mood in the White House. The presidency was adrift.

In this context, McCloy was asked by Ike's chief of staff, Sherman

Adams, to find a replacement for Jackson. But by early August, after going through a "well-thumbed list," he was unenthusiastic about any of the possible candidates. And the more he talked to Jackson, the more convinced he was that Jackson should return to Washington. The sticking point was that Henry Luce was unwilling to relinquish his right-hand man. Then, over the last weekend in July, McCloy huddled with Sherman Adams and the president in Washington and came up with the idea that Jackson should return to Washington as a two-day-a-week special adviser. He conveyed this idea to Luce, who then discussed it with Jackson. The Time-Life executive noted in his diary that day, "Luce advised that despite his best efforts, Washington was closing in on me again through McCloy. . . ."[102]

By this point, Jackson felt that, if he was going to have his arm twisted to go back to Washington, he would take the opportunity to lay out his complaints about Eisenhower's passive leadership style. He called up McCloy and shocked him with the vehemence of his criticisms. He told McCloy that Eisenhower had repeatedly accepted "bad political advice" and naïvely thought he could run U.S. foreign policy by occasionally giving a speech. Jackson thought the whole White House operation looked "like a bunch of frightened amateurs, adhoc-ing themselves out of business."[103]

McCloy agreed with Jackson that the White House should be taking more initiatives in foreign affairs and that the Cold War should be fought vigorously with every nonmilitary weapon at hand. Specifically, he and Jackson wanted to see the administration implement more of the covert-action programs recommended by Task Force C of Project Solarium. This meant more money had to be spent on national security. As Jackson defined it in 1951, the "three big ingredients of psychological warfare are 1) money, 2) no holds barred and 3) no questions asked."[104] McCloy was himself a foreign-policy activist and saw nothing wrong with encouraging Jackson to pressure the president into taking a higher profile.

On August 11, 1954, Jackson went to the White House for a meeting with the president and Sherman Adams. Buttressed by his talks with Luce and McCloy, he was determined to tell Ike some "unpleasant truths." To make sure he didn't get flustered, Jackson brought notes. When Ike walked in from a press conference for the meeting, Jackson slapped his notes on the table, took a deep breath, and said, "I have had several talks with Jack McCloy about the idea of coming down here. I have also talked with the Governor [Adams], the Dulles brothers . . . Bobby Cutler, Beedle [Bedell Smith], [Ambassador] Clare Luce when she got back from Italy, on various aspects of the general situation—and the word for it is 'crisis.' " Jackson listed the president's inadequacies: ". . . foreign policy by Presidential speech, with no follow-through afterwards"; a belief that "it is possible to separate foreign policy climate and impact from domestic political actions"; and a perception "that you, Mr. President, don't like your job." At this, Jackson noticed "a little red rising on Prexy's neck, but he didn't blow." When Jackson was finished, Eisenhower gently defended his leadership, saying that "we ought first of all be content with little steps. . . . Many people have the vision to see what should be done; the difficulty is what is possible at home. . . ."[105] Money was limited, Eisenhower insisted, and one therefore couldn't conduct an activist foreign policy on all fronts simultaneously. Nevertheless, the president indicated he'd like to have Jackson back on board, if only for a couple of days a week.

Jackson agreed to the arrangement worked out by McCloy, and for almost another year worked part-time out of the White House. But neither he nor McCloy ever succeeded in persuading Eisenhower to become more of an activist president. It just wasn't Ike's style. Eisenhower was content with his "little steps," one of which had just occurred in Guatemala, where the CIA had orchestrated a covert operation—consisting largely of sheer military bluff—to topple a left-of-center elected government. Jackson applauded the Guatemalan operation; he just wished the administration would commit greater resources to similar ventures in places more important to U.S. interests than Central America. McCloy could hardly disagree; the Guatemalan intervention was an operation one of his own study groups at the Council on Foreign Relations had recommended in 1953.[106]

McCloy's role as a private adviser to the president on national-security and intelligence issues was not widely known in the mid-1950s. A few columnists—James Reston, Arthur Krock, and Drew Pearson—occasionally referred to his influence on the White House. And as Joseph McCarthy's power receded in late 1954 and 1955, conservative columnists like George Sokolosky sometimes made a point of identifying McCloy as a behind-the-scenes power-broker for the liberal wing of the Republican Party. But to the public at large, McCloy was seen only as the former high commissioner and current chairman of Chase National Bank. His public profile as one of the country's most powerful bankers rose dramatically when, in early 1955, he succeeded in pushing through the merger of Chase with the Bank of Manhattan. Thereafter, if his name appeared in the newspapers at all it was invariably in connection with his actions as chairman of the second-largest bank in the country.

Business for the newly merged Chase Manhattan Bank was booming. In the three years 1954–57 the bank's loans to commercial and industrial ventures nearly quadrupled from $1.0 billion to $3.9 billion.[107] By the spring of 1955, the stock market was experiencing a tremendous rise in prices. Some economists expressed worries that the frenzy of speculation on the market was reminiscent of the autumn of 1929. That spring, John

Kenneth Galbraith gave such pessimistic testimony before a congressional committee that his comments precipitated a temporary break in the market. As it happened, McCloy followed Galbraith's testimony a few days later and jokingly told the committee that there was some conjecture on Wall Street as to whether "there was a new economic policy from Harvard. . . ."[108]

Though he shared some of the same concerns as Galbraith—for instance, that there were dangers of a "certain hysteria" on the market—McCloy said he believed the economy was fundamentally sound. He pointed out that since 1929 Congress had passed a number of laws protecting investors from such panics. At this point, Senator William Fulbright (Democrat from Arkansas) interrupted to ask, "Are you endorsing that New Deal legislation?" McCloy laughingly answered that he "wouldn't go as far as that," but he could praise the creation of the Securities and Exchange Commission. "Isn't that enough for a staunch Republican?" Senator Paul Douglas (Democrat from Illinois) agreed, and suggested that for such remarks McCloy might "lose his union card in the Republican Party."[109]

As the stock market spiraled upward throughout 1955, McCloy happened to be working on what would become the largest stock offering ever to hit Wall Street. In May 1955, the president of the Ford Foundation, Rowan Gaither, announced that the trustees were considering a sale of Ford Motor Company stock controlled by the Foundation. McCloy, a new trustee, thought this move long overdue. The Foundation had 3,089,908 shares of Class A nonvoting stock in the Ford Motor Company, worth at least $1 billion, and represented 88 percent of all outstanding shares in the automobile company. Of the remaining 12 percent controlled by the Ford family, 5 percent was Class B voting stock. This arrangement had been devised in 1936 by Henry Ford's lawyers as a means of avoiding the New Deal's 70-percent inheritance tax on any estates worth more than $50 million. As a result, when Henry Ford, Sr., and his son Edsel Bryant Ford died, respectively, in 1947 and 1943, the family saved itself $321 million in taxes and retained its control over both the Ford Motor Company and the Foundation. Unlike John D. Rockefeller, Jr., Henry Ford, Sr., possessed no grand philanthropic philosophy. He viewed the massively endowed Foundation merely as a vehicle to preserve the Ford fortune. Shortly before he died, a reporter asked if the Ford Motor Company would ever have a public stock offering. Rising from his sickbed, the old man swore, "I'll take my factory down brick by brick before I'll let any of those Jew speculators get stock in the company."[110]

His grandson, however, had different ideas. Henry Ford II realized that, to compete with General Motors, his company could not remain a privately held corporation. The huge sums necessary to modernize assembly lines could only be raised by launching a public offering of Ford stock. For the young Ford, it was only a question of how to go public without losing control of the company. Ford was chairman of the board of trustees of the Foundation, and although he had taken little interest in the Foundation's activities, he had attended enough trustee meetings in 1955 to know that sentiment was rising among his fellow trustees to sell at least a portion of the Foundation's portfolio.

In McCloy's view, the Ford Foundation could not be run on a professional basis without control over its investment portfolio. With virtually all of its assets in one stock, the Foundation was extremely vulnerable; should the Ford family decide one year to defer all stock dividends, the Foundation's entire annual budget would disappear. In addition, the trustees might be held accountable in some legal sense for allowing their entire portfolio of stocks to rest on the fortunes of one automobile company. For McCloy, the arrangement symbolized what he perceived as an atmosphere of immaturity within the Foundation, particularly when compared with the "well established" Rockefeller Foundation. The people at the Ford Foundation, he thought, were more "loquacious" and naïve. "I didn't think the Ford Foundation had the seasoning, knowledge, and judgment of the people at the Rockefeller Foundation. . . . [By contrast] Every time John D. Rockefeller, Jr. addressed the philosophy of philanthropy, I thought he made good sense."[111]

By the spring of 1955, the Ford Foundation trustees had precipitated the issue by deciding that at least a portion of the Foundation's Ford stock should be sold. McCloy was elected to a special four-member finance committee charged with developing a plan for the sale of the stock. Throughout that summer and autumn, he and fellow trustees Charles E. Wilson (a former chairman of General Electric), James F. Brownlee, and H. Rowan Gaither conducted lengthy negotiations with Henry Ford II and his lawyers. As legal counsel for the Foundation, McCloy hired his former HICOG colleague, Eli Whitney Debevoise.[112]

With stock-market prices rising across the board, this was obviously an opportune moment to offer the public a large block of Ford shares. The problem was how to sell the Foundation's Class A stock without the Ford family's losing control over the company. If the remaining shares controlled by the Foundation were sold as voting shares—as they would have to be on the New York Stock Exchange—Henry Ford was not satisfied that the family's 12 percent would be enough to retain control. The family hired Wall Street lawyer Sidney J. Weinberg to negotiate with the Foundation trustees. Initially, Weinberg proposed and the Fords accepted a deal whereby their 12 percent of stock received 25 percent of all voting rights. Henry Ford thought this sufficient. But after the trustees had agreed to this formula, Henry's brother Bill Ford came to him and said,

"I don't think 25 percent will keep us in the position of calling the shots." Henry Ford told his brother, "Look, I've already told Sidney what the percentages are. If you want to change, you take him on." Weinberg was skeptical and told Bill Ford that if he insisted on a higher ratio "the thing will never fly."[113]

But Bill Ford refused to relent, and so Weinberg finally went back to the Foundation trustees with the following offer: the Foundation's Class A shares would be sold to the public as voting stock, representing 60 percent of the company's value; simultaneously, the Ford family would be allowed to convert their 12-percent holdings into shares representing 40 percent of all outstanding voting shares. This way, in the unlikely event of a hostile takeover attempt, the Fords would only have to buy another 11 percent to assure absolute control. The whole idea rested on the quite arbitrary decision that stock owned by members of the Ford family was worth more than three times the value of stock held by the Foundation. Logically, this plan subverted the original intent of the 1936 arrangement, whereby 88 percent of Henry Ford's wealth had been deeded to the Ford Foundation in order to keep it out of the hands of the Internal Revenue Service. Now the Ford family would suddenly be given back a large chunk of their tax-exempt inheritance. Though tax lawyers might have debated the legality of the scheme, Wall Street was not about to pass up the largest single stock offering in the history of the exchange.[114]

The New York Stock Exchange quickly approved the plan, and on November 11, 1955, *The Wall Street Journal* reported in a front-page story, "The Ford Foundation yesterday lifted the lid on one of business' most tantalizing secrets—how big, privately-owned Ford Motor Co. will become a publicly-owned corporation." In somewhat of an understatement, the newspaper suggested that preparations for the public offering of Ford stock was "probably one of the most complicated financial undertakings in many a year."[115] McCloy and other Foundation trustees, of course, wished to receive as much as they could for the sale of the Ford stock. To dump too much of the stock on the market all at once might have depressed the price, so McCloy decided to sell only 15 percent of the Foundation's holdings in the first offering. In addition, to assure the Ford family control, he arranged for an extraordinarily large number (722) of underwriters across the country to broker the stock sale. This ensured that Ford stock would be widely distributed among many thousands of investors, making it difficult for any one bloc of stockholders to challenge Henry Ford II's management of the company.[116]

In large measure, the success or failure of the stock offering depended on public relations. In the eighty days between the announcement and the actual distribution of the stock, a whirl of publicity swept the country. Newspapers and stockbrokers reported an unusual interest in the stock from first-time small investors who were simply attracted by the mystique of the Ford name. Only a handful of critics voiced any objections to the fact that the Ford family's 12 percent of equity was nevertheless going to give it 40 percent of all voting shares in the company. Senator Joseph C. O'Mahoney of Wyoming suggested that all financial instruments like nonvoting stock be made illegal. But in the rush to get in on a good deal, such old-line populist sentiments seemed anachronistic to most Americans. Here was a private company with assets of more than $2.4 billion; its current annual sales of $4.042 billion made it the fourth-largest corporation in the country, after General Motors, Standard Oil, and AT&T. "I have news for Sen. O'Mahoney," wrote the columnist Max Lerner. "Most Americans don't worry about the giant corporations. What they want is to be cut in—on even a small slice of them."[117]

By the start of the new year, the price of Ford stock had risen, thousands of investors had been lined up, and publicity couldn't have been better. Everything seemed set for a most successful launching of the stock when suddenly, just three weeks before the event, Henry Ford II threatened to cancel the entire deal. Despite everything that had been done to advance his interests, the auto manufacturer now wanted a pledge of full indemnification for any misstatements or omissions contained in the official registration statement filed by Ford Motor Company with the SEC. Such a registration statement was legally required before the sale of stock on the open market could proceed. But in the opinion of McCloy's lawyer, Eli Debevoise, the Foundation should not be held liable for actions performed by officers of the Ford Motor Company. It was, after all, the responsibility of Henry Ford to file a correct registration statement. With McCloy's concurrence, Debevoise had rejected Ford's request in August. Now his lawyers were raising the matter once again.

McCloy and Debevoise brought the dispute to the full board of trustees on January 4, 1956. Judge Charles E. Wyzanski, an old friend of McCloy's who had married Eric Warburg's sister, took the lead in arguing against any concession to Ford. In an emotional appeal to the board, Wyzanski argued that the "most conspicuous charity" in the country should not be held hostage to the private interests of one family. If Henry Ford or his brother Benson ran the risk of a stockholders' suit, "either one of them can afford to bear it . . . especially because the reorganization gives them . . . a considerable sum of money."[118]

Debevoise at this point was willing to concede to Ford's demands. But, given Wyzanski's eloquent appeal, Gaither called Ford that evening and tried to explain the trustees' reluctance. The auto executive emphatically rejected Gaither's explanation and threatened over the phone to call the whole deal off. Upon hearing this the next morning, a shocked group of trustees quickly agreed to surrender. Even Judge Wyzanski backed down: "I assumed if we maintained a firm position there would be a cave-in on the other side. . . . I was mistaken. . . . Frankly, I think there might be a national disaster, nothing less, if this negotiation now got hung up, taking into account the magnitude of the stock issue, the delicacy of the financial markets, and the consequences not merely national but international." McCloy himself weighed in with similar sentiments, citing the "potential consequences to the Foundation and indeed to the financial markets of the country. . . ." He now felt it was their duty to vote Ford his personal indemnification; in quick order, the trustees so voted.[119] Private interests had once again prevailed.

On the afternoon of January 17, 1956, trading opened for the first time on the New York Stock Exchange for shares of Ford Motor Company. The stock offering was greatly oversubscribed, and very soon afterward a smiling McCloy posed for cameramen as the underwriters handed him a check for the astonishing figure of $640,725,445. This represented the sale of only 22 percent of the motor company's total stock; under McCloy's direction, the Foundation retained some 67 percent of the company's equity and only gradually sold off this stock, milking it for all it was worth. The last piece of Ford stock wasn't disposed of until 1974.[120] The successful stock flotation of 1956, however, secured for the Ford Foundation a financial legacy unmatched by any other philanthropic institution in the world. It had become, in the words of Dwight Macdonald, writing in *The New Yorker,* a whale among a school of tuna fish. Among his colleagues on the board, McCloy received considerable credit for the success of the venture. In terms of crude financial criteria, shepherding this unprecedented stock offering to its successful conclusion was a remarkable feat for any lawyer or banker. McCloy was both. Through a combination of his patience, his legal abilities, and his intimate knowledge of Wall Street, he could claim credit for helping to create a major American institution of the postwar years. That he did so while simultaneously preserving the private power and wealth of the Ford dynasty is not incidental.

CHAPTER 22

Ike's Wise Man

"Don't ever underestimate John McCloy's power."

SAMUEL KOPPER, 1956

Soon after the January 1956 flotation of Ford stock, McCloy found himself flying across the Atlantic, bound for an extensive tour of the Middle East. He had been planning such a trip for many months. Deposits in Chase accounts by oil-producing countries in the Middle East were a small but growing part of the bank's business. Since the successful merger of Chase National and the Bank of Manhattan, resistance within the bank to expansion abroad had weakened. Late in 1955, McCloy hosted a large dinner meeting attended by Baker, Ebbott, Champion, and other Chase officials. In the words of one Chase officer, ". . . the decision was taken and orders given: we were going to expand abroad."[1]

There were other good reasons for making the trip in early 1956. McCloy's predecessor, Winthrop Aldrich, had toured the Middle East in 1950; though this led to the opening of a Chase branch in Beirut in 1952, Aldrich had failed in his attempts to persuade the Saudi royal family to allow Chase to open a branch in Jedda. Chase did, however, become the personal banker for King Abdul-Aziz Ibn Saud, and the kingdom's central bank began using Chase as a foreign depository. Oil royalties from ARAMCO were rising, but at the same time expenditures by the royal family and the government increased at such a rate in the early 1950s that the kingdom was frequently forced to apply to ARAMCO for advances on future royalty payments. (ARAMCO actually regarded these sums as foreign taxes which could then be deducted from its U.S. tax bill, a ploy known in the business as the "Golden Gimmick.") The situation became even worse when King Abdul Aziz died in 1953 and was succeeded by his eldest son, Saud, who by 1956 was engaged in a major spending spree. ARAMCO officials in Dhahran initially agreed to pay early royalties to King Saud only on the condition that the funds be deposited with Chase Manhattan. When, sometime in late 1955 or early 1956, ARAMCO officials heard that Saud intended to transfer one such large Chase account to a Swiss bank, they quickly went to McCloy with the news. In the interest of preserving the oil consortium's amiable relations with the King, ARAMCO's officers asked McCloy to intercede. Would he, they asked, consent to be the bearer of bad tidings and as diplomatically as possible inform the king that (a) if he withdrew funds from the Chase account for deposit in Switzerland, ARAMCO would no longer be willing to pay royalties in advance, and (b) he would have to restrict the kingdom's expenditures?[2]

McCloy agreed, and on February 7, 1956, he and his party arrived in Beirut. Accompanying him was his good friend and fellow banker Henry C. Brunie, president of the Empire Trust Co. Also along for part of the trip were two Chase officials, Vice-President Kenneth Hill and oil consultant Joseph Pogue. Chase's representative in Beirut, Frank Howard, checked everyone into the Saint George, an elegant hotel perched on a corner of the city's beautiful corniche. The Saint George's seaside bar was then the watering hole for local journalists, diplomats, and spies—of which there were plenty in Lebanon in those years.[3] McCloy quickly discovered that a fellow Council on Foreign Relations member, Samuel K. C. Kopper, was in town and had also taken a suite at the Saint George. Trained as a lawyer, Kopper had worked on Palestinian affairs as deputy director of the State Department's Bureau of Near Eastern Affairs from 1947 to 1949. He had resigned in disgust over Truman's Middle East policies, which he perceived as too pro-Israeli. During the 1952 campaign, he served as a foreign-policy adviser to Adlai Stevenson, and later was hired by ARAMCO as a political adviser and troubleshooter. Kopper was a man who knew his way around the Middle East.[4]

One day that week, while McCloy and Kopper were sitting on the terrace of the Saint George, sipping their drinks and gazing over the blue-green waters of the Mediterranean, a young acquaintance of Kopper's appeared on the terrace. Kopper introduced him to McCloy as Colonel Wilbur Crane Eveland. Ostensibly attached to the U.S. Embassy as a military attaché, Eveland had actually been personally hired by Allen Dulles as a free-lance, roving agent, authorized to report directly to Dulles back in Washington. An Arabic linguist, Eveland could tell stories about rendezvous with various Arab leaders, including Egypt's Gamal Abdel Nasser and Lebanon's Camille Chamoun. He was a classic CIA "bagman" who on at least one occasion during his intelligence career drove to Damascus with a suitcase filled with cash in order to finance a coup d'état. He also happened to have worked with McCloy's favored old aide from the War Department, Colonel Al Gerhardt, so the two men quickly felt at ease with each other. Years later, Eveland remembered McCloy as the "bustling, bald guy" whom he had heard so much about from Gerhardt.[5]

Like McCloy, Eveland was scheduled to be in Damascus in a couple of days, so, when McCloy offered him a seat on the DC-3 plane he had chartered, Eveland accepted. During the short flight across the Lebanese mountains, McCloy openly discussed his mission. The conversation drifted into a discussion of the Saudis, their border dispute with the British over the Buraimi oasis, and King Saud's willingness to fund the destabilization of the Hashemite monarchies in Jordan and Iraq. He told Dulles's agent that Chase was receiving "constant" requests for loans against future oil royalties and that the king's interference against the Hashemites was undermining long-term U.S. interests.

In Damascus they parted company, and Eveland immediately cabled Allen Dulles an account of his conversation with McCloy. When he later told this to Kopper, the ARAMCO official laughed and said, "Colonel, you've still got so much to learn. . . . Don't ever underestimate John McCloy's power." He then explained to the young agent that McCloy had no doubt talked to Dulles before leaving New York and would be speaking to King Saud and other heads of state with the full knowledge of Washington.[6]

After briefly seeing the U.S. ambassador in Damascus, McCloy flew on to Saudi Arabia, where he first met with ARAMCO officials in Dhahran. U.S. Ambassador James J. Wadsworth joined them from Jedda for these discussions. On the agenda were a number of complicated political and economic problems. There was the delicate matter of the rumored Saudi intention to transfer one of their large Chase accounts to Switzerland. Then there was the problem of the king's erratic foreign policies: motivated by a combination of both fear and admiration for Colonel Nasser's brand of Arab nationalism, King Saud was at the moment trying to place himself in the good graces of the charismatic Egyptian leader. Intelligence reports suggested that Saudi money was behind some of Nasser's latest arms purchases and various covert operations in Jordan and Iraq aimed at destabilizing these Hashemite monarchies, traditionally the tribal rivals of the House of Saud. It was clear that such displays of Saudi meddling abroad could prove to be troublesome. The Saudi claim to the Buraimi oasis on their border with the British-controlled Trucial States had recently resulted in armed clashes with British-led troops. McCloy had been briefed on all of these issues back in Washington. One recent intelligence report had concluded that the House of Saud was "a tribal dynasty trying to play the role of a twentieth century nation-state." The results, said the report, "are contradictory policies and growing instability."[7]

One could, of course, attempt to rein in King Saud by restricting the flow of oil money. Strong-arm tactics like that were actually contemplated by such influential opinion-makers as Henry Luce. About the same time McCloy was visiting Saudi Arabia, Luce wrote a private memo in which he observed, "If the fact is that Saudi Arabia is acting as an enemy of the

United States and her allies, the U.S. is entitled to take steps to put an end to such hostile action. If that means turning off the ARAMCO taps then we turn them off."[8]

McCloy was not inclined to such rash threats. For one thing, it made no economic sense. Forecasts of rising world oil consumption over the next ten years suggested that Saudi oil production must double from its current level of one million barrels per day. Though at the moment there might be some temporary budgetary shortfalls because of King Saud's excessive spending, in the years ahead the king could count on large oil revenues. Clearly, the long-term solution was to find some way to commit the Saudis to an ambitious economic-development scheme in order to keep their revenues at home—and out of mischief.[9] With this goal in mind, McCloy flew on to Riyadh for meetings with the king, Crown Prince Faisal, and the Saudi finance minister. The capital of Saudi Arabia in those years was nothing but a mud-brick village, which was being torn apart by construction crews. They were demolishing Saud's old palace—built at a cost of 4 million English pounds—and had built a self-contained royal township, complete with traffic lights, a hospital, several mosques, gardens, and a palace modeled after the Beverly Hills Hotel. The entire complex was surrounded by a seven-mile pink-washed wall standing fifteen feet high. McCloy's entourage was driven to this desert Disney World and entered the complex through a huge triumphal archway. Inside, they were taken to the king's conference room, where the negotiations commenced. As gently as possible, McCloy delivered his message: a budget would have to be followed; credits on advance ARAMCO "taxes" could not be extended unless these monies were kept in Chase accounts, where they could be monitored; and Saud was urged to join the World Bank, which could then help him mount an ambitious development program for his people. McCloy emphasized throughout his presentation that, though present finances might be short, the kingdom could expect to see its oil revenues rise dramatically in the near future. All that was required was patience and cooperation with their American friends in ARAMCO. This was a message the Saudis could digest.

McCloy was put up in the king's Nasariyah Palace long enough to learn a few details of Saud's legendary sexual appetite and his ability to imbibe vast quantities of alcohol. Henry Luce described what McCloy must have seen, in a memo he wrote from the king's Jedda palace two months later: "The preoccupation of the palace is copulation and since the life of the nation is centered on the King, it is the King's Kinsey report that is at the center of Saudi life. You will be pleased to hear that the number of pregnancies in the harem at the moment is exactly 22. . . . By the way, girls are also supplied to the harem from the U.S."[10]

From Riyadh, McCloy flew to Baghdad on February 19, 1956. Over the next three days, he saw the king, the crown prince, the ministers of economics, finance, and development, and the real power in the country at the time, Prime Minister Nuri Said. The prime minister himself had requested the meeting with McCloy, and in advance of the meeting had told a U.S. diplomat that he specifically wished to discuss the credits extended by Chase to the Saudis. Forewarned, McCloy entered the meeting and immediately volunteered to explain Chase's position in Saudi Arabia. Nuri Said obviously wanted to know why Chase was giving the Saudis the money they needed to fund antigovernment activities in Iraq. McCloy first tried to explain that Chase's credits to the Saudis were not really loans, but merely advance payments on taxes owed by ARAMCO. But then, according to the State Department's report on the meeting, McCloy "freely admitted that the huge royalties Saudi Arabia was deriving from oil, unless channeled in productive enterprises, posed a serious problem for Saudi Arabia and the area." He assured Said that he had told King Saud as much earlier in the week.[11]

Such high-level conversations with foreign leaders constituted a special form of private diplomacy. King Saud, Prince Faisal, and Prime Minister Nuri Said were all quick to appreciate McCloy's power—the power of money. This was not merely another representative of the U.S. government, or even a private envoy of the U.S. president. This was a man who on the basis of his own authority and contacts could provide material aid to a country desperate for Western investments. The Iraqi prime minister had other expectations of McCloy. After making his pitch to see that Chase would do what it could to restrict Saudi intelligence operations in his country, Nuri Said pressed McCloy to use his influence to see that Iraq's most recent request to the World Bank for development loans would be approved.[12]

Upon returning to the United States in late February, McCloy quickly scheduled a meeting with the president. Over lunch on March 20, he regaled Ike for more than an hour with exotic stories about his trip.[13] In the meantime, he had already arranged for Eugene Black, president of the World Bank, to visit Saudi Arabia and arrange for Saudi membership in the Bank. Black happened to be in the Middle East already, negotiating with Nasser over possible World Bank funding for the Aswan High Dam. Extending his trip to Iran, Black suddenly received an invitation from King Saud to visit Riyadh. One of the royal family's own planes flew to Teheran and ferried him back to Arabia for an audience with the king. Saud's eagerness to join the Bank rather puzzled Black until he returned to Washington and learned of McCloy's intervention. The kingdom formally signed the World Bank protocols in August 1957.[14]

This was only the first of many trips McCloy made out to the Middle East. A success in terms of protecting Chase's ARAMCO interests in Saudi Arabia, the trip had also exposed him to the rising tide of Arab nationalism in the region. For some time, he had felt that Foster Dulles's efforts to enlist various Arab and Asian countries to join military pacts against the Soviet Union were apt to backfire. In the wake of his trip to the Middle East, he was now convinced that such military pacts would bring U.S. policy into conflict with the basic forces of nationalism sweeping these countries. That spring, he expressed these criticisms of Dulles's policies in a book generated by the Council on Foreign Relations' Study Group on U.S.-Soviet Relations. McCloy had been meeting with this group for more than two years at the CFR. Edited by Henry L. Roberts, director of the Russian Institute at Columbia University, the book was scheduled for publication in May 1956 by Harper & Brothers. As chairman of the Council, and a major participant in the study group's deliberations, McCloy wrote the foreword.

McCloy's foreword drew far more attention and newspaper headlines, particularly in Europe, than the book itself. Among other things, he argued that the United States should accept the "neutrality" of many Asian and African countries, shift away from the current emphasis on military alliances, and move in the direction of offering these countries "constructive political and economic solutions" to their problems. In the Middle East, he said, a new effort should be made to resolve the Israeli-Arab conflict over Palestine. In a not very veiled criticism of Foster Dulles's demand that countries pass an ideological litmus test before becoming eligible for U.S. economic assistance, McCloy again suggested, as he had in earlier speeches critical of Joe McCarthy, that there should be more to U.S. foreign policy than a crusade against communism. "The American public has good reason to guard against subversion," he wrote, "but we must not shrink from our own faith that free exchanges of ideas are our strength and that ultimately they will prevail."

Turning to Europe, McCloy recommended a similar de-emphasis of the military component in U.S. policy. Though suggesting that the European allies might find it prudent to equip themselves with nuclear weapons by 1960, he said that a major effort should be made to end the arms race through active exploration of "the most far-reaching proposals, including those for total disarmament—universal, enforceable and complete with international control and inspection." He argued that Western Europe's security could be better enhanced by building strong economies. In his most shocking departure from official wisdom, McCloy suggested that NATO offer the Soviet Union firm guarantees to recognize the boundaries and security of communist Poland and Czechoslovakia. For the first time since leaving Germany as high commissioner, he suggested that, in return for recognition of the Oder-Neisse Line, Germany might be reunified. That was not all. Peaceful trade should be revived between Eastern and Western Europe, while a broad program of cultural, educational, and personal exchanges should be implemented with the Soviet

Union itself. Though McCloy said he didn't believe long-term Soviet goals had changed, he suggested that "some very radical and important changes had taken place in Soviet methods." (Ten days after the publication of the book and McCloy's foreword, *The New York Times* published the full text of Nikita Khrushchev's speech denouncing Stalin and his crimes.)

At the time, such unorthodox views were hotly debated in the German Bundestag and inside the editorial pages of many European newspapers. *The New York Times* headlined its news story on the release of the book, "Policy of Reality Urged upon West: Unit Headed by McCloy Bids Allies Meet Soviet Shifts with Flexible Outlook."[15] McCloy's views, particularly his remarks urging a greater tolerance and flexibility toward "neutralism," contrasted sharply with Foster Dulles's official pronouncements. Only a couple of weeks after the release of McCloy's essay, Dulles told an audience in Iowa that neutralism "is an immoral and shortsighted conception."[16] Such public differences with the secretary of state inevitably revived speculation in both Europe and Washington that McCloy might soon replace Foster Dulles.[17]

Speculations of this sort had not been confined to the possibility of a Cabinet post. The previous autumn, when Eisenhower had a heart attack, leaving in doubt whether he would run for re-election in 1956, *The New York Times* had added McCloy to the list of "dark-horse" candidates for the Republican nomination.[18] For some time, various columnists had identified him as a member of Eisenhower's "unofficial Cabinet," a label McCloy fiercely disclaimed. Now, in the midst of the 1956 presidential campaign, he was branded by Drew Pearson and Fulton Lewis, Jr., as a member of the "Dump Dick" movement. Describing him as "a potent power in GOP politics," Pearson reported in July that McCloy "has added his weight to those trying to maneuver Vice President Nixon off the ticket. . . ."[19] Fulton Lewis reported that McCloy, Paul Hoffman, Lucius Clay, Bedell Smith, and Harold Stassen were all trying to get Nixon off the ticket, fearing that if he someday were to become president they would be barred from their "side door influence with the White House." McCloy denied this charge as a "vicious misstatement" and protested in a letter to Lewis that he had never talked about the vice-presidential nomination with any of these men.[20]

Pearson had exaggerated when he labeled McCloy a "potent power" in Republican Party politics. McCloy had never dabbled in party politics in the manner of a Tom Dewey or a Lucius Clay. Like Eisenhower, he felt a personal distaste for the mundane aspects of party politics and was never seen at New York Republican affairs or in the back rooms of the state or national party bosses. This was not his style. Lewis was also incorrect to report that McCloy was part of any organized lobby to get

Nixon off the ticket. McCloy didn't have to operate through someone like Lucius Clay; if he had felt strongly enough about the issue, he would have gone straight to the president.

There is no record that he raised the matter with Ike in any of their private meetings. But there is no doubt that McCloy was not personally enamored of Nixon; he and Eisenhower had been angered by Nixon's mimicry of McCarthy's "generation-of-treason" language during the 1954 congressional campaign. Like many of his colleagues in the Council on Foreign Relations, McCloy found Nixon transparently ambitious and unsound in his political judgments. And though Pearson and Lewis missed the story at the time, the president himself was indeed quietly trying to persuade Nixon to take a Cabinet post instead of running on the ticket in 1956. Nixon firmly resisted Eisenhower's arguments that a Cabinet post would give him better exposure and experience to run for the presidential nomination in 1960. In the end, Ike couldn't bring himself to fire his young vice-president.[21]

That summer, the Middle East was drifting into war. In McCloy's view, the road to this war had begun with a miscalculation on the part of Foster Dulles. Egypt's Gamal Abdel Nasser had been trying to persuade the Americans—and if not the Americans then the Russians—to help finance his proposed Aswan High Dam, a project Nasser was determined to make the centerpiece of his economic-development program. For months he had been negotiating with the Americans on the financing of the dam, which was slated to cost some $500–600 million. By the spring of 1956, Nasser's hopes for Western funding rested with the World Bank. Eugene Black had become an ardent advocate of the project, and had agreed to contribute $200 million if the United States and Britain matched that figure. In December 1955, Foster Dulles had given his approval to the scheme—but he attached certain conditions, including a pledge by the Egyptian government that it would not assume any other foreign loans without the permission of the World Bank. This Nasser regarded as an infringement on Egyptian sovereignty and a thinly veiled attempt to prevent any further purchases of Eastern-bloc arms. Still, Black was convinced he could negotiate a compromise, and left for Egypt in early 1956.

McCloy did what he could that spring to help Black push the dam project along. Black, who consulted with his old friend quite frequently on World Bank matters, argued that whoever financed the dam would essentially determine Egypt's political orientation for the next two decades. Nasser might be difficult, he said, but he was an Arab leader the United States could work with over the long term. Nasser's professed neutralism didn't bother McCloy. When Black came back from his February negotiations with Nasser on the dam, McCloy arranged for Black to give Eisenhower a private briefing on the Egyptian leader. But this was one issue that Eisenhower had delegated entirely to Foster Dulles. And when Nasser, in May 1956, recognized the People's Republic of China, Dulles was firmly convinced that Egypt, not merely neutralist, was drifting into the communist camp. On July 19, 1956, he called in the Egyptian ambassador and, in a manner even Eisenhower later said was "abrupt," withdrew the U.S. offer to help finance the dam. Black was mortified, particularly since Nasser had just agreed to accept all the terms of the U.S. offer. He later called it "the greatest disappointment of my professional life. . . ." Nasser himself was angered, and a week later announced in a three-and-a-half-hour speech to the Egyptian people that he had nationalized the Suez Canal in order to finance the construction of the High Dam. Dulles was shocked, and the British were outraged. The London *Times* called it "an act of international brigandage."[22]

Foster Dulles had believed that, by denying Nasser the means to build his dam, he could deal the Egyptian leader a humiliating blow. He had received tentative permission from Eisenhower to develop the same kind of destabilization program used by the CIA to overthrow Arbenz in Guatemala. But it quickly became clear that Nasser's nationalization of the Suez Canal was a bold political stroke. It galvanized pent-up nationalist emotions and made Nasser the indisputable leader of the Arab world.[23]

In the wake of the nationalization, the British and French signaled to Washington their readiness to use force against Egypt. Eisenhower sent Foster Dulles on two hours' notice to London with a message designed to calm the European powers and make them understand that U.S. military forces would not support such an operation. Simultaneously, the U.S. Treasury ordered the assets of both the Egyptian government and the Suez Canal Company frozen. The latter had sizable accounts with Chase Manhattan Bank in both New York and London. McCloy had met the chairman of the Suez Canal Company, Jacques Georges-Picot, in New York on several occasions. The Frenchman had once briefed the Council on Foreign Relations on the company's operations in Egypt, and McCloy was aware that Georges-Picot had talked extensively with Eugene Black about a possible World Bank loan for modernization of the canal. Now, as tensions rose, Georges-Picot occasionally called McCloy to talk about the disposition of the company's frozen account and other aspects of the crisis.[24] Between his trip to the Middle East in February and his frequent contacts with both Black and Georges-Picot, McCloy was well informed about the developing crisis.

Throughout that summer and early autumn, Foster Dulles acted as if he were the legal adviser to the French and British in their case against Nasser. By October, he had lost control of events. Behind his back, his clients (so to speak) had taken the matter out of his hands. Dulles picked up only the barest hints of the collusion between the British, French, and Israelis, who by late October had already set the date for an invasion of

Egypt. Shortly before hostilities commenced, Dulles phoned McCloy in the middle of the night and asked if he had noticed any major transfers of British sterling that could signal a war. McCloy called back the next morning to say that he saw no evidence of any large financial shifts.[25]

Soon afterward, the Israelis launched a ground attack across the Sinai Peninsula toward the Suez Canal while the British and French bombed Port Said. Dulles was devastated by what he regarded as a betrayal of trust on the part of the British. He again phoned McCloy from Washington and had him pulled out of a meeting of the Ford Foundation trustees in order to discuss whether Israel should be restrained.[26] Three days later, the secretary awoke with severe intestinal pains. Exploratory surgery discovered cancer; Dulles was to spend the next two months hospitalized. That same week, Eisenhower won a second resounding victory at the polls over Adlai Stevenson. The war crisis had killed whatever was left of Stevenson's losing but dynamic campaign.

The New York Times immediately reported that McCloy's name was again circulating in administration circles as Eisenhower's favored replacement for the ailing secretary of state.[27] In fact, for the next several months Eisenhower himself took charge of the crisis. He would, however, find a low-profile role for McCloy to play from New York.

Venting his anger at his European allies and Israel, Eisenhower demanded and got a cease-fire and a pledge from the tripartite aggressors to withdraw their troops from both the canal zone and the Sinai. By the time the fighting stopped, however, the canal was blocked by at least a dozen sunken vessels and two bridges. The United Nations' secretary general, Dag Hammarskjöld, was given the task of clearing the canal. Within days, the newspapers announced that McCloy was working as an unpaid consultant for Hammarskjöld. Salvage vessels, tugs, and dredgers had to be found and brought to Egypt; in the meantime, the canal might be closed for as long as six months, a blow not only to Egypt's economy but also to that of Western Europe, which depended for much of its oil on tankers transiting the canal. Washington thus had a strategic-economic interest in seeing the canal—which Bismarck once called "the world's neck"—reopened as quickly as possible. Though the chairman of Chase Manhattan Bank obviously had the right contacts to raise loans for the operation, Hammarskjöld also knew that McCloy had Eisenhower's trust and support.

In short order, McCloy got the operation moving. To start with, he hired an old friend, Lieutenant General Raymond A. Wheeler, to supervise the project on the ground in Egypt. Wheeler had once been in charge of maintenance for the Panama Canal, and McCloy had known him during the war as the man who built the Burma Road. More recently, he had persuaded Eugene Black to hire him as a consultant to the World Bank.[28] "Spec" Wheeler flew out to Cairo immediately and began assemblying the necessary crews and salvage equipment to clear the canal. Within five weeks, McCloy had a financial plan put together; the major Western countries whose shipping fleets used the canal pledged to contribute \$2–3 million each toward the operation. Throughout late November and December, McCloy met with Hammarskjöld and Herbert Hoover, Jr., the undersecretary of state who was running the State Department in Dulles's absence. Shortly before Christmas, U.N. Ambassador Henry Cabot Lodge reported to Hoover, "Hammarskjöld advises me that McCloy is pulling the whole problem together as you desired, but is doing it in such a way that he does not get too far out in front and thereby make it appear that the United States is running the whole show."[29]

In fact, the salvage operation involved a number of delicate political problems. Almost as soon as Wheeler got out to Egypt, he reported that the British were trying to use the salvage operation as a cover for keeping their naval force in the canal. Wheeler cabled that their goal was "how to make a withdrawal not a withdrawal."[30] Nasser, in the meantime, decreed that no salvage operation could even begin until all three invading forces were out. The British and the French were gone by the end of the year. But the Israelis held on to pieces of the Sinai until March 1957 and only retreated when Eisenhower threatened to cut off all U.S. governmental and private aid to the country.

McCloy juggled these political problems in the midst of his fund-raising campaign. In early January 1957, he was able to report that he had firm commitments from Germany, Norway, Sweden, and Denmark to contribute \$1 million each to the canal clean-up fund. He now thought the entire operation would cost less than the originally projected \$40 million, and as things turned out, the canal was cleared of all obstacles by March 1956, well ahead of schedule. Late that month, McCloy flew to Egypt. Cairo was devoid of its usual throngs of tourists, and he found himself the only guest at one of the city's main hotels. General Wheeler gave him a quick tour of the canal zone and the Palestinian refugee camps in the Gaza Strip, where his party escaped unscathed from an exploding mine. But the high point of the trip was a nearly five-hour talk with Gamal Abdel Nasser. Now that the canal was cleared of obstructions, McCloy was instructed by Hammarskjöld and the Eisenhower administration to negotiate an understanding with Nasser on how the canal would be operated. He brought with him a draft of a statement of principles and policies that the Western users wanted Nasser to recognize. The Egyptian was willing to be accommodating, even to the extent of agreeing that canal tolls might initially be collected by the World Bank.

It was clear, however, that on some issues Nasser himself would be making the decisions. He told McCloy, for instance, that no Israeli ships would be allowed to transit the canal, "as he would require troops along the whole distance to prevent tossing of hand grenades back and forth."

(McCloy actually thought there was "some degree of truth" to this statement.) But the two men got along quite well, and by the end of the meeting, Nasser was confiding to McCloy that he was "worried about falling down on [the] operation of the Canal." He needed loans to buy tugs, without which the largest oil tankers could not be guided through the narrow channel. McCloy said he had been talking to Eugene Black about a World Bank loan for Egypt, but he indicated to Nasser that this was probably contingent on the Egyptians' reaching a settlement with the stockholders of the old Suez Canal Company. Speaking as if McCloy were an official representative of Washington, and not a private, unpaid consultant to the U.N. secretary general, Nasser told him that he was quite grateful for the help he had received from the Eisenhower administration in getting the British, French, and Israelis out of Egypt. But he said he now had the impression that "the tide is turning" and that the United States was "now becoming more pro-British, pro-French, and pro-Israeli."[31] McCloy enjoyed parrying such rhetorical thrusts. Like many Americans who had had a chance to talk with Nasser at length, he came away from this first encounter highly impressed with the charismatic Egyptian leader. He sensed, as one CIA agent later wrote, that this was a leader with whom one could reason: "One could discuss any subject with Nasser, including the possibility of peace with Israel, with the feeling that he was listening intelligently to what was said and was using his brains rather than his emotions as he offered his rebuttals."[32]

Upon his return to the United States, McCloy gave Foster Dulles a full briefing in New York on his conversation with Nasser. He also sat down with his colleagues at the Council on Foreign Relations and gave an off-the-record evaluation of the Egyptian president. More than two hundred members showed up to hear McCloy's briefing, including Henry Kissinger, Nelson Rockefeller, Reinhold Niebuhr, Walter J. Levy, C. D. Jackson, and such old friends as Benjamin Buttenwieser, Ben Shute, Shep Stone, Emilio Collado, and Don Price. McCloy gave a highly favorable description of the man who had so recently caused the West such grief. He reported that he found the Egyptian to be "healthy, athletic, friendly and courteous." Though Nasser was "bitter, suspicious and strongly politically minded," McCloy clearly liked him. "A man with a pleasing smile and disarming manner, Nasser did not appear," McCloy said, "to be a ranter, nor did he remind one of a Hitler or Mussolini; he seemed instead to be a typical army officer." No topic was dismissed as "too sensitive to permit frank treatment." Nasser bluntly asserted that he "had no illusions" about the Soviet aid he received and noted that he had only accepted such arms and bread after the West had refused to come to his assistance. When McCloy questioned whether communist influence on his regime was becoming "excessive," Nasser assured him that, "after saving his head from the British noose, he had no intention of putting it into the Soviet's."

McCloy concluded his talk by giving his fellow Council members what in retrospect must be seen as a fairly astute assessment of the Egyptian leader: "Nasser is apparently very conscious of the nature of his popular support and he feels that his actions are limited by his own demagogic speeches. The Egyptians strongly feel the need of asserting their independence. They don't want to be pushed around though they know that they need outside help if their plans for progress are to materialize."[33] In McCloy's view, Nasser and other nonaligned leaders like him were the kind of men whom Washington had to work with if the United States was to conduct a sound foreign policy, grounded in the political realities of postcolonial nationalism. But what may have persuaded many influential Council members up in New York, left Foster Dulles unmoved down in Washington. There was no room in Dulles's neat little game of global alliances for mavericks like Gamal Abdel Nasser.

By 1957, it might easily have appeared to Chase stockholders that their chairman was moonlighting with the State Department, the Council on Foreign Relations, the Ford Foundation, and a half-dozen other institutions around the country. But if his outside activities were remarkably varied, no one doubted the impact of McCloy's presence on the bank. Not only had he achieved the merger of Chase with the Bank of Manhattan, but he was now well on his way to creating both a new home for the bank and a distinctive architectural landmark on the tip of Manhattan Island. Back in 1953, he had found Chase's operations distributed among nine different buildings around the city. Winthrop Aldrich told him he should make it a priority to consolidate all Chase employees under one roof. To do so, McCloy first had to decide whether to construct a new bank building in the downtown tip of Manhattan or to follow the migration of many other corporate headquarters to midtown Manhattan. It was a difficult decision. The wave of the future seemed to be the posh new Park Avenue business district uptown. "Every day one heard of a new concern that was moving uptown," he recalled. But McCloy himself was sentimentally attached to the Wall Street district. "We had a big investment downtown," he said a few years later. "The Stock Exchange was downtown, so was the Federal Reserve Bank. Besides, it was the hearthstone, so to speak, of the city. . . . The tip of Manhattan had a great tradition and it had real beauty at the confluence of two great rivers. It seemed to me that it had some significance not only to the city but to the nation to keep in existence this area, where, in and out of those narrow streets for a period of a century, the progress of the country had been financed."[34]

Having decided to remain on Wall Street, McCloy had then determined that he wanted to construct a building so distinctive that it would "tend to fix the financial district downtown as well as adorn the City of New York." Early in 1955, he authorized the payment of $4.4 million for an abandoned lot immediately behind 18 Pine Street. This was considered to be an enormous sum at the time, but he made the decision on his own and consulted with the Chase board only after the fact. As one Chase official said, "He didn't hem or haw, he just did it." Having committed the bank to this building site, he then delegated to David Rockefeller the task of dealing with William Zeckendorf, the city's leading real-estate broker and developer. Architects from the firm of Skidmore, Owings & Merrill were contracted to come up with a number of designs. "We told them we wanted a building of stature," recalled McCloy. Early on, he and Rockefeller conceived of the idea that there should be an open plaza around the building, an architectural feature unseen at the time on Wall Street. The plaza would create some much-needed open space in a part of the city characterized by narrow streets and dark skyscraper canyons. In return for creating a little public space with the plaza, McCloy thought he could obtain some concessions from City Hall on the building's specifications. In particular, the city's most powerful planning official, Robert Moses, agreed to waive the requirement that new skyscrapers be built with "setbacks." This concession was necessary if the bank wished to construct a building with a modern "flush" exterior, straight up and down. The combination of a "flush" exterior and the ability to build underground, beneath the plaza, would more than make up for the space lost to the public plaza. As McCloy put it, ". . . what, so to speak, we lost on the 'oranges,' we could make on the bananas." Rockefeller in particular pushed for an ultramodern glass-and-aluminum skin for the building, a look at least half of the board thought inappropriate. But after much debate, McCloy sided with Rockefeller, and soon the architects came up with a plan for a towering shaft of glass and steel, the most distinctive feature of which was rows of aluminum-sheathed columns rising sixty stories from the plaza.[35]

McCloy enjoyed one aspect of the construction of One Chase Plaza: the building's art program. The building's interior layout provided a large central open area on each floor with blank walls devoid of the plaster moldings one saw in traditional office buildings. The architects intended that some warmth would be given to these cold, austere interiors by modern furnishings and displays of abstract art. An avid collector of abstract art, Rockefeller enthusiastically endorsed this scheme.[36] McCloy agreed that David should serve as chairman of the art-selection committee, but he specified that both he and George Champion would also serve on the committee. The considerable sum of $500,000 was set aside to acquire original paintings and sculptures. Chase's art program had a major impact on the New York art world, benefiting such leading artists as Pierre Soulages, Adolph Gottlieb, Jack Youngerman, Larry Rivers, and Alfred Jensen, as well as other, lesser-known artists.

McCloy had to admit to Rockefeller that there was much abstract art that he didn't understand. But he enjoyed listening to the leading art curators' appraisals. "The more they talked and the more they judged," McCloy recalled, "the more confidence I gained." George Champion, however, never reconciled himself to the abstract works of art so favored by Rockefeller, and McCloy often found himself mediating between the two. In deference to Champion's tastes, some of the more avant-garde pieces of sculpture were kept out of view of his office.[37]

When the building was finally finished, it received rave reviews in the press. It was then the seventh-tallest building in the world and housed a 985-ton bank vault, longer than a football field. *Architectural Forum* ran a thirty-page spread on the building, which it said "is already proving to be one of the boldest, and quite possibly one of the soundest, investments to be made on Wall Street in many years." To the surprise of not a few skeptics, including some on Chase's board, twenty-four of the building's sixty floors were profitably leased out to more than fifty major Wall Street business and legal firms. *Forbes* editorialized that One Chase Plaza had given a "hopeful cast . . . to the old financial district," and *Time* ran color photos highlighting the modern artworks adorning the walls of the bank. Senior Chase bank officers wryly referred to the building as "the house that Jack built." It was indeed a personal triumph for the chairman.[38]

Disagreements between McCloy's two most senior colleagues—Rockefeller and Champion—extended beyond art. As one Chase executive put it, "Champion worries about where the bank will be ten minutes from now and Rockefeller about where it will be ten years from now." Their personalities and contrasting banking strategies fueled an open rivalry. Champion was a stickler for details. He could glance down a column of numbers and pick out the footnote with a typo in it. Rockefeller was invariably annoyed by Champion's probing questions, which seemed to reflect his general unhappiness with whatever project was at hand. Not surprisingly, each man developed his own group of loyal associates within the bank, which would sometimes accuse the other group of "cronyism." This situation created natural tensions. In the words of one Chase official, "There would have to be, if not clashes, a lot of strain and tension."[39]

McCloy got along with both men, in part by compartmentalizing their responsibilities. But Rockefeller, who at the time served as one of four executive vice-presidents, was clearly tagged to head the bank someday. As early as 1955, *Business Week* had observed, "Among the top men, it is David Rockefeller who is heir apparent."[40]

For the moment, however, Champion was still the most experienced and senior of McCloy's executives. He could display a prickly personality, and McCloy did not share his Christian fundamentalism. (Champion regularly contributed to Reverend Billy Graham's crusades.) But on a professional level, McCloy made it clear to Champion that he could largely run his own show in the U.S. department of the bank. "If we had any policy decision," recalled Champion, "that we felt he ought to have a part in, why, we'd take them to him. But there weren't too many of them."[41]

On the international side, McCloy found Rockefeller an ally for his view that Chase should expand its branches and clients abroad. By the end of the 1950s, Chase had twenty-five branches operating in eleven foreign countries, many of them in the Caribbean. In addition, McCloy and Rockefeller believed the bank not only should act in the national interest, but could help define the national interest. Rockefeller would later say that it "was impossible to be involved in business with a great international bank without being involved in government and politics."[42] In this respect, they were taking their lead from Winthrop Aldrich, who had sometimes run the Chase as if it were an arm of the U.S. government. During the war, when Eisenhower's troops in North Africa needed banking facilities, Aldrich opened a branch for them. When Tito broke with Stalin, and Washington wished to encourage his independence, Chase—not without Washington's concurrence—became the principal corresponding bank for the National Bank of Yugoslavia.[43]

McCloy always acted in close collusion with Washington, even when this might benefit Chase's competitors. In the summer of 1957, the Paris branches of First National City Bank and the Bank of America were handling short-term "acceptances" for the Soviet Union to purchase Western goods. Chase had an opportunity to get a cut of the same business with the Soviets, but before proceeding, McCloy called Washington and made it clear that he would not approve the transactions without the State Department's approval.[44] Dulles, of course, discouraged the idea.

The fact that Rockefeller had early on cast himself as an ally of McCloy in the decision to expand the bank's branches abroad did not by itself explain their close relationship. Despite their differences in age and background, the two men shared habits and values. Like McCloy, Rockefeller was never brusque, never confrontational, and always polite in his dealings with people. His favorite word was "appropriate." He was always a good listener. As one friend explained, "David could listen to a bore go on and on explaining something which was obvious to everyone listening and still give that bore his whole undivided attention because he just might say something which David would not know." His slow, stolid temperament caused one colleague to call him a "phlegmatic forty-year-old." Of the five Rockefeller sons, David most resembled his father. His bland, open-faced demeanor masked a willingness to work eighteen-hour days. Such patience matched McCloy's characteristic persistence. Rockefeller's stamina was motivated by a desire to prove that "there was something there besides a famous family name." The chemistry was thus perfect: with McCloy as chairman, David could prove his professional worth as a banker under the supervision of an individual who respected the Rockefeller name. The relationship was only helped by McCloy's personal friendship with David's father. In addition, they shared extracurricular interests: David gave not only his money ($25,000 annually) but a great deal of his time to the Council on Foreign Relations, where he served as a vice-president and participated every year in one of the Council's study groups. It was plain for all to see that Rockefeller was a McCloy protégé.[45]

In addition to serving as vice-president of the Council, Rockefeller chaired the Council on Foreign Relations' membership committee. Virtually the youngest officer in the Council, he used his position to lobby for the admission of more and younger members. In this he was supported by the Council's executive director, George Franklin, Jr., a sometime lawyer who had been his college roommate and later married a Rockefeller cousin.[46] Rockefeller's views were not always endorsed by his elders within the Council. On one occasion in 1954, Hamilton Fish Armstrong vigorously opposed his suggestion that they should "seek out younger men." (The Council's membership until 1969 was all male.) Armstrong thought that, for the Council's purposes, men in their late thirties or early forties could be considered young. At a board meeting, Rockefeller submitted a list of prospective candidates only to have them rejected out of hand because they were all corporate executives. Frank Altschul told Rockefeller that his list "would be more appropriate for an organization like the National Association of Manufacturers. . . ."[47]

McCloy favored broadening the CFR's membership to include academicians and men from professions outside law and business. But he certainly did not wish to dilute the "select" quality of the Council's deliberations at Pratt House. Conferring resident-membership status on any individual was a serious matter; some candidates found their nominations deferred from one year to the next. This happened even to such well-connected individuals as Leo Cherne, the executive director of the Research Institute of America, whose partner, William Casey—the future CIA director—was then a close acquaintance of McCloy's.[48]

Resident members (those living or working within fifty miles of Manhattan) were limited to 675 men, whereas the less prestigious nonresident category could number as high as five hundred. Dues ran a hefty $200 annually for resident members. In 1956, the elite inner circle of this exclusive club included, besides McCloy and Rockefeller, such influential men as Henry M. Wriston, Frank Altschul, Allen Dulles, Arthur Dean, Grayson L. Kirk, Lewis W. Douglas, and Hamilton Fish Armstrong, who also served as the editor of the Council's well-read quarterly, *Foreign Affairs.* The list of resident members included men from a wide range of New York's leading business, legal, and cultural institutions. There were, of course, many lawyers, bankers, and corporate executives. But there were also such men as Simon Michael Bessie and Cass Canfield, both highly influential book editors. Ralph Bunche was one of the few blacks.* Also included were such academics as Professor J. C. Hurewitz, a Middle East specialist, and Henry Kissinger, then a lecturer at Harvard University. To the outsider, it might seem that the same old Wall Street crowd still dominated the Council's membership in these years. But there were subtle differences in the Council's makeup from the 1920s and '30s, when the Council was both smaller and less diverse.

Many members gave voluntary contributions of $1,000 or more annually. But the Council's needs were now growing so rapidly that McCloy inaugurated a "Corporation Service," whereby various corporations were persuaded to pay $1,000 or more for special corporate memberships. By 1956, this program was contributing $50,000 a year to the CFR's budget. As the Council's activities mushroomed in the 1950s, McCloy used his foundation connections to raise large sums for a budget that quickly grew to more than $700,000 annually. In 1955, the Rockefeller Foundation gave $500,000, and the Ford Foundation regularly funded specific study projects until early 1958, when it gave $1.1 million in unearmarked grants to cover general operating expenses. (McCloy also persuaded the board in 1954 to transfer the Council's $1-million investment portfolio from the New York Trust Company to Chase.[50])

McCloy devoted a great deal of his intellectual energy to the Council's meetings and study groups. He could be found at the Council's Harold Pratt (of Standard Oil) House on East 68th Street at Park Avenue several afternoons each month. With its book-lined walls, worn Persian carpets, and Old World elegance, Pratt House created an atmosphere of weightiness. The Council usually scheduled two or three events each

*Other members included Henry T. Heald, the president of the Ford Foundation; Joseph Johnson, president of the Carnegie Endowment for International Peace; Don Price, in charge of the Ford Foundation's international program; Dean Rusk, president of the Rockefeller Foundation; petroleum consultant Walter J. Levy; David Lilienthal; publicist Herbert Bayard Swope (the man who coined the phrase "Cold War"); Arthur Hays Sulzberger, publisher of *The New York Times;* authors and journalists William L. Shirer, Theodore H. White, and James P. Warburg; Adolph Berle; Nelson Rockefeller; John D. Rockefeller III; and business tycoons like Najeb Halaby, Harold K. Hochschild, Henry Luce, Harry F. Guggenheim, Roger Blough, Marshall Field, and John Whitney.[49]

week, which often began in the late afternoon and broke up in time for those attending to catch their trains to their suburban homes. (In 1955, McCloy himself began to commute to Connecticut, where he had built a comfortable but not particularly ostentatious home on a plot of five acres in Cos Cob.) The chosen speaker would talk for no more than forty-five minutes, leaving enough time for a few questions from the floor. In the mid-1950s, McCloy moderated such meetings as Allen Dulles talking on "U.S. Intelligence Organization," James B. Conant speaking on Germany, and Lester Pearson addressing the "New Challenges in East-West Relations." Foreign heads of state and numerous foreign ministers gradually came to regard the opportunity to give a CFR talk as one of the requirements for an American tour. In a typical year, three prime ministers, six foreign ministers, and one president addressed the Council.[51] Though all CFR meetings were and are off the record, all too frequently these speakers gave such lackluster performances that George Franklin had to reprimand members for departing before the end of a meeting.[52]

One exception occurred during Fidel Castro's visit to New York in April 1959. The CFR's membership turned out in large numbers to hear the Cuban revolutionary speak. Afterward, Castro was repeatedly questioned about civil liberties and the expropriation of foreign property. Finally, one Council member stood and asked, "How much does Cuba want?" Insulted, Castro replied angrily, "We don't want your money. We want your respect." Faced with further hostile questions, Castro eventually drew himself up and announced, "I can see that I am not among friends," and walked out.[53]

But it was a rare occasion when a speaker actually chose to use the Council's platform to say something candid or unorthodox. A recitation of facts, laced with the usual platitudes, was the norm. As John Kenneth Galbraith wryly put it, such exercises could result in a "frank appreciation of the support to self-esteem that comes from being in the presence of the great." (Galbraith later resigned, he said, for "reasons of boredom.") In short, under McCloy's direction the Council was rarely a center for debate or the airing of controversies. Instead, it became a venue for a meeting of minds, the construction of a consensus, or, at worst, a mechanical ratification of conventional wisdom.

Lew Douglas, a Council director since 1940, thought the Council under McCloy "was becoming a protagonist of the views of the government, no matter which party was in power." Men who bothered to raise "legitimate questions" about basic assumptions of a given policy were "given little credence, if indeed they were not occasionally referred to with a not too well concealed contempt." As an example of the Council's being run as a mouthpiece of Washington, Douglas cited a Council meeting in which Soviet productivity figures were discussed. Douglas noted that "the statement was made that, although the C.I.A. source of the figures could not be disclosed, it was hoped that the figures themselves would be widely used."[54] Douglas believed the Council should not have been so eager to disseminate what he suspected were inflated estimates of Soviet productivity.

McCloy certainly did everything he could to create a congenial relationship between the Council and Washington. He frequently hosted smaller dinners at the Pratt House to which a select number of CFR members would be invited to dine with a State Department official or a visiting foreign dignitary. These were formal, black-tie affairs, but he made sure that the conversation, even in the presence of a foreign official, was always relaxed and informal. Issues of great moment might well be discussed, but so too might the conversation drift toward a discussion of fly-fishing or reminiscences of the war years. In terms of the stature of those invited and the ambience created by Pratt House, these dinners represented a private counterpart to Eisenhower's stag dinners. In such relaxed settings, the Council's members could take the measure of a Guy Mollet, a Harold Macmillan, or an Abba Eban.[55]

By 1958, Joseph Kraft was describing the Council as "an incubator of men and ideas."[56] Few of the speakers McCloy brought to the Council were particularly brilliant or entertaining, but they often could bring a firsthand report on a major news event. If nothing else, a great body of dry factual material was conveyed to the CFR's membership. The Council emphasized the importance of understanding the "factual situation" of any foreign-policy problem.[57] By this it meant to stress the complexity of foreign affairs and the value of experienced, expert leadership in the making of U.S. foreign policy. The unspoken assumption, of course, was that foreign policy was a subject that could not be left solely in the hands of the average American voter or his elected representatives in Congress.[58]

Next to the quarterly publication of *Foreign Affairs,* the most important activity carried on at the Council during these years was the institution of the study group. Much of the initial foundation money raised by McCloy soon after he became chairman was used to expand the number and quality of these study groups. The earliest of such projects—the study of U.S.-Soviet relations—had been chaired by McCloy and was without a doubt the Council's most ambitious and most expensive undertaking. Six full-time researchers were financed by the Ford Foundation, and McCloy, Dean Rusk, McGeorge Bundy, and Walt W. Rostow participated in the group's deliberations, which were also attended by observers from the CIA, the State Department, and the armed services. Its relative success set the standard for subsequent study groups. Soon the Council was publishing an average of four books or pamphlets a year. By 1956, there were six study groups at work and five less intensive "discussion groups" regularly meeting.

These discussions were not meant to be merely academic exercises; the purpose of the Council's "study group method" was to ensure that the "views and experience of Council members of different backgrounds can be brought to bear on a foreign policy. . . ."[59]

Some CFR study groups were, of course, more influential than others. The most important such project became a study of "Nuclear Weapons and Foreign Policy," which was begun late in 1954. Earlier that year, McCloy and many other Pratt House regulars had been extremely disquieted by John Foster Dulles's CFR speech, in which the Eisenhower administration endorsed the doctrine of massive nuclear retaliation. McCloy bluntly dismissed Dulles's doctrine as "rather contrived."[60]

Since then, he had given considerable thought to the problem of nuclear strategy. Like anyone who was aware of the technical developments in nuclear weaponry and delivery systems, McCloy was particularly disturbed by the potential for a Soviet first strike. That same autumn, he gave a speech warning that guided missiles armed with nuclear warheads are "only a matter of time and ballistics." He told his Atlantic City audience, five thousand members of the National Gas Association, that he wondered whether the American people understood the dangers. "The shortest distance to our heartland from an aggressive Soviet," he said, "is by way of the North. Ice blocks to the North are no longer a barrier to aggression."[61]

McCloy was already chairing the CFR Study Group on U.S.-Soviet Relations, so he did not formally participate in the nuclear-weapons study group. But through Robert Bowie, who flew up from his job at the State Department to attend the meetings, McCloy kept himself informed of its progress. Not surprisingly, the group floundered for nearly a year, getting caught up in the convoluted logic of nuclear warfare. Hanson Baldwin suggested that the credibility of a doctrine of massive retaliation ultimately required one to convince the Soviets that U.S. strategic thinkers were capable of the final irrational act. Baldwin concluded this was not credible. Paul Nitze disagreed, saying, "Even if war were to destroy the world as we know it today, still the U.S. must win that war decisively." This sounded to David Rockefeller like a veiled call for a "preventive war," a charge Nitze denied. The study group nevertheless went on to discuss whether "an initial attack by the United States could succeed in destroying the Soviet potential for retaliation."[62]

After almost half a year, the group's chairman, Gordon E. Dean (the same man who had sat in judgment of J. Robert Oppenheimer at his security hearing), decided to bring in an outside academic to serve as study director. Henry Kissinger quickly became the leading candidate. The young Harvard lecturer had recently written an article for *Foreign Affairs*, and both his Harvard mentor, Professor William Elliot, and Arthur Schlesinger, Jr., were promoting him for a job opening at *Foreign Affairs*.

When interviewed for the position of managing editor, Kissinger impressed the men he met at the Council, but the magazine's patrician editor, Hamilton Fish Armstrong, realized Kissinger's writing style was too ponderous. When Kissinger was rejected by Armstrong, George Franklin steered him toward the nuclear-weapons study group. On the basis of strong letters of recommendation from both Schlesinger and Harvard Dean McGeorge Bundy, Kissinger was then given the appointment, which marked a major turning point for both Kissinger's career and the Council.[63]

Beginning in the spring of 1955, Kissinger began working out of a small office in Pratt House. McCloy already knew him as the editor of *Confluence,* a quarterly magazine distributed largely in Western Europe and devoted to promoting unity inside the Atlantic alliance. *Confluence* aimed to influence the same audience of West European intellectuals targeted by such CIA-funded publications as Melvin Lasky's *Der Monat.* Founded in 1952 with seed money from the Rockefeller Foundation, the magazine was assured of survival in 1953 by a grant from the Ford Foundation, arranged by McCloy.[64]

Over the next two years, Kissinger spent twelve and sixteen hours a day in the Council, attending late-afternoon sessions of the study group, writing and rewriting his manuscript. Intellectually, the work he produced was his own, but he owed much to the men who made up the study group. Kissinger learned which arguments they found *sound.* In addition, he received informal access to what amounted to highly classified information. High-ranking Washington officials like General Lyman Lemnitzer and Air Force Major General James McCormack, Jr., came to these sessions and openly discussed the circumstances under which the U.S. military establishment contemplated battlefield use of nuclear weapons. In one such meeting, a former assistant secretary of defense stated that, if the situation in Korea "had continued to deteriorate, the U.S. would have used atomic bombs."[65] In no other setting outside of government could Kissinger have had the opportunity to hear such a frank exchange of views concerning the most sensitive defense secrets.

This extraordinary access to various defense and intelligence officials was reflected in the authoritative tone of Kissinger's final manuscript. The Council had produced numerous dry, soporific books over the years, but Kissinger's *Nuclear Weapons and Foreign Policy* sold seventeen thousand copies in its first year and remained on the best-seller list for fourteen weeks. It was easy to see why. Though his prose was far from graceful, the critique he presented of the Truman and Eisenhower strategic policies was bound to generate controversy. Nuclear weapons, he argued, had indeed changed the world, but not quite in the manner that had come to be accepted by Washington policy-makers. Because total war meant the end of all civilization, both the Soviets and the Americans would avoid waging total war except as a last resort. Indiscriminate thermonuclear warfare, and even a surprise attack, was therefore a remote possibility. But this did not mean, Kissinger said, that the Soviets could not hope to undermine the critical U.S. position in Western Europe by means of subversion and political warfare.

Echoing some of McCloy's own speeches, Kissinger argued that the Cold War would be won or lost in a political arena, not on the battlefields of Western Europe. But, should things come to a military confrontation, the Soviets could announce their intention to seize a limited objective, such as the disarming and neutralization of West Germany, and they could proceed to wage a conventional war in pursuit of that objective. They might even use limited nuclear weapons in such a conflict without precipitating general thermonuclear warfare. Would Washington risk the destruction of fifty American cities to defeat a limited Soviet objective in West Germany? One had to conclude that John Foster Dulles's threat of massive retaliation in such a situation would have no credibility, and therefore it provided little deterrence to Soviet aggression. What was required, Kissinger argued, was a much more flexible doctrine. The United States had to announce its readiness to fight limited conventional wars and even limited nuclear wars. Specifically, NATO had to become more than a "trip-wire" presence in Western Europe.

The apocalyptic nature of nuclear weapons themselves had not made diplomacy obsolete. The Soviets had pursued their political objectives in the world as if Hiroshima had never happened. They had consolidated their empire in Eastern Europe and invaded Hungary in 1956. On military grounds, Kissinger argued, the United States must be prepared "to fight local actions on our own terms and to shift to the other side the risk of initiating all-out war." The United States had to be willing to risk war: "I would suggest you cannot avoid war except by the willingness to fight one." Washington policy-makers must not allow the Soviets to "paralyze us with the argument that any limited war must automatically lead to all-out war."[66]

Kissinger also criticized Dulles's legalistic approach to dealing with America's allies. Imposing "obligations" upon them to join in support of various U.S. objectives outside the arena of their central national interests only generated unnecessary resentments. Similarly, Washington should become much more tolerant of anticolonial nationalism and neutralist sentiments in Asia, Africa, and Latin America. There was no need for Washington policy-makers to treat every change from the *status quo* as a crisis. In a similar vein, Kissinger suggested that the string of military pacts Dulles had created around the world was greatly overrated. Much of the book, in fact, constituted an assault on what Kissinger considered to be an overly legalistic approach to foreign-policy making by men trained as lawyers. Such men acted "as if a course of action were eternally valid, as if a policy which might meet exactly the needs of a given moment could not backfire if adopted a year later." In short, Americans had to lead the free world with a greater sense of realism and understanding of foreign sensibilities than had been displayed by John Foster Dulles.[67]

All of these thoughts had been articulated by McCloy over the first four years of the Eisenhower administration. Though Kissinger wrote his critique of Dulles within a broader intellectual framework, the world-view expressed was shared by the chairman of the Council on Foreign Relations. McCloy had always felt that "we had to be much more flexible in this strategic [nuclear] business" and that "the legalities that seemed to intrigue" Dulles were actually quite irrelevant.[68] What Kissinger had to say about greater tolerance of neutralist attitudes had already been voiced by McCloy a full year earlier, in his foreword to the Council's book on U.S.-Soviet relations. McCloy also had lobbied for the building up of a larger and more modern conventional force within NATO. In fact, Kissinger's ideas regarding the need for a versatile conventional-force structure borrowed heavily from a controversial talk General Maxwell Taylor gave at the Council in May 1956. The celebrated book that so helped to launch Kissinger's subsequent career as a foreign-policy consultant was very much a creature of the Council on Foreign Relations.

Of course, not everyone liked the book. At the White House, General Andrew Goodpaster, Jr., had Eisenhower read extensive excerpts of it. Ike thought Kissinger's arguments were "over-simplified"; besides, "What he urges we are attempting to do. We are ready to use force in a limited way, that we have showed in Formosa, in the Mid-East." To do any more would just be too "expensive."[69]

Still, if Ike didn't like it, Kissinger's book was widely enough read in the foreign-policy community during the summer of 1957 to identify the Council on Foreign Relations as an alternative school of thought to John Foster Dulles's stewardship. Now, more than ever before, McCloy's name was frequently mentioned in the press and in letters to the president as a suitable replacement for Dulles. Liberal Republicans and internationalist Democrats both claimed as their own the Council's tough new realism in dealing with foreign-policy issues.

By the time Kissinger's book came out in the summer of 1957, McCloy had arranged for him to do a little part-time work for Nelson Rockefeller. The most charismatic of the Rockefeller brothers was at that time serving as the president's special assistant for national-security affairs. Simultaneously, he chaired one of the family's philanthropic institutions, the Rockefeller Brothers Fund. In 1956, Rockefeller was looking for someone to head a "Special Studies Project," an ambitious effort financed by the Fund to define the nation's major problems and opportunities over the next ten to fifteen years. On McCloy's recommendation, Rockefeller hired Kissinger to direct the study. "He wanted to get close to the Rockefellers," McCloy remembered, "[and so] took up the offer as a trout takes to bait."[70] Rockefeller enjoyed Kissinger's sardonic wit, and over the next year they saw a great deal of each other over meals at his home or in meetings at the Rockefeller Brothers Fund. Kissinger sometimes talked of what he was learning at the CFR's meetings on nuclear weapons, and from these conversations, Rockefeller gradually became obsessed with the idea that the country was in dire need of a massive civil-defense program. At a luncheon with Eisenhower in March 1957, he urged the president to establish a special commission to study the whole problem.[71]

Eisenhower was skeptical, but gave his assent to the formation of a commission empowered to develop a "broad brush opinion of the relative values of various active and passive measures to protect civil population in case of nuclear attack." Rowan Gaither, chairman of the Ford Foundation, was named as chairman. McCloy was selected as a member of the Gaither Commission's top advisory panel.

Gaither quickly expanded the scope of the Commission's investigation when he became persuaded that one could not come to any sensible conclusions on the scope of a civil-defense program without studying the overall balance of power between the United States and the Soviet Union. After studying reams of classified material, McCloy and the other panel members concluded that U.S. strategic defenses were unprepared for the deployment of Soviet intercontinental ballistic missiles. By October, McCloy and most others on the Gaither Commission were convinced that the United States had to increase defense expenditures dramatically if the nuclear deterrent was to remain credible.

On October 4, 1957, just as the steering committee was about to sit down and write a final report for the president, the Soviets launched a 184-pound satellite into orbit. Overnight, the country's national self-esteem plunged. Eisenhower's ratings in the Gallup opinion poll dropped twenty-two points.[72] Clare Booth Luce quipped that Sputnik's distinctive radio "beep" was "an intercontinental outer-space raspberry to a decade of American pretensions. . . ."[73] However, Sputnik handed the Gaither Commission a timely opportunity to underscore the urgency of their recommendations. Paul Nitze quickly drafted the final report, and it was presented to the president in the Oval Office on November 4 by McCloy and other members of the advisory panel.

This twenty-nine-page report was clearly written with the intention of alarming the president so that he would sweep aside his conservative budgetary principles and endorse a massive defense buildup. Eisenhower had cut the defense budget in 1954 from $41.3 billion to $36 billion; the Gaither Report proposed spending an additional $44.2 billion over five years: $19 billion on offensive weapons and missiles and $25.1 billion on an ambitious civil-defense program. The authors of "Deterrence and Survival in the Nuclear Age" recommended that U.S. production of ICBMs be increased from eighty to six hundred Atlas and Titan missiles by 1963. In addition, the Polaris submarine intermediate-range ballistic missile (IRBM) program should be accelerated. Looking ahead to the 1970s, the authors predicted that there would be a "continuing race" and that "There will be no end to the technical moves and counter-moves." Anticipating the "Star Wars" program of the 1980s, they even suggested that an active missile defense system designed to intercept incoming warheads would someday prove to be feasible and therefore now required a "high-priority research and test program."

On the "passive-defense" side of the ledger, the Gaither panel proposed spending an astonishing $25 billion on civilian fallout shelters. This was justified largely on the grounds that it would "forcibly augment" the credibility of the U.S. nuclear deterrent "by reinforcing his [the enemy's] belief in our readiness to use, if necessary, our strategic retaliatory power."[74]

All of this, of course, sounded quite bleak. McCloy, Nitze, and other civilian members of the Commission were coming to grips with the sobering realities of the intercontinental missile. To men who could remember the shock of Pearl Harbor, a mere sixteen years in the past, the idea that the Soviet Union would soon be able to wipe out whole American cities on thirty minutes' notice was a nightmare. Three members of the group actually believed Washington should consider launching a preventive war, before the Soviets acquired a full-blown ICBM capability.[75]

In his meeting with the Gaither advisory panel on November 4, 1957, Eisenhower listened calmly while Gaither outlined the group's draconian recommendations. By the time Gaither finished, it was clear that the president was unconvinced. Not only did he assume that the Strategic Air Command was a much more survivable force than the Gaither group believed, but he also said he was inclined to think that fallout shelters were "rather low in the list of priorities." At this, McCloy interrupted to argue that the cost of such shelters would be only $100 per life saved. A few days later, he again tried to assure the president that the economy could support the proposed defense expenditures.

Eisenhower was willing to acknowledge that down the road the country would probably have to make a greater investment in missile technology. But in his view, the missile program was progressing just about as fast as was necessary, and he made it clear that his administration was not going to adopt the fantastic spending increases endorsed by the panel. Having firmly sidestepped the Gaither panel's recommendations, Eisenhower politely urged the group to keep themselves together and "review the matter every now and then."[76]

Despite this presidential dismissal, the Gaither panel did influence the administration on some defense policies. Eisenhower ordered SAC to have at least one-third of its strategic bomber fleet either in the air or on fifteen-minute alert at all times. The Polaris submarine-based missile program was accelerated. Only a few weeks later, the administration acted on one of the report's recommendations by broaching the idea of stationing nuclear armed missiles in Germany with West Germany's defense minister, Franz-Josef Strauss. And eventually some money was appropriated to educate the public about various civil-defense measures. Starting in the late 1950s, a whole generation of American schoolchildren periodically were asked to hide beneath their desks during practice atomic alerts.

Ironically, all the bellicose rhetoric about demonstrating a "will to survive" and building hundreds of new missiles masked the panel's most significant conclusion. Though McCloy and his colleagues had identified a window of vulnerability—which they believed would last from 1957 to 1961—they also said there would soon be a window of opportunity for serious arms-control negotiations. "This could be the best time to negotiate from strength," wrote the authors, "since the U.S. military position vis-à-vis Russia might never be so strong again."[77] According to their timetable, this window of opportunity would probably occur sometime in the early 1960s. (In fact, the Soviets took much longer to develop their ICBM force.) The panel emphasized that, beyond the early 1960s, the Soviets and the United States could expect to achieve nuclear parity in both weapons and delivery systems. At this point, it would be much more difficult to stop the arms race. McCloy and several other members of the Gaither group, including Isidor Rabi, were particularly impressed by this argument. Rabi went so far as to argue that the impending Soviet ICBM threat was such that the United States should (a) build an emergency defensive-missile system, and (b) negotiate "immediately a world-wide moratorium on nuclear explosions."[78] A ban on nuclear testing would go far to slow the arms race and therefore prolong America's overall military superiority to the Soviets. McCloy too became persuaded of the advantages to be gained from a ban on nuclear testing. Ironically, his strong interest in arms-control negotiations thus dated from his experiences with the Gaither Commission, a group soon to be associated in the public mind with those calling for major increases in the defense budget.

Inevitably, someone leaked the Gaither Report to the ubiquitous Drew Pearson, and the ensuing controversy led to another round of speculation on John Foster Dulles's continued tenure at the State Department. Those who had leaked the report knew very well that Dulles had scoffed at its alarmist conclusions. Simultaneously, Dulles was being criticized for his opposition to a U.S.-Soviet summit and for the refusal of the Eisenhower administration to halt atmospheric nuclear testing. In December 1957, the Soviets had proposed a two-or-three-year moratorium on nuclear testing, but Dulles had insisted that the United States could not agree to any moratorium without an outright ban on further production of nuclear weapons. This stance was not a serious negotiating position, since neither side could possibly verify that the other was not engaging in clandestine production. Verification of a test-ban treaty, however, was quite feasible. The scientists were already certain they could detect an atmospheric test.[79]

From the point of view of many critics—such as Paul Nitze, the primary author of the Gaither Report—Dulles combined the worst of two positions: not only was he unwilling to support the increased defense expenditures recommended, but he seemed to have an inflexible approach to disarmament negotiations with the Soviets. By contrast, McCloy had signed on to the Gaither Report's budgetary recommendations and yet was known to be a realistic advocate of arms control. Characteristically, he had maneuvered himself into a position that blended tough military preparedness with a willingness to negotiate. On January 6, 1958, the debate within the Eisenhower administration over how to respond to the Soviet proposal for a test moratorium came to a head in an acrimonious National Security Council meeting. Eisenhower's disarmament adviser, Harold Stassen, presented the argument for accepting the Soviet proposal. Eisenhower rejected Stassen's arguments, and within a month asked for his resignation.[80]

In the meantime, a public campaign emerged in the press to have Dulles replaced by McCloy. On January 12, 1958, Philip Graham and his wife, Katharine, dined with Drew Pearson, and the publisher of the *Washington Post* confided that he was "working to get Jack McCloy in Dulles's job. . . ." He told Pearson that Lucius Clay and Milton Eisenhower had lent their support. *The New York Time*'s Cy Sulzberger wrote that the secretary of state was a "tragic-comic figure." Senator Jacob Javits told Undersecretary of State Christian Herter that he thought McCloy should be given some position in the administration, even if not in the Cabinet. About this time, Eisenhower himself complained of Dulles's "practice of becoming a sort of international prosecuting attorney" in his dealings with the Soviets. But the president was still reluctant to move against his secretary of state.[81]

But if Dulles was not to be removed, Eisenhower nevertheless had to contend with an increasingly vocal public campaign mounted in Congress and by private citizens' groups like SANE to force the administration to negotiate a test-ban treaty. Harold Stassen's dismissal as the president's disarmament adviser only made things worse. So, two weeks after Stassen's resignation, McCloy, Alfred M. Gruenther, Bedell Smith, and Robert Lovett were named to advise Dulles on disarmament policy. In

Europe, the London *Times* reported that these appointments meant that "Washington's disarmament policies will now flow directly from the State Department and that means from Mr. Dulles." In Moscow, *Izvestia,* citing the fact that McCloy and Lovett had both signed their names to the Gaither Report, characterized the panel of disarmament advisers as "bulls let loose in a china shop."[82]

But McCloy and his three colleagues were actually rather inclined to push the process along. Twice in April 1958, McCloy and the other members of the disarmament panel met with Dulles to discuss whether the administration should support a test-ban treaty with the Soviets. McCloy strongly favored such a treaty and did not believe the U.S. nuclear deterrent could be harmed by a ban on atmospheric testing. In this he was vigorously opposed by AEC Chairman Lewis Strauss. Dulles and Eisenhower were beginning to waver. World public opinion was such that the administration was under heavy pressure to demonstrate its willingness to negotiate with the Soviets. In March 1958, Khrushchev announced a unilateral halt to their own series of nuclear tests. Washington had to respond. So, at the end of April 1958, Eisenhower and Dulles finally agreed to drop their insistence that no progress could be made on a test-ban treaty without a simultaneous ban on production of nuclear weapons. In response to a letter from Eisenhower, Khrushchev agreed to send a delegation to Geneva, where preliminary talks on the technical aspects of a test-ban agreement commenced in July. McCloy and Eisenhower's other disarmament advisers could claim at least part of the credit for this first concrete breakthrough in U.S.-Soviet arms-control negotiations.[83]

Early 1958 was a low point for the Eisenhower presidency. Ike was recovering from his second heart attack, which some of his friends believed had been brought on by the wave of criticism he received in the wake of the Sputnik affair. Though he had made a remarkable recovery by January, for the rest of his life he had to struggle with a mild speech impediment in which he occasionally transposed the syllables of a long word.[84] He was severely embarrassed by this affliction and even considered resigning the presidency. Aware of his friend's self-consciousness on this score, McCloy made a point of praising Ike's State of the Union speech in early January. He wrote him that his ninety-two-year-old mother, Anna, had watched the speech on television: "In order to give you some idea of the high regard in which she holds you, I would say she ranks you just a little above me. She was so relieved, not only by the content of your speech but also by the vigor and manner of your delivery of it, that she burst into tears just after it was over in pure thankfulness."

Ike was touched by this little gesture and responded with a note to Anna assuring her "that I value highly the opinion of the mother of my good friend."[85]

A few months later, Eisenhower invited his old friend to a White House dinner in honor of Prime Minister Harold Macmillan. It was an intimate gathering, attended by Foster Dulles, Bedell Smith, Al Gruenther, Robert Lovett, C. D. Jackson, Lewis Strauss, and a couple of British officials and their wives. After cocktails were served, the men adjourned to a stag dinner and their wives ate in a separate room. Later, while the women watched a movie, the men sat around and had a serious discussion on the issues of atomic testing, disarmament, and whether to have a summit conference with Khrushchev. Dulles led the discussion by going around the room and calling on each individual to express his opinion. It became apparent to all that Dulles's hard-line views were shared by very few, if any, other men in the room. He began by turning to the president's committee of advisers on disarmament issues: McCloy, Smith, Gruenther, and Lovett. They made it clear that they thought a summit was inevitable, an opinion Dulles disputed. Dulles was still looking for any excuse to avoid a summit, which he felt could only result in a propaganda coup for the Soviets. McCloy, Macmillan, Smith, and others argued that, realistically speaking, there was no way the United States could avoid such high-profile negotiations. Macmillan put it rather bluntly by saying the British people were not panicking at the thought that eight or nine bombs could exterminate their society, but they "jolly well feel that it is only fair to have a go at a conversation on the subject" [of a test ban and disarmament].[86]

McCloy tried to explain to Dulles that, though a summit was probably inevitable, one could take steps to ensure that it wasn't confined simply to a discussion of the Soviet proposal for a unilateral ban on testing. The Americans could put forward proposals for mutual on-site inspections in order to verify such a test-ban treaty, and a discussion of outstanding European problems could be placed on the agenda. Jackson suggested the administration should try to steal the initiative from the Soviets by announcing not only a suspension of nuclear testing, but a suspension of the production of fissionable material, provided the Soviets did the same. Dulles again expressed his displeasure at such an idea.

Throughout this little debate, Eisenhower sat "visibly puzzled." As Jackson reported to his diary, "Several times he blurted the kind of interruption that clearly showed he just had not understood." Altogether, it was a discouraging evening for men who were, after all, some of the president's closest friends and advisers. McCloy, Jackson, and others came away feeling that, in the face of Khrushchev's aggressive diplomacy on disarmament issues, Foster Dulles was hamstringing the administration's ability to break out of a defensive mode.[87]

McCloy and the other disarmament advisers, however, underestimated their influence over the administration. Dulles's objections focused on a summit meeting, with all its attendant publicity, and not the idea of a test-ban treaty. To be sure, Strauss and other AEC officials continued to argue that a test ban, or even a suspension of testing, should not be declared unless the Soviets were prepared to pledge a halt to all nuclear-weapon production. But with the encouragement of McCloy, Bedell Smith, Lovett, and Gruenther, both Dulles and Eisenhower began drifting toward a decision to press ahead for full-fledged negotiations on a test ban. When the team of Soviet and American experts negotiating in Geneva determined in August that it was "technically feasible" to detect violations of a test-ban treaty, the president announced his willingness to suspend all nuclear tests for one year if the Soviets agreed to have formal negotiations begin on the treaty by the end of October. Khrushchev quickly agreed, but between August and October 31, when the suspension took effect, the two superpowers exploded another thirty-three nuclear weapons—drenching the globe in record-breaking levels of radioactivity.[88]

That autumn, McCloy finally accepted an invitation to attend one of the exclusive and highly confidential meetings of the Bilderberg Group. This organization had been founded in 1952–53 by Dr. Joseph Retinger and Prince Bernhard of the Netherlands, the consort to Queen Juliana. Until then, Retinger, a former adviser to the Polish government-in-exile during the war, had served as the secretary general of the European Movement, a coalition of institutions dedicated to promoting European political and economic unity. Nearly half of the European Movement's budget was provided by the CIA-funded American Committee for a United Europe.[89] In 1952, Retinger, alarmed by the rise of anti-Americanism in Western Europe, persuaded Prince Bernhard to head a new organization designed to influence public opinion by bringing together leading American and European personalities once a year for a free-wheeling discussion of their differences. As Retinger later explained it to Prince Bernhard's official biographer, the idea was "to get the leaders of opinion in the most important European countries to make an appraisal of where the Americans were wrong" and then "at a completely private meeting of top-level people from both continents . . . to present this frank critique to leaders of American opinion and give them an opportunity to answer the indictment."[90]

In late 1952, Retinger went to America to try the idea out on his American contacts. Among others, he saw such old friends as Averell

Harriman, David Rockefeller, and Bedell Smith, then director of the CIA. After Retinger explained his proposal, Smith said, "Why the hell didn't you come to me in the first place?" He quickly referred Retinger to C. D. Jackson, who was about to become Eisenhower's special assistant for psychological warfare. It took a while for Jackson to organize the American wing of the group, but finally, in May 1954, the first conference was held in the Hotel de Bilderberg, a secluded hotel in Holland, near the German border. Prince Bernhard and Retinger drew up the list of invitees from the European countries, while Jackson controlled the American list. As Retinger later explained, invitations were "only sent to important and generally respected people who through their special knowledge or experience, their personal contacts and their influence in national and international circles can help to further the aims set by Bilderberg."[91]

Americans like David Rockefeller, Dean Rusk, and Joseph Johnson turned up in Bilderberg to meet with such influential Europeans as Denis Healey, Guy Mollet, and Alcide de Gasperi, the architect of postwar Italy. That first meeting was dominated by a fierce discussion of McCarthyism. Some of the Europeans suggested America "was heading for a Fascist dictatorship," a charge Jackson vigorously dismissed.[92]

In subsequent years, the Bilderberg Group focused on negotiations with the Soviets in the wake of Stalin's death, relations with the nonaligned nations, and the future of NATO. In 1957, the Bilderbergers "almost came to blows" discussing the Suez crisis of the previous year. Some of these discussions actually resulted in concrete steps. One regular Bilderberger, George McGhee, an oil-company executive and former assistant secretary of state, later said, "I believe you could say the [1957] Treaty of Rome which brought the Common Market into being, was nurtured at these meetings."[93]

But in general, the purpose of the Bilderberg meetings was less a matter of elite decision-making than yet another attempt to sketch the boundaries of an Atlantic consensus. In this respect, Prince Bernhard's meetings were little more than an extension of the Council on Foreign Relations. Indeed, the steering committee of the American section of the Bilderberg Group consisted entirely of CFR members.[94]

McCloy had been invited to the first meeting, in 1954, but could not come. And though he accepted an invitation to come to the 1957 session, at the last minute he had to cancel. He finally made it to the group's meeting at an oceanside resort in Buxton, North Carolina, for three days in mid-September 1958. Seventy-five men attended this session with McCloy, including Hermann J. Abs, Dean Acheson, George Ball, David Rockefeller, Giovanni Agnelli, and Paul Nitze. Prince Bernhard presided, as usual, and the discussion ranged over such broad issues as NATO conventional-force strategy, European monetary policy, the character of foreign aid for the developing nations, and the possibility of benign evolution within the Soviet Union. The minutes of the meeting report that the Bilderbergers that year "sometimes felt that a general relaxation of tension in the world could help that trend of evolution which we hope for inside the Soviet Union." And yet, as C. D. Jackson put it, "we used to have such a useful ally in the simple, byzantine brutality of Stalin. You knew where you were, and you also knew that if you bumbled your way into trouble, you would be rescued by Stalin. That is no longer true today with Mr. Khrushchev, who is an infinitely more subtle character." Still, a consensus emerged that the "seeming Russian interest in preventing the spread of atomic weapons could lead them to conclude some limited agreements."[95]

The most contentious issue discussed that year, however, concerned the Europeans' criticism of Washington's China policy. Only three weeks earlier, Chiang Kai-shek had again instigated another crisis over Quemoy and Matsu. After he had steadily infiltrated a hundred thousand of his troops onto the two offshore islands, the Chinese communists had first protested and then initiated an artillery bombardment of the islands. Eisenhower was aware that Chiang had provoked the crisis, but he was unwilling to have the Chinese communists overrun the islands. Publicly, he announced that he had ordered two additional aircraft carriers to join the Seventh Fleet in the Formosa Straits. Privately, he was considering the use of tactical nuclear weapons, an action Foster Dulles fully advocated. Only two days before the Bilderberg Conference opened in Buxton, Eisenhower went on national television and warned that the United States was pledged to defend Formosa: "There is not going to be any appeasement." Few people at home or abroad thought Quemoy and Matsu were worth going to war over. Most Europeans thought the whole crisis was absurd, and it frightened them to think that their American allies could even contemplate allowing Chiang Kai-shek to drag them into a war with China.[96]

It was in this context that McCloy and the other American invitees to the Bilderberg Group found themselves subjected to blistering criticism. The Europeans felt the two islands "should be treated as part of the mainland, and that the conflict over them was in reality a further episode in the Chinese Civil War. . . . Moreover, the islands were important to the Nationalists, not as a bastion for the defense of Formosa, but as a forward base for possible invasion of the mainland." They believed the survival of Chiang's regime was of "little importance" and the best that could happen would be to see a "transformation of the Nationalist regime into an independent state of Formosa, following some kind of popular consultation or plebiscite. . . ." In Quemoy and Matsu the United States had dug itself into an "untenable position." The islands should be abandoned.

This was not all. Most of the European Bilderbergers favored seating communist China at the United Nations. This should be done, they said, not only because it was realistic, but because to do so might help the West to "break" the alliance between China and the Soviet Union.[97]

McCloy was not a stranger to these arguments. His old friend from Sullivan & Cromwell, Arthur Dean, had been saying much the same thing for several years. As chairman of the Council on Foreign Relations' study group on Sino-Soviet relations, Dean had publicly linked the CFR to a "two-Chinas" policy.[98] As early as 1955, David Rockefeller was saying that it was simple "political foolishness" to pretend that the Chinese didn't exist.[99] McCloy was also aware of his brother-in-law's views. Lew Douglas, in fact, was writing the president that week to suggest that Quemoy and Matsu be "conceded to be a part of the mainland." Eisenhower promptly wrote back, saying this would amount to "appeasement," an argument Douglas thought was mere "sophistry."[100]

For McCloy, the issue was simply pragmatism. How could one run a foreign policy in the Far East while ignoring the existence of "this mighty empire on the mainland"? He could remember speaking with General George C. Marshall after the general's unsuccessful postwar mediation effort in China. Chiang had been rude and obstinate, and the trip had damaged Marshall's reputation with the powerful China lobby back home. But Marshall had impressed upon McCloy that "the idea of ostracizing China even after they became communist" just wasn't the right way to work things out.[101] So, as McCloy sat in the Bilderberg meeting listening to the Europeans, he couldn't help thinking that their criticism was directed not at himself or other like-minded members of the Council on Foreign Relations, but at C. D. Jackson, who was, after all, the personal representative of Henry Luce, the man probably more responsible than anyone else for what the Bilderbergers called America's "emotional attitude" on this issue.[102] McCloy thought the Eisenhower administration's China policy was as wrong as the Europeans believed it to be.

So it was with some irony that upon his return to New York McCloy learned that Foster Dulles wanted to speak to him about Quemoy and Matsu. First they had a number of phone conversations about the ongoing crisis. The secretary told McCloy that, in the wake of this most recent war-scare, perhaps it was time to persuade Chiang to moderate his demands. Dulles was unsure, however, just how far he wanted to press Chiang. Disaffection with Chiang was such that some officials within the administration actually muttered veiled threats about having the Chinese leader assassinated.[103] But Dulles just wanted to rein Chiang in, not eliminate him. The situation was further complicated by the fact that highly secret meetings were then taking place on an ambassadorial level between the Americans and the communist Chinese in Warsaw.[104] Dulles briefed McCloy on these negotiations, which had taken place off and on since 1955.

Late in September, Dulles flew up to New York to continue his talks with McCloy in person. With Eisenhower's approval, he had decided to ask the Chase chairman to fly to Formosa and "try to talk Chiang into giving up the islands."[105] McCloy took time out that day from a meeting of the Ford Foundation trustees to have lunch with Dulles. After listening to Dulles give his pitch, McCloy returned to his Ford Foundation meeting, where his colleagues voted to have him replace Rowan Gaither as chairman of the Foundation. (Gaither's health had declined precipitously in the last year, since he had been diagnosed with cancer.) Several times that day, McCloy was again called out of the trustees' deliberations to take phone calls from the president himself and other administration officials, all urging him to undertake the China mission. Some of the Ford Foundation trustees, however, advised their new chairman not to accept the assignment. Given Chiang's disposition, they believed McCloy could not expect to accomplish anything.[106]

McCloy had his own doubts, and after pondering over the matter for twenty-four hours, he wrote Dulles a memo explaining why he had decided to decline. Too many times during World War II, he had been the bearer of negative replies to Chiang's requests for more money and arms: "If he recalls me at all clearly it is probably in connection with unpleasant decisions." He was also inclined to "go further in the way of concessions respecting Quemoy and Matsu than the Department or you feel it is wise to go." Finally, he feared the "China Lobby": "I must confess that I see something akin public relations–wise to the ill-fated mission of General Marshall to Chiang. Again a friend of the President's is called upon to induce Chiang to moderate his attitude toward the Communists. The parallelism would not be lost on the China block and the columnists. . . ."[107]

Dulles was disappointed, and even more so when Eisenhower ordered him out to Formosa in McCloy's place. In the event, he offered Chiang some American amphibious landing craft, necessary for any invasion of the mainland, in return for a withdrawal of the garrisons on Quemoy and Matsu. Chiang refused, but eventually he agreed to issue a statement renouncing force. The Chinese communists responded by agreeing to a cease-fire, and gradually the crisis receded.[108] In the meantime, the Warsaw negotiations, which McCloy thought should have been given priority by the administration, dragged on without result. The strategic opening to communist China—which McCloy and many of his colleagues in the CFR and the Bilderberg Group thought so necessary—would not happen for another thirteen years.[109]

By the end of 1958, Cold War tensions in Germany were once again on the rise, and, inevitably, McCloy's counsel was sought. On November 10,

1958, Khrushchev announced that he intended to sign an early peace agreement with East Germany, a political entity the West refused to recognize. Washington feared such a treaty would become the first step to an abrogation of Allied rights in the free city of West Berlin. Indeed, later that month Soviet troops began harassing U.S. Army trucks transporting supplies to West Berlin across the *Autobahn.* Eisenhower told Christian A. Herter, his undersecretary of state, that his "instinct was to make a very simple statement to the effect that if the Russians want war over the Berlin issue, they can have it."[110]

McCloy thought the crisis atmosphere in Washington over the issue was rather overblown. He had been through this kind of thing with the Russians before. After discussing Berlin at some length with Lucius Clay one day in November, McCloy felt "it seemed like old times." The next day he wrote the president, "I have a certain confidence that it is going to come out without too serious consequences."[111] And so it did, though Khrushchev's posturing made for many a newspaper headline over the next few months. In the end, Khrushchev let one deadline after another pass, without ever moving against the Allied presence in West Berlin. Ultimately, the jockeying over the city's peculiar status would not end until after Eisenhower left the White House.

In the midst of the 1958 Berlin crisis, Foster Dulles again checked into Walter Reed Hospital, and this time the doctors told him that his cancer had returned. Surgery would be required. Eisenhower's secretary, Ann Whitman, noted in her diary, ". . . my hunch . . . is that this may be finis for Dulles as Secretary of State."[112] Dulles was a very sick man. But he insisted on postponing treatment of his cancer until early February 1959, when he returned from a trip to Europe. In the meantime, Christian Herter began to assume more of his duties, and so too did McCloy. The Chase chairman saw the president in mid-December, and a few days later was appointed to yet another panel of consultants, this time to the National Security Council. Joining him on this *ad hoc* panel were more than the usual number of Council on Foreign Relations types, including Hamilton Fish Armstrong, Robert Bowie, Arthur Dean, C. D. Jackson, Robert Lovett, and Dean Rusk. For the remainder of the Eisenhower administration, these consultants were frequently brought down to Washington from New York to discuss the Berlin situation, the Geneva arms-control talks, and planning for the upcoming Eisenhower-Khrushchev summit.[113] Later that year, Eisenhower was told that McCloy had criticized a National Security Council report for assuming that the United States had to shoulder the "full burdens of the entire free world." He disliked what he called an "Atlas complex" in some of the NSC's assumptions and invariably argued that the West Europeans could and should be encouraged to participate more fully in the Cold War.[114]

In early 1959, McCloy met with the ailing secretary of state to talk again about the now stalled disarmament talks in Geneva. And later that spring, as Dulles's health deteriorated, Christian Herter requested Eisenhower's permission to reconvene the small committee of disarmament advisers. So once again McCloy, Gruenther, Smith, and Lovett were summoned to Washington for meetings. McCloy complained that the administration was drifting, giving the appearance of disarray. Foster Dulles was trying to conduct State Department business out of his hospital bed; his doctors had decided that surgery was no longer possible and instead placed the secretary of state on a debilitating course of radiation treatment. Finally, on April 15, 1959, Eisenhower accepted his resignation.

The president's trusted former aide General Al Gruenther urged him to appoint McCloy to the position: "I have seen a good deal of McCloy in the past year," Gruenther wrote. "He is very sound, and his associates have a high opinion of him always. . . . He keeps in close touch with foreign affairs; he goes around the world each year in connection with bank business. Foreign visitors of political importance constantly come to see him."[115] Gruenther wasn't the only one pushing McCloy's nomination. Drew Pearson reported that he was among the top four candidates to replace Dulles.[116]

Eisenhower never explained why he did not chose McCloy, but he later told a friend that there were only four candidates—and McCloy was not one of them. Herter, he said, was the "obvious choice," but all the men he had in mind either were already in the Cabinet or worked in the State Department.[117] Eisenhower knew he could exercise direct control over these men. Having just accepted the resignation of a strong-willed secretary of state, the president now wanted to run his own foreign policy. McCloy, he knew, would be as strong a secretary of state as Foster Dulles had been.

McCloy himself was not any longer so interested in the job as he had been earlier. There was too little time left in the Eisenhower administration for a new secretary of state to accomplish much. He had his own commitments to Chase, where he was due to retire at the mandatory age of sixty-five in 1960. Besides, he too thought Herter was the obvious successor. That spring, he told Frankfurter, "I cannot see how they could have made any other appointment under the circumstances."[118]

He was, in fact, much closer to Herter than he had ever been to Foster Dulles. Born in the same year as McCloy, Herter had been a Foreign Service officer in his younger days, and then went on to become a congressman and governor of Massachusetts. But his personality was less that of a politician than the image of a soft-spoken Boston Brahmin. His six-foot-five-inch frame, crippled by osteoarthritis, made him walk slowly, with the gait of a man who lived in constant pain. He had none of the self-righteousness of Foster Dulles, or, as Eisenhower's press aide later put it, he was "a little less arbitrary in his beliefs."[119] The new secretary frequently phoned McCloy to discuss various matters, particularly anything to do with Germany and the test-ban talks. McCloy continued to come down to Washington for meetings of the president's panel of consultants to the National Security Council. Herter also consulted him on Middle East developments, China, the Soviet Union, and such broader policy questions as the U.S. balance-of-payments problem. McCloy made several trips to Germany that year, and each time he checked in with Herter. On one occasion, Herter used McCloy to carry a personal message to Adenauer, reassuring the German chancellor of Washington's commitment to defend Berlin. On another trip, he was instructed to try to persuade Adenauer to patch up his relations with the British.

One of these trips was made to attend a conference in October 1959 organized by the American Council on Germany, a group dedicated to promoting German-American relations. Ellen McCloy served as vice-president, and McCloy's old friend Eric Warburg handled the Council's finances as treasurer. (Inevitably, the Ford Foundation funded some of the Council's functions.) The previous year, the Council had sponsored Dean Acheson's rebuttal of George Kennan's much-publicized Reith Lectures in Great Britain, given during the autumn of 1957. Kennan had argued in these controversial lectures that the West should seriously consider the Soviet Union's offer to demilitarize a reunified Germany.* The Council's annual report that year charged that Kennan's comments had "sparked a movement in Germany and Britain for steps toward Disengagement and German neutralization." McCloy, Warburg, Shep Stone, and other men associated with the Council believed this kind of talk was somehow responsible for Khrushchev's ultimatum on Berlin. Though men like Adenauer and McCloy paid lip service to the principle of German unification, they certainly did not wish to achieve this goal at the cost of seeing West Germany fall out of the NATO military alliance.[121] For these reasons, the American Council on Germany during this period devoted itself to building up "confidence in the NATO nuclear shield in Germany" and generally shoring up the Atlantic alliance.[122]

On this particular occasion, McCloy was joined by Henry Kissinger, James Conant, Shep Stone, Dean Acheson, and an equally prominent list of Germans. Kissinger gave an address on the general military balance between the NATO and Warsaw pacts, and McCloy presided over an

*The Soviet proposal, outlined by Polish Foreign Minister Adam Rapacki, envisioned a demilitarized zone consisting of the two Germanys, Poland, and Czechoslovakia. Rapacki floated his plan in various forms from 1957 through March 1962. But the Western powers repeatedly rejected the plan, even though it provided for on-site inspection and a phased reduction of both conventional and nuclear forces.[120]

open debate. Afterward, Adenauer hosted a reception for the conferees. Such gatherings resulted in no high-level decision-making. But they served, like the Bilderberg meetings, as a forum for cementing elite friendships and establishing the boundaries of an unofficial consensus on the issues of the day.

On one of his trips to Germany, in the summer of 1959, McCloy visited Villa Hugel, the three-hundred-room limestone Krupp castle perched atop a mountain overlooking Essen. Since walking out of Landsberg Prison, Alfried Krupp had done quite well. In 1957, *Time* put him on its cover and described him as "the wealthiest man in Europe—and perhaps the world."[123] McCloy was not surprised by Krupp's business successes: "Given the base from which he had to move and the resurgence of Germany, it was almost inevitable."[124] Now Krupp had extended an invitation to McCloy to join him for lunch at Villa Hugel. This was not, however, to be a social occasion. McCloy had come to attend to some quite distasteful business.

A year earlier, McCloy had been approached by an old friend, Jacob Blaustein, to use his influence on Krupp to resolve a difficult problem. An oil man of substantial wealth, Blaustein also served as senior vice-president of the Conference on Jewish War Material Claims Against Germany, the organization that had McCloy's old friend Benjamin Ferencz as its counsel. Ferencz had been persuaded to stay on in Germany after McCloy's departure, and over the next few years he negotiated a reparations agreement with the Germans. Under the terms of the 1956 indemnification law, Israel was to receive some $700 million over a ten-year period. In addition, the Germans agreed to pay about $10 million each year over the same time period to rehabilitate Jewish communities in Europe. Ferencz was pleased with this settlement, but he was troubled that it provided no compensation for the Jewish and gentile survivors of slave camps operated by various German industrialists. Ferencz reasoned that the Krupp, Flick, and I. G. Farben industries could now well afford to compensate survivors of their slave camps. After quietly broaching the matter with the companies that had inherited I. G. Farben's assets, he had obtained an out-of-court settlement of $1,200 for each surviving slave worker who had worked in that firm. It wasn't much, but it was something for the few hundred survivors, many of whom were still destitute and in broken health.

When Ferencz turned his attention to the case of Krupp slave workers, he received a blunt refusal even to consider the question of compensation. Handed a fifteen-thousand-word legal brief that meticulously documented Alfried Krupp's personal responsibility for the horrendous conditions under which his slave workers lived and died, Krupp's chief aide, Berthold Beitz, turned white with anger, cried out, *"Erpressung"* ("blackmail"), and then stomped out of the room.[125]

At this point, Ferencz had Blaustein formally approach McCloy. Ferencz was confident that McCloy would intercede with the German industrialist. In all the years he had known McCloy, the lawyer had never said no: "Whatever I proposed, he said yes to. . . . I found him to be the kind of man who liked to say yes."[126]

But though McCloy was willing to help Ferencz and Blaustein win what compensation they could for the surviving slave workers, he did not want it to appear that Krupp had relented only out of consideration for the man who had given him his freedom and restored his personal fortune. "He was very hesitant," Ferencz later recalled, "about approaching Krupp directly. He didn't want Krupp to feel [that he was saying], 'I turned you loose, now you have to pay the Jews.' "[127]

So, when first asked to intercede with Krupp in the summer of 1958, McCloy let it be known through one of his German friends that he thought it wise for Krupp to settle the Jewish claims. There may have been the barest hint of a threat that he might be willing to issue a pointed public statement on the issue unless Krupp began negotiations in earnest.[128] Within weeks, Beitz flew to New York and in a meeting with McCloy, asked to see a detailed proposal for such a settlement. Blaustein quickly messengered a document to McCloy's Chase office which outlined a settlement modeled after the modest compensation paid by the I. G. Farben companies. But before real negotiations could begin, Beitz told McCloy that, though Krupp could be interested, any such settlement had to be seen as something voluntarily initiated by Krupp himself. Beitz then returned to Germany, and McCloy told Blaustein and Ferencz to give the Germans time to come up with a proposal of their own.[129]

Months went by with no word from Krupp. Finally, in June 1959, Beitz informed the Jewish Claims Conference that Krupp was breaking off all negotiations. Upon hearing of this, Ferencz decided to strike out at the heart of Krupp's business assets. Krupp had one vulnerable point in 1959. When McCloy had restored Krupp's fortune in 1951, he had stipulated that Krupp would have to divest himself of the massive steel plant at Rheinhausen. On top of this, in the "Krupp Treaty" of March 1953, Alfried Krupp himself had given his word of honor to divest himself of his coal and steel holdings by 1959. Since then, he had done anything but try to sell these holdings, and his manager, Beitz, had given his own pledge as early as 1954 that, as long as he was associated with the firm, "Not a stone shall be sold." Each year thereafter, Alfried Krupp had managed to obtain an extension from the Mixed Commission empowered to enforce the Allied laws on industrial deconcentration. These laws were now being openly flouted, and by 1957 Adenauer himself formally requested that the Krupp Treaty be allowed to lapse without implementing its decartelization provisions. All this caused some annoyance to McCloy, who felt he had placed his own personal prestige behind the Krupp Treaty. "I've said, and I still say," he told one reporter, "that he [Krupp] volunteered to sign it and he should stick to it. He says it was extorted from him under duress. That's absolutely untrue."[130] Well aware of McCloy's unhappiness with Krupp over this issue, Ferencz thought that he could use the threat of a divestment order to compel Krupp to pay what was, after all, a paltry sum of $2.38 million to the slave workers.

McCloy in any case thought it would be "good business" if Krupp settled the claims, and now told Blaustein that during his upcoming trip to Germany that summer he would investigate the matter. True to his word, once in Germany, McCloy discussed the issue with his old friend David Bruce, who was now serving as the U.S. ambassador to Bonn. A short time before McCloy's arrival, Bruce had gone pheasant-hunting with Alfried Krupp and Berthold Beitz, and he encouraged McCloy to talk with Krupp directly. So it was that McCloy found himself being driven to Krupp's Villa Hugel estate one day in July 1959.[131]

Over lunch, he tried to impress upon Krupp and Beitz that a settlement on purely humanitarian grounds would only enhance the company's image and moral stature. The two Germans admitted that the amount of money involved was small indeed. But they told McCloy that they had promised other private companies, facing similar claims, that they would not prejudice their court battles by settling out of court. McCloy reported to Ferencz that Krupp needed more time.

But Ferencz could brook no further delays. If McCloy's "velvet glove" could not produce results immediately, Ferencz had decided it was time to file a case in New York, suing Krupp for $100,000 for each slave worker, and attaching Krupp's accounts in Chase Manhattan Bank. Just before the case was filed, some of the more incriminating documents were shown to Beitz by Eric Warburg. Warburg told the Krupp manager that things were getting out of hand. He again urged Beitz to fly at once to New York and settle the claims before a torrent of bad publicity jeopardized Krupp's standing with the U.S. government.

Warburg's arguments—and the documents proving Krupp's guilt—finally persuaded Beitz that he had to act. At the same time, Krupp had been waiting for the claims commission to recommend a cancellation of the divestiture order concerning his coal and Rheinhausen steel holdings. The claims commission did this during the autumn of 1959, so, by the time Krupp agreed to reopen negotiations on the Jewish slave-worker claims in November, all that remained was for the State Department to approve the recommendation.

Obviously, the timing was such that Krupp's willingness, finally, to talk compensation payments for the Jews was intimately tied to whether the U.S. government agreed to waive the divestiture order. Whether McCloy played any direct role in this trade-off is not clear. But it is known that Beitz first flew to Washington, where he met with State Department officials. Then, on Thanksgiving Day, he flew to New York, where McCloy had reserved a conference room in Chase's midtown office. There Beitz offered Blaustein the following deal: Krupp would pay up to $2.38 million, enough, it was thought, to give each surviving slave worker $1,250 in compensation. In return, the Jewish Claims Conference had to pledge that Krupp would no longer be subject to any further claims by Jewish survivors of the Holocaust. The slave workers would receive a paltry sum, and Krupp would be allowed to retain his coal and steel holdings. But after so much haggling, Blaustein felt it was all they could hope for, and so quickly initialed a preliminary agreement. A little more than a month later, on the day before Christmas, a final document was released to the press. *The New York Times* reported that Krupp had rejected any legal liability and was only paying the compensation in order to help "heal the wounds suffered during World War II." In London, the *Sunday Dispatch* noted how little the surviving slave workers were to be compensated and called the settlement "mean-spirited and tawdry."[132]

In the end, everyone had greatly underestimated the number of surviving Krupp slave workers. Consequently, instead of the $1,250 Ferencz had budgeted for each survivor, most claimants received no more than $500.[133] Still, in retrospect, Ferencz believed his efforts were worthwhile, and he always credited McCloy for whatever meager compensation was extracted from Krupp in behalf of the former slave workers. So too did prominent Jewish leaders like Nahum Goldmann. Because of his role in the restitution of these Jewish slave workers, the following year the American Jewish Committee and the B'nai B'rith singled him out for a Human Rights Award.[134] Just a few short years before, he had angered many of these same Jewish leaders for giving Krupp his freedom. But that was ancient history.

During these sunset years of the Eisenhower administration, McCloy's counsel was sought by a remarkably broad range of influential and powerful men in and out of government. Journalists like "Scotty" Reston and Joe Alsop used him for background information in their widely read columns. From time to time, he still received summonses to appear in Washington for one of Frankfurter's "tête-à-tête dinner[s]." Typically, the justice's invitations explained only that a "matter that is, I think, of as much concern to you as it is to me makes me anxious to see you. . . ."[135] Once—in a reference to his Harvard years, when Frankfurter never called on him in class—McCloy joked, "I am impressed that at long last (some thirty-nine years) you have gotten around to calling on me."[136]

He seemed to be everywhere—in Washington, New York, Bonn, London, and Paris—and to know everything. When Eisenhower was contemplating a round-the-world trip that summer, McCloy advised him that it would be a mistake to pass up the Philippines, for he had heard from one of his contacts that this would cause serious injury to America's political allies there. As the country's foremost banker, he regularly served on the Federal Advisory Council of the Federal Reserve Board. His responsibilities now included the chairmanship of the Chase Manhattan Bank, the Ford Foundation, and the Council on Foreign Relations. Among his charitable activities during the late 1950s he and the Rockefellers raised money for the Metropolitan Opera and its new home in the modernistic Lincoln Center on the West Side of Manhattan. In addition, he sat on the board of directors of such major American corporations as Westinghouse, United Fruit, AT&T, Metropolitan Life Insurance Co., Squibb Corporation, and a half-dozen other corporations. College students across the country were just then beginning to know him as one of those named in C. Wright Mills's best-selling book, *The Power Elite.* The "inner core of the power elite," wrote Mills, "consists, first, of those who interchange commanding roles at the top of one dominant institutional order with those in another. . . ."[137] The professor couldn't have cited a better example of this phenomenon than John J. McCloy.

In the summer of 1959, just before McCloy took his family for an extended trip to Europe, C. D. Jackson wrote to remind McCloy that later that summer a World Youth Festival was scheduled to take place in Vienna. Jackson asked McCloy to contribute an article, perhaps on the "benign and constructive aspects" of the U.S. occupation of Germany. The piece would appear in a daily newspaper to be published in Vienna in conjunction with the festival. McCloy agreed, and the article was published (in five languages) in a newspaper distributed by a twenty-five-year-old Smith graduate named Gloria Steinem.[138]

McCloy's connection to Steinem went beyond contributing an article to the propaganda operation of which she was an editor in Vienna. Late in 1958, he and Jackson had discussed how the United States should respond to the expected Soviet propaganda blitz in Vienna. Previous gatherings of this kind had always been held in Moscow, East Berlin, or other cities in Eastern Europe. These events were major propaganda circuses, and the CIA was determined, in the words of Cord Meyer, a career CIA officer, "to compete more effectively with this obviously successful Communist apparatus."[139]

Washington expected some twenty thousand students and young

scholars from all over the world to converge on Vienna that summer for the three-week festival. Consequently, the CIA wanted an organized student presence in Vienna in order to counter Soviet propaganda.

C. D. Jackson recognized the Vienna Youth Festival as "an extremely important event in the Great Game." He explained, "This is the first time commies have held one of these shindigs on our side of the iron curtain; and what goes on, how it goes on, and what the follow-up will be is, I think, extremely important."[140]

By the time Jackson first approached McCloy, in the autumn of 1958, he and Cord Meyer, head of the CIA's International Organizations division (IO), had a plan. The Agency would provide discreet funding to an "informal group of activists" who would constitute themselves as an alternative American delegation to the festival. The CIA would not only pay their way but also assist them to distribute books and publish a newspaper in Vienna. Among other individuals, Jackson and Meyer hired Gloria Steinem to work with them. Steinem had recently returned from a two-year stint in India, where she had been a Chester Bowles Asian Fellow.

"I came home in 1958," Steinem later explained, "full of idealism and activism, to discover that very little was being done. . . . Private money receded at the mention of a Communist youth festival."[141] Convinced that a contingent of liberal but anticommunist American students should go to Vienna, she heard through her contacts at the National Student Association that there might be funding available to finance American participation in the festival. Working through C. D. Jackson and Cord Meyer, Steinem then set up an organization in Cambridge, Massachusetts called the Independent Service for Information on the Vienna Youth Festival. She obtained tax-exempt status, and Jackson helped her raise contributions from various American corporations, including the American Express Company. But most of the money came from the CIA, to be managed by Jackson in a "special account." The entire operation cost in the range of $85,000, a not inconsiderable sum in those years.[142] (Steinem's organization, later renamed the Independent Research Service, continued to receive support from the CIA through 1962, when it financed an American delegation to the Helsinki Youth Festival.[143])

Steinem ended up working closely with Samuel S. Walker, Jr., vice-president of the CIA-funded Free Europe Committee. Because the Austrians did not want to be associated with the Free Europe Committee, the Agency set up a commercial front called the Publications Development Corporation (PDC). Walker was made president of this dummy corporation, funded in part by "a confidential one-year contract" worth $273,000 from the Free Europe Committee.[144] His job was to supervise the book-and-newspaper operation at the Youth Festival.[145]

McCloy was brought into the entire operation when Jackson needed to arrange a procedure for paying expenses in Vienna. As Jackson explained it to Cord Meyer, "I have been in touch with Jack McCloy on handling of funds, on a non-attributable basis. He told me that the Chase Bank had done it in the past and gave me the name of the man in Chase who knew all about such things."[146]

McCloy told Jackson that the "money would have to do quite a lot of traveling—from Chase to Switzerland in one of the numbered accounts; from Switzerland to Breisach & Co. in Liechtenstein. . . ." From there, Jackson arranged to have *Time* reporter Klaus Dohrn pick up the Liechtenstein funds in cash, stuff them into a suitcase, and drive to Vienna.

How often McCloy allowed the CIA to use Chase Manhattan Bank in this fashion is not known. He probably had fewer qualms about the Agency's using Chase Bank facilities than he did about the much more delicate relationship between the Agency and the Ford Foundation. Chase's accounts and its network of corresponding banks overseas were there for any client, private or governmental, to use. Given the tenor of the times, and McCloy's close relationship to Allen Dulles, it would be surprising if Chase's contacts with the CIA were not frequent and friendly. About the same time that McCloy helped the Agency with its covert operation at the Vienna Youth Festival, Cord Meyer began fundraising for the American Institute for Free Labor Development (AIFLD), a new organization designed to train labor-union officials from Latin America on how to combat communism. Chase Manhattan Bank, Standard Oil of New Jersey, and several other large corporations subsidized AIFLD's activities.[147]

Upon his return from Europe in the summer of 1959, McCloy had his first chance to meet Nikita Khrushchev. Eisenhower had finally extended an invitation to the Soviet Communist Party chairman, who promptly accepted and announced that he would spend a full ten days in America. He wanted to see as much of the country as possible. When Khrushchev arrived in New York, Averell Harriman hosted an exclusive reception for him in the library of his New York town house at 16 East 81st St. The previous autumn, Harriman had been bitterly disappointed to lose his gubernatorial re-election race to Nelson Rockefeller. Finding himself essentially unemployed, Harriman had set off on a private visit to the Soviet Union, where he spent an extraordinary ten hours in conversation with Khrushchev. "I never realized," he said later, "that you could learn so much about a man in one long session."[148] He came away from Moscow highly impressed with the voluble Soviet premier.

When Khrushchev agreed to come to a reception, Harriman consulted McCloy on who should be invited. It was Harriman's thought to introduce the Russian to "leading bankers and businessmen."[149] McCloy suggested a dozen names, including Frederick Ecker (Metropolitan Life Insurance Co.), Rogers Herod (International General Electric) and W. Alton "Pete" Jones, an oil man and a member of Eisenhower's informal "kitchen Cabinet." All together, twenty-nine corporate executives, foundation presidents, and politicians came to Harriman's home on the evening of September 17, 1959. In addition to those whom McCloy had suggested, Harriman had invited such personalities as John D. Rockefeller III, David Sarnoff, Dean Rusk, Henry Heald, William C. Foster, and John Kenneth Galbraith. Afterward, Harriman calculated that the men assembled in his library controlled among themselves some $38.9 billion in corporate or foundation assets.[150]

Khrushchev was properly impressed when Harriman introduced him to this imposing assemblage of the capitalist world. "You rule America," he quipped. "You are the ruling circle." Indeed, like Stalin before him, Khrushchev always displayed a greater willingness to deal with recognized "capitalists" than with the politicians who represented them.[151] In his memoirs, Khrushchev vividly recalled meeting Harriman's guests, who looked to him "like typical capitalists, right out of the posters painted during our civil war—only they didn't have the pigs' snouts our artists always gave them."[152]

In the presence of this "ruling circle," Khrushchev tried to be blunt. The United States, he said, would be wise "not to be tough with the USSR" and "not to push the USSR around." He tried to convey the confidence he felt in his country's strength and the pride he felt for its accomplishments. But, though insisting that America treat his country as an equal, he also tried to convey his willingness to deal realistically with Washington. Most of the businessmen present came away rather frightened at the prospect of negotiating with such an intelligent adversary. Peter Jones thought him a "clever, cunning fellow." General Electric's Rogers Herod wrote Harriman afterward that the Russian impressed him as "a quick, shrewd thinker. . . . I came away with some misgivings as to the results of his visit to the USA if he impresses others as he did me."[153]

McCloy too thought Khrushchev was a formidable opponent. When, at one point during the reception, Khrushchev warned, "You had better write off the socialist countries from your balance sheet," McCloy shot back, "Are you ready to write off the rest of the world from your balance sheet?" Ever "quick on his feet," Khrushchev diverted attention from the question and, more or less as a "ward politician would do," gave McCloy an "evasive" answer.[154] But the exchange gave McCloy the impression that this was a Soviet leader with whom the United States could negotiate. Khrushchev seemed to imply that all the Soviets wanted was an assurance of nonintervention in their bailiwick, a "sphere of influence" that McCloy himself had recognized in the wake of Yalta.

Khrushchev had actually been much more explicit with Harriman three months earlier. Only on the issue of Allied rights in West Berlin, which he said he would someday unilaterally terminate, did Khrushchev talk tough. On the broader issues of peaceful coexistence and arms control, he made it clear that he sought to work out some kind of détente with Washington. Referring to the start of the Cold War, he said, "We don't consider Stalin without blame. . . . In the last years he had a bad influence both internally and in international affairs." The Soviets were willing to prohibit all nuclear explosions, and he pointed out that the technical experts at Geneva had found no obstacle to verifying a test-ban treaty. He wanted to sign a nonaggression pact with the United States and afterward negotiate a "reduction in forces" with "the most thorough control with inspection by both armies." When Harriman asked him why he hadn't accepted Eisenhower's 1955 "Open Skies" proposal, Khrushchev replied that it was not "realistically fair," because the United States had so many military bases outside its borders. However, if this was such a good idea, the Soviets "would agree to air reconnaissance but not as a start." Khrushchev also brought up the subject of George Kennan's Reith Lectures and confessed that the ideas outlined by Kennan "coincided with his own." Harriman's confidential notes of the meeting reported, "He [Khrushchev] liked particularly the idea of a gradual withdrawal in Central Europe."[155]

This extraordinary interview with the Soviet premier convinced Harriman that the next administration, if not Eisenhower's, would probably have the opportunity to achieve a major breakthrough in relations with Moscow. As for McCloy, his exchange with Khrushchev in 1959 merely reinforced his gut feeling not only that arms-control treaties were a desirable necessity in the nuclear age, but also that the Soviets had come to the same conclusion. The Geneva negotiations had a future.

Early in 1960, McCloy went to Gordon Gray, the president's special assistant, to express his concern about all the talk of an alleged "missile gap." Ever since the leaking of the Gaither Report a year earlier, a number of newspaper columnists had been emphasizing the report's assumptions regarding Soviet ICBM capabilities. This theme was about to become a major element in the presidential campaign of Senator John F. Kennedy. "Mr. McCloy had said," Gray reported to the president, "he was getting increasing reports from around the country and from prominent and responsible people that they were confused and in some cases concerned." Gray said he thought Eisenhower "should take seriously the concern of such individuals as Jack McCloy as distinguished from much of the political talking that is going on."[156] Eisenhower knew these concerns to be groundless, because photointelligence obtained during U-2 overflights of the Soviet Union demonstrated that the Soviets were, in fact, way behind the Americans in deployment of ICBMs.[157] The president felt he could not reveal the existence of the top-secret U-2 program. But, on hearing about the worries of men like McCloy, Eisenhower acknowledged to Gray that he would have to do something to respond to his critics.

Two days later, at a press conference, Eisenhower once again denied that there was a missile gap and then made a dramatic announcement: he now favored a test-ban treaty covering nuclear explosions in the air, in the sea, in outer space, and those among the underground tests "which can be monitored." Five weeks later, the Soviets said they would agree to such a treaty, including on-site inspection, if the United States would also agree to an indefinite moratorium on low-kiloton, unverifiable underground tests. Eisenhower's critics reacted in near hysteria to the prospect of such an agreement with the Soviets. *The New York Times* suggested that such an unverifiable test-ban treaty would "leave the Soviets free to continue experiments behind the Iron Curtain to develop Premier Khrushchev's fantastic weapons." Eisenhower's AEC chief, John McCone, bluntly told him that such an agreement "was a surrender of our basic policy." But men like Herter and McCloy encouraged the president, whose last ambition before leaving office was to negotiate a test ban. So, at the end of March, Eisenhower suggested a compromise proposal for a limited two-or-three-year moratorium on such unverifiable testing, to be followed by further negotiations. The Soviets indicated their agreement, and an Eisenhower-Khrushchev summit meeting was scheduled for that May.[158]

The president's commitment on this issue was such that he now wanted to set up within the bureaucracy an autonomous unit devoted to the control of armaments. He felt there was such opposition to disarmament talks among the military establishment that such an arms-control agency should be located within the State Department. But he wanted a man to head it who "would have stature roughly equivalent to that of the Secretary of Defense." In short, he wanted McCloy. Once again an effort was mounted to persuade the Chase chairman to come back to Washington. Eisenhower, Herter, and Gruenther all talked to McCloy, who acknowledged that he was "tremendously interested" in the disarmament job. Under Chase's rules, he was supposed to have retired on March 31, 1960, his sixty-fifth birthday. But because of an unresolved dispute between David Rockefeller and George Champion on the division of their responsibilities in the wake of McCloy's departure, the Chase chairman had agreed to stay on for another six months. In the end, McCloy called the president back to say "that overriding personal considerations, along with his Bank commitments, would make it impossible for him to take on a full-time job before the first of the coming year."[159] The creation of the Arms Control and Disarmament Agency would have to wait until the next administration.

On the eve of what Eisenhower thought was to be a major triumph for his administration, the president committed a most serious blunder. Pressed by the CIA to authorize one more U-2 overflight, Eisenhower agreed, provided no flights occurred past May 1, 1960, two weeks before his scheduled departure for the Paris summit. On that day, Gary Powers took off from a U.S. base in Turkey, and shortly later a Soviet anti-aircraft missile shot his U-2 down.[160] Had Eisenhower acknowledged responsibility for the flight, and explained to the American people the existence of the U-2 project (which the Soviet government had known since 1956), the summit might still have proceeded. All Khrushchev needed was a bland statement of regret for the flight, the kind of statement the administration had in fact made on previous overflight incidents. But Eisenhower engaged in a cover-up, thinking that the downed U-2 had been destroyed and its pilot with it. The president denied that there had been any spy plane and suggested that the plane shot down had been a weather aircraft that accidentally drifted off course. Within days, Khrushchev caught him in this lie, producing not only a very much alive Powers, but also reams of the plane's surveillance photos.

The severely embarrassed president had been caught lying to his own people. To make matters worse, the administration now issued a series of conflicting nondenial denials. Admitting that the plane was equipped for photosurveillance, the State Department denied that the president himself had authorized the flight. James Reston concluded the next day in *The New York Times* that Washington was "caught in a swirl of charges of clumsy administration, bad judgment and bad faith." Eisenhower finally held a press conference and admitted to the whole project, but refused to offer the Soviets any apologies. Spying, he said, "is a distasteful but vital necessity."[161]

Khrushchev was certainly angry about the whole incident, but in retrospect some historians have suggested that as a matter of political necessity the Soviet premier needed to carry back an official apology to his own military establishment.[162] Equally compelling political factors precluded Eisenhower from dramatizing his humiliation by bringing any kind of apology to Paris. The summit was therefore doomed even before it began, and with it any hopes for a test-ban treaty. Before finally walking out, Khrushchev savaged the Americans and ridiculed the president in the most personal manner.

McCloy was extremely upset by these developments. As the U-2 crisis unfolded in early May, he talked with a variety of administration officials on how to limit the damage. When Khrushchev verbally assaulted the president in Paris, McCloy quickly cabled Eisenhower, "I do not know when I have been more distressed over anything than the news of the treatment you received at the hands of the Soviet President in Paris. . . . To have him deliver the invectives that he did against you angered and saddened me. You behaved with the greatest dignity and restraint."[163] Later, Ike sent a note to McCloy, referring to his "amazing experience in Paris," and thanked him for his "extremely heart-warming" message, which arrived "at a most opportune moment."[164]

The president was shaken by his encounter with the temperamental Khrushchev, and his critics at home had a field day. Many of them, including Democratic presidential candidate John F. Kennedy, blamed the president for the collapse of the summit. Kennedy said that Ike had "let the risk of war hang on the possibility of an engine failure," and that he should have "expressed regret" for the overflight if that would have kept the summit talks alive.[165] McCloy quickly responded to Kennedy's comments in a commencement speech a few days later. He complained that a "spate of gratuitous and inappropriate comments" had been made by "some political aspirants."[166]

Nevertheless, it was true that the Eisenhower presidency was terribly wounded by the disastrous collapse of the summit and its bitter aftermath. Eisenhower himself complained how the "stupid U-2 mess had ruined all his efforts" to end the Cold War with a test-ban treaty. The president even told one aide that he saw "nothing worthwhile left for him to do now until the end of his presidency."[167]

McCloy too was disappointed that nothing was going to come of all his efforts in the disarmament committee, and he was disturbed by the general drift in the administration. With the election just a few months away, Eisenhower was a lame-duck executive, and he acted the part. McCloy did not play any public role in the presidential campaign that year, feeling the same ambivalence about Nixon as did Eisenhower himself; both men just hoped the vice-president had matured during the last eight years. McCloy was willing to vote for Nixon, mainly out of loyalty to the Republican Party and Eisenhower. (He contributed $500 to the Nixon campaign.) He was partisan enough to dislike Kennedy's attacks on Eisenhower's handling of the failed summit, but, on the other hand, many in McCloy's circle of friends at the Council on Foreign Relations and on Wall Street were working for the Massachusetts senator. At the end of August, Kennedy announced the formation of a bipartisan panel of consultants to advise him on national-security issues. He cited Franklin Roosevelt's and Harry Truman's appointment of "many outstanding Republicans" to positions of influence on foreign-policy matters, and specifically mentioned McCloy, Lovett, and Stimson. Eisenhower, he pointed out, had not appointed many Democrats to his administration.

Kennedy proposed to "start the renewal of that tradition right now," and therefore he was naming to his panel of advisers Paul Nitze, David Bruce, Roswell L. Gilpatric, and James Perkins.[168] All of these individuals, of course, had worked with McCloy in various capacities and considered themselves good friends of the Chase chairman.

Soon after Kennedy won the election by a paper-thin margin, Drew Pearson reported that McCloy was being considered for a Cabinet post.[169] The Eisenhower administration was seeing its last days, but McCloy's influence in Washington, particularly on the central issue of nuclear warfare and arms control, was actually on the rise.

BOOK V

The Kennedy Administration

CHAPTER 23

Arms Control Czar

". . . the only way you can make a man trustworthy is to trust him."

HENRY STIMSON

Having won the presidency, John F. Kennedy thought he would take great satisfaction in naming his Cabinet. But in the weeks after the election, he found the process an exercise in frustration. He was particularly annoyed by "the loud claque of Stevenson's liberal admirers who wanted Adlai to head the State Department."[1] Stevenson, he thought, had shown himself to be indecisive, and the most he would offer the former presidential nominee was the ambassadorship to the United Nations. He would give the liberals some of the minor Cabinet posts. But for the three most powerful positions—State, Defense, and Treasury—Kennedy wanted the best-qualified men he could find. And by this he meant men of Henry Stimson's stature, men whose experience in the New York financial community and the country's legal establishment afforded them, he thought, a certain soundness of mind and bipartisan common sense.

Given the narrow margin of Kennedy's election mandate, it made political sense, of course, to reach out beyond the Democratic Party's liberal constituency. But, then, it was also clear that John Kennedy was essentially a much more cautious and conservative politician than either his supporters or his detractors thought. The forty-three-year-old president-elect had reached adulthood at a time when men like Henry Stimson, John McCloy, and Robert Lovett were running a global war, the war in which Kennedy became a hero. He felt a certain awe for these Stimsonians; they were men of substance who had made commanding decisions in the greatest war of all time. He also knew from his father, who had been almost a pariah on Wall Street, that people like McCloy and Lovett were Wall Street insiders. Indeed, part of his attraction to these men stemmed from the fact that they came from an elite slice of society from which the Irish Catholic Kennedys had always been excluded.

So Kennedy's good Irish American friend and aide, Kenneth O'Donnell, was somewhat taken aback one day in late November when the president-elect remarked that he wanted to become acquainted with Lovett. O'Donnell argued that Lovett and others in his crowd were Republicans, and certainly not liberals. But Kennedy responded, "Henry Stimson was one of those New York Republicans, and Roosevelt was glad to get him. I'm going to talk with Lovett and see what he can do for me. . . . I can use a few smart Republicans. Anyway, we need a Secretary of the Treasury who can call a few of those people on Wall Street by their first names."[2]

Kennedy may have wanted them, but men like Lovett and McCloy had only skepticism for the new regime. Lovett had a positive dislike for Kennedy's father, dating back to his knowledge of the financier's questionable practices on Wall Street during the 1920s. McCloy associated the elder Kennedy with pre–World War II appeasement and isolationism. And as for his son, he knew the young senator had made no effort to institute any connections to the Council on Foreign Relations or other Establishment institutions. All in all, the president-elect seemed to be a man of little experience or substance.

Kennedy approached Lovett first, phoning the investment banker at a corporate board meeting in New York on the morning of December 1, 1960. Invited to lunch, Lovett caught the next plane for Washington and within hours found himself shouldering past a crowd of reporters outside Kennedy's tiny town house at 3307 N Street in Georgetown. Inside, he was first greeted by three-year-old Caroline Kennedy, carrying a football and dressed in overalls bearing the letter "H." Lovett turned to Kennedy as he walked in and said, "That's a hell of a way to treat a Yale man." The ice broken, the two men took to each other surprisingly well, considering their differences in age, background, and politics. Lovett saw that the younger man was as much a skeptic as himself. Kennedy, in turn, was charmed by Lovett's bluntness and wit. He just grinned when Lovett immediately volunteered that he had not voted for him. And when the president-elect asked what the New York financial community thought of John Kenneth Galbraith, Lovett wryly said his colleagues believed the Harvard professor to be a fine novelist.[3] Unlike most of the men Kennedy had been seeing since the election, this one sought no favors and wanted no office.

Offered his choice of State, Defense, or Treasury, Lovett firmly rejected any Cabinet post, saying, "No, sir, I can't. My bearings are burnt out."[4] Though his friends knew him to be a hypochondriac, and he would live many more years, he did have bleeding ulcers, and the doctors had recently removed a portion of his stomach. But the truth of the matter was that Lovett simply had no desire for such public power. Like McCloy, he had turned down similar requests from Eisenhower, and there seemed no reason to make an exception for this president. When Kennedy then complained that he just didn't know enough of the "right people," Lovett assured him that he and his colleagues could introduce him to any number of qualified men.[5] For example, Lovett said, someone from one of the New York banks should receive the Treasury post. Why not Jack McCloy from Chase, Henry Alexander from Morgan's, Eugene Black from the World Bank, or Douglas Dillon, who was currently serving as Eisenhower's undersecretary of state? For secretary of state, Lovett proposed Dean Rusk, currently president of the Rockefeller Foundation. And for the Defense post, he suggested McCloy or Robert McNamara, who had just become president of Ford Motor Company.

Kennedy himself had first mentioned McCloy's name in connection with a Cabinet post only a week after the election. Vacationing in Palm Beach on November 14, he turned to an aide and speculated on whether there were any Republicans he could appoint to head a proposed new disarmament agency. After throwing around a few names, he concluded "that when one mentions the names of (David) Rockefeller, (Douglas) Dillon and McCloy one has about exhausted the supply of 'good Republicans' . . ."[6] When he began to focus on who should take the Treasury spot, a number of advisers suggested that the current gold-drain crisis might be reason enough to bow to "tradition" and choose a Treasury secretary from the financial community. Richard Neustadt, a Harvard professor who had been recruited to advise Kennedy on the transition period, listed McCloy, Lovett, and Dillon as men who fit this description. He warned Kennedy, however, that if he chose a Republican, he should be sure it was a Republican with whom he could work. "Among Republicans, Stimsons and Lovetts are not met with every day; and superficial resemblances can be deceiving."[7]

If there were evidently not many men left in the Stimson mold, and with Lovett pleading poor health, an increasingly frustrated Kennedy was determined to recruit McCloy. On the evening of December 7, 1960, while attending a dinner party, McCloy received a message to call the president-elect at the Carlyle Hotel in New York City. When he dialed the number, he heard a voice promptly answer, "This is Jack Kennedy." There was a long pause as McCloy, in some confusion, hesitated. Finally, the voice said, "the President-elect."[8] McCloy hastily apologized, explaining he had not expected Kennedy to answer the phone himself. When Kennedy then asked if McCloy could come right over to his hotel suite, McCloy abruptly left the dinner, grabbing a dirty old raincoat to keep himself warm. Arriving at the Carlyle, he passed unrecognized by a throng of reporters, a fact he attributed to his scruffy appearance.[9] Inside, he was greeted by an equally informal Kennedy, who paced the suite barefoot as he tried to talk his visitor into joining his administration.

First he mentioned the secretary-of-defense slot. McCloy promptly dismissed the idea by saying, "I've already done that." Then Kennedy said he understood from Lovett that he had a contractual relationship with Chase Bank that "might represent a certain conflict of interest if you were to take, say, the Secretaryship of the Treasury." McCloy said yes, he had a pension arrangement with Chase which "was definitely a handicap if I should go to Treasury." Still, Kennedy pressed him several times about the Treasury job, until finally McCloy said that he feared, as a Republican who had "just finished as head of a large bank," he would be too visible a political target in a Democratic administration. "Whatever you do," he told Kennedy, "don't pick a Republican for your Secretary of the Treasury."[10] Instead, he urged Kennedy to consider Eugene Black, a good Southern Democrat, for the Treasury post. As for himself, the one position he coveted, secretary of state, was the one position that Kennedy had decided he wanted to fill with a Democrat. So, instead of offering McCloy the top post at State, he asked what he thought of Dean Rusk for that position. McCloy diplomatically replied that Rusk "has a fine mind and is experienced." Actually, he thought Rusk merely "a competent man, but never a leader."[11] As the conversation petered to an end, Kennedy played his last card, a job as the president's disarmament adviser, a position that didn't even exist. If McCloy couldn't become secretary of state, he really didn't want to leave New York for anything else. But the disarmament position was something different. Its requirements were undefined, so he might do with it exactly as he pleased.

Later, in a second conversation at the Carlyle, they discussed the details of the job. Kennedy assured him that he would report directly to the Oval Office. Twisting his arm, he told the sixty-five-year-old banker that he just couldn't find younger men with the "guts and toughness" of McCloy's generation.[12] Actually, Kennedy's motives were probably strictly political; as Arthur Schlesinger later put it, he desperately needed "a conservative to execute a liberal policy."[13] The creation of a disarmament agency had been a prominent issue in the presidential campaign, and if it was going to happen, Kennedy would need a Republican of McCloy's stature to get the legislation past Congress. The president-elect explained he would have three priorities: (1) the legislative establishment of a formal disarmament agency, (2) the formulation of a broad policy on negotiating disarmament issues with the Soviets, and (3) the resumption of negotiations on a test-ban treaty. The latter had been in abeyance ever since the U-2 incident. McCloy had taken a strong interest in the test-ban talks and in various disarmament schemes ever since his exposure to these problems during the Gaither Commission's deliberations. So, after a brief discussion, he told Kennedy he would tentatively agree to take on what he regarded as a short-term assignment. McCloy said he didn't know, but the work might even be done on a part-time basis, which would suit him, because he was intent on returning to his old firm of Milbank, Tweed, Hadley & McCloy. Once the new disarmament agency had been set up, McCloy said, he would return to New York, and in any case he would not spend more than nine months on the job.[14] With this understanding, McCloy shook hands with the young president-elect and left.

When the appointment was announced a few days later, Nikita Khrushchev in Moscow quipped, "That's like sending a goat to guard the cabbage patch."[15] The writer Barbara Ward complained that McCloy had a "banker's soul" and was therefore an inappropriate choice for the position of disarmament adviser.[16] When a prominent religious leader visiting the White House made a similar criticism of McCloy, Kennedy responded with a little humor: "You believe in redemption, don't you?"[17]

By the first of the year, Kennedy had made most of his major appointments. Accepting Lovett's recommendation, he named Robert McNamara to the Defense post and Dean Rusk as secretary of state.[18] Many more of Kennedy's appointments came from McCloy's circle of friends and colleagues. Of some eighty-two State Department appointments initially made by Kennedy, sixty-three were members of the Council on Foreign Relations.[19] McGeorge Bundy was named national-security adviser. His brother, and Dean Acheson's son-in-law, William Bundy, was made a deputy assistant secretary of defense. Because Kennedy thought Averell Harriman too old and too deaf, the seventy-year-old former governor was given the decorative title of "roving ambassador" in the State Department. George Kennan was named ambassador to Yugoslavia. Dean Acheson turned down an ambassadorship to NATO but promised to be available to the young president for private consultation. Allen Dulles was retained as CIA director. And, ignoring McCloy's advice not to select a Republican, Kennedy named Douglas Dillon to the Treasury post. The new administration was to be a government of the Establishment.

Turning to his own task, McCloy quickly began to assemble a staff to work with him in creating a disarmament agency. The loyal Shep Stone agreed to serve as his special assistant. Stone soon recruited a liberal Democrat, Betty Goetz, a young woman who had just spent five years working on disarmament issues for Senator Hubert Humphrey. Another old friend from the war years, Adrian "Butch" Fisher, agreed to serve as McCloy's deputy. McCloy and his skeleton staff began to go to work even before Kennedy was inaugurated. They worked closely with the State Department's own disarmament staff, headed by Edmund A. Gullion, a veteran Foreign Service Officer. Over the next nine months, McCloy saw

Dean Rusk at least once a week and often two or three times a week.[20]

After attending the Inauguration and listening to Kennedy's speech, which he thought eloquent, McCloy met with Rusk on the secretary's first full working day in office. They lunched in the secretary's private dining room, and discussed how to revive the test-ban talks. The next morning, at ten-thirty, he went to the White House, where it became clear there was no consensus in the new administration on how to handle arms-control issues. For an hour and a half, he batted around ideas with Kennedy, Rusk, McNamara, "Mac" Bundy, Paul Nitze, and the president's science adviser, Jerome Wiesner. Afterward, he and Rusk went with Kennedy into the Oval Office for a short private meeting.[21] Later, McCloy wrote his old wartime friend Bedell "Beetle" Smith, "All I can say from my discussions of the past week or so is that if confusion is the beginning of wisdom, I shall be wise before too long."[22] There were many problems. McCloy sensed that Kennedy had backtracked and now was not even committed to the piece of legislation he had introduced during the campaign to establish an independent disarmament agency. The president's "superficial preference" was for now merely to issue an executive order placing the proposed new organization inside the White House. This would make it possible to avoid what was certain to be a partisan congressional battle if a bill was introduced to establish an independent agency. McCloy's own staff was divided on this issue, with professional Foreign Service officers like Edmund A. Gullion arguing strongly that the director of the new disarmament agency should report directly to the secretary of state.[23] Liberals within the administration, however, wanted a congressionally mandated independent agency, located outside both the State Department and the White House. After much discussion, a compromise suggested by Richard Neustadt and supported by McCloy was agreed upon. Legislation would be drafted to create an autonomous arms-control agency located within the State Department, but reporting directly to both the president and the secretary of state. This solution preserved the secretary's role as ultimate coordinator, but it simultaneously gave disarmament affairs a new prominence.[24]

That spring, McCloy continued to meet with Kennedy once or twice a month to discuss the formulation of a general disarmament policy. This too proved to be a controversial issue. Skeptics like Dean Rusk told McCloy, "Many dangerous problems were involved in disarmament; one was the tendency of democracies to disarm at the drop of a hat."[25] The whole idea aroused emotions reminiscent of the debates over the atomic bomb between the scientific community and the military establishment. As Shep Stone summarized it for McCloy, the military believed the whole concept of total disarmament should be flatly rejected as a "Soviet propaganda trick." By contrast, the scientists, Stone said, "agree that our security will decrease each year unless there are disarmament controls."[26]

McCloy's intuitive response was to remember Oppenheimer's warnings and side with the scientists. But there were also some stark political reasons to play the disarmament game. The Soviets had scored impressive public-relations gains with their proposal for "general and complete disarmament" in four years. McCloy regarded the Soviet plan as utopian at best and consciously propagandistic at worst. As a standard-bearer for the Stimsonian tradition of preparedness, he was instinctively repelled by such language. But he and Stimson had also agreed, after Hiroshima, that the rules of human conflict had changed; great nation-states could no longer expect to resolve their disputes by resorting to total warfare. Early in the nuclear age, the U.S. nuclear monopoly may have kept the peace, but in the long run, the dangers of an arms race made the arguments for some kind of international control over such apocalyptic weapons more and more compelling. He also knew that the Gaither panel had predicted that a window of opportunity for placing a cap on the arms race would open up in the early 1960s. The time to act was now. Though he and others in the Kennedy administration disliked the simplistic and unverifiable character of the Soviet disarmament plan, they felt a credible U.S. disarmament plan had to be placed on the negotiating table. Disarmament was not only a public-relations game; America's long-term security would in fact be increasingly threatened as the Soviets began to achieve nuclear parity. Ultimately, arms control and disarmament would be the only sane game in town.

Barely a month in office, McCloy explored some of these issues in a speech he gave at Phillips Andover Academy. Since the occasion for his presence at the elite prep school was the dedication of an Andover dormitory in Stimson's name, McCloy used Stimson's attitude toward the Soviets in 1945 to explain his own thinking about disarmament policy. Stimson, he reminded his audience, had initially argued in a September 11, 1945, memo (which McCloy had helped draft) that "the only way you can make a man trustworthy is to trust him. . . ." For this reason, Stimson had then wanted Truman to share the bomb with the Soviets by placing it under the control of some international authority. But by 1947, after Soviet actions in Poland and elsewhere made their intentions clear, McCloy said Stimson had changed his mind. One cannot extend trust to an adversary "who is determined to make you his dupe." Today, he said, "If we cannot trust, we are compelled to erect inspection systems and control procedures, which, by their very extent and character, may introduce irritations and instability in any agreements we reach." He concluded that "general and complete disarmament" could only occur when "agreed and reliable procedures are set up for the just settlement of disputes. . . ."[27]

Late one night, after downing numerous toasts with Andrei Gromyko, he told the Soviet foreign minister that general disarmament would come just as peace had come to the Western frontier: the cowboys had only agreed to check their guns outside the saloon "when they had a sheriff and a court and a jail." Trust had to be nurtured, and that meant the Soviets had to discard their "fetish" for secrecy. "With all this secrecy," he complained, "we were compelled to arm against every weapon of which we had the remotest report. We were compelled to credit Khrushchev's statement that the missiles were coming out like sausages, even if they were not. . . ." Gromyko retorted that the United States had "no moral right to talk about their (Soviet) secrecy when we still held our bases overseas." McCloy insisted that disarmament could only be achieved in a step-by-step fashion, over many years. Gromyko insisted just as strongly that such "half measures would only result in imbalances. . . ."[28] It was all or nothing.

McCloy was disheartened by such encounters. And yet, though few realized it, the Kennedy administration's "tough" Republican was inching toward an extremely liberal and internationalist position on disarmament. Not many Democrats, let alone Republicans, were ready to subject the most basic of sovereign powers, the ability to maintain a standing army, to the authority of an international body. But McCloy was willing to cede such rights to an international body that possessed the legal power and arms to enforce the peace. Ever since his Black Tom litigation, he had always believed the United States should subject itself to the decisions of the World Court or similar international institutions.[29] If disarmament was necessary, then it should occur within the framework of an agreed-upon body of international law.

Some of Kennedy's advisers thought this approach was overly complicated and highly legalistic. Arthur Schlesinger, the president's special assistant, complained that McCloy was trying to work toward "a somewhat vague conception of the 'rule of law.' "[30] U.N. Ambassador Adlai Stevenson worried that McCloy's emphasis on legalities would leave the impression in the United Nations that the administration was backing away from disarmament talks. Stevenson believed the United States "must appear second to none in its desire for disarmament."[31] For his part, McCloy did not want Washington to commit itself to general disarmament in the absence of his complicated legalities.

Though McCloy found Stevenson an adversary in this instance, he actually had a better relationship with the liberal Democrat than did Kennedy. He had known Stevenson ever since the Illinois lawyer had worked in the Navy Department during the war. He enjoyed Stevenson's wit and genuinely respected his political views. Stevenson himself so admired McCloy that during the 1952 presidential campaign he told George Ball that his only candidate for the job of secretary of state was McCloy.[32] And when Stevenson lost the 1952 election, McCloy wrote him a long letter congratulating him on running a campaign full of intellect. Since then, the two men had continued to correspond and occasionally had dinner together in New York.[33] There was genuine warmth and respect shared between them even as they took opposite sides in a policy debate. By contrast, the generational gap between Kennedy and Stevenson, and their recent political rivalry, made their relationship strained. Kennedy found Stevenson wooden and indecisive, while the U.N. ambassador thought Kennedy brash and arrogant.

Their dispute came to a head in March 1961. On the 12th, McCloy made his case in a one-hour private meeting with Kennedy on a Middleburg, Virginia, farm.[34] Then, six days later, a full-dressed debate was held in the White House, with Stevenson making his argument that world public opinion demanded a commitment from the administration to "general and complete disarmament." Kennedy, impressed by the public-relations factors, ruled in Stevenson's favor, though McCloy convinced him to use the phrase "total and universal disarmament" so as not to appear to endorse the Soviet plan.[35]

Throughout that spring, McCloy commuted between Manhattan and Washington. Earlier that year, he had moved from the top of One Chase Plaza down to Milbank, Tweed's thirty-sixth-floor offices, where he was given a corner suite. He could look out across the southern tip of Manhattan and see the Statue of Liberty and Ellis Island; far off to the right, near the Jersey shore, he had a view of what remained of the old Black Tom railroad terminus. His arrangement with Milbank, Tweed was very informal. He served the firm not as a partner, but as "of counsel," a term usually used in the legal community to describe a senior lawyer and former partner who has reached retirement age. In McCloy's case, it was recognized that he had no intention of retiring. In fact, he had told his former partners that he intended to become quite active in the firm. But because of his nine-month commitment to the president, he would take a little longer to work his way back into the business. In addition, he had not relinquished his chairmanships of the Council on Foreign Relations and the Ford Foundation. He also remained on the board of directors of a dozen corporations. In May, he was elected vice-president of the New York City Bar Association, a largely ceremonial post but one that occasionally required his presence at functions.[36] Still, despite these outside activities and his commuting to Washington, he gradually eased himself back into the law, acquiring a number of corporate retainers on behalf of Milbank, Tweed.

When not in Washington, he spent as much time as possible with Ellen in their apartment on 79th Street, which occupied one floor of a large town house. On the weekends, they moved up to their country home in Cos Cob, Connecticut, which they had built in 1958 on a five-acre lot.[37] There was a pool in the backyard which they shared with their neighbors. On one side lived McCloy's old fishing partner Henry Brunie, his wife, and their daughters, who considered McCloy an adopted uncle. On the other side lived Freddie Warburg and his wife. There was a housekeeper, and a butler who drove McCloy into Manhattan each morning. McCloy's son, Johnny, had graduated from Princeton, where he had written his senior thesis on the German resistance to Hitler, and was now serving a two-year stint with the U.S. Army back in Germany. His daughter, Ellen, to whom McCloy was very close, was now a twenty-year-old student at her mother's alma mater, Smith College. His thirty-one-year marriage to Ellen was as solid and comfortable as ever. She was active in a large number of charitable ventures, most prominently as a member of the board of Bellevue Hospital. He displayed the same vigor as always on the tennis court, and on two or three occasions a year he found the time to pack himself off to Vermont, Arizona, Texas, or some other stretch of wilderness for a few days of fishing or hunting. Occasionally, he and Freddie Warburg went horseback-riding together on Warburg's horse farm near Middleburg, Virginia. He had ample income, considerable material assets, and the admiration and respect of his peers. As McCloy celebrated his sixty-sixth birthday that March, his personal life seemed to lack nothing.

That spring, the Kennedy administration faced the first of a string of foreign-policy crises: the fiasco known as the Bay of Pigs. It is not clear if McCloy was aware that the Eisenhower administration had been planning a covert operation involving the invasion of Cuba by a band of CIA-trained and -equipped Cuban exiles. Robert Lovett, however, had been briefed on the project in late 1960 and had expressed strong disapproval of the scheme. But the new president was unaware of Lovett's skepticism and did not consult anyone outside his immediate intelligence and military advisers. (Arthur Schlesinger justified the invasion in a White Paper written shortly before the fiasco.[38]) In the event, the Cuban exiles landed on the beaches at the Bay of Pigs and were quickly defeated. Publicly humiliated, the young president told Clark Clifford, "I've made a terrible mistake. . . . I would hope that I could live it down, but it is going to be difficult." Called down from New York to assess what went wrong, Lovett told Kennedy what he had told the Eisenhower administration in January 1961, that the CIA's covert-action programs were not always "worth the risk or the great expenditure of manpower, money, and other resources involved."[39] The fiasco sealed Allen Dulles's fate. In a few months, he was replaced by McCloy's West Coast business acquaintance John McCone.

McCloy regarded the Bay of Pigs as a singular example of bad presidential decision-making. He was inclined to be less critical of the CIA's covert operations than was Lovett. But for him the Cuban affair raised troubling legal questions. How could we protest Khrushchev's arming of Laotian or Vietnamese rebels if we ourselves armed anti-Castro rebels? It was also a matter of misplaced priorities. Why risk so much presidential prestige over a Caribbean island of so little strategic importance? The Bay of Pigs venture, McCloy thought, had diverted the White House from the far more weighty issues of NATO defense, Berlin, and arms-control negotiations with the Soviets. As he told the president's speechwriter Theodore Sorensen, he hoped that, "no matter what the provocations or jingoistic pressures, any further action against Castro will be prayerfully considered."[40]

It was understood that McCloy would concentrate on the broader problem of developing a disarmament policy and setting up a new agency; meanwhile, negotiations over a test-ban treaty were revived in Geneva. McCloy selected his old friend Arthur Dean, a Sullivan & Cromwell partner, to go to Geneva that spring.[41] The talks quickly became stalemated, however, partly because of Soviet insistence that there be a "troika" of three administrators with inspection powers, each one of whom could veto an inspection of a suspicious explosion. Washington wanted one administrator, believing that a troika of inspectors would only paralyze the inspection system.[42]

For its part, the United States was making the negotiations difficult by insisting on the right to explode certain outdated nuclear-weapon designs in order to refine its seismic capabilities. Such tests, the Soviets responded, would only provide a cover for the testing of new weapon designs. Among themselves, the Americans could admit that there "was some validity" to the charge that "these shots would teach us how to evade the test ban agreement." But this was something they were unwilling to concede to the Soviets.[43]

In addition, the two parties were at loggerheads over the number of on-site inspections each side would be entitled to in the course of a year. On-site inspections were thought to be necessary to distinguish low-level nuclear explosions from minor earthquakes. The United States demanded twenty such on-site inspections, while the Soviets insisted that three inspections a year would be entirely sufficient. In fact, the two positions were not so far apart. McCloy told Rusk in March that the scientists now believed their seismic instruments were sensitive enough that ten on-site inspections "would be an acceptable deterrent."[44] Ultimately, Washington would have accepted as few as seven or eight inspections. And it is known today from Soviet sources that they were prepared to go to at least four or five inspections.[45] In retrospect, it seems clear that a test-ban treaty was much more attainable in 1961 than either party thought.

Faced with what they perceived as a stalemate on the test-ban talks, Stevenson and other liberals in the administration persuaded Kennedy that spring to shift the focus of negotiations from a test ban to an agreement on general disarmament principles. McCloy was initially reluctant on this score, since he thought he needed more time to develop a legal framework for a general disarmament agreement. But early in June, Kennedy met with Khrushchev in Vienna for a mini-summit. The Soviet leader took a hard line on Berlin and other matters, but on the issue of disarmament he suggested there was room for radical progress. "In view of the fact," Khrushchev told the president, "that apparently no agreement can be reached on the question of nuclear tests this question should be linked to disarmament. If agreement could be reached on disarmament, then the USSR could agree to any controls and it would then drop the troika arrangement and the requirement for unanimity." With a disarmament agreement, he promised, controls "must be most extensive so that no country could arm itself clandestinely."[46] In other words, if the two superpowers could trust each other enough to go for a sweeping disarmament package, the Soviets would agree to all the verification provisions Washington wanted. Without disarmament, however, there could be no progress on such limited arms-control measures as a test-ban treaty.

Needless to say, the Kennedy administration was not politically prepared to end the Cold War so precipitously. Nor could McCloy make the leap in trust that would have been required for a breakthrough. Later that week, he told a commencement audience at Williams College, "Every time Russia pulls a new weapon advance out of its sleeve, the United States tries to do the same. And the whole grim sequence leads to a sense of instability and insecurity."[47]

He could describe the cycle of distrust between the two superpowers, but he could not himself break it. On the contrary, he now decided it was time to take a tough position. Several days later, he went in to see Kennedy, armed with a memo recommending that the United States unilaterally break the moratorium on nuclear testing. He said Khrushchev had made it clear in Vienna that the Soviets were not about to change their position on either the test ban or general disarmament. He warned Kennedy that the Soviets might soon or already be engaging in "clandestine testing," and concluded that so long as the U.S. respected the moratorium "the USSR is under no pressure to come to an agreement involving any inspection." He even suggested that the United States give no prior announcement of the resumed tests.[48] For the time being, Kennedy rejected this advice, though he made sure that preparations continued for the tunnels necessary for a series of underground tests. And he did accept McCloy's recommendation to send a signal to the Soviets by recalling Arthur Dean from the Geneva test-ban talks.

McCloy's tough line on a resumption of testing did not mean he wished to break off the general disarmament talks. In fact, he wished to proceed with these negotiations and reiterated his concept of a "rule of law": "We should press for . . . an acceptance of the concept of the rule of law in international disputes which involves a true acceptance of the principle of international arbitration, the extension of the jurisdiction of the International Court, the application of international sanctions by impartial tribunals not subject to veto."[49]

Soon after seeing Kennedy, he had his first session with the Soviet disarmament negotiator, Valerian A. Zorin. After they had met for 110 minutes in the State Department, McCloy told the press the opening session went "OK." But in a series of meetings between June 19 and 30, the two men made no progress at all. When McCloy tried to confine the discussion to the mechanics of setting up a multinational disarmament conference, Zorin expressed "surprise" that the United States did not wish to discuss matters of substance.[50] The Russian kept pressing McCloy for unilateral steps toward actual disarmament. One day that month, McCloy scrawled a note to Eisenhower, "I feel like a maiden in need of prayer. . . ."[51]

The disarmament talks seemed unrealistic enough as it was, but to make matters worse, McCloy's meetings with Zorin occurred at a time of heightened tensions over Berlin. *The New York Times* that week reported that administration officials expected a difficult summer, "replete with talk of war."[52] Berlin was heavy on everyone's minds. Refugees were streaming across from East Germany through the city's unguarded lines into West Berlin, and Khrushchev was repeatedly warning that the abnormal status of West Berlin had to be altered. At an NSC meeting called to discuss the crisis on June 28, a hawkish Dean Acheson recommended that Kennedy send a division of army troops down the *Autobahn* to West Berlin and declare a national emergency. Afterward, a shocked Averell Harriman complained to Arthur Schlesinger that Acheson, a "frustrated and rigid man," was "leading us down the road to war."[53] In such an atmosphere, McCloy was not likely to achieve much on the disarmament front. At the end of the month, he took Zorin to the White House to introduce him to the president, but this presidential meeting led to no breakthrough. Clearly, if McCloy was to meet with any success, he would have to find it in the Moscow round of talks, scheduled for mid-July.

Before taking off for Moscow, he "bummed a ride" with the Army chief of staff, General Lyman L. Lemnitzer, for two days of good "dry-fly" fishing on the north shore of the Saint Lawrence. "The salmon are smaller than on the south shore," he wrote Eisenhower, "but they were active and in many ways more exciting. . . . It was a real relaxation." He said that he really did not "relish" the prospect of another session with the Russians, and reported to the retired president that he had just received a "rather surly and unpleasant" note from the Russians on the test-ban issue. "I suppose one must expect as much."[54]

After six months on the job, the only concrete accomplishment McCloy could claim was that he and his staff had finally drafted the legislation necessary for establishing an autonomous Arms Control and Disarmament Agency within the State Department. Before leaving for Moscow, McCloy presented it to Kennedy, who then sent it on to Congress for what would later prove to be a contentious debate.[55]

After two further meetings with Kennedy, McCloy finally boarded a plane for Frankfurt, where he planned to spend a day or two before going on to Moscow.[56] He traveled with what Dean Acheson told Justice Frankfurter was "quite a harem": Ellen McCloy; their daughter, Ellen; and his niece, the pretty thirty-two-year-old Sharman Douglas. When he arrived in Moscow, the talks with Zorin resumed in what *The New York Times* reported was an atmosphere of "gloom."[57] Zorin informed McCloy that the Soviets were not prepared to participate in a multinational disarmament conference until some broad bilateral agreement on general principles was reached with the United States. For a week, the two men argued over language, mechanically reading prepared speeches to each other. Zorin continued to insist on the phrase "general and complete disarmament," while McCloy held to his own formulation of "total and universal disarmament." The Russian translations of the two phrases were actually identical, so the argument seemed rather nonsensical. The only light moment in their discussions occurred when the Soviet interpreter once mistakenly translated Zorin as saying that the Soviet Union was unalterably wedded to "total and universal disarmament." At this Zorin interrupted and, speaking in English for the first time, said, "You know, Mr. McCloy, it looks as if he is going over to your side."[58]

This charade continued until finally, on July 25, McCloy left unexpectedly for the resort town of Sochi, on the Black Sea. Khrushchev had invited him and his family to join him at his vacation dacha. The boisterous Soviet leader warmly greeted the McCloy party, and laughingly apologized for having called McCloy a "goat sent to guard the cabbage patch" when he was appointed Kennedy's disarmament adviser. McCloy replied, "No, no, that's all right," and, pointing to the rows of old war medals emblazoned across Khrushchev's chest, "I see you're something of an old goat yourself."[59] The two men laughed, and then Khrushchev talked in reassuring terms about the diplomatic sparring McCloy had just put himself through. It was, he joked, like kicking a football back and forth. Perhaps the ball would be kicked around like this until the Soviets sent in a new ball, and then a treaty would be signed. But the next day, having read a translation of a speech President Kennedy had given on the Berlin crisis, Khrushchev exploded. He told McCloy that the speech constituted "a preliminary declaration of war."[60]

Kennedy had not taken Acheson's advice to send in troops, and he had not declared a national emergency. But he had announced in bellicose language that he was calling out 150,000 reservists and was asking Congress for a dramatic increase in the defense budget. Whereas Eisenhower had steadfastly refused to frighten the American people with talk of bomb shelters, Kennedy now endorsed a program to build fallout shelters nationwide. Nuclear warfare, he seemed to be saying, could be right around the corner. "We cannot and will not," he said, "permit the Communists to drive us out of Berlin, either gradually or by force."[61]

Kennedy's speech escalated the war of words over Berlin's status. In part, he was motivated by the widespread perception that his reputation had been damaged by the Bay of Pigs episode and press reports that Khrushchev had browbeaten him at their meeting in Vienna. He now had to look tough. But he could also threaten to fight for Berlin because he knew now that the alleged "missile gap" did not exist. Earlier that year, the Defense Department had shown him satellite photos demonstrating that the Soviets had only a "handful" of ICBMs.[62] McCloy, of course, had not heard Kennedy's speech, but he was quite alarmed by Khrushchev's reaction and worried that the two powers might actually be drifting into war.

That evening, however, Khrushchev acted the gracious host and held a dinner in McCloy's honor. Vast quantities of food were served, accompanied by plenty of wine and vodka. The more they talked, the less rhetorical became their exchanges. On the following morning, Khrushchev took a motorboat ten minutes across the Black Sea to the villa where the McCloy party was lodged. Arriving a half-hour earlier than expected, he caught Mrs. McCloy and her niece, Sharman Douglas, sunning themselves in bathing suits on the dock. Embarrassed, the two women scrambled inside as Khrushchev politely turned his back. A few moments later, McCloy and his now fully clothed ladies joined Khrushchev for the boat ride back to the general secretary's own dacha. Quite proud of his indoor pool with its retractable glass doors, Khrushchev insisted they go for a swim. He loaned McCloy a pair of his large black boxer-style swimming trunks, and shortly later the two men were photographed bobbing around together in the pool. Grinning broadly, with Khrushchev's arm wrapped around McCloy's shoulder, the Russian and the American looked the closest of friends. Afterward, they played some tennis together and then went for a walk in Khrushchev's garden. The next day, McCloy hinted to reporters that the arms talks might be making some progress: "Maybe we are further along."[63]

But when their conversation turned to substantive topics, Khrushchev again took a hard line. Regarding the stalled test-ban treaty talks, he confided that he was subject to strong pressure from his own military establishment to resume nuclear testing.[64] The crisis over Berlin was only making it more difficult to fend off this pressure. McCloy tried to assure Khrushchev that the United States was not secretly preparing another series of atomic tests in the Nevada desert. (In fact, the tunnels for such a series of underground tests were being dug that very month.) If Moscow would reciprocate, he said, Washington would invite Soviet scientists to inspect the Nevada test sites. Khrushchev harshly responded, "I will never agree to inspection. You would only come over and spy on what we were doing."[65] In the absence of a major arms-control agreement, both sides were obviously edging toward a resumption of nuclear testing.

At one point, Khrushchev tried to give McCloy a lesson on how the Soviets view Europe. "We are Europeans," he asserted. "We are here to stay. . . . Napoleon, then Hitler came and gave us problems. And now the Americans." McCloy protested that the United States would never attack Russia. But when Khrushchev reminded him that Woodrow Wilson had sent American troops after the October Revolution, McCloy had to concede that he had forgotten about this intervention.[66]

Turning to Berlin, Khrushchev frightened McCloy. "You know and I know that when war starts there [in Germany] with conventional weapons, if you are losing, you will use atomic weapons. If we are losing, we will use atomic weapons."[67] Though this might be the hard truth, McCloy thought it ominous that Khrushchev should be saying such things to him in the midst of the Berlin crisis. It also greatly disturbed him, as he later told Soviet Ambassador Anatoly Dobrynin, that he "had never talked with any national leader who talked so much about his weapons as did Mr. Khrushchev. He seemed enamored of them; it was like a farmer with a new set of tractors. . . ."[68] Once, in the presence of McCloy's daughter, Khrushchev began boasting that his scientists were ready to test a hundred-megaton bomb. Ellen was so distraught about Khrushchev's description of the weapon that, to the surprise of both men, she suddenly burst into tears.[69] McCloy was also shocked by the premier's behavior. Khrushchev was an enigma to him. To some extent, the Soviet leader's earthy language and candor were reassuring, and certainly a refreshing change from the impenetrable hardness of Stalin. But even if there was nothing really new in what Khrushchev was saying, the emotion with which he said it was somehow alarming.

The next day, McCloy returned to Moscow for one more two-hour meeting with Zorin. The Soviet negotiator finally consented that, back in New York in September, they could try to reach agreement on a joint statement on disarmament principles. But in every other respect, the talks had reached an impasse. Before leaving Moscow, McCloy sent a long cable back to Washington summarizing his talks with Khrushchev. Emphasizing as it did Khrushchev's more extremist statements, the cable created quite a stir in Washington. Dean Acheson disapproved, telling Justice Frankfurter, "McCloy has caused quite a flurry [sic]. He repaired to the Black Sea . . . and had a weekend of talks in which Khrushchev said nothing whatever that he has not said at least a dozen times. . . . I should have thought the way to treat this quite unpleasant discussion was with 'intelligent neglect.' . . . Instead of this, he appears as a sort of modern Paul Revere, flapping his way through the sky to warn us that the Russians are coming, and giving everyone the idea that we are in quite a dither about something, though God knows what."[70]

Acheson could so casually dismiss Khrushchev's blustering threats only because his own position on Berlin was extremely hard-line. Believing the Soviets would never go to war over Berlin, he was prepared for the brashest kind of brinkmanship and felt increasingly frustrated that Kennedy had not sent a division of army troops down the *Autobahn*. But, though rejecting the specifics of Acheson's advice, the president had been acting throughout the crisis as if he agreed that Berlin was a "simple conflict of wills." This ignored the substance of the problem: Berlin was an abnormality, but so was the division of Germany. And this artificial division of Germany had to be preserved to maintain the postwar peace. But now West Berlin's very success as an outpost of freedom and economic opportunity threatened continued Soviet control over East Germany. Thousands of educated workers, technicians, and scientists were leaving East Germany through Berlin. The East German state could not sustain this loss of human resources. The specter arose of a collapse in the East that would lead inexorably to the reunification of Germany under NATO's banner, something Khrushchev's constituency in the Kremlin would not tolerate.[71]

When the situation is viewed from this perspective, it is not hard to understand what happened next. On the evening of Friday, August 12, East German troops moved up to the line dividing the city and began building a wall. The flow of refugees from East to West would now be halted. At the time, the president was sailing up on Cape Cod, and didn't come back to Washington until after the weekend. Some of his political enemies, such as Eleanor Dulles, sister of the late secretary of state and an Eisenhower-administration expert on German affairs, bitterly criticized Kennedy for not having done something promptly to dramatize Washington's opposition to the wall.[72]

Over the years, rumors have persisted that one of the reasons Kennedy did not break off his vacation earlier and rush back to Washington was that he had been informed in advance by McCloy of Khrushchev's intentions. McCloy repeatedly denied these reports and said he had no foreknowledge of Khrushchev's plan. There seems little reason to doubt him. The wall, however, was not the complete surprise Western governments made it out to be. "We could see the stream of refugees," recalled Wilhelm Grewe, a high-ranking aide to Adenauer, "and we knew something would happen."[73] The ugly wall splitting the city soon became a symbol of Soviet repression, but it was remarkable how quickly tensions began to recede in the weeks and months immediately after it was built. Khrushchev had defused the explosive German problem by forcefully demonstrating that the issue of reunification had been settled: there would be two Germanys—at least for this generation of Germans.

For McCloy and his generation, who had twice fought a world war against Germany, this was not the worst outcome. George Kennan and Chip Bohlen certainly felt this way and advised the president not to overreact to the building of the wall.[74] As for McCloy, he could not publicly say such things without touching a raw nerve among his West German friends. But that Germany was best left divided, even if half of it had to live under communism, was the unspoken truth. And certainly there was no point in going to war over the wall, which, after all, had become a necessity if Germany was to remain divided. Averell Harriman said it bluntly to Kennedy in a secret letter written to the president a few weeks after the wall went up: "Since Potsdam, I have been satisfied that Germany would be divided for a long time. . . . In addition, I believe Khrushchev is sincerely concerned with the remilitarization of Germany, particularly with the prospect of her eventually getting independent nuclear capability. . . . He feels Adenauer is safe enough, but he said to me, 'What will happen if Strauss or someone else gets control?' . . . She [Germany] will have the strongest army in Europe, and who can stop her if some leader determines that she shall produce her own nuclear weapons?" Harriman then urged Kennedy to negotiate a "denuclearized control zone of West Germany and East Germany. . . ."[75]

McCloy felt the same way about the permanency of the Potsdam divisions, though he disagreed with Harriman's proposal for a nuclear-free Germany. But the difference of opinion is explained by their respective expertise: Harriman came to this position in trying to convey to the president how much the Soviets still feared the Germans. McCloy could talk about giving the Germans access to nuclear weaponry only because he saw it as a means to retain their loyalty and confidence in NATO. Implicit in both views was the commitment to the postwar structure of peace that required the division of Germany between East and West.

Back in Washington, McCloy had four meetings with the president over the course of the next month. He testified on the Hill a number of times about both the disarmament talks and his conversations with Khrushchev on the Berlin issue. He was a guest on "Meet the Press," where he told a national television audience that the United States was prepared to unveil its own comprehensive disarmament plan in the autumn. In fact, he had not come back from Moscow entirely empty-handed. He and Zorin had talked about the feasibility of setting up a direct and reliable communication link between the Kremlin and the White House. McCloy liked the idea; it seemed a logical and practical thing to have in the age of intercontinental missiles. One day, he astonished his security-conscious staff by announcing that he had discussed the feasibility of a "hot line" at a meeting of the AT&T board on which he sat. Security precautions were unusually tight for McCloy's small staff, but it was characteristic of the man that he felt free to talk to anyone on any subject. (The "hot line" was eventually installed in the summer of 1963.)[76]

He also had to spend considerable time on Capitol Hill lobbying for passage of legislation to create an Arms Control and Disarmament Agency. While McCloy had been in Moscow, Senator Hubert Humphrey had told Kennedy that in his opinion the legislation had no chance of passage. Important swing-voting senators such as Fulbright and Willis Robertson were opposed to the bill. Humphrey and Kennedy agreed the new agency might just have to be established by presidential fiat. Upon his return from Moscow, McCloy agreed with his staff, particularly Adrian Fisher and Betty Goetz, that the agency would have no clout without a congressional mandate. So he told the president that this was worth a fight. In testimony before the House Foreign Affairs Committee, he bluntly warned that a nuclear war could only be averted in the long run by disarmament. "Such a disaster," he said, "could happen. It could happen if the world does not disarm and it could happen if we proceed to disarm unwisely. We may suffer such a disaster despite our best efforts to prevent it."[77] In late August, just prior to the critical vote, Goetz heard a rumor that the relevant Senate committee had just about decided in executive session to turn the bill back to the White House. This would have meant there could have been no legislation at all in that year. Goetz persuaded her old boss, Senator Humphrey, to leak her a copy of the transcript of the executive session; this enabled her to go to McCloy with a list of the problem senators and the right arguments to address their concerns. McCloy then went around to their offices and personally twisted arms. Conservative senators like Virginia's Willis Robertson, and even liberals like Fulbright, had long-standing personal relationships with McCloy. McCloy had been going to Robertson's favorite fishing streams with the senator ever since the 1930s. And he had seen Fulbright off and on throughout the 1950s in various sessions on the Hill or at the Council on Foreign Relations. McCloy got both their votes and a number of others at the last minute, despite fierce opposition from a number of other Southern Democrats. He was also responsible for getting Eisenhower's written endorsement of the bill, which in turn won some critical votes on the Republican side of the aisle. "The legislation just would not have passed without him," said Goetz of McCloy's lobbying efforts.[78]

In the meantime, McCloy was scheduled to begin another series of negotiations with Zorin in New York. Just a few days before their talks resumed, however, the Soviets broke the *de facto* three-year moratorium on open-air nuclear testing by exploding a large bomb somewhere north of China. That same afternoon, McCloy met with Kennedy and others in the White House to discuss the U.S. response. The president came out of his bedroom wearing a dressing gown and seemed impatient as he listened to his advisers argue. McCloy felt strongly that the administration should immediately announce its intention to resume U.S. testing. Arthur Schlesinger, who attended the meeting, recalls McCloy telling Kennedy that he had to demonstrate "hard and tough leadership—that he could not continue to stand by and let the communists kick us in the teeth." When someone suggested that resumed U.S. testing would have an ill effect on world opinion, McCloy interrupted sharply to say, "World opinion? I don't believe in world opinion. The only thing that matters is power. What we have to do now is to show that we are a powerful nation and not spend our time trailing after the phantom of world opinion."[79]

Kennedy ultimately accepted this advice, telling Stevenson, who again opposed McCloy's position, "We couldn't possibly sit back and do nothing at all." Breaking the moratorium had become a test of wills, and now Washington had to respond in kind. Neither McCloy nor Kennedy believed there was any military necessity to test. Earlier that summer, after listening to a panel of scientists and military officers debate the issue, McCloy concluded that a decision to resume testing could easily be postponed to the first of the year without risk to the nation's nuclear-weaponry program.[80] For him, the question of whether to test or not was always a matter of negotiating tactics. Instinctively, he felt that a decision to break the moratorium would pressure the Soviets to negotiate in good faith a verifiable test-ban treaty. When the Soviets broke the moratorium on their own initiative instead, he believed the only practical response was to resume U.S. testing. Nor was he particularly surprised by the Soviet decision, since Khrushchev had warned him in July that he was under severe pressure from his own military to resume testing. The Soviet testing did not, in any case, prevent McCloy from proceeding to negotiate an agreement on disarmament principles.

During the next month of frenetic negotiations, he continued to display an odd combination of both toughness and the most utopian form of internationalism. In this he was strongly influenced by another Stimsonian, his old friend Grenville Clark. Now seventy-nine years old, Clark had written a book in 1958, *World Peace Through World Law,* which had received considerable attention in the media.[81] Co-authored by Harvard Law Professor Louis Sohn, Clark's book was a remarkable blend of idealism and legalistic prescriptions for a global government encompassing a unicameral parliament apportioned by population figures, a world court, and an international police force.[82] Now, as McCloy began his wranglings with Zorin over a joint U.S.-Soviet statement of disarmament principles, he borrowed liberally from Clark's ideas.[83]

Dispensing with their little games of semantics, McCloy quickly told Zorin that the United States would agree to use the "general-and-complete-disarmament" terminology. In return, Zorin reported that Moscow would acquiesce to McCloy's insistence that disarmament take place in stages supervised by an international body, and that each stage be accompanied by the development of an international police force. By September 20, the two men had drafted a "Joint Statement of Agreed Principles for Disarmament Negotiations." The thousand-word document was quickly adopted by the U.N. General Assembly and became known as the McCloy-Zorin Agreed Principles. Its language was both utopian and specific: "The programme for general and complete disarmament shall ensure that States will have at their disposal only those nonnuclear armaments, forces, facilities and establishments as are agreed to be necessary to maintain internal order and protect the personal security of citizens; and that States shall support and provide agreed manpower for a United Nations peace force." To implement the various stages of disarmament, inspectors from an International Disarmament Organization would "be assured unrestricted access without veto to all places as necessary for the purpose of effective verification."

In the years since its signing, historians have found it difficult to know what to make of this first Soviet-American accord on disarmament. Some observers have simply ignored it or labeled it a transparent exercise in superpower propaganda. Certainly, it had little effect at the time and contained no concrete timetables for achieving any specific steps toward reversing the arms race. But as a definition of disarmament and the principles whereby it could be achieved, the document has survived irrelevancy. At the time, McCloy believed it was no mean achievement to have persuaded the Soviets to agree to the principle of unrestricted verification by an international disarmament organization. Arthur Schlesinger and others in the Kennedy administration may have belittled McCloy's "faith in the rule of law," but to him this was fundamental to any agreement.[84]

Actually, the McCloy-Zorin Agreed Principles might have contained concrete arms-control provisions had not an earlier draft been vetoed by the Joint Chiefs and various officials in the White House.[85] In preparation for his negotiations with Zorin, McCloy had earlier set up a panel of consultants that included such outside experts as Henry Kissinger, Robert Bowie, and Jerome Wiesner. This panel prepared a plan that focused on the stabilization and then elimination of nuclear-weaponry delivery vehicles. The "Foster Panel," as it became known, first tried to determine how many delivery vehicles—missiles or bombers—would be necessary to maintain nuclear deterrence. Assuming that deterrence would be maintained if each side could wipe out half of its adversary's population, they concluded that no more than two to five hundred delivery vehicles were necessary. To provide for a sure margin of safety, they doubled their high figure and therefore proposed that a ceiling of one thousand be placed on the number of delivery vehicles in each country's arsenal. Had it been accepted, this proposal would have dramatically altered the arms race in the decades ahead. But the president himself thought it went too far and too quickly, and McGeorge Bundy simply labeled it "too radical."[86] Once again, an opportunity to achieve some meaningful constraints over the nuclear-arms race was lost. All that was left was a theoretical scheme for what everyone assumed was far in the future.

Kennedy had hired McCloy nine months previously to accomplish three tasks: the creation of an arms-control agency, the formulation of a disarmament policy, and the negotiation of a test-ban treaty. McCloy now retired, having accomplished only the first two of these tasks. He told the press that his failure to achieve a test-ban agreement was the most "discouraging exercise in disarmament negotiations" since World War II.[87] He was disillusioned, even bitter, at what he felt had been a lack of candor on the part of the Soviets. But in the eyes of the Soviets, at least, his negotiations with Khrushchev and Zorin had established him as an important channel of communication. About this time, he struck a friendship with the Kremlin's new ambassador in Washington, Anatoly Dobrynin. This suave, English-speaking Russian regularly used McCloy as a sounding board, and McCloy was blunt and candid with the Russian. They would talk about everything, from the collapse of the stock market in 1962 to why the United States was supporting the creation of the European Common Market. (Dobrynin thought the Common Market would only hurt U.S. exports, and couldn't understand why Washington was supporting its creation.) McCloy, in turn, would complain about Khrushchev's attitude on Berlin. Why not, he asked, leave Berlin's status unchanged? "It was, of course, annoying to Ulbrecht but who was Ulbrecht to allow him to play with fire?" Dobrynin valued such banter, and their relationship became an important source of information for him on America's ruling circles.[88]

On October 6, 1961, McCloy had his last meeting with Kennedy as the president's disarmament adviser. William Foster, whom he had selected to succeed him, was now designated to become director of the new Arms Control and Disarmament Agency. Kennedy was reluctant to see McCloy go, and had offered to make him undersecretary of state in place of Chester Bowles, who had been coaxed to take up his old posting as ambassador to India. But McCloy once again turned down this job, not wanting to work under Rusk.[89] Instead, he agreed to serve in the part-time role of chairman of the newly created President's Advisory Committee on Disarmament. In this way, he could keep his hand in arms-control matters, and simultaneously go back to his Wall Street practice in earnest.

He had, in fact, already brought a major piece of business to Milbank, Tweed. Important changes were occurring in the global petroleum industry, controlled for so many years by the "Seven Sisters," the largest of the international oil companies. In 1959, Congress had passed mandatory oil-import control legislation, which had quickly reduced the amount of oil that could be imported from the Middle East and Venezuela. In addition, the Soviets had begun dumping cheap oil on West European markets. In response to reduced demand, the companies in August 1960 unilaterally cut the posted price, a move that galvanized the oil-producing governments to form a cartel the following month in Baghdad.[90] From his experience in the 1940s, McCloy was sensitive to the power that the new cartel, the Organization of Petroleum Exporting Countries (OPEC), could theoretically exert on the market. Sometime in 1961, a number of oil-company executives from the "Seven Sisters" approached McCloy to inquire whether they might retain his counsel on how to deal with the infant cartel. "We thought it only logical," recalled John Loudon, the CEO of Royal Dutch Petroleum Company (part of the Shell group), "then that the seven of us at once get together to see how we could defend ourselves against the common united front of the governments of the producing countries."[91] McCloy was asked to become chairman of a small committee representing the five U.S. international oil companies, British Petroleum, and the Royal Dutch Petroleum Company. The problem with any such legal counsel given by one law firm to more than one oil company was the risk of an antitrust suit. So, in one of his meetings with Kennedy after returning from his summit with Khrushchev, McCloy raised the matter with the president. After McCloy explained the national-security implications of a foreign cartel controlling some 80 percent of the free world's known petroleum reserves, Kennedy automatically picked up the phone and called his brother the attorney general. Shortly afterward, in a meeting with Robert Kennedy, McCloy emerged with a "business review letter" signifying the Justice Department's acquiescence to McCloy's representation of more than one oil company. As McCloy explained it years later, "My job was to keep them out of jail." Now the chief executive officers of these firms could meet together in McCloy's law office at One Chase Plaza without any real risk of an antitrust suit.[92]

Actually, the threat from OPEC was not very immediate. A CIA assessment of the cartel in February 1961 had concluded that it would be "extremely difficult, if not impossible" for the member countries to muster enough discipline to limit their production, share the market, and thereby increase oil prices.[93] McCloy could, however, make a credible argument in the early 1960s that the dumping of cheap Soviet oil on the world market was a national-security threat. "The Free World international oil industry," he wrote in 1962, "has become the principal target of this Soviet economic and political offensive." The Soviets were trying to destabilize Western oil markets and support OPEC in the hope that Western oil interests in the Middle East would eventually be nationalized.[94] Twenty years earlier, during the war, he had used the same arguments with Stimson to justify an invasion of North Africa. He was still Stimson's "Mid-Easterner," determined to defend Western access to cheap Middle Eastern oil.

If, in retrospect, his fears of OPEC were premature by a decade, McCloy had nevertheless identified a good piece of business for Milbank, Tweed. Over the next ten years, he met with various attorney generals on twenty-seven different occasions to discuss his oil clients and OPEC.[95] He was the perfect intermediary; he knew the Middle East, and through his associations with such Texas oil men as Sid Richardson (who had recently died), he knew the domestic oil industry. In addition, he obviously had a special reputation in Washington. There were probably only a handful of men the federal government would trust with such a peculiar arrangement. Though a lawyer representing private interests, he was somehow also an untitled, unsalaried civil servant, the rare kind of man everyone assumed could watch out for the public's national-security interests while simultaneously serving his corporate clients. For precisely this kind of access to Washington, the oil companies paid sizable retainers. The seven majors now began paying Milbank, Tweed $1,000 a month each, or a total of $84,000 a year.[96] In addition to the security of having McCloy's antitrust waiver in their pockets, the companies received other services. Throughout the next few years, the CEOs from all of the majors attended confidential briefings arranged by McCloy with the CIA and the State Department. At these meetings, both parties—the government's Middle East experts and the oil-company officers—informally traded information. Though these contacts were not a matter of public knowledge at the time, if they had been, few would have questioned the arrangement or McCloy's participation. It was all a matter of national security.[97]

Soon after returning to New York in the autumn of 1961, McCloy became embroiled in a power struggle for control of the Ford Foundation. In the previous year, the Foundation had given away some $161 million, dwarfing other philanthropic ventures. Dwight Macdonald aptly described the Foundation as "a large body of money entirely surrounded by people who want some."[98] With so much money available, there was considerable contention about the Foundation's funding priorities.

As one Foundation officer put it, "McCloy chose to be the first among equals and regarded all the other [board] members around as potentates and he was simply the first baron among barons."[99] He never hesitated to push his own agenda, urging funding for such projects as the Free University in Berlin, the Council on Foreign Relations, and various "Atlanticist" projects such as conference grants for things like the Bilderberg Group gatherings. And he still thought of the Foundation as a quasi-extension of the U.S. government. It was his habit, for instance, to drop by the National Security Council in Washington every couple of months and casually ask whether there were any overseas projects the NSC would like to see funded.[100]

The Foundation's president, Henry Heald, could not hide his annoyance at such instances of interference by the trustees. With his academic background, Heald was inclined to give priority to university funding. Over the years, McCloy began to feel that Heald "was a little too prone to confine the benefactions of the Ford Foundation to conventional university academic areas. . . ."[101] Moreover, as chairman, McCloy felt no compunction about holding Heald personally accountable for grant decisions he felt to be inappropriate. This was illustrated in an incident that took place in late 1959. The *New York Herald Tribune* ran a front-page story reporting that the Ford Foundation had commissioned a communist to compose an opera on the Sacco-Vanzetti case and had requested the Metropolitan Opera to produce it. That morning, McCloy happened not to have read the newspaper, and when he arrived at his luncheon club he was immediately collared by one of his Wall Street friends, who said, "So this is how the Ford Foundation wastes its money; getting 'commie' operas written and reopening the whole damn Sacco-Vanzetti case." McCloy was visibly upset and "raised Cain" with Heald.[102] There were many other conflicts.

As president of the Foundation, Heald made it clear that he thought funding decisions should be initiated only out of his office. The board of trustees received the impression that his attitude toward them was, "Take it or leave it."[103] As the years passed, the Foundation's professional staff found themselves drifting into Heald or McCloy factions, depending on whether their particular program had the backing of the president or the chairman. One Foundation officer who more often than not was identified as a Heald supporter recollected McCloy and his exercise of power over the Foundation: "That coalition of power that the Ford Foundation trustees represented both was an asset and a liability. The assets were that these were men of affairs, were wired in, that when Ford moved everybody knew there was more than its money that was going; it was symbolic; if, for example, they would go into social affairs, that was a powerful statement that this was important. The liabilities of it were all equally obvious. . . . McCloy was a guy who had to be accepted at the White House. He loved his role of running around the world and being the God. He watched everything from that point of view. . . . Clearly those guys thought politically. There's no question about it."[104]

Eventually, tensions between Heald and the trustees were such that McCloy felt he had to do something to reassert control over the Foundation's policies. So, one day, he walked into Heald's office in New York and announced that he wanted to make a statement to the principal officers of the Foundation. A few minutes later, in the presence of Heald, McCloy told a gathering of some eighteen program directors that he had a statement to make about his role and the role of the president in the operating of the Foundation. He then announced that henceforward *the* doctrine of the Foundation would be a policy of direct fraternization between themselves and the trustees. Small groups of trustees, he said, would regularly meet with individual program officers to discuss their priorities and needs. When he finished, McCloy turned to Heald and asked him if he had anything to add. Obviously shocked, the president muttered, "No," and walked out of the room. But he still did not resign, despite this open usurpation of his authority.[105]

For the next eighteen months, Heald hung on to his job. He had, however, little authority within the Foundation. Most program officers felt that he was on his way out. Morale was dismal. Only those program directors who had cultivated their own constituencies within the board of trustees had the power to get things done. An uneasy truce developed between Heald and the trustees, but as a result the Foundation began to drift, hiring few new personnel and developing even fewer new programs.[106] One of the exceptions was a grant to fund a campaign to save the redwood forests of California, a pet project of McCloy's. He rammed it through the board of trustees over the objections of Heald. Finally, in the spring of 1965, more than four years after the conflict had begun, McCloy told Heald he had to go.[107] They agreed that Heald could publicly announce that he was simply retiring in six months, and that in the interregnum McCloy would head a search committee to select his successor. In the event, McCloy made the decision himself, selecting his old friend McGeorge Bundy, who had finally decided to leave his job as national-security adviser.

Though he was absorbed by these intermittent problems at the Ford Foundation, the years of the Kennedy presidency still found McCloy active in a number of quasi-public roles. Early in 1962, he made a quick trip to Germany, where he held talks with Adenauer on the status of Berlin. Germany was always on his mind. But there were other issues as well. As usual, he presided over various seminars at the Council on Foreign Relations, and wrote an article for *Foreign Affairs* criticizing the neutral bloc of nations' reaction to the Soviet resumption of nuclear-weapons testing the previous autumn. In early April, he had a short meeting with Kennedy, and on the following day was formally sworn in as the chairman of the General Advisory Committee to the Arms Control and Disarmament Agency, a post he would occupy for the next fifteen years. This was a part-time position, which only required him to attend meetings in Washington three or four times a year. But it gave him access to the most secret of national-security information and entitled him to briefings in the CIA and the Defense Department on the status of American and Soviet nuclear arsenals.

In September 1962, Kennedy tried to persuade McCloy to take on a full-time job as his trade representative. But the lawyer preferred to stay in New York, where he could keep his hand in many issues and not become ensnared in the federal bureaucracy. On the other hand, he was always willing to undertake temporary assignments, particularly if they involved issues of concern to his Milbank, Tweed clients. So, with the administration's encouragement, he planned a trip to Europe in which he intended to hold discussions with various European oil companies and their governments on the still-troublesome matter of Soviet oil exports. On October 5, 1962, a State Department cable went out to a number of U.S. embassies in West European capitals informing them that McCloy was "proceeding to Europe on matter in which Government is interested. Would appreciate anything you can do for him. . . ."[108] The following evening, McCloy boarded a Pan Am flight for London, where he planned to spend a week meeting with British and Dutch oil-company officials before moving on to Rome and then Germany.

CHAPTER 24

The Cuban Missile Crisis

"Well, Mr. McCloy, we will honor this agreement. But I want to tell you something. The Soviet Union is not going to find itself in a position like this ever again."

VASILY KUZNETSOV
DECEMBER 1962

Shortly after nine o'clock on one of those balmy Indian-summer mornings peculiar to Washington in mid-October, John Kennedy called his brother over at the Justice Department and asked him to come right over to the White House. When he arrived, Bobby Kennedy was told that a U-2 photoreconnaissance mission over Cuba had just come back with evidence that the Soviets were installing medium- and intermediate-range missiles on the island. "I had no doubt," recalled the thirty-six-year-old attorney general, "we were moving into a serious crisis."[1]

The Kennedy brothers were both surprised and puzzled by the Soviet move. The CIA had for some months monitored the shipment of Soviet weapons to Cuba. But in the wake of the failed Bay of Pigs invasion, and the subsequent numerous strafings of Cuban ports by CIA-backed Cuban exiles in high-speed motorboats, it was no surprise that the Soviets were building up the Castro regime's military defenses. However, as recently as mid-September, the president had publicly warned Khrushchev against the installation of anything more than defensive weaponry. Now he could not understand why the Soviet leader, who he thought had "demonstrated a sense of caution" during the Berlin crisis the previous year, would risk so much over Cuba.[2]

Whatever Khrushchev's intentions, the president immediately knew that the discovery of Soviet nuclear missiles ninety miles offshore was political dynamite. The country was less than three weeks away from a congressional midterm election. It had been a hard-fought campaign so far, and the Republicans had made the Kennedy administration's apparent tolerance of Castro's regime a major issue. Only a week earlier, the Republican senator from New York, Kenneth Keating, had announced that he knew from his own sources of information that the Soviets were constructing six intermediate-range missile sites in Cuba.[3] This had elicited a firm denial from McGeorge Bundy, the president's national-security adviser, that there was "no present evidence" or likelihood that the Soviets would attempt to install an offensive capability in Cuba. If, in fact, it now turned out to be true that the Soviets had covertly managed to sneak such missiles into Cuba, the Democrats could pay a heavy price at the polls.

Baffled and disturbed, the president told "Mac" Bundy to call together an abbreviated session of the National Security Council (NSC) for a meeting in strictest secrecy at 11:45 A.M. He told Bundy he wanted only a few men present and listed Dean Rusk, Bob McNamara, and a dozen other top officials. Then, in an effort to get his bearings before meeting with them, Kennedy asked his secretary to track down private citizen John McCloy. By this time, McCloy was in Rome, halfway through his quick tour, seeing a variety of European officials. It was late afternoon in Rome when Kennedy was put on the phone with his former disarmament adviser. The president informed him in guarded language of what he had learned only a couple of hours earlier. McCloy's initial judgment was characteristically uncomplicated and sharp: he favored an air strike to take out the missile sites, to be followed up, if necessary, by a full-scale invasion.[4] After a brief discussion, Kennedy told McCloy to keep in touch, that he might be needed in the next few days. The president already sensed that, as a matter of domestic politics, the missiles could not remain in Cuba. But this brief phone conversation confirmed to him that the country's foreign-policy establishment would regard the introduction of such missiles into the Western Hemisphere as a grave development.

On one level, McCloy instinctively regarded the Cuban missiles as a new and dramatic military challenge. Sometime after talking to Kennedy, he wrote out his thoughts in longhand: "The size, character and speed of the nuclear build-up really staggers the imagination." But more frightening than the missiles themselves was that the Soviets obviously thought they could get away with this challenge. He was absolutely appalled that they could think the world would accept this "dagger at our throat" as a defensive maneuver. "What do they take us for?" he wrote. He had already forgotten that only the year before he had written the president's speechwriter Theodore Sorensen and asked, "Even if the Soviet Union had missiles in Cuba—which it hasn't—why would we have any more right to invade Cuba than Khrushchev has to invade Turkey—where we do have missiles?" Instead, the Soviet challenge now brought to his mind the 1938 lessons of Munich, and this time the West had to stand firm.

The missiles had to come out, and fast. There could be "no doubt about our willingness to accept the risk of nuclear conflict rather than to permit this massive attempt to disturb the nuclear balance."[5]

In this sense, his hard-line assessment was just as political as Kennedy's. The president had his eye on the domestic implications, but in McCloy's mind the worst aspect of the news was the psychological impact on America's NATO allies of what would clearly be seen as a Soviet coup. Cuba had become another test of wills, and if Washington did not prevail, morale in Western Europe could be affected terribly. Worse, the Soviets might even be able to extract some kind of concessions over West Berlin in return for removing their missiles from Cuba. As it happened, Chancellor Adenauer at that very moment found himself in the center of a storm of controversy known as the "*Spiegel* affair." The editors of the German equivalent of *Time* magazine had recently shocked the German people by publishing highly secret NATO documents that in stark language described the inability of the German Army and NATO forces to resist Soviet aggression in Europe. McCloy and others already feared that the chancellor's political credibility as a loyal champion of NATO might be "permanently damaged" by *Spiegel*'s revelations.[6] If the United States was now seen backing down before the Soviet challenge in Cuba, how much credibility would West Europeans place in the NATO deterrent? Political concerns for the Atlantic alliance, more than fear of the military threat posed by the Cuban missiles, explains McCloy's initial advice to the president.

He knew, as did Kennedy, that a few more missiles in Cuba could not appreciably alter the United States' overwhelming nuclear superiority. In his capacity as chairman of the president's Advisory Committee on Arms Control and Disarmament, he had been briefed with the most highly classified information on American and Soviet nuclear arsenals. In October 1962, the United States had some 172 ICBM launchers versus about 44 Soviet launchers. All told, the United States had some 3,000 nuclear warheads, which could be delivered to targets in the Soviet Union by 1,450 long-range strategic bombers. In contrast, the Soviets only had an estimated 250 warheads and a bomber fleet of no more than 155.[7] Kennedy, McCloy, and others privy to this classified information knew that they possessed an overwhelming superiority. Naturally, there were differences of opinion about what this meant. Some of the president's military advisers, such as Air Force chief General Curtis LeMay, believed the United States capable of delivering a credible first strike in which most, if not all, of the Soviet nuclear arm could be destroyed. McNamara himself publicly said in June 1962 that the American missile force was so accurate that in a nuclear war the United States could afford to target only Soviet military installations, sparing the civilian population. This implied that the United States was capable of launching a first strike, a suggestion the president had said that spring was a possibility under certain circumstances.[8] These statements must have worried Soviet military planners, who were well aware of their own missile gap and, worse, now knew that the American president knew.[9] In fact, Robert McNamara, for one, believed that, despite their numerical deficiency in nuclear warheads, the Soviets nevertheless possessed essential parity with the United States. In any nuclear exchange, McNamara reasoned, at least a few Soviet warheads would probably be delivered on American cities, killing millions. "No responsible political leader," McNamara wrote later, "would expose his nation to such a catastrophe."[10]

Fortunately for Kennedy, he had not been caught unawares. The American public did not know of the construction going on at the Cuban missile sites, and the president thought the Soviets still seemed to think their activities there were a secret.[11] So he had time—not much, perhaps only a week—time enough to do something about the missiles before they became operational and before the news of their existence put him and his administration on the political defensive, both at home and abroad.[12] The problem was how to manage the crisis.

This may seem, in retrospect, too cool an assessment of how Kennedy and his advisers felt at the time. But it is borne out by the most reliable of historical documents, a transcript of their first two meetings on the crisis. Kennedy had a surreptitious tape recorder running during these meetings, and from the partially released transcripts of these verbatim conversations it is clear that, even in the first heat of the crisis, most of the president's advisers understood that the Cuban missiles in themselves had not substantially altered the strategic balance.[13]

Of course, McNamara had to report that the Joint Chiefs believed the missiles "substantially" affected the strategic balance. But he immediately discounted this by saying that he personally felt there was no change at all. In his view, a missile was a missile.[14] Bundy chimed in his agreement, and no one else in the room took issue with McNamara except Chief of Staff General Maxwell Taylor. Even Taylor prefaced his mild objections by saying, "You're quite right in saying that these, these are just a few more missiles, uh, targeted on the United States." Later in the conversation, the president himself observed, "You may say it doesn't make any difference if you get blown up by an ICBM flying from the Soviet Union or one that was ninety miles away. Geography doesn't mean that much. . . ." The problem, as Kennedy pointed out, was that it "makes them look like they're coequal with us and that . . . [Doug Dillon finishes the president's sentence:] We're scared of the Cubans."[15]

There may have been some arguable strategic reasons, but the bottom line was that U.S. domestic political considerations alone required the administration to find a way to remove the missiles. As McNamara said that day, "I don't think there is a military problem here. . . . This is a domestic, political problem." The administration had previously announced that it would do something if the Soviets placed offensive weaponry in Cuba. Now, said the defense secretary, the administration had to act. That meant some kind of concrete military action. As George Ball remarked, "Yeah, well, as far as the American people are concerned, action means military action."[16]

Actually, though Khrushchev had misled Kennedy about his intentions, he had not done anything that the Americans had not themselves already done. In one of the more telling exchanges during the entire crisis, Kennedy questioned the "advantage" the Russians would gain from their gamble: "It's just as if we suddenly began to put a major number of MRBM's [Medium Range Ballistic Missiles] in Turkey. Now that'd be goddam dangerous, I think." Bundy then said, "Well, we *did,* Mr. President." Kennedy lamely replied, "Yeah, but that was five years ago."[17] Kennedy was in fact mistaken. NATO had made the decision in 1957 to install intermediate-range missiles in Britain, Italy, and Turkey. But the fifteen Jupiter missiles destined for Turkey had not become operational until July 1962; indeed, though Kennedy did not realize it, a ceremony was scheduled for the following week in which the Jupiters were to be formally turned over to Turkish control.[18] This had to be viewed by the Soviets as a provocation, and it is not unreasonable to assume that the deployment of the Turkish missiles played an important part in motivating Soviet military leaders to reply in kind. A few days later, Averell Harriman sent Kennedy a memo further emphasizing the link between the Turkish and Cuban missiles: "There has undoubtedly," wrote Harriman, "been great pressure on Khrushchev for a considerable time to do something about our ring of bases, aggravated by our placing Jupiter missiles in Turkey."[19]

But even if everyone recognized these facts that first day of the crisis, it was also known that the Kennedy administration could not afford any reciprocity. The missiles had to come out. U.S. nuclear superiority was such that the risks were worth taking. The only question was how the missiles should be taken out. Many options were discussed, and the gut reaction on the part of many if not most of the men in the room favored the same choice as McCloy's: a surprise air strike to be followed by an invasion. But McNamara and Rusk in particular made strong arguments for a moderated response. McNamara spoke about a "blockade against offensive weapons entering Cuba" in which every ship would be searched and any offensive weapons seized. By the end of the day, during their final evening session, McNamara had fully fleshed out his blockade strategy.[20]

That was Tuesday evening. By Thursday, October 18, 1962, Kennedy was telling his chief speechwriter, Theodore Sorensen, to draft a speech announcing the blockade. But nothing was firmly decided. All the President's advisers, now known as the "Executive Committee" or "Excomm," switched positions a number of times. Some, like Mac Bundy, were still arguing for an air strike as late as Sunday. But as a group they kept coming back to the idea of a blockade. The lawyers among them, particularly George Ball, argued that, of all the alternatives, a naval blockade had the most "color of legality."[21]

Up to this point, McCloy, who was still traveling in Europe, took no part in the deliberations. But then an incident occurred that resulted in a decision by the Kennedy brothers to have him return from Europe immediately. On Saturday, October 20, U.N. Ambassador Adlai Stevenson flew down from New York to take part in Excomm's meeting that day. Stevenson favored the naval-blockade option, and he suggested that the administration could enhance the legality of the blockade by having the Organization of American States formally vote its approval. Kennedy accepted this suggestion. But then Stevenson reiterated several diplomatic concessions he had proposed in a handwritten note to Kennedy on the previous Wednesday. Perhaps, he said, the United States should offer to withdraw from its Cuban naval base in Guantanamo as part of a deal to demilitarize the entire island. Maybe Washington should further offer to guarantee the territorial integrity of Cuba. In addition, many in the U.N. were going to question why the United States could not tolerate Soviet missiles in Cuba when U.S. missiles had been stationed on the Soviet Union's border in Turkey for five years. The president, he argued, should offer to withdraw the Jupiter missiles in Turkey.[22]

Kennedy had already been annoyed by these proposals. Now he flatly rejected them. Everyone else in the room opposed Stevenson's arguments, and Robert Kennedy came away from the meeting that afternoon with the distinct impression that Stevenson was soft. The attorney general recommended to his brother, "He's [Stevenson] not strong enough or tough enough to be representing us at the U.N. at a time like this."[23] He suggested that McCloy or Herman Phleger, a California Republican who had worked under Foster Dulles, be brought to New York to ensure that Stevenson displayed some backbone.[24] Either Republican, thought Robert Kennedy, would make the administration's efforts at the U.N. look bipartisan.[25]

The next day, Sunday, President Kennedy consulted Robert Lovett about the matter. Aside from McCloy on that first day, Kennedy had sought counsel from only two other outsiders, Robert Lovett and Dean Acheson. Lovett had been present when Stevenson made his pitch for diplomatic concessions, and now Kennedy wanted to know whether Lovett thought Stevenson would not take a tough enough stance at the U.N. Lovett recommended that McCloy be brought back to the U.N. Kennedy agreed. Lovett called McCloy's secretary at home and got her to track McCloy down in Europe. He was reached in the middle of a business meeting in Frankfurt, and after taking the phone call McCloy turned to his colleagues and said, "Sorry, boys, I hate to drop names, but the President needs me."[26] He had been scheduled to hunt partridges in Spain that week, but instead a U.S. Air Force plane was dispatched to ferry him to New York.[27]

The obvious tensions between Stevenson and the Kennedy brothers placed McCloy in a delicate spot when he arrived in New York. "In some respects," McCloy later recalled, "this was a rather awkward relationship because I am sure that President Kennedy's motive in asking me to come to New York was to counteract what he thought might be a too soft attitude on the part of Adlai." Ironically, things were not what they seemed. "When I got to New York," McCloy said, "I did not find that he had any such attitude. . . . I even found him tougher than I was prepared to be. . . ."[28]

For the first couple of days, McCloy concentrated on taking aside small groups of U.N. delegates and briefing them on the crisis.[29] Many people, including some of Washington's European allies, still needed to be convinced that even a naval blockade was necessary. After talking to several of his banking friends in London and Zurich, Lovett told Michael Forrestal, an aide to Mac Bundy on the National Security Council, that "documentary evidence is essential, since a number of countries—some of them our friends—will not take the President's word alone."[30]

Consequently, two days later, Stevenson spoke to the Security Council and this time went through the exercise of displaying U-2 photos of the missile sites. The focus of the mounting crisis was now rapidly shifting from the White House to the United Nations. Since Kennedy had imposed the "quarantine" of Cuba and issued his ultimatums on Monday evening, tensions had risen considerably. More than two dozen Soviet freighters and submarines were steaming toward the quarantine line; an incident on the high seas might occur at any moment, which could lead to the death of Soviet sailors and thus precipitate another round of escalation in the crisis. To postpone this confrontation, the acting secretary general of the U.N., U Thant, proposed on Wednesday, October 24, that Khrushchev should voluntarily agree to suspend further arms shipments into Cuba while Kennedy simultaneously lifted the quarantine for a period of two or three weeks.[31] This proposal set the scene for another debate within the administration.

To McCloy's astonishment, a strong current of opinion within the U.S. delegation to the U.N. now favored a suspension of the quarantine. Stevenson himself called the president from New York to urge him to accept U Thant's proposal. McCloy was thoroughly "disgusted" by Stevenson's position and concerned that the administration might "back down on the quarantine in the face of blandishments from [Khrushchev] and U Thant."[32]

He need not have worried, for later that afternoon the president sent

U Thant an answer to his proposal: the United States was willing to engage in some form of negotiations with Soviets at the U.N., but the quarantine would remain in place. The same day, Khrushchev fully accepted the proposal, and halted any further shipment of arms into Cuba. This was certainly a concession, but it was not enough, in the view of Kennedy's advisers, to change the situation.

That day, George Ball arranged for McCloy to come down for an Excomm meeting. Though McCloy had initially favored forceful military action, he had done so with the assumption that the Soviets would never risk nuclear war for the sake of Cuba. But now, ten days into the crisis, things seemed to be getting out of hand. He left for Washington on Thursday evening, October 25, in a somber mood, thinking to himself that he might just possibly be saying goodbye to Ellen for the last time.[33] On arriving at the State Department in time for a rump session of Excomm, he found the atmosphere extremely tense.[34] Thirteen Soviet ships were still steaming toward the quarantine line. The next morning, for the first time, a U.S. destroyer stopped and inspected a third-country freighter, and in Moscow Khrushchev told a visiting U.S. businessman that his submarines would sink any U.S. ship that interfered with Soviet shipping.[35] None of this weakened McCloy's resolve that the quarantine must continue.

In the Excomm meeting on Friday morning, the president's advisers once again divided themselves into two camps: those who advocated a lessening of military pressure, and those who argued against any compromise until the Russians began dismantling their missiles. When Dean Rusk suggested that perhaps the U.S. quarantine could be replaced by a U.N.-administered quarantine, McCloy interjected "that our quarantine was vital and should be kept in place until the Russians had accepted all of our conditions."[36]

McCloy's uncompromising position had the attraction of seeming tough-minded and clear-cut. But as the discussion continued, it also became clear that, unless Khrushchev intended to engage in general nuclear warfare, the Soviet premier at some point would make Washington a counteroffer. Again and again the men in the room that morning had to ask themselves what concessions they would be willing to give in exchange for the removal of the Cuban missiles. Stevenson predicted the Soviets would ask for a pledge from the United States not to invade Cuba in the future and the dismantlement of U.S. strategic missiles in Turkey. CIA Director John McCone vigorously objected to this linking of the Cuban and Turkish missiles. But the president himself confessed that he doubted the quarantine alone could produce a withdrawal of the missiles. The missiles would come out, he said, "only by invading Cuba or by trading."[37] McCloy himself finally muttered something about how they had to "get them (the missiles) out or trade them out."[38]

Kennedy observed that there was little support for Stevenson's negotiating track. No one else in the room, including McCloy, wanted to concede anything by way of loosening the quarantine until the Soviets capitulated on the major issue and actually began to dismantle their missiles. McCloy returned to New York reassured that the quarantine would stay in place. But though once a "hawk"—a term that came into usage during the missile crisis—by October 26 McCloy was beginning to go through the process of reconsidering his outlook. Later that day, at the U.N., Secretary General U Thant suggested to him that an American pledge not to invade Cuba might be traded for a Soviet commitment to withdraw the missiles.[39] McCloy was not automatically inclined to dismiss the idea. In his eyes, the Castro regime may have been a nuisance and reprehensible, but its removal was not essential to U.S. security. As long as Cuba did not become a Soviet nuclear base, McCloy did not on ideological grounds rule out a noninvasion pledge.

In the meantime, however, preparations in Washington were gathering speed for a full-scale invasion of Cuba, and later that day Robert Kennedy warned Soviet Ambassador Dobrynin that an air strike could not be held off longer than two days.[40] Pressures were also escalating from outside the government to launch an air strike. Zbigniew Brzezinski, then a Harvard professor, cabled his White House friend Arthur Schlesinger, "Any further delay in bombing missile sites fails to exploit Soviet uncertainty."[41] But within hours the situation began to change. At 6:00 P.M., the president received a long, rambling letter obviously dictated personally by Khrushchev, and probably sent without the knowledge of his Politburo colleagues. McNamara called it the "most extraordinary diplomatic message I have ever seen." Running six or seven feet in length, the teletyped message seemed to suggest the basis for a settlement.[42]

First the Soviet leader asserted once again that the missiles in Cuba were there purely to defend Castro's regime from his powerful North American neighbor. "You can be calm in this regard," he wrote, "that we are of sound mind and understand perfectly well that if we attack you, you will respond the same way. . . . Only lunatics or suicides, who themselves want to perish and destroy the whole world before they die, could do this." Khrushchev then said that, if the United States would pledge itself not to invade Cuba and to lift the quarantine, there would be no need for Soviet military forces to be deployed in the defense of Cuba. "If you have not lost your self-control," he pleaded, ". . . then, Mr. President, we and you ought not now to pull on the ends of the rope in which you have tied the knot of war, because the more we pull, the tighter the knot will be tied."[43] This was an altogether encouraging personal statement, and the Kennedy brothers retired that night feeling that the crisis had eased.

But then, the following morning, another Khrushchev letter—this time sounding as though it had been written by his Foreign Office—was broadcast on Moscow radio. This letter added to the deal a public demand that the United States reciprocate by removing the Jupiter missiles stationed in Turkey. Stevenson had been right all along: the Soviets viewed the Turkish missiles as no different from the missiles they had placed in Cuba. A few days earlier, Walter Lippmann had suggested such a swap in a column the Soviet newspaper *Izvestia* had reprinted. It had all along been an obvious solution to the crisis, and now Kennedy told his advisers that he was ready to make the deal. Excomm hard-liners, particularly Paul Nitze and Mac Bundy, again argued that he should not link the two issues. Kennedy replied that he was concerned that, if "we wouldn't take the missiles out of Turkey, then maybe we'll have to invade or make a massive strike on Cuba, which may lose Berlin."[44] At another point in the debate, he complained, "We are in a bad position if we appear to be attacking Cuba for the purpose of keeping useless missiles in Turkey."[45]

Later in the day, tensions mounted once again when news came that a Soviet SAM anti-aircraft missile had shot down a U-2 reconnaissance plane and killed its pilot. At this McNamara said that they should be prepared to attack Cuba, that an "invasion had become almost inevitable."[46] CIA Director McCone suggested that Kennedy send an ultimatum by "fast wire" to Khrushchev, and "demand that he stop this business and stop it right away or we're going to take those SAM sites out immediately."[47]

McCone, like McCloy, often expressed a blend of toughness and pragmatism. He had changed his mind overnight, and now told Kennedy that, while threatening the Soviets with an air strike, he should also tell Khrushchev that he'd deal on the Turkish bases. "I'd trade these Turkish things out right now. I wouldn't even talk to anybody about it."[48] That's exactly what the Kennedy brothers decided to do, and they were going to do it in secrecy. That evening, the attorney general went to tell Soviet Ambassador Dobrynin that, although there could be no public "quid pro quo," the Russians could be assured that the Turkish missiles would be out within four to five months. "You have my word on this," the attorney general told Dobrynin, "and that is sufficient. . . . If you should publish any document indicating a deal then it is off. . . ."[49]

These private assurances were given to Dobrynin by the Kennedy brothers on Saturday night without the knowledge of most Excomm advisers. Yet it was the heart of the deal; together with the public pledge that the United States would not invade Cuba, the secret concession on the Turkish bases allowed Khrushchev to face down his own hard-liners in the Politburo.[50] Ironically, it was the one concession that Adlai Stevenson had predicated would be necessary. But for domestic political reasons, it was also the one concession the Kennedy brothers thought was best done in secrecy. Furthermore, if Khrushchev and his colleagues had not been satisfied with a secret pledge, President Kennedy was prepared to endorse a public swap of missiles.[51]

On that Saturday, October 27, 1962, Kennedy had brought the country to the very brink of an invasion of Cuba. But the next morning, a radio broadcast brought welcome news: the Soviet premier was taking his missiles home. However, even though tensions at last began to recede, this did not mean that the crisis was over. Most accounts of the Cuban missile crisis end their narratives at this point. But behind closed doors, the crisis—including the danger of war—stretched out for another two months. As the man responsible for negotiating the details of the missile withdrawals from Cuba, McCloy was center-stage throughout this period. Among the terms of the agreement was a provision for U.N. inspections of the missile sites and an accounting of the dismantled missiles to be shipped back to the Soviet Union. Only then, the Kennedy administration said, would it issue a noninvasion pledge to Cuba and end the quarantine. There were other details to be worked out concerning the fate of forty-two IL-28 bombers, which the Americans regarded as offensive weapons since they were capable of carrying nuclear bombs.

All these issues were now to be debated at the U.N., where McCloy was appointed chairman of a three-man committee to handle the negotiations. Working with him were George Ball and Roswell Gilpatric. A number of U.N. delegates expressed surprise that McCloy seemed to be superseding Stevenson's authority. *The New York Times* observed, however, that the same thing had happened to the Soviet's chief U.N. delegate, Valerian A. Zorin, whose negotiating responsibilities were now assumed by Deputy Foreign Minister Vasily Kuznetsov. McCloy's new counterpart was a tall, white-haired man who spoke fluent English from his studies as a young man at the Carnegie Institute of Technology in Pennsylvania. A veteran diplomat, Kuznetsov got along well with McCloy over the next two months of hard bargaining.

The first snag in the McCloy-Kuznetsov talks occurred over Khrushchev's agreement to an on-site inspection in Cuba of the dismantled missiles. When an angry Castro learned that Khrushchev had backed down, he reportedly kicked the wall and broke a mirror.[52] He then warned that "whoever tries to inspect Cuba must come in battle array."[53] After visiting Cuba for two days at the end of October, U Thant told McCloy that the missiles would all be dismantled within days, a fact confirmed by aerial photography. But as regards on-site inspection, Castro was demanding strict reciprocity. The Cuban leader wanted the right to inspect the Cuban exile camps in the United States, from which numerous attacks on Cuba had been launched. (Ironically, a few days later a CIA-dispatched sabotage team funded by Operation Mongoose successfully blew up a

Cuban factory.[54]) Short of such reciprocity, U Thant said Castro would not allow ground inspection by U.N. observers or anyone else. The White House at this point really didn't expect to win on-site verification. As of October 31, McCloy's written instructions stated that "Kuznetsov's insistence on no physical inspection of dismantling and removal of Soviet weapons is essentially non-negotiable." It was "probable," he was told, that he would have to settle for aerial inspections.[55]

U Thant had learned quite a bit about the situation in Cuba. He told McCloy that relations between the Soviets and the Cubans were "unbelievably bad." Castro had boasted that Cubans, not Russians, had fired the SAM that had brought down the American U-2 earlier in the week.[56] The Cuban leader warned that "his boys are trigger happy." The secretary general then conveyed a quite remarkable piece of information: the commander of all Soviet forces in Cuba, a General Stazenko, had told a U.N. official that the Americans ought to vary the pattern of their surveillance flights, since the Cubans "had established what they believed to be the standard routine for reconnaissance flights." This U.N. official came away from his conversation with the Soviet general convinced that the Cubans would take every opportunity to fire on U.S. planes. Washington had trouble digesting this news. Rusk fired off an "eyes-only" cable to McCloy's colleague George Ball saying that the United States could not accept that sophisticated weapons like surface-to-air-missiles could be operated by Cubans. McCloy thought all this was a serious complication. But it didn't stop him from cabling Rusk that, though any further attacks on U.S. reconnaisance planes "would again put us face to face," aerial surveillance was absolutely essential.[57] Despite the risks, the reconnaissance continued.

On November 3, McCloy went back down to Washington for further instructions. He attended the Excomm meeting with Kennedy present, and later that evening he and Stevenson spent a half-hour alone with the president.[58] By this time, yet another problem had arisen: aerial photoreconnaisance confirmed that the Soviets were continuing to assemble IL-28 bombers. Early in the crisis, President Kennedy himself had mentioned to his advisers that the presence of the IL-28 bombers did not bother him.[59] Indeed, the eight-year-old, first-generation jet bombers were universally regarded as an outmoded nuclear-delivery vehicle.[60]

Despite his own doubts on the matter, Kennedy now insisted that they should be regarded as falling within the definition of the offensive weapons that Khrushchev had agreed to withdraw. The Soviets had only been informed of this American interpretation the evening before.[61] They understandably thought the Americans were interpreting the phrase "offensive weapon" in an entirely "arbitrary fashion."[62] Far from trying to avoid further humiliation to Khrushchev, as some court historians have argued, President Kennedy at this point in the crisis dug in his heels.

McGeorge Bundy later recalled that at this point the president was actually "irritated" with his New York negotiators and worried that his tactical instructions were being ignored.[63] He now told McCloy and Stevenson in rather severe language that he could not be satisfied with a "mere gentlemen's agreement relating only to visible missiles on identified launch pads."[64] They had to insist on both on-site inspection and the removal of the IL-28s. Furthermore, said Kennedy, McCloy was to tell Kuznetsov that no Soviet military base of any kind could remain in Cuba.[65]

Back in New York, McCloy had lunch with Kuznetsov and told him that the United States had evidence that the Soviets were building a submarine base. He said the president regarded this as a violation of the agreement barring offensive weaponry. McCloy also raised the matter of the presence in Cuba of a Soviet "combat brigade," which he said Washington also wanted out. In response, Kuznetsov denied that they were building anything like a submarine base. Regarding the combat brigade, the Russian diplomat only went so far as to say that any Soviet military personnel associated with offensive weaponry would be withdrawn. McCloy didn't pursue the matter, and the Soviets never committed themselves to withdrawing all their troops from Cuba.[66]

Nor was McCloy any more successful in pinning Kuznetsov down on the issue of on-site inspection. Instead, the Soviet diplomat proposed an alternative to a ground inspection of the missile sites. Why not, he suggested, perform the inspection on the high seas, and count all forty-two missiles on the decks of the freighters as they return to the Soviet Union? Following his new instructions from the president, McCloy insisted that on-site inspection was "of the gravest importance."[67] The United States would not be satisfied with a simple inspection of vacant missile sites; the designated inspectors had to have the "freedom to investigate reports of concealed weapons in caves or elsewhere."[68] Once again, Kuznetsov explained that Castro was not going to allow inspections on this basis. The talks were stalemated, and time was running out. By now, the missiles had all been trucked into various seaports and were waiting to be shipped out aboard Russian freighters. Frustrated by the impasse, McCloy felt that it was time to have his instructions changed. At one Excomm meeting, he got into a vigorous debate with Edwin M. Martin, assistant secretary of state for inter-American affairs. Citing his experience in Germany, McCloy insisted that aerial photography was the best possible verification system. Martin was unconvinced, but the president nevertheless authorized McCloy to have a second look at Kuznetsov's proposals.[69]

Over the next few days of intensive talks with Kuznetsov, he finally worked out detailed procedures for an inspection at sea. U.S. destroyers would be allowed to pull alongside the Russian freighters once they had steamed out of Cuban waters. The tarpaulins covering the missiles, which all had to be laid out on the ships' upper decks, would then be pulled back so that the missiles could be photographed. Crates containing missile equipment would be pried open, and American helicopters would be allowed to hover overhead to take additional photographs.[70]

As Kuznetsov and McCloy now actually began to accomplish something concrete in working out these details, the two men acquired a grudging admiration for each other. Years afterward, McCloy had Kuznetsov in mind when he frequently told interviewers, "I never had a session with the Russians in which I didn't think the fellow on the other side was almost as fair as I was."[71] With his excellent English and aristocratic bearing, Kuznetsov seemed to McCloy a most reasonable negotiator. Soon they had worked out all the procedures for an inspection at sea, and by November 9, McCloy reported that thirty-eight of the forty-two missiles had been observed leaving Cuba.[72] The four remaining missiles departed the next day.

This was a major accomplishment, but it was not the end of their encounters. Nor was it the end of the crisis; U.S. forces were still on the exceedingly high Defcon-2 alert level as late as November 12.[73] And McCloy's negotiations with Kuznetsov sometimes became as nerve-racking as at the height of the crisis. One Sunday in mid-November, he drove out to the old George Pratt property in Locust Valley on Long Island, where the Soviet mission to the U.N. maintained a country estate for their diplomats. There he joined Kuznetsov and Zorin for a game of Russian billiards and a luncheon. It was a cordial affair; McCloy had brought Ellen along, together with his son, John, Jr. After lunch, the men adjourned for coffee and a long talk about their problems. On instructions from Kennedy, McCloy again pressed his host for on-site inspection of the original missile sites, if only as a matter of principle. The Kennedy administration, he explained, would not give the Soviets the promised no-invasion pledge until they were allowed the on-site inspection promised by Khrushchev.[74] Kuznetsov accused the United States of "stalling" and once again explained that Castro would not submit to such inspections unless Washington could agree to his conditions.[75] These now included, in addition to the principle of inspection reciprocity, such demands as the abandonment of Guantanamo, a suspension of the trade embargo, and an end to "subversive" activity inside Cuba.[76] Kennedy, of course, was not about to make such concessions to Castro. He was still hoping, in fact, that the Soviet humiliation in Cuba might somehow lead to Castro's collapse.[77] And as far as the no-invasion pledge was concerned, the president had decided that the domestic political cost of such a pledge was too high. He wanted to avoid any clear-cut pledge not to invade. McCloy was fully aware of these domestic political considerations, but he personally felt that the principle of obtaining a ground inspection was irrelevant now that the missiles had been withdrawn and counted at sea. He favored an end to the quarantine and, together with Stevenson, was quite willing to drop the whole idea of a U.N.-supervised ground inspection. McCloy even thought that the United States should now pledge not to invade Cuba, in the hopes that this might help persuade the recalcitrant Cubans to give up the IL-28 bombers.[78] Having started out the crisis as an instinctive "hawk," McCloy had now become a verifiable "dove." Once the missiles were out of Cuba, he simply regarded anything to do with Cuba as a "minor issue." U.S. leverage on the Soviets should be used, he thought, to obtain agreements on such critical national-security issues as the status of Berlin and substantive arms-control measures.[79] He told Kuznetsov that he was anxious to "wind up this transaction," because there were plenty of other "things we ought to be discussing in order to keep this situation from arising again." Today it was "this bearded figure who is dictator in Cuba and (a) certain miscalculation on (the) part of (the) Soviet Union that almost brought us to war. Tomorrow it may be something else." He wanted to discuss not only broader arms-control measures but such specific topics as the current Chinese-Indian war, which he thought was the kind of regional conflict that might get out of hand.[80]

Kennedy was disinclined to open the discussions up to such far-flung issues, and felt he repeatedly had to instruct McCloy and Stevenson not to talk to the Russians about these larger issues. The president was heard one day complaining that he was spending more time worrying about McCloy and Stevenson than he did about the Russians.[81]

The longer McCloy listened to his adversary's position, the more willing he was to make a few concessions. On November 15, he became so frustrated with the deadlocked talks that he proposed to Rusk that, in exchange for a one-shot on-ground inspection in Cuba, the United States and some Latin American countries might allow the Cubans an inspection of their territories so as to ascertain whether there were any "refugee training camps preparing for attack on Cuba." Even Stevenson realized that such an idea was "politically intolerable," and the McCloy proposal was quietly ignored.[82]

The question of the IL-28 bombers was a different matter. McCloy told Kuznetsov that the president was not going to back down on this issue: the bombers had to be crated up and shipped out under the same procedures as the missiles. Otherwise, he said, Kennedy was prepared not only to continue the naval quarantine but also to take some other, unspecified measures. The crisis suddenly threatened to escalate once again to the point of armed conflict. This was McCloy's most sobering encounter with Kuznetsov, and he did not leave the Soviet estate that day until 5:00 P.M.[83]

Kennedy was, in fact, warning his European allies that air strikes and a toughening of the quarantine were a possibility. Ominously, a press conference was scheduled for the evening of November 20 to announce his intentions. Kuznetsov must have taken the warnings he received through McCloy quite seriously, for a few hours before the press conference Khrushchev informed the president that the IL-28s would be out of Cuba within thirty days. A relieved Kennedy then appeared before the reporters to announce the news and to say that he had finally ordered a suspension of the quarantine. With Thanksgiving being celebrated the next day, he said the country had "much for which we can be grateful, as we look back to where we stood only four weeks ago."[84]

The crisis was now more or less over. Both sides had residual problems. From the Soviet perspective, the most serious of these was the matter of a no-invasion pledge. In his press conference, Kennedy waffled, observing only that, "if Cuba is not used for the export of aggressive Communist purposes, there will be peace in the Caribbean." Of course, the United States had to fight subversion from Cuba and could not abandon its "hope that the Cuban people shall some day be truly free." But these policies, he said, "are very different from any intent to launch a military invasion of the island."[85] Not surprisingly, the Soviets found this a less than satisfactory fulfillment of the no-invasion pledge.

So far, Washington had won every round with the Soviets, and the Kennedy administration was not about to tie its hands with regard to further interventions in Cuba. The day after Kennedy's press conference, McCloy was told by Rusk: "Recent indications from Soviets make clear their intention: to disengage militarily from Cuba, but to stick to their story that they have saved the Castro regime from US invasion. Our interest lies in speeding the disengagement process, while avoiding the kind of commitment that unduly ties our hands in dealing with the Castro regime while it lasts."[86]

Off and on throughout the rest of November and December, McCloy continued to meet with Kuznetsov to discuss loose ends. The Russian kept pressing McCloy for little crumbs, minor concessions that might help Khrushchev save face with his own military establishment. He reiterated the Soviet demand for a definitive no-invasion pledge, and he "almost pleaded" with McCloy to leave out any mention of U.S. overflights in the administration's report to the U.N. on ending the crisis. The overflights, of course, were an embarrassment to both the Cubans and the Soviet military, and if they continued, the Soviets at least wanted no public mention made of them. As McCloy put it, "In essence, he kept asking us to find a way to maintain our position without rubbing their noses in it." On instructions from Washington, McCloy refused Kuznetsov on both counts, insisting that the Soviets had not fulfilled their pledge for on-site inspections.[87]

He knew that this was a pointless argument. In fact, he had been told by the State Department that a stalemate was actually preferable, that "the absence of on-site verification" allowed the U.S. "to retain full freedom of action as regards aerial surveillance and other means of keeping a close eye on Cuban behavior and any evidence of renewed Soviet intrusion in the Hemisphere."[88] As McCloy had predicted, the camera was proving to be the best inspector of all. On December 6—the day the last of the IL-28 bombers left Cuba—McCloy met for two hours with Kuznetsov, and they had the same old conversation.[89] Both men were entirely weary of the argument, if not of each other.

McCloy was by now so fed up with his instructions from Washington that he and Stevenson sent an "eyes-only" cable to Rusk and the president pleading for an end to the demand for on-site inspection. They reported their "growing impression that effects of victory in public mind are being gradually effaced by prolonged and inconclusive negotiation which gives impression we are still seeking vital objective. . . . If public presumes this objective is on-site inspection, more and more importance will be attached to such inspection as negotiation continues." McCloy and Stevenson warned that, "if and when we emerge from negotiation without achieving that objective, even though it may have been otherwise successful, we will risk seeming to have failed rather than to have succeeded."[90]

It was not advice the White House wanted to hear, but, with considerable reluctance, McCloy was now authorized to negotiate with Kuznetsov wording on an official statement to be read at the Security Council. The nuclear confrontation was over, though both sides would agree to disagree on the terms of the settlement. The United States would not get on-site inspection, and the Soviets failed to obtain from the United States an unqualified pledge not to invade Cuba. But, true to Bobby Kennedy's promise to Dobrynin at the height of the crisis, the Jupiter missiles in Turkey were withdrawn. From the Soviet point of view, an understanding had been reached with the Americans; Soviet officials spoke of how the crisis had demonstrated that "mutual concessions" could resolve disputes between the two powers without going to war. The Soviets even began to suggest that, in the wake of the missile crisis, superpower agreements could be reached on a number of Cold War issues, such as the status of Berlin and Germany, a nuclear-test-ban treaty, nuclear-free zones, and other steps toward disarmament. McCloy and Stevenson reiterated their view that further agreements could be negotiated and cabled Washington that it was important to close up their Cuban "transactions" on a "relatively harmonious note . . . thus maintaining momentum for possible subsequent agreements on other subjects."[91]

In Washington, however, the men around the president were chary. One Excomm memo at the time complained of the "air of détente" that had settled in since the negotiations in New York had eased the crisis: the " 'mutual concessions' theme is being played to the hilt by the Russians. . . ." This was dangerous, it was suggested, because it implied a linkage between Cuba and East-West questions, "and very often takes the line that since the USSR has made concessions in Cuba it is only right and proper that the West now give some ground elsewhere."[92] The Kennedy administration simply was not ready to take advantage of the momentum achieved by McCloy's negotiations.

Late in December, McCloy invited Kuznetsov up to his country home in Cos Cob, Connecticut. It was to be one of their final sessions. Despite the cold, Kuznetsov suggested they take a walk outside. Perched uncomfortably atop the wood-rail fence surrounding McCloy's home, Kuznetsov leaned over to his companion and said, "Well, Mr. McCloy, we will honor this agreement. But I want to tell you something. The Soviet Union is not going to find itself in a position like this ever again."[93] McCloy understood exactly what Kuznetsov meant, and quickly reported the conversation to Washington. The Soviets had been humiliated on the world stage, certainly in part because they had taken a risk in an area of the world far from the focus of their own conventional military strength. (They had no real naval deterrent at the time to counter Kennedy's naval quarantine of Cuba.) But in the view of Soviet military planners, it was America's great strategic nuclear superiority that had allowed Kennedy to take the risks that he did in Cuba.[94] Khrushchev had gambled on a temporary shortcut to rectify that imbalance. Now the Soviets would invest the resources necessary to acquire a credible countervailing nuclear force. A megatonnage race had now begun in earnest.[95]

With the crisis over, the Soviet ambassador to Washington, Anatoly Dobrynin, had Averell Harriman and his wife over for dinner. Dobrynin asked a series of what Harriman thought were "leading questions." He wanted to know if the administration was divided now between those who wanted to "make progress" on U.S.-Soviet relations and those who were content just to sit back and see what happened in the wake of Cuba. When Harriman deflected this parry, Dobrynin began naming names, and specifically asked "whether McCloy represented the business and banking group" in the country. Harriman tried to say that McCloy represented no one but himself; the Russian commented, "We find him frank, objective and have confidence in his statements."[96] (For his part, McCloy always thought Dobrynin was one of "those pretty fair and reasonable people."[97])

It is not hard to understand why the Soviets found McCloy "objective." He may have started out as a hawk, urging the president to launch an air strike against the missile sites and later counseling against a relaxation of the quarantine until the Soviets backed down. But, characteristically, as soon as he was exposed to other points of view, particularly those of doves like Stevenson and George Ball, he began to reassess his initial reactions. He was altogether more flexible and less driven by ideological prejudices than most of his colleagues during the crisis. For him, Castroism was not the bugbear that it was for some of the president's other advisers. He favored a no-invasion-of-Cuba pledge even before the Soviets agreed to withdraw their IL-28 bombers. He also recommended that "if the Cubans want to normalize relations we are ready and willing to talk to them about it."[98] Most important, at the height of the crisis he gave his acquiescence to the president for a trade of the Jupiter missiles in Turkey.

During the course of the negotiations in New York, McCloy demonstrated a willingness to deal on a substantive level with the Soviets. Once he had arranged for aerial inspection of the departing missiles, he knew further U.S. demands for on-site inspection were both impractical (because of Castro's opposition) and unnecessary. When the Kennedy administration nevertheless pressed for such ground inspections, he was willing to make the case for Cuban inspections of U.S. territory as a matter of reciprocity. Similarly, when Kennedy demanded that no Soviet troops should be allowed to stay in Cuba, McCloy got the most pragmatic deal he could from Kuznetsov: a promise that all troops associated with the offensive weaponry would leave the island.

In short, the Soviets recognized that McCloy was the kind of negotiator who wanted to solve problems. A lifetime of legal experience had taught him that no set of negotiations could be a one-way street. By the end of his sessions with Kuznetsov, he thought "a considerable record of conciliation and performance on both sides" had been established.[99] The Soviets had demonstrated their willingness to abide by complicated contractual arrangements, and McCloy was convinced that further steps toward détente could be right around the corner.[100]

Throughout early 1963, as the missile crisis petered out, McCloy continued to come down to Washington to see Kennedy, Rusk, and other officials. But the focus of his work now returned to the law. On the first day of the new year, Milbank, Tweed mailed out a nicely embossed card announcing that "John J. McCloy has again become a member of the firm." This meant that, after two years of very part-time work, he had graduated from semiretirement status—"of counsel"—to the much more remunerative position of a full-time partner. It was unusual, though not extraordinary, for a major Wall Street firm to take back a sixty-seven-year-old former partner. McCloy himself had been just a little hesitant about returning to the law in 1960; he had not, after all, practiced any law for nearly fifteen years. "I had a real question in my mind if I could come back to the law," he recalled. "[But] You have a feeling of where the red flags are and where the thin ice is that sticks with you. After I got into it again, I had the feeling of coming home."[101] Indeed, through his corporate connections, particularly to the oil companies, McCloy had quickly re-established his reputation as a "rainmaker," a lawyer who brought high-paying clients to the firm.

In connection with his oil-company clients, early in the year he decided to plan a month-long trip to the Middle East. In February, he wrote President Kennedy that, in addition to Egypt and Saudi Arabia, "I hope to stick my head into Baghdad if I am not too apt to get it shot off."[102] When Rusk found out McCloy was on his way to the Middle East, he gave him a few discreet assignments. In Egypt, he had a highly secret and, as it turned out, unsatisfactory meeting with Nasser, who refused McCloy's plea that the Egyptians abandon a missile program staffed with ex-Nazi scientists. In Saudi Arabia, McCloy developed friendships with Crown Prince Faisal, Petroleum Minister Zaki Yamani, and—with a recommendation from David Rockefeller—the real power behind the throne, Prince Abd-Allah bin Abd al-Rahman. The brother of the late king, "Uncle Abbie" had the reputation of a vizier, the man who literally stood behind the throne and whispered counsel into the ear of the king. When McCloy flew into Riyadh to see him in 1963, Uncle Abbie was thought to be using his influence within the royal family to replace the profligate King Saud with the far more suave and intelligent Prince Faisal. (A year later, the palace coup succeeded.) Typically, McCloy used his visits to these Middle Eastern countries to combine discussions of U.S. foreign-policy goals with his own business interests. Specifically, he discussed the effect on his oil-company clients of OPEC's latest demands for increased oil revenues, and such matters as Chase Manhattan Bank's desire to handle the investment of Saudi and ARAMCO pension funds. Somehow he managed in these conversations to blend private and national issues in a seamless web of common interests.

Later in the spring of 1963, McCloy had numerous meetings with German and American officials to discuss an ominous trend in the Atlantic alliance. He was shocked by France's withdrawal from the military aspects of NATO and disappointed that Adenauer seemed to be climbing aboard General De Gaulle's platform of European independence. The French general's anti-British sentiments were blocking any chance for British entry into the Common Market, and this in turn threatened McCloy's vision of a European union based on the American-dominated Atlantic alliance. With his usual persistence, he urged Adenauer, the British, and various officials in Washington to halt the drift in NATO affairs.

McCloy was, of course, always worried about relations with Europe, and Germany in particular. He had warned Washington so many times of impending crises in German-American relations that his credibility on the subject sometimes wore thin. But Washington rarely ignored him. When he learned from Ball that the president intended to confine his visit to Germany in the summer of 1963 to a simple stop in Bonn, McCloy insisted that Kennedy go to West Berlin. Though the White House feared some incident might occur in the divided city, Kennedy reluctantly agreed to risk the visit. It became, of course, the scene of his famous *"Ich bin ein Berliner"* speech, a personal triumph for the president and a high point in German-American relations.

That summer, McCloy relaxed more than he had for many years. He hunted whitewings with Clint Murchison on the Texas oil man's Mexico farm.[103] Over Memorial Day weekend, he went fishing on one of his favorite Adirondack rivers, the West Branch of the Ausable, and caught several good-sized browns.[104]

Uncharacteristically, he seemed that summer rather pessimistic about the state of the world and unhappy with both the Kennedy administration and the caliber of presidential candidates already running for the Republican nomination. After lunching with Dick Nixon—for the first time since the former vice-president had moved to New York City—he wrote Eisenhower that he doubted either Nixon or Nelson Rockefeller would be a factor in the Republican nomination. Barry Goldwater, he thought, was going to be the nominee, and he wasn't pleased by the prospect. He thought Goldwater "a fine character," but "quite naïve" and "overconservative." He complained to Ike, "I do feel that both domestically and internationally the country is face-to-face with some deeply disturbing issues and I very much wish that we could have Republican leadership at this time that would give promise of being able to cope with them."[105]

He was thinking not only of the troubled Atlantic alliance but also of Vietnam. When Kennedy had first considered sending "combat advisors" to South Vietnam, he had sought McCloy's counsel. The lawyer had cautioned him to "consider this very carefully because once committed, there would be no turning back." Kennedy had gone ahead and dispatched eighteen thousand troops to support the Saigon government. Now, when the Diem regime seemed incapable of prosecuting the war, the administration was wavering, and it disturbed McCloy that Kennedy seemed to feel he could place the prestige of American troops on the line "without making an irretrievable commitment."[106]

He was also disturbed by the domestic racial upheavals that were beginning to rock American society. Martin Luther King and other civil-rights leaders were at that moment planning a mammoth "march on Washington." Early in June, he wrote Lew Douglas, "The racial problem, if you read the newspapers, is causing everyone a lot of concern. No one knows where the next outbreaks are going to occur and how serious they will be." Despite his role in desegregating the army during the war, he rather thought, like Eisenhower, that racial equality could not easily be legislated. On such domestic issues, McCloy could be quite conservative, and he doubted the Kennedy brothers' ability to contain the pent-up emotions of this potentially explosive social problem. "It does seem to be clear," he warned Douglas, "that on both sides more radical elements are taking control."[107] The great American consensus—built on a postwar ideology of corporate liberalism at home and unprecedented imperial strength abroad—seemed to be coming undone.

He was now even pessimistic on the prospects for achieving some kind of test-ban accord with the Soviets. So, when Rusk asked him early that summer if he would be willing to go to Moscow in a final attempt to negotiate a test-ban treaty with Khrushchev, McCloy turned him down flat. He said he was planning an Aegean cruise with his daughter and suggested that Rusk send Harriman in his place.[108] He thought, in fact, that the timing of such negotiations was all wrong. "Mr. Khrushchev is just about to go into a plenary session of the Soviet Council and next month he has the Chinese confrontation in Moscow," he wrote Lew Douglas by way of explanation. "I do not think, in the light of either of these events, that he is apt to make any new concessions now and there is absolutely no chance of effecting an agreement on the basis of three on-site inspections which is all that he will now agree to."[109]

He was wrong. Harriman arrived in Moscow in July and discovered that Khrushchev was willing to sign a partial agreement banning nuclear explosions underground, in the sea, or in outerspace. Within two weeks, Harriman had the initialed treaty in his pocket and was on his way home. It was a diplomatic coup that greatly pleased the president, and one that by all rights could have belonged to McCloy. He always thought, with good reason, that he had laid the foundation for the Atmospheric Test Ban Treaty during his negotiations with the Soviets in the previous two years.

Ironically, instead of negotiating with Khrushchev that summer, McCloy found himself once again across the table from Gamal Abdel Nasser. When Rusk had learned that McCloy intended to take his daughter, Ellen, and one of her college classmates on an Aegean cruise, he persuaded him to take a detour into Cairo and Tel Aviv.[110] So again McCloy tried to cajole Nasser into abandoning his missile program, this time with the promise that he would ask the same thing of the Israelis. Nasser seemed a little more receptive now, but when McCloy saw Israeli leaders in Jerusalem, he found them unimpressed with the whole idea. Once more he returned empty-handed from the Middle East.

In his absence, *The New York Times* had announced that President Kennedy had named him and some thirty other individuals as recipients of the nation's highest civilian honor, the Freedom Medal. Describing him as a "diplomat and public servant, banker to the world, and Godfather to German freedom," Kennedy said, "He has brought cheerful wisdom and steady effectiveness to the tasks of war and peace." Other recipients of the Freedom Medal that year were such old friends as Felix Frankfurter, Alexander Meiklejohn, Robert Lovett, Jean Monnet, and Ralph Bunche. The *Times* reported that Kennedy would personally award the medals at a ceremony scheduled for December 6, 1963.[111]

On the morning of November 22, 1963, McCloy had breakfast with Dwight Eisenhower, and shortly afterward heard the news from Dallas. The young president he had served in so many different ways was dead.

Early the next morning, he cabled Lyndon Johnson that he was "stunned and shocked at the terrible loss to the nation. . . . If I can do anything to help, you know I am available."[112]

BOOK VI

LBJ's Wise Man

1

McCloy's strong-willed mother, Anna, was widowed when he was only six years old. She went to work as a hairdresser for the well-to-do families living on the right side of Philadelphia's "Chinese Wall." It was a social barrier Anna was determined her son would cross.

2

[ABOVE, RIGHT] She insisted on young Jack's getting a private education, first at the Peddie Institute in Hightstown, New Jersey, and later at Amherst College. McCloy as a freshman at Amherst in 1916, flanked by Theodore Edwards (left) and Amzi Hoffman (right).

3

While at Amherst, McCloy joined the Plattsburg military preparedness movement. His World War I identity card records First Lieutenant McCloy's middle initial as "S," for Snader, his mother's maiden name, but by that time he had already begun to call himself John Jay McCloy, renaming himself after his father. (The "black eye" is an ink splotch on the card.)

McCloy sat in the back of the Harvard Law School class of Felix Frankfurter (left), while Dean Acheson (right) was a "front-row boy." Years later, McCloy became Frankfurter's eyes and ears in the War Department.

4

5

Two of McCloy's clients from the investment banking firm of Kuhn, Loeb—Otto H. Kahn (left) and Benjamin J. Buttenwieser (right)—testifying before the Senate in the 1930s. The Senate investigating committee criticized McCloy's role in handling the bankruptcy of various railroads in the 1920s and '30s, while Buttenwieser admitted taking profits on insider trading. McCloy complained that the New Deal investigations of Wall Street were fanning the fires of class resentment.

6

In July 1916, a thousa[nd] tons of munitions exploded on Black Tor[m] Island in New York Harbor. In 1939, after nine years of sleuthing, McCloy proved that German secret agents had been responsible. The case convinced McCloy and many oth[er] Americans of the need for "an efficient counter-espionage system in time of peac[e] as well as war."

[RIGHT] As War Secretary Henry L. Stimson's (left) favorite troubleshooter, McCloy (right) "got his nose into everything," handling such issues as Lend-Lease legislation, war production planning, the use of Magic and Ultra intelligence intercepts, and deciding where and when to open up a second front against Nazi-occupied Europe.

7

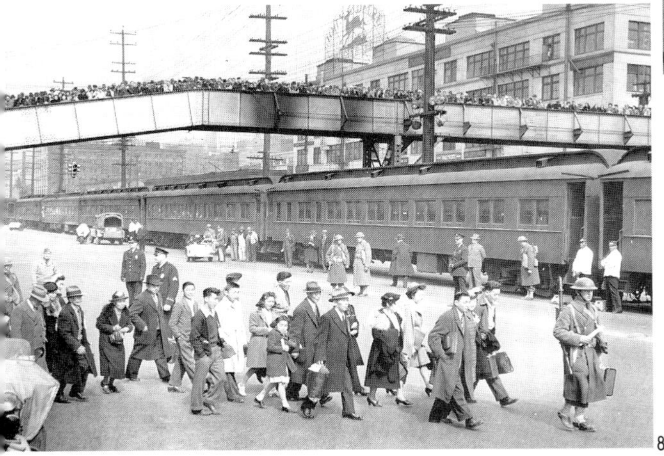

Fears of sabotage convinced McCloy of the necessity of interning more than one hundred thousand Japanese Americans in 1942: "if it is a question of safety of the country . . . why the Constitution is just a scrap of paper to me."

8

Stimson called McCloy (left) and Robert A. Lovett (right) his two "Imps of Satan." Like other Wall Street lawyers and investment bankers such as Averell Harriman, James Forrestal, Lewis Strauss, and "Wild Bill" Donovan, McCloy and Lovett emerged from World War II as part of an identifiable Establishment, "Stimsonians" dedicated to building a Pax Americana.

9

10

General George S. Patton (left) and Assistant Secretary of War McCloy (right) on the Italian front in 1943. The press created a furor when Patton slapped a soldier. After that, McCloy wrote General Eisenhower, "Lincoln's remark when they got after Grant comes to mind when I think of Patton—'I can't spare this man—he fights.' "

11

McCloy and his wife, Ellen, with their five-year-old son, Johnny, commissioning a new troopship in 1943.

12

13

[ABOVE] Lieutenant General Mark Clark (left) and Secretary of the Treasury Henry Morgenthau (right) on the Italian front in late 1943. McCloy and Morgenthau argued over the Treasury secretary's postwar plans for a pastoral, demilitarized Germany, and Morgenthau once went so far as to call McCloy an "oppressor of the Jews" because the assistant secretary was reluctant to divert any military resources away from the war effort to the rescue of European Jewry.

[LEFT] In the Bavarian Alps, July 1945, with his nephew, Lieutenant James Stuart Douglas. The fishing party also included General of the Army George C. Marshall, Field Marshal Bernard Montgomery, General Omar Bradley, and General Walter Bedell Smith, Eisenhower's chief of staff.

14

15

[ABOVE] At the Potsdam Conference in July 1945, McCloy and Stimson, pictured here standing to the left of General George S. Patton during the playing of "The Star-Spangled Banner," tried to persuade a new and inexperienced president, Harry Truman, that the war against Japan was over.

[ABOVE, RIGHT] But following the advice of Secretary of State James F. Byrnes, Truman ordered the atomic bombing of Hiroshima without either the specific warning or the redefinition of the surrender terms that McCloy believed would have ended the war weeks earlier.

[RIGHT] After Hiroshima, Truman sent McCloy out to Tokyo, where he got into a shouting match with the new proconsul of occupied Japan, General Douglas MacArthur. "I fought to get my words in and by sheer might and main succeeded."

16

17

[ABOVE] In 1949, Truman (left) made McCloy proconsul of occupied Germany. Dean Acheson (right) instructed McCloy to solve the "German problem" by building a West German state firmly aligned with NATO, even if this meant an end to de-Nazification and eventual rearmament.

[RIGHT] While McCloy ruled Germany, his brother-in-law, Lewis Douglas (wearing his trademark eyepatch), served as Truman's ambassador in London.

[BELOW] The two men worked closely with General Dwight Eisenhower (left), Secretary of Defense Robert A. Lovett (center), and W. Averell Harriman (right) in building the Atlantic alliance. In the end, McCloy believed, "We made unthinkable another European civil war."

18

19

20

22

[ABOVE, LEFT] The McCloys became occupied Germany's "first family." Ellen McCloy stands behind the high commissioner, who had broken his ankle while skiing a week earlier.

[ABOVE, RIGHT] At Munich Town Hall, McCloy downs a huge stein of beer in support of Bavarian export week. While encouraging the reconstruction of the German economy, McCloy sometimes had to fight back his "revulsions." He once angrily lectured a group of German industrialists, "remember the war and all the misery that followed it . . . was born and bred in German soil. . . . Don't weep in your beer."

[LEFT] Germany was then the anvil of the Cold War. East German communists parade with a caricature of McCloy dictating orders to West German Chancellor Konrad Adenauer.

23

24

25

[ABOVE, LEFT] McCloy, flanked by his son Johnny and daughter Ellen, walks through Rothenburg, the medieval walled city he saved from Allied bombardment during the war.

[ABOVE, RIGHT] McCloy's press agent, former *New York Times* man Shepard Stone, helps McCloy kick off a football game against a team of newspaper correspondents. McCloy's "Hicoggers" beat the writers 10–0.

[LEFT] McCloy's prep school coach always told him to "run with the swift." Tennis became his game, and he once beat Wimbledon champion "Big Bill" Tilden in one set. Here, McCloy is on the court with Gussie Moran, another Wimbledon pro.

26

[LEFT] Alfried Krupp was convicted of war crimes at Nuremburg. In 1951, McCloy granted Krupp clemency and restored his private fortune. A shocked Eleanor Roosevelt wrote McCloy: "Why are we freeing so many Nazis?"

27

[ABOVE] Chancellor Konrad Adenauer (right, with W. Averell Harriman and McCloy) was a cold, aloof man, "full of distrust." But McCloy and "Der Alte"—the Old Man—became the closest of allies.

[LEFT] By the time McCloy and his family returned to New York in 1952, the "German problem" had been solved, and Germany would remain divided for another thirty-seven years.

28

29

[ABOVE AND LEFT] As chairman of Chase Bank, McCloy—flanked by David Rockefeller (left), George Champion, and Stewart J. Baker—turned the Rockefeller-dominated bank into the second largest bank in the country by merging it with the Bank of Manhattan in 1955 to form Chase Manhattan Bank. Afterward, he went fly-fishing.

[BELOW] During Eisenhower's presidency, McCloy served as Ike's private secretary of state, providing a counterpoint to the hard-line Cold War views of John Foster Dulles (right).

30

31

32

[RIGHT] President-elect John F. Kennedy wanted McCloy as his Treasury or defense secretary, but McCloy consented to serve only as his disarmament adviser. [BELOW] Accompanied by his two "Ellens," McCloy arrived back in New York in July 1961 after negotiating with Nikita Khrushchev about Berlin and nuclear disarmament.

33

34

[RIGHT] During the Cuban missile crisis, Kennedy assigned McCloy to work with U.N. Ambassador Adlai Stevenson (left) in negotiating an end to the crisis. Afterward, Soviet diplomat Vasily Kuznetsov warned McCloy, "The Soviet Union is not going to find itself in a position like this ever again."

[RIGHT] After Kennedy's assassination, President Lyndon Johnson appointed McCloy to the Warren Commission. lcCloy thought it important to "show e world that America is not a banana republic, where a government can be hanged by conspiracy." Despite some doubts, he brokered the compromise language that allowed the commissioners to conclude unanimously that Lee Harvey Oswald was probably the sole assassin. McCloy (right) is pictured with Senator John Cooper (left) and Commission investigator David Belin (center) in front of the xas School Book Depository in Dallas.

[BELOW] McCloy (far left) watches as Chief Justice Earl Warren hands the Commission's report to President Johnson in the fall of 1964.

37

[ABOVE] Lyndon Johnson continued to seek McCloy's counsel. Although he initially supported the president's Vietnam policies, by 1968, McCloy had grown weary of the war. He also served as Johnson's secret emissary to the Middle East. Here, he reports to Johnson about his latest secret talks with Egypt's Gamal Abdel Nasser.

[BELOW] As chairman of the President's Advisory Committee on Arms Control and Disarmament, McCloy meets with President Richard M. Nixon. Lucius D. Clay, Thomas E. Dewey, and Dean Acheson (left to right) were the other committee members. McCloy clashed with Henry Kissinger over the decision to place multiple warheads on American missiles.

38

39

[ABOVE] Well into his eighties, McCloy continued to advise presidents. Here he presents Jimmy Carter with a gift in the early days of Carter's presidency. Together with David Rockefeller and Henry Kissinger, McCloy would organize a private lobbying campaign, code-named "Project Alpha," to convince the Carter administration to give the shah of Iran asylum in 1979.

[BELOW] David Rockefeller and Richard Nixon congratulate McCloy on his ninetieth birthday at a party thrown by the Chase Manhattan Bank.

40

41

42

[ABOVE, LEFT AND RIGHT] McCloy loved the outdoors all his life and took great pleasure in introducing his grandchildren to fishing and hunting. McCloy and his son flank John Jay McCloy III in 1975, and McCloy in the field with his youngest grandson, Rush Middleton McCloy, 1986.

[RIGHT] McCloy with Ronald Reagan at the White House Rose Garden celebration of his ninetieth birthday, at which he was also made an honorary citizen of Germany.

43

CHAPTER 25

The Warren Commission, a Brazil Coup, Egypt Again, and the 1964 Election

"The Commission is going to be criticized . . . no matter what we do. . . ."

JOHN J. MCCLOY, 1963

On November 24, Lee Harvey Oswald was himself shot dead before a live television audience. A shocked and grieving nation instinctively suspected a conspiracy had taken the life of John Kennedy. As McCloy later told CBS's Eric Sevareid, "Here the President was shot, and a couple of days later the fellow that shot him was killed. It was a strange sort of thing."[1] Lyndon Johnson knew that such suspicions could quickly diminish his authority. "I became President," Johnson later told his chosen biographer. "But for millions of Americans I was still illegitimate, a naked man with no presidential covering, a pretender to the throne, an illegal usurper."[2] It was soon learned that Oswald had been a self-proclaimed Marxist and had once defected to the Soviet Union. His killer, Jack Ruby, was the owner of a strippers' bar in Dallas and boasted years of associations with mobsters in Chicago, Dallas, New Orleans, and Miami. And all of this had taken place in Lyndon Johnson's Texas, a hotbed of anti-Catholic, antiliberal, and anti-Kennedy passions. Not even the new president was exempt from suspicion.[3]

Before Kennedy was even buried, both Senate and House committees announced their intention to investigate the assassination. On top of this, the FBI, the Dallas police, and the Texas attorney general were all beginning their own independent investigations. Johnson was well aware that such multiple investigations might only entrench the country's skepticism by coming to different conclusions as to what happened on November 22, 1963. He felt he had quickly to persuade most Americans that whatever had happened in Dallas was finished. A single investigation, carried out swiftly by a blue-ribbon presidential commission, was most likely to dispel the country's worries. Eugene Rostow, then a professor at Yale Law School, first suggested the idea to Johnson on the day Oswald was killed. Abe Fortas, Dean Rusk, and Joe Alsop gave him the same advice.[4]

Johnson recalled that the last time a shocking event had so disrupted the nation's collective psychic had been in the aftermath of the surprise attack on Pearl Harbor. Many Americans had then suspected Franklin Roosevelt of having foreknowledge of the Japanese attack, a conspiratorial theory laid to rest by a presidential commission led by Supreme Court Justice Owen Roberts. To Johnson's mind, there could be no better choice to lead a similar investigation than the chief justice of the Supreme Court, Earl Warren. The chief justice, however, didn't want the job. The president only persuaded him to serve when he insisted that it was a matter of war and peace. No one but the country's highest judicial officer, Johnson said, could "dispel these rumors." Otherwise, "if the public became aroused against Castro and Khrushchev, there might be war."[5] And, to turn the screws a bit more, the president claimed that the other commissioners he had selected—John McCloy, Allen W. Dulles, Representative Gerald R. Ford, Representative Hale Boggs, Senator Richard B. Russell, and Senator John Sherman Cooper—had only agreed to serve if Warren chaired the Commission.[6]

In fact, only after wheedling a reluctant promise from Warren to chair the Commission did Johnson approach McCloy. As a Republican who had served Kennedy, the Milbank, Tweed lawyer was an ideal choice.[7] Johnson's chief behind-the-scenes adviser, Abe Fortas, suggested McCloy's name.[8] Fortas had known McCloy ever since their occasional tiffs during World War II over the internment of the Japanese Americans. He was also aware of McCloy's prewar detective work on the Black Tom case. In addition to everything else that McCloy symbolized—bipartisanship, a deep and long familiarity with the law, and a reputation for sound and sober judgment in serving four previous presidents—his Black Tom credentials made him peculiarly suited for the purpose at hand. Later, the famed trial lawyer Louis Nizer, in a preface for Doubleday's 1964 unabridged version of the Commission's final report, cited McCloy's role during the 1930s in unmasking "German secret agents" as evidence that "if there was conspiratorial chicanery [in the Kennedy assassination], he could cast an experienced eye on the scene."[9]

Early in the Commission's deliberations, in fact, McCloy demonstrated that he was the one man most inclined to look for the threads of a conspiracy. Allen Dulles opened one early Commission meeting by passing out copies of a ten-year-old book about seven previous attempts on the lives of various presidents. The author argued that presidential assassins typically are misfits and loners. Dulles told his colleagues, ". . . you'll find a pattern running through here that I think we'll find in this present case." To this McCloy retorted, "The Lincoln assassination was a plot."[10] And when Chief Justice Warren announced at the first meeting that he didn't think it would be necessary for the Commission to request subpoena powers, McCloy convinced his colleagues that without such investigative powers the Commission's credibility would be "somewhat impaired."[11]

But if his Black Tom experience thirty years earlier prepared him temperamentally to ferret out any conspiracy, circumstances did not favor the exercising of these investigative instincts. There was neither the time nor the political will to conduct a thorough investigation. McCloy acknowledged these political pressures during the commissioners' very first meeting, on December 5, 1963, when he muttered something about how the Commission had been "set up to lay the dust . . . not only in the United States but all over the world. It is amazing the number of telephone calls I have gotten from abroad."[12] He was disturbed by how many of his friends in Europe assumed that some kind of conspiracy was behind the assassination. He thought it was important to "show the world that America is not a banana republic, where a government can be changed by conspiracy."[13] On the other hand, he, of all the commissioners, was best equipped to know that an investigation that really intended to establish the truth or nontruth of a larger conspiracy would require more than a few months. It had taken him nine years to prove the Black Tom conspiracy. It would be that much harder to prove the *absence* of a conspiracy. "The Commission," he said in that first meeting, "is going to be criticized . . . no matter what we do. . . ."[14]

Neither the country nor the president could wait nine years for an exhaustive investigation. Johnson wanted the Commission's conclusions published before the November 1964 elections, and so a deadline was set for all drafts of the report to be completed by June 1. Despite this looming deadline, the Commission was slow to gear up. They met twice in a room in the National Archives during December 1963, but there was not another meeting until the third week of January. This delay worried an impatient McCloy. One evening, over dinner with John McCone, he told the CIA director that he feared with the passage of time "trails [of evidence] will be lost." He thought the commissioners should be interviewing witnesses right away and asked McCone to see if he could get the president to exert a little pressure on Chief Justice Warren. The next day, McCone wrote a short note to Johnson recommending that he call the chief justice.[15]

To be fair, Warren was already working hard to assemble a staff. Because each of the commissioners had a full-time job, the bulk of the actual investigative work would have to be done by a team of lawyers. But many of these lawyers came from prestigious firms and could give only part of their time to the Commission. The lawyers did not begin their actual investigations until March, leaving themselves with only three months to interview witnesses and write their reports. The commissioners themselves regarded their commitment to the investigation as a part-time responsibility. McCloy attended only sixteen out of the fifty-one formal sessions and heard fewer than half of the witnesses who testified.[16]

He had a number of weighty business affairs on his mind when he began working on the assassination investigation. In their very first meeting, McCloy told Chief Justice Warren that he had "a terrific schedule, it's just piled up at this time."[17] The next day, at noon, he went to the White House to receive his Freedom Medal from Johnson in the State Dining Room. Then he flew to London for a day, to give a major address attacking the rise of European nationalism and its Gaullist manifestations in particular for undermining the Atlantic alliance.

Upon his return to New York, he began to prepare for a business trip to Brazil he had scheduled for later in the month. One of Milbank, Tweed's corporate clients, the M. A. Hanna Mining Company, the largest producer of iron ore in the country, was facing some serious legal difficulties in Brazil. George Humphrey, Hanna's chief executive officer, and a man McCloy knew as Eisenhower's Treasury secretary, wanted him to see what he could do to protect Hanna's Brazilian investments. Two years earlier, a left-of-center government led by President João Goulart had issued an expropriation decree against Hanna's iron-ore concession. Humphrey had appealed the decree, but by the autumn of 1963 it looked as if the Brazilian federal courts would uphold the nationalization.[18] In the late 1950s, Humphrey had paid no more than $8 million to acquire the mineral rights to one of the richest Brazilian concessions, and he was desperate to retain this concession.[19]

In late September, he sent his right-hand man, Jack W. Buford, to Washington to explain how serious matters had become. Buford told the State Department that the whole conflict had now entered the "political arena." Pointing to the "constant agitation and activity against Hanna on the part of the Communists and leftist elements in Brazil," Buford said the "United States must now stand and be counted." By referring to the "close past collaboration of Hanna with conservative and military groups in Brazil," he hinted that the company was preparing to intervene directly in the country's political contest.[20]

Despite this blunt language, Humphrey and Buford feared that their appeal to Washington for some kind of intervention was not being heard. So, on the recommendation of a mutual friend, Leo Model, a Wall Street investment banker with close ties to Rothschild interests, Buford went to see McCloy. He immediately recognized that McCloy had "a little more 'oomph' than the usual lawyer."[21]

McCloy quickly set about educating himself on the situation by seeing all the appropriate officials at the State Department, the World Bank, the IMF, and the CIA. As it happened, one of the men he had worked with in Germany after the war, Lincoln Gordon, was now the U.S. ambassador to Brazil. Gordon was back in Washington temporarily that week and gave McCloy his own highly pessimistic assessment of the situation.[22] He told him things were so bad that contingency planning for a coup had begun as early as September 1963.[23]

In preparation for the worst, McCloy set up a channel of communication between the CIA and Hanna's man, Buford. Thereafter, whenever Buford returned from one of his frequent trips to Rio de Janeiro, he would drive out to the CIA's headquarters in Langley, Virginia, for a debriefing. According to Buford, McCloy also arranged for him to meet periodically with the CIA station chief in Rio. "Through this fellow," recalled Buford, "we had many, many meetings with the military people who were opposing Goulart behind the scenes."[24]

Goulart had forged a broad political alliance with the left. But he was far from being a communist. A large landowner, Goulart was described by Colonel Vernon Walters, the U.S. military attaché in Rio, as "basically a good man with a guilty conscience for being rich."[25] And as long as he was in power, McCloy thought it was worth the effort to try to strike a deal with him. In late November, he told Harriman that he thought Humphrey "should face the new trends" and invite the Brazilians to negotiate some kind of joint participation in Hanna's mining concessions.[26]

But as political tensions rose, Hanna became an obvious target for anti-American sentiment. In January, signs began to appear in city streets that read, "Out with Hanna. . . ."[27] Passions were such that the Goulart government went to great lengths to ensure that McCloy's arrival in Rio on February 28 received no publicity. The next day, he met with President Goulart.

The Brazilian president was actually looking forward to meeting the famous American. He was so curious to learn what McCloy had to say about the Kennedy assassination that it was some time before Hanna's troubles were discussed. But then McCloy pulled two proposals out of his suit pocket. Plan "A" guaranteed that, if Hanna was allowed to mine the Minas Gerais iron-ore fields, the company would make a $18-million investment in the construction of a modern ore-and-coal maritime terminal on the Brazilian coast. Alternatively, Plan "B" proposed that Hanna lease at a nominal cost 50 percent of its current iron-ore reserves to a new joint-venture company of which Hanna would have a minority share. In either case, Hanna retained control of the majority of its iron-ore reserves, while the government could advertise either deal as a major American concession. Goulart bought this pitch and agreed that a six-man committee of Hanna and government representatives could commence detailed negotiations in a week.[28]

By the time McCloy boarded a Pan Am flight back to the United States, his presence in Rio had been detected. One pro-Goulart newspaper reported that McCloy, "considered the highest asset of the American government in any international deal," was in Rio. In another article, headlined "The Great Negotiator," readers were told that McCloy was insisting on "taking back that which belongs exclusively to our people. . . . The main thing in this fight is not to give up what is legitimately ours. . . . Even if conversations are carried out by the great expert in negotiations, McCloy."[29]

Despite this negative publicity, he left hoping that he had brokered a deal both acceptable to Hanna and politically palatable to the Brazilians. A few days later, Harriman told him that he "had heard that he did a good job." McCloy replied that he "didn't know yet whether they were out of the woods."[30] Three days later, the political landscape changed dramatically when Goulart, addressing a mammoth leftist rally, announced the expropriation of all private oil refineries and some landholdings. The Brazilian right-wing opposition responded by organizing a counterdemonstration. Rhetoric on all sides escalated, and many private citizens, including Hanna's American employees in Brazil, began arming themselves.[31] The political crisis was such that no further progress was made on the tentative agreement worked out by McCloy in early March.

Hanna officials were now very worried. Back in their Cleveland headquarters, Humphrey and Buford considered sending McCloy down to Rio once again. But McCloy knew from his contacts in the intelligence community that the time for deal-making was over. On March 27, 1964, Colonel Walters cabled Washington that General Castello Branco had "finally accepted [the] leadership" of the anti-Goulart "plotters."[32] Three days later, he told Ambassador Gordon that a military coup was "imminent."[33] The following morning, Washington's contingency plan for a Brazilian coup, code-named Operation Brother Sam, was activated as a

U.S. naval-carrier task force was ordered to station itself off the Brazilian coast. Well before the coup began, the Brazilian generals were told that the U.S. Navy would provide them with both arms and scarce oil.[34]

The Goulart regime, however, collapsed so quickly that the protracted civil war predicted by the CIA on March 31 never developed.[35] The generals who planned and executed the coup did not need the arms or oil supplies waiting for them off the coast. Hanna Mining Company, in fact, ended up giving the generals more direct assistance than did Operation Brother Sam. The initial army revolt occurred in Minas Gerais, the state in which Hanna had its mining concession. When these troops began marching on Rio, some of them rode in Hanna trucks.[36] In Rio itself, Jack Buford was in constant touch with the local CIA station chief, who kept him informed by phone on Goulart's movements.[37]

McCloy was back in New York when the coup occurred, but he and his Hanna clients were tremendously relieved at this turn of events. As *Fortune* magazine put it, "For Hanna, the revolt that overthrew Goulart . . . arrived like a last minute rescue by the First Cavalry."[38] The generals who now ruled the country soon saw to it that Hanna's concession was restored.

The 1964 Brazilian coup marked a turning point for U.S. policy in Latin America. The Johnson administration had made clear its willingness to use its muscle to support any regime whose anticommunist credentials were in good order.[39] Later that year, millions of dollars were funneled by the CIA to influence the Chilean elections. And the following year, President Johnson intervened with troops in the Dominican Republic to oust a similar left-of-center government. In Brazil, thousands of citizens were arbitrarily arrested, many newspapers were closed down, and press censorship was imposed. But one had to be understanding, Ambassador Gordon told Dean Rusk only a week after the coup, because there had been a "very narrow escape from Communist-dominated dictatorship."[40] For McCloy, it was just a matter of creating the right kind of business climate. As he explained to the regime's new leader, General Castello Branco, he had agreed to represent Hanna "only because he was convinced that such an arrangement would be in the public interest—of benefit to Brazil and to Brazilian-American relations as well as to the company."[41] What was good for Hanna was good for Brazil and its relations with Washington.

Throughout late 1963 and early '64, Brazil was a mere sideshow on McCloy's calendar. The main event was his frustrating experience on the Warren Commission. By mid-December 1963, a number of things had already prejudiced the assassination probe. Various arms of the federal bureaucracy had made up their minds on the basic facts. Only two hours after Oswald was shot on November 24, J. Edgar Hoover phoned the White House and left a message for Johnson: "The thing I am most concerned about . . . is having something issued so we can convince the public that Oswald is the real assassin."[42] Hoover ordered his men to concentrate exclusively on making the case against Oswald as the lone assassin.[43] Without wasting any time, on December 9, Hoover handed the commissioners the FBI's Summary Report on the assassination. It concluded that Oswald had acted alone in firing three shots at the presidential party, two of which hit Kennedy and one of which hit Governor John Connally.[44]

In describing the president's wounds, the report said that one of the bullets had entered "just below his shoulder" at a downward angle of forty-five to sixty degrees. It had penetrated to a distance of less than a finger length, and there was no point of exit. Furthermore, the bullet was not in his body.[45] The report described the fatal head wound but made no mention at all of the wound in the front of Kennedy's neck.

Almost immediately, the commissioners saw some major problems with the FBI Summary Report. Its description of the entry wound in the president's shoulder as being nearly six inches below the base of the neck flatly contradicted the Bethesda Naval autopsy report submitted by Dr. James J. Humes. The navy autopsy had placed this same entry wound at the base of the neck, high enough for the bullet to have exited through the wound at the front of Kennedy's neck. If the FBI description of the shoulder wound was correct, the bullet could not have entered Kennedy at a 40-percent downward angle and then climbed enough to exit through the front of his neck.

When the commissioners sat down behind closed doors to discuss the FBI's conclusions, McCloy said, "Let's find out about these wounds, it is just as confusing now as could be. It left my mind muddy as to what really did happen. . . . Why did the F.B.I. report come out with something which isn't consistent with the autopsy when we finally see the autopsy?"[46] He also couldn't understand why there was no mention of Governor Connally's wounds. The evidence as to how the bullets hit Kennedy, he said, "is looming up as the most confusing thing that we've got."[47] At this point, McCloy was not ruling out a second assassin. He said he wanted to go to the Dallas assassination site "to see if it is humanly possible for him [Kennedy] to have been hit in the front. . . ."[48]

But even as they complained about the report, the commissioners found reasons to excuse the FBI's behavior. "It does leave you some loopholes in this thing," McCloy said, "but I think you have to realize they put this thing together very fast."[49] What McCloy didn't know was that the FBI chief was withholding evidence from the Commission. Hoover had been unhappy that Johnson had even appointed an outside body to investigate the assassination. He regarded the Commission as a threat to the Bureau, particularly since he was soon informed that the Bureau's handling of the Oswald case in the months prior to the assassination could be severely criticized. Among other things, soon after the assassination the FBI ordered one of its agents to destroy a threatening note written to the Bureau by Oswald just a few weeks before the assassination.[50] In addition, Hoover had conducted his own internal investigation of why Oswald hadn't been listed on the FBI's Security Index, a list of more than twenty thousand potentially disloyal citizens. On December 10, he was told that Oswald should have been on the list, and that the FBI's investigation of Oswald should have escalated when the Bureau learned from the CIA that Oswald had made an appointment to see a KGB officer in the Soviet Embassy in Mexico less than two months prior to the assassination. An angry Hoover immediately acted upon this internal report by disciplining seventeen FBI agents, including William Sullivan, the assistant director. But this action was to remain secret, since Hoover felt that, if the Bureau's deficient handling of the Oswald case became known, the FBI's reputation would be compromised.[51] Indeed, Hoover believed there was "no question" that the Bureau "failed in carrying through some of the most salient aspects of the Oswald investigation."[52] But he was not about to admit this to the Warren Commission. Instead, he withheld information critical of the Bureau's handling of Oswald. And just in case the Commission began to attack the Bureau, he asked his men to dig out "all derogatory material on Warren Commission members and staff contained in FBI files."[53] Finally, he did everything he could to find out how its investigation was being conducted. To this end, an obliging Congressman Ford soon began giving confidential briefings to the FBI on the commissioners' top-secret deliberations.[54]

The FBI was not the only agency withholding information from the Commission. The CIA had numerous critical facts in its possession concerning the possible motives various foreign powers may have had to assassinate the president. Among other things, on the very day of Kennedy's murder a CIA agent had met in Paris with a Cuban official who claimed he was willing to assassinate Fidel Castro. The Cuban, whom the CIA later determined was probably a double agent, was actually given an assassination weapon, a poison pen with a hidden syringe.[55] This was only the most recent of numerous plots to kill Castro, but neither it nor any previous attempts were revealed to the Warren Commission. (Some of these CIA plots involved the use of various Mafia networks, a highly relevant fact given Jack Ruby's underworld associations.) Of course, one commissioner, Allen Dulles, was aware that the Agency had targeted Castro during his tenure as Director of Central Intelligence (DCI). Whether he shared this information with McCloy or any of the other commissioners is not known. Like everyone else, McCloy knew that both the Eisenhower and Kennedy administrations had wanted to destroy

Castro's regime, and in his mind this alone might have given Castro reason to retaliate.[56] But, given Oswald's defection to the Soviet Union, he also thought the accused assassin may have been recruited by the KGB. He had talked about the case with Ellen, who thought it "pretty suspicious" that Oswald had found it so easy to obtain an exit visa from the Soviets for his Russian wife.[57] (Unknown to him at the time, a December 1963 CIA memo gave voice to the same speculation.[58]) Alternatively, he thought the possibility that Oswald may never have been a genuine defector, that he might have been sent to the Soviet Union by the CIA, was "a very realistic rumor" and worthy of investigation.[59] In short, he thought anything was possible.

This was underscored for him when, on the afternoon of January 22, 1964, he received an unexpected call from the Commission's newly appointed general counsel, J. Lee Rankin. The lawyer informed him that an emergency meeting had been scheduled for five o'clock that afternoon in the Veterans of Foreign Wars Building on Capitol Hill. Canceling his other appointments, McCloy flew down from New York and arrived just as the meeting began.[60] Taking his seat around an eight-foot oblong table with the other commissioners, McCloy heard Rankin report some shocking news: the Texas attorney general had just forwarded an allegation that Oswald had been an undercover agent of the FBI, that he had been paid $200 a month since September 1962, and that his agent number was 179.[61]

The commissioners were aware of the explosive nature of this news. Representative Ford later wrote, "I cannot recall attending a meeting more tense and hushed."[62] By the time they parted two and a half hours later, the commissioners had agreed that Rankin should with the greatest secrecy interview the Texas attorney general and report to the Commission on what he learned. Five days later, the commissioners met once again in the Veterans of Foreign Wars Building, where they now had taken over two floors of office space.

Rankin told them that the source of the allegation against the FBI was a Dallas reporter, and that the allegation probably could not be substantiated. "We do have a dirty rumor," he said, "that is very bad for the Commission. . . . It must be wiped out insofar as it is possible to do so by this Commission." But as they discussed the problem, it gradually dawned on the commissioners that this was something that was going to be very hard to disprove.

"This is going to build up," McCloy said. "In New York, I am already beginning to hear about it. I got a call from Time-Life about it. . . ." Dulles then interrupted to explain that if Oswald had been an FBI informant there might be no records of the fact, and if you interviewed the FBI agent who recruited him, he would be unlikely to admit the fact, even under oath.

"Wouldn't he tell it to his own chief?" McCloy asked.

"He might," Dulles replied, "or might not. . . . What I was getting at, I think under any circumstances, I think Mr. Hoover would say certainly he didn't have anything to do with this fellow. . . . You can't prove what the facts are."[63]

In other words, if Oswald had been on the FBI payroll, Hoover might not have known, or might lie about it. At this point, McCloy suggested that they either go to Hoover himself with the information or ask another intelligence agency to investigate the rumor. In the end, knowing that whatever course of action they took, the truth of the allegations could not be proved or disproved, the commissioners decided just to inform Hoover of the rumor. The FBI chief responded that there was nothing to it, and there the matter was allowed to rest.

The crisis passed, and though the allegations that Oswald had been an FBI informant were almost certainly false, the Commission's handling of the problem underscored a central dilemma in the conduct of its investigation. The Commission had two possibly contradictory purposes: it was supposed to expose the facts of the assassination, but the commissioners—and, indeed, most Americans—hoped the facts would reassure the nation that the assassination was the work of a lone gunman. What would happen if any of the "dirty rumors" were discovered to be true? Would the national interest be served if an unresolved conspiracy was all that could be known?

This first crisis also made it clear that, unless they took the time and expense to establish an independent team of investigators, the Commission would remain absolutely dependent on the FBI. McCloy pointed out the inherent problem of this dependency: "There is a potential culpability here on the part of the Secret Service and the FBI, and their reports, after all, human nature being what it is, may have some self-serving aspects in them."[64] But, again, the Commission decided to live with this problem.

By this time, McCloy was full of doubts about almost every aspect of the case. Even before the crisis over Oswald's alleged ties to the FBI, he had been brooding about the unresolved contradictions between the FBI's Summary Report and the Bethesda Naval Hospital's autopsy report on the president. Sometime in mid-January, he discussed these concerns with C. D. Jackson. The Time-Life executive had just bought the rights to an 8mm movie shot by Abraham Zapruder, a Dallas businessman who had chanced to catch most of the assassination sequence on film. Zapruder's film was to become a key piece of evidence for both the Commission and its critics in the years to come.

On January 20, 1964, Jackson sent McCloy a series of blown-up transparencies reproduced from Zapruder's film sequence of the assassination. In an accompanying note, he told McCloy, "Our scrutiny of these stills indicates one thing we did not notice when looking at the movie, and one other thing that you seemed to be in doubt about. I think there is no question but that the first shot actually took place behind the sign [a traffic sign that blocked Zapruder's view], inasmuch as the first frame of the car emerging from behind the sign shows Kennedy's hands just beginning to come up [to grasp his wounded throat]."[65]

McCloy's doubts were only heightened when he and the other commissioners viewed the Zapruder movie. As C. D. Jackson's transparencies made clear, the Zapruder film shows that Kennedy had already been shot once as he emerged from behind the traffic sign. But it also showed clearly enough that Governor Connally had not yet been wounded—or at least he had not yet reacted, even though his rib and his wrist bone were shattered. This suggested that Connally could not have been hit by the same bullet that wounded Kennedy in the neck. After viewing the film, McCloy had the following exchange with Allen Dulles:

". . . you would think," Dulles said, "if Connally had been hit at the same time [as Kennedy, he] would have reacted in the same way, and not reacted much later as these pictures show."

"That is right," said McCloy.

"Because the wounds would have been inflicted," Dulles said.

"That is what puzzles me," said McCloy.

McCloy later asked the doctor who had treated Connally's wounds whether the governor could have had a delayed reaction to the impact of the bullet. The doctor replied, "Yes, but in the case of a wound which strikes a bony substance such as a rib, usually the reaction is quite prompt."[66] (Connally later confirmed this view in his testimony before the Commission: he stated that it was his firm belief that he was hit after Kennedy and by a second bullet.)

The film was puzzling. When it was finally released in 1975, most viewers had the same reaction as McCloy and Dulles. Kennedy seems to have been shot first, and Connally wounded a second and a half later. This time frame seriously undermined a lone-gunman theory of the assassination, since the Commission had already established that Oswald's vintage 1940 bolt-action Italian rifle could not be fired more than once every 2.3 seconds. If Oswald was a lone assassin, the bullet he presumably fired through Kennedy's neck must also have hit Connally. If a single bullet was not responsible for the wounding of both men, there had to be a second assassin. McCloy and the other commissioners, some reluctantly, adopted the explanation that Connally had had a delayed reaction to his wounds. If Oswald was the lone assassin, he had fired three shots, one of which passed through both Kennedy and Connally.

This became the heart of the Warren Commission's conclusions. But to reach this verdict, the commissioners had to embrace the Bethesda Naval autopsy description of Kennedy's wounds and discount the FBI Summary Report. The latter placed the rear entry wound nearly six inches below the base of Kennedy's neck, too low for the bullet to have exited through the president's neck. This contradiction, and much of the ensuing controversy over the Commission's conclusions, could have been resolved by a look at some definitive evidence. Dozens of color photographs and X-rays were taken during the Bethesda autopsy, and a close inspection of these photos could have resolved the dispute.

But, in what was perhaps the Commission's major mistake, Chief Justice Warren decided, out of deference to the Kennedy family, not to allow the Commission access to the photos and X-rays. If such photos became a part of the record, Warren said, "it would make it a morbid thing for all time to come." McCloy agreed at the time with this decision, on condition that at least one commissioner, accompanied by a doctor, be allowed to inspect this critical evidence.[67] In the event, Warren reviewed the photos in private and then allowed the autopsy doctors to testify before the Commission without producing the material.[68] Just three years later, after a number of books throwing doubt on the Commission's conclusions had been published, McCloy told a television audience on "Face the Nation," "I think there's one thing I would do over again. I would insist on those photographs and the X-rays having been produced before us." He still believed the "best evidence" on the autopsy came from the sworn testimony of the naval doctors who conducted it. "We couldn't have interpreted the X-rays if we'd had them," he said. "But probably it would have been better to have had them for the sake of completeness in view of all the to-do that's occurred since."[69]

Fifteen years later, McCloy's retrospective assessment was confirmed by the House of Representatives' Select Committee on Assassinations. The Select Committee reopened the case in 1976–78 and made a point of having a medical panel examine the autopsy photos and X-rays. Although the panel reported that the entry wound in the back was two inches lower than claimed by the Warren Commission, it concluded that the wound was high enough to have allowed the bullet to exit from Kennedy's throat.[70] Obviously, if this information had been released in a clear and definitive fashion in 1964, the Warren Commission Report would have met with much less skepticism in subsequent years.

The controversy over the autopsy was only one of several issues that the Commission found troubling. As late as August 1964, just a few weeks before the report was submitted to President Johnson, the commissioners expressed skepticism about elementary pieces of evidence.[71] McCloy was startled one day to hear testimony from a Dallas police officer that he couldn't make a positive identification of Oswald's palm print on the alleged assassination rifle.[72] His frustration with the case mounted as he and his colleagues listened to a barrage of confusing and sometimes contradictory testimony. Some of the most curious statements concerned the "grassy knoll" to the right of the assassination site. Numerous witnesses swore they had heard shots fired from this direction, and some said they had seen puffs of smoke in the same location. Others claimed to have talked to men on the grassy knoll who had flashed Secret Service badges and told them to move on. But there had been no Secret Service personnel near the grassy knoll. As for the "puffs of smoke," McCloy knew from his knowledge of hunting rifles that modern ammunition was virtually smokeless: "There haven't been any 'puffs of smoke' like they say since the Gettysburg battle during the Civil War."[73]

Certainly the most intriguing story to come before the Commission involved an important Russian defector who had come to the United States in February 1964. At the time, Yuri Nosenko was the highest-ranking KGB officer to have crossed over to the West. He told his CIA debriefers that he had, coincidentally, seen Lee Harvey Oswald's KGB file, dating from his 1959 defection to Moscow. Nosenko reported that the KGB had never even debriefed Oswald, and, indeed, had never used him for operational purposes. If Nosenko's testimony was to be accepted, the KGB had nothing to do with Kennedy's accused assassin. But as the Warren Commission soon learned, there were many within the CIA who believed Nosenko was a disinformation agent, sent by the KGB to reassure the Americans that Oswald had not been their man. Placed in solitary confinement and relentlessly interrogated by the Agency's counterintelligence chief, James Jesus Angleton, Nosenko never changed his story. Angleton became obsessed with the Nosenko case; it seemed to him incredible that the KGB would not have debriefed an American defector with Oswald's credentials. As a radar operator in the Marines, Oswald had been stationed in Japan, where he had had access to classified information about the U-2 spy planes. Angleton and his allies within the Agency convinced Richard M. Helms, the CIA's deputy director for plans, that there were enough subtle inconsistencies in Nosenko's story to warrant his continued detention and interrogation.*

Helms—who had been designated the CIA's liaison to the Warren Commission—naturally became alarmed when he learned that the Commission intended to rely on Nosenko's story to exonerate the Soviets from any involvement in the assassination. So, one humid day in late June, he asked for a private meeting with Chief Justice Warren and told him that

*If Nosenko's story was true, it not only exonerated the KGB of any responsibility for Kennedy's murder, but also discredited the bona fides of another KGB defector, Anatoliy Golitsyn, who had been providing Angleton with information that in retrospect we know greatly inflated the operational capabilities of Soviet intelligence. Among other things, Golitsyn claimed the KGB possessed a master plan to infiltrate the West, and would send just such a "disinformation" agent as Nosenko to discredit Golitsyn. By 1964, Angleton was so ensnared in Golitsyn's web of paranoia that he had every reason to prevent Nosenko from testifying before the Warren Commission. In 1969, after five years of illegal imprisonment by the CIA, Nosenko was released, and his story is now accepted as true by most observers of the intelligence business.

the Agency could not vouch for Nosenko and did not want him to testify before the Commission. The chief justice reacted to this news with visible annoyance. He had been given to understand by J. Edgar Hoover that Nosenko's bona fides had checked out. Helms replied that he could only speak for the CIA, but that there was a division of opinion within his Agency over Nosenko. At this, Warren curtly thanked Helms, and later the same day the commissioners met behind closed doors to discuss this new problem.[74]

The minutes of this extraordinary meeting are still classified, but we know McCloy, for one, had all along thought there were legitimate reasons to suspect Oswald had some kind of relationship with Soviet intelligence. By the summer of 1964, Warren Commission lawyers William Coleman and David W. Slawson had concluded that Oswald probably began planning his defection while stationed in Japan. They pointed out that he could have established contact with Soviet agents through an active Japanese Communist Party.[75] After his defection, Oswald had lived in Minsk, next door to a school for training Soviet Army intelligence agents. He had been paid well by the Soviets and given a spacious apartment. He had married a Russian woman, whose uncle was an army-intelligence colonel. The Soviets had then allowed Oswald to redefect to the United States, together with his Russian bride. McCloy thought all of these facts suspicious. But neither he nor any of the Warren Commission's later critics concluded that the Soviets had sent Oswald to kill the president. Rather, if Oswald had been recruited, he may well have been sent back as a "sleeper," an agent instructed to lie low until activated in a crisis or for some specific operation. This theory did not rule out the possibility that Oswald was being used by more than one intelligence agency. Theoretically, he could have been recruited in the Marines as a sleeper for U.S. military intelligence or the CIA when he initially defected to the Soviets. The Soviets, suspicious of the genuineness of his defection, could have sent him back to the United States ostensibly as one of their own sleepers, but with the intention of feeding disinformation to his U.S. intelligence handlers.[76] Whomever he worked for, once he arrived in the United States, according to this theory, Oswald went awry and eventually acted alone in killing the president. If this is what happened, any or all of the intelligence agencies he ever had a relationship with would have been frantic to cover up their connection to him. It would also explain Nosenko's timely defection only two months after the assassination with the news that the KGB had nothing to do with Oswald. This was a line of speculation McCloy found plausible.[77]

He knew that in the business of intelligence one found many men of unsavory character. Earlier in the year, he had amused his colleagues on the Commission by observing, "Well, I can't say that I have run into a fellow comparable to Oswald, but I have run into some very limited mentalities in the CIA and FBI." Everyone laughed at this, and then Warren chimed in, "It almost takes that kind of man to do a lot of this intelligence work."[78] Neither McCloy nor the other commissioners were naïve men. They knew, to use one of McCloy's favorite words, that they were grappling with one of those "imponderables." The puzzle of Oswald's life would probably never be solved. All that really mattered now was to determine if there was enough evidence that Oswald had pulled the trigger.

None of the other evidence concerning Oswald's possible foreign connections could ever be verified. McCloy was impatient to have the Commission's report out, if only to "lay the dust," as he had said on the first day of their investigation. He was annoyed by the publicity generated by Mark Lane, an early conspiracy theorist, who had embarked on a lecture tour of Europe that spring. On the afternoon of April 30, 1964, McCloy told his fellow commissioners, ". . . Generally speaking, from the reports that come to me from all over Europe, what with Mr. Lane's visits over there—there is a deep-seated feeling that there is a deep conspiracy here. . . . Let's to the best of our ability search these out and attack them."[79]

Later that spring, McCloy and Allen Dulles went to Dallas to look at the scene of the murder.[80] The trip became a turning point for McCloy. Whereas before he had sometimes described himself as "a doubting Thomas," he came back from Dallas prepared to endorse the lone-assassin theory.[81] Oswald, he decided, fit the pattern of a "loner" rather than a "plotter."[82] He also reconciled his doubts about Connally's wounds and accepted that one of the three bullets fired from Oswald's rifle had hit both Kennedy and Connally.[83] Having made up his mind, McCloy was disappointed when the Commission decided it had to extend its deadline for submission of first-draft chapters of the report from June 1 to July 1. The "ugly rumors" in Europe would "spread like wildfire," he feared, if the publication of the report was delayed much longer.[84]

Adding to McCloy's concerns about the drift in European opinion was the fact that Senator Barry Goldwater seemed assured of being the Republican Party's presidential nominee in the November elections. Goldwater's foreign-policy views, particularly on the Atlantic alliance, were strongly isolationist. McCloy recognized that, from a European perspective, both the assassination and Goldwater's impending nomination cast doubt on America's ability to lead the Atlantic alliance. So, for the first time since the Willkie campaign in 1940, he became active in Republican Party politics. In late June, Drew Pearson reported that McCloy was "working backstage" for Goldwater's strongest remaining opponent, Governor William Scranton of Pennsylvania.[85] There was pressure for

McCloy to endorse Scranton, a political act he thought inappropriate for a man in his position. He was watching "Meet the Press" on July 12, 1964, when Scotty Reston asked Scranton why such men as McCloy and Lovett, who represented a certain high tradition in the Republican Party, had not come out forcefully against Goldwater. Scranton diplomatically replied that he knew McCloy and had a high regard for him, but that he didn't think it was appropriate for such a man to engage in party politics. As soon as the program was over, McCloy received a message from Scranton, and when he returned the call, Henry Kissinger came on the line and said he was speaking for the governor. Would McCloy help the Scranton campaign draft a platform plank on the control of nuclear weapons? McCloy said he would be happy to do this.[86] He would go that far, but he never allowed his name to be used at the convention in association with any "stop-Goldwater" effort.

By mid-July, it was too late: Goldwater's grass-roots organization of conservative Republicans easily gave him the nomination at San Francisco. Shortly after the convention, McCloy took a swing out to California and Illinois to gauge Goldwater's strength. He told Averell Harriman afterward that he had found evidence of "some nationalization of [the] Goldwater business. . . . Most of the businessmen were for him." He saw a real danger of an "overwhelming collapse of the [Republican] party."[87] He felt himself being dragged into partisan political matters, and he didn't like it. But he had already confessed in an earlier conversation with Harriman that "in the course of the campaign I may want to come out for the Democratic nominee. . . ."[88] Harriman called Mac Bundy, Johnson's national-security adviser, with this piece of political intelligence. He told Bundy that McCloy was "disturbed" and "almost ready to do anything within his dignity to help."[89] He advised Bundy, however, against organizing a "Republicans for Johnson" committee. McCloy would never have anything to do with something so publicly partisan. Instead, Harriman suggested that the White House get liberal and moderate Republicans like McCloy to sign on to an elite bipartisan committee. (McCloy wasn't the only distinguished Republican to feel so disaffected. Robert Lovett told McCloy he was going to vote for Johnson.[90])

Shortly before the Democratic convention in Atlantic City, Bundy took Harriman's advice. He wrote the president a memo entitled "Backing from the Establishment." Bundy has always disclaimed the existence of any "Establishment." But as the result of a satirical article by Richard Rovere in the May 1962 issue of *Esquire,* the term was in vogue among Bundy's circle of friends. Rovere had written that John Kenneth Galbraith, challenged to name the chairman of the Establishment, had by "sheer intuition" named John J. McCloy. The *Esquire* article had been written tongue in cheek; but even as men like Bundy had a good laugh reading Rovere's spoof, they had to admit that, as with all good satire, there was some truth in his description of a foreign-policy establishment.[91]

So, in all seriousness, Bundy told Lyndon Johnson, a man he knew to be profoundly self-conscious around "Eastern Establishment" types, that "the key to these people is McCloy." Bundy defined "these people" as "the very first team of businessmen, bankers et al." McCloy, he wrote, "is for us, but he is under very heavy pressure from Eisenhower and others to keep quiet. I have told him that this is no posture for a man trained by Stimson, and I think he agrees in his heart, but I also think that in the end the person to whom he will want to say 'yes' is you. He belongs to the class of people who take their orders from Presidents and nobody else." Bundy also told the president that he knew McCloy's personal choice for the vice-presidential spot was Senator Hubert Humphrey, and "if in fact that is your decision, you might make a lot of money by telling McCloy just before you tell the country."[92]

McCloy did think that Humphrey had "grown a great deal and has a good bit of sense."[93] There is no indication that the secretive Johnson let McCloy in on his choice of Humphrey as vice-president, but one can imagine him savoring the idea that the Establishment was closing ranks behind his campaign. Late in July, Harriman moved things along by planting a story idea with *New York Times* columnist C. L. Sulzberger. Why not urge the president to send Jack McCloy across the Atlantic to calm European concerns about both the assassination and Goldwater's nomination?[94] A week later, Sulzberger's widely read column reported, ". . . personalities high in the Government are giving serious thought to efforts to calm opinion in certain allied lands. There has been private talk of encouraging distinguished Republican moderates who do not sympathize with Senator Goldwater's more extreme views, to travel overseas during coming weeks and explain American realities and the underlying constancy of our national position." Sulzberger named McCloy as the ideal candidate for such a mission, not only because he was so "highly respected in Europe," but also because he was a member of the Warren Commission, "which is expected to lay the ghost of any suspicion Mr. Kennedy was killed by organized conspiracy."[95] In the event, McCloy was already too busy with other matters to take time off for a trip to Europe. (Unknown to Sulzberger, the president was talking to McCloy about a secret mission to the Middle East.)

Sulzberger may have expected the Warren Commission to bury all the "vicious speculation" about assassination plots, but even as he wrote his column, McCloy and the other commissioners were having trouble reaching consensus.[96] They discovered they were more or less evenly divided on such critical issues as the "single-bullet" theory. Russell, Boggs, and

Cooper had "strong doubts." McCloy, Ford, and Dulles felt no other theory could satisfactorily explain what had happened. When Russell said he would not sign a report that stated flatly that one of the bullets had hit both Kennedy and Connally, McCloy mediated a compromise. He told Russell that the Commission could not afford the luxury of issuing majority and minority reports. The country had to have a unanimous report. Reaching for his yellow legal pad, McCloy began to scribble out some alternative language: he suggested saying that there was "very persuasive evidence from the experts to indicate that the same bullet which pierced the President's throat also caused Governor Connally's wounds." However, Connally's testimony and "certain other factors have given rise to some difference of opinion as to this probability but there is no question in the mind of any member of the Commission that all the shots which caused the President's and Governor Connally's wounds were fired from the sixth floor window of the Texas School Book Depository."[97] This language acknowledged the doubts of Russell, Boggs, and Cooper, but made their dissent irrelevant to the critical issue of whether a lone gunman in the Book Depository was responsible for Kennedy's assassination. In the discussion that followed, which McCloy later called the "battle of the adjectives," Ford and Russell argued over McCloy's language. Ford wanted to strengthen the conclusion by saying that there was "compelling" evidence. Russell wanted to say only that there was "credible" evidence. In the end, they agreed to McCloy's description of "very persuasive evidence."[98]

McCloy also brokered the wording of the Commission's primary conclusion, that Oswald had acted alone. The staff's initial draft stated that there had been "no conspiracy." Ford suggested it say that the Commission had found "no evidence" of a conspiracy. McCloy's language was finally agreed upon: "Because of the difficulty of proving a negative to a certainty the possibility of others being involved with either Oswald or Ruby cannot be rejected categorically, but if there is any such evidence it has been beyond the reach of all investigative agencies and resources of the United States and has not come to the attention of this Commission."[99] This was lawyers' language, and it laid "the dust" on all the "ugly rumors" of conspiracy without forcing the Commission to make a categorical denial, to "prove a negative." On the other hand, McCloy's language is categorical in its assertion that any such evidence of a conspiracy was beyond its reach. The commissioners, after all, had expressed doubts about the full cooperation of the CIA and the FBI. They had admitted among themselves that, if Oswald had had any kind of relationship with a U.S. intelligence agency, that fact probably could not be proved. They had been told by the CIA's Richard Helms that the Agency could not vouch for the testimony offered by the KGB defector Yuri Nosenko, that Oswald was not a KGB asset. They knew that Oswald's career, from the time he joined the Marines, was filled with mystery. Similar problems arose in the Commission's final report in dealing with Jack Ruby's connections to organized crime, the one group in the country with an unequivocal motive to kill the brother of the attorney general.

The public, however, was not to be privy to these doubts. When the report was released in late September, the eight hundred–plus pages, based on twenty-six volumes of testimony and thousands of field interviews by the FBI and the Selective Service, seemed quite definitive. *The New York Times* called it "comprehensive and convincing."[100] But in the end, the long-term credibility of the report was undermined as much by what it said as by what it left out. Reasonable people still could have concluded that in all probability Lee Harvey Oswald alone fired the shots that killed Kennedy. But too many questions arose in the course of its investigation for the Commission to state this or any other conclusion with finality.*

Over the years, McCloy was distressed whenever doubts were raised about the Commission's central verdict, that Oswald had acted alone. But on occasion, some of the Commission's own members voiced such doubts. Senator Russell told the press in 1970, "I have never believed that Oswald planned that [the assassination] altogether by himself."[102] Lyndon Johnson himself privately told one of his aides in 1967 that "he was now convinced that there was a plot in connection with the assassination." The president suspected the CIA had "something to do with this plot."[103] As McCloy knew from his conversations with Johnson, the president had arrived at this conclusion when he was informed by the FBI of the CIA's plotting with the Mafia to assassinate Castro.[104] Later, McCloy told an interviewer of his own "frustration" with "the testimony of the C.I.A. before the Commission." He had a feeling the CIA could be telling the commissioners only "what they wanted us to hear."[105]

For McCloy, the experience had been an exercise in frustration, and it pained him that his attempts to construct a consensus both within the Commission and, through its report, with the public at large, had unraveled over the years. Instead of putting the whole tragic business behind the country, the Warren Commission Report unintentionally planted the seeds of an enduring controversy. As Arthur Schlesinger put it, the Kennedy assassination had become a "quagmire for historians."[106]

*Fifteen years later, the case was reinvestigated by the Select Committee on Assassinations of the House of Representatives. The Select Committee endorsed many of the Warren Commission's findings, but on the central question it concluded that Kennedy "was probably assassinated as a result of a conspiracy."[101] In the same breath, the Committee admitted it was "unable to identify the other gunman or the extent of the conspiracy." The Committee's evidence was hardly definitive, and its conclusions never won credibility with scholars of the assassination.

McCloy was in Cairo, waiting for an appointment with President Nasser, the day the Warren Commission Report was released. Johnson had sent him once again to use his charms on the Egyptian president in an effort to revive Egyptian-American relations. Since McCloy's last visit, in June 1963, Nasser had hosted a highly publicized state visit to Egypt by Nikita Khrushchev. The Johnson administration feared that Nasser was providing the Soviets with a solid foothold in the Middle East. Washington was also unhappy over Nasser's intervention in the Yemeni civil war, where fifty thousand Egyptian troops were backing the Republican government. Worse, U.S. intelligence sources had determined that the Egyptian surface-to-surface-missile program was progressing, a development that threatened a major new Arab-Israeli arms race. McCloy had been instructed by Johnson to raise all these issues with Nasser.

Given the upcoming election, Johnson had not wanted it known that he had sent a high-level emissary to talk with the controversial Egyptian leader. McCloy's mission, and even his presence in Cairo, were supposed to have been a secret, but there was a leak, and the Egyptian press reported on September 29, 1964, that Nasser would be seeing John McCloy as a "special representative of President Johnson." The U.S. Embassy quickly tried to cover the slip by releasing a statement to the wire services that McCloy was in Cairo on one of his "periodic visits" to discuss Ford Foundation projects with various Egyptian officials. He was to see Nasser only as a courtesy, to convey President Johnson's "personal greetings."[107] When questioned by newsmen after he had spent an hour with Nasser in his suburban Cairo villa, McCloy told them that he had given him a copy of the Warren Commission report and that they had discussed "a variety of world issues."[108]

This was McCloy's fourth or fifth session with Nasser since 1957, and he found the Egyptian president "less suspicious and more willing to talk about the arms problem" than on his last visit. But his mission was no more successful than on previous visits. McCloy had been authorized by the State Department to tell Nasser that, if he froze the Egyptian missile program, Washington would persuade the Israelis to do the same. McCloy also assured Nasser that the Israelis were not refining bomb-grade plutonium. (This turned out to be incorrect: it later became clear that the Israelis had acquired a nuclear-weapons capability.) Nasser listened politely to these assurances, but gave no indication that he would respond positively. When the conversation turned to the still-festering Palestinian problem, Nasser confessed he had no solution to offer and implied that another war was no answer.[109]

At the end of their talks, McCloy raised an issue of concern to Chase

Manhattan Bank, where he was still a board director. He asked what Nasser could do to keep Chase off the Arab Boycott Committee's list of proscribed companies.[110] Earlier that summer, in response to a report that the bank was being investigated by the Committee, Chase officials had submitted documentation of their contention that Chase had not acted directly as a financial agent for Israel.[111] Nasser listened with more than polite interest to this plea. Egypt already had a $10-million commercial loan from Chase, and he wanted to be able to extend his lines of credit with Chase and other New York banks. (McCloy's representation seems to have convinced Nasser, since, with the exception of Syria, most Arab states thereafter continued to deal with Chase Bank.[112])

Back in Washington, McCloy told Harriman and other State Department officials that he was not optimistic that Nasser would freeze his missile program. "We were asking him something," he said, "that was very hard for him to do." But he thought the talks worthwhile, and if "we kept working on Nasser, we might eventually get some results." Harriman agreed, though he felt it was going to be tough to get the Israelis and their domestic "supporters to think of the long-range aspects of our policy and understand why it was desirable for us to continue frank discussions with Nasser."[113]

By the time McCloy returned from the Middle East, Lyndon Johnson was poised to win his own electoral mandate for the presidency. The Democrats had convinced many Americans that Senator Goldwater should not have his finger on the nuclear button. By contrast, Johnson was presented as a peace candidate, committed to keeping the United States out of a ground war in Vietnam, and dedicated to preventing the proliferation of nuclear weapons. On such weighty issues, Johnson seemed to have bipartisan support. This was reinforced for the voters that autumn by the formation of two panels of foreign-policy advisers: the President's Panel of Foreign Policy Consultants and a special task force to study nuclear proliferation. McCloy agreed to have his name associated with both groups, which included all the familiar names: Arthur Dean, Allen Dulles, Robert Lovett, Eugene Black, Roswell Gilpatric, and others. *The New York Times* dryly observed that Johnson was "eager" to "project an image of bipartisanship and unity in foreign affairs."[114] Despite the overt political purpose, McCloy was happy to loan his reputation to Johnson. Like 61.2 percent of the American electorate that November, he voted Democratic—for only the second time in his life.

CHAPTER 26

McCloy and Vietnam: 1965–68, NATO Crisis, Secret Middle East Negotiations

"We're organizing for victory over there, McCloy, and I want you."

LYNDON JOHNSON, 1964

Even as a young congressman, Lyndon Johnson knew that foreign policy was not his strength. His earliest political mentor, Alvin J. Wirtz, wrote him in 1940, "I will admit you are a whiz on domestic problems, but I still think that on international problems you should listen to the elder statesmen."[1] Twenty-five years later, Johnson still lacked the confidence to rely on his own instincts when it came to foreign affairs. He knew pork-barrel politics; he knew how to bring running water and electricity to his Texas hill-country constituents; he knew how to make deals; and in 1965 he was ramming through Congress the most sweeping body of domestic legislation since Roosevelt's New Deal. But even as Johnson savored these domestic triumphs, he feared that Vietnam was threatening his Great Society. He had inherited this troubling guerrilla war from the Kennedys after November 1963, when President Ngo Dinh Diem was murdered in a coup d'état just before John F. Kennedy's assassination. Coup followed coup, and the Vietnamese communists expanded their control of the countryside. Johnson's foreign-policy advisers—all of whom had been John Kennedy's men—would tell him he had to stand firm, that Vietnam could not be lost. But he had no illusions. Two days after Kennedy's death, upon listening to a particularly gloomy assessment of the situation by Ambassador Henry Cabot Lodge, Johnson said he felt like a catfish that had just "grabbed a big juicy worm with a right sharp hook in the middle of it." He nevertheless told Lodge to "go back and tell those generals in Saigon that Lyndon Johnson intends to stand by our word. . . ."[2]

More troops were sent to enable the shaky military regime to survive. When Kennedy died, eighteen thousand "advisers" were in Vietnam; by the summer of 1964, the U.S. commitment had risen to 23,300.[3] Johnson wanted just enough troops to make the difference, but not enough to make it seem that America was going to war. That June, he began casting about for someone to replace Henry Cabot Lodge as his ambassador in Saigon. Remembering Alvin Wirtz's advice to "listen to the elder statesmen," Johnson told Dean Rusk to sound out McCloy about the Saigon job.

One Saturday in late June, Rusk sat down with his former boss and gave him a long briefing on the situation and why his services were so needed in Southeast Asia. But McCloy was unimpressed. He could not see why he should give up his lucrative legal practice for a mere ambassadorship. He told Rusk that at the age of seventy he was "without independent income" and would therefore have to earn his livelihood for the rest of his life. (All told, he was earning close to $200,000 a year from Milbank, Tweed, the Ford Foundation, Chase Manhattan, and his other corporate directorships.[4]) In the last year, he explained, he had built up a "modest law practice" and he had assured his clients that he would not be taking another government job. Rusk reported back to Johnson that McCloy felt "Saigon is not the place. If there were an over-riding crisis about Germany . . . he would consider making whatever personal sacrifice is involved to help in that situation. He knows . . . nothing about South Vietnam, and does not feel a sureness of touch about such matters which would give him personal confidence that he could do a good job." In sum, he couldn't contribute enough to justify "making such a drastic personal sacrifice."[5]

Johnson nevertheless thought he saw an opening. If McCloy were willing in principle to make a financial sacrifice for Germany, all the president had to do was convince him that Vietnam was of equal importance. So he called him to the White House and took him into the small sitting room off the Oval Office where he liked to have intimate conversations. He began by saying the Saigon ambassadorship was "almost as powerful as the Presidency," and he wanted McCloy, the "finest proconsul ever," to take the job. McCloy laughed good-naturedly, imagining himself dressed as a Roman proconsul, complete with toga and laurel wreath. But he told the president that the Saigon post wasn't for him, that he wished to remain on Wall Street. Besides, he didn't know anything about Vietnam, and what he did know only reminded him of Ike's belief that America should never become involved in a land war in Asia. It was not a problem he personally cared to handle.[6]

This was an attitude Johnson could not understand. Leaning so close now that McCloy could feel his breath across his face, Johnson said, "We're organizing for victory over there, McCloy, and I want you. You are the only one now who is going to lead us to victory." When McCloy tried to back away and politely repeated that the job really wasn't for him, Johnson placed his hand atop the lawyer's head and, drawing him close again, said it was his patriotic duty to take the job. He was ordering him—as an old soldier—to obey his commander-in-chief. And if he refused, why, he must be lacking the courage he had once had as an artillery captain. Maybe, said Johnson, "you're just yellow." Shocked, McCloy protested that he had served his country in two world wars and had sacrificed his legal career for many long years of public service. Calmly backing away, he said he would not go to Vietnam, and abruptly left the room.[7]

Johnson ended up appointing McCloy's colleague from Germany, General Maxwell Taylor. Barely a month later, in the Gulf of Tonkin, two U.S. destroyers were allegedly attacked by North Vietnamese gunboats. And though Johnson later admitted, "For all I know, our Navy was shooting at whales out there," he sought and obtained from Congress a resolution authorizing him to "take all necessary steps, including the use of armed force" to defend Vietnam.[8] The first air strikes against North Vietnam were launched, and a policy of gradual escalation set in motion. By January 1965, additional American troops were required to shore up the unstable Saigon regime.

Three-quarters of all Americans were still not aware that their country had twenty-three thousand military "advisers" stationed in Vietnam. Most Americans could not even have located South Vietnam on a map. And yet Johnson feared the political consequences of being labeled by the Republican right wing as the president who lost South Vietnam. He remembered too well how the Democratic Party and men like General George Marshall had been pilloried by the McCarthyites for the "loss" of China. If this began to happen again, he risked losing congressional support for his cherished Great Society legislation. Out of such insecurities came the gradual escalations of 1964; the president and his closest advisers, particularly Mac Bundy and Bob McNamara, had convinced themselves that one more show of force—one more round of bombing, a few thousand more troops—would convince Hanoi that the Americans were determined to deny them a military victory in the South. Then some kind of truce could be negotiated, as had been achieved in South Korea.

McCloy had observed Johnson's growing commitment to the war with increasing unease. Unlike America's security interests in Western Europe, where the United States had identifiable allies with strong domestic constituencies, the situation in Southeast Asia seemed so much more vague. From one month to the next, it was hard to know who in Saigon was an ally and who was not. South Vietnam wasn't so strategically important in itself as it was as the symbol of the U.S. commitment. If pressed in early 1965, McCloy was willing to have the administration use a display of U.S. military muscle to lend credibility to that commitment. But he did not wish to see Vietnam overshadow the centrality of Washington's more important commitments in Western Europe. Vietnam just wasn't that important. If he had thought otherwise, he would have seen to it that the Council on Foreign Relations grappled with the problem. But throughout the period 1960–68, the Council organized no study groups on the subject of Southeast Asia.[9]

His attitude was pretty much mirrored by a poll of his colleagues at the Council. Early in 1965, six hundred of the Council's twenty-one hundred members responded to a questionnaire on U.S. policy in Vietnam. The results—published in a small pamphlet entitled *American Dilemma in Viet-Nam,* constituted less than a ringing endorsement by the "Establishment" of the U.S. effort in Vietnam: a quarter of the membership advocated an expansion of the war, a quarter supported disengagement, and half seemed to hope that the administration could muddle through with continued American aid to the Saigon regime.[10]

As these sentiments suggest, the foreign-policy establishment in 1965—the year of decision for Vietnam—was much more divided than has been supposed.[11] Most of McCloy's peers were pessimistic about the prospects for the war and had no firm conviction about how to resolve the conflict. Moreover, McCloy was also well aware that some of his closest friends were quite vigorously dissenting against any further escalation. Two days after the Viet Cong killed a number of U.S. Marines at Pleiku on February 7, 1965, Lew Douglas phoned Johnson and urged him not to retaliate. He followed this up with a cable arguing the merits of submitting the whole problem for negotiation at the United Nations. Douglas thought the South Vietnamese lacked the will to fight, and that the United States could not ultimately win "without making South Viet Nam an American Province for, at least, half a century." When Johnson ordered B-52 raids on North Vietnam, Douglas told Arthur Krock that this decision was "nuts." And after the first U.S. combat troops landed at Danang in March 1965, he wrote a friend, "That we are there at all is one of the residual heritages from John Foster Dulles."[12]

Douglas was not alone in these thoughts. That spring, Undersecretary of State George W. Ball repeatedly tried to make the case for a negotiated withdrawal. So too did George Kennan, who in testimony before Congress flatly stated that Vietnam was not an area of "vital importance to this country," and suggested that the best the United States could probably hope for was some kind of "Titoist" solution.[13] Yet another close friend of McCloy's, Averell Harriman, privately complained in March, "We have got to have a settlement. . . . We are applying the stick without the carrot."[14]

McCloy more or less agreed with the basic premise behind these views; if possible, America should not be drawn into another land war in Asia. He also had reason to think the country could live with a "Titoist" solution in South Vietnam. Beginning in 1962, the Ford Foundation had generously funded a Council on Foreign Relations study on the possibility of opening up a new relationship with communist China. McCloy and other Council members had long thought Washington's China policy unrealistic. If a civil relationship could be established with Peking, the symbolic importance of drawing the line in Vietnam became quite academic.[15]

These were sound instincts. And yet, as the war unfolded over the summer of 1965, McCloy's characteristic willingness to reconsider his views—combined with his natural deference to presidential authority—led him astray. The visits of administration spokesmen to Council meetings in 1964–65 were like missions of seduction. In this period, for instance, Henry Cabot Lodge, General Maxwell Taylor, and McGeorge Bundy all gave the Council long briefings on the reasons behind the U.S. intervention. William Bundy (Mac's elder brother) became a director of the Council at the same time he was appointed assistant secretary of state for Far Eastern affairs.[16]

McCloy, of course, had known the Bundy brothers for a quarter-century. He had hosted a breakfast reception when William Bundy had married Dean Acheson's daughter. These were men he regarded as friends, and if they now had become the chief architects of a policy of gradual escalation, they had also made it painfully clear that they believed this course was the least objectionable path to the achievement of U.S. goals. In the policy debate that spring, the Bundys had positioned themselves, as McCloy might have if he had been in their shoes, right in the center. While George Ball and Lew Douglas argued for disengagement, General Westmoreland was asking for 150,000 troops, which he said were needed immediately to stave off the Viet Cong's monsoon offensive. Bob McNamara favored the mining of Haiphong harbor, a complete naval quarantine of North Vietnam, virtually unlimited bombing, and the introduction of whatever force levels were necessary to demonstrate to Hanoi that the Viet Cong could not hope to win.[17]

McNamara and Westmoreland thus made the Bundys look quite

cautious. William Bundy favored trying to hold on with no more than eighty-five thousand troops, and then seeing how the situation looked in two months. Mac Bundy was prepared to send more troops sooner than that.[18] But in their conversations with McCloy, both Bundys left an impression of the gravity of the situation. They told him that the administration was fully aware of all the risks associated with Vietnam. These were risks, however, that men of sound judgment had to face. In February 1965, upon returning from an inspection trip to Saigon, Mac Bundy wrote Johnson, "To be an American in Saigon today is to have a gnawing feeling that time is against us. . . . At its very best the struggle in Vietnam will be long. It seems to us important that this fundamental fact be made clear and our understanding of it be made clear to our own people and to the people of Vietnam."[19]

But as the bombing escalated, and as more combat troops were introduced, Johnson ordered his officials to "minimize any appearance of sudden changes in policy."[20] The war would escalate, but Johnson wanted to hide this fact from the American people as long as possible. With time, he thought, each step in the escalation would appear to be a natural and reasonable response to the enemy's actions. The politician who was so successful at coaxing cooperation from his constituency on contentious domestic issues was sure that he could do the same on Vietnam. In late April, this belief was reinforced when his popularity ratings rose after he sent twenty-one thousand troops to suppress an alleged communist rebellion in the Dominican Republic.[21] Johnson chose to dismiss the rising number of antiwar demonstrations on university campuses as the expressions of a noisy minority.

McCloy, however, found these student demonstrations—one had recently taken place outside his office at Chase Manhattan Bank Plaza—both gratifying and disturbing. He thought they were evidence that the students cared about matters of public policy. But he had to wince at the extreme rhetoric used in some of the protests. In early June 1965, he gave the commencement address at Haverford College, in Pennsylvania. In preparation for the speech, he spent a few days on the campus, talking to members of the Class of '65. It was a sobering experience, for he was challenged to defend the U.S. interventions in both Vietnam and the Dominican Republic. He was shocked to see that many of the students who pressed him vigorously on these issues were brimming with cynicism about the fundamental motivations of postwar U.S. policy.

In his address a few days later, he tried to answer these critics. "I am troubled," he said, "as are a great many, as to where our actions may lead us and I do not yet see clearly, in either case [Vietnam or the Dominican Republic], light through the tunnel. . . ." This was a significant admission. But he went on to say that he could not accept "the thesis so vigorously put forward by some that in each case what we have done is only the expression of outright imperialism. . . ." The sending of the Marines, he said, was an honest attempt to defend ordinary liberties. The effort might be "beyond our means" or even "maladroit." He didn't really know enough to say. But he did know that recent history was full of examples in which tough decisions had to be made to preserve our liberties. Munich was again the unspoken theme. The determination of the Soviet Union to take over Western Europe after World War II "was no myth." Nor was the Cuban missile crisis, when he had had to "look down the gun barrel of nuclear disaster." At such critical moments of history, he said, our leaders sometimes have to make a "leap in the dark . . . where no amount of education nor doctrine [can] fully bridge the gap to sound decision."

He then tried to explain why he thought the youthful critics of the war should place their trust in men like Johnson, Rusk, the Bundy brothers, and, by implication, himself. "The Romans would have understood what I am trying to say. They had a word for it—'gravitas'—and the one who possessed it had the respect and regard of his countrymen, whether he was in the forum or on the farm. 'Gravitas' did not imply age nor brilliance, and, least of all, a style or school of thought. It means a core, a weight of judgment and honest appraisal."

Gravitas. This word explains much about how McCloy saw himself on the stage of public service. Certain men had it, that "weight of judgment," that ability of honest, objective appraisal. They need not be brilliant, and they must not be the creatures of any ideological doctrine. Both brilliance and ideology got in the way of objectivity. They needed to be men who knew how—as Paul Cravath had taught him so many years ago—to break a problem down into all its pieces and put it back together again. These few men of *gravitas* were entitled to the public's trust, for only they were capable of dealing with the "imponderables" of public policy.

McCloy cited his late mentor, his "hero statesman," Henry L. Stimson, as one such man. And then, in the same breath, he suggested that similar men were making the hard decisions on Vietnam. "President Johnson and Secretary Rusk," he told his Haverford audience, "are faced with similar tests today and they deserve our understanding."[22]

The speech was a hit with all of his friends. Arthur Krock devoted a column in *The New York Times* to it. Dean Rusk congratulated him for a "masterful handling of a controversial subject." Averell Harriman "thoroughly approved" of it and wrote his friend, "The assumption nowadays that when we try to stop communism we are imperialists 'interfering with the course of social justice' should be hit as you did."[23]

Shortly after this speech, the men of *gravitas* were called to Washington to consult with the president. Vietnam was at a turning point. Should

Washington accede to Westmoreland's request for a major commitment of combat troops to save the Saigon regime? Or should George Ball's proposal for a political solution be accepted, knowing that it probably meant an eventual communist takeover of the South? Johnson now asked Mac Bundy to assemble his "Wise Men"—the members of his foreign-policy consultants' panel. On July 8, 1965, nearly twenty of these consultants gathered on the seventh floor of the State Department for a series of briefings. Only a few—McCloy, General Omar Bradley, Roswell Gilpatric, George B. Kistiakowsky, and Arthur Larson—were assigned to a special panel to discuss Vietnam. After several hours of briefings by Rusk, McNamara, Ambassador Llewellyn Thompson, and William Bundy, the Vietnam Panel emerged ready to endorse a policy of controlled escalation.

That afternoon, the Vietnam panelists met with the rest of the consultants in a plenary session. McCloy spoke at some length, telling his colleagues that he was now impressed with "the toughness of the situation." Merely blunting the Viet Cong's current monsoon offensive, he thought, would not persuade Hanoi to negotiate.[24] The war would probably go on for a long time, but he nevertheless told Rusk and McNamara, "You've got to do it. You've got to go in."[25] He and the other panelists thought the "stakes were very high indeed." South Vietnam was a "crucial test" in the Cold War; if the free world could not cope with the "Communist tactic" of wars of national liberation, then U.S. commitments everywhere would be questioned. If South Vietnam fell, Thailand could not be held, and the loss of Southeast Asia would have dire consequences for India and even Japan. Worse, from McCloy's perspective, was that "de Gaulle would find many takers for his argument that the US could not now be counted on to defend Europe."[26]

It was true that Germany's new chancellor, Christian Democrat Ludwig Erhard had recently told the administration that the people of West Berlin would be concerned if the United States opted for a "compromise" out of its commitment to Saigon. McCloy was such a Germanophile that he took Erhard literally. By contrast, George Ball, a man just as devoted to the Atlantic alliance as McCloy, suggested the chancellor was probably "telling us what he believed we wanted to hear." The principal anxiety of our NATO allies, Ball argued, was "that we have become too preoccupied with an area which seems to them an irrelevance. . . . Moreover, they have a vested interest in an easier relationship between Washington and Moscow. By and large, therefore, they will be inclined to regard a compromise solution in South Vietnam more as new evidence of American maturity and judgment than of American loss of face. . . ."[27] In just a few years, McCloy would take the same position and publicly complain that the administration had lost sight of the "primacy of Europe."[28] But in the summer of 1965, he convinced himself that disengagement from Vietnam would be misinterpreted by the European allies.

In the general discussion that followed, most of the "Wise Men" endorsed whatever combat-force increases McNamara wanted. They also generally approved of the bombing campaign in the North. It was not as if these hard-line positions were arrived at without some argument. Arthur Larson, a university professor who had served in the Kennedy administration, argued the merits of taking the whole issue to the United Nations. Dean Acheson quickly shot down this idea by harshly interrupting to say that this was no time to "turn over our Far East policy to the UN." McCloy and others thought there would be time for negotiations later, after the United States had taken control of the military situation. But at the present time, UN talks would only be a "dangerous sign of weakness."

McCloy's concern with the appearances of looking tough, of being fully prepared militarily, goes a long way toward explaining his hard-line positions in this crucial meeting. His old instincts were too deep-rooted to be overwhelmed by doubts concerning the viability of fighting a war on the Asian mainland. American prestige was already on the line: he knew that, as he spoke, nearly ninety thousand American soldiers were already stationed in Vietnam, and some of them were dying. For him, this fact weighed heavily, and arguing the merits of the original commitment to the Saigon regime was pointless. As he later told Arthur Dean, "We are committed in Vietnam because we are there and there is nothing to be gained and considerably [sic] to be lost in rearguing the commitment or dragging in the actions of former Presidents."[29]

Only one man in the room, Arthur Larson, provided any coherent dissent. He said he had "grave doubts that we would get a truly viable and democratic Vietnam even by causing Hanoi to pull out. . . ." This argument only momentarily caused the "Wise Men" to pause and wonder whether what the United States could achieve in Vietnam would be much improved after years of combat. No one suggested that the Viet Cong might be tapping into a nationalism or a collectivist cultural tradition so virulent as to make the U.S. goal of a "democratic" society irrelevant. No one asked why Americans should now succeed in a venture where the French had so recently failed. Lew Douglas would have forcefully raised these arguments, but he had not been invited. Instead, as William Bundy reported to the president, ". . . it was clear that the group thought we needed to look hard at just what we did expect to come out in South Vietnam—and equally clear that none of the other members of the group were prepared to buy Larson's basic thesis."[30]

The "Wise Men" sanctioned "whatever amounts of military power may be needed, perhaps as much as [was] brought to bear in Korea fifteen years ago."[31] But they admittedly had no idea what political outcome could be expected of such an effort in a country of which they had no personal knowledge. As if to underscore their confusion, Robert Lovett said it was "not useful to talk about 'victory,' that what was really involved was preventing the expansion of Communism by force; in a sense, avoiding defeat."[32]

There was something of a staged quality to the exercise the "Wise Men" were put through at the State Department that day. True, they were being "consulted." But by virtue of the assumptions presented by Rusk, McNamara, and the Bundy brothers, the decision to escalate had already been made. The only questions now were how many combat troops would be sent and how would the intervention be explained to the American people. Arthur Dean and most of the others favored a massive, decisive intervention, believing that "there was a great deal of sentiment in the country for doing whatever it took, if we were going to go on at all."[33] All or nothing. "They were for bombing the be-Jesus out of them [North Vietnam]," recalled one official.[34]

At the end of the day, a select group, including McCloy, were ushered into the White House to see Johnson himself. If the meetings during the day had been slightly staged, the conversation in the Cabinet Room was positively surreal. After everyone settled in with a cocktail in hand, Johnson subjected them all to a performance they found quite disturbing. As he complained about everything—fate, the press, Congress, the intellectuals—it became clear that the real purpose of their "consultation" was to assuage the president's insecurities. Johnson had gone on for some time, complaining that no one was supporting him on Vietnam and that no course of action seemed right, when Acheson finally exploded. "I blew my top," he wrote Harry Truman, "and told him he was wholly right on Vietnam, that he had no choice except to press on, that explanations were not as important as successful action."

Acheson, in fact, only a month earlier had worked with George Ball on his proposal for a political settlement, and, like McCloy, hadn't ever really thought Vietnam itself was critical to U.S. national security. But, as with McCloy, the appearance of strength was important to him. McCloy and others in the room now echoed Acheson's sentiments: "With this lead my colleagues came thundering in like the charge of the Scots Greys at Waterloo. They were fine; old Bob Lovett, usually cautious, was all out. . . . I think . . . we scored." The next day, Mac Bundy reported to his aides, "The mustache was voluble."[35]

Despite this shot in the arm, Johnson was still agonizing over the impending escalation. He acted as if he knew the war would destroy his administration. A week after seeing the "Wise Men," he walked into a staff meeting and, when he had listened to the discussion for a few minutes, said, "Don't let me interrupt you. But there's one thing you ought to know. Vietnam is like being in a plane without a parachute when all the engines go out. If you jump, you'll probably be killed, and if you stay in you'll crash and probably burn. That's what it is." With that he abruptly stood up and walked out of the room.[36]

The "Wise Men" too began to ponder the implications of their advice. McCloy and Arthur Dean were invited back to Washington for a second meeting on July 22, 1965. In the interim, they had not had second thoughts, but they wondered why, if the country was going to war, it could not do so without any restrictions. "The country is looking," McCloy told Johnson, Rusk, McNamara, and the other officials assembled in the Cabinet Room, "to getting on with the war." He wanted to know why Hanoi and Haiphong couldn't be bombed, why the North Vietnamese were being left a "sanctuary." When Rusk explained they thought the Soviets would intervene if Hanoi was bombed, Arthur Dean pointedly asked, "What do you do if the war drags on—with mounting casualties—where do we go? The people say if we are not doing what is necessary to end it, why don't we do what is necessary?" McNamara replied that bombing Haiphong wouldn't win the war. This led to a poignant discussion on the ultimate direction of the war:

DEAN: "If this carries on for some years, we'll get in the same fix we were in Korea and the Yalu."

RUSK: "We were under no pressures to make it [Korea] a larger war until the war was practically over."

MCCLOY: "If we could define our objectives specifically, what are our objectives in a discussion [peace negotiations]? What do we have to negotiate?"

RUSK: "1. Infiltration from the North must stop.
"2. We have no interests in a permanent military base there.
"3. 1954–1962 agreements ought to be solved by peaceful means and not . . ." [Rusk is interrupted.]

MCCLOY: "When do the troops get withdrawn?"

RUSK: "When proof of infiltration—stopping."

BUNDY: "If we really were the ones for free elections, it would be good. It is difficult for Saigon to sign on."

MCCLOY: "Would we be willing to take a Tito government or a VC victory [at the polls]?"

BUNDY: "That's where our plan begins to unravel."[37]

Obviously, Bundy was not prepared for any compromise short of an American victory. This conversation, remarkable for what it should have revealed about Bundy's thinking, did not dissuade McCloy from signing on to the war effort. A few days later, just minutes before Johnson went before a press conference, Bundy called McCloy to inform him of the president's final decision: Westmoreland would be allowed to have a total of 125,000 troops immediately (an addition of thirty-five thousand), and it was recognized that this would not be the end. Bundy reported to the president that McCloy "understood and approved of the international reasons for not blowing the thing way up to the level of option 4."[38] Option 4 was an all-out bombing campaign of Hanoi and the critical harbor facilities at Haiphong. That, thought Johnson, "would be rape rather than seduction. . . ."[39] Instead, the nation was going to wage a calibrated war, a reasonable war, a war of gradual escalation accompanied at each step by peace proposals. As he explained it to McCloy, "It's like a prize fight. Our right is our military power, but our left must be our peace proposals. Every time you move troops forward, you move diplomats forward."[40]

Johnson thus made his July 1965 decision to escalate the war appear to be a moderate, cautious step. It was certainly a reluctant step. Watching him announce the decision at his press conference, Joe Alsop observed, "It must be said there is a genuine element of pathos (and pray God, the pathos does not turn into tragedy) in the spectacle of this extraordinary man in the White House wrestling with the Vietnamese problem, which is so distasteful to him, and all the while visibly longing to go back to the domestic miracle-working he so much enjoys."[41] Johnson had every reason to know that he was embarking on a tragic endeavor. The same day he saw McCloy, his old friend and adviser Clark Clifford repeated the warnings he had written him on May 17: "This could be a quagmire. It could turn into an open end commitment on our part that would take more and more ground troops, without a realistic hope of ultimate victory."[42]

Over the next three years, thirty thousand young American soldiers, most of them draftees from blue-collar and lower-middle-class families, would die fighting the "limited" war. Throughout these early years of the war, McCloy stubbornly maintained that, once American soldiers were fighting and dying, one couldn't just renounce the U.S. commitment to South Vietnam. It would be too much like Munich. True, the situation inside Vietnam was murky, and maybe in a free election the Vietnamese people would vote for the Viet Cong. But the president would just have to see this one through to some kind of honorable resolution. McCloy's attitude was reinforced each time he heard an exposition of the administration's case. After listening to Dean Rusk explain Vietnam to a group of his peers at a Bohemian Grove retreat in late July, McCloy reported to the White House that Rusk had been an "outstanding success."[43]

But he still had doubts. One day soon after Johnson's press conference, McCloy found himself seated on the Washington–New York air shuttle next to Marcus Raskin, a former NSC aide with whom he had worked on disarmament issues during 1961. Inevitably, they got to talking about Vietnam, and Raskin criticized the escalation decision. McCloy listened as Raskin outlined his views and then said, yes, it was a difficult problem and "it looks as if we're going to get our nose bloodied."[44] But what had to be done had to be done.

McCloy had counseled Johnson to use whatever force was necessary, to go in decisively with the intention of quickly bringing Ho Chi Minh to the negotiating table. But when Johnson chose a middle course, McCloy did not try to warn him against half-measures. If this was what the president had decided, he would support him. Among other things, he agreed to associate himself publicly with the war by lending his name to a public-relations campaign organized out of the White House. He did so reluctantly, telling Mac Bundy that the formation of a Committee for an Effective and Durable Peace in Asia might only "stimulate the formation of an opposing group."[45] (He had been talking to Hamilton Fish Armstrong, the editor of *Foreign Affairs,* who feared that such tactics would attract criticism "against the control of government policy by reactionaries, Wall Street, the East, the Establishment or whatever critics of the policy choose to call it."[46]) He also questioned whether the administration really needed to drum up support: "The people have now faced the fact that this is a very messy situation but the country has determined that what has to be done will be done in spite of intermittent opposition from irresponsible groups."[47] But these arguments did not convince Bundy or the president whom he served. Johnson had a desperate craving for any approbation, particularly if it came from the Eastern Establishment. So, in the end, McCloy agreed to join the Committee. Together with such friends as Arthur Dean, David Rockefeller, Dean Acheson, James Conant, and Eugene Black, he signed a full-page newspaper advertisement endorsing "the President's policy of doing no more and no less than what is necessary militarily in Vietnam to bring about a viable peace."[48]

Between July and the end of 1965, the American public slowly came to realize that an enormous military expedition was required just to keep the Saigon regime in place. By December, there were nearly two hundred thousand U.S. troops committed on the ground. "In the South," reported Malcolm Browne in *The New York Times,* "huge sectors of the nation have been declared 'free bombing zones,' in which anything that moves is a legitimate target. . . . If only by the laws of chance, bloodshed is believed to be heavy in these raids."[49] And in the North, the air war had also greatly accelerated, with the number of sorties tripling to some seventy-nine thousand flights in 1966.[50] The bombing took its toll on Hanoi's infrastructure, but it also led to rising civilian casualties. This in turn fueled antiwar sentiments at home. In October and November 1965, critics of the war organized mass demonstrations in Washington. About the same time, McCloy sounded out Mac Bundy about leaving his job as national-security adviser in the White House to become president of the

Ford Foundation. He knew that the younger man was tiring in his White House job. Both Bundy brothers were still just as committed to prosecuting the war as they had been in the summer. But now it was becoming a daily, gruesome grind, so when McCloy mentioned the Ford job, Mac Bundy jumped at the opportunity.

Johnson hated it when any man left his employ, but the departure of Bundy, just as the war was getting nasty, was a particular blow. The president had always felt that the Eastern Establishment would invariably give Bundy credit for any foreign-policy victories—and blame him for any failures. Vietnam was not exactly a failure yet, but it looked as if it was becoming a tar baby. In December, the same month Bundy announced that he would leave his post in the near future, Johnson decided to announce a trial pause in the bombing campaign. This would demonstrate, Johnson thought, once and for all whether Hanoi was willing to respond to Washington's peace feelers. If nothing happened, Bundy and the president's other advisers on the war hoped that at least the administration's critics would be silenced.

More than a month passed, during which emissaries were sent all over the world in a relentless search for "signals" that Hanoi might be prepared for peace talks. It quickly became apparent that this whirlwind of diplomatic activity was quite pointless. It was already widely known that Hanoi had only one precondition for comprehensive negotiations: the bombing had to stop for good. After that, Hanoi said it wished to negotiate the withdrawal of all foreign troops and the establishment of a coalition government in the South that would include both the National Liberation Front and the Saigon junta. Peace talks could begin prior to the withdrawal of any U.S. troops—but first the bombing had to stop. Washington, however, was opposed to the establishment of a coalition government, since this was seen by all as a sure formula for an eventual takeover of the South by the NLF. So the Johnson emissaries were instructed to say that Washington would stop the bombing permanently only if Hanoi would halt its infiltration of troops and supplies into the South. This effectively sabotaged any hopes for real negotiations, because it rejected Hanoi's only condition to the commencement of peace talks—the unconditional cessation of the bombing.[51]

As the bombing pause entered its fifth week, pressures from the Pentagon mounted on Johnson to resume the air war. In a meeting on January 24, 1966, with his principal advisers, the president was basically told he had to get on with it. So first Johnson called in the congressional leaders, who, with the exception of Fulbright and Mike Mansfield, argued that the administration had to "do what is necessary to win."[52]

The next afternoon, Bundy sounded out McCloy and Lovett over the phone. They both favored a "prompt resumption" of the bombing. Citing his "painful memories of Korea," Lovett told Bundy that he was a "charter member of the Never Again Club." He wished Washington had never gotten involved, but now that it was, he favored not only a resumption of the bombing, but the imposition of a "friendly blockade" of North Vietnamese ports. Unlike Lovett, McCloy thought the pause had done some good on both political and military grounds. But since Hanoi had not responded to Washington's peace feelers, "it makes no sense now to let the highways and bridges be repaired and put in use again after we spent so much time bombing them." The risks of escalation, he said, were low.[53]

Needing more reassurance, Johnson wanted to hear this in person, and so he instructed Bundy to call another session of the "Wise Men." Lovett declined, believing he had nothing more to add to what he had told Bundy over the phone. He always seemed to recognize that these little gatherings were a bit staged and usually held only when the president wished the "Wise Men" to ratify a decision that had already been made. Once, when the White House sent him a photo of himself and McCloy sitting in on one of these meetings, looking particularly sleepy-eyed, Lovett sent it on to McCloy with the caption "Bored of Advisers."[54]

But McCloy invariably answered these presidential summonses, and so, two days later, he found himself once again in the White House Cabinet Room facing Johnson and his men. Vice-President Hubert Humphrey was present, in addition to Rusk, McNamara, Harriman, the Bundy brothers, Ball, Allen Dulles, Arthur Dean, and Clark Clifford. The agenda was clear from the beginning: the bombing would be resumed, even though everyone present voiced various reasons not to escalate. Read today, the transcript seems to portray a remarkable degree of cynicism; at the very least, these were men resigned to a course of action that they knew to be of doubtful wisdom, domestically unpopular, and certainly bloody. But Hanoi had called their bluff, and now they were trapped. Mac Bundy set the tone early on when he stated, ". . . we did not expect any serious response to the pause. . . ." McCloy himself admitted to being "puzzled" that "Hanoi hasn't thrown us off balance with some phony probe."

Instead, the North Vietnamese were continuing to reinforce their troops in the South. McNamara admitted that Hanoi was now capable of infiltrating forty-five hundred men per month—three times the rate of last year. When Arthur Dean asked whether stepped-up bombing could deter the enemy's supply operations, McNamara flatly stated that not even the mining of Haiphong harbor would markedly cut down on the supplies reaching the South. "[I] Don't think we can affect their will through bombing. . . . No matter what bombing we do we need more men [on the ground]." McCloy then asked the same question in a different way: "What can we accomplish by doubling [bombing] sorties? Would this bring us victory?" To this, McNamara responded that "doubling our force over a period of six months might be sufficient to break their will." But when McCloy asked whether the current ground offensive could bring about a pacification of the countryside, McNamara said, "No."

In short, McCloy was being told that the bombing should be resumed even though in the past it had not stopped infiltration into the South, that more ground troops would be needed, but that they would not pacify the countryside. But neither he nor anyone else in the room questioned the logic of the escalation they were being asked to approve. Instead, McCloy's questions tended to be of a technical or factual nature. He asked General Wheeler whether the army had developed anything "in the way of tactics or weapons that give you hope?" Wheeler responded by boasting of the army's tactical mobility.

McCloy summed up their sentiments toward the end of the meeting when he suggested that the administration's peace offensive and the bombing pause had made Washington appear too eager for negotiations. "We've been too excited," he said, "too panicky—an indication of weakness to the enemy. [The] general impression abroad is we overdid it. But I'm not criticizing it. It helped us here at home. I think I would resume the bombing after having made these efforts—and saying we would if we didn't get [a] response—talks would be diminished if we don't resume. Insofar as Hanoi is concerned, they are confirmed in their estimate that we are weak and feeling the pressures at home."

Arthur Dean, Clark Clifford, and Allen Dulles agreed with these sentiments, leaving only Arthur Goldberg to make a case for prolonging the bombing pause. Even Vice President Humphrey favored a resumption. A moment later, the president ended the meeting with the words: "I am not happy about Vietnam but we cannot run out—we have to resume bombing."[55]

The same day, Senator J. William Fulbright—whom Johnson was now derisively calling "Senator Halfbright"—began holding hearings on the war. By early February, some of the television networks were broadcasting the hearings live, which so infuriated Johnson that he allegedly used his friendship with CBS President Frank Stanton to have that network cancel live coverage. George Kennan's critique of administration policy was replaced by reruns of the "I Love Lucy" show.[56] Fulbright nevertheless succeeded in showing that opposition to the war was no longer confined to a vocal minority of "longhair" students and leftist professors on elite university campuses. At the hearings' conclusion, Lew Douglas congratulated Fulbright for his "great courage."[57]

As the war continued—five thousand American soldiers would be killed in 1966—the debate entered the confines of Pratt House, where McCloy still presided over the Council on Foreign Relations. Professor Hans J. Morgenthau, a known critic of the war who had testified with Kennan at the Fulbright hearings, was invited that year to be a senior fellow at the Council. McCloy regularly debated the merits of the war at the Council's off-the-record dinner meetings with Morgenthau, Zbigniew Brzezinski, Averell Harriman, George Ball, Asian specialist A. Doak Barnett, Francis Plimpton, and many others. If there was some room for critics like Morgenthau at Pratt House, McCloy also made sure that the administration was allowed to make its case. Dean Rusk, Henry Kissinger—who was a hawk on the war—and Walt W. Rostow, who had replaced Mac Bundy as the president's NSC adviser, all spoke at the Council in 1965–66.[58]

The Council's house organ, *Foreign Affairs,* similarly opened its pages to such administration spokesmen as Mac Bundy and the CIA's George Carver. Ten months after leaving the White House, Bundy was still an unabashed defender of the war: ". . . the argument on Viet Nam turns on tactics, not fundamentals," although he warned, ". . . there are wild men in the wings." The president and his advisers, wrote Bundy, deserve the "understanding support of those who want restraint," in part because it was these men who were responsible for the fact that "the bombing of the North has been the most accurate and the most restrained in modern warfare."[59] The journal's editor, Hamilton Fish Armstrong, did not let such administration spokesmen go unanswered. In the autumn of 1966, Armstrong published a long piece by veteran French reporter Bernard B. Fall which effectively destroyed many of the arguments used by Washington to justify the war. After Lew Douglas read the piece, he wrote his friend Thomas Lamont at Morgan Guaranty Trust that in his opinion Fall had made an "unimpeachable argument" against the escalating war.[60]

By then, Douglas firmly believed that "the position that we have been driven into is a dangerous one—dangerous to us and to the whole world. I hope with great urgency that we will escalate no further. . . ."[61] McCloy was used to his brother-in-law's strong opinions—and tended to dismiss them. The two old friends, in fact, were arguing quite a bit in the mid-sixties, and not only about Vietnam. Ever suspicious of the Germans, the Anglophile in Douglas thought Washington was allowing Bonn to "dictate [American] foreign policy."[62] He knew McCloy to be notoriously soft on the Germans; he was aghast that McCloy supported giving West Germany some kind of control over the nuclear weapons stationed on her soil. He just refused to believe that "the leopard has changed its spots." The Germans should not be trusted with the ultimate weapon.[63]

McCloy was having similar disagreements with Harriman. In late January 1966, he had what Harriman described as a "hot argument" over breakfast at his Georgetown home. The Germans were indeed asking for some control over NATO nuclear weaponry, and McCloy thought they should get it, even though Washington was then trying to negotiate a Non-Proliferation Treaty (NPT) with the Soviets. He knew the Germans believed the proposed NPT was primarily aimed at them; indeed, former

Chancellor Adenauer soon created a political rumble by calling the NPT "a Morgenthau plan raised to the 2nd power." Adenauer thought that, if West Germany signed the treaty, it would be signing its own death warrant.[64] McCloy "deplored such emotional statements" but as he now told Harriman, he just didn't think such a treaty was important enough to sacrifice "NATO for the benefit of the Russians."[65] He bluntly criticized the administration, saying that it was letting "NATO go to hell in a hack." Echoing Douglas's sentiments, Harriman said McCloy was allowing Germany to "dictate" U.S. foreign policy. "We can't take a corporals' guard out of Germany without a crisis," he complained. He joshingly told his old friend that he ought to "get up to date and not live in the past when Germany was his ward."[66]

It was true, McCloy was soft on the Germans; he always thought them to be "our best ally."[67] He had also begun to think that "the general acceptance of the desirability of non-proliferation may be more instinctive than analytical." Perhaps Washington, inclined to give up too much in pursuit of absolute nonproliferation, might have to resign itself to the emergence of new nuclear powers in certain regional settings.[68] In order to preserve the credibility of NATO's deterrence, West Germany, the fulcrum state in the Atlantic alliance, might someday have to be given control over the bomb.

With the president almost completely absorbed by the Vietnam mess, McCloy was also worried that the administration was ignoring a far more dangerous crisis. On February 21, 1966, de Gaulle had once again surprised Washington by announcing that France was withdrawing from the military provisions of the NATO alliance. Starting in July 1966, he said, French troops stationed in Germany or elsewhere would no longer be under the command of NATO's supreme commander, always an American general. Furthermore, de Gaulle stated that his troops would respond only to "unprovoked aggression," not the mere outbreak of hostilities between the NATO and Warsaw pacts.[69] To McCloy, all of this was practically heresy. To make matters worse, there were indications that, with the weakening of the British pound, London might soon withdraw its own troops from Germany unless someone paid for them. But the U.S. Congress was unlikely to approve such expenditures. The rising costs of the Vietnam War, combined with a worsening U.S. trade balance, had led to pressure on Capitol Hill to bring some of the troops home from Europe. McCloy thought the very existence of NATO, and therefore the entire structure of the postwar peace, threatened to disintegrate.

Having just relinquished his job as chairman of the Ford Foundation, he decided to focus his energies on NATO's problems. Just a few days after de Gaulle's announcement, McCloy accepted an appointment as chairman of the board of governors of the Atlantic Institute, a Paris-based nonprofit group dedicated to promoting unity inside the Atlantic alliance.

In addition to Harriman, he made the rounds among his old colleagues, seeing Dean Acheson, George Ball, Robert Lovett, and others. Something had to be done, he told them, to save NATO. In early March, he went to see Dean Rusk, and a month later the president designated him a "special consultant" on the NATO crisis.[70]

McCloy immediately left for Bonn, where he encouraged the Germans to be tough in their dealings with de Gaulle. German Chancellor Ludwig Erhard, however, feared a confrontation. Was it, he asked, really "worthwhile to bring about a deterioration in Franco-German relations and a weakening of NATO simply because of questions of form and legality?" Weren't there many Americans, let alone Europeans, who rather agreed with de Gaulle and believed it was time for the Europeans to stand alone?

McCloy was shocked and disheartened by Erhard's question, but he tried to reply as best he could. Yes, there were Americans who thought the issue was not worth the risk of a break with France. "Walter Lippman, for one," McCloy said, "could be expected to follow this line, but Lippman . . . had been notoriously wrong on almost every important issue, beginning back in the days of Hitler." Some intellectuals and scientists would take the same view. In a way, he said, their attitude was a little like that of Khrushchev, who had once told him, "We don't want a strong united Western Europe. Why do you?" But most Americans, McCloy assured Erhard, had long ago rejected this view of the world. True, there was still some antagonism remaining from the war, but the general view among his countrymen today was that "de Gaulle is trying to set the clock back."[71]

McCloy was certainly underestimating both the appeal and the legitimacy of de Gaulle's brand of European nationalism. Most Europeans interpreted détente differently from the policy-makers in Washington and Moscow: for men like McCloy and Rusk, détente meant only a further consolidation within secure borders of each power's sphere of influence. But for the Europeans, détente held the promise of a gradual, mutual withdrawal of the two superpowers from Europe.[72] The policy changes of "*Ostpolitik*" were still four years distant, but the political rumblings in this direction could already be heard in the German Social Democratic Party. After his conversation with McCloy, however, Erhard ignored these signs of change and proceeded to take an extremely pro-American stance. In a very few months, this would cost him the chancellorship.

Back in Washington, McCloy was disturbed to find that the Johnson administration didn't seem so concerned about the NATO crisis as he thought they should be. The president himself had told Bob McNamara, "When a man asks you to leave his house, you don't argue; you get your hat and go." Johnson thought the "only way to deal with de Gaulle's fervent nationalism was with restraint and patience.[73]

McCloy, however, was not one to give up, and certainly not on an issue so close to his heart as the German alliance. That spring, he testified before a Senate subcommittee and complained of the "reinfection of Europe with nationalism" and "discriminatory" attitudes toward Germany: "Kept from any form of sharing nuclear potentials and denied an equal place at the table because of the claim that Germany is still not a sovereignty in the same sense as France, we have the seeds of ill will, reminiscent to me of the discriminatory provisions of Versailles. This attitude to me is like a fire bell in the night."[74]

"Difficult adjustments" would have to be made in order to preserve NATO; American troops had to remain in Europe, if not in France, and "a new expenditure of energy and thought" was required in order to refashion the alliance.[75] Many in Congress were not so sure. Later that summer, the House majority leader, Mike Mansfield, introduced a resolution stating that "a substantial reduction of U.S. forces permanently stationed in Europe can be made without adversely affecting either our resolve or ability to meet our commitment under the North Atlantic Treaty. . . .[76]

Critics charged that behind the Mansfield Amendment lay deep-rooted isolationist sentiments. McCloy certainly regarded it thus. The American troops in Europe, he believed, represented the "lynchpin of our Alliance."[77] But he was also aware that NATO's critics could marshal sound fiscal reasons for bringing home some of the 225,000 American soldiers stationed in Europe.[78] America's postwar dominance of world trade was coming to an end; the United States' share of trade was declining, partly in relation to the recovery of the Japanese and German economies. The country's trade surplus in 1966 was half what it had been in 1964. Simultaneously, because of America's many expenditures abroad, the world was being flooded with American dollars. As the U.S. balance of trade declined, many foreigners began to doubt the value of those dollars. Not surprisingly, the dollar soon came under attack. In 1965, there was a run on gold, and de Gaulle accused the United States of exporting its inflation to Europe.[79]

McCloy was aware that something had to be done to rectify this imbalance: Washington obviously could no longer afford to carry alone the costs of defending Europe. De Gaulle's solution—that the United States should retire from Europe—was not even to be considered, in McCloy's view. He believed NATO had to be saved, and this meant the allies had to recognize that the military and fiscal aspects of the alliance were intertwined. Ideally, the solution lay in persuading the Europeans to share the fiscal burden. For years, the United States' overall current account had been consistently thrown into deficit by overseas military expenditures, foreign aid, tourist expenditures, and direct capital investments abroad by U.S. corporations. The latter was the most significant factor, but the costs of maintaining America's military commitments overseas was not insignificant. U.S. troops in West Germany alone spent some $800 million a year on German goods and services. This foreign-exchange drain meant, of course, that the Germans were accumulating that many more U.S. dollars each year—dollars that contributed to the U.S. current-account deficit and weakened the value of the American currency. Beginning in the early 1960s, U.S. authorities persuaded the Germans to "off-set" this foreign-exchange drain by making large purchases of U.S. military arms.[80] This was to prove a temporary solution.

By 1966, many Germans tended to view these payments to offset the cost of U.S. troops stationed on their soil as a form of tribute to an occupation force.[81] Political pressures mounted on the Erhard government to renege on the payments. In the summer of 1966, his government had increased expenditures on social welfare. Then he informed the Americans there was no money to purchase further U.S. arms. The offset arrangement seemed dead.[82]

So, by the summer of 1966, as McCloy immersed himself in these problems, NATO seemed to be falling apart from within: de Gaulle had withdrawn his troops from NATO command, the British were threatening to bring their fifty-one thousand troops home from Germany, and now the Germans themselves were refusing to pay their share of the defense burden.

Robert McNamara reported to the president that the Germans owed the United States $1.35 billion in offset payments, and only $261 million of this had been paid. McNamara ridiculed the German claim that they had neither the budget nor the need to buy additional American military equipment. Among other comparisons, he pointed out that, whereas the United States currently had 230,000 tons of bombs either in or in transit to Vietnam, the West German Air Force's entire inventory of bombs ran to no more than forty-four hundred tons—"an obviously inadequate amount."

"Unless something is done," McNamara warned, "there will be a very large gap between the foreign exchange costs of US deployments to Germany . . . and German foreign exchange expenditures on the military account in the US. . . ." He estimated this gap would run to $500 million per year over the next five years. McNamara believed the Germans had to be squeezed.[83]

McCloy could not dispute McNamara's numbers, but he thought the United States had to be more flexible in dealing with the Germans.[84] It was tactically wrong, he thought, to link the number of American troops stationed in Germany with German payments. He agreed with his old friend Jean Monnet, who blamed "the association of cash with troops" for the current deterioration in German-U.S. relations.[85] Such a linkage only fueled German insecurities and doubts about the ultimate nature of the American commitment. And this in turn made them less willing to pay for the American nuclear umbrella. Erhard himself, in a recent conversation with Dean Rusk and George Ball, had conjured up the image of a small-scale Soviet attack on Germany. "Somewhere along the line of escalation," Erhard said, "the Soviets would have to be told: one more step will unleash the full nuclear force. With all our trust in the US and our allies will we and the man in the street be sure the rest of the world would be ready to die for the sake of saving Germany?" The answer was obvious, at least to Erhard's "man in the street." The rest of the world was not inclined to sacrifice itself for Germany. That was why, chimed in Erhard's foreign secretary, Gerhard Schröder, "the presence of U.S. troops was so important as a symbol of U.S. involvement. . . . Frankly, the thesis of 'massive retaliation' never made any military sense. . . ."[86] Now, if the Americans were prepared to withdraw some of their troops merely for fiscal reasons, perhaps the U.S. deterrent was no longer credible. To combat this trend in German thinking, McCloy felt Washington should isolate the issue of troop levels from the crass question of money. Only by re-creating the original spirit of mutual defense could the Americans persuade the Germans to do what was required.

The problem was that, as secretary of defense, McNamara had naturally taken the lead on this defense issue. To alter the cash-for-troops policy, McCloy would have to go up against the most powerful of Cabinet secretaries. A short time later, on October 7, 1966, McCloy saw Johnson alone in New York City for twenty minutes, just before the president gave a major address on the state of the Atlantic alliance.[87] In their talk, Johnson asked McCloy to go back to Europe as the U.S. representative in a series of "trilateral negotiations" with Germany and Britain. Assured that he had the authority to negotiate a deal, McCloy quickly agreed, and two weeks later flew to Bonn. This was one occasion when the Germans were not happy to see him. They felt on the defensive, put upon by their Anglo-Saxon allies. Scarcely had they begun the talks when Erhard's government of Christian Democrats collapsed. A major factor in the government's fall was the opposition of the German business community to any further offset payments. McCloy was particularly sensitive to the views of such Germans. Shortly before Erhard's fall, his friend of nearly forty years, Jean Monnet, reported through State Department channels that ". . . German big business interests have decided to withdraw their support from Erhard. . . . This could explain the generally noncooperative attitude of the Bundesbank on the offset problem. Industrial circles with an influence on the Bank may be urging a hard line in the expectation that this would bring about Erhard's fall."[88] The chancellor's government had fallen in large part because he seemed incapable of standing up to the Americans.[89]

Certainly the "Great Coalition" government of Chancellor Kurt Kiesinger, which for the first time shared power with Germany's Social Democrats, was less willing to follow Washington's lead than Adenauer's or Erhard's had been. The new government took until the end of January 1967 before reluctantly agreeing to continue the trilateral negotiations. In the interim, McCloy began to have second thoughts. He had been shocked by the "German feeling of concern bordering on distrust that followed the collapse of the Erhard government."[90] He was even more unsettled by the willingness of all the major players to stand by and watch while NATO unraveled. The British were setting deadlines for the removal of all their troops. Powerful congressional leaders such as Majority Leader Mike Mansfield and Senator Stuart Symington were calling for a substantial reduction of U.S. troops. McCloy feared a "stampede" was about to occur in which British troop withdrawals would be quickly followed by the complete disintegration of NATO as a military force.[91] In his view, the administration had to step down from McNamara's demand that the Germans fully offset the foreign-exchange costs of maintaining U.S. troops in Germany. So, on January 11, 1967, he came down to Washington to sound out various officials; in one day, he had private meetings with Dean Rusk, a half-dozen other State Department officials, Bob McNamara, and Treasury Secretary Henry H. Fowler.[92] Referring to his role as a "Wise Man," he confessed to Fowler that he found his status as a private citizen difficult; he did not wish to "pursue his own views, or try to defend them in the future, if the decisions are being made elsewhere—or are already made."[93] The implication was clear that, if the various wings of the bureaucracy did not take their lead from him, he would end his participation in the talks.

The message got through, and by the time the talks resumed, McCloy had persuaded the principal players within the administration—McNamara, Rusk, and Fowler—that the whole idea of offsetting the full foreign-exchange costs of the U.S. troops with German procurement of American military hardware had "become a serious political liability" in West Germany.[94] A new formula had to be designed, with respect to both military requirements and monetary cooperation. To begin with, a way had to be found to reduce the offset payments owed by Germany. To this end, the United States would play a game of musical chairs with its troops stationed in Germany. Instead of sending any complete divisions home, Washington would station two of the three brigades in a division back in the United States. The third brigade would remain in its German base and periodically rotate with one of its sister brigades Stateside. By this sleight of hand, the United States could save an estimated $100 million in foreign exchange that otherwise would have been spent by these soldiers in Germany. Of course, what was saved abroad would have to be spent at home, and more.[95] But the "dual-basing" and rotation scheme would allow the Johnson administration to claim that roughly the same number of U.S. troops were "based" in Germany, familiar with its potential battlefields, and equipped at a moment's notice to be shipped to the front.[96]

McCloy endorsed the rotation scheme, and quickly set about negotiating the details with the Germans and British. He drove a hard bargain. The Germans, after all, wanted to remain under the protective American military umbrella; they just wanted to pay as little for it as possible. With McCloy cajoling them along, they finally agreed, in late April, to a package deal whereby the Americans would rotate one army division and no more than ninety-six aircraft. In return, Bonn agreed to buy $500 million worth of medium-term U.S. government bonds. The British were given similar financial assistance and with great reluctance agreed to withdraw only sixty-five hundred of their fifty-one thousand troops from Germany. But, most significant of all, the Germans pledged never to knock on the U.S. Treasury's door and request the conversion of their enormous dollar holdings into gold. In effect, McCloy had negotiated an important step toward taking the U.S. currency off the gold standard.[97] A complete break with the gold standard would not come until 1971, but in the meantime he had successfully neutralized the massive German holdings of U.S. dollar reserves.[98]

That the Johnson administration could get away with writing such special currency exemptions for itself was a sign of both Washington's weakness and its strength. In 1966, there was no alternative to the dollar as the currency of the international marketplace. But the fact that the United States could not afford to convert the dollar reserves of one of its major allies into gold was a sign that Pax Americana was in decline. Even so, a superpower in decline is still a superpower. As the London *Times'* Washington correspondent observed, "Mr. McCloy's duty as the representative of a super-power was to remind them [the Germans and British] of their duty to the super-power as well as the alliance, and to persuade them that they can afford to go on doing what the super-power wants them to do. There can be no doubt of Mr. McCloy's success."[99]

Just a week before McCloy finally clinched the deal, Konrad Adenauer died. President Johnson decided to attend the funeral and took with him as part of his official delegation McCloy, Dean Rusk, Lucius Clay, Allen Dulles, and Eleanor Dulles.[100] A major chapter in German-American relations was closing. And, ironically, for the first time since the start of the Cold War, American troops were about to be withdrawn from continental Europe. McCloy was not happy to see this happen, but he could console himself that, thanks to the rotation scheme, he had managed to keep the withdrawals down to only thirty thousand.[101] Johnson, in any case, was pleased that "NATO was still in business," and congratulated McCloy for a "very important job well done."[102] In Germany, the press generally concluded that the trilateral talks had demonstrated that "despite its global problems the U.S. remains ready to pay heed to Germany's concerns."[103]

The U.S. press hailed the agreement as "a near-miracle," and McCloy was complimented for having "somehow brought tripartite agreement out of tripartite chaos."[104] But in the end, the arrangement turned out to be a stopgap measure; Bonn could not forever accept U.S. dollars without doing something with them. Only two months later, McCloy had to fly back to Germany for secret talks with a group of German bankers—including Hermann Abs—to persuade them to agree to the formation of a new monetary reserve designed to support the dollar.[105] Eventually, either the U.S. military presence in Germany would have to be cut, or the Germans would have to pay for their defense. McCloy had merely engineered a lawyer's postponement of the inevitable.

Over the next few years, largely due to the requirements of Vietnam, more American troops were brought home from Europe. Gradually, the Germans were persuaded to replace these troops and further ease Washington's foreign-exchange costs. With considerable reluctance, the British too kept more than a "trip-wire" force stationed in Germany. By 1971, the actual balance-of-payments costs of maintaining the Seventh U.S. Army in Germany was lower than it had been in 1967. But even if this had not been the case, McCloy would have continued to argue that NATO was worth any price.[106]

NATO was not an end in itself—though McCloy's constant arguments sometimes made it seem so. He was not in principle opposed to what would later be known as the *Ostpolitik* of the West German Social Democrats. But he believed that whatever hopes existed for improved East-West relations "must rest on a firm NATO foundation—not one which was seen to be unraveling."[107] In 1966–67, the unfortunate coincidence of four events—a U.S. balance-of-payments crisis, the collapse of the British pound, a budget crisis in Germany, and the introduction of the Mansfield Amendment in the U.S. Congress—converged to threaten the unraveling of the Atlantic alliance. McCloy would not let it happen.

The fate of the Atlantic alliance, of course, did not make for front-page headlines in these years. The Vietnam War squeezed these issues off to the back pages, which explains McCloy's growing annoyance with the war. He and other Europeanists had initially signed on to the war precisely because it was presented as symbolic of America's commitments elsewhere—specifically in Western Europe. Now the war in Southeast Asia was contributing to the United States' foreign-exchange drain problems and causing domestic inflation. And despite the heavy commitment of more than four hundred thousand troops, there seemed no end in sight.[108]

By 1967, the war had settled into a dreadful quagmire. Washington was spending $2 billion a month to support a half-million American soldiers in South Vietnam. More than thirteen thousand Americans had died. Draft calls in the summer of 1967 were running at thirty thousand per month. More bombs had been dropped on the country than in all the theaters of World War II, and civilian casualties in the North were as high as a thousand per month. And yet, according to American estimates, the North Vietnamese had still been able to raise their rate of infiltration into the South from thirty-five thousand men in 1965 to some ninety thousand in 1967.[109] Washington had miscalculated the endurance and determination of the North Vietnamese to outlast the Americans.

To make matters worse, it was becoming clear that, as the Americans took over the ground war, the South Vietnamese were fighting less. The following year, when the U.S. commitment rose to 525,000 troops, more soldiers of the South Vietnamese 25th Division died in traffic accidents than in combat.[110] The Vietnamese had handed the war over to the Americans.

The men running the war from Washington were not blind to the facts. As early as the summer of 1966, Robert McNamara had expressed his doubts privately. These doubts had grown in part as a result of his argument with McCloy over force levels in Europe. He had to acknowledge that the war had gotten out of hand and its further expansion threatened America's ability to maintain its war-fighting capabilities in Europe.[111] By the autumn of 1967, 40 percent of America's combat-ready divisions, half of its tactical air power, and a third of its navy was bogged down in Southeast Asia.[112]

In a candid series of conversations with Averell Harriman, the strait-laced Defense Secretary McNamara confessed his deepest worries. In October 1966, he asked Harriman why he hadn't been able to "open up channels of communication with Hanoi." Harriman responded that opening up channels of communication was not the problem: "It is what we say that closes them down. We have nothing of any interest to Hanoi to tell them." Johnson still wanted what amounted to a victory. But as Harriman told McNamara that day, "Ho Chi Minh had been fighting for a quarter of a century for the independence and unification of his country. He thought that he had been cheated by the '54 agreements, and didn't want to give up now." The North Vietnamese leader, he said, "still thinks that we will get tired. . . ."[113] A month later, McNamara confided to Harriman that he believed Johnson would be beaten in the '68 election unless the war was settled soon. "It must be settled this year," McNamara said. "Well," Harriman replied, "early next year."[114]

McNamara and Harriman, however, were exceptions. Most of the president's advisers were stubbornly insisting that the war was being won. Harriman thought that men like Walt Rostow, who had replaced Bundy as national-security adviser, were "reckless" and downright "maniacal" in their determination to escalate the war.[115]

McCloy knew from his own occasional conversations with Harriman that the war was not going well. But he stayed away from Vietnam. Unlike Harriman or McNamara, he did not try to immerse himself in the subject, so he never really gave himself the opportunity to reconsider his earlier views. McCloy's natural deference to professional military opinion made it unlikely that he would question the tactics or strategy of the military commander in the field. So, even as casualties mounted, he refused to second-guess General Westmoreland's "search-and-destroy" strategy. In committing his forces to fight a ground war in Asia, Westmoreland assumed that his highly mobile forces could inflict intolerable losses on the enemy while sustaining a level of U.S. casualties acceptable to the American public. Even as the Vietnamese communists demonstrated that they were prepared to match the U.S. escalation step by step, Westmoreland assured the civilians in Washington that American firepower would ultimately prevail.[116]

McCloy's position on the war remained essentially unchanged from what it had been in 1965–66. Once the commitment of American prestige had been made, the country and the president had to await an honorable resolution.[117] He sometimes even encouraged Johnson to think that things would get better. In the spring of 1967, when the president sent his old friend Ellsworth Bunker as ambassador to Saigon, McCloy wrote that he was "delighted" with the appointment. Bunker, he thought, was a man with "a habit of success," so perhaps he could find a solution to the war: "I believe this augurs very well."[118]

Lyndon Johnson was a deeply troubled man, exhausted emotionally and physically by the strain of the war. He was beginning to feel abandoned by his closest advisers. Also in the spring of 1967, McNamara proposed not only a halt to most bombing, but a recognition that a settlement could not be achieved without the inclusion of the Viet Cong in some kind of coalition government. The Joint Chiefs threatened to resign en masse if the president accepted this advice. Johnson soon began complaining that "that military genius, McNamara, has gone dovish on me."[119] But he could not stomach the Joint Chiefs' proposal for a greatly expanded war either. "Bomb, bomb, bomb, that's all you know," he complained. In the end, he again chose a "middle" course, approving an increase of only fifty-five thousand troops—instead of the two hundred thousand Westmoreland had requested.[120]

McNamara was thoroughly disillusioned. He told Harriman that the president's advisers were terribly unrealistic. Dean Rusk, in particular, was "much too optimistic over what could be achieved, much too rigid. . . . Rusk didn't seem to understand that his position was asking for unconditional surrender of North Vietnam and the VC. . . ." McNamara now unequivocally thought that "it is impossible for us to win the war militarily," and that Saigon would just have to negotiate with the National

Liberation Front.[121] (The defense secretary would admit this only in private; in public he said quite a different thing.[122])

That summer, McCloy was well aware of the intensity of the divisions within the administration. But from his position on the outside he was often more upset by the harsh rhetoric of the war's critics. The cynicism and generational distrust he had seen among a minority of students in 1965 now seemed pervasive.[123] McCloy had firsthand experience with some of the student protests at Amherst College, where he served as chairman of the board of trustees. In June 1966, for instance, he had been greatly embarrassed when a group of Amherst students protesting the war staged a walkout at commencement ceremonies. Sitting next to him that day on the podium as the students walked out was McNamara, whom he had invited to give the commencement address.[124] The defense secretary was pained to note that the brightest students—those graduating *summa* and *magna*—were all wearing antiwar arm bands.[125]

McCloy was offended by the tenor of the public debate over the war and feared that the demonstrators were giving succor to the enemy. He told Bob Lovett that he was worried about Dean Rusk, whom the antiwar demonstrators were vilifying as a war criminal. Why didn't Rusk fight back and respond to his critics?[126] Later in 1967, he was at a Council on Foreign Relations meeting when his frequent tennis partner Cass Canfield complained that the war was alienating American youth. McCloy shot back that the British had put up with dissent during the long Boer War and so could we.[127]

He was also taken aback by criticism from intellectuals like Richard Falk of Princeton University and Arthur Schlesinger.[128] Late in 1966, Schlesinger had published a widely read pamphlet entitled *The Bitter Heritage* in which he suggested that the "so-called Establishment" in general and McCloy in particular had not done all they could to keep the United States out of the war. Schlesinger argued that the architects of the war, men such as the Bundy brothers and Dean Rusk, had all been heavily influenced by Henry Stimson's "powerful advocacy" of the doctrine of collective security. But in Vietnam they had expanded this "Stimsonianism" to what was essentially a civil war in a country of tenuous strategic importance. He accused this Establishment of "cowardice for its fear of acting as an Establishment should." Unlike the "original Establishment in Great Britain," wrote Schlesinger, the American version could not be relied on "to provide support for the established values and institutions of society." As an example, Schlesinger reminded his readers that the American Establishment had "crumpled up before McCarthy." Specifically, the reputed chairman of the Establishment (he did not actually name McCloy) had once "suggested in a public speech that the inquiries of the McCarthy committee were no worse than Senator Black's investigations into the public utility holding companies in 1935." Schlesinger then snidely concluded: "No doubt such leaders of respectable opinion became anti-McCarthy once the crisis was over; but whatever the retrospective courage, let us avoid the illusion that the American Establishment will be much braver the next time around."[129]

McCloy let this personal attack go unanswered. He thought such polemics unseemly, and it pained him to see the war so undermine the country's bipartisan consensus on foreign policy. He was immobilized by the fact that American soldiers were fighting and dying on a foreign battlefield. One could not walk away from such a commitment. And yet he did not wish to join in the public fray over the war either. Late in the spring of 1967, James Rowe, a Washington lawyer and an old friend of Johnson's, wrote a memo to the president suggesting the formation of an independent citizens' committee "to answer the Galbraiths, the Schlesingers, the Percys, the Fulbrights and the McGoverns." In addition to some "tough-minded liberals" like Thurman Arnold and Dean Acheson, Rowe suggested it would be "helpful to have some of the 'Establishment,' such as John McCloy, McGeorge Bundy and a few others. Lots of people are still influenced by the 'Establishment.' In this particular battle of public opinion, it has been silent. It has not joined the intellectuals but it certainly is not breaking its back for the Administration."[130] Rowe said it would take the president's tacit support to sign up the kind of people who should head the committee, but he warned that the operation should not appear to have been instigated by the White House.

An ardent White House aide, John Roche, thought this a wonderful idea. A former head of Americans for Democratic Action, Roche believed that too many liberals in the 1960s had lost their anticommunist fervor. He took Rowe's proposal to Johnson, who quickly approved the project with the caveat: "But don't get surfaced."[131] Because both Roche and Johnson realized that the committee would lack any credibility if it appeared to be run out of the White House, they had former Senator Paul Douglas of Illinois front the operation. Douglas approached Eisenhower, Truman, George Meany, and eventually McCloy to sign on as officers of the new organization, to be called the Citizens Committee for Peace with Freedom in Vietnam.

Initially, McCloy indicated support for the idea. He even passed on to Douglas his suggestions for other members of the Committee: Acheson, Lovett, and Dillon.[132] But soon afterward, perhaps after speaking with Lovett, he had a change of heart. Throughout that summer, he procrastinated, refusing to commit himself. He was torn. Old friends like Dwight Eisenhower, Omar Bradley, Dean Acheson, and James Conant had agreed to join the new organization. But Lovett and Mac Bundy were dragging their feet. By October, the White House knew that McCloy was "something of a problem along with Mac Bundy."[133]

Shortly before the Committee was scheduled to surface, Cabot Lodge and James Conant tried one more time to get McCloy and Mac Bundy on board. But their arguments left McCloy unconvinced.[134] Afterward, McCloy wrote Lodge to remind him that he had already lent his name to one such citizens' committee on Vietnam in 1965. To do so again now would be "rather redundant." Moreover, he said, "I am always reluctant to have my name spread around on broadsides in any event. It is something you may be justified in doing two or three times in a lifetime, but not intermittently." He reassured Lodge that he was, of course, always ready to help the president "bring this Vietnam affair to a constructive conclusion," but adding his name to another committee was not going to help matters.[135]

Nor did Mac Bundy, Robert Lovett, or Arthur Dean join the Committee. As Jim Rowe had observed that spring, the Establishment was not siding with the war's intellectual critics, but now it was no longer prepared to associate itself publicly with the war effort. On November 1, 1967, Johnson convened another meeting of the "Wise Men," but McCloy and Bob Lovett declined to attend. Of those who showed up, Acheson, Bundy, and others conveyed to the president their doubts about the bombing campaign.[136] It was clearly unrealistic, they said, to expect the North Vietnamese to negotiate on Washington's terms simply because of the bombing. They were convinced by McNamara's arguments that the bombing, if anything, hardened the enemy's resolve. On the other hand, evidence presented to them by General Wheeler and the CIA's Richard Helms and George Carver led them to hope that the war was finally being won on the ground. General Westmoreland was insisting that the "crossover point" had been reached in this war of attrition. The enemy, he claimed, was losing men faster than they could be replaced. The weekly body counts were up, and the Saigon regime controlled more territory and a higher percentage of the population than ever before. Given these optimistic statistics, the "Wise Men" encouraged the president to carry on the struggle, though they urged him to find a ground strategy that would give the South Vietnamese a larger role in actual combat operations.[137] Acheson and Mac Bundy urged Johnson to mount a new public-relations campaign to sell the war to the American people: "Emphasize the 'light at the end of the tunnel,' " Bundy advised, "instead of battles, deaths and danger."[138] Only George Ball spoke for a sharp disengagement. At the end of one of their briefings, Ball could not restrain himself from bursting out, "I've been watching you across the table. You're like a flock of buzzards sitting on a fence, sending the young men off to be killed. You ought to be ashamed of yourselves."[139] These were strong words, but men like Ball and Acheson could argue vehemently and at the end of the day go to Acheson's townhouse in Georgetown to sip whiskey sodas.

If he had been there, McCloy would have gone along with Acheson,

Rusk, and the other hard-liners. Only a few days after this "Wise Men" meeting, he found himself sitting next to Endicott Peabody on the New York–Boston air shuttle. The former governor of Massachusetts turned the conversation to Vietnam. McCloy surprised Peabody with his tone of resignation. Johnson had no choice, he said, but to press ahead. He blamed President Kennedy for the initial decision to send troops to Vietnam. Kennedy, he said, had thought he could do this "without making an irretrievable commitment." But, looking back, McCloy thought "the die was cast at that point." Once they were committed, there could be no turning back.[140]

This did not mean that McCloy thought the war a good or even a necessary thing in his scheme of national-security priorities. On the contrary, he emphatically agreed with George Ball's premise that America's most important interests lay in Europe. But as the war dragged on, he found it difficult to accept the obvious import of Ball's position: a defeat in Vietnam would advertise to all that there were indeed limits on the ability of the United States to exercise its will. To McCloy's mind, this was a dangerous proposition, particularly at a time when the whole framework of a collective defense in Western Europe seemed to be unraveling. How could Washington rejuvenate the kind of foreign policy of a "heroic scale" that had emerged from the rubble of World War II? What were the limits of U.S. power and the minimum needs of U.S. national security?

It was these kinds of questions that concerned McCloy when he met his colleagues at the Council on Foreign Relations to discuss Vietnam. Many Council events in 1967–68 began to focus on Vietnam; men like Henry Cabot Lodge, the former ambassador to Saigon; Herman Kahn, the Rand Corporation war-games strategist; Robert G. K. Thompson, the British counterinsurgency specialist; Chester Cooper, a former CIA analyst and an aide to Averell Harriman; and Major General William G. DuPuy—all of whom in one way or another had been involved in the war—gave the Council off-the-record briefings that year. These discussions culminated in early December, when George Ball and William Bundy were invited to present their opposing views in two successive meetings. Ball belittled Vietnam's strategic importance to the United States in a talk entitled "Viet-Nam from the Perspective of U.S. Global Responsibilities." Bundy followed two days later with a speech emphasizing the "progress" made in achieving U.S. objectives in Vietnam. These sessions were well attended, and the questioning afterward was lively and pointed.[141]

Out of these Council discussions, McCloy began, finally, to come to a few conclusions about Vietnam's lessons for the rest of U.S. foreign policy. In early January 1968, he gave a speech in Chicago in which he cautiously criticized Washington's "preoccupation with the frustrations of Vietnam." Significantly, he chose to speak out publicly at a meeting of the Table Ronde, an elite group of some ninety European government officials, businessmen, and intellectuals: "I am prepared to admit that we seem to be overcommitted at the present time and perhaps in view of the uncertain and complicated world we face in the next decade, we should take a more modest view of our individual ability to shape the world. I am not prepared to debate the point as to where we should draw the line—certainly not to go into the problem of Vietnam. I have no doubt, however, that the line should include Western Europe." The crisis in NATO, the withdrawal of France from the military alliance, the resurgence of "hoary" nationalisms—all these trends were undermining the West's "sense of community in all of our international affairs." If NATO should disappear, he warned, "The tensions which could, and probably would, arise under such circumstances might make the present tribulations in respect to Vietnam appear trivial."[142]

As cautious as these words may seem in retrospect, for McCloy to state publicly that the United States seemed "to be overcommitted" was a major signal that the war was finally causing the foreign-policy community to question the administration. Publications across the country, from *The New York Times* to the *Los Angeles Times,* noted the speech. In an editorial headlined "Disaffected Establishment," the liberal *Nation* observed, ". . . McCloy is troubled by the overshadowing effect of the Vietnamese War on our role in Europe. . . . With no dovelike sentiments in their [the foreign-policy establishment's] make-up, they see the United States overextended and would like us to revert to prudent policy in the Pacific."[143]

Harriman, impatient with his efforts to nudge Johnson toward a negotiated settlement, wrote McCloy to applaud him for putting in a plug for NATO: "It's well that people realize where the center of power in the world resides and our fundamental interests."[144] Two weeks later, on the very eve of the Tet holidays in Vietnam, Harriman complained to his old friend, "I wish you would take a hand in settling Vietnam. It's a frustrating business."[145]

On January 30, 1968, Johnson was sitting in on his regular Tuesday luncheon meeting with his closest advisers when the phone rang at 2:33 P.M. Walt Rostow took the call on the kitchen phone and listened quietly to an urgent dispatch from Saigon. When he got off the phone, he turned to the president and reported, "We are being mortared heavily in Saigon. The Presidential Palace and BOQ's [bachelor officers' quarters] are being hit."[146] The Viet Cong had brought the war to the doors of the U.S. Embassy. Just minutes earlier, a team of nineteen Viet Cong sappers had blown a hole in the wall surrounding the embassy compound in Saigon. After rushing inside, they took up positions inside the courtyard in front of the chancellory and for the next six hours pounded the building with rockets and machine-gun fire. The suicide attack ended at 9:15 A.M., when all nineteen men were killed or wounded. But that was only the beginning. Within twenty-four hours, the Viet Cong had struck thirty-six of forty-four provincial capitals and five out of six of the country's largest cities. They actually seized the ancient city of Hue and occupied it for the next three weeks. Altogether, the Tet Offensive cost the United States eleven hundred killed. The South Vietnamese lost twenty-three hundred soldiers and an estimated 12,500 civilians. One million new refugees were created, and for a time the country appeared on the verge of collapse. The Viet Cong had hoped that their attacks would precipitate a civilian uprising. This did not happen. Instead, the enemy suffered as many as forty thousand battle deaths; the Viet Cong regular units were so decimated that in the future the North Vietnamese would have to bear the brunt of the war.

Most Americans could not believe what had happened. Walter Cronkite exclaimed, "What the hell is going on? I thought we were winning the war."[147] McCloy was not so much shocked as depressed by this turn of events. Five days into the Tet Offensive, he called up his old friend Lewis L. Strauss and said he was so "blue" that he needed to commiserate with a "kindred spirit." The moral fiber of his fellow Americans, he complained, seemed to have deteriorated, a trend he blamed on the media. The war was bad enough, but the film clips of the war shown on television "day after day placed the worst possible complexion on our troops and their conduct in that country." He and Strauss agreed that the worst part of the whole mess was not the war itself but the "loss of prestige" at home and abroad.[148] America's credibility as a global power seemed to be evaporating.

Lyndon Johnson was determined to avoid a collapse in Saigon. He immediately ordered an additional 10,500 men to Vietnam and instructed Westmoreland that if he needed more troops he should ask for them. This led quickly to a Wheeler-Westmoreland request for an additional 206,000 troops. Wheeler reported that Tet had been a "very near thing," and that without a major escalation on the ground the war might be lost.[149]

This request shocked the president's closest advisers and precipitated a full-scale review of the administration's war plans. In early March 1968, Clark Clifford, who had replaced McNamara, persuaded Johnson that he had to reject Westmoreland's request for another major escalation. Events then moved very quickly. On March 12, Senator Eugene McCarthy rocked the country by unexpectedly winning 42 percent of the New Hampshire Democratic primary for president. Four days later, an even more formidable challenger, Senator Robert Kennedy, declared his own candidacy for the presidency. The mood of the country had dramatically changed.

Some of the president's advisers—Walt Rostow and Dean Rusk in particular—still urged him to "hang in there."[150] But by the third week of March, Clifford was arguing for a methodical de-escalation of the war. Johnson was still undecided when Clifford suggested that the "Wise Men" be brought in for yet another consultation. Johnson agreed, and so another series of briefings were held for a group of the "elder statesmen" on the war. McCloy was again not invited for this session on March 26, 1968—even though he had been in Washington the previous day to see Harriman.[151]

Johnson already knew that McCloy—and Lovett, for that matter—were tired of the war and would only complain that it had distracted the administration from the much more serious problems of Europe and NATO.[152] But he also knew that McCloy and Lovett had no idea how to end the war. Besides, the president stubbornly refused to abandon his ultimate goal, telling a group of businessmen on March 17, "We shall and we are going to win."[153] He fully expected the other "Wise Men"—including such hawks as Acheson, Arthur Dean, Cabot Lodge, and Omar Bradley—to reject Clifford's arguments for a de-escalation. He was wrong. To his surprise, a majority announced that they favored an immediate de-escalation of the conflict. Mac Bundy told the president that he had expected slow and steady progress from their briefings the previous November.[154] Instead, the CIA's George Carver had given them a gloomy assessment of the post-Tet situation. Despite their heavy losses, the North Vietnamese were prepared to match whatever force levels the United States committed to the war.[155] Acheson bluntly concluded that the United States could "no longer do the job we set out to do in the time we have left and we must begin to take steps to disengage."[156] Only a few of the standard hard-liners favored another escalation. General Maxwell Taylor couldn't explain why his colleagues had changed their minds, except perhaps that "my Council on Foreign Relations friends were living in the cloud of *The New York Times.*"[157]

Johnson was shocked and embittered by this betrayal. "The establishment bastards have bailed out," he muttered after the "Wise Men" had filed out.[158] Still, he knew these to be "steady and balanced" men. "If they had been so deeply influenced by the reports of the Tet offensive," he later wrote in his memoirs, "what must the average citizen in the country be thinking?"[159] So, five days later, he went on television to make the dramatic announcement that he would not seek a second term in office. He said he wished to avoid "the partisan divisions that are developing in this political year" and concentrate on bringing peace to Vietnam. The bombing of North Vietnam would stop above the 20th parallel. Averell Harriman was designated his personal representative in any future peace talks. In retrospect, one sees that Johnson's speech signaled not a change of strategy but a change in tactics. All he had abandoned was the tactic of gradual escalation, not the goal of an independent South Vietnam. As Hanoi's representatives to the Paris peace talks soon learned, unless they negotiated a cease-fire in place, leaving the Thieu-Ky regime intact, the war would continue. Only from now on, the South Vietnamese would be forced to shoulder a larger and larger share of the combat. "Vietnamization" had begun.[160]

This was a solution to which McCloy had no objection. As long as the conflict did not continue to escalate and drain resources and attention away from Europe, he remained publicly silent. In the years to come, McCloy would have nothing to do with the war. Nor, however, did he do anything to stop what Lew Douglas called "one of the craziest, maddest adventures this country has ever embarked upon."[161] Indeed, in contrast to Douglas and many of his other friends, including Walter Lippmann, his attitude was cool and unemotional. Lippmann had come to the conclusion that "decent people could no longer support the war."[162] But whereas the elderly columnist wrote impassioned pieces on the immorality of the war, McCloy confined his reservations to geopolitical arguments.

It has become commonplace to observe that Vietnam destroyed the Establishment. This judgment is too easy. The influence of men like McCloy continued unabated. The war polarized the nation, and the bipartisan consensus on foreign-policy issues broke down for a time. But this was a temporary phenomenon; in any case, the Establishment itself had been first ambivalent, then divided over the war. The commitment to Vietnam was never important to the Establishment except as a symbol of America's willingness to fight the Cold War anywhere and everywhere.

McCloy had refused Johnson's pleadings to be his "proconsul" in Saigon, and yet, when asked to approve the major intervention of 1965, had gone along with the policy. In the crucial two years that followed, the "Wise Men" never seriously questioned Johnson's gradual escalation of the American commitment into a major ground war. Should they have known better? McCloy, Lovett, Ball, Acheson, Clifford, and others repeatedly demonstrated that they were aware of the folly of fighting a war on the Asian mainland. But that was an abstract notion. In practice, they could not condone a defeat to an American commitment of military strength. They deferred too easily to the assessments of the military professionals. And with few exceptions, the generals kept saying that this war of attrition was being won. In the words of Lieutenant Colonel John Paul Vann, who had arrived in Vietnam in 1962, it was all a "bright, shining lie."[163]

McCloy insisted for a long time that there could be no turning back. In the end, he brought himself to question the war publicly only when it threatened America's standing in Europe. He did not openly question the administration's war goals, only the country's capacity for waging this war. Johnson was poorly served by such ambivalent counsel.

In McCloy's view, there were more strategic regions of the world than Vietnam, and one of them was the oil-rich Middle East. Throughout the 1960s, he had regularly brought his oil-company clients down to Washington to exchange information with the government. In the spring of 1967, shortly after concluding his negotiations with the Germans over NATO's troubles, he turned his attention to a growing crisis between Egypt and Israel. Relations with Egypt had soured since his 1964 trip. In response to the lobbying efforts of McCloy, Harriman, and others, Congress had agreed to resume shipments of foreign aid food grains to Egypt, stipulating that Nasser would have to renegotiate the wheat deal every six months. Not surprisingly, Nasser resented this calculated effort to keep him on a short leash. In an effort to counter this pressure from the West, he resumed negotiations with the Kremlin for shipments of Soviet arms and wheat, and simultaneously allowed Palestinian resistance fighters greater freedom to launch guerrilla attacks on Israel from Egyptian-occupied Gaza. Similar border raids from the Syrian Golan Heights had led to Israeli retaliation.

By the spring of 1967, tensions had so escalated that the region seemed headed for war. Challenged by the Syrians to support them against the Israeli retaliations in the Golan, Nasser ordered Egyptian Army units into the Sinai desert and closed the Strait of Tiran to Israeli shipping. The Israelis then ordered a general mobilization. Late in May 1967, McCloy called Harriman to say that he was "worried." What was Washington doing to prevent a war that could jeopardize U.S. access to Arab oil? Harriman confessed that the administration hadn't been able to give this "vital" region the attention it deserved.[164] Two weeks later, McCloy's fears were realized when the Israelis launched a surprise attack against Egypt. Syria and Jordan soon joined in the war, but within six days the Israelis had conquered the entire Sinai Peninsula, the West Bank, and a good portion of the Golan Heights.

This humiliating defeat led Egypt, Syria, and most other Arab states to break off diplomatic relations with Washington. In the weeks following the war, some twenty-four thousand American expatriates—businessmen, diplomats, and their dependents—were thrown out of the Middle East.[165] Anti-American demonstrations swept the Arab world, and brief strikes occurred in the Arabian oil fields. American interests in the region had never been in such jeopardy. Believing it important to maintain some informal channels of communication, the Johnson administration decided to encourage a number of American businessmen with corporate ties to the Arab world to visit the region from time to time. Soon after the war,

Assistant Secretary of State for Near-Eastern Affairs Lucius "Luke" Battle persuaded David Rockefeller, Robert B. Anderson (Eisenhower's Treasury secretary), James Linen (a Time-Life officer), and McCloy to make periodic visits to the region.

McCloy already had business reasons to go to the Middle East. Both Chase Manhattan Bank and the Allied Chemical Co., of which McCloy was a board director, had significant investments in Iran. Chase had made an investment in a local development corporation, and Allied had recently signed a $173-million contract to build five chemical plants. But in the winter of 1968, McCloy learned from Allied's president, John Connor, that the project was in trouble. Cost overruns of $20–25 million might force Allied to eliminate two of the five projected plants. The Iranians were beginning to level "accusations of bad faith. . . ."[166] In addition, the American oil consortium in Iran, which included a number of McCloy's clients, was facing increasing pressures from the shah to raise its offtake of oil in order to finance the regime's ambitious development budget.

So, in March 1968, he flew out to the region, accompanied by George Ballou, the head of Standard Oil of California (SOCAL). They allotted three weeks to visit Iran, Kuwait, Saudi Arabia, Jordan, Lebanon, and Egypt.[167] So, on the day Lyndon Johnson announced his decision not to run for a second term, McCloy was being driven from Teheran to the shah's palace on the Caspian Sea. He arrived at noon and found the shah dismayed by the news. The Iranian monarch said he hoped the president's decision did not foreshadow a "shirking" of Washington's "key responsibilities in Vietnam" and elsewhere. This, he warned McCloy, could lead to a "loss of faith in U.S. commitments. . . ."[168]

McCloy nodded his agreement and then listened patiently as the monarch went through a familiar litany of complaints about British misbehavior in the Persian Gulf, the Saudis and the Arab Emirates on the Trucial Coast. When the lecture was done, McCloy got down to business. He urged him to demonstrate a bit of statesmanship himself. Iran was a "big progressive country" and the shah a "respected leader who could afford to be big in dealing with his neighbors." As such, he should "collaborate" with the Saudis. McCloy warned that it was "particularly important to Iran that there be no rupture with the West, meaning the oil companies." This point was critical. In this and further conversations with the shah's prime minister, McCloy explicitly identified the oil companies with Western interests. There could be no relationship with Washington if the shah failed to maintain his deal with the oil companies.[169]

The oil companies, of course, did not wish to increase Iran's royalties or production quota; either measure would harm their relationship with other producing countries and disrupt markets. But McCloy could see that the Iranian ruler's dream of turning his country into a modern military and economic power would someday require greatly increased oil revenues. His assignment from the oil companies was to postpone any such reckoning. The companies' argument against a unilateral attempt by the producers to alter oil production rates and pricing was the threat of a withdrawal of political support from Washington.

His message delivered, McCloy went back to Teheran to deal with Allied Chemical's problems. He told Prime Minister Amir Abbas Hoveyda that Allied was doing its best to keep the chemical-plant project on a sound economic footing. "It [Allied] did not appreciate," McCloy said, "having its efforts met with charges of bad faith. . . ." Hoveyda accepted these assurances. Confidentially, however, McCloy told the American ambassador that the enterprise was now not $25 million over cost, but as much as $75 million over the original estimate.[170] The project would probably never be economical, and critics would later cite it as one of those "white elephants" that drained the country's resources and contributed to the revolutionary upheavals of the 1970s.

On the Arabian Peninsula, McCloy continued his mission of private diplomacy. In Bahrein, he assured the ruler, Sheikh Isa, that the shah "had no intention of using force to take Bahrein."[171]

In Riyadh, capital of Saudi Arabia, he had an audience with King Faisal and tried to persuade the Saudi monarch that he could patch up his differences with the shah. He suggested that the shah just needed to be "more fully consulted on future decisions on Gulf" issues. All the parties in the region needed to exercise a little "statesmanship." Faisal indicated that his real concerns lay not with the Iranians but with the general threat of communism in the region. U.S. policies regarding the Arab-Israeli conflict were only giving the communists greater popular support. McCloy argued with Faisal. Later, he met with Petroleum Minister Zaki Yamani and a number of influential Saudi princes. Breaking with protocol, McCloy refused to allow the American ambassador, Herman Eilts, to sit in on all his meetings with the Saudis. He wanted to be able to speak privately and with the kind of frankness most diplomats avoid. Based on what he later heard from the Saudis, Eilts reported that McCloy's visit, "even though private, was very useful. From what I hear . . . McCloy stood up strongly and effectively, yet sympathetically, to Saudi critics of U.S. policies. Saudis, including Faisal, welcome such opportunities [to] air their worries to distinguished private Americans."[172]

Actually, Eilts would have been astonished if he had known just how far McCloy had gone in his conversations with Faisal. In his free-wheeling style, McCloy had explored the possibility of a comprehensive settlement of the Arab-Israeli dispute. Subjected to the lawyer's gentle prodding, the Saudi king had said he could accept a settlement with Israel based on U.N. Resolution 242, which called for a peace settlement based on Israeli withdrawal from the occupied territories and mutual recognition. Significantly, Faisal was willing to compromise on such contentious issues as the continued Israeli occupation of the Golan Heights and the status of Jerusalem. He proposed a complicated formula whereby Jerusalem would remain united, while simultaneously allowing for the creation of a free Islamic sanctuary within the Holy City. McCloy was excited by these proposals and eager to see if he could extract similar concessions from other Arab leaders.

Over the next ten days, he saw King Hussein of Jordan, the president of Lebanon, and finally Nasser. The latter appointment was fixed only at the last minute, and an official record of his conversation with the mercurial Egyptian leader does not seem to exist. But it is clear from McCloy's private correspondence that Nasser was eager to have the United States broker a peace settlement. The Egyptian suggested that, since Johnson was no longer a candidate for president, perhaps he would be freed politically to implement a solution to the Arab-Israeli conflict on the basis of an "equitable interpretation" of U.N. Resolution 242. McCloy then carefully extracted from Nasser what he thought would constitute the details of a comprehensive settlement. By the time he left Egypt, he felt he had a "package" peace settlement practically in his pocket.[173] "It included," he later wrote George Ball, "Israeli use of the Canal, Resolution 242 supplemented by demilitarized zones, continued Israeli occupation of the [Golan] Heights with Feisal ready to work out a free Moslem sanctuary in Jerusalem, with Egypt's recognition of Israel and support by the Western European countries as well as the Soviet Union in the settlement. I really had a package in regard to which I was quite optimistic after my talks with Nasser, Hussein and Feisal."

Here was a chance, he thought, to restore American interests in the Arab world. Upon arriving in New York, he immediately called Walt Rostow in the White House and scheduled an appointment with the president. In the meantime, he lined up support from Siegmund Warburg and a few other Jewish leaders who endorsed the broad outlines of the package. One week later, he went to the White House and for forty minutes briefed the president, Dean Rusk, Clark Clifford, and Joseph Sisco, an assistant secretary of state. McCloy tried to make the case for a major change in U.S. policy. Everyone acknowledged that he had brought back dramatic concessions from the Arabs, but Clifford said bluntly that a broad U.S. peace initiative could not be launched in an election year.

McCloy thought the president was at first eager to pursue the matter, "but he simply faded away after Clifford's discouragement." Rusk, as usual, sat in silence. McCloy came away from the meeting thinking he had "failed rather completely" in making his point. Back in New York, he sat down at his desk and drafted a long letter to Rusk. The president, he wrote, seemed to think the only problem at hand was the rupture in diplomatic relations. This was really inconsequential to the main problems: the need to avoid another Arab-Israeli war and the need to "repair our power and influence in what is probably the most strategic area in the world." Another war might lead to another Arab defeat, but it could just as easily lead to a superpower confrontation. He then predicted:

> Nasser has had his [military] material replenished, but he is not yet ready for another gamble. He intends, I think, to undergo a long period of training with his Soviet technicians before he tries the game again. He doesn't have the pilots now, but he does think seriously in terms of renewed war as long as Arab territory is occupied by the Israelis, and, in my judgment, it will come some day if steps are not taken during this interim period to avoid it.

The Soviets were exploiting "our partiality to Israel" in order to achieve their century-old ambition to turn the Mediterranean into a Soviet sea. There was a danger that they would in a few short years replace the British as the hegemonic power in the region, thus outflanking NATO from the south. Seventy percent of all the oil consumed by Western Europe and 80 percent of that consumed by Japan came from the Middle East. He warned that if the United States lost control over the marketing of this oil, America's already discouraging balance-of-payments picture would be "radically impaired."

Things should not be allowed to deteriorate any further. "The simple fact," he wrote, "is our Israeli policy is not operating in favor of our national interest in the Middle East. . . . We cannot afford to have our national interest overridden by a policy which would preclude us from taking any position opposed to further Zionist ambitions." Though Israel deserved to have firm international guarantees of her security, she had to be confined to within her pre–June 1967 boundaries. "The issue, in short, is really one of [Israeli] expansion. Moreover, it is, I believe, entirely in the long range interests of Israel that such ambitions be curbed. . . ." The president should appoint someone of experience and stature, some one like former under secretary of state Livingston Merchant, to implement a settlement based on U.N. Resolution 242. To be sure, the Arab states would have to end their attitude of belligerency and recognize Israel. Portions of the Golan Heights, the Sinai, and the West Bank should be demilitarized, and then something would have to be done about the Palestinian refugees. Such a high-level effort at a comprehensive settlement might not succeed, but McCloy concluded that "the situation should not be permitted to drift without a sustained and imaginative effort on our part to anticipate the coming trouble and further loss of United States position in an area vital to us and to our allies."[174]

This was, of course, a succinct exposition of the views held by his oil-company clients. But it was an opinion McCloy had personally held ever since he first visited Jerusalem in 1943. The important thing to U.S. national interests in the Middle East was not Israel but oil. In McCloy's view, the creation of Israel, and Truman's hasty recognition of it in 1948, had not altered those strategic interests. The Jewish claims on Palestine had been a complication then, and, unfortunately, they were still a complication. The solution, seen from McCloy's legalistic approach to the problem, was to treat Israel's cease-fire lines as an internationally recognized boundary. "The whole concept," he told Rusk, "of the Palestinian homeland, and Israel itself, precluded expansion. It was a limited area carved for outside settlement from an already occupied area." Now that Israel had expanded beyond those cease-fire lines, she should be asked to exchange the newly occupied territories for a comprehensive peace settlement.

It would have taken any administration a great deal of political courage, self-confidence, and determination to accept such recommendations. But in April 1968, barely a month after the war in Vietnam had ended Lyndon Johnson's hopes for a second term, this administration had none of those qualities. McCloy's letter was knocked around the State Department for three weeks before Rusk finally responded with a short note thanking him for his "thought-provoking comments. . . ." The administration, however, was going to wait and see what became of a new round of U.N. talks. Realizing that McCloy would hardly be satisfied with such a meager response, Rusk agreed to have Luke Battle call up the lawyer and explain the administration's position in more detail. Battle then had to carry out the awkward job of explaining to McCloy over the phone that the administration felt his proposal was too risky. Failure to make real progress toward a settlement might itself stimulate another war, a Soviet-U.S. confrontation, and "long-term losses to the U.S. position." The State Department would play it safe.

McCloy was severely disappointed, and later blamed Clifford, the president's "white-haired boy at that time," and Rusk, who "simply failed as usual to seize the initiative."[175] The Johnson administration was, in any case, on its way out. Since the Republicans certainly had a good chance of winning the White House in November, he thought perhaps his advice would be listened to more closely by those who succeeded Johnson.

BOOK VII

Elder Statesman 1969–1989

CHAPTER 27

The Establishment at Bay: The Nixon–Kissinger Administration

[McCloy was] "a reliable pilot through treacherous shoals. . . . He was always available. He was ever wise."

HENRY KISSINGER

Though his memories of Richard M. Nixon's red-baiting during the 1954 congressional campaign had not faded, McCloy still thought of himself as a loyal Republican. As he cast his vote in 1968 for the Republican nominee, he only hoped the "New Nixon" had become a more mature and seasoned politician. When Nixon narrowly won the election, McCloy had no expectations that he would become part of the new administration's inner circle. The new president was insecure among the men who ranked as elder statesmen in the Eastern Establishment. As Henry Kissinger would later write, these were men whom Nixon "revered and despised, whose approbation he both cherished and scorned."[1] Nixon had not forgotten how some of these Wall Street Republicans had tried to ease him off the ticket in 1956; he was suspicious of them, though his political instincts told him that he needed to be seen seeking their counsel. So, for rather ambivalent reasons on both sides, McCloy found himself on

Nixon's postelection foreign-policy transition team. His presence was mere window-dressing.

Henry Kissinger was another matter. Here was a man who had all the necessary Establishment credentials—Harvard, the Council on Foreign Relations, and a long-standing relationship with Nelson Rockefeller, who had been Nixon's only real rival for the nomination. And yet Nixon sensed in Kissinger a kindred spirit, a desperately ambitious man who as an immigrant would always remain an outsider, insecure about his standing with the Establishment. He knew that Kissinger had called his thirty-two-year-old foreign-policy adviser, Richard V. Allen, and offered to keep him informed during the campaign about the Paris peace talks. Kissinger had said their contacts would have to be secret, so as not to close off his access to the Democrats. Allen's major worry that autumn had been that Johnson's envoy to Paris, Averell Harriman, might suddenly achieve a breakthrough in the talks and bring home the kind of peace settlement that could throw the election to Hubert Humphrey. So he was more than grateful that Kissinger was willing to use his friendship with Harriman to keep the campaign informed on any last-minute "October surprises."[2] Kissinger served Nixon well, all the while assuring his Democratic friends that he favored Humphrey.[3]

McCloy had been unaware of Kissinger's activities that autumn. He recognized that the younger man had a "fine mind." But he always thought him a bit too calculating, and occasionally he would complain to friends about "Henry's opportunism."[4] Years later, when Kissinger brought out his two volumes of memoirs, McCloy judged them "defensive and not good history."[5]

Kissinger went to great lengths to associate himself with men like McCloy, Acheson, Lovett, and Harriman. These were men, he said, who "represented a unique pool of talent—an aristocracy dedicated to the service of this nation on behalf of principles beyond partisanship." Of all these men, Kissinger wrote, there were none he saw more frequently during the transition period than McCloy, whom he described as "a reliable pilot through treacherous shoals. . . . He was always available. He was ever wise." Such flattery aside, the truth was that neither during the transition nor afterward did Kissinger very often act upon McCloy's counsel. He thought McCloy's "penchant for anecdotes" "time-consuming" and his intelligence was "balanced rather than penetrating."[6]

Early in the Nixon administration, McCloy took David Rockefeller and a number of his oil-company clients in to see the new president. Oil-company executives like Rawleigh Warner of Mobil and Robert Anderson of Arco had contributed heavily to Nixon's campaign and expected his administration to protect their interests. McCloy briefed the president and Kissinger on his conversations with Nasser, and the oil men urged Nixon to launch a major initiative to achieve a comprehensive Middle

East peace settlement before the situation deteriorated further. Nixon seemed sympathetic; he boasted that this was one president who was not indebted to the Jewish vote. But nothing happened, and later Warner complained, "We could always get a hearing, but we felt we might just as well be talking to that wall."[7]

Kissinger had already decided not to stick his neck out on the Middle East. Early in 1969, he did everything he could to block the State Department's efforts to launch a major peace initiative. When Nasser wrote a personal letter to Nixon, suggesting that diplomatic relations could be restored if only the United States would "break the ice" with some gesture such as holding up the sale of F-4 Phantom jets to Israel, Kissinger persuaded the president to dismiss this overture as nothing more than the machinations of a "Soviet client state."[8] When McCloy heard from his own sources what had happened, he was appalled by Kissinger's misjudgment of Egyptian intentions. He felt that, if Washington continued to remain aloof from the conflict, another war would result, which would further jeopardize U.S. control of Arab oil. He thought Kissinger shortsighted.

McCloy's uneasiness about Kissinger was not mollified by his dealings with the White House aide on arms-control matters. As chairman of the President's General Advisory Committee on Arms Control and Disarmament—a position he had held since 1961—McCloy was supposed to sign off on any major recommendations to the president concerning arms-control measures. He and his fellow committee members—Dean Rusk, Cyrus R. Vance, Harold Brown, U.S. Air Force General Lauris Norstad, William C. Foster, a former chief of the Arms Control and Disarmament Agency, and William W. Scranton, former governor of Pennsylvania—were given regular top-secret briefings on U.S. and Soviet strategic weapons. By law, McCloy reported directly to the president, and his Committee's reports had usually been accepted as the consensus in the defense community. But in 1969–70, Kissinger systematically deflected the recommendations of what was informally known around Washington as the "McCloy Advisory Committee."

In retrospect, many arms-control experts and historians judge that the United States lost an opportunity in these years to place a cap on the arms race. With the opening of the first Strategic Arms Limitation Talks (SALT) in 1969, two critical issues had to be decided by Soviet and American negotiators: whether to ban defensive antiballistic missiles (ABMs) and whether a similar ban should be imposed on the deployment of multiple independently targetable re-entry vehicles (MIRVs). Both questions dealt with the issue of whether the two superpowers could control technologies that threatened to lower the threshold of nuclear war. The Soviets were eager to negotiate an ABM treaty and gave every indication that they would also agree to ban MIRVs. But by the spring of 1969, Kissinger said, he had concluded that a ban on MIRVs was politically unpalatable.[9]

On March 10, 1970, the McCloy Advisory Committee strongly recommended a ban on both ABMs and MIRVs. Kissinger was extremely upset, recognizing that McCloy's conservative credentials would lend considerable support to the arms controllers in the administration. In his memoirs, he suggests that McCloy was merely reflecting the prevailing mood. Actually, McCloy had adopted this position after considerable thought. In part, he was influenced by a January 1969 Council on Foreign Relations report to the president-elect which had concluded that an early arms-control agreement with the Soviets was "imperative." Significantly, the report recommended a unilateral moratorium on MIRVs. McCloy felt that, though the United States was ahead in MIRV technology, it would only be a matter of years before the Soviets began placing multiple warheads on their missiles. Besides, he knew that MIRV technology had been developed in response to the Soviet deployment of antimissile defense systems. If the Soviets were now ready to limit such systems with an ABM treaty, there was no need to deploy U.S. MIRV missiles. Multiple warheads not only represented a quantum leap in the nuclear-arms race, but also made any future arms-control agreements difficult to monitor. One would not know, from counting missiles, how many independently targetable warheads existed. Worse, in a few years there would be so many multiple warheads that each superpower might be able to threaten the survivability of the other's land-based ICBMs in a surprise first strike.[10] When Paul Nitze argued that the United States should not give up a technology in which it was ahead, McCloy brusquely commented that he was "crazy."[11] There was no doubt in his mind that, if the Soviets were willing, the Nixon administration should jump at the chance to ban the technology.[12]

Kissinger was aware of these arguments, but, like many in the Pentagon, he found it difficult to reconcile himself to the fact of nuclear parity with the Soviets. In addition, he decided that, in order to assert his control over the pace of the emerging SALT negotiations, he had to scuttle any viable MIRV ban supported by the arms-control community. In deference to the force of McCloy's arguments, he allowed U.S. negotiators to put forward a proposal to ban MIRVs. But he weighed the proposal down with what some military experts regarded as an irrelevant and unnecessary demand for on-site inspection. Kissinger's own NSC aides later admitted that the on-site-inspection provision was designed to make the MIRV ban "unacceptable" to the Soviets.[13] Another Kissinger aide, William G. Hyland, later concluded that his boss had made a mistake. It was, he told reporter Strobe Talbot, "the key decision in the entire history of SALT

. . . that changed strategic relations, and changed them to the detriment of American security."[14]

When McCloy found out about Kissinger's linkage of a MIRV ban to on-site inspections, he requested access to all NSC documentation on the matter. But in a letter that McCloy must have found extremely insulting, Kissinger refused. Saying that he had "given careful thought" to the request, he informed McCloy that his staff would periodically determine which documents should be made available to the Advisory Committee. This procedure, he explained, "will be more workable than a blanket release of all the papers. . . ."[15] Clearly, McCloy was to be kept out of the loop.

Late in 1970, McCloy went over Kissinger's head and had his Advisory Committee send Nixon a formal written recommendation, appealing for a major shift in the administration's negotiating position. He stated that Kissinger's requirement for on-site inspection was unnecessary.[16] Nixon refused the advice, and, to no one's surprise, the Soviets subsequently rejected the on-site verification procedures. But the Soviet negotiators at the SALT sessions told the American delegates that they were sorry that "more hadn't been done on MIRV."[17] McCloy was shocked by Kissinger's cynicism, and years later sarcastically observed, "Some people thought the MIRV was hot stuff . . . gold at the end of a rainbow. They acted as if it was always a sign of weakness if you tried to concede anything."[18] He did not understand it, and felt alienated from the increasingly poisonous atmosphere of bureaucratic back-stabbing that seemed to prevail in Washington.

By 1970, he was a very unhappy man. At seventy-five, he felt his world crumbling. The bipartisan consensus on foreign-policy issues that he had worked so hard to build in the aftermath of World War II seemed to have collapsed. There was little decorum in public debate, and the deference with which his counsel had once been received on Capitol Hill or by the media was now lost in bitter partisanship. He recognized that Vietnam had a lot to do with the divisiveness that prevailed in much of the country. On this issue too he was unimpressed by the Nixon administration's performance. Just before the Inauguration, he had invited Averell Harriman to speak at a Council on Foreign Relations dinner. Harriman had left him with the impression that, if Washington were to seek an end to the U.S. military commitment in Vietnam, such a solution could emerge from the Paris peace talks. Yet, after Nixon had spent more than a year in office, the American people were only beginning to learn what the president meant by his promise of "peace with honor." The Kissinger-Nixon team had done nothing to end the war. Instead, the administration had instituted "Vietnamization," and then, in May 1970, widened the war with the "incursion" into Cambodia. McCloy might have been shocked if he had heard what Kissinger was saying in private about the war. In December 1970, at a point when even some administration officials thought Nixon's conduct of the war made it doubtful that he could be re-elected, Kissinger told a friend over lunch that ". . . anytime we want to get out of Vietnam, we can, and that we will get out of Vietnam before the election."[19]

McCloy wanted to see the war ended. He felt, as always, that the merits of keeping communism out of South Vietnam were far outweighed by the damage to the country's domestic equilibrium and its critical national-security interests in Europe. But appearances were still important, and he did not wish to associate himself with anything that smacked of a "cut and run policy."[20] He also felt that the president's ability to negotiate a way out of the war was severely hampered by the growing strength and vociferousness of the antiwar movement. Moreover, he was offended by the tenor of the debate.

The angry debate over the Vietnam War affected McCloy's most cherished club and the citadel of the Establishment, the Council on Foreign Relations. By 1970, the Council membership was sharply divided on the failure of the Nixon administration to end the war. Discussion groups were becoming heated, contentious affairs, and even McCloy uncharacteristically once lost his temper. It happened when some of the new, younger members invited Richard Falk to speak about his recent visit to North Vietnam. A professor of international law at Princeton, and a Council member, Falk was a well-known antiwar activist. Falk told his Pratt House audience that he had talked with almost all of Hanoi's senior leadership, and he argued that the cease-fire terms they demanded were not unreasonable. He reported that Hanoi was not insisting on the right to maintain any of its regular troops in South Vietnam (a condition that became part of the eventual 1973 peace accords). The gist of Falk's talk was similar to Harriman's lecture to the Council earlier that year, but McCloy nevertheless became agitated, and during the question-and-answer period he lost his temper. "He seemed to think," Falk recalled, "that what I was saying just made it harder to fight the war. It was the first time I had seen McCloy become visibly upset." It did not become a shouting match only because McCloy finally stood up and walked from the room. Afterward, he told the Council staff that Falk should never have been invited to speak.[21]

McCloy had now personified the Council for more than sixteen years, and he held proprietary feelings for everything that went on inside its headquarters. Under his tutelage, the Council's budget had grown from $360,000 to over $2 million annually.[22] The Ford Foundation continued to fund many of the Council's study groups, but McCloy's solicitations from corporations had also grown dramatically. By 1969, 112 major corporations—including such Milbank, Tweed clients as ARAMCO, Chase Bank, Texaco, IT&T, and Mobil—were contributing $2,000 to $15,000 annually. That year, in a fund-raising letter to Lew Douglas, McCloy wrote that the Council was the "leading private organization" studying U.S. foreign policy, and the number of its members who were now in high government posts was proof of its influence.[23]

Douglas, as usual, was more than skeptical of these claims, and though he did not say so to his brother-in-law, he believed that the Council had "unwittingly deviated from the fundamental purposes for which it was organized fifty years ago. . . ." It was in danger of losing its objectivity and becoming a "propaganda" organization.[24] Douglas's views might be dismissed as those of an inveterate grouser, but a growing number of Council members thought McCloy took himself and the Council entirely too seriously.[25] About this time, John Kenneth Galbraith let his membership lapse, calling the Council "the seat of boredom. . . ."[26] Things were about to change, however, even within the rarefied atmosphere of Pratt House. By 1969, growing dissension within the Council over Vietnam began to generate pressure for reform of the Council's homogeneous membership. A committee recommended a special effort to recruit younger members and a greater number of minorities. That October, Council members in New York crowded into a second-floor chamber of Pratt House to discuss whether women should be invited to join the Council. Some said that women couldn't keep secrets, and one member thought that "inviting ladies to join the Council would be like the Union League taking in Communists."[27] Though one man was reduced to tears, the meeting decided by a margin of one vote to admit a few qualified women—though no wives. (The membership agreed that wives would only turn Council functions into social affairs.[28]) McCloy endorsed these reforms, but in the spring of 1970 he told the board that after seventeen years it was time for him to retire as chairman. He would step down that autumn. Simultaneously, Hamilton Fish Armstrong, who had been associated with the Council since 1925, announced that he too wished to retire.

There was no need for a search committee to select McCloy's successor. For the second time in his life, David Rockefeller quickly agreed to replace his mentor. McCloy was given the title of "honorary chairman," and he would remain an active director of the Council for years to come. The matter of choosing a new editor for *Foreign Affairs,* however, turned out to be the cause of considerable controversy. McCloy appointed a balanced search committee which included Bill Moyers, Armstrong, and several other Council members. But that autumn, Rockefeller pre-empted the process when he offered the job to William Bundy while the two men sat in the bleachers in Cambridge, watching the Harvard-Yale football game. "David wasn't authorized to make even a tentative commitment like that to Bundy," complained one board director. "[But] when the chairman of your club goes out on a limb, you don't saw it off."[29]

That Rockefeller had acted unilaterally was bad enough. But to many Council members, Bundy's record in government as one of the chief architects of the Vietnam War was morally and politically repugnant. It was not so to McCloy, who, like Rockefeller, counted the Bundy brothers as among his oldest friends. But to his consternation, a group of dissident Council members led by Richard Falk, Ronald Steel, and Richard J. Barnet, a cofounder with Marcus Raskin of the Institute for Policy Studies, publicly protested Bundy's appointment. Meetings were held to discuss the issue, and one-third of the Council's membership voted against Bundy.[30] The debate became acrimonious. Some said Bundy was a "war criminal."[31] His critics, in turn, were accused of being "left McCarthyites."[32] Harvard Professor Francis Bator thought Falk was leading a "witch hunt."[33] Barnet received hate mail, including some anti-Semitic letters from Council members.[34] Richard Ullman, a Princeton academic, argued that the Council would be handicapped in playing any role in the postmortem on Vietnam if a man with Bundy's record became editor of *Foreign Affairs.*[35] But McCloy, Rockefeller, and the rest of the Council's leadership stood their ground and confirmed the appointment. Rockefeller explained, "Why, I know all the Bundys, they're a fine, upright family."[36]

Four days after McCloy and his fellow board directors confirmed Bundy's appointment, *The New York Times* published the Pentagon Papers, leaked by an ex–Rand Corporation analyst, Daniel Ellsberg.* Bundy's critics charged that the Pentagon Papers demonstrated that he and Johnson had deceived Congress about their intentions in 1964. Specifically, the documents revealed that Bundy had drafted a contingency resolution authorizing the use of military force in Vietnam five months prior to the Gulf of Tonkin crisis. This made it appear that Congress had been manipulated into approving the Vietnam commitment on a contrived pretext.

The controversy caused the press to take a critical look at the Council's activities. Later in 1971, a former Council fellow, John Franklin Campbell, wrote a biting piece in *New York* magazine entitled "The Death Rattle of the Eastern Establishment":

> If you can walk—or be carried—into Pratt House, it usually means that you are a partner in an investment bank or law firm—with occasional "trouble-

*The Pentagon Papers originated as a result of Robert McNamara's request for a team of analysts to review how the United States had become involved in Vietnam. The resulting multivolume report contained thousands of pages of top-secret documents.

> shooting" assignments in government. You believe in foreign aid, NATO and bipartisan foreign policy. You've been pretty much running things in this country for the last 25 years and you know it.
>
> But today your favorite club is breaking up, just on the eve of its fiftieth anniversary. The same vulgar polarizations that have popped up elsewhere—young against old, men against women, hawks against doves—have at last invaded the secluded Pratt House sanctuary and citadel of the establishment itself."[37]

The Council was not breaking up, but it was true that its credibility as an independent and nonpartisan voice on foreign-policy issues was not what it used to be. Over the next few years, the Council began the process of building a new consensus within a less exclusive Establishment. Younger men and women were invited to join its ranks, including a significant number of liberals and critics of the Cold War consensus. Richard Ullman, one of those who had opposed Bundy's appointment, was selected in 1973 as director of studies. The Council held fewer of its proceedings behind closed doors and made an effort to seem less secretive. William Bundy turned out to be a far more liberal editor than his critics had expected, opening the pages of *Foreign Affairs* to controversy by occasionally publishing authors who stood outside the usual bipartisan consensus. Winston Lord, an old Kissinger aide who eventually became president of the Council, explained, "Ideologically, it's important that we have not just the safe center but some spice from the left and right as well." McCloy did not object to these changes, and continued to participate in the Council's affairs. But it was not the same, and he probably quietly agreed with *The Wall Street Journal* when it headlined a story about the Council in the 1980s "Club That Is Ghost of Former Self."[38]

Halfway through his eighth decade, McCloy could look about him and see that the order and equanimity of his world was slipping away. Vietnam had broken the bipartisan consensus on foreign policy. The Council on Foreign Relations was no longer accorded the deference that had given it such influence in Washington for nearly fifty years. He now also had cause to worry that the security system he had worked so hard to build and sustain in Western Europe was about to unravel. NATO had recovered somewhat from the balance-of-payments crisis of 1966–67, but with the arrival of East-West détente, a new wind was blowing over Germany. The SPD's Willy Brandt was chancellor, and in McCloy's view, the charismatic Social Democrat was repudiating Adenauer's policy of keeping West Germany firmly facing the West. He feared that Brandt's campaign to open up contacts with East Germany and the Soviet Union ultimately threatened the basis of the Atlantic alliance. Brandt's *Ost-*

politik (Eastern policy) climaxed in August 1970, when the German chancellor signed a nonaggression pact with the Kremlin. A few months later, he signed a treaty with Poland and began negotiations with the East Germans on trade and travel rights between the two Germanys.

On the day Brandt signed the agreement with the Poles, which recognized the Oder-Neisse border between Poland and East Germany, McCloy went to the White House. Joined by Dean Acheson and Lucius Clay, McCloy complained that the administration was ignoring these dramatic developments in Europe. Western Europe and the Soviet Union, the three suggested, should command Nixon's attention, not the war in Vietnam. McCloy pointed out that, until Brandt had come along, West Germany had been governed by men from the Rhineland, men like Adenauer, who had been reconciled to the division of Germany and were absolutely loyal to the Atlantic alliance. Now, he said, it was unfortunate that Bonn was being run by "people from eastern Germany, who are seeking to experiment with relations with the Soviet Union."[39] McCloy was not opposed to détente *per se;* he just didn't like the idea of the Germans' leading the way. In the same meeting, for instance, he could criticize Kissinger's handling of the MIRV issue in the SALT negotiations and emphasize the urgency of achieving some kind of arms-control agreement with the Soviets. But he thought *Ostpolitik*—and Brandt's popular slogan about Germany being "one country, but two states"—threatened the postwar security system.

Kissinger and Nixon listened politely to this sermon, but they tended to think there were more opportunities than dangers in a European détente. Besides, it seemed to them that McCloy had become a "Cassandra" on the issue of Germany. For years, he had been running to the White House with warnings about one crisis or another that he claimed threatened the Atlantic alliance. They listened and did nothing.

It was a different matter when, in the spring of 1971, Senator Mike Mansfield reintroduced his amendment to the selective-service bill requiring the administration to withdraw 150,000 U.S. troops from Western Europe. When it became clear that the vote on the Mansfield Amendment could be close, Kissinger decided that, for the first time during the Nixon administration, it was necessary to mobilize "the Establishment figures who had been responsible for so many of America's great postwar achievements." He called Dean Acheson, who suggested that what was needed was "a little volley firing and not just a splattering of musketry." Why not, he said, assemble as many of those who were "present at the creation" of the postwar system and have them meet with the president?* Afterward, they could emerge with a statement opposing the Mansfield Amendment. Nixon was greatly taken with the idea, and so, on May 13,

*Acheson had titled his 1969 memoir *Present at the Creation.*

1971, Acheson, McCloy, George Ball, Cy Vance, Henry Cabot Lodge, Lucius Clay, former NATO Supreme Commander General Alfred M. Gruenther, Air Force General Lauris Norstad, and former Joint Chiefs of Staff Chairman General Lyman Lemnitzer gathered in the Cabinet Room to discuss the issue.

Nixon said a few appropriate words about NATO, and then opened up the floor to discussion. To Kissinger's discomfort, a few of these old "Wise Men" suggested the merits of proposing a compromise. Acheson firmly rejected this and eventually persuaded everyone to sign a statement categorically opposing any troop cuts. After a longer-than-expected meeting, Acheson led everyone out to greet the press. With characteristic acerbity, he told the assembled reporters that any unilateral troop reductions would be "asinine." When asked why the meeting with Nixon had taken so long, he quipped, "We are all old and we are all eloquent."[40]

McCloy then flew to Bonn, where he managed to have Willy Brandt issue a timely statement saying that any troop reductions would leave "the irradicable impression that the United States is on its way out of Europe." These efforts had their intended effect. As Kissinger later wrote, "The media reaction showed that the old foreign policy Establishment still carried quite a wallop." Major newspapers across the country editorialized against "Senator Mansfield's Folly," and finally, on May 19, the Senate voted the measure down by a hefty sixty-one-to-thirty-six margin.[41]

McCloy was relieved, but the episode underscored for him what he felt was an "apparent malaise of spirit and will which the Vietnam war, the demonstrations, the violence and the lack of community and individual responsibility in this country seem to have induced." He thought Mansfield had simply forgotten that U.S. troops were sent to Europe in the first place for political, not military reasons. "If anything," he wrote in an article *The New York Times* decided not to publish, "the political need which was the primary cause for placing the troops in Europe is perhaps greater now than it was then. Contrary to some present contentions, we did not then fear a Soviet ground attack in spite of all the harassments in Berlin. . . . What we did fear was the political and psychological effect in Western Europe of the presence in Eastern Europe of large undemobilized Soviet ground forces with nothing more convincing to offset their influence than the rather illusory commitments of the NATO pact alone." In other words, the troops were always needed in order to shore up America's political allies in Western Europe, and not because Washington ever thought the Kremlin intended to wage aggressive warfare.[42]

Throughout the 1970s and '80s, McCloy used whatever platform he could to preach his "Atlanticist" message of West European unity. Each year, he visited Germany, and as chairman or board director of the Council on Foreign Relations, the Atlantic Council, the American Council on Germany, the German-Marshall Fund, and the Aspen Institute he continued to exert his influence on journalists, academics, and selected politicians. Conveniently, it just happened that these particular public-policy organizations controlled most of the travel funds, the conference monies, and the publication subsidies that financed the policy debates on NATO's future, German-American relations, and the course of the Cold War. McCloy presided over their activities, setting the tone and general direction, while men closely identified with his career, such as Shepard Stone, who headed the Aspen Institute's Berlin office; Joseph Slater, another Aspen Institute officer; and David Klein, who headed the American Council on Germany, did the day-to-day staff work. Well into the 1980s, these elite opinion-making institutions continued to set the parameters of what the Establishment considered to be "legitimate" debate on America's European policies.

Kissinger might regard him as a "jovial gnome," an old man with a "time-consuming . . . penchant for anecdotes," but in New York McCloy was not treated with condescension.[43] He was still the single most powerful partner at Milbank, Tweed, and the law firm's premier rainmaker. Well into his late seventies, he still played a hard game of tennis and several times a year waded into frigid Canadian and New England streams for a few days of fly-fishing. One summer, he took a trip to Alaska, where he shot an enormous Kodiak bear, which he had stuffed and placed at the entrance of his son's Vermont hunting cabin. In the summer of 1970, he took his family on a hunting safari in Botswana.

In September 1970, Egypt's Gamal Abdel Nasser suddenly died of a heart attack, and Nixon asked McCloy to attend the funeral as part of an official U.S. delegation. On a few hours' notice, McCloy packed a bag and boarded a windowless U.S. Air Force 707 oil-refueler plane converted for passenger use. On the long flight to Cairo, he stayed up all night, entertaining his companions with old war stories. Accompanying him were retired Ambassador Robert Murphy, Undersecretary of State Elliot Richardson, Special Assistant to the President Donald Rumsfeld, and a Foreign Service officer named Michael Sterner. When they arrived in Cairo, more than a million people were in the streets mourning the popular Arab nationalist. At the funeral, McCloy went through the receiving line inside a large tent set up for dignitaries and shook hands with Anwar Sadat. Egypt's new president had fainted during the chaotic funeral procession and was sweating profusely. Afterward, McCloy and his colleagues were given a chance to talk privately with Sadat.[44] They also had a chance to meet the young Libyan leader, Colonel Muammar Qaddafi, who had come to power in a coup d'état the previous year. Shaking hands with the colonel was an unforgettable experience. Sterner remembered he had a dreamy, faraway look in his eyes and seemed distracted and genuinely grief-stricken at the sudden death of his political idol. Sterner told himself, "This man is the first deranged Middle East head of state."[45]

McCloy had an interest in sizing up the mercurial Libyan leader: a number of his Milbank, Tweed clients were currently having considerable difficulties with the colonel. Earlier in the year, he had demanded a 40-cent-per-barrel increase in the royalty paid by all the oil companies pumping Libyan oil. The State Department's chief oil expert, James E. Akins, told the companies that this was not an entirely unreasonable increase. A tall, imposing man, Akins had Quaker attitudes and blunt opinions that had won him a reputation in the Foreign Service as an iconoclast. As he later explained to the Senate's Subcommittee on Multinational Corporations, he had "the same slide rules that the Libyans" used to calculate the value of Libyan oil as compared with Persian Gulf oil. In fact, for some time the companies had been lying to the native producers. While telling the Libyans that their low-sulfur oil gave them a 10-cent-per-barrel price differential, they simultaneously told the Venezuelans that their high-sulfur oil was worth 50 to 70 cents less than Libyan oil. Akins worried that, if the Libyans "concluded they were being cheated," it might lead to a complete breakdown in relations. The Saudis, Venezuelans, and other OPEC producers were not only more educated and sophisticated in the mores of the industry than ever before, but they could see that Western consumer demand for imported oil had risen dramatically. In the previous decade, the U.S. market had absorbed more oil than all the oil produced in the previous one hundred years. Akins knew it was in the U.S. consumers' interest to keep the price of oil "fairly low." But he also thought it was in the U.S. interest to have a "reasonable working relationship with the Libyans" and other producers.[46]

The companies, led by Exxon, ignored Akins's recommendation and announced they would not pay more than 5 cents per barrel extra. Qaddafi shrewdly responded by singling out one of the smaller independent oil companies, Armand Hammer's Occidental Oil Company, and ordered a cutback in its production quota. Unlike Exxon or the majors, Occidental depended entirely on Libyan oil, and by July 1970 Hammer was desperate. He had to get access to other oil supplies to honor his contracts, or cave in to Qaddafi's price demands. In a grim mood, he went to see Ken Jamieson, CEO of Exxon, and asked if Exxon could supply Occidental with oil at cost. There had always been bad blood between the "Seven Sisters" and the independents, and Jamieson was suspicious of Hammer's request. He told the seventy-two-year-old oil man that he needed some time to think about the matter. After two weeks, he sent word to Hammer that he would not sell at cost, but would be willing to sell him oil "at our lowest third-party price." By this time, Hammer had given up on Jamieson and, fearing that Qaddafi might nationalize his operations at any minute, flew off in his company jet to make a deal with the Libyans. On September 4, 1970, Qaddafi announced that Occidental had agreed to a 30-cent price increase, with an additional 2 cents over each of the next five years. Henry Schuler, an oil man then working for Bunker Hunt, thought this was the beginning of the end. "Maybe Hammer was right that prices had been too low," Schuler later said. "But the way he did what he did set in train the oil price rises of the 1970s."[47]

Three days after Hammer's capitulation, McCloy flew to Washington with a group of his oil-company clients for a meeting with Secretary of State William Rogers, Undersecretary U. Alexis Johnson, and Jim Akins. He was alarmed by what Hammer had done. Libya was producing 3.6 million barrels per day and was supplying 25 percent of Western Europe's oil. The twenty-eight American companies operating in Libya had a $1.5-billion investment at stake, and their profits were contributing over $700 million to the U.S. balance of payments.[48] McCloy felt the Libyan demands confronted the American oil industry with a fundamental challenge. It was a question of control over a global industry essential to U.S. national security and economic well-being. Price was another issue. He favored low prices, but in the long run it was much more important that the major oil companies—the "Seven Sisters"—maintain a reasonable working relationship with the native producers and control over the marketing of this essential resource.

It was no accident that the crisis had erupted in Libya, since that was the one major oil-producing country where the independents had managed to establish a significant foothold. A disproportionate number of oil concessions had been parceled out by the Libyans to small independents in the belief that such companies had a greater interest in aggressively exploring for oil and marketing it once it had been discovered. Companies like Occidental had every reason to pump as much oil as they could. This was not necessarily true for the majors, who always had more oil than they wished to sell. Historically, the industry had been plagued by profit-cutting episodes of overproduction which were only solved when the majors became large enough to establish what were essentially worldwide production quotas. For decades, the global price for oil generally mirrored the production quotas set by the Texas Railroad Commission, which was run as an unofficial industry association. For a long time, the majors were able to reject any demands for higher production in one country simply by threatening to raise production in another.

As the crisis broke in the wake of Occidental's September 4 settlement with Qaddafi, it was McCloy's intention to invoke his Justice Department antitrust waiver, and persuade the companies to form a common front.

Qaddafi, however, moved quickly. Within two weeks, a consortium of three other independents—Continental, Marathon, and Amerada-

Hess—capitulated. Only in late September, when the Libyan colonel turned his attention to one of the majors, did he encounter resistance. The chairman of Shell Oil, Sir David Barran, a Briton who wore a monocle and affected the pose of an English country gentleman, was determined to try "to stem the avalanche." When he refused to capitulate, Qaddafi ordered a complete shut-in of Shell's production quota of 150,000 barrels per day. Barran happened to be in New York that day and told the British foreign secretary, who was attending the annual U.N. General Assembly, that he felt the companies could hold out—if the British and American governments stood firmly behind them.[49]

McCloy agreed with him, and the very next day he led another delegation of oil-company executives down to Washington for a meeting with Undersecretary Johnson. The oil men were severely disappointed with what Johnson had to say. When the SOCAL and Texaco executives repeatedly asked "what the U.S. government would do to back up the companies in any stand they might take," Johnson kept telling them that the United States had "virtually no economic or political leverage in Libya" and that "in our view the Libyans are in a very strong position in their confrontations with the companies both financially and geographically."[50] It seemed there was nothing the U.S. government was willing to do to encourage the companies to hold the line.

Afterward, McCloy flew back to New York in an Exxon jet, together with Jamieson and Shell's Sir David Barran. The British oil man was in a black mood and told him that he thought the game was up, that his American colleagues would soon concede. This happened only a few weeks later, when Texaco and SOCAL agreed to the large price hikes demanded by Qaddafi. McCloy now feared that other OPEC member countries would demand a renegotiation of their contracts. This OPEC did on December 28, 1970, when it called for a "general uniform increase in the posted price" of oil and gave the companies only two weeks to begin negotiations. If these negotiations failed, OPEC warned it would enforce a price increase "through a concerted and simultaneous action by all Member countries."[51]

Upon hearing this news, McCloy rushed back down to Washington and told Attorney General John Mitchell, "Unified action by the governments required unified action by the companies."[52] He requested written assurances that the Justice Department did not contemplate any antitrust actions if his oil-company clientele met to negotiate jointly as an industry with OPEC. Mitchell gave his oral approval, and a few days later the antitrust division drafted a "business review letter" with the language McCloy wanted.[53] A Justice Department lawyer, Dudley Chapman, and the State Department's energy man, James E. Akins, were assigned to monitor the talks.

So it was that on Monday, January 11, 1971, Chapman took the noon shuttle flight to New York with McCloy. Akins joined them at the airport, and the three men were driven to McCloy's plush offices at One Chase Plaza, where a meeting of oil-company chiefs was already in progress.[54] Instead of taking them into the meeting, however, McCloy ushered Akins and Chapman into his office, where they chatted briefly. The room was decorated with memorabilia of McCloy's long years of public service. Above the couch hung a painting by Alice Acheson, depicting a view of the Rhine McCloy had so loved during his years as high commissioner. The walls were adorned with black-and-white photos—McCloy jokingly referred to them as his "rogues' gallery"—of Lyndon Johnson, John Kennedy, Dwight Eisenhower, Richard Nixon, Jerry Ford, Dean Rusk, Henry Kissinger, George C. Marshall, General George S. Patton, James Forrestal, Konrad Adenauer, General John J. "Blackjack" Pershing, Lucius Clay, Omar Bradley, and his beloved "Stimmie," Henry Stimson. With the notable exception of Nixon's photo, each one was autographed with a personal inscription.[55] After hanging up his winter coat, McCloy escorted his two guests into an anteroom adjoining Milbank, Tweed's expansive reception room. The oil men were gathered in another room, opposite the reception room. Despite this curious arrangement, neither Akins nor Chapman asked why they had not been invited to listen to the actual deliberations. Akins was "uncomfortable" about it, but said nothing.[56] And though Chapman was there to make sure the oil executives confined their discussions to dealing with OPEC, he and his Justice Department colleagues knew these oil men had been meeting in private with McCloy for years.[57]

The unspoken assumption was that private citizen McCloy could watch out for the public's interest. It wasn't until 1974, when Congress was investigating the energy crisis, that any questions were asked about this remarkable arrangement. Even then, Senator Clifford Case only in passing wondered aloud how McCloy could have "represented everybody, including the U.S. government without the U.S. government knowing what was being done until you [McCloy] told them about it." But in January 1971, the fact that one man could "wear so many hats," as Senator Case put it, did not seem inappropriate. On McCloy, all the hats fit.[58]

The rest of that afternoon, McCloy shuttled back and forth between the meeting of the oil-company executives and the anteroom where Akins and Chapman sat. From time to time, he came out to show the government representatives drafts of two documents, the first a public statement informing OPEC that the companies would only negotiate as a group, not individually, and the second a secret agreement specifying that all the companies would share in any cutbacks in production ordered against any one company in Libya. Chapman and Akins reviewed both documents and suggested some minor amendments. At the end of the day, the two officials returned to Washington, and later that week the Justice Department officially gave McCloy its blessing for the arrangements. In the meantime, McCloy continued his meetings with the oil men, sometimes in his office, sometimes in the ornate University Club, and sometimes in Mobil's skyscraper on 42nd Street.[59]

McCloy was relieved that he had cajoled the oil men into taking a common stand. But he felt their collective-bargaining strategy with OPEC would be greatly helped if the U.S. government used its influence to pressure the OPEC governments, many of whom, after all, were close allies. So, on January 15, he took another delegation of oil-company CEOs to see the secretary of state. He told Rogers that "it would be wise if the government could enter into this thing and get the heads of the countries involved to moderate their demands." A "person of dignity, with clout," he said, should be sent to the Middle East.[60] The very next day, Undersecretary of State John N. Irwin II boarded a plane bound for the Middle East. He carried in his pocket a personal message from Nixon to the shah of Iran, King Faisal of Saudi Arabia, and the sheikh of Kuwait, encouraging them to moderate their demands.

The trip did not, however, have the intended effect. A Sullivan & Cromwell corporate lawyer, Irwin was a political appointee with no experience in the oil business or the Middle East. When he and Jim Akins arrived in Teheran, they were met by the U.S. ambassador, Douglas MacArthur II, who reported that the Iranians were unhappy about the letter the oil companies had sent insisting upon a single set of negotiations with OPEC. In their meeting with the shah, the Iranian monarch made it clear that there had to be two sets of negotiations. Convinced that the companies had no choice in the matter, Irwin cabled Washington and recommended that there be two sets of negotiations, one in Teheran for the Persian Gulf producers, and one in Tripoli for Libya. McCloy thought this a serious blow to his collective-bargaining strategy, because there was nothing to prevent the OPEC countries from "leapfrogging" their price demands. An agreement reached in Teheran might easily set the stage for increased demands in the second set of negotiations, in Tripoli. And though he knew that the shah could be stubborn, he was disturbed that Irwin and MacArthur had caved in so quickly to the monarch's demands. MacArthur, he thought, was acting "more Persian than the Persians."[61]

Within days of Irwin's capitulation, the companies agreed to hold dual negotiations. They had decided to accept at face value the shah's pledge that there would be no "leapfrogging" of demands, even though McCloy told his clients that he placed "little faith" in the shah's word. The first set of talks nevertheless opened in Teheran on January 28, 1971.[62] Back in New York, the CEOs of all the companies gathered each day in McCloy's law offices to monitor the negotiations. After clearing it with the Justice Department, McCloy also arranged to have technical and financial specialists from the companies meet in a "London Policy Group." These talks were held in British Petroleum's "Britannic House" headquarters and were monitored daily by McCloy's law partner Bill Jackson. Over the next two weeks, hundreds of telexes flew back and forth between Teheran, London, and New York. McCloy sat in on most but not all of the meetings in New York. He saw himself not as one of the negotiators, but as "sort of a watchdog, to see that these fellows were moving in the right areas."[63]

Despite all this elaborate coordination, things did not go well. It quickly became clear that OPEC was setting the pace. On February 2, 1971, the cartel suspended negotiations and then announced that, if the companies did not settle by February 15, the governments of each of the producing countries would simply legislate new terms. If necessary, OPEC would impose a total embargo. The game was up, for without strong government direction, it became apparent that the companies had no desire to fight the producers. In Teheran, the shah told the BBC that "the all powerful six or seven sisters have got to open their eyes, and see that they're living in 1971, and not in 1948 or 1949."[64] So, on Valentine's Day, February 14, 1971, a new agreement was signed in Teheran, giving the Persian Gulf producers an extra 30 cents per barrel with an additional 20 cents by 1975. It would be known in the industry as the "Second Saint Valentine's Day Massacre."

Six weeks later, when the second set of talks adjourned in Tripoli, the Libyans achieved a settlement that gave them a 91-cent-per-barrel increase—three times the increase negotiated in Teheran. Both agreements were supposed to last five years, at least providing the industry and Western consumers with a measure of stability. But everyone in the industry knew the agreements could easily unravel. Even McCloy, who told the Justice Department that the agreements were a "milestone in the effort to achieve stabilization in relations with the oil-producing countries," acknowledged that they were "fragile and delicate. . . ."

The Justice Department was not entirely happy with McCloy's report on his actions. They had requested copies of any notes, tapes, or other company documents that described the meetings of the oil companies that took place under his supervision. These he had not provided. This was worrisome to the department's antitrust lawyers, for they only had McCloy's word that the oil-company executives had confined their discussions to dealing with OPEC. Moreover, McCloy's own report admitted that he had not attended all the meetings, and that on three occasions the oil executives had met on short notice without the presence of any Milbank, Tweed lawyer. In order to coordinate "technical information," McCloy explained that an "Economic Evaluation Committee" had been established which researched "exports and imports and related data concerning inflation. . . ."[65] As a practical matter, there was probably no way the companies could have negotiated a "common front" against OPEC without exchanging such information. Being a good lawyer, McCloy was now making sure that he covered himself by apprising the Justice Department of what had happened and making it seem that such activities were well within the scope of the department's original business review letters. Dudley Chapman, the Justice Department lawyer responsible for monitoring McCloy's activities, complained to his superiors, ". . . there is much in the [McCloy] report that is slanted or self-serving, or just ambiguous."[66]

To those experts who were following the oil industry, it seemed only a matter of time before the producers would make another set of price demands. McCloy was unhappy about how quickly things had slipped out of control, and he blamed the government for not stepping in and providing the companies with leadership. The companies, in the meantime, were showing signs of renewed disunity. In the two years after the 1971 concessions, OPEC did everything it could to bind the interests of the oil companies to those of the producing nations. And the companies, no doubt welcoming the opportunity for higher profits, put up little resistance.[67] A new oil regime was evolving out of the old private cartel. As the Saudis, the Iranians, and other OPEC members pressed their demands for greater participation, they created fissures in the private cartel. Those companies with major oil concessions in the Middle East were reluctant to risk their exclusive access to these supplies by acting in concert. So they were the first to concede.[68] These concessions encouraged further concessions across the industry, and by 1972 some Americans were beginning to brand the companies "agents of a foreign power."[69]

OPEC's strength as a cartel was also growing as a result of oil shortages in America. Whereas the industry had historically always had to grapple with overproduction, by the early 1970s consumer demand in the United States for the first time seemed to be exceeding available supplies. Globally, there was still plenty of oil around, and if there had been a free market in this essential commodity there would still be abundant supplies. But government oil-import restrictions—imposed now for many years to protect domestic oil producers—had encouraged the draining of American reserves and now made it impossible to import enough foreign oil to cover increased consumer demand.[70] In combination with the fact that OPEC was increasingly able to dictate production levels abroad, this factor now created the necessary ingredients for an energy crisis. Something could have been done by the government to combat both the domestic and foreign interests driving the country in this direction. But the Nixon administration, its attentions focused elsewhere, never developed a cohesive energy strategy.

McCloy always felt the government could have done much more, both to encourage the companies to act in concert, and to exert pressure on the producing countries to moderate their demands. He recognized what many did not: that maintaining access and control over Middle Eastern oil was a matter of national interest, and that government involvement in the dispute was justified. But he would not acknowledge that the confluence of interests between the producing countries and the oil companies might become such that the companies no longer acted in the American national interest. Instead, they began behaving strictly as multinationals, and the era of relatively cheap oil ended in an abrupt and harsh fashion. Admittedly, the demands by the producing countries for a greater share of the profits derived from their only natural resource could not have been flatly rejected. The oil companies had been cheating the producing countries for years, giving them less than 10 percent of the value of the commodity as charged to the consumer.[71] Ironically, for years consuming countries in Europe had earned twice as much from oil taxes as producer countries had received for their only resource. But there is no reason to doubt that closer regulation of the industry and early government intervention in the dispute with the producing nations could have resulted in a more equitable arrangement than was struck by the companies in 1971–74. This did not happen because no one in Washington wished to take on the oil companies. Even McCloy, who had been telling presidents ever since the formation of OPEC in 1960 that this was a matter of national interest, was ambivalent about involving the government too directly in the affairs of a private cartel.

In 1974, after yet another round of unprecedented oil price rises, Senator Stuart Symington asked McCloy at a U.S. Senate hearing, "Why shouldn't this [the oil industry] be considered a public utility just as much as other energy, like electricity, is considered a public utility? Why should the Government come in and help these people [the companies] out when they get in trouble in other countries and then allow them to make high profits and benefit from that support?"

"That is a very philosophical question," McCloy replied. "The oil companies are a tricky business—are a very risky business. . . . You have to spend so much money and take so many risks that I question whether it can be well regulated like a company that is going to give you so much electricity per day. . . . The fact that it has a political aspect and a very deep economic aspect would lead me to feel that it is something that the Government has to know a lot more about and follow more closely than it has in the past."[72] McCloy's ambivalence stemmed from the confusion of attempting simultaneously to represent both private and public interest. With such indecisiveness emanating from a major spokesman for the Establishment, it is no wonder that Washington sat more or less paralyzed during the energy crisis of the early seventies.

McCloy continued to represent the companies in the years after the 1971 capitulation. But his agenda shifted—as did the companies'—from the attempt to take a common stand vis-à-vis OPEC, to easing the political strains between Washington and the Arabs. In large measure, this meant lobbying Washington to address a settlement of the Arab-Israeli conflict. The oil companies had never stopped conveying to Washington their views on this subject. Inevitably, growing Arab economic muscle would begin to flex itself in the political arena. To protect their interests, the companies were not averse to using whatever influence they had in Washington to bring about a settlement of the Arab-Israeli conflict.

By the end of 1972, the perceived oil shortages and the upward pressure on oil prices in the spot market gave OPEC additional incentives to exact further concessions from the companies. At the same time, the companies were passing these higher prices directly on to Western consumers and registering record-breaking profits. The new alliance between the companies and the producing countries seemed to be ushering in a new era of high profits and control over production.

The new cartel still had to worry, just as the old cartel did, about the dangers of overproduction. The difference was that now one Arab producing country, Saudi Arabia, could choose to shut in its production enough to create a shortage, or, alternatively, produce so much oil as to create a glut on the market. The Saudis were finding it impossible to spend their growing dollar reserves. In the words of one Foreign Service officer stationed in Jedda, a way had to be found to turn the kingdom into a "spending machine"; otherwise, the Saudis would be accumulating dollar reserves of $100 billion by the early 1990s.[73]

The kingdom's wealth and pivotal ability to shut in its oil production without harming its own interests actually placed enormous political pressures on King Faisal. By early 1973, his fellow Arabs were asking him to use this "oil weapon" in the Israeli-Arab conflict. On May 3, 1973, Frank Jungers, the genial head of ARAMCO, was ushered in to see King Faisal for a thirty-minute social call. Faisal was notorious for subjecting his foreign visitors to long-winded sermons on the "Zionist-Communist conspiracy." But this time, the king quietly warned Jungers that, though American interests in Saudi Arabia were relatively safe, it "would be more and more difficult to hold off the tide of opinion." Afterward, the king's intelligence chief, Kamal Adham, told Jungers that Egypt's Sadat would "have to embark on some sort of hostilities" if U.S. policy didn't change. Three weeks later, the four directors of ARAMCO met with Faisal, who gave them an even more explicit warning: time was running out, he said, and if America did not repudiate Israeli policies, "you will lose everything." The oil men had never heard Faisal speak so plainly, and felt ARAMCO's future in Saudi Arabia was at risk as never before.[74]

Back in Washington, the ARAMCO directors repeated Faisal's warnings to high-ranking officials in the State Department and the White House. But everyone claimed their fears were unfounded: the latest CIA estimate concluded that Faisal would resist Sadat's appeals to join him in another war. And though the CIA had discovered in May that Sadat had ordered his General Staff to develop a coherent plan for launching an attack across the Suez Canal, the Agency's analysts told Kissinger that these preparations were for psychological purposes only. So, when the oil men asked for an appointment to see Kissinger, the national-security adviser said he was too busy to meet with them.[75]

While the Egyptian president secretly prepared for his October gamble, McCloy impatiently tried to get Washington to focus on the Middle East. The power vacuum created by the growing Watergate scandal, however, made any dramatic initiatives unlikely. In August, in an effort to shore up his administration, Nixon nominated Kissinger to be his new secretary of state. Early that September, just after Colonel Qaddafi nationalized the remaining foreign oil companies in Libya, Kissinger asked Averell Harriman to pay him a visit. The elderly Democrat spent a leisurely hour at the White House, talking about the state of the world. The Middle East, he said, was going to prove to be Kissinger's "greatest immediate difficulty." Harriman was in an aggressive mood, and complained vigorously that "it was tragic that between the British and ourselves we had let this crazy Colonel take over in Libya." Now he bluntly told Kissinger he "had to get involved in economic matters." Kissinger, who once had told Harriman that he just didn't like economics, agreed that it was "part and parcel of his job. . . ." Harriman urged him to support a high gasoline tax, strong conservation policies, and a crash program to develop nonpetroleum energy sources. "We had," Harriman said, "to get ourselves in the position where the Arabs recognize they better sell their oil now rather than hold us up."[76]

It was too late. On the morning of October 6, 1973, Egyptian troops stormed across the Suez Canal while Syria attacked in the Israeli-occupied Golan Heights. Two days later, a delegation of oil-company officers, operating under the authority of McCloy's "London Administrative Group," began negotiations with OPEC on the cartel's new price demands. Once again McCloy had cleared the companies' collective-bargaining strategy with the Justice Department's antitrust division. A Milbank, Tweed lawyer monitored the meetings of the London group, and McCloy was consulted on almost a daily basis. Yamani began the negotiations by suggesting doubling the price to $6 per barrel. The companies countered, first with an offer of $3.45, and then $3.75. In the midst of the negotiations, with the newspapers full of news from the battlefronts in the Sinai, the Arab members of OPEC announced they would soon be meeting in Kuwait to discuss using their oil power as a weapon in the war. In this atmosphere, it was clear there could be no bridging of the wide gap between the companies' position and that of the oil cartel. In short order, the oil-company delegates broke off the talks, and Yamani flew back to Saudi Arabia.

Back in New York, McCloy sat down with a group of ARAMCO officials and drafted an "eyes-only" memo to Nixon, appealing to the president not to side with the Israelis in the current war. The memo warned Nixon that supplying Israel with military assistance at this time would "have a critical and adverse effect on our relations with the moderate Arab producing countries. . . . The whole position of the United States is on the way to being seriously impaired, with Japanese, European, and perhaps Russian interests largely supplanting United States presence in the area. . . . Much more than our commercial interest in the area is now at hazard. The real stakes are both our economy and our security."[77] On October 12, McCloy took the memo—with his own cover letter—and delivered it into the hands of General Alexander Haig, the president's chief of staff. Haig, however, sat on the memo for three days, and in the meantime Nixon and Kissinger decided to airlift large quantities of military supplies to Israel.

This was the last straw. On October 16, 1973, OPEC announced a 70-percent price increase—to $5.12 per barrel—and a 5-percent cutback in production. Three days later, the Saudis went even further and ordered a unilateral 10-percent cutback. Furthermore, the Saudis imposed an embargo on oil shipments to the United States and the Netherlands. In Riyadh, Yamani sat down with ARAMCO's Jungers and discussed how the company should implement his embargo orders. Jungers reported to New York that the Saudis were "looking to ARAMCO to police it [the embargo]." ARAMCO's directors implemented the embargo in the strictest possible manner. The company even went so far as to bar supplies of Saudi oil to U.S. military installations. McCloy's oil-company clients were now very much partners of the producing nations' cartel.[78] Gradually, the companies shifted their profit centers downstream to the refining-and-distribution end of the business. Though they no longer dictated price decisions, they quickly saw that OPEC's higher prices could translate into much higher profit margins for themselves. McCloy had failed in his attempt to have the companies stave off OPEC's challenge, and in the process he had helped to bring about a new oil regime. The companies became richer than ever, and so too did the native producers, while the world economy and consumers everywhere suffered from higher energy prices.

The energy crisis of 1971–74 did not spell the end of McCloy's active representation of various oil interests. While representing the Seven Sisters in their negotiations with OPEC, he simultaneously provided legal counsel to Occidental's Armand Hammer. In the spring of 1971, the mercurial independent oil man began what turned out to be a decade-long battle with the SEC, which charged him with filing "false and misleading earnings reports" to Occidental shareholders. McCloy advised Hammer to sign a consent decree, because a protracted and costly legal battle would make it difficult to sell a major Occidental bond offering in Europe. However, once Hammer signed the consent decree, at least twenty class-action suits were filed by disgruntled shareholders. Eventually, Hammer settled out of court for about $11 million. In 1975, when Hammer got into legal trouble again over an illegal campaign contribution to the Nixon presidential campaign, McCloy interceded and wrote a letter to the judge in the case urging "sympathetic consideration of his case." In March 1976, Hammer was given a suspended one-year sentence and fined $3,000.[79]

In a far more public fashion, McCloy performed similar services in 1975–76 for Gulf Oil Corporation when the firm was implicated in a foreign bribery scandal. In order to avert a court battle, Gulf's executives signed a consent decree which acknowledged that the company had paid more than $10 million in illegal political campaign contributions and bribes in the United States and abroad since 1959. As part of the settlement, Gulf agreed to appoint McCloy and two nonmanaging directors of Gulf to a special review committee to investigate what had happened to this money and which of its officers had known of the political slush fund. McCloy told reporters that Gulf needed an "independent figure," and "I guess I was the only person they could find in a short time they could all agree on."[80]

Ten months later, he and his two colleagues submitted a 298-page report with six appendixes to the SEC. By law, the report was a public document, and though such reports are not usually popular fare, an enterprising publisher quickly recognized its commercial value as a remarkably readable exposé of the scandal. In the atmosphere of the mid-1970s, the American public was more than receptive to an accounting of corporate misdeeds. Issued in paperback, *The Great Oil Spill: The Inside Report—Gulf Oil's Bribery and Political Chicanery* became a national best-seller. It described Gulf's contributions to dozens of politicians in the United States, South Korea, and Italy as "shot through with illegality." Altogether, some $12.3 million had been laundered through a Bahamian dummy corporation.[81]

Fifteen days after the report's release, the president of Gulf Oil, Robert R. Dorsey, and two other executives were fired. Once this was done, McCloy began giving interviews to reporters in which he attempted to limit the damage. The report included tantalizing allusions to the fact that Gulf's practices were not unique. Other oil companies, including Shell and Exxon, were apparently involved in similar operations in Italy.

But when Congress began making noises about enacting tough new reporting requirements on corporate payments of foreign commissions, McCloy testified that such laws would go too far. "Gratuities" given to low-level foreign officials, he said, shouldn't be compared to secret slush funds. American corporations had already reformed their practices overseas: "The barn door is now well fastened," he said.[82]

In the end, Gulf was fined a mere $5,000, a minuscule amount for a corporation that ranked seventh in the nation, with annual sales of over $16 billion. By following McCloy's counsel, and disciplining itself, the company probably averted legal and regulatory consequences far more serious than the dismissal of its chief executive officer. Gulf weathered the scandal precisely because it had in McCloy a man whose reputation as a guarantor of the public trust allowed him to wear two hats simultaneously, as public prosecutor and as corporate defender.

By the spring of 1973, as the Watergate cover-up began to unravel, Richard Nixon became obsessed with saving his presidency. In an effort to restore a measure of his credibility, he swallowed some of his pride and reached out to the Establishment network he had always distrusted. That April, he assured Elliot Richardson—a Boston Brahmin lawyer who had served him as undersecretary of state, secretary of health, education, and welfare, and secretary of defense—that if he took the job of attorney general he would be empowered to "get to the bottom" of the Watergate case. Nixon affirmed his innocence and suggested that Richardson might approach a man like John J. McCloy for the job of special prosecutor. Such an appointment, he indicated, would demonstrate that he was willing to see justice done.[83] When Richardson did select a special prosecutor, he turned to his Harvard law professor Archibald Cox, a Democrat.

As Cox's investigations subsequently linked the scandal closer to the White House, McCloy and other Establishment figures agonized over what was becoming a constitutional crisis. On May 17, 1973—the day the Senate's Watergate hearings opened on nationwide television—Averell Harriman called McCloy from Washington to say he thought "the New York Republican establishment should review the seriousness of the White House situation and take some action." It had a responsibility "to get the President to clean up and put in some honorable people" to restore the White House's credibility. "A General [Alexander Haig] and John Connolly is not doing it." Someone like Barry Goldwater, he said, should talk to the president.

McCloy said he would think about it, and called back four days later to say that he agreed something "ought to be done." For one thing, the scandal was worrying international bankers: the dollar, he said, "couldn't stand another devaluation without serious consequences." He had tried to phone Herbert Brownell and David Rockefeller, but both men were out of town. He said he would talk to Nelson Rockefeller, and he agreed that someone should contact Goldwater. The Arizona senator wasn't McCloy's favorite politician, but he and Lew Douglas thought Goldwater might now be in a position to influence Nixon.[84]

Later that summer, Goldwater went to see Nixon and, like Richardson, he came away convinced by the president's assurances that he had not been involved in either the break-in or the cover-up. Though the Senate hearings continued to reveal an appalling story of deceit, pettiness, and vindictiveness, Nixon would manage to hold on to power for more than another year.[85]

McCloy felt ambivalent about the scandal. He rather agreed with an editorial in the London *Times* that attacked the American media in general, the *Washington Post* in particular, and the Senate Democrats for blowing Watergate out of proportion.[86] But after he watched some of the televised hearings early that summer, he wrote Lew Douglas, "The Watergate business is horribly depressing. The hearings go on with a succession of young men testifying to a mishmash of chicanery, intrigue and dissembling which casts a deep reflection on the leadership in the White House. Perhaps much of it is the usual pattern of politics in these days of 'sophisticated' techniques but it is very discouraging, disillusioning and really damaging, domestically and internationally."[87]

Douglas's assessment was, as usual, more emotional. He saw the roots of the whole affair in the gradual accumulation of power in the White House, begun, he said, by Franklin Roosevelt, and now taken to an extreme by Nixon. But he could not have imagined "such a perfectly outrageously stupid and incalculably great act of deception and dishonesty as the Watergate affair." He decided Nixon had to go, either by resignation or, if necessary, by impeachment.[88]

McCloy, ever more cautious, wrote Douglas, "Impeachment would be a very damaging episode and how one would govern during the impeachment which could last from six to eight months I don't know. I think no one contemplates this seriously. Resignation is another alternative which would also be damaging but perhaps less so than impeachment. The third alternative would be a reorganization of the Government either in coalition form or at least by gathering together in Washington a number of people in whose integrity the country would have full confidence and who would present such a real contrast to the group of young, irresponsible and power-minded kids that Nixon seems thus far to have gravitated toward."

McCloy seemed to be thinking that, if only one could surround the president with a few good "Stimsonians," and thereby reassure the country that the Establishment, not Richard Nixon, was at the helm, then perhaps this distasteful Watergate business would go away. There were many problems with such an approach, not the least of which was that Nixon himself would have none of it. But, more to the point, the president faced serious legal charges which were not going to fade away, even if the entire roster of the Establishment moved into the White House as a caretaker government. "At some point," McCloy admitted, "he [Nixon] has to make his defense, but just in what form, I really don't know. If I were counsel to the President, I would not know what advice to give at this point. I do think it would be inappropriate and probably unwise for him to attempt to answer the charges before the full case is really in. . . ."

To some extent, McCloy treated the affair as a public-relations problem, and he was tempted to rationalize what the Nixon White House had done as no worse than the political skulduggery of previous administrations. When John Dean testified that Nixon had ordered the Internal Revenue Service to audit the tax returns of his "political enemies," McCloy wrote Douglas, "I seem to remember that there was some White House stimulation for similar audits in the Roosevelt Administration. . . ." But he had to admit that, "whatever Administration undertook it, it was a poisonous instinct."[89]

For McCloy, Watergate was a matter of gross incompetence and simple buffoonery. This may explain why men like McCloy, Harriman, and other elder statesmen of the Establishment could do nothing to cut short the nightmare called Watergate. They had no standing with this peculiar president, a man who envied and hated what they represented.[90]

"Mr. President," Elliot Richardson had told Nixon when he accepted the job of attorney general, "I believe your real problem is that you have somehow been unable to realize that you have won—not only won, but been reelected by a tremendous margin. You are the President of *all* the people of the United States. There is no 'they' out there—nobody trying to destroy you. Even the people who didn't vote for you want you to succeed."[91] Richard Nixon sat expressionless, and said nothing. He thought he knew otherwise.

Six months later, Richardson resigned in the "Saturday Night Massacre" rather than fire Special Prosecutor Archibald Cox. Eventually, he became one of McCloy's law partners at Milbank, Tweed and opened the law firm's Washington office.

Throughout the remainder of the 1970s, McCloy continued to represent some of Milbank, Tweed's most lucrative corporate clients. He defended his oil-company clients before Senator Frank Church's (Democrat from Idaho) Senate Subcommittee on Multinational Corporations, which spent months investigating the Seven Sisters. As a consequence, his monthly retainer from each of the five major American oil companies increased from $1,500 to $2,250 per month. In addition to the oil companies, he worked with AT&T, Westinghouse, and Olin Mathieson Chemical Corporation. Often such clients needed McCloy's assistance in fending off antitrust threats from the Justice Department. But in the case of Westinghouse, McCloy was hired to do what he had done for Gulf Oil, conduct an in-house investigation of allegations that the company had paid large bribes, in this case to one of Philippine President Ferdinand Marcos's cronies. As in the Gulf case, the SEC allowed Westinghouse to investigate itself, and McCloy was selected to do the job. He wrote a report that has never been released, and the SEC decided, after several years, not to prosecute the case.[92]

In addition to this legal work, McCloy continued to serve on the boards of Dreyfus Corporation, the Mercedes Benz Corporation of North America, Olinkraft Inc., and the Squibb Corporation. These activities kept him busy and pretty much out of the limelight. After the publicity associated with the Gulf Oil scandal, he seemed to recede into the corporate woodwork of Wall Street. And when Jimmy Carter brought the Democrats back into control of the White House in 1976, McCloy had even less cause to be seen in the public eye. Carter and his people did not make any attempt to bring him within their inner circle. He was occasionally invited down to the White House, but as McCloy would learn, these invitations were more window-dressing than anything else. And as the Carter presidency began to flounder, McCloy found himself annoyed and angered by what he considered its incompetence.

CHAPTER 28

McCloy and the Iran-Hostage Crisis

"To hell with Henry Kissinger. I am the President of this country."

JIMMY CARTER, 1979

"National honor is more important than American lives."

JOHN J. MCCLOY, 1980

Nothing so alarmed McCloy about the Carter administration as its handling of the Iran crisis in the autumn of 1978. McCloy regarded the Pahlevi regime as a loyal ally of more than three decades. It seemed to him that Carter's people, with their emphasis on human rights and liberalization, had sapped the shah's will to rule. McCloy regarded the shah as a U.S. strategic asset, a force for gradual modernization and stability in a region of the world notorious for instability. He saw great value in the Iranian military buildup of the 1970s, since it was rapidly turning the country into a strong regional power, capable of defending U.S. interests in the Persian Gulf.

He also had long-standing private interests with the Pahlevi regime. Milbank, Tweed provided legal counsel not only to Chase Bank, but also to the shah himself.[1] The Chase International Investment Corporation, which McCloy had established back in the 1950s, had several joint ventures in Iran. The shah maintained a personal account with Chase, and so too did his private family trust, the Pahlevi Foundation. Each year, the bank handled some $2 billion in Iranian Eurodollar transactions, and throughout the 1970s Iran had at least $6 billion on deposit at various Chase branches around the world. As one financial analyst put it, "Iran became the crown jewel of Chase's international banking portfolio."[2] Chase also had on its books several outstanding loans to the regime, amounting to over $500 million. On a personal level, over the course of two decades McCloy had gotten to know the shah "very well." He had attended his extravagant self-coronation at Persepolis in 1967, and he genuinely liked the monarch: "I always found him to be a statesmanlike fellow. . . . He wasn't as anti-Jewish as the Arabs."[3] As a token of their friendship, each Christmas the shah sent the McCloys five pounds of fine Beluga caviar.[4]

So, when mass demonstrations erupted in January 1978 and continued with such growing violence that it seemed the regime might collapse, McCloy thought Washington should be doing something to help the shah keep his throne. He was sure the only alternative to the shah was a communist regime. This was a country, after all, that bordered the Soviet Union. Fundamentalist Muslim clerics might at present be leading the demonstrations, but everything McCloy heard from the CIA and his own contacts in Iran suggested that the mullahs could not govern. That autumn, after a bloody massacre of civilian demonstrators by the shah's troops, David Rockefeller told a private meeting of Chase Manhattan Bank employees that communists were directing the revolution.[5] Rockefeller was not McCloy's only source for this assessment of what was happening. In November, his old friend Robert Bowie—who was now serving as deputy director of the CIA—returned from Iran convinced that such left-wing forces as the Fedayeen and Mujahadeen guerrilla organizations and the communist Tudeh Party were managing the demonstrations from behind the scenes.[6] Rockefeller and Bowie strongly reinforced McCloy's presumption that the Carter administration should do something to stiffen the shah's spine.

McCloy, Kissinger, and both David and Nelson Rockefeller made their unhappiness known to the administration. Operating through the Council on Foreign Relations and their own network of contacts within the government, this private foreign-policy establishment began buttonholing administration officials and providing background briefings for the press. The Pahlevi regime, they argued, was still an "oasis" of stability and rationality. The shah's opponents were extremists who could be handled with strong police action. And if the shah was displaying any lack of will, it was probably because he was receiving mixed signals from our embassy in Teheran.[7] An Iran without the shah was unthinkable, and any analysis that failed to conform to this "shared view" was unsound.[8]

This "group-think" became a critical factor in the bureaucratic tussle inside the Carter administration over Iran policy. Carter's NSC adviser, Zbigniew Brzezinski, unreservedly endorsed the Establishment's view of what should be done. Brzezinski aggressively used the crisis to strengthen his grip over the administration's foreign policy, cutting out Secretary of

State Cyrus Vance, another Establishment figure, who nevertheless disagreed with those who insisted there was no alternative to the shah.

By the end of October 1978, Iranian troops had killed some ten thousand demonstrators, and even the shah considered further repression fruitless. Back in Washington, however, few officials were ready to comprehend how far the situation had deteriorated.

On November 2, 1978, Brzezinski reported in a meeting at the White House situation room that he had received a phone call from Nelson Rockefeller. The former vice-president was worried and urged a "clear-cut U.S. stand in support of the Shah."[9] In response, Brzezinski proposed that a message be sent to Ambassador Sullivan instructing him to tell the shah that President Carter supported him "without reservation in the present crisis." Brzezinski even managed to block suggestions from the State Department that the message should make some reference to elections or a coalition government. The shah, Brzezinski argued, should be free to take whatever action he thought necessary to stabilize the situation. Brzezinski won this argument and persuaded the president to link his prestige unequivocally to the shah's survival.

As late as May 1978, Carter's ambassador in Teheran had reported that the regime was firmly in place, but by the autumn William Sullivan had changed his mind. On November 9, 1978, he wrote a cable entitled "Thinking the Unthinkable," and recommended that private talks be opened with the Ayatollah Khomeini's entourage in an attempt to broker a peaceful transition to a new coalition government composed of moderate elements in the opposition.[10] Sullivan was not alone in this view. Henry Precht, one of the Foreign Service's most knowledgeable Iran experts, believed the shah was completely isolated. But these views were not the administration's.

On December 12, 1978, Carter told the press, "I fully expect the Shah to maintain power in Iran. . . . I think the predictions of doom and disaster that come from some sources have certainly not been realized at all. The Shah has our support and he also has our confidence."[11]

A little more than a month later, the shah fled his country, leaving behind a civilian government that would collapse just eleven days after the Ayatollah Khomeini returned from exile on February 1, 1979. Partly because the Carter administration had supported the shah until the bitter end, relations with the new revolutionary government in Teheran were difficult. To make matters worse, the fate of the shah quickly became a bone of contention in Iranian-U.S. relations. Though the Carter administration had initially offered the shah, Queen Farah Diba, and their family sanctuary in America, the monarch had decided first to visit Anwar Sadat in Egypt. After only six days in Egypt, the royal party left for Morocco. More than two months later, when it was clear he had worn out his welcome in Morocco, the shah wanted to seek permanent refuge in

America. But by then, the Carter administration had decided the timing was wrong. Anti-Americanism in Iran was such that the U.S. diplomats were warning Washington that their embassy might be stormed by mobs if the shah were permitted to go to America.

The State Department put out discreet inquiries everywhere, but only two countries offered him sanctuary—South Africa and Paraguay—and the shah did not want to go to either. Nevertheless, Secretary of State Vance called Henry Kissinger and David Rockefeller and asked if either of them would be willing to tell the shah that it would be best if he postponed any visit to America. Both men indignantly refused, and began to make their own calls around the world in search of a haven for the shah.[12] Hours before the Pahlevi party was virtually pushed onto a plane in Morocco, Rockefeller arranged for a haven in the Bahamas. He sent his late brother Nelson's public-relations man, Robert Armao, to greet the shah. Armao would thereafter serve as the monarch's spokesman, accompanying him throughout his journeys in exile. Rockefeller's personal assistant at Chase Manhattan, Joseph V. Reed, was assigned to handle the shah's finances and the logistics of his security needs. And later, when the shah's health deteriorated, Rockefeller dispatched a close personal friend, Dr. Benjamin Kean, to supervise his medical care.

With the shah temporarily ensconced in a beach-front villa in the Bahamas, Rockefeller and Kissinger turned their attention back to Washington, where they were determined to persuade the Carter administration to allow their friend permanent U.S. asylum. To this end, they organized a "special project," code-named Project Alpha. David Rockefeller dipped into his private funds to pay Chase Bank and Milbank, Tweed employees for the time they spent working on Project Alpha. Milbank, Tweed lawyers like McCloy and Jackson deducted the hours they spent on the project from their daily log sheets. Thousands of dollars were spent on phone, travel, and legal expenses over the next year. At one point, they paid an academic specialist on the Middle East $40,000 to write a short book intended to answer the shah's critics.[13] It was a remarkable effort, something only a Rockefeller could have mounted. Frequent strategy meetings were held at One Chase Plaza, and the ever exuberant Joseph Reed kept everyone informed of the latest developments through a flurry of "personal and confidential" memos. The shah was given his own code name—the "Eagle"—and Reed referred to Rockefeller, Kissinger, and McCloy as the "Triumpherate" (sic).[14]

Over the next seven months, Project Alpha pestered the Carter administration into providing sanctuary for the "Eagle." Kissinger fired the first volley. On April 7, 1979, he called Brzezinski in the White House and berated him "in rather sharp terms" for the administration's stance.[15] Kissinger disliked Brzezinski, and Brzezinski knew it. Just three months earlier, Kissinger had entertained the entire first-class lounge of a Pan Am

747 flight crossing the Atlantic with his caustic comments on the "amateurishness" and "incompetence" of the Carter administration. Brzezinski, he had loudly said, was the kind of man who "knows everything and understands nothing."[16]

But Brzezinski happened to agree with Kissinger's belief that Carter's emphasis on human rights and liberalization was "naive."[17] He also agreed that the shah should have been offered sanctuary. At the end of their conversation, Brzezinski encouraged Kissinger to call the president directly. Kissinger did this almost immediately and reminded Carter that he had an appointment to see David Rockefeller in two days. He told the president that he would be behind whatever Rockefeller had to say about the shah's predicament. "I said," Kissinger recalled, "I felt very strongly about this." Two days later, Brzezinski reported to Carter *his* conversation with Kissinger and irritated the president by saying that the asylum matter was a question of principle: "We simply had to stand by those who had been our friends."[18]

Carter heard the same sentiments from Rockefeller when the Chase chairman visited the White House on April 9, 1979. The president sat "stiff and formal" as he listened to Rockefeller tell him that a "great power such as ours should not submit to blackmail." Rockefeller left with the "impression that the president didn't want to hear about it." On one level, Carter was certainly sympathetic to the shah's personal plight. But he was annoyed by the not-so-subtle lobbying. That night, he wrote in his diary of Rockefeller's visit: "The main purpose of this visit, apparently, is to try to induce me to let the Shah come into our country. Rockefeller, Kissinger, and Brzezinski seem to be adopting this as a joint project." He felt there were good reasons to keep the shah out. "Circumstances had changed since I had offered the Shah a haven. Now many Americans would be threatened, and there was no urgent need for the Shah to come here."[19] As he told his chief of staff, Hamilton Jordan, ". . . it makes no sense to bring him [the shah] here and destroy whatever slim chance we have of rebuilding a relationship with Iran. It boils down to a choice between the Shah's preferences as to where he lives and the interests of our country."[20]

Kissinger and company, however, were not about to accept Carter's evaluation of the national interest. After learning from Rockefeller that the president had been unmoved by their private appeals, Kissinger decided to go public. That same evening, he told a Harvard Business School dinner in Manhattan that "a man who for 37 years was a friend of the United States should not be treated like a Flying Dutchman looking for a port of call." It was all too apt a metaphor—though not the one Kissinger intended—since the Flying Dutchman of the legend was condemned to his eternal wanderings at sea for high crimes against man and God. But Kissinger had made his point, and the press picked up on the phrase and broadcast it widely. The conservative columnist George Will castigated the administration in his April 19 column: "It is sad that an Administration that knows so much about morality has so little dignity."[21]

This was only the beginning of a well-orchestrated and persistent revolt by a private foreign-policy establishment against the Carter administration.[22] On the same day Will's critical column appeared, the president's wife, Rosalynn Carter, noted in her diary, "We can't get away from Iran. Many people—Kissinger, David Rockefeller, Howard Baker, John McCloy, Gerald Ford—all are after Jimmy to bring the shah to the United States, but Jimmy says it's been too long, and anti-American and anti-shah sentiments have escalated so that he doesn't want to. Jimmy said he explained to all of them that the Iranians might kidnap our Americans who are still there. . . ."[23]

McCloy thought Carter's refusal to provide sanctuary to an old U.S. ally was "ungentlemanly," and he did not take seriously Carter's fears that American lives in Iran might be jeopardized.[24] So, even though he'd had his differences with Kissinger as secretary of state, McCloy now became a determined foot soldier in the campaign to challenge Carter's efforts to normalize relations with revolutionary Iran. The same week Kissinger let loose his broadside at the administration, he called McCloy and asked him to see what he could do. Over Easter weekend, McCloy talked on the phone with Brzezinski, Vance, and Dean Rusk. Vance told him to write a memo with his views on the matter to his deputy, Warren Christopher.

This McCloy did at considerable length, writing a four-page single-spaced letter to the undersecretary of state. He said that, though he was well aware of the "difficult dilemma" involved, he nevertheless believed the United States could not afford to be seen turning its back on the shah. To do so, he argued, would be "taken as persuasive evidence of our unreliability as a protector of our former friends. . . . It could seriously impair our ability in the future to obtain the support of those of whom we might well stand in need." It was, McCloy believed, precisely the conspicuous character of the shah, and "his pronounced support of United States interests," that made it imperative to respond favorably to his request for asylum.

Having marshaled his arguments, he told Christopher how the whole matter ought to be handled. Referring to Rockefeller's Project Alpha, he said, "It cannot be left to a group of private citizens to cope with it." The administration should appoint someone to deal with "whatever logistics may be involved in acting promptly in response to the Shah's request." He had in mind a soldier with substantial staff experience: "I think of Lucius Clay when he was a young major on the general staff." Perhaps a "young Bob Murphy" should accompany this envoy to the Bahamas to handle the political aspects. The two men should reconnoiter the situation, confer with the shah, and arrange for the logistics of the shah's next move. Some "reasonable form of security" should be offered the monarch. McCloy concluded his memo by admitting that "many awkward consequences" might follow from acting upon this advice, but the administration had to meet its "responsibilities." There was "no time to lose. . . ."[25]

He had his memo hand-delivered to Christopher the same day to underscore the urgency of his message. But the State Department official replied two days later with a note that was obviously designed to put McCloy off. Although Christopher acknowledged many of McCloy's points regarding the shah's past services to the United States, he pointed out that the department was "deeply concerned" about the safety of Americans residing in Iran. "Now the risks to these Americans are great, but they could lessen over time, and we do not exclude the possibility of the Shah's coming here at a future time." Christopher thanked McCloy for his concerns, and closed by saying, ". . . you are one of those distinguished Americans to whom we look for insight and wisdom."[26]

McCloy did not let the matter drop. He immediately wrote Christopher another letter, saying that, in his judgment, the matter could not be "postponed to an indefinite date." He felt "time may soon be running out and events may well overtake us and restrict our options." And even if it wasn't a "propitious" moment to admit the shah to the United States, McCloy suggested that his idea of appointing a "planner" to go to meet with the shah in the Bahamas was not inconsistent with "your quite proper concern for the safety of our personnel in Iran."[27]

Even though he received no reply to this second overture, McCloy did not give up. Vance later recalled, "John is a very prolific letter writer. The morning mail often contained something from him about the Shah."[28] McCloy felt no inhibitions about picking up the phone and calling the secretary of state; Vance was, after all, an old friend, a fellow Wall Street lawyer, and a member of his intimate luncheon club, Nisi Prius. McCloy claimed no special knowledge, but Vance recalled he always spoke with "passion" on the issue of the shah. " 'Right or wrong,' he told me," recalled Vance, 'he's our ally, and if you treat him otherwise, you could appear wobbly.' " Vance argued with his friend, telling him that the situation had changed, and that much of the shah's predicament was of his own making. "But this just never penetrated McCloy's thinking." Vance thought McCloy's attitude was a sign of the "rigidity that came with old age."[29] McCloy thought Vance "too timid."[30]

He pestered not only Vance and Christopher, but also Undersecretary of State David Newsom, whom he had frequently seen during the early 1970s on Middle East oil issues. He was beginning to sound like a broken record. "To a certain extent," recalled Newsom, "he was a man who lived in the past. I remember him saying, 'I have been in contact with some of the chancellors in Europe about this issue and they are outraged at our conduct." When Newsom asked him which chancellors he was speaking of, McCloy replied breezily, "Oh, I was talking the other day with [Harold] Macmillan." At this point, Macmillan had been out of office for over twelve years. Newsom didn't by any means think the eighty-four-year-old McCloy was senile, just that he was out of touch.[31] McCloy had never been very knowledgeable about the Third World, and he had no clue as to the deep-rooted hatred the Iranian people felt for their exiled monarch. He acted as if the issue were strictly a matter of personal loyalty. "The shah wasn't as enlightened a despot as he might have been," he admitted in 1985, "but we did importune him so many times to assist in guarding our interests that we owed him a certain decency when he got in trouble."[32]

Later in the crisis, McCloy began seeing Carter's U.N. ambassador, Donald F. McHenry. On five or six occasions, he called McHenry and asked to see him on short notice. He insisted that the meetings should be entirely secret, that even McHenry's secretary should not be aware of where he was going. And so, though McHenry thought it all rather curious, he would leave his office and meet McCloy in some Manhattan restaurant. There he would be subjected to the same speeches McCloy had made before Brzezinski, Vance, and Christopher. McCloy repeated his arguments, McHenry recalled, "ad nauseam." He wanted to know if McHenry was aware of all the shah's "good deeds." No honorable nation, he said, "would turn its back on a man who had been so helpful to it." McHenry listened politely to these little sermons, but privately he thought the old man had a "myopic view of the shah's deeds." McCloy exhibited no interest in Iran *per se;* he was concerned only with appearances and what he thought were "unseemly" aspects of U.S. policy.[33]

He didn't restrict his campaign to only the highest-ranking officials. Gary Sick was a relatively junior officer attached to Brzezinski's office. But when McCloy learned that Sick, a retired Navy captain, was Brzezinski's point man on the Middle East, he called him up. Sick was startled to receive a call from someone who he knew was in the habit of calling presidents, not lowly NSC aides. After clearing it with Brzezinski, Sick accepted McCloy's invitation to a private luncheon, which he thoroughly enjoyed. What McCloy had to say about the shah was all very familiar, but Sick was greatly flattered that the old man had bothered to "track me down to make a point."[34]

By midsummer of 1979, the campaign was beginning to have an effect on the administration. After a final push from Kissinger, Vice-President Walter Mondale told Carter that he had changed his mind, and now supported asylum for the shah. In a late-July meeting, Brzezinski and Mondale so annoyed the president with their arguments that he finally cut them off by saying, "Fuck the Shah. I'm not going to welcome him here when he has other places to go where he'll be safe."[35] According to Brzezinski, he complained that "Kissinger, Rockefeller and McCloy had been waging a constant campaign on the subject. . . ." Prophetically, he said he did not want the shah "here playing tennis while Americans in Teheran were being kidnapped or even killed."[36]

It was not so easy, however, to dismiss all this high-powered lobbying. Carter needed the cooperation of men like McCloy and Kissinger on other issues of immediate concern to his administration. Like presidents before him, Carter had used McCloy on occasion as a private emissary—to Germany and, surprisingly, to China, in the autumn of 1978.[37] McCloy had already lent his prestige to helping the administration win Senate ratification of the Panama Canal Treaty in the spring of 1978. He and Harriman had formed a "Committee of Americans for the Canal Treaties," and McCloy's testimony on Capitol Hill had been forceful and persuasive.[38] Now Carter was encountering stiff resistance in the Senate regarding ratification of SALT II, the arms-control treaty he had just signed with the Soviets in June 1979. Through an organization called the Committee on the Present Danger, a coalition of the Republican old guard and a number of prominent conservative Democrats had succeeded in casting doubt on the treaty. The support that summer of an elder "Wise Man" like McCloy was a powerful counterbalance to the anti-SALT testimony of Paul Nitze and other critics of the measure. The president could not afford to alienate McCloy.

Unfortunately, relations between the two men had never been very good. Reflecting the personal dislike Germany's Helmut Schmidt felt for Carter, McCloy had gotten it into his head that the Carter administration was snubbing his German friends. The president, he thought, was just not sensitive enough to West European concerns. To make matters worse, Carter had offended McCloy when he made the mistake of inviting the eighty-four-year-old lawyer to the White House, ostensibly to discuss SALT II. When McCloy arrived at the White House, on May 16, 1979, he found himself herded into the East Room with an eclectic assortment of fifty-odd private citizens. "It was a cattle show," McCloy later told *Time* columnist Hugh Sidey.[39]

A month later, the president tried to make amends by inviting McCloy to a private lunch. They met first in the Oval Office, where McCloy presented the president with a gift, an antique hunting rifle. Carter then escorted his elderly, slightly stooped guest outside, where the two men sat down at a small round table on the terrace and lunched alone. They spent an hour talking about the state of the world, and once again McCloy outlined his reasons for providing the shah with sanctuary. Carter listened politely. Afterward, he scrawled a short note to McCloy, saying, "Enjoyed having lunch with you today."[40]

Such efforts on Carter's part to build bridges to the Establishment failed to stem the pressure to do something to help the shah. By the summer of 1979, the Carter administration found itself on the defensive on several fronts. Taking advantage of the Iran crisis, the oil companies and OPEC once again were forcing major price increases on Western consumers. High fuel prices and long lines at gasoline stations around the country inevitably reflected poorly on the administration. Republicans began capitalizing on this disgruntlement by blaming Carter for having "lost Iran." Carter was being depicted as a weak president, a man who had also given away too much in the SALT II Treaty. The administration responded by making SALT II ratification its number-one priority.[41] This in turn made the administration even more vulnerable to pressure from the Kissinger-McCloy campaign to accommodate the shah. At the end of July 1979, Kissinger made the linkage explicit when he bluntly told Brzezinski that his continued support for SALT II was linked to a "more forthcoming attitude on our part regarding the Shah."[42] Carter was thoroughly annoyed by this linkage, but he decided to allow Vance to begin working on contingency plans to bring the shah into the country.

Then, in September 1979, the administration stumbled into another foreign-policy crisis, in which it again needed McCloy's assistance. Someone in the administration leaked the news that the intelligence community had "discovered" a Soviet combat brigade in Cuba. Conservatives alleged that such a force was a violation of the agreement reached during the October 1962 missile crisis, whereby the Soviets agreed not to introduce offensive weaponry into Cuba in exchange for a pledge by the United States not to invade the island. The "news," of course, was old news, and anyone who was familiar with the 1962 negotiations, as McCloy was, knew that the Soviets had maintained a small combat brigade in Cuba for years.[43] Nevertheless, there was considerable furor, both in the press and in Congress, about a new Soviet threat in Cuba.

Before ascertaining the facts, President Carter rashly pledged that his administration would not tolerate the presence of a Soviet combat brigade in Cuba. This neatly boxed him into a hard-line position, and by the time he learned that there was considerable doubt as to whether the Soviet brigade was really anything new, his pledge not to accept the *status quo* was threatening to sour Soviet-American détente and derail ratification of the SALT II Treaty. To extract himself from this political dilemma, Carter made a public show of calling together a panel of "Wise Men" to advise him on the matter.

McCloy was one of the initial group of seven "Wise Men"—later expanded to sixteen—who flew down to Washington to consult with the intelligence community. He was joined by such other Establishment luminaries as John A. McCone, McGeorge Bundy, Brent Scowcroft, Henry Kissinger, George W. Ball, Roswell Gilpatric, Dean Rusk, William P. Rogers, Clark Clifford, and Averell Harriman. McCloy, however, was in a unique position to reconstruct for the administration what had been promised during the Cuban missile crisis. Only he and the late Adlai Stevenson had conducted the phase of the negotiations with the Soviets relevant to the question of what kind of Soviet military personnel would be allowed to remain in Cuba after the withdrawal of the missiles.

Among other things, McCloy flatly asserted, the subject of Soviet military personnel "arose only incidentally" in the 1962 negotiations. He had merely told the Soviets that any troops associated with the missiles would have to be removed; he had not requested or obtained a ban on all Soviet troops in Cuba. The presence in Cuba of a Soviet combat brigade was therefore not a violation of the 1962 "understanding." As to the troops that were there, after spending nine hours one day at the CIA scrutinizing the evidence, "McCloy said he was not worried about a few thousand Soviet troops in Cuba since they presented no strategic threat to the United States."[44] His unequivocal opinion quickly put an end to any effort by conservative Republicans to make an issue of the brigade. McCloy and the other "Wise Men" went to the White House at the end of September 1979 to report their conclusions to Carter, and after the administration promised to monitor Soviet military activity in Cuba, the issue died down.[45]

On all these issues—SALT, Cuba, the Panama Canal Treaty, Germany, China—the Carter administration had called upon McCloy for advice and assistance. Not surprisingly, by the autumn of 1979 it was becoming harder to resist his insistence that the shah be given a haven in America. That September, Cy Vance went up to New York and visited the Council on Foreign Relations. In an off-the-record private session before the Council's membership, he tried to explain why the shah was being denied an entry visa. McCloy was not impressed, and in private even Vance was beginning to have second thoughts. In Iran, the conservative Muslim clergy were in the political ascendancy, making it less likely that normal relations could be achieved with Iran anytime soon. Then, in mid-October, David Rockefeller's assistant, Joseph Reed, called the State Department and revealed that the shah had cancer and needed immediate treatment in a U.S. medical facility.[46] By then, the shah had found another temporary haven in Cuernavaca, Mexico.

Upon hearing this news, Vance changed his mind and told the president that, as a matter of "common decency," the shah should be admitted to the United States. Even Carter's chief of staff, Hamilton Jordan, found domestic political reasons to reverse the administration's decision.

"Mr. President," Jordan argued, "if the Shah dies in Mexico can you imagine the field day Kissinger will have with that? He'll say that first you caused the Shah's downfall and now you've killed him."

"To hell with Henry Kissinger," Carter responded, "I am the President of this country."[47]

But, faced with the now unanimous opposition of his closest advisers, the president reluctantly agreed to admit the shah. He instructed his aides to make sure that the shah's medical condition required treatment in the United States, and he asked that the embassy in Teheran be apprised of the decision so they could make their own security preparations. Then he turned to everyone in the room and asked, "What are you guys going to advise me to do if they overrun our embassy and take our people hostage?"[48]

His fears were shortly realized. The shah checked into New York Hospital on October 22, 1979, whereupon Joseph Reed circulated a memo to McCloy and other members of Project Alpha, congratulating them: "Our 'mission impossible' is completed. . . . My applause is like thunder."[49] Less than two weeks later, Iranian militants stormed the U.S. Embassy in Teheran and took hostage almost seventy Americans. During the next 444 days, the hostage crisis mesmerized America and took hostage the remaining days of the Carter administration.

It is easy to see that the decision to admit the shah to the United States created the political atmosphere in which the Ayatollah Khomeini could purge the revolutionary government of any figures—religious or secular—who opposed the creation of a harsh Islamic theocracy. It was a disaster for both the American and Iranian peoples. Soon after the hostages were taken, the Establishment's perennial dissenter, George Ball, told "Meet the Press" that, "had it not been for Mr. Kissinger and a few others making themselves enormously obnoxious for the administration, trying to force the Shah into this country, maybe we wouldn't even have done it, even for reasons of compassion."[50]

But McCloy, Kissinger, and Rockefeller always refused to say they might have misjudged the situation. Kissinger immediately blamed the Carter administration for the embassy's takeover, and told the press that Americans were "tired of getting pushed around. . . ."[51] Rockefeller suggested that, if the embassy couldn't be protected, it should have been closed down before the shah came to America.[52] Four days after the hostages were seized, McCloy met with Undersecretary Newsom and Ambassador McHenry and warned them that "any negotiation with the Iranians must be preceded by the release of the hostages." Furthermore, he said it was "quite clear" that the administration "must take charge of the situation," and communicate directly with the shah. The next day, he visited the hospitalized shah and reassured him that Washington had no intention of pressuring him to leave the country.[53] After more than a month in the hospital, the shah was flown to a Texas air base, and then on to yet another temporary haven in Panama.

As the hostage crisis stretched into 1980, McCloy was defiantly unrepentant, and he continued to lobby various administration officials to take a tough line with the Iranians.[54] In retrospect, it is difficult to distinguish when McCloy was acting in his public role as elder "Wise Man" and when he was simply representing the private interests of his legal clients. The Rockefeller-Kissinger-McCloy team, after all, represented Chase Manhattan Bank, an institution that was particularly exposed as a result of the Iranian revolution.[55] In the first eight months of 1979, the new government in Teheran transferred some $6 billion out of Chase accounts. It became apparent by the summer of 1979 that Chase would soon not have enough Iranian funds on deposit to cover the bank's loans to the Pahlevi regime. Chase was the lead syndicator of a $500-million loan that might easily be repudiated by the revolutionary government. Chase had approved the loan in 1977 even though its own Iranian lawyers pointed out that the shah had not won Parliament's endorsement as required by Article 25 of the Iranian Constitution. Technically, it was unconstitutional. If Teheran were to repudiate the loan, Chase would have to answer to the other banks that had participated in the syndicate. Chase's good name was at stake, as well as its loans.[56]

Despite this exposure, Chase made out remarkably well as a direct result of the hostage crisis. So too did McCloy's law firm, which represented Chase and in some instances directed its strategy. The day after the embassy was seized, Chase received a telex from the Iranian government authorizing the payment of $4.05 million in interest due on the $500-million loan. Chase was to take the payment, due on November 15, from one of Iran's accounts in its London branch. Chase did not acknowledge these instructions. In the meantime, Milbank, Tweed lawyers consulted with the Treasury Department on freezing Iranian assets. This contingency had been considered by both Treasury Department and Chase officers as early as February 1979, when Khomeini came to power. But now it took on a certain urgency. And when, early on the morning of November 14, it was reported that Iran's acting foreign-affairs minister, Abol Hassan Bani Sadr, had announced that his country was going to withdraw all deposits from American banks, the Carter administration froze all Iranian assets in any American banks, both in the United States and abroad. The foreign banking community was taken aback by the sweeping nature of the order. It was one thing to freeze Iranian assets within the United States, but to extend the freeze order to U.S. banks operating under foreign jurisdiction was highly unusual.

Guided by its Milbank, Tweed counsel, Chase went a step further. Since Carter's freeze order had taken effect one day prior to the day on which Iran's $4.05-million interest payment was due, the payment was not made from Chase's London branch. Over the vigorous objections of the foreign banks in the syndicate, Chase then declared Iran's $500-million loan in default. Moving with deliberate haste—and even before receiving the required Treasury Department authorization—Chase seized all of Iran's Chase accounts and used those monies to "offset" any outstanding Iranian loans. "When the dust had cleared," wrote financial analyst Mark Hulbert, "Chase had no loans to Iran left on its books."[57]

All of these steps were taken with the close supervision of Chase's legal counsel at Milbank, Tweed, which of course included McCloy. And so, while the firm's leading name partner was once again attempting to advise Washington, he was also representing a private interest that had a major financial stake in the outcome. In McCloy's mind, there was no conflict of interest; the interests of Chase Bank and the interests of the country were pretty much the same. America, he thought, should not appear to be weak or on the defensive in its dealing with the revolutionary regime. He even went so far as to tell one State Department official in 1980 that "national honor is more important than American lives."[58] Simultaneously, Chase's fiduciary responsibilities required it to do everything it could to retrieve its Iranian loans.

Until negotiations finally led to a settlement on January 20, 1981, the hostage crisis seemed on the face of it to be driven by deep-rooted anti-American passions and Shia religious intrigue. But over time it became clear that the fate of the hostages was intimately bound up with Teheran's desire to retrieve its frozen assets, and the demands of the American and European bankers, led by Chase, to be repaid on their Iranian loans. One lawyer involved in the negotiations later commented, "It was obvious that there would be no hostage release without a financial settlement." One of McCloy's senior Milbank, Tweed partners, Francis D. Logan, forty-nine, who sat on the firm's ten-member governing "Firm Committee," was one of the handful of lawyers who made secret trips to London and Algiers to negotiate the deal. In the end, not only Chase, but all the banks walked away with a generous settlement. Iran eventually paid out $3.7 billion; when the American bankers learned their loans were to be repaid in full, they "nearly fell off their chairs."[59] Wall Street's lawyers—and none more so than the lawyers at Milbank, Tweed—earned millions of dollars in legal fees. The hostage crisis, in the words of author and legal reporter Paul Hoffman, was nothing less than a "bonanza for the bar."[60]

Twilight Years

When Ronald Reagan won the November 1980 presidential election, McCloy was greatly relieved to see Jimmy Carter out of the White House. He thought the Georgian had been a weak and indecisive president. And even though the Goldwater-Reagan ideologues were not his kind of Republicans, he hoped he would have an inside track to the new administration. The president-elect's campaign manager was William Casey, an old friend and fellow member of the Council. No doubt at Casey's urging, Reagan appointed McCloy to his foreign-policy transition team. So, during the late autumn, the eighty-five-year-old McCloy took the shuttle to Washington twice a week to participate in meetings at the State Department. The transition team had a fair number of Reaganites, such as Richard V. Allen, Jeane J. Kirkpatrick, and Anne Armstrong, but there were also old friends and Establishment figures like Kissinger, Eugene Rostow, George Schultz, and Edward Bennett Williams, a prominent Washington corporate attorney.

McCloy's presence on the transition team was not merely window-dressing; this was to be an extremely conservative administration, but not so rigid as entirely to exclude liberal Republicans like McCloy. There were some complaints from within Reagan's "New Right" constituency that this leading member of the Eastern Establishment should not be advising the new administration. Any worries, however, that McCloy would be too liberal proved groundless. The Carter years, and the humiliating experience of the Iran-hostage crisis, had convinced him that America had to reassert its control over global events. Working with the transition team, he signed on to a foreign-policy "strategy" which endorsed a "long term rebuilding of military strength." He believed America's position in the world was now "a dangerous one—balance is shifting against us in terms of military strength, cohesion of alliances, perception of leadership and economic competitiveness. . . ." Reagan, he recommended, should "get out a coherent message to the world to re-establish purpose and confidence." New monies had to be invested in cruise missiles, the B-1 bomber, and even an antimissile defense.[1] Reagan accepted this blueprint for his foreign policy, and McCloy was gratified in the early 1980s by what he thought was a restoration of America's image abroad. From time to time, he saw the president, but his only real friend in the administration was William Casey, the new CIA director, with whom he occasionally socialized.[2] The two men shared a love for reminiscing about the OSS and the early days of the CIA.

McCloy generally approved of Reagan's policies, though he was disturbed by the administration's fixation on Central American issues. In one Council on Foreign Relations meeting, he was heard to grumble, "El Salvador doesn't amount to a hill of beans."[3] He still believed that Germany, and not various Third World conflicts, should be Washington's first priority. As he had told Cy Vance at the beginning of Carter's term in office, "The Germans can be exasperatingly nervous about their security. . . . If not a super power, they are certainly emerging as a great European power and with thoughtful effort they can continue to be a really friendly power."[4] He had been disappointed by the Carter administration's coolness with Helmut Schmidt's Germany, and now, at the beginning of a new administration, he emphasized to Reagan's secretary of state, Alexander Haig, the importance of getting "off on the right foot, in the way the last administration was unable to do."[5]

Although too old to serve any longer as a discreet conduit for the private views of German chancellors, McCloy was considered an institution in German-American relations. Through the Council on Foreign Relations, the American Council on Germany, the Atlantic Council, and a new foundation called the McCloy Fund, his influence on German-American relations continued to be felt long after he was able to play any active personal role in these organizations. The McCloy Fund was established in 1975 with a grant from the German government. In 1982, the chairman of the Krupp Foundation, Berthold Beitz, gave the Fund a $2-million grant, nearly tripling its capital base.[6] With this money, the McCloy Fund organized symposiums between German and American policy-makers, and funded academic studies on policy issues of importance to the West German government.

As the Cold War seemed to revive under Reagan, McCloy once again began emphasizing his faith in international law and arbitration as a means of settling sovereign disputes. He was displeased when the Reagan administration refused to recognize the World Court's jurisdiction over a case brought about by the CIA's mining of Nicaraguan harbors. He disliked the Sandinista regime in Nicaragua as much as his friend Bill Casey, but he thought it a bad precedent for the United States to ignore the World Court.[7]

McCloy also made his influence felt on one other issue of long-standing personal interest. He had supported the Reagan defense buildup as a necessary response to the Brezhnev regime's invasion of Afghanistan. But by the end of Reagan's first term in office, he was worried about the president's extreme rhetoric and the failure to achieve any kind of arms-control agreement with the Soviets. The Soviets may have been an ideological adversary—even an "evil empire," in the president's words—but in the nuclear era McCloy believed that a refusal to negotiate seriously on arms control was not in the U.S. national interest. "We seem to be talking past each other," he complained to visitors in his Milbank, Tweed office. "We should have the best people on both sides meet, instead of figuring out the best missile to throw at each other. . . . No two countries have more to lose by having bad relations, or to gain by good relations. We need to figure out what we have in common, and enter a period of more cooperative attitudes." He thought "especially a president as popular as Reagan" should be able to take such an initiative.

In the spring of 1986, Robert McNamara called him up and invited him to join such veterans of previous arms-control negotiations as Paul Warnke, Gerard Smith, and George Kennan in urging President Reagan to take a less adversarial approach in his dealings with the Soviets. But McCloy was uncomfortable with the idea; he did not want to seem partisan, and he did not want to force himself on the president, particularly in the company of a group of prominent Democrats. Instead, he sat down and wrote the president a letter that repeated to Reagan what he had told numerous friends in and out of government: that in all his encounters with the Soviets, he had always found someone on the other side of the table who could be reasonable. Surely, he told Reagan, your administration should be able to negotiate some sort of agreement with the Soviets which could serve to ease tensions.[8]

Partly because the Soviets had a new, dynamic leader in Mikhail Gorbachev, and partly in response to Reagan's growing domestic problems, the Reagan administration in 1987 finally began to show a genuine interest in arms-control negotiations. McCloy was pleased when, at the end of that year, the administration signed the INF treaty, which eliminated intermediate-range nuclear missiles from the European continent. He hoped further such agreements could be made in the future.

In March 1985, on McCloy's ninetieth birthday, President Reagan invited him to the White House for a celebration in the Rose Garden. It was a crisp spring day when McCloy arrived at the front gate in his pale-blue Mercedes limousine. (He still served as a board director of Mercedes-Benz of North America, Inc.) With him were his son, John, an investment banker, and his daughter-in-law, Laura, and his two grandsons, Jay and Rush. His wife of fifty-five years, Ellen, had been ill for some time and could not attend. Inside, more than a hundred friends and colleagues—including the chairman of the Federal Reserve, Paul Volcker; Vice-President George Bush; and Secretary of State George Shultz—

watched as the president of Germany, Richard von Weizsäcker, conferred honorary German citizenship on McCloy. Weizsäcker, the son of the same man whose war crimes sentence McCloy had commuted in 1950, praised McCloy's "human decency in helping the beaten enemy to recover" and his efforts to build "one of the free and prosperous countries in the world. . . ."[9]

President Reagan congratulated the old man, saying, "John McCloy's selfless heart has made a difference, an enduring difference, in the lives of millions." Afterward, McCloy stood up against a chill wind, hatless and without an overcoat, and joked with the president: "Compared to me, what a spring chicken you are." He admitted that he was a little sensitive about his age. "A friend of mine—I'm sure he was a friend—once said to me, 'Jack, did you ever stop to think . . . in a few years your life will represent one-half the life of the entire country. . . ." America, he said, was still "a young country. . . . Its great destinies are ahead of it." He then reminisced briefly about his long life, and particularly his experience in two world wars. He recalled his service in World War I under Brigadier General Guy H. Preston, "a man who had fought Indians on the Plains."[10]

The following evening, he was the guest of honor at a black-tie dinner hosted by the Council on Foreign Relations. Former West German Chancellor Helmut Schmidt was there, as were Henry Kissinger, David Rockefeller, and dozens of other old friends. Rockefeller anointed him "the first Citizen of the Council on Foreign Relations," and unveiled a plaque beneath a portrait of McCloy hung in the Council's ornate meeting hall which read, "Statesman, Patriot, Friend." Then Kissinger rose to speak. Quoting Bismarck, he intoned, "John McCloy, I believe, heard the footsteps of God as he went through history. And those of us who were not humble enough or whose ears were not sharp enough had the privilege of knowing that if we followed in his footsteps we were in the path of doing God's work."

McCloy responded to this outlandish flattery with better-measured words: "I know that many of the things said tonight were exaggerated, but they made me feel warm. My record has its pluses and minuses. I only hope that it has been credible, that people can say of me: he did his damnedest, the angels can do no more."[11]

To his distress, however, his last years were stalked by the kind of controversy and personal animus that he had managed to avoid most of his life. Outside of the Council on Foreign Relations and similar Establishment turfs, strident voices were sometimes heard, disputing the soundness of his judgment and protesting the awards and honors heaped upon him. When Harvard University accepted Volkswagen money funneled through the McCloy Fund, a coalition of students and some faculty organized a vigorous protest. Articles appeared in campus publications recounting McCloy's role in the internment of the Japanese Americans during World War II and his decision not to bomb Auschwitz. The *Washington Post, The New Republic, Commentary,* and numerous other national magazines re-examined the controversy, while old friends came to his defense, including Nahum Goldmann's son, Guido, who happened now to be on the Harvard faculty.

But the debate persisted, partly because McCloy refused to stay above the fray. In 1981, when a congressional commission investigating the Japanese American internment invited him to testify, he eagerly agreed, thinking he would be able to explain why such tough decisions had been made in the midst of the war. He mistakenly thought he would be accorded the usual deference and courtesy of an elder statesman. Things did not work out that way. When he tried to describe conditions in the internment camps as "very pleasant," the audience, many of whom had lived in those camps, burst into sarcastic laughter. Later, one of the commission members, a Japanese American who was then serving as a judge in Pennsylvania, literally screamed at him, "What other Americans, Mr. McCloy, fought for this country while their parents, brothers and sisters were incarcerated?"

McCloy angrily responded, "I don't like the word 'incarcerated.' "[12] He then astonished everyone by warning the commission that Congress should do nothing to tie the hands of a president in a future crisis. One could not predict what might have to be done in the name of national security. The next war, he suggested, could be waged against Cuba, and it might be necessary to detain large numbers of Cuban Americans in southern Florida. Not surprisingly, such testimony was punctuated by hissing and booing. McCloy thought the whole proceedings were a "disgrace," and told a friend, "Money, money, money. Why don't they dun the Japanese government? We didn't attack Pearl Harbor, they did."[13] Few were convinced by his arguments, and eventually Congress issued a formal apology to the Japanese American community and promised to pay $20,000 in compensation to each surviving internee. McCloy was crestfallen when President Reagan signed the bill into law.

The controversy even invaded the private confines of Milbank, Tweed, where one of the firm's associates, a Japanese American whose parents had been interned, confronted McCloy in the hallway outside his office. It quickly turned into a shouting match, and though the associate was not dismissed, he soon left Milbank, Tweed for another firm.

McCloy felt misunderstood. He told reporters who came around to his One Chase Plaza office that he was never such an important figure. He didn't understand why anyone would think he had ever had the power to decide these issues. "I was just a leg man," he protested. He was further annoyed when *Harper's* magazine profiled him in a long cover story as "the most influential private citizen in America." He tried to stop the publication of the article and, failing that, vigorously protested its treatment of his role in the internment, Auschwitz, and Krupp decisions.

Unhappy as he was with these public recriminations, McCloy's private life had taken a tragic turn. In the mid-1970s, Ellen had begun noticing that her hands sometimes trembled. Eventually, she was diagnosed with Parkinson's disease, a degenerative nerve disorder. By 1976, she could no longer take care of herself, and McCloy hired a live-in nurse. Over the years, the disease steadily advanced, clouding Ellen's mind so that at times she couldn't even recognize her husband of fifty years.[14] Once, McCloy returned home from his Milbank, Tweed offices late at night and found Ellen hallucinating. To his shock, he realized that she thought he was some Nazi general who had come to take her away. On another occasion, a doctor asked her to name the current president of the United States, and she replied, referring to Jimmy Carter, "Oh, you know, that Peanut." These spells came and went, but her condition never improved.

Watching his once strong-willed wife deteriorate pained McCloy greatly. Ellen had always been the one who had pushed him in his career. He had relied on her judgment and scheduled his social life around her desires. In the presence of others, McCloy tried to hold his emotions in. He never sobbed, or broke down, but sometimes he would softly cry, and mumble quietly that it hurt him that he couldn't do anything to help her. Finally, though the idea was awful to him, he realized he would have to put Ellen in a nursing home where she could receive round-the-clock care. A place was found thirty minutes from Cos Cob, and Ellen, now generally unaware of her surroundings, was moved into a large pleasant room. (McCloy told his old friend Benny Buttenwieser that the nursing home was costing him $75,000 a year.)

Every day after work, he came and sat by her; they would hold hands for hours, while he read aloud from a biography or history book from his large library. At times he thought of retiring and spending his whole day looking after Ellen. But though by most standards he was a relatively rich man, he felt he had to keep on working in order to meet Ellen's medical expenses and to maintain the household. He told his friends that he realized that retirement wouldn't do him or Ellen any good.[15]

Ellen finally died in the spring of 1986, at the age of eighty-seven. By then McCloy's own health, at the age of ninety-one, was beginning to deteriorate. He had suffered a mild heart attack in 1982, but after a brief hospitalization, he returned to work. Even though he found little corporate legal work to do, Milbank, Tweed allowed him to retain his office and the use of a secretary. Nearly every day, he was driven to One Chase Plaza, where he answered his correspondence and talked with old friends. With the assistance of Shep Stone and the Harvard diplomatic historian, Ernest

May, he attempted for a time to write a short memoir. It didn't work out, but it gave him the excuse to reminisce on tape with such old friends as Robert Lovett, Averell Harriman, and Benny Buttenwieser. After Ellen died, he spent more time at his Cos Cob home, where his daughter took care of him. Off and on for five years, he suffered from congestive heart failure. Then one day, just a couple of weeks before his ninety-fourth birthday, he awoke and found it difficult to breathe. His doctor was called from nearby Greenwich and quickly determined that the patient was suffering an attack of pulmonary edema.[16] In lay terms, his heart was simply giving out, and his lungs were filling with fluid. For three hours, he struggled to find the strength to breathe, and then, at 12:15 P.M. on March 11, 1989, he was gone. The Chairman was dead.

At the very beginning of the Cold War, in 1946, John J. McCloy unabashedly wrote his earliest mentor, Philadelphia lawyer George Wharton Pepper, "In the light of what has happened, I would take a chance on this country using its strength tyrannously. . . . We need, if you will, a Pax Americana, and in the course of it the world will become more receptive to the Bill of Rights viewpoint than if we do no more than devoutly wish for peace and freedom." This imperial vision of a beneficent America attempting to impose its values on a hostile world became the rationale for a prolonged Cold War, fought not only in Europe, but throughout the developing world.

It also required an enormous investment of American resources in building a military establishment the likes of which the world has never seen. As Henry Stimson's lieutenant during World War II, McCloy was instrumental in mobilizing the American economy to wage total war. This may have been his greatest service to the country. But when the war ended, he and his peers in the American foreign policy establishment provided the rationale for continuing this mobilization, this time to build a peacetime national security state. America would turn outward and assume global responsibilities. The costs of building this military and intelligence apparatus have been staggering; the end of the Cold War has left America with an uncompetitive economy burdened with debt, high unemployment, low growth, and income levels more unevenly divided than at any time since the beginning of the Cold War.

The Establishment always assured the American people that the burdens of the national security state were affordable while the risks of isolationism were not. Like many in his generation, McCloy had overlearned the lessons of Munich. He equated neutrality with isolationism, and isolationism with appeasement. He shared with most members of the Establishment a worldview that ultimately set the stage for America's disastrous intervention in the Vietnamese civil war.

McCloy himself candidly stated that his career had "its pluses and minuses." Foremost among his many attractive qualities was his flexible legal mind. Studying the law required patience, persistence, and humility. One had to be able to see another man's point of view and understand how two people could arrive at opposing opinions. The man who staged "reading debates" for himself on the issues of the day also had the ability to convince two adversaries that he could represent the interests of both. Through sheer hard work he became remarkably adept at "yellow-padding" complicated legal agreements between contentious parties. No one disliked this man except from a distance.

McCloy had a reservoir of patience and enough persistence to prevail in almost any endeavor. But he was not a stubborn man. He could change his mind. He even possessed the ability to admit he was wrong, a rare quality in men of his stature and power.

Through persistence, not brilliance, he crossed over Philadelphia's "Chinese Wall" and elbowed his way into elite society. The son of a hairdresser earned a position for himself as lawyer–servant for some of the most powerful private interests in America. Men like John D. Rockefeller, Jr., Felix Warburg, and Sid Richardson sought his counsel, in part because he was just a very good lawyer, but also because they knew he was the kind of man who could tell rich men what he really thought. He could be disarmingly frank, even critical, and yet they also sensed that his loyalties were to their class. He was exactly the kind of man a Rockefeller could trust to run his bank or teach his sons how to sail.

On occasion, McCloy's pragmatism led to his most troubling decisions. He could justify almost anything in the name of national security, including the wholesale internment of Japanese Americans during World War II. Similarly, his determination not to divert military resources away from the war effort blinded him to the opportunity of rescuing thousands of doomed European Jews from the gas chambers of Auschwitz. And even some of his admirers find it difficult to understand his clemency decisions on behalf of Alfried Krupp and dozens of other convicted Nazi war criminals.

Often, however, his instincts were sound. As assistant secretary of war he helped the U.S. Army take the first halting steps toward racial integration. As high commissioner in Occupied Germany he nurtured democratic institutions and encouraged a robust free press. He had gambled that if Germany could be kept divided for at least one generation, eventually the powerful German nation could be reunited within a democratic European union. To an extraordinary degree, he won this gamble. As an adviser to the president during the Cuban missile crisis, he patiently negotiated the withdrawal of Soviet missiles from Cuba and urged the Kennedy administration to place arms control high on the national agenda. From the dawn of the nuclear era, he understood that after

Hiroshima, mankind would someday have to take the path to a disarmament system or not survive.

As men possessing a measure of *gravitas,* McCloy and other Establishment figures always claimed they could rise above the private interests they represented and discern the larger public good. Ultimately, this claim is not sustainable. But it is nevertheless remarkable how the postwar Establishment managed for so long to fulfill that promise. Before he died, McCloy himself observed of the new generation, "These big salaries lawyers are getting make it much harder for them to consider government as part of their careers. When I was young, the idea of serving in Washington was the most exciting prospect I could imagine."

McCloy's career compares so favorably to the opportunism of his successors that many observers have taken to voicing a certain nostalgia for the pre-Vietnam Establishment. But even McCloy, at critical moments in his stewardship, blurred the boundaries between private and public interests.

The Establishment symbolized by John J. McCloy's life remains a useful metaphor for understanding how power works in America at the end of the twentieth century. Lawyers trained in the Wall Street tradition still constitute American democracy's only natural aristocracy.

Admittedly, this Establishment is no longer the narrow, male-only, Wall Street private club of McCloy's time. The old Philadelphia Establishment is dying out. Elite institutions are no longer exclusively dominated by white Anglo-Saxon Protestants from the Eastern seaboard. Reflecting the splintering of interests within society at large, the *club* itself displays more divisiveness and less bipartisanship than at any time in this century.

Like the country at large, the Establishment today is suffering a sustained crisis of confidence. But it still exists in many of the same institutions McCloy chaired, and it continues to define the parameters of *sound* thinking on the great imponderables of public policy.

The ideas that the American Establishment stood for are still the driving ideas of the republic. Liberal internationalism abroad and a moderate social compact based on a free market economy at home still define what is considered legitimate political thought. Like his mentor, Henry Stimson, and his scion, George Bush, John J. McCloy ardently believed it was America's destiny to lead the world. And it was this modest man's own destiny to "run with the swift" through the course of the American Century.

NOTES

BOOK ONE

ONE: A PHILADELPHIA YOUTH: 1895–1912

1. E. Digby Baltzell, *Philadelphia Gentlemen: The Making of a National Upper Class* (Glencoe, Ill.: The Free Press, 1958).

2. *Semi-Centennial Celebration: The Penn Mutual Life Insurance Co.* (privately printed, Penn Mutual Life Insurance Co., Philadelphia), p. 131.

3. McCloy interview, June 23, 1983.

4. McCloy interview, Sept. 14, 1984.

5. George Wharton Pepper, *Philadelphia Lawyer: An Autobiography* (Philadelphia: J. B. Lippincott, 1944), p. 341.

6. Pepper, *Philadelphia Lawyer,* p. 342.

7. McCloy interview, June 23, 1983.

8. Penn Mutual Life Insurance Co., minutes of meeting, 1901.

9. Russell F. Weigley, *Philadelphia* (New York: W. W. Norton, 1982), pp. 498–99.

10. McCloy interview, Sept. 14, 1984.

11. Katherine Bingham, *The Philadelphians,* p. 61.

12. McCloy interviews, June 23, 1983, and Sept. 5, 1984.

13. Bingham, *Philadelphians,* p. 55.

14. McCloy interview, Sept. 14, 1984.

15. McCloy speech, Pennsylvania Club, 1948.

16. Weigley, *Philadelphia,* pp. 519, 534.

17. McCloy interview, June 23, 1983.

18. Stephen Birmingham, *Our Crowd* (New York: Futura Books, 1967), p. 208.

19. Pepper, *Philadelphia Lawyer,* p. 318.

20. McCloy interview, June 23, 1983.

21. Ibid.

22. Ibid.

23. Swetland letter to Amzi Hoffman, Oct. 8, 1912; Amzi Hoffman interview, Dec. 6, 1982, Amzi Hoffman Papers.

24. *Peddie Chronicle,* vol. 40, pp. 327–28.

25. Ibid.

26. *The Old Gold and Blue,* 1911, p. 72.

27. *Peddie Chronicle,* Winter 1961, p. 3.

28. Amzi Hoffman interview, Dec. 6, 1982.

29. Ibid.

30. McCloy interview, May 26, 1983.

31. McCloy speech, published in *Peddie Chronicle,* vol. 90 (May 1955), p. 4; McCloy interview, June 23, 1983.

32. Amzi Hoffman to "Herb," Jan. 7, 1957, Amzi Hoffman Papers; Guy Preston to McCloy, 11/29/42, box PA 1, folder 70, JJM.

33. *Peddie Chronicle,* vol. 90 (May 1955), p. 4.

34. Crawford H. Droege letter to author, Aug. 9, 1982.

35. McCloy interview, June 23, 1983.

36. *Peddie Institute Bulletin,* May 1912, p. 41.

37. Walter Isaacson and Evan Thomas, *The Wise Men: Six Friends and the World They Made* (New York: Simon & Schuster, 1986), p. 68.

38. Amzi Hoffman interview, Dec. 6, 1982; McCloy interview, Sept. 14, 1984.

39. *Peddie Chronicle,* vol. 40, p. 329.

40. Ibid., Jan.-Feb. 1909, p. 71.

41. Swetland to Hoffman, July 19, 1919, Amzi Hoffman Papers.

42. *Peddie Chronicle,* vol. 90, no. 3, p. 5.

43. C. Wright Mills, *The Power Elite* (New York: Oxford University Press, 1957).

44. *Peddie Chronicle,* vol. 90, no. 3, p. 9; Crawford H. Droege letter to author, Aug. 9, 1982.

TWO: AMHERST YEARS: 1912–16

1. *Essays on Amherst's History* (Amherst, Mass.: The Vista Trust, 1978), p. 194.

2. Alexander Meiklejohn, "The Theory of the Liberal College," in Meiklejohn, *Freedom and the College* (New York: Century, 1923), pp. 155–56.

3. Julius Seelye Bixler, "Alexander Meiklejohn: The Making of the Amherst Mind," *New England Quarterly,* June 1974, pp. 182–83.

4. J. S. Bixler letter to author, Aug. 4, 1982.

5. John J. McCloy, "Champion of Freedom in Higher Education," *Amherst Student,* Jan. 21, 1965, p. 5.

6. Ibid.

7. Ibid.

8. Bixler, "Making of the Amherst Mind," p. 184.

9. Walter Isaacson and Evan Thomas, *The Wise Men: Six Friends and the World They Made,* p. 68.

10. J. S. Bixler letter to the author, Aug. 4, 1982.

11. Bixler, "Making of the Amherst Mind," p. 191; Robert Paul Browder and Thomas G. Smith, *Independent: A Biography of Lewis W. Douglas* (New York: Alfred A. Knopf, 1986), p. 21.

12. Browder and Smith, *Independent,* pp. 19–20.

13. Claude Moore Fuess, *Amherst: The Story of a New England College* (Boston: Little, Brown, 1935), p. 349; Craig P. Cochrane, phone interview, Sept. 12, 1982.

14. Isaacson and Thomas, *Wise Men,* p. 69; Fuess, *Amherst,* pp. 348–49.

15. McCloy letter to the author, Sept. 5, 1984.

16. John Garry Clifford, *The Citizen Soldiers: The Plattsburg Training Camp Movement, 1913–1920* (Lexington: University Press of Kentucky, 1972), p. 52.

17. Isaacson and Thomas, *Wise Men,* p. 70.

18. List of students, Plattsburg Barracks Training Camp, 1915, Records of U.S. Army, Continental Commands, 1821–1920, RG 393, box 13, NA.

19. Ralph Barton Perry, *The Plattsburg Movement* (New York: E. P. Dutton, 1921), p. 37.

20. Ibid., p. 13.

21. Clifford, *Citizen Soldiers,* p. 73.

22. John S. McCloy, "Why Not the Camp?," *Amherst Monthly,* Nov. 1915, p. 178.

23. Clifford, *Citizen Soldiers,* p. 64.
24. Ibid., p. 65.
25. Ibid., p. 67.
26. Ibid., p. 63.
27. McCloy letter to author, Sept. 5, 1984.
28. Clifford, *Citizen Soldiers,* p. 79.
29. Perry, *Plattsburg Movement,* p. 43.
30. Clifford, *Citizen Soldiers,* p. 83
31. George Wharton Pepper, *Philadelphia Lawyer: An Autobiography,* p. 111.
32. Clifford, *Citizen Soldiers,* pp. 83–85.
33. "The Plattsburg Idea," *New Republic,* vol. 4 (Oct. 9, 1915), pp. 247–49.
34. Anna May McCloy letter to War Department, October 10, 1915, RG 94, box 7982, AGO Doc. No. 2331877, NA.
35. McCloy, "Why Not the Camp?," pp. 176–80.
36. Ibid.
37. McCloy interview, June 23, 1983. McCloy apparently never considered any career other than law. Although a large number of Amherst men went into law, an equal number pursued careers in finance. During these years, for instance, Amherst graduates Dwight W. Morrow, '95; Mortimer L. Schiff, '96; Charles E. Mitchell, '99; and Charles D. Norton, '93, were partners or presidents of Wall Street's four major financial institutions: J. P. Morgan & Co., Kuhn, Loeb & Co., National City Bank, and the First National Bank. See Albert W. Atwood's "Amherst Men in Finance," *Amherst Graduates' Quarterly,* vol. VIII, no. 2 (Feb. 1919), p. 40.
38. *Amherst College Campaign Reporter,* May 1983; Scott Buchanan, *So Reason Can Rule: Reflections on Law and Politics* (New York: Farrar, Straus & Giroux, 1982), p. 15.
39. Isaacson and Thomas, *Wise Men,* p. 70; John S. McCloy and Lewis W. Douglas descriptive cards, Records of U.S. Army, Continental Commands 1821–1920, RG 393, boxes 13, 15, NA.
40. Clifford, *Citizen Soldiers,* p. 167.
41. Ibid., p. 123.
42. Ibid., p. 169.

THREE: HARVARD LAW SCHOOL AND THE WAR YEARS: 1916–21

1. Dr. Harlan B. Phillips, *Felix Frankfurter Reminisces: An Intimate Portrait as Recorded in Talks with Dr. Harlan B. Phillips* (New York: Reynal, 1960), p. 19.
2. McCloy's class of 335 first-year students was decidedly Ivy League, but there was also considerable diversity: fully 41 percent came from Harvard, Yale, Princeton, Brown, and Dartmouth; 71 percent had their homes outside of New England; and there was a high percentage of Jews, though very few blacks. By 1922, the year after McCloy graduated, Jews represented 22 percent of Harvard's undergraduate population, a statistic that prompted President Lowell to impose a quota on Jewish admissions. (See Richard Norton Smith, *Harvard Century* [New York: Simon & Schuster, 1986], pp. 87–89; Ronald Steel, *Walter Lippmann and the American Century,* [Boston: Atlantic/Little, Brown, 1980], pp. 193–95; *Harvard Law Review,* Dec. 1916, p. 160.)
3. Phillips, *Felix Frankfurter Reminisces,* pp. 26–27.
4. McCloy interview, June 23, 1983.
5. Charles A. Wolfe letter to the author, Aug. 1, 1983. Wolfe wrote that McCloy shared a room with an Amherst classmate whose name he could not remember. Robinson is the only one of McCloy's classmates to enter Harvard that year. Wolfe later spent fifty-one years with the prestigious Philadelphia law firm founded by Justice Owen J. Roberts.

6. Phillips, *Felix Frankfurter Reminisces,* p. 29.

7. McCloy interview, June 23, 1983; Lee C. Bradley, Jr., letter to the author, Aug. 17, 1983.

8. Wallace C. Chandler letter to the author, June 6, 1983.

9. "Notes," *Harvard Law Review,* Nov. 1916.

10. McCloy interview, June 23, 1983.

11. Walter Isaacson and Evan Thomas, *The Wise Men: Six Friends and the World They Made,* p. 93.

12. Michael E. Parrish, *Felix Frankfurter and His Times* (New York: Free Press, 1982), p. 72.

13. Phillips, *Felix Frankfurter Reminisces,* p. 81.

14. Ibid. p. 21.

15. McCloy interview, June 23, 1983.

16. Edgar J. Schoen letter to the author, Aug. 4, 1983.

17. Otto C. Stegemann letter to the author, Sept. 3, 1983. "Bull" Warren was, in fact, the prototype for "Professor Kingsfield" in the popular novel and film *The Paper Chase.* (See *New York Times* [hereafter *NYT*], April 30, 1984.)

18. Isaacson and Thomas, *Wise Men,* p. 71.

19. Phillips, *Felix Frankfurter Reminisces,* p. 18.

20. Edgar J. Schoen letter to the author, June 9, 1983.

21. Parrish, *Felix Frankfurter,* p. 79.

22. R. N. Smith, *Harvard Century,* p. 77; "Harvard War Activities: A Report of the Harvard University Board of Overseers Committee on Military Science and Tactics," Harvard University, 1917.

23. Postcard from Lieutenant Colonel Wolf to McCloy, found in McCloy scrapbook, "Memorabilia Regarding John J. McCloy kept by Mrs. John J. McCloy, Sr.," JJM.

24. McCloy to Anna McCloy, 6/27/17, JJM.

25. McCloy to Anna McCloy, n.d. (c. spring 1918), JJM.

26. McCloy to Anna McCloy, March 26, 1918, JJM.

27. Isaacson and Thomas, *Wise Men,* p. 70; McCloy interview, March 19, 1986.

28. Isaacson and Thomas, *Wise Men,* p. 70.

29. Guy Preston to McCloy, 4/3/42, box PA 1, folder 70, JJM.

30. Frederick S. Meade, ed., *Harvard's Military Record in the World War* (Boston: Harvard Alumni Association, 1921), p. 606.

31. McCloy letter to the author, Sept. 5, 1984.

32. McCloy interview, June 23, 1983.

33. Isaacson and Thomas, *Wise Men,* p. 71.

34. *Harvard Law Review,* Feb. 1920, p. 515.

35. Smith, *Harvard Century,* p. 79.

36. Parrish, *Felix Frankfurter,* p. 119.

37. "Persecution and Americanism," *Harvard Advocate,* Jan. 29, 1920, p. 166.

38. Archibald MacLeish, "The Liberalism of Herbert Hoover," *Harvard Advocate Supplement,* April 1, 1920, pp. 6–7.

39. Peter Collier and David Horowitz, *The Rockefellers: An American Dynasty* (New York: Holt, Rinehart & Winston, 1976), p. 94.

40. McCloy letter to the author, Sept. 5, 1984.

41. Parrish, *Felix Frankfurter,* p. 58.

42. Lewis J. Paper, *Brandeis: An Intimate Biography of One of America's Truly Great Supreme Court Justices* (Secaucus, N.J.: Citadel, 1983), pp. 92–93.

43. Phillips, *Felix Frankfurter Reminisces,* p. 81.

FOUR: WALL STREET: 1921–30

1. McCloy interview, June 23, 1983.

2. Geoffrey Perrett, *America in the Twenties* (New York: Simon & Schuster, 1982), p. 321.

3. McCloy interview, Sept. 5, 1984.

4. Richard N. Crockett, *The Lighter Side of the Practice of Law by a Wall Street Law Firm from 1929 to 1979* (privately printed, 1979), p. 4; notes from Keith Kane Papers, miscellaneous folders, CWT.

5. McCloy interview, June 23, 1983; Henry W. Taft, *Cadwalader, Wickersham & Taft* (privately printed, 1938), p.11.

6. Crockett, *Lighter Side,* pp. viii–ix.

7. McCloy interview, June 23, 1983; Walter Isaacson and Evan Thomas, *The Wise Men: Six Friends and the World They Made,* p. 121.

8. Benjamin Buttenwieser interview, July 15, 1982.

9. Keith Kane Papers, CWT.

10. Wiseman to Strauss, 3/28/23, Strauss Papers, HH.

11. Robert T. Swaine, *The Cravath Firm and Its Predecessors, 1819–1948,* vol. II (privately printed, 1948), p. 4.

12. Francis Plimpton interview, June 23, 1982.

13. J. D. Robb letter to author, Nov. 25, 1983.

14. Milton Mackaye, "Public Man," *New Yorker,* Nov. 1, 1931, p. 21.

15. Priscilla Mary Roberts, "The American 'Eastern Establishment' and World War I: The Emergence of a Foreign Policy Tradition," unpublished thesis, King's College, Cambridge University, 1982, p. 40.

16. Swaine, *The Cravath Firm,* p. 256.

17. Ibid., pp. 257–58.

18. Paul Hoffman, *Lions in the Street: The Inside Story of the Great Wall Street Law Firms* (New York: Saturday Review Press, 1973), p. 8.

19. McCloy interview, March 19, 1986.

20. Ibid.

21. James F. Simon, *Independent Journey: The Life of William O. Douglas* (New York: Harper & Row, 1980), p. 81.

22. McCloy interview, March 19, 1986.

23. Isaacson and Thomas, *Wise Men,* p. 119.

24. Simon, *Independent Journey,* p. 84.

25. U.S. Senate, Committee on Interstate Commerce, *Investigation of Railroads, Holding Companies and Affiliated Companies: Hearings Before a Subcommittee,* pt. 15, Nov. 10, 12, 17, 18, 1937, pp. 7015–20.

26. Max Lowenthal, *The Investor Pays* (New York: Alfred A. Knopf, 1933), pp. 6–12, 113.

27. Ibid., p. 306.

28. Swaine, *The Cravath Firm,* p. 425.

29. Benjamin Buttenwieser interview, July 15, 1982.

30. Lowenthal, *Investor Pays,* p. 355.

31. Ibid., p. 352.

32. Ibid., p. 355.

33. Simon, *Independent Journey,* p. 89.

34. Ibid.

35. Swaine, *The Cravath Firm,* p. 430.

36. Simon, *Independent Journey,* p. 86.

37. Swaine, *The Cravath Firm,* p. 442.

38. Thomas W. Lamont, *Henry P. Davison: The Record of a Useful Life* (New York: Harper & Brothers, 1933), p. 241; Isaacson and Thomas, *Wise Men,* p. 78.

39. Isaacson and Thomas, *Wise Men,* p. 91; Robert Paul Browder and Thomas G. Smith, *Independent: A Biography of Lewis W. Douglas,* p. 53.

40. McCloy interview, March 19, 1986.

41. Isaacson and Thomas, *Wise Men,* p. 121.

42. Swaine, *The Cravath Firm,* pp. 440–41.

43. McCloy interview, May 26, 1983; Swaine, *The Cravath Firm,* p. 507.

44. Swaine, *The Cravath Firm,* p. 441.

45. Roberts, "American 'Eastern Establishment,'" pp. 481–83.

46. Gabriel Kolko, *Main Currents in Modern American History* (New York: Pantheon, 1976), p. 208.

47. Roberts, "American 'Eastern Establishment,'" p. 444.

48. Isaacson and Thomas, *Wise Men,* p. 122; McCloy interview, May 26, 1983.

49. Roberts, "American 'Eastern Establishment,'" pp. 544–50.

50. Ibid., p. 332.

51. U.S. Senate, Committee on Banking and Currency, *Stock Exchange Practices: Hearings,* pt. 3, 1933, p. 965.

52. Ibid., p. 964.

53. Ibid., pp. 1011, 1032.

54. John J. McCloy, oral-history interview by Robert Cubbedge, 12/2/70, p. 1, HH; press release, Office of Eastern Treasurer, Republican National Committee, 10/16/28, C&T—Camp, Lit. Press Releases—Elihu Root, HH.

55. Roberts, "American 'Eastern Establishment,'" p. 556.

56. John Kenneth Galbraith, *The Great Crash: 1929* (New York: Houghton Mifflin, 1954), p. 77.

57. Perrett, *Twenties,* pp. 321–24.

58. Swaine, *The Cravath Firm,* p. 449.

59. Benjamin Buttenwieser interview, April 29, 1982.

60. U.S. Senate, Committee on Interstate Commerce, *Investigation of Railroads, Holding Companies, and Affiliated Companies: Hearings Before a Subcommittee,* 75th Cong., Jan. 4, 1938, p. 8376; U.S. Securities and Exchange Commission, *Investment Trusts and Investment Companies,* pt. three, 1940, p. 936; Galbraith, pp. 152–54.

61. Isaacson and Thomas, *Wise Men,* p. 121.

62. Elizabeth Luce Moore interview, Oct. 21, 1983.

63. Perrett, *Twenties,* p. 324.

64. J. D. Robb letter to the author, Nov. 25, 1983.

65. Elizabeth Luce Moore interview, Oct. 21, 1983.

66. Swaine, *The Cravath Firm,* p. 449.

67. McCloy interview, March 19, 1986.

68. *NYT,* Nov. 12, 1961.

69. Benjamin Buttenwieser interview, July 15, 1982.

70. Mrs. Frederick Warburg interview, April 10, 1984.

71. Judge Charles Wyzanski letter to the author, Nov. 23, 1982.

72. McCloy letter to the author, Sept. 5, 1984; McCloy interview, March 19, 1986.

73. McCloy interview.

74. *NYT,* April 26, 1930.

75. McCloy interview, March 19, 1986.

76. Ibid.

77. John Zinsser to Douglas, May 15, 1930, LD.
78. John Zinsser to Douglas, May 24, 1930, LD.
79. Plimpton interviews, March 16, 1982, June 23, 1982.
80. "Period Piece Fellow," *New Yorker,* Dec. 4, 1971, p. 6.
81. Mrs. Mary Paulsen (formerly Mrs. Mary Weicker) interview, Aug. 7, 1985.
82. Douglas to F. C. Brophy, Nov. 26, 1930, LD.
83. Amos Peaslee and Admiral Reginald Hall, *Three Wars with Germany* (New York: G. P. Putnam's, 1944).
84. McCloy interview, July 10, 1986.

FIVE: BLACK TOM: MCCLOY'S WILDERNESS OF MIRRORS

1. Lincoln Steffens letter to Laura Steffens, Aug. 1, 1916, in Ella Winters and Granville Hicks, eds., *The Letters of Lincoln Steffens* (New York: Harcourt, Brace, 1938), vol. I, p. 382; Amos Peaslee and Admiral Reginald Hall, *Three Wars with Germany,* p. 72.
2. McCloy memo: "Chronology Re Filing of Lyndhurst Testimony," 1/24/39, NA (Suitland).
3. McCloy interview, May 26, 1983; Robert T. Swaine, *The Cravath Firm and Its Predecessors, 1819–1948,* vol. II, p. 638.
4. Walter Isaacson and Evan Thomas, The Wise Men: *Six Friends and the World They Made,* p. 123.
5. Benjamin Shute interview, June 24, 1983.
6. *Liberty Magazine,* April 4, 1931, p. 56.
7. Martin to Friedman, May 13, 1931, NA (Suitland).
8. Testimony of Fred Herrmann, April 4, 1930, NA (Suitland).
9. Swaine, *The Cravath Firm,* vol. II, p. 638.
10. Ibid.
11. Martin to McCloy, May 28, 1931, NA (Suitland).
12. McCloy interview. July 10, 1986.
13. Benjamin Shute interview, June 24, 1983.
14. McCloy interview, May 26, 1983.
15. Benjamin Shute interview, June 24, 1983.
16. Henry Stimson diary, Jan. 14, 1933, LOC.
17. Martin to McCloy, Dec. 12, 1933, NA (Suitland).
18. McCloy affidavit, contained in Oral Arguments, May 15, 1936, pp. 250–63, NA (Suitland); see also Oral Argument, Jan. 1939, p. 490, NA (Suitland).
19. McCloy affidavit.
20. Franz Ernst Hanfstaengl, *The Unheard Witness* (Philadelphia: Lippincott, 1957), p. 197.
21. *NYT,* July 5, 1936; McCloy interview.
22. Langbourne M. Williams letter to the author, Aug. 10, 1983; Langbourne M. Williams interview, April 1, 1986.
23. Jules Witcover, *Sabotage at Black Tom* (Chapel Hill, N.C.: Chapel Hill Press, 1989), p. 301.
24. *NYT,* Aug. 14, 1936.
25. Martin to McCloy, Feb. 2, 1937, NA (Suitland).
26. Memo for Assistant Attorney General McMahon from William Ramsey, July 10, 1937, file 227675, Record Group 60, Department of Justice Straight Numerical files, NA.
27. Ramsey memo to Assistant Attorney General McMahon, October 19, 1937, file 227675, RG 60, Department of Justice Straight Numerical, NA.
28. McCloy interview, July 10, 1986.

29. Peaslee to McCloy, July 30, 1938, with attached memo, "The Collapse of Carl Ahrendt's testimony," NA (Suitland).

30. Mrs. Mary Paulsen interview, Aug. 7, 1985.

31. Mrs. Pauline Plimpton interview, March 16, 1982.

32. Peaslee to McCloy, August 25, 1938, NA (Suitland).

33. "Proposed Outline of Sabotage Brief," July 21, 1938, NA (Suitland).

34. Final Oral Arguments, Jan. 16, 1939, vol. I, p. 12, NA (Suitland).

35. McCloy to Martin, May 12, 1939, with attached memo, NA (Suitland).

36. Benjamin Shute interview, June 24, 1983.

37. Martin to Christopher B. Garnett, May 3, 1941, NA (Suitland).

38. McCloy interview, March 19, 1986; Personal Affairs, JJM.

39. Witcover, *Black Tom,* p. 308.

SIX: CRAVATH, THE NEW DEAL, AND THE APPROACH OF WAR

1. Benjamin Shute interview, June 24, 1983.

2. Howard Petersen interview, Aug. 30, 1982.

3. Jean Monnet, *Memoirs* (Garden City, N.Y.: Doubleday, 1978), p. 109.

4. Benjamin Shute interview, June 24, 1983.

5. George Ball interview, Dec. 5, 1985.

6. Lewis Douglas to Evan S. Stallcup, 12/4/30, LD.

7. Thomas Ferguson, "From Normalcy to New Deal: Industrial Structure, Party Competition, and American Public Policy in the Great Depression," *International Organization,* vol. 38, no. 1 (Winter 1984).

8. Ted Morgan, *FDR* (New York: Simon & Schuster, 1985), p. 361.

9. Douglas had a poor opinion of FDR. Prior to the convention, he had sent out to the Arizona delegation copies of a column in which Walter Lippmann called Roosevelt "a pleasant man who, without any important qualifications for office, would very much like to be President." (Robert Paul Browder and Thomas G. Smith, *Independent: A Biography of Lewis W. Douglas,* p. 73.)

10. McCloy to Douglas, 2/24/33, LD.

11. Browder and Smith, *Independent,* p. 78.

12. McCloy to Douglas, 3/7/33, LD.

13. Browder and Smith, *Independent,* p. 96.

14. Morgan, *FDR,* p. 382.

15. Robert T. Swaine, *The Cravath Firm and Its Predecessors, 1819–1948,* p. 469.

16. Leon Harris, "Clubs for the Cognoscenti," *Town & Country,* Sept. 1982.

17. McCloy to Hoover, 11/13/40, PPS File, Anglers' Club; Anglers' Club Membership Book, PPS, Subject: Anglers' Club of New York, HH.

18. McCloy to Herbert Hoover, 6/5/63, HH.

19. Dean Acheson to Douglas, 6/15/35, LD.

20. Douglas to Honorable Leonard P. Moore, 12/31/63, LD.

21. Browder and Smith, *Independent,* pp. 106–7.

22. Swaine, *The Cravath Firm,* p. 452.

23. Ibid., p. 557.

24. McCloy interview.

25. Browder and Smith, *Independent,* p. 111.

26. Douglas to W. R. Matthews, 9/6/34, LD.

27. Morgan, *FDR,* p. 408.

28. Browder and Smith, *Independent,* p. 119.

29. Frankfurter Memo regarding Crimson Dinner, 5/8/35, Ballantine Correspondence, reel no. 13, Frankfurter Papers, LOC.

30. Swaine, *The Cravath Firm,* p. 453.

31. Browder and Smith, *Independent,* p. 128.

32. Benjamin Shute interview, June 24, 1983.

33. Thomas Ferguson, "From Normalcy to New Deal: Industrial Structure, Party Competition and American Public Policy in the Great Depression," *International Organization,* vol. 38, no. 1 (Winter 1984), p. 91.

34. Swaine, *The Cravath Firm,* pp. 546–47.

35. U.S. Senate, Committee on Interstate Commerce, *Investigation of Railroads, Holding Companies, and Affiliated Companies: Hearings Before a Subcommittee,* 75th Cong., pt. 13, Nov. 4–5, 1937, Feb. 17, 1938, p. 5604.

36. Ibid., p. 6777.

37. Ibid., p. 8838.

38. Ibid., pp. 8376–77.

39. U.S. Senate, Committee on Banking and Currency, *Stock Exchange Practices: Hearings,* 73rd Cong., pt. 3, June 27–30, July 5, 1933, p. 1011.

40. U.S. Senate, *Investigation of Railroads, Holding Companies, and Affiliated Companies,* p. 8379.

41. Lewis Strauss cable, 10/21/37, Strauss Papers, Warburg, Felix M. & Frieda, Funeral of Felix, HH.

42. McCloy interview, March 19, 1986.

43. Ibid.

44. Lawrence H. Shoup and William Minter, *Imperial Brain Trust* (New York: Monthly Review Press, 1977), p. 130.

45. Leonard Mosley, *Dulles: A Biography of Eleanor, Allen, and John Foster Dulles and Their Family Network* (New York: Dial, 1978), p. 90.

46. Thomas Schwartz, "From Occupation to Alliance: John J. McCloy and the Allied High Commission in the Federal Republic of Germany, 1949–52," unpublished thesis, Harvard University, June 1985, p. 15; Browder and Smith, *Independent,* pp. 148–56.

47. Thomas Ferguson interview.

48. Howard Petersen interview, Aug. 30, 1982.

49. Henry L. Stimson and McGeorge Bundy, *On Active Service in Peace and War* (New York: Harper & Row, 1947), p. 303.

50. Morgan, *FDR,* p. 534.

51. Philip H. Burch, Jr., *Elites in American History: The New Deal to the Carter Administration* (New York: Holmes & Meier, 1981), p. 66.

52. Ronald Steel, *Walter Lippmann and the American Century,* p. 386.

53. Benjamin Shute interview, June 24, 1983.

54. Morgan, *FDR,* p. 540; Browder and Smith, *Independent,* p. 152; Langbourne M. Williams interview, April 1, 1986.

55. Morgan, *FDR,* p. 535.

56. McCloy to Dean Acheson, 9/13/40, folder 261, box 21, Acheson Papers, Sterling Library, Yale University; Schwartz, "From Occupation to Alliance," p. 16.

57. Shoup and Minter, *Imperial Brain Trust,* p. 123; Robert Divine, *Reluctant Belligerent: American Entry into World War II* (New York: Wiley, 1965), p. 90.

58. Lewis Douglas to James Conant, 10/9/40, LD.

59. James Conant to Lewis Douglas, 10/4/40, LD.
60. Morgan, *FDR,* p. 539.
61. Henry Stimson diary, 10/23/39, LOC.
62. Henry Stimson diary, 9/16/40, LOC.
63. *PM,* Oct. 1, 1940, Sept. 2, 1940, Sept. 15, 1940.
64. Henry Paynter, "What Set Off Power Blast?," *PM,* Sept. 13, 1940.
65. Morgan, *FDR,* p. 540.

BOOK TWO
SEVEN: IMPS OF SATAN

1. Henry Stimson diary, 9/25/40, LOC.
2. Thomas F. Troy, *Donovan and the CIA: A History of the Establishment of the Central Intelligence Agency* (Washington, D.C.: Altheia Books, University Publications of America, 1981), pp. 14–15.
3. McCloy had been briefly consulted sometime that summer regarding the establishment of Hoover's SIS. See J. Edgar Hoover to McCloy, 2/4/41, folder ASW 044.2, FBI, RG 107, Formerly Security Classified, box 11, NA.
4. McCloy to Miles, 11/2/40, folder ASW 000.24, Propaganda, RG 107, box 1, NA.
5. Miles to McCloy, 2/26/41, folder ASW 000.24, Propaganda, RG 107, box 1, NA.
6. McCloy memo, 11/7/40, folder ASW 000.24, Propaganda, RG 107, box 1, NA.
7. McCloy to Marshall, 2/2/41, folder ASW 000.24, Propaganda, RG 107, box 1, NA.
8. McCloy to Hoover, 11/18/40, folder ASW 044.2, FBI, RG 107, box 11, NA.
9. Geoffrey Perrett, *Days of Sadness, Years of Triumph: The American People, 1939–1945* (Madison: University of Wisconsin Press, 1985), p. 87.
10. "Sabotage, Spying and Plotting Found Rife on West Coast," *PM,* Nov. 8, 1940.
11. McCloy to Hoover, 11/18/40, folder ASW 044.2, FBI, RG 107, box 11, NA.
12. Henry L. Stimson and McGeorge Bundy, *On Active Service in Peace and War,* p. 342.
13. Arthur E. Palmer to McCloy, 11/22/40, folder ASW 021, Air Force, RG 107, box 10, NA.
14. John Morton Blum, *Years of Urgency,* p. 209.
15. McCloy picked up the phrase from his friend Jean Monnet, who was then working with the British Supply Council in Washington.
16. Max Freedman, *Roosevelt and Frankfurter: Their Correspondence 1928–1945* (Boston: Little, Brown, 1967), pp. 573–74. Freedman reports that Jean Monnet also used the phrase at lunch one day with Frankfurter.
17. Forrest Pogue, *George C. Marshall: Ordeal and Hope, 1939–1942* (New York: Viking, 1966), p. 44.
18. Walter Isaacson and Thomas Evans, *The Wise Men: Six Friends and the World They Made,* pp. 192–95.
19. Ibid., p. 194.
20. Henry Stimson diary, 12/18/40, NA.
21. McCloy testimony, Commission on Wartime Relocation and Internment, Washington, D.C., 11/3/81.
22. Accountant's statement, Personal Affairs, JJM; McCloy to Douglas and Brunie, 2/24/41, LD.
23. Memorandum for the secretary of war from JJMcC, 12/28/40, folder ASW 004.401, Overall Balance Sheet, RG 107, box 4, NA.
24. Henry Stimson diary, 12/17/40, LOC.
25. Henry Stimson diary, 12/29/40, LOC.

26. John Morton Blum, *Years of Urgency,* p. 212; Warren F. Kimball, *The Most Unsordid Act: Lend-Lease, 1939–1941* (Baltimore: Johns Hopkins University Press, 1969), p. 135; Bruce Allen Murphy, *The Brandeis/Frankfurter Connection* (New York: Oxford University Press, 1982), pp. 217–18.

27. Stephen E. Ambrose, *Rise to Globalism: American Foreign Policy, 1938–1980* (New York: Penguin Books, 1971), p. 34.

28. Henry Stimson diary, 3/3/41, 3/4/41, LOC; Blum, *Years of Urgency,* p. 227.

29. Henry Stimson diary, 3/7/41, 3/8/41, LOC; Blum, *Years of Urgency,* pp. 227–28.

30. Kimball, *The Most Unsordid Act,* p. 233.

31. Merlo J. Pusey, *Eugene Meyer* (New York: Alfred A. Knopf, 1974), p. 310.

32. McCloy interview, July 10, 1986.

33. Ibid.

34. McCloy to Lippmann, 6/26/42, box 48, RG 107, NA.

35. Bruce A. Murphy, *Brandeis/Frankfurter* p. 227.

36. Ibid., p. 204.

37. Henry Stimson diary, 3/21/41, LOC; Elliot Roosevelt, ed., *F.D.R.: His Personal Letters, 1928–1945* (New York: Duell, Sloan & Pearce, 1950), vol. II, p. 1151.

38. Isaacson and Thomas, *Wise Men,* p. 193.

39. Eric Larrabee, *Commander in Chief: Franklin Delano Roosevelt, His Lieutenants and Their War* (New York: Harper & Row, 1987), p. 147.

40. Stimson and Bundy, *On Active Service,* p. 344.

41. Leon Pearson, "Did You Happen to See—John J. McCloy?" *Washington Post* (hereafter *WP*), April 23, 1941.

42. McCloy memorandum of conversation with Mr. J. Edgar Hoover on April 26, 1941; memorandum for the secretary of war, "Subject: Proposed sabotage investigations, 5/1/41," ASW, 383.4, Espionage & Sabotage General, RG 107, box 36, NA.

43. Athan Theoharis, *Spying on Americans: Political Surveillance from Hoover to the Huston Plan* (Philadelphia: Temple University Press, 1978), pp. 98–99. Hoover himself was on record as having disapproved of wiretapping as an investigative tool. In a letter dated Feb. 9, 1940, he wrote that wiretapping "has proved a definite handicap or barrier in the development of ethical, scientific, and sound investigative technique." (*Harvard Law Review,* vol. 53 [March 1940], p. 870.)

44. McCloy, memorandum for the secretary of war, "Subject: Proposed sabotage investigations, 5/1/41," ASW 383.4, Espionage & Sabotage General, RG 107, box 36, NA.

45. Jackson memorandum for the president, 4/29/41, ASW 383.4, Espionage & Sabotage General, RG 107, box 36, NA.

46. McCloy to attorney general, 5/6/41, ASW 383.4, Espionage & Sabotage General, RG 107, box 36, NA.

47. Jackson to McCloy, 5/16/41, ASW 383.4, Espionage & Sabotage General, RG 107, box 36, NA.

48. Perrett, *Days of Sadness,* p. 101.

49. David Kahn, *Hitler's Spies: German Military Intelligence in World War II* (New York: Macmillan, 1978), pp. 331–33.

50. Ibid; Michael Sayers and Albert E. Kahn, *Sabotage: The Secret War Against America* (New York: Harper & Brothers, 1942), pp. 16–17, 24–32.

51. McCloy to La Guardia, 6/20/41, ASW 383.4, Fifth Column Activities, RG 107, box 35, NA.

52. Troy, *Donovan and the CIA,* pp. 55–56, 59, 81.

53. "Charges Contained in Letter of February 10, 1941," ASW 371.1, General, RG 107, box 34, NA.

54. Troy, *Donovan and the CIA,* p. 42.

55. McCloy to Stimson, 6/3/41, ASW 371.1, General, RG 107, box 34, NA.

56. Henry Stimson diary, 7/3/41, LOC.

57. Troy, *Donovan and the CIA,* p. 68. Even as he was negotiating the formation of the country's first centralized intelligence service, he established a new branch within G-2 called the "Special Study Group" (SSG) to "study the psychology of Americans, neutrals, and conquered peoples and the impact on them of certain proposed operations." (Troy, *Donovan and the CIA,* p. 130.) SSG never really became an operational unit, but its existence was yet another indication of the priority McCloy placed on counterintelligence and propaganda.

58. Stimson and Bundy, *On Active Service,* pp. 343–44.

59. McCloy to Jesse H. Jones with attached memo, "The Problem of War Organization and Post-War Readjustment," 4/23/41, ASW 388, Peace Preserving, RG 107, box 39, NA.

60. Ibid.

61. Ted Morgan, *FDR,* p. 666.

62. Douglas to Frankfurter, 6/19/41, LD.

63. Perrett, *Days of Sadness,* p. 116.

64. Gordon W. Prange, *Pearl Harbor* (New York: McGraw-Hill, 1986), p. 138; Henry Stimson diary, 7/2/41, LOC.

65. Douglas to Connally, 8/19/41; Connally to Douglas, 8/23/41; Robertson to Douglas, 7/25/41; Douglas to Robertson, 7/18/41, LD.

66. McCloy to Clark, 8/14/41, ASW 014.3, Civil Status and Relations—Public Relations, RG 107, box 6, NA. McCloy had sent an army lawyer, Captain Karl R. Bendetsen, to work with Rayburn on the draft-bill vote. In the midst of the debate, Bendetsen reported to McCloy on the phone that an amendment had been proposed that would bar the president from sending any of the draftees outside of the forty-eight continental states. McCloy told Bendetsen to tell Rayburn that the amendment was unacceptable, saying, "If the Congress wants to terminate our defenses, it will be their responsibility." (Karl R. Bendetsen interview, Nov. 10, 1983.)

67. "All U.S. Defense Efforts Aimed at Nazis, McCloy Says," *WP,* Sept. 20, 1941.

68. *NYT,* Sept. 20, 1941.

69. Perrett, *Days of Sadness,* pp. 194–95.

70. Ibid., p. 189; "From McCloy, Additional Notes on Reduction of Size of Army, 10/1/41?," LD.

71. "Notes on the Lippmann-Lindley theory," n.d., LD.

72. Ibid.

73. McCloy to Gerow, 7/31/41, ASW 004.401, Victory Program, RG 107, box 4, NA.

74. Albert C. Wedemeyer, *Wedemeyer Reports* (New York: Henry Holt, 1958), p. 73.

75. Gerow to McCloy, 8/5/41, ASW 004.401, Victory Program, RG 107, box 4, NA.

76. Stimson to Roosevelt, 8/18/41, ASW 004.401, Victory Program, box 4, RG 107, NA.

77. Wedemeyer, *Wedemeyer Reports,* p. 21; Albert C. Wedemeyer interview, Nov. 11, 1983.

78. McCloy memo, n.d., 8 pages, ASW 004.401, Victory Program, box 4, RG 107, NA.

79. Henry Stimson diary, 8/12/41, LOC.

80. McCloy to Hugh A. Moran, 11/15/41, ASW 014.3, Civil Status and Relations—Public Relations, RG 107, box 6, NA.

81. John U. Terrell, "Naval Officer Warns of Threat of Japanese Agents on the Coast," *PM,* Aug. 14, 1941.

82. Peter Irons, *Justice at War: The Story of the Japanese American Internment* (New York: Oxford University Press, 1983), p. 5.

83. Gordon W. Prange, *At Dawn We Slept* (New York: McGraw-Hill, 1981), p. 58.

84. Ibid., p. 256.

85. Richard Gid Powers, *Secrecy and Power: The Life of J. Edgar Hoover* (New York: Free Press, 1987), p. 255; *Personal Justice Denied: Report of the Commission on Wartime Relocation and Internment of Civilians* (Washington, D.C.: U.S. Congress, 1982), p. 62.

86. Anthony Cave Brown, *Wild Bill Donovan: The Last Hero* (New York: Times Books, 1982), p. 193.

87. McCloy interviews, May 26, 1983, June 23, 1983; Ladislas Farago, *The Game of the Foxes: The Untold Story of German Espionage in the United States and Great Britain During World War II* (New York: David McKay, 1971), p. 552; Ronald Lewin, *The American Magic: Codes, Ciphers and the Defeat of Japan* (New York: Farrar, Straus & Giroux, 1982), p. 67; Thomas Parrish, *The Ultra Americans: The U.S. Role in Breaking the Nazi Codes* (New York: Stein & Day, 1986), p. 70.

88. For a thorough discussion of the role of Magic intercepts in the Pearl Harbor attack, see David Kahn's seminal book, *The Codebreakers: The Story of Secret Writing* (New York: Macmillan, 1967), pp. 1–67. Magic is also extensively discussed in the U.S. 79th Congress's multivolume *Hearings Before the Joint Committee on the Investigation of the Pearl Harbor Attack.*

89. Prange, *At Dawn We Slept,* p. 81

90. Ibid., pp. 249–50; McCloy interview, May 26, 1983. The early revisionist historian Charles Beard published a book after the war charging that Roosevelt consciously provoked the Japanese to attack Pearl Harbor. (Charles A. Beard, *President Roosevelt and the Coming of the War, 1941* [New Haven, Conn.: Yale University Press, 1948.]) More recently, John Toland, in his book *Infamy: Pearl Harbor and Its Aftermath* (Garden City, N.Y.: Doubleday, 1982), argues a similar thesis. Stimson's diary notes, the Magic intercepts, and many other sources make it clear that Roosevelt, Stimson, McCloy, and other high-ranking administration officials were convinced that war with Japan was a very near-term prospect. But the evidence suggests that they were indeed caught unawares by the attack on Pearl Harbor. Stimson's Nov. 25 diary comment actually lends credence to this balanced view: ". . . the Japs are notorious for making an attack without warning. . . . The question was how we should maneuver them into firing the first shot without allowing too much danger to ourselves." A surprise attack on Pearl Harbor, resulting in the severe crippling of the Pacific fleet, was certainly not a price Stimson was willing to pay.

91. Prange, *At Dawn We Slept,* pp. 402–4.

92. Memorandum for the chief of staff from Miles, 11/25/41, ASW 371.1, General, RG 107, box 34, NA.

93. Leonard Mosley, *Marshall: Hero for Our Times* (New York: Hearst Books, 1982), p. 156.

94. Henry Stimson diary, 12/4/41, LOC.

95. Dean Rusk interview, Nov. 17, 1982; Farago, *Game of the Foxes,* pp. 556–58. The Potsdam Club officers were probably as anti-British as they were pro-German, an attitude that often stemmed from their distrust of British imperial policies, particularly in the Pacific, where they believed American political and commercial interests were impeded

by British colonial interests. Ironically, McCloy himself had been accused of "pro-Nazi" views upon his return from Germany in 1936. (See McCloy to Clark, 8/14/41, ASW 014.3, Civil Status and Relations [Public Relations], box 6, RG 107, NA.)

96. Wedemeyer, *Wedemeyer Reports,* p. 21; Albert C. Wedemeyer interview, Nov. 11, 1983.

97. Albert C. Wedemeyer interview, Nov. 11, 1983.

98. Wedemeyer, *Wedemeyer Reports,* p. 27; Mosley, *Marshall,* p. 157.

99. Wedemeyer, *Wedemeyer Reports,* p. 6.

100. John Toland, in *Infamy,* credits an Army Air Corps captain as the source of the leak. So too does Ladislas Farago in *The Game of the Foxes.* Both authors say the captain, who worked with Wedemeyer and attended some of the same social gatherings hosted by Captain Truman Smith, gave the Victory Plan to Senator Burton Wheeler, who turned it over to the *Chicago Tribune.* Yet another source, William Stevenson, the biographer of Sir William Stephenson, otherwise known as "Intrepid," asserts that British intelligence fabricated a fake set of plans which were leaked through Senator Wheeler in the hope that they might provoke Hitler into declaring war on the United States. This latter thesis is certainly wrong. (See Toland, *Infamy,* p. 288; Farago, *Game of the Foxes,* p. 562; William Stevenson, *A Man Called Intrepid,* p. 328.)

101. Mosley, *Marshall,* p. 157; Toland, *Infamy,* p. 293.

102. McCloy interview, May 26, 1983.

103. Toland, *Infamy,* p. 305; U.S. Congress, Joint Committee on the Investigation of the Pearl Harbor Attack, *Hearings,* 79th Cong., pt. 7, p. 4517; McCloy diary, 12/7/41, DY box 3, folder 3, JJM.

104. Prange, *At Dawn We Slept,* p. 486.

105. Ibid., pp. 491–95; Richard Collier, *The Road to Pearl Harbor* (New York: Atheneum, 1981), pp. 232–33; Toland, *Infamy,* p. 310.

106. McCloy interview, May 26, 1983; Irons, *Justice at War,* pp. 5–6.

107. McCloy interview, May 26, 1983.

108. Irons, *Justice at War,* p. 6.

109. Henry Stimson diary, 12/7/41, LOC.

110. Ibid.

111. Brown, *Wild Bill Donovan,* p. 194.

112. Ibid., p. 200; Henry Stimson diary, 1/19/41.

113. Henry Stimson diary, 12/16/41, LOC.

114. Henry Stimson diary, 12/8/41, LOC.

115. Irons, *Justice at War,* p. 19.

116. Roger Daniels, *Concentration Camps USA: Japanese Americans and World War II* (New York: Holt, Rinehart & Winston, 1972), p. 35; Irons, *Justice at War,* p. 6.

117. General Joseph "Vinegar Joe" Stilwell wrote in his diary on Dec. 11, "Had the Japs only known, they could have landed anywhere on the coast, and after our handful of ammunition was gone, they could have shot us like pigs in a pen." (Joseph W. Stilwell, *The Stilwell Papers,* ed. Theodore H. White [New York: William Sloane Associates, 1948], p. 4.)

118. Martin Gilbert, *Winston S. Churchill: Road to Victory* (Boston: Houghton Mifflin, 1986), vol. VI, p. 2.

119. Henry Stimson diary, 12/17/41, 12/20/41, LOC.

120. McCloy memo to the secretary of war, 12/20/41, ASW 381, Strategic Objective, box 35, RG 107, NA.

121. John Grigg, *1943: The Victory That Never Was* (London: Eyre Methuen, 1980), pp. 18–20.

122. McCloy memo to secretary of war, 12/20/41, ASW 381, Strategic Objective, box 35, RG 107, NA.

123. Robert Dallek, *Franklin D. Roosevelt and American Foreign Policy, 1932–1945* (New York: Oxford University Press, 1979), p. 321.

124. Dallek, *Franklin D. Roosevelt,* p. 322.

125. Grigg, *1943,* p. 21.

126. Dallek, *Franklin D. Roosevelt,* p. 321.

127. Henry Stimson diary, 12/28/41, LOC.

128. Gilbert, *Winston S. Churchill,* p. 35.

129. McCloy interview, June 23, 1983.

130. Henry Stimson diary, 1/6/42, LOC; *Philadelphia Inquirer,* Jan. 9, 1942.

EIGHT: INTERNMENT OF THE JAPANESE AMERICANS

1. Gordon W. Prange, *At Dawn We Slept,* p. 589.

2. *Personal Justice Denied: Report of the Commission on Wartime Relocation and Internment of Civilians,* p. 55. For a detailed account of the internment decision, see Roger Daniels, *Concentration Camps USA: Japanese Americans and World War II,* pp. 42–73.

3. Bill Hosokawa, *JACL in Quest of Justice: The History of the Japanese American League* (New York: William Morrow, 1982), p. 142.

4. *Personal Justice Denied,* p. 70.

5. McCloy to Frankfurter, 1/13/42; Frankfurter to McCloy, 1/17/42, ASW 014.3, Civil Status and Relations (Public Relations), box 6, RG 107, NA.

6. Francis Biddle, *In Brief Authority* (Garden City, N.Y.: Doubleday, 1962), p. 215.

7. Susan G. Goldmark, "The Japanese in America," unpublished paper, Hunter College, 1970, p. 26.

8. Karl R. Bendetsen interview, Nov. 10, 1983.

9. Peter Irons, *Justice at War: The Story of the Japanese American Internment,* p. 43.

10. *Personal Justice Denied,* pp. 64–65.

11. Major Bendetsen, General Gullion, and General Clark phone conversation, 2/4/42, RG 389 (CWRIC 5936–40), NA (courtesy of Jack Herzig); this document was first cited by Roger Daniels in *Concentration Camps USA,* p. 56. In the Gullion-Clark phone conversation, Gullion attributes this quote to McCloy three days after the Feb. 1, 1942, meeting. In his wartime diary, Ickes attributes to McCloy the same attitude regarding the Constitution. (Ickes diary, 7/12/42, LOC.) Nearly forty years after the fact, McCloy told a congressional commission that as a lawyer he could never have made such a statement. (See McCloy testimony before the Commission on the Wartime Relocation of Japanese Americans, 11/3/81, p. 17.)

12. *Personal Justice Denied,* pp. 74–75; Irons, *Justice at War,* pp. 44–45.

13. Major Bendetsen, General Gullion, and General Clark phone conversation, 2/4/42, RG 389 (CWRIC 5936–40), NA.

14. *Personal Justice Denied,* p. 75.

15. McCloy–De Witt telephone transcript, 2/3/42, ASW 014.311, E.D.C. Exclusion Order Reports, box 6, RG 107, NA.

16. Roger Daniels, *The Decision to Relocate the Japanese Americans* (Philadelphia: J. B. Lippincott, 1975), p. 104; Irons, *Justice at War,* p. 53; Allan R. Bosworth, *America's Concentration Camps* (New York: W. W. Norton, 1967), p. 102.

17. Henry Stimson diary, 2/10/42, LOC.

18. Ibid. Only a few days earlier, General Mark Clark and Admiral Stark had both discounted a West Coast invasion in testimony before Congress. Stark went so far as to

state flatly that it would be "impossible for the enemy to engage in a sustained attack on the Pacific Coast at the present time." (See Irons, *Justice at War,* p. 52.)

19. Irons, *Justice at War,* p. 57.

20. McCloy testimony, Commission on Wartime Relocation, 11/3/81, p. 59.

21. *Personal Justice Denied,* p. 79.

22. Irons, *Justice at War,* p. 58.

23. Robert Dallek, *Franklin D. Roosevelt and American Foreign Policy: 1932–1945,* p. 335.

24. Roosevelt to chief of operations, 8/10/36, folder A 8-5, box 216, RG 80, NA (courtesy of Jack Herzig).

25. Biddle, *In Brief Authority,* p. 219.

26. *Personal Justice Denied,* p. 80; Ronald Steel, *Walter Lippmann and the American Century,* p. 394; Irons, *Justice at War,* p. 60. Daniels, *Concentration Camps USA,* pp. 42–73.

27. Irons, *Justice at War,* p. 61.

28. Stetson Conn et al., *Guarding the United States and Its Outposts* (Washington, D.C.: U.S. Army Center of Military History, 1980), p. 135.

29. McCloy diary, 8:55 A.M., Tuesday, 2/17/42, as cited in McCloy testimony, Congressional Commission on the Wartime Relocation, 11/3/81, p. 105.

30. Biddle, *In Brief Authority,* pp. 218–19.

31. Irons, *Justice at War,* p. 62; Biddle, *In Brief Authority,* p. 219; Conn et al., *Guarding the United States,* p. 135.

32. Irons, *Justice at War,* p. 63.

33. Ibid., p. 349.

34. "Japanese Americans and 'Magic,' " Statement of Lt. Col. John A. Herzig, U.S. Army (Ret.) to the House Committee on the Judiciary, Subcommittee on Administrative Law and Governmental Relations, 9/12/84, p. 19. Citing Don Whitehead, *The FBI Story* (New York: Random House, 1956), p. 193, Herzig reports that ninety-one persons were convicted of espionage from 1938 to 1945, and none of these individuals were Japanese Americans.

35. Herbert Wechsler, assistant attorney general during the war, told this to Irons. (*Justice at War,* p. 358.)

36. Years afterward, McCloy told reporter Jules Witcover that Roosevelt "knew all about Black Tom. He said to me, 'We don't want any more Black Toms.' " As assistant secretary of the navy during the Wilson administration, Roosevelt certainly was aware of Black Tom, but I could find no evidence that McCloy talked with the president about either the old sabotage case or the decision to intern the Japanese Americans. (See Jules Witcover, *Sabotage at Black Tom,* p. 311.)

37. Frankfurter to McCloy, 3/5/42, Frankfurter Papers, LOC.

38. *Personal Justice Denied,* p. 113.

39. See U.S. House of Representatives, *Hearing on H.R. 4110 by the House Judiciary Subcommittee on Administrative Law and Governmental Relations,* David D. Lowman testimony, Washington, D.C., June 27, 1984. Lowman is a retired National Security Agency official.

40. John J. McCloy, written testimony prepared for appearance before the Commission on Wartime Relocation and Internment of Civilians, Nov. 3, 1981, p. 2.

41. The Magic Background to Pearl Harbor, (Washington, D.C.: Department of Defense, 1977), vol. I, no. 174, as cited by David D. Lowman, testimony, *House Judiciary Subcommittee on Administrative Law and Governmental Relations,* Washington, D.C., June 27, 1984.

42. Lieutenant Colonel John A. Herzig, "Japanese Americans and Magic," *Amerasia*, vol. 11, no. 2 (1984), pp. 56–58, provides a detailed rebuttal of the congressional testimony regarding Magic made by David D. Lowman, a retired National Security Agency official.

43. Gordon W. Prange, *Pearl Harbor*, pp. 541–42.

44. The Magic Background to Pearl Harbor, vol. II, Appendix A-124–125. The same cable includes a request for another $500,000 "for the development of intelligence." No indication is made as to whether the request was approved.

45. Michi Weglyn, *Years of Infamy: The Untold Story of America's Concentration Camps* (New York: Morrow Quill Paperbacks, 1976), p. 43.

46. McCloy diary, 12/1/41, JJM.

47. K. D. Ringle to chief of naval operations, 1/26/42, ASW 014.311, W.D.C., box 8, RG 107, NA.

48. Ibid.

49. Clark to McCloy, 2/12/42, cited in appendix of David D. Lowman, testimony, Commission on Wartime Relocation and Internment of Civilians.

50. Biddle, *In Brief Authority*, p. 226.

51. Daniels, *Decision to Relocate*, p. 121.

52. *Personal Justice Denied*, pp. 100–102.

53. McCloy testimony before the Congressional Commission on Wartime Relocation and Internment of Civilians, 11/3/81, Washington, D.C., p. 10; McCloy to Stimson, 3/6/42, ASW 014.311, E.D.C. Exclusion Order Reports, box 6, RG 107, NA.

54. McCloy to Francis Biddle, 3/21/42, ASW 014.311, E.D.C. Exclusion Order Reports, box 6, RG 107, NA.

55. Hosokawa, *JACL*, p. 155.

56. Ibid., p. 166.

57. Ibid.

58. Ibid., p. 363.

59. Ibid., p. 362.

60. Irons, *Justice at War*, pp. 70–71; Hosokawa, *JACL*, p. 171.

61. John J. McCloy, "The Challenge Before Us," Amherst College speech, May 16, 1942, reprinted in *Congressional Record*, vol. 88, p. A1929.

62. *NYT*, March 28, 1942; *Philadelphia Inquirer*, March 28, 1942. McCloy still had constitutional doubts about what he was doing. The day after this press conference, he wrote General Dwight Eisenhower, "There are also some grave legal difficulties in placing American citizens, even of Japanese ancestry, in concentration camps. All we have done, thus far, in the West Coast is to remove them from certain areas, which I think can clearly be done as a matter of law." (McCloy to General Eisenhower, 3/28/42, ASW 014.311, Hawaii, box 6, RG 107, NA.)

63. Daniels, *Decision to Relocate*, p. 56.

64. McCloy to Bendetsen, 4/6/42, ASW Defense Command, Western, Bendetsen, OASW Reference-Subject File 1940–47, Da-Dm, Box 159, RG 107, NA.

65. Lieutenant General John L. DeWitt, "Final Report: Japanese Evacuation from the West Coast," Department of the Army, Washington, D.C., 1942, p. 145.

66. Colonel Joel F. Watson and W. F. Magill, Jr., to DeWitt, 4/11/42, 014.31, Aliens, vol. II, RG 338-7, NA (courtesy of Michi Weglyn).

67. Stephen Ambrose and Richard Immerman, *Milton S. Eisenhower: Educational Statesman* (Baltimore: Johns Hopkins University Press, 1983), p. 62.

68. Milton Eisenhower interview, Aug. 5, 1982; Ambrose and Immerman, *Milton S. Eisenhower*, p. 63.

69. *Personal Justice Denied*, p. 139.

70. Ickes diary, 7/12/42, LOC.

71. Ickes diary, 6/7/42, LOC.

72. Milton Eisenhower, *The President Is Calling* (Garden City, N.Y.: Doubleday, 1974), p. 114. As early as April 1, 1942, Eisenhower had written a friend, "I feel most deeply that when the war is over . . . we as Americans are going to regret the avoidable injustices that may have been done." (Weglyn, *Years of Infamy,* p. 114.) On June 15, 1942, Harold Ickes wrote FDR, "I have it from several sources that Eisenhauer [sic] is sick of the job." (Weglyn, *Years of Infamy,* p. 114.)

73. Ultimately, some forty-three hundred Nisei students were allowed out of the camps to attend college. (See Ambrose and Immerman, *Milton S. Eisenhower,* p. 64.)

74. Richard Drinnon, *Keeper of Concentration Camps: Dillon S. Myer and American Racism* (Berkeley: University of California Press, 1987), pp. 7–8.

75. *Personal Justice Denied,* p. 149.

76. Daniels, *Decision to Relocate,* p. 56.

77. Biddle, *In Brief Authority,* pp. 325–27.

78. McCloy to Elmer Davis, 8/9/42, ASW 383.4, Espionage etc. (Alphabetically), box 36, RG 107. This letter was never sent to Davis.

79. McCloy to Stimson, 8/9/42, ASW 383.4, Espionage etc. (Alphabetically), box 36, RG 107, NA.

80. McCloy to Elmer Davis, 8/9/42, ASW 383.4, Espionage etc. (Alphabetically), box 36, RG 107, NA.

81. James Rowe, Jr., to attorney general, 10/31/42, folder James H. Rowe, Jr., box 3, Biddle Papers, FDR.

82. Alexander Meiklejohn to Roger Baldwin, 3/17/42, vol. 2363, pp. 196–97, ACLU Papers, PU.

83. Roger Baldwin to Alexander Meiklejohn, 6/30/42, vol. 2363, pp. 29–30, ACLU Papers, PU.

84. Drinnon, *Keeper of Concentration Camps,* p. 123.

85. Baldwin to Meiklejohn, 6/30/42, vol. 2363, ACLU Papers, PU.

86. John Hall memo to adjutant general, 9/17/42, ASW 333.1, Military Post, Hospitals, depots, etc., box 18, RG 107, NA.

87. Drinnon, *Keeper of Concentration Camps,* p. 36.

88. McCloy to Myer, 11/6/42, ASW 014.311, Segregation of Japs, classif. no. ASW 254, Minidoka, RG 107, NA (courtesy of Aiko Herzig).

89. Drinnon, *Keeper of Concentration Camps,* p. 53.

90. Ibid., p. 124.

91. Irons, *Justice at War,* p. 129. Such prominent board members as Morris Ernst, Corliss Lamont, John Dos Passos, and Max Lerner had all decided that, if military necessity required it, they could support Executive Order 9066. A liberal such as Freda Kirchwey, editor of *The Nation,* had written Roger Baldwin that she felt the "federal authorities have been doing their best to handle moderately and without hysteria an extremely explosive and dangerous problem." Later that autumn, the ACLU's chairman actually wrote General DeWitt a letter expressing his "congratulations on so difficult a job accomplished with a minimum of hardship, considering its unprecedented character." (Freda Kirchwey to Roger Baldwin, 3/18/42, vol. 2363, p. 188, ACLU Papers, PU; ACLU chairman et al. to DeWitt, 11/3/42, vol. 2444, p. 119, ACLU Papers, PU.) Only a few socialist and pacifist organizations actually took a firm stand against the internment, and for this they were closely monitored by the FBI and military intelligence. That

autumn, for instance, McCloy sent Myer an excerpt from an intelligence report suggesting that the American Friends Service Committee and the Fellowship of Reconciliation "are either deliberately, or unwittingly, hindering the war effort . . . [by] encouraging Japanese evacuees to resist restrictions placed upon them." (McCloy to Myer, 10/15/42, ASW 014.311, WDC Gen., RG 107, NA [courtesy of William Hohri].)

92. McCloy to the judge advocate general, 9/17/42, ASW 012.2–013.1 / 013.3–013.-37, box 5, RG 107, NA.

93. Irons, *Justice at War,* p. 160.

94. McCloy to General M. C. Cramer, 11/25/42; McCloy to General DeWitt, 11/28/42, ASW 012.2–013.1 / 013.3–013.37, box 5, RG 107, NA.

95. Weglyn, *Years of Infamy,* pp. 122–24.

96. Hosokawa, *JACL,* p. 210.

97. Irons, *Justice at War,* p. 269.

98. McCloy to DeWitt, 2/11/43, ASW 014.311, WDC Exclusion Orders, box 8, RG 107, NA.

99. There were actually major disturbances at some camps, where the army had to move in to restore order. The *San Francisco Chronicle* reported one official as saying, "You can't imagine how close we came to machine-gunning the whole bunch of them. The only thing that stopped us, I guess, were the effects such a shooting would have had on the Japs holding our boys in Manila and China." (Weglyn, *Years of Infamy,* p. 151.) Irons, *Justice at War,* p. 201; Hosokawa, *JACL,* p. 214.

100. Weglyn, *Years of Infamy,* pp. 143–44, 306n.

101. Irons, *Justice at War,* p. 209.

102. Ibid., pp. 208–10.

103. Ibid., p. 210.

104. Ibid., p. 239.

105. *Personal Justice Denied,* p. 202.

106. Biddle to Ickes, 12/31/44 with enclosed Biddle to FDR, 12/30/43, Harold Ickes Papers, LOC.

107. Irons, *Justice at War,* pp. 272–73.

108. Ickes diary, 1/1/44, LOC. In early 1944, McCloy, Marshall, and other War Department officials were still solicitous about the overwhelming Soviet contribution to the war against Hitler. McCloy's attitude changed markedly in the aftermath of the successful cross-Channel invasion of France.

109. Irons, *Justice at War,* pp. 274, 276.

110. Ibid., p. 286.

111. Ibid., p. 288.

112. Ibid., pp. 290–91, 287.

NINE: POLITICAL COMMISSAR

1. Early in the war, McCloy put a halt to the Justice Department's attempts to prosecute a number of large U.S. corporations for antitrust violations. Thurman Arnold, assistant attorney general in charge of antitrust matters at the Justice Department, was an uncompromising populist and made no secret of his dislike for big business. Now, in early 1942, despite the war, he was determined to press ahead with the prosecution of such corporate giants as General Electric, Bausch & Lomb Optical Co., Remington Arms Co., Bendix Aviation Corporation, and Dow Chemical Co. for price-fixing, and Standard Oil for having collaborated with the German chemical company I. G. Farben, to withhold

synthetic-rubber technology from the government during the years immediately prior to Pearl Harbor. McCloy and Stimson warned Roosevelt that Arnold's investigations had to stop if essential war-production targets were to be met. McCloy drafted a letter to the president for Stimson's signature that complained, "Mr. Hitler himself could hardly have chosen a surer way to embarrass our munitions production today. . . ."

Inevitably, the War Department's position prevailed, and most of Arnold's investigations were allowed to die. Only after the war did the public learn the full extent of Standard Oil's collaboration with the enemy. In 1947, an appeals-court judge declared, "Standard Oil can be considered an enemy national in view of its relationships with I.G. Farben. . . ." (McCloy to Patterson, 3/6/42, ASW 004.401, Capital & Output, box 4, RG 107, NA; Stimson to Roosevelt, 3/4/42, ASW 004.401, Capital & Output, box 4, RG 107, NA.) In the case of Standard Oil, Arnold was successful in persuading the government to seize the company's synthetic-rubber patents. When, at the end of the war, Standard Oil sued the government in an attempt to regain control of the valuable patents, Judge Charles E. Wyzanski, a good friend of McCloy's, ruled against Standard. (See Charles Higham, *Trading with the Enemy* [New York: Delacorte, 1983], pp. 45, 62.)

2. Arthur Krock to McCloy, 7/27/42, McCloy Correspondence, Arthur Krock Papers, PU.

3. *Time,* Aug. 10, 1942.

4. Lenore Fine and Jesse A. Remington, *United States Army in World War II: The Technical Services, The Corps of Engineers: Construction in the United States* (Washington, D.C.: Office of the Chief of Military History, U.S. Army, 1972), pp. 435–37.

5. McCloy interview Sept. 14, 1984; Walter Isaacson and Evan Thomas, *The Wise Men: Six Friends and the World They Made,* pp. 201–2. Hanfstaengl thereafter spent the better part of the war in a Virginian estate, requisitioned by the War Department, near the Civil War battlefield of Bull Run. There he was placed under the "guard" of his son, a U.S. Army sergeant, and occasionally interviewed by German experts from Bill Donovan's organization. (See Anthony Cave Brown, *Wild Bill Donovan: The Last Hero,* p. 211; Ernst Hanfstaengl, *The Unheard Witness,* pp. 310–13. Hanfstaengl reports he didn't arrive in Washington until June 30, 1942.)

6. Henry Stimson diary, 4/25/41, LOC; Ickes diary, 11/29/42, LOC; Isaacson and Thomas, *Wise Men,* p. 201.

7. Drew Pearson, "Washington Merry-Go-Round," Nov. 25, 1942.

8. Martin Gilbert, *Winston S. Churchill: Road to Victory,* p. 123.

9. Henry L. Stimson and McGeorge Bundy, *On Active Service in Peace and War,* p. 423; Robert Dallek, *Franklin D. Roosevelt and American Foreign Policy, 1932–1945,* p. 344.

10. Henry Stimson diary, 6/22/42, LOC.

11. Gilbert, *Winston S. Churchill,* p. 129.

12. Ibid.

13. Ibid.; John Grigg, *1943: The Victory That Never Was,* pp. 39–40; Dallek, *Franklin D. Roosevelt,* p. 347.

14. Ickes diary, 7/5/42, LOC. McCloy's views were shared by many army generals. General Joseph Stilwell, for instance, believed that, "Besides being a rank amateur in all military matters, FDR is apt to act on sudden impulses." (Joseph W. Stilwell, *The Stilwell Papers,* p. 16.)

15. Ickes diary, 7/5/42, LOC.

16. Ickes diary, 9/12/42, LOC; Henry Stimson diary, 7/12/42, LOC.

17. Gilbert, *Winston S. Churchill,* p. 144.

18. Stimson and Bundy, *On Active Service,* p. 424.

19. Henry Stimson diary, 7/12/42, LOC.

20. Stimson and Bundy, *On Active Service,* p. 425.

21. Gilbert, *Winston S. Churchill,* p. 150.

22. Ibid., p. 152.

23. Even Joseph Stalin approved of the Darlan agreement, cabling Roosevelt on Dec. 17, "I think it a great achievement that you succeeded in bringing Darlan and others into the waterway of the Allies fighting Hitler." (Gilbert, *Road to Victory,* p. 276.)

24. Merry Bromberger and Serge Bromberger, *Jean Monnet and the United States of Europe* (New York: Coward-McCann, 1969), p. 193.

25. Ronald Steel, *Walter Lippmann and the American Century,* p. 398.

26. John Morton Blum, ed., *Public Philosopher: Selected Letters of Walter Lippmann* (New York: Ticknor & Fields, 1985), pp. 425–30.

27. Gilbert, *Winston S. Churchill,* p. 260.

28. Piers Brendon, *Ike: His Life and Times* (New York: Harper & Row, 1986), p. 100.

29. McCloy to Lippmann, 12/29/42, ASW 371, Operations, Field of, box 34, RG 107, NA.

30. Steel, *Walter Lippmann,* p. 402.

31. Stephen E. Ambrose, *Eisenhower: Soldier, General of the Army, President-Elect, 1890–1952* (New York: Simon & Schuster, 1983), p. 204.

32. Henry Stimson diary, 1/13/43, LOC.

33. Henry Stimson diary, 2/5/43, LOC.

34. Ickes diary, 1/2/43, LOC.

35. McCloy memo to Eisenhower, 3/1/43, DDE.

36. Harold Macmillan, *War Diaries: The Mediterranean 1943–1945* (New York: St. Martin's Press, 1984), p. 27.

37. Ibid., p. 179.

38. McCloy to Eisenhower, 3/8/43, DDE.

39. Henry Stimson diary, 3/14–3/23/43, p. 2, LOC.

40. Isaacson and Thomas, *Wise Men,* p. 202.

41. Henry Stimson diary, 5/17/43, LOC.

42. Dallek, *Franklin D. Roosevelt,* p. 403.

43. Richard Rhodes, *The Making of the Atomic Bomb* (New York: Simon & Schuster, 1986), pp. 486–87.

44. When Undersecretary of War Robert Patterson found out about the secret work that was being conducted at Oak Ridge, he sent an engineer to look the place over. The engineer, a contractor named Jack Madigan, came back from Tennessee and reportedly told Patterson that if the device ever exploded it would go off with such a bang that no one would stop to consider how much it cost. On the other hand, he told Patterson, if the bomb didn't work, Congress would never stop to investigate anything else. McCloy heard this story at the time in the War Department. McCloy interview, Sept. 14, 1984.

45. Ickes to Stimson, 4/19/43; Stimson to Ickes, 4/26/43, Harold Ickes Papers, LOC.

46. Colonel John T. Bissell memo to undersecretary of war, 3/8/43, ASW 322.14, Brigades, box 17, RG 107, NA.

47. Brigadier General Edward S. Greenbaum to McCloy, 6/12/43, ASW 322.14, Brigades, box 17, RG 107, NA.

48. Ickes diary, 9/5/43, LOC.

49. Major General George V. Strong to McCloy, 7/31/43, ASW 322.14, Brigades, box 17, RG 107, NA.

50. Morris J. MacGregor, Jr., *Integration of the Armed Forces: 1940–1965,* Defense Studies Series (Washington, D.C.: Center of Military History, U.S. Army, 1981), p. 39.

51. Ibid.

52. Ibid., p. 35.

53. Ibid., pp. 20–21.

54. The chief of staff objected that Judge Hastie's proposals "would be tantamount to solving a social problem which has perplexed the American people throughout the history of this nation. The Army cannot accomplish such a solution. . . ." (Ibid., pp. 21–22.)

55. Bernard C. Nalty and Morris J. MacGregor, Jr., eds., *Blacks in the Military: Essential Documents* (Wilmington, Del.: Scholarly Resources, 1977, 1981), p. 118.

56. MacGregor, *Integration of the Armed Forces,* p. 51.

57. Bernard C. Nalty, *Strength for the Fight* (New York: Free Press, 1967), p. 148.

58. Nalty and MacGregor, eds., *Blacks in the Military,* p. 122; MacGregor, *Integration of the Armed Forces,* pp. 41–42; Nalty, *Strength for the Fight,* pp. 156–57.

59. Nalty, *Strength for the Fight,* pp. 156–57.

60. MacGregor, *Integration of the Armed Forces,* p. 43.

61. Early in 1944, the McCloy Committee quietly distributed a unique pamphlet entitled *Command of Negro Troops.* For its time, this tract was a remarkably sophisticated piece of integrationist propaganda. The pamphlet boldly stated that "competent scholars" were "almost unanimous in the opinion that race 'superiority' and 'inferiority' have not been demonstrated. . . ." Army officers in command of Negro troops were told that "scientific investigations" left no doubt that "most of the differences revealed by intelligence tests and other devices can be accounted for in terms of differences in opportunity and background." In what must have been one of the earliest pleas within the government for affirmative action, the McCloy Committee flatly concluded, "The important consideration at this point, then, is how to offer increased opportunities—both physical and cultural—to all handicapped groups, regardless of race, since these variables account in large part for poor performance and achievement in every group." (See Nalty and MacGregor, eds., *Blacks in the Military,* p. 129.)

62. MacGregor, *Integration of the Armed Forces,* p. 46.

63. Henry Stimson diary, 6/14/43, LOC.

64. Gilbert, *Winston S. Churchill,* p. 449.

65. Ickes diary, 9/5/43, LOC.

66. Rhodes, *Atomic Bomb,* p. 474.

67. Ickes diary, 9/5/43, LOC.

68. Henry Stimson diary, 11/12/43, LOC.

69. McCloy scrapbook, "Memorabilia Regarding John J. McCloy Kept by Mrs. John J. McCloy, Sr.," JJM.

70. McCloy scrapbook, "Memorabilia," JJM. Sir John Dill told Churchill two weeks later that he predicted the Germans would collapse by March 1944. (Gilbert, *Winston S. Churchill,* p. 601.)

71. "Directory of the Mena Conference—Third Edition," 11/24/43, AH.

72. McCloy to Stimson, 11/22/43, ASW 333.9, Cairo, box 18, RG 107, NA.

73. Major Paul L. E. Helliwell to McCloy, 12/6/43, ASW 333.9, Cairo, box 18, RG 107, NA; Robert Paul Browder and Thomas G. Smith, *Independent: A Biography of Lewis W. Douglas,* p. 205.

74. McCloy scrapbook, "Memorabilia," diary entry 11/21/43, JJM.

75. Macmillan, *War Diaries,* p. 304.

76. Hilldring to McCloy, 11/25/43, reproduced in *Foreign Relations of the United*

States: The Conferences at Cairo and Teheran 1943 (Washington, D.C.: Government Printing Office, 1961), p. 423.

77. McCloy to Hopkins, 11/25/43, ASW 333.9 Cairo, box 18, RG 107, NA. General Marshall shared McCloy's concern regarding any attempt "to remove the center of gravity from Washington to London. . . ." (*FRUS*, p. 198.)

78. McCloy to Colonel Stimson, 12/2/43, ASW 333.9, Cairo, box 18, RG 107, NA.

79. Lord Moran, *Churchill—Taken from the Diaries of Lord Moran: The Struggle for Survival 1940–1965* (Boston: Houghton Mifflin, 1966), pp. 140–42.

80. McCloy to Stimson, 12/2/43, ASW 333.9, Cairo, box 18, RG 107, NA.

81. Henry Stimson diary, 12/5/43, LOC.

82. "Until he [Churchill] came here," wrote Lord Moran in his diary at Teheran, "the P.M. could not bring himself to believe that, face to face with Stalin, the democracies would take different courses. Now he sees he cannot rely on the President's support. What matters more, he realizes that the Russians see this too. It would be useless to try to take a firm line with Stalin. He will be able to do as he pleases. Will he become a menace to the free world, another Hitler? The P.M. is appalled by his own impotence." (Moran, *Churchill*, p. 151.)

83. Ibid., p. 153.

84. McCloy scrapbook, "Memorabilia," diary entry 12/14/43, JJM.

85. McCloy to Eisenhower, 12/13/43, ASW 333.9, Cairo, box 18, RG 107, NA.

86. Martin Blumenthal, ed., *The Patton Diaries* (New York: Houghton Mifflin, 1984), vol. II, p. 387.

87. McCloy scrapbook, diary entry 12/14/43, JJM.

88. McCloy scrapbook, "Memorabilia," diary entry 12/15/43, JJM.

89. *FRUS*, pp. 484–85.

90. McCloy to Stimson, 1/13/44, ASW 370.8, France 1943 through June 1944, box 25, RG 107, NA.

91. Henry Stimson diary, 1/14/44, LOC.

92. McCloy to Stimson, 1/17/44, ASW 370.8, France, box 25, RG 107, NA.

93. Henry Stimson diary, 1/13/44, LOC.

94. Henry Stimson diary, 1/21/44, LOC.

95. Henry Stimson diary, 2/28/44, 2/29/44, 3/1/44, 3/15/44, LOC.

96. Ted Morgan, *FDR*, pp. 717–24.

97. Donovan memo to the president, 7/6/44, PSF France, No. 42, Degaulle, 1944–45, FDR; Brown, *Wild Bill Donovan*, pp. 561–62.

98. John S. D. Eisenhower, *Allies: Pearl Harbor to D-Day* (Garden City, N.Y.: Doubleday, 1982), p. 457.

99. Telephone transcript, McCloy and General Holmes, 6/13/44, ASW 370.8, France 1943 through June 1944, box 25, RG 107, NA.

100. McCloy to the president, 6/13/44, ASW 370.8, France 1943 through June 1944, box 25, RG 107, NA.

101. Henry Stimson diary, 6/14/44.

102. Telephone transcript, Stimson and Marshall, 6/15/44, ASW 370.8, France 1943 through June 1944, box 25, RG 107, NA.

103. Marshall to Eisenhower, 4/3/44, ASW 333.9, ETO England 5 April–22 April 1944, box 18, RG 107, NA.

104. David Eisenhower, *Eisenhower at War* (New York: Random House, 1986), p. 229.

105. McCloy diary, 4/20/44, folder 13, box 1/3, JJM.

106. Ibid; McCloy interview, March 19, 1986; Gilbert, *Winston S. Churchill,* p. 760; Isaacson and Thomas, *Wise Men,* p. 202. Isaacson and Thomas place this midnight visit to the House of Commons in 1943, but there's no evidence that McCloy had a chance to see Churchill in London in 1943.

107. Henry Stimson diary, 4/22/44, LOC.

108. McCloy to Marshall, 4/26/44, ASW 333.9, Eto England 5 April–22 April 1944, Box 18, RG 107, NA.

TEN: McCLOY AND THE HOLOCAUST

1. David S. Wyman, *The Abandonment of the Jews: America and the Holocaust, 1941–1945* (New York: Pantheon, 1984), pp. 204, 209.

2. Deborah E. Lipstadt, *Beyond Belief: The American Press and the Coming of the Holocaust, 1933–1945* (New York: Free Press, 1985), p. 157.

3. Gerald Fleming, *Hitler and the Final Solution* (Berkeley: University of California Press, 1982), pp. 59–60, 91–92.

4. Lipstadt, *Beyond Belief,* pp. 162–64.

5. Ibid., p. 175.

6. Ibid., p. 188.

7. Ibid., p. 186.

8. Ibid., p. 194.

9. Ibid., p. 186.

10. Wyman, *Abandonment of the Jews,* pp. 185–87.

11. Ibid., p. 187. The brother of Alger Hiss, Donald, was the State Department official who leaked the cable to Morgenthau.

12. Henry Stimson diary, 1/26/44, LOC.

13. "Accomplishments to date," 2/2/44, ASW 400.38, War Refugee Board, box 44, RG 107, NA.

14. Henry Stimson diary, 2/1/44, LOC.

15. "Accomplishments Since February 2, 1944," ASW 400.38, War Refugee Board, box 44, RG 107.

16. Major General J. H. Hilldring to McCloy, 1/25/44, ASW 400.38, War Refugee Board, box 44, RG 107, NA; Wyman, *Abandonment of the Jews,* p. 293.

17. Wyman, *Abandonment of the Jews,* p. 267.

18. Ibid., p. 293. Soon after the formation of the WRB, Pehle proposed that the Yugoslav partisans be asked to provide local currency so that the Rab Jews might hire private boats to take them to Italy. In return, the War Department would promise the partisans eventual reimbursement in hard currency. Even this proposal was referred by Stimson to the Joint Chiefs, where it languished. Eventually, most of the Jews were evacuated from Rab by Tito's partisans without any assistance from the U.S. military. Several hundred, however, were captured by the Germans and deported to death camps. (Ibid., p. 407.)

19. Ibid., p. 292.

20. Martin Gilbert, *Auschwitz and the Allies* (New York: Holt, Rinehart & Winston, 1981), p. 94.

21. Jan Karski, *Story of a Secret State* (Boston: Houghton Mifflin, 1944), p. 387; Jan Karski phone interview, April 21, 1987.

22. Jan Karski speech, Washington, D.C., March 29, 1987. Harvey Bundy, not McCloy, happened to sit in on Karski's briefing of Stimson on Aug. 12, 1943. From Stimson's cursory diary entry that day, it is possible to conclude that in this luncheon

meeting Karski did not dwell on the fate of the Jews, but spent most of his time talking about the exploits of the Polish underground. Thus, even though three of his closest friends—Stimson, Bundy, and Frankfurter—were briefed by the Polish courier, it is possible that McCloy was never told of Karski's visit to Belzec. A year later, however, Karski told his story for the general public in *Story of a Secret State.* Selected by the Book-of-the-Month Club, it became a best-seller and was excerpted by a number of national magazines.

23. Wyman, *Abandonment of the Jews,* p. 323.

24. Carey McWilliams, *A Mask for Privilege: Anti-Semitism in America* (Boston: Little, Brown, 1948), pp. 118–19.

25. Ellen McCloy's brother, John S. Zinsser, wrote Lew Douglas in 1945 concerning a possible buyer for the family chemical business: "Dad will have absolutely nothing to do with him because he is Jewish." (J. S. Zinsser to Lew Douglas, 9/10/45, LD.)

26. Author's interview with anonymous Wall Street lawyer, June 22, 1983. This story was told to me with considerable reluctance. The lawyer emphasized that he believed the incident reflected less on McCloy personally than on the tenor of society at the time.

27. Henry Stimson diary, 3/8/44, LOC.

28. Senate resolution 247, 1/24/44, ASW 291.2, Jews, box 16, RG 107, NA.

29. Henry Stimson diary, 3/8/44, LOC.

30. McCloy to Marshall, 2/22/44, ASW 291.2, Jews, box 16, RG 107, NA.

31. Ibid.

32. Wyman, *Abandonment of the Jews,* pp. 173–75, 253.

33. Ibid., pp. 219–20.

34. Pehle to McCloy, "Report of Accomplishments for the Week of February 14–19, 1944," and other weekly reports submitted to McCloy in the spring of 1944, ASW 400.38, War Refugee Board, box 44, RG 107, NA.

35. Henry Stimson diary, 3/31/44, LD; Wyman, *Abandonment of the Jews,* p. 262.

36. Richard Breitman and Alan M. Kraut, *American Refugee Policy and European Jewry, 1933–1945* (Bloomington: Indiana University Press, 1987), p. 173.

37. Wyman, *Abandonment of the Jews,* pp. 290–91; Gilbert, *Auschwitz and the Allies,* p. 237.

38. Wyman, *Abandonment of the Jews,* p. 236.

39. Gilbert, *Auschwitz and the Allies,* p. 194.

40. Wyman, *Abandonment of the Jews,* p. 289.

41. Harrison (McClelland) to sec. of state for War Refugee Board, 6/24/44, ASW 400.38, Jews, box 44, RG 107, NA.

42. Ibid.

43. Gilbert, *Auschwitz and the Allies,* p. 238.

44. Pehle to McCloy, 6/29/44, ASW 400.38, Jews, box 44, RG 107, NA.

45. Wyman, *Abandonment of the Jews,* pp. 292, 407n.; Ray S. Cline, *Washington Command Post: The Operations Division* (Washington, D.C.: Office of the Chief of Military History, Department of the Army, 1951), pp. 300–301.

46. Major General J. E. Hull (signing for Major General Thos. T. Handy) to director, Civil Affairs Division, 6/26/44, ASW 400.38, Jews, box 44, RG 107, NA; also cited in Wyman, *Abandonment of the Jews,* pp. 292–94.

47. Gerhardt to McCloy, 7/3/44, ASW 400.38, Jews, box 44, RG 107, NA.

48. McCloy to Pehle, 7/4/44, ASW 400.38 Jews, box 44, RG 107, NA.

49. Dino A. Brugioni and Robert C. Poirier, *The Holocaust Revisited: A Retrospective Analysis of the Auschwitz-Birkenau Extermination Complex* (Washington, D.C.: Central Intelligence Agency, 1979), p. 5.

50. Gilbert, *Auschwitz and the Allies,* p. 315.

51. Primo Levi, *Survival in Auschwitz* (New York: Summit, 1986), p. 118.

52. Wyman, *Abandonment of the Jews,* p. 290; Gilbert, *Auschwitz and the Allies,* p. 256.

53. Gilbert, *Auschwitz and the Allies,* p. 248.

54. Levi, *Survival in Auschwitz,* p. 388.

55. Pehle to War Refugee Board, with attachments, 7/15/44, ASW 400.38, Jews, box 44, RG 107, NA.

56. Johnson (Olsen) to secretary of state, 7/1/44, ASW 400.38, Jews, box 44, RG 107, NA.

57. Murray Green, "Why We Didn't Bomb Auschwitz," *WP,* June 18, 1983. Years later, when McCloy came under criticism for the decision, he authorized a friend, Edward T. Chase, to write an article that reported his recollection of having "had some discussions with Harry Hopkins, Sam Rosenman and either Air Force Gen. Hap Arnold or one of his aides" about whether to bomb the death camps. No record of these discussions can be found.

58. Wyman, *Abandonment of the Jews,* p. 295.

59. Gilbert, *Auschwitz and the Allies,* p. 265.

60. Ibid., p. 270.

61. Churchill and Eden may have seen other evidence on the death camps. In 1980, Peter Calvocoressi, a British veteran of Bletchley Park, the site in Britain where intercepts of German Enigma traffic were decoded, published a memoir in which he asserts that his fellow cryptologists at some point during the war began intercepting the daily statistics radioed to Berlin from each concentration camp. The intercepts reported the number of new arrivals, the number killed, and the number of inmates remaining in each camp. Calvocoressi reports that special attention had to be paid to these figures, because it was discovered that the German cryptologists were using the daily numbers to determine the random settings for their constantly changing Enigma cipher. It is hard to believe that Bletchley Park did not inform British policy-makers of these grisly statistics. But there is no evidence that McCloy himself saw these intercepts. (Peter Calvocoressi, *Top Secret Ultra* [New York: Ballantine Books, 1981], p. 16.) In addition, it is known that British cryptologists broke the German railway code in 1941 and therefore were able to track the unusually large number of trains carrying Jews to the Silesian death camps. Some historians have concluded that the intelligence services suppressed this information. (Walter Laqueur, *The Terrible Secret: Suppression of the Truth About Hitler's* "Final Solution" [Boston: Little, Brown, 1980], pp. 84–86.)

62. Gilbert, *Winston S. Churchill,* p. 847.

63. Gilbert, *Auschwitz and the Allies,* pp. 272, 285, 341.

64. Wyman, *Abandonment of the Jews,* pp. 307, 410.

65. Ira Hirschmann memo to Ambassador Steinhardt, 6/22/44, ASW 400.38, Jews, box 44, RG 107, NA.

66. Clayton Bissel to McCloy, 7/25/44; Pehle to McCloy, 7/20/44 with attached transcripts, memos, and correspondence relating to interrogation of Joel Brand, ASW 400.38, Jews, box 44, RG 107, NA; see also Breitman and Kraut, *American Refugee Policy,* p. 215; Amos Elon, *Timetable: The Story of Joel Brand* (London: Hutchinson, 1980), p. 212.

67. Wyman, *Abandonment of the Jews,* p. 296.

68. Gilbert, *Auschwitz and the Allies,* p. 321.

69. Pehle to McCloy, 10/4/44, ASW 400.38, Jews, box 44, RG 107, NA; Gerhardt to McCloy, 10/5/44, ASW 400.38, Jews, box 44, RG 107, NA. Though McCloy and

Gerhardt repeatedly turned down or deflected requests for bombing Auschwitz, they were willing to issue another war-crimes warning. This time, at the suggestion of Jewish groups, Eisenhower was asked to issue a statement warning the Nazis against the extermination of concentration-camp inmates, "whether they are Jewish or otherwise." Yet, when this language was wired to Eisenhower in mid-October, he replied that his Psychological Warfare Division believed that any direct reference to Jews "would give Germans powerful propaganda line [sic]." McCloy personally approved alternative language, specifying those of any "religious faith," and this warning was subsequently broadcast under Eisenhower's name. Even warning the Nazis against the destruction of Jews, let alone rescuing Jewry from the death camps, was sometimes thought unseemly. (Supreme Headquarters to War Department, 10/14/44, ASW 400.38, Countries—Germany, box 44, RG 107, NA.)

70. Wyman, *Abandonment of the Jews,* p. 324.

71. Pehle to McCloy, 11/8/44, ASW 400.38, Countries—Germany, box 44, RG 107, NA.

72. Major General J. E. Hull to McCloy, 11/14/44, ASW 400.38, Countries—Germany, box 44, RG 107, NA.

73. McCloy to Pehle, 11/18/44, ASW 400.38, Countries—Germany, box 44, RG 107, NA.

74. Martin Gilbert, *The Holocaust: A History of the Jews of Europe During the Second World War* (New York: Holt, Rinehart & Winston, 1986), p. 745.

75. Wyman, *Abandonment of the Jews,* p. 304.

76. Ibid., p. 292.

77. Laqueur, *Terrible Secret,* p. 100.

78. Henry Morgenthau, *Morgenthau Diary.* Prepared by the Subcommittee to Investigate the Administration of the Internal Security Act and Other Internal Security Laws, Committee on the Judiciary, U.S. Senate, 11/20/67 (Washington, D.C.: U.S. Government Printing Office, 1967), vol. I, pp. 393–98.

79. Ickes diary, 8/6/44, LOC.

80. Morgenthau, *Diary,* vol. I, U.S. Senate, pp. 440–42.

81. Ibid., p. 424; see also David Eisenhower, *Eisenhower at War,* pp. 402–3.

82. Morgenthau, *Diary,* vol. I, U.S. Senate, pp. 436, 438.

83. Ibid., pp. 443–45.

84. Henry Stimson diary, 9/4/44, LOC.

85. Morgenthau, *Diary,* vol. I, U.S. Senate, pp. 521, 524.

86. Ibid., p. 529.

87. Henry Stimson diary, 9/7/44, LOC.

88. Henry Stimson diary, 9/9/44, LOC.

89. Henry Stimson diary, 9/14/44, LOC.

90. Henry Stimson diary, 9/16–17/44, LOC.

91. Ickes diary, 9/17/44, LOC.

92. Morgenthau, *Diary,* vol. I, U.S. Senate, p. 40.

93. Henry Stimson diary, 9/27–10/1/44, LOC.

94. Henry L. Stimson and McGeorge Bundy, *On Active Service in Peace and War,* p. 581.

ELEVEN: VICTORY IN EUROPE

1. McCloy to chief of staff, 6/9/44, ASW 000.2, Communism, box 1, RG 107, NA.

2. McCloy to assistant chief of staff, G-2, 12/23/44, ASW 000.2, Communists, box 1, RG 107, NA.

3. McCloy to Senator Kenneth S. Wherry, 2/21/45; McCloy to Francis Biddle, 3/14/45, ASW 000.2, Communists, Hearings—Subcommittee of House Military Affairs Committee, box 1, RG 107, NA.

4. Ickes diary, 11/24/44, LOC.

5. Henry Stimson diary, 12/19/44, LOC.

6. Henry Morgenthau, *Morgenthau Diary,* vol. I, U.S. Senate, pp. 52–53.

7. John Morton Blum, *Roosevelt and Morgenthau: A Revision and Condensation from the Morgenthau Diaries* (Boston: Houghton Mifflin, 1970), p. 616.

8. Ibid., p. 619.

9. Walter Isaacson and Evan Thomas, *The Wise Men: Six Friends and the World They Made,* p. 236.

10. Blum, *Roosevelt and Morgenthau,* pp. 623–24.

11. Morgenthau, *Diary,* vol. I, U.S. Senate, p. 61.

12. Isaacson and Thomas, *Wise Men,* p. 202.

13. Mary Ellen Crane Rossiter interview, Oct. 31, 1987.

14. Isaacson and Thomas, *Wise Men,* p. 196. General Jacob Devers was McCloy's landlord at the time. (McCloy interview, July 10, 1986.)

15. Ladislas Farago, *Patton: Ordeal and Triumph* (New York: Dell Publishing, 1970), p. 762.

16. Martin Blumenthal, ed., *The Patton Diaries,* vol. II, p. 685.

17. Isaacson and Thomas, *Wise Men,* pp. 254–55; "Proposed Itinerary Mr. John McCloy and Party," ASW 333.9, ETO, box 18, RG 107, NA; McCloy diary, 4/12/45, box 1/3/55M.

18. Blum, *Roosevelt and Morgenthau,* p. 630.

19. Major General Ralph C. Smith, "Military Attaché Report: Conversation with General De Gaulle on Economic Problems and War Criminals," 4/18/45, ASW 333.9, ETO, box 18, RG 107, NA.

20. McCloy interview, July 10, 1986; Martin Gilbert, *Winston S. Churchill: The Road to Victory,* p. 1301; McCloy to Chuck Weeden, 3/12/74, JJM, Amherst.

21. Henry Stimson diary, 4/19/45, LOC.

22. Nelson M. Shepard, "Problem of Feeding Germany Unsolved, McCloy Says on Return," *Washington Star,* April 26, 1945; "U.S. Opens Action to Punish Nazis," *NYT,* April 26, 1945.

23. Warren F. Kimball, *The Juggler: Franklin Roosevelt as Wartime Statesman* (Princeton, N.J.: Princeton University Press, 1991), p. 159.

24. Harry S. Truman, *Year of Decisions* (Garden City, N.Y.: Doubleday, 1955), pp. 77–78.

25. Henry Stimson diary, 4/23/45, LOC.

26. Truman, *Year of Decisions,* p. 82.

27. Ibid., pp. 85–86; Melvyn P. Leffler, "Adherence to Agreements: Yalta and the Experiences of the Early Cold War," *International Security,* Summer 1986.

28. Truman, *Year of Decisions,* p. 102.

29. Ibid., p. 64.

30. Peter Wyden, *Day One: Before Hiroshima and After* (New York: Simon & Schuster, 1984), pp. 133–34.

31. McCloy diary, 4/30/45, box 1/3, JJM.

32. Gabriel Kolko, *The Politics of War: The World and United States Foreign Policy, 1943–1945* (New York: Random House, 1968), pp. 470–73.

33. Henry Stimson diary, 4/27–29/45, 5/10/45, LOC. The next day, over lunch, McCloy told Ickes that Stettinius "has no real leadership and no real ideas. He tries to

keep everybody happy by jollying them and inviting them to cocktails." (Ickes diary, 5/20/45, LOC.)

34. Henry Stimson diary, 5/10/45, LOC.

TWELVE: HIROSHIMA

1. Gar Alperovitz, *Atomic Diplomacy: Hiroshima and Potsdam* (New York: Penguin, 1985), pp. 347–48.

2. Martin Sherwin, *A World Destroyed: The Atomic Bomb and the Grand Alliance* (New York: Vintage Books, 1977), p. 190.

3. Henry Stimson diary, 5/15/45, LOC. Stimson was mistaken to think that a date for the Potsdam meeting had already been set. Almost two more weeks would pass before it was set.

4. Stimson to acting secretary of state (Grew), 5/21/45, top secret, folder: Soviet Union, Memcons & Ltrs, 1945, AH.

5. Henry Stimson diary, 5/15/45, LOC.

6. Stimson to President Truman, 5/16/45, PSF, HST. Stimson reported in his diary on May 16, 1945, that McCloy helped him prepare this memo.

7. Sherwin, *World Destroyed,* p. 191. Joseph E. Davies noted in his diary on May 21, 1945, that Truman had confided in him that he did not want to meet in June because the "test was set for June, but had been postponed to July."

8. Alperovitz, *Atomic Diplomacy,* p. 44.

9. On May 19, 1945, Stimson told McCloy over the phone that he thought simple geography and "our position in the world, made it perfectly possible for us to get along [with the Soviets] without fighting. . . . This was the time to put up with a good bit of ill mannered behavior with the Russians in a sincere attempt to work out such a relationship rather than form what would be construed as a close military alliance against them." (memo of telephone conversation with the secretary of war, 5/19/45, box WD 1, folder 29, JJM.)

10. Alperovitz, *Atomic Diplomacy,* p. 156.

11. Donovan to president, 5/12/45, Confidential Files, HST; see also Allen Dulles, *The Secret Surrender* (New York: Harper & Row, 1966), p. 255.

12. On May 28, 1945, Grew bluntly told Truman, "The greatest obstacle to unconditional surrender by the Japanese is their belief that this would entail the destruction or permanent removal of the Emperor and the institution of the throne." Grew believed the idea of depriving the Japanese of their emperorship simply "unsound." See Joseph C. Grew, *Turbulent Era* (Boston: Houghton Mifflin, 1952), vol. II, pp. 1428–29.

13. McCloy to Colonel Stimson, 5/28/45, box WD 1, folder 29, JJM.

14. Memorandum of conversation with General Marshall and the secretary of war—May 29, 1945, McCloy diary, 5/29/45, DY box 1, folder 17, JJM.

15. In fact, McCloy's Kuhn, Loeb friend Lewis Strauss a few weeks later suggested to Forrestal a quite practical demonstration. Strauss remembered seeing in a Siberian forest the 1908 effects of a large meteor hit which had "knocked down forests for miles around its point of impact and the trees lay in windrows radiating like spokes of a wheel from the center." Troubled by the idea of dropping such a "cataclysmic weapon" on a crowded metropolis filled with women and children, Strauss suggested targeting the bomb over a large grove of cryptomeria trees near the village of Nikko on Honshu Island. There is no record of whether Forrestal tried to pursue the idea or not. (Lewis L. Strauss, *Men and Decisions* [Garden City, N.Y.: Doubleday, 1962], pp. 192–93.)

16. Sherwin, *World Destroyed,* p. 302. Ironically, it was James B. Conant, the president of America's leading institution of higher learning, Harvard University, who proposed

targeting civilian workers' quarters. At the time, Conant was serving as deputy science adviser to the White House.

17. Ibid., p. 210.

18. Ibid., p. 205.

19. Ibid., p. 301.

20. Charles S. Cheston, acting director, OSS, to president, 5/31/45, Confidential Files, HST; Henry Stimson diary, 6/1/45, LOC. The most destructive air raid over Tokyo actually occurred on March 9–10, when some eighty-three thousand people were killed. The Japanese capital was repeatedly firebombed in the months afterward.

21. Peter Wyden, *Day One: Before Hiroshima and After,* p. 171.

22. John Toland, *The Rising Sun: The Decline and Fall of the Japanese Empire* (New York: Random House, 1970), vol. II, p. 943; Wyden, *Day One,* pp. 171–72.

23. Toland, *Rising Sun,* vol. II, p. 943.

24. John J. McCloy, *The Challenge to American Foreign Policy* (Cambridge, Mass.: Harvard University Press, 1953), p. 40.

25. Toland, *Rising Sun,* vol. II, p. 944.

26. Ibid.

27. Alperovitz, *Atomic Diplomacy,* p. 159; McCloy, *Challenge to American Foreign Policy,* p. 41.

28. Wyden, *Day One,* p. 172.

29. Walter Mills, ed., *The Forrestal Diaries* (New York: Viking Press, 1951), p. 70.

30. McCloy recalled that he went to see Byrnes, who was then working in the White House, and pitched the idea to him. But Byrnes dismissed the idea without explanation: "He said," recalled McCloy, "my proposal was not possible." McCloy left with the impression that Byrnes was angry about not having been invited to the meeting. (McCloy interview, Sept. 14, 1984.)

31. Wyden, *Day One,* p. 173.

32. Alperovitz, *Atomic Diplomacy,* p. 37.

33. Wyden, *Day One,* p. 173.

34. Toland, *Rising Sun,* vol. II, p. 945; Wyden, *Day One,* pp. 172–74; McCloy, *Challenge,* pp. 40–43.

35. In a private meeting with Joseph Grew the same morning, Truman said he favored the acting secretary of state's suggestion to issue a similar explanation of what the United States meant by "unconditional surrender." But he told Grew that he wished to delay any such statement until the Big Three meeting at Potsdam. (See Grew, *Turbulent Era,* vol. II, p. 1437.)

36. Minutes of meeting of the Committee of Three, 6/19/45, ASW 334.8, Committee of Three Minutes, box 19, RG 107, NA.

37. Minutes of meeting of the Committee of Three, 6/26/45, ASW 334.8, box 19, RG 107, NA.

38. McCloy to Colonel Stimson, 6/29/45, ASW 387, Japan, box 38, RG 107, NA.

39. Toland, *Rising Sun,* vol. II, p. 946.

40. McCloy to Colonel Stimson, 6/29/45, ASW 387, Japan, box 38, RG 107, NA.

41. George L. Harrison to McCloy, 7/2/45, ASW 387, Japan, box 38, RG 107, NA.

42. Nuel Pharr Davis, *Lawrence and Oppenheimer* (New York: Simon & Schuster, 1968), p. 247. Discouraged by his lack of influence, and tired of his four-year service as undersecretary of the navy, Bard resigned on July 1, 1945.

43. Charles L. Mee, Jr., *Meeting at Potsdam* (New York: Evans, 1975), pp. 4–5.

44. Harry S. Truman, *Year of Decisions,* p. 87.

45. Alperovitz, *Atomic Diplomacy,* p. 43.

46. Ickes diary, 7/8/45, LOC.

47. Cordell Hull, *The Memoirs of Cordell Hull* (New York: Macmillan, 1948), vol. II, p. 1594.

48. David Kahn, *The Codebreakers: The Story of Secret Writing,* p. 610; Richard Rhodes, *The Making of the Atomic Bomb,* p. 685.

49. Walter Isaacson and Evan Thomas, *The Wise Men: Six Friends and the World They Made,* pp. 299–300.

50. McCloy to Grew, 7/5/45, ASW 387, Japan, box 38, RG 107, NA.

51. McCloy to chief of staff, 7/17/45; memorandum for the president, 7/16/45, ASW 387, Japan, box 38, RG 107, NA.

52. Rhodes, *Atomic Bomb,* pp. 685–86.

53. McCloy diary, 7/16/45, 7/23/45, DY box 1, folder 18, JJM.

54. Mee, *Meeting at Potsdam,* p. 88.

55. Alperovitz, *Atomic Diplomacy,* p. 32; Herbert Feis, *Japan Subdued* (Princeton, N.J.: Princeton University Press, 1961), p. 59.

56. Alperovitz, *Atomic Diplomacy,* p. 33.

57. McCloy diary, 7/16–17/45, DY box 1, folder 18, JJM; Gar Alperovitz, "Did We Have to Drop the Bomb?," *NYT,* Aug. 3, 1989. On July 17, McCloy wrote in his diary, "The delivery of a warning now would hit them at *the* moment. It would probably bring what we are after—the successful termination of the war. . . ." Stalin himself had told Harry Hopkins as early as May 30, 1945, "the Japs were on the verge of collapse and know they are doomed; they were putting out peace feelers. . . ." As Hopkins paraphrased Stalin, "Perhaps we [the U.S.] can get a surrender without using the words 'unconditional surrender' but give them 'the works' once we get to Japan." (McCloy memo to the secretaries of war and navy, 6/10/45, no. 2698, reel 116, GCM.)

58. Churchill noted on July 23, 1945, at Potsdam: "It is quite clear that the United States do not at the present time desire Russian participation in the war against Japan." (See Alperovitz, "Drop the Bomb?")

59. McCloy diary, 7/23/45, DY box 1, folder 18, JJM.

60. Alperovitz, *Atomic Diplomacy,* p. 54. A California oil man and Democratic Party treasurer, Pauley was in Potsdam to negotiate German reparation payments with the Soviets.

61. Isaacson and Thomas, *Wise Men,* p. 304.

62. Allen Dulles's foreword to Per Jacobsson's pamphlet *The Per Jacobsson Mediation,* Basle Centre for Economic and Financial Research, ser. C, no. 4, published about 1967, on file in Allen Dulles Papers, box 22, folder John J. McCloy 1945, PU.

63. McCloy diary, 7/20/45, DY box 1, folder 18, JJM.

64. McCloy diary, 7/27/45, DY box 1, folder 18, JJM.

65. Alperovitz, *Atomic Diplomacy,* p. 30.

66. McCloy to Ellen McCloy, n.d. (July), Potsdam, JJM.

67. W. Averell Harriman and Elie Abel, *Special Envoy* (New York: Random House, 1975), p. 48.

68. Rhodes, *Atomic Bomb,* p. 688. Eisenhower probably made the same pitch to Truman, but the president brushed aside what he thought were familiar arguments. In the words of his brother, Milton, Eisenhower thought that for the United States to introduce atomic weapons into the war as late as Aug. 1945 might be viewed by the Soviets as a "supreme provocation." (See David Eisenhower, *Eisenhower at War,* p. 692.)

69. Margaret Truman, *Harry S. Truman* (New York: William Morrow, 1973), p. 280; John McCloy to Ellen McCloy, two undated letters written from Potsdam, n.d. (July 1945), McCloy scrapbooks, JJM.

70. Isaacson and Thomas, *Wise Men,* p. 306.

71. McCloy to Ellen McCloy, n.d., Potsdam, JJM. Papers.

72. McCloy diary, 7/25/45, DY box 1, folder 18, JJM; Isaacson and Thomas, *Wise Men,* p. 305.

73. McCloy to Ellen McCloy, n.d., Potsdam, JJM.

74. Ibid.

75. Alperovitz, *Atomic Diplomacy,* pp. 216–18.

76. Isaacson and Thomas, *Wise Men,* p. 306. "I feel that this situation [a divided Germany] is better than the constant distrust and difficulty we would have with the Russians over their being in our zones. . . ." (McCloy diary, 7/23/45, DY box 1, folder 18, JJM.)

77. Walter Lippmann made some of these arguments in a series of articles shortly after the war. See Alperovitz, *Atomic Diplomacy,* p. 56.

78. Isaacson and Thomas, *Wise Men,* p. 306

79. McCloy to Ellen McCloy, n.d., Potsdam, JJM.

80. Harriman and Abel, *Special Envoy,* p. 488.

81. McCloy diary, 7/16/45, DY box 1, folder 18, JJM.

82. McCloy diary, 7/28/45, DY box 1, folder 18, JJM.

83. Gabriel Kolko, *The Politics of War: The World and United States Foreign Policy, 1943–1945,* p. 561; Mee, *Meeting at Potsdam,* p. 209.

84. Sherwin, *World Destroyed,* p. 227; McCloy diary, 7/25/45, DY box 1, folder 18, JJM.

85. Alperovitz, *Atomic Diplomacy,* p. 108.

86. McCloy diary, 7/20/45, DY box 1, folder 18, JJM; Isaacson and Thomas, *Wise Men,* p. 303.

87. Mee, *Meeting at Potsdam,* pp. 235–36.

88. "Biweekly Political Analysis of the Far East," 7/26/45, ASW 371.1, Service of Information Alpha, box 34, RG 107, NA; see also Colonel Truman Smith to Brigadier General John Weckerling, chief, Intelligence Division, G-2, 7/3/51, file: Russian Declaration of War on Japan, Truman Smith Papers, HH.

89. After the war, Lewis L. Strauss wrote in a private letter that he thought Forrestal hoped these intercepts would convince Truman and Byrnes that "the war was essentially over and that little more than a question of semantics separated the terms which the victors would impose and those which the vanquished were eager to accept." (Lewis Strauss to Dr. Robert G. Albion, 12/19/60, Agro-American Committee on United Europe, Strauss Papers, HH.)

90. McCloy diary, 7/30/45, DY box 1, folder 18, JJM.

91. Mee, *Meeting at Potsdam,* p. 247.

92. Ibid., p. 272.

93. Isaacson and Thomas, *Wise Men,* p. 308.

94. McCloy to Ellen McCloy, n.d., Potsdam, JJM.

95. Kolko, *Politics of War,* pp. 449, 498.

96. Isaacson and Thomas, *Wise Men,* p. 315; Wyden, *Day One,* p. 289.

97. "Note Received from Swiss Government August 10, 1945," ASW 387, Japan, box 38, RG 107, NA.

98. Rhodes, *Atomic Bomb,* pp. 733–34, 740.

99. Ibid., p. 742.

100. John Morton Blum, ed., *The Price of Vision: The Diary of Henry A. Wallace, 1942–1946* (Boston: Houghton Mifflin, 1973), p. 474.

101. Byrnes-McCloy telcon, 8/11/45, ASW 387 Japan, box 38, RG 107, NA; Henry Stimson diary, 8/11/45, LOC.

102. Rhodes, *Atomic Bomb,* p. 743.

103. Blum, ed., *Price of Vision,* p. 474. It is interesting to note that at the end of this Cabinet meeting Henry Wallace concluded that Truman, Byrnes, Stimson, and Forrestal were already moving away from strengthening the U.S.-Soviet relationship. "Their attitude," he warned, "will make for war eventually." (Ibid., p. 475.)

104. Harriman, Kennan, Stalin, Molotov memorandum of conversation, 8/8/45, AH.

105. Stimson and Bundy, *On Active Service,* p. 641; McCloy interview, Sept. 14, 1984.

106. McCloy diary, 9/2/45, box 1, folder 18, JJM; Henry Stimson diary, 8/12–9/3/45, LOC.

107. McCloy diary, 9/2/45, box 1, folder 18, JJM.

108. Henry Stimson diary, 8/12–9/3/45, with attached phone records, LOC.

109. Stimson and Bundy, *On Active Service,* p. 642.

110. Memorandum for the president, "Proposed Action for Control of Atomic Bombs," signed by Henry Stimson, 9/11/45, found in McCloy diary, 9/2/45, DY box 1, folder 18, JJM.

111. Alperovitz, *Atomic Diplomacy,* p. 55.

112. James F. Byrnes, *Speaking Frankly* (New York: Harper & Brothers, 1947), p. 203.

113. Millis, ed., *Forrestal Diaries,* p. 70. After Hiroshima, the Truman administration did everything it could to control the history of the bomb decision. Henry Stimson and McGeorge Bundy, for instance, agreed to eliminate several paragraphs from their 1948 book, *On Active Service in Peace and War,* which explicitly discussed the bomb "as a diplomatic weapon." They rewrote this and several other critical passages at the urging of George Kennan and General Marshall, who by then was secretary of state. Kennan explained to Bundy that these passages "would play squarely into the hands of the Communists who so frequently speak of our 'atomic diplomacy' . . ." (George Kennan to McGeorge Bundy, 12/2/47, box 86, folder 17, GCM.)

114. McCloy interview, Sept. 14, 1984.

115. McCloy diary, 7/20/45, DY box 1, folder 18, JJM.

116. McCloy interview, Sept. 14, 1984.

117. McCloy diary, 7/21/45, DY box 1, folder 18, JJM.

118. "Dr. Freeman's Impressions," McCloy diary, box DY 1/3, folder 19, JJM; McCloy interview, Sept. 14, 1984.

119. Isaacson and Thomas, *Wise Men,* p. 336.

120. McCloy diary, 9/30/45, box DY 1/3, folder 19, JJM.

121. Isaacson and Thomas, *Wise Men,* p. 330.

122. Ibid., p. 331.

123. McCloy to George Wharton Pepper, 10/15/46, box PA 1, folder 69, JJM.

124. McCloy diary, 10/22–25/45, JJM.

125. McCloy cable to secretaries of war and state, n.d., box DY 1/3, folder 19, JJM.

126. Isaacson and Thomas, *Wise Men,* p. 335.

BOOK THREE
THIRTEEN: A BRIEF RETURN TO WALL STREET

1. Walter Isaacson and Evan Thomas, *The Wise Men: Six Friends and the World They Made,* p. 336.

2. Paul Hoffman, *Lions in the Street: The Inside Story of the Great Wall Street Firms,* p. 10.

3. Maurice "Tex" Moore interview, Oct. 21, 1983.

4. Isaacson and Thomas, *Wise Men,* pp. 335–36.

5. James B. Stewart, *The Partners: Inside America's Most Powerful Law Firms* (New York: Simon & Schuster, 1983), p. 288.

6. Alexander Forger, speaking at McCloy Memorial Service, March 21, 1989.

7. Harrison Tweed, "Extra Curricular Opportunities and Activities of Lawyers," *New Jersey State Bar Association Yearbook,* 1947, pp. 84–85 (speech, Jan. 18, 1947).

8. George Martin, *Causes and Conflicts: The Centennial History of the Association of the Bar of the City of New York 1870–1970* (Boston: Houghton Mifflin, 1970), p. 249.

9. Hoffman, *Lions in the Street,* p. 19.

10. Ibid., p. 77.

11. John D. Rockefeller, Jr., to Tom Debevoise, 2/24/47, Rockefeller Family Collection, RG 2 OMR, ser. 87.1S4, box 122, folder Standard Oil / Davies-Ickes, RF.

12. Robert Engler, *The Politics of Oil* (Chicago: University of Chicago Press, 1961), p. 288.

13. Thomas M. Debevoise to Albert G. Milbank, 3/26/46; memo, "Twenty-five Largest Stockholders as of April 10, 1946," Rockefeller Family Collection, RG 2 OMR, box 122, folder Standard Oil / Davies-Ickes, RF. A close inspection of these documents shows that the Rockefeller family or the Rockefeller Foundation owned at least 12 percent of Standard Oil of California shares in 1946. Most stock analysts would regard this share as a controlling interest.

14. Frankfurter to McCloy, 2/6/46, Frankfurter Papers, LOC.

15. McCloy to Frankfurter, 2/13/46, Frankfurter Papers, LOC.

16. Robert D. Schulzinger, *The Wise Men of Foreign Affairs: The History of the Council on Foreign Relations* (New York: Columbia University Press, 1984), p. 120.

17. Isaacson and Thomas, *Wise Men,* p. 337.

18. Schulzinger, *Wise Men of Foreign Affairs,* p. 121.

19. E. J. Kahn, Jr., *The World of Swope* (New York: Simon & Schuster, 1965), p. 405.

20. J. Edgar Hoover to George E. Allen, 5/29/46, PSF, HST.

21. John Newhouse, *War and Peace in the Nuclear Age* (New York: Alfred A. Knopf, 1989) p. 61.

22. Dean Acheson oral history, PPS Files, HST; Newhouse, *War and Peace,* p. 62.

23. Dean Acheson, *Present at the Creation* (New York, W. W. Norton, 1969), p. 153.

24. McCloy to Frankfurter, 2/13/46, Frankfurter Papers, LOC.

25. J. Robert Oppenheimer, "Atomic Explosives," 4/6/46, PU.

26. Gregg Herken, *The Winning Weapon: The Atomic Bomb in the Cold War, 1945–1950* (New York: Alfred A. Knopf, 1980), pp. 155–57.

27. Joseph I. Lieberman, *The Scorpion and the Tarantula: The Struggle to Control Atomic Weapons, 1945–1949* (Boston: Houghton Mifflin, 1970), pp. 253, 255; Acheson, *Present at the Creation,* p. 152; Herken, *Winning Weapon,* p. 158.

28. Herken, *Winning Weapon,* p. 158.

29. Frankfurter to McCloy, 4/5/46, Frankfurter Papers, LOC; Herken, *Winning Weapon,* pp. 159–60.

30. Herken, *Winning Weapon,* p. 171; Daniel Yergin, *Shattered Peace: The Origins of the Cold War and the National Security State* (Boston: Houghton Mifflin, 1978), p. 238.

31. Herken, *Winning Weapon,* p. 366.

32. Ibid., p. 162.

33. Ferdinand Eberstadt diary, 3/25/46, Truman Library.

34. J. Anthony Panuch memorandum to Mr. Russell, 11/14/45, Papers of J. Anthony Panuch, HST.

35. Ibid.

36. Acheson, *Present at the Creation,* pp. 161–62.

37. Athan G. Theoharis and John Stuart Cox, *The Boss: J. Edgar Hoover and the Great American Inquisition* (Philadelphia: Temple University Press, 1988), pp. 199–200.

38. J. Edgar Hoover to George E. Allen, 5/29/46, PSF, FBI Atomic Bomb, HST. In 1945, Elizabeth Bentley told the FBI that Nathan Gregory Silvermaster, a Department of Agriculture economist, was the ringleader of an intelligence-gathering group in Washington.

39. Herken, *Winning Weapon,* p. 162.

40. Searls admitted to Lilienthal that he thought the resource survey could serve as a cover for espionage. "Searls said that in this way we would find out what was going on in Russia. And if the Russians refused to accept this proposal, then we would know that they would not go along on any international scheme, and . . . he didn't finish the statement, but his eyes indicated what he thought should then be recommended, and it was anything but pleasant." (Ibid., p. 165.)

41. Lieberman, *Scorpion and Tarantula,* pp. 282–83; Frankfurter to McCloy, 5/14/46, Frankfurter Papers, LOC.

42. Acheson oral history, n.d., PPF, HST.

43. For further discussion of the Baruch Plan, see D. F. Fleming, *The Cold War and Its Origins: 1917–1960* (Garden City, N.Y.: Doubleday, 1961), vol. I, pp. 370–75.

44. McCloy to Eugene Meyer, 6/13/46, box 35, Meyer Papers, LOC.

45. Merlo J. Pusey, *Eugene Meyer,* pp. 352–53.

46. Russell C. Leffingwell to Meyer, 12/23/46, box 32, Meyer Papers, LOC.

47. *Financial Times,* Dec. 9, 1946.

FOURTEEN: THE WORLD BANK: "MCCLOY ÜBER ALLES"

1. Emilio Collado oral history, p. 48, HST.

2. Emilio "Pete" Collado interview, Aug. 18, 1982.

3. Mrs. Frederick Warburg interview, April 10, 1984.

4. Robert W. Oliver, *International Economic Cooperation and the World Bank* (London: Macmillan, 1975), p. 239.

5. Robert L. Garner diary notations, 2/13/47, 2/15/47, 2/16/47, HST.

6. *Time,* Feb. 17, 1947.

7. Oliver, *International Economic Cooperation,* p. 237.

8. Edward S. Mason and Robert E. Asher, *The World Bank Since Bretton Woods* (Washington, D.C.: The Brookings Institution, 1973), p. 46.

9. Eugene Black interview, July 24, 1984.

10. Grigg cable to British Foreign Office, 2/18/47, *Assumption of Presidency,* PRO.

11. Minister of state to foreign secretary, 2/21/47, PRO.

12. *Financial Times,* Feb. 24, 1947.

13. Robert W. Oliver, "Early Plans for a World Bank," unpublished paper, Princeton University International Finance Section, Department of Economics, 1971, pp. 4–5, 17, 45.

14. Bolton to Mr. Rowe-Dutton, 5/13/47, PRO.

15. *New York Herald Tribune,* Feb. 28, 1947.

16. Hugh Dalton, M.P., to John Snyder, 3/3/47, Snyder Papers, HST.

17. Washington to London, 3/27/47, PRO.

18. Parsons to Foreign Office, 4/8–9/47, PRO.

19. Eugene Black interview, July 24, 1984.

20. Ibid.; Robert L. Garner diary, 3/17/47, HST.

21. Oliver, *International Economic Cooperation,* p. 238.

22. *NYT,* March 1, 1947.

23. *Time,* Feb. 17, 1947; Oliver, *International Economic Cooperation,* p. 241.

24. James Morris, *The Road to Huddersfield: A Journey to Five Continents* (New York: Pantheon, 1963), p. 24.

25. *Herald Tribune,* April 1947; Oliver, *International Economic Cooperation,* p. 249; Eugene Black interview, July 24, 1984.

26. *NYT,* May 27, 1947.

27. Harry S. Truman, *Years of Trial and Hope, 1946–52* (Garden City, N.Y.: Doubleday, 1956), p. 106.

28. Fleming, *Cold War and Origins,* vol. I, p. 443.

29. David Mayers, *George Kennan and the Dilemmas of U.S. Foreign Policy* (New York: Oxford University Press, 1988), p. 109.

30. Oliver, *International Economic Cooperation,* p. 260.

31. Mason and Asher, *World Bank Since Bretton Woods,* pp. 51–52.

32. Robert L. Garner diary, 3/19/47, HST.

33. Oliver, *International Economic Cooperation,* p. 242.

34. Charles L. Mee, Jr., *The Marshall Plan: The Launching of the Pax Americana* (New York: Simon & Schuster, 1984), pp. 118–19; Daniel Yergin, *Shattered Peace: The Origins of the Cold War and the National Security State,* p. 312; see also Catherine Gavin, *Liberated France* (New York: St. Martin's Press, 1955), pp. 167, 177.

35. Oliver, *International Economic Cooperation,* pp. 247–48.

36. *Newsweek,* July 28, 1947.

37. The British thought the French loan's 4.25-percent interest rate was "rather steep." (5/21/47, PRO.)

38. *Newsweek,* July 28, 1947.

39. Mason and Asher, *World Bank Since Bretton Woods,* p. 132. It would be a full decade before Wall Street deigned to give World Bank securities a triple-A rating.

40. Ibid., p. 131.

41. Privy Council to Hugh Dalton, 6/23/47, PRO.

42. Yergin, *Shattered Peace,* p. 236; Forrest C. Pogue, *George C. Marshall: Statesman 1945–1959* (New York: Viking, 1987), pp. 194–95.

43. *The Times* (London), June 17, 1947.

44. *NYT,* Jan. 16, 1948.

45. *Philadelphia Evening Bulletin,* Aug. 26, 1947.

46. *WP,* Sept. 11, 1947.

47. Yergin, *Shattered Peace,* pp. 327–28.

48. *Washington Star,* Sept. 13, 1947.

49. George Sokolsky, *Philadelphia Inquirer,* April 2, 1948.

50. Oliver, *International Economic Cooperation,* p. 239.

51. McCloy to Foster Dulles, 11/21/47, Dulles Papers, PU.

52. British Foreign Office memo, 5/29/47, PRO.

53. Oliver, *International Economic Cooperation,* p. 245.

54. Thomas Alan Schwartz, "From Occupation to Alliance: John J. McCloy and the Allied High Commission in the Federal Republic of Germany, 1949–52," unpublished thesis, Department of History, Harvard University, June 1985, p. 41; Mason and Asher, *World Bank Since Bretton Woods,* pp. 170–71. While McCloy was in Poland, his vice-president, Bob Garner, went over to the State Department to discuss the "various political difficulties" of the loan with Bob Lovett. Garner frankly told Lovett that the Bank would "need positive backing by the State Department . . . before the Bank

could afford to go into this ticklish situation." (Robert L. Garner diary, 9/30/47, HST; Robert Garner–Llewellyn E. Thompson memo of conversation, 9/30/47, John Snyder Papers, HST.)

55. Foreign Office cable to Washington, 11/10/47, PRO.

56. Foreign Office to Munro in Washington, 10/28/47, PRO.

57. Munro to Rowe-Dutton, 12/17/47, FO 371/62351 xc/a/54435, PRO.

58. Robert L. Garner, *This Is the Way It Was* (Chevy Chase, Md.: Chevy Chase Printing, 1972), p. 211.

59. CIA intelligence memorandum no. 167, 4/21/49, HST.

60. *NYT,* March 3, 1949.

61. Averell Harriman memo, 6/28/71, Harriman oral history Truman Era, AH.

62. Fleming, *Cold War and Origins,* vol. I, p. 293.

63. Mayers, *George Kennan,* p. 99.

64. *NYT,* April 6, 1948.

65. John J. McCloy, address, Economic Commission of the 9th International Conference of American States, 11:00 A.M., Monday, April 5, 1948.

66. Alexander Fleming, *Private Capital Flows to Developing Countries and Their Determination: Historical Perspectives, Recent Experience, and Future Prospects,* World Bank Staff Working Paper No. 484 (Washington, D.C.: The World Bank, 1981), p. 2.

67. *Time,* June 20, 1949; Robert Garner diary, 12/13/48, HST.

68. Mason and Asher, *World Bank Since Bretton Woods,* pp. 496–98.

69. John J. McCloy memorandum to the president, 1/7/49, Dean Acheson Papers, HST.

70. Robert L. Garner diary, 1/24/49, HST; Marquis Childs, *New York Post,* Jan. 24, 1949.

71. *NYT,* Feb. 1, 1949.

72. McCloy to Baruch, 2/21/49, Baruch Papers, PU.

73. Mason and Asher, *World Bank Since Bretton Woods,* pp. 61, 96; *Time,* June 20, 1949.

74. Garner, *The Way It Was,* pp. 220, 218.

75. Phillip Knightley, *The Master Spy: The Story of Kim Philby* (New York: Alfred A. Knopf, 1989), p. 153.

76. James Rowe, Jr., to Dean Acheson, 5/13/48, HST.

77. James Rowe, Jr., to Dean Acheson, 5/7/48, HST.

78. Commission on Organization of the Executive Branch of the Government, Committee on the National Security Organization, morning meeting of June 9, 1948, Strauss Papers, Hoover Committee, National Security Task Force Minutes, HH.

79. Gregory F. Treverton, *Covert Action: The Limits of Intervention in the Postwar World* (New York: Basic Books, 1987), pp. 35–36; U.S. Senate, *Final Report of the Select Committee to Study Governmental Operations with Respect to Intelligence Activities,* bk. IV, 4/23/76, p. 31.

80. John Ranelagh, *The Agency: The Rise and Decline of the CIA from Wild Bill Donovan to William Casey* (New York: Simon & Schuster, 1986), p. 115; William R. Corson, *The Armies of Ignorance: The Rise of the American Intelligence Empire* (New York: Dial, 1977), pp. 295, 299.

81. Walter Isaacson and Evan Thomas, *The Wise Men: Six Friends and the World They Made,* pp. 457–59.

82. Morning meeting, 9/9/48, Committee on National Security Organization, Meck Papers, Intelligence Gathering–Interview Sessions, p. 452, HH; see also Corson, *Armies of Ignorance,* p. 292.

83. Report on the Central Intelligence Agency, Sutherland and Bross for Eberstadt, 9/20/48, Meck Papers, Intelligence Gathering, National Security Task Force, HH.

84. Rhodri Jeffreys-Jones, *The CIA and American Democracy* (New Haven, Conn.: Yale University Press, 1989), p. 58.

85. Final Report, Senate Select Committee on Intelligence, "CIA History," bk. IV, p. 31; Ranelagh, *The Agency*, p. 218; Harriman cable to Hoffman, 3/28/49, AH.

86. McCloy to Baruch, 2/21/49, Baruch Papers, PU.

87. Robert Paul Browder and Thomas G. Smith, *Independent: A Biography of Lewis W. Douglas*, p. 326; Douglas cable re: McCloy travel plans, 4/6/49, LD.

88. Isaacson and Thomas, *Wise Men*, p. 515; McCloy interview.

89. Oliver, *International Economic Cooperation*, p. 240; Lew Douglas to McCloy, 5/11/49, LD.

90. Schwartz, "From Occupation to Alliance," pp. 72–74. When Harriman, who had objected to Clay's attempt to control ECA funds in Germany, learned that McCloy was to be Clay's successor, he said his old friend could "write his own ticket."

91. McCloy to Truman, 5/18/49, Official File, HST.

92. *The World Bank Annual Report 1988* (Washington, D.C.: The World Bank, 1989), p. 9.

93. John J. McCloy, "The Lesson of the World Bank," *Foreign Affairs*, July 1949.

FIFTEEN: GERMAN PROCONSUL: 1949

1. *NYT*, May 21, 1949.

2. Ibid., May 20, 1949.

3. Ronald Steel, *Walter Lippmann and the American Century*, p. 452.

4. Ibid., p. 451.

5. Richard Hiscocks, *The Adenauer Era* (Philadelphia: J. B. Lippincott, 1966), pp. 18–20, 24.

6. D. F. Fleming, *The Cold War and Its Origins: 1917–1960*, vol. I, p. 506.

7. Steel, *Walter Lippmann*, p. 453.

8. Thomas Alan Schwartz, "From Occupation to Alliance: John J. McCloy and the Allied High Commission in the Federal Republic of Germany, 1949–52," unpublished thesis, Department of History, Harvard University, June 1985, p. 65.

9. Lippmann to Kennan, Feb. 1, 1949, in John Morton Blum, ed., *Public Philosopher: Selected Letters of Walter Lippmann*, p. 528.

10. Axel von dem Bussche interview, April 5, 1984. Von dem Bussche, a member of the German resistance, remembers having long conversations with McCloy about the resistance and Germany's collective guilt.

11. For a general discussion of the Allied attitude toward the division of Germany, see Wolfram F. Hanrieder, *Germany, America, Europe: Forty Years of German Foreign Policy* (New Haven, Conn.: Yale University Press, 1989), pp. 6–11.

12. *Time*, June 20, 1949.

13. Ibid.

14. *Washington Star*, June 19, 1949.

15. "Excerpts from Conference on the Future of the Jews in Germany, Remarks by John J. McCloy, High Commissioner," McCloy HICOG Papers, NA (Suitland).

16. Allen Dulles to McCloy, 6/9/49, box 41, John J. McCloy 1949, Dulles Papers, PU.

17. *NYT*, June 30, 1949.

18. *WP*, July 2, 1949.

19. *NYT*, July 3, 1949.

20. *Newsweek,* July 11, 1949.

21. *Washington Star,* July 27, 1949.

22. Shepard Stone interview, March 1, 1984.

23. Edward M. M. Warburg to McCloy, 7/1/49, McCloy HICOG Papers, NA (Suitland); Jacques Attali, *A Man of Influence: The Extraordinary Career of S. G. Warburg* (Bethesda, Md.: Adler & Adler, 1987), p. 188.

24. Harry Greenstein to McCloy, 7/19/49, McCloy HICOG Papers, NA (Suitland).

25. "Introduction of Mr. McCloy by Harry Greenstein at the Conference on the Future of the Jews in Germany, Heidelberg, 31 July 1949," McCloy HICOG Papers, NA (Suitland).

26. Text of McCloy remarks, Heidelberg, 7/31/49, McCloy HICOG Papers, NA (Suitland).

27. Benjamin Buttenwieser oral history, Nov. 10–11, 1982, Columbia University.

28. Saul Sherman interview, Feb. 3, 1984; Benjamin Buttenwieser oral history, Columbia University.

29. Dean Acheson, *Sketches from Life of Men I Have Known* (New York: Harper & Brothers, 1959), p. 167.

30. Ibid., p. 168.

31. Mrs. Frederick Warburg interview, April 10, 1984.

32. Saul Sherman interview, Feb. 3, 1984.

33. Gates Davison interview, Nov. 5, 1986.

34. Acheson, *Sketches from Life,* p. 177.

35. Mrs. Frederick Warburg interview, April 10, 1984.

36. Dean Acheson, *Present at the Creation,* p. 288.

37. McCloy to Acheson, eyes only, 9/16/49, McCloy HICOG Papers, NA (Suitland).

38. Schwartz, "From Occupation to Alliance," p. 101.

39. *Washington Star,* Aug. 7, 1949.

40. *NYT,* Aug. 15, 1949.

41. *The Times* (London), Aug. 15, 1949.

42. *NYT,* Aug. 16, 1949.

43. James Warburg, *Germany: Key to Peace* (Cambridge, Mass.: Harvard University Press, 1953), p. 121.

44. Terence Prittie, *Adenauer: A Study in Fortitude* (Chicago: Cowles, 1971), p. 124. Prittie points out that in 1934 Adenauer wrote a letter to the Nazi minister of the interior in which he used rather obsequious language to request the payment of his pension of 12,000 marks a year and compensation for two homes requisitioned by the party in Cologne. Adenauer stated that he was "nationally reliable" and that his dealings with the Nazis had always been "correct." His plea was successful, and he used these monies to build the house he owned in the village of Rhondorf, where he was left alone up to 1944. Until very late, Adenauer had always thought the communists more dangerous than the Nazis. After his dismissal as mayor of Cologne, he never made any demonstration of his opposition to Hitler and never joined the resistance. (Ibid., pp. 94–95.)

45. Schwartz, "From Occupation to Alliance," p. 89.

46. Prittie, *Study in Fortitude;* William Manchester, *The Arms of Krupp* (Boston: Little, Brown, 1964), p. 307.

47. Charles Wighton, *Adenauer: A Critical Biography* (New York: Coward-McCann, 1963), pp. 109–10.

48. Benjamin Buttenwieser oral history, Columbia University; Charles W. Thayer, *The Unquiet Germans* (New York: Harper & Brothers, 1957), p. 120.

49. Schwartz, "From Occupation to Alliance," p. 88.

50. Acheson, *Sketches from Life,* p. 169.

51. Wilhelm Grewe interview, Feb. 9, 1984.

52. Prittie, *Study in Fortitude,* p. 153.

53. T. H. Tetens, *The New Germany and the Old Nazis* (London: Secker & Warburg, 1962), p. 63.

54. Warburg, *Germany: Key to Peace,* p. 120.

55. Transcript of 23rd meeting of the military governors in Frankfurt, 9/2/49, McCloy HICOG Papers, NA (Suitland).

56. Transcript of HICOG staff conference, 9/22/49, McCloy HICOG Papers, NA (Suitland).

57. HICOG staff-meeting transcript, 11/18/49, McCloy HICOG Papers, NA (Suitland).

58. Schwartz, "From Occupation to Alliance," pp. 124–25.

59. Ibid., pp. 125–26; Paul Weymar, *Adenauer: His Authorized Biography* (New York: E. P. Dutton, 1957), pp. 286–87; Konrad Adenauer, *Memoirs 1945–1953* (Chicago: Henry Regnery, 1966), p. 184; Prittie, *Study in Fortitude,* p. 154. It is possible that McCloy confused his "Canossa" anecdote with a later meeting between Adenauer and the high commissioners.

60. Weymar, *Authorized Biography,* pp. 288–89.

61. Prittie, *Study in Fortitude,* p. 153.

62. Ibid., p. 129.

63. Memo of conversation with American labor leaders, 3/14/50, DOS FOIA.

64. C. L. Sulzberger, *A Long Row of Candles* (Toronto: Macmillan, 1969), p. 893.

65. Walter Isaacson and Evan Thomas, *The Wise Men: Six Friends and the World They Made,* p. 516.

66. *NYT,* Sept. 14, 1949; McCloy cable to Acheson, 9/14/49, re: dismantling and his meeting with Adenauer and Schumacher, McCloy HICOG Papers, NA (Suitland).

67. Schwartz, "From Occupation to Alliance," p. 146; Axel von dem Bussche interview, April 5, 1984; Eric Warburg interview, March 10, 1986; see also Eric Warburg to Allen Dulles, 10/6/49, Allen Dulles Papers, box 42, PU.

68. *WP,* 10/10 49; Schwartz, "From Occupation to Alliance," pp. 153–54.

69. Schwartz, "From Occupation to Alliance," p. 148.

70. Ibid., p. 162.

71. Meeting of ambassadors at Paris, summary record, 10/21–22/49, HST.

72. Summary meeting between Adenauer and the high commissioners at Bonn-Petersberg, 10/28/49, McCloy HICOG Papers, NA (Suitland).

73. Prittie, *Study in Fortitude,* p. 152.

74. Secret memorandum of conversation of luncheon with Adenauer, McCloy, Acheson, et al., 11/13/49, McCloy HICOG Papers, NA (Suitland).

75. Acheson, *Sketches from Life,* pp. 172–73.

76. Ibid., p. 178.

77. Prittie, *Study in Fortitude,* pp. 154–55.

78. *NYT,* Nov. 30, 1949, Dec. 17, 1949; Prittie, *Study in Fortitude,* p. 156; Schwartz, "From Occupation to Alliance," p. 172.

79. McCloy cable to Acheson and Byroade, 12/2/49, McCloy HICOG Papers, NA (Suitland).

80. McCloy letter to Maurice Leon, 12/12/49, McCloy HICOG Papers, NA (Suitland).

81. "Possibility of Soviet Troop Withdrawal from Germany before the Summer of 1949," CIA report ORE 51-48; "The Possibility of Direct Soviet Military Action During

1949," CIA report ORE 46-48; "Review of the World Situation," July 1949, CIA report to the president, pp. 5–6, HST.

82. *NYT,* Nov. 8, 1949.

83. Secret memorandum of conversation of luncheon with Adenauer, McCloy, Acheson, et al., 11/13/49, McCloy HICOG Papers, NA (Suitland).

84. Prittie, *Study in Fortitude,* p. 158.

85. McCloy to Acheson, 12/22/49, McCloy HICOG Papers, NA (Suitland).

86. *The Times* (London), Dec. 23, 1949.

87. *NYT,* Dec. 24, 1949.

88. Shepard Stone interview, March 1, 1984.

89. Tetens, *New Germany and Old Nazis,* p. 100.

90. Schwartz, "From Occupation to Alliance," p. 169.

91. Tetens, *New Germany and Old Nazis,* p. 51.

92. Robert Wistrich, *Who's Who in Nazi Germany* (London: Weidenfeld & Nicolson, 1982), pp. 93–94. Adenauer had offered Globke the powerful post of state secretary of the Chancellory in 1949, but Globke turned it down on the grounds that the position was too prominent. He accepted the same post in 1953. (Prittie, *Study in Fortitude,* p. 217.)

93. Benjamin Buttenwieser oral history, Columbia University; Axel von dem Bussche interview, April 5, 1984.

94. Tetens, *New Germany and Old Nazis,* p. 253.

95. Edwin Hartrich, *The Fourth and Richest Reich: How the Germans Conquered the Postwar World* (New York: Macmillan, 1980), pp. 68–70.

96. Transcript of HICOG staff meeting, 11/30/49, McCloy HICOG Papers, NA (Suitland).

97. Memo by Mortimer Kollender, acting chief of the HICOG Administrative Justice Division, to the general counsel, 10/11/49, McCloy HICOG Papers, NA (Suitland).

98. McCloy memo to McClain, 12/9/49, with attachments: McCloy memo to McCloy, 12/9/49; draft letter from McCloy to Joseph Cardinal Frings, archbishop of Cologne, 12/9/49; and archbishop to McCloy, 11/17/49, McCloy HICOG Papers, NA (Suitland).

99. Telford Taylor to McCloy, 12/27/49, McCloy HICOG Papers, NA (Suitland).

SIXTEEN: THE DILEMMA OF GERMAN REARMAMENT

1. T. H. Tetens, *The New Germany and the Old Nazis,* p. 100.

2. McCloy extended a dinner invitation to Frau Elizabeth Struenck at the urging of Allen Dulles. Struenck's husband had served as one of Dulles's underground couriers during the war and had informed Dulles about the plot to assassinate Hitler. (Dulles to McCloy, 8/31/49; McCloy to Dulles, 9/30/49, Allen Dulles Papers, box 41, PU.)

3. Drexel Sprecher interview, May 25, 1984; McCloy to Eugene Meyer, 12/14/49, Meyer Papers, box 35, LOC.

4. *NYT,* Jan. 12, 1950.

5. Draft statement regarding formation of a clemency board, 1/19/50, McCloy HICOG Papers, NA (Suitland).

6. McCloy to Acheson, 1/7/46, HST.

7. *Stars and Stripes,* Feb. 2, 1950.

8. McCloy to Acheson, 2/17/50; Acheson to McCloy, 2/23/50, McCloy HICOG Papers, NA (Suitland).

9. *NYT,* Jan. 27, 1950.

10. Ibid., Feb. 7, 1950.

11. *WP,* Feb. 8, 1950.

12. *New York Post,* Feb 8, 1950; *New York Compass,* Feb. 8, 1950.

13. Thomas Alan Schwartz, "From Occupation to Alliance: John J. McCloy and the Allied High Commission in the Federal Republic of Germany, 1949–52," unpublished thesis, Department of History, Harvard University, June 1965, p. 192.

14. *NYT,* April 19, 1950.

15. McCloy to Adenauer, 4/25/50, McCloy HICOG Papers, NA (Suitland).

16. Drexel Sprecher interview, July 11, 1984.

17. William Manchester, *The Arms of Krupp,* pp. 647–48.

18. *NYT,* April 3, 1950.

19. Schwartz, "From Occupation to Alliance," p. 199.

20. *NYT,* April 5, 1950.

21. Schwartz, "From Occupation to Alliance," p. 236.

22. *NYT,* May 15, 1950; Schwartz, "From Occupation to Alliance," p. 201.

23. *NYT,* May 3, 1950.

24. Ibid., May 23, 1950.

25. Ibid., June 17, 1950; *WP,* June 17, 1950.

26. Schwartz, "From Occupation to Alliance," p. 237.

27. McCloy to Stimson, 6/28/50, McCloy HICOG Papers, NA (Suitland).

28. *NYT,* July 4, 1950.

29. Charles W. Thayer, *The Unquiet Germans,* pp. 210–11.

30. *NYT,* July 5, 1950; Schwartz, "From Occupation to Alliance," p. 298.

31. Schwartz, "From Occupation to Alliance," p. 242.

32. *NYT,* Aug. 23, 1950; Don Cook, *Forging the Alliance* (New York: Arbor House/William Morrow, 1989), p. 224.

33. Schwartz, "From Occupation to Alliance," pp. 299–301.

34. Ibid., pp. 305–6, 312–13.

35. Ibid., pp. 301, 323.

36. *NYT,* Aug. 24, 1950.

37. John Dornberg, *The New Germans: Thirty Years After* (New York: Macmillan, 1975), p. 55.

38. That summer, McCloy's office hired a political scientist, James Pollack, to sample German political opinions. Among other things, Pollack had concluded that the German people had "lost its military ardor and would not, without considerable difficulty, cooperate in the revival of any kind of military force." (Schwartz, "From Occupation to Alliance," pp. 389–90.)

39. Thayer, *Unquiet Germans,* pp. 223–24.

40. *NYT,* Sept. 7, 1950.

41. Ibid., Sept. 6, 1950.

42. Schwartz, "From Occupation to Alliance," pp. 332–33.

43. McCloy to Acheson, Sept. 20, 1950, cited in Schwartz, "From Occupation to Alliance," pp. 368, 424. The French would have been shocked had they known that, sometime in late September or early October 1950, McCloy quietly met with Adenauer's defense adviser, General Hans Speidel, who during the war had served as Rommel's chief of staff. Speidel revealed that recently a group of former Wehrmacht generals like himself had secretly met in a secluded monastery and had drawn up a blueprint of a new German army. They envisioned a twelve-division army of 250,000 men, complemented by naval and air defenses. (Schwartz, "From Occupation to Alliance," p. 398.)

44. Schwartz, "From Occupation to Alliance," pp. 390, 396.

45. Ibid., pp. 332, 358.

46. Top-secret intelligence report, n.d., AH.

47. McCloy to Acheson cable, 12/27/50, DOS FOIA declassified 9/7/82.

48. McCloy to Acheson, 12/18/50, McCloy HICOG Papers, NA (Suitland).

49. Schwartz, "From Occupation to Alliance," pp. 406–7.

50. Stephen E. Ambrose, *Eisenhower: Soldier, General of the Army, President-Elect,* p. 508.

SEVENTEEN: McCLOY AND U.S. INTELLIGENCE OPERATIONS IN GERMANY

1. Christopher Simpson, *Blowback: America's Recruitment of Nazis and Its Effects on the Cold War* (New York: Weidenfeld & Nicolson, 1988), pp. 187–88. Erhard Dabringhaus, *Klaus Barbie: The Shocking Story of How the U.S. Used This Nazi War Criminal as an Intelligence Agent* (Washington, D.C.: Acropolis Books, 1984), p. 79.

2. HICOG staff meetings, Aug. 1, 1950, July 25, 1950, Aug. 22, 1950, McCloy HICOG Papers, NA (Suitland).

3. Magnus Linklater, Isabel Hilton, and Neal Ascherson, *The Nazi Legacy: Klaus Barbie and the International Fascist Connection* (New York: Holt, Rinehart & Winston, 1984), p. 177.

4. Justice Department Ryan Report, Klaus Barbie and the United States Government, August 1983, p. 93, and tab 53, p. 99.

5. Ibid., p. 101.

6. Tom Bower, *Klaus Barbie: The "Butcher" of Lyon* (New York: Pantheon, 1984), p. 170.

7. Justice Department Ryan Report, p. 104.

8. Ibid., p. 107.

9. Ibid., p. 108.

10. Justice Department Ryan Report Exhibits, tab 77. Another State Department document, declassified and released only after the Ryan Report was published, confirms that Byroade "talked the matter over with McCloy and Riddleberger. . . ." (Courtesy of Christopher Simpson.)

11. Justice Department Ryan Report Exhibits, tab 58.

12. Brendan Murphy, *The Butcher of Lyon: The Story of the Infamous Nazi Klaus Barbie* (New York: Empire Books, 1983), p. 251.

13. Justice Department Ryan Report Exhibits, tab 77.

14. Ibid., tab 80.

15. Justice Department Ryan Report, p. 97.

16. Justice Department Ryan Exhibits, tab 58.

17. Murphy, *Butcher of Lyon,* p. 250.

18. Linklater et al., *Nazi Legacy,* p. 180.

19. Justice Department Ryan Report, pp. 121–22.

20. Linklater et al., *Nazi Legacy,* p. 181.

21. Justice Department Ryan Report, p. 132.

22. Ibid., p. 147.

23. Allan A. Ryan, Jr., *Quiet Neighbors: Prosecuting Nazi War Criminals in America* (New York: Harcourt Brace Jovanovich, 1984), pp. 26–27.

24. A year later, in August 1951, McCloy himself assisted one such recruitment when he certified that a former SA general, Kurt Blome, was "not likely to become [a] security threat to the U.S." Blome had confessed to interrogators in 1945 that he had once appealed to Himmler for SS funds to finance a medical institute where he intended to experiment with a plague vaccine on concentration camp inmates. He was narrowly

acquitted of war crimes at Nuremberg when prosecutors were unable to prove that he had acted on his expressed intention. He was hired by the U.S. Chemical Corps in August 1951 at a salary of $6,800 annually. Such cases were common. (Tom Bower, *The Paperclip Conspiracy: The Hunt for Nazi Scientists* [Boston: Little, Brown, 1987], p. 254.)

25. Ibid., p. 152.

26. There is some evidence that Shute himself was a knowing participant in the cover-up. In late August 1950, when the CIC learned that a request for Barbie's arrest had finally been issued, CIC's commanding officer, Colonel David G. Erskine, cabled EUCOM to remind them that back in May 1950 CIC had "coordinated" the Barbie case with Shute and several other intelligence officials: "The decision reached on subject case [Barbie] at that time is well known to the above-mentioned persons." The May decision, of course, was the one in which CIC decided not to turn Barbie over to the French. If Shute was fully informed of this decision in early May, then he must be considered a central player in the cover-up. The Justice Department's Ryan Report investigation of the affair argues that no weight should be given this cable, because Erskine had no personal contact with Shute. Instead, the Ryan Report speculates that the Erskine cable was merely an attempt to muddy the waters and slow down the extradition process. This explanation seems unnecessarily complicated. If it wasn't true, why would Erskine name Shute as a party to the decision, and thereby risk having the matter bucked all the way up to the high commissioner's intelligence coordinator? That could have led to the unraveling of the entire cover story.

27. McCloy HICOG daily journal, 3/30/50, McCloy HICOG Papers, NA (Suitland).

28. John Loftus, *The Belarus Secret* (New York: Alfred A. Knopf, 1982), p. 59. Loftus reports that Gehlen was impressed with the work of Radislaw Ostrowsky, who had been mayor of Nazi-occupied Smolensk when Gehlen had his headquarters in that city. Ostrowsky had returned to Byelorussia in June 1941 with the Einsatzgruppen killing squads, and later became president of Nazi Byelorussia. After the war, Ostrowsky worked closely with Gehlen's "Org," providing him with the names of Belarus SS Brigade veterans willing to work for American intelligence. (Ibid., p. 57.)

29. Simpson, *Blowback,* p. 44.

30. Michael Burke interview, Sept. 23, 1985; Charles Whiting, *Gehlen: Germany's Master Spy* (New York: Ballantine, 1972), p. 130; Rhodri Jeffreys-Jones, *The CIA and American Democracy,* p. 104.

31. A professor with a doctorate in law from the University of Berlin, Dr. Six was a cold, calculating Nazi intellectual who as late as 1944 could tell a conference on the "Jewish Question," "The physical elimination of Eastern Jewry would deprive Jewry of its biological reserves. The Jewish Question must be solved not only in Germany but also internationally." Six was closely associated with the Wannsee Institute, where the Final Solution was planned in January 1942, and where Germany's top academic experts on the Soviet Union gathered during the war to plan the strategic aspects of the war on the Eastern front.

32. Simpson, *Blowback,* pp. 46–49. McCloy reduced Six's twenty-year sentence to ten years in January 1951.

33. Otto John, *Twice Through the Lines* (New York: Harper & Row, 1972), p. 210; Whiting, *Gehlen,* pp. 127–28; Loftus, *Belarus Secret,* p. 60.

34. Though he confirmed an ex-Nazi like Reinhard Gehlen as Adenauer's external-intelligence adviser, at the end of 1950 McCloy chose an individual with quite a different background as head of the newly created Federal Internal Security Office. Otto John was one of the few surviving members of the July 20, 1944, plot to assassinate Hitler. A lawyer and a confirmed democrat, he had narrowly escaped execution and after the war had the

courage to assist the Allies in the trial of various war criminals at Nuremberg. McCloy was fascinated by the German resistance and enjoyed talking with John about his exploits during the war. But Adenauer and John's counterpart, General Gehlen, did not share the high commissioner's enthusiasm for the new head of internal intelligence. Adenauer knew that John had close links to the British, whom the chancellor had disliked ever since they had rudely dismissed him from office as mayor of Cologne in 1945. As for Gehlen, he quite simply regarded John as a traitor for his involvement in the July 20 plot. Needless to say, John's tenure was a rocky one. It was finally brought to an abrupt end in 1954, when Gehlen handed Adenauer a dossier on John alleging that the internal-security chief was a homosexual and possibly a Soviet double agent. Shortly afterward, John mysteriously disappeared into East Berlin, where ten days later he appeared at a press conference to say that he had defected. Later, he reappeared in West Berlin, claiming that he had been kidnapped and forced to cooperate with the Soviets. Though the West Germans tried him and sentenced him to four years in prison, the CIA today has concluded that the evidence, on balance, supports John's story. (Otto John interview, Feb. 20, 1984; John Ranelagh, *The Agency: The Rise and Decline of the CIA from Wild Bill Donovan to William Casey*, p. 749.) Don Cook, a *New York Herald Tribune* reporter, interviewed John shortly before his "defection" or "kidnapping" to East Berlin. John surprised Cook by suddenly exclaiming that Gehlen was creating a "potential Gestapo organization." Cook ascribed John's disappearance to a combination of emotional exhaustion and frustration at having lost his bureaucratic struggle with Gehlen. (Don Cook interview, Dec. 19, 1983.)

35. Officially, there was a ban on the hiring of Nazis. But even some of the earliest Labor Service units in 1946 had a large number of SS veterans. In 1950, when someone in the bureaucracy proposed regulations that would strictly prohibit the recruitment of all former SS officers, McCloy's personal assistant and old Cravath colleague, Chauncey G. Parker, overturned the regulation. By this time, there were some thirty thousand Labor Service recruits armed with light infantry weapons, ostensibly prepared to wage guerrilla warfare inside the Soviet bloc in the aftermath of a nuclear attack. These Labor Service units had also become a warehouse for some of Gehlen's networks of Baltic and Ukrainian Nazi collaborators. (Simpson, *Blowback*, pp. 142–45.)

36. Ibid., pp. 123–24, 145.

37. Michael Burke interview, Sept. 23, 1985.

38. Ibid.; Michael Burke, *Outrageous Good Fortune: A Memoir* (Boston: Little, Brown, 1984), pp. 139–44, 149–53, 160. Nicholas Bethell, *Betrayed* (New York: Times Books, 1984), pp. 119–23.

39. Michael Burke interview, Sept. 23, 1985.

40. Simpson, *Blowback*, pp. 146–47; William Blum, *The CIA: A Forgotten History* (London: Zed Books, 1986), p. 66.

41. On McCloy's wiretapping, see McCloy cable to State Department, 10/19/51, control no. 5899, McCloy HICOG papers, NA (Suitland). For RFE/RL budget, see Ranelagh, *The Agency*, p. 216.

42. HICOG staff meeting, 1/30/51, McCloy HICOG Papers, NA (Suitland).

43. Ambassadors' conference, Frankfurt, Feb. 5–8, 1951, item 7, Coordination of Psychological Warfare Programs, U.S. High Commissioner, McCloy HICOG Papers, NA (Suitland). See also top-secret memo from Allen Dulles to director of the CIA and chairman of the Psychological Strategy Board, "Analysis of the power of the Communist Parties of France and Italy and of measures to counter them," AH.

44. Blum, *CIA: A Forgotten History*, p. 114. Murray Waas reported in *The Nation* (June 19, 1982) that Springer received $7 million in the early 1950s.

45. Thomas Schwartz, "From Occupation to Alliance: John J. McCloy and the Allied

High Commission in the Federal Republic of Germany, 1949–52," unpublished thesis, Department of History, Harvard University, June 1965, pp. 332–33.

46. Peter Coleman, *The Liberal Conspiracy* (New York: Free Press, 1989), pp. 27–32.

47. Ibid., p. 9.

48. Ranelagh, *The Agency,* p. 246; McCloy to Paul G. Hoffman, 12/31/51, McCloy HICOG Papers, NA (Suitland). By this time, McCloy already had a close relationship to the Ford Foundation, which in the summer of 1951 contributed $25,000 to the McCloy Fund, a charitable trust consisting of funds contributed by various corporations and McCloy friends. McCloy was given exclusive control over the distribution of these private funds. (Paul Hoffman to McCloy, 7/16/51, Fund for the Republic Papers, box 16, PU.)

49. Ranelagh, *The Agency,* p. 194.

50. Ibid., p. 246.

51. McCloy was partially influenced by theoreticians of psychological warfare like Edward Meade Earle of Princeton's Institute for Advanced Study. A prominent historian, Earle had served on the OSS's Board of Analysts and had helped Bill Donovan recruit academics for intelligence work during the war. By the early 1950s, Earle was working with Allen Dulles and C. D. Jackson on various intelligence projects, including "some of the problems of 'psychological warfare' directed toward our allies." McCloy and Earle had been personal friends for some time, and from their correspondence it is clear that the Princeton academic helped provide McCloy with a theoretical framework for HICOG's intelligence activities. A typical anticommunist liberal, Earle emphasized the importance of public relations. He thought rewarding and promoting liberal-thinking Germans and critical institutions such as newspapers and labor unions was a positive tactic, and McCloy agreed, particularly when he felt he had so little time left. Financing Axel Springer's press empire was a case in point: Springer was chosen because he gave evidence of liberal attitudes and a willingness to publish American-style critical, muckraking journalism. Similarly, McCloy favored the funding of SPD labor unions and individual Social Democratic politicians in order to build a credible anticommunist opposition to Adenauer's Christian Democrats. (Edward Meade Earle to Lieutenant General Al Gruenther, 10/1/51; McCloy to Earle, 12/22/49, Edward Meade Earle Papers, PU; Robin W. Winks, *Cloak and Gown: Scholars in the Secret War, 1939–1961* [New York: William Morrow, 1987], p. 70; *Who's Who in America,* 1936–37, vol. 19, p. 784.)

EIGHTEEN: THE CLEMENCY DECISIONS

1. William Manchester, *The Arms of Krupp,* p. 377.

2. Benjamin B. Ferencz, *Less Than Slaves: Jewish Forced Labor and the Quest for Compensation* (Cambridge, Mass.: Harvard University Press, 1979), p. 70.

3. Some of the beatings took place in the cellar of the Main Administration Building, in which Krupp had his office. The journalist Bernard Fall later reported, "Sometimes, the German employees on the first floor complained about the screams and cries that emanated from those cellars, but the directing members of the Krupp firm had their offices on the third floor. . . ." (Bernard B. Fall, "The Case of Alfried Krupp," *Prevent World War III,* Summer 1951, published by the Society for the Prevention of World War II, pp. 39–40.)

4. Manchester, *The Arms of Krupp,* pp. 644–45.

5. Conrad E. Snow to Jack Tate, 7/26/50, DOS FOIA.

6. J. M. Raymond memo to Robert Bowie, 9/11/50, DOS FOIA.

7. John Bross memo to McCloy, 8/18/50, McCloy HICOG Papers, NA (Suitland).

8. Thomas Schwartz, "From Occupation to Alliance: John J. McCloy and the Allied High Commission in the Federal Republic of Germany, 1949–52," unpublished thesis, Department of History, Harvard University, June 1965, p. 451.

9. *NYT,* Aug. 26, 1950.

10. Ferencz, *Less Than Slaves,* p. 74.

11. *NYT,* Sept. 14, 1950.

12. On Jan. 2, 1951, Adenauer reiterated his hope for a "great clemency." (See McCloy to State Department, 1/3/51, DOS FOIA; Schwartz, "From Occupation to Alliance," pp. 453–54.)

13. Schwartz, "From Occupation to Alliance," pp. 453–54.

14. Meeting between Mr. McCloy and delegation from Bundestag, 1/9/51, McCloy HICOG Papers, NA (Suitland).

15. T. H. Tetens, *The New Germany and the Old Nazis,* p. 206.

16. Manchester, *The Arms of Krupp,* p. 648.

17. But there was no doubt about his guilt. Von Weizsäcker's own son, who in the 1980s became president of West Germany, later publicly acknowledged the seriousness of his father's crimes.

18. *NYT,* Oct. 15, 1950. On Oct. 17, 1950, Buttenwieser told a HICOG staff meeting, "I guess Mr. McCloy was impressed by the letters [on behalf of Weizsäcker] because they came from the type of people whose influence you couldn't buy. . . . It is true that there was the letter [signed by Weizsäcker] that sent some 6,000 people to some concentration camp and he okayed it, but there was considerable evidence to say that in some ways he had not been as bad as he might have been; therefore, Mr. McCloy said that there ought to be some indication that with so many people speaking in his behalf, they should not be unheard." (HICOG staff meeting, 10/17/50, McCloy HICOG Papers, NA (Suitland).

19. Acheson cable to McCloy, 11/16/50, McCloy HICOG Papers, NA (Suitland); Acheson memorandum of conversation with Truman, 11/16/50, HST.

20. Schwartz, "From Occupation to Alliance," pp. 401–2.

21. Adenauer to McCloy, 12/5/50; McCloy to Adenauer, 12/19/50, McCloy HICOG Papers, NA (Suitland).

22. To complicate matters for McCloy, the expropriation order had never been carried out, so the Krupp companies lay intact, operating under the original Krupp-appointed managers. Earlier in the year, several American politicians had written McCloy, protesting this fact and urging him to seize the properties and redistribute them to new owners. In answering these appeals, McCloy's legal counsel had discovered a problem. In March 1949, shortly before leaving Germany, General Clay had found cause to amend the confiscation order. The original order had specified that Krupp property would be "delivered to the Control Council for Germany. . . ." This would have given the Soviets grounds for a claim to at least a portion of the confiscated Krupp assets in the Ruhr. So HICOG lawyers rewrote the order, providing that the zone commander in each of the four occupied sectors would take control of Krupp property in that sector. This gave the Soviets no claim to properties in West Germany. But the new language also stated that Krupp assets would only be "subject to forfeiture," which was different from outright confiscation. John Bross, HICOG's deputy legal counsel, told McCloy in the spring of 1950 that his office would study the matter, but, clearly, McCloy realized now that, if the Nuremberg expropriation judgment was to be carried out, he would have to issue a confiscation order in the American sector and persuade his fellow commissioners to do the same in their

sectors. To further complicate matters, the Krupp family was attempting to block any expropriation order on the grounds that the Nazi law under which Bertha Krupp had transferred sole ownership to her son was illegal. In the spring of 1950, with the appointment of the Peck Panel, McCloy simply allowed the matter to slide. (John Bross memo to Chester McClain, 1/19/50; General Hays to Governor Lehman, 3/20/50; Senator Joseph C. O'Mahoney to Hays, 3/10/50, McCloy HICOG Papers, NA (Suitland).

23. Manchester, *The Arms of Krupp,* p. 649.

24. Charles W. Thayer, *The Unquiet Germans,* pp. 234–35.

25. Schwartz, "From Occupation to Alliance," p. 458.

26. Manchester, *The Arms of Krupp,* pp. 646, 653.

27. Schwartz, "From Occupation to Alliance," pp. 459–60.

28. Eugene Davidson, *The Trial of the Germans* (New York: Collier, 1966), p. 255.

29. McCloy to Javits, 4/18/51, McCloy HICOG Papers, NA (Suitland).

30. Manchester, *The Arms of Krupp,* p. 649.

31. Ibid., pp. 656–57.

32. Christopher Simpson, *Blowback: America's Recruitment of Nazis and Its Effects on the Cold War,* p. 191.

33. Schwartz, "From Occupation to Alliance," p. 445.

34. Manchester, *The Arms of Krupp,* p. 654.

35. Ibid.

36. Ferencz, *Less Than Slaves,* p. 6.

37. Wellington Long, *The New Nazis of Germany* (Philadelphia: Chilton, 1968), p. 29.

38. Tragically, the one Krupp director who had been an anti-Nazi, Ewald Löser, was left off the clemency list in what McCloy later called a "dreadful mistake." Löser had risked his life in several conspiracies to get rid of Hitler, including the ill-fated July 20 plot. (Manchester, *The Arms of Krupp,* pp. 652, 434–35.)

39. Ibid., pp. 659–62.

40. *NYT,* Aug. 17, 1950; Simpson, *Blowback,* p. 192.

41. Manchester, *The Arms of Krupp,* p. 642.

42. Ibid., p. 652.

43. Schwartz, "From Occupation to Alliance," p. 516. Schwartz cites an interview with Abs as evidence of the "importance of the Krupp pardon to German economic leaders."

44. Ibid., p. 462.

45. Transcript of Jan. 9, 1951, HICOG staff meeting, McCloy HICOG Papers, NA (Suitland).

46. McCloy to Judge David W. Peck, 2/5/51, McCloy HICOG Papers, NA (Suitland).

47. There were three capital cases in which the Peck Panel recommended the death penalty but McCloy nevertheless commuted the sentences to life imprisonment. In at least two of these cases, the defendants claimed they had evaded orders to round up and kill Jews. Both the Nuremberg tribunal and the Peck Panel dismissed this defense, and nowhere in McCloy's HICOG Papers is there any indication of the "new evidence" on which he decided to commute these death penalties.

48. Landsberg, "A Documentary Report," p. 9, McCloy HICOG Papers, NA (Suitland).

49. Ferencz, *Less Than Slaves,* p. 74.

50. McCloy cable to State Department, 3/5/51, McCloy HICOG Papers, NA (Suitland).

51. Report of the Advisory Board (Peck Panel), p. 8, DOS FOIA.

52. *Trials of War Criminals before the Nuremberg Military Tribunals,* vol. IV: "The Einsatzguppen Case," p. 559.

53. Nor was there any consistency in McCloy's application of this criterion for clemency. Otto Ohlendorf, one of the men who McCloy said should die, had himself, for a time in the summer of 1941, resisted carrying out a Himmler order to execute a large number of Jews near Odessa. (Robert E. Conant, *Justice at Nuremberg* (New York: Harper & Row, 1983).

54. J.M. Raymond to Robert Bowie, 9/11/50, DOS FOIA, no. 123.

55. Report of the Advisory Board on Clemency, p. 24, DOS FOIA, no. 123.

56. Excerpt From H. A. Byroade's testimony, House Appropriations Committee hearing, 2/28/51, DOS FOIA no. 123.

57. Transcript of staff meeting, 1/9/51, McCloy HICOG Papers, NA (Suitland).

58. John M. Raymond memo, "Memorandum Regarding Review of Subsequent Nuremberg Proceedings," June 29, 1950, DOS FOIA, no. 123.

59. Schwartz, "From Occupation to Alliance," p. 463; Ferencz, *Less Than Slaves,* p. 72.

60. On the contrary, Adenauer's closest aide, Herbert Blankenhorn, went so far as to submit a memorandum to McCloy questioning his judgment in the Pohl case and in two of the Einsatzgruppen cases, involving Erich Naumann and Werner Braune. Blankenhorn's memo displayed utter ignorance of the facts in all three of these cases, and had to be dismissed out of hand. (Memorandum re: Blankenhorn memo of Feb. 12, 1951, 2/22/51, McCloy HICOG Papers, NA [Suitland].)

61. McCloy to Cardinal Frings, 3/15/51, McCloy HICOG Papers, NA (Suitland).

62. McCloy to Axel Kolbe, 5/15/51, McCloy HICOG Papers, NA (Suitland).

63. *NYT,* Feb. 20, 1951.

64. Frankfurter to McCloy, 3/5/51, Frankfurter Papers, LOC.

65. McCloy to Frankfurter, 7/11/51, Frankfurter Papers, LOC.

66. Schwartz, "From Occupation to Alliance," p. 457; Manchester, *The Arms of Krupp,* p. 658.

67. Jack Fishman, *Long Knives and Short Memories: Lives and Crimes of the 7 Nazi Leaders Sentenced at Nuremberg* (New York: Richardson & Steirman, 1986), pp. 176–77, 306, 388.

68. Matthias Schmidt, *Albert Speer: The End of a Myth* (New York: St. Martin's Press, 1984).

NINETEEN: NEGOTIATING AN END TO OCCUPATION

1. Dean Acheson, *Present at the Creation,* p. 589.

2. Thomas Schwartz, "From Occupation to Alliance: John J. McCloy and the Allied High Commission in the Federal Republic of Germany, 1949–52," unpublished thesis, Department of History, Harvard University, June 1965, pp. 419–20.

3. Memorandum by Mr. McCloy, September 4, 1951, Paris, McCloy HICOG Papers, NA (Suitland).

4. Richard J. Barnet, *The Alliance: America-Europe-Japan, Makers of the Postwar World* (New York: Simon & Schuster, 1983), p. 137.

5. *Washington Star,* Nov. 4, 1951.

6. *WP,* Dec. 18, 1951.
7. McCloy cable, personal for Byroade, 8/28/51, DOS FOIA.
8. McCloy to Department of State, 11/6/51, McCloy HICOG Papers, NA (Suitland).
9. D. F. Fleming, *The Cold War and Its Origins: 1917–1960,* vol. I, p. 517.
10. *The Times* (London), Jan. 13, 1952.
11. Schwartz, "From Occupation to Alliance," p. 589.
12. Ibid., p. 591.
13. Ibid., p. 593.
14. Ibid., p. 594.
15. Ibid., p. 605.
16. HICOG staff meeting, 3/11/52, p. 1, McCloy HICOG Papers, NA (Suitland).
17. Schwartz, "From Occupation to Alliance," p. 618.
18. Wolfram F. Hanrieder, *Germany, America, Europe: Forty Years of German Foreign Policy,* p. 152.
19. Ibid., p. 154.
20. Alan Brinkley, "The Most Influential Private Citizen in America: Minister Without Portfolio," *Harper's,* February 1983, p. 40.
21. Acheson, *Present at the Creation,* p. 640; Dean Acheson, *Sketches from Life of Men I Have Known,* p. 178.
22. Schwartz, "From Occupation to Alliance," p. 626.
23. Edwin Hartrich, *The Fourth and Richest Reich: How the Germans Conquered the Postwar World,* p. 152.
24. McCloy later admitted as much to Acheson: "The final conventions bear little resemblance to those which were initially proposed, and the differences are primarily due to Allied concessions to the German negotiators and to Allied recognition that in the new relationship the Federal Republic was justified in demanding full equality." (Acheson, *Present at the Creation,* p. 640.)
25. Lily Gardner Feldman, *The Special Relationship Between West Germany and Israel* (Winchester, Mass.: Allen & Unwin, 1984), pp. 62–65; Nahum Goldmann, *The Autobiography of Nahum Goldmann: Sixty Years of Jewish Life* (New York: Holt, Rinehart & Winston, 1969), pp. 265–67.
26. Walter LaFeber, *America, Russia and the Cold War: 1945–1975* (New York: John Wiley and Sons, 1976), p. 132.
27. Acheson, *Present at the Creation,* pp. 645, 647.
28. Schwartz, "From Occupation to Alliance," p. 628; *The Times* (London), May 24, 1952.
29. McCloy cable to State Department, 5/2/52, McCloy HICOG Papers, NA (Suitland).
30. Henry A. Kissinger, "Notes on Germany," 1952, records of the Psychological Strategy Board, HST (courtesy of Dennis Bilger).
31. Hanrieder, *Germany, America, Europe,* pp. 156, 162.
32. Schwartz, "From Occupation to Alliance," p. 659.
33. *Philadelphia Evening Bulletin,* June 12, 1952.
34. *New York Herald Tribune,* June 14, 1952.
35. Schwartz, "From Occupation to Alliance," p. 629.
36. C. L. Sulzberger, *A Long Row of Candles,* p. 950.
37. Closing remarks by Mr. John J. McCloy, Third U.S. Resident Officers' Conference, McCloy HICOG Papers, NA (Suitland).
38. Shep Stone to Paul Hoffman, 8/29/52, Hoffman Papers, HST.

39. Townsend Hoopes, *The Devil and John Foster Dulles* (Boston: Little, Brown, 1973), p. 136; Peter Collier and David Horowitz, *The Rockefellers: An American Dynasty,* p. 271.

40. McCloy interview, Sept. 14, 1984; Hoopes, *Devil and Dulles,* pp. 135–37; see also McCloy oral-history interview, 12/18/70, p. 18, DDE.

BOOK FOUR

TWENTY: CHAIRMAN OF THE CHASE MANHATTAN BANK: 1953–60

1. *NYT,* n.d. (Jan. 1953).

2. Crawford Wheeler, ed., "The Chase Manhattan Story;" McCloy oral-history interview, 2/63, p. 307, CMB.

3. *NYT,* Dec. 7, 1952.

4. McCloy to Arthur A. Kimball, 1/5/53, DDE.

5. Frankfurter to McCloy, 1/2/53; McCloy to Frankfurter, 1/19/53; Frankfurter to McCloy, 1/22/53, Frankfurter Papers, LOC; *NYT,* Jan. 3, 1953; Dean Acheson, *Present at the Creation,* pp. 711–13.

6. John J. McCloy, *The Challenge to American Foreign Policy; NYT,* Jan. 15, 1953.

7. *Philadelphia Evening Bulletin,* July 5, 1953; *Washington Star,* July 19, 1953.

8. McCloy, *Challenge,* pp. 79–80.

9. "McCloy of the Chase," *Fortune,* June 1953, p. 141; McCloy oral history, 2/63, pp. 308–10, CMB.

10. *NYT,* n.d. (Jan. 1953).

11. John Donald Wilson, *The Chase: The Chase Manhattan Bank, N.A., 1945–1985* (Boston: Harvard Business School Press, 1986), pp. 44–45.

12. *NYT,* n.d. (Jan. 1953).

13. "McCloy of the Chase," p. 141; McCloy oral history, 2/63, p. 310, CMB.

14. "McCloy of the Chase," p. 141.

15. Ibid.

16. Metropolitan Life Insurance Co. had for many years been closely aligned with Rockefeller interests through reciprocal directorships with Chase National Bank. See Philip H. Burch, Jr., *Elites in American History: The New Deal to the Carter Administration,* vol. III, p. 16.

17. Wilson, *The Chase,* pp. 54–55.

18. Ibid., p. 51; George Champion oral history, 7/7, 7/12/79, p. 46, CMB.

19. George Champion oral history, 7/7, 7/12/79, p. 59, CMB.

20. Wilson, *The Chase,* pp. 55–56.

21. Victor E. Rockhill oral history, 9/13, 10/5/79, p. 22, CMB.

22. Ibid., p. 22.

23. Wilson, *The Chase,* p. 56.

24. John J. McCloy oral history, 2/63, p. 316, CMB.

25. Ibid., pp. 317–18.

26. The Dartmouth case, argued before the Supreme Court by Daniel Webster, established that the federal or state government could not abrogate contractual rights between private parties. Though the case has never been overturned, the courts have implicitly recognized, particularly since the New Deal, the right of the government to regulate certain private contractual relationships.

27. Wilson, *The Chase,* p. 61.

28. Alvin Moscow, *The Rockefeller Inheritance* (Garden City, N.Y.: Doubleday, 1977), p. 218.

29. *Wall Street Journal,* Jan. 14, 1955.

30. Wilson, *The Chase,* pp. 64, 67.
31. *WP,* Jan. 26, 1955; *NYT,* Jan. 26, 1955.
32. *Wall Street Journal,* July 6, 1955.
33. Collier and Horowitz, *The Rockefellers,* p. 208. The letter cited is dated July 25, 1945.
34. Wilson, *The Chase,* pp. 70, 91. In 1960, Nelson Rockefeller alone held eighteen thousand shares of Chase Manhattan stock.
35. McCloy to Frankfurter, 3/28/55, Frankfurter Papers, LOC.
36. Harold van B. Cleveland and Thomas F. Huertas, *Citibank: 1812–1970* (Cambridge, Mass.: Harvard University Press, 1985), pp. 239–41.
37. Wilson, *The Chase,* p. 73.
38. Ibid., p. 72.

TWENTY-ONE: McCLOY, McCARTHYISM, AND THE EARLY EISENHOWER PRESIDENCY

1. *NYT,* Jan. 27, 1953; James B. Conant, *My Several Lives: Memoirs of a Social Inventor* (New York: Harper & Row, 1970), pp. 536–39.
2. *NYT,* April 3, 1953.
3. Telford Taylor, *Grand Inquest* (New York: Simon & Schuster, 1955), p. 82.
4. *NYT,* April 4, 1953.
5. Ronald Steel, *Walter Lippmann and the American Century,* pp. 484, 499.
6. Fred I. Greenstein, *The Hidden-Hand Presidency* (New York: Basic Books, 1982), p. 169.
7. *Manchester Guardian,* April 9, 1953.
8. *NYT,* April 11, 1953.
9. *Manchester Guardian,* April 9, 1953.
10. Lately Thomas, *When Even Angels Wept: An Objective Reappraisal of the Senator Joseph McCarthy Affair* (New York: William Morrow, 1973), p. 313. Benjamin Buttenwieser claims that at the time he and McCloy also received reports that HICOG electronic surveillance of Cohn and Schine's hotel room revealed evidence of homosexual behavior, or what Buttenwieser euphemistically called "pillow fights." (Benjamin Buttenwieser interview, July 15, 1982.)
11. *NYT,* May 13, 1953.
12. John J. McCloy to the president, 5/26/53, DDE.
13. *NYT,* May 27, 1953.
14. Ibid., June 11, 1953.
15. Drew Pearson, "Washington Merry-Go-Round," *Philadelphia Evening Bulletin,* March 13, 1954.
16. *NYT,* June 15, 1953.
17. Piers Brendon, *Ike: His Life and Times,* p. 251.
18. Eisenhower diary, 1/10/57, Eisenhower Archives.
19. One such shipment, in December 1953, amounted to 940 pounds of prime rib, sirloin strips, lamb racks, smoked bacon, sausage, shrimp, walnuts, and Texas Ruby Red grapefruit. (Amos G. Carter to Eisenhower, 12/29/53, Eisenhower Archives.)
20. A mark of their friendship was the fact that Eisenhower had once entrusted Richardson with his life savings. Sometime in 1951, he gave Richardson $20,000 to invest in one of the oil man's ventures. Late that year, at a time when he was publicly denying any intention to run for the presidency, he had second thoughts and wrote Richardson to return the money without any of the profit that might already have accrued. He told Richardson that a "public official should, under no circumstances, be involved in anything

that might even *look* unreasonably profitable. . . ." (Eisenhower to Richardson, 12/26/51, DDE.)

21. Harry A. Bullis memo, 6/22/53, "Dinner with President Eisenhower at the White House," DDE. For evidence that McCloy on this or some previous occasion had urged Eisenhower to defend his civil servants, see McCloy to Foster Dulles, 7/13/53, DDE.

22. Richardson to Eisenhower, 7/2/53; Eisenhower to Richardson, 8/8/53, DDE.

23. *NYT*, Aug. 29, 1953, June 12, 1953.

24. Conant, *My Several Lives*, pp. 576–77; *WP*, June 27, 1953.

25. McCloy to Foster Dulles, 7/13/53; Dulles to McCloy, 7/20/53, DDE.

26. William P. Rogers to J. Edgar Hoover, 12/21/53, DDE; Webster/Eisenhower letters, 7/17/53, 8/7/53, DDE.

27. FBI memo, 11/21/52, quoting Nichols memo to Tolson, 11/5/52, FBI FOIA document, file no. 94-4sub4666.

28. FBI memo, 12/27/50, quotes 9/28/45 anonymous letter to Truman, FBI FOIA document, file no. 121-27291. In the summer of 1953, one informant reported to the Bureau that she had had an argument with Ellen McCloy, who had told her that "the Russians were a grand people, intelligent, kind and considerate." (FBI memo, 7/8/53, p. 10, FBI FOIA document, file no. 116-382-159.) One can see from McCloy's FBI security file that, throughout the postwar period, the Bureau repeatedly dredged up the fact that McCloy had vigorously defended his decision to give officer commissions to some American communists during the war.

29. FBI memo, Jones to Deloach, 12/1/60, quoting FBI memos from 1945 and 1950, FBI FOIA document, file no. 94-4sub4666. In 1955, Hoover himself scrawled on a security report, "McCloy is no friend of the F.B.I." (FBI memo, 4/8/55, FBI FOIA document, File No. 94-4sub4666. Hoover's dislike of McCloy clearly stemmed from the lawyer's championing of a central intelligence agency and his willingness to second-guess Hoover's judgment on various security issues during the war.

30. ". . . Mr. McCloy does considerable work for Mr. [Allen] Dulles." (Nease memo to Tolson, 8/4/58, FBI FOIA document, file no. 94-4sub4666.

31. Sidney Zion, *The Autobiography of Roy Cohn* (Secaucus, N.J.: Lyle Stuart, 1988), p. 61; Nicholas von Hoffman, *Citizen Cohn: The Life and Times of Roy Cohn* (New York: Doubleday, 1988), pp. 123–24, 282–84.

32. David M. Oshinsky, *A Conspiracy So Immense* (New York: Free Press, 1983), p. 257; Richard Gid Powers, *Secrecy and Power: The Life of J. Edgar Hoover*, p. 318.

33. Westbrook Pegler to Lewis Douglas, n.d., LD. For background on Anthony Panuch's charges, see William F. Buckley, Jr., and L. Brent Bozell, *McCarthy and His Enemies: The Record and Its Meaning* (Chicago: Henry Regnery, 1954), pp. 234–36. Pegler didn't know it, but, as high commissioner, McCloy had once quietly refused to disinvite Helen Buttenwieser from accompanying him on his official plane back to Germany, even though Helen was at the time serving as a defense counsel to Alger Hiss. She thought this little act of courtesy displayed considerable political courage on McCloy's part. (Helen Buttenwieser interview, March 17, 1983.)

34. During the early 1950s, the CIA helped create West Germany's largest media conglomerate by funneling an estimated $7 million to Axel Springer. (William Blum, *The CIA: A Forgotten History*, pp. 114–16.) Tom Braden, who headed the Agency's International Organizations Division during these years, has estimated that the Congress of Cultural Freedom received $800,000 to $900,000 annually from the CIA. (John Ranelagh, *The Agency: The Rise and Decline of the CIA from Wild Bill Donovan to William Casey*, p. 246.)

35. William B. Pickett, "The Eisenhower Solarium Notes", *Society for Historians of*

American Foreign Relations Newsletter, vol. 16, no. 2 (June 1985), pp. 1–10; Christopher Simpson, *Blowback: America's Recruitment of Nazis and Its Effects on the Cold War,* p. 244; *FRUS, 1952–1954: National Security Affairs,* vol. II, pt. 1, pp. 349–34.

36. Blanche Wiesen Cook, *The Declassified Eisenhower: A Divided Legacy of Peace and Political Warfare* (Garden City, N.Y.: Doubleday, 1981), p. 177.

37. Eisenhower to McCloy, 8/15/53, DDE.

38. Stephen E. Ambrose, *Eisenhower the President: 1952–1969* (London: George Allen & Unwin, 1984), p. 113. List of invitees, stag dinner at the White House, 9/23/53, DDE.

39. Memorandum by John J. McCloy to the secretary of state, 3/16/53, *FRUS, 1952–1954,* vol. V, pt. 1, pp. 770–73.

40. *NYT,* Oct. 18, 1953, Oct. 22, 1953.

41. *New York Herald Tribune,* May 30, 1953; see also M. S. Handler, "Germans Look to Future," *NYT,* Aug. 9, 1953.

42. *NYT,* Oct. 29, 1953; *WP,* Oct. 29, 1953.

43. Thomas C. Reeves, *The Life and Times of Joe McCarthy: A Biography* (New York: Stein & Day, 1982), p. 530; Oshinsky, *Conspiracy So Immense,* pp. 349–50; Richard M. Fried, *Men Against McCarthy* (New York: Columbia University Press, 1976), pp. 273–77.

44. C. D. Jackson diary, 11/27–12/2/53, DDE; Oshinsky, *Conspiracy So Immense,* p. 352; Fried, *Men Against McCarthy,* p. 274; Reeves, *Life and Times of Joe McCarthy,* pp. 530–31. At this point, the only public figure associated with the army willing to challenge McCarthy by name was retired Brigadier General Telford Taylor, then practicing law in New York. In a speech at West Point, Taylor courageously called McCarthy a "dangerous adventurer." For this, McCarthy promptly showed reporters a copy of Taylor's confidential civil-service form, which he pointed out contained a security "flag" indicating an "unresolved question of loyalty." Taylor's commission as a reserve officer, McCarthy demanded, should be revoked. Once again the senator had displayed an uncanny ability to produce leaked security documents which, however unsubstantiated, somehow lent credence to his slanderous charges. (Reeves, *Life and Times of Joe McCarthy,* p. 524.)

45. *NYT,* Nov. 27, 1953.

46. Reeves, *Life and Times of Joe McCarthy,* p. 525.

47. Oshinsky, *Conspiracy So Immense,* p. 360.

48. Philip M. Stern, with the collaboration of Harold P. Green, *The Oppenheimer Case: Security on Trial* (New York: Harper & Row, 1969), p. 223.

49. AP, *NYT,* Feb. 7–8, 1954.

50. *WP,* Feb. 10, 1954; *Washington Star,* Feb. 10, 1954.

51. Tyler Abell, ed., *Drew Pearson: Diaries 1949–1959* (New York: Holt, Rinehart & Winston, 1974), p. 297.

52. *Washington Star,* Feb. 17, 1954; *NYT,* Feb. 17, 1954.

53. Frankfurter to McCloy, 3/3/54, McCloy to Frankfurter, 3/8/54, Frankfurter Papers, LOC.

54. Frankfurter to McCloy, 3/10/54, Frankfurter Papers, LOC.

55. Telcon: Eisenhower and Lucius Clay, 2/25/54, DDE.

56. H.C. Lodge to Eisenhower, 2/23/54, DDE.

57. In his 1945 congressional testimony, McCloy said, "I was responsible as much as anyone." (George E. Sokolsky, *WP,* March 22, 1954.)

58. Thomas, *When Even Angels Wept,* p. 465.

59. Drew Pearson, *Philadelphia Evening Bulletin,* March 13, 1954.

60. Oshinsky, *Conspiracy So Immense,* p. 401.

61. *NYT,* March 19, 1954.

62. *Washington Star,* March 19, 1954.

63. McCloy interview, July 10, 1986.

64. E. Murphy to Mr. Franklin, 6/4/56, "Facts on Dr. Oppenheimer's connection with the Council's study group on U.S.-Soviet Relations," CFR.

65. *NYT,* June 20, 1954.

66. McCloy to Frankfurter, 4/13/54, Frankfurter Papers, LOC.

67. He told Ike there were so few qualified scientists to work on the Manhattan Project that "we would have put a pro-German to work who had these qualities . . . or even a convicted murderer." (McCloy-Eisenhower, 4/16/54, 4/23/54, DDE; McCloy interview, March 19, 1986.)

68. Stern, *The Oppenheimer Case,* p. 197.

69. Arthur Krock, *NYT,* July 1, 1954. Lloyd Garrison believed that McCloy was "one of the two or three strongest witnesses." (Lloyd Garrison interview, Jan. 31, 1984.)

70. *NYT,* July 1, 1954, June 20, 1954; John Crosby, *WP,* July 2, 1954; Stern, *The Oppenheimer Case,* p. 346.

71. Though Chevalier apparently had already rejected the British engineer's overture, he nevertheless thought it was something Oppenheimer should "know of." (Stern, *The Oppenheimer Case,* pp. 44–45.)

72. Ibid., p. 347; *NYT,* June 20, 1954; John Crosby, *WP,* July 2, 1954.

73. Stern, *The Oppenheimer Case,* pp. 381–83.

74. McCloy to Frankfurter, "Tuesday," n.d., Frankfurter Papers, LOC.

75. Frankfurter to McCloy, 7/16/54, Frankfurter Papers, LOC.

76. On April 24, 1953, a Ford Foundation officer visited C. D. Jackson in his White House office and said that "Ford Foundation policy has shifted again and [we] may be able to do something in [the] cold war." A few days later, McCloy was formally elected a trustee of the Foundation.

The Foundation's officers had for some time been uncertain about how to respond to requests from the CIA to fund various projects. Back in the spring of 1951, Bedell Smith, Allen Dulles, and Frank Wisner visited New York and met with Foundation President Rowan Gaither. The Agency's officials wished to feel out Gaither concerning whether the Foundation could support seven different CIA projects: the CCF, the University of Free Berlin, the National Committee for Free Asia, the University of Teheran, an unnamed research institute in Cambridge, Massachusetts, and a proposal made by George Kennan to fund Russian and East European defectors. Minutes of the meeting indicate Gaither listened sympathetically to the Agency's pitch.

A few weeks later, the Foundation seemed to have decided on a policy in dealing with the CIA: Foundation officer Bernard L. Gladieux wrote Gaither that such requests from the Agency should first be cleared with Tex Moore, McCloy's old friend from Cravath who now was the Foundation's chief outside counsel. If Moore saw no legal problems, the request would be sent through the Foundation's normal staff channels. Only a few days later, however, vigorous objections from the Foundation's lower-ranking staff led Gaither, for the moment, to turn down the Agency's requests.

This was not the end of the matter. By late 1952, after McCloy had joined as a consultant on international projects, the Foundation's leadership evidently had undergone a change of heart: at least one grant of $150,000 was awarded that year to the National

Committee for a Free Europe, which as a CIA front ran Radio Free Europe. (C. D. Jackson diary, 4/24/53, DDE; conference memo, 4/3/51, folder "Central Intelligence Agency," box one, Gaither Presidential Papers, FF; Bernard L. Gladieux to Rowland Gaither, 4/23/51; Gaither to Gladieux, 4/27/51, folder "Central Intelligence Agency," box one, Gaither Presidential Papers, FF; Blum, *Forgotten History,* p. 356.)

77. McCloy interview, July 10, 1986.

78. Ibid.; Ranelagh, *The Agency,* p. 218.

79. Don Price oral history, pp. 61–62, FF. Bob Bowie, then director of the State Department's Policy Planning Staff, also weighed in, encouraging the Foundation to finance exchange programs involving lawyers, public administrators, doctors, and engineers. The idea, he said, would be "to strengthen in the underdeveloped countries the institutional structure and growth of the middle class. . . . We should be doing business with private institutions, quality institutions on an elite basis, and hook in with a local selection apparatus."

80. Don Price oral history, p. 63, FF.

81. McCloy interview, July 10, 1986.

82. Don Price memo, May 21, 1954, found in appendix to Don Price oral history, FF.

83. McCloy interview, July 10, 1986. Price himself later justified the arrangement by saying, "I don't think we could have kept clean if our policy had been never to talk to the government." (Don Price oral history, 6/22/72, p. 70, FF.)

84. Ibid., p. 70.

85. Memo, n.d., Congress for Cultural Freedom file; Don Price oral history, 6/22/72, p. 69, FF. Some Foundation monies were funneled directly to CIA-sponsored publications. Melvin Lasky, editor of the German-language magazine *Der Monat* (and later the London-based and CIA-funded *Encounter* magazine), recalled how he visited McCloy at his Chase office in the spring of 1954 and explained that he needed to find a private source of funding to replace Agency subsidies. "McCloy was crucial to getting us new funding," recalled Lasky. "He took the proposal to the Ford Foundation board and arranged three years of funding for the magazine. I thought that was quite a lot at the time." Altogether, the Foundation replaced some $60,000 to $70,000 of CIA subsidies for *Der Monat.* (Melvin Lasky phone interview, Jan. 2, 1987; Don Price oral history, p. 56, FF; *New York Herald Tribune,* July 9, 1954.

86. Don Price oral history, 6/22/72, p. 58, FF; Cleon O. Swayzee to Donald Mulcahy, CIA, 4/30/59 et al., General Correspondence, 1959, reel 1316, FF.

87. Charles Merrill, *The Checkbook: The Politics and Ethics of Foundation Philanthropy* (Boston: Oelgeschlager, Gunn & Hain, 1986), pp. 447–50.

88. The Bricker Amendment was an attempt by isolationist Republicans to restrict the power of the executive branch to conduct foreign policy. McCloy bluntly warned Ike that "there can be no compromise" on the issue, that as the "trustee of the executive powers of the President" he could not relinquish his constitutional prerogatives. After a lengthy exchange of correspondence, Eisenhower—who had been tempted to compromise—was persuaded by McCloy to stonewall the Congress. (McCloy cable to Eisenhower, 1/54; Eisenhower to McCloy, 1/13/54; McCloy to Eisenhower, 1/18/54, DDE.)

89. McCloy to Eisenhower, 1/21/54, DDE.

90. McCloy to DDE, 4/16/54; DDE to McCloy, 4/23/54; telcon, 4/29/54, DDE.

91. Ambrose, *Eisenhower the President,* p. 73.

92. Eisenhower to Joseph McConnell, 1/16/61, DDE.

93. Ambrose, *Eisenhower the President,* p. 75; McCloy to DDE, 1/21/54, DDE.

94. Robert Griffith, "Dwight D. Eisenhower and the Corporate Commonwealth," *American Historical Review,* vol. 87, no. 1 (Feb. 1982), pp. 87–122.

95. Eisenhower to F. Dulles, 1/16/54, DDE.

96. *NYT,* March 11, 1954; Matthew Josephson, *The Money Lords* (New York: Weybright & Talley, 1972), pp. 242–45.

97. CFR list of members attending dinner in honor of J. F. Dulles, 1/12/54, AH; *NYT,* Jan. 13, 1954.

98. DDE to C. D. Jackson, 5/17/54, DDE.

99. C. D. Jackson diary, 7/8/53, DDE.

100. Robert Cutler to DDE, 8/18/54, DDE.

101. C. D. Jackson diary, 8/7/54, DDE.

102. C. D. Jackson log, 8/4/54, DDE.

103. Ibid.

104. Cook, *Declassified Eisenhower,* p. 177.

105. C. D. Jackson diary, 8/11/54; untitled memo, 8/11/54, DDE.

106. Laurence Shoup and William Minter, *Imperial Brain Trust,* p. 197.

107. John Donald Wilson, *The Chase: The Chase Manhattan Bank, N.A., 1945–1985,* p. 79.

108. *Wall Street Journal,* March 14, 1955; *London Times,* March 14, 1955.

109. *WP,* March 11, 1955.

110. Robert Lacey, *Ford: The Men and the Machine* (Boston: Little, Brown, 1986), p. 452.

111. McCloy interview, July 10, 1986.

112. *Wall Street Journal,* Nov. 7, 1955.

113. Peter Collier and David Horowitz, *The Fords: An American Epic* (New York: Summit Books, 1987), pp. 258–59.

114. Lacey, *Men and Machine,* pp. 453–54.

115. *Wall Street Journal,* Nov. 7, 1955.

116. Allan Nevins and Frank Ernest Hill, *Ford: Decline and Rebirth 1933–1962* (New York: Charles Scribner's Sons, 1962), p. 422; Dr. G. van Hall to Rowan Gaither, 11/23/55, Rowan Gaither Files, box VI, file "Ford Motor Co. Correspondence," FF.

117. Nevins and Hill, *Decline and Rebirth,* pp. 422–23.

118. Judge Wyzanski statement at board-of-trustees meeting, 1/4/56, Rowan Gaither Files, box VI, file "Ford Motor Co. Correspondence," FF.

119. Statements at board-of-trustees meeting, 1/5/56, Rowan Gaither Files, box VI, file "Ford Motor Co. Correspondence," FF.

120. Lacey, *Men and Machine,* pp. 454, 658, 705; Nevins and Hill, *Decline and Rebirth,* p. 424.

TWENTY-TWO: IKE'S WISE MAN

1. Victor E. Rockhill oral history, 9/13/79, 10/5/79, p. 21, CMB.

2. John D. Wilson, *The Chase: The Chase Manhattan Bank, N.A., 1945–1985,* p. 41; Wilbur Crane Eveland, *Ropes of Sand: America's Failure in the Middle East* (New York: W. W. Norton, 1980), p. 142; State Department cable from Gallman in Baghdad to secretary of state, 2/21/56, DOS FOIA; Eisenhower telcon with Herbert Hoover, Jr., 3/15/56, DDE ("President said McCloy went over unquestionably to keep King Saud from transferring big account to Switzerland").

3. Later that year, in September 1956, Kim Philby arrived in Beirut and met his future wife, Eleanor, in the Saint George bar. Eleanor was then married to *New York Times* correspondent Sam Pope Brewer.

4. Eveland, *Ropes of Sand,* p. 75.

5. Wilbur Crane Eveland interview, July 25, 1982. In his memoirs, Eveland would

later write that McCloy told him he was "going to see King Saud to explain the extent to which his foolish policies were making it difficult for Chase to continue the very loans upon which Saud was almost dependent." (Eveland, *Ropes of Sand,* p. 142.)

6. Eveland, *Ropes of Sand,* pp. 142–43.

7. Robert Lacey, *The Kingdom: Arabia and the House of Saud* (New York: Harcourt Brace Jovanovich, 1981), p. 312. The official view in Washington was, in retrospect, overly alarmist. The Saudi royal family was certainly not anti-Western or even pro-Nasser. Within two years, King Saud would be caught red-handed in a plot to assassinate Nasser.

8. Henry Luce, "To Pin Down One Point of American Policy," 4/22/56, DDE.

9. Wadsworth cable to secretary of state, no. 370, 2/16/56, DOS FOIA.

10. "Dispatches," *The Nation,* June 22, 1985.

11. Gallman to secretary of state, 2/21/56, State Department cable 852, Baghdad, DOS FOIA.

12. McCloy's private brand of diplomacy was usually regarded as a most useful intervention by U.S. Embassy officials. After his trip to Iraq, one Foreign Service officer wrote a friend, "Jack McCloy made a great contribution in Iraq even though he was in Baghdad only three days." (Clarence B. Randall to McCloy, 10/17/56, DDE.) McCloy also spent a short time in Teheran on this trip, before returning to New York. (State Department cable 767, Teheran-Washington, "Visit to Teheran of Mr. John J. McCloy," 3/10/56, DOS FOIA.)

13. Presidential schedule, 3/20/56, DDE.

14. Eugene Black interview, July 24, 1984.

15. *America,* June 16, 1956; *London Times,* May 24, 1956, May 30, 1956; *NYT,* May 23, 1956, June 3, 1956; Henry L. Roberts, *Russia and America: Dangers and Prospects* (New York: Harper & Brothers, 1956). A paperback edition of this book was published in the fall of 1956 with a first print run of a hundred thousand. (See AH, McCloy: 1956.)

16. Kennett Love, *Suez: The Twice Fought War* (New York: McGraw-Hill, 1969), p. 319.

17. *America,* June 16, 1956.

18. *NYT,* Oct. 9, 1955.

19. Drew Pearson, "Washington-Merry-Go-Round," July 27, 1956, July 11, 1956.

20. McCloy to Fulton Lewis, Jr., 8/3/56, DDE.

21. George Whitney to president, 3/9/56, DDE diary, 9/18/54, 10/10/55, 2/9/56, 3/13/56, 4/9/56, 5/25/55, DDE. Ike's first choice for the vice-presidential spot was always Robert Anderson of Texas. See also Stephen E. Ambrose, *Eisenhower the President: 1952–1969,* pp. 319–26.

22. Kennett Love, *Suez,* pp. 297, 360. Not everyone in official Washington was taken by surprise. Frank Wisner, deputy director of the CIA, asked one of his subordinates a week before the crisis whether Nasser would nationalize the Canal if the United States reneged on its promise of aid for the High Dam. (See Miles Copeland, *The Game of Nations* [London: Weidenfeld & Nicolson, 1969], p. 24.)

23. If McCloy and Black seemed overly tolerant of Nasser's concept of a "positive neutrality," both the Dulles brothers were, by contrast, easily provoked by the Egyptian leader's actions. At one point during the crisis that summer, Allen Dulles ran out of patience listening to an intelligence officer's attempt to convey how Nasser saw the situation, and angrily threatened, "If that colonel of yours pushes us too far, we will break him in half." (Thomas Powers, *The Man Who Kept the Secrets: Richard Helms and the CIA* [New York, Alfred A. Knopf, 1979], pp. 85, 127.) Miles Copeland reports that Foster Dulles was so angered by Nasser's nationalization of the Canal that he ordered the CIA to blow up a famous television and radio tower built by Nasser in 1954 with $3 million

in CIA funds meant to bribe him. The explosives planted by the Agency, however, were found and defused by an Egyptian intelligence officer. (See Miles Copeland, *The Real Spy World* [London: Weidenfeld & Nicolson, 1974], p. 63.) Citing a retired CIA officer, John Marks says that the Agency sent three assassination teams to Egypt during this period with instructions to eliminate Nasser. Nothing happened. The Church Committee later confirmed that it had investigated this allegation but never came to a conclusion as to whether the assassination attempts actually took place. (See Powers, *Man Who Kept Secrets,* pp. 335–36.)

24. Jacques Georges-Picot, *The Real Suez Crisis* (New York: Harcourt Brace Jovanovich, 1978), pp. 55, 59, 101, 123–24, 133–36, 163.

25. Walter Isaacson and Evan Thomas, *The Wise Men: Six Friends and the World They Made,* p. 572.

26. Judge Charles E. Wyzanski, Jr., letter to author, Nov. 23, 1982.

27. *NYT,* Nov. 7, 1956; see also Drew Pearson, "Washington Merry-Go-Round," Nov. 10, 1956.

28. Eugene Black interview, July 24, 1984.

29. Lodge to Hoover, 12/17/56, State Department cable released to DOS FOIA, 1/30/85.

30. Lodge to secretary of state, 12/11/56, State cable, DOS FOIA, 1/30/85.

31. Memorandum of conversation, McCloy, 4/4/57, State Department memo, DOS FOIA; CFR meeting, 4/5/57.

32. Copeland, *Game of Nations,* p. 130.

33. CFR meeting, John J. McCloy, "Report on the Suez Problem," 4/5/57, CFR.

34. John J. McCloy oral history, p. 328, CMB.

35. Wilson, *The Chase,* pp. 106–7; John J. McCloy oral history, pp. 330–31, CMB; Victor E. Rockhill oral history, p. 111, CMB.

36. David Rockefeller made his first major purchase of a painting, Renoir's *Gabriel,* in 1951, for $50,000. (See Alvin Moscow, *The Rockefeller Inheritance,* p. 224.)

37. John J. McCloy oral history, p. 339, CMB; Peter Collier and David Horowitz, *The Rockefellers: An American Dynasty,* p. 408.

38. Wilson, *The Chase,* pp. 110–11; John J. McCloy oral history, 2/63, p. 351, CMB; Moscow, *Rockefeller Inheritance,* p. 232.

39. Moscow, *Rockefeller Inheritance,* p. 238; Victor E. Rockhill oral history, pp. 112–13, CMB.

40. Collier and Horowitz, *The Rockefellers,* p. 312.

41. *Newsday,* Jan. 9, 1957; John J. McCloy oral history, 2/63, pp. 348–49, CMB; George Champion oral history, pp. 53, 67, CMB; Collier and Horowitz, *The Rockefellers,* p. 408.

42. Collier and Horowitz, *The Rockefellers,* p. 318.

43. Wilson, *The Chase,* p. 35; Collier and Horowitz, p. 318.

44. Christian Herter memo to Douglas Dillon, 6/4/57, DDE.

45. Moscow, *Rockefeller Inheritance,* pp. 214–16, 226; Collier and Horowitz, *The Rockefellers,* p. 312.

46. Philip H. Burch, Jr., *Elites in American History: The New Deal to the Carter Administration,* vol. III, p. 125.

47. Minutes of the 106th meeting of the board of directors of the CFR, 10/28/54, AH.

48. Minutes of the 107th meeting of the CFR, 2/28/55, AH.

49. Robert D. Schulzinger, *The Wise Men of Foreign Affairs,* p. 124; *Annual Report of the Council on Foreign Relations, 1955–1956* (New York: Council on Foreign Relations, 1956).

50. Minutes of the 106th annual meeting of the board of directors of the CFR, 10/28/54, AH; "Contributions and Pledges Received to date . . . ," 1/7/53, confidential CFR document; Walter H. Mallory to Averell Harriman, 4/25/55; CFR document, "Comparison of Budget with Actual Receipts and Disbursements, 4/30/55"; Shoup and Minter, *Imperial Brain Trust,* p. 96.

51. *CFR Annual Report, 1955–1956,* p. 1.

52. George S. Franklin, Jr., "Notice to Members," 12/63, LD.

53. Shoup and Minter, *Imperial Brain Trust,* pp. 42–43.

54. Lewis Douglas to Frank Altschul, 12/7/53, LD. This letter was apparently written but never mailed to Altschul.

55. Leonard Silk and Mark Silk, *The American Establishment* (New York: Basic Books, 1980), p. 184; Stephen R. Graubard, *Kissinger: Portrait of a Mind* (New York: W. W. Norton, 1973), pp. 60–62; John Kenneth Galbraith, "Staying Awake at the Council on Foreign Relations," *The Washington Monthly,* Sept. 1984, p. 42; *NYT,* Oct. 30, 1982; *CFR Annual Report, 1955–1956.*

56. Silk and Silk, *American Establishment,* p. 184.

57. *CFR Annual Report, 1955–1956,* p. 9.

58. Ibid., p. 1.

59. Shoup and Minter, *Imperial Brain Trust,* pp. 38–40; CFR *Annual Report, 1955–56,* p. 7.

60. McCloy oral history, p. 26, DDE; Schulzinger, *Wise Men of Foreign Affairs,* pp. 150–51.

61. *NYT,* Oct. 14, 1954.

62. Schulzinger, *Wise Men of Foreign Affairs,* pp. 153–54.

63. Marvin Kalb and Bernard Kalb, *Kissinger* (Boston: Little, Brown, 1974), pp. 50–51; Graubard, *Portrait of a Mind,* p. 60.

64. James Laughlin memo to Don Price, 10/15/53, Rowan Gaither Files, box III, "Intercultural Publications," 3/5/53–1/8/55, FF; Kissinger–Milton Katz correspondence, 6/15/53 et al., Grant File, PH 52-86, PA 54-137, roll no. 1027, FF.

65. Confidential study-group report, digest of discussion, "Nuclear Weapons and Foreign Policy," 2/21/55, CFR.

66. By the time the book came out, Kissinger had already urged one such limited war in the Middle East. One day, while working on the book, he happened to be in Washington when the Czech arms deal to Nasser's Egypt was announced. "My recommendation at the time," he later told a symposium hosted by Bill Casey's Research Institute of America, "was that the Soviet [sic] arms deal had to be stopped by all means—even by the use of force." (Confidential transcript of remarks by Henry A. Kissinger before the board of the Research Institute of America," 10/57, DDE.)

67. Graubard, *Portrait of a Mind,* pp. 80–104; Schulzinger, *Wise Men of Foreign Affairs,* pp. 155–56.

68. McCloy oral history, pp. 21, 26, DDE.

69. Henry Cabot Lodge to Eisenhower, 7/25/57; Ann Whitman diary, 7/31/57; Eisenhower memo to acting secretary of state, 7/31/57, DDE.

70. McCloy interview, Sept. 14, 1984.

71. Graubard, *Portrait of a Mind,* pp. 106–10; Fred Kaplan, *The Wizards of Armageddon* (New York: Simon & Schuster, 1983), p. 127; Moscow, *Rockefeller Inheritance,* p. 172; David Landau, *Kissinger: The Uses of Power* (Boston: Houghton Mifflin, 1972), pp. 53–54; Henry Kissinger, *White House Years* (Boston: Little, Brown, 1979), p. 4.

72. Michael R. Beschloss, *May-Day: Eisenhower, Khrushchev and the U-2 Affair* (New York: Harper & Row, 1986), p. 148.

73. Kaplan, *Wizards of Armageddon,* pp. 135–36.

74. "Deterrence and Survival in the Nuclear Age," report to the president by the Security Resources Panel of the Science Advisory Committee, 11/7/57, DDE.

75. Ambrose, *Eisenhower the President,* p. 434.

76. Memorandum of conference with the president, 11/4/57, DDE; Richard Barnet, *The Alliance: America-Europe-Japan, Makers of the Postwar World,* p. 153; Kaplan, *Wizards of Armageddon,* p. 152.

77. "Deterrence and Survival in the Nuclear Age," 11/7/57, DDE.

78. I. I. Rabi to Gordon Gray "re advantages of an agreement to cease nuclear testing, portions exempted, MR 81-429 No. 1," 10/28/57, Ann Whitman file, DDE.

79. Ambrose, *Eisenhower the President,* p. 452.

80. Ibid., p. 447.

81. Tyler Abell, ed., *Drew Pearson: Diaries 1949–1959,* p. 417; Ambrose, *Eisenhower the President,* p. 443; Ann Whitman diary, 1/24/58, DDE; Christian A. Herter memo to the secretary, 12/27/57, DDE.

82. *NYT,* Feb. 27, 1958; *London Times,* Feb. 28, 1958; *NYT,* March 6, 1958.

83. Foster Dulles to president, 4/30/58, DDE; Ann Whitman diary, 4/11/58, DDE; Philip J. Farley to General Smith, 4/3/58, DDE; *NYT,* April 9, 1958; Ambrose, *Eisenhower the President,* p. 453; *NYT,* April 27, 1958; Robert A. Divine, *Blowing on the Wind: The Nuclear Test Ban Debate, 1954–1960* (New York: Oxford University Press, 1978), pp. 180–81, 210.

84. Ambrose, *Eisenhower the President,* p. 438.

85. McCloy to president, 1/10/58; Eisenhower to Mrs. John J. McCloy, 1/13/58, DDE.

86. C. D. Jackson log, 6/10/58, DDE.

87. Ibid.

88. Ambrose, *Eisenhower the President,* pp. 477–80.

89. Peter Thompson, "Bilderberg and the West," in Holly Sklar, ed., *Trilateralism: The Trilateral Commission and Elite Planning for World Management* (Boston: Southend Press, 1980), p. 184.

90. Ibid., p. 164.

91. Ibid., p. 168.

92. Ibid., p. 167.

93. Ibid., pp. 170–74.

94. Shoup and Minter, *Imperial Brain Trust,* p. 80.

95. Bilderberg Group, Buxton Conference, 9/13–15/58, preliminary report; C. D. Jackson to Dr. Joseph H. Retinger, 10/23/58, with attached comments by Jackson, DDE.

96. Ambrose, *Eisenhower the President,* pp. 484–85.

97. Bilderberg Group, Buxton Conference, preliminary report, 9/13–15/58, DDE.

98. Shoup and Minter, *Imperial Brain Trust,* p. 209.

99. William Hoffman, *David: Report on a Rockefeller* (New York: Lyle Stuart, 1971), p. 127.

100. Robert Paul Browder and Thomas G. Smith, Independent: *A Biography of Lewis W. Douglas,* pp. 390–91.

101. McCloy oral history, 12/18/70, p. 24, DDE.

102. Bilderberg Group, Buxton Conference, preliminary report, 9/13–15/58, DDE.

103. Ambrose, *Eisenhower the President,* p. 485.

104. Kissinger, *White House Years,* p. 165.

105. Eisenhower phone calls, 9/26/58, DDE.

106. *WP,* Oct. 4, 1958.

107. McCloy memo to Foster Dulles, 9/27/58, DDE.

108. Ambrose, *Eisenhower the President,* p. 485.

109. Henry Kissinger's account of his 1971 Chinese initiative gives no credit to his colleagues in the CFR for having advocated a rapprochement with China as early as 1955. Indeed, Kissinger claims sole intellectual authorship for recognizing that the Chinese themselves had a strategic incentive to move toward the U.S. as a counterweight to the Soviet Union. (Kissinger, *White House Years,* p. 165.)

110. Herter-Eisenhower telcon, 11/22/58, DDE.

111. McCloy to Eisenhower, 11/28/58, DDE.

112. Ann Whitman diary, 12/6/58, DDE.

113. Herter to Gordon Gray, 12/20/58, with attachments, DDE.

114. Memo of meeting with the president, 6/29/59, DDE.

115. Al Gruenther to Eisenhower, 2/14/59, DDE.

116. Drew Pearson syndicated column, 2/13/59.

117. Eisenhower later told Livingston Merchant that the only four men he considered for the post were Merchant, Herter, Robert Anderson, and Doug Dillon. He may also have considered Henry Cabot Lodge and Allen Dulles. (Eisenhower to Merchant, 12/28/60, DDE; Ambrose, *Eisenhower the President,* p. 524.

118. McCloy to Frankfurter, 5/12/59, Frankfurter Papers, LOC.

119. Beschloss, *May-Day,* pp. 244–46.

120. Jonathan Steele, "The Forgotten Hope for a Safer Europe," *Manchester Guardian,* Jan. 29, 1982.

121. "Report of Activities, 1958–1959," American Council on Germany, AH.

122. Later that year, Khrushchev told Averell Harriman, "We will not agree to your taking over Eastern Germany, and I know you will not agree to a united Germany that does not have your system. In fact, no one wants a united Germany. De Gaulle told us so; the British have told us so; and Adenauer himself when he was here said he was not interested in unification. Why then, do you insist on talking about it?" (Confidential conversation of Governor Harriman with Mr. Khrushchev, June 23, 1959, AH.)

123. Benjamin B. Ferencz, *Less Than Slaves: Jewish Forced Labor and the Quest for Compensation,* p. 76; William Manchester, *The Arms of Krupp,* pp. 5, 663.

124. Manchester, *The Arms of Krupp,* p. 735.

125. Ibid., p. 754.

126. Benjamin B. Ferencz interview, Sept. 15, 1984. Ferencz sent McCloy a long memo documenting Krupp's personal guilt. He bluntly told him that Krupp "did in fact exercise effective control of the Krupp company and all its enterprises, that they deliberately sought concentration camp labor for the Krupp industries, that there was absolutely no requirement that such labor be used, that the inmates were employed as slaves without pay under the most inhuman conditions and that Alfried Krupp was personally aware of all this, and encouraged it." McCloy did not respond. (Benjamin B. Ferencz to McCloy, June 23, 1959, with attached "Memorandum: Claims of Former Slave Laborers Against Alfried Krupp and the Krupp Company," copy given to author by Ferencz.)

127. Ferencz interview, Sept. 15, 1984.

128. Manchester, *The Arms of Krupp,* p. 755.

129. Ferencz, *Less Than Slaves,* p. 78.

130. Manchester, *The Arms of Krupp,* pp. 674–79, 732; Ferencz, *Less Than Slaves,* p. 85.

131. Ferencz, *Less Than Slaves,* pp. 82–83.

132. Ibid., p. 86.

133. Manchester, *The Arms of Krupp,* p. 756.

134. *NYT,* Oct. 11, 1960.

135. Frankfurter to McCloy, 11/2/59, Frankfurter Papers, LOC.

136. McCloy to Frankfurter, 10/16/59, Frankfurter Papers, LOC.

137. C. Wright Mills, *The Power Elite* (New York: Oxford University Press, 1957), pp. 288–90.

138. C. D. Jackson to McCloy, 6/12/59, DDE; Cord Meyer, *Facing Reality: From World Federalism to the CIA* (New York: Harper & Row, 1980), p. 103.

139. Meyer, *Facing Reality,* p. 102.

140. C. D. Jackson to Frank Stanton, 7/13/59, DDE.

141. *NYT,* Feb. 21, 1967.

142. C. D. Jackson to Cord Meyer, 12/16/58; Samuel S. Walker, Jr., to C. D. Jackson, 2/2/59; Gloria Steinem to C. D. Jackson, 3/19/59, DDE.

143. When this covert operation was revealed by *Ramparts* magazine in 1967, Steinem told *The New York Times* that she approved the Agency's role. "Far from being shocked by this involvement, I was happy to find some liberals in government in those days who were far-sighted and cared enough to get Americans of all political views to the Festival." (*NYT,* Feb. 21, 1967.) Steinem's definition of a liberal then included such young men as Zbigniew Brzezinski, an assistant professor at Harvard, and Tom Garrity, a lawyer with Donovan & Leisure. She arranged through Jackson funding for both men to attend the festival. (She also tried to get Michael Harrington to attend, but he dropped out at the last minute.) Steinem's politics then appeared to be typical of many 1950s anticommunist liberals. She told the *Times* in 1967, "I was never asked to report on other Americans or assess foreign nationals I had met." But in fact, in response to a query from C. D. Jackson, Steinem wrote Jackson in great detail on the left-wing affiliations of various Americans associated with the allegedly Soviet-backed U.S. Festival Committee. (Gloria Steinem to C. D. Jackson, 3/19/59, DDE; *NYT,* Feb. 21, 1967.)

144. S. S. Walker to C. D. Jackson, "Status Report," DDE.

145. Samuel Walker eventually made a career out of publishing, becoming president of Walker & Co., a New York City publishing firm founded in the same year as the CIA funded Publications Development Corporation.

In Vienna, he and Steinem worked well together. Their organizing efforts led to a split in the official American delegation. Their propaganda machine pumped out four hundred thousand copies of a daily newspaper for three weeks with articles by McCloy, Irving Kristol, Czeslav Milosz, Hubert Humphrey, Willy Brandt, Isaac Deutscher, and a broad range of other intellectuals and politicians. They also distributed some thirty-six thousand books by such left-of-center but anti-Soviet writers as George Orwell and Milovan Djilas. In the midst of it all, Walker reported back to Jackson, "Gloria's group continues to do yeoman service, distributing books etc. to the point where the cry has gone up 'Never before have so many Young Republicans distributed so much Socialist literature with such zeal.' " Walker praised Steinem's "female intuition" and wrote, "Gloria is all you said she was, and then some. She is operating on 16 synchronized cylinders and has charmed the natives. . . ." (C. D. Jackson to Cord Meyer, 7/14/59, with attached Walker diary; Walker to Jackson, 7/31/59, DDE.)

146. The Chase officer in question was Alfred W. Barth, a vice-president and the number-two man in charge of Chase's international division in 1959. (See C. D. Jackson Papers, file Youth Festival—Financial, box 95, DDE.) Barth evidently had acquired expertise in such laundering operations when he conducted banking business for the U.S. government in Spain during World War II. (See Wilson, *The Chase,* p. 371.)

147. John Ranelagh, *The Agency: The Rise and Decline of the CIA from Wild Bill Donovan to William Casey,* p. 249.

148. W. Averell Harriman, *American and Russia in a Changing World: A Half Century of Personal Observation* (Garden City, N.Y.: Doubleday, 1971), p. 61.

149. Ibid.

150. "Reception for Khrushchev," guest list 9/17/59, AH.

151. Harriman, *America and Russia,* p. 61. Khrushchev once described all American politicians as "representatives of the Duponts, Rockefellers and Harrimans." (Mark Frankland, *Khrushchev* [New York: Stein & Day, 1967], p. 160.)

152. Beschloss, *May-Day,* p. 197.

153. These comments reflected a general assumption among such people that nothing was so dangerous as a Russian capable of making himself seem like a reasonable fellow to the American people. Any "possible easing of tension as a result of this [Khrushchev's] trip," said Herod, worried him. It made it all the more difficult to rouse the American people to do what was necessary to fight the Cold War. Herod and Pete Jones actually hoped Khrushchev would display a bit of his temper, if only to "awaken some Americans to the kind of shrewdness . . . which we have to deal with in the Kremlin. . . ." (W. Alton Jones to A. Harriman, 9/18/59; W. R. Herod to A. Harriman, 9/19/59, AH.)

154. Averell Harriman to George S. Franklin, Jr., 12/9/59; W. R. Herod to A. Harriman, 12/19/59, AH.

155. Confidential conversation of Governor Harriman with Mr. Khrushchev, June 23, 1959, AH.

156. Memorandum of meeting with the president, 2/10/60, DDE.

157. Beschloss, *May-Day,* pp. 152–53; Ambrose, *Eisenhower the President,* p. 563.

158. Ambrose, *Eisenhower the President,* pp. 564–67.

159. Herter to James Killian, 4/23/60; memorandum of meeting with the president, 4/27/60, DDE.

160. There is still some mystery about whether Powers's U-2 was brought down by engine failure or a Soviet missile. But Powers's own testimony indicates that it was a missile that disabled his plane. (Beschloss, *May-Day,* p. 403.)

161. Ambrose, *Eisenhower the President,* pp. 575–76.

162. Frankland, *Khrushchev,* p. 169; Ambrose, *Eisenhower the President,* p. 577.

163. Telegram from John J. McCloy, n.d., DDE.

164. Eisenhower to McCloy, 5/24/60, DDE.

165. Beschloss, *May-Day,* p. 319.

166. *NYT,* June 16, 1960.

167. Ambrose, *Eisenhower the President,* p. 580.

168. Press release, Office of Senator John F. Kennedy, 8/30/60, DDE.

169. Drew Pearson, "Washington Merry-Go-Round," Nov. 14, 1960.

BOOK FIVE

TWENTY-THREE: ARMS CONTROL CZAR

1. Kenneth P. O'Donnell and David F. Powers with Joe McCarthy, *Johnny, We Hardly Knew Ye: Memories of John Fitzgerald Kennedy* (Boston: Little, Brown, 1970), p. 236.

2. Ibid., p. 235.

3. Walter Isaacson and Evan Thomas, *The Wise Men: Six Friends and the World They Made,* p. 592; David Halberstam, *The Best and the Brightest* (New York: Fawcett Crest, 1972), p. 15.

4. Isaacson and Thomas, *Wise Men,* p. 594.

5. Halberstam, *Best and Brightest,* p. 16.

6. Arthur M. Schlesinger, Jr., *A Thousand Days* (Boston: Houghton Mifflin, 1965), p. 156.

7. Ibid., p. 133.

8. McCloy memo of conversation with President-elect Kennedy, 12/8/60, box PA 1, folder 9, JJM; Betty Goetz Lall interview, Feb. 20, 1985; Isaacson and Thomas, *Wise Men,* p. 599.

9. Mrs. Frederick Warburg interview, April 10, 1984.

10. McCloy interview, Sept. 14, 1984; Betty Goetz Lall interview, Feb. 20, 1985; McCloy memo of conversation with President-elect Kennedy, 12/8/60, box PA 1, folder 9, JJM.

11. McCloy interview, Sept. 14, 1984.

12. Halberstam, *Best and Brightest,* p. 33.

13. Schlesinger, *Thousand Days,* p. 472.

14. Betty Goetz Lall interview, Feb. 20, 1985.

15. Ibid.

16. John Bartlow Martin, *Adlai Stevenson and the World: The Life of Adlai Stevenson* (Garden City, N.Y.: Doubleday, 1977), p. 556.

17. Theodore C. Sorensen, *Kennedy* (New York: Harper & Row, 1965), p. 518.

18. When Rusk complained that a government salary would not cover his large mortgage or pay for the college education of his children, Lovett and McCloy quickly assured him that the Rockefeller trustees would pay him a sizable bonus. (Isaacson and Thomas, *Wise Men,* p. 595.)

19. Leonard Silk and Mark Silk, *The American Establishment,* p. 202.

20. Dean Rusk appointment books, Rusk Papers, LBJ.

21. McCloy was prepared to tell the president that, on the question of whether to seek a test ban agreement, "all things considered, including the chance of detection and the relatively limited advantage which the Soviets could gain by surreptitious testing, it is probably better for us to seek this agreement." (Notes for talk with President Kennedy at White House conference, 1/24/61, box DA 1, folder 44, JJM.)

22. McCloy to General W. Bedell Smith, 1/24/61, DDE.

23. Edmund A. Gullion memo to McCloy, 4/28/61, "Comments on Draft Report to the President on Disarmament Organization, Arms Control and Disarmament Agency" (ACDA) document, DOS FOIA.

24. Schlesinger, *Thousand Days,* p. 473.

25. Memorandum of conversation, "Meeting of Principals," 3/2/61, State Department document obtained from ACDA under FOIA.

26. Shepard Stone memo to JJ McCloy on the subject of disarmament, dated about Jan. 6, 1961, an ACDA memo obtained by the author under FOIA.

27. John J. McCloy speech at Phillips Andover Academy, Feb. 25, 1961, JJM.

28. Meeting with Andrei Gromyko, 3/30/61, box DA 1, folder 11, JJM. McCloy told Gromyko, "I was sure that we were over-armed viz-a-viz [sic] the Soviets if we really knew the facts, and probably they were against us."

29. *WP,* July 4, 1963.

30. Schlesinger, *Thousand Days,* p. 474.

31. Ibid., p. 469.

32. Martin, *Adlai Stevenson and the World,* p. 24.

33. Ibid., p. 165.

34. Kennedy appointment book, 3/12/61, JFK.

35. Schlesinger, *Thousand Days,* p. 474.

36. *NYT,* May 10, 1961.

37. "The Fine Qualities of Mrs. McCloy," *New York Herald Tribune,* Nov. 5, 1962.

38. Walter LaFeber, *America, Russia and the Cold War,* p. 218.

39. Arthur Schlesinger, *Robert Kennedy and His Times* (New York: Ballantine, 1979), pp. 492–93.

40. McCloy to Sorensen, 4/27/61, box DA 1, folder 35, JJM.

41. Dean was a poor choice. Averell Harriman later commented of the Sullivan & Cromwell lawyer that he was the kind of negotiator you sent to the Soviets when "the American objective is to make a record and not to reach an agreement." (Harriman memo, 5/2/67, AH.)

42. *NYT,* May 20, 1961.

43. Memorandum of conversation, "Meeting of Principals," 3/2/61, DOS FOIA; Arthur Dean to McCloy, 4/18/61, DOS FOIA.

44. Memorandum of conversation, McCloy, Rusk, McNamara et al., 3/2/61, DOS FOIA.

45. Betty Goetz Lall interview, Feb. 23, 1985. By late 1962, with the advent of new satellite technology, the United States was willing to reduce its annual inspection quota to only six. (Albert Carnesale, "Learning from Experience with Arms Control," final report submitted to the U.S. Arms Control and Disarmament Agency, John F. Kennedy School of Government, Harvard University, Sept. 1986, Contract AC5PC101, pp. 2–8. This report mistakenly asserts that the Soviets did not offer to have two or three inspections until December 1962. Its source is Glenn Seaborg, *Kennedy, Khrushchev and the Test Ban,* pp. 179, 187–88. But 3/2/61 memorandum of conversation, meeting of principals, ACDA FOIA document, p. 5, refers to "Soviet proposal of 3.")

46. "Extract From Transcript of Vienna Talks Between President Kennedy and Chairman Khrushchev, Conversation at the Soviet Embassy June 4, 1961," secret document, AH. The Vienna summit has always been painted officially as a harsh confrontation. This document, however, shows that Khrushchev was not entirely the blustering hard-liner that we thought.

47. *NYT,* June 11, 1961.

48. McCloy memo for the president, 6/7/61, taken to the president by JJM on June 13, 1961, at about twelve noon. ACDA FOIA.

49. McCloy to Kennedy, 6/7/61, ACDA FOIA.

50. *NYT,* June 24, 1961.

51. McCloy to Eisenhower, 6/23/61, DDE.

52. *NYT,* June 24, 1961.

53. Isaacson and Thomas, *Wise Men,* p. 611.

54. McCloy to Eisenhower, 7/7/61, DDE.

55. *NYT,* June 29, 1961, June 30, 1961.

56. Kennedy appointment book, 7/10/61 & 7/13/61, JFK.

57. *NYT,* July 16, 1961.

58. Schlesinger, *Thousand Days,* p. 475.

59. Betty Goetz Lall interview, Feb. 20, 1985.

60. Schlesinger, *Thousand Days,* p. 392; Isaacson and Thomas, *Wise Men,* p. 613.

61. Schlesinger, *Thousand Days,* p. 391; Schlesinger, *Robert Kennedy and His Times,* p. 460.

62. LaFeber, *America, Russia and the Cold War,* p. 220.

63. *NYT,* July 27, 1961; see also Ronald Steel, *Walter Lippmann and the American Century,* pp. 526–27, for a description of Khrushchev's Sochi dacha.

64. Schlesinger, *Thousand Days,* p. 454.

65. Senator Willis Robertson statement, 9/16/63, *Congressional Record.* Robertson reported that, after returning from Sochi, McCloy had given him an account of his talks with Khrushchev. The senator was now using McCloy's account to argue against ratification of the test-ban treaty in the summer of 1963.

66. McCloy interview, Sept. 14, 1984.

67. Senator Willis Robertson statement, 9/16/63, *Congressional Record.*

68. Memorandum of conversation with Ambassador Dobrynin, 7/3/62, box C1, folder DB 1, JJM.

69. Andrei Sakharov, *Memoirs* (New York: Alfred A. Knopf, 1990), as excerpted in *Time,* May 14, 1990, p. 70.

70. Acheson to Frankfurter, n.d., Frankfurter Papers, LOC; also quoted in Isaacson and Thomas, *Wise Men,* p. 614.

71. LaFeber, *America, Russia and the Cold War,* pp. 219–20.

72. Eleanor Lansing Dulles interview, April 7, 1982. But even Dulles had personally told Dean Rusk in the month before the wall was built that something had to be done to stop the refugee flow through Berlin.

73. Wilhelm Grewe interview, Feb. 9, 1984.

74. Isaacson and Thomas, *Wise Men,* pp. 614–15.

75. Harriman to JFK, 9/1/61, AH.

76. Betty Goetz Lall interview, Feb. 23, 1985; Schlesinger, *Thousand Days,* p. 920.

77. *NYT,* Aug. 25, 1961.

78. Betty Goetz Lall interview, Feb. 23, 1985.

79. Schlesinger, *Thousand Days,* pp. 460, 481.

80. Ibid., p. 458.

81. Clark's research had been financed by a Ford Foundation grant, obtained as a result of McCloy's intervention. When it was finally published, the Foundation spent an extraordinary $2 million to give it the widest possible circulation. It was translated into Russian, Chinese, French, German, and a number of other languages. (Judge Charles E. Wyzanski, Jr., letter to the author, Nov. 23, 1982; Gerald T. Dunne, *Grenville Clark: Public Citizen* [New York: Farrar, Straus & Giroux, 1986], p. 214.)

82. Dunne, *Grenville Clark,* p. 189. The following year, Clark in turn used the McCloy-Zorin Agreement as the blueprint for his "Draft of a Proposed Treaty on General and Complete Disarmament in a Peaceful World."

83. Shepard Stone memo to J. J. McCloy, "Disarmament," about Jan. 6, 1961: Stone told McCloy one of the first things he had to do was "A review of the Grenville Clark proposals." (ACDA FOIA.)

84. Schlesinger, *Thousand Days,* p. 477; John J. McCloy, "Balance Sheet on Disarmament," *Foreign Affairs,* April 1962, pp. 339–59.

85. Schlesinger, *Thousand Days,* pp. 476–77.

86. Betty Goetz Lall interview, Feb. 23, 1985. Lall later confronted Bundy on why the Foster Panel proposals to limit delivery vehicles had been turned down by the White House, and Bundy admitted in retrospect that it might have been a mistake.

87. *NYT,* Oct. 6, 1961.

88. Memorandum of conversation with Ambassador Dobrynin, 7/3/62, box C 1, folder DB 1, JJM.

89. Sorensen, *Kennedy,* p. 288.

90. Albert L. Danielsen, *The Evolution of OPEC* (New York: Harcourt Brace Jovanovich, 1982), p. 128.

91. John Loudon oral history, pp. 1–2, FF. Loudon, the chief executive officer of the

Royal Dutch Petroleum Company (Shell), was later selected by McCloy to go on the board of the Ford Foundation.

92. Isaacson and Thomas, *Wise Men,* p. 730. McCloy's success in so quickly obtaining this dispensation from the Justice Department was all the more remarkable since an antitrust suit dating back to 1953 was still pending against three of the five American companies in question. Not only that, but the companies already had a venue in which to discuss their relationship with OPEC. Back in 1956, when the Suez crisis disrupted international oil supplies, the Eisenhower administration had activated the Foreign Petroleum Supply Committee. The Committee allowed oil-company officers to sit in the presence of government observers and share the kind of information necessary to ensure the delivery of emergency supplies of petroleum to U.S. allies in Europe. The Committee still existed in 1961 and could have served as a forum for the kind of discussions the oil majors claimed were necessary to deal with OPEC. One difference, of course, was that they would have been compelled to hold their discussions in the presence of Justice Department observers. Another was that the companies were barred from exchanging marketing data in their meetings with the Committee.

When McCloy went in to see Robert Kennedy, a debate was taking place within the Justice Department as to whether the Foreign Petroleum Supply Committee should even continue to function. As one Justice Department official in the Antitrust Division explained to the attorney general, "The ability of these five major international oil companies to sit as a governmentally sponsored Committee, to discuss and perhaps arrange details of their foreign operations, all with full antitrust immunity, certainly conflicted with our objectives in the oil cartel case."

In the event, Robert Kennedy decided that "national-security" needs had to prevail over antitrust considerations and authorized the continued meetings of the Committee. He made this decision about the same time that he gave the companies a dispensation to meet in the privacy of McCloy's law office. (Lee Loevinger, assistant attorney general, Antitrust Division, memo to Deputy Attorney General Byron R. White, 10/16/61, Justice Department memo obtained by the author under FOIA; memorandum for the attorney general from W. Wallace Kirkpatrick, acting assistant attorney general, 2/2/61, obtained by the author under FOIA from the Justice Department; attorney general to Frank B. Ellis, Office of Emergency Planning, 10/18/61, Justice Department FOIA.)

93. "Middle East Oil Developments," Current Intelligence Weekly Summary, CIA, OCI no. 0265/61, 2/2/61, CIA FOIA.

94. "Strategic Threats to Free World Petroleum," 8/29/62, box Oil 1, folder 9, JJM. McCloy even suggested that he should arrange with the U.S. government and the EEC to erect a "quota wall which would limit Russian oil imports [into Western Europe]. . . ." Such a quota would have been directly targeted at Italy's government-owned oil company, ENI, led by the charismatic Enrico Mattei, who was killed in a mysterious plane crash that autumn. (McCloy memo, "Specific Current Problems," 8/28/62, box Oil 1, folder 9, JJM.)

95. "List of Dates Mr. McCloy Saw the Attorney Generals," box Oil 3, folder 28, JJM.

96. McCloy memo to Miss Lamkin, 8/16/62, box Oil 1, folder 12, JJM.

97. As McCloy put it, in order to "develop unified policies to resist expropriations . . . a Consultant is needed. Through this mechanism the views of the companies could be coordinated and common denominators could be found for a united industry front. The Consultant would represent the industry before the United States, United Nations and other appropriate governments and organizations to represent the industry's views." ("Representational Problems," 8/29/62, box Oil 1, folder 9, JJM.)

98. *NYT,* March 16, 1962.

99. Laurence M. Gould oral history, FF.

100. Marcus Raskin interview, April 28, 1985.

101. John J. McCloy oral history, FF.

102. W. McNeil Lowry oral history, FF.

103. Ibid.

104. Paul Ylvisaker oral history, FF.

105. W. McNeil Lowry oral history, pp. 103–5, FF.

106. Ibid., p. 106, FF.

107. John J. McCloy oral history, FF, and Judge Charles E. Wyzanski, Jr., letter to the author, Nov. 23, 1982.

108. State Department cable, 10/5/62, DOS FOIA.

TWENTY-FOUR: THE CUBAN MISSILE CRISIS

1. Elie Abel, *The Missile Crisis* (New York: J. B. Lippincott, 1966), p. 45.

2. Transcript of tape of National Security Council Executive Committee meeting, 10/16/62, 6:30 P.M.–7:55 P.M., mandatory review case, NLK-82-131, JFK. The CIA's intelligence estimate in early Oct. had predicted that the Soviets would not install ground-to-ground missiles in Cuba. (John Ranelagh, *The Agency, The Rise and Decline of the CIA from Wild Bill Donovan to William Casey,* p. 394.)

3. This information was leaked to Keating by low-ranking intelligence officials who believed the Kennedy administration was for political reasons disregarding human-intelligence reports that gave circumstantial evidence of the presence of such missiles as early as Aug. and Sept. (Raymond L. Garthoff, *Reflections on the Cuban Missile Crisis* [Washington, D.C.: The Brookings Institution, 1987], p. 14.)

4. Robert F. Kennedy, *Thirteen Days: A Memoir of the Cuban Missile Crisis* (New York: W. W. Norton, 1971), pp. 35–36; Abel, *The Missile Crisis,* p. 45. Abel reports that the president reached McCloy in New York shortly before McCloy departed for Europe. But an Oct. 5, 1962, State Department cable obtained by the author under FOIA shows that McCloy was scheduled to leave New York on Oct. 6 and was supposed to be in Rome Oct. 13–17. Walter Isaacson and Evan Thomas, in *The Wise Men: Six Friends and the World They Made,* p. 802, report McCloy's recollection that he was called by the president in Frankfurt. This apparently was not true, for it was McCloy's secretary who reached him later in Frankfurt and conveyed the president's desire that he return immediately. It is reasonable to assume that McCloy's memory was essentially accurate, but that the call took place when he was in Rome, not in New York.

5. Handwritten McCloy notes, Oct. 1962, "Main thing . . . ," box CMC 1, folder 12, JJM. Lovett wrote him a letter during the crisis, quoting from a book about the lessons of Munich. (Lovett to McCloy, 10/31/62, box CMC 1, folder 9, JJM.) See also McCloy to Sorensen, 4/27/61, box DA 1, folder 35, JJM.

6. Colonel Burris to the vice-president, "Highlights of World Activities and Situations," 11/5/62, LBJ.

7. Garthoff, *Reflections,* p. 142.

8. Walter LaFeber, *America, Russia and the Cold War: 1945–1975,* p. 226; Roger Hilsman, *To Move a Nation* (Garden City, N.Y.: Doubleday, 1967), p. 163.

9. According to the CIA's top spy in Moscow, Colonel Oleg Penkovsky, the entire Soviet ballistic-missile program had recently suffered a serious setback when one of their ICBMs exploded at a test site and killed the head of the program along with three hundred officers. (Abel, *The Missile Crisis,* p. 52; Ranelagh, *The Agency,* p. 402; see also Andrei Sakharov, *Memoirs.*)

10. Robert S. McNamara, *Blundering into Disaster: Surviving the First Century of the Nuclear Age* (New York: Pantheon, 1986), pp. 44–45.

11. More probably, the Soviets were aware that U.S. U-2 flights over Cuba had discovered the missile sites but believed that Kennedy was postponing any response until after the Nov. elections.

12. There is some dispute about whether four of the six medium-range ballistic missiles (MRBMs) might not already have been operational. (Barton J. Bernstein, "We Almost Went to War," *Bulletin of Atomic Scientists,* Feb. 1976, citing an Oct. 23, 1962, declassified CIA report.) A handwritten undated note found in the vice-president's files concerning the missile crisis suggests that thirty-two MRBMs were expected to be operational by Nov. 1. (Handwritten notes, C, LBJ.)

13. Until recently, most accounts of the Cuban missile crisis have had to rely on the memoirs of various participants in the crisis, such as those written by Robert Kennedy, Roger Hilsman, and Arthur Schlesinger. The release of the secret White House transcripts now requires historians to reconsider these accounts, which in more than one instance either are self-serving or leave out critical parts of the story. (See Professor Marc Trachtenberg's introduction to the published excerpts of the transcripts, "The Influence of Nuclear Weapons in the Cuban Missile Crisis," *International Security,* Summer 1985, pp. 164–70.)

14. Hilsman, *To Move a Nation,* p. 195. Hilsman, a State Department official and a participant in Kennedy's deliberations, suggests that others disagreed with McNamara's assertions. This disagreement, however, is not reflected in the transcripts. Hilsman himself, in his later account of the crisis, states that, even if McNamara's assessment was correct, "the United States might not be in mortal danger but the administration most certainly was." (Ibid., p. 197.)

15. Evening transcript, NSC Excomm meeting, 10/16/62, pp. 12, 14, JFK. Today there is still a debate concerning whether the Cuban missiles substantially altered the strategic equation. At one point that evening, the transcripts show Kennedy saying, "What difference does it make? They've got enough to blow us up now anyway." But it is also true that the president and others felt that the missiles might be an "opening wedge," a prelude to another installment of many more missiles. (See Trachtenberg, "Influence of Nuclear Weapons.")

16. Evening transcript, NSC Excomm meeting, 10/16/62, p. 48, JFK.

17. Ibid., p. 26.

18. Garthoff, *Reflections,* p. 43. Previous accounts of the Oct. crisis have downplayed the role of the Turkish missiles; in fact, they are a central explanation of the entire crisis and its ultimate resolution. The Turkish parallel certainly was not lost on the president's advisers, who on that very first day of the crisis speculated that Khrushchev was merely trying to rectify somewhat his own missile gap. As Bundy told his colleagues, "I'm sure his generals have been telling him for a year and a half that he had, was missing a golden opportunity to add to his strategic capability." (Evening transcript, NSC Excomm meeting, 10/16/62, p. 26, JFK.)

19. Bernstein, "We Almost Went to War," p. 13. Khrushchev wrote in his memoirs, "We hadn't given the Cubans anything more than the Americans were giving to their allies." (Nikita Khrushchev, *Khrushchev Remembers* [Boston: Little, Brown, 1970], p. 496.)

20. Evening transcript, NSC Excomm meeting, 10/16/62, p. 47, JFK.

21. Abel, *The Missile Crisis,* pp. 72–73.

22. Theodore C. Sorensen, *Kennedy,* p. 695; Abel, *The Missile Crisis,* p. 95. In a memo to the president on Oct. 22, 1962, Averell Harriman also suggested a trade of the

Jupiter missiles in Turkey for the Cuban missiles. (Barton J. Bernstein, "The Cuban Missile Crisis: Trading the Jupiters in Turkey?," *Political Science Quarterly,* vol. 95, no. 1 (Spring 1980), p. 106.

23. David Detzer, *The Brink: Cuban Missile Crisis, 1962* (New York: Thomas Y. Crowell, 1979), p. 159; Abel, *The Missile Crisis,* p. 96.

24. Arthur M. Schlesinger, Jr., *Robert Kennedy and His Times,* p. 556.

25. Kennedy, *Thirteen Days,* pp. 35–36.

26. Abel, *The Missile Crisis,* pp. 113–14. McCloy was scheduled to see Hermann Abs that day in Frankfurt. ("Memo to Mr. McCloy—European trip," box Oil 1, folder 10, JJM.)

27. Isaacson and Thomas, *Wise Men,* p. 627; "Memo to Mr. McCloy—European trip," box Oil 1, folder 10, JJM.

28. Walter Johnson, ed., *The Papers of Adlai E. Stevenson* (Boston: Little, Brown, 1979), vol. 8., p. 307.

29. Mahmoud Riad interview, Nov. 22, 1983.

30. Michael V. Forrestal secret memo to Bundy, 10/23/62, AH.

31. Johnson, ed., *Papers of Adlai E. Stevenson,* vol. 8, p. 325.

32. Michael V. Forrestal confidential memo to Bundy, 10/25/62, AH.

33. Judge Charles E. Wyzanski, Jr., letter to the authors, Nov. 23, 1982.

34. Dean Rusk appointment book, 10/25/62, box 1, Rusk Papers, LBJ. McCloy joined a meeting in Rusk's office at 7:20 P.M. with Rusk, Ambassador Llewellyn Thompson, Edwin M. Martin, Harland Cleveland, George Ball, and U. Alexis Johnson.

35. Abel, *The Missile Crisis,* p. 151.

36. Summary record of NSC Excomm meeting no. 6, Oct. 26, 1962, 10:00 A.M., JFK.

37. Ibid., p. 6.

38. Notes of Excomm meeting taken by Colonel Burris for Lyndon Johnson, 10:00 A.M., 10/26/62, LBJ.

39. Garthoff, *Reflections,* p. 51.

40. Abel, *The Missile Crisis,* p. 174.

41. Detzer, *The Brink,* p. 234.

42. McNamara, *Blundering into Disaster,* p. 10.

43. Kennedy, *Thirteen Days,* pp. 65–67.

44. *WP,* Oct. 22, 1987.

45. Summary record of NSC Excomm meeting no. 7, Oct. 27, 1962, 10:00 A.M., JFK.

46. Summary record of NSC Excomm meeting no. 8, Oct. 27, 1962, 4:00 P.M., JFK.

47. *WP,* Oct. 22, 1987. According to Seymour Hersh, the National Security Agency cracked a Soviet military code several years later and learned that the SAM site in question was in the hands of Cuban, not Soviet troops. (Seymour Hersh, "Was Castro Out of Control in 1962?," *WP,* Oct. 11, 1982.) Castro, fed up with the Soviet response to the blockade, had reportedly ordered the firing of the SAM to take down the U-2 over Cuban skies. If Kennedy had followed McCone's advice, he would have been retaliating against the Soviets for an act performed by a recalcitrant Soviet ally. (Garthoff, *Reflections,* p. 53.) Soviet sources deny that any of the SAM sites were ever in the hands of the Cubans. (Richard Bernstein, "Meeting Sheds New Light on Cuban Missile Crisis," *NYT,* Oct. 14, 1987.)

48. *WP,* Oct. 22, 1987.

49. Schlesinger, *Robert Kennedy and His Times,* p. 564.

50. Herbert S. Dinerstein, *The Making of a Missile Crisis: October 1962* (Baltimore: Johns Hopkins University Press, 1976), pp. 228, 236.

51. On the evening of Oct. 27, President Kennedy instructed Dean Rusk to phone

a Columbia University professor, Andrew Cordier, who had discreet but ready access to U Thant. Rusk dictated a statement to Cordier proposing the removal of the missiles in both Turkey and Cuba. Cordier was to have U Thant propose the swap only after a signal from Washington. Thus, if Khrushchev had not capitulated the next morning, Kennedy had prepared for himself a face-saving method of accepting a public swap of the missiles through U.N. auspices. (James Blight, Joseph Nye, Jr., and David A. Welch, "The Cuban Missile Crisis Revisited," *Foreign Affairs,* Fall 1987, p. 179; Thomas J. Schoenbaum, *Waging Peace and War: Dean Rusk in the Truman, Kennedy and Johnson Years* [New York: Simon & Schuster, 1988], p. 324.)

52. Detzer, *The Brink,* p. 260.

53. Schlesinger, *Robert Kennedy and His Times,* p. 550.

54. Raymond L. Garthoff, "The Cuban 'Contras' Caper," *WP,* Oct. 25, 1987.

55. State Department memo to USUN, "Subject: New York Negotiations," 10/31/62, LBJ. Ralph Bunche, the undersecretary general of the U.N., frankly told McCloy and Stevenson that "what is being asked of Cuba on verification has never been granted by any sovereign country and he doubted Castro would accept." (Stevenson cable to secretary of state, 11/5/62, LBJ.)

56. U.S. intelligence later learned that Cuban troops had actually encircled the four Soviet missile bases on Oct. 28, the day after Khrushchev's capitulation, and continued to threaten Soviet control over the sites for as long as three more days. (Garthoff, *Reflections,* p. 63.)

57. State Department cable nos. 1584 (11/1/62); 1588 (11/1/62); 1579 (10/31/62); 1585 (11/1/62; and Rusk, eyes only, for George Ball, 11/1/62, LBJ.

58. *NYT,* Nov. 4, 1962.

59. On Oct. 28, Kennedy "agreed that we should read offensive weapons to include bombers, but should not get hung up on this issue." [NSC Excomm record of action, 10/28/62, LBJ.)

60. Betty Goetz Lall interview, Feb. 23, 1985. The IL-28s had been decommissioned out of the Soviet Air Force in 1960, and the United States had not protested when some of these planes were given to Egypt and Indonesia. (Garthoff, *Reflections,* p. 65.)

61. Johnson, ed., *Papers of Adlai E. Stevenson,* vol. 8, p. 337.

62. Ronald R. Pope, ed., *Soviet Views on the Cuban Missile Crisis* (Washington, D.C.: University Press of America, 1982), contains a translation of Anatolii A. Gromyko's article "The Caribbean Crisis" on p. 221.

63. John Bartlow Martin, *Adlai Stevenson and the World: The Life of Adlai Stevenson,* p. 739.

64. Eyes only for Stevenson and McCloy from the president, 11/3/62, LBJ.

65. Garthoff, *Reflections,* p. 76.

66. Ibid., pp. 76–77. Early in 1963, the CIA estimated that seventeen thousand Soviet troops remained in Cuba after the departure of five to six thousand troops closely associated with operating and defending the missile and bomber systems. (Colonel Burris to vice-president, 2/5/63, LBJ.)

67. Stevenson to secretary of state, 11/5/62, LBJ.

68. Stevenson to secretary of state, 11/14/62, cable no. 1781, LBJ. In fact, President Kennedy had been told that such refugee reports could not be substantiated and instructed White House officials to brief various reporters on the unreliability of such rumors.

69. Edwin M. Martin, unpublished manuscript, pp. 102–3. McCloy believed the U-2 overflights of Cuba had "probably saved us from war and they might do so again." (McCloy-Kuznetsov meeting, 11/18/62, box CMC 1, folder 7, JJM.)

70. Defense Department officials were quite unhappy with the procedures McCloy

worked out, believing they left the Soviets plenty of opportunity to cheat. (Colonel Burris to LBJ, 11/2/62, LBJ.)

71. McCloy interview, March 19, 1986.

72. State Department cable no. 1710, 11/9/62, LBJ.

73. NSC Excomm record of action, 11/12/62, LBJ.

74. *NYT,* Nov. 19, 1962; eyes only for the secretary, meeting between McCloy and Kuznetsov, 11/18/62, box CMC 1, folder 7, JJM.

75. Garthoff, *Reflections,* p. 72.

76. These Soviet-Cuban conditions had been initialed by Mikoyan in Havana just a few days before, and Rusk told McCloy they were "obviously unacceptable." He even suggested McCloy might want to tell Kuznetsov that Washington understood that it may have been necessary for the Soviets to sign this protocol with the Cubans "in order to get Mikoyan out with a whole skin, [but] they can hardly expect us to take it seriously." (Rusk to McCloy, 11/17/62, box CMC 1, folder 6, JJM.)

77. A Nov. 7, 1962, State Department document referred to a U.S. strategy of aiming at the "elimination" of the "Castro regime including its old line communist hardcore." (W. W. Rostow memo, 11/7/62, LBJ.)

78. Schlesinger, *Robert Kennedy and His Times,* p. 567.

79. Martin, unpublished manuscript, p. 104.

80. Eyes only for the secretary, meeting between McCloy and Kuznetsov, 11/18/62, box CMC 1, folder 7, JJM.

81. Martin, *Adlai Stevenson and the World,* p. 739.

82. Stevenson to Rusk, 11/15/62, LBJ.

83. *NYT,* Nov. 19, 1962.

84. Sorensen, *Kennedy,* p. 721.

85. Kennedy, *Thirteen Days,* p. 176.

86. Rusk, eyes only for Stevenson and McCloy, "Next Steps in New York Negotiations," 11/21/62, LBJ.

87. Draft cable, "Correction to ourtel 1941," 11/25/62, box CMC 1, folder 16, JJM.

88. State Department eyes-only cable for Stevenson and McCloy, "Next Steps in New York Negotiations," 11/21/62, LBJ.

89. *NYT,* Dec. 7, 1962.

90. New York eyes-only cable to secretary of state, no. 2140, 12/5/62, LBJ.

91. New York to secretary of state, cable no. 2183, 12/7/62, LBJ.

92. Memo for Excomm meeting, 11/29/62, "Information and Public Affairs Matters Growing Out of Cuban Situation—Part II: East-West Aspects," mandatory-review case no. 84-6, doc. no. 18, LBJ.

93. Ranelagh, *The Agency,* p. 398; Isaacson and Thomas, *Wise Men,* p. 630.

94. Garthoff, *Reflections,* p. 122.

95. Raymond L. Garthoff, *Détente and Confrontation: American-Soviet Relations from Nixon to Reagan* (Washington, D.C.: The Brookings Institution, 1985), p. 77.

96. Averell Harriman memo of conversation, 12/28/62, AH.

97. McCloy interview, March 19, 1986.

98. Harland Cleveland to the secretary (Rusk), "Conversation with Mr. McCloy on Cuba," mandatory-review case no. NLJ 84-6, doc. no. 13, LBJ, declassified 5/4/84.

99. Ibid.

100. The vague nature of the "understandings" that ended the crisis led a number of right-wing critics years later to charge that McCloy and the Kennedy administration had failed to define exactly what kind of Soviet military presence would be permitted in Cuba. (See George F. Will, "Romanticizing the Cuban Missile Crisis," *WP,* Sept. 3,

1987.) Thus, in the midst of the "Soviet combat-brigade" affair of 1978, McCloy was consulted by the Carter administration and questioned as to what exactly had been negotiated. He reported, of course, that no agreement had been reached barring Soviet troops from the island, only that the Soviets had promised to withdraw those troops associated with the operating of the missiles. Similarly, critics in recent years have mistakenly charged that McCloy gave the Soviets a firm pledge not to invade Cuba. In fact, Henry Kissinger told the Soviets in 1970 that the Nixon administration believed that the understandings of 1962 "were still in force" and that the United States had pledged that it "would not use military force to bring about a change in the governmental structure of Cuba." If anything, Kissinger's statement represented an expansion of the McCloy-Kuznetsov understandings. (Martin, unpublished manuscript, p. 133.) Finally, twenty-five years after the crisis, Jack Anderson and Dale Van Atta charged that the Soviets had violated the "understandings" by placing a dozen TU-95 Bear bombers and some 40 MiG-23 or MiG-27 fighter-bombers in Cuba. Such planes, they point out, are all capable of carrying nuclear weapons. (Jack Anderson and Dale Van Atta, "Cuban Missile Crisis Facts Under Wraps," *WP,* Oct. 9, 1987.) If such reports are true, they merely underscore the limited nature of the understandings reached by McCloy in 1962 and remind us that what was unacceptable on the domestic political stage in 1962 is today merely a redundant fact of life in the age of nuclear parity.

101. Paul Hoffman, *Lions in the Street: The Inside Story of the Great Wall Street Law Firms,* p. 41.

102. McCloy to President Kennedy, 2/21/63, JFK.

103. Lew Douglas to Clint Murchison, 4/15/63, LD.

104. McCloy to Lew Douglas, 6/7/63, LD; McCloy to Herbert Hoover, 6/5/63, HH.

105. McCloy to Eisenhower, 6/6/63, DDE.

106. Endicott Peabody memo to the president, "John McCloy on Vietnam and the Presidency," 11/6/67, NSF, Memos to the President, vol. 53, box 26, LBJ. Robert McNamara claims that before his death Kennedy had already made the decision to withdraw U.S. troops from Vietnam. (Robert S. McNamara interview, March 7, 1990.)

107. McCloy to Lew Douglas, 6/7/63, LD.

108. McCloy interview, March 19, 1986.

109. McCloy to Lew Douglas, 6/7/63, LD.

110. Rusk cable to Cairo, Rome, et al., re: McCloy itinerary, 6/18/63, DOS FOIA.

111. *NYT,* July 4, 1963.

112. McCloy to Johnson, 11/23/63, LBJ.

BOOK SIX

TWENTY-FIVE: THE WARREN COMMISSION, A BRAZIL COUP, EGYPT AGAIN, AND THE 1964 ELECTION

1. *Baltimore Sun,* July 21, 1975 (courtesy of Harold Weisberg).

2. Doris Kearns, *Lyndon Johnson and the American Dream* (New York: Harper & Row, 1976), p. 170.

3. Lyndon Baines Johnson, *The Vantage Point: Perspectives of the Presidency 1963–1969* (New York: Holt, Rinehart & Winston, 1971), p. 26.

4. Johnson, *Vantage Point,* p. 26; Alfred Steinberg, *Sam Johnson's Boy: A Close-up of the President from Texas* (New York: Macmillan, 1968), p. 625. Fortas was the lawyer who ensured Johnson's election to the Senate in 1948 by an eighty-seven-vote margin. The first phone call Johnson made in Dallas immediately after the assassination was to Fortas. (Jack Harrison Pollack, *Earl Warren: The Judge Who Changed America* [Englewood Cliffs, N.J.: Prentice-Hall, 1979], p. 260.)

5. Steinberg, *Sam Johnson's Boy,* p. 626.

6. Pollack, *Earl Warren,* p. 229.

7. Johnson later claimed that Bobby Kennedy specifically asked him to appoint both McCloy and Allen Dulles to the Commission. This seems unlikely, since the attorney general at the time acted as if he was emotionally incapable of involving himself in any investigation of who killed his brother. (Johnson, *Vantage Point,* p. 27; Arthur M. Schlesinger, Jr., *Robert Kennedy and His Times,* p. 662.

8. Steinberg, *Sam Johnson's Boy,* p. 625.

9. *The Official Warren Commission Report on the Assassination of President John F. Kennedy,* with special analysis and commentary by Louis Nizer (Garden City, N.Y.: Doubleday, 1964), p. vi-a.

10. Warren Commission meeting transcript, 12/16/63, p. 52, JFK.

11. Warren Commission meeting transcript 12/5/63, p. 37, JFK. On the other hand, McCloy decided that the power to grant immunity to hostile witnesses was unnecessary to the Commission's work. This decision has been attacked by critics of the Warren Commission. (Ibid., p. 61.)

12. Warren Commission meeting transcript, 12/5/63, p. 37, JFK.

13. Edward Jay Epstein, *Inquest: The Warren Commission and the Establishment of the Truth* (New York: Bantam, 1966), p. 30.

14. Robert Sam Anson, *"They've Killed the President": The Search for the Murderers of John F. Kennedy* (New York: Bantam, 1975), p. 39.

15. John A. McCone to Lyndon Johnson, 1/9/64, LBJ.

16. Mark Lane, *Rush to Judgment* (New York: Holt, Rinehart & Winston, 1966), p. 7; Henry Hurt, *Reasonable Doubt: An Investigation into the Assassination of John F. Kennedy* (New York: Henry Holt, 1985), pp. 28–29.

17. Warren Commission meeting transcript, 12/5/63, p. 58, JFK.

18. Jan Black, "Linkage Groups and Denationalization: Denationalizing Business Elites, United States Penetration of Brazil," unpublished manuscript, p. 87.

19. Edie Black and Fred Goff, *The Hanna Industrial Complex* (New York: North American Congress on Latin America, 1969), p. 8.

20. Memo of conversation, 9/20/63, DOS FOIA.

21. Jack W. Buford interviews, Jan. 17, 1985, Feb. 1, 1985.

22. John W. F. Dulles, "Hanna in Brazil," unpublished manuscript, pt. IX, pp. 337, 340. As recently as Aug. 21, 1963, for instance, Gordon had cabled Washington, "If God really is Brazilian, Goulart's heart trouble of 1962 will soon become acute. . . . Goulart will almost certainly do his best to institute some form of authoritarian regime."

23. "Proposed Short Term Policy: Brazil," State Department secret report, 9/30/63, AH. This document mentions such activities as initiating a "covert program" to "assure U.S. penetration of the non-commissioned officers of all three [Brazilian military] services." The report also recommends "quick recognition and support to any regime which the Brazilians install to supplant Goulart's regime. . . ." See also Ruth Leacock, "JFK, Business, and Brazil," *Hispanic American Historical Journal,* vol. 59, no. 4 (Nov. 1979), p. 667. Not everyone was as pessimistic as Ambassador Gordon. Tom Hughes, director of the State Department's Intelligence and Research Bureau, argued with his colleagues that Goulart was simply a "social reformer" and that Gordon's analysis lacked "validity." (Thomas L. Hughes secret memo to Mr. Martin, State Department, 8/29/63, AH.)

24. Jack W. Buford interview, Jan. 18, 1985.

25. Vernon Walters, *Silent Missions* (Garden City, N.Y.: Doubleday, 1978), p. 388.

26. McCloy-Harriman telcon, 11/4/63; McCloy-Harriman telcon, 11/29/63, AH; Frederic L. Chapin to McCloy with enclosures, 12/16/63, AH.

27. Dulles, "Hanna in Brazil," p. 355.

28. Ibid., pp. 346–47, 359.

29. Ibid., p. 360.

30. Harriman-McCloy telcon, 3/10/64, AH.

31. Dulles, "Hanna in Brazil," p. 366.

32. Walters to ACSI, Department of State cable, 3/27/64, LBJ.

33. Walters, *Silent Missions,* p. 386.

34. Top-secret Joint Chiefs of Staff cable to CINCSTRIKE, 3/31/64, LBJ; Ruth Leacock, "Promoting Democracy: The United States and Brazil, 1964–68," *Prologue,* 1981, p. 79; see also Department of State cable from American Consulate in São Paulo, 3/30/64, LBJ.

35. CIA intelligence-information cable, 3/30/64, LBJ.

36. Jan Black, "Linkage Groups and Denationalization, Denationalizing Business Elites," p. 87, unpublished manuscript.

37. Jack W. Buford interviews, Jan. 17, 1985, Feb. 1, 1985.

38. Black and Goff, *Hanna Industrial Complex,* p. 4; Philip Siekman, "When Executives Turned Revolutionaries," *Fortune,* Sept. 1964, p. 221.

39. When Arthur Schlesinger expressed his puzzlement as to why the United States had "rushed to embrace the new Brazilian regime," he received a firm rebuke from McGeorge Bundy, who said Johnson was "considerably annoyed" by this criticism. Bundy explained that Johnson was extremely sensitive to the suggestion that his administration's policies in Brazil represented a reversal of John Kennedy's support for democratic forces in Latin America. (McGeorge Bundy to Schlesinger, 5/12/64; Schlesinger airgram to State Department, 4/23/64, LBJ.)

40. Ruth Leacock, "Promoting Democracy," p. 81.

41. State Department airgram, 11/10/64, reporting on McCloy's call on President Branco, 11/5/64, DOS FOIA.

42. Hurt, *Reasonable Doubt,* p. 19.

43. Ibid., p. 327.

44. David S. Lifton, *Best Evidence: Disguise and Deception in the Assassination of John F. Kennedy* (New York: Macmillan, 1980), p. 106.

45. Ibid., pp. 83–84.

46. Ibid., p. 85.

47. Warren Commission meeting transcript, 12/16/63, p. 55, JFK; Hurt, *Reasonable Doubt,* p. 43.

48. Warren Commission meeting transcript, 12/16/63, p. 35, JFK.

49. Ibid., p. 12.

50. Hurt, *Reasonable Doubt,* p. 252.

51. Edward J. Epstein, *Legend: The Secret World of Lee Harvey Oswald* (New York: Reader's Digest Press, 1978), p. 17.

52. Ibid., p. 264.

53. David E. Scheim, *Contract on America: The Mafia Murder of President John F. Kennedy* (New York: Shapolsky Publishers, 1988), p. 218; *NYT,* Nov. 29, 1985.

54. Hurt, *Reasonable Doubt,* p. 32.

55. Epstein, *Legend,* p. 254.

56. Ibid., p. 232. The CIA also withheld Agency documents reporting that a Cuban agent named Miguel Casas Saez was in Dallas on Nov. 22, 1963, on a "sabotage and espionage mission." (Hurt, *Reasonable Doubt,* pp. 420–22.)

57. Warren Commission meeting transcript, 12/16/63, p. 39, JFK.

58. Hurt, *Reasonable Doubt,* p. 214.

59. McCloy interview, BBC Panorama, March 6, 1978.
60. Pollack, *Earl Warren*, p. 237.
61. Lane, *Rush to Judgment*, p. 368.
62. Ibid., p. 367–68.
63. Anson, *"They've Killed the President,"* pp. 46–47.
64. Pollack, *Earl Warren*, p. 235.
65. C. D. Jackson to McCloy, 1/20/64, DDE.
66. Lifton, *Best Evidence*, p. 73.
67. Warren Commission meeting transcript, 4/30/64, pp. 33–35, JFK.
68. Pollack, *Earl Warren*, p. 245.
69. *Long Beach Independent Press*, July 3, 1967.
70. *The Final Assassinations Report*, House Select Committee on Assassinations (New York: Bantam, 1979), p. 34; Hurt, *Reasonable Doubt*, pp. 53–54.
71. Hurt, *Reasonable Doubt*, p. 108.
72. David W. Belin, Esq., *November 22, 1963: You Are the Jury* (New York: Times Books, 1973), p. 194.
73. Pollack, *Earl Warren*, p. 244. In fact, the House Select Committee on Assassinations concluded in 1978 that such "smokeless" gunpowder can indeed be seen when fired. (Hurt, *Reasonable Doubt*, p. 117.)
74. Tom Mangold, *Cold Warrior James Jesus Angleton: The CIA's Master Spy Hunter* (New York: Simon & Schuster, 1991), pp. 174–75; Epstein, *Legend*, pp. 47–48.
75. Epstein, *Legend*, p. 49.
76. Nosenko actually brought with him some documentation of his story, including some papers from Oswald's KGB file. These documents testified that the Soviets indeed feared that Oswald was a sleeper agent under the control of U.S. intelligence. Nosenko said orders were given for Oswald to be kept under surveillance but not recruited. He claimed that, when Oswald was accused as Kennedy's assassin, KGB officials feared that someone in their organization might nevertheless have recruited him. A bomber was quickly dispatched to Minsk, Nosenko says, to retrieve Oswald's file, and KGB officials were relieved to read that the ex-Marine had never been recruited. (Anson, *"They've Killed the President,"* p. 164.)
77. McCloy interview, BBC Panorama, March 6, 1978; see also McCloy questioning of Alan H. Belmont, assistant to the director of the FBI, in *The Witnesses: Selected and Edited from the Warren Commission's Hearings by the New York Times* (New York: McGraw-Hill, 1964), pp. 604–13, 526, 551.
78. Anson, *"They've Killed the President,"* p. 154.
79. Warren Commission meeting transcript, 4/30/64, p. 18, JFK.
80. Ibid., p. 31.
81. *Baltimore Sun*, July 21, 1975 (interview of McCloy on CBS by Eric Sevareid).
82. *The Witnesses*, p. 553.
83. Pollack, *Earl Warren*, p. 250.
84. Epstein, *Inquest*, p. 81.
85. Drew Pearson, Bell-McClure Syndicate, June 22, 1964.
86. McCloy-Harriman telcon, 7/13/64, AH.
87. McCloy-Harriman telcon, 8/4/64, AH.
88. McCloy-Harriman telcon, 7/13/64, AH.
89. Harriman–Mac Bundy telcon, 7/13/64, AH.
90. Harriman-McCloy telcon, 8/4/64, AH.
91. In a 1978 postscript to his famous essay, Rovere wrote, "There was no American Establishment; of course there wasn't, yet in a way there was, and in any case the chairman

of the board had to be John J. McCloy." (Richard Rovere, "The American Establishment," *Wilson Quarterly*, Summer 1978, pp. 170–84.)

92. McGeorge Bundy memo to the president, "Backing from the Establishment," 8/24/64, Bundy Memos, LBJ.

93. Harriman-McCloy telcon, 8/4/64, AH.

94. Cyrus Sulzberger–Harriman telcon, 7/23/64, AH.

95. *NYT*, Aug. 1, 1964.

96. Ibid.

97. *Official Warren Commission Report*, p. 19.

98. Epstein, *Inquest*, p. 122.

99. Ibid., p. 124.

100. Pollack, *Earl Warren*, p. 253.

101. *The Final Assassinations Report*, House Select Committee on Assassinations (New York: Bantam, 1979), p. 104.

102. Hurt, *Reasonable Doubt*, p. 30.

103. FBI memo, C. D. De Loach to Mr. Tolson, 4/4/67, FBI FOIA.

104. McCloy told an interviewer in 1978, "I must assume he [Johnson] knew it at the time when I was sort of visiting with him and we were talking about these matters—that there had been an effort, on behalf of the CIA, to assassinate Fidel Castro, and that therefore this was logical that Fidel Castro was retaliating and had retaliated." (McCloy interview, BBC Panorama, March 6, 1978.)

105. Ibid.

106. Scheim, *Contract on America*, p. vii.

107. Ambassador Lucius Battle cable to secretary of state, 9/29/64, DOS FOIA.

108. *NYT*, Sept. 29, 1964.

109. "McCloy's Impressions of His Meeting with President Nasser on September 28," State Department memorandum of conversation, 10/6/64, AH.

110. Ibid.

111. *NYT*, Dec. 19, 1964.

112. Eugene Bird interview, Aug. 11, 1988; Ben Read memo to Mac Bundy, 1/8/65, LBJ.

113. "McCloy's Impressions of His Meeting with President Nasser on September 28," State Department memcon, 10/6/64, AH.

114. *NYT*, Sept. 10, 1964, Nov. 2, 1964.

TWENTY-SIX: McCLOY AND VIETNAM: 1965–68, NATO CRISIS, SECRET MIDDLE EAST NEGOTIATIONS

1. Alvin Wirtz to LBJ, 5/20/40, LBJ (courtesy of Robert Dallek).

2. George C. Herring, *America's Longest War: The United States and Vietnam 1950–1975* (New York: Alfred A. Knopf, 1979, 2nd ed. 1986), p. 110; NSC action memo no. 273, 11/26/63, LBJ.

3. Herring, *America's Longest War*, p. 116.

4. *NYT*, n.d. (1965) reports McCloy receiving $30,000 from the Ford Foundation; *Wall Street Journal*, March 1, 1965, reports he was paid $49,914 by Chase in 1964, and he must have drawn a minimum of $100,000 from his Milbank, Tweed partnership. Finally, he was being paid thousands of dollars as a board director for numerous corporations.

5. Dean Rusk memorandum of conversation with Mr. John J. McCloy, 6/20/64, LBJ.

6. Endicott Peabody memo to the president, 11/6/67, NSF, Memos to the President, vol. 53, box 26, LBJ.

7. McCloy interview, Sept. 14, 1984; McCloy oral history, LBJ Library; Walter Isaacson and Evan Thomas, The Wise Men: *Six Friends and the World They Made,* pp. 647–48; Alan Brinkley, "John J. McCloy," *Harper's,* Feb. 1982.

8. Larry Berman, *Planning a Tragedy: The Americanization of the War in Vietnam* (New York: W. W. Norton, 1982), p. 33.

9. Lawrence H. Shoup and William Minter, *Imperial Brain Trust,* p. 238.

10. George S. Franklin, Jr., to Lew Douglas, 1/28/65, LD.

11. Godfrey Hodgson, "The Establishment," *Foreign Policy,* Spring 1973.

12. Lew Douglas cable to LBJ, 2/10/65; Douglas to the earl of Swinton, 7/8/65; Douglas to Congressman A. Willis Robertson, 7/30/65, LD. Douglas told anyone who would listen that South Vietnam was a "mouse trap" and the problem now was to find an "acceptable" way of escaping it. The whole notion of a monolithic communist menace was an "antiquated idea," and he believed that a country, "though it might be communistic, need not necessarily be the handmaiden and the servant of Peking, any more than we thoroughly understand that Tito is not necessarily orbiting around the Kremlin." (Robert Paul Browder and Thomas G. Smith, *Independent: A Biography of Lewis W. Douglas,* p. 396.)

13. Marcus Raskin and Bernard B. Fall, eds., *The Viet-Nam Reader* (New York: Random House, 1965), pp. 15–17.

14. Harriman to Arthur Schlesinger, 3/20/65, AH.

15. Shoup and Minter, *Imperial Brain Trust,* p. 210.

16. Ibid., p. 239.

17. Berman, *Planning a Tragedy,* p. 80.

18. Ibid., pp. 89–91.

19. Mac Bundy to LBJ, 2/7/65, LBJ.

20. NSC action memo no. 328, 4/6/65, LBJ.

21. Berman, *Planning a Tragedy,* p. 63.

22. "Commencement Address by John J. McCloy," Haverford College, 6/4/65, AH.

23. Dean Rusk to McCloy, 6/14/65; Harriman to McCloy, 6/28/65, AH.

24. William Bundy memo on Vietnam Panel, 7/10/65, LBJ.

25. Isaacson and Thomas, *Wise Men,* p. 650.

26. William Bundy memo on Vietnam Panel, 7/10/65, LBJ.

27. *The Pentagon Papers* (New York: Bantam, 1971), pp. 453–54.

28. Isaacson and Thomas, *Wise Men,* p. 691.

29. McCloy to Arthur Dean, 8/20/65, LBJ. On March 24, 1965, McNamara's chief aide, John T. McNaughton, wrote a memo to his boss in which he asserted that 70 percent of the U.S. aim in Vietnam was "to avoid a humiliating U.S. defeat. . . ." (*Pentagon Papers,* p. 432.)

30. William Bundy memo on Vietnam Panel, 7/10/65, LBJ.

31. Roswell Gilpatric to Mac Bundy, 7/9/65, LBJ.

32. William Bundy memo on Vietnam Panel, 7/10/65, LBJ.

33. Ibid.

34. Hodgson, "The Establishment," p. 21.

35. Isaacson and Thomas, *Wise Men,* p. 652.

36. Richard N. Goodwin, "The War Within," *NYT Magazine,* Aug. 21, 1988, p. 38.

37. Transcript of Cabinet Room meeting, 7/22/65, Meeting Notes File, box 1, LBJ.

38. Mac Bundy memo to the president, 7/28/65, LBJ.

39. Doris Kearns, *Lyndon Johnson and the American Dream,* p. 265.

40. Transcript of Cabinet Room meeting, 7/22/65, Meeting Notes File, box 1, LBJ.

41. Berman, *Planning a Tragedy,* pp. 151–52.

42. Clark Clifford to president, 5/17/65, LBJ.

43. Bundy memo to the president, 7/28/65, LBJ.

44. Marcus Raskin interview, April 28, 1985; Ralph Stavins, Richard J. Barnet, and Marcus G. Raskin, *Washington Plans an Aggressive War: A Documented Account of the United States' Adventure in Indochina* (London: Davis-Poynter, 1972), p. 192.

45. Bundy to president, 8/2/65, LBJ.

46. Hamilton Fish Armstrong to Arthur Dean, 8/9/65, LBJ. Nearly half of the Committee's membership overlapped with the Council on Foreign Relations. (Shoup and Minter, *Imperial Brain Trust,* p. 240.)

47. McCloy to Arthur Dean, 8/10/65, LBJ.

48. "Statement of Principles of Committee for an Effective and Durable Peace in Asia," 9/9/65, LBJ. The statement was actually drafted by members of the White House staff and State Department officials working under William Bundy. (Jonathan Moore memo to William Bundy, 8/3/65, LBJ.)

49. Noam Chomsky, *American Power and the New Mandarins* (New York: Pantheon, 1969), pp. 335–36.

50. Melvin Small, *Johnson, Nixon and the Doves* (New Brunswick, N.J.: Rutgers University Press, 1988), p. 61.

51. Chomsky, *American Power,* p. 303.

52. Meeting in Cabinet Room, 1/25/66, LBJ.

53. Mac Bundy to the president, 1/26/66, LBJ.

54. Isaacson and Thomas, *Wise Men,* p. 669.

55. Meeting in Cabinet Room, 1/28/66, LBJ.

56. Small, *Johnson, Nixon and the Doves,* p. 78.

57. Lew Douglas to Senator Fulbright, 7/23/66, LD.

58. Shoup and Minter, *Imperial Brain Trust,* p. 239.

59. Chomsky, *American Power,* p. 335.

60. Lew Douglas to Thomas Lamont, 10/17/66, LD.

61. Douglas to Fulbright, 7/23/66, LD.

62. Douglas to Lord Salter, 11/27/67, LD.

63. Douglas to Walden Moore, 10/12/67, LD.

64. Glenn T. Seaborg with Benjamin S. Loeb, *Stemming the Tide: Arms Control in the Johnson Administration* (Lexington, Mass.: Lexington Books, 1987), p. 359.

65. McCloy's meeting with Kissinger, State Department cable, 3/5/67, DOS FOIA.

66. Notes on conversation with John J. McCloy, 1/22/66, AH. In the same breakfast meeting, McCloy said that, as far as Germany was concerned, he was prepared to "settle the Oder-Neisse line with an agreement with the Russians that we would protect it from attack in either direction." Harriman thought this was a startling suggestion coming from McCloy, and so he immediately asked why McCloy hadn't posed it before. McCloy said he had. And it was true: he had done so back in 1956, when he wrote the preface to the Council on Foreign Relations' book on U.S.-Soviet relations. Harriman was skeptical and noted in a memo for his files, "I doubt whether he has put it that specifically, as the Germans would have a fit since they would think we would be giving up support for unification, this being their last card to play in return for Soviet agreement to unification."

67. Ibid.

68. Seaborg with Loeb, *Stemming the Tide,* pp. 139–40.

69. Secret McCloy cable to secretary of state, 4/15/66, DOS FOIA.

70. Dean Rusk appointment book, 3/7/66, LBJ; *NYT,* April 12, 1966.

71. Memo of conversation, McCloy, Erhard, et al., 4/17/66, State Department, DOS FOIA.

72. David P. Calleo, *The Imperious Economy* (Cambridge, Mass.: Harvard University Press, 1982), p. 10.

73. Lyndon B. Johnson, *The Vantage Point: Perspectives of the Presidency, 1963–1969,* p. 305.

74. John J. McCloy, "Statement on the Atlantic Alliance," 5/25/66, Subcommittee on National Security and International Operations, AH.

75. McCloy, "Statement on the Atlantic Alliance," 5/25/66, AH.

76. Johnson, *Vantage Point,* p. 307.

77. John J. McCloy testimony, 5/14/71, LD.

78. *NYT,* Oct. 27, 1966.

79. Calleo, *Imperious Economy,* pp. 21, 47, 60.

80. Johnson, *Vantage Point,* pp. 306–7.

81. Calleo, *Imperious Economy,* p. 55.

82. Johnson, *Vantage Point,* p. 307.

83. McNamara memorandum to the president, 9/19/66, LBJ.

84. McCloy's meeting with Kissinger, State Department cable, 3/5/67, DOS FOIA; Louis Heren, "The Duties in London of a Philadelphia Lawyer," *The Times* (London), March 14, 1967.

85. "Conversation with Jean Monnet," confidential State Department cable, Ambassador George McGhee to secretary of state, 10/14/66, AH.

86. Secret memo of conversation: Rusk, Ball, McGhee, Erhard, Schroder, et al., Blair House, 9/25/66, AH.

87. LBJ diary cards, 10/7/66, LBJ.

88. McGhee State Department cable to secretary of state, 10/14/66, AH.

89. Heren, "Duties in London." Heren, *The Times'* Washington correspondent, blamed McNamara's tough position on obtaining full payment on the offset deal for Erhard's downfall.

90. McCloy to President Johnson, 5/17/67, DOS FOIA.

91. *The Reporter,* May 18, 1967.

92. Raymond J. Albright memo to the secretary, 1/11/67, Treasury Department FOIA.

93. Memorandum of conversation, Secretary Fowler, McCloy, et al., 1/12/67, Treasury Department FOIA.

94. *The Reporter,* May 18, 1967.

95. In fact, the Pentagon estimated that the dual-basing, rotation scheme would be very costly. One 1966 study estimated that over a five-year period such rotations would add $9–25 to the Defense Department budget for every $1 improvement in the U.S. balance of payments. ("Balance of Payments Impact of Offset Arrangements and Troop Deployments," Alfred Puhan memo to Mr. Leddy, State Department, 9/29/66, with attached summary of Institute for Defense Analyses study, DOS FOIA.)

96. State Department cable to London and Bonn, 3/1/67, FOIA.

97. Johnson, *Vantage Point,* pp. 310–11.

98. McCloy later wrote the president that the German "gold letter" "protects US gold stocks against much more than defense expenditures in Germany." (See McCloy to Johnson, 5/17/67, State Department FOIA; see also "Deming Option Roman Two," 1/18/67, State Department FOIA.

99. *The Times* (London), March 14, 1967. McCloy was described in this dispatch as an "ornament of the Establishment."

100. *NYT,* April 24, 1967.

101. Ibid., April 29, 1967.

102. Johnson, *Vantage Point,* p. 311.

103. "The McCloy Visit," State Department cable, 3/6/67, FOIA.

104. *The Reporter,* May 18, 1967.

105. "Talking Paper for Mr. McCloy's meetings with Minister Schiller, Mr. Abs, Governor Blessing, and Minister Strauss: International Monetary Negotiations," 6/5/67, Treasury Department, FOIA.

106. When the Mansfield Amendment was reintroduced in the spring of 1971, McCloy again lobbied vigorously against any troop reductions, telling Congress: "To those who say that the presence of our troops in NATO simply extends the aspects of the Cold War, precisely because it does confirm and solidify the Alliance, I would simply reply that perhaps at another period in history the Alliance in its present convincing nature would be unnecessary and unproductive, but it is vital now. While it functions in full vigor, it, itself, contributes to the damping down of the cold war." (John J. McCloy testimony, 5/14/71, LD.)

107. "Report to NATO on Tripartite Talks," 6/7/67, State Department cable from Paris to secretary of state, DOS FOIA.

108. Frances FitzGerald, *Fire in the Lake: The Vietnamese and the Americans in Vietnam* (Boston: Atlantic/Little, Brown, 1972), p. 303.

109. Herring, *America's Longest War,* pp. 145, 147, 149, 174.

110. FitzGerald, *Fire in the Lake,* pp. 320, 354.

111. Herring, *America's Longest War,* p. 176; The Pentagon Papers (NYT), p. 485.

112. Townsend Hoopes, *The Limits of Intervention* (New York: David McKay, 1969), p. 57.

113. Secret memorandum of conversation with Secretary McNamara, 10/10/66, AH.

114. Secret memorandum of conversation with Secretary McNamara, 11/26/66, AH.

115. In the spring of 1966, Rostow told Harriman, "The President is going to stick it out. The bombing will escalate." When Harriman expressed the opinion that one had to be careful that the bombing campaign didn't eventually place us in a nuclear confrontation with the Soviet Union, Rostow demurred: "Oh, yes," he said, "we will probably have to get there [to that point] because it is only in extreme crises that some settlement will come." Such conversations only confirmed Harriman's worst fears about the advice the president was receiving. (Secret memorandum of conversation with the president, 5/30/66, AH.) Senator Fulbright agreed with Harriman's assessment of Walt Rostow, calling him the president's "Rasputin." (Fulbright to Lew Douglas, 1/9/68, LD.) Townsend Hoopes, the undersecretary of the air force, thought Rostow was a "fanatic in sheep's clothing." (Hoopes, *Limits of Intervention,* p. 61.)

116. Hoopes, *Limits of Intervention,* pp. 63, 89.

117. Endicott Peabody memo to the president, "John McCloy on Vietnam and the Presidency," 11/6/67, National Security File, Memos to the President, vol. 53, box 26, LBJ.

118. McCloy to LBJ, 3/16/67, LBJ.

119. Hoopes, *Limits of Intervention,* p. 90; David Halberstam, *The Best and the Brightest,* p. 783.

120. Herring, *America's Longest War,* pp. 178–79.

121. Top-secret memorandum of conversation with Secretary McNamara, 7/1/67, AH.

122. As late as Oct. 1967, McNamara told reporters at a Pentagon press conference, "I do not know any qualified military observer, national or foreign, who believes that there is a military stalemate." He felt compelled to maintain the fiction that the war could be won. The hypocrisy of his position led his own wife to observe that year that he was "at

war with himself." (Paul Hendrickson, "Self-inflicted Pain," *WP Magazine,* June 12, 1988, p. 23; Hoopes, *Limits of Intervention,* p. 86.)

123. Lew Douglas to Calvin Plimpton, 10/8/69, LD.

124. Hendrickson, "Self-inflicted Pain," *WP Magazine,* June 12, 1988.

125. Myra MacPherson, *A Long Time Passing* (Garden City, N.Y.: Doubleday, 1984), p. 145.

126. Halberstam, *Best and Brightest,* p. 771.

127. Isaacson and Thomas, *Wise Men,* p. 673.

128. Richard Falk interview, March 28, 1985.

129. Arthur M. Schlesinger, Jr., *The Bitter Heritage: Vietnam and American Democracy 1941–1968* (Greenwich, Conn.: Fawcett, 1968), p. 124.

130. James Rowe memorandum for the president, 5/17/67, LBJ.

131. John Roche eyes-only memo to the president, 5/26/67, LBJ.

132. Paul H. Douglas to McCloy, 7/28/67, LBJ.

133. Walt Rostow to the president, 10/9/67, LBJ.

134. Henry Cabot Lodge to Walt Rostow with attached "Memorandum Regarding my Several Conversations with Dr. James B. Conant Concerning His Joining the Committee for Peace with Freedom in Viet-Nam," LBJ; Walt Rostow to the president, 10/9/67, LBJ.

135. McCloy to Henry Cabot Lodge, 10/16/67, LBJ.

136. The "Wise Men" were unaware that McNamara's disaffection extended far beyond his criticism of the bombing. The day before the "Wise Men" met, McNamara told Johnson of his "belief that continuation of our present course of action in Southeast Asia would be dangerous, costly in lives, and unsatisfactory to the American people." (McNamara to the president, 11/1/67, LBJ.)

137. Herring, *America's Longest War,* p. 184.

138. Neil Sheehan, *A Bright Shining Lie: John Paul Vann and America in Vietnam* (New York: Random House, 1988), p. 695.

139. George Ball interview, Dec. 4–5, 1985; Isaacson and Thomas, *Wise Men,* p. 680.

140. Endicott Peabody memo to the president, 11/6/67, NSF, Memos to the President, vol. 53, box 26, LBJ.

141. Shoup and Minter, *Imperial Brain Trust,* pp. 240–41.

142. John J. McCloy to Averell Harriman, with attached speech, "Challenge in Europe," 2/5/68, AH; see also *The Nation,* Feb. 5, 1968.

143. *The Nation,* Feb. 5, 1968; *NYT,* Jan. 13, 1968; *Los Angeles Times,* Jan. 15, 1968.

144. Harriman to McCloy, 2/8/68, AH.

145. Harriman to McCloy, 1/30/68, AH.

146. Tom Johnson notes, daily diary, 1/30/68, LBJ.

147. Herring, *America's Longest War,* p. 191.

148. "Memorandum for the Files of Lewis L. Strauss," 2/5/68, Strauss Papers, AEC Series—McCloy, John J., HH.

149. Herring, *America's Longest War,* p. 194.

150. Ibid., p. 204.

151. Harriman appointment diary, 3/25/68, AH. Many historians have mistakenly placed McCloy at this March 26, 1968, "Wise Men" meeting. See Herring, *America's Longest War,* p. 206; Halberstam, *Best and Brightest,* p. 794; Hoopes, *Limits of Intervention,* p. 215.

152. Lovett soon began echoing McCloy's argument that Washington was "overcommitted." In 1968, Lovett told Harriman's personal assistant that the war had demonstrated that "we had neither the manpower nor the financial ability to support activities all around

the world at the rate we were accumulating. . . . I have always believed that you never ought to go to war unless you are prepared to fight full out." (Confidential interview of Robert Lovett by Mark L. Chadwin, 7/10/68, AH.)

153. Johnson, *Vantage Point*, p. 417.

154. Isaacson and Thomas, *Wise Men*, p. 695.

155. CIA memo, "Questions Concerning the Situation in Vietnam," 3/1/68, LBJ.

156. Herring, *America's Longest War*, p. 206.

157. Isaacson and Thomas, *Wise Men*, pp. 700–701.

158. Herring, *America's Longest War*, p. 206.

159. Johnson, *Vantage Point*, p. 418.

160. Herring, *America's Longest War*, pp. 208–11.

161. Lew Douglas to Dr. Calvin H. Plimpton, 10/8/69, LD.

162. Ronald Steel, *Walter Lippmann and the American Century*, p. 571.

163. Sheehan, *Bright Shining Lie*, p. 695.

164. Harriman confidential memorandum for personal files, 5/24/67, AH.

165. Mohamed Heikel, *The Cairo Documents: The Inside Story of Nasser and His Relationship with World Leaders, Rebels, and Statesmen* (Garden City, N.Y.: Doubleday, 1973), p. 249.

166. State Department memorandum of conversation, 4/2/68, DOS FOIA.

167. State Department cable, 3/23/68, DOS FOIA.

168. State Department cable, "McCloy and Shah," 4/1/68; 4/3/68, DOS FOIA.

169. State Department confidential memorandum of conversation, "Highlights of McCloy-Hoveyda Conversation," 3/31/68; State cable, "Shah reviewed with John McCloy . . . ," 4/3/68; State cable, "Saudi-Iranian Relations," 4/1/68, DOS FOIA.

170. State Department confidential memorandum of conversation, "Highlights of McCloy-Hoveyda Conversation," 3/31/68; McCloy-Mostofi memorandum of conversation, 4/2/68, DOS FOIA.

171. State Department cable, Dhahran to secretary of state, "McCloy Visit to Bahrein," 4/6/68, DOS FOIA.

172. Eilts cable to secretary of state, 4/10/68, DOS FOIA; Roger P. Davies to Dwight J. Porter, 4/29/68, DOS FOIA.

173. McCloy to Dean Rusk, 4/30/68, DOS FOIA; McCloy to George Ball, 2/17/76 (courtesy of David L. Dileo).

174. McCloy to Dean Rusk, 4/30/68, DOS FOIA; McCloy to George Ball, 2/17/76 (courtesy of David L. Dileo).

175. Lucius D. Battle memo to the secretary, 5/17/68, with attached talking points; Rusk letter to McCloy, 5/23/68, DOS FOIA; McCloy to George Ball, 2/17/76 (courtesy of David L. Dileo).

BOOK SEVEN

TWENTY-SEVEN: THE ESTABLISHMENT AT BAY: THE NIXON–KISSINGER ADMINISTRATION

1. Henry Kissinger, *White House Years*, p. 944.

2. Harriman was unaware of Kissinger's perfidy and completely misjudged what Kissinger would do with the national-security-adviser job. On Dec. 4, 1968, he told Robert Kleiman, a member of *The New York Times'* editorial board, "Off the record, I think Henry Kissinger is a fine appointment. . . . He won't try to make this into the same kind of job as Rostow and Bundy did, but will try to coordinate planning, and I think he'll do it well." (Harriman-Kleiman telcon, 12/4/68, AH.)

3. At a critical juncture, he called Allen from a phone booth in Paris and warned him

that the Johnson administration had negotiated a bombing pause. The tip allowed the Nixon campaign to prepare for the news and encourage the Thieu regime in Saigon to repudiate the Paris negotiations. Three days before the election, Thieu did exactly that, which publicly undermined the chances for an early cease-fire. This in turn dented Humphrey's late surge in the opinion polls, and may have cost him the narrow election. Kissinger's information, according to John Mitchell, was "basic." Richard Allen later told Seymour Hersh, "My attitude was that it was inevitable that Kissinger would have to be part of our administration. . . . Kissinger had proven his mettle by tipping us. It took some balls to give us those tips." It was, after all, "a pretty dangerous thing for him to be screwing around with the national security." (Seymour Hersh, *The Price of Power: Kissinger in the Nixon White House* [New York: Summit, 1983], pp. 11–22; Stephen E. Ambrose, *Nixon: The Triumph of a Politician 1962–1972* [New York: Simon & Schuster, 1989], pp. 196, 208.)

4. McCloy to George Ball, 2/17/76 (courtesy of David L. Dileo); McCloy interview, Sept. 14, 1984; Stephen R. Graubard, *Kissinger: Portrait of a Mind* (New York: W. W. Norton, 1973), p. 115.

5. McCloy interview, May 26, 1983.

6. Henry Kissinger, *White House Years,* pp. 22–23.

7. Anthony Sampson, *The Seven Sisters: The Great Oil Companies and the World They Shaped* (New York: Viking, 1975), pp. 245–46.

8. Kissinger, *White House Years,* pp. 341, 360–61.

9. Raymond L. Garthoff, *Détente and Confrontation: American-Soviet Relations from Nixon to Reagan* (Washington, D.C.: The Brookings Institution, 1985), p. 135; John Newhouse, *War and Peace in the Nuclear Age* (New York: Alfred A. Knopf, 1989), pp. 216, 222.

10. McGeorge Bundy, *Danger and Survival* (New York: Random House, 1988), pp. 551–52. Bundy acknowledges that the "destabilizing character of MIRV is not so hard to understand that it was not noticed before it was deployed." But he argues that the "cause of stopping MIRV never had top priority for more than a few" and makes no mention of McCloy's vigorous opposition to MIRVing.

11. Kissinger, *White House Years,* pp. 543, 131.

12. McCloy interview, Dec. 3, 1985. McCloy's position was supported by the CIA's estimates, which concluded that the Soviets were not seeking a "first-strike" capability and were not intending to MIRV their new SS-9 missile. Kissinger, however, forced the Agency to change its estimate. (Hersh, *Price of Power,* pp. 495–97.)

13. Garthoff, *Détente and Confrontation,* p. 136; Hersh, *Price of Power,* p. 165; Kissinger, *White House Years,* p. 540. Kissinger himself, four years later, admitted, "I would say in retrospect that I wish I had thought through the implications of a MIRVed world more thoughtfully in 1969 and in 1970 than I did." (Newhouse, *War and Peace,* pp. 222–23.)

14. Strobe Talbot, *The Master of the Game: Paul Nitze and the Nuclear Peace* (New York: Alfred A. Knopf, 1988), p. 124.

15. Kissinger to McCloy, 12/12/69, NSC FOIA.

16. Hedrick Smith, "Panel Urges U.S. to Yield on Missile Site Inspection," *NYT,* Jan. 9, 1971.

17. Hersh, *Price of Power,* p. 166.

18. McCloy interview, Dec. 3, 1985.

19. Averell Harriman memorandum of conversation, 12/2/70, AH. Harriman was told this by Ed Williams, who had recently lunched with Kissinger.

20. McCloy to Hamilton Fish Armstrong, 2/28/68, PU.

21. Richard Falk interview, March 28, 1985.

22. Minutes of the 153rd annual meeting of the board of directors, 11/4/70, LD.

23. McCloy to Lew Douglas, 1/29/69, LD.

24. Lew Douglas to Bayless Manning, 8/10/72, LD.

25. Richard J. Barnet, Roots of War: *Men and Institutions Behind U.S. Foreign Policy* (Baltimore, Penguin, 1973), p. 49.

26. Robert D. Schulzinger, *The Wise Men of Foreign Affairs: The History of the Council on Foreign Relations* p. 209.

27. Ibid., p. 214.

28. Rolland Bushner memo to all committee chairmen, 12/4/69, LD.

29. Richard Falk interview, March 28, 1985; Laurence H. Shoup and William Minter, *Imperial Brain Trust,* p. 46; Schulzinger, *Wise Men of Foreign Affairs,* p. 211.

30. Richard J. Barnet interview, Dec. 1, 1989.

31. Schulzinger, *Wise Men of Foreign Affairs,* p. 211.

32. James H. Billington to Bayless Manning, 1/15/73, LD.

33. Francis M. Bator to Bayless Manning, 1/19/73, LD.

34. Richard J. Barnet interview, Dec. 1, 1989. Barnet was first sponsored as a Council member in 1968, by Arthur Dean.

35. Francis M. Bator to Bayless Manning, 1/19/73, LD.

36. Shoup and Minter, *Imperial Brain Trust,* p. 46.

37. Ibid., pp. 46–47.

38. Schulzinger, *Wise Men of Foreign Affairs,* p. 242.

39. Ambrose, Nixon, p. 386.

40. Kissinger, *White House Years,* pp. 942, 944–45.

41. Ibid., pp. 945–46.

42. McCloy to Hamilton Fish Armstrong, with attachment, 5/17/71, PU. McCloy once told James Chace, then the managing editor of *Foreign Affairs*, "We had no fear of the Soviets at the end of the war. NATO wasn't constructed merely out of the Soviet threat." (James Chace interview, March 3, 1982.)

43. Kissinger, *White House Years,* p. 22.

44. Michael Sterner interview, Aug. 14, 1984.

45. Ibid.

46. Testimony of James E. Akins, 10/11/73, executive session of hearings before the Senate Subcommittee on Multinational Corporations, pt. 5, pp. 1–28; John M. Blair, *The Control of Oil* (New York: Pantheon, 1976), p. 221.

47. Steven Weinberg, *Armand Hammer: The Untold Story* (New York: Little, Brown, 1989), pp. 210–13.

48. Secret State Department doc., "Current Foreign Relations," issue no. 16, April 22, 1970.

49. Sampson, *Seven Sisters,* pp. 254–55.

50. Secret State Department memorandum of conversation, "Libyan Oil Negotiations," 9/26/70, DOS FOIA,

51. Confidential and private letter from McCloy to Richard McLaren, assistant attorney general, 7/23/71, Justice Department FOIA.

52. Private and confidential letter from McCloy to McLaren, 7/23/71, Justice Department FOIA.

53. Justice Department memo, "Business Review Letters Issued in Connection with OPEC Negotiations January-February 1971," 1/28/72, p. 6, Justice Department FOIA.

54. Dudley H. Chapman memo to Richard W. McLaren, 2/1/71, attached to Justice Department memo on business-review letters, 1/28/72, Justice Department FOIA.

55. Author's visit to McCloy's office, May 26, 1983.

56. Senate Multinational Hearings, pt. 5, p. 14.

57. Justice Department memo, "Business Review Letters Issued in Connection with OPEC Negotiations January-February 1971," 1/28/72, p. 4, Justice Department FOIA.

58. Senate Multinational Hearings, pt. 5, pp. 69–70.

59. Sampson, *Seven Sisters,* p. 259.

60. Senate Multinational Hearings, pt. 5, p. 263; Sampson, *Seven Sisters,* pp. 260–63.

61. Senate Multinational Hearings, pt. 5, pp. 265–66.

62. Ibid., p. 265.

63. Ibid., p. 271.

64. Sampson, *Seven Sisters,* p. 269.

65. McCloy to McLaren, 7/23/71, Justice Department FOIA.

66. Dudley H. Chapman memo to Richard W. McLaren, 8/25/71, Justice Department FOIA.

67. Robert Engler, *The Brotherhood of Oil* (Chicago: University of Chicago Press, 1977), p. 119.

68. Sampson, *Seven Sisters,* p. 283.

69. Ibid., p. 279. Sampson is quoting Professor Maurice Adelman, *Foreign Policy,* Autumn 1972.

70. Robert Sherrill, *The Oil Follies of 1970–1980: How the Petroleum Industry Stole the Show (and Much More Besides)* (Garden City, N.Y.: Anchor-Doubleday, 1983), p. 145.

71. Ibid., p. 103.

72. Senate Multinational Hearings, pt. 5, p. 276.

73. The Foreign Service officer in question, Eugene H. Bird, is my father. The cable, "The Saudi Oil Income Spending Machine," dated Aug. 26, 1972, was obtained from DOS FOIA. Actually, the Saudis would accumulate about $120 billion in dollar reserves by 1982.

74. Sampson, *Seven Sisters,* pp. 291–92.

75. Henry Kissinger, *Years of Upheaval* (Boston: Little, Brown, 1982), pp. 461–62; Sampson, *Seven Sisters,* pp. 292–93.

76. Harriman-Kissinger memorandum of conversation, Sept. 7, 1973, referring to a conversation of the previous day, AH. Later that autumn, after the October War, McCloy went to see Kissinger and, among other things, suggested there ought to be a "common policy" between Washington and Europe on a solution to the Arab-Israeli conflict. In notes he jotted down in preparation for the meeting, he asked, "What does Europe want to see accomplished there? Would it prefer to see Israel liquidated in return for the continued flow of oil? If not, what?" ("Notes for Meeting with Secretary Kissinger on November 28, 1973," box NA 1, folder 1, JJM.)

77. Sherrill, *Oil Follies,* p. 195; Sampson, *Seven Sisters,* p. 300.

78. As the chairman of Standard Oil of California said in 1974, "Who owns certain assets is not the important thing. The international companies still have a role to play in the Persian Gulf. The important things were access to oil and the incentive given us to go on producing it and developing new fields." (Engler, *Brotherhood of Oil,* pp. 123, 121.)

79. McCloy to Chief Judge William B. Jones, 9/24/75, Joint Collection, University of Missouri Western Historical Manuscript Collection–Columbia and State Historical

Society of Missouri Manuscripts, provided to the author by Steven Weinberg; see also Weinberg, *Armand Hammer,* The Untold Story, pp. 3–10, 285.

80. *NYT,* Dec. 31, 1976.

81. *Washington Star,* Dec. 31, 1975; *NYT,* Jan. 4, 1976; Jack Sunderland interview, Sept. 26, 1985.

82. *Philadelphia Inquirer,* April 6, 1976.

83. Elliot Richardson, *The Creative Balance* (New York: Holt, Rinehart & Winston, 1976), pp. 4–5; George Higgins, *The Friends of Richard Nixon* (New York: Ballantine, 1975), pp. 251–52; Theodore H. White, *Breach of Faith: The Fall of Richard Nixon* (New York: Atheneum, 1975), p. 220.

84. Harriman, "Notes for Files," 5/21/73, AH.

85. White, *Breach of Faith,* p. 21; Fawn M. Brodie, *Richard Nixon: The Shaping of His Character* (New York: W. W. Norton, 1981), p. 19.

86. McCloy to Douglas, 6/15/73, LD.

87. Ibid.

88. Robert Paul Browder and Thomas G. Smith, *Independent: A Biography of Lewis W. Douglas,* p. 399.

89. McCloy to Douglas, 6/29/73, LD.

90. Nixon would have felt his paranoia vindicated had he known, for instance, that someone like Lew Douglas was lunching with Alger Hiss, the very same Harvard-trained, East Coast lawyer whose perjury conviction had jump-started Nixon's political career.

91. Richardson, *Creative Balance,* p. 5.

92. Christopher Paine interview, Oct. 9, 1986.

TWENTY-EIGHT: McCLOY AND THE IRAN-HOSTAGE CRISIS

1. James A. Bill, The Eagle and the Lion: *The Tragedy of American-Iranian Relations* (New Haven, Conn.: Yale University Press, 1988), p. 334.

2. Mark Hulbert, *Interlock* (New York: Richardson & Snyder, 1982), p. 85; Robert D. McFadden, Joseph B. Treaster, and Maurice Carroll, *No Hiding Place: New York Times Inside Report on the Hostage Crisis* (New York: Times Books, 1981), p. 153. Chase also owned 35 percent of the International Bank of Iran. ("Recent History of Chase and Iran," memo, n.d., box SH 1, folder 1, JJM.)

3. McCloy interview, Dec. 3, 1985.

4. This information comes from a friend of John J. McCloy II.

5. Bill, *Eagle and Lion,* p. 508. However, William Sullivan reports that Bowie left Iran with the impression that the shah "was not a man who was prepared to take vigorous action to defend his position." (William H. Sullivan, *Mission to Iran* (New York: W. W. Norton, 1981), p. 198.) David Rockefeller himself had visited the shah in Iran on March 1, 1978, soon after the first demonstrations in Qum erupted.

6. Gary Sick, *All Fall Down: America's Tragic Encounter with Iran* (New York: Random House, 1985), p. 105.

7. Sullivan, *Mission to Iran,* p. 199.

8. Bill, *Eagle and Lion,* p. 436.

9. Bill, *Eagle and Lion,* p. 251; Zbigniew Brzezinski, *Power and Principle: Memoirs of the National Security Adviser 1977–1981,* (New York, Farrar, Straus & Giroux, 1983), p. 363.

10. William Sullivan, *Mission to Iran,* pp. 203–4.

11. Bill, *Eagle and Lion,* p. 259.

12. McFadden et al., *No Hiding Place,* p. 152, 154.

13. Memo for the record re: Professor Lenczowski, 12/10/79, box SH 1, folder 2, JJM. The book was apparently never published.

14. Joseph V. Reed memo to "Volunteer Team on the Project Eagle,'" 10/23/79; McCloy memo to Mr. Reilly, 5/7/80, box SH 1, folder 2, JJM. In the spring of 1980, Reed informed members of Project Alpha that he had just discovered that his phone lines at One Chase Plaza were being wiretapped. There is no indication in McCloy's papers whether they determined who was responsible.

15. Brzezinski, *Power and Principle,* p. 473.

16. Overheard by James E. Akins, whom Kissinger had fired as ambassador to Saudi Arabia in 1975, the conversation was reported to Brzezinski the very next day. (Akins to Brzezinski, 12/6/78, Mandatory review 5/4/89, JC.)

17. James E. Akins to Brzezinski, 12/6/78, JC.

18. Brzezinski, *Power and Principle,* p. 473; William Shawcross, *The Shah's Last Ride: The Fate of an Ally* (New York: Simon & Schuster, 1988), p. 153.

19. Shawcross, *Shah's Last Ride,* p. 154; Jimmy Carter, *Keeping Faith: Memoirs of a President* (New York: Bantam, 1982), p. 452.

20. Hamilton Jordan, *Crisis: The Last Year of the Carter Presidency* (New York: G. P. Putnam's Sons, 1982), p. 29.

21. Bill, *Eagle and Lion,* p. 335; Shawcross, *Shah's Last Ride,* p. 13.

22. Jimmy Carter says "the question was brought to me at least weekly from some source." (Carter, *Keeping Faith,* p. 453.)

23. Rosalynn Carter, *First Lady from Plains* (New York: Ballantine, 1984), p. 292

24. Donald F. McHenry interview, March 12, 1982.

25. McCloy "personal and confidential" memo to Warren Christopher, 4/16/79, declassified 3/16/88, JC.

26. Warren Christopher to McCloy, 4/18/79, declassified 3/16/88, JC.

27. McCloy to Christopher, 4/20/79, declassified 3/16/88, JC.

28. McFadden et al., *No Hiding Place,* p. 159; Bill, *Eagle and Lion,* p. 335. On May 31, 1979, McCloy again wrote Christopher a memo, warning him of a "rather sordid denouement to this whole affair" if the government didn't act. "I cannot predict its form, but it could be tragic." (McCloy to Christopher, 5/31/79, box SH 1, folder 12, JJM.)

29. Cyrus Vance interview, Oct. 10, 1985.

30. McCloy interview, Dec. 3, 1985.

31. David Newsom interview, Feb. 15, 1984.

32. McCloy interview, Dec. 3, 1985.

33. Donald F. McHenry interview, March 12, 1982.

34. Gary Sick interview, Aug. 5, 1985. George Ball had urged McCloy to see Sick as early as Jan. 1979. (Memo re: meeting with George Ball, 1/28/79, box SH 1, folder 9, JJM.)

35. McFadden et al., *No Hiding Place,* p. 159; Shawcross, *Shah's Last Ride,* pp. 240–41.

36. Brzezinski, *Power and Principle,* p. 474.

37. McCloy to Cyrus Vance, 10/23/78, State Department FOIA.

38. McCloy to Senator Edward Zorinsky, 2/27/78, AH; "Notables Unite in Endorsing Canal Treaties," *WP,* Oct. 16, 1977. One senator, Charles Mathias of Maryland, thought McCloy's testimony "made the difference." (McCloy to Harriman, 5/10/78, AH.) See also letter from Carter thanking McCloy for his assistance in passage of Panama Canal Treaty, 3/27/78, WHCF, Name File, McCloy I-P, JC.

39. Walter Isaacson and Evan Thomas, *The Wise Men: Six Friends and the World They Made,* p. 733.

40. Carter daily diary, 6/12/79, and photos of lunch, JC.

41. Hamilton Jordan observed, "SALT was the background for all our discussions in those days." (McFadden et al., *No Hiding Places,* p. 157.)

42. Brzezinski, *Power and Principle,* p. 474.

43. "Notes from Admiral Gayler," Harriman memo, Sept. 1979, AH. Gayler told Harriman, "The Brigade probably has been in Cuba for many years, and there has been no change and there is no danger to the United States." See also censored Defense Intelligence Agency "Intelligence Appraisal / Cuba: Soviet Brigade(U) 8 December 1979, DIAIAPPR 224-79," DIA FOIA. At the height of the Cuban missile crisis, the Soviets had some twenty thousand troops in Cuba. (*NYT,* Sept. 30, 1979.)

44. Robert Perito and John McCloy memorandum of conversation, Sept. 24, 1979, Metropolitan Club, Washington, D.C., State Department FOIA, declassified Feb. 22, 1985; *NYT,* Sept. 30, 1979; *Philadelphia Inquirer,* Sept. 28, 1979.

45. Carter daily diary, 9/29/79, JC.

46. Confusion arose later over the shah's medical condition. Carter said he was informed that the shah was near death and that the only treatment possible existed in New York. Rockefeller's physician, Dr. Benjamin Kean, in fact only said that the shah should be treated in a matter of weeks and listed a number of hospitals outside the United States that could handle the case. (Hulbert, *Interlock,* p. 145; Shawcross, *Shah's Last Ride,* p. 250.)

47. Jordan, *Crisis,* p. 31. Carter's annoyance may have been stimulated by an angry message he received indirectly from the shah. In Sept. 1979, the shah told two Rockefeller-McCloy associates in Mexico, "I ask President Carter directly why I am not welcome in the United States. . . . I cannot accept this insult. . . . I cannot ignore the fact that I have been mistreated by President Carter." (Memo for the record, 9/9/79, box SH 1, folder 2, JJM.)

48. Jordan, *Crisis,* p. 32.

49. Reed memo to "Volunteer Team on the 'Project Eagle,' 10/23/79, box SH 1, folder 2, JJM.

50. Bill, *Eagle and Lion,* p. 335.

51. Ibid.

52. Hulbert, *Interlock,* p. 143.

53. Memo of conversation, 11/12/79, box SH 1, folder 12, JJM.

54. David Newsom interview, Feb. 15, 1984.

55. Chase Bank was not the only one of McCloy's legal clients threatened by developments in revolutionary Iran. By the summer of 1979, Iranian oil production had climbed back to four million barrels per day, and most of this oil was being marketed independently of the major oil companies. This threatened the companies' and OPEC's control over price and production quotas globally. (See Kai Bird, "The Workers' Committees Are Pumping Iran," *The Nation,* April 21, 1979; Hulbert, *Interlock,* p. 144.)

56. Bill, *Eagle and Lion,* pp. 342–48; Hulbert, *Interlock,* p. 144.

57. Hulbert, *Interlock,* pp. 156, 171–72, 174.

58. David Newsom interview, Feb. 15, 1984.

59. James B. Stewart, *The Partners: Inside America's Most Powerful Law Firms,* pp. 36, 344.

60. Paul Hoffman, *Lions of the Eighties* (Garden City, N.Y.: Doubleday, 1982), p. 313.

TWILIGHT YEARS

1. William Casey memo to "All members of the interim Foreign Policy Advisory Board," 12/23/80; "A Strategy for Foreign Policy and National Security," n.d., box C1, folder RT 1, JJM.

2. William Casey conversation with author, Eisenhower Conference, Hofstra University, March 29–31, 1984.

3. Interview with anonymous member of Council on Foreign Relations, Aug. 1982.

4. McCloy to Cyrus Vance, April 25, 1977, DOS FOIA.

5. McCloy to Al Haig, 2/10/81, DOS FOIA.

6. Richard Burt memo to the secretary, 6/16/82, State Department FOIA.

7. McCloy interview, March 19, 1986.

8. McCloy interviews, Sept. 14, 1984, March 19, 1986; John Newhouse, *War and Peace in the Nuclear Age,* p. 375. Newhouse dates the McCloy letter to Reagan as late 1984 or early 1985. In an interview with the author, McCloy referred to the possibility of writing such a letter to Reagan in March 1986.

9. *WP,* April 3, 1985; author's notes.

10. The author was present at the ceremony. See also Isaacson and Thomas, *Wise Men,* p. 734; *WP,* April 3, 1985.

11. Isaacson and Thomas, *Wise Men,* p. 734.

12. *NYT,* Nov. 4, 1981.

13. Dan Charles, memorandum of conversation, June 21, 1984.

14. Mrs. Mary Paulsen interview, Aug. 7, 1985.

15. Author's interview with a member of the McCloy household who prefers to remain anonymous.

16. *WP,* March 12, 1989. The details of McCloy's death are taken from "Certificate of Death, State of Connecticut, Dept. of Health Services, No. 212, Stamford Town Clerk's Office."

ARCHIVAL SOURCES

Cadwalder, Wickersham & Taft Archives, Brooklyn, N.Y. (CWT)
Jimmy Carter Presidential Library, Atlanta, Ga. (JC)
Chase Manhattan Bank Archives, N.Y., N.Y. (CMB)
Council on Foreign Relations Archives, N.Y., N.Y. (CFR)
Lewis W. Douglas Papers, University of Arizona, Tucson, Ariz. (LD)
Dwight D. Eisenhower Presidential Library, Abilene, Kan. (DDE)
Ford Foundation Archives, N.Y., N.Y. (FF)
Gerald Ford Presidential Library, Grand Rapids, Mich. (GF)
Averell Harriman Papers, Washington, D.C. (AH)
Amzi Hoffman Papers
Herbert Hoover Presidential Library, West Branch, Iowa (HH)
Lyndon B. Johnson Presidential Library, Austin, Tex. (LBJ)
John F. Kennedy Presidential Library, Boston, Mass. (JFK)
Library of Congress Manuscript Collection, Washington, D.C. (LOC)
George C. Marshall Library, Lexington, Va. (GCM)
Papers of John J. McCloy, Amherst College Manuscript Collection (JJM)
National Archives, Washington, D.C., and Suitland, Md. (NA)
Vice-Presidential Papers of Richard Nixon, Calif. (RN)
Peddie School Archives, Hightstown, N.J. (PS)
Penn Mutual Life Insurance Co. Archives, Philadelphia, Pa. (PML)
Princeton University Manuscript Library, Princeton, N.J. (PU)
Public Records Office, London (PRO)
Rockefeller Family Archives, Pocantico, N.Y. (RF)
Franklin D. Roosevelt Presidential Library, Hyde Park, N.Y. (FDR)
Harry S Truman Presidential Library, Independence, Mo. (HST)
U.S. Military Archives, Carlyle Barracks, Pa. (CB)
World Bank Archives, Washington, D.C. (WB)

In addition, hundreds of government documents were obtained under the Freedom of Information Act (FOIA) from the State Department, the Central Intelligence Agency, the Treasury Department, the Federal Bureau of Investigation, the Securities and Exchange Commission, the National Security Agency, the National Security Council, and the Defense Department.

INTERVIEWS

Alice Acheson, 6/15/84
James Akins, 3/9/83
Herve Alphand, 12/22/83*
Egon Bahr, 12/13/83*
George Ball, 12/4–5/85
Richard J. Barnet, 12/1/89
Lucius Battle, 3/9/83
Doug Bazata, 10/9/84
Karl R. Bendetsen, 11/10/83
Armand Berard, 12/20/83*
Donald C. Bergus, phone interview, 6/15/83
Kurt Birrenbach, 2/14/84*
Eugene Black, 7/24/84
Herbert Blankenhorn*
Jack Blum, 2/16/83
Judge Dudley Bonsal, 12/6/85
Robert Bowie, 8/29/84
John Bross, 7/16/84
Irving Brown, 4/2/84
Herbert Brownell, 3/17/86
Jack W. Buford, 1/17–18/85, 2/1/85*
Michael Burke, 9/23/85
Axel von dem Bussche, 4/5/84
Benjamin Buttenwieser, 4/29/82, 7/15/82, 11/11/82
Helen Buttenwieser, 3/17/83
Henry Byroade, 4/11/84
William Casey, 3/30/84
George Champion, 2/20/85
Ramsey Clark, phone interview, 7/22/83
Eugene "Pete" Collado, 8/18/82
Lucien Conein, 10/9/84
Don Cook, 12/19/83*
William Crago, phone interview, 10/3/83
Richard N. Crockett, 6/17/83
Ernest Cuneo, 8/1/85
John Paton Davies, 6/2/84
Dorothy "Dot" Davison, 11/5/86
Gates Davison, 11/5/86
Eli Debevoise, 7/15/82
Francis Dickman, 9/12/82
Grafin Donhoff, 11/28/83*
Eleanor Lansing Dulles, 4/7/82
John F. Dulles, Jr., 5/1/85*
Harry Dunn, 2/7/85*
John Eichler, 6/22/83
Milton Eisenhower, 8/5/82
John Eliff, phone interview, 5/19/83
Edward J. Ennis, 10/23/81, 9/20/84, 8/4/85
Erhard Eppler, 3/5/84*
Wilbur Crane Eveland, 7/25/82
Richard Falk, 3/28/85
Benjamin B. Ferencz, 9/15/84
Alexander Forger, 12/6/85
Michael Forrestal, 10/10/85
William C. Foster, 8/5/82
Lloyd Garrison, 1/31/84
Mrs. Colonel Al Gerhardt, 7/10/84
Leo Gottlieb, 6/22/83
Wilhelm Grewe, 2/9/84*
Morton Halperin, 7/22/85
Averell Harriman, 3/25/82
Ambassador Parker T. Hart, 7/31/84
Sir William Hayter, 1/29/84*
Mohamed Heikel, 12/82
Struve Hensel, 1/26/84
Aiko and John Herzig, 2/2/83
Alger Hiss, 1/12/82
Amzi Hoffman, 12/6/82*
Jean Holke, 3/14/83
William Horhi, 8/17/82*
Stefan Heym, 11/7/83*
Joseph Iseman, 6/22/83
Senator Jacob Javits, 11/9/82
Otto John, 2/20/84*

Joseph E. Johnson, 6/21/83
Jan Karski, phone interview 4/21/87, speech 3/29/87
Henry Kellerman, 10/3/84*
Robert Kempner, 11/24–25/83*
Bernard Knox, 10/9/84
Otto Kranzbuhler, 2/21/84*
Betty Goetz Lall, 2/20/85, 2/23/85
William John Lamont, phone interview, 2/9/83
Fran Lapinski, 8/9/84
Melvin Lasky, phone interview, 1/2/87
Jerome Levinson, 12/11/80
Walter J. Levy, 12/5/85
Robert Lochner, 2/28/84*
John Loftus, phone interview, 5/18/83
Angus Macbeth, 7/9/84
Harry Magdoff, 2/27/82
Edwin M. Martin, 7/10/84
John J. McCloy, 5/26/83, 6/23/83, 6/25/83, 9/5/84, 9/14/84, 10/9/85, 12/3/85, 3/19/86, 7/10/86
John W. McDonald, Jr., 3/8/83
George McGhee, 6/14/83
Donald F. McHenry, 3/12/82
Robert S. McNamara, 3/7/90
Martin Mendelsohn, 8/21/84
Elizabeth Luce Moore, 10/21/83
Maurice "Tex" Moore, 10/21/83
David Newsom, 2/15/84
James E. O'Brien, 1/85*
Robert Oliver, 1/15/85*
Sir Con O'Neill, 2/1/84*
Marcel Ophuls, 4/13/85
Christopher Paine, 10/9/86
Mrs. Mary Paulsen (formerly Mrs. Mary Weicker), 8/7/85
Judge David W. Peck, 9/20/84
John Pehle, 8/9/84
Mrs. John "Madge" Pendelton, 7/18/82
Martin Peretz, 4/14/86
Howard Petersen, 8/30/82
Walter L. Pforzheimer, 7/8/84
Francis Plimpton, 3/16/82; 6/23/82
Mrs. Pauline Plimpton, 3/16/82
Milt Pollen, 8/21/84*
Marcus Raskin, 4/28/85
Joseph Rauh, 11/1/83
James Reston, 8/9/84
Mahmoud Riad, 11/22/83,
Gerhardt Riegner, 12/16/83*
Mary Ellen Crane Rossiter, 10/31/87
James Rowe, Jr., 10/12/83
Dean Rusk, 12/16/87; 11/17/82
Arthur Schlesinger, Jr., 12/6/85
Helmut Schmidt, 12/14/83*
Lord Shawcross, 2/2/84*
Saul Sherman, 2/3/84
Benjamin Shute, 6/24/83
Gary Sick, 8/5/85
Davidson Sommers, 7/20/84
Drexel Sprecher, 5/25/84, 7/11/84
Michael Sterner, 8/14/84
Dietrich Stobbe, 11/22/83*
Phil Stoddard, 12/12/84
I. F. Stone, 1/15/82
Shepard Stone, 3/1/84, 3/3/84*
Jack Sunderland, 9/25–26/84*
Maxwell Taylor, 11/7/83
Telford Taylor, 11/11/82
Stefan Thomas, 2/27/84, 2/25/84*
Thomas Troy, 4/4/86
Cyrus Vance, 10/10/85
Eric Warburg, 3/10/86
Mrs. Frederick Warburg, 4/10/84
Bethuel M. Webster, 12/4/85
Herbert Wechsler, 10/23/81*
Albert Wedemeyer, 11/11/83
Senator Lowell Weicker, 3/5/85
Langbourne M. Williams, 4/1/86

Note: Those interviews marked with an asterisk were conducted by a former colleague. In addition, I have consulted scores of oral-history interviews on file at the various archives.

BIBLIOGRAPHY

Abel, Elie. *The Missile Crisis.* New York: J. B. Lippincott, 1966.

Abell, Tyler, ed. *Drew Pearson: Diaries 1949–1959.* New York: Holt, Rinehart & Winston, 1974.

Acheson, Dean. *Sketches from Life of Men I Have Known.* New York: Harper & Brothers, 1959.

———. *Present at the Creation.* New York: W. W. Norton, 1969.

———. *Morning and Noon.* Boston: Houghton Mifflin, 1965.

Adenauer, Konrad. *Memoirs, 1945–1953.* Chicago: Henry Regnery, 1966.

Alperovitz, Gar. *Atomic Diplomacy: Hiroshima and Potsdam.* New York: Penguin, 1985.

Ambrose, Stephen E. *Rise to Globalism: American Foreign Policy, 1938–1980.* New York: Penguin, 1971.

———. *Ike's Spies: Eisenhower and the Espionage Establishment.* Garden City, N.Y.: Doubleday, 1981.

———. *Eisenhower: Soldier, General of the Army, President-Elect, 1890–1952.* New York: Simon & Schuster, 1983.

———. *Eisenhower the President: 1952–1969.* London: George Allen & Unwin, 1984.

———. *Nixon: The Triumph of a Politician 1962–1972.* New York: Simon & Schuster, 1987, 1989.

Ambrose, Stephen E., and Immerman, Richard. *Milton S. Eisenhower: Educational Statesman.* Baltimore: Johns Hopkins University Press, 1983.

Amrine, Michael. *The Great Decision: The Secret History of the Atomic Bomb.* New York: G. P. Putnam's Sons, 1959.

Anson, Robert Sam. *"They've Killed the President:" The Search for the Murderers of John F. Kennedy.* New York: Bantam, 1975.

Armstrong, Hamilton Fish. *Fifty Years of Foreign Affairs.* New York: Praeger, 1972.

Attali, Jacques. *A Man of Influence: The Extraordinary Career of S. G. Warburg.* Bethesda, Md.: Adler & Adler, 1987.

Backer, John H. *Winds of History: The German Years of Lucius DuBignon Clay.* New York: Van Nostrand Reinhold, 1983.

Baker, Leonard. *Brandeis and Frankfurter.* New York: Harper & Row, 1984.

Ball, George. *The Past Has Another Pattern.* New York: W. W. Norton, 1982.

Baltzell, E. Digby. *Philadelphia Gentlemen: The Making of a National Upper Class.* Glencoe: Ill.: Free Press, 1958.

———. *The Protestant Establishment: Aristocracy and Caste in America.* New York: Random House, 1964.

———. *Puritan Boston and Quaker Philadelphia.* New York: Free Press, 1979.

Barnet, Richard J. *Roots of War: Men and Institutions Behind U.S. Foreign Policy.* Baltimore: Penguin, 1973.

———. *The Alliance: America-Europe-Japan, Makers of* the Postwar World. New York: Simon & Schuster, 1983.

Beard, Charles A. *President Roosevelt and the Coming of the War, 1941.* New Haven, Conn.: Yale University Press, 1948.

Beesly, Patrick. *Room 40: British Naval Intelligence 1914–18.* (New York: Harcourt Brace Jovanovich, 1982.

Belin, David W., Esq. *November 22, 1963: You Are the Jury.* New York: Times Books, 1973.

———. *Final Disclosure: The Full Truth About the Assassination of President Kennedy.* New York: Charles Scribner's Sons, 1988.

Berman, Larry. *Planning a Tragedy: The Americanization of the War in Vietnam.* New York: W. W. Norton, 1982.

———. *Lyndon Johnson's War: The Road to Stalemate in Vietnam.* New York: W. W. Norton, 1989.

Beschloss, Michael R. *May-Day: Eisenhower, Khrushchev and the U-2 Affair.* New York: Harper & Row, 1986.

Bethell, Nicholas. *Betrayed.* New York: Times Books, 1984.

Biddle, Francis. *In Brief Authority.* Garden City, N.Y.: Doubleday, 1962.

Bill, James A. *The Eagle and the Lion: The Tragedy of American-Iranian Relations.* New Haven, Conn.: Yale University Press, 1988.

Birmingham, Stephen. *Our Crowd.* New York: Future Books, 1967.

Blackett, P. M. S. *Fear, War and Bomb: Military and Political Consequences of Atomic Energy.* New York: McGraw-Hill, 1948, 1949.

Blair, John M. *The Control of Oil.* New York: Pantheon, 1976.

Blum, John Morton, ed. *From the Morgenthau Diaries* (3 vols.). Boston: Houghton Mifflin, 1959–67.

———, ed. *Roosevelt and Morgenthau: A Revision and Condensation from the Morgenthau Diaries.* Boston: Houghton Mifflin, 1970.

———, ed. *The Price of Vision: The Diary of Henry A. Wallace, 1942–1946.* Boston: Houghton Mifflin, 1973.

———, ed. *Public Philosopher: Selected Letters of Walter Lippmann.* New York: Ticknor & Fields, 1985.

Blum, William. *The CIA: A Forgotten History.* London: Zed Books, 1986.

Blumenthal, Martin, ed. *The Patton Diaries.* New York: Houghton Mifflin, 1984.

Bohlen, Charles E. *Witness to History, 1929–1969.* New York: W. W. Norton, 1973.

Bosworth, Allan R. *America's Concentration Camps.* New York: W. W. Norton, 1967.

Bower, Tom. *Klaus Barbie: The "Butcher" of Lyon.* New York: Pantheon, 1984.

———. *The Paperclip Conspiracy: The Hunt for Nazi Scientists.* Boston: Little, Brown, 1987.

Brands, H. W. Jr. *Cold Warriors: Eisenhower's Generation and American Foreign Policy.* New York: Columbia University Press, 1988.

Breitman, Richard, and Kraut, Alan M. *American Refugee Policy and European Jewry, 1933–1945.* Bloomington: Indiana University Press, 1987.

Brendon, Piers. *Ike: His Life and Times.* New York: Harper & Row, 1986.

Brodie, Fawn M. *Richard Nixon: The Shaping of His Character.* New York: W. W. Norton, 1981.

Bromberger, Merry, and Bromberger, Serge. *Jean Monnet and the United States of Europe.* New York: Coward-McCann, 1969.

Browder, Robert Paul, and Smith, Thomas G. *Independent: A Biography of Lewis W. Douglas.* New York: Alfred A. Knopf, 1986.

Brown, Anthony Cave. *Wild Bill Donovan: The Last Hero.* New York: Times Books, 1982.

Brzezinski, Zbigniew. *Power and Principle: Memoirs of the National Security Adviser 1977–1981.* New York: Farrar, Straus & Giroux, 1983.

Buchanan, Scott. *So Reason Can Rule: Reflections on Law and* Politics. New York: Farrar, Straus & Giroux, 1982.

Buckley, William F., Jr., and Bozell, L. Brent. *McCarthy and His Enemies: The Record and Its Meaning.* Chicago: Henry Regnery, 1954.

Bundy, McGeorge. *Danger and Survival.* New York: Random House, 1988.

Burch, Philip H., Jr. *Elites in American History: The New Deal to the Carter Administration.* New York: Holmes & Meier, 1981.

Burke, Michael. *Outrageous Good Fortune: A Memoir.* Boston: Little, Brown, 1984.

Burns, James MacGregor. *Roosevelt: The Lion and the Fox.* New York: Harcourt, Brace & World, 1956.

Burt, Nathaniel. *The Perennial Philadelphians: The Anatomy of an American Aristocracy.* Boston: Little, Brown, 1963.

Byrnes, James F. *Speaking Frankly.* New York: Harper & Brothers, 1947.

Callahan, David. *Dangerous Capabilities: Paul Nitze and the Cold War.* New York: Harper Collins, 1990.

Calleo, David P. *The Imperious Economy.* Cambridge, Mass.: Harvard University Press, 1982.

Calvocoressi, Peter. *Top Secret Ultra.* New York: Ballantine, 1981.

Calvocoressi, Peter, and Wint, Guy. *Total War: The Story of World War II.* New York: Pantheon, 1972.

Carter, Jimmy. *Keeping Faith: Memoirs of a President.* New York: Bantam, 1982.

Carter, Rosalynn. *First Lady from Plains.* New York: Ballantine, 1984.

Caute, David. *The Great Fear: The Anti-Communist Purge Under Truman and Eisenhower.* New York: Simon & Schuster, 1978.

Chadwin, Mark. *The Hawks of World War II.* Chapel Hill: University of North Carolina Press, 1968.

Chernow, Ron. *The House of Morgan: An American Banking Dynasty and the Rise of Modern Finance.* New York: Atlantic Monthly Press, 1990.

Chomsky, Noam. *American Power and the New Mandarins.* New York: Pantheon, 1969.

Clark, Grenville. *Memoirs of a Man.* New York: W. W. Norton, 1975.

Cleveland, Harold van B., and Huertas, Thomas F. *Citibank: 1812–1970.* Cambridge, Mass.: Harvard University Press, 1985.

Clifford, Clark. *Counsel to the President.* New York: Random House, 1991.

Clifford, John Garry. *The Citizen Soldiers: The Plattsburg Training Camp Movement, 1913–1920.* Lexington: University Press of Kentucky, 1972.

Coleman, Peter. *The Liberal Conspiracy.* New York: Free Press, 1989.

Collier, Peter, and Horowitz, David. *The Rockefellers: An American Dynasty.* New York: Holt, Rinehart & Winston, 1976.

———. *The Fords: An American Epic.* New York: Summit Books, 1987.

Collier, Richard. *The Road to Pearl Harbor.* New York: Atheneum, 1981.

Conant, James B. *My Several Lives: Memoirs of a Social Inventor.* New York: Harper & Row, 1970.

Conant, Robert E. *Justice at Nuremberg.* New York: Harper & Row, 1983.

Conn, Stetson, et al. *Guarding the United States and Its Outposts.* Washington, D.C.: U.S. Army Center of Military History, 1980.

Conway, James. *The Texans.* New York: Alfred A. Knopf, 1976.

Cook, Blanche Wiesen. *The Declassified Eisenhower: A Divided Legacy of Peace and Political Warfare.* Garden City, N.Y.: Doubleday, 1981.

Cook, Don. *Forging the Alliance.* New York: Arbor House/William Morrow, 1989.

Cookridge, E. H. *Gehlen: Spy of the Century.* New York: Random House, 1971.

Cooper, Chester. *The Lost Crusade: America in Vietnam.* New York: Dodd, Mead, 1970.

Copeland, Miles. *The Game of Nations.* London: Weidenfeld & Nicolson, 1969.

———. *The Real Spy World.* London: Weidenfeld & Nicolson, 1974.

Corson, William R. *The Armies of Ignorance: The Rise of the American Intelligence Empire.* New York: Dial, 1977.

Crockett, Richard N. *The Lighter Side of the Practice of Law by a Wall Street Law Firm from 1929 to 1979.* Privately printed, 1979.

Cumings, Bruce. *The Origins of the Korean War.* Princeton: Princeton University Press, 1981.

Current, Richard N. *Secretary Stimson: A Study in Statecraft.* New Brunswick, N.J.: Rutgers University Press, 1954.

Dabringhaus, Erhard. *Klaus Barbie: The Shocking Story of How the U.S. Used This Nazi War Criminal as an Intelligence Agent.* Washington, D.C.: Acropolis Books, 1984.

Dallek, Robert. *Franklin D. Roosevelt and American Foreign Policy, 1932–1945.* New York: Oxford University Press, 1979.

Daniels, Roger. *Concentration Camps USA: Japanese Americans and World War II.* New York: Holt, Rinehart & Winston, 1972.

———. *The Decision to Relocate the Japanese Americans.* (Philadelphia: J. B. Lippincott, 1975.

———. *American Concentration Camps* (9 vols.). New York: Garland, 1989.

Danielsen, Albert L. *The Evolution of OPEC.* New York: Harcourt Brace Jovanovich, 1982.

Davidson, Eugene. *The Trial of the Germans.* New York: Collier, 1966.

Davis, John H. *Mafia Kingfish: Carlos Marcello and the Assassination of John F. Kennedy.* New York: New American Library, 1989.

Davis, Nuel Pharr. *Lawrence and Oppenheimer.* New York: Simon & Schuster, 1968.

Destler, I. M.; Gelb, Leslie; and Lake, Anthony. *Our Own Worst Enemy.* New York: Simon & Schuster, 1984.

Detzer, David. *The Brink: Cuban Missile Crisis, 1962.* New York: Thomas Y. Crowell, 1979.

Dileo, David L. *George Ball: Vietnam and the Rethinking of Containment.* Chapel Hill: University of North Carolina Press, 1991.

Dinerstein, Herbert S. *The Making of a Missile Crisis: October 1962.* Baltimore: Johns Hopkins University Press, 1976.

Divine, Robert A. *Reluctant Belligerent: American Entry into World War II.* New York: Wiley, 1965.

———. *Blowing on the Wind: The Nuclear Test Ban Debate, 1954–1960.* New York: Oxford University Press, 1978.

———. *Eisenhower and the Cold War.* New York: Oxford University Press, 1981.

Donovan, Robert. *Conflict and Crisis: The Presidency of Harry S. Truman.* New York: W. W. Norton, 1977.

Dornberg, John. *The New Germans: Thirty Years After.* New York: Macmillan, 1975.

Dower, John. *War Without Mercy: Race and Power in the Pacific War.* New York: Pantheon, 1986.

Drinnon, Richard. *Keeper of Concentration Camps: Dillon S. Myer and American Racism.* Berkeley: University of California Press, 1987.

Dugger, Ronnie. *The Politician: The Life and Times of Lyndon Johnson.* New York: W. W. Norton, 1982.

Dulles, Allen. *The Secret Surrender.* New York: Harper & Row, 1966.

Dulles, Eleanor. *Chances of a Lifetime.* Englewood Cliffs, N.J.: Prentice-Hall, 1980.

Dunlop, Richard. *Donovan: America's Master Spy.* New York: Rand McNally, 1982.

Dunne, Gerald T. *Grenville Clark: Public Citizen.* New York: Farrar, Straus & Giroux, 1986.

Eisenhower, David. *Eisenhower at War.* New York: Random House, 1986.

Eisenhower, John S. D. *Allies: Pearl Harbor to D-Day.* Garden City, N.Y.: Doubleday, 1982.

Eisenhower, Milton S. *The President Is Calling.* Garden City, N.Y.: Doubleday, 1974.

Elon, Amos. *Timetable: The Story of Joel Brand.* London: Hutchinson, 1980.

Engler, Robert. *The Politics of Oil.* Chicago: University of Chicago Press, 1961.

———. *The Brotherhood of Oil.* Chicago: University of Chicago Press, 1977.

Epstein, Edward Jay. *Inquest: The Warren Commission and the Establishment of the Truth.* New York: Bantam, 1966.

———. *Legend: The Secret World of Lee Harvey Oswald.* New York: Reader's Digest Press, 1978.

Essays on Amherst's History. Amherst, Mass.: The Vista Trust, 1978.

Evangelista, Matthew. "Stalin's Postwar Army Reappraised." *International Security,* vol. 7 (Winter 1982/83), p. 135.

Eveland, Wilbur Crane. *Ropes of Sand: America's Failure in the Middle East.* New York: W. W. Norton, 1980.

Ewald, William Bragg, Jr. *Who Killed Joe McCarthy?* New York: Simon & Schuster, 1984.

Farago, Ladislas. *Patton: Ordeal and Triumph.* New York: Dell, 1970.

———. *The Game of the Foxes: The Untold Story of German Espionage in the United States and Great Britain During World War II.* New York: David McKay, 1971.

Fairlie, Henry. *The Kennedy Promise: The Politics of Expectation.* Garden City, N.Y.: Doubleday, 1973.

Farrer, David. *The Warburgs: The Story of a Family.* New York: Stein & Day, 1975.

Feis, Herbert. *Japan Subdued.* Princeton: Princeton University Press, 1961.

———. The Atomic Bomb and the End of World War II. Princeton: Princeton University Press, 1966.

Feldman, Lily Gardner. *The Special Relationship Between West Germany and Israel.* Winchester, Mass.: Allen & Unwin, 1984.

Ferencz, Benjamin B. *Less Than Slaves: Jewish Forced Labor and the Quest for Compensation.* Cambridge, Mass.: Harvard University Press, 1979.

Fine, Lenore, and Remington, Jesse A. *United States Army in World War II: The Technical Services, The Corps of Engineers: Construction in the U.S.* (Washington, D.C.: Office of the Chief of Military History, U.S. Army, 1972).

Fishman, Jack. *Long Knives and Short Memories: Lives and Crimes of the 7 Nazi Leaders Sentenced at Nurembeurg.* New York: Richardson & Steirman, 1986.

FitzGerald, Frances. *Fire in the Lake: The Vietnamese and the Americans in Vietnam.* Boston: Atlantic-Little, Brown, 1972.

Fleming, D. F. *The Cold War and Its Origins: 1917–1960.* Garden City, N.Y.: Doubleday, 1961.

Fowler, W. B. *British-American Relations, 1917–1918: The Role of Sir William Wiseman.* Princeton: Princeton University Press, 1969.

Frankland, Mark. *Khrushchev.* New York: Stein & Day, 1967.

Freedman, Max. *Roosevelt and Frankfurter: Their Correspondence* 1928–1945. Boston: Little, Brown, 1967.

Fried, Richard M. *Men Against McCarthy.* New York: Columbia University Press, 1976.

Frieden, Jeffry A. *Banking on the World: The Politics of American International Finance.* New York: Harper & Row, 1987.

Fuess, Claude Moore. *Amherst: The Story of a New England College.* Boston: Little, Brown, 1935.

Fuller, Helen. *Year of Trial: Kennedy's Crucial Decisions.* New York: Harcourt, Brace & World, 1962.

Gaddis, John Lewis. *The U.S. and the Origins of the Cold War.* New York: Columbia University Press, 1972.

———. *Strategies of Containment.* New York: Oxford University Press, 1982.

Galbraith, John Kenneth. *The Great Crash: 1929.* New York: Houghton Mifflin, 1954.

Garner, Robert L. *This Is the Way It Was.* Chevy Chase, Md.: Chevy Chase Printing, 1972.

Garthoff, Raymond L. *Détente and Confrontation: American-Soviet Relations From Nixon to Reagan.* Washington, D.C.: The Brookings Institution, 1985.

———. *Reflections on the Cuban Missile Crisis.* Washington, D.C.: The Brookings Institution, 1987.

Gehlen, Reinhard. *The Service: The Memoirs of General Reinhard Gehlen.* New York: World Publishing, 1972.

Georges-Picot, Jacques. *The Real Suez Crisis.* New York: Harcourt Brace Jovanovich, 1978.

Gilbert, Martin. *Auschwitz and the Allies.* New York: Holt, Rinehart & Winston, 1981.

———. *The Holocaust: A History of the Jews of Europe During the Second World War.* New York: Holt, Rinehart & Winston, 1986.

———. *Winston S. Churchill: Road to Victory.* vol. VI. Boston: Houghton Mifflin, 1986.

Goldman, Eric, *The Tragedy of Lyndon Johnson.* New York: Alfred A. Knopf, 1969.

Goldmann, Nahum, *The Autobiography of Nahum Goldmann: Sixty Years of Jewish Life.* New York: Holt, Rinehart & Winston, 1969.

Goodman, Walter. *The Committee: The Extraordinary Career of the House Committee on Un-American Activities.* New York: Farrar, Straus & Giroux, 1968.

Goodwin, Doris Kearns. *The Fitzgeralds and the Kennedys: An American Saga.* New York: Simon & Schuster, 1987.

Goodwin, Richard N. *Remembering America.* Boston: Little, Brown, 1988.

Gormly, James L. *From Potsdam to the Cold War: Big Three Diplomacy 1945–47.* Wilmington, Del.: Scholarly Resources Books, 1990.

Graubard, Stephen R. *Kissinger: Portrait of a Mind.* New York: W. W. Norton, 1973.

Greenstein, Fred I. *The Hidden-Hand Presidency.* New York: Basic Books, 1982.

Grew, Joseph C. *Ten Years in Japan.* New York: Simon & Schuster, 1944.

———. *Turbulent Era* (2 vols.). Boston: Houghton Mifflin, 1952.

Grigg, John. *1943: The Victory That Never Was.* London: Eyre Methuen, 1980.

Halberstam, David. *The Making of a Quagmire.* New York: Random House, 1964, 1965.

———. *The Best and the Brightest.* New York: Fawcett Crest, 1972.

Halle, Louis. *The Cold War as History.* New York: Harper & Row, 1967.

Hanfstaengl, Franz Ernst. *The Unheard Witness.* Philadelphia: J. B. Lippincott, 1957.

Hanrieder, Wolfram F. *Germany, America, Europe: Forty Years of German Foreign Policy.* New Haven, Conn.: Yale University Press, 1989.

Harriman, W. Averell. *America and Russia in a Changing World: A Half Century of Personal Observation.* Garden City, N.Y.: Doubleday, 1971.

Harriman, W. Averell, and Abel, Elie. *Special Envoy.* New York: Random House, 1975.
Hart, Liddel. *History of the Second World War.* New York: G. P. Putnam's Sons, 1970.
Hartrich, Edwin. *The Fourth and Richest Reich: How the Germans Conquered the Postwar World.* New York: Macmillan, 1980.
Heikel, Mohamed. *The Cairo Documents: The Inside Story of Nasser and His Relationship with World Leaders, Rebels, and Statesman.* Garden City, N.Y.: Doubleday, 1973.
Herken, Gregg. *The Winning Weapon: The Atomic Bomb in the Cold War, 1945–1950.* New York: Alfred A. Knopf, 1980.
Herring, George C. *America's Longest War: The United States and Vietnam 1950–1975.* New York: Alfred A. Knopf, 1979, 2nd ed. 1986.
Hersey, John. *Hiroshima.* New York: Alfred A. Knopf, 1946.
Hersh, Seymour. *The Price of Power: Kissinger in the Nixon White House.* New York: Summit, 1983.
Hewlett, Richard, and Anderson, Oscar, Jr. *The New World.* University Park: Pennsylvania State University Press, 1962.
Higgins, George. *The Friends of Richard Nixon.* New York: Ballantine, 1975.
Higham, Charles. *Trading with the Enemy.* New York: Delacorte, 1983.
Hilsman, Roger. *To Move a Nation.* Garden City, N.Y.: Doubleday, 1967.
Hiscocks, Richard. *The Adenauer Era.* Philadelphia: J. B. Lippincott, 1966.
Hodgson, Godfrey. *America in Our Time.* Garden City, N.Y.: Doubleday, 1976.
———. *The Colonel.* New York: Alfred A. Knopf, 1990.
Hoffman, Nicholas von. *Citizen Cohn: The Life and Times of Roy Cohn.* New York: Doubleday, 1988.
Hoffman, Paul. *Lions in the Street: The Inside Story of the Great Wall Street Law Firms.* New York: Saturday Review Press, 1973.
Hoffman, William. *David: Report on a Rockefeller.* New York: Lyle Stuart, 1971.
Hohne, Heinz, and Zolling, Hermann. *The General Was a Spy: The Truth About General Gehlen and His Spy Ring.* New York: Coward, McCann & Geoghegan, 1972.
Hoopes, Townsend. *The Limits of Intervention.* New York: David McKay, 1969.
———. *The Devil and John Foster Dulles.* Boston: Little, Brown, 1973.
Hosokawa, Bill. *JACL in Quest of Justice: The History of the Japanese American League.* New York: William Morrow, 1982.
Hulbert, Mark. *Interlock.* New York: Richardson & Snyder, 1982.
Hull, Cordell. *The Memoirs of Cordell Hull.* New York: Macmillan, 1948.
Hurt, Harry, III. *Texas Rich: The Hunt Dynasty from the Early Oil Days Through the Silver Crash.* New York: W. W. Norton, 1982.
Hurt, Henry. *Reasonable Doubt: An Investigation into the Assassination of John F. Kennedy.* New York: Henry Holt, 1985.
Hyde, H. Montgomery. *Room 3603: The Story of the British Intelligence Center in New York During World War II.* New York: Farrar, Straus & Co., 1962.
Ickes, Harold L. *The Secret Diary of Harold L. Ickes* (3 vols.). New York: Simon & Schuster, 1953–54.
Irons, Peter. *Justice at War: The Story of the Japanese American Internment.* New York: Oxford University Press, 1983.
Isaacson, Walter, and Thomas, Evan. *The Wise Men: Six Friends and the World They Made.* New York: Simon & Schuster, 1986.
Janis, Irving L. *Group Think: Psychological Studies of Policy Decisions and Fiascoes.* Boston: Houghton Mifflin, 1983.
Jeffreys-Jones, Rhodri. *The CIA and American Democracy.* New Haven, Conn.: Yale University Press, 1989.

Jessup, Philip C. *Elihu Root* (2 vols.). New York: Dodd, Mead, 1938.

John, Otto. *Twice Through the Lines.* New York: Harper & Row, 1972.

Johnson, Lyndon B. *The Vantage Point: Perspectives of the Presidency, 1963–1969.* New York: Holt, Rinehart & Winston, 1971.

Johnson, U. Alexis. *The Right Hand of Power: The Memoirs of an American Diplomat.* Englewood Cliffs, N.J.: Prentice Hall, 1984.

Johnson, Walter, ed. *The Papers of Adlai E. Stevenson,* vol. 8. Boston: Little, Brown, 1979.

Jordan, Hamilton. *Crisis: The Last Year of the Carter Presidency.* New York: G. P. Putnam's Sons, 1982.

Josephson, Matthew. *The Money Lords.* New York: Weybright & Talley, 1972.

Kahn, David. *The Codebreakers: The Story of Secret Writing.* New York: Macmillan, 1967.

———. *Hitler's Spies: German Military Intelligence in World War II.* New York: Macmillan, 1978.

Kahn, E. J., Jr. *The World of Swope.* New York: Simon & Schuster, 1965.

Kalb, Marvin and Kalb, Bernard. *Kissinger.* Boston: Little Brown, 1974.

Kaplan, Fred. *The Wizards of Armageddon.* New York: Simon & Schuster, 1983.

Karnow, Stanley. *Vietnam.* New York: Viking, 1983.

Karski, Jan. *Story of a Secret State.* Boston: Houghton Mifflin, 1944.

Kearns, Doris. *Lyndon Johnson and the American Dream.* New York: Harper & Row, 1976.

Kennan, George W. *Memoirs: 1925–1950.* Boston: Little Brown, 1967.

———. *Sketches from a Life.* New York: Pantheon, 1989.

Kennedy, Robert F. *Thirteen Days: A Memoir of the Cuban Missile Crisis.* New York: W. W. Norton, 1971.

———. *Robert Kennedy in His Own Words: The Unpublished Recollections of the Kennedy Years.* New York: Bantam, 1988.

Kersaudy, François. *Churchill and De Gaulle.* New York: Atheneum, 1982.

Khrushchev, Nikita. *Khrushchev Remembers.* Boston: Little, Brown, 1970.

Kimball, Warren F. *The Most Unsordid Act: Lend-Lease, 1939–1941.* Baltimore: Johns Hopkins University Press, 1969.

———. *The Juggler: Franklin Roosevelt as Wartime Statesman.* Princeton: Princeton University Press, 1991.

Kissinger, Henry. *White House Years.* Boston: Little, Brown, 1979.

———. *Years of Upheaval.* Boston: Little, Brown, 1982.

Knightley, Phillip, *The Master Spy: The Story of Kim Philby.* New York: Knopf, 1989.

Kolko, Gabriel. *The Politics of War: The World and United States Foreign Policy, 1943–1945.* New York: Random House, 1968.

———. *Main Currents in Modern American History.* New York: Pantheon, 1976.

Krock, Arthur. *Memoirs: Sixty Years on the Firing Line.* New York: Funk & Wagnalls, 1968.

Kurzman, Dan. *Day of the Bomb: Countdown to Hiroshima.* New York: McGraw-Hill, 1986.

Lacey, Robert. *The Kingdom: Arabia and the House of Saud.* New York: Harcourt Brace Jovanovich, 1981.

———. *Ford: The Men and the Machine.* Boston: Little, Brown, 1986.

LaFeber, Walter. *America, Russia and the Cold War: 1945–1975.* New York: John Wiley and Sons, 1976.

Lamont, Lansing. *Day of Trinity.* New York: Atheneum, 1965.

Lamont, Thomas W. *Henry P. Davison: The Record of a Useful Life.* New York: Harper & Brothers, 1933.

Landau, David. *Kissinger: The Uses of Power.* Boston: Houghton Mifflin, 1972.

Landau, Henry. *The Enemy Within.* New York: G. P. Putnam's, 1937.

Lane, Mark. *Rush to Judgment.* New York: Holt, Rinehart & Winston, 1966.

Laqueur, Walter. *The Terrible Secret: Suppression of the Truth About Hitler's "Final Solution."* Boston: Little, Brown, 1980.

Larrabee, Eric. *Commander in Chief: Franklin Delano Roosevelt, His Lieutenants and Their War.* New York: Harper & Row, 1987.

Larson, Deborah Welch. *Origins of Containment: A Psychological Explanation.* Princeton: Princeton University Press, 1985.

Latham, Earl. *The Communist Controversy in Washington: From the New Deal to McCarthy.* Cambridge, Mass.: Harvard University Press, 1966.

Leffler, Melvyn P. *A Preponderance of Power: National Security, the Truman Administration and the Cold War, 1945–52.* Palo Alto, Calif.: Stanford University Press, 1992.

Levi, Primo. *Survival in Auschwitz.* New York: Summit, 1986.

Lewin, Ronald. *The American Magic: Codes, Ciphers and the Defeat of Japan.* New York: Farrar, Straus & Giroux, 1982.

Lieberman, Joseph I. *The Scorpion and the Tarantula: The Struggle to Control Atomic Weapons, 1945–1949.* Boston: Houghton Mifflin, 1970.

Lifton, David S. *Best Evidence: Disguise and Deception in the Assassination of John F. Kennedy.* New York: Macmillan, 1980.

Lilienthal, David E. *The Journals of David E. Lilienthal.* (5 vols.). New York: Harper & Row, 1970.

Linklater, Magnus; Hilton, Isabel; and Ascherson, Neal. *The Nazi Legacy: Klaus Barbie and the International Fascist Connection.* New York: Holt, Rinehart & Winston, 1984.

Lipstadt, Deborah E. *Beyond Belief: The American Press and the Coming of the Holocaust, 1933–1945.* New York: Free Press, 1985.

Loftus, John. *The Belarus Secret.* New York: Alfred A. Knopf, 1982.

Long, Wellington. *The New Nazis of Germany.* Philadelphia: Chilton, 1968.

Love, Kenneth. *Suez: The Twice Fought War.* New York: McGraw-Hill, 1969.

Lowenthal, Max. *The Investor Pays.* New York: Alfred A. Knopf, 1933.

MacGregor, Morris J., Jr. *Integration of the Armed Forces: 1940–65.* Washington, D.C.: Center of Military History, U.S. Army, 1981.

Macmillan, Harold. *War Diaries: The Mediterranean 1943–1945.* New York: St. Martin's Press, 1984.

Manchester, William. *The Arms of Krupp.* Boston: Little, Brown, 1964.

Mangold, Tom. *Cold Warrior James Jesus Angleton: The CIA's Master Spy Hunter.* New York: Simon & Schuster, 1991.

Marrus, Michael R. *The Holocaust in History.* Hanover, N.H.: University Press of New England, 1987.

Martin, George. *Causes and Conflicts: The Centennial History of the Association of the Bar of the City of New York 1870–1970.* Boston: Houghton Mifflin, 1970.

Martin, John Bartlow. *Adlai Stevenson and the World: The Life of Adlai Stevenson.* Garden City, N.Y.: Doubleday, 1977.

Masaoka, Mike, with Hosokawa, Bill. *They Call Me Moses Masaoka.* New York: William Morrow, 1987.

Mason, Edward S., and Asher, Robert E. *The World Bank Since Bretton Woods.* Washington, D.C.: The Brookings Institution, 1973.

Matz, Mary Jane. *The Many Lives of Otto Kahn.* New York: Macmillan, 1963.

Maurer, Harry. *Strange Ground: Americans in Vietnam, 1945–1975.* New York: Henry Holt, 1989.

Mayers, David. *George Kennan and the Dilemmas of U.S. Foreign Policy.* New York: Oxford University Press, 1988.

McCloy, John J. *The Challenge to American Foreign Policy.* Cambridge, Mass.: Harvard University Press, 1953.

McFadden, Robert D.; Treaster, Joseph B.; and Carroll, Maurice. *No Hiding Place: New York Times Inside Report on the Hostage Crisis.* New York: Times Books, 1981.

McGhee, George. *At the Creation of a New Germany.* New Haven, Conn.: Yale University Press, 1989.

McJimsey, George. *Harry Hopkins: Ally of the Poor and Defender of Democracy.* Cambridge, Mass.: Harvard University Press, 1987.

McNamara, Robert S. *Blundering into Disaster: Surviving the First Century of the Nuclear Age.* New York: Pantheon, 1986.

McWilliams, Carey. *A Mask for Privilege: Anti-Semitism in America.* Boston: Little, Brown, 1948.

Mead, Walter Russell. *Mortal Spleandor: The American Empire in Transition.* Boston: Houghton Mifflin, 1987.

Meade, Frederick S., ed. *Harvard's Military Record in the World War.* Boston: Harvard Alumni Association, 1921.

Medvedev, Roy. *Khrushchev: A Biography.* Garden City, N.Y.: Anchor Press, 1983.

Mee, Charles L., Jr. *Meeting at Potsdam.* New York: Evans, 1975.

———. *The Marshall Plan: The Launching of the Pax Americana.* New York: Simon & Schuster, 1984.

Meiklejohn, Alexander. "The Theory of the Liberal College." In Meiklejohn, *Freedom and the College.* New York: Century, 1923.

Merrill, Charles. *The Checkbook: The Politics and Ethics of Foundation Philanthropy.* Boston: Oelgeschlager, Gunn & Hain, 1986.

Messer, Robert L. *The End of the Alliance: James F. Byrnes, Roosevelt, Truman and the Origins of the Cold War.* Chapel Hill: University of North Carolina Press, 1982.

Meyer, Cord. *Facing Reality: From World Federalism to the CIA.* New York: Harper & Row, 1980.

Miller, Aaron David. *Search for Security: Saudi Arabian Oil and American Foreign Policy, 1939–1949.* Chapel Hill: University of North Carolina Press, 1980.

Millis, Walter, ed. *The Forrestal Diaries.* New York: Viking, 1951.

Mills, C. Wright. *The Power Elite.* New York: Oxford University Press, 1957.

Monnet, Jean. *Memoirs.* Garden City, N.Y.: Doubleday, 1978.

Moran, Lord. *Churchill—Taken from the Diaries of Lord Moran: The Struggle for Survival 1940–1965.* Boston: Houghton Mifflin, 1966.

Morgan, Ted, *FDR.* New York: Simon & Schuster, 1985.

Morgenthau, Henry. *Morgenthau Diary,* vol. I, U.S. Senate. Washington, D.C.: U.S. Government Printing Office, 1967.

Morison, Elting. *Turmoil and Tradition.* Boston: Houghton Mifflin, 1960.

Morris, James. *The Road to Huddersfield: A Journey to Five Continents.* New York: Pantheon, 1963.

Morris, Roger. *Richard Milhous Nixon: The Rise of an American Politician.* New York: Henry Holt, 1990.

Morse, Arthur D. *While Six Million Died: A Chronicle of American Apathy.* New York: Random House, 1967.

Moscow, Alvin. *The Rockefeller Inheritance.* Garden City, N.Y.: Doubleday, 1977.
Mosley, Leonard. *Marshall: Hero for Our Times.* New York: Hearst Books, 1982.
Murphy, Brendan. *The Butcher of Lyon: The Story of the Infamous Nazi Klaus Barbie.* New York: Empire Books, 1983.
Murphy, Bruce Allen. *The Brandeis/Frankfurter Connection.* New York: Oxford University Press, 1982.
Murphy, Robert. *Diplomat Among Warriors.* Garden City, N.Y.: Doubleday, 1964.
Nalty, Bernard C. *Strength for the Fight.* New York: Free Press, 1986.
Nalty, Bernard C., and MacGregor, Morris J., Jr., eds. *Blacks in the Military:* Essential Documents. Wilmington, Del.: Scholarly Resources Inc., 1977, 1981.
Navasky, Victor S. *Naming Names.* New York: Viking, 1980.
Neff, Donald. *Warriors at Suez.* New York: Simon & Schuster, 1981.
Nevins, Allan, and Hill, Frank Ernest. *Ford: Decline and Rebirth 1933–1962.* New York: Charles Scribner's Sons, 1962.
Newhouse, John. *War and Peace in the Nuclear Age.* New York: Alfred A. Knopf, 1989.
Nielsen, Waldemar A. *The Big Foundations.* New York: Columbia University Press, 1972.
———. *The Golden Donors: A New Anatomy of the Great Foundations.* New York: E. P. Dutton, 1982.
O'Donnell, Kenneth P., and Powers, David F., with McCarthy, Joe. *Johnny, We Hardly Knew Ye: Memories of John Fitzgerald Kennedy.* Boston: Little, Brown, 1970.
Oliver, Robert W. *International Economic Cooperation and the World Bank.* London: Macmillan, 1975.
Oshinsky, David M. *A Conspiracy So Immense.* New York: Free Press, 1983.
Paper, Lewis J. *Brandeis: An Intimate Biography of One of America's Truly Great Supreme Court Justices.* Secaucus, N.J.: Citadel, 1983.
Paris, Erna. *Unhealed Wounds: France and the Klaus Barbie Affair.* New York: Grove Press, 1985.
Parmet, Herbert S. *Eisenhower and the American Crusade.* New York: Macmillan, 1972.
Parrish, Michael E. *Felix Frankfurter and His Times.* New York: Free Press, 1982.
Parrish, Thomas. *The Ultra Americans: The U.S. Role in Breaking the Nazi Codes.* New York: Stein & Day, 1986.
Patterson, Thomas G. *Soviet-American Confrontation: Postwar Reconstruction and the Origins of the Cold War.* Baltimore: Johns Hopkins University Press, 1973.
———. *On Every Front: The Making of the Cold War.* New York: W. W. Norton, 1979.
Pearson, Drew. *Diaries: 1949–1959.* Ed. Tyler Abell. New York: Holt, Rinehart & Winston, 1974.
Peaslee, Amos, and Hall, Admiral Reginald. *Three Wars with Germany.* New York: G. P. Putnam's, 1944.
Pepper, George Wharton. *Philadelphia Lawyer: An Autobiography.* Philadelphia: J. B. Lippincott, 1944.
Perrett, Geoffrey. *America in the Twenties.* New York: Simon & Schuster, 1982.
———. *Days of Sadness, Years of Triumph: The American People, 1939–1945.* Madison: University of Wisconsin Press, 1985.
Perry, Ralph Barton. *The Plattsburg Movement.* New York: E. P. Dutton, 1921.
Personal Justice Denied: Report of the Commission on Wartime Relocation and Internment of Civilians. Washington, D.C.: U.S. Congress, 1982.
Phillips, Dr. Harlan B. *Felix Frankfurter Reminisces: An Intimate Portrait as Recorded in Talks with Dr. Harlan B. Phillips.* New York: Reynal, 1960.
Pilat, Oliver. *Drew Pearson: An Unauthorized Biography.* New York: Harper & Row, 1973.

Pogue, Forrest. *George C. Marshall* (4 vols.). New York: Viking, 1966, 1973, 1987.

Pollack, Jack Harrison. *Earl Warren: The Judge Who Changed America.* Englewood Cliffs, N.J.: Prentice-Hall, 1979.

Pope, Ronald R., ed. *Soviet Views on the Cuban Missile Crisis.* Washington, D.C.: University Press of America, 1982.

Powers, Richard Gid. *Secrecy and Power: The Life of J. Edgar Hoover.* New York: Free Press, 1987.

Powers, Thomas. *The Man Who Kept the Secrets: Richard Helms and the CIA.* New York: Alfred A. Knopf, 1979.

Prados, John. *Presidents' Secret Wars: CIA and Pentagon Covert Operations Since World War II.* New York: William Morrow, 1986.

Prange, Gordon W. *At Dawn We Slept.* New York: McGraw-Hill, 1981.

———. *Pearl Harbor.* New York: McGraw-Hill, 1986.

Prittie, Terence. *Adenauer: A Study in Fortitude.* Chicago: Cowles, 1971.

———. Willy Brandt. *Portrait of a Statesman.* London: Weidenfeld & Nicolson, 1974.

Pruessen, Ronald W. *John Foster Dulles: The Road to Power.* New York: Free Press, 1982.

Pusey, Merlo J. *Eugene Meyer.* New York: Alfred A. Knopf, 1974.

Ranelagh, John. *The Agency: The Rise and Decline of the CIA from Wild Bill Donovan to William Casey.* New York: Simon & Schuster, 1986.

Raskin, Marcus, and Fall, Bernard B., eds. *The Viet-Nam Reader.* New York: Random House, 1965.

Reeves, Thomas C. *The Life and Times of Joe McCarthy: A Biography.* New York: Stein & Day, 1982.

Rhodes, Richard. *The Making of the Atomic Bomb.* New York: Simon & Schuster, 1986.

Richardson, Elliot. *The Creative Balance.* New York: Holt, Rinehart & Winston, 1976.

Roberts, Henry L. *Russia and America: Dangers and Prospects.* New York: Harper & Brothers, 1956.

Rogow, Arnold. *James Forrestal.* New York: Macmillan, 1963.

Roosevelt, Elliot, ed. *F.D.R.: His Personal Letters, 1928–1945,* vol. II. New York: Duell, Sloan & Pearce, 1950.

Rovere, Richard H. *Senator Joe McCarthy.* New York: Harcourt, Brace & World, 1959.

———. *The American Establishment and Other Reports, Opinions and Speculations.* New York: Harcourt, Brace & World, 1962.

Ryan, Allan A., Jr. *Quiet Neighbors: Prosecuting Nazi War Criminals in America.* New York: Harcourt Brace Jovanovich, 1984.

Saikal, Amin. *The Rise and Fall of the Shah.* Princeton: Princeton University Press, 1980.

Sakharov, Andrei. *Memoirs.* New York: Alfred A. Knopf, 1990.

Sampson, Anthony. *The Seven Sisters: The Great Oil Companies and the World They Made.* New York: Viking, 1975.

———. *The Money Lenders.* New York: Viking, 1982.

Sayers, Michael, and Kahn, Alfred E. *Sabotage: The Secret War Against America.* New York: Harper & Brothers, 1942.

Schacht, Hjalmar. *My First Seventy-six Years.* London: Allan Wingate, 1955.

Scheim, David E. *Contract on America: The Mafia Murder of President John F. Kennedy.* New York: Shapolsky Publishers, 1988.

Arthur M. Schlesinger, Jr. *The Vital Center.* Boston: Houghton Mifflin, 1949.

———. *A Thousand Days.* Boston: Houghton Mifflin, 1965.

———. *The Bitter Heritage: Vietnam and American Democracy 1941–1968.* Greenwich, Conn.: Fawcett, 1968, revised edition, originally published by Houghton Mifflin, 1966.

———. *Robert Kennedy and His Times.* New York: Ballantine, 1979.
Schmidt, Matthias. *Albert Speer: The End of a Myth.* New York: St. Martin's Press, 1984.
Schoenbaum, Thomas J. *Waging Peace and War: Dean Rusk in the Truman, Kennedy and Johnson Years.* New York: Simon & Schuster, 1988.
Schulzinger, Robert D. *The Wise Men of Foreign Affairs: The History of the Council on Foreign Relations.* New York: Columbia University Press, 1984.
Schwartz, Thomas Alan. *America's Germany: John J. McCloy and the Federal Republic of Germany.* Cambridge, Mass.: Harvard University Press, 1991.
Seaborg, Glenn, with Loeb, Benjamin S. *Stemming the Tide: Arms Control in the Johnson Administration.* Lexington, Mass.: Lexington Books, 1987.
Seligman, Joel. *The High Citadel: The Influence of Harvard Law School.* Boston: Houghton Mifflin, 1978.
Shawcross, William. *The Shah's Last Ride: The Fate of an Ally.* New York: Simon & Schuster, 1988.
Sheehan, Neil. *A Bright Shining Lie: John Paul Vann and America in Vietnam.* New York: Random House, 1988.
Sherrill, Robert. *The Oil Follies of 1979–1980: How the Petroleum Industry Stole the Show (and Much More Besides).* Garden City, N.Y.: Anchor-Doubleday, 1983.
Sherwin, Martin. *A World Destroyed: The Atomic Bomb and the Grand Alliance.* New York: Vintage, 1977.
Sherwood, Robert E. *Roosevelt and Hopkins: An Intimate History.* New York: Harper & Brothers, 1948.
Shoup, Lawrence H., and Minter, William. *Imperial Brain Trust.* New York: Monthly Review Press, 1977.
Sick, Gary. *All Fall Down: America's Tragic Encounter with Iran.* New York: Random House, 1985.
Silk, Leonard, and Silk, Mark. *The American Establishment.* New York: Basic Books, 1980.
Simon, James F. *Independent Journey: The Life of William O. Douglas.* New York: Harper & Row, 1980.
Simpson, Christopher. *Blowback: America's Recruitment of Nazis and Its Effects on the Cold War.* New York: Weidenfeld & Nicolson, 1988.
Sklar, Holly, ed. *Trilateralism: The Trilateral Commission and Elite Planning for World Management.* Boston: Southend Press, 1980.
Small, Melvin. *Johnson, Nixon and the Doves.* New Brunswick, N.J.: Rutgers University Press, 1988.
Smith, Gaddis. *Dean Acheson.* New York: Cooper Square, 1972.
———. *American Diplomacy During the Second World War, 1941–45.* New York: Alfred A. Knopf, 1985.
Smith, Jean Edward. *Lucius D. Clay: An American Life.* New York: Henry Holt, 1990.
Smith, Richard Norton. *Harvard Century.* New York: Simon & Schuster, 1986.
Sorensen, Theodore C. *Kennedy.* New York: Harper & Row, 1965.
Stavins, Ralph; Barnet, Richard J.; and Marcus G. Raskin. *Washington Plans an Aggressive War: A Documented Account of the United States' Adventure in Indochina.* London: Davis-Poynter, 1972.
Steel, Ronald. *Pax Americana.* New York: Viking, 1967.
———. *Walter Lippmann and the American Century.* Boston: Atlantic-Little, Brown, 1980.
Steinberg, Alfred. *Sam Johnson's Boy: A Close-up of the President from Texas.* New York: Macmillan, 1968.

Stern, Philip M. with the collaboration of Harold P. Green. *The Oppenheimer Case: Security on Trial.* New York: Harper & Row, 1969.

Stewart, James B., *The Partners: Inside America's Most Powerful Law Firms.* New York: Simon & Schuster, 1983.

Stilwell, Joseph W. *The Stilwell Papers.* Ed. Theodore White. New York: William Sloane Associates, 1948.

Stimson, Henry L., and Bundy, McGeorge. *On Active Service in Peace and War.* New York: Harper & Row, 1947.

Strauss, Lewis L. *Men and Decisions.* Garden City, N.Y.: Doubleday, 1962.

Sullivan, William H. *Mission to Iran.* New York: W. W. Norton, 1981.

Sulzberger, C. L. *A Long Row of Candles.* Toronto: Macmillan, 1969.

Swaine, Robert T. *The Cravath Firm and Its Predecessors, 1819–1948,* vol. II. Privately printed, 1948.

Taft, Henry W. *Cadwalader, Wickersham & Taft.* Privately printed, 1938.

Taheri, Amir. *Nest of Spies: America's Journey to Disaster in Iran.* New York: Pantheon, 1988.

Talbot, Strobe. *Deadly Gambits.* New York: Alfred A. Knopf, 1984.

———. *The Master of the Game: Paul Nitze and the Nuclear Peace.* New York: Alfred A. Knopf, 1988.

Taubman, William. *Stalin's American Policy: From Entente to Détente to Cold War.* New York: W. W. Norton, 1982.

Taylor, Telford. *Grand Inquest.* New York: Simon & Schuster, 1955.

Tetens, T. H. *The New Germany and the Old Nazis.* London: Secker & Warburg, 1962.

Thayer, Charles W. *The Unquiet Germans.* New York: Harper & Brothers, 1957.

———. *Diplomat.* New York: Harper & Brothers, 1959.

Theoharis, Athan. *Spying on Americans: Political Surveillance from Hoover to the Huston Plan.* Philadelphia: Temple University Press, 1978.

Theoharis, Athan, and Cox, John Stuart. *The Boss: J. Edgar Hoover and the Great American Inquisition.* Philadelphia: Temple University Press, 1988.

Thomas, Lately. *When Even Angels Wept: An Objective Reappraisal of the Senator Joseph McCarthy Affair.* New York: William Morrow, 1973.

Thorne, Christopher. *Allies of a Kind: The United States, Britain and the War Against Japan, 1941–1945.* New York: Oxford University Press, 1978.

Tocqueville, Alexis de. *Democracy in America.* New York: New American Library, 1956.

Toland, John. *The Rising Sun: The Decline and Fall of the Japanese Empire,* vols. I and II. New York: Random House, 1970.

———. *Infamy: Pearl Harbor and Its Aftermath.* Garden City, N.Y.: Doubleday, 1982.

Treverton, Gregory F. *Covert Action: The Limits of Intervention in the Postwar World.* New York: Basic Books, 1987.

Trewhitt, Henry L. *McNamara: His Ordeal in the Pentagon.* New York: Harper & Row, 1971.

———. *Trials of War Criminals Before the Nuremberg Military Tribunals,* vol. IV. Washington, D.C.: U.S. Government Printing Office, 1946–1949.

Troy, Thomas F. *Donovan and the CIA: A History of the Establishment of the Central Intelligence Agency.* Washington, D.C.: Altheia Books, University Publications of America, 1981.

Truman, Harry S. *Year of Decisions.* Garden City, N.Y.: Doubleday, 1955).

———. *Years of Trial and Hope, 1946–52.* Garden City, N.Y.: Doubleday, 1956.

Truman, Margaret. *Harry S. Truman.* New York: William Morrow, 1973.

Vance, Cyrus. *Hard Choices.* New York: Simon & Schuster, 1983.

Walters, Vernon. *Silent Missions.* Garden City, N.Y.: Doubleday, 1978.
Walton, Richard J. *Henry Wallace, Harry Truman and the Cold War.* New York: Viking, 1976.
Warburg, James. *Germany: Key to Peace.* Cambridge, Mass.: Harvard University Press, 1953.
Wedemeyer, Albert C. *Wedemeyer Reports.* New York: Henry Holt, 1958.
Weglyn, Michi. *Years of Infamy: The Untold Story of America's Concentration Camps.* New York: Morrow Quill Paperbacks, 1976.
Weigley, Russell F. *Philadelphia.* New York: W. W. Norton, 1982.
Weinberg, Steve. *Armand Hammer: The Untold Story.* Boston: Little, Brown, 1989.
Weymar, Paul. *Adenauer: His Authorized Biography.* New York: E. P. Dutton, 1957.
White, Theodore H. *Breach of Faith: The Fall of Richard Nixon.* New York: Atheneum, 1975.
Whitehead, Don. *The FBI Story.* New York: Random House, 1956.
Whiting, Charles. *Gehlen: Germany's Master Spy.* New York: Ballantine, 1972.
Wighton, Charles. *Adenauer: A Critical Biography.* New York: Coward-McCann, 1963).
Williams, William Appleman. *The Tragedy of American Diplomacy.* New York: Dell, 1962.
Wills, Garry. *The Kennedy Imprisonment.* New York: Pocket Books, 1981, 1982.
Wilson, John Donald. *The Chase: The Chase Manhattan Bank, N.A., 1945–1985.* Boston: Harvard Business School Press, 1986.
Winks, Robin W. *Cloak and Gown: Scholars in the Secret War, 1939–1961.* New York: William Morrow, 1987.
Winters, Ella, and Hicks, Granville, eds. *The Letters of Lincoln Steffens,* vol. 1. New York: Harcourt, Brace, 1938.
Wise, Stephen. *Challenging Years: The Autobiography of Stephen Wise.* New York: G. P. Putnam's 1949.
Wistrich, Robert. *Who's Who in Nazi Germany.* London: Weidenfeld & Nicolson, 1982.
Witcover, Jules. *Sabotage at Black Tom.* Chapel Hill, N.C.: Chapel Hill Press, 1989.
Wofford, Harris. *Of Kennedys and Kings.* New York: Farrar, Straus & Giroux, 1980.
Wyden, Peter. *Day One: Before Hiroshima and After.* New York: Simon & Schuster, 1984.
Wyman, David S. *Paper Walls: America and the Refugee Crisis, 1938–1941.* New York: Pantheon, 1968, 1985.
———. *The Abandonment of the Jews: America and the Holocaust, 1941–1945.* New York: Pantheon, 1984.
Yergin, Daniel. *Shattered Peace: The Origins of the Cold War and the National Security State.* Boston: Houghton Mifflin, 1978.
———. *The Prize: The Epic Quest for Oil, Money, and Power.* New York: Simon & Schuster, 1991.
Zion, Sidney. *The Autobiography of Roy Cohn.* Secaucus, N.J.: Lyle Stuart, 1988.

ACKNOWLEDGMENTS

In the decade that it took me to write this book, I was encouraged by scores of people. Victor Navasky, the editor of *The Nation,* is a man endowed with more good-natured wisdom than anyone I know. Watching Victor write one of his own books, *Naming Names,* at the same time that he edited the country's oldest political weekly, gave me the confidence to write this book. Victor was my guide and counsel throughout this project. He introduced me to Elaine Markson, a literary agent who promptly sold the idea to Alice Mayhew at Simon & Schuster.

Alice is a magnificent editor, whose line-editing is reflected on every page of this book. But I will always be in her debt for another reason. I began this project with a coauthor—who prefers to remain anonymous—and when we regrettably parted company, Alice had the patience to stand by me through a difficult period. Also at Simon & Schuster, Ari Hoogenboom guided me through the editing process with his easy wit. Marcia Peterson and Terry Zaroff performed a miracle with their meticulous copyediting of a lengthy and difficult manuscript.

Gar Alperovitz, Eric Alterman, Richard Barnet, Patrick Breslin, David Corn, Steve Dagget, Roger Daniels, Steve Emerson, Bill Metz, Marcus Raskin, John Rosenberg, Caleb Rossiter, Christopher Simpson, and Don Wilson read portions of the manuscript. Arthur Samuelson read an early version of the entire manuscript and was unsparing in his critique of what needed to be done to complete the book. I owe him a heavy debt and treasure his friendship.

Many other friends and colleagues encouraged me over the years, including: Fouad Ajami, Jocelyn Albert, Mercedes Arnold, Scott Armstrong, James A. Bill, Norman Birnbaum, Jan Knippers Black, Helma Bliss, Jack Blum, James Boyce, Howard Bray, Frank Browning, Axel von dem Bussche, the late Benjamin Buttenwieser, Gordon Chang, Blair Clark, the late Thomas Collier, Robert Dallek, David L. Dileo, Reinhard Doerries, Carolyn Eisenberg, Joseph Eldridge, Robert Engler, Richard Falk, Terry Fehner, Benjamin Ferencz, Thomas Ferguson, Hamilton Fish III, the late Michael Forrestal, Jeff Frieden, Pie Friendly, Charles Glass, Andrea Giles, Richard Gonzalez, Bill Goodfellow, Bernd Greiner, Betsy Hartmann, Jean Holke, Mark Hulbert, Peter Irons, Peter Iseman, Brennon Jones, Jim Klumpner, Deborah Larson, Maya Latynski, Jerome I. Levinson, Lawrence Lifschultz, Richard Lingeman, Ed Long, Donald F. McHenry, Harry Magdoff, Harry Maurer, Emily Medine, Martin Mendelsohn, George Metcalf, Jim Morrell, Robert Naper, Paula Newberg, Pamela Norick, Kit O'Donohue, Ralph Oman, Marcel Ophuls, David Painter, David & Beth Pollazo, Richard Powers, the late Donald Ranard, Virginia Ranard, Priscilla Roberts, Joel Rogers, Henry Schwarzchild, Gitta Sereny, Tara Siler, Joseph Speer, Dietrich Stobbe, the late I.F. Stone, Corrine Whitlatch, and James Wilkins III.

I also wish to thank the many professional archivists who guided me through the paper trail of McCloy's life, particularly Daria D'Arienzo and Cheryl A. Gracey at the Amherst College archives; Samuel Butler of Cravath, Swaine & Moore, Grant D. Hering and John Eichler of Cadwalader, Wickersham & Taft; David Haight and John E. Wickman at the Dwight D. Eisenhower Library; Anne van Kamp of Chase Manhattan Bank's archives; Carl E. Geiger of the Peddie School Archives; Dwight Miller at the Herbert Hoover Presidential Library; Benedict K. Zobrist and Dennis Bilger of the Harry S. Truman Presidential Library; John Taylor, Wilbur Mahoney, Cindy Fox, and Richard Boylan of the National Archives; Nancy Bressler and Jean Holliday of the Mudd Manuscript Library at Princeton University; Ann Newhall of the Ford Foundation archive; Fred Edson of the University of Arizona Library; Thomas Rosenbaum and Darwin H. Stapleton of the Rockefeller Archive Center; Edward J. Boone of the Douglas MacArthur Memorial Library; John N. Jacob of the George C. Marshall Foundation Library; Martin Elzy and Donald Schewe of the Jimmy Carter Library; Robert Wood, John T. Fawcett, Shirley Sondergard, and Dwight M. Miller of the Herbert Hoover Library; David Humphrey of the Lyndon B. Johnson Library; Georgene Cassels, Sharon Kotok, Frank Maichak, Peter Shields, and many other over-worked officials of the State Department's Freedom of Information Act office.

Viken Berberian, Gwen Bondi, Michael Brownrigg, Dan Charles, Sam Fromartz, Stephen Harvey, and Nicholas Targ volunteered their time as interns to do basic research on various aspects of McCloy's career.

I am especially grateful to Benjamin Buttenwieser who first introduced me to McCloy and gave generously of his time in reminiscing about his own life. William Hohri of the National Council for Japanese American Redress and Aiko and Jack Herzig went out of their way to guide me through the archival records on the Japanese American internment. Thomas A. Schwartz was generous with his time in educating me about McCloy's tenure as High Commissioner in Germany; I relied on his thesis, which was later published as *America's Germany: John J. McCloy and the Federal Republic of Germany.* Jacques Morgan, the proprietor of Idle Time Books in Washington, D.C., kept my library well-stocked, and

Jill Hinckley's pottery class gave me more Washington gossip than I can reveal here. Mark Lynch and Allen Adler advised me on all my Freedom of Information Act requests. Gail Ross is an author's lawyer, a terrific agent, and good friend. She rescued this book and made it possible for me to finish the manuscript.

Biographies are perhaps the best but also the most expensive form of history, and without generous foundation funding, I could not have done much of the research. I am grateful to Cathy Trost, Margaret Engel, Helen McMaster Coulson, and Joseph Albright of the Alicia Patterson Foundation, Peter R. Weitz of the German Marshall Fund, and G. Thomas Tanselle of the John Simon Guggenheim Memorial Foundation for providing substantial fellowships. Anne Zill of the Fund for Constitutional Government, along with the Rockefeller Archive Center, the Harry S. Truman Library Institute, the Lyndon B. Johnson Library Foundation, the Hoover Presidential Library Association, and the Dwight D. Eisenhower Institute for World Affairs provided additional travel and research funds.

My parents, Eugene and Jerine Bird, gave me the passion for history that got me started on this project. From them I learned to love books. And from them I learned the persistence that made it possible for me to write another man's life. Shelly Bird kept my Kaypro computer running long after it should have been retired. My other sisters, Nancy and Christina, put up with my endless stories about McCloy and his world.

This book is dedicated to Susan Goldmark, who took time out from her own career to read the first draft and the last. She has been my best critic, a steadfast partner, and my closest friend. I have relied on her good judgment, sharp intelligence, and patience for almost two decades. All biography is part obsession, and she gave me the perspective, humor, and love to sustain the work. No wife could have done more.

INDEX

ABMs (antiballistic missiles), 615–17
Abraham Lincoln Brigade, 185–86, 211, 418
Abs, Hermann J., 329, 366, 368–69, 382, 383, 403, 593
Acheson, Alice, 628
Acheson, Dean, 49, 50, 102, 103, 112, 249, 264, 276–78, 290, 293, 299, 301, 302, 320, 386, 408, 499, 507, 509, 527
  "German problem" as viewed by, 305, 311, 318, 324, 325–26, 328, 333, 339, 342, 349, 363, 374, 376, 378, 379, 380, 381, 383, 478, 587, 621, 623
  McCloy's relationship with, 54, 99, 100, 111, 131, 132, 305, 311, 312, 316, 317, 318, 392, 393, 508, 510
  Vietnam War as viewed by, 577, 578, 581, 597, 598
Acheson Committee, 276–82
Acheson-Lilienthal Plan, 278–82
Adams, John, 419–20, 421
Adams, Sherman, 408, 433–34
Adenauer, Gussi Zinsser, 319, 320
Adenauer, Konrad, 329, 354
  background of, 318–19
  as chancellor, 318, 321, 326–27, 335, 336, 344, 380, 479, 480–81, 512, 524, 541, 591
  death of, 592
  economic policies of, 337
  German rearmament supported by, 339–40, 342–43, 344, 586
  German reunification as viewed by, 335, 336, 378, 379, 621, 622
  McCloy's relationship with, 314, 319–22, 323, 324–27, 334, 340–41, 342, 362, 363, 372, 377, 382, 383, 384, 403–4, 414, 415, 478, 520
Adenauer, Paul, 319
Adham, Kamal, 633
Adler, Julius Ochs, 106, 110
Advisory Committee on Negro Troop Policy, 187, 188
Agudath Israel World Organization, 211
Ahrendt, Carl, 92, 93
Akins, James E., 625, 626, 627–29
Akzin, Benjamin, 214–15
Albania, 354–55
Aldrich, Winthrop, 98, 107, 274, 388, 391, 393, 394, 395, 397, 441, 453, 456
Alexander, Henry, 497
Allen, George E., 281
Allen, Richard V., 614
Allied Advisory Council, 266–68
Allied Chemical Co., 15, 605, 606
Allied High Commission for Occupied Germany (HICOG), 314, 317, 321, 328, 330, 331, 336, 347–50, 351–53, 363, 369, 370, 372, 406, 407, 408, 410, 416, 426
Alsop, Joseph, 112, 125, 313, 482, 548, 580
Altschul, Frank, 108, 110, 111, 276, 457, 458
America First, 109, 135, 136
American Banker, 289
American Black Chamber (Yardley), 85
American Civil Liberties Union (ACLU), 154, 165, 166
American Committee for a United Europe, 471
American Council on Germany, 15, 478–79, 624
American Cyanamid & Chemical Corporation, 102
American Dilemma in Viet-Nam, 572
American Express Company, 484
American Friends Service Committee, 162
American Institute for Free Labor Development (AIFLD), 485
American Jewish Committee, 482
American Jewish Joint Distribution Committee, 314
American Protective League, 94
Amerika Haus, 407–8
Amherst Monthly, 40, 44

Anderson, Dillon, 429
Anderson, Robert B., 605, 614
Anglers' Club, 15, 99
Angleton, James Jesus, 560
Anti-Defamation League of B'nai B'rith, 482
antitrust legislation, 55, 58, 62, 175, 274–75, 402, 404–5, 517, 518, 627–29, 630–31, 634, 640
Arab Boycott Committee, 568
ARAMCO, 441–45, 541, 633–35
Arcadia Conference, 144–46
Architectual Forum, 455
Armao, Robert, 644
Armour, Ogden, 65
arms control, 282, 465–69, 487–91, 498–503, 505–8, 512–18, 521, 615–17, 622, 655, 657, 662–63
Arms Control and Disarmament Agency, 488–89, 508, 513–14, 516, 521
Armstrong, Hamilton Fish, 63, 109, 457, 458, 462, 581, 585, 619
Army, U.S.:
  Communists in, 185–86, 228–29
  desegregation of, 175, 186–89, 211, 542–43, 662
  Intelligence operation (G-2) of, 117, 118, 125, 129, 130, 142, 156, 228–29, 257, 353, 411, 417
  Japanese-Americans in, 168–69
Army Air Corps, U.S., 125–26, 134
Army-McCarthy hearings, 409, 415, 419, 421, 426
Arnold, Henry H. "Hap," 217, 303
Arnold, Thurman, 274, 597
Aspen Institute, 15, 624
Astor, John Jacob, 42
Aswan High Dam, 445, 448–49
AT&T, 15, 396, 439, 513
Atlantic Charter, 257
Atlantic Institute, 15, 586–87
atomic bomb:
  development of, 185, 234, 240, 246–47
  Eisenhower's views on, 253–54, 264
  international control of, 237, 275–82
  McCloy's views on, 185, 246–47, 251, 262–64, 275–82, 423
  political impact of, 241, 249, 262–64, 500
  Soviet response to, 237–38, 242, 256, 278–79, 281–82
  Stimson's views on, 237–38, 239, 240, 256, 261, 262–63
  targets for, 243, 244–45, 257
  Trinity test of, 251–52, 253, 255, 263
  Truman's views on, 238, 247, 251, 252, 279, 310, 462, 501
  U.S. monopoly of, 255, 261–62, 278–79, 281, 282, 303, 501
  see also Hiroshima bombing
Atomic Energy Commission (AEC), 276, 279, 417, 422
Attlee, Clement, 256
Auerbach, Sol, 404
Ausable Club, 29, 113
Auschwitz concentration camp, 211–23, 315, 354, 359–60, 367, 659, 660, 662

Baker, James A., III, 16
Baker, J. Stewart, 394, 398, 399–400, 402, 441
Baldwin, Hanson, 461
Baldwin, Roger, 87, 165
Ball, George W., 502, 526, 527, 529, 532, 533, 539, 541, 572–73, 576, 578, 585, 587, 590, 598, 599, 652
Ballantine, Arthur, 107
Balli Kombetar, 354
Ballou, George, 605
Bank for International Settlements, 252
Bank Holding Company Act (1956), 402
Bank Merger Act (1960), 402
Bank of America, 399, 400, 456
Barbie, Klaus, 345, 346–53
Bard, Ralph A., 243*n,* 248–49
Barnet, Richard J., 620
Barnett, A. Doak, 585
Barran, David, 627
Baruch, Bernard, 41, 182, 279, 281–82, 300, 302, 304, 409
Baruch Plan, 282
Bass, Perry Richardson, 16
Bator, Francis, 620
Battle, Lucius, 605, 609
Bay of Pigs invasion, 504–5, 509, 522
Beale, Joseph H., 48, 49
Begin, Menachem, 202
Beitz, Berthold, 480, 481, 482, 656
Bendetsen, Karl, 148–49, 150, 152, 153, 154, 156, 157, 158, 159, 161, 165, 169
Bentley, Elizabeth, 287*n*
Bergson, Peter, 202, 207, 209
Berlin, 303, 310, 313, 476, 478, 487, 536
  Kennedy's policies on, 506, 509, 511–12, 524, 531, 541–42
  Khrushchev's policies on, 507, 509, 510, 511, 516, 522
Berlin Wall, 511–12
Bernays, Murray C., 258
Bessie, Simon Michael, 458
Bethe, Hans, 423
Bethlehem Steel Co., 60, 62, 77, 79, 101
Bevin, Ernest, 324

Bidault, Georges, 292
Biddle, Francis, 128, 148, 149, 150, 151, 152, 153, 155, 156, 162, 164–65, 171
Bilderberg Group, 471–74, 475, 479
Birrenbach, Kurt, 369
Bismarck, Otto von, 154, 319, 323, 450, 658
Bissell, Clayton, 229, 428–29
Bitter Heritage, The (Schlesinger), 596–97
Bixler, Julius Seelye, 38
Black, Eugene, 285–86, 289, 295, 305, 445, 448, 449, 450, 452, 497, 498, 581
Black Tom Island case, 46, 78–95
  appeal filed in, 83–86
  destruction investigated in, 78–79
  documentary evidence in, 80, 81, 82, 83–85, 87–88, 93
  Hermann Message and, 84–85, 93
  incendiary pencils as evidence in, 81, 85, 92, 113
  international arbitration in, 93–94
  lawsuit as result of, 77, 92–93
  McCloy's investigation of, 77, 78–95, 96, 108, 113, 119, 126, 154, 163, 176, 278, 302, 345, 347, 353, 427, 502, 503, 548–49
  sabotage as issue in, 77, 80–82, 85, 87, 88, 91
  Zimmermann cable on, 80, 81, 82, 93
Blankenhorn, Herbert, 322
Blaustein, Jacob, 479, 480, 482
Blobel, Paul, 370
Blue Book, 84, 85
Blum, Léon, 111
Boggs, Hale, 548, 564–65
Bohlen, Chip, 512
Bohr, Niels, 277
Bond Club, 15, 290
Bonesteel, Charles S., 171
Bovenizer, George W., 104
Bowie, Robert R., 348, 349, 352, 360–61, 423, 461, 515, 642,
Bowles, Chester, 516–17
Bowman, Isaiah, 276
Boy-Ed, Karl, 88
Boyle, Kay, 406
Braden, Tom, 358
Bradley, Omar N., 233, 327, 576
Brand, Joel, 218
Brandeis, Louis D., 55–56, 67
Brandt, Willy, 358, 621–22, 623
Bratton, Rufus C., 138, 140
Braun, Eva, 254
Brazil, 550–53
Bretton Woods conference, 282, 285, 286, 292, 296, 297
Brezhnev, Leonid, 656
Bridges, Harry, 128
British Broadcasting Company (BBC), 202
British Secret Operations Executive, 181
British Security Coordination, 129
Bross, John, 349, 352, 361, 363, 412
Browder, Earl, 404
Browne, Malcolm, 581
Brownell, George, 106
Brownell, Herbert, Jr., 409, 415, 417, 638
Brownlee, James F., 437
Bruce, David, 325, 481, 491
Brunie, Henry C., 69, 75, 99, 442, 504
Bryan, William Jennings, 43
Brzezinksi, Zbigniew, 530, 585, 642–43, 644–45, 646, 648, 649, 650
Buchanan, Scott, 38
Buford, Jack W., 550–53
Bunche, Ralph, 458
Bundy, Harvey H., 121, 132, 143, 185, 239, 243*n,* 251
Bundy, McGeorge, 16, 423, 460, 462, 520, 563, 564, 581–82, 585, 596
  as Kennedy's national security advisor, 499, 500, 516, 523, 526, 527, 531, 534
  Vietnam policy of, 571, 573–74, 575, 576, 578, 581–83, 597, 598, 602
Bundy, Mary Acheson, 182
Bundy, William, 182, 412, 413, 499, 573–74, 575, 576, 577, 578, 596, 599, 619–20, 621
Bunker, Ellsworth, 595
Burgess, Randolph, 285
Burke, Michael, 355, 356
Burling, John, 172
Bush, George, 16, 657, 663
Bush, Vannevar, 243*n,* 276, 278, 423
Business Week, 455
Buttenwieser, Benjamin, 59, 60, 64, 66, 72, 74, 104, 105, 207, 318, 328, 405, 412, 660
Byrnes, James F., 123, 242, 243*n,* 244, 246, 249–58, 261–63, 272, 276, 279, 280, 292
Byroade, Henry, 340, 349, 371–72, 379–80

Cadwalader, Wickersham & Taft, 15, 58–61, 62
Cairo Conference, 190–95
Cairo Declaration, 257
Campbell, John Franklin, 620–21
Canfield, Cass, 458, 596
Carnegie, Andrew, 79
Carstens, Karl, 16
Carter, Jay Franklin, 155
Carter, Jimmy, 640–54, 660
  Establishment and, 649–50
  Iranian hostage crisis and, 641, 655

Carter *(cont.)*
shah of Iran as viewed by, 641–52
Carter, Rosalynn, 646
Carver, George, 585, 598, 602
Case, Clifford, 628
Casey, William, 457, 656
Castro, Fidel, 459, 522, 523, 530, 532, 533, 534, 535, 536, 537, 540, 548, 555–56, 566
Cecil, Robert, 61
Celler, Emmanuel, 400, 402
Central Intelligence Agency (CIA), 130, 295, 301, 352*n*
covert activities of, 302–4, 353, 354, 355–56, 413, 414, 435, 449, 504–5, 551, 553
Dulles as director of, 412, 413, 426, 429, 459, 499, 504
front organizations of, 357–58, 483–85
as information source, 459–60, 634, 642
International Organizations (IO) Division of, 412, 484
Kennedy assassination and, 555–56, 560–61, 562, 565–66
McCarthy's investigations of, 412–13
McCloy's contacts with, 302–4, 426–29, 518, 521, 651, 656
Nazi war criminals and operations of, 352*n*
Office of Policy Coordination of, 304, 355, 427
Soviet military threat analyzed by, 327–28
Century Group, 111–12, 124
Chafee, Zachariah, Jr., 53, 55
"Challenge to American Foreign Policy, The" (McCloy), 392–93
Chamoun, Camille, 442
Champion, George, 396–98, 441, 454, 455–56, 488
Chandler, Wallace C., 48
Chapman, Dudley, 627–29, 631
Chartered Life Underwriters, 289
Chase International Investment Corporation, 641
Chase Manhattan Bank:
Bank of Manhattan merger and, 394, 398–402, 435, 441, 453
charter of, 399, 402
CIA involvement with, 485
headquarters of, 453–55
international loans of, 396–98, 449, 456, 567–68, 605, 641–42, 653–54
McCloy as chairman of, 18, 387–88, 391–402, 412, 430–32, 435–36, 443, 444, 445, 450, 453–57, 458, 477, 488, 498
retail banking facilities of, 394, 398, 402
Rockefeller control of, 395, 401
shareholders' meeting of, 393–95, 400, 401
Chase National Bank, 91, 93, 103, 274, 481
Chemical Corn Exchange Bank, 400
Cherne, Leo, 457
Chevalier, Haakon, 424
Chiang Kai-shek, 192, 241, 473–75
Chicago Daily News, 67
Chicago, Milwaukee & St. Paul Railroad, 64–67, 104–5
Chicago Tribune, 138
Childs, Marquis, 300
China, People's Rupublic of, 241, 449
U.S. relations with, 473–75, 571, 573
China lobby, 474, 475
Christian Aid Committee, 362
Christian Democratic Union (CDU), 318, 323, 326–27, 590
Christopher, Warren, 646, 647, 648
Church, Frank, 639
Churchill, Mary, 200
Churchill, Winston, 129, 132, 143, 197
at Cairo Conference, 192
German occupation as viewed by, 226
Holocaust and policy of, 217–18
McCloy's relationship with, 199–200, 364
military strategy of, 177, 178, 179, 181, 190, 192–93, 200
Roosevelt and, 143, 178, 182, 184–85, 193–94, 225, 235, 236, 258
Stalin's relationship with, 251, 338
Truman's relationship with, 241, 251, 252
World Bank as viewed by, 294–95
Citizens Committee for Peace with Freedom in Vietnam, 597–98
civil-defense program, 465, 466, 467, 509
Clark, Grenville, 19, 41, 43, 44, 45, 80, 107, 110, 133, 141, 408, 514–15
Clark, Mark, 153, 195
Clark, Tom, 153
Clay, Lucius, 233, 303, 305, 309–10, 313, 330, 333, 360, 365, 386, 419, 447, 448, 468, 476, 622, 646
Clayton, William L., 112, 232, 243*n*, 292
Cleveland *Plain-Dealer,* 327
Clifford, Clark, 504, 580, 584, 601, 602, 607, 609
Cohen, Ben, 125
Cohn, Roy, 405–6, 407, 412, 413, 417, 419–20, 421, 422
Cold War, 262, 263, 276, 576
"German problem" and, 310–11, 360, 378, 381, 385, 475–76, 592

intelligence operations in, 302, 303, 347, 356, 357, 434
international finance and, 306, 307
McCloy's views on, 290, 300, 336, 476, 624
U.S. strategy for, 413–14, 506, 538–39, 603
as "war of ideas," 393, 408, 428, 463
Coleman, William, 561
Collado, Emilio G. "Pete," 283, 284–85, 286
Commission on Foreign and Economic Policy, 411
Commission on Organization of the Executive Branch of the Government, 301–2
Committee for an Effective and Durable Peace in Asia, 581
"Committee of Three," 229, 240–41, 247
Committee on the Present Danger, 649
Committee to Defend America by Aiding the Allies, 109, 112
Common Market, 379, 472, 516, 541
Communist Party, French, 290, 291, 293, 302, 350
Communist Party, German (KPD), 347, 352
Communist Party, Italian, 302
Communist Party, U.S., 185, 186, 229, 421
Communists:
McCloy's views on, 185–86, 271, 280, 296, 300, 356–57, 385, 393, 411, 412, 416, 417, 418, 420, 423, 446
in military service, 185–86, 228–29
Compton, Arthur, 243*n*
Compton, Karl T., 243*n*, 423
Conant, James, 112, 243–44, 276, 278, 391–92, 403–4, 406, 410, 459, 478, 581
"Concentration Camp: U.S. Style," 162
Conference on Jewish War Material Claims Against Germany, 479
Confluence, 462
Congress for Cultural Freedom (CCF), 357–58, 412–13, 428
Connally, John, 554, 558, 562, 565, 637
Connally, Tom, 133
Connor, John, 605
Coolidge, Calvin, 54, 99
Cooper, Chester, 599
Cooper, John Sherman, 548, 565
Corcoran, Tommy, 124
Cotton, Joseph, 107
Council for Democracy, 109
Council of Europe, 326
Council of Foreign Ministers, 259
Council on Foreign Relations, 112, 124, 457, 616
CIA involvement with, 426, 459–60
Corporation Service for, 458
as discussion group, 459–64, 618–21
Establishment represented in, 619–21
founding of, 59, 63
Franklin Report of, 275–76
McCloy as chairman of, 18, 416, 432–33, 452–53, 457–64, 503, 521, 584–85, 618–19
McCloy as member of, 108, 275–76, 312, 403, 423, 424, 448, 449, 658
membership of, 457–58, 472, 499
political agenda of, 108–9, 287, 435
"two-Chinas" policy of, 474, 475
Vietnam War studied by, 572, 573, 584–85, 596, 599–600, 618, 619–20, 621
War and Peace project of, 109
Counter-Intelligence Corps (CIC), 345, 346–53
Cox, Archibald, 637, 639
Cravath, Henderson & de Gersdorff, 60, 61–77, 79, 94, 100–101, 103–4, 106, 122, 207, 271–72
Cravath, Paul, 17–18, 57, 61, 62–63, 65, 71, 72, 73, 102, 108, 405, 575
"Cravath system," 61–62, 267, 273, 575
Cronkite, Walter, 601
CROWCASS directory, 346
Cuban Missile crisis, 522–40, 575, 650–51
Cummings, Homer, 101
Cutler, Robert, 433, 434
Czechoslovakia, 296, 304, 306, 308, 446

Dalton, Hugh, 288
Darkness at Noon (Koestler), 358
Darlan, Jean, 180, 181, 199
Dartmouth College case, 399
Davies, John Paton, 407, 415, 416
Davies, Ralph K., 274, 275
Davis, John W., 63
Davis, Norman H., 109
Davis, Pierpont V., 66, 106
Davison, Dorothy Peabody, 68
Davison, F. Trubee, 68–69, 71, 75, 316
Davison, Gates, 316–17
Davison, Henry, 68, 399
Dean, Arthur, 423, 458, 474, 505, 507, 577, 578, 579, 581, 583, 584, 598
Dean, Gordon E., 461
Dean, John, 639
"Death Rattle of the Eastern Establishment, The" (Campbell), 620–21
Debevoise, Eli Whitney, 437, 439
Debevoise, Thomas M., 274

de Gasperi, Alcide, 472
de Gaulle, Charles, 541
German occupation as viewed by, 234–35, 385
as leader of Free French, 180, 181, 183, 184, 195–96, 197–99, 200
NATO abandoned by, 586, 587, 588, 589, 600
Roosevelt and, 180, 183, 196–99, 234
de Gersdorff, Carl, 60, 62
Dehler, Thomas, 329, 334
Democratic Party, 98, 103, 571
de Neufville, Lawrence, 354, 355, 356
Depression, Great, 96, 98, 99, 103
"destroyer-for-bases" deal, 120–21, 133
Deutsche Bank, 329
Deva, Xhafer, 355
Devers, Jacob, 233–34
Dewey, Tom, 447
DeWitt, John, 148, 149, 150–51, 153, 156, 157, 158–59, 160, 165, 168, 169, 172, 173
Diem, Ngo Dinh, 542, 569–70
Dies, Martin, 137
Dill, John, 190, 191, 219
Dillon, Douglas, 497, 499, 525
Disston, Samuel, 28
Dobrynin, Anatoly, 510, 516, 530, 531, 538, 539
Dohrn, Klaus, 485
Dominican Republic, 553, 574
Donovan, William J., 52, 129, 130, 142, 165, 191, 198, 206, 242, 302, 411
Dorsey, Robert R., 636
Dosti, Hasan, 355
Douglas, Lewis W., 190, 191, 325, 412, 458, 459–60, 474, 638
McCloy's relationship with, 19, 38, 39–40, 45, 68, 74, 75, 76, 101–2, 131, 132, 285, 304–5, 387, 414, 542, 543
New Deal policies as viewed by, 98–100, 101–3, 106, 108, 109, 111, 112
Vietnam War as viewed by, 572, 573, 577, 585, 602
Douglas, Paul, 436, 597
Douglas, Peggy Zinsser, 68, 74–75, 77
Douglas, Sharman, 508, 509
Douglas, William O., 64, 65, 66, 67, 68, 173
Dulles, Allen W., 108, 109, 112, 212, 242, 252, 458, 548, 584
as CIA director, 412, 413, 426, 429, 459, 499, 504
McCloy's relationship with, 76–77, 253, 414, 427, 428, 485
on Warren Commission, 549, 555, 557, 558, 562, 565
Dulles, Eleanor, 511
Dulles, John Foster, 72, 107, 109, 294, 430, 572
China policy of, 473, 474–75
foreign policy of, 433, 447, 448–53, 461, 463–64, 467, 468–71, 476, 477–78
McCarthyism and, 392, 404, 407, 415, 416
McCloy's relationship with, 386–87, 442, 443, 444–45, 450, 456, 474–75, 476–77
Dumbarton Oaks conference, 228, 278
DuPuy, William G., 599

Eastern Forwarding Co., 91–92
East Germany, *see* German Democratic Republic
Eban, Abba, 460
Ebbott, Percy J., 393, 395, 431, 441
Eberstadt, Ferdinand, 279, 281, 301–2
Eberstadt Task Force, 301–4, 354
Ecker, Frederick H., 66
Economic Cooperation Administration (ECA), 305–6
Eden, Anthony, 217, 218, 240
Edwards, Theodore "Gus," 35, 39
Egypt, 448–53, 604, 606–9
Eichmann, Adolf, 218
Eilts, Herman, 606
Einsatzgruppen squads, 332, 354, 367, 369–71, 373
Eisenhower, Dwight D., 157, 179, 180, 386, 403–91
atomic bomb as viewed by, 253–54, 264
China policy of, 473–75
defense budget of, 465–66
de Gaulle and, 195–96
European military campaign of, 197, 198, 200, 227, 233–34
foreign policy of, 413, 415, 433–35, 445–47, 448–53, 473, 477–78, 504, 555–56, 571
German occupation policy of, 224, 404
heart attacks of, 447, 469–70
Khrushchev's relationship with, 467, 470–71, 476, 487–91
McCarthyism as viewed by, 403, 405, 408–10, 415–16, 417, 418, 419–21, 433, 448
McCloy's relationship with, 146, 181–82, 193, 195, 199, 225, 344, 386, 391–92, 403, 407–11, 414, 421, 423, 429–30, 435, 445, 447–48, 469–70, 477, 483, 490, 497, 507, 513–14, 542, 544, 564
North African military campaign of, 181–82, 190, 456

nuclear strategy of, 461, 462–64, 465–71
Oppenheimer security case and, 423, 425
Eisenhower, Milton, 157, 160–61, 162–63, 409, 468
Eliot, Charles W., 30
Eliot, T. S., 88
Elliott, William, 461
Ellsberg, Daniel, 620
Elman, Philip, 170
Emergency Committee to Save the Jewish People of Europe, 202–3, 209
Encounter, 358, 413
Endo, Mitsuye, 166–67, 173
Ennis, Edward J., 149, 153, 172
Equitable Trust Company, 274
Erhard, Ludwig, 576, 587, 589, 590, 591
Esquire, 563–64
Establishment:
British Establishment vs., 18
McCloy as "chairman" of, 15, 17, 19, 20, 563–64, 596–97
McCloy as member of, 15–20, 47, 107, 661, 663
in Philadelphia, 23–27, 663
political outlook of, 312, 619–21
prep-school credentials for, 35–36
Vietnam War and, 603–4
in Washington, D.C., 499, 613, 622–23, 637–39, 649–50
EUCOM (European Command, U.S. Army), 345, 350
Europe, Eastern, *see specific countries*
Europe, Western:
anti-Americanism in, 392–93, 471
postwar reconstruction in, 235, 292–94, 306
Soviet threat to, 303, 308–9, 327–28, 339–44, 356, 357, 360, 378, 524, 623
union for, 336–37, 379, 385
U.S. military presence in, 265, 344, 381, 384, 588–93, 621–24
see also specific countries
European Defense Force (EDF), 340, 341, 344, 364, 368, 378, 379, 381, 385
European Economic Community (EEC), 379, 472, 516, 541
European Movement, 471
European Recovery Program (ERP), *see* Marshall Plan
Evans, Ward V., 422
Eveland, Wilbur Crane, 442–43
Excomm (Executive Committee), 526–27, 529, 531, 533, 538–39
Executive Order 9066, 153–54, 156
Export-Import Bank (Eximbank), 298–99
Exxon, 625
'Face the Nation," 559
Fahy, Charles, 172
Faisal, King of Saudi Arabia, 444, 445, 541, 606–7, 633–34
Falk, Richard, 596, 618, 620
Fall, Bernard B., 585
I. G. Farben, 214, 219, 309, 316, 368, 479
Federal Bureau of Investigation (FBI):
intelligence operations of, 118, 126, 280–81
Kennedy assassination and, 548, 554–55, 556–59, 562, 565–66
McCloy investigated by, 411–12
sabotage investigated by, 117, 119, 128, 136, 137, 142–43, 163–65
Security Index of, 555
Special Intelligence section of, 118
wiretapping by, 127, 128, 162
Federal Reserve, 58, 72, 402, 453
Fee, James A., 167
Ferencz, Benjamin B., 336, 362, 368, 479, 480, 481
Fermi, Enrico, 243*n*, 423
"Fifth Column on the Coast, The" (Lippmann), 152–53
Final Report, Japanese Evacuation from the West Coast, 169, 172–73
Financial Times, 283, 287
Fish, Hamilton, Jr., 46
Fisher, Adrian, 172, 173, 499, 513
Fleming, Ian, 129
Flick, Friedrich, 361, 365, 367, 479
Flyfishers Club, 99
Forbes, 455
Ford, Benson, 439
Ford, Bill, 437–38
Ford, Edsel Bryant, 436
Ford, Gerald R., 548, 556, 565
Ford, Henry, 88, 436, 438
Ford, Henry, II, 414, 426, 436–40
Ford, Leland M., 147
Ford Foundation, 15, 358, 458, 478
board of trustees of, 437, 438, 439–40, 519–20
CIA involvement with, 426–29, 485
McCloy as chairman of, 18, 475, 503, 518–20, 586
McCloy as consultant to, 386, 391, 403
McCloy as trustee of, 416, 426–29, 436, 437, 438
projects funded by, 518–20, 567, 573, 618
stock offering by, 436–40
Ford Motor Company, 436–40
Foreign Affairs, 63, 306, 307, 458, 460, 461–62, 521, 585, 619–20, 621
Forger, Alexander, 16
Formosa, 464, 473–75

Forrestal, James V., 103, 130–31, 229, 239, 240–41, 247, 257, 260, 263, 264, 301, 302–3, 308
Forrestal, Michael, 528
Fortas, Abe, 274, 275, 548
Fortune, 391, 395, 396, 553
Forum, 413
Foster, William, 516
Foster Panel, 515–16
Fowler, Henry H., 591
France:
  intelligence operations in, 347, 348, 350–51
  Jewish community in, 346
  in NATO, 586, 587, 588, 589, 600
  occupation currency in, 197, 198
  postwar reconstruction of, 290–91, 292, 293, 296
  resistance groups in, 196, 197, 198, 199, 207, 221, 346, 350
  U.S. relations with, 347, 348
  Vichy, 180–81, 196, 197
  West Germany's relations with, 342, 344, 376–78, 379, 380, 383, 385, 393
Frankenstein, Joseph M., 406, 407, 410
Frankfurter, Felix, 76, 102, 104, 120, 183, 205–6, 392, 401, 423, 477, 508, 511
  McCloy's relationship with, 47–48, 49–50, 54, 55, 56, 121, 125, 131, 132, 148, 154, 170, 207, 219, 275, 282, 373, 374, 380, 418–19, 425, 482–83
Franklin, George S., Jr., 107, 275–76, 457, 459, 462
Frasheri, Midhat, 355
Free French Committee, 180, 181, 183, 184, 195–96, 197–99, 200
Freemantle Diary, 429
Friedman, William, 142
Frischer, Ernest, 218
Fulbright, J. William, 436, 513, 582, 584
Furland, Richard M., 16
Furness, H. H., 28

Gaither, H. Rowan, 436, 437, 439, 465, 475
Gaither Commission, 465–68, 469, 487, 498, 501
Galbraith, John Kenneth, 19, 435–36, 459, 496, 619
Garner, Robert L., 286, 289, 298, 300, 301, 305
Garrison, Lloyd K., 422, 423, 425
Gehlen, Reinhard, 353–54, 355–56
General Advisory Committee to the Arms Control and Disarmament Agency, 521, 524
General Motors, 59, 132, 436, 439
George VI, King of England, 235
Georges-Picot, Jacques, 449
Gerhardt, Al, 213, 218, 220, 221, 355, 442
German-American Mixed Claims Commission, 79–80, 82–83, 85, 86, 89, 90–91, 93
German Democratic Republic (East Germany):
  government of, 323–24
  military forces of, 327
  refugees from, 338, 511–12
  Soviet control of, 380, 511
Germany, Federal Republic of (West Germany):
  Allies' "contractual relationship" with, 343–44, 376, 378, 379–85, 404
  anti-Semitism in, 334–35
  Basic Law for, 310, 322, 335
  Bonn Constitution of, 311
  British troops in, 586, 591, 593
  Bundestag of, 314, 315, 356–57, 404, 447
  Constitution of, 362
  currency reform in, 303, 309–10, 323
  demilitarization of, 326, 327–28, 336, 415, 512
  de-Nazification program in, 309, 317, 328–30, 337, 347–48, 367
  dismantling of industry in, 324–25, 326, 332, 368–69, 383, 480–81, 482
  economy of, 360, 380
  French relations with, 342, 344, 376–78, 379, 380, 383, 385, 393
  General Claims Law for, 314–15
  industrialists in, 332, 337–39, 368–69
  intelligence operations in, 334, 345–58
  Jewish affairs in, 314–15, 328, 334–35, 337, 382–83, 479–82
  Labor Service units in, 354–55
  McCarthyism as viewed in, 410, 414–15
  McCloy's agenda for, 318–19, 336–44, 371, 379–82, 414–15, 478, 585–93, 621–24
  McCloy's staff in, 317–18
  Marshall Plan for, 309
  in NATO, 585–93
  Nazi war criminals in, 330–36, 346–56
  neutrality of, 342, 343, 380, 381, 384, 463, 478
  nuclear weapons in, 467, 585–86
  Occupation Statute for, 321–22, 323, 337, 343
  occupation zones in, 309, 318, 320–21, 325, 326, 334, 337, 338, 376, 377, 379
  Ostpolitik of, 587, 593, 621–22

as parliamentary democracy, 310, 311, 313, 318, 320, 326–27, 328, 334, 335, 337, 338, 374, 379–80, 385
postwar reconstruction of, 309, 324–25
rearmament of, 339–44, 363, 376–79, 380, 381, 385
reparations paid by, 314–15, 317
Secret Service of, 353
sovereignty of, 342, 379–80, 381, 383
Soviet opposition to, 323–24, 336, 339, 590
Soviet "peace offensives" and, 380–82, 383, 384, 415
taxation in, 337, 338
"trilateral negotiations" in, 590–93
U.S. relations with, 341, 586, 592
U.S. troops in, 376, 381, 384, 586, 588–93, 594, 621–24
Germany, Occupied:
demilitarization of, 311, 343, 478
dismemberment of, 230, 308, 310
European stability dependent on, 295
McCloy as high commissioner of, 16, 18, 268, 305–6, 308–86, 446, 570, 662
McCloy's inspection tour of, 232–35
nationalism in, 309, 377
neutrality of, 310, 378
occupation zones of, 192, 254, 255, 258, 259, 308, 310–11, 342
pastoralization of, 230, 287
postwar reconstruction of, 224–27, 231, 232, 233, 234–35, 255, 295
Prussian militarism in, 310, 319
reparations paid by, 231, 232, 255, 382–83, 479–82
reunification of, 311, 319, 323, 324, 325, 335, 336–37, 342, 376, 377–78, 380–82, 384, 446, 478, 511–12, 662
Soviet zone in, 224, 225, 267, 308, 310–11
U.S. occupation policy on, 223–27, 230, 254
Germany, Weimar, 70–71, 324
Gerow, Leonard T., 135, 139, 146, 233
Gestapo, 361, 369
Gettel, Raymond, 39
Gettysburg, Battle of, 429
Gilpatric, Roswell L., 491, 532, 576
Giraud, Henri, 180, 181, 182, 183
Globke, Hans, 329
Godkin, Edwin L., 392
Goering, Hermann, 89, 90, 324
Goetz, Betty, 499, 513, 514
Goldberg, Arthur, 584
Goldmann, Guido, 659
Goldmann, Nahum, 219, 222, 382–83, 482, 659
Goldwater, Barry, 542, 562–64, 568, 637, 638
Golitsyn, Anatoliy, 560*n*
Goodpaster, Andrew, Jr., 464
Gorbachev, Mikhail S., 657
Gordon, Lincoln, 551, 552
Gottlieb, Leo, 49
Goulart, João, 550–53
Graham, Billy, 456
Graham, Katharine, 468
Graham, Philip, 468
Gray, Gordon, 422, 424–25, 487, 488
Gray Board, 422–26
Great Oil Spill (McCloy et al.), 636
Greco, El, 278
Greece, 237, 290
Greenstein, Harry, 314, 315
Gregory VII, Pope, 322
Grew, Joseph, 239, 240–41, 247
Grewe, Wilhelm, 320, 512
Grigg, James, 289
Gromyko, Andrei, 250, 501–2
Grotewohl, Otto, 323–24
Groves, Leslie R., 243*n*, 244, 276, 278
Gruenther, Alfred M., 468, 470, 471, 477, 488
Guatemala, 435, 449
Gulf of Tonkin resolution, 571, 620
Gulf Oil Corporation, 636–37, 640
Gullion, Allen W., 148, 149, 150, 151, 153, 154
Gullion, Edmund A., 499, 500

Haig, Alexander, 635, 637, 656
Hall, W. Reginald, 80, 84, 85, 94
Hamilton, Andrew, 26
Hamilton, Walton, 39
Hammarskjöld, Dag, 450, 451
Hammer, Armand, 625–26, 636
Hammett, Dashiell, 404
Hanauer, Jerome J., 60, 66
Hancock, John, 279
Hand, Learned, 49, 392
Handy, Thomas T., 119, 178, 213, 374
Hanfstaengl, Ernst Franz "Putzi," 88–89, 95, 176–77
M. A. Hanna Mining Company, 550–53
Hanrieder, Wolfram, F., 384
Harding, Warren G., 54–58
Hardy, René, 348, 350
Harper's, 19, 263, 659–60
Harriman, Averell, 103, 239, 256, 260–61, 296, 305, 423, 471–72, 499, 507, 512, 526, 539, 634, 637, 639
Khrushchev and, 485–87, 543
McCloy's relationship with, 19, 69, 191, 228, 250, 253, 265, 300, 340, 485–87, 551, 552, 563, 564, 568,

Harriman *(cont.)*
575, 586, 587, 600, 649
Vietnam War and, 573, 585, 594, 600, 602, 614, 617, 618
Harriman, Edward H., 69
Harris, George L., 37, 185, 243*n*, 251
Harrison, Pat, 124
Harvard Advocate, 53–54
Harvard Crimson, 50, 102
Harvard Law Review, 48, 50, 53
Harvard University, 658–59
Hastie, William H., 187–88
Hays, George P., 314, 315, 318
Haywood, "Big" Bill, 87
Heald, Henry, 519–20
Healey, Denis, 472
Hearst, William Randolph, 61
Heinemann, Gustav, 343
Helms, Richard M., 560–61, 565, 598
Henry, Bayard, 57
Heritage Foundation, 414
Hermann, Frederick Laurent, 81–83, 84–85, 93, 95
Herod, Rogers, 486
Herter, Christian A., 468, 476, 477–78, 488
Hess, Rudolf, 89, 374
Heusinger, Adolf, 364
Heydrich, Reinhard, 201
Hilken, Paul, 81–83, 84, 92, 95
Hill, Kenneth, 442
Hillenkoetter, Roscoe H., 302
Hinsch, Friedrich, 81–82, 83, 84
Hirabayashi, Gordon K., 166–67, 170
Hirohito, Emperor of Japan, 242, 243, 245, 246, 248, 250, 251, 252–53, 257, 258, 259–60, 263
Hiroshima bombing, 240–68, 463
intelligence information and, 242, 251, 252, 263
Japanese surrender and, 242–43, 263
McCloy's opposition to, 16–17, 240, 242–43, 259, 263–64, 501, 663
moral consequences of, 254, 263–64
Stalin's views on, 260–61
Stimson's views on, 240–48, 251, 263, 501
Truman's policy on, 241, 244, 254, 257, 259, 260, 263
U.S. invasion and, 244–48
Hirschmann, Ira, 218
Hiss, Alger, 281, 283, 404–5, 412, 413
Hitler, Adolf, 86, 88, 90, 108–9, 132, 143, 144, 176, 276, 316, 319
dictatorial powers of, 329, 419
industrialists as supporters of, 359–60, 366–67, 372
McCloy's views on, 133, 254, 452
military strategy of, 179
opposition to, 332–33, 374–75, 504
as responsible for Nazi crimes, 330, 361
Roosevelt vs., 89, 171
Ho Chi Minh, 581, 594
Hoffman, Amzi, 32, 34, 35, 39
Hoffman, Paul, 294, 447, 654
Holmes, Oliver Wendell, Jr., 47
Holocaust:
concentration camps in, 359–60, 361, 362, 366, 367, 369
gas chambers in, 205, 211–12, 214–17
Jewish-Americans and, 175, 202, 205, 207, 208, 209, 218, 222
Jewish emigration and, 203, 208–11
McCloy's policies on, 201–27
military force and, 204–5, 207, 212–23
Nuremberg trial and, 331
reports of, 201, 202, 205–6, 207, 211–12, 215, 217, 220, 221, 309, 334
rescue efforts and, 175, 203–4, 209–10, 216
slave labor in, 479–82
Soviet military strategy and, 214, 218, 219, 220
see also Auschwitz concentration camp
Hook, Sidney, 357
Hoover, Herbert, 18, 71–72, 97–98, 99, 103, 109, 139, 301, 430
Hoover, Herbert, Jr., 451
Hoover, J. Edgar, 118, 119, 126, 127, 128, 129, 137, 147, 149, 162, 164–65, 276, 301
Kennedy assassination and, 554–55, 557, 561
McCloy's relationship with, 271, 280–81, 411–12
Hope, Walter, 107
Hopkins, Harry, 144, 179, 184, 192, 193, 194–95, 224, 225
House of Morgan, 60, 66, 98
House of Representatives, U.S.:
Committee on Government Operations, 406
Foreign Affairs Committee, 513–14
Foreign Relations Committee, 123, 208
Select Committee on Assassinations, 559, 566*n*
Howard, Frank, 442
Howe, Louis, 101
Hulbert, Mark, 654
Hull, Cordell, 103, 140, 192, 225, 250
Hull, John E., 213, 221
Humes, James J., 554
Humphrey, George, 550–53
Humphrey, Hubert H., 499, 513, 564, 583, 584, 614
Hurewitz, J. C., 458
Hyland, William G., 616–17

ICBMs (intercontinental ballistic missiles), 465, 466, 467, 487, 488, 509, 524, 525, 616
Ickes, Harold L., 110, 118, 119, 124, 137, 161, 171, 177, 182, 185, 190, 223, 226, 229, 272, 274, 275, 417
IL-28 bombers, 533, 534, 537, 538, 540
Independent Research Service, 484
insider trading, 72, 105, 404–5
Institute for Policy Studies, 620
intelligence operations:
  centralized, 84, 94, 118, 129–30, 279–80
  counter-, 128, 137, 164, 351
  covert operations and, 353–58, 384, 411, 413–14
  ex-Nazis used in, 346–53
  illegal methods used in, 126–28, 130, 136, 155
  McCloy's views on, 84, 85, 94, 95, 118–19, 126–30, 141–42, 279, 301–4, 345, 347, 350, 355, 356–57, 411–12, 414, 427, 429, 561–62
  in Pearl Harbor attack, 140, 141–42
  against Soviets, 345, 347, 353–57
  see also Central Intelligence Agency
Interim Committee, 237, 242, 243–44, 249, 276
Internal Revenue Service (IRS), 438, 639
International Acceptance Bank, 71
International Bank for Reconstruction and Development, *see* World Bank
International Monetary Fund (IMF), 228, 282, 287, 292, 295, 296, 397
Interstate Commerce Commission (ICC), 67, 432
Investor Pays, The (Lowenthal), 65
Iran, 17, 605–6
Iranian hostage crisis, 641, 655
Iraq, 444–45
IRBMs (intermediate-range ballistic missiles), 466, 467
Irons, Peter, 170
Irwin, John N., II, 629
Israel, 446, 449–50, 451–52, 479, 567, 568, 604, 606–9, 615, 633–35
Italy, 254–55, 259, 302
Izvestia, 469, 531

Jackson, Baxter, 285
Jackson, Bill, 630
Jackson, C. D., 109, 387, 411, 413, 414, 416, 419, 433–35, 470, 472, 473, 474, 483, 484–85, 557, 558
Jackson, Robert, 126–28
Jacobsson, Per, 252
Jamieson, Ken, 625, 627
Japan, Imperial:
  Soviet declaration of war against, 246, 251, 252, 260
  surrender of, 242–54, 257–58, 259–61, 263, 264
  see also Hirohito, Emperor of Japan; Hiroshima bombing
Japan, Occupied, 266–68
Japanese American Citizens League (JACL), 157–58, 167
Japanese-Americans, 147–74
  in concentration camps, 147, 152, 157, 158–59, 161, 162, 165, 171
  constitutional rights for, 147, 149–50, 151, 152, 153, 154, 156, 159–60, 161–62, 166–73, 175
  detention of, 142–43, 156
  disloyal vs. loyal, 150–51, 157–58, 159, 168, 170–71, 173
  as foreign agents, 136–38, 147, 150
  in Hawaii, 136–37, 159
  internment of, 147–74, 228, 548
  legal process for, 166–73
  McCloy's policies on, 148, 149–63, 165–69, 173–74, 176, 302, 659, 660, 662
  mass evacuation of, 148–54, 156–61, 172–73
  in military units, 168–69
  military zones closed to, 150–51, 152, 153–54, 157, 171
  national security and, 154, 161, 167
  property of, 156–57
  questionnaire for, 168–69, 170
  sabotage and, 152–53, 154, 155, 172
  writ of *habeas corpus* for, 166–67
Javits, Jacob, 365, 468
Jay, Delancey K., 42
Jay, John, 34, 42
Jewish Claims Conference, 480, 482
Jewish War Veterans of America, 333
Jews:
  Final Solution and, 201, 204, 209, 215, 218
  McCloy's views on, 206–7, 210, 222–23
  in "Our Crowd," 60, 102
  Vichy decrees on, 181, 182
  West Germany and, 314–15, 328, 334–35, 337, 382–83, 479–82
  see also Holocaust
Johnson, George, 30
Johnson, Joseph, 472
Johnson, Lyndon B., 409, 547–609
  domestic programs of, 569, 571
  foreign policy of, 569, 570, 582
  Kennedy's assassination and, 544, 547, 548, 549, 554, 566
  McCloy's relationship with, 544, 550,

Johnson (cont.)
563, 567, 568, 569, 570–71
Middle East policy of, 604–9
presidential campaign of, 542, 562–64, 567, 568
Vietnam policy of, 568, 569–85, 593–604, 609, 620
Warren Commission authorized by, 548, 549, 550, 554–55
Johnson, U. Alexis, 626
Joint Chiefs of Staff (JCS), 193, 204, 244, 246, 247, 251–52, 525, 595
Joint Intelligence Committee, 242
Jones, Robert Tyre, 429
Jones, W. Alton, 103, 429, 486
Jordan, Hamilton, 645, 651
Josselson, Michael, 357
Jungers, Frank, 633, 635
Justice Department, U.S.:
banking probe of, 400–401
Japanese-American internment and, 148, 149, 153, 156, 172, 173
oil company consortium allowed by, 627–29, 630–31, 634
sabotage prosecuted by, 164–65, 169

Kaghan, Theodore, 406, 407
Kahn, Herman, 599
Kahn, Otto H., 60, 70, 71, 72, 105
Kaiser, Jacob, 380
Karski, Jan, 205–6, 207
Kase, Shunichi, 242
Kean, Benjamin, 644
Keating, Kenneth, 523
Kennan, George, 260, 290, 293, 296–97, 302, 308, 310, 311, 340, 376, 381, 423, 478, 487, 499, 512, 573, 584
Kennedy, Caroline, 496
Kennedy, John F., 495–544
arms control policies of, 490–91, 498–99, 500, 503, 506–7, 508, 514
assassination of, 544, 547–50, 552, 553–62, 564–66
autopsy report on, 557–59
Bay of Pigs invasion and, 504–5
Cabinet of, 495–98, 499
Castro opposed by, 555–56
in Cuban Missile crisis, 522–39
foreign policy of, 504–5
Khrushchev's relationship with, 509, 530–31
McCloy's relationship with, 18, 490, 491, 497–99, 540, 541, 543–44, 662
presidential campaign of, 487, 490–91
Vietnam policy of, 542, 599
West Berlin visited by, 541–42
Kennedy, Joseph P., 496
Kennedy, Robert F., 517, 522, 527, 530, 531, 538, 601
Keynes, John Maynard, 287
KGB, 556, 560–61, 565
Khomeini, Ayatollah Ruhollah, 643, 652, 653
Khrushchev, Nikita, 447, 469, 473, 478, 485–87, 499, 548, 567
arms control policies of, 502, 506, 510, 543
in Cuban Missile crisis, 522, 523, 526, 528, 529, 530–32, 533, 535, 537
Eisenhower's relationship with, 467, 470–71, 476, 487–91
foreign policy of, 505, 507, 509, 510, 511, 516, 522, 587
Kennedy's relationship with, 509, 530–31
McCloy's meeting with, 508–11
Kido, Saburo, 157
Kiesinger, Kurt, 590–91
King, Ernest J., 178, 179
King, Martin Luther, Jr., 542
Kirk, Alexander C., 191
Kirk, Grayson, 458
Kirkpatrick, Lyman, 302
Kissinger, Henry, 458, 461–65, 478, 515, 585, 623, 634, 635
McCloy's relationship with, 16, 17, 383–84, 563, 613, 614, 615–17, 622, 624, 658
Nixon's relationship with, 613, 614
shah of Iran supported by, 644–46, 649, 650, 651–52, 653
Vietnam War as viewed by, 617–18
Kistiakowsky, George B., 576
Kitchel, William Lloyd, 58, 71
Klarsfeld, Bette, 346–47
Klein, David, 624
Knox, Frank, 129, 140, 147
Koenig, Paul, 81
Koestler, Arthur, 357, 358
Kook, Hillel, *see* Bergson, Peter
Kopper, Samuel, 441, 442, 443
Korean War, 338, 339, 341, 343, 352*n*, 357, 358, 360, 363, 368, 396, 409, 462, 572, 577, 579, 582
Korematsu, Fred T., 166–67, 170, 172, 173
Kraft, Joseph, 460
Kristoff, Michael, 84
Krock, Arthur, 125, 176, 226, 435, 572, 575
Krupp, Alfried, 359–62, 363, 364, 365–67, 368, 372, 374, 479–82, 660, 662
Krupp, Gustav, 359, 365, 366
Krupp Treaty, 480–81
Kubowitzki, A. Leon, 206, 214, 218
Kuhn, Loeb & Co., 15, 59, 60, 61, 62, 63, 64, 65, 66, 67, 71, 72, 97, 104–5

Kuznetsov, Vasily, 522, 523, 533, 534–39, 540

La Guardia, Fiorello H., 129
Lamont, Thomas, 70, 110, 399, 585
Landon, Alfred, 102–3
Lane, Mark, 562
Langdell, Christopher Columbus, 48
Larkin, James, 87–88, 93, 95
Larson, Arthur, 576, 577
Lasky, Melvin, 357, 358, 462
Latin America, development loans to, 297–300, 306–7
law, international, 93–94, 258, 278, 365, 502, 515–16, 656
Lawrence, Ernest O., 243*n*
League of Nations, 18, 63, 80
League of Young Germans, 356
Leahy, William D., 245–46, 247
Leffingwell, Russell C., 108, 283
LeMay, Curtis, 524
Lemnitzer, Lyman L., 462, 507
lend-lease, 123–24, 133, 136, 140
Lenglen, Suzanne, 52
Lerner, Max, 439
"Lesson of the World Bank, The," (McCloy), 306–7
Levi, Primo, 214
Lewis, Fulton, Jr., 423, 447, 448
"Liberalism of Herbert Hoover, The" (MacLeish), 54
Libya, 624–27, 628, 630
Lightner, E. Allan, Jr., 351
Lilienthal, David, 276, 277–82
Lincoln, Abraham, 195, 549
Lindbergh, Charles, 109
Lindsay, Franklin, 355
Linen, James, 605
Lippmann, Walter, 88, 98, 125, 134, 135, 152, 180–81, 206, 207, 310, 313, 405, 531, 587, 603
List, Eugene, 254
Lodge, Henry Cabot, 419–20, 451, 570, 573, 597–98, 599
Logan, Francis D., 654
London Policy Group, 629–30, 634
London *Times,* 319, 324, 449, 469, 592, 638
Long, Breckinridge, 203, 206, 222
Long, Huey, 396
Lord, Winston, 621
Los Angeles Times, 142, 143
Loudon, John, 517
Lovett, Robert Abercrombie, 106, 293, 423, 477, 490, 563, 587
  as assistant to Stimson, 121, 125, 126, 132, 141, 143, 185, 264, 418
  disarmament as viewed by, 468, 469, 470, 471
  Kennedy's relationship with, 495–97, 499, 504, 505, 527
  McCloy's relationship with, 68, 105
  Vietnam War as viewed by, 577–78, 582–83, 598, 602
Lowell, A. Lawrence, 50
Lowenthal, Max, 65, 104, 105
Luce, Clare Booth, 434, 465
Luce, Henry, 73, 109, 136, 411, 434, 443–44, 474

McAdoo, Francis, 107
MacArthur, Douglas, 52, 141, 146, 189, 260, 264, 266–68, 343, 363
MacArthur, Douglas, II, 629
McCarthy, Eugene, 601
McCarthy, Joseph, 392, 408–9, 412, 415, 416–18, 420–21, 435
McCarthyism, 392, 403–22, 433, 448, 571
  European views on, 410, 414–15, 472
  McCloy's opposition to, 393, 403–22, 426, 446, 596–97
McClain, Chester, 69, 73, 99, 282–83, 317, 331
McClelland, Roswell, 212, 213, 214
McCloy, Amelia Conrad (grandmother), 24–25
McCloy, Anna Snader (mother), 25, 26, 35, 50, 51, 54, 57, 58, 233, 312
  as hairdresser, 19, 28, 29–30, 60
  McCloy's relationship with, 19, 27–31, 53, 75, 469–70
McCloy, Edward T. (cousin), 27
McCloy, Ellen (daughter), 132, 315, 316, 385, 504, 508, 510, 543, 657, 661
McCloy, Ellen Zinsser (wife), 97, 99, 111, 122, 125, 146, 182, 228, 235, 248, 253, 254, 255, 262, 272, 320, 392, 478, 503–4, 508, 509, 529, 535, 556
  illness and death of, 657, 660, 661
  McCloy's first meeting with, 74
  McCloy's marriage to, 75–76, 77, 83, 86, 132–33
  in Nazi Germany, 89, 90, 316
  pregnancies of, 77, 92
  in West Germany, 311, 315–17, 344, 385, 412
McCloy, John Jay:
  on Acheson Committee, 276–82
  air power supported by, 125–26
  at Amherst College, 35, 37–46
  ancestry of, 24–25
  "Atlanticist" message of, 623–24
  Barbie case and, 349–50, 352–53
  birth of, 25
  as business leader, 429–30

McCloy *(cont.)*
at Cairo Conference, 190–95
as candidate for Secretary of State, 386–87, 415, 468, 477, 502
as "chairman" of Establishment, 15, 17, 19, 20, 563–64, 596–97
charitable activities of, 483, 504
charm of, 231–32
childhood of, 23–36, 190
civil rights as viewed by, 542–43
class acculturization of, 35, 42–43, 69
clemency board established by, 331, 333–36
clubs of, 59, 99, 107–8, 207, 423
code name of, 199
congressional relations of, 123–24, 415
constitutional rights as viewed by, 95, 119, 147, 149–50, 151, 154, 156, 159–60, 161–62, 164, 173–74
as corporate board director, 18, 396, 483
as corporate lawyer, 17–18, 34, 57–77, 106–7, 122, 271–75, 282, 503, 517–18, 540–41, 570, 571, 662
in Cuban Missile crisis, 523, 527–40, 650–51, 662
death of, 661
détente as viewed by, 540, 621, 650
diary of, 251, 252, 256–57, 264–65, 266, 267
Distinguished Service Medal awarded to, 264
as "dove" vs. "hawk," 530, 536, 539
education of, 27–56
as elder statesman, 659–60
energy crisis and, 624–37
fishing as pastime of, 99–100, 133, 262, 282, 312, 504, 507–8, 513, 542, 624
Freedom Medal awarded to, 543–44, 550
free market supported by, 312
funeral of, 15–20
German culture as viewed by, 40, 52, 205, 310, 312, 338–39, 403
Godkin lectures given by, 392–93
gravitas as value of, 19, 575, 663
Greek studied by, 26, 27, 30, 32–34, 39
at Harvard Law School, 45, 46, 47–50, 52–56
hunting as pastime of, 431, 504, 542, 624
idealism of, 266, 514
illnesses of, 69–70, 660, 661
"imponderables" of public policy as viewed by, 19, 259, 426, 562, 575, 663
informality of, 176, 313, 395–96
intelligence of, 17–18, 38–39
internationalism of, 307, 387, 416, 430, 502, 507, 514, 663
as interventionist, 44–45, 132, 133–35, 140, 146
as law firm partner, 68, 73, 96–97, 122
liberalism of, 38, 54, 102
as managing partner, 96–97, 101
memoir of, 660–61
Middle East trips of, 441–46, 541, 543, 567–68, 604–9, 624–25
military mind-set of, 164
military service of, 50–53
military strategy as viewed by, 135–40, 143–44, 177–85, 192–93
national security as important to, 95, 124, 128, 154, 161, 164, 174, 175, 210, 423–25, 435, 517, 518, 521, 578, 659, 661, 662
Nazis as viewed by, 89–90, 366–67
Nazi war criminals as judged by, 330–36, 359–75, 376
neutrality as viewed by, 446, 447, 448, 464
ninetieth birthday of, 657–58
nuclear strategy as viewed by, 464, 466, 487–88
occupation policy handbook of, 223–27
oil companies represented by, 18, 517–18, 604, 608, 624–37, 639–40
pacifism as viewed by, 45
pension of, 391, 498
physical appearance of, 33, 117, 176
at Plattsburg camp, 40–46, 50, 78, 110
political ambitions unimportant to, 19, 447–48
political influences on, 18–19, 40, 44
at Potsdam Conference, 249–59
power of, 18, 19–20, 176, 317, 429, 441, 443, 445, 447–48, 482–83, 491, 623–24
pragmatism of, 19, 127, 181, 199, 256–57, 266, 307, 474, 662
at preparatory school, 30–36, 48
as Presbyterian, 24
press coverage of, 124–25, 159, 176, 235, 285, 288, 308, 311–12, 313–14, 315, 318, 333, 340, 341–42, 391, 395, 435, 447, 512–13, 593, 600, 659
railroads represented by, 58, 59, 60, 62, 64–67, 96, 104–6
reputation of, 106–7, 171, 435–36, 657–60
residences of, 58, 122, 125, 131, 312, 316, 459, 503–4
as sabotage expert, 91, 113, 117–18, 119, 126, 136–37, 141, 142, 154, 163–64
salary of, 58, 73, 94, 122, 317, 391, 639–40
secret war plans studied by, 135–40
as senior partner, 271–75

skiing as pastime of, 380
social life of, 17, 34, 40, 48, 59, 68, 72–73, 99–100, 182, 662
sports as interest of, 29, 31–32, 33
as storyteller, 99–100, 117
Stuttgart speech of, 334
tennis played by, 17, 33, 34, 39, 52, 58–59, 64, 75, 76, 107, 117, 165, 191–92, 193, 303, 316, 319, 504, 509
U.S.-Soviet relations as viewed by, 228, 237–38, 239, 241–42, 254–57, 265–66, 268, 276
war production as viewed by, 123–24, 131–32, 134–36
on Warren Commission, 548–50, 554–62, 565–66
Watergate scandal as viewed by, 637–39
Wheeler-Truman hearings and, 105–6
in "Wise Men" group, 575–80, 583–84, 603, 623, 649, 650, 651, 653
world tour of, 265–68
McCloy, John Jay (father), 24–26, 27, 30
McCloy, John Jay, II (son), 16, 17, 92, 122, 262, 272, 315, 316, 332, 385, 504, 535, 657
McCloy, Rush Middleton (grandson), 17
McCloy, William (grandfather), 24–25
McCloy, William Snader (brother), 25, 27
McCloy Committee, 187, 188
McCloy Fund, 656, 658–59
"McCloy's Folly," 177
McCloy-Zorin Agreed Principles, 515–16
McCone, John, 488, 504, 529, 531, 550
McCormack, Alfred, 142, 165, 279–80
McCormack, James, Jr., 462
McCormack, John, 133
McCormack Plan, 279–80
Macdonald, Dwight, 440, 518–19
McGhee, George, 472
McGraw, James, 349
McHenry, Donald F., 648, 652
MacLeish, Archibald, 49, 50, 54, 75
Macmillan, Harold, 175, 183, 192, 460, 470, 648
McNamara, Robert, 497, 499, 500, 523, 524–25, 526, 530, 587, 589–90, 657
Vietnam policy of, 571, 573, 576, 577, 578, 579, 583–84, 594, 595–96, 601, 620*n*
Magic intercepts, 137, 138, 140, 141–42, 154–55, 253
Maguerre, Frederick, 84
Malenkov, Georgi M., 328
Mallory, Walter H., 109
Manchester, William, 363, 368, 374
Manhattan Project, 185, 230, 240, 246, 251, 264, 277
Mansfield, Mike, 582, 588, 591, 622
Mansfield Amendment, 593, 622–23
Manufacturer's Trust, 400
Maplewood Institute, 30–31
Marks, Herbert S., 281
Marshall, George C., 52, 119, 125, 137, 138, 139, 140, 141, 191, 192, 228–29, 239, 240, 264, 266, 292, 293, 308, 474
desegregation of military and, 187, 188–89
Hiroshima bombing as viewed by, 241, 243, 244, 245
Holocaust as viewed by, 205, 208, 209
McCloy's relationship with, 129, 130, 178, 187, 191, 192, 421
military strategy of, 145, 146, 177, 179, 181, 184, 194, 199, 227
Marshall Plan, 71, 292–94, 296, 297, 298, 299, 300, 304, 306
Martin, Edwin M., 534
Masaoka, Mike, 158, 168
May, Ernest, 660–61
May, Stacy, 112
"Meet the Press," 512–13, 563, 652
Meiklejohn, Alexander, 37–39, 40, 165, 166
Merchant, Livingston, 608
Merk, Kurt, 346
Metropolitan Life Insurance Co., 15, 396
Metropolitan Opera, 72, 99, 483, 519
Meyer, Cord, 483, 484, 485
Meyer, Eugene, 124, 229, 282–83
Middleton, Drew, 373
Milbank, Albert G., 273
Milbank, Jeremiah, 103, 111
Milbank, Tweed, Hadley & McCloy, 15, 16, 273–75, 282, 386, 499, 503, 517–18, 521, 540–41, 624, 625, 628, 630, 634, 639, 641, 653, 654, 659, 660
Miles, Sherman, 113, 118, 119, 129, 137, 138, 141
military-preparedness movement, 19, 40–46, 50, 80, 154, 501
Miller, Bert, 160
Miller, Francis P., 112
Mills, C. Wright, 35, 483
MIRVs (multiple independently targetable re-entry vehicles), 615–17, 622
"missile gap," 487, 488, 509
Mitchell, Charles E., 71
Mitchell, John, 627
Mitchell, William, 93
Model, Leo, 551
Moffat, Douglas M., 62
Moffett, James A., 98
Mohammad Reza Pahlavi, shah of Iran, 414, 605–6, 629, 630, 641–52

Mollet, Guy, 460, 472
Molotov, V. M., 235–36, 238, 250, 255
Monat, Du, 357, 358, 413, 462
Mondale, Walter, 648
Monde, Le, 336
Monnet, Jean, 17, 72, 97, 105, 180, 182, 183, 196, 197, 225, 234, 336, 337, 344, 377, 405, 589, 590
Monnet, Sylvia, 97
Monroe Doctrine, 109, 238, 239
Moore, Elizabeth Luce, 73
Moore, Hoyt A., 60, 62, 63, 405
Moore, Maurice, 73, 75, 271, 272, 386
Moran, Frederick A., 335
Morgan, J. P., 62
Morgan, Thomas Alfred, 422, 425
J. P. Morgan & Co., 398–99, 400
Morgenthau, Hans J., 584–85
Morgenthau, Henry, Jr.:
  German occupation as viewed by, 230–33, 287, 586
  McCloy's relationship with, 222–23, 230–33, 234
  as Secretary of the Treasury, 100, 102, 120, 123, 124, 197, 198, 203, 210, 214, 219
Morgenthau Plan, 225–27, 228, 287, 586
Morrow, Dwight, 42
Moses, Robert, 454
Mossadegh, Mohammed, 427
Moulin, Jean, 346, 348
Moyers, Bill, 619
Muench, A. J., 333
Munich agreement (1938), 109, 523, 575, 661
Munich Beer Hall Putsch (1923), 88
Munson, Curtis B., 155
Murchison, Clint, 103, 430–32, 542
Murphy, Robert, 175, 180, 183, 624
Murrow, Edward R., 420
Myer, Dillon S., 162–63, 166, 167

Nadolny, Rudolf, 84
Nagasaki bombing, 257, 259
Nasser, Gamal Abdel, 442, 443, 445, 448–53, 541, 543, 567–68, 604, 607, 608, 614, 615, 624–25
Nation, 44, 364, 600
National Banking System, 399, 402
National City Bank, 65, 66, 67, 71, 398, 400, 402, 456
National Committee for a Free Albania, 355
National Committee for a Free Europe, 414
National Industry Recovery Act (NIRA), 101
National Liberation Front (NLF), 582, 595–96
National Security Act (1947), 301
National Security Council (NSC), 229, 302, 468, 476, 478, 507, 519, 523, 528
National Student Association, 484
Naumann, Erich, 373
Nelidoff, Alexander, 83–84, 95
Neustadt, Richard, 497, 500
New Deal, 98–104, 108–12, 287, 307
  McCloy's views on, 106, 387, 404–5, 418–19, 426, 430, 436
New Republic, 42, 44, 162
Newsom, David, 647–48, 652
Newsweek, 291, 313
New York Central Railroad Company, 431–32
New York City Bar Association, 15, 59, 99, 503
New York *Compass,* 334
New Yorker, 59, 62–63, 77
New York Herald Tribune, 201, 519
New York Post, 334
New York State Chamber of Commerce, 404
New York Stock Exchange, 289, 291, 437, 438, 440, 453
New York Times, 41, 66, 79, 202, 211, 219, 221, 226, 289, 294, 300, 313, 315, 318, 328, 333–34, 356, 393, 395, 405, 407, 410, 422, 432, 447, 450, 482, 488, 507, 532, 543, 544, 566, 568, 620, 623
Nicaragua, 298, 656
Niemoller, Martin, 336, 343
Nisi Prius club, 15, 107–8, 423
Nitze, Paul, 340, 461, 465, 466, 468, 491, 500, 531, 616, 649
Nixon, Richard M., 15–16, 413, 613–40
  arms control policies of, 615–18
  energy crisis and, 629, 631–32
  Establishment as viewed by, 613, 622–23, 637–39
  foreign policy of, 621–24
  Kissinger's relationship with, 613, 614
  McCloy's relationship with, 447–48, 490, 542, 613–15
  Middle East policy of, 614–15, 633–35
  re-election campaign of, 636, 639
  Vietnam policy of, 614, 617–18, 622
  in Watergate scandal, 634, 637–39
Nizer, Louis, 549
Non-Proliferation Treaty (NPT), 585–86
North Atlantic Treaty Organization (NATO), 310, 328, 342, 343, 344, 381, 385, 446, 463, 472, 478, 505, 511, 524, 526, 541, 576, 586–600, 621–24

Nosenko, Yuri, 560–61, 565
nuclear weapons, 461–64
on-site inspection of, 505–6, 510, 515, 616–17
proliferation of, 585–86
see also arms control; atomic bomb
Nuclear Weapons and Foreign Policy (Kissinger), 461–64
Nuremberg trials, 228, 258, 330–31, 333, 334, 335–36, 360–61, 363, 365, 366–67, 370, 371, 372, 374, 375
Nuri Said, 445

Occidental Oil Company, 625–26, 636
O'Donnell, Kenneth, 496
Office of Naval Intelligence (ONI), 118
Office of Strategic Services (OSS), 130, 198, 231, 244, 252, 279–80
Ohlendorf, Otto, 367, 370, 371
oil prices, 626, 627, 630, 632, 634–35, 650
Old Philadelphia Rabbit Club, 24
Olsen, Iver C., 216
O'Mahoney, Joseph C., 439
"Open Skies" proposal, 487
Operation Bolero, 145, 177–78, 184
Operation Brother Sam, 552–53
Operation Husky, 184
Operation Mongoose, 532–33
Operation Overlord, 190, 194, 195, 196, 199, 200
Operation Paperclip, 352*n*, 425
Operation Rankin, 192
Operation Roundup, 145, 184
Operation Sledgehammer, 145, 178, 179
Operation Super-Gymnast, 145, 178
Operation Torch, 179
Oppenheim, E. Phillips, 77
Oppenheimer, J. Robert, 243, 277–78, 279, 281, 417, 422–26, 461, 501
Organization of American States (OAS), 527
Organization of Petroleum Exporting Countries (OPEC), 517–18, 541, 625, 627–35, 650
Orwell, George, 357
Oswald, Lee Harvey, 547, 554, 556–62, 565–66
Otis, Harold, 107
"Our Relations with Darlan" (Lippmann), 180–81
Oxford Book of Verse, 312

Page, Arthur W., 243*n*
Page, Ralph W., 42
Palestine, 207, 208–9, 446, 609
Palmer, A. Mitchell, 53
Panuch, John Anthony, 271, 280
Papen, Franz Joseph von, 80, 82, 86, 87, 88, 89, 95
Parker, Chauncey, 99
Parker, Dorothy, 121
Patterson, Robert P., 127, 141, 418
Patton, George S., 193, 195, 233, 234
Pauley, Edwin, 252
Pax Americana, 19, 108, 266, 592, 661
Peabody, Endicott, 31, 599
Pearl Harbor attack, 138, 140–43, 147, 152, 154, 156, 158, 252, 303, 466, 548, 659
Pearson, Drew, 125, 177, 193, 208, 226, 408, 410, 412, 418, 420–21, 435, 447, 448, 467, 468, 491, 562
Pearson, Leon, 126
Pearson, Lester, 459
Peaslee, Amos, 79, 81, 82, 84, 94
Peck, David W., 335
Peck Panel, 335–36, 360–62, 363, 365, 368, 369, 370, 371
Pecora, Frederick, 105
Peddie Institute, 31–36, 48
Pegler, Westbrook, 412
Pehle, John, 203, 205, 209, 210, 211, 212–13, 214, 215–17, 220–21, 222, 223, 224
Penn Mutual Life Insurance Company, 25–26, 27, 28
Penrose, Boies, 57
Pentagon Papers, 620
Pepper, Charlotte, 28, 30
Pepper, George Wharton, 26, 28, 30, 35, 41, 42, 44, 46, 54, 57–58, 661
Perkins, James, 491
Pershing, John J., 52
Pétain, Henri, 180, 196
Peters, Gerhard, 356
Petersberg Agreement, 326–27
Petersen, Howard C., 97, 110, 281
Petersen Bureau, 346
Peterson, Peter G., 16
Pfeffer, Hauptmann von, 89, 90, 91
Pferdmenges, Robert, 329
Philadelphia, Pa.:
"Chinese Wall" of, 23, 25, 26, 29, 36, 57, 58, 662
McCloy's childhood in, 23–36, 190
upper class in, 23–24, 57–58
Philby, Kim, 355
Phleger, Herman, 527
Plant, John D., 33
Plattsburg camp, 40–46, 50, 78, 110
Pleven Plan, 344, 378
Plimpton, Francis T., 62, 76, 585
Plimpton, Pauline, 76, 77
Plympton, Noah, 27
PM, 113, 119

Pogue, Joseph, 442
Pohl, Oswald, 331, 370, 372–73
Point Four program, 299–300
Poland:
death camps in, 201–2, 204, 205–6, 219–20, 228
Lublin government of, 236–37, 258
Nazi invasion of, 108–9
postwar reconstruction in, 294–96, 306
Soviet control of, 242, 446
Polk, Frank L., 107, 108, 112
Poncet, François, 322, 325, 377
Porter, Sylvia, 292
Potsdam Conference, 242, 249–59, 290, 323, 343
Potsdam Proclamation, 253, 257–59, 260, 263, 310, 512
Pound, Roscoe, 48, 53
Power Elite, The (Mills), 483
Powers, Gary, 489
Precht, Henry, 643
President's Advisory Committee on Arms Control and Disarmament, 18, 517, 615–17
President's Panel of Foreign Policy Consultants, 568
Preston, Guy H., 51–53, 658
Price, Don, 426, 427–29
"Problem of War Organization, Post-War Readjustment, The" (McCloy), 131–32
Project Alpha, 644–47, 652
Project 63, 352*n*
Project Solarium, 413–14, 434
Proskauer, Joseph, 408
Psychological Strategy Board, 384, 411
Publications Development Corporation (PDC), 484
PURPLE machine, 118, 137–38

Qaddafi, Muammar, 624–27, 634
Quakers, 24, 30
Quebec Conference, 225–26, 231, 258
Quemoy and Matsu islands, 473–75

Rabi, Isidor I., 277, 423, 426, 467
Rankin, J. Lee, 556
Rapacki, Adam, 478*n*
Raskin, Marcus, 580–81, 620
Rats, Lice and History (Zinsser), 74
Rauh, Joseph L., 120, 125
Rayburn, Sam, 133
Raymond, John M., 360–61, 368
Reagan, Ronald, 16, 655–58, 659
Reams, R. Borden, 202
Reber, Sam, 351, 364, 406, 407
receiverships, railroad, 64–67, 96, 104–6
Reconstruction Finance Corporation (RFC), 123
Reed, John, 88
Reed, Joseph V., 644, 651, 652
Reed, Lansing P., 107
Renger, Annemarie, 322–23
Repplier, Agnes, 28
Republican Party, 102–3, 110–11, 112
liberal wing of, 18–19, 430, 464
McCloy as member of, 54, 103, 111, 133, 312, 430, 436, 447–48, 490–91, 502, 542, 562–64, 568, 613, 655
"Taft" wing of, 386–88
Reston, James, 125, 308, 313, 318, 416, 422, 435, 482, 489, 563
Retinger, Joseph, 471–72
Reuter, Ernst, 358
Richardson, Elliot, 624, 637, 639
Richardson, Sid, 103, 409, 410, 429, 430–32, 518, 662
Riddleberger, James D., 317, 348, 349, 350
Riegner, Gerhardt, 211
Ringle, Kenneth D., 136, 155–56, 157
Rintelen, Franz von, 94–95
Rittenhouse Club, 24, 26
Robb, J. D., 62
Robb, Roger, 424
Roberts, George, 107, 113
Roberts, Henry L., 446
Roberts, Owen, 86, 93, 548
Robertson, Brian, 314
Robertson, Willis, 133, 513
Robinson, Homans, 48
Robinson, William, 429, 430
Roche, John, 597
Rockefeller, Abby, 55, 274
Rockefeller, David, 275, 461, 472, 474, 488, 497, 541, 581, 605, 614, 619–20, 638
McCloy's relationship with, 16–17, 55, 395, 397–98, 454–57, 658
shah of Iran supported by, 642, 644, 645, 652, 653
Rockefeller, John D., Jr., 54, 55, 106, 274–75, 388, 395, 401, 436, 437, 662
Rockefeller, John D., Sr., 55
Rockefeller, John D., III, 55
Rockefeller, Laurance, 55
Rockefeller, Nelson, 55, 272–73, 289, 464–65, 485, 542, 614, 638, 642, 643
Rockefeller, Percy, 65
Rockefeller, William, 65
Rockefeller, Winthrop, 55
Rockefeller Brothers Fund, 464–65

Rockefeller family, 91, 98
McCloy's association with, 19–20, 54–55, 272–75, 387–88, 395, 483
Rockefeller Foundation, 15, 109, 387, 388, 416, 428, 458, 462
Rogers, William P., 411, 626, 629
Rommel, Erwin, 177, 179, 183
Roosevelt, Archie, 42, 43
Roosevelt, Eleanor, 187, 365, 366
Roosevelt, Franklin D., 16, 18, 88, 117–235
"brain trust" of, 101
budget of, 98–99, 101, 102, 110
at Cairo Conference, 19
as chief executive, 112–13, 122, 124
Churchill and, 143, 178, 182, 184–85, 193–94, 225, 235, 236, 258
death of, 234, 235, 239, 249
de Gaulle and, 180, 183, 196–99, 234
economic policies of, 99–100
foreign policy of, 112–13, 490, 496
German occupation as viewed by, 224, 225–26, 230, 231, 232
Hitler vs., 89, 171
Holocaust and policies of, 203, 206, 210, 218
intelligence activities and, 119
isolationism opposed by, 108, 111
Japanese-American internment as viewed by, 152, 154, 171
McCloy's relationship with, 98, 106, 111, 113, 130–31, 171, 182, 196–97, 234, 305, 318, 638, 639
military strategy of, 113, 143–45, 146, 178, 179, 181, 245
New Deal policies of, 98–99, 100–101, 102, 104, 106, 110, 175, 436
Pearl Harbor attack and, 140–43, 548
Pentagon project and, 176–77
re-election campaign of (1944), 171, 430
Stalin and, 194–95, 338
at Teheran Conference, 193–94, 196
U.S.-Soviet relations as viewed by, 228, 235–36
Wall Street and, 99–106, 109–13
wiretapping as viewed by, 127, 128, 129
at Yalta Conference, 255
Roosevelt, Kermit, 414, 427
Roosevelt, Theodore, 18, 41, 43–45, 62, 80, 102
Root, Elihu, 27, 41, 46, 47, 88, 107, 264–65, 302
Rosenheim, Jacob, 211, 213
Rostow, Eugene, 548
Rostow, Walt W., 460, 585, 594, 600, 601–2, 607
Rovensky, Joseph C., 91
Rovere, Richard, 563–64
Rowe, James H., Jr., 148, 149, 153, 154, 155, 164, 165, 301–2, 597, 598
Ruby, Jack, 547–48, 555, 565, 566
Ruhr Valley industries, 224, 225, 231, 234–35, 309, 318, 326, 337, 338, 360, 368, 369
Rumsfeld, Donald, 624
Runyon, Damon, 147
Rusk, Dean, 139, 338, 423, 428, 460, 472, 548, 553, 587, 590, 591, 597, 599, 607, 609, 646
as Kennedy's Secretary of State, 497, 498, 499–500, 505, 517, 523, 526, 533, 536, 537, 538, 540, 541, 543
Vietnam policy of, 570, 575, 576, 578, 579, 580, 585, 596, 601–2
Russell, Bertrand, 357
Russell, Donald, 279–80, 281
Russell, Richard B., 548, 564–65, 566
Russell Plan, 279–80
Ryan, Allan A., Jr., 347, 352

Sadat, Anwar, 624, 633, 634, 643
SALT Treaty, 615–17, 622
SALT II Treaty, 649, 650
Santayana, George, 121
Sartre, Jean-Paul, 357, 408
Satow, Masao, 158
Saud, Abdul-Aziz Ibn, King of Saudi Arabia, 441–45, 541
Saudi Arabia, 441–45, 541, 606–7, 633–35
Scandrett, Jay J., 42
Schacht, Hjalmar, 91
Schelabrendorff, Fabian von, 332
Schiff, Jacob, 29, 60, 62, 63
Schiff, Mortimer L., 60
Schine, G. David, 405–6, 419–20, 422
Schlesinger, Arthur, Jr., 461, 462, 489, 502, 504, 507, 515, 530, 566, 596–97
Schmidt, Helmut, 16, 649, 656, 658
Scholl, Inge, 332
Schram, Emil, 291
Schröder, Gerhard, 590
Schubert, Heinz Hermann, 371
Schuler, Henry, 626
Schumacher, Kurt, 305, 322–23, 326, 327, 328, 335, 336, 341, 343, 344, 362, 378, 379, 383
Schuman, Robert, 378, 383
Schuman Plan, 337, 379
Schwartz, Thomas, 366
Scott, Austin, 48, 55
Scott, Ernest, 57
Scott, J. Allison, 25–26, 57
Scranton, William, 562–63
Searls, Fred, Jr., 279
Sebold, William G., 128
Secret Service, 557, 560

Securities and Exchange Commission (SEC), 72, 274–75, 289, 436, 439, 636–37, 640
Seebohm, Hans Christoph, 329
"See It Now," 420
Selective Service, 133, 168
Senate, U.S.:
 Committee on Interstate Commerce, 104–6
 Foreign Relations Committee, 123, 133
 Permanent Subcommittee on Investigations, 413
 Subcommittee on Multinational Corporations, 625, 639
Sevareid, Eric, 17, 547
"Seven Sisters" oil companies, 18, 517–18, 625–37, 639–40
Shepardson, Whitney H., 109, 112
Short, Walter C., 138
Shultz, George, 658
Shute, Ben, 86, 94, 97, 111, 348, 351, 352, 353, 354, 355
Sick, Gary, 648
Sidey, Hugh, 649
Silvermaster, Nathan G., 281
Sinclair, Archibald, 217
Sisco, Joseph, 607
Six, Franz, 354
Slater, Ellis, 430
Slawson, David W., 561
Smith, Alfred E., 71, 87
Smith, Walter Bedell, 387, 414, 426, 434, 447, 468, 470, 471, 472, 477, 500
Snader, Lena M. (aunt), 28, 29, 74
Snader, Sarah "Sadie" M. (aunt), 28, 74
Snow, Conrad E., 335
Snyder, John W., 284, 285, 288
Social Democratic Party (SPD), 305, 318, 323–24, 325, 328, 335, 356–57, 363, 380, 406, 418, 587, 591, 593
Socialist Commentary, 413
Sohl, Hans-Gunther, 369
Sohn, Louis, 514–15
Sokolosky, George, 435
Somoza, Anastasio, 298
Sorensen, Theodore, 523, 526
Soviet Union:
 atomic weapons of, 257, 261–62
 disarmament proposals of, 500, 501–2, 503
 German invasion of, 132, 144, 331
 lend-lease credits for, 255, 296
 McCloy's trip to, 508–11
 McCloy's views on, 132, 228, 308–9
 military strength of, 295, 303
 nuclear capability of, 461–64, 465, 467
 oil production of, 517, 518
 political repression in, 262
 uranium resources of, 281
 U.S. relations with, 63, 194–95, 228, 235–42, 249, 254–57, 265–66, 268, 276, 296–97, 463–64, 465, 469, 506, 523–24, 538, 539, 540, 587, 621, 650, 656–57
Speer, Albert, 374–75
Speer, Hilda, 374
Speidel, Hans, 364
Speidel, Wilhelm, 364
Spiegel, Der, 329
Spiegel affair, 524
Springer, Axel, 357
Sputnik, 465, 469
E. R. Squibb & Sons, 15, 72
Stalin, Joseph, 171, 364, 380, 381, 447, 456, 473, 486, 487, 510
 Churchill's relationship with, 251, 338
 death of, 472
 military strategy of, 179, 184, 189
 nuclear policy of, 260–61, 278
 at Potsdam Conference, 251, 252, 253, 255, 256, 258
 Roosevelt and, 194–95, 338
 at Teheran Conference, 193, 194, 196
 Truman's relationship with, 236–37, 238, 241, 251, 252, 256, 257, 258
Standard Oil of California (SOCAL), 272, 274–75, 439, 605, 627
Stanley, Harold, 285
Stanton, Frank, 584
Stassen, Harold, 447, 468
State Department, U.S.:
 anti-Communist policy of, 291, 295
 "Black Chamber" of, 85, 95
 German occupation policy of, 230–33
 Jewish refugee rescue and, 203, 204
 McCarthyite attacks on, 392, 393, 404, 407, 410
 political influence of, 175, 301
State-War-Navy Coordinating Committee (SWNCC), 193, 229–30
Steel, Ronald, 620
Steffens, Lincoln, 79
Steinem, Gloria, 483, 484
Stephenson, William, 129
Sterner, Michael, 624, 625
Stettinius, Edward R., 229
Stevenson, Adlai, 442, 450, 495, 502–3, 506, 528, 529–30, 531, 533, 534, 536, 538, 539, 651
Stewart, Walter, 39
Stimson, Henry Lewis, 18–19, 45, 46, 47, 55, 85, 86, 103, 187, 189, 264, 332, 490, 495
 atomic bomb as viewed by, 237–38, 239, 240, 256, 261, 262–63
 collective security doctrine of, 596

German occupation as viewed by, 224–27
Hiroshima bombing as viewed by, 240–48, 251, 263, 501
Holocaust and policies of, 206, 210, 215, 222–23
Japanese-American internment as viewed by, 149, 150–51, 153, 156, 157
Lend-Lease supported by, 123
Lovett as assistant to, 121, 125, 126, 132, 141, 143, 185, 264, 418
McCloy as assistant to, 113, 117, 119–26, 131, 137–40, 143, 145, 181–84, 194, 196, 199, 200, 201, 229, 235, 242, 253, 262–65, 268, 302, 308, 321, 338–39, 418, 421, 518, 575, 661, 663
military strategy of, 144, 145, 177–78, 179, 180, 194, 197
at Potsdam Conference, 249–50, 252, 253, 255
resignation of, 262, 264–65
as Secretary of War, 110, 185, 496
U.S.-Soviet relations as viewed by, 237, 238–39, 241–42
Victory Parade war plans and, 138–40
Stimson, Mabel, 121, 262
stock market crash (1929), 72, 73–74, 105
Stone, Shepard, 16, 314, 335, 338, 392, 403, 414, 426, 478, 499, 660–61
Straight, Willard, 42, 44, 46
Strategic Air Command (SAC), 466, 467
Strauss, Franz-Josef, 467, 512
Strauss, Lewis L., 60, 61, 106, 417, 422, 425, 469, 470, 471, 601
Strong, Benjamin, 70
Struenck, Elizabeth, 332
Study Group on Soviet-U.S. Relations, 423, 424, 426, 446, 460
Suez Canal Company, 449, 452
Suez Canal crisis, 448–53, 472
Sullivan, William, 555, 643
Sulzberger, Arthur Hays, 314, 409
Sulzberger, C. L., 323, 385, 468, 564
Sunday Dispatch (London), 482
Supreme Court, U.S., 60, 67, 80, 101, 127
Japanese-American internment reviewed by, 168, 169–73
Nazi war criminal appeals before, 373–74
Suzuki, Kantaro, 242–43
Swaine, Robert, 61, 62, 63, 64, 65, 67, 70, 71, 72, 96, 97, 100, 101, 103–4, 106, 107, 271–72
Swatland, Donald, 50, 60, 62, 64, 65, 67, 73, 97, 271, 272, 273
Swetland, Roger W., 31–32, 34–35
Swope, Herbert Bayard, 276
Symington, Stuart, 591, 632
Tachibana, Itaru, 136, 137, 155–56
Taft, Henry W., 58
Taft, Robert, 110–11, 123, 294, 386–88
Taft, William Howard, 18, 58
Talbot, Strobe, 616
Tamm, Edward, 127
Taylor, Maxwell, 464, 525, 571, 573, 602
Taylor, Robert, 351
Taylor, Telford, 331, 336, 361, 364–65, 366, 405, 416
Tempo Presente, 413
Ter Meer, Fritz, 368
test-ban treaty, 467–68, 469, 470, 471, 478, 487, 488, 490, 498, 500, 505–8, 510, 514, 516, 538, 543
Texaco, 627
Texas Railroad Commission, 626
Thant, U, 528–29, 530, 532, 533
Thayer, Charles W., 339, 341, 363–64, 407
Thompson, Llewellyn, 576
Thompson, Robert G. K., 599
Tilden, William, Jr., 59
Time, 109, 136, 176, 285, 311–12, 455, 479
Tocqueville, Alexis de, 96, 106, 107
Togo, Shigenori, 250, 257
Towers, Graham F., 284
Treaty of Rome (1972), 472
Trevor-Roper, Hugh, 357
Trident Conference, 184–85
Truman, Harry S., 18, 235–83, 578
Churchill's relationship with, 241, 251, 252
foreign policy of, 290, 296–97, 298, 299–300, 303, 306, 310, 341, 442, 490, 609
Japanese occupation policy of, 266
Japanese surrender as viewed by, 246, 248, 249, 251
Korean War and, 358
McCarthy's attacks on, 415
McCloy's relationship with, 106, 237, 247, 249–50, 254, 263, 264, 299–300, 305, 306, 312, 317, 318, 363, 392, 411, 412
Marshall Plan and, 293
nuclear policy of, 238, 241, 244, 247, 251, 252, 254, 257, 259, 260, 263, 279, 310, 462, 501
at Potsdam Conference, 249–59
re-election campaign of, 304
Stalin's relationship with, 236–37, 238, 241, 251, 252, 256, 257, 258
U.S.-Soviet relations as viewed by, 235–38, 249
in Wheeler-Truman hearings, 104–6
World Bank as viewed by, 293, 295, 299, 300

Truman Doctrine, 290
Tsuji, Keizo, 159–60
Tugwell, Rex, 101
Turkey, 526, 527, 529, 531, 538, 540
Tweed, Harrison, 107, 273

U-boats, 163–64
Ullman, Richard, 620, 621
United Nations (UN), 18, 230, 296, 473–74
  atomic policy set by, 276, 279, 280
  Charter of, 238–39
  Cuban Missile crisis and, 527, 528–30, 532
  disarmament and, 502, 515
  founding of, 236, 238
  General Assembly of, 515
  "German problem" and, 381
  McCloy's involvement with, 238–39, 267, 307
  regional issues in, 238–39, 267
  Resolution 242 of, 606, 607, 608
  Security Council of, 239
  Vietnam War and, 572, 577
United Nations Refugee and Relief Agency (UNRRA), 223
United States:
  as "arsenal of democracy," 121, 122–23, 134
  British Empire replaced by, 112, 124
  centralization of power in, 131
  "command economy" in, 131
  global influence of, 18–19, 71, 112, 124, 238–39, 268, 303, 476, 592, 601, 655, 661, 663
  gold standard of, 99, 588, 592
  isolationism in, 108–9, 132, 133, 140, 146, 210, 265, 414–15, 416, 496, 562, 588, 661
  nuclear capability of, 255, 261–62, 278–79, 281, 282, 303, 378, 501, 524–25, 526, 539
  prosperity in, 72
  protectionism in, 98
  trade balance of, 586, 588–92, 593, 608, 621, 626
  war production in, 123–24, 131–32, 134–36, 145–46
U.S. v. *Schechter Poultry,* 100–101
U-2 crisis, 489–91, 498
U-2 overflights, 487–91, 498, 522, 528, 531, 533, 560

Vance, Cyrus R., 16, 643, 644, 646, 647, 648, 650, 651, 656
Vandenberg, Arthur, 433
Vann, John Paul, 603
Versailles Treaty, 63, 226, 588
"Victory Parade" war plan, 135–40, 143
Viet Cong, 573, 576, 577, 579, 580, 595, 600–601
Vietnam War:
  bombing campaigns in, 573, 574, 579, 580, 581, 582–84, 594, 595, 602
  cost of, 593–94
  Establishment affected by, 603–4
  foreign policy affected by, 593, 599–600, 602, 603, 621
  French period of, 296
  Johnson's strategy for, 568, 569–85, 586, 593–604, 609, 620
  Kennedy's strategy for, 542, 599
  Kissinger's views on, 617–18
  McCloy's views on, 542, 571–85, 595–604, 617–18, 661
  media coverage of, 584
  Nixon's strategy for, 614, 617–18, 622
  opposition to, 574–75, 581, 584–85, 596, 618, 623
  peace negotiations on, 582, 583, 594, 614, 617, 618
  Tet offensive in, 600–602
  'Titoist" solution to, 573, 579
  Vietnamization of, 598, 603, 617
Villard, Oswald Garrison, 43–44
Vincent, John Carter, 392
Viner, Jacob, 109
Visser't Hooft, W. A., 222
Voice of America (VOA), 404, 409
Volcker, Paul A., 16, 657
Vrba, Rudolf, 211–12, 215, 217, 220, 221

Wadsworth, James J., 443
Waldman, Morris, 106
Walker, Samuel S., Jr., 484
Wallace, Henry, 249, 260, 281, 287
Wallenberg, Raoul, 215
Wall Street:
  congressional investigations of, 103–6, 404–5, 418–19, 596
  McCloy's activities on, 57–77, 106–8, 265
  Roosevelt and, 99–106, 109–13
  World Bank and, 288, 289, 293, 295, 298, 306
Wall Street Journal, 438, 621
Walters, Vernon, 551, 552
Wambaugh, Eugene, 48
Wanamaker, John, 28, 385
Warburg, Edward M. M., 314–15
Warburg, Eric, 207, 324, 369, 403, 478, 481
Warburg, Felix M., 60, 72, 106, 662
Warburg, Frederick, 63–64, 207, 284, 285, 317, 504
Warburg, Frieda Schiff, 60

Warburg, James, 98, 102, 103, 112
Warburg, Paul M., 60, 70, 71, 72
Warburg, Siegmund, 607
Ward, Barbara, 499
War Department, U.S.:
  foreign policy directed by, 229–30
  intelligence channels in, 130
  Operations and Planning Division (OPD) of, 213, 221
  Pentagon built for, 176–77
  political influence of, 164, 175
  War Plans Division of, 135, 146
  see also Stimson, Henry Lewis
Warner, Rawleigh, 614, 615
War Refugee Board (WRB), 201, 203–4, 205, 207, 211, 212, 215, 219–20
War Relocation Authority (WRA), 157, 160–61, 162–63, 168, 170, 171, 173
Warren, Earl, 548, 549, 550, 559, 560–61, 562
Warren, Edward H., 48, 49
Warren Commission, 547, 548–50, 553–62, 564–66
Warsaw pact, 478, 586
Washington, George, 99
Washington Evening Star, 78, 95
Washington Post, 126, 189, 229, 364, 420, 638
Washington Star, 313, 421
Webster, Bethuel M., 410–11
Wechsler, Herbert, 172–73
Wedemeyer, Albert C., 135, 139, 140, 143
Weicker, Lowell, 77
Weicker, Mary, 77, 92
Weinberg, Sidney J., 103, 106, 111, 437, 438
Weizsäcker, Ernst von, 362–63
Weizsäcker, Richard von, 658
Welch, Joseph Nye, 421
Welt, Die, 414, 415
West Germany, *see* Germany, Federal Republic of
Westinghouse, George, 62
Westinghouse Corp., 15, 62, 396, 411, 640
Westmoreland, William, 573, 576, 579–80, 595, 598, 601
Wetzler, Alfred, 211–12, 215, 217, 220, 221
Wheeler, Burton K., 104–6
Wheeler, Raymond A., 450–51, 584, 598, 601
White, Harry Dexter, 224, 231, 283, 287, 307, 415
White, Theodore, 320, 408
White, William Allen, 109
Whitman, Ann, 476
Whitney, George, 285, 386, 398–99
"Why Not the Camp?" (McCloy), 44–45
Wickersham, George W., 58, 59, 71
Wiesner, Jerome, 500, 515
Wiley, Alexander, 404
Will, George, 646
Williston, Samuel, 48, 49
Willkie, Wendell, 110–11, 112–13
Willoughby, Charles A., 142
Wilson, Charles, 420, 421
Wilson, Woodrow, 38, 40, 41, 43, 53, 510
Winters, Herbert, 32–33
Wirtz, Alvin J., 569, 570
Wise, Stephen, 207, 209, 211
Wiseman, William, 60–61, 85, 94
Wisner, Frank G., 302, 304, 353, 354, 426, 427
Wolfe, Charles A., 48
Wolfe, Glen, 410
Wood, Leonard, 41, 43, 46, 50
Wood, Robert, 109
Woodring, Harry H., 110
Woodruff, Bob, 429
Woods, Arthur, 42
World Bank, 282–307
  Articles of Agreement for, 285, 286
  board of directors of, 283, 285–86, 289, 300
  bonds issued by, 283, 286, 287–92, 306
  British participation in, 286–87, 289, 292, 295
  bylaws of, 285
  creation of, 228, 282
  development loans by, 283, 288, 290–91, 293, 297–300, 448–49, 452
  financial resources of, 288
  international role of, 286–89, 291, 299, 300
  McCloy as president of, 15, 18, 282–307, 398
  Marshall Plan and, 292–94, 297, 298, 299, 300, 306
  membership in, 444, 445
  as New Deal proposal, 287, 307
  political agenda of, 294–96, 307
  Soviet participation in, 296–97
  staff of, 300–301
  underdeveloped countries aided by, 297–300, 306–7
  U.S. participation in, 287, 288
  Wall Street reaction to, 288, 289, 293, 295, 298, 306
  West German participation in, 326
World Court, 18, 63, 502, 507, 656
World Jewish Congress, 203, 204, 211, 382–83
World Peace Through World Law (Clark and Sohn), 514–15
World War I:
  McCloy's military service in, 50–53

World War I: *(cont.)*
  U.S. arms shipments in, 78–79
  war reparations after, 63, 70
World War II, 117–268
  air war in, 125–26, 134, 190, 214, 217, 220–21
  British armament needs in, 119–21, 123–24
  cross-Channel invasion in, 145, 177–79, 184, 190, 191, 193, 194, 198, 199, 200
  European theater in, 143–44, 145, 177–79, 184, 197, 198, 200
  Italian front in, 184, 189–90, 193, 195
  North African theater in, 143, 144, 145, 177, 178, 179–84, 518
  oil supplies as factor in, 143, 178, 179, 208–9
  Pacific theater in, 143, 152, 189, 267
  peace terms in, 225–27
  second front in, 184, 191, 194
  Soviet front in, 177, 189, 266
World Youth Festival, 483–85
Wozniak, Theodore, 84
Wright, Edwin, 303–4
Wriston, Henry M., 409, 458
Wyman, David S., 209
Wyzanski, Charles E., 439–40

Yalta Conference, 231, 235–36, 240, 241, 255, 265, 266, 290, 486
Yamani, Zaki, 541, 606, 634–35
Yardley, Herbert, 85
Yasui, Minoru, 166–67, 170
Young, Robert R., 431–32

Zapruder, Abraham, 557
Zapruder film, 557–58
Zeckendorf, William, 454
Zenger, John Peter, 26
Zhukov, Georgi K., 256
Zimmermann, Arthur, 80, 81, 82, 93
Zinsser, Frederick G., 74
Zinsser, Hans, 74
Zinsser, John, 74
Zionism, 191, 207, 208, 209
Zorin, Valerin A., 507, 510, 513, 514, 515–16, 532, 535

PICTURE CREDITS

Amherst College Archives 2
AP / Wide World 3, 5, 12, 20, 22, 23, 24, 27
UPI / Bettmann 4, 6, 7, 8, 9, 11, 14, 16, 17, 18, 19, 21, 25, 26, 28, 31, 32, 33, 34, 35, 36, 38
Bettmann Archive 15
Courtesy of the Chase Manhattan Archives 29, 30, 40
Lyndon Johnson Library 37
Jimmy Carter Library 39
Ronald Reagan Library 43